Civilization Past & Present,
Eleventh Edition, Primary Source Edition
Volume I

It has everything students need to master the course!

A highly readable text that examines all aspects of world history. A wealth of original primary source documents (at the end of this text) help make the material come alive by supporting the chapter content. Accompanying *Document Analysis* questions encourage students to delve deeper into the documents and explore how they relate to the events of the time. Documents are organized to correlate with chapter material.

TO DO

☐ Review text material for exams.

☐ Put together a study plan for midterm.

☐ Stop by professor's office for extra help.

☐ Pick up supplementary books at the bookstore.

Longman has something to make your *To-Do* list a whole lot shorter.

You have a lot to do to be successful in your history course.

myhistorylab™

Where it's a good time to connect to the past!

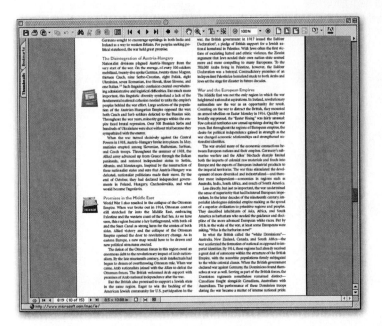

Would your life be easier if you had an electronic version of your textbook?

MyHistoryLab contains the complete text with icons that link to selected sources. You can print sections of the text to read anytime, anywhere.

Are you overwhelmed by the time it takes to find primary source documents, images, maps, and other sources for your research papers?

MyHistoryLab contains hundreds of primary sources, images, and maps— all in one place —to help make writing your research paper easier and more effective, and to help you better understand the course material.

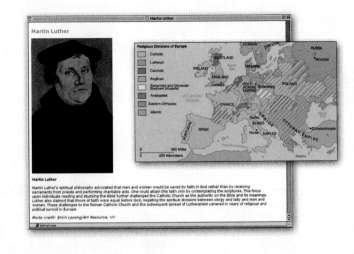

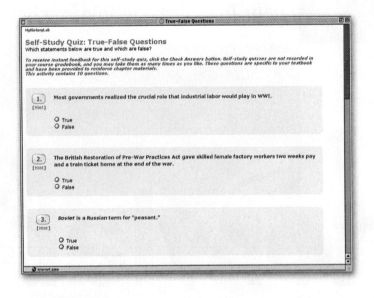

Are you sometimes overwhelmed when you study for exams?

MyHistoryLab gives you a quizzing and testing program that shows what you've mastered, as well as where you need more work. Look for these icons on MyHistoryLab:

Need extra help during evening hours?

Get help from The Tutor Center when your instructor is often unavailable — 5 pm to midnight, Sunday through Thursday, Spring and Fall terms (Sunday through Wednesday, Summer term). Tutors can help you navigate MyHistoryLab or review your paper for organization, grammar, and mechanics.

The Tutor Center

Addison-Wesley • Allyn & Bacon • Benjamin Cummings • Longman

Did your professor assign other books to read?

MyHistoryLab allows you to read, download, or print over twenty of the most commonly assigned works for this course – all at no additional cost!

Now, flip through *Civilization Past & Present*. You will find the icons shown on the opposite page. Each icon will direct you to a place in MyHistoryLab to help you better understand the material. For example, when reading about classical China or 19th century European politics, you may find an icon that links you to an original source document by Confucius or Karl Marx.

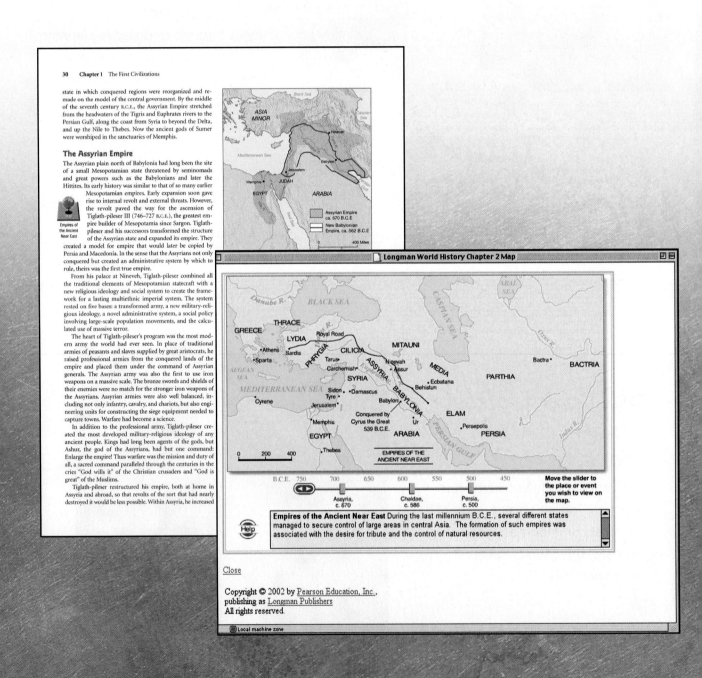

DOCUMENT

This icon will lead you to primary source documents, so you can see the original documents that pertain to the people and events you're studying.

CASE STUDY

Analyze and interpret two or more primary sources on a similar theme or topic. Includes critical thinking questions.

IMAGE

You'll find photos, cartoons, and artwork that relate to the topic you're reading.

MAP

Interactive maps will help you visualize the geography you are exploring in this course. You will also find printable map activities from one of Longman's workbooks.

History Bookshelf Listing

1. *Aesop's Fables*; date unknown
2. *The Iliad*, Homer; 800 BCE
3. *The Upanishads*; 800 BCE
4. *The Analects*, Confucius; circa 500 BCE
5. *The Tao of Teh King*, Lao-Tze;
6. *Histories*, Herodotus; 440 BCE
7. *The Oedipus Trilogy*, Sophocles; circa 400 BCE
8. *The Republic*, Plato; 360 BCE
9. *The Art of War*, Sun Tzu; 100 BCE
10. *The Arabian Nights*; 10 AD
11. Plutarch's *Lives*; 100 AD
12. *The Bhagavad-Gita*; 200 AD
13. *The Holy Koran*; circa 630 AD
14. *Beowulf*; 1100 AD
15. *The Prince*, Machiavelli; 1505 AD
16. *95 Theses*, Martin Luther; 1517 AD
17. *Gulliver's Travels*, Jonathan Swift; 1726 AD
18. *The Communist Manifesto*, Karl Marx; 1848 AD
19. *Origin of Species*, Charles Darwin; 1859 AD
20. *20,000 Leagues Under the Sea*, Jules Verne; 1869 AD
21. *To the Gold Coast for Gold*, Sir Richard Burton; 1883 AD
22. *The Jungle Book*, Rudyard Kipling; 1894 AD
23. *Heart of Darkness*, Joseph Conrad; 1899 AD

PRIMARY SOURCE EDITION
Civilization
Past & Present
Eleventh Edition

Volume I: To 1650

Palmira Brummett
UNIVERSITY OF TENNESSEE

Robert R. Edgar
HOWARD UNIVERSITY

Neil J. Hackett
ST. LOUIS UNIVERSITY

George F. Jewsbury
CENTRE D'ÉTUDES DU MONDE RUSSE
  ÉCOLE DES HAUTES ÉTUDES EN SCIENCES SOCIALES

Barbara Molony
SANTA CLARA UNIVERSITY

THIS BOOK HAS BENEFITED FROM THE CONTRIBUTIONS
OVER MANY EDITIONS OF THE FOLLOWING AUTHORS:

T. Walter Wallbank (Late)

Alastair M. Taylor (Late)

Nels M. Bailkey

Clyde J. Lewis

PEARSON
Longman

New York Boston San Francisco
London Toronto Sydney Tokyo Singapore Madrid
Mexico City Munich Paris Cape Town Hong Kong Montréal

Executive Editor: Michael Boezi
Senior Acquisitions Editor: Janet Lanphier
Senior Development Editor: Dawn Groundwater
Development Editor: Adam Beroud
Executive Marketing Manager: Sue Westmoreland
Media and Supplements Editor: Kristi Olson
Senior Media Editor: Patrick McCarthy
Production Manager: Eric Jorgensen
Project Coordination, Text Design, and Electronic Page Makeup: Electronic Publishing Services
    Inc., NYC
Photo Research: Photosearch, Inc.
Cover Designer/Manager: Nancy Danahy
Cover Photograph: Image: Western Han Dynasty Ceramic Male Figure. © Asian Art &
    Archaeology, Inc./CORBIS.
Manufacturing Buyer: Roy L. Pickering, Jr.
Printer and Binder: Courier Corporation
Cover Printer: Coral Graphic Services

For permission to use copyrighted material, grateful acknowledgment is made to the copyright
holders on pp. C-1–C-3, which are hereby made part of this copyright page.

Library of Congress Cataloging-in-Publication Data

Civilization past & present / Palmira Brummett ... [et al.].— 11th ed.
    p. cm.
 Includes bibliographical references and index.
 ISBN 0-321-23613-0 — ISBN 0-321-23627-0 — ISBN 0-321-23628-9
 1. Civilization. I. Brummett, Palmira Johnson

CB69.C57 2005
909—dc22   2004029985

Visit us at http://www.ablongman.com.

ISBN 0-321-42332-1 (Primary Source Edition, Complete Edition)
ISBN 0-321-42838-2 (Primary Source Edition, Volume I)
ISBN 0-321-42837-4 (Primary Source Edition, Volume II)

1 2 3 4 5 6 7 8 9 10—CRK—07 06 05

Brief Contents

Detailed Contents

*Each chapter ends with a Conclusion, Suggestions for Web Browsing, Literature and Film, and Suggestions for Reading.

CHAPTER 6
Byzantium and the Orthodox World

CHAPTER 7
Islam

GLOBAL ISSUES   RELIGION AND
GOVERNMENT   222

CHAPTER 8
African Beginnings

CHAPTER 9
The European Middle Ages, 476–1348 C.E.   256

CHAPTER 10
Culture, Power, and Trade in the Era of Asian Hegemony, 220–1350   286

CHAPTER 11
The Americas to 1492   322

Documents

Maps

Global Issues

Discovery Through Maps

Chapter Opening Image Descriptions

CHAPTER 1

Gold and lapis lazuli Goat and Tree in the form of an offering stand to the Sumerian fertility god Tammuz, from the royal burials at Ur, c. 2600–2500 B.C.E.

CHAPTER 2

The details of the lives of individual human beings in ancient times sometimes become lost in the broader discussions of economic, military, and political events. This image of a Chinese couple playing a board game shows that ordinary life with its amusements remained, and that an artisan thought it moving enough to portray it.

CHAPTER 3

The Lion capital of Sarnath, from an Ashoka column placed at the site of the Buddha's first sermon. This Lion capital is used today as a national emblem of the Republic of India.

CHAPTER 4

A view of the Acropolis of Athens, dominated by the Parthenon, the temple dedicated to the goddess Athena.

CHAPTER 5

The Forum of Rome, with the ruins of the Temple of Vesta and the Column of Phocas.

CHAPTER 6

The gold and silver domes of the Cathedral of Hagia Sophia, Novgorod, built in the mid eleventh century. Though Novgorod lies some 1000 miles to the north of Constantinople, Byzantine cultural influence penetrated deeply into the region that would one day form the heartland of Russia.

CHAPTER 7

Qur'an page with gold lettering by the fifteenth-century calligrapher Sheykh Hamdullah. For Muslims the Qur'an is eternal; craftsmen created beautiful, elaborate Qur'ans for various Muslim rulers.

CHAPTER 8

Brass statue of a queen mother, from the Court of Benin, sixteenth century.

CHAPTER 9

The Gothic-style Benedictine abbey of Mont St. Michel, constructed between the eleventh and sixheenth centuries and built on a rocky inlet amid the sandbanks and tides between Brittany and Normandy, France.

CHAPTER 10

Refined gentlemen of the Tang and Song dynasties, seen in this detail from a scroll by tenth-century artist Gu Hongzhong, displayed their taste and culture in banquets in their own homes. Entertainment by female musicians and courtesans enhanced the opulent foods and rich decorations.

CHAPTER 11

Detail from painted Mayan vase depicting a ceremonially dressed ball player. The ball game served important social, political, and religious functions in Mayan civilization. On a very basic level, it provided the Mayan polity with entertainment. The construction of stone-paved courts, the training of players, and the holding of games also reinforced the prestige of the community. Finally, the game and its players could serve as religious offerings, with losing players sometimes being sacrificed to the gods.

CHAPTER 12

The Ottoman army under Lala Mustafa Pasha parading before the captured fortress of Tiflis. Some janissaries, carrying their gunpowder weapons, are shown in the center of the image.

CHAPTER 13

The Temple of the Golden Pavilion was commissioned by the Japanese shōgun Ashikawa Yoshimitsu in 1397. The building was intimate in scale and designed as part of a garden in which the shōgun could meditate. The building, destroyed by an arsonist in 1950, was rebuilt exactly as the original.

CHAPTER 14

Detail from *The Creation of Adam*, painted by the master Renaissance artist Michelangelo Buonarroti. Ceiling of the Sistine Chapel (1511–1512), in Rome.

CHAPTER 15

The Armada Portrait of Queen Elizabeth I was painted in 1588 to commemorate the English naval victory over the Spanish Armada. Against considerable odds, Elizabeth succeeded in mobilizing her nation to withstand Spanish diplomatic and military pressures. At the same time, she managed to maintain a certain unity in her socially and religiously diverse realm.

CHAPTER 16

This ivory saltcellar, with its carved figure of a Portuguese sailor in crow's nest, makes clear the influence of the West on the artists of Benin.

To the Instructor

The eleventh edition of *Civilization Past & Present* continues to present a survey of world history, treating the development and growth of civilization as a global phenomenon in which all the world's culture systems have interacted. This new edition, like its predecessors, includes all the elements of history—social, economic, political, military, religious, aesthetic, legal, and technological—to illustrate that global interaction. One of the most significant changes in the eleventh edition is the addition of our new Asian scholar and co-author, Barbara Molony. Barbara is a professor of history at Santa Clara University and is director of Santa Clara's Program for the Study of Women and Gender. Well-versed in modern Asia, she significantly revised the book's Asian chapters.

With the accelerating tempo of developments in business, communication, and technology, every day each part of the world is brought into closer contact with other parts: economic and political events that happen in even the most remote corners of the world affect each of us individually. An appreciation for and an understanding of all the civilizations of the world must be an essential aim of education. Thus, the eleventh edition of *Civilization Past & Present* emphasizes world trends and carefully avoids placing these trends within a Western conceptual basis.

CHANGES TO ORGANIZATION AND CONTENT

The eleventh edition maintains the many strengths that have made *Civilization Past & Present* a highly respected textbook. As the authors revised the text, they relied on the latest historical scholarship and profited from suggestions from adopters of the text and reviewers. Maintained throughout this compelling survey are a fluid writing style and consistent level of presentation seldom found in multi-authored texts.

While the text retains the basic organization of its predecessors, all chapters have been reviewed and revised in light of the globalization of today's changing world. The authors have carefully evaluated, revised, combined, and rewritten chapters to provide balanced coverage of all parts of the world throughout history.

One of the major changes in the eleventh edition is a new chapter, "Latin America: Independence and Dependence, 1825–1945" (Chapter 25). This new chapter provides detailed coverage of Latin America, including the political, social, and economic challenges following independence and into the twentieth century and relations between the Latin American nations and the United States.

Other chapter changes are as follows:

- **Chapter 1:** "Stone Age Societies and the Earliest Civilizations of the Near East" provides coverage of human prehistory, Egyptian civilization, and the development of smaller Near Eastern states.
- **Chapter 2:** "Ancient China—Origins to Empire: From Prehistory to 220 C.E." and **Chapter 3:** "Ancient India: From Origins to 300 C.E." both include expanded coverage of gender and social history.
- **Chapter 6:** "Byzantium and the Orthodox World: Byzantium, Eastern Europe, and Russia, 325–1500" has been revised to stress the independent development of East Rome and includes enhanced information on the development of the Balkan States.
- **Chapter 9:** "The European Middle Ages: 476–1348 C.E." combines the tenth edition's Chapter 9 and Chapter 10, examining the political, religious, and social history of the entire European Middle Ages in one chapter rather than two.
- **Chapter 10:** "Culture, Power, and Trade in the Era of Asian Hegemony, 220–1350" and **Chapter 13:** "East Asian Cultural and Political Systems, 1300–1650" have been thoroughly revised and expanded, with particular attention to gender and social history.
- **Chapter 14:** "European Cultural and Religious Transformations: The Renaissance and the Reformation 1300–1600" combines the tenth edition's Chapter 15 and Chapter 16, exploring the political, religious, and social connections between the European Renaissance and Reformation in one chapter rather than two.
- **Chapter 15:** "The Development of the European State System: 1300–1650" is a new chapter that examines the growth of the European nation-states from the late Middle Ages through the religious wars of the seventeenth century.
- **Chapter 17:** "Politics in the First Age of Capitalism: 1648–1774: Absolutism and Limited Central Power" places more emphasis on the social crises of the first phase of capitalism.
- Reorganized **Chapter 18:** "New Ideas and Their Political Consequences: The Scientific Revolution,

the Enlightenment and the French Revolutions" combines the tenth edition's Chapter 19 and with content from Chapter 22, as the authors believethat intellectual transformations represented by the Enlightenment are directly connected to the political upheavals of French Revolutions and so should be discussed as such in one chapter.

- A recast **Chapter 19:** "Africa, 1650–1850" provides detailed coverage of Africa, including the Atlantic Slave Trade, Islamic Africa, the settlement of South Africa by Africans and Europeans, and state formation in the east and northeast of the continent.
- A recast **Chapter 20:** "Asian and Middle Eastern Empires and Nations, 1650–1815" examines political, social, and cultural developments across Asia, including the Ottoman Empire, Persia, India, China, Korea, Japan, Southeast Asia, and the Pacific.
- **Chapter 21:** "The Americas, 1650–1825: From European Dominance to Independence" offers expanded treatment of the Haitian Revolution.
- Reorganized **Chapter 22:** "Industrialization: Social, Political, and Cultural Transformations," focuses exclusively on the social, ideological, religious, and cultural effects of the Industrial Revolutions in Great Britain, Continental Europe, and the United States.•
- **Chapter 23:** "Africa and the Middle East During the Age of European Imperialism" provides expanded coverage of Islam and Christianity in Africa during the colonial era.
- **Chapter 24:** "Asia, 1815–1914: India, Southeast Asia, China, and Japan" provides expanded coverage of Asian civilizations, with particular emphasis on gender and social history.
- **Chapter 26:** "Politics and Diplomacy in the West: 1815–1914" combines the tenth edition's Chapter 23 and Chapter 27, examining the political changes in Europe between the Congress of Vienna and World War I in one chapter rather than two.
- Expanded **Chapter 28:** "The USSR, Italy, Germany, and Japan: The Failure of Democracy in the Interwar Period" adds coverage of Japan.
- A recast **Chapter 29:** "Forging New Nations in Asia, 1910 to 1950" examines political and social transformations in China, Korea, Southeast Asia, and India.
- A recast **Chapter 30:** "Emerging National Movements in the Middle East and Africa, 1920s to 1950s" explores the rising tide of nationalism in Africa and the Middle East following World War I through the start of the Cold War.
- Expanded **Chapter 31:** "World War II: Origins and Consequences, 1919–1946" adds coverage of

the postwar settlements that followed the defeat of the Axis powers in 1945.

- Reorganized **Chapter 32:** "The Bipolar World: Cold War and Decolonization 1945–1991" prefaces its examination of the Cold War by examining the competing economic systems of the United States and the USSR. It also provides a more detailed treatment of decolonization and its relationship to the Cold War.
- Reorganized **Chapter 33:** "The United States and Europe Since 1945: Politics in an Age of Conflict and Change" now stresses the relationship between technology and social change in the United States and Europe and also provides expanded coverage of the Soviet Union and the Russian Republic.
- Reorganized **Chapter 35:** "Asia Since 1945: Political, Economic, and Social Revolutions" integrates coverage of China, Hong Kong, Taiwan, and Singapore.

The eleventh edition of *Civilization Past & Present* is a thorough revision in both its narrative and its pedagogical features. It is intended to provide the reader with an understanding of the legacies of past eras and to illuminate the way in which the study of world history gives insight into the genesis, nature, and direction of global civilization. Given the growing interdependence of the world's nations, the need for this perspective has never been greater.

NEW SPLIT

The split for the two-volume edition has changed for the eleventh edition: Volume I, To 1650, contains Chapters 1–16; Volume II, From 1300, contains Chapters 12–35. The start of Volume II at 1300 accommodates those courses that cover materials beginning earlier than 1650. The eleventh edition also includes a three-volume split edition for schools operating on the quarter system: Volume A, To 1500, contains Chapters 1–11; Volume B, From 500–1815, contains Chapters 9–20; and Volume C, From 1775, contains Chapters 18–35.

FEATURES AND PEDAGOGY

The text has been developed with the dual purpose of helping students acquire a solid knowledge of past events and, equally important, of helping them think more constructively about the significance of those events for the complex times in which we now live. A number of pedagogical features—some well tested in earlier editions and lightly revised here, and a few new ones—will assist students in achieving these goals.

MIGRATION

Why do people move from one place to another?

The history of migration is in a sense the history of humankind. All migrations involve the movement of peoples, cultures, languages, and ideas. As a result, they have shaped history around the world and played a major role in the growth of civilization. The reasons why people migrate vary. Changing environmental conditions, population pressures, economic shifts, political and religious controversies, and war and violence have all compelled people to move from one place to another. Whatever the triggering circumstance may be, the decision to migrate is ultimately driven by the human necessity or desire to find a better or more secure place to live.

Migrations have been an integral part of human experience since our early ancestors took their first tentative steps on the African savanna and began exploring and adapting to new environments. *Homo erectus* migrated from the African continent to Eurasia. Members of *Homo sapiens* followed their predecessor out of Africa and traveled further still, showing considerable ingenuity in overcoming obstacles such as the open sea to reach Australia and the cold of the northern latitudes to traverse the Bering Strait and enter the Americas.

These earliest human movements were small in scale. Extended families or clans would move into a new area and live off the land. Even with small populations, humans often placed considerable environmental strain on the land after only a short time. From 3000 B.C.E. to 500 C.E., Bantu communities migrating into central, eastern, and southern Africa could cultivate an area for only a few years before the soils were exhausted and they had to move to new land.

While environmental degradation caused by human activity has often forced people to migrate, so too have acts of nature such as droughts, floods, cold spells, and crop failures. Severe drought from around 1300 to 1100 B.C.E. likely initiated political disruptions in the eastern Mediterranean and the migrations of the Sea Peoples, Philistines, Sicilians, Sardinians, and Etruscans that followed.[1] More recently, potato blight destroyed the potato crop in Ireland between 1846 and 1850, creating widespread famine and economic hardship.

New! *Global Issues* **Essays** These new essays explore seven topics of unique transcultural and transhistorical significance: Migration, Religion and Government, Location and Identity, Technological Exchange, Slavery, Gender, and War and International Law. Each essay employs examples that span both history and the world's many civilizations. As pedagogical tools, the essays are intended to do more than just inform students about global topics; they also reveal challenges that have confronted and still confront civilizations the world over. The essays carefully avoid discussing their topics from a Western conceptual basis and instead strive to examine them using a global framework. Each essay uses art to illustrate its ideas and ends with critical thinking questions. Evenly distributed throughout the book, the essays appear on two-page spreads between chapters.

global economy due to transatlantic discoveries and the rise of oceanic merchant empires like those of the Dutch and the English.

The Age of the Köprülü Vizirs

Mehmed IV became sultan in 1648, facing rampant inflation, a Venetian blockade of the Dardanelles, rebellion in the provinces, and a violent struggle among palace factions, including his mother, Turhan (TOOR-hahn) Sultan, and her rival, the old Valide Sultan Kösem (KOO-sem). These senior women wielded considerable influence and controlled considerable wealth in the palace system. In 1651 Turhan ended Kösem's long-term dominance of the harem by having her strangled, but Mehmed remained enmeshed in factional politics. This internal strife was compounded by a vehement struggle between groups of conservative mullahs representing the *ulama* (oo-LAH-mah) and **sufis,** both of which were contending for spiritual authority and influence in the capital. By 1656 Istan-

ulama—Islamic religious authorities; men versed in Islamic sciences and law.

sufis—Islamic mystics who sought contact with Allah through prayer and ritual dance; considered a heretical movement by conservative Muslims.

New! Pronunciation Guide This new feature will help students correctly pronounce key foreign words. Pronunciations appear in parentheses immediately after the first use of a key foreign term in the text.

New! On-page Glossary This new feature provides students with concise definitions of key historical terms. Glossary definitions appear in the footer of the page in which they are discussed.

CHAPTER
10

Culture, Power, and Trade in the Era of Asian Hegemony, 220–1350

Chapter Opening Pages Chapter opening pages again feature an illustration relevant to a major chapter topic, a chapter outline, and a newly designed, easy-to-read chronology of key events—political, social, religious, and cultural—that are discussed in the chapter. Students can easily refer back to the timeline as they read the chapter.

A short text introduction previews the civilizations and themes to be discussed in the chapter. The chronology then sets the major topics within a framework easy for the student to comprehend at a glance. Chapter opening images reflect a wide range of genres, including sculpture, painting, mosaics, tapestries, and illuminated manuscripts. The images have been carefully selected to invoke a particular culture and engage the student visually.

CHAPTER CONTENTS

- India in the Classical and Medieval Eras
  DOCUMENT: *Faxian: A Chinese Buddhist Monk in Gupta India*
- China: Cultural and Political Empires
  DOCUMENT: *Bo Juyi (772–846): "The Song of Everlasting Sorrow"*

DISCOVERY THROUGH MAPS: *Gog and Magog in the Ebstorf Mappamundi*
- Korea: From Three Kingdoms to One
- The Emergence of Japan in East Asia
  DOCUMENT: *Sei Shônagon: The Pillow Book*

Asia served as an incubator and transmitter of cultures and religions with global reach from 220 to 1350. As empires consolidated and expanded their boundaries, trade and commerce accompanied cultural diffusion. Human cultures had long migrated globally, but during this long millennium, the pace of international contacts accelerated. Religions, philosophies, and arts deepened their roots in areas that had spawned them, and at the same time, new ideas spread throughout the region.

The first half millennium was, in some ways, Asia's Buddhist Age. In South Asia, Hinduism, and in East Asia, Daoism and Confucianism as well as indigenous religions continued to play important roles. But a Buddhist traveler from East Asia would find co-religionists in lands with remarkably distinct cultures. Buddhism was spread by both missionary activity and commercial activity along the Silk Roads. The second half of the millennium was likewise influenced by a global religion—Islam. South and Southeast Asian rulers either adopted Islam or resisted it, and power and trade networks were influenced by Islamic missionary and commercial activities. China and Northeast Asia felt the impact of nomadic cultures throughout the millennium, and in the twelfth and thirteenth centuries much of East and Central Asia was integrated into a trade and power network controlled by originally nomadic Mongols. Disease—bubonic plague—took advantage of these networks to spread the hand of death throughout Eurasia in the mid-fourteenth century, and ironically, fatally weakened the Mongols, whose dominance in China created fourteenth-century globalism. While Asian power and culture were in many ways hegemonic until that time and Asia would

300
c. 300 Yamato clan emerges in central Japan
320–515 Gupta dynasty in India
380s Buddhism adopted in Korea

400
439–534 Northern Wei dynasty in China

500
515 Huna seize northwestern India

600
606–647 Reign of Harsha in north India
618–907 Tang dynasty in China
676 Tang driven out of Korea; Silla unifies Korea

700
710–784 Nara period in Japan
755–763 An Lushan Rebellion in China
788–820 Hindu philosopher Shankara
794–1181 Heian period in Japan

900
900–1279 Song dynasty in China
c. 978–1016 Murasaki Shikibu, writer of *The Tale of Genji*

1100
1130–1200 Zhu Xi, Neo-Confucian scholar in China
1185 Minamoto clan establishes Kamakura Shogunate in Japan

1200

The Great Schism of the Roman Catholic Church

In response to pressure from churchmen, rulers, scholars, and commoners throughout Europe, the papacy returned to Rome in 1377, it seemed for a time that its credibility would be regained. However, the reverse proved true. In the papal election held the following year, the **College of Cardinals** elected an Italian pope. A few months later the French cardinals declared the election invalid and elected a French pope, who returned to Avignon. During the Great **Schism** (1378–1417), as the split of the church into two allegiances was called, there were two popes, each with his college of cardinals and capital city, each claiming complete authority, each sending out papal administrators and collecting taxes, and each excommunicating the other. The nations of Europe gave allegiance as their individual political interests influenced them.

The Great Schism continued after the original rival popes died, and each group elected a replacement. Doubt and confusion caused many Europeans to question the legitimacy and holiness of the church as an institution.

The Conciliar Movement

Positive action came in the form of the Conciliar Movement. In 1395 the professors at the University of Paris proposed that a general council, representing the entire church, should meet to heal the schism. A majority of the cardinals of both factions accepted this solution, and in 1409 they met at the Council of Pisa,

The Conciliar Movement represented a reforming and democratizing influence in the church. But the movement was not to endure, even though the Council of Constance had decreed that general councils were superior to popes and that they should meet at regular intervals in the future. Taking steps to preserve his authority, the pope announced that to appeal to a church council without having first obtained papal consent was heretical. Together with the inability of later councils to bring about much-needed reform and with lack of support for such councils by secular

Religious Reforms and Reactions

1415	John Hus, Bohemian reformer, burned at the stake
1437–1517	Cardinal Ximenes carried out reforms of Spanish Catholic Church
c. 1450	Revival of witchcraft mania in Europe
1452–1498	Savonarola attempted religious purification of Florence
1483–1546	Martin Luther
1484–1531	Ulrich Zwingli, leader of Swiss Reformation
1491–1556	Ignatius Loyola, founder of Society of Jesus (Jesuits)
1509–1564	John Calvin, leader of Reformation in Geneva
1515–1582	St. Teresa of Avila, founder of Carmelite religious order
1517	Luther issues Ninety-Five Theses
1521	Luther declared an outcast by the Imperial Diet at Worms
1534–1549	Pontificate of Paul III
1545–1563	Council of Trent
1561–1593	Religious wars in France

College of Cardinals—Cardinals are the highest-ranking churchmen serving under the pope in the Catholic Church. Collectively, they constitute the Sacred College of Cardinals, and their duties include electing the pope, acting as his principal counselors, and aiding in governing the church.

Schism—Literally a split or division (from the Greek *schizein* = to split). The word is usually used in reference to the Great Schism (1378–1417), when there were two, and later three, rival popes, each with his own College of Cardinals.

Chronology Tables Throughout each chapter, brief chronology tables once again highlight the major events occurring within a text section. Whether focusing on general trends, as does Religious Reforms and Reactions (Chapter 14), or on a single country, as does China in the Imperialist Era (Chapter 24), the chronology tables give the student an immediate summary view of a topic, at its point of discussion.

Discovery Through Maps This special feature focusing on primary maps in many chapters offers a unique historical view—be it local, city, country, world, or imagined—of the way a particular culture looked at the world at a particular time. Students tend to take the orientation of a map for granted; however, "An Islamic Map of the World" (Chapter 7) makes clear that not all peoples make the same assumptions. The world map of the famous Arab cartographer al-Idrisi is oriented, as was common at the time, with south at the top. Chapter 19's "The Myth of the Empty Land" shows how European settlers of South Africa laid claim to the South African interior by asserting that they were moving into an unpopulated area.

The discussions accompanying these maps have been expanded to emphasize their connection with the text itself; the addition of review questions help students better understand the concepts presented by the maps.

Discovery Through Maps

Map of China's Ancient Heartland, circa 1500 C.E.

It is one of the marks of human nature that the center of the world is found in one's self-consciousness, and then in concentric circles in the family, community, and nation. This trait extends across civilizations and continents and can be seen not only in this Chinese map depicting the area known as the *Zhongyuan* (ZHONG-yoo-AHN) or heartland of ancient China, but also in maps created around the same time by Europeans as they made their voyages of discovery. The Chinese map is particularly informative because it reminds its viewers that even within China itself, the heartland was the repository of culture and power.

The map has political implications, in that it shows its viewers that the original heartland of China was the same place as the home of the Ming. This portrayal is difficult, however, for those trained to see geography in terms of a Mercator projection (see, e.g., p. 467). The Mercator projection, like the Ming map, also reflects a worldview that places the map's creators in the center—in the Mercator case, the center is in Europe. Is there any particular reason, for example, why the Greenwich Meridian (from which all longitudes on the surface of the earth are presently measured) should be the central part of the world's geography.

Excerpts from Primary Source Documents Seventeen of the more than 100 primary source documents are new. In "Muslim and Christian: Two Contemporary Perspectives" (Chapter 9), first the Christian knight, then the Muslim physician, write of the bloody fall of Jerusalem with the certainty of religious justification for his cause, and of cultural superiority. Simón Bolívar, in his powerful Proclamation to the People of Venezuela (Chapter 21), addresses his fellow-countrymen to reestablish a republican form of government in the state.

Almost every chapter now includes a document concerning the status of women in general during a particular era or details the accomplishments of a specific woman. In Chapter 35, Benazir Bhutto, Pakistan's first female prime minister, relates the dilemma of being a "foreign" student at Harvard during an era of political turmoil for both Pakistan and the United States.

Headnotes to all have been expanded to better link the documents to the text itself. Several discussion questions now follow each excerpt.

Document   Letter from Abigail Adams

Abigail Adams, with her husband John, served as the embodiment of the American republican virtues of plain speaking, lack of ostentation, and sometimes brutal honesty. Her letter to her husband speaks to the openness and strength of their relationship. Her spelling represents the usage of the time.

31 Mar. 1776

I wish you would ever write me a Letter half as long as I write you; and tell me if you may where your Fleet are gone? What sort of Defence Virginia can make against our common Enemy? Whether it is so situated as to make an able Defence? Are not the Gentry Lords and the common people vassals, are they not like the uncivilized Natives Brittain represents us to be? I hope their Riffel Men who have shewen themselves very savage and even Blood thirsty; are not a specimen of the Generality of the people.

I am willing to allow the Colony great merrit for having produced a Washington but they have been shamefully duped by a Dunmore.

I have sometimes been ready to think that the passion for Liberty cannot be Eaquelly Strong in the Breasts of those who have been accustomed to deprive their fellow Creatures of theirs. Of this I am certain that it is not founded upon that generous and christian principal of doing to others as we would that others should do unto us. . . .

I long to hear that you have declared an independancy—and by the way in the new Code of Laws which I suppose it will be necessary for you to make I desire you would Remember the Ladies, and be more generous and favourable to them than your ancestors. Do not put such unlimited power into the hands of the Husbands. Remember all Men would be tyrants if they could. If perticular care and attention is not paid to the Laidies we are determined to foment a Rebellion, and will not hold ourselves bound by any Laws in which we have no voice, or Representation.

That your Sex are Naturally Tyrannical is a Truth so thoroughly established as to admit of no dispute, but such of you as wish to be happy willingly give up the harsh title of Master for the more tender and endearing one of Friend. Why then, not put it out of the power of the vicious and the Lawless to use us with cruelty and indignity with impunity. Men of Sense in all Ages abhor those customs which treat us only as the vassals of your Sex. Regard us then as Beings placed by providence under your protection and in immitation of the Supreem Being make use of that power only for our happiness.

Questions to Consider

1. Why does Abigail Adams fear that the coming political changes will not benefit women?

2. What is Adams's rationale for her critique of the way men sometimes go about doing business?

3. Would Abigail Adams think her descendants living today have fulfilled her hopes for a "proper" place for women in society?

From Abigail Smith Adams, *The Book of Abigail and John: Selected Letters of the Adams Family, 1762–1784*, eds. L. H. Butterfield, et al. (Cambridge, Mass.: Harvard University Press, 1975).

254   CIVILIZATION PAST AND PRESENT

tapping Muslim trading networks. The kingdom of Aksum became a major Red Sea power, serving as a bridge between the Mediterranean and the Indian Ocean. The Swahili city-states on the East African coast and the states of the Zimbabwe Plateau carried on extensive relations with Indian Ocean trading networks. West African savanna kingdoms created the most extensive trading network through their position overseeing trade between North Africa, the savanna, and forest regions to the south. However, within these long-distance trading networks, African states were primarily producers of raw materials.

Although most Africans remained faithful to their traditional religious beliefs and practices, many con-

verted to Christianity and Islam in specific areas. Egypt became an early center of Christianity, while Ethiopia's rulers firmly established Christianity as their kingdom's state religion. Islam became the dominant religion of North Africa, while some rulers and traders in the West African savanna, northeastern Africa, and along the Swahili coast adopted Islam. However, until the eighteenth century, Islam remained primarily a religion of court and commerce in sub-Saharan Africa. It won few followers in small-scale societies that did not have ruling elites. This pattern is similar to other places such as Indonesia where Muslim traders established themselves but did not initially win many converts.

Suggestions for Web Browsing

You can obtain more information about topics included in this chapter at the websites listed below. See also the companion website that accompanies this text, http://www.ablongman.com/brummett, which contains an online study guide and additional resources.

Internet African History Sourcebook
http://www.fordham.edu/halsall/africa/africasbook.html
Extensive online source for links about the history of ancient Africa, including the kingdoms of Ghana, Mali, and Songhai.

Art of Benin
http://www.si.edu/ofg/Units/sorsnmafa.htm
Site of the Smithsonian Institution's National Museum of African Art displays art objects from the kingdom of Benin before Western dominance.

Great Zimbabwe
http://www.mc.maricopa.edu/~reffland/anthropology/anthro2003/legacy/africa/zimbabwe/
A 23-slide series, with commentary, that will take you through the ruins of Great Zimbabwe in southern Africa.

The Story of Africa
http://www.bbc.co.uk/worldservice/africa/features/storyofafrica/index.shtml
The radio service of the BBC presents a history of Africa from the origins of humankind to modern nation-states.

African Voices
http://www.mnh.si.edu/africanvoices/

Suggestions for Reading

The best detailed coverage of African history can be found in two multivolume series, each containing chapters by leading scholars: *The Cambridge History of Africa*, 8 Vols. (Cambridge University Press, 1982–1984) and *The UNESCO General History of Africa*. Among other general surveys of African history are Robert July, *A History of the African People*, 4th ed. (Waveland Press, 1992); Erik Gilbert and Jonathan Reynolds, *Africa in World History from Prehistory to the Present* (Pearson Education, 2004); and Christopher Ehret, *The Civilizations of Africa: A History to 1800* (University Press of Virginia, 2002).

The best general reference work on early African history is Joseph Vogel, ed., *Encyclopedia of Precolonial Africa: Archaeology, History, Languages, Cultures, and Environments* (AltaMira Press, 1997). Another general work that examines Africa's history with a disciplinary focus is James Newman, *The Peopling of Africa: A Geographic Interpretation* (Yale University Press, 1995). A general synthesis on women in African history is Iris Berger and E. Frances White, *Women in Sub-Saharan Africa: Restoring the history of Ethiopian royal literature, see G. W. B. Huntingford, ed., Royal Chronicles of Abyssinia: The Glorious Victories of Amu Seyon King of Ethiopia* (Clarendon Press, 1965).

Caravans of Gold (Home Vision, 1984) treats the gold trade between the Sudanic kingdoms of West Africa and the Muslim and European worlds. It is one film in an eight-part series, *Africa: The Story of a Continent*, presented by Basil Davidson, a British writer on African issues. *Lost Cities of the South* (PBS, 1999) presents a discussion of African civilizations of southern Africa, such as Mapungubwe and Great Zimbabwe. It is part of a six-part series, *Wonders of the African World*, narrated by Harvard professor Henry Louis Gates, Jr.

Suggestions for Reading To give the student an additional view of the various cultures and time-frames, a *Literature and Film* section at the end of each chapter offers a listing of novels, poetry, films, and videos. Readings have been updated and carefully trimmed of dated entries. Students can consult these general interpretations, monographs, and collections of traditional source materials to expand their understanding of a particular topic or to prepare reports and papers. *Suggestions for Web Browsing* have also been updated throughout.

---

silkworms were smuggled out of China about 550 C.E., silk production flourished and became a profitable state monopoly. The state paid close attention to business: controlling the economy through a system of guilds to which all tradesmen and members of professions belonged; setting wages, profits, work hours, and prices; and even organizing bankers and doctors into compulsory corporations.

Justinian and Theodora

The dream of reclaiming the Mediterranean basin and reestablishing the Roman Empire to its former glory, however, did not die until the end of the reign of Justinian (r. 527–565). Aided by his forceful wife, Theodora, and a corps of competent assistants, he made long-lasting contributions to Byzantine and Western civilization, but gained only short-term successes in his foreign policy.

In the 520s and 530s, after earthquakes devastated much of his realm, Justinian carried out a massive

Emperor Justinian. Justinian bequeathed a splendid architectural and legal legacy to Europe. However, his attempt to reclaim the former glory of the Roman Empire gained only temporary success and bankrupted his treasury.

CHAPTER 6 • *Byzantium and the Orthodox World*   171

project of urban renewal throughout the empire. He strengthened the walls defending Constantinople and built the monumental Hagia Sophia, which still stands. Forty windows circle the base of this great church's dome, producing a quality of light that creates the illusion that the ceiling is floating.

Justinian also reformed the government and ordered a review of all Roman law. This project led to the publication of the **Code of Justinian**, a digest of Roman and church law, texts, and other instructional materials that became the foundation of modern Western law. Following Constantine's example, Justinian saw himself as the thirteenth apostle and par-

---

Photographs The text's more than 500 photos, most in full color, have been carefully revised to present a diverse range of images from all of the world's civilizations. Special care has again been taken to include images of the lifestyles and contributions of women for all eras and areas.

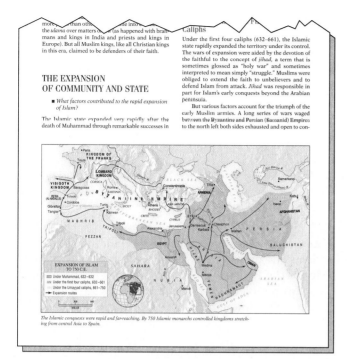

more... than oth... ...e into...
the *ulama* over matters o... ...(as happened with brahmans and kings in India and priests and kings in
Europe). But all Muslim kings, like all Christian kings
in this era, claimed to be defenders of their faith.

THE EXPANSION OF COMMUNITY AND STATE

■ *What factors contributed to the rapid expansion of Islam?*

The Islamic state expanded very rapidly after the
death of Muhammad through remarkable successes in

Caliphs
Under the first four caliphs (632–661), the Islamic
state rapidly expanded the territory under its control.
The wars of expansion were aided by the devotion of
the faithful to the concept of *jihad*, a term that is
sometimes glossed as "holy war" and sometimes
interpreted to mean simply "struggle." Muslims were
obliged to extend the faith to unbelievers and to
defend Islam from attack. *Jihad* was responsible in
part for Islam's early conquests beyond the Arabian
peninsula.

But various factors account for the triumph of the
early Muslim armies. A long series of wars waged
between the Byzantine and Persian (Sasanid) Empires
to the north left both sides exhausted and open to con-

The Islamic conquests were rapid and far-reaching. By 750 Islamic monarchs controlled kingdoms stretching from central Asia to Spain.

Maps The use of full color allows students more readily to see distinctions on the more than 100 maps in
the text. Some maps make clear the nature of a single
distinctive event; others illustrate larger trends. For
example, Trade and Cultural Interchange, c. 50 B.C.E.
(Chapter 2), makes clear that an interconnected world
economy existed long before the advent of modern
communication and technology. The specific focus of
The Persian Gulf Region, c. 1900 (Chapter 23), fore-
tells some of today's complexities in this area of the
world. A caption accompanying each map highlights
the significance of the map and its relevance to a specific text topic. Many of the maps have been revised,
updated, and/or increased in size. Most of the maps
also include insets that show where their territory fits
within a larger hemisphere or the globe.

FOR QUALIFIED COLLEGE ADOPTERS

Supplements for Instructors

MyHistoryLab With the best of Longman's multimedia solutions for history in one easy-to-use place,
MyHistoryLab offers students and instructors a state-
of-the-art interactive instructional solution for the
World History survey course. Delivered in Course
Compass™, Blackboard™, or WebCT™, MyHistory-
Lab is designed to be used as a supplement to a traditional lecture course, or to administer a completely
online course. MyHistoryLab provides helpful tips,
review materials, and activities to make the study of
history an enjoyable learning experience. Icons in the
book lead students to specific assets.

MyHistoryLab includes the following features, all
organized according to the text's table of contents:

- **E-Sources:** Each chapter of the book has its own
  collection of images, individual documents, and
  case studies.
- **History Bookshelf:** Read, download, or print
  more than 20 of the most commonly assigned
  works like Plato's *The Republic*, Machiavelli's *The
  Prince*, or Confucius' *The Analects*.
- **History Toolkit:** Guided tutorials help students
  learn to analyze several types of sources.
- **Map Activities:** Each chapter contains a map
  activity in which students assess a map from the
  time period covered and take a brief geography
  quiz for the chapter.
- **Pre-Test and Post-Test Self-Study Quizzes with
  Targeted Feedback:** Two quizzes per chapter
  allow students to review their knowledge of the
  material and concepts. Chapter feedback provides
  links that take students directly to the relevant
  section of the textbook online.
- **Chapter Review Materials:** The Study Guide,
  PowerPoint™ presentations, flashcards, and other
  features will help students master the contents of
  the textbook and prepare for exams.
- **The Textbook Online:** Students can read the
  book online, or print out sections of the book to
  read anywhere.
- **Chapter Exam:** Each chapter has a chapter exam
  whose results report to the CourseCompass™,
  Blackboard™, or WebCT™ online gradebook.
- **Test Bank:** Create your own exams using the Test
  Bank from your text, and place them right in
  MyHistoryLab for your students to take as prac-
  tice quizzes or as graded exams.
- **The Tutor Center:** On-call qualified help is avail-
  able to answer student questions about MyHisto-
  ryLab when an instructor may not be available.
  The Tutor Center is open Sunday through Thurs-
  day from 5 PM to midnight, EST.
- **Unlimited use of Pearson's Research Naviga-
  tor™:** The EBSCO ContentSelect, Academic
  Journal & Abstract Database, *The New York Times*
  Search by Subject Archive, "Best of the Web"
  Link Library, and *Financial Times* Article Archive
  and Company Financials offer thousands of credible and reliable articles and websites to get the
  research process started.
- **A wealth of instructor support material:** Text-
  specific materials, such as instructor's manuals,
  test banks, and PowerPoint™ presentations sim-
  plify and enrich the teaching experience.

www.LongmanWorldHistory.com This website offers
all the best of MyHistoryLab without course management features or the online e-book. As with MyHisto-

ryLab, icons in the book lead students to specific assets on the website.

Instructor's Manual by Rick Whisonant of Winthrop University. This collection of resources includes chapter outlines, definitions, discussion suggestions, critical thinking exercises, term paper and essay topics, and audiovisual suggestions.

Companion Website (www.ablongman.com/brummett).This online course companion provides a wealth of resources for both students and instructors using *Civilization Past & Present,* Eleventh Edition. Students will find chapter summaries, test questions, and links for further research.

SafariX. SafariX Textbooks Online is an exciting new choice for students looking to save money. As an alternative to purchasing the print textbook, students can subscribe to the same content online and save up to 50% off the suggested list price of the print text. With a SafariX WebBook, students can search the text, make notes online, print out reading assignments that incorporate lecture notes, and bookmark important passages for later review. For more information, or to subscribe to the SafariX Web Book, visit www.safarix.com.

Test Bank and Test Generator by Susan Hellert of the University of Wisconsin at Platteville. This easy-to-customize test bank presents a wealth of multiple-choice, true-false, short-answer, and essay questions. Free to qualified college adopters.

Civilization Past & Present PowerPoint™ Presentations. Updated by Pamela Marquez of Metropolitan State College of Denver, these easy-to-customize Power-Point™ slides outline key points of each chapter of the text and are available for download from the Companion Website (www.ablongman.com/brummett). Free to qualified college adopters.

The History Digital Media Archive CD-ROM. This CD-ROM contains hundreds of images, maps, interactive maps, and audio/video clips ready for classroom presentation, or downloading into PowerPoint™ or any other presentation software. Free to qualified college adopters.

Overhead Transparency Acetates to Accompany Civilization Past & Present. These text-specific acetates are available to all adopters. Every map is represented. Free to qualified college adopters.

Guide to Teaching World History by Palmira Brummett of the University of Tennessee at Knoxville. This guide offers explanations of major issues and themes in world history, sample syllabi and instructions on how to create a manageable syllabus, ideas for cross-cultural and cross-temporal connections, a pronunciation guide, and tips on getting through all the material. Free to qualified college adopters.

Discovering World History Through Maps and Views Overhead Transparency Acetates by Gerald Danzer of the University of Illinois at Chicago. This unique resource contains more than 100 full-color acetates of beautiful reference maps, source maps, urban plans, views, photos, art, and building diagrams. Free to qualified college adopters.

Longman World History Atlas Overhead Transparency Acetates. These acetates are available to instructors who select the *Longman World History Atlas* for their students. Free to qualified college adopters.

Historical Newsreel Video. This 90-minute video contains newsreel excerpts examining U.S. involvement in world affairs over the past 60 years. Free to qualified college adopters.

Longman-Penguin Putnam Inc. Value Bundles. Students and professors alike will love the value and quality of the Penguin books offered at a deep discount when bundled with *Civilization Past & Present,* Eleventh Edition, for qualified college adopters.

Supplements for Students

Companion Website (www.ablongman.com/brummett). This online course companion provides a wealth of resources for both students and instructors using *Civilization Past & Present,* Eleventh Edition. Students will find chapter summaries, test questions, and links for further research.

Student Study Guide in two volumes: Volume 1 (Chapters 1–17) and Volume 2 (Chapters 13–35) revised by Norman Love of El Paso Community College. Each chapter includes chapter overviews, lists of themes and concepts, map exercises, multiple-choice practice tests, and critical thinking and essay questions.

Study Card for World History. Colorful, affordable, and packed with useful information, the *Study Card for World History* makes studying easier, more efficient, and more enjoyable. Course information is distilled down to the basics, helping students quickly master the fundamentals, review a subject for understanding, or prepare for an exam. Because they are laminated for durability, Study Cards can be kept for years to come and be pulled out whenever they are needed for a quick review.

Mapping World History. This workbook was created for use in conjunction with *Discovering World History Through Maps and Views.* Designed to teach students to interpret and analyze cartographic materials as historical documents.

World History Map Workbooks, Second Edition, Volumes I and II. These workbooks, created by Glee Wilson, Kent State University, are designed to explain the correlations between historical events and geography through assignments that involve reading and interpreting maps.

Longman World History Atlas. A comprehensive collection of historical maps that reflects truly global coverage of world history. Each of the atlas's 56 maps are designed to be readable, informative, and accurate as well as beautiful.

Longman Library of World Biography Series. Each interpretive biography in the new Library of World Biography series focuses on a figure whose actions and ideas significantly influenced the course of world history. Pocket-sized and brief, each book relates the life of its subject to the broader themes and developments of the times. Series titles include:

- *Alexander the Great: Legacy of a Conqueror* by Winthrop Lindsay Adams, University of Utah
- *Benito Mussolini: The First Fascist* by Anthony L. Cardoza, Loyola University of Chicago
- *Fukuzawa Yukichi: From Samurai to Capitalist* by Helen M. Hopper, University of Pittsburg
- *Ignatius of Loyola: Founder of the Jesuits* by John Patrick Donnelly, Marquette University
- *Jacques Coeur: Entrepreneur and King's Bursar* by

Kathryn L. Reyerson, University of Minnesota
- *Kato Shidzue: A Japanese Feminist* by Helen M. Hopper, University of Pittsburg
- *Simón Bolívar: Liberation and Disappointment* by David Bushnell, University of Florida
- *Vasco da Gama: Renaissance Crusader* by Glenn J. Ames, University of Toledo

Longman World History Series. These books focus on the historical significance of a particular movement, experience, or interaction. Concise and inexpensive, they bring the global connections and consequences of these events to the fore, showing students how events that happened long ago or far away can still affect them. Titles include:

- *Colonial Encounters in the Age of High Imperialism* by Scott B. Cook, Rhode Island School of Design.
- *Environmentalism: A Global History* by Ramachandra Guha
- *Expansion and Global Interaction: 1200–1700* by David Ringrose, University of California at San Diego

ACKNOWLEDGMENTS

A special note of appreciation goes to the following reviewers for providing thorough and expert advice for the *Global Issues* essays. Their suggestions have been of tremendous help in the writing of this new feature:

Milan Andrejevich
Indiana University Northwest

Charles E. Bashaw
College of Charleston

Kevin W. Caldwell
Blue Ridge Community College

Peter Fraunholtz
Northeastern University

James C. Godwin II
University of Delaware

Elizabeth P. Hancock
Gainesville College

Frank Karpiel
College of Charleston

Thomas O. Kay
Wheaton College

Laurence W. Marvin
Berry College

Donald T. McGuire
SUNY Buffalo

Fannie T. Rushing
Benedictine University

Mark B. Tauger
West Virginia University

Rick Whisonant
Winthrop University

We are most grateful to the following reviewers who gave generously of their time and knowledge to provide thoughtful evaluations and many helpful suggestions for the revision of this edition.

Henry Abramson
Florida Atlantic University

Lee Annis
Montgomery College—Rockville

Daniel Ayana
Youngstown State University

James W. Brodman
University of Central Arkansas

Thomas Cary
City University

Edward R. Crowther
Adams State College

Cole P. Dawson
Warner Pacific College

Dr. Michael de Nie
State University of West Georgia

Shannon L. Duffy
Loyola University New Orleans

Charles T. Evans
Northern Virginia Community College

Ronald Fritze
University of Central Arkansas

Richard M. Golden
University of North Texas

Elizabeth P. Hancock
Gainesville College

Eric J. Hanne
Florida Atlantic University

Caroline Hoefferle
Wingate University

Roger L. Jungmeyer
Lincoln University of Missouri

Jeffrrey W. Myers
Avila University

William R. Rogers
Isothermal Community College

Daniel E. Schafer
Belmont University

Roger Schlesinger
Washington State University

William Seavey
East Carolina University

Deborah A. Symonds
Drake University

Mark B. Tauger
West Virginia University

Ted Weeks
Southern Illinois University

Rick Whisonant
Winthrop University

We also thank the many conscientious reviewers who reviewed previous editions of this book.

Henry Abramson
Florida Atlantic University

Wayne Ackerson
Salisbury State University

Jay Pascal Anglin
University of Southern Mississippi

Lee Annis
Montgomery County Community College—Maryland

Joseph Appiah
J. Sargeant Reynolds Community College

Michael Auslin
Yale University

Mark C. Bartusis
Northern State University

Charlotte Beahan
Murray State University

Martin Berger
Youngstown State University

Joel Berlatsky
Wilkes College

Jackie R. Booker
Kent State University

Mauricio Borrero
St. John's University

Darwin F. Bostwick
Old Dominion University

Robert F. Brinson Jr.
Santa Fe Community College

Robert H. Buchanan
Adams State College

Nancy Cade
Pikeville College

Michael L. Carrafiello
East Carolina University

James O. Catron Jr.
North Florida Junior College

Mark Chavalas
University of Wisconsin

William H. Cobb
East Carolina University

J. L. Collins
Allan Hancock College

J. R. Crawford
Montreat-Anderson College

Edward R. Crowther
Adams State College

Lawrence J. Daly
Bowling Green State University

Demoral Davis
Jackson State University

Anne Dorazio
Westchester Community College

Dawn Duensing
Maui Community College

Ellen Emerick
Georgetown College

William Edward Ezzell
Georgia Perimeter College

John D. Fair
Auburn University at Montgomery

Nancy Fitch
California State University

Robert B. Florian
Salem-Teikyo University

Nels W. Forde
University of Nebraska

Joseph T. Fuhrmann
Murray State University

Lydia Garner
Southwest Texas State University

Robert J. Gentry
University of Southwestern Louisiana

Paul George
Miami Community College, Dade

David Gleason
Armstrong Atlantic State University

Richard Golden
University of North Texas

Oliver Griffin
Weber State University

Michael Hall
Armstrong Atlantic State University

Paul Halsall
University of North Florida

Jeffrey S. Hamilton
Old Dominion University

Donald E. Harpster
College of St. Joseph

Gordon K. Harrington
Weber State University

J. Drew Harrington
Western Kentucky University

Janine Hartman
University of Cincinnati

Geoff Haywood
Beaver College

Thomas Hegarty
University of Tampa

Madonna Hettinger
McHenry County College

David Hill
McHenry County College

Conrad C. Holcomb, Jr
Surry Community College

Thomas Howell
Louisiana College

Clark Hultquist
University of Montevallo

Scott Jessee
Appalachian State University

Roger L. Jungmeyer
Lincoln University of Missouri

Daniel R. Kazmer
Georgetown University

Bernard Kiernan
Concord College

David Koeller
North Park University

Michael L. Krenn
University of Miami

Teresa Lafer
Pennsylvania State University

Harral E. Landry
Texas Women's University

George Longenecker
Norwich University

Norman Love
El Paso Community College

Marsha K. Marks
Alabama A&M University

Caroline T. Marshall
James Madison University

Eleanor McCluskey
Broward Community College

Robert McCormick
Newman University

Christopher McKay
University of Alberta

David A. Meier
Dickinson State University

Arlin Migliazzo
Whitworth College

William C. Moose
Mitchell Community College

Zachary Morgan
William Patterson University

Wayne Morris
Lees-McRae College

John G. Muncie
East Stroudsburg University

Justin Murphy
Howard Payne University

David Owusu-Ansah
James Madison University

George Pesely
Austin-Peay State

Al Pilant
Cumberland College

Jana Pisani
Texas A&M International University

Sr. Jeannette Plante, CSC
Notre Dame College

Norman Pollock
Old Dominion University

J. Graham Provan
Millikin University

George B. Pruden Jr.
Armstrong State College

John D. Ramsbottom
Northeast Missouri State University

Ruth Richard
College of Lake County

Charles Risher
Montreat College

Hugh I. Rodgers
Columbus College

Ruth Rogaski
Princeton University

William Rogers
Isothermal Community College

Patrick J. Rollins
Old Dominion University

Chad Ronnander
University of Minnesota

R. A. Rotz
Indiana University

Robert Rowland
Loyola University

Barry T. Ryan
Westmont College

Bill Schell
Murray State University

Louis E. Schmier
Valdosta State College

William M. Simpson
Louisiana College

Paul J. Smith
Haverford College

Barbara G. Sniffen
University of Wisconsin—Oshkosh

Lawrence Squeri
East Stroudsburg University

Lawrence Stanley
McHenry County College

Terrence S. Sullivan
University of Nebraska at Omaha

John Swanson
Utica College of Syracuse

Edward Tabri
Columbus State Community College

Gordon L. Teffeteller
Valdosta State College

Malcolm R. Thorp
Brigham Young University

Helen M. Tierney
University of Wisconsin—Platteville

Leslie Tischauser
Prairie State College

Arthur L. Tolson
Southern University

Joseph A. Tomberlin
Valdosta State University

Marcia Vaughan
Murray State University

Thomas Dwight Veve
Dalton College

Chris Warren
Copiah-Lincoln Community College

Mary Watrous
Washington State University

David L. White
Appalachian State University

Thomas Whigham
University of Georgia

John R. Willertz
Saginaw Valley State University

To the Student

We set two goals for ourselves when we wrote *Civilization Past & Present*. The first is to provide you with an understanding of the contributions of past eras in all parts of the globe to the shaping of world history. The second is to illuminate the way in which the study of world history gives us insights into the genesis, nature, and direction of our own civilization.

These are challenging tasks. However, given the globalization of all aspects of our lives, they are essential. When economies in East Asia or Latin America are in a state of crisis, the impact is felt on Wall Street. The culture of the New World—especially music and movies—has spread around the globe. When tragedies occur in the Middle East, we are all affected. Long gone are the days when an occurrence that took place far away could be isolated.

Now you are taking a course in world history to understand the development of the cultures of the world—cultures that are coming together to form a multifaceted world civilization. By understanding how and why other civilizations have chosen differing routes to their future, you can gain an understanding of why your part of civilization has succeeded or failed in attaining its potential. With an understanding of world history, you will be able to respond more knowledgeably to the changes through which you will live and to make informed choices as a world citizen.

History is the study of change over time. A historian is a person who focuses on one aspect of changes in the past, poses questions about why a particular event has taken place, proposes answers—hypotheses—and tests those hypotheses against the evidence—all of the evidence. We do not expect you to be historians at this point in your careers—to form your own hypotheses and write monographs. We have written this book, however, to enable you to study change over the entire course of human history.

We have included a number of tools to help you on your voyage through this text. The new **Global Issues essays** explore seven topics of unique trans-cultural and trans-historical significance: Migration, Religion and Government, Location and Identity, Technological Exchange, Slavery, Gender, and War and International Law. The essays carefully examine these topics using a global framework, employing examples that span both history and the world's many civilizations. The essays are intended to do more than just inform you about global topics; however, they also reveal challenges that have and still confront civilizations the world over.

As you begin each chapter, take five or ten minutes to look at the **chapter opening pages.** These two pages at the beginning of each chapter reveal what is to come: a photo conceptualizes a main theme of the chapter, and a chapter outline and a timeline allow you to fix beginning and end points in this part of your trip. The chapter introduction sets the stage for the content that follows and indicates the chapter's overall themes—sometimes political or economic, sometimes religious, social, or artistic. Take time to read the introduction and then thumb to the end of the chapter to read the conclusion. Next, go through the chapter reading only the main and secondary headlines. Finally, return to the beginning of the chapter and start to read—knowing in advance where you have come from and which way you are going.

Within each chapter we offer you other tools to gain an understanding of the past. Events take place in a location, and each location has particular features that affect what will happen. Thus the text includes more than 100 full-color **maps,** each with its own explanatory caption. Shaded **insets** on most of the maps help you to locate its territory on its larger hemisphere or the globe. Some maps are designed to make clear the nature of a single distinctive event; others illustrate larger trends.

Each chapter also offers new features to help you better engage with the content. The new **pronunciation guide** will help you correctly pronounce key foreign terms—after each such word within the text a pronunciation appears in parentheses. The new on-page **glossary** provides concise definitions of key historical terms and appears in the footer of the pages in which terms are discussed.

Different civilizations have different visions of themselves and their place in the world. The **Discovery Through Maps** boxes in many of the chapters will give you a notion of the way that various cultures in the world have seen themselves and their relation to the rest of the globe. For example, al-Idrisi's "An Islamic Map of the World" is oriented, as was common in Arab maps of his time, with south at the top; it is centered on the world of his own experience, the sacred city of Mecca in Arabia and the civilized realm of the Mediterranean. A late-nineteenth-century map of southern Africa perpetuated "The Myth of the Empty Land," by which white settlers would claim that they were moving into an unpopulated land and that they had just as much right to it as Africans did.

We also include one or more excerpts from **primary source documents** in each chapter. These excerpts from original sources offer you a window into the way that the people of the time expressed themselves. The documents cover a variety of viewpoints: political, economic, legal, religious, social, artistic, and popular. For example, in "That Was No Brother," two documents—one by an African chief and the other by the English explorer Henry Morton Stanley—give two very different perceptions of the same battle.

The text's 500 **photos,** most in full color, give balanced pictorial coverage of all parts of the world and enhance the reading of each chapter by giving additional context and bringing to life the matters under discussion. For this edition, we have paid special attention in these photos to the lifestyles and contributions of women.

After you have finished each chapter you will find three features to help you prepare a paper or project or simply to learn more. The **Literature and Film** listings offer a listing of novels, poetry, films, and videos. The annotated bibliographies of **Suggestions for Reading** indicate useful general studies, monographs, and source materials. Also included is a list of **Suggestions for Web Browsing** to allow you to hook up to databases, sounds, images, or discussion groups dealing with the topics under consideration.

Robert R. Edgar
Neil J. Hackett
George F. Jewsbury
Barbara Molony

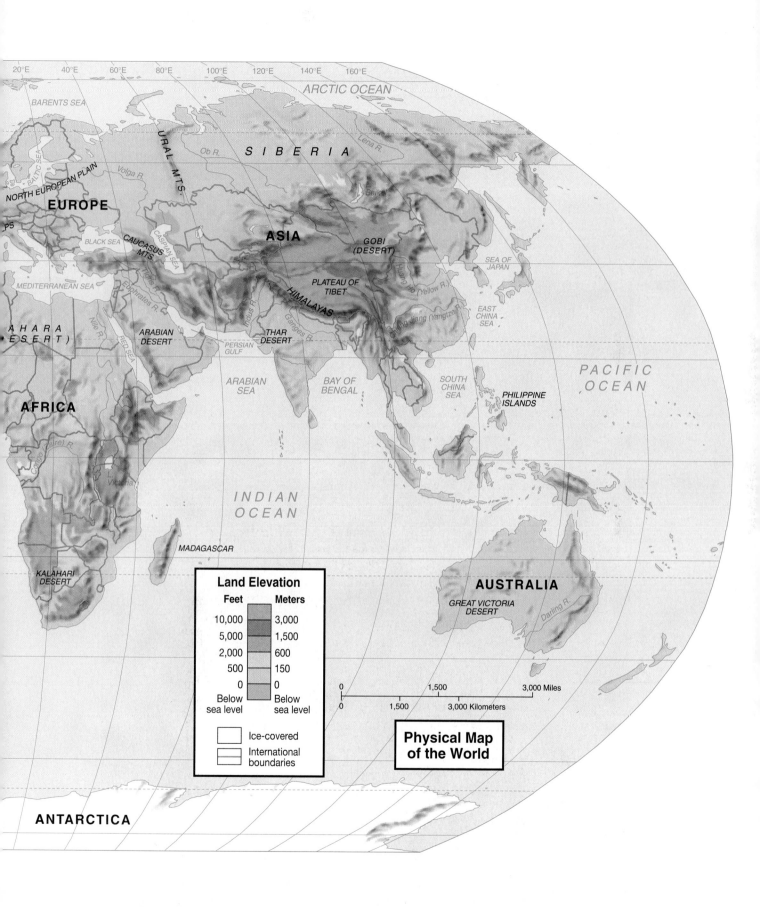

ARCTIC OCEAN

BARENTS SEA

SIBERIA

Lena R.

Ob R.

URAL MTS.

Volga R.

NORTH EUROPEAN PLAIN

Baikal

BALTIC SEA

EUROPE

PS

ASIA

BLACK SEA

CAUCASUS MTS.

CASPIAN SEA

GOBI (DESERT)

SEA OF JAPAN

MEDITERRANEAN SEA

Tigris R.

Euphrates R.

PLATEAU OF TIBET

Huang Ho (Yellow R.)

EAST CHINA SEA

SAHARA (DESERT)

Nile R.

RED SEA

ARABIAN DESERT

Indus R.

HIMALAYAS

Ganges R.

THAR DESERT

Chang Jiang (Yangtze)

PERSIAN GULF

AFRICA

ARABIAN SEA

BAY OF BENGAL

SOUTH CHINA SEA

PACIFIC OCEAN

PHILIPPINE ISLANDS

Congo (Zaire) R.

L. Victoria

INDIAN OCEAN

KALAHARI DESERT

MADAGASCAR

AUSTRALIA

GREAT VICTORIA DESERT

Darling R.

Land Elevation

Feet	Meters
10,000	3,000
5,000	1,500
2,000	600
500	150
0	0
Below sea level	Below sea level

Ice-covered

International boundaries

0   1,500   3,000 Miles

0   1,500   3,000 Kilometers

Physical Map of the World

ANTARCTICA

Stone Age Societies and the Earliest Civilizations of the Near East

This chapter begins with an overview of the evolution of humankind on the African continent and examines the longest period of human life on the planet when our earliest ancestors invented basic tools and social structures on which all succeeding cultures would build. The skills necessary for survival were mastered over many hundred millennia as humans spread around the world, culminating in the breakthrough to farming with the domestication of plants and animals, and a settled life in villages.

Over the passage of many thousands of years, human societies located throughout Africa, Asia, and Europe continued to develop distinct cultural and technological patterns of life, but change in the patterns of everyday life was something most of the earth's early cultures avoided as frightening and disruptive. Profound change, even if extremely slow in comparison to social change in our modern world, seems to have taken place first in southwestern Asia and northeastern Africa (the Near East), where social developments were accelerated especially by the development of farming and the domestication of animals. There, along the banks of great rivers, villages evolved into towns and cities, and after the fourth millennium B.C.E. the complexity and sophistication of those cultures has led experts to label them as the world's earliest civilizations. The study of these earliest civilizations should furnish us with insights into the nature of some of humankind's most ancient institutions and oldest cultural legacies.

50,000

c. 50,000 B.C.E. *Homo sapiens*

10,000

c. 10,000 End of last ice age

c. 10,000–6000 The Aquatic Age in the Sahara

8000

c. 8000 Neolithic Revolution

6000

c. 6000 Agricultural Revolution: Occupation of Çatul Hüyük

4000

c. 3200 Emergence of civilization in Mesopotamia and Egypt

c. 2800–2300 Old Sumerian Period

c. 2700–2200 Old Kingdom of Egypt (Pyramid Age)

c. 2300–2150 Akkadian Empire

c. 2050–1800 Middle Kingdom of Egypt

2000

c. 2000–1600 Old Babylonian Empire

c. 1570–1090 New Kingdom of Egypt

c. 1450–1200 Hittite Empire

c. 745–612 Assyrian Empire

c. 586–538 Babylonian Captivity of the Jews

c. 550–332 Persian Empire

3

THE ORIGINS OF HUMANKIND

■ *What role did the African environment play in the evolution of* Homo sapiens?

Who are we? Where do we come from? Human beings have probably asked these questions ever since they have had the ability to communicate through language. For thousands of years, humans turned to religion to answer such questions. Indeed, it has only been within the last 150 years that science has put forth the theory that the human species evolved out of lower life forms. The controversy surrounding the theory of evolution continues up to today, although with decreasing intensity as more and more fossil evidence comes to light supporting the theory. Of course, the fossil record will never be complete, and paleontologists (scientists who study fossil remains in order to understand the life of past geological periods) have only skeletal remains to analyze. Nevertheless, the case for evolution appears overwhelming.

According to the theory of evolution, humans belong to the Primate order, which also includes lemurs, tarsiers, monkeys, and apes. A crucial development occurred when the ape family split into branches: tree-dwelling apes and ground-dwelling apes known as *hominids* ("prehumans" or "protohumans"). Over time and in response to environmental pressures, the hominids learned to walk upright, their

legs grew longer than their arms, and their hands—no longer required for locomotion—became more dexterous. Most important, the prehuman head gradually shifted toward a more upright position, rendering superfluous much of the muscle at the back of the neck. This favored expansion of the brain, which ultimately led to modern *Homo sapiens* ("thinking man"), the only survivor of the many-branched hominid tree.

Paleontologists have discovered all of the fossil remains of the earliest ancestors of *Homo sapiens* in Africa. These include *Australopithecus africanus* (ah-STRAH-loh-pi-THEE-kuhs ah-fri-KAH-nus; "southern African ape"). First discovered in South Africa in 1924, it had an erect posture but apelike brain. In 1964 the first representative of the genus *Homo* was found at Olduvai Gorge in Tanzania at a site some 1.75 million years old. In 1973 the partial skeleton of a female named "Lucy" (for the Beatles' hit song "Lucy in the Sky with Diamonds") was found in Ethiopia and dated to about 3.8 to 3 million years ago. One of the most recent discoveries came in 1998, when South African paleontologists discovered a hominid 4 feet tall and some 3.5 million years old, whose virtually complete remains provide uniquely detailed information on the transition from ape to human.

Homo habilis ("skillful man") was the first toolmaker. Dating from about two and a half to two million years ago, *H. habilis* was less than 5 feet tall, walked

An Introduction to the Elements of the Earth

Aerial view of Olduvai Gorge in Tanzania, the site of findings by Mary Leakey and Louis S. B. Leakey, including the first representative fossils of the genus Homo.

erect, and had a well-developed opposable thumb that allowed the species to fashion tools. These fossil remains were found in association with crude tools—rocks cracked and flaked into specialized tools to cut meat and softer plants and to ward off predators. These tools expanded the nutritional options of *H. habilis*.

Later and more advanced species included *Homo ergaster*, which emerged perhaps as long as 2.3 million years ago in Africa. This species was labeled *Homo erectus* in Asia and is more widely known by that name. *H. erectus* had an upright posture, a physique very similar to modern humans, and a brain size of about 1000 cubic centimeters. *Erectus* learned to control and use fire—a major step in extending human habitation into colder latitudes—and perfected the first major standardized all-purpose tool, the Acheulean hand ax. Dubbed the Paleolithic "Swiss army knife" because it could be used for cutting, scraping, chopping, and digging, this ax remained a favorite tool long after the extinction of the species. *Erectus* was the first species to live its life primarily on the ground rather than in the trees and to demonstrate the ability to adapt to varied environments.

Around 1.6 million B.C.E. this species took the bold step of migrating out of Africa, into the Near East and Asia and eventually to the colder climate of Europe. Several theories have been advanced to explain why this movement took place out of Africa. One is that an extended dry period in the region of the present-day Sahara desert may have forced *H. erectus* to move over a wider area to collect foodstuffs. Another argument is that *H. erectus* could have moved into other regions as the species developed an ability to adapt to different environments.

From about 200,000 to 40,000 years ago, during the last ice age, a subspecies of *H. erectus*, the Neanderthals, were the principal inhabitants of Europe and spread to adjacent parts of Asia and Africa. Named for the Neander valley in western Germany where their remains were unearthed in 1856 (*thal* is the German word for "valley"), Neanderthals were slightly taller than 5 feet and had sloping foreheads, with prominent brow ridges, and thickset bodies. They were especially suited to coping with the colder climes of Europe. The inventors of many specialized tools, they were able hunters and adapted to extreme cold by using fire, wearing clothes, and living in caves. One school of thought contended that Neanderthals were the ancestors of modern Europeans until recent DNA testing of a Neanderthal skeleton showed very little overlap with the DNA of *H. sapiens*. Consequently, though sharing a common ancestor, the Neanderthals were probably not a subspecies of *sapiens*.

The culminating phase of the development of the genus *Homo* occurred around 150,000 to 100,000 years ago with the gradual emergence of *H. sapiens*. Up until a few years ago, scientists were engaged in a vigorous debate between the proponents of the "Out of Africa" school—who contend that *H. sapiens* originated exclusively in Africa and spread from there to other continents—and the multiregionalists—who argue that *H. sapiens* evolved independently in Africa, Asia, and Europe. Recent testing of mitochondrial DNA, however, strongly supports the argument for an African origin for *H. sapiens*. Mitochondrial DNA is passed on only through a mother to her offspring. By comparing DNA samples from individuals around the world and calculating the rate of mutations, geneticists have traced our human ancestors back to a hypothetical "Eve" whom they believe lived in eastern Africa some 200,000 years ago.

There is also a lively debate about the interaction between *H. sapiens* and the species of *H. erectus*. In Europe, the Cro-Magnons—*H. sapiens* named after a locality in southern France where their bones were unearthed in 1868—and Neanderthals coexisted for 50,000 years. Around 40,000 years ago, however, the Neanderthals died out, leaving the Cro-Magnons as the only hominids in Europe. Perhaps Cro-Magnons' superior brainpower and communications skills ultimately gave them a decisive advantage over Neanderthals in controlling and using food resources. We don't know for certain, but paleontologists have established that Cro-Magnon skeletons are virtually indistinguishable from those of humans today. Skillfully made flint and bone tools and polychrome paintings found on cave walls indicate that the Cro-Magnon possessed an advanced culture. By 20,000 B.C.E. Cro-Magnon and other representatives of *H. sapiens* inhabited Europe, Asia, Africa, and Australia and had moved into Americas by migrating across the Bering Strait on foot or by traveling in small boats along the coast. Today there is but one existing species of the genus *Homo*.

DOCUMENT

The Long Journey

PRELITERATE CULTURES

■ *What distinguishes Paleolithic from Neolithic culture?*

In many respects we humans are eclipsed in physical endowments by numerous other creatures—in an all-species Olympic Games, we might not qualify for a medal. We cannot compete with the strength of the elephant or the speed of the antelope on land or any number of marine creatures. Our ability to defy gravity is dwarfed by insects that can jump higher and farther in terms of their size, to say nothing of birds, whose specialized structures enable them to fly and soar. Yet, a number of attributes functioning in concert allowed our species to forge ahead of all others.

They include erect posture, an opposable thumb ideal for fashioning tools, stereoscopic and color vision capable of close visual attention, and a brain whose size and multiple capabilities have enabled it to be termed the "organ of civilization."

Like other creatures, humans possess a practical intelligence for making meaningful responses to the environment. In addition, we are capable of thinking and communicating symbolically through language. The principle of symbolism gives everything a name and makes its functioning universally applicable, rather than restricting it to particular cases. By means of this capability to engage in symbolic thought and communication, humankind has created patterns of behavior and learning that can be termed *culture*. Unlike other creatures, we live also in a symbolic universe that draws on language, myth, art and religion to express aspects of human experience.

Paleolithic Culture

Making and using tools provide the first evidence of humankind's ability to employ reason to solve problems. Stone implements were the most distinctive feature of early human culture; thus, this stage is known as the **Paleolithic** or Old Stone Age. Our earliest ancestors made use of *eoliths* ("dawn stones"), bits of

---

Paleolithic—An era associated with the early Stone Age and the use of simple stone implements and weapons.

As human beings faced an ever-expanding set of challenges to their existence, they invented even more sophisticated tools, as evidenced by these examples of Paleolithic toolmaking.

stone picked up to perform an immediate job. This simple utilization of what lay at hand was the first major step in toolmaking. The second consisted of *fashioning*, the haphazard preparation of a tool as need arose. The third step was *standardization*, making implements according to certain set traditions. It is with this third stage that we see the importance of symbolic thought in creating patterns of learning and behavior, transmitted in turn from one generation to the next.

In later Paleolithic cultures, toolmaking became progressively sophisticated and efficient. It was marked by a wide range of specialized tools and weapons, including implements whose primary purpose was to make other tools. The fashioning of small, specialized flints, known as *microliths*, represents a compact use of materials—indeed, the ancestor of present-day technological miniaturization. In late Paleolithic cultures, too, our ancestors applied mechanical principles to the movement of weapons. Throwers to launch spears worked on the lever principle to increase the propelling power of a hunter's arm. The bow was also invented to concentrate muscular energy to propel an arrow; it was soon also used to provide a means of twirling a stick, and this led to the invention of the rotary drill. Strictly speaking, *Paleolithic* is a cultural and not a chronological term. In fact, much of our knowledge of Paleolithic culture comes from groups surviving into modern times— for example, indigenous peoples in the rain forests

DOCUMENT
The Tool Maker

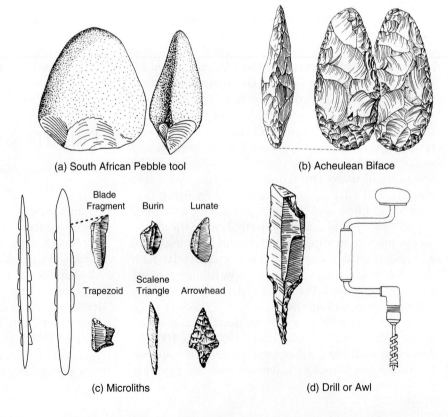

(a) South African Pebble tool

(b) Acheulean Biface

Blade Fragment   Burin   Lunate

Trapezoid   Scalene Triangle   Arrowhead

(c) Microliths

(d) Drill or Awl

Prehistoric art in Los Toldos, Argentina, includes representations of deer and hands. Archaeologists have dated the art to around 15,000 B.C.E.

of Brazil. From an economic standpoint, the Paleolithic is also a food-gathering stage, when humans hunted, fished, and collected wild foodstuffs. Labor was divided according to sex. Men hunted, fished, and protected the group. Women picked wild plants, fruits, and nuts and prepared the food for eating; they also processed animal hides and wood into household objects and cared for the children. Men and women shared such tasks as building dwellings, making ornaments and tools, and training children for adult life.

A special achievement of late Paleolithic cultures around the world was their art. For instance, animated, realistic paintings of bison, reindeer, primitive horses, and other animals, colored in shades of black, red, yellow, and brown, have been found in more than a hundred Cro-Magnon caves in Spain and France dating from about 28,000 to 10,000 B.C.E. Cave art rivals that of civilized artists not only stylistically but also as an expression of significant human experiences. Universal in appeal, the pictures reflect the Paleolithic dependence on an abundance of game animals and success in hunting them. In addition, the artists may have believed they could wield a magical power over the spirits of animals to ensure their availability. Paleolithic artists also chiseled pictures on rock and bone and modeled figures out of clay.

DOCUMENT
A Need to Remember

The Neolithic Revolution and Advent of Agriculture

A development of enormous consequence for human societies—the shift to food-producing—took place in the ancient Near East. There, on the flanks of the

mountains bordering the **Fertile Crescent,** an area of rich soil stretching northeast from the Nile River to the Tigris in what is now northern Iraq and then southeast to the Persian Gulf, was adequate rainfall to nourish wild forms of wheat and barley and provide grass for wild sheep, goats, and pigs. By 7000 B.C.E., people in that region had domesticated these grains and animals and lived in villages near their fields and herds. This momentous change ushered in the **Neolithic** or New Stone Age. The best-preserved village so far uncovered is Çatal Hüyük (chah-tahl HOO-yook; "forked mound") in southern Turkey. This 32-acre site, occupied from around 6500 to 5400 B.C.E., contains some of the most advanced features of Neolithic culture: pottery, woven textiles, mud-brick houses, shrines honoring a mother goddess, and plastered walls decorated with murals and carved reliefs. The most recent archaeological excavations at the site have raised questions about whether settled village life happened at the same time as the domestication of agriculture and whether the community had a political and religious elite.

CASE STUDY
The Neolithic Village

Neolithic artisans ground and polished stones to produce axes, adzes, and chisels with sharp cutting edges. They devised methods for drilling holes in stone, used boulders for grinding grain, and made stone bowls for storage. Skilled in their earlier role as wild food gatherers, women were responsible now for cultivating the prepared fields. They also made clay pots—decorated with geometric designs—and spun and wove textiles from cultivated flax and animal wool. The Neolithic revolution, with its "migration of skills," spread to the Balkan Peninsula by 5000 B.C.E., Egypt and Central Europe by 4000 B.C.E., and Britain and northwest India by 3000 B.C.E. The Neolithic cultures of sub-Saharan Africa, East Asia, Mesoamerica, and the Andes all developed independently from the Neolithic culture of the Fertile Crescent.

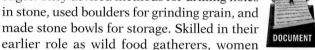
DOCUMENT
The Iceman

PRELITERATE SOCIETY AND RELIGION

▪ *What were the characteristics of religious beliefs among the earliest human societies?*

How can we know about those features of early cultures that are not apparent from the remains of tools and other objects? In addition to our being able to observe cultures similar to Paleolithic and Neolithic

---

Fertile Crescent—A geographic region that stretches in a semicircular arc from the eastern Mediterranean to the Persian Gulf.

Neolithic—A time period associated with the later Stone Age and the use of polished stone implements and weapons.

The Oldest Known Map: Çatal Hüyük

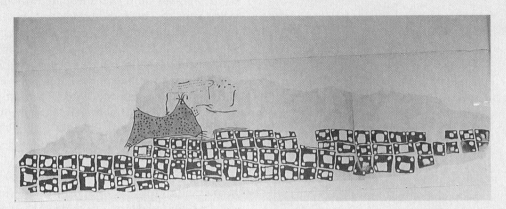

This wall painting is perhaps the oldest known map. It is also, for modern viewers, one of the most easily understood ancient maps. It is a city plan painted on two walls of a room in a Neolithic community in south-central Anatolia, near what is still the major land route in Turkey between Europe and the Near East. Radiocarbon dating has placed the image around 6200 B.C.E. It is a very large figure, nearly 9 feet wide.

By the 1960s archaeologists had uncovered 139 rooms in the complex and decided that at least 40 were used for special rites, probably of a religious nature. One of these special rooms, whose walls had often been replastered, contained this large image featuring rows of boxlike shapes. Archaeologists were amazed at the similarity between their own carefully drawn site maps and the painting on the wall. It soon became apparent that the Neolithic image was a map of the community or perhaps of the town that immediately preceded the one the dig was uncovering.

A great deal of information can be gleaned from this map:

- The town site was on a slope, with rows of houses or buildings set on graded terraces.

- The rectangular buildings and the streets set at right angles provide a gridiron look that has characterized much town planning throughout history.

- The elongated, or linear, pattern of the settlement may reflect an orientation to a major road.

- The large figure that looks like a mountain with two peaks beyond the town is, no doubt, Hasan Da-g, a volcano that was active until about 2000 B.C.E. The volcano was the source of the obsidian that was the basis of the settlement's wealth. The glassy, volcanic rock was used for making cutting tools, knives, scrapers, weapons, jewelry, ornaments, and a variety of other artifacts.

The complete map contains about 80 rooms or buildings, somewhat fewer structures than were found in the actual town that was excavated. Since the wall was replastered several times, perhaps the map was "updated." Or it may have served a ceremonial purpose for which the absolute accuracy of a civic map was unnecessary.

This map, certainly the oldest example of landscape art in addition to its function as a map, has perplexed the experts since its excavation in the 1960s. The painting certainly depicts an urban landscape, 2000 years earlier than archaeologists expected such a settlement in the area. Further excavation revealed that the town was very large by contemporary standards—perhaps home to a population exceeding 6000. A settlement of that size could not have grown enough food to support itself while accomplishing all the other tasks that Çatal Hüyük's residents did. Trade and an extensive commercial network had to be present, but there is no archaeological evidence from the site of specialized tools. Yet there is very clear proof that Çatal Hüyük possessed good pottery, well-fashioned textiles, and outstanding artwork. Some experts have speculated that the city may have served primarily as a religious center for an extensive area. In one section of the excavated town, an area of about one acre, archaeologists believe that as many as one of every three buildings may have served as a religious shrine or cult center of some sort.

Questions to Consider

1. What do you think may have been the purpose of the artist or artists who painted this map? Do you think it was intended to impart information?

2. Could the map have been constructed for a religious or ceremonial reason?

3. Why do you think that the volcano plays such a dominant part of this landscape? Could its depiction have a ceremonial or religious significance?

that still exist, the myths of Stone Age peoples throw light on their beliefs and customs. Like ourselves, our Stone Age ancestors sought to account for the origin of the universe and the meaning of existence. In often ascribing the behavior of natural phenomena to supernatural causes, Stone Age mythmakers were nonetheless seeking to make sense of what was familiar in their own lives—such as thunder and lightning and the cycle of the seasons.

Social Organization

Among all peoples, the basic social unit appeared to be the *elementary family*—parents and their offspring. In early human societies, the *extended family* was an individual family, together with a circle of related persons who usually traced their descent through their mothers and were bound together by mutual loyalty. The extended family strengthened the elementary unit in obtaining food and protecting its members against other groups. Land was communally owned but allocated to separate families. A *clan* was a group of extended families that believed that they had a common ancestor. Many peoples identified their clans by a **totem**—an animal or other natural object that was revered. Examples of totemism exist today in military insignia and the emblems of fraternal and sports organizations.

A fourth grouping, the *tribe*, comprised a number of clans. Such a community was characterized by a common speech or distinctive dialect, common cultural heritage, specific inhabited territory, and tribal chief. No community could exist or hold together unless rules governing relations among its members were recognized as binding upon all. Such rules crystallized into precedent or customary law, often attributed to a divine origin.

Correct behavior in preliterate societies consisted of not violating custom. Justice in a group acted to maintain equilibrium. Because theft disturbed economic equilibrium, justice was achieved by a settlement between the injured person and the thief. If the latter restored what had been stolen or its equivalent, the victim was satisfied, and the thief was not punished. Murder and wounding were also private matters, to be avenged by the next of kin on the principle of "an eye for an eye." Certain acts, however, such as treason, witchcraft, and incest were considered dangerous to the whole group and required punishment by the entire community—if need be, by death.

As a general rule, government in these early societies was of a democratic character. Older males—the council of elders—played a dominant role in decision-making because of their greater experience and knowledge of the group's customs and folklore. Serious decisions, such as going to war or electing a chief, required the consent of a general assembly of all adult males. The elected chief was pledged to rule in accordance with custom and in consultation with the council of elders.

Undoubtedly, the strongest single force in the life of preliterate peoples, past and present, has been religion. Religious sensibilities apparently originated in feelings of awe, as our ancestors became conscious of the universe about them. Awe and wonder led to the belief, usually called **animism,** that life exists in everything in nature—winds, stones, animals, and humans. A natural extension was belief in the existence of spirits separable from material bodies. Neanderthal people placed food and implements alongside their carefully buried dead, indicating that they believed in an afterlife and treated their forebears with affection and respect.

Late Paleolithic people revered the spirits of the animals they hunted as well as the spirit of fertility upon which human and animal life depended. Associated in particular with Neolithic cultures was the worship of a fertility deity, the Earth Mother (or Mother Goddess), known to us from many carved female figures with exaggerated sexual features. Fertility figurines have been excavated from Neolithic sites all over the world. At Çatal Hüyük, 33 representations of the Mother Goddess have been found, but only eight of a god who was either the goddess's son or consort. The relative scarcity of representations of male gods, together with evidence that the cult of the goddess was administered by priestesses rather than priests, supports the view that women occupied a central position in Neolithic society.

Closely associated with ancient religion was the practice of magic. In addition to revering spirits, people wanted to compel them to provide favors. For this purpose they employed magic and turned to shamans to ward off droughts, famines, floods, and plagues through what they believed to be magic powers of communication with the spirits.

Traditionally, magic has been regarded as diametrically opposed to science. Yet, as scholars are increasingly recognizing, both our ancestors and contemporary scientists believe that nature is orderly and that what is immediately perceived by the senses can be systematically classified—such as by the present-day subsistence-level Hanunóo of the Philippines. They have recorded 461 animal types and classified insect forms into 108 named categories,

DOCUMENT

Early Art: Religion or Worship?

---

totem—A symbol or emblem, usually an animal or natural object, that is associated with a family or clan.

animism—Generally, the belief that everything in the world is endowed with its own spirit.

including 13 for ants and termites.[1] Preliterate peoples must therefore be credited with a desire to acquire knowledge, both for practical purposes and for its own sake.

Further indications of this avid search for knowledge have been provided by studies of large stone monuments constructed by Neolithic peoples in at least two continents. With a computer, one astronomer found an "astonishing" number of correlations at Stonehenge in England between the alignments of stones, stone holes, and mounds and the solar and lunar positions as of 1500 B.C.E. when Stonehenge was built. These made possible a more accurate calendar and the prediction of the rising and setting of the sun and moon. But the construction of Neolithic astronomical structures had occurred long before Stonehenge. Ancient sandstone monuments in the Nile delta of Egypt indicate that their builders possessed a surprisingly complex knowledge of geometry and astronomy. Between 5000 and 7000 years old, this earliest known astronomical complex shows slabs in various configurations, including a circle that allowed the inhabitants to anticipate sunrise during the summer solstice.[2]

Before we conclude our overview of preliterate cultures, a brief summary is in order. During the first period of humankind's cultural evolution, the Paleolithic or Old Stone Age, our ancestor's toolmaking capability advanced from reliance on very simple implements—such as the standardized, all-purpose hand ax—to ever more sophisticated tools and techniques of operation. This technological evolution enabled *Homo sapiens* to move into and adapt to different environments around the world. By the time of the last glacial phase, our forebears had spread over most of the world.

Paleolithic cultures had food-gathering economies. Then, perhaps about 10,000 years ago, the Neolithic, or New Stone Age, emerged with the appearance of food-producing communities first in the Fertile Crescent of southwestern Asia and then elsewhere. Neolithic cultures are characterized by the cultivation of grains, the domestication of animals, pottery making, and the fashioning of polished stone tools. These advances occurred in different places on earth and at different times.

MESOPOTAMIA: THE FIRST CIVILIZATION

■ *What factors contributed to the development of civilization in Mesopotamia?*

Historians do not agree on how best to define the term *civilization*. But most would accept the view that a civilization is a culture that has attained a degree of complexity, characterized by urban life and the interdependence of those urban residents. In other words, a civilization is a culture capable of sustaining a great number of specialists to furnish the economic, social, political, and religious needs of a large social unit. Other components of a civilization are a system of writing (originating from the need to keep records); monumental, permanent architecture in place of simple buildings; and art that is not merely decorative, like that on Neolithic pottery, but representative of people and their activities. All these characteristics of civilization first appeared together in the southern part of Mesopotamia, which came to be called Sumer.

The Beginnings of Civilization in the Ancient Near East: City States and International Empires

Around 6000 B.C.E., after the agricultural revolution had begun to spread from its origins on the northern edge of the Fertile Crescent, Neolithic farmers began making their homes in the valleys of the Tigris and Euphrates Rivers themselves. Although the broad plain created by these rivers received insufficient regular rainfall to support agriculture, the eastern section was able to benefit from both rivers as sources of irrigation. Known to the Greeks as Mesopotamia (Greek for "between the rivers"), the lower sections of this plain, beginning near the point where the two rivers nearly converge, was called Babylonia. Babylonia included two geographical areas—Akkad in the north and Sumer, the delta of this river system, in the south.

Sumer had tremendous agricultural potential as long as natural environmental problems could be addressed. The rivers sometimes flooded in uncontrollable torrents. Spring and summer storms were often severe. The valley was virtually exposed on all sides to potential invaders, with no formidable natural boundaries to reduce the possibility of invasion. From the very beginning of habitation, cooperation was necessary for life to succeed. Swamps had to be drained, canals had to be dug to bring water to remote fields, and safeguards had to be constructed against flooding. These and many other related problems were solved by cooperative effort; yet the Mesopotamians continued to live in awe of their gods, whose whims might at any time bring destruction down on them.

In spite of the unpredictable nature of their gods, the Sumerians struggled to bring stability to their society. Sumerian metal workers discovered that copper, when combined with tin, produced an alloy, bronze, which was harder than copper and provided a sharper edge. The beginning of civilization in Sumer is associated with the beginning of this Bronze Age, and the new technology soon spread to Egypt, and later to Europe and Asia. Between 3500 and 3100 B.C.E. the foundations were established for a complex economy and a social order more sophisticated than any previously developed. This far more complex culture, based on large urban centers populated by interdependent and specialized workers, is what experts define as civilization.

Since the Mesopotamian plain had no stone, no metals, and no timber except its soft palm trees, these materials had to be imported, most often from the north. Water transport down the Tigris and Euphrates aided in this process. The oldest sailing boat known is represented by a model found in a Sumerian grave dating to around 3500 B.C.E. Soon after this date, wheeled vehicles appear in the form of war chariots drawn by donkeys. Another important invention was the potter's wheel, first used in Sumer soon after 3500 B.C.E.

The Emergence of Civilization in Sumer, c. 3200–2800 B.C.E.

By 3200 B.C.E. the urban centers in the region known as Sumer had developed the majority of the characteristics required to be called a civilization. Because these included the first evidence of writing, this first phase of Sumerian civilization, to about 2800 B.C.E., is called the **Protoliterate** (meaning "before literate") period.

The Sumerian language is not related to **Semitic** or **Indo-European,** the major language families that appear later in the Near East. The original home of the Semitic-speaking peoples was most likely the Arabian peninsula, and the Indo-Europeans seem to have migrated from regions around the Black and Caspian Seas. A third, much smaller language family, sometimes called Hamitic, included the Egyptians and other peoples of northeastern Africa. But the origin of the Sumerians remains a subject of speculation: Some suggest that migration from the Indus River valley might account for their arrival.

A number of the inventions and innovations of protoliterate Sumer eventually made their way to both the Nile and the Indus valleys, most likely through trade and commercial contacts. Among these inventions were wheeled vehicles and the potter's wheel. The discovery in Egypt of cylinder seals similar in shape to those used in Sumer attests to contact between the two cultures toward the end of the fourth millennium B.C.E. Certain early Egyptian art themes and architectural forms are also thought to be of Sumerian origin. And it is probable that the example of Sumerian writing stimulated the Egyptians to develop a script of their own.

The symbols on the oldest Sumerian clay tablets, the world's first writing, were pictures of concrete things such as a person's face, a sheep, a star, or a measure of grain. Some of these pictographs also represented ideas; for example, the picture of a foot was used to represent the idea of walking, and a picture of a mouth joined to that for water meant "to drink." This early pictographic writing developed into phonetic (or syllabic) writing when the scribes realized that a sign could represent a sound as

This small but beautifully crafted black diorite statue represents Gudea, the powerful king of the Sumerian city of Lagash in the late third millenium B.C.E. Contemporary poetry and inscriptions indicate that Gudea possessed great wealth and honored his gods by constructing numerous temples and shrines.

well as an object or idea. Thus, the personal name Kuraka could be written by combining the pictographs for mountain *(kur),* water *(a),* and mouth *(ka).* By 2800 B.C.E. the use of syllabic writing had reduced the number of Sumerian signs from nearly 2000 to 600.

When writing, Mesopotamian scribes used a reed stylus to make wedge-shaped impressions in soft clay tablets. This *cuneiform* system of writing (from the Latin *cuneus,* "wedge") was adopted by many other peoples of the Near East, including the Babylonians, the Assyrians, the Hittites, and the Persians.

protoliterate—Meaning "before literacy"; the period in a society's development that precedes the development and use of a written language.

Semitic—A group of related languages that include Akkadian, Arabic, Aramaean, Canaanite, and Hebrew. The presumptive source language of these languages is thought to have originated in the Arabian Peninsula, from whence, beginning about 2500 B.C.E., Semitic-speaking tribes migrated to the Mediterranean coast, Mesopotamia, and the Nile delta. The term *Semitic* also refers to the cultures of those who speak Semitic languages.

Indo-European—A family of languages that descended from a single unrecorded language spoken in the Caucasus region more than 5000 years ago. Carried by migrating tribes to Europe and Asia, dialects of the source language eventually evolved into such varied languages as English, German, French, Spanish, Latin, Greek, Persian, and Hindi.

The Old Sumerian Period, c. 2800–2300 B.C.E

By 2800 B.C.E. the Sumerian cities had fully emerged into complex civilizations. This first historical age, called the Old Sumerian period, was characterized by constant warfare as each city attempted to protect or enlarge its land and guarantee its access to water and irrigation. Each city-state was a theocracy, a state in which the chief local god was believed to be the actual ruler. The god's earthly representative was the *ensi*, the high priest and city governor, who acted as the god's caretaker in both religious and civil functions. Though given the power to act for the god by virtue of being the human agent of the divine ruler, the *ensi* was not himself considered a divine being.

The *ensis* were powerful and sometimes autocratic rulers. Most famous is the semilegendary Gilgamesh, ruler of Uruk about 2700 B.C.E., who is known only from several epic tales. Although Gilgamesh is portrayed as an extremely powerful ruler, the epic poem also shows that Sumerian rulers could be questioned, even opposed, by some of the nobles who served as advisers in the city's council.

Early Sumerian society was highly stratified, with priests and officials of the city god and subordinate deities assuming great authority. Each temple administered extensive land holdings; that land served as the god's "estate on earth." In addition to the temple lands, a considerable part of a city's territory originally consisted of land collectively owned by clans, kinship groups comprising a number of extended families. By 2600 B.C.E. these clan lands were becoming the private property of great landowners called *lugals* (literally, "great men"). Deeds of sale record the transfer of clan lands to private owners in return for substantial payments in copper to a few clan leaders and insignificant grants of food to the remaining clan members. These private estates were worked by "clients" whose lives were regulated by the temple authorities.

In time, priests, administrators, and *ensis* began confiscating temple land and other property and asserting their authority over the common people. Their ambitions frequently led to the rise of autocratic leaders who came to power on a wave of popular discontent. Since these despots were usually *lugals*, the term *lugal* became a political title and is now generally translated as "king."

The Sumerians, like their Mesopotamian successors, made extensive use of the institution of slavery, and slaves are recorded to have worked in many capacities—as farm and urban laborers, as servants in homes and temples, and in civic positions, such as in public administration. In some cities, slaves accounted for 40 to 50 percent of the population. Slaves in Mesopotamia were not without rights, and in many cases they were treated with care. Slavery was not based on racial characteristics or cultural differences; people of the same culture became enslaved through conquest or to pay off debt. Perhaps because of the possibility that any city-state might be overtaken and its residents enslaved at the pleasure of the gods, the treatment of slaves in Mesopotamia seems generally to have been more humane than at other times and places in human history.

Sumerian women were able to attain high social prominence, usually depending on the rank of their own or their husbands' families. Men were given the greater authority than their wives in economic and legal matters, and only the husband could initiate divorce proceedings against his wife. Children were under the complete control of their parents until 20 or 21 years of age.

The Akkadian Period, c. 2300–2150 B.C.E.

To the immediate north of Sumer was the region of Akkad, inhabited by Semites who had adopted much of Sumerian culture. Appearing late in the fourth millennium B.C.E., the Akkadians were among the earliest of the Semitic peoples who migrated into Mesopotamia from the Arabian peninsula. Sargon I (2370–2315 B.C.E.), the first Akkadian ruler, conquered Sumer and went on to establish an empire that extended from the Persian Gulf almost to the Mediterranean Sea—the first true empire in history.

Very proud of his lower-class origins, Sargon boasted that his humble, unwed mother had been forced to abandon him, placing him in a reed basket and floating the basket down the river. Rescued and brought up by a gardener, Sargon rose to power through the army. As *lugal*, Sargon claimed to look after the welfare of the lower classes and to aid the rising class of private merchants. At the merchants' request, he once sent his army to far-off Asia Minor to protect a colony of them from interference by a local ruler. Sargon reputedly was a tireless worker on behalf of his people's prosperity and expanded his influence in neighboring lands through almost unending campaigns of conquest.

Early Sumer and Akkad

c. 3200–2800 B.C.E.	Protoliterate period in Sumer
c. 2800–2300 B.C.E.	Old Sumerian period
c. 2370–2315 B.C.E.	Reign of Sargon of Akkad
c. 2300–2150 B.C.E.	Akkadian dominance
c. 2150–2000 B.C.E.	Neo-Sumerian period
c. 2000–1600 B.C.E.	Old Babylonian period
c. 1792–1750 B.C.E.	Reign of Hammurabi
c. 1595 B.C.E.	Sack of Babylon by Hittites

Sargon's successors, however, were unable either to repel the attacks of hostile mountain peoples or to overcome the desire for independence of the priest-dominated Sumerian cities. As a result, the dynasty founded by Sargon collapsed about 2150 B.C.E.

The Neo-Sumerian Period, c. 2150–2000 B.C.E

Order and prosperity were restored by the *lugals* of the powerful Sumerian city of Ur. By creating a highly centralized administration in Sumer and Akkad, these rulers solved the problem of internal rebellion that had been of great concern for Sargon and his successors. The formerly temple-dominated cities became provinces administered by closely regulated governors. Religion became an arm of the state: the high priests were state appointees, and careful oversight and regulation by temple officials gave protection to a newly developing free enterprise economy that Sargon had encouraged. At the head of this bureaucratic state stood the *lugal* of Ur, now considered a living god and celebrated as a heaven-sent authority who brought order and security to the people, who were considered to be his servants.

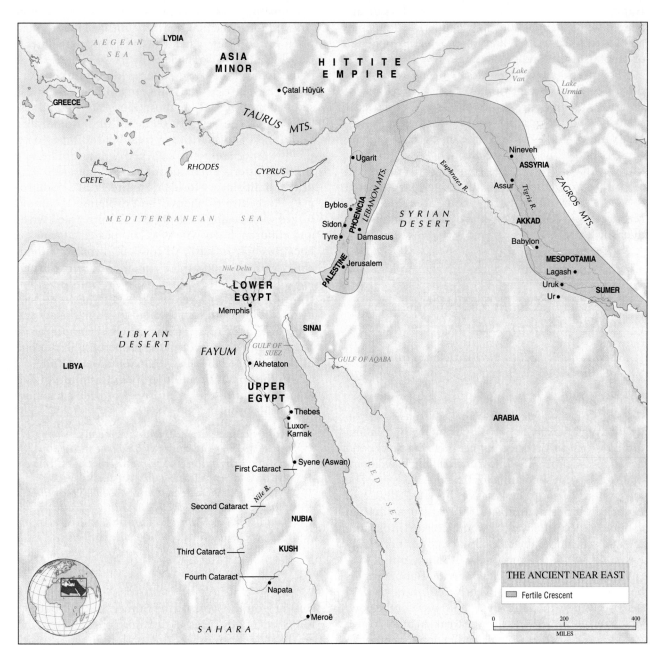

The earliest of humankind's great civilizations developed in the area that came to be called the Fertile Crescent—where rainfall was adequate to nourish wild forms of grain and grazing animals could find sufficient food.

The *lugals* of Ur, who called themselves the "vigilant shepherds" of their people, presided over a highly centralized and efficient administration. Thousands of records have been preserved from this period, detailing the meticulous regulation of commerce, agriculture, and social standards by the powerful overlords of the city. In addition, Sumerian literature and culture flourished under their direction. But the greatness of Ur lasted for little more than one hundred years.

Disaster struck Ur about 2000 B.C.E., when Elamites from what is now Iran destroyed the city. The Sumerians were never again a dominant force politically, but their cultural influence continued to be powerful throughout all subsequent civilizations in the Tigris-Euphrates valley. The Sumerians themselves disappeared as a people, but the Sumerian language continued to be written and to serve as the language of scholarship and religious ritual.

For more than two centuries following the destruction of Ur, disunity and warfare again plagued Mesopotamia, along with economic stress, a lack of security, and acute hardship for the lower classes. Many merchants, however, used the absence of state controls to become aggressive capitalists who amassed fortunes that they invested in banking operations and land. The stronger local rulers of the period attempted to assert their authority by seizing access to water resources and working toward the establishment of dynastic control.

THE BABYLONIAN EMPIRE, c. 2000–1600 B.C.E.

■ *What distinguished the Babylonians from their Sumerian predecessors?*

Semitic Amorites (from the Akkadian word *Amurru*, "West"), produced one dynasty that based its power on its control of the city of Babylon. This new Babylonian family of rulers defeated its neighboring rivals and began to build their city into a capital that would dominate most of Mesopotamia for the next 300 years. The most outstanding of the kings of this Old Babylonian Empire was Hammurabi (c. 1792–1750 B.C.E.), an extremely successful warrior who succeeded in expanding and securing Babylon's military power north into Assyria, south into Sumer, and east into Elam.

Although he was a tireless warrior, Hammurabi is best known for the code of nearly 300 laws that were given by the king "in order to prevent the powerful from oppressing the weak, in order to give justice to the orphans and widows, in order to give my land fair decisions and to give rights to the oppressed. . . ."[3] The Code of Hammurabi is

DOCUMENT
Hammurabi's
Law Code

a compilation of laws covering a wide variety of topics, such as property disputes, adultery, slavery, prostitution, inheritance, and public order. The collection was not exhaustive, but most likely served as guideposts for judges, as well as educated subjects, in their attempts to administer or anticipate the law. Such compilations of law date back to Sumerian codes 1400 years before Hammurabi's time, and much of the king's code echoes ancient Sumerian precedent. Hammurabi's Code made wide use of corporal punishment for offenses: based on the "eye for an eye, tooth for a tooth" principle of dispensing justice; in many cases Babylonian law was more harsh in its administration of mutilation or death as fitting punishment for crime than that by Sumerian judges, who often levied fines instead of corporal punishment. Babylonian law also made clear the privileged status of the upper classes, who suffered less severe penalties for their offenses as the common citizen, and far less severe punishments than those administered to slaves.

IMAGE
Hammurabi
Receives His
Law Code
from the
Gods

Despite the severity of much of Hammurabi's Code, and the disparities in treatment it imposed on the lower classes and slaves, Hammurabi's Code shows an attempt to reduce abusive interest rates and prices, limit slavery for debt to three years, and provide more care to widows and orphans. Minimum wages were established. Other laws protected wives and children; but a wife who had neglected care for her household or husband could be divorced without alimony, or the husband could take another wife and force the first to remain as a servant. Unless a son committed some grave offense, his father could not disinherit him. If the state failed to maintain law and order, the victim of that failure received compensation from the state: the value of the property stolen, or one mina of silver to the relatives of a murder victim.

In the conclusion to the Code, Hammurabi eloquently summed up his efforts to provide social justice for his people:

> *Let any oppressed man, who has a cause, come before my image as king of righteousness! Let him read the inscription on my monument! Let him give heed to my weighty words! And may my monument enlighten him as to his cause and may he understand his case! May he set his heart at ease! (and he will exclaim): Hammurabi indeed is a ruler who is like a real father to his people. . . .*[4]

Mathematics and Science

Building on the work of the Sumerians, the Babylonians made advances in arithmetic, geometry, and algebra. For ease in working with both whole numbers and fractions, they compiled tables for multiplication and division and for square and cube roots.

They knew how to solve linear and quadratic equations, and their knowledge of geometry included the theorem later formulated by the Greek philosopher Pythagoras: The square of the hypotenuse of a right-angled triangle is equal to the sum of the squares of the other two sides. They used the Sumerian system of counting based on the unit 60 (sexagesimal) rather than that based on the number 10 (decimal). The remnants of this sexagesimal system is found today in computing divisions of time—60-minute hours—and the 360-degree circle. They also adopted the Sumerian principle of place-value notation that gave numbers a value according to their position in a series. To represent zero, they employed the character for "not," which is the same as our "naught," still used colloquially for "nothing."

The Babylonians achieved little that today can be called pure science. They were most concerned with observing the natural world so that the future could be predicted. They did observe nature and collect data, the first requirement of the scientific method; but to explain natural phenomena, they were satisfied with the formulation of myths that defined things in terms of the unpredictable whims of the gods. They thought the sun, moon, and five visible planets to be gods who were able to influence human lives; accordingly, their movements were watched, recorded, and interpreted—more the study of astrology than the science of astronomy. But through their study of the world around them in an effort to predict the future, the Mesopotamians were attempting to impose an order on what they found to be a chaotic universe. Through proper reading of the signs given by the gods, some stability in the world might be achieved.

Literature and Religion

The Babylonians borrowed from the Sumerians a body of literature ranging from heroic epics that compare in scope and themes with the *Iliad* and the *Odyssey* to wisdom writings that have their counterparts in the Hebrew Old Testament. The Sumerian *Epic of Gilgamesh* records the great adventures of the heroic ruler of Uruk who supposedly lived about 2700 B.C.E. The epic poem reflects the values of a heroic age, in which great heroes seek to earn undying fame and glory. The supreme value is the eternal reputation achieved through the performance of heroic deeds. After Gilgamesh slays the fierce Bull of Heaven, he stops to proclaim his victory:

> *What man is most impressive now:*
> *Who is finest, firmest, and most fair?*
> *Isn't Gilgamesh that man above men . . . ?*
> *Who is most glorious among men?*[5]

What Gilgamesh fears most is death, which, in the Mesopotamian viewpoint replaces a glorious life on earth with a dismal existence in the House of Dust, "where dust is their fare and clay their food." The epic's central theme is Gilgamesh's search for everlasting life. He seeks out and questions Utnapishtim (oot-nah-PISH-tim), who was granted eternal life because he saved all living creatures from a great flood. (Utnapishtim's story has many similarities with the Hebrew account of Noah and the Flood). But Gilgamesh's search in not successful, and he finally concludes that he must die like all other mortals:

> *There is darkness which lets no person*
> *again see the light of day;*
> *There is a road leading away from*
> *bright and lively life. There dwell those who eat*
> *   dry dust*
> *and have no cooling water to quench their*
> *   awful thirst.*
> *As I stood there I saw all those who've died*
> *and even kings among those darkened souls*
> *have none of their remote and former glory.*[6]

The ancient Mesopotamians never moved far beyond this early view that immortality was reserved for the gods, and that life after death, if it existed at all, was a gloomy and terrible existence where spirits haunted the world in a continual search for food and water. Unlike the Egyptians, they did not develop an expectation of an attractive life after death as a reward for good behavior on earth. They did come to believe in divine rewards for moral conduct, but these were rewards to be enjoyed in this life—increased worldly goods, numerous offspring, long life.

The ethical content of Babylonian religion was never well developed. Numerous priesthoods—more than 30 different types of priests and priestesses are known—became preoccupied with an elaborate set of rituals, particularly those designed to ward off evil demons and predict the future through observing omens and portents. Good deeds, the priests insisted, could not protect a person from demons that have the power to make their part-human and part-animal bodies invisible. Only the proper spells, incantations, and offerings could ward off evil.

While one large class of priests provided amulets inscribed with incantations and magic formulas to expel demons, another group dealt with predicting the future. Almost anything could be viewed as an omen, but most popular were dreams, the movements of birds and animals, the internal organs of sacrificed animals, the shape taken by oil poured on the surface of water, the casting of dice, and astronomical phenomena. Such practices, called superstitions in the modern world, were in reality attempts

Worshipper statues from the square temple, Eshnunna (now Tel Asmar, Iraq).

by the Mesopotamians to obtain some semblance of control and predictability over a world ruled by chaotic and random forces.

Collapse and Disorder, c. 1600–1200 B.C.E.

The pattern of disunity and warfare, all too familiar in Mesopotamia, reasserted itself following Hammurabi's death. In 1595 B.C.E. the Hittites, an Indo-European people who had established control in Asia Minor, mounted a daring raid down the Euphrates, sacking Babylon and destroying the weakened dynasty of Hammurabi. The swift success of the Hittite raid was made possible by a new means of waging war: the use of lightweight chariots drawn by horses instead of donkeys or oxen. The next five centuries in Mesopotamia were years of disorder about which little is known; political unity dissolved, yet the cultural foundations of Mesopotamian society, and the inheritance that culture owed to the Sumerians, continued to influence the shaping of later Mesopotamian societies.

The beginnings of civilization in Egypt, and the continuous development of that great early civilization, was a development for the most part contemporary with the origins and development of civilization in Mesopotamia. Yet the circumstances under which Egyptian culture took shape, and the very nature of

the Egyptian civilization, stands in contrast to the Mesopotamian achievement.

EGYPT: GIFT OF THE NILE

■ *What effect did the waters of the Nile have on ancient Egyptian political and religious institutions?*

Egypt, one of Africa's earliest civilizations, is literally "the gift of the [Nile] river," as the ancient Greek historian Herodotus observed. The Nile River stretches for 4100 miles, but it is its last valley, extending 750 miles from the First **Cataract** to the Nile delta, that was the heartland of Egyptian civilization. Egyptians called the Nile valley *Kemet* ("the black land") because its soils were renewed annually by the rich black silt deposited by the floodwaters of the Blue Nile and the Apara, rivers descending from the Ethiopian highlands. Unlike the unpredictable floods of Mesopotamia, the Nile's floods rose and fell with unusual precision, reaching Aswan (ahs-WAHN) by late June and peaking in September before beginning to subside. The perennial key to successful farming was con-

---

cataract—Large waterfall or a series of rapids on a river such as the Nile.

trolling the Nile by diverting its floodwaters along the 10- to 20-mile-wide floodplain for irrigation. Egyptian farmers achieved this by building an elaborate network of dikes and canals.

Predynastic Egypt

The first Nile settlers were likely people who moved to the river valley as climatic changes transformed the savanna grasslands west of the Nile into desert. By 4800 B.C.E. the earliest farming communities began to appear in the western Nile delta and spread to the rest of Egypt over the next eight centuries. Recognizing the advantages of creating larger social groupings and the need to cushion themselves from the impact of droughts, floods, and plagues, farming communities started banding together to form regional chiefdoms in Lower Egypt, the area comprising the broad Nile delta north of Memphis, and Upper Egypt, which extended southward along the narrow Nile valley as far as the First Cataract at Aswan. A kingdom emerged in Upper Egypt, while Lower Egypt was divided into a number of districts (later called *nomes*) that had formerly been ruled by independent chieftains.

The Predynastic period ended soon after 3100 B.C.E. when King Menes (also known as *Narmer*) united Upper Egypt and started gradually incorporating Lower Egypt into a new kingdom with its capital at Memphis. This period has become known as the First **Dynasty,** and it marks the beginning of one of the longest-lasting civilizations in history, lasting for 3000 years.

---

dynasty—A series of rulers who belong to the same family or line.

Ancient Egypt

c. 3100 B.C.E.	Menes unites Upper Egypt
c. 2700 B.C.E.	Construction of Step Pyramid
c. 1720 B.C.E.	Hyksos conquer Egypt
c. 1600 B.C.E.	Oldest medical text
c. 1479–1458 B.C.E.	Regency of Queen Hatshepsut
c. 1458–1436 B.C.E.	Reign of Thutmose III
c. 1363–1347 B.C.E.	Reign of Amenhotep IV (Akhenaton)
c. 1290–1224 B.C.E.	Reign of Ramses II
c. 700s B.C.E.	Conquest of Egypt by Kush

The Old Kingdom, c. 2700–2200 B.C.E.

The kings of the Third through Sixth Dynasties—the period called the Old Kingdom or Pyramid Age—firmly established order and stability, as well as the basic elements of Egyptian civilization. The nobility lost its independence, and all power was centered in the king, or *pharaoh* (*per-ao*, "great house," originally signified the royal palace but during the New Kingdom began to refer to the king). The king had a character both divine and human. Considered a god, he also represented humans before the gods. He had the responsibility to maintain **maat,** that is, truth, justice, and order.

The king, along with his relatives, owned extensive tracts of land (from which he made frequent grants to temples, royal funerary cults, and private persons) and received the surplus from the crops produced on the huge royal estates. This surplus supported a large corps of specialists—administrators, priests, scribes, artists, artisans, and merchants—who labored in the pharaoh's service. The pharaoh's power and legitimacy were based on his ability to offer protection and sustain prosperity through abundant harvests. In return, his subjects gave their absolute devotion to the god-king, and Egyptians generally felt a sense of security that was rare in Mesopotamia.

The belief that the pharaoh was divine led to the construction of colossal tombs—pyramids—to preserve the pharaoh's embalmed body for eternity. The ritual of mummification was believed to restore vigor and activity to the dead pharaoh; it was his passport to eternity. The pyramid tombs, especially those of the Fourth Dynasty at Giza near Memphis, which are the most celebrated of all ancient monuments, reflect the great power and wealth of the Old Kingdom pharaohs. Although pyramid building was year-round, most construction took place during the months when the Nile overflowed its banks, and the pharaoh could expect farmers to provide their labor on construction crews. The Egyptian masses performed it primarily as an act of fidelity to their god-king, on whom the security and prosperity of Egypt depended.

IMAGE

The Pyramids at Giza

Security and prosperity came to an end late in the Sixth Dynasty. The burden of building and maintaining pyramid tombs for each new king exhausted the state. The Nile floods failed, and famines ensued. As the state and its god-king lost credibility, provincial rulers assumed the prerogatives of the pharaohs, including the claim to immortality, and districts became independent. Inscriptions, known as coffin texts, also began to appear in nonroyal coffins. Among other things, the

DOCUMENT

Two Accounts of an Egyptian Famine

---

maat—A goddess who represented the balance and harmony of the universe as well as a set of ethical concepts that encompassed "truth," "order," and "cosmic balance." One's life and personal behavior should contribute to universal order. Hence, a pharaoh maintained *maat* by ruling justly and serving the gods.

Pharoah Ra-Hotep and his wife Nofret. Ra-Hotep was a pharaoh of the Seventeenth Dynasty who ruled around 1650 B.C.E. as Egypt was under Hyksos rule. These statues raise questions of whether it is fruitful to apply modern racial classifications to ancient Egyptians.

inscriptions expressed the hope that the deceased would be reunited with their families in the afterlife. For about a century and a half, known as the First Intermediate Period (c. 2200–2050 B.C.E.), the pharaoh's central authority weakened as civil war raged among contenders for the throne and local rulers reasserted themselves. Outsiders raided and infiltrated the land. The lot of the common people became unbearable as they faced famine, robbery, and oppression. "All happiness has vanished," related a Middle Kingdom commentary on this troubled era. "I show you the land in turmoil. . . . Each man's heart is for himself. . . . A man sits with his back turned, while one slays another."[7]

The Middle Kingdom, c. 2050–1800 B.C.E

Stability was restored by the pharaohs of the Eleventh and Twelfth Dynasties, who reunited the kingdom.

Stressing their role as watchful shepherds of the people, the Middle Kingdom pharaohs promoted the welfare of the downtrodden. One of them claimed, "I gave to the beggar and brought up the orphan. I gave success to the poor as to the wealthy."[8] The pharaohs of the Twelfth Dynasty revived the building of pyramids as well as the construction of public works. The largest of these, a drainage and irrigation project in the marshy Fayum (fai-YOOM) district south of Memphis, resulted in the reclamation of thousands of acres of arable land.

During the Thirteenth Dynasty, the Hyksos (HIK-sohs; "rulers of foreign lands"), a Semitic people from western Asia, assumed power over much of Egypt. The Hyksos are often portrayed as invaders who conquered Egypt around 1720 B.C.E., but now it is understood that the Hyksos migrated into Lower Egypt during the Middle Kingdom and established trading networks. During the Second Intermediate Period (c. 1800–1570 B.C.E.), they took advantage of weaknesses in the Egyptian state and gradually took control over all of Lower Egypt and many parts of Upper Egypt. The Hyksos did not sweep aside Egyptian institutions and culture. They adapted to existing Egyptian government structures, copied architectural styles and the **hieroglyphic** ("sacred carvings") system of writing, and incorporated Egyptian cults into their religious pantheon. The Hyksos army also introduced new weaponry to the Egyptians: the horse-drawn chariot and bronze weapons such as the curved sword and body armor and helmets.

The New Kingdom or Empire, c. 1570–1090 B.C.E.

Hyksos rule over Egypt lasted several centuries before a resurgent Egyptian dynasty based at Thebes challenged it. Adopting the new weapons introduced by their rulers, the Egyptians expelled the Hyksos and pursued them northwards into Phoenicia. The pharaohs of the Eighteenth Dynasty, who reunited Egypt and founded the New Kingdom, made Phoenicia the nucleus of an Egyptian empire in western Asia and conquered Nubia to the south.

The outstanding representative of this aggressive state was Thutmose III. When the union of Thutmose II and his half-sister, Hatshepsut (hat-SHEP-soot), failed to produce a male heir, Thutmose II fathered Thutmose III with a concubine. When Thutmose II died in 1479 B.C.E., Thutmose was still a child, and Hatshepsut was to act as co-regent until he came of age. Mindful of the Egyptian ideal that a son inherited the throne from the pharaoh, she legitimized her suc-

hieroglyphics—The mode of writing of ancient Egyptians that featured signs or figures to represent words.

cession by claiming that she was the designated successor of Thutmose I. She also stated that she had a divine origin as a daughter of Amon and had an oracle proclaim that Amon had chosen her to become king. She adopted all the customary royal titles; and in many of her statues and helmets, she was even depicted sporting the royal beard.

Because Hatshepsut had her own ambitions, Thutmose III had to wait for more than two decades before he assumed the throne on his own. Toward the end of his reign, he ordered Hatshepsut's name and inscriptions erased, her reliefs effaced, and her statues broken and thrown into a quarry. Historians still speculate whether he was expressing his anger at Hatshepsut or promoting his own accomplishments. Thutmose III is most noted for leading his army on 17 campaigns as far as Syria, where he set up his boundary markers on the banks of the Euphrates, called by the Egyptians "the river that runs backwards." Under his sway, Thutmose III allowed the existing rulers of conquered states to remain on their thrones, but their sons were taken as hostages to Egypt, where they were brought up, thoroughly Egyptianized, and eventually sent home to succeed their fathers as loyal vassals of Egyptian rule. Thutmose III erected *obelisks*—tall, pointed shafts of stone—to commemorate his reign and to record his wish that "his name might endure throughout the future forever and ever." The Egyptian Empire reached its peak under Amenhotep III (c. 1402–1363 B.C.E.). The restored capital at Thebes, with its temples built for the sun-god Amon east of the Nile at Luxor and Karnak, became the most magnificent city in the world. Tribute flowed in from conquered lands, and relations were expanded with Asia and the Mediterranean. To improve ties, the kings of Mitanni and Babylonia offered daughters in marriage to Amenhotep III in return for gold.

During the reign of the succeeding pharaoh, Amenhotep IV (c. 1363–1347 B.C.E.), however, the empire went into a sharp decline as the result of an internal struggle between the pharaoh and the powerful and wealthy priests of Amon, "king of the gods." The pharaoh undertook to revolutionize Egypt's religion by proclaiming the worship of the sun's disk, Aton, in place of Amon and all the other deities. Often called the first monotheist (although, as Aton's son, the pharaoh was also a god and he, not Aton, was worshipped by the Egyptians), Amenhotep changed his name to Akhenaton (akh-NAHT-in; "he who is effective for the Aton"), left Amon's city to found a new capital (Akhetaton,"horizon of Aton"), and concentrated on religious reform. By demoting Amon to a lesser status and taxing his temples, Akhenaton provoked strong opposition from Amon's priesthood. Most of Egypt's tributary princes in Asia defected when their appeals for aid against invaders went unheeded.

Akhenaton's monotheism did not survive his reign. When Akhenaton died, his 9-year-old brother, Tutankhamen (tu-tan-KAHM-in; "King Tut," c. 1347–1338 B.C.E.)—now best remembered for his small but richly furnished tomb, discovered in 1922—returned to the worship of Amon and to Memphis. Amon's priests gained revenge against Akhenaton as Tutankhamen and his successors destroyed Akhenaton's statues and tried to erase all memory of him. When Tutankhamen died in his late teens with no heir, one of his advisers, Horemheb, a general from the Nile delta region, founded the Nineteenth Dynasty (c. 1305–1200 B.C.E.).

Taking the name Ramses I, he sought to reestablish Egyptian control over Palestine and Syria. The result was a long struggle with the Hittites, who in the meantime had pushed south from Asia Minor into Syria. This struggle reached a climax in the reign of Ramses II (c. 1290–1224 B.C.E.) Ramses II regained Palestine, but when he failed to dislodge the Hittites from Syria, he agreed to a treaty. Its strikingly modern character is revealed in clauses providing for nonaggression, mutual assistance, and extradition of fugitives.

The long reign of Ramses II was one of Egypt's last periods of national grandeur. The number and size of Ramses' monuments rival those of the Pyramid Age. Outstanding among them are the great Hypostyle Hall, built for Amon at Karnak, and the temple at Abu Simbel in Nubia, with its four colossal statues of Ramses, which was raised in the 1960s to save it from inundation by the waters of the High Dam at Aswan. After Ramses II, royal authority gradually decayed as the power of the priests of Amon rose.

Third Intermediate Period, 1090–332 B.C.E.

The Third Intermediate Period was another period of transition in which the Amon priesthood at Thebes became so strong that the high priest was able to found his own dynasty and to rule over Upper Egypt. At the same time, merchant princes set up a dynasty of their own in the Nile delta. Libyans from the west moved into central Egypt, where in 940 B.C.E. they established a dynasty whose founder, Shoshenq, was a contemporary of King Solomon of Israel. Two centuries later, Egypt was conquered by the rulers of the kingdom of Kush, who established the Twenty-Fifth Dynasty. Kush's rule came to an end around 670 B.C.E. when the Assyrians of Mesopotamia made Egypt a province of their empire.

Egypt enjoyed a brief reprise of revived glory during the Twenty-Sixth Dynasty (c. 663–525 B.C.E.), which expelled the Assyrians with the aid of Greek mercenaries. The revival of ancient artistic and literary forms proved to be one of the most creative periods in Egyptian history. After attempts to expand into Syria were blocked by Nebuchadnezzar's (neh-boo-kad-NE-zahr) Babylonians, Egypt's rulers concentrated on expanding their commercial linkages throughout the region. To achieve this end, Pharaoh Necho II (c. 610–595 B.C.E.) created the first Egyptian navy. He encouraged the Greeks to establish trading colonies in the Nile delta; he put 12,000 laborers to work, digging a canal between the Nile mouth and the Red Sea (it was completed later by the Persians); and he commissioned a Phoenician expedition to search for new African trade routes.

Egypt came under Persian rule in 525 B.C.E. but was able to regain its independence in 404 B.C.E. After three brief dynasties, Egypt again fell under the Persians before coming within the domain of Alexander the Great (see Chapter 4).

Nubia and the Kingdom of Kush

Egypt's most enduring relationship was with its neighbor to the south, Nubia (NOO-bee-ah; derived from *nub*, the Egyptian word for gold), an area that stretches almost 900 miles from the town of Aswan to Khartoum, the point where the Blue and White Niles converge. The Nile gave Nubian civilization a distinctive character but in ways different from those in Egypt. As the Nile flows northward, its course is interrupted six times by cataracts that served as barriers to river traffic and Nubia's commercial contacts with Egypt. Like Egypt, many parts of Nubia east and west of the Nile are barren, so Nubian agricultural production depended on the Nile's two-mile wide floodplain.

Emerging around 4000 B.C.E., the earliest Nubian culture was made up of hunters, fishermen, farmers, and semi-nomadic pastoralists. This culture was distinguished for its highly skilled sculptures, ceramics, and clay figurines. Nubia also developed a healthy trade with Egypt. After a centralized state emerged in Egypt, Egyptian dynasties regarded Nubia as a source of slaves and raw mate-

rials such as gold, timber, and ivory and made several attempts to colonize Nubia. This state of hostility did not prevent Nubians from marrying into Egyptian royal families and the Egyptian state and army from recruiting Nubian administrators and archers.

Centered in a fertile area of the Nile around the Third Cataract, the Kingdom of Kush emerged around 1600 B.C.E. Its capital was at Kerma, an urban center renowned for its sophisticated temples and palaces. Kush prospered most when Egypt's fortunes declined. Although the basis of Kush's society was agriculture and animal husbandry, Kush engaged in extensive trade with Egypt to the north and African societies to the south and east.

After expelling the Hyksos, Egyptian forces reasserted their dominion over northern Nubia as far south as the Fourth Cataract, including Kerma. For the next four centuries, Egyptian administrators exploited Nubian gold to finance military campaigns in Asia and created an Egyptianized Nubian elite who spoke the Egyptian language and adopted Egyptian deities such as Amon and ritual and burial practices, including erecting pyramids.

Kush did not regain its autonomy until the eighth century B.C.E., when a new line of rulers established themselves at Napata (nah-PAH-tah) between the Third and Fourth Cataracts. The high point of Kush's power came a short time later. Taking advantage of strife in Egypt, the armies of Kush's King Piye swept through Egypt, conquering territory as far north as the Nile Delta. Although Piye proclaimed himself pharaoh

Sections of a wall painting from the tomb chapel of the treasurer Sebekhotep at Thebes show Nubians presenting gold nuggets and rings to King Thutmose IV. It dates from around 1400 B.C.E.

over Egypt and Nubia, he allowed local rulers in Egypt a measure of independence, and he cultivated the priests of the temple of Amon. His brother and successor, Shabaqo, was not so benign. He brought Egypt under the direct control of Kush and moved his capital to Thebes. He and the three pharaohs who succeeded him established the Twenty-Fifth Dynasty, which ruled Kush and Egypt for the next half century until they were forced to retreat following an Assyrian invasion. Kush's capital then moved to Meroe (MEHR-oh-wee), situated at the confluence of the Nile and APara Rivers. This site enjoyed annual rainfalls and supported a larger population. Meroe became a noted center for ironworking and weaving and exporting cotton cloth.

Kush remained in existence until 400 C.E., when it was absorbed into the Ethiopian kingdom of Aksum (ak-soom). Around the second century B.C.E. Kush's rulers started recording their royal annals in a script based on hieroglyphics and a cursive script also derived from hieroglyphics. This language, known as Meroitic, has not been translated to this day.

Egyptian Society and Economy

Egyptian society was highly stratified. Most Egyptians were poor peasants subject to forced labor for the rulers and who paid taxes to those who owned the land—the pharaoh, temples, or wealthy landowners—based on the yields of harvests.

However, class distinctions were not rigid. People could rise to a higher rank in the service of the pharaoh by joining the tiny literate elite. Pupils—usually boys—attended a scribal school for many years in which they learned to read and write hieratic script, a cursive form of hieroglyphics. Students practiced with reed pens on limestone chips or clay tablets. Scribes were in demand by the state for many tasks—writing letters, recording harvests, tracking taxes collected and owed, and keeping accounts for the Egyptian army. The most scholarly scribes assumed positions as priests, doctors, and engineers. Scribes enjoyed secure positions and were free from labor service.

Compared with the Greeks and Romans, Egyptian women enjoyed more rights, although their status at all levels of society was generally lower than that of men. Few women could qualify as scribes and thus were largely excluded from administrative positions. However, women could serve as temple priestesses, musicians, gardeners, farmers, and bakers. Some royal women, because of their positions as wives or mothers of pharaohs, had great influence in royal courts. Business and legal documents show that women shared many of the economic and legal rights of men. Women generally had rights to own, buy, sell, and inherit property without reliance on male legal

Many tomb paintings depict everyday life in Egypt. Here, two servants pick figs at the tomb of Khnumhotpes at Bani Hasan.

guardians; to negotiate legal settlements; to engage in business deals; to make wills; and to initiate litigation and testify in court. In a divorce, a woman kept any property she brought into a marriage as well as one-third of a couple's community property. When Egypt came under Greek rule, most Egyptian women preferred the option of maintaining their legal rights under Egyptian rather than Greek law.

The economy of Egypt was dominated by the divine pharaoh and his state, which owned most of the land and monopolized its commerce and industry. Because of the Nile and the proximity to the Mediterranean and Red seas, most of Egypt's trade was conducted by ships. Boats regularly plied up and down the Nile, which, unlike the Tigris and the Euphrates, is easily navigable in both directions up to the First

Document   "The Great Hymn to the Aton" and Psalm 104

A notable example of New Kingdom Egyptian literature is the pharaoh Akhenaton's "Hymn to the Sun," which was found carved on the tombs of his followers. Akhenaton's Hymn reflected his dramatic break with Egyptian religious beliefs that stressed prayers to gods for health and well-being and prepared the way for "blessed" afterlife. Akhenaton conceived one omnipotent and beneficent Creator and that he was the guarantor of the afterlife. Some scholars argue that his religious reforms may have had a formative effect on the development of monotheism on the Hebrews, many of whom were perhaps enslaved in Egypt at the time of Akhenaton's reforms. The style and subject of Psalm 104 bear a striking resemblance to the king's hymn to the sun:

The Great Hymn to the Aton

Splendid you rise in heaven's lightland,
O living Aton, creator of life!
When you have dawned in eastern lightland,
You fill every land with your beauty.
You are beauteous, great, radiant,
High over every land;
Your rays embrace the lands. . . .
How many are your deeds,
Though hidden from sight;
O Sole God beside whom there is none!
You made the earth as you wished, you alone.
All peoples, herds, and flocks;
All upon earth that walk on legs,
All on high that fly on wings, . . .
You set every man in his place,
You supply their needs;
Everyone has his food,
His lifetime is counted. . .

From Miriam Lichtheim, *Ancient Egyptian Literature: A Book of Readings (Volume II: The New Kingdom)* (Berkeley: University of California Press, 1976, pp. 96–98.

Psalm 104

Bless Yahweh, my soul,
Yahweh my God, how great you are!
Clothed in majesty and glory,
wrapped in a robe of light!
You stretch the heavens out like a tent,
you build your palace on the waters above;
using the clouds as your chariot,
you advance on the wings of the wind;

you use the winds as messengers
and fiery flames as servants.
You fixed the earth on its foundations,
unshakable for ever and ever;
you wrapped it with the deep as with a robe,
the waters overtopping the mountains. . . .
The sun rises, they retire,
going back to lie down in their lairs,
and man goes to work, and to labour until dusk.
Yahweh, what variety you have created
arranging everything so wisely!
Earth is completely full of the things you have made. . . .
Glory for ever to Yahweh!
May Yahweh find joy in what he creates,
at whose glance the earth trembles,
at whose touch the mountains smoke!

From "Psalm 104," *The Jerusalem Bible*, ed. Alexander Jones (Daarton, Longman & Todd, Ltd., and Doubleday: 1966), pp. 886–888, as quoted in Perry M. Rogers, *Aspects of Western Civilization*, Vol. I (Prentice Hall: 2000), pp. 33–35.

Questions to Consider

1. How do you account for the striking similarities between Akhenaton's Hymn and Psalm 104? Do you think the Hymn might have inspired the writer of Psalm 104?
2. What are the similarities between the Aton and Yahweh? Are there any differences in the manner in which they are described?
3. Why did Akhenaton's monotheism not last beyond his reign, while the Hebrew's monotheism was sustained?

Cataract at Aswan. The current carries ships downstream, and the prevailing north wind enables them to sail upstream easily. Trade reached its height during the empire (c. 1570–1090 B.C.E.), when commerce traveled along four main routes: the Nile River to and from the south; the Red Sea, which was connected by caravan to the Nile bend near Thebes; a caravan route to Mesopotamia and southern Syria; and the Mediterranean Sea, connecting northern Syria, Cyprus, Crete, and Greece with the Nile delta. Egypt's primary imports were timber, copper, tin, and olive oil, paid for with gold from its rich mines, linens, wheat, and **papyrus** rolls made from reeds—the preferred writing materials of the ancient world (the word *paper* is derived from the Greek *papyros*).

Egyptian Religion

Religion played a central role in the everyday life of Egyptians, who attributed everything from the annual cycles of the flooding of the Nile to personal illnesses to acts of gods. The Egyptian pantheon included hundreds of gods and goddesses. Male gods usually represented rulers, creators, and insurers of fertility, while goddesses assumed roles as nurturers, magicians, and sexual temptresses. People made sacrifices and prayed to household gods to protect the well-being and health of their families. They also worshipped deities on a local and regional basis. When the Old Kingdom came into being, ruling families elevated certain local gods and religious centers such as Heliopolis (hel-YOH-POH-lis) and Thebes (in the Middle Kingdom) gained national prominence. The most important gods—such as Osiris, Horus, Re', Amun, and Hathor—had their own temples and priesthoods that conducted rituals, sacrifices, and festivals honoring the god they served. The temples owned vast properties, and the income they generated paid for the salaries and upkeep of priests.

---

papyrus—An early form of writing material made from the stem of the papyrus plant.

Egypt's most popular religious cult was devoted to Osiris, the fertility god of the Nile, whose death and resurrection symbolized the planting of grain and its sprouting. The Egyptian myth of fertility and life after death, according to the priests at Heliopolis, was that Osiris had been murdered by Seth, his brother, who cut the victim's body into many pieces and scattered them around Egypt. When Isis, his bereaved widow, collected all the pieces and wrapped them in linen, Osiris was resurrected so that he could father Horus, the Nile floods resumed, and vegetation revived. The Osiris cult taught that Seth was the god of violence and disorder, that Osiris was the ruler of the dead in the netherworld, and that every mummified Egyptian could become another Osiris, capable of resurrection from the dead and a blessed eternal life.

However, only a soul free of sin would be permitted to live forever. In a ceremony called "counting up character," Osiris presided over a court of 42 gods that weighed the heart of the deceased against the Feather of Truth. If the virtues of the heart were outweighed by the Feather of Truth, a horrible creature devoured it. Charms and magical prayers and spells were sold to the living as insurance policies guaranteeing them a happy outcome in the judgment before Osiris. They constitute much of what is known as the *Book of the Dead*, which was placed in tombs and coffins.

Mathematics and Science

The Egyptians were much less skilled in mathematics than the Mesopotamians. Their arithmetic was limited to addition and subtraction, which also served them when they needed to multiply and divide. They could cope with only simple algebra, but they did have considerable knowledge of practical geometry; the obliteration of field boundaries by the annual flooding of the Nile made the measurement of land a necessity. Knowledge of geometry was also essential in computing the dimensions of ramps for raising stones during the construction of pyramids. In these and other engineering projects, the Egyptians were superior to their

In this scene from the Book of the Dead, *a princess stands in the Hall of Judgment in the Underworld before a set of scales on which the jackal-headed god Anubis weighs her heart against the Feather of Truth. The baboonlike god Thoth records the result. On the left, Isis presents the princess, who has also aided her cause, with an offering to Osiris, a haunch of beef.*

Mesopotamian contemporaries. Like the Mesopotamians, the Egyptians acquired a "necessary" technology without developing a truly scientific method. Yet what has been called the oldest known scientific treatise (c. 1600 B.C.E.) was composed during the New Kingdom. Its author, possibly a military surgeon or a doctor who treated pyramid-building laborers, described cases of head and spinal injuries, dislocations, and broken bones and recommended treatments or, in the case of more serious complications, nothing at all. Other medical writings considered a range of ailments, from pregnancy complications to hippopotamus bites. To Egyptian practitioners, the causes of medical conditions had to be dealt with holistically on a spiritual as well as a physical level. Thus they prescribed a combination of medicines, rituals, magical spells, and amulets.

The Old Kingdom also produced the world's first known solar calendar, the direct ancestor of our own. In order to plan their farming operations in accordance with the annual flooding of the Nile, the Egyptians kept records and divided the calendar into three seasons—flooding, planting and growing crops, and harvesting. Each season contained four months with 30 days in each month. They observed that the Nile flood coincided with the annual appearance of the Dog Star (Sirius) on the eastern horizon at dawn, and they soon associated the two phenomena.

Monumentalism in Architecture

Because of their impressive, enduring tombs and temples, the Egyptians have been called the greatest builders in history. The earliest tomb was the mud-brick Arab *mastaba* (MAS-tuh-buh), so called because of its resemblance to a low bench. By the beginning of the Third Dynasty, stone began to replace brick, and an architectural genius named Imhotep, now honored as the "father of architecture in stone," constructed the first pyramid by piling six huge stone *mastabas* one on top of the other. Adjoining this Step Pyramid was a temple complex whose stone columns were not freestanding but attached to a wall, as though the architect were tentatively feeling his way in the use of the new medium.

The Step Pyramid of Zoser, which was built by piling six huge stone mastabas, *one of top of the other.*

The most celebrated of the true pyramids were built for the Fourth Dynasty pharaohs Khufu, Khafre, and Menkaure. Khufu's pyramid, the largest of the three, covers 13 acres and originally rose 481 feet. It is composed of 2.3 million limestone bricks, some weighing 15 tons, and all pushed and pulled into place by human muscle. This stupendous monument was built without mortar, yet some of the stones were so perfectly fitted that a knife cannot be inserted in the joints. The Old Kingdom's 80 pyramids are a striking expression of Egyptian civilization. Their dignity and massiveness reflect the religious basis of Egyptian society—the dogma that the king was a god who owned the nation and that serving him was the most important task of the people.

Just as the glory and serenity of the Old Kingdom can be seen in its pyramids, constructed as an act of loyalty by its subjects, so the power and wealth of the empire survive in the Amon temples at Thebes, made possible by the booty and tribute of conquest. On the east side of the Nile were built the magnificent temples of Karnak and Luxor. The Hypostyle Hall of the temple of Karnak, built by Ramses II, is larger than the cathedral of Notre Dame in Paris. Its forest of 134 columns is arranged in 16 rows, with the roof over a central aisle raised to allow the entry of light. This technique was later used in Roman basilicas and in Christian churches.

Sculpture and Painting

Egyptian art was essentially religious. Tomb paintings and relief sculpture depict the everyday activities that the deceased wished to continue enjoying in the afterlife, and statues glorify the god-kings in all their serenity and eternity. Since religious art is inherently conservative, Egyptian art seldom departed from the classical tradition established during the vigorous and self-assured Old Kingdom. Sculptors idealized and standardized their subjects, and the human figure is shown either looking directly ahead or in profile, with a rigidity very much in keeping with the austere architectural settings of the statues.

Yet, on two occasions an unprecedented realism appeared in Egyptian sculpture. The faces of some of the Middle Kingdom rulers appear drawn and weary, seemingly reflecting the burden of reconstructing Egypt after the collapse of the Old Kingdom. An even greater realism is seen in the portraits of Akhenaton and his queen, Nefertiti, which continued into the following reign of Tutankhamen. The portraits realistically depict the pharaoh's physical appearance such as his ungainly paunch and his happy but far from god-like family life in informal settings—the pharaoh playing with one of his young daughters on his knee or munching on a bone. The "heretic" pharaoh, who insisted on what he called "truth" in religion, seems also to have insisted on truth in art.

Painting shows the same precision and mastery of technique that are evident in sculpture. No attempt was made to show objects in perspective, and the scenes seem flat. The effect of distance was conveyed by making objects in a series or by putting one object above another. Another convention employed was to depict everything from its most characteristic angle. Often the head, arms, and legs were shown in side view while the eyes, shoulders, and chest were shown in front view.

Writing and Literary Texts

In Egypt, as in Sumer, writing began with pictures. But unlike the Mesopotamian signs, the Egyptian hieroglyphics remained primarily pictorial. At first, the hieroglyphics represented a mix of pictorial signs and one- and two-consonant signs that later came to stand for ideas and syllables. Early in the Old Kingdom the Egyptians took the further step of using alphabetical characters for 24 consonant sounds. Although they also continued to use the old pictographic and syllabic signs, the use of sound symbols had far-reaching consequences. It influenced their Semitic neighbors in Syria to produce an alphabet that, in its Phoenician form, became the forerunner of our own.

The earliest Egyptian literary works generally recorded the accomplishments of rulers or expressed religious beliefs through prayers, hymns, and funerary inscriptions. Among the latter are the *Pyramid Texts*, a collection of magic spells and ritual texts inscribed on the walls of the burial chambers of Old Kingdom pharaohs. Their recurrent theme is an affirmation that the dead pharaoh is really a god and that no obstacle can prevent him from joining his fellow gods in the heavens.

Old Kingdom literature went on to achieve a classical maturity of style and content—it stresses a "truth" that is "everlasting." Hence *The Instructions of Ptah-hotep*, addressed to the author's sons, insists that "it is the strength of truth that it endures long, and a man can say, 'I learned it from my father.'" Ptah-hotep's maxims stress the values and virtues that are important in fostering positive human relationships. To him, honesty is a good policy because it will gain one wealth and position, while affairs with other men's wives is a bad policy because it will impede one's path to success in life.[9]

DOCUMENT

Elders' Advice
to Their
Successors

The troubled times that followed the collapse of the Old Kingdom produced the highly personal writings of the First Intermediate Period and the Middle Kingdom. They contain protests against the ills of the day and demands for social justice. In the New Kingdom, writers composed love poems as a means of forgetting misery. The universal appeal of this literature is illustrated by the following lines.

> *I think I'll go home and lie very still,*
> *feigning terminal illness,*
> *Then the neighbors will all troop over to stare,*
> *my love, perhaps among them*
> *How she'll smile while the specialists snarl in*
> *   their teeth!—*
> *She perfectly well knows what ails me.*[10]

MESOPOTAMIAN SUCCESSORS TO BABYLON, c. 1600–550 B.C.E.

■ *What is the legacy left by the states that succeeded the Babylonian Empire?*

The Babylonian Empire came to an end in the sixteenth century B.C.E., most probably through the raids of chariot driving invaders known as the Kassites. Primarily warriors and raiders, they ruled as a minority of conquerors over the native population. Their concern was not with the establishment of lasting political control, but rather with the accumulation of wealth for the dominant warrior class.

The Hittites

Gradually, a people known as the Hittites began to migrate into the region now known as Turkey, settle themselves as a ruling class over the native population, and establish a kingdom that by 1400 B.C.E. became the strongest power in the region and the greatest rival of the Egyptian empire. Very little was known about the Hittites until archaeologists began to unearth the remains of their civilization in Turkey at the beginning of the twentieth century. By 1920 C.E. Hittite writing had been deciphered, and it proved to be the earliest example of an Indo-European language, closely related to Greek, Latin, and Sanskrit. The Hittites began migrating into Asia Minor from the northeast as early as 2000 B.C.E. Their superior military, in particular their mastery of horse-drawn chariot warfare and mass attacks by archers using long-range bows, enabled them to conquer the native people of central Asia Minor and establish a centralized kingdom with its capital city at Hattushash (HAHT-teu-shahsh), which is near the present Turkish capital city, Ankara.

The kings of the early Hittite kingdom were aggressive monarchs who were frequently at odds with their nobles and struggled to establish an orderly succession to the throne. The early effectiveness of the Hittite monarchy was severely limited by this pattern of constant internal strife.

After 1450 B.C.E. a series of energetic Hittite kings succeeded in limiting the independence of their nobles and creating a more centralized empire that included Syria and northern Palestine, which had been left virtually undefended by the Egyptian pharaoh Akhenaton. The pharaoh Ramses II moved north from Palestine in an unsuccessful attempt to reconquer the region in the battle of Kadesh (1285 B.C.E.). Ambushed and forced back to Palestine after a bloody standoff, the pharaoh agreed to a treaty of "good peace and good brotherhood" with the Hittites in 1269 B.C.E.

The Hittite Civilization

The Hittite state under the empire differed in its organization and reflected the traditions of its Indo-European origins rather than the governmental patterns set by the older monarchies of Mesopotamia and Egypt. The king was thought to be the greatest of the nobles, but not a living god or even a god's representative on earth. Hittite nobles held large estates granted by the

The Hittites dedicated animal-shaped drinking vessels to their gods for their own private use. This vessel in the shape of a stag, made of silver with gold inlays, is 7 inches high and dates between the fifteenth to the thirteenth centuries B.C.E.

king and in return provided warriors and served on a council to advise the king and limit his arbitrary power.

The Hittites adopted the Mesopotamian cuneiform script in order to write their Indo-European language. In addition to preserving their own cus-

DOCUMENT

Near Eastern
Law Codes

toms, the Hittites readily incorporated features of earlier Mesopotamian civilization that they found appealing. Sumerian and Mesopotamian literature were preserved, and Mesopotamian gods and goddesses were honored with temples and placed on equal footing with their own traditional deities. While their law codes showed great similarity to the Code of Hammurabi, they differed in prescribing more humane punishments. Instead of retaliation ("an eye for an eye"), the Hittite code made greater use of restitution and compensation.

The Hittites left their mark on later peoples of the region primarily as intermediaries. Their skills in metalworking, especially in iron, were passed eventually to their neighbors. Not especially creative in the formulation of law or literature and art, they borrowed extensively from other cultures and in turn passed their knowledge on to others, in particular to the neighboring Phrygians, Lydians, and Greeks.

The Sea Peoples

The Hittites may have been eager for the peace they concluded with Egypt in after the battle at Kadesh because of threats posed by new movements of raiding and displaced peoples—Indo-Europeans and others. A series of disruptions all over the eastern Mediterranean resulted in the overthrow of previously stable regimes now sacked and destroyed. Many survivors of these upheavals, which possibly included the fall of Troy (c. 1150 B.C.E.), fled by sea to seek new lands to plunder or settle. Collectively known as the Sea Peoples, these uprooted people included Philistines (FI-le-steens), Sicilians, Sardinians, and Etruscans. Many gave their names to the areas where they eventually settled. The collapse of the Hittite Empire, shortly after 1200 B.C.E., was partially a result of these migrations and attacks.

Scholars still hotly debate the causes behind the collapses of so many regimes for around 200 years after 1200 B.C.E. Some experts now believe that changes in warfare— especially the reliance on mobile infantry using short swords and javelins in place of the extensive use of chariots—account for the destruction of stable governments and the resulting displacement of peoples.

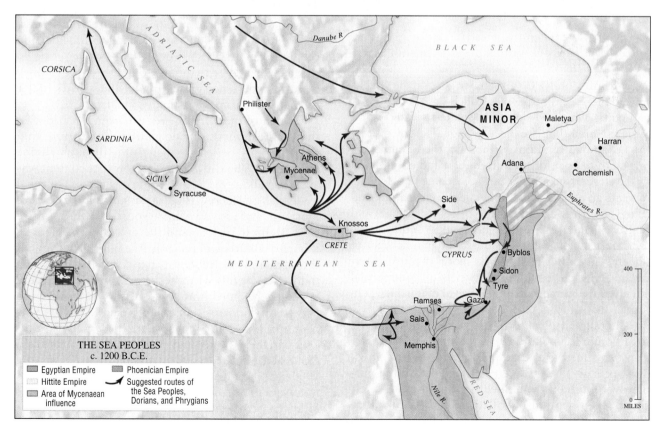

Population movements, the fall of established states, and even the introduction of new and more effective techniques of producing iron weapons may be some of the reasons for the disruption of the eastern Mediterranean around 1200 B.C.E.

The Beginnings of the Iron Age, c. 1100 B.C.E.

Shortly after the disruptions culminating with the invasion of the Sea Peoples, scholars mark the beginning of the Iron Age in the eastern Mediterranean. In fact, iron had been present in small amounts in Mesopotamia as early as one thousand years before, but the metal was seen as too precious to be employed extensively and not initially more effective than bronze. Iron weapons were used by the Hittites as early as 1400 B.C.E., and the technology used to produce iron was a fiercely guarded secret. Many scholars now suggest that, around 1100 B.C.E., partially because of the collapse of the Hittite Empire, the employment of carbonization in the production of iron tools and weapons, and a shortage in the supply of tin to aid in the manufacture of bronze, the use of iron spread from north to south in the eastern Mediterranean.

After 1200 B.C.E, with the Hittite Empire destroyed, the disorder brought by the incursions of the Sea Peoples, and Egypt in decline, the Semitic peoples of Syria and Palestine were able to assert their territorial claims in the power vacuum created by the weakness of once dominant states. For nearly 500 years, until they were conquered by the Assyrians, these peoples played a significant role in the history of the eastern Mediterranean and southwestern Asia.

The Phoenicians

Phoenicians (foh-NEE-shee-ans) is a name the Greeks gave to those Semitic peoples, called Canaanites (KAY-nah-naits), who lived along the Mediterranean coast of Syria, an area that is today Lebanon. Hemmed in by the Lebanon Mountains to the east, the Phoenicians turned to the sea for their livelihood and empire and by the eleventh century B.C.E. had become the Mediterranean's greatest traders, shipbuilders, navigators, and colonizers. To obtain silver and copper from Spain and tin from Britain, they established Gades (Cadiz) on the Atlantic coast of Spain. Carthage, one of a number of Phoenician trading posts on the shores of the Mediterranean, was a remarkably successful commercial colony and became Rome's chief rival in the third century B.C.E. (see Chapter 5).

Although the Phoenicians were essentially traders, their home cities—notably Tyre, Sidon, and Byblos—also produced manufactured goods. Their most famous export was woolen cloth dyed with the purple dye obtained from shellfish found along their coast. They were also skilled makers of furniture (made from the famous cedars of Lebanon), metalware, glassware, and jewelry. The Greeks called Egyptian papyrus rolls *biblia* ("books") because Byblos was the shipping point for this widely used writing material; later the Hebrew and Christian Scriptures were called "the Book" (Bible).

Culturally, the Phoenicians were not particularly original. They left behind no literature and little innovative art. Yet they made one of the greatest contributions to human progress, the perfection of the alphabet, which had a direct influence on the development later western European scripts. Between 1800 and 1600 B.C.E. Phoenician and neighboring Semitic peoples, influenced by Egypt's semi-alphabetical writing, started to evolve a simplified method of writing. The Phoenician alphabet of 22 consonant symbols (the Greeks later added signs for vowels) is related to the 30-character alphabet of Ugarit, a Canaanite city, which was destroyed about 1200 B.C.E. by the Sea Peoples.

The half-dozen Phoenician cities never united to form a strong state, and in the second half of the eighth century B.C.E. all but Tyre were conquered by the Assyrians. Tyre fell to the Chaldean (kahl-DEE-an) Empire in 571 B.C.E., and the one-time fiercely independent status of the Phoenicians ended with their subjugation first to the Chaldeans, and later to subsequent empires—those of the Persians, Greeks, and Romans.

The Hebrew Kingdoms

In war, diplomacy, technology, and art, the Hebrew contributions to history are of small significance; in religion and ethics, however, their contribution to world civilization was momentous. Out of the Hebrew cultural experience grew three of the world's major religions: Judaism, Christianity, and Islam.

Much of that Hebrew experience is recorded in the Old Testament, the collection of literature that the Hebrews believe was written through divine inspiration. The Old Testament's present content was approved about 90 C.E. by a council of rabbis (spiritual leaders). The Hebrew Bible is an outstanding work of literature and also a valuable source for the study of early Hebrew history and the evolution of Hebrew thought, culture, and religion. The biblical account of the history of the Hebrews (later called Israelites, and then Jews) begins with the account of a **patriarchal** clan leader named Abraham, called "the Hebrew" (a nomad or wanderer). Abraham is said to have led his people out of Ur in Sumer, where they had settled for a time in their wanderings. Most biblical scholars suggest that the date of such a migration should be around 1900 B.C.E. Abraham is then credited with leading his followers to northwestern Mesopotamia. He and his followers remained nomadic—the Bible records that Abraham moved his people to Egypt and back again to

---

patriarchal—"Father rule"; of or relating to a social system in which familial and political authority is wielded exclusively by men.

the north, and Abraham's grandson Jacob (later called Israel, and from whom the Israelites derive their name) eventually led a migration into the land of Canaan, later called Palestine.

Historians and archaeologists have raised many questions about the accuracy of biblical accounts for the early Hebrew community. No archaeological proof exists for a migration of peoples into northern Palestine around 1900 B.C.E. although no evidence exists to negate the possibility. Recently archaeologists have suggested that the culture of the age of the founders of the Hebrew community—that culture described in the early books of the Bible—best describes Hebrew culture around 1100 B.C.E., and not that probably in existence 800 years earlier.[11]

The Old Testament suggests that about 1550 B.C.E., driven by famine, some Hebrews followed Abraham's great-grandson Joseph into Egypt. Joseph's possible rise to power in Egypt and hospitable reception of his people there may be attributed to the presence of the largely Semitic Hyksos, who had conquered Egypt about 1720 B.C.E. Following the expulsion of the Hyksos by the pharaohs of the Eighteenth Dynasty, the biblical account states that the Hebrews were enslaved by the Egyptians. Shortly after 1300 B.C.E. a Hebrew leader named Moses led them out of bondage and into the wilderness of Sinai, where they entered into a pact or covenant with their God, Yahweh. The Sinai Covenant bound the people as a whole—the nation of Israel, as they now called themselves—to worship Yahweh before all other gods and to obey his Law (Torah). In return, Yahweh made the Israelites his chosen people, whom he would protect and to whom he granted Canaan, the Promised Land "flowing with milk and honey." The history of Israel from this time on is held by Jewish people to be the account of the fulfillment of this covenant.

There are no indications in Egyptian sources of a large number of Hebrews enslaved in Egypt after the Hyksos were expelled; at the same time, there are no reasons to believe that such treatment of Semitic peoples who remained in Egypt after the Hyksos did not occur. Hebrew tradition identifies Moses as the leader and eventual liberator of the Hebrews in Egypt and their leader during the Exodus (the "Road Out" in Greek), but Egyptian records give no mention of him, the demands he made of Pharaoh, or the plagues the Hebrew god supposedly visited on Egypt.

The Old Testament account of the Exodus from Egypt ends when the Israelites are led through the Sinai and arrive after 40 years of wandering in sight of Palestine. Here, they had to contend with the Canaanites, whose Semitic ancestors had migrated from Arabia early in the third millennium B.C.E. Joined by other Hebrew tribes already in Palestine, the Israelites formed a **confederacy** of 12 tribes, led by leaders called judges, and in time succeeded in subjugating the Canaanites. The biblical account of the conquest of Palestine records a bloody history of conquest and destruction of those Canaanite cities that resisted Hebrew domination—a feat mainly accomplished through the brilliant military leadership of a hero named Joshua. Recent archaeology reveals a different view: that the Hebrew occupation of Palestine was a long and slow process and that the massive destruction of Canaanite cities by Israelites as recorded in the Old Testament is not affirmed by archaeological remains. Rather, the Hebrews seemed to have absorbed, to have been absorbed, and at times to have lived in peace along with already established Canaanite communities in the region.

Leadership of the Israelites in this effort to claim their promised land seems to have been exercised by both men and women called judges—individuals among the twelve tribes of Israel who had shown uncommon degrees of courage (Judith), strength (Sampson), or divine inspiration (Samuel). The active

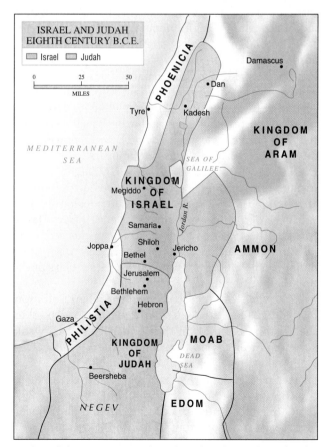

ISRAEL AND JUDAH
EIGHTH CENTURY B.C.E.

☐ Israel ☐ Judah

0   25   50
MILES

PHOENICIA

Damascus

• Dan

Tyre •   • Kadesh

MEDITERRANEAN SEA

KINGDOM OF ARAM

SEA OF GALILEE

KINGDOM OF ISRAEL
Megiddo •

Jordan R.

Samaria •

Joppa •   Shiloh •
        Bethel •   Jericho •
    Jerusalem •
        Bethlehem •
            • Hebron

AMMON

PHILISTIA

Gaza •

KINGDOM OF JUDAH
    Beersheba •

MOAB

DEAD SEA

NEGEV   EDOM

In the eighth century B.C.E., the Hebrew kingdoms of Israel and Judah often found themselves in opposition to each other, as well as being surrounded by potentially more powerful enemies.

confederacy—A system of government in which power is shared between existing political units with no single unit having authority over the others.

and decisive role the Old Testament attributes to Israelite women reflects the great influence they must have exercised in early Israel. Genesis describes the two sexes as being equal and necessary for human livelihood: "So God created mankind in his image, . . . male and female he created them. And God blessed them and said to them, 'Be fruitful and multiply and fill the earth and subdue it [together]'" (1:27–28). And in the Song of Songs the maiden and the youth share equally in the desire and expression of love; there is no sense of subordination of one to the other. But the continuing dangers that faced the nation led to the creation of a strong centralized monarchy, and with it came male domination and female subordination.

As the Israelites were contesting the Canaanites for dominance of the region, an even more formidable opponent appeared. The Philistines, Sea Peoples that had tried unsuccessfully to invade Egypt, and from whom the name Palestine comes, settled along the coast of Israel about 1175 B.C.E. Aided by the use of iron weapons, which were new to the region and the Hebrews, the Philistines captured the Ark of the Covenant, the sacred chest described as having mysterious powers, in which Moses had placed stone tablets inscribed with the Ten Commandments entrusted to him by Yahweh. By the middle of the eleventh century B.C.E. the Philistines appear to have been on course to dominate the entire land.

Lacking a central authority, the loose 12-tribe confederacy of Israel could not hope to ward off the Philistine danger, and a king, Saul, was chosen to unify resistance to the Philistines.

According to the Bible, Saul's reign (c. 1020–1000 B.C.E.) was not successful. Continuously undercut by tribal rivalries and overshadowed by the fame of the boy hero David, who came to prominence by slaying the Philistine giant Goliath in single combat, Saul made no attempt to transform Israel into a centralized monarchy. Saul's successor, the popular David (c. 1000–961 B.C.E.), is credited with restricting the Philistines to a narrow coastal strip to the south of Israel, and also with the consolidation of an impressively large and unified state. David also won Jerusalem from the Canaanites and made it the private domain of his royal court, separate from the existing 12 tribes. His popularity was enhanced when he placed the recovered Ark of the Covenant in his royal chapel, to which he attached a priesthood.

David was succeeded by his son Solomon (961–922 B.C.E.), under whom the Bible says Israel reached its highest degree of power and splendor as a monarchy. But the price of Solomon's vast bureaucracy, building projects (especially the palace complex and the Temple at Jerusalem), standing army (1400 chariots and 12,000 horses), and harem (700 wives and 300 concubines) was great. High taxes, forced labor, and tribal rivalries led to dissension.

Recently, archaeologists have called the Old Testament accounts of the glorious reigns of David and Solomon into question. Some scholars even suggest that a united monarchy never existed, and that even if it did, the extent of its influence is vastly overstated by the Bible. Experts also suggest that the biblical accounts of David's glory and Solomon's wealth are the work of later rulers, dating in particular to the seventh century in the Kingdom of Judah, whose rulers were searching for a glorious past upon which to base their claims of legitimacy.[12] Most archaeologists now concur that the biblical description of David's power and might is exaggerated. Jerusalem appears to have been a hill town of probably no more than 5000 inhabitants in the tenth century B.C.E., and traces of Solomon's great temple have so far evaded the archaeologists. The existence of a dynasty of kings descended from David (the so-called House of David) has been claimed to be proven by the recent discovery of several inscriptions dating to the eighth century, but other scholars question their authenticity.

The Old Testament records that when Solomon died in 922 B.C.E., the kingdom split in two—Israel in the north and Judah in the south. These two weak kingdoms were in no position to defend themselves when new, powerful empires rose again in Mesopotamia. In 722 B.C.E. the Assyrians captured Samaria, the capital of the northern kingdom, taking 27,290 Israelites into captivity (the famous "ten lost tribes" of Israel; two remained in the southern kingdom) and settling other subjects of their empire. The resulting population, called Samaritans, was ethnically, culturally, and religiously mixed, as well as deprived of any political role.

The Hebrews

c. 1800 B.C.E.	Migration of Hebrews to Palestine
c. 1550 B.C.E.	Migration to Egypt
c. 1300–1200 B.C.E.	Exodus from Egypt
c. 1020–1000 B.C.E.	Reign of Saul
c. 1000–961 B.C.E.	Reign of David
961–922 B.C.E.	Reign of Solomon
722 B.C.E.	Northern kingdom destroyed by Assyria
586 B.C.E.	Southern kingdom destroyed by Chaldeans
586–538 B.C.E.	Babylonian Captivity

The southern kingdom of Judah held out until 586 B.C.E., when Nebuchadnezzar, the Chaldean ruler of Babylon, destroyed Jerusalem and carried away a large number of its residents to his capital city. This deportation began the so-called Babylonian Captivity of the Jews (Judeans), which lasted until 538 B.C.E. While held in Babylon, the Jews were considered to be free people, allowed to engage in commerce and industry, and to practice their own religion. Some Jews abandoned their religious traditions, but most seem to have held strongly to them. It was in Babylon that the first synagogues (Greek for "gathering together") came into existence, as the Jewish communities assembled for worship and study.

DOCUMENT

Suffering
Explained

In 538 B.C.E. Cyrus the Great, the king of Persia, conquered Babylon, and allowed the captives to return to Jerusalem. In 515 B.C.E. the returning exiles completed the reconstruction of the Temple destroyed by Nebuchadnezzar. But large numbers of believers never returned to Judah, which was now referred to as Judea by the Persian governors who administered it. These Jews, scattered all over the region, formed communities of worship in their cities of residence, and membership in these communities of believers became an essential component in the lives of the participants. By 500 B.C.E. the majority of Jewish believers lived outside Palestine. This "scattering" (*diaspora* in Greek) was to be a significant characteristic of Jewish existence from this time forward in their history.

The mostly peaceful Persian rule in Judea was followed by the conquest of Palestine by Alexander the Great in 332 B.C.E. After Alexander's death Judea was part of the empire ruled by the Ptolemaic dynasty of Egypt, and in 63 B.C.E. it became a Roman protectorate. Roman administration proved especially rigid and unpopular with the Jews. In 70 C.E. a revolt of the Jews against their Roman rulers was crushed, the city of Jerusalem and the temple destroyed, and the history of the Jews as a political entity ended until the twentieth century. The resulting *diaspora* from their troubled homeland sent the Jews to all the major cities of the Mediterranean, where many became influenced by the culture of the Greco-Roman world, even while others strictly adhered to their traditional beliefs and customs emphasized through instruction in the synagogues.

Hebrew Religion

The Bible states that from the time of Abraham, the Hebrews worshiped one stern, warlike tribal god whose name was not revealed to the Hebrews until the time of Moses. Yet there are traces in the Old Testament of an earlier stage of religious development that shows evidence of animism and a reverence for spirits associated with the winds, stones, and sacred springs. Gradually, beliefs became more sophisticated and developed into a worship of **anthropomorphic** gods. The god of Abraham was a god closely associated with Abraham's clan or tribe. Hebrew religion entered a more sophisticated stage of development around the thirteenth century B.C.E., when Moses is credited with directing the Hebrews toward the worship of a national god, the god of Abraham now revealed to be named Yahweh. The religion of Moses may be called monolatry—the belief that there is one god for that god's select people, but that there may exist other gods for other peoples.

Moses is credited in the Bible with being the recipient of God's law in the form of the Ten Commandments, and the leader who, with Yahweh's assistance, led the Hebrews from Egypt to the Promised Land. After their entrance into Palestine, many Hebrews adopted the **polytheism** of the Canaanites as well as the luxurious Canaanite manner of living. As a result, prophets arose who "spoke for" Yahweh (*prophetes* is Greek for "one who speaks for God"), insisting on strict adherence to the laws delivered by Moses. Between 750 and 550 B.C.E. a series of these prophets wrote down their messages and insisted that disaster would result if Yahweh's chosen people strayed from proper worship. They also developed the idea of a coming Messiah (the "anointed one" of God), a descendant of King David, who would begin a reign of peace and justice.

The destruction of Jerusalem in 586 B.C.E. and the exile in Babylon was another formative event in the evolution of Jewish thought. In accord with the prophetic warnings, Yahweh had punished his chosen people, yet the prophets also foretold that they would be allowed to return to Jerusalem and be reconfirmed as the chosen of God. Many scholars believe that the time spent in Babylon was crucial to the final achievement of true monotheism by Jewish thinkers: the destruction of Yahweh's holy city was not a sign of His weakness, but rather a sign of His power and universality, and His people's journey would serve as proof to all mankind of His glory. The Jews who returned from the Babylonian Captivity were provided a renewed faith in their destiny and a new understanding of their significance in human history.

The Aramaeans

Closely related to the Hebrews were the Aramaeans (ah-rah-MAY-ens), who occupied Syria east of the Lebanon Mountains. The most important of their little kingdoms was centered at Damascus, one of the oldest

---

anthropomorphic—Literally, "human shaped"; endowed with human characteristics.

polytheism—Belief in many gods. Though Judaism, Christianity, and Islam are monotheistic, most other religions throughout history have been polytheistic. The numerous gods may be dominated by a supreme god or a group of gods.

continuously inhabited cities in the world. The Aramaeans dominated the camel caravan trade connecting Mesopotamia, Phoenicia, and Egypt and continued to do so even after Damascus fell to the Assyrians in 732 B.C.E. The Aramaic language, which used an alphabet similar to the Phoenician, became the international language of the Mesopotamian region and the northeastern Mediterranean coast by the fifth century B.C.E. In Judea it was more commonly spoken than Hebrew among the lower classes, and was the language spoken by Jesus and his disciples.

The Assyrian Empire, c. 550–331 B.C.E.

By 700 B.C.E. the era of small states had ended with the emergence of a powerful Assyrian Empire. Two of the greatest achievements of the Assyrians were the forcible unification of weak, unstable regions of Mesopotamia and the establishment of an efficient and centralized imperial organization.

For two centuries before 700 B.C.E. the Assyrians had been attempting to transform the growing economic prosperity of northern and central Mesopotamia into a political unity. The Assyrian attempt to dominate the region began in the ninth century B.C.E; after a short period of weakness, the Assyrian monarchy regained its effectiveness in the eighth century, when the state also took over Babylon. By 671 B.C.E. the Assyrians had annexed Egypt and were the masters of the entire Fertile Crescent.

A Semitic people long residing in the hilly region of the upper Tigris, the Assyrians had experienced a thousand years of constant warfare. But their matchless army was only one of several factors that explain the success of Assyrian imperialism: a policy of calculated terrorism, an efficient system of political administration, and the support of the commercial classes that wanted political stability and unrestricted trade over large areas.

The Assyrian army, with its chariots, mounted cavalry, and sophisticated siege engines, was the most powerful ever seen in the ancient world before 700 B.C.E. Neither troops nor walls could long resist the Assyrians, whose military might seemed unstoppable. Conquered peoples were held firmly in control by systematic policies designed to terrorize. Mass deportations, like that of the Israelites, were employed as an effective means of destroying national feeling.

The well-coordinated Assyrian system of political administration was another factor in the success of the empire. Conquered lands became provinces ruled by governors who exercised extensive military, judicial, and financial powers. Their chief tasks were to ensure the regular collection of tribute (payments demanded by the conquerors) and the raising of troops for the per-

Assyria	
c. 1350 B.C.E.	Assyrian rise to power
704–681 B.C.E.	Military power at height
669–626 B.C.E.	Reign of Ashurbanipal
612 B.C.E.	Fall of Nineveh

manent and professional army that eventually replaced the native militia of sturdy Assyrian peasants. An efficient system of communications carried the "king's word" to the governors as well as the latter's reports to the royal court—including one prophetic dispatch reading: "The king knows that all lands hate us." Nevertheless, the Assyrians should be credited with laying the foundations for some elements of the later more humane administrative systems of their successors, the Persians and Alexander the Great of Macedonia.

Assyrian Culture

The Assyrians borrowed from the cultures of other peoples and unified the elements into a new product. This is evident in Assyrian architecture and sculpture, the work of subject artisans and artists. Both arts glorified the power of the Assyrian king. The palace, serving as both residence and administrative center, replaced the temple as the characteristic architectural form. A feature of Assyrian palace architecture was the structural use of the arch and the column, both

This ancient Assyrian relief, The Dying Lion, is an example of a common theme in royal Assyrian sculpture. The prowess of the Assyrian king as hunter and leader was often emphasized through such artistic themes.

borrowed from Babylonia. Palaces were decorated with splendid relief sculptures that glorified the king as warrior and hunter. Assyrian sculptors were especially skilled in portraying realistically the ferocity and agony of charging and dying lions.

Assyrian kings were interested in preserving written as well as pictorial records of their reigns. King Ashurbanipal (ah-shoor-BAH-ni-pahl; 669–626 B.C.E.), for example, left a record of his great efforts in collecting the literary heritage of Sumer and Babylon. The 22,000 clay tablets found in the ruins of his palace at Nineveh (NI-neh-vah), in today's northern Iraq, provided modern scholars with their first direct knowledge of the bulk of this literature, which included the Sumerian *Epic of Gilgamesh*.

Downfall of the Assyrian Empire

Revolt against Assyrian terror and tribute was inevitable when Assyria's strength weakened and united opposition to Assyrian terror arose. By the middle of the seventh century B.C.E. the Assyrians had been destroyed by wars, and the Assyrian kings had to use unreliable mercenary troops and conscripted subjects. Egypt regained its independence from the Assyrians under the Twenty-Sixth Dynasty, and the Medes to the north refused to pay further tribute. The Chaldeans, tribal groups of Semites who had migrated into Babylonia, revolted in 626 B.C.E. In 612 B.C.E. they joined the Medes in destroying Nineveh, the Assyrian capital. With the fall of the capital city, Assyrian dominance was ended, much to the general satisfaction of the subjects of the Assyrian overlords.

The Lydians and the Medes

The fall of Assyria left four states to struggle over the remains of their empire: the Chaldeans and Egypt fought for control of Syria and Palestine, and Media and Lydia clashed over eastern Asia Minor.

After the collapse of the Hittite Empire about 1200 B.C.E., the Lydians succeeded in establishing a kingdom in western Asia Minor. When Assyria fell, the Lydians expanded eastward until stopped by the Medes at the Halys River, in central Turkey. Lydia profited from being in control of part of the commercial land route between Mesopotamia and the Aegean Sea, and from the possession of valuable gold-bearing streams. About 675 B.C.E. the Lydians invented coinage, which replaced the silver bars in general use up to that time. Lydia's most famous king was Croesus (KREE-sus), a monarch whose wealth was legendary. With the king's defeat by the Persians in 547 B.C.E., Lydia ceased to exist as an independent state.

The Medes were an Indo-European people who by 1000 B.C.E. had established themselves on the Iranian plateau east of Assyria. By the seventh century B.C.E. they had created in Media a strong kingdom with Ecbatana (ek-bah-TAH-nah) as its capital and with the Persians, their kinsmen to the south, as their subjects. Following the collapse of Assyria, the Medes expanded into Armenia and eastern Asia Minor, but their short-lived empire ended in 550 B.C.E. when they, too, were absorbed by the Persians.

The Chaldean (New Babylonian) Empire

While the Median kingdom controlled the northern Iranian plateau, the Chaldeans, with their capital at Babylon, became masters of the fertile crescent. Nebuchadnezzar, who had become king of the Chaldeans in 604 B.C.E., raised Babylonia to another epoch of brilliance after more than a thousand years of eclipse. By defeating the Egyptians in Syria, Nebuchadnezzar ended Egyptian hopes of recreating their empire. As we have seen, he destroyed Jerusalem in 586 B.C.E. and took thousands of captured Jews to Babylonia.

Nebuchadnezzar rebuilt the city of Babylon, making it the largest and most impressive urban center of its day. The tremendous city walls were wide enough at the top to have rows of small houses on either side. In the center of Babylon ran the famous Procession Street, which passed through the Ishtar Gate. This arch, which was adorned with brilliant tile animals, is the best remaining example of Babylonian architecture. The immense palace of Nebuchadnezzar towered terrace upon terrace, each decorated with masses of ferns, flowers, and trees. These roof gardens, the famous Hanging Gardens of Babylon, were so beautiful that they were regarded by the Greeks as one of the seven wonders of the ancient world.

Nebuchadnezzar was the last great Mesopotamian ruler, and Chaldean power quickly crumbled after his death in 562 B.C.E. Chaldean priests, whose interests included political intrigue as well as astrology, continually undermined the monarchy. Finally, in 539 B.C.E. they opened the gates of Babylon to Cyrus the Persian, allowing him to add Babylon to his impressive new empire.

THE PERSIAN EMPIRE, 550–331 B.C.E.

■ *In what ways were the Persians innovators, and how did they also incorporate the legacies of earlier Mesopotamian societies?*

Cyrus the Persian was the greatest conqueror in the history of the ancient Near East. In 550 B.C.E. he ended Persian subjugation to the Medes by captur-

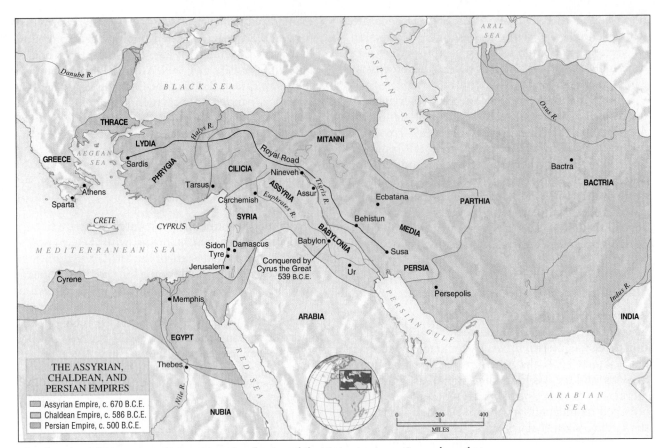

After the seventh century B.C.E. three great empires dominated the Mesopotamian region and sought to extend their control. The Assyrian Empire extended its might into Egypt, the Chaldean into the region of the Fertile Crescent, and the Persian from Egypt in the west to the Indus River in the east.

ing Ecbatana and ending the Median dynasty. Most of the Medes readily accepted their vigorous new ruler, who soon demonstrated that he deserved to be called "the Great." When King Croesus of Lydia moved across the Halys River in 547 B.C.E. to pick up some of the pieces of the collapsed Median Empire, Cyrus defeated him and annexed Lydia, including Greek cities on the coast of Asia Minor that were under Lydia's nominal control. Then he turned his attention eastward, establishing his power as far as the frontier of India. Babylon and its empire were also annexed to the great Persian Empire.

After Cyrus died, his son Cambyses (cam-BAI-seez; 530–522 B.C.E.) conquered Egypt. The next ruler, Darius I (522–486 B.C.E.), added the Punjab region in India and Thrace in Europe. He also began a conflict with the Greeks that continued intermittently for more than 150 years until the Persians were conquered by Alexander the Great in 331 B.C.E.

DOCUMENT

Darius the Great

Persian Government

Although built on the Assyrian model, the Persian administrative system was far more efficient and humane. The empire was divided into 20 *satrapies*, or provinces, each ruled by a governor called a *satrap*. To check the satraps, a secretary and a military official representing the "Great King, King of Kings" were installed in every province. Also, special inspectors, "the Eyes and Ears of the King," traveled throughout the realm. Imperial post roads connected the important cities. Along the Royal Road between Sardis and Susa there was a post station every 14 miles, where the king's couriers could obtain fresh horses, enabling them to cover the 1600-mile route in a week.

The Persian Empire was the first to attempt to govern many different racial groups on the principle

Persia

c. 600 B.C.E.	Union under Achaemenid kings
559–530 B.C.E.	Reign of Cyrus the Great
550 B.C.E.	Conquest of Median Empire
539 B.C.E.	Conquest of Babylon
530–522 B.C.E.	Reign of Cambyses
522–486 B.C.E.	Reign of Darius I

of equal responsibilities and rights for all peoples. So long as subjects paid their taxes and kept the peace, the king did not interfere with local religion, customs, or trade. Indeed, Darius was called "the shopkeeper" because he stimulated trade by introducing a uniform system of gold and silver coinage on the Lydian model.

Persian Religion and Art

The humaneness of the Persian rulers may have stemmed from the ethical religion founded by the prophet Zoroaster, who lived in the early sixth century B.C.E. Zoroaster attempted to replace what he called "the lie"—ritualistic, idol-worshipping cults and their Magi priests—with a religion centered on the sole god Ahura-Mazda ("Wise Lord"). This "father of Justice" demanded "good thoughts of the mind, good deeds of the hand, and good words of the tongue" from those who would attain paradise (a Persian word). This new higher religion made little progress until first Darius and then the Magi adopted it. The Magi revived many old gods as lesser deities, added much ritual, and replaced monotheism with dualism by transforming what Zoroaster had called the principle or spirit of evil into the powerful god Ahriman (the model for the Jewish Satan), the rival of Ahura-Mazda, "between which each man must choose for himself."

The complicated evolution of Zoroastrianism is revealed in its holy book, the Avesta ("The Law"), assembled in its present form between the fourth and sixth centuries C.E. Zoroastrian **eschatology**—the "doctrine

---

eschatology—Theological doctrine of the "last things," or the end of the world.

Document   The Majesty of Darius the Great: A Persian Royal Inscription

The Persian kings ruled their vast empire with absolute authority. But these kings were not regarded as divine beings ruling without responsibility. The power of the king had to be exercised in a reasonable and ethical manner, and in accord with the precepts of the great god of the Persians, Ahura-Mazda. The following inscription, attributed to King Darius the Great, was intended to show the Persian people that the king was an able and powerful monarch, but in addition a just and merciful administrator of his responsibilities:

A great god is Ahuramazda who created this excellent work which one sees; who created happiness for man; who bestowed wisdom and energy upon Darius the king. Says Darius the king: by the favour of Ahuramazda I am of such a kind that I am a friend to what is right, I am no friend to what is wrong. It is not my wish that to the weak is done wrong because of the mighty, it is not my wish that the weak is hurt because of the mighty, that the mighty is hurt because of the weak. What is right, that is my wish. I am no friend of the man who is a follower of the lie. I am not hot-tempered. When I feel anger rising, I keep that under control by my thinking power. I control firmly my impulses. The man who co-operates, him do I reward according to his co-operation. He who does harm, him I punish according to the damage. It is not my wish that a man does harm, it is certainly not my wish that a man if he causes damage be not punished. What a man says against a man, that does not convince me, until I have heard testimony(?) from both parties. What a man does or performs according to his powers, satisfies me, therewith I am satisfied and it gives me great pleasure and I am very satisfied and I give much to faithful men.

I am trained with both hands and feet. As a horseman I am a good horseman. As a bowman I am a good bowman, both afoot and on horseback. As a spearman I am a good spearman, both afoot and on horseback. And the skills which Ahuramazda has bestowed upon me and I have had the strength to use them, by the favour of Ahuramazda, what has been done by me, I have done with these skills which Ahuramazda has bestowed upon me.

Questions to Consider

1. What might have been the purpose of this inscription? What might have been its effect on the king's subjects who read it?

2. How does the inscription give the impression that the king's authority is unquestioned?

3. Why do you think that references to the king's skill as a hunter and a bowman are included? Are his exploits overstated or modestly listed? What purpose did these references to physical skills have?

From B. Gharib, "A Newly Found Inscription of Xerxes," *Iranica Antiqua,* 1968, as quoted in Amélie Kuhrt, *The Ancient Near East: c. 3000–330 B.C.E.,* Vol. 2 (London: Routledge, 1995), p. 681.

of final things" such as the resurrection of the dead and a last judgment—also influenced later Judaism. Following the Muslim conquest of Persia in the seventh century C.E., Zoroastrianism virtually disappeared in its homeland. It exists today among the Parsees in India and in scattered communities worldwide.

In art the Persians borrowed largely from their predecessors in the fertile crescent, particularly the Assyrians. Their most important contribution was in palace architecture, the best remains of which are now found at Persepolis. Built on a high terrace in southern Iran, the royal residence was reached by a grand stairway faced with beautiful reliefs. Instead of the warfare and violence that characterized Assyrian sculpture, these reliefs depict hundreds of soldiers, courtiers, and representatives of 23 nations of the empire bringing gifts to the king for the festival of the new year.

CONCLUSION

During the Paleolithic and Neolithic periods, several technological and agricultural advances gave humans the opportunity to spread and adapt to different parts of the world. Increasingly sophisticated tools and techniques of operation allowed humans to hunt and gain control over diverse environments, while the transition from good gathering to food production made it possible for the development of the first significant civilizations along the banks of rivers.

In the second half of the fourth millennium B.C.E., the first major civilizations, Mesopotamia and Egypt, originated in river valleys: one by the Tigris and Euphrates and one by the Nile. In each instance, the complex society we call a civilization was the result of organized and cooperative efforts that were necessary to make the rivers useful to humans living along them.

Cooperation and centralized leadership resulted in interdependent urban living—the quest for order in a challenging, disorderly world. Through centralized control of religion, these early civilizations sought to understand the gods and establish harmony with them.

Through creativity and inventiveness—bronze tools and weapons, the wheel, writing, and law, either in written form or revealed through the person of pharaoh—social order was established in the first cities.

Mesopotamian civilization originated in the land called Sumer. The achievements of the Sumerians served as a foundation for later Mesopotamian civilizations established by Semitic peoples migrating into the river valleys. The most significant of these later Semitic civilizations was the Babylonian Empire ruled by Hammurabi. Babylon was sacked by the Indo-European Hittites of Asia Minor, who went on to duel with Egypt over control of Syria and Palestine.

In Egypt a great civilization arose on the banks of the Nile, a civilization both monumental and timeless. The temples and tombs of the Egyptian monarchs were designed to endure forever and to preserve the satisfying and stable existence of this world into eternity. Egypt centered on the absolute rule of the pharaohs—god-kings who eventually extended their domain from Nubia to the Euphrates River.

By 1200 B.C.E. the great Near Eastern empires—Babylonian, Egyptian, and Hittite—had weakened, allowing the Semitic peoples of Syria and Palestine more opportunity to make their own cultural contributions. Although never a powerful political force in the ancient world, Israel would have a momentous impact on the future through its development of a sophisticated and influential religious tradition. Political diversity had ended by the rise of the Assyrian Empire, which unified the ancient Near East for the first time. After the fall of Assyria, the Chaldean Nebuchadnezzar constructed a new Babylonian Empire, but it was soon engulfed by the expansion of Persia. Stretching from India to Europe, the Persian Empire gave the Near East its greatest extension and power.

The achievements of these early civilizations would become the inheritance of the Greeks and eventually the Romans. Much of the social and cultural legacy of the ancient Near East remains preserved in the fabric of those Mediterranean societies, which rose to political and cultural prominence after the first civilizations declined in vitality.

Suggestions for Web Browsing

You can obtain more information about topics included in this chapter at the websites listed below. See also the companion website that accompanies this text, http://www.ablongman.com/brummett, which contains an online study guide and additional resources.

Fossil Hominids: Mary Leakey
http://www.talkorigins.org/faqs/homs/mleakey.html

Discussion, with images, of the life and findings of one of the twentieth century's most famous archaeologists. Links to husband Louis Leakey, son Richard Leakey, Olduvai Gorge, and fossil findings.

Human Prehistory: An Exhibition
http://users.hol.gr/~dilos/prehis.htm

Walk through six rooms of text and vivid images that discuss the works of Lyell, Huxley, and Darwin; the first humans; the first human creations; the first villages, including Çatal Hüyük, and artworks of Neolithic Greece.

Chauvet Cave
http://www.culture.gouv.fr/culture/arcnat/chauvet/en/

A French government site on a major discovery of prehistoric cave art. Contains information about the findings and many views of cave paintings at this location and others in France.

Neanderthal Museum
http://www.neanderthal.de/

Site of a German museum whose goals are to maintain and popularize the cultural heritage of the Neanderthals.

Oriental Institute Virtual Museum
http://www-oi.uchicago.edu/OI/MUS/QTVR96/QTVR96.html

An integral part of the University of Chicago's Oriental Institute, the Oriental Institute Museum offers a virtual showcase of the history, art, and archaeology of the ancient Near East.

Hammurabi
http://home.echo-on.net/~smithda/hammurabi.html

A short biography of Hammurabi, in addition to a discussion of the legal concepts he espoused in his code and a virtual recreation of the Hanging Gardens of Babylon.

Egyptian Museum
http://www.egyptianmuseum.gov.eg/

Website of the Egyptian Museum in Cairo, highlighting images of accessories and jewelry, sculptures, furniture, mummies, and written documents of ancient Egypt from the museum's enormous collection.

Museums of the Vatican: Gregorian Egyptian Museum
http://www.christusrex.org/www1/vaticano/EG-Egiziano.html

The Vatican Museum's Egyptian Museum provides images and descriptions of many of the significant objects in one of the world's best ancient Egyptian museums.

Nubia: The Land Upriver
http://ancientneareast.tripod.com/Nubia.html

The geography and early history of the Nubian peoples, from prehistoric times to the kingdom of Kush.

The Hittite Home Page
http://www.asor.org/HITTITE/HittiteHP.html

A website devoted to all things Hittite, including a useful list of links to various universities conducting excavations of Hittite sites.

Material Culture of the Ancient Canaanites, Israelites, and Related Peoples: An Information Database from Excavations
http://www.bu.edu/anep/

This site contains hundreds of images of artifacts such as weapons, tools, and jewelry, with brief histories of the cultures described.

World Cultures: Mesopotamia and Persia
http://www.wsu.edu:8080/~dee/MESO/PERSIANS.HTM

This site gives valuable information on the influence of geography on early Persian civilization, reviews Persian military history, and discusses the importance of Persian religion.

Literature and Film

Selections of Egyptian literature are presented in John Foster, *Echoes of Egyptian Voices: An Anthology of Ancient Egyptian Poetry* (University of Oklahoma Press, 1992), and R. B. Parkinson, trans. and ed., *Voices from Ancient Egypt: An Anthology of Middle Kingdom Writings* (University of Oklahoma Press, 1991).

Stephanie Dalley, ed., *Myths from Mesopotamia: Creation, the Flood, Gilgamesh, and Others* (Oxford University Press, 1998), is an excellent compilation from a variety of Mesopotamian cultures. Danny Jackson et al., eds., *The Epic of Gilgamesh* (Bolchazy Carducci, 1997), is a unique modern translation of the epic poem.

Two excellent videos are *Ancient Mesopotamia* (Schlessinger Media, 1998), and the six-video set presented by Bill Moyers on

Genesis (PBS, 1998), in which an impressive array of experts discuss the implications and meaning of the biblical account.

Three other videos stand out: *Egypt—Beyond the Pyramids* (History Channel, 2001). This film investigates recent archaeological discoveries in Egypt, including tombs of pharaohs, temples, and cemeteries. *In Search of Human Origins* (NOVA PBS, 1994) is a three-part documentary that explores the search for human origins by scientists. *In search of History: Akhenaten: Egypt's Heretic King* (Arts and Entertainment, 1998) is a documentary portrait of Akhenaton's life and his impact on Egyptian religion and art and an exploration of his capital city, Akhetaton.

Suggestions for Reading

For comprehensive accounts of the human fossil record, the evolution of the human brain and cognitive powers, and the significance of lithic art, see Ian Tattersall, *Becoming Human: Evolution and Human Uniqueness* (Harcourt Brace, 1998), and Donald C. Johanson and Blake Edgar, *From Lucy to Language* (Simon & Schuster, 1996).

On human evolution and the spread of humankind from Africa to the rest of the world, see Noel T. Boaz, *Eco Homo: How the Human Being Emerged from the Cataclysmic History of the Earth* (HarperCollins, 1997); Ian Tattersall, *The Last Neanderthal: The Rise, Success, and Mysterious Extinction of Our Closest Relatives* (Westview Press, 1999); and Christopher Stringer and Robin McKie, *African Exodus: The Origins of Modern Humanity* (Henry Holt, 1997). Jared Diamond's *Guns, Germs and Steel: The Fates of Human Societies* (W. W. Norton, 1997) examines the impact of environment on the development of human societies in different parts of the world.

A work that deals with the origins of toolmaking in a broad cultural matrix is Kathy Schick and Nicholas Toth, *Making Silent Stones Speak: Human Evolution and the Dawn of Technology* (Simon & Schuster, 1993). On early communities, see Tim Megarry, *Society in Prehistory: The Origins of Human Culture* (New York University Press, 1996).

Fundamental forms of expression in primeval art, symbolization, the role of animals, depiction of the human figure (including fertility figurines), and the conception of space in prehistory are dealt with in Sigfried Giedion's *The Eternal Present: The Beginnings of Art* (Pantheon, 1962).

The debate between the "Out of Africa" and multiregional schools is treated in Milford Wolpoff and Rachel Caspari, *Race and Human Evolution: A Fatal Attraction* (Simon & Schuster, 1997) and Christopher Stringer and Rachel McKie, *African Exodus: The Origins of Modern Humans* (Henry Holt, 1997).

Amélie Kuhrt, *The Ancient Near East*, 2 vols. (Routledge, 1995), is an outstanding and useful overview of Mesopotamia to 330 B.C.E. William W. Hallo and William Kelly Simpson, *The Ancient Near East: A History* (Harcourt Brace, 1998), remains a good standard text. Jean Bottero et al., *Everyday Life in Ancient Mesopotamia* (Johns Hopkins University Press, 2001) gives an excellent account of the culture. Surveys of Egyptian history include Nicolas Grimal, *A History of Ancient Egypt*, trans. Ian Shaw (Blackwell, 1992), and the 14-volume *Cambridge Ancient History* (Cambridge University Press, 1970–1997). The history of Nubia and the kingdom of Kush is examined in Derek Welsby, *The Kingdom of Kush* (Wiener, 1998) and Stanley Burstein, ed., *Ancient African Civilizations: Kush and Axum* (Wiener, 1998). For the history and significance of the Hittites, see Trevor Bryce, *The Kingdom of the Hittites* (Oxford University Press, 1998). For two contrasting but well-researched interpretations of ancient Israel, see David J. Goldberg and John D. Rayner, *The Jewish People: Their History and Their Religion* (Viking, 1987), and I. Finkelstein and N. A. Silberman, *The Bible Unearthed* (The Free Press, 2001). Don Nardo, *The Persian Empire* (Lucent Books, 1998) and J. M. Cook, *The Persian Empire* (Barnes & Noble, 1998), are two of the best studies on ancient Persian history and culture.

Ancient China—Origins to Empire

Prehistory to 220 C.E.

The Neolithic Chinese people were a series of distinct, regional groups or cultures that have been traced back almost 10,000 years. By 200 C.E., the Chinese people belonged to an empire supported by trade routes in Asia and Africa, by a written history, and by rule by kings: they had a sense of commonality as Chinese. They also shared legendary heroes and heroines. Within both the empire and contending philosophies, there were strong attempts to maintain social differences—to keep an order that distinguished between Chinese and non-Chinese, rich and poor, and the feminine and the masculine both inside and outside the household. Such attempts at establishing and maintaining these distinctions did not always work.

Even with the maintenance of social differences during this formative period, in the face of often cataclysmic disasters, the Chinese maintained a zest for life. They reacted to human suffering by pursuing religious answers and by instituting ambitious innovations in all aspects of society from philosophy to economics. Throughout, the state retained its theoretical focus toward the amelioration of social evils and the relief of distress.

THE ORIGINS OF CHINA, 6500–221 B.C.E.

■ *What developments in culture, politics, and philosophy molded prehistoric China into a civilization?*

The Neolithic Age: c. 6500–c.1600 B.C.E.

As in other parts of the world, there were tool-using humanoids *(homo erectus)* some 600,000 to 800,000 years ago on the Chinese subcontinent. Modern humans *(homo sapiens)* appeared in China around 100,000 years ago, and were hunters and gatherers during the Paleolithic period (c. 100,000–10,000 B.C.E.). They lived in a vast watershed, extending over 1000 miles from north to south and east to west and drained by two river systems that rise on the high

Tibetan plateau and flow eastward to the Pacific. Three mountain ranges crisscross the river systems, diminishing in altitude as they slope eastward. The Huanghe (HWAHNG-HUH) or Yellow River crosses the highlands of the west, the deserts of the north, the hills filled with yellow silt called "loess," and the entire alluvial plain. The silt gradually builds up along the river bottom, requiring extensive dykes and river control to permit the development of agriculture. The Yangzi (YAHNG-zih) River forms the second river system. Emerging from the Tibetan highlands, it moves through gorges with cliffs 1000 or more feet high. Extensive drainage of the Yangzi valley over several centuries allowed rice agriculture to emerge in China's heartland.

Within the Chinese subcontinent, geographers have identified at least eight different ecosystems, ranging from the semitropical southeast, receiving as much as 5 feet of rain each year, to the desert-like northwest, which gets less than 4 inches of rain annu-

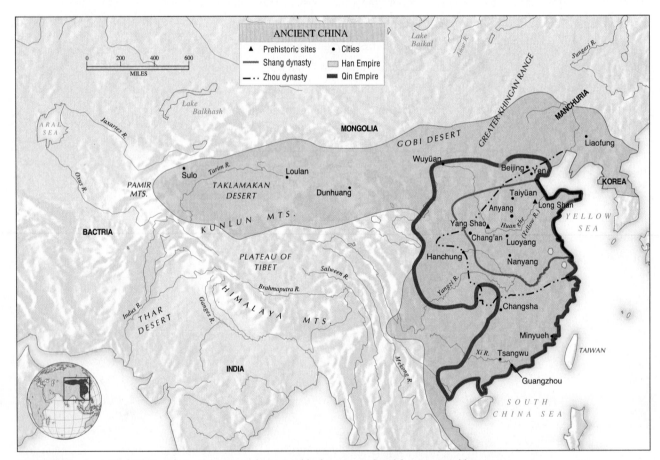

Ancient China's establishment and expansion were determined by key geographical factors. In addition to such divisions as those separating northern and southern cultures, determined by the Huanghe and Yangzi Rivers, there was geographic expansion incorporating independent peoples and states into one bureaucratic entity. By the end of the Han Empire, China had come close to achieving its natural geographic frontiers from the South China Sea to the Eurasian Steppes to the north, and the Himalayan mountains to the west. China was thus open to invasion from the north, west, and south, but conflict with "barbarians" was a stimulus to enormous cultural change.

ally. Geography, along with shifts in climate, determined the emergence of two main regional cultures by the Neolithic era.

Archaeological discoveries confirm the presence of Neolithic settlements in China before 5000 B.C.E. In each region, climate and rainfall affected the kinds of crops that were domesticated. Rice and water plants such as lotus and water chestnuts were grown in the warm, moist Yangzi valley and south of the Yangzi. Millet and wheat grew well in the drier climate of the north. In both north and south China, dogs, cattle, and pigs were raised, while buffalo were more common in the north and sheep in the south. Domestication of plants and animals in the Neolithic period may have been influenced by similar developments in West Asia, showing a sophisticated ability to adopt and develop techniques used elsewhere in Eurasia. Neolithic culture can also be divided into eastern and western geographic regions. The Yangshao (yahng-SHOW) culture of the western region (5000–3000 B.C.E.) produced geometrically painted pottery. The eastern region's culture produced beautifully crafted jade figurines and jewelry. By the late Neolithic period (3000–2000 B.C.E.), the techniques and skills were blended, as geometric designs moved westward and styles of pottery were shared. Interpreting cracks on heated bones inscribed with questions, called oracle bones, was also practiced in both areas. There is evidence that metallurgy began to be used to make weapons in this period.

Settlements surrounded by packed-earth walls appeared throughout North China. Located along the rivers, they sheltered their residents from aggressive actions of other communities. China's communities were very diverse in the Neolithic era. Some people lived in towns; some were nomadic. While the towns made institutional and technological advances, especially in the area of defense, the nomadic bands created their own effective weapons. The tension between the settled communities and the more nomadic bands had a decisive effect on the development of Chinese politics and culture.

Historians do not agree if a well-organized dynasty existed in China before the Shang dynasty in the

Preimperial History

before 1600 B.C.E.	"Xia"
c. 1600–1027 B.C.E.	Shang
1027–770 B.C.E.	Western Zhou
770–256 B.C.E.	Eastern Zhou
722–481 B.C.E.	Spring and Autumn period
403–221 B.C.E.	Warring States period

Bronze Age. But the founding myths of China constructed a country defined by government and technology bequeathed by sage rulers. According to these myths, the earliest sages were Fu Xi (FOO SHEE), the Ox-tamer, credited with inventing the family and domesticating animals; Shen Nong, the Divine Farmer, who invented farming; and Huang Di (hoo-AHNG DEE), the Yellow King, who invented writing, silk, and pottery and was deemed the first of the **Five Sover-**

The sophistication of c. 4000 B.C.E. artisans can be seen in this Neolithic vessel. At the same time practical and pleasing to the eye, this bowl testifies to the aesthetic standards of everyday Chinese civilization.

eigns. The last two of these five were Yao, who invented rituals, and Shun, a paragon of filial piety, who appointed wise officials. Shun's successor, Yu, is credited with developing flood control. Early historians considered Yu and his son the founders of a dynasty called Xia (shee-AH). Though such a centralized dynasty may not have existed (and is the object of debate among historians in China), the kinds of values attributed to its kings and sagely men before them created lasting Chinese institutions.

Five Sovereigns—Mythical ancient kings who are believed to have ruled before hereditary dynastic succession was established.

The Bronze Age: The Shang Dynasty (c. 1600–c. 1027 B.C.E.)

The diverse cultures of northern China gave rise to a complex Bronze Age civilization sometime in the centuries after 2000 B.C.E. Several cultures remained in North China for a few centuries while one, the Shang, came to predominate by 1600 B.C.E. The Shang supposedly arose to conquer a particularly oppressive Xia overlord; the idea that sagely rule could give way, in later generations, to rule by corrupt descendents, had begun to take root. Over the 600 years of Shang rule, China developed even more complex systems of government, cities, writing, class and occupational stratification, religious ritual as the basis of the state, and sophisticated metallurgy.

Shang territorial control was not extensive, being located primarily around the Huanghe. But the spread of Shang culture stretched all the way to the Yangzi valley. In the area of Shang control, archaeological evidence of Shang capitals such as Zhengzhou (juhng-JOH) and, later, Anyang, indicates that the kings could exercise enormous power. They could demand the work of a large number of laborers and craftsmen to build their palaces and tombs. Zhengzhou, for instance, was surrounded by walls 2385 feet long, 60 feet wide, and 30 feet high. As their political and military fortunes varied, the rulers moved their capitals frequently during the six centuries of the Shang dynasty. The final Shang capital was at Anyang where the marshaling of resources and skills for the production of bronze artifacts also points to a concentration of power.

The Shang dynasty differed from its predecessors in more than simply the development of a sophisticated bronze metallurgy. Shang artisans, who lived in production centers surrounding the capital's power core with its palaces and temples, used bronze to make elaborate ceremonial and drinking vessels, weapons, pottery, and stone carvings. Not only were the bronze and other productions practical, but they were also works of art with both incised and high-relief designs. A common design was the animal mask, or *taotie* (TOW-tee-eh).

The Shang people used a system of writing that probably originated before their rule, as graphs are

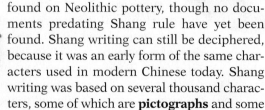

DOCUMENT

Oracle Bones and Chinese Characters

found on Neolithic pottery, though no documents predating Shang rule have yet been found. Shang writing can still be deciphered, because it was an early form of the same characters used in modern Chinese today. Shang writing was based on several thousand characters, some of which are **pictographs** and some of which represent sounds or meanings. Some Chinese characters consisted of two parts: one part indicating the topic of the word and the second expressing the

sound. An example of the combination of two elements is the word for "family" or "home," which consists of the character for pig placed under a roof.

The Chinese writing system in later centuries served as the foundation for other written languages in East Asia, including Korean and Japanese. Because the writing system was not phonetic, it could be used to represent other languages as well as variations of Chinese in different locations and across the centuries. It could be imposed on conquered peoples who already spoke Chinese or a related language. Shang culture could even be extended beyond the boundaries of the king's control—including to those who spoke different languages—through transmission of ideas written in Chinese characters. Over the next three millennia, a certain degree of ideological conformity could be maintained even as diverse cultures and technological advances produced fundamental differences within China. Writing also served to advance government functions and increasingly sophisticated intellectual activities.

IMAGE

An Inscribed Oracle Bone

Most Shang writing is found on thousands of oracle bones, fragments of animal bones and tortoise shells. The religious diviners of the Shang kings dried the shells and bones and dug hollows in them to make the bones crack more easily. After the king relayed his question, the priests put a hot poker to the bones and interpreted the resulting cracks. Engravers then recorded these interpretations onto the bones. The written questions were directed at the ancestral spirits, who were believed to be closely tied to their living descendants as members of the family group. The living would ask the dead such questions as "Will the king's child be a son?" and "If we raise an army of 3000 men to drive X away from Y, will we succeed?" The practice of oracle bone divination was a form of religious ritual, accompanied by music, dancing, and animal or human sacrifices.

As the state and its activities grew more complex, the kings had to oversee not only fighting but also taxing and governing, processes facilitated by writing and record keeping. The leaders needed to record their decisions and to transmit them to their often distant subjects. These tasks were done by scribes, who became increasingly useful to the kings. Later, the scribes would grow in power to become trusted officials who would defend the monarch's power when the kings were off fighting wars or interacting with communities outside the region around the capital.

Religion played the key connective role in the maintenance of social order. The king was at the top of the Shang power structure because his ancestors were deemed best able to communicate with the supreme deity, Di, and the Shang king himself was best able to communicate with his own ancestors. The king and people worshipped other deities, including the gods controlling the Huanghe River and the mountains as well as the long-dead ancestors and recently deceased members

---

pictographs—Characters that depict an object or idea; thus, the character for "tree" originated in a drawing of a tree.

of the royal family. Ancestor worship, a key element of Shang royal power, continued in later times as veneration of ancestors and, in a particular case, as filial piety, or veneration of one's parents, the closest ancestors.

No distinction was made between the king's religious and secular powers, and his government was replicated in the structure of the patriarchal family—the state was a household that had to be managed. The Shang kings were to communicate with Di via dialogue with deceased royal kin. Such communication was accompanied by offerings to the king's ancestors in a ceremony. Offerings took various forms, including sacrifice of humans or offerings of rich foods to ancestors. Below the king on the social ladder were members of his family line or lineage who comprised the Shang aristocracy, court officials, lords who owned land, and finally what the oracle bones termed "the multitude"—common people who, unlike the kings and nobles, had no recorded ancestors and did not belong to a clan. Common people included artisans who worked in jade, bronze, wood, or leather; spun and wove silk; and devised a rich material culture, as well as peasants who lived in villages in houses partially below ground level. At the very bottom of the social order were the prisoners of war who were enslaved and forced to work on massive building projects. After their work was completed, many prisoners' heads and limbs were cut off before burial. Members of the nobility often accompanied the king to his death, and oracle bone inscriptions reveal that over 7000 captive slaves, many from the neighboring Qiang (chee-AHNG) people, were sacrificed in order to win the aid or avoid the displeasure of the spirits. As part of the ritual of human and animal sacrifice, a beerlike liquor was poured on the ground.

Unlike the common people, the kings and nobles had recorded ancestors and belonged to a clan. They were the descendants in the male line from a common ancestor whom they worshipped. The lesser levels of society each had their local gods, to whom requests to guarantee good harvests and long life were addressed. The peasants belonged to no clans, and there is no evidence that they worshipped their ancestors. Instead, their gods were the fundamental forces of nature, such as rivers, mountains, earth, wind, rain, and the stars and planets.

During the Shang period, a special group of Chinese became skilled in the use of magic, with which they attempted to manipulate the two forces of the world. They called these two opposed but complementary forces *yang* and *yin*. Yang was associated with the sun and all things male, strong, warm, and active; yin was associated with the moon and all things female, dark, cold, weak, and passive. Many centuries later, in the fourth century B.C.E., scholars speculated about these forces. In later ages Chinese thinkers would also employ these concepts to compel greater obedience and passivity from women.

The power of the kings and nobles rested on their ownership of the land, their monopoly of bronze metallurgy, their chariots, the king's religious functions and his frequent visits to subordinate domains, and a bureaucracy that was considered divine. We can see proof of the power of the Shang kings and their nobles in their imposing buildings, military superiority, and tombs. They often entered into battle across North

Chariots, whose appearance around 1200 B.C.E. attests to contact with cultures to the west of China, were a symbol of kingly power in the Shang and Zhou and were therefore sometimes buried with rulers, as in this pit in Hebei.

China and, for centuries, gained victory by using chariots, a potent technological advantage around the year 1200 B.C.E. that suggests contact with other chariot-using societies in western Asia. After death, the Shang kings' power continued when they were buried in sumptuous tombs along with those chariots and still-living servants and war captives.

Peasants might be legally free, but they had little mobility. They rarely owned land and worked plots periodically assigned to them by royal and noble landowners. They collectively cultivated the fields retained by their lords. Farming methods were primitive, not having advanced beyond the Neolithic level. Bronze was used for weapons and artwork, but not for farm tools or implements, and the peasants continued to reap wheat and millet with stone sickles and till their allotted fields with wooden plows. The inequity between the power of the king and the powerlessness of his impoverished subjects was evident by the eleventh century B.C.E. It was replaced by a new power that claimed political legitimacy due to its greater virtue.

The Zhou Dynasty (1027?–221 B.C.E.)

Around 1050 B.C.E. the Zhou frontier state, which had adopted the material advances of the Shang while preserving the cultural traditions of pre-Shang Neolithic societies, overthrew the Shang dynasty. An early Zhou history, *The Book of Documents*, later included among the classics, explained that the Shang had become corrupt and dissolute and their conquest by the virtuous Zhou was to be expected. The Zhou leader announced that Heaven *(Tian)* had given him a mandate to replace the Shang. Because the concept that Heaven indicated its will through uprisings and natural disasters was new in China, the Zhou seizure of power as *Tian*'s will was probably, in part, a rationalization for the Zhou overthrow of Shang rule. The idea of a mandate of Heaven introduced a new and very long-lasting aspect of Chinese thought: The cosmos is ruled by an impersonal and all-powerful Heaven that sits in judgment over the human ruler who links Heaven's commands and human fate. Without approval or mandate from Heaven, in other words, kingly rule was not possible. The king came to be called the "Son of Heaven."

The Zhou were a powerful western frontier tribe that took advantage of the opportunities of the wealth and increasing weakness of Shang rule. Given the Zhou's military strength, the other Chinese tribes wisely switched their loyalty to them. The Zhou went on to establish a dynasty that lasted, in one form or another, for almost 900 years (c. 1027–221 B.C.E.).

Three Zhou rulers are credited in early texts with establishing the stable Zhou state. The founder, King Wen, formed alliances with neighboring states while the Shang ruled with cruelty; Wen's son, King Wu, moved the capital eastward to Luoyang (lo-YANG) and began to fight the Shang; and the Duke of Zhou, Wu's brother, intelligently and benevolently ruled as regent for Wu's young son. After building a beautiful capital at Luoyang and conquering other states in the Yangzi valley, the Duke of Zhou stepped down to let his nephew rule.

Spread out over most of North China and the Yangzi valley, the very size of the Zhou domain made it impossible to be ruled directly from the center. States on the periphery were either ruled by Zhou relatives sent out as their representatives or allowed to stay under the jurisdiction of local chiefs. These chiefs were given hereditary titles and sent tribute to the Zhou. They also had armies that fought alongside the Zhou king's army. The king and these subordinate lords (later called vassals) were linked by kinship. Some were partrilineally related; others were related through marriage. The num-

Bronze vessels, such as this one from the early tenth century B.C.E., were designed to contain water, wine, meat, or grain used during the sacrificial rites in which the Shang and Zhou prayed to the spirits of their ancestors. Animals were a major motif of ritual bronzes.

bers of these subordinate rulers fluctuated greatly over the long centuries of Zhou rule. Around 800 B.C.E., there were approximately 200 domains, of which 25 or so were large enough to be important. With their hereditary officials and various types of aristocrats, Zhou society was hierarchically arranged from the Son of Heaven on top, down through domain lords, great officials, lesser officials, and ordinary commoners.

The early Zhou kings were strong leaders who kept the allegiance of their vassals, the lords of the peripheral territories, while fighting off attacks on the frontiers. However, after two centuries, complacency set in, and a succession of weak kings led to a reduction in the central throne's power over its subordinates; taking advantage of advances in military technology, the vassals became more independent. By the eighth century B.C.E. the vassals no longer went to the Zhou capital for investiture by the Son of Heaven. As the Zhou monarchs became weaker, court officials increased their influence. Under the feudal politics of the Zhou, bureaucratic documentation became ever more complex, as the center had to define its relations with the 50 major vassal dependencies and continually changing foreign contacts. The kings' scribes, clerks, and officials wrote the documents that defined hierarchy and order and mastered the political precedents that the military men needed to exercise legitimate authority. As the state became more complex, the qualifications for state servants became more specific. Now the officials of the state, along with the nobles, could gain rank, land, wealth, and an assured future for their family, but such a bureaucracy did not ensure the strength of the reign.

The remnants of Zhou royal power disappeared completely in 771 B.C.E., when an alliance of disloyal vassals and border-area tribesmen destroyed the capital and killed the king. Part of the royal family managed to escape eastward to Luoyang, however, where the dynasty survived for another five centuries (until around 250 B.C.E.), doing little more than performing state religious rituals as the Sons of Heaven. The period before 771 is often called the "Western Zhou" to distinguish it from the era after 771 B.C.E., referred to as the "Eastern Zhou" for the location of the capital. In 335 B.C.E. some of the stronger vassals began calling themselves "kings" *(wang)*, thereby ending the sovereignty of the Zhou monarchs. Some conquered their weaker neighbors. Some pioneered new policies, based on new schools of thought developed in the East. Warfare among emerging states was incessant. During the early Eastern Zhou, also called the Spring and Autumn Period (722–481 B.C.E.), warfare often took a chivalrous form, but it turned more violent during the two and a half centuries known as the period of Warring States (403–221 B.C.E.). By 221 B.C.E. the ruler of the Qin (CHIN), the most successful of the seven largest states still existing in 300 B.C.E., had conquered all of his rivals and established a unified empire over which he was the absolute ruler.

The art of horseback riding, common among the nomads of Central Asia, greatly influenced later Zhou military strategies, supplanting the chariot-based strategy of earlier centuries. Rulers in the north developed cavalry as a defense against nomadic forces and later used their new cavalry against other Chinese states. Infantry forces drafted from the farm population were also effective against chariots. Rulers of the Warring States period began constructing increasingly complex defensive walls. The infantry adapted to new conditions by wearing tunics and trousers adopted from the nomads, an example of the interactions of non-Chinese and Chinese culture. In later centuries, the mutual influence of Chinese and "barbarian" culture would encompass military, political, intellectual and material culture. Large populations were essential to build defensive walls and raise armies. Effective rulers devised new economic and sociopolitical ways to enrich their growing populations and their resources.

Zhou Economy and Society

The contestants for power—the Jin (divided during the Warring States era into Han and Wei) in the north, the Qi (CHEE) in the east, the Chu in the Yangzi region, and the Qin in the west—recognized the connection between wealth and power. Prosperous rulers could field large armies of soldiers and laborers. New lands were claimed for agriculture from marginal fields and marshes, and the states encouraged trade in textiles, metals, woods, jade, bamboo, seafood, pearls, and animal products. During the seventh century B.C.E., the Chinese mastered the use of iron and mass-produced cast iron objects from molds, which were in wide use by the end of the third century B.C.E. The ox-drawn iron-tipped plow, together with the use of manure and the growth of large-scale irrigation and water-control projects, led to a more dependable and productive food supply and greater population growth. Zhou-era rulers also understood the necessity to build canals to improve their realm's economy and communication. The canals made it possible to move food and useful items dependably over long distances. Commerce and wealth thus grew rapidly. At the beginning of the Zhou dynasty, brightly colored shells, bolts of silk, and ingots of precious metals were used as forms of exchange; by the end of the dynasty, small round copper coins with square holes had taken their place.

Under the Zhou dynasty, merchant and artisan classes played an economically prominent, if not socially recognized, role as wealth spread beyond the nobles and court servants. Indicative of the rise in the general economic level, chopsticks and finely lacquered objects, today universally considered as symbols of Chinese and East Asian culture, were in general use by the end of the period. The continued importance of the intertwining of political power and cultural beliefs, as in the Shang era, is evident from inscriptions on bronzes. From them we know that Zhou kings, like the Shang kings, worshipped their ancestors. The Zhou kings had elaborate rituals in family temples, where they made offerings to their ancestors. The nobility, for their benefit, recorded honors they had received from the Zhou kings onto commissioned pieces of bronze. These messages were inscribed inside food containers or hidden on the backs of bells because they were meant only for the eyes of the ancestors.

Other vessels, no longer shaped in the *taotie* or animal mask form of the Shang dynasty, appear to have been used in rituals viewed by an audience. Many were inscribed with texts, suggesting their owners may have been thinking about their descendants.

The early Zhou years gave birth to the first collection of poetry, *The Book of Songs*, later canonized as one of China's great classics. The poems, composed between 1000 B.C.E. and 600 B.C.E., included love poems, poems about government officials, and poems that depict everyday lives of commoners. One poem laments the role played in the Zhou court by the powerful wives of rulers, which was a reflection of their role in the frequent disputes over succession to the throne:

> *Clever men build cities,*
> *Clever women topple them . . .*
> *Disorder does not come down from heaven;*
> *It is produced by women.*[1]

Not all royal women, however, were so poorly regarded by their contemporaries. The excavation of the tomb of Lady Hao, wife of King Wu (c. 1200 B.C.E.) contains oracle bones showing she led military expeditions, managed an estate, and carried out rituals.

It was during the time of political and social disruption of the Eastern Zhou that teachers and philosophers, longing for an idealized "good old days" of social stability of the Western Zhou, played an important role in defining and teaching values that, in continually evolving forms, would dominate Chinese society into the twentieth century. This new form of leadership found a willing audience among the people who had the most to gain from order and hierarchy, the clerks and officials who increased their influence, wealth, and legal privileges during the Zhou dynasty.

Nostalgia for the imagined past led to the conceptualizing of an entire hierarchical social order developed around an idealized monarch, with each inferior in the descending scale owing respect and obedience to his superior.

The peasant masses stood at the bottom of the hierarchy. They were controlled by government officials, landed gentry, and rural moneylenders, although, ostensibly, they were free to buy and sell land or change occupation. Most, like peasants elsewhere, were tied to their villages, where they worked as tenants or serfs and struggled to eke out an existence. Some were forced into debt slavery. To increase production and control of farmers, some rulers used their own officials rather than local intermediaries to govern the farm population. Officials gained opportunities for advancement through good performance in these jobs, and farmers were increasingly rewarded by freedom from serfdom by their own good performance. By the end of the Warring States era, rulers with more effective centralized bureaucratic control and increasingly free peasants found themselves emerging on top.

The Philosophical Schools

The rich streams of thought that appeared during the latter part of the Zhou period emerged from the very disquiet and instability of the times. During the next three centuries, some great teachers and philosophers thought deeply about the nature of humanity and the problems of society. They created a range of philosophies on how people should live. These ideas went from the extremes of living for society to living for one's own soul, and they continued to change through the centuries and shape Chinese society even today.

Confucianism: The Foundation

The first, most famous, and certainly most influential Chinese philosopher and teacher was Kong Fuzi (KONG FOO-dzih; "Master Kong, the Sage," c. 551–c. 479 B.C.E.), known in the West as Confucius after Jesuit missionaries to China in the seventeenth century Latinized his name. He was one in a line of teachers who tried to explain the universe and the place of the Chinese people within it as well as the appropriate behavior among human beings in society. Eventually viewed as the central figure in orthodox Chinese philosophy, many of his students believed the master composed or edited what were often called the Confucian classics—*The Book of Songs*, *The Book of Poetry*, *The Book of Documents*, *The Analects*, and other texts. The only work that can be accurately attributed to Confucius is *The Analects* ("Selected Sayings"), a collection of his responses to questions posed by his disciples that was passed on after his death.

Confucius belonged to the lower aristocracy of a minor state, Lu, which had been under the Duke of Zhou, idealized by Confucius and later made into a model by the master's students. Confucius was more or less a contemporary of the Buddha in India,

Document The Wisdom of Confucius

The wisdom of Confucius is celebrated across the world. Unlike some wise ancient texts that seem limited to the time in which they were written, the thoughts of the great Chinese philosopher have a relevance that transcends the moment they were expressed. In these extracts, Confucius reflects on the notions of family, power, and education.

1:1 The Master said, "To learn, and at due times to practice what one has learned, is that not also a pleasure? To have friends come from afar, is that not also a joy? To go unrecognized, yet without being embittered, is that not also to be a noble person?"

1:2 Master You [You Ruo] said, "Among those who are filial toward their parents and fraternal toward their brothers, those who are inclined to offend against their superiors are few indeed. Among those who are disinclined to offend against their superiors, there have never been any who are yet inclined to create disorder. The noble person concerns himself with the root; when the root is established, the Way is born. Being filial and fraternal—is this not the root of humaneness?"

1:3 The Master said, "Those who are clever in their words and pretentious in their appearance, yet are humane, are few indeed."

1:4 Zengzi said, "Each day I examine myself on three things: In planning on behalf of others, have I failed to be loyal? When dealing with friends, have I failed to be trustworthy? On receiving what has been transmitted, have I failed to practice it?"

1:5 The Master said, "In ruling a state of a thousand chariots, one is reverent in the handling of affairs and shows himself to be trustworthy. One is economical in expenditures, loves the people, and uses them only at the proper season."

1:7 Zixia said, "One who esteems the worthy and has little regard for sexual attraction, who in serving his parents is able to summon up his entire strength, who in serving his ruler is able to avoid himself with utmost devotion, who in interacting with friends shows himself trustworthy in his words—though it may be said of him that he has not studied. I would definitely call him learned."

1:8 The Master said, "If the noble person is not serious, he will not inspire awe, nor will his learning be sound. One should abide in loyalty and trustworthiness and should have no friends who are not his equal. If one has faults, one should not be afraid to change." . . .

1:16 The Master said. "One should not grieve that one is unrecognized by others; rather, one should grieve that one fails to recognize others." . . .

2:1 The Master said. "One who governs through virtue may be compared to the polestar, which occupies its place while the host of other stars pay homage to it." . . .

2:11 The Master said, "One who reanimates the old so as to understand the new may become a teacher."

2:12 The Master said, "The noble person is not a tool."

2:14 The Master said, "The noble person is inclusive, not exclusive: the small person is exclusive, not inclusive."

2:15 The Master said, "To learn without thinking, is unavailing; to think without learning is dangerous."

Questions to Consider

1. What do you think Confucius considers to be the traits of a "serious" person?
2. Does your professor fit the qualification expressed in 2:11? If so, why? If not, why not?
3. According to Confucius, what should be the ruler's attitude toward his people?

From the *Analects*, in William Theodore de Bary et al., eds., *Sources of Chinese Tradition*, 2nd ed., Vol. 1 (New York: Columbia University Press, 1999).

Zoroaster in Persia, and the early philosophers of Greece. To achieve his goal of improving society, Confucius did not look to the gods and spirits for assistance; he accepted the existence of Heaven *(Tian)* and spirits, but he insisted in the *Analects* that it was more important "to know the essential duties of man living in a society of men."

"We don't know yet how to serve men," he said, "How can we know about serving the spirits?" And, "We don't yet know about life, so how can we know about death?" Confucius hoped to become an adviser to a ruler, but he turned to teaching after traveling from court to court in an unsuccessful search for a ruler who would make use of his ideas.

He tried to inspire his students to be moral and prepared them to serve in government even if he himself was unable to do so. He honored the roles of learned men who served their rulers in ritual practice, record keeping, divination, and reception of guests and envoys from other rulers. He stressed that following honorable conventions and accepting hierarchy produced social harmony. Confucius advocated a fairly conservative order, though his words were reinterpreted constantly over the centuries to offer a variety of approaches to organizing the state and society.

Confucius was deeply disappointed with the condition of his own society, which he viewed as characterized by selfishness, lack of benevolence, and greed. Nobility, he contended, was not transmitted by birth but by acquiring wisdom and virtue. The ideal man was a *junzi* (JOON-zih), often translated as "gentleman," though without the hereditary connotations with which the word is associated in English. A *junzi* should be virtuous, righteous, humane, wise, and brave. Interactions among people should be governed by *li,* a term which covers the modern English-language connotations of propriety, manners, and ceremonial and sacred ritual. *Li* performed with a sincere heart rendered an individual human. Though *li* was manifested in each of the Five Relationships—the relationships between parent and child, ruler and subject, husband and wife, elder brother and younger brother, and friend and friend—it was most important in the family. Confucius emphasized filial piety, the respect of a child for his or her parents, above all. If the interests of one's ruler and one's parents conflicted, one's support of the parent came first. A son should never turn his father in for theft, for example.

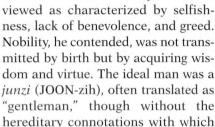
DOCUMENT
Government and the Superior "Man"

At the same time, Confucius believed that the improvement of society was the responsibility of the ruler and that the quality of government depended on the ruler's moral character: "The way (Dao) of learning to be great consists in shining with the illustrious power of moral personality, in making a new people, in abiding in the highest goodness," he wrote.[2] Confucius's definition of the Dao as "moral personality" and the "highest goodness" was in decided contrast to the old premoral Dao, in which gods and spirits, propitiated by offerings and ritual, regulated human life for good or ill. Above all, Confucius's "new way" meant a concern for the rights of others, an adherence to a type of Golden Rule. When a disciple asked, "Is there any

Throughout the ages, Confucius became idealized as the authority to whom one could look for instruction on proper government and behavior.

saying that one can act on all day, every day?" Confucius replied, "Perhaps the saying about consideration: 'Never do to others what you would not like them to do to you.'"

Confucius's view of society was hierarchical. Even though four of the Five Relationships connected a superior and an inferior (only the relationship of friend to friend was equal), all relationships were to be grounded in *ren* (often translated as benevolence, humanity, or human-relatedness), a virtue applied to all without any hierarchical dimensions.

Although Confucius called himself "a transmitter and not a creator," his redefinition of Dao and his teachings produced an ethical program for this world, by this world.[3] His desire to reemphasize the propriety and humanity of *li,* which he felt were being ignored in his day, and his redirecting of the concept of the *junzi*, or gentleman, to one whose character rather than birth defined his nobility, underscore his new ethical emphasis. As he noted, "The noble man understands what is right; the inferior man understands what is profitable."[4]

Mozi (MOH-dzih; c. 490–391 B.C.E.), born around the time of Confucius's death, took issue with Confucius's placing of priority on one's family. Mozi stressed universal love instead, though he also believed in a hierarchy headed up by those who were capable and educated. Mozi disdained wars of aggression for territorial gain and excessive mourning rituals. Though Mozi, like numerous other philosophers of the Spring and Autumn era, had a lively following in his day, his school of thought did not survive the end of the Warring States period. In the end, historians stress the contributions of Confucianists, Daoists, and Legalists because of their continuing influence on Chinese thought, but scholars like Mozi were part of a very active intellectual climate.

Mencius: The Mandate of Heaven

Mencius, or Mengzi (MUNG-dzih; c. 372–c. 289 B.C.E.) was one of two scholars whose work was largely responsible for the emergence of Confucianism as the most widely accepted philosophy in China. Born a century after the death of Confucius, Mencius was raised by a mother who, according to legend, sacrificed her own happiness to support her son's education in scholarship and righteous behavior. Mencius's mother, revered as a paragon of virtue, is supposed to have expressed the long-lasting prescription for women's position in the family: as a child, a girl is subordinate to her father; as a young adult, a woman is subordinate to her husband; and as a widow, to her son.

Mencius is best known for adding important new dimensions to Confucian thought in terms of conceptions of human nature and of the right to govern. Whereas Confucius had only implied that human nature is good, Mencius emphatically insisted that all people are innately good and tend to seek the good, just as water tends to run downhill. But goodness must be cultivated by virtuous and wise rulers. He compared human nature to a mountain, once beautiful and lush, made barren by humans and animals denuding it of vegetation. Just as the mountain's nature was not to be barren, so, too, human nature was not to be corrupt. But both needed the right conditions to flourish.

Mencius believed good kings had ruled benevolently in the past and urged rulers of his day to practice benevolence as well, by reducing taxes and making punishments less severe. In that way, he stressed, kings would gain their people's support and be invincible. Mencius went further, proposing a system of land distribution believed to have been used by ancient sage rulers. This system, called the "well-field" system, called for eight families to farm fields shaped like the Chinese character for *well* (like a modern day tic-tac-toe board), with one field in the middle farmed by all eight families for taxes. This way, Mencius argued, everyone's needs would be satisfied fairly. When the people were happy, they would support their ruler.

If the ruler was not wise and benevolent, government would be corrupt, the people hungry, and natural disasters destructive of the people's livelihood. This, Mencius averred, was Heaven's sign that the ruler was not really a true ruler. By the Confucian principle of "rectification of names," a person who was not a ruler should be removed. Such a ruler had lost the mandate of Heaven. If the Son of Heaven ruled by virtue of the permission (or mandate) of Heaven, Heaven also had the right to withdraw the mandate. Mencius's great contribution to Confucian thought was his suggestion that people's rebellion was a sign of the loss of the mandate. In fact, the phrase "removing the mandate" became the basis for the modern Chinese and Japanese terms for "revolution."

As we have seen, this concept had been used by the Zhou to justify their revolt against the Shang whom they considered corrupt. On that occasion the concept had a religious meaning. The people were to obey the Zhou ruler as the Son of Heaven, just as they worshipped Heaven through rites and rituals. Mencius, however, secularized the mandate of Heaven when he declared, "Heaven hears as the people hear; Heaven sees as the people see."[5] By redefining the concept of a heavenly mandate in this way, Mencius made the welfare of the people the ultimate standard for judging the virtue of government. Mencius advocated responsible monarchy, supporting this concept because he believed there was a need for a new, unifying leadership that could end the warring between regional states during the late Zhou period, not, however, because he believed that people had a right to express their political views. Nonetheless, the idea of the mandate of Heaven came to be associated with the idea of the people's right to rebel and to overthrow the unjust leadership of a leader who had "lost the mandate of Heaven."

Xunzi: Human Nature as Antisocial

Xunzi (SHOON-dzih; c. 310–c. 220 B.C.E.), like Mencius, interpreted and extended Confucius's ideas. Contrary to Mencius, however, Xunzi argued that human nature tended to be antisocial and needed guidance to turn toward virtue. Wise leadership, proper rituals, and even strict laws (which Mencius rejected) would make humans capable of living good lives, filled with filial piety and morality. Once a person recognizes what is good, Xunzi argued, he or she will practice goodness. Xunzi differed from some other Confucianists by arguing that an impartial Heaven did not respond to prayers or ritual: It will rain whether or not one prays for rain. But he did not reject ritual and prayer; rather he stated that ritual, like music, was an excellent way for people to express their emotions, to provide social harmony, and to order social hierarchy.

Legalism

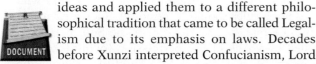

Legalism: The Way of the State

Xunzi is appropriately considered a Confucian thinker. Two of his students, however, took some of his ideas and applied them to a different philosophical tradition that came to be called Legalism due to its emphasis on laws. Decades before Xunzi interpreted Confucianism, Lord Shang (d. 338 B.C.E.), a minister in the state of Qin, described his work as Legalist. He got rid of Qin's aristocracy; determined his subordinates' military rank by the number of heads they cut off in battle; organized territory into counties; attracted farmers to those counties by offering them houses, land, and freedom from serfdom; made people responsible for crimes committed by members of their mutual responsibility groups; and codified laws, applying them harshly without consideration for rank.

Xunzi's student Han Feizi (HAN FAY-dzih; d. 233 B.C.E.) followed in Lord Shang's tradition. He advocated harsh application of laws, unmodified by family concerns. It was shocking to Confucianists that he suggested that rulers should not be expected to be moral leaders who treated their subjects with kindness. Indeed, he said, since even parents treated their newborn sons and daughters differently, thereby showing little parental love for their own daughters, how could a ruler be expected to rule subjects, with whom they had no familial bond, with morality and virtue? Equal application of the law was the only answer. Han Feizi's contemporary, Li Si (d. 208 B.C.E.), also a former student of Xunzi, put Legalist political theory into practice in Qin as its leading minister.

The Legalists argued for an elaborate system of laws defining fixed penalties for each offense, with no consideration for rank, class, or circumstances, with the important exception of the ruler, who was above the law. Judges were not to use their own consciences in estimating the gravity of a crime and arbitrarily deciding on the punishment. Their task was solely to define the crime correctly; the punishment was provided automatically by the code of law. This clashed with Confucian prioritization, in the name of human kindness, of the family, and with the notion that *ren* (benevolence) itself was a motivation for the people to support their ruler.

Daoism

A third, lasting school of thought emerged in the late Zhou era. **Daoism** contrasted greatly with Confucian ideals and practices, as it focused on natural harmony rather than social harmony. In its very earliest forms, Daoism had some political aspects, but in the third century B.C.E. its leading philosopher, Zuangzi (JWAHNG-dzih) (c. 369–c. 286 B.C.E.), embraced relativism and spiritual freedom and was adamantly apolitical. Daoists, unlike Confucianists, did not welcome rulers' intervention to improve people's livelihoods. For Confucianists, the Dao ("the way") was the ethical path for rulers' humanity in a human-centered world; for Daoists, the Dao was the way of nature with which humans should seek harmony rather than dominance.

Daoism: The Way and Virtue

Two Daoist texts survive. The earliest, the *Daodejing* (DOW-deh-JING) or *Laozi* (LOW-dzih), is often attributed to Lao Dai, a sixth-century contemporary of Confucius. Most likely the book was compiled three centuries later. This poetic text is cryptic and paradoxical and open to many interpretations, because, as it suggests, the Dao itself cannot be defined. There are a few ideas that are strongly encouraged, however: that nonaction and nonbeing triumph over action and being and that silence is superior to words. Rulers should not take actions, but rather allow nature to take its course. As the *Laozi* explained, "Do not honor the worthy, and the people will not compete. Do not value rare treasures, and the people will not steal. . . A sage governs this way: He empties people's minds and fills their bellies. . . . Engage in no action and order will prevail."[6]

The other Daoist text, the *Zhuangzi*, goes much farther in rejecting politics and engagement with society. While the *Laozi* had some political uses—for instance, some rulers believed that by doing nothing their state or society could be strengthened—the *Zhuangzi* strongly rejected politics. Zhuangzi himself, believed to be the book's author, turned down government jobs and titles, preferring, he said, to drag his tail in the mud like a turtle rather than having his bones venerated after his death. Here Zhuangzi rejects both political power, which he likens to the impotence of dead bones, and social respect, suggested by his rejection of the veneration ("ancestor worship") of his bones.

Daoism was a revolt not only against society but also against the intellect's limitations. Intuition, not reason, was the source of true knowledge; and books, Daoists said, are "the dregs and refuse of the ancients." Zhuangzi even questioned the reality of the world of

Daoism—A philosophical school, later a religion, focusing on natural harmony and nonaction.

Document   Legalism: The Theories of Han Feizi (d. 233 B.C.E.)

Throughout history, philosophers and leaders have generally differed in their notions of human nature. Some, like Confucius, counseled a due respect for the people, while others like Mencius saw the need for the people's consent in the affairs of state. The thinker Han Feizi disagreed with both Confucius and Mencius, viewing human nature as essentially evil and the average human being as incompetent.

When the sage rules the state, he does not count on people doing good of themselves, but employs such measures as will keep them from doing any evil. If he counts on people doing good of themselves, there will not be enough such people to be numbered by the tens in the whole country. But if he employs such measures as will keep them from doing evil, then the entire state can be brought up to a uniform standard. Inasmuch as the administrator has to consider the many but disregard the few, he does not busy himself with morals but with laws.

. . . Therefore, the intelligent ruler upholds solid facts and discards useless frills. He does not speak about deeds of humanity and righteousness, and he does not listen to the words of learned men.

Those who are ignorant about government insistently say: "Win the hearts of the people." If order could be procured by winning the hearts of the people, then even the wise ministers Yi Yin and Guan Zhong would be of no use. For all that the ruler would need to do would be just to listen to the people. Actually, the intelligence of the people is not to be relied upon any more than the mind of a baby. If the baby does not have his head shaved, his sores will recur; if he does not have his boil cut open, his illness will go from bad to worse. However, in order to shave his head or open the boil someone has to hold the baby while the affectionate mother is performing the work, and yet he keeps crying and yelling incessantly. The baby does not understand that suffering a small pain is the way to obtain a great benefit.

. . . The sage considers the conditions of the times . . . and governs the people accordingly. Thus though penalties are light, it is not due to charity; though punishment is heavy, it is not due to cruelty. Whatever is done is done in accordance with the circumstances of the age. Therefore circumstances go according to their time, and the course of action is planned in accordance with the circumstances.

. . . Now take a young fellow who is a bad character. His parents may get angry at him, but he never makes any change. The villagers may reprove him, but he is not moved. His teachers and elders may admonish him, but he never reforms. The love of his parents, the efforts of the villagers, and the wisdom of his teachers and elders—all the three excellent disciplines are applied to him, and yet not even a hair on his shins is altered. It is only after the district magistrate sends out his soldiers and in the name of the law searches for wicked individuals that the young man becomes afraid and changes his ways and alters his deeds. So while the love of parents is not sufficient to discipline the children, the severe penalties of the district magistrate are. This is because men become naturally spoiled by love, but are submissive to authority. . . .

That being so, rewards should be rich and certain so that the people will be attracted by them; punishments should be severe and definite so that the people will fear them; and laws should be uniform and steadfast so that the people will be familiar with them. Consequently, the sovereign should show no wavering in bestowing rewards and grant no pardon in administering punishments, and he should add honor to rewards and disgrace to punishments—when this is done, then both the worthy and the unworthy will want to exert themselves.

Questions to Consider

1. What is the function of the law, according to Legalist thinker Han Feizi?
2. What does the author believe to be the intellectual capacity of "the people?"
3. According to Han Feizi, how should a leader behave in regard to those who do good and those who do not?

From *Sources of Chinese Tradition*, 2nd ed., Vol. 1, eds. William Theodore de Bary, et al. Copyright © 1999 Columbia University Press. Reprinted with the permission of the publisher.

the senses. He said that he once dreamed that he was a butterfly, "flying about enjoying itself." When he awakened, he was confused: "I do not know whether I was Zhuangzi dreaming that I was a butterfly, or whether now I am a butterfly dreaming that I am Zhuangzi."

Anecdotes and allegories abound in both texts, as in all mystical teachings that deal with subjects that are difficult to put into words. As the *Daodejing* put it, "The one who knows does not speak, and the one who speaks does not know." In later centuries, Daoism, which was primarily philosophical in its formative years, adopted a religious aspect. At the end of the Han dynasty, also discussed in this chapter, Daoism took on a religious coloration, and Daoists then used their beliefs in political movements and in the quest for immortality through alchemy and sexual practices. Although Confucianism and Daoism frequently sniped at each other, they never became mutually exclusive outlooks on life. Daoist intuition complemented Confucian rationalism in the search for the true way, and during the centuries to come, Chinese often attempted to follow Confucianist precepts in their social relations, while at the same time maintaining Daoist beliefs.

The diverse philosophers of the Warring States centuries reflected not only a variety of responses to the brutality of war but also the different cultural or regional environments in which they emerged. Those that left a record in the form of silk scrolls were not only attached to their time and place but also were able, through the constancy of the Chinese written language, to transcend their time. In time, these written works became part of the "Classics" considered to be the heart of Chinese philosophy.

THE QIN AND HAN EMPIRES, 221 B.C.E.–220 C.E.

■ *How did Chinese leaders use Confucian and Daoist ideas to justify conflicting state policies in the name of promoting the people's welfare and the growth of the state?*

The Qin Dynasty: Unification

Two dynasties, the Qin and the Han, unified China and created a centralized empire. The Qin dynasty collapsed soon after the death of its founder, but the Han lasted for about four centuries. Together, these dynasties transformed China, but the changes were the culmination of earlier philosophical, political, and economic developments that had emerged during the turmoil of the Warring States period.

Throughout the Warring States period, there had been a widely shared hope that a king would unite China and inaugurate a great new age of peace and stability. Whereas the Confucianists believed that such a king would accomplish the task by means of his outstanding moral virtue, the Legalists substituted kingly power and rule of law as the essential elements of effective government. The rise to preeminence of the Qin state began in 361 B.C.E. when its ruler selected Lord Shang, a man imbued with Legalist principles, to be chief minister. Recognizing that the growth of Qin power depended on a more efficient and centralized bureaucratic structure, Lord Shang undermined the old hereditary nobility and created a new aristocracy based on military merit. He also undermined their privileged place in society by introducing a universal draft beginning at approximately age 15. This produced an effect of leveling social difference, as chariot and cavalry warfare, in which the nobility had played the leading role, was replaced in importance by masses of peasant infantry equipped with iron weapons. Economically, Lord Shang further weakened the old landowning nobility by granting peasants ownership of the plots they tilled. Thereafter, the peasants paid taxes directly to the local state, thus increasing its wealth and power. These reforms were essential to Qin's rise to power during the Warring States period.

Nearly a century later, King Zheng ascended the throne as a boy of nine in 247. Nine years earlier, the last Zhou king had been deposed. Aided by two ministers, former merchant Lu Buwei (LOO boo-WAY; d. 235 B.C.E.) and Li Si, King Zheng conquered the neighboring states of Han, Zhao, Wei, Chu, and Qi, thereby unifying China in 221 B.C.E. The king then declared himself *Shi Huangdi* (SHIH HWAHNG-dee) or the "First August Supreme Ruler" of the Qin, or First Emperor, as his new title is more commonly translated. Huangdi ("emperor") endured as the royal title until 1911. Shi Huangdi also enlarged China—a name derived from the word Qin—by conquests in the south as far as the coast of South China. Military expeditions

The Early Empires	
221–206 B.C.E.	Qin
206 B.C.E.–9 C.E.	Former (Western) Han
9–23 C.E.	Reign of Wang Mang
23–220 C.E.	Later (Eastern) Han

entered Vietnam and Inner Mongolia as well. The emperor stated that his dynasty would endure 10,000 generations. Although it lasted just 15 years, the idea of a united China ruled by an emperor would persist into the twentieth century.

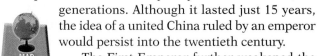

China's Struggle for Cultural and Political Unity, 400 B.C.E. to 400

The First Emperor further weakened the power of the nobility by moving hundreds of thousands of leading families to the capital at Xianyang (shee-AHN-yahng), near Xi'an, where they could be closely watched. To block rebellion, he ordered the entire civilian population to surrender their weapons to the state. A single legal code replaced all local laws. Modeled on the social structure of Lord Shang, the population was organized into groups of ten families, and each person was held responsible for the actions of all the members of the group. This structure ensured that all crimes would be reported; it also increased loyalty to the state at the expense of loyalty to the family.

As part of the unifying process, the entire realm was divided into 36 commanderies which were subdi-vided into counties directly ruled by the emperor's centrally controlled civil and military appointees sent to replace the local families who had been moved to Xianyang. To destroy the source of the aristocracy's power and to permit the emperor's agents to tax every farmer's harvest, private ownership of land by peasants, promoted a century earlier in the state of Qin by Lord Shang, was decreed for all of China. Thus the Qin Empire reflected emerging social forces at work in China: the peasants freed from serfdom, a new military and administrative upper class, and merchants eager to increase their wealth within a larger political arena. In place of the hereditary power of the nobility, the entire population was divided into 20 ranks, each entitled to different rights, including access to a certain type of clothing and a specified amount of land, slaves, and housing. The new bureaucracy was a meritocracy in both the civil and military realms. As late as the early Zhou period, cowrie shells and cloth had been used as currency, but money had begun to circulate broadly around 500 B.C.E., and by the outset of

The tombs of the First Emperor, 210 B.C.E., have yielded most of the surviving art of that period in China. The more than 6000 figures, including these terra-cotta warriors, were not discovered until 1974 in one of the greatest archaeological finds in history.

Qin rule, the centuries of unrest had stimulated an economic boom manifested not only in support for military endeavors, but in trade routes and networks, regional specialization, and the growth of cities.

Economic growth under the First Qin Emperor's short reign was also stimulated by public works, the standardization of the written language and of currency, and the erecting of walls to keep non-Chinese nomads out. All construction was by forced labor, and under the First Emperor, 4000 miles of roads and thousands of miles of canals and waterways, one of which connected the Yangzi to the Xi River and Guangzhou (gwahng-JOH), were completed. (This surpassed the system of the Roman Empire, which was estimated to be somewhat shorter—3740 miles.) The standardization of writing entailed the introduction of new, simpler written language, and no variation was allowed. These Chinese characters, central to unification, would be used until 1949, when an even more streamlined method of writing was created.

The new, unified currency could be threaded together in strings. Moreover, weights and measures and even the length of axles (so that cart wheels would

IMAGE
The Great
Wall of China

fit the grooves cut in the highways) were made uniform. Although the First Emperor, like some Warring States rulers before him, built walls to impede the incursion of nomadic tribes from central Asia, it is no longer believed that he built the 1400-mile Great Wall of China. In its present form the Great Wall was mainly the work of the sixteenth-century Ming dynasty.[7]

DOCUMENT
Li Si and
Legalist
Policies of Qin
Shi Huang

The First Emperor tried to enforce intellectual conformity and to cast the Qin Legalist system as the only natural political order. He suppressed all other schools of thought, especially the Confucianists, who idealized the Zhou political order. To break the hold of the past, the emperor put into effect a Legalist proposal requiring that all privately owned books reflecting past traditions be burned and that opponents of government in the name of antiquity be beheaded. Books burned included the Confucian classics and any statements of political philosophy that countered the Qin concern for control. Legend has it that the Qin emperor had 460 Confucian scholars buried alive, but the anti-Qin hostility of later generations of Confucian scholars makes it impossible to prove whether this really happened.

The First Emperor created a new cultural elite of state-appointed teachers who would give an approved reading of the traditions and lessons of history. This set in motion the precedent that "imperial governments would henceforth insist that approved texts and suitable interpretations would be used for this purpose and that teaching would be conducted along recognized lines." As recent scholarship has argued, however, much of Chinese thought was based on oral traditions handed down, and therefore the burning of books and state control of intellectual life did not eradicate late Zhou learning.[8]

The First Emperor's control of the lives of his subjects did not erase his fear of death. Three assassination attempts gave him reason to be concerned. He dispatched a group of young men and women on a fruitless quest for the mythical islands of immortality. In addition, his fear of death, along with the Qin need to demonstrate its power, led to the emperor's employment of over half a million laborers to construct a huge burial mound near the Qin capital. The location of the mound was to be kept a secret from the people, however. All artisans and laborers involved in the construction of the tomb were locked inside the tomb while alive. Nearby, over 6000 terra-cotta soldiers were presented in military formation, in three large pits. These sculptures represented figures of the Emperor's imperial guard, and no two faces of these life-size figures are alike—each head is a personal portrait.

When the First Emperor took ill and died in 210 B.C.E. while on one of his frequent tours of inspection to control his realm, he was succeeded by an inept son who was unable to control the rivalry among his father's chief aides. Qin policies had alienated not only the intellectuals and the old nobility but also the peasants, who were subjected to ruinous taxation and forced labor. Rebel armies thus rose in every province of the empire; some led by peasants, others by aristocrats. Anarchy followed, and by 206 B.C.E. the Qin dynasty had disappeared. But the idea of a unified Chinese empire, though it often failed to be created, would last until 1912, when China became a republic.

At issue in the fighting that continued for another 4 years after the end of the Qin dynasty was not only the question of succession to the throne but also the form of government. The peasant and aristocratic leaders, first allied against the Qin, became engaged in a ruthless civil war. The aristocrats, led by the brilliant general Xiang Yu (shee-AHNG YOO; 233 B.C.E.–202 B.C.E.), sought to restore the power they had possessed before the Legalist consolidation of imperial rule. Their opponents, whose main leader was Liu Bang (LEE-oo BAHNG), a peasant who became a minor government functionary, desired a centralized state. In this contest between the old order and the new, the new was the victor—China would stay united under the Han emperors and by a bureaucratic culture, based on merit, and dedicated to rule from the center.

The Han Dynasty

The Empire Consolidated

In 206 B.C.E. Liu Bang, known to history as the Emperor Gaozu (GOW-dzoo; r. 202–195 B.C.E.), defeated his aristocratic rival and established the Han dynasty, building a capital at Chang'an (modern Xi'an). It lasted for more than 400 years and is traditionally divided into two parts: the Former Han (206 B.C.E.–8 C.E.) and the Later Han (23–220 C.E.).

Classical China

The impact of these four centuries is illustrated by the fact that ethnic Chinese still call themselves "people of Han."

The empire and power sought by Gaozu and his successors were those of the Qin, but they succeeded where the Qin had failed because they attempted to balance *wu* ("military power") with *wen* ("ethical civilian rule"). To indicate his opposition to the centralized rule of the tyrannical Qin, Gaozu had initially distributed domains to supporters who would govern them as somewhat autonomous vassal states. He soon realized, however, that effective rule required centralization. He then appointed officials to carry out legal and administrative functions in the provinces. To placate the peasants, Gaozu lowered taxes and reduced forced labor. The Han tied the empire together physically as well. By 100 B.C.E., the Han had established a road system that made it possible for a traveler to go from the far north to the far south in 56 days on foot or in 32 days on horseback. But the most effective tool to gain acceptance was to enlist the support of the Confucian intellectuals. The emperors recognized that an educated bureaucracy was necessary for governing their vast empire. They lifted the Qin ban on the Confucian classics and other Zhou literature. The way was open for a revival of intellectual life that had been suppressed under the Qin, and the result was yet another reformulation of Confucian thought.

In accordance with Legalist principles, now tempered by Confucian insistence on the ethical basis of government, the Han emperors established administrative organs, staffed by a salaried bureaucracy with as many as 20 levels, to rule their empire. Government officials hailed mainly from rich families who were able to educate their sons, but the door to a government career was, in principle, open to all capable men. Emperor Wudi (r. 141–87 B.C.E., "Martial Emperor"), the Han dynasty's most vigorous emperor, established a university to train future officials. The first student body numbered 50. By 8 B.C.E., there were 3000 students; the number increased to 30,000 in the Later Han. The curriculum focused on Confucianism, endearing the emperor to many scholars and legitimizing the dynasty in their skeptical eyes. The formal examination system to select officials (developed in later centuries) did not yet exist; all officials were selected after they gave evidence of their scholarly abilities. Though these officials owed their positions to political appointments, they were men of conviction. Many suffered when their convictions differed with the opinions of their rulers.

The Han dynasty devised effective ways to maintain control of power, but they were unable to address one major challenge to their control. The families of emperors' wives emerged as powerful political actors. Gaozu's widow ruled and promoted her family's interests for 15 years after Gaozu's death. At the end of the Former Han, Wang Mang, a relative of an emperor's widow, came to power briefly, attempting to establish his own dynasty, the Xin (SHIN; 9 C.E.–23 C.E.).

Wudi

After 60 years of consolidation, the Han dynasty achieved its greatest size and zenith of achievements during the long reign of Wudi. At the same time, however, Wudi raised the peasants' taxes. In addition, he increased the amount of labor and military service the peasants were forced to contribute to the state. Those taxes were lowered after his death.

Even before Wudi's reign, Han officials were concerned about the burden of taxes on the ordinary peasants. Estate holders could generally evade taxation, so peasants began to turn their land over to estate holders to whom they paid rents that were lower than

Officials conspicuously indicated their rank by the retinues of attendants that accompanied them on their travels to their posts. Officials' tombs often contained paintings, statues, or friezes depicting these retinues. This scene, carved on a tomb brick during the Later Han, shows carriages, horses, and runners.

official taxes. The government responded by lowering taxes on peasants and finding new revenue sources. To pay for his military expansion, Wudi increased taxes on businesses, confiscated some nobles' lands, and most controversially, started government monopolies in salt and iron production in 119 B.C.E. Salt and iron were both necessities, and the government monopolies raised a lot of money. Confucianists were horrified, however, that the Son of Heaven should be involved in something they disdained—the quest for profits. A great debate about the economic role of the state—should the state promote profit making for the people's benefit or should it stay away from enterprise for the benefit of government morality?—engaged scholars in 81 B.C.E. This classic debate is still the basis of discussions on the role and scope of government, in China and throughout the world. Should the government play an economic role, or are laissez-faire policies more effective?

Wudi may also have initiated policies concerning grain, but the timing of those policies is unclear. Certainly by 51 B.C.E. (after Wudi's death), the Ever-Normal Granary Policy had the government buy grain when it was plentiful, allowing farmers to earn a good profit, and storing it until shortfalls hit, as they always did, saving the people from famine. The price and the quantity of rice available were, thus, stabilized.

Wudi justified his expansionist policies in terms of self-defense against nomadic tribes, including the Xiongnu (SHONG-noo), known later to Europeans as the Huns. The nomads' threats had caused the Emperor Gaozu to construct a wall and to send the nomads gifts and imperial princesses as brides. In 133 B.C.E., Wudi reversed the conciliatory policy and sent huge armies to the far west, establishing military colonies there and forcing local chieftains to send their sons to China for education, in effect making them hostages. Wudi annexed a large corridor extending through the Tarim River basin of central Asia to the Pamir Mountains, close to Bactria.

Wudi sent an envoy westward to seek allies against the Xiongnu. Captured and held prisoner for ten years, this envoy eventually reached Bactria and Ferghana. His reports of the interest shown in Chinese silks by the peoples of the area is an excellent example of increasing Chinese cultural, economic, and political interaction with non-Chinese. Commercial exchanges between China and other civilizations farther west were already underway. By 101 B.C.E., Wudi conquered Ferghana, thus controlling trade routes across Central Asia. This was the beginning of centuries of what came to be called "Silk Roads," major trade routes that carried a variety of products in addition to the popular silks.

Wudi also outflanked the Xiongnu in the east by the conquest of southern Manchuria and northern Korea. In addition, he completed the conquest of South China, begun by the Qin, and added northern Vietnam to the Chinese Empire. Chinese settlers moved into all the conquered lands. In fact, just as the armies of the Roman Republic were laying the foundation of the Pax Romana in the West, the Martial Emperor was consolidating power in the East.

Han Decline

Wudi's conquests led to overextension of the empire. As costs increased and many peasants fled to the protection of the great estates, taxes on the remaining peasants increased. Advances in agricultural technology, especially new plows and irrigation systems, permitted increased output. The donkey, brought from the west by the Xiongnu, was a helpful pack animal. These improvements led to population growth—the Han Empire had more people than Rome in 2 B.C.E.—but life for farmers was precarious. The custom of multiple inheritance led to tiny farms. The central government had to rely more and more on local military commanders and great landowners for control of the population, giving them great power and prestige at its own expense. More and more peasants fell behind in their rents and were forced to sell themselves or their children into debt slavery. This decline after an initial period of increasing prosperity and power made it appear that the Han were in danger of losing the mandate of Heaven.

Wudi was followed by less powerful rulers. Two child emperors, with Wang Mang as their regent, weakened Han control. At the same time, the rise of a messianic religious movement inspired by the cult of a goddess called the Queen Mother of the West suggested that the end of the dynasty was near. Wang Mang took over the throne in 9 C.E., seeming to fulfill the cult's prophecy. Wang Mang united Confucian ethics with Legalist practice. His goal was the rejuvenation of society by employing the power of the state. Because the number of large tax-free estates had greatly increased while the number of tax-paying peasant holdings had declined in the decades before Wang Mang's rise to power, he resurrected the well-field system, cut court expenses, issued new coins, abolished slavery, and reinvigorated the Ever-Normal Granary Policy. He tried to bring back Zhou-style offices. (In 1938 a chance reading of Wang Mang's proposal inspired the "ever-normal granary" program of the American New Deal!)[9]

Wang Mang's reform program failed. The conservative bureaucracy was unequal to the difficult administrative task. The powerful landowners rebelled against the ruler who proposed to confiscate their land. To make matters worse, in 11 C.E., the Huanghe changed course dramatically, flooding enormous tracts of land. The peasants joined the wealthy in opposition to Wang Mang. Although Wang Mang rescinded his reforms, he was killed by the rebels in 23 C.E. The conflicts over landownership and tenancy, along with the concentration of power of great families, became—and remained—a major problem in Chinese history.

The Later Han dynasty never reached the heights of its predecessors. Warlords who were members of the rich landowner class seized more and more power, and widespread peasant rebellions sapped the state's resources.

Religious uprising abounded, including one led by Daoist Mother Lu. Rivalries between Confucian scholars and court **eunuchs** had always been a problem, but in the second century of the Later Han, these erupted in murderous attacks on one another. Eunuchs were in control of the throne by the 170s. The previous decades saw plagues of locusts and horrific floods. By the 180s, rebellions were occurring everywhere. The uprising of the Yellow Turbans (so named because of the yellow scarves they wore) in 184 C.E. was particularly destructive to the Later Han. This was a messianic movement joined by thousands of poverty-stricken people, who believed in what they called *Taipingdao* (tai-PING-DOW) or "The Way of Great Peace." Emerging from economic need, this movement combined folk religious Daoism with the political goal of ending the dynasty. The Yellow Turbans did not achieve their goal, but they left behind a legacy in terms of setting a precedent for other grassroots revolts.

The general who subdued the Yellow Turbans went on to slaughter over 2000 eunuchs, along with beardless men mistaken for eunuchs. Luoyang was sacked in 189.

Surviving in name only during its last 30 years, the Han dynasty ended in 220 C.E., when the throne was usurped by the son of a famous warlord. Three and a half centuries of disunity and turbulence followed—the longest period of strife in China's long history. But China eventually succeeded in reuniting. In 589 the Sui dynasty united China again. By the end of the sixth century, as a result of centuries of political and cultural transformation, China had been created.

Han Scholarship, Art, and Technology

Scholarship flourished under the Han. A major concern of scholars was the collecting and interpreting of the classics of Chinese thought produced in the Zhou period. Many of the texts destroyed under the Qin were reproduced by scholars who had memorized

them earlier. When some documents assumed to be original classics were unearthed in the first century B.C.E., disputes over authenticity arose. The recovered volumes were venerated as a repository of past wisdom, while the texts written down from memory accorded more closely with scholarly currents of the Han dynasty. This encouraged studies of the past, including historical studies and the production of the world's first dictionary. This dictionary, containing 9000 characters with their meanings and pronunciations, was written by Xu Shen (SHOO SHEN; c. 54–120 C.E.). Han scholars venerated Confucius, who moved in the popular imagination from being a teacher, a man like any other, to becoming the ideal thinker and a being regarded as in some ways divine. Confucianism became the official philosophy of the state. Antiquarian interest spurred the research of Sima Qian (SIH-mah CHEN; c.145–90 B.C.E.) and Ban Gu (BAHN GOO; d. 92 C.E.). Sima Qian's work, a comprehensive history of China, the *Historical Records (Shiji)*, is a huge and highly detailed work of 130 chapters beginning with the Xia dynasty, including narratives of political events, chronological tables, and biographies. Sima Qian carefully quoted from documents, weighing evidence and bringing sophisticated historical methods to his study. He was so dedicated to his work that he chose castration over death for the crime of defending a general who had surrendered to an enemy in order to complete the *Historical Records*. Ban Gu's *History of the Former Han* was the first dynastic history written during and later approved by the following dynasty. Ban Gu, like Sima Qian, strove for historical accuracy and objectivity. Thereafter, it became customary for each dynasty to write the official history of its immediate predecessor.

DOCUMENT

Sima Qian on Qin Shi Huang

Other scholars made an important mark as well. Dong Zhongshu (DONG JONG-shoo; c. 179–104 B.C.E.), Wudi's adviser, stressed the ruler's central role in leading the people to understand the goodness in their nature. He also stressed that earthquakes, eclipses, and weather disasters were signs of a ruler's immorality and pending loss of the mandate of Heaven. The Chinese believed that the successes and failures of the past provided guidance for one's own time and for the future. As stated in the *Historical Records*, "Events of the past, if not forgotten, are teachings about the future." The state-sponsored Chinese historians wrote to affirm the intimate and unchanging and essential link—the emperor—between the heavenly order and politics, caught up in supposedly predictable cycles.[10]

Han scholars also made use of archaeological investigation as an aid to the writing of history. One scholar anticipated modern archaeologists by more than a thousand years in classifying human history by

---

eunuchs—Castrated men used to guard the Emperor's wives and concubines because they posed no sexual threat.

"ages": "stone" (Old Stone Age), "jade" (New Stone Age), "bronze," and "the present age" when "weapons are made of iron."[11]

Han art was clearly creative. The largely decorative art of the past, which served a religious purpose, was replaced by a realistic pictorial art (foreshadowed earlier by the individually sculpted soldiers buried near the First Emperor's tomb) portraying ordinary life. The result was the first great Chinese flowering of sculpture. Some of the finest examples of this realistic secular art are the models of the tall and spirited horses that Wudi imported from Bactria. The Han greatly admired these proud "celestial" and "blood-sweating" horses from the west, and their artists brilliantly captured the beasts' high spirit. Human figures, models, and tiles depicting everyday life are among

A masterpiece nearly 2000 years old is this lively horse of bronze, galloping and neighing with its head and tail high. To show its speed, the unknown artist, with bold imagination, placed its left hind hoof on a flying swallow, and the other three hooves in the air. The craftsmanship is extremely fine and conforms to the principles of mechanics.

Because Han buildings were made largely of wood, none remain. Ceramic models show us how houses and towers were constructed. This Han-era model of a tower, which might have been part of a single- or multistory housing compound surrounding a courtyard, indicates the use of tile, plaster, wood, and other materials.

the fine art forms. The flair for ornamentation in the visual arts and architecture are replicated in the vibrant poetry.

During the Han period, China surpassed the level of technological development in the rest of the world. Notable inventions included a simple seismograph capable of indicating earthquakes several hundred miles away; the use of water power to grind grain and to operate a piston bellows for iron smelting; the horse collar, which greatly increased the pulling power of horses; paper made from cloth rags, which replaced cumbersome bamboo strips and expensive silk cloth as a writing surface; a sophisticated, labor-saving plow; and the humble but extremely useful wheelbarrow. By the end of the first century B.C.E., the Han Chinese had recognized sunspots and accurately determined the length of the calendar year, an example of the high level gained in their mathematical and observational astronomy.[12]

The Confucian Woman of the Han

Confucius had placed wives in a position subordinate to their husbands, and yin-yang theory had held that men and women were fundamentally different, but few scholars discussed women before the Han dynasty. Poetry and art had depicted women, but two writers in the Han wrote works that had the most long-lasting effects on the status of women. The first work, *Biographies of Heroic Women* by Liu Xiang (lee-OO SHANG; 79–8 B.C.E.), is a major collection of biographies of 125 exemplary women, notable for their filial piety, wise counsel to their husbands, and valor in the defense of their chastity. Such biographies were common didactic vehicles for men, and Liu Xiang's work parallels those with examples of women.

The other work was by Ban Zhao (BAN JOW; 45–116 C.E.), sister of Ban Gu, and a teacher to the girls and women in the palace. Her *Lessons for Women* were strict rules for the separation of men's and women's spheres. She elaborated on what propriety meant for women, listing four "womanly qualifications": womanly virtue, womanly words, womanly bearing, and womanly work that included sewing, weaving, and the ordering of wine and food for guests. Women were to guard their chastity and exhibit modesty and self-control, to choose their words with care, to wear clean clothing and ornaments, and to keep their bodies clean. She stated that wives should be obedient to their husbands, parents-in-law, and brothers- and sisters-in-law.

Because she knew that courtesy and righteousness could only be attained if women were educated, she stressed education. She asked: "Only to teach men and not to teach women, is that not ignoring the essential relation between them?"[13] *Lessons for Women* was passed down from Chinese men and women to girls into the twentieth century, and Ban Zhao's approach to womanhood influenced ideas in Japan and Korea as well as China.

Religious Daoism and Buddhism

The philosophical Daoism of the late Zhou era was joined by a new form of religious Daoism in the Han. While it was not until the last century of the Later Han that religious Daoism developed a written body of sacred texts and clergy able to interpret them—concepts that would have seemed alien to Zhuangzi and Laozi—other uses of Daoism emerged as early as the founding of the Qin. Both the first emperor of the Qin and Wudi of Han consulted Daoist specialists on extending their lives through elixirs, diet, and talismans in addition to sexual practices and breathing exercises. These techniques were performed by men in power and were not yet a form of popular religious expression.

By the second century of the Later Han, these Daoist-inspired practices for extending longevity were joined by an interest in alchemy to produce elixirs and combined with folk beliefs in local gods and shamanistic rituals to create a more organized religion. From these roots, religious Daoism produced several leaders able to transform peasant discontent into massive religious movements, such as the Red Eyebrows and the Yellow Turbans. Religious Daoism continued to evolve in the next several centuries.

The breakdown of the political and social order during the Later Han also produced an upsurge in philosophical Daoism. Because they had no faith in the political order or in social action that could eradicate the widespread discontent and were discouraged with Confucianism and its concern for society, educated Chinese began to turn inward. The Mahayana school of Buddhism, first mentioned in China around 66 C.E. and brought in by missionaries and traders through central Asia, provided another answer to the need for religious assurance. (For the history and beliefs of Buddhism in its country of origin, India, see the next chapter.) At first, Buddhism in China was practiced by foreigners and was not a single system of beliefs but a wide array of sects and approaches. Mahayana Buddhism came to China along with meditation, monasticism, and magic. About 148 C.E. a Buddhist missionary established a center for the translation of Buddhist writings into Chinese at the Later Han capital. Relatively few Chinese, however, were attracted to the religion during the Han dynasty. Buddhism's great attraction to converts and its influence on Chinese culture came after the fall of the Han dynasty when renewed political turmoil made its emphasis on otherworldly salvation appealing to the great majority of Chinese and its stress on compassion, transcending gender and ethnicity, particularly attractive to women. Indeed, some scholars refer to the next half millennium as China's Buddhist age, when the religion permeated culture, arts, and governance. Ten thousand temples transformed the Chinese countryside within 300 years of the fall of the Han. Religious Daoism became increasingly sophisticated and experienced great growth, too, but new Chinese developments in Buddhism particularly endeared the latter to the masses.

China and Foreign Trade

Chinese leaders had ambivalent feelings about trade with foreigners. On the one hand, they did not want to provide "the barbarians" with the means to become richer or the technology to become stronger. But to ensure stability on the northern frontier and with their

Document   From *The Book of Songs:* "A Simple Rustic You Seemed"

Every Confucian gentleman was expected to memorize *The Book of Songs*, one of the five Chinese Confucian classics, along with *The Book of History, The Book of Rites,* and *The Book of Change.* The poems of *The Book of Songs* were composed between 1000 and 600 B.C.E. This particular poem is attributed to the Daoist "old master" Laozi.

A Simple Rustic You Seemed

A simple rustic you seemed,
Carrying cloth to barter for silk.
But you did not come to buy silk;
You came with a design on me.
I saw you off, wading the river Ch'i
As far as Tun-ch'iu.
"It is not that I'd put off the date,
But no good go-between you have,
Please, do not be angry;
Autumn is the time we meet again."
I climbed that ruined wall
To look towards Fu-kuan.
I did not see Fu-kuan;
My tears flowed in streams.
After I had seen Fu-kuan,
How I laughed and talked!
You'd consulted the shell and the stalks,
And there was nothing inauspicious.
You came with your carriage
And carried me away and my goods.
Before shedding from the mulberry tree,
How glossy green the leaves are!
Alas, you turtledove,
Eat not the mulberries!
Alas, you women,
Do not dally with men!
When a man dallies,
He will still be pardoned;
But when a woman dallies,
No pardon will she have.
The mulberry leaves have fallen,
All yellow and sere.
Since I came to you,
Three years I have lasted poverty.
The waters of the Ch'i are full;
They wet the curtains of my carriage.
The woman remains constant,
But the man has altered his ways;
He is lacking in faith

And changeable in his conduct.
Three years I was your wife,
I never tired of household chores.
Early I rose and late I went to bed
Not a morning was I without work.
First you found fault with me,
Then treated me with violence,
My brothers, not knowing this,
Jeered and laughed at me.
Quietly I brood over it
And myself I pity.
Together with you I was to grow old;
Old, it has made me wretched!
The Ch'i, at least, has its banks,
And the swamp, its shores.
At the feast of the "tufted hair,"
We talked and laughed gaily.
You pledged solemnly your truth,
Little reckoning that it would be broken.
No, I never thought that it could be broken,
And that this should be the end.

(Trans. Wu-chi Liu)

Questions to Consider

1. This poem gives us an indication of the role of gender in classical China. What sense do you now have regarding how expectations for women differed from expectations for men?
2. *The Book of Songs* contained folk songs, military songs, religious hymns, and love songs. The poem "A Simple Rustic" is one of the love songs. Do you think the ideas and emotions expressed here can be compared to the thoughts and sentiments in contemporary love songs? If so, why and if not, why not?
3. Do you think that this poem can be read as an expression of protest, or do you see it more as an acceptance of the composer's personal history?

From Wu-chi Liu and Irving Yuchang, eds., *Sunflower Splendor. Three Thousand Years of Chinese Poetry* (Garden City: Anchor Books, 1975), pp. 97–101.

Central Asian neighbors, the Chinese engaged in trade, especially in silk. In return they received the horses and woolen goods they needed. The Han government began to actively promote the silk business in the first century B.C.E. Some of the caravans carrying silk reached the Mediterranean basin via middlemen along trade routes stretching from Rome to China. In late nineteenth-century Europe the idea of the existence of one Silk Road was first popularized, but, in fact, there were numerous routes, most of which led to India or Persia. We have evidence of the trade from the Roman writer Pliny who criticized the decadence of those in Rome who were purchasing silk. The Latin word *serica* ("silk") came from *Seres,* the Greek word for China. Just as China was forced to form relationships beyond its borders, others were beginning to formulate images and policies for China.

In 138 B.C.E. the Han emperor Wudi sent an envoy to Bactria to seek allies against the Xiongnu. The information he brought back amounted to the Chinese discovery of western Eurasia. Intrigued above all by his envoy's report of interest in Chinese silks and his description of Central Asia's magnificent horses, Wudi resolved to open trade relations with his western neighbors. His armies pushed across the Pamir Mountains to a location close to Alexandria Eschate (Khojend), founded by Alexander the Great as the northern limit of his empire. Shortly after 100 B.C.E. silk began arriving in the Mediterranean basin, conveyed by the Parthians. Wealthy private merchants carried on this trade, which required large outlays of capital. They organized their cargoes into caravans of shaggy pack-horses and two-humped Bactrian camels. When the Chinese armies moved back across the Pamirs, the

Kushans of India became their middlemen, selling the silk to the Parthians and later to European merchants coming by sea to India.

It was not until about 120 C.E. that the Parthians allowed some merchants from the west to cross their land. The information they brought back about the Chinese was used by Ptolemy in constructing his map of the world. During the first and second centuries C.E.—the prosperous years of the Pax Romana—the peoples of the Roman Empire had a voracious appetite for Chinese silk, which the Romans believed was produced from the leaves of trees. In 166 C.E., according to the *History of the Later Han Dynasty,* some merchants from Da Qin ("Great Qin," the Chinese name for Rome), claiming to represent "King Antun" (Emperor Marcus Aurelius Antoninus), arrived in South China by sea across the Bay of Bengal and around the Malay peninsula.

To satisfy the Roman world's insatiable appetite for luxury goods, trade with China grew immensely in the first two centuries of the Common Era. But because such Roman exports to the East as wool, linen, glass, and metalware did not match in value Rome's imports of silk, spices, perfumes, gems, and

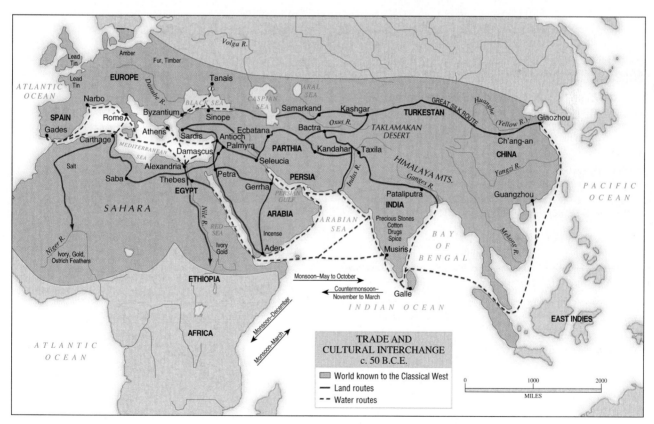

An interconnected world economy existed long before the advent of modern communications and technology. During the first century B.C.E., *Africa, Asia, and Europe were drawn together in a trade cycle of raw materials and finished goods. Many items were traded across Eurasia, but the predominance of silk in the trade between the Han and Roman empires led to the routes across Central Asia being dubbed the "Silk Road."*

other luxuries, the West suffered seriously from an adverse balance of trade. Gold and silver had to be continually exported to Asia. Late in the first century C.E., Pliny estimated that China and Arabia drained away annually at least 100 million sesterces (the daily wage of an unskilled Roman laborer was 4 sesterces).

For the Chinese, trade with what would come to be Europe was the least important aspect of its international commerce during the Han dynasty and continued to be so until the nineteenth century. There were, however, relations between China and the West through central Asia. Indochina, Korea, Japan, India, and the lands to the north would all come together in the next millennium to form the first global trading zone, in conjunction with the Arab markets, and would enrich and stimulate China.[14]

Early China

CONCLUSION

China was created because of, not in spite of, constant turmoil over the centuries. By the third century C.E. institutions of kingship, kinship, and empire would be in place. These would take highly different forms throughout the centuries. Nonetheless, the idea of a centralized kingdom under the mandate of Heaven was now a powerful force.

Confucian presumptions about social relationships, including the interaction between women and men in the family and between the dead and the living, had taken a strong hold. So had the Daoist philosophical and religious stream of thought that provided a counterpoint to Confucianism because of its emphasis on nonaction over social interaction and on supernatural beliefs. Buddhism was beginning to transform the entire religious landscape. The Chinese state was based primarily on Confucian concerns, however, focusing on the secular amelioration of social evils and the relief of distress.

Finally, a domestic bureaucratic model that relied on both Confucian and Legalist goals and methods was in place by the beginning of the Common Era. China was seen as a united entity inhabited by a people with shared culture and power. The imperial ambitions that had coalesced many kingdoms into one was channeled into a lively trade with the outside world, and the dynamic interaction between China and its neighbors resulted in cultural innovations and enormous social change.

Suggestions for Web Browsing

You can obtain more information about topics included in this chapter at the websites listed below. See also the companion website that accompanies this text, http://www.ablongman.com/brummett, which contains an online study guide and additional resources.

Ancient Dynasties

http://www-chaos.umd.edu/history/ancient1.html

Images and text present a view of early China, from prehistory to the era of the Warring States, 221 B.C.E.

China the Beautiful

http://www.chinapage.com/chinese.html

Extensive site exploring the art, calligraphy, poetry, literature, and music of China throughout its lengthy history.

Ancient China

http://www.wsu.edu:8080/~dee/ANCCHINA/ANCCHINA.HTM

Chinese history from 4000 to 256 B.C.E., with details about philosophy and culture.

Literature and Film

Selected Poems of Chu Yuan, ed. Dayu Sun (Universe Inc., 1999) presents a translation of representative poems by the man considered the first great Chinese poet. In the classic *Pan Chao: Foremost Woman Scholar of China* (published 1932; reprinted with an introduction by Susan Mann, Center for Chinese Stud-

ies, 2001), Nancy Lee Swann paints an insightful picture of the famous Chinese woman intellectual—a sketch of the Eastern Han period when Pan Chao (Ban Zhao) lived and wrote, of her family background, and of the literary milieu of which she was a part. In addition, Swann provides translations of writings definitively identified with Ban that survive from the years when she was active (c. 89–105 C.E.).

The Tomb of the Terra Cotta Warriors offers viewers a detailed look at one of the most surprising and important archaeological discoveries in history (The History Channel, 2001).

Suggestions for Reading

Insightful surveys and analyses of ancient China include John K. Fairbank, *China: A New History* (Belknap, 1998); Jacques Gernet, *A History of Chinese Civilization*, 2nd ed. (Cambridge University Press, 1996); Derk Bodde, Charles le Blanc, and Dorothy Borei, *Essays on Chinese Civilization* (Princeton University Press, 1981); Charles Holcombe, *The Genesis of East Asia* (University of Hawaii Press, 2002); David Keightly, ed., *The Origins of Chinese Civilization* (University of California Press, 1983); Michael Loewe, *The Pride That Was China* (St. Martin's Press, 1990); Kwang-Chih Chang, *The Archaeology of Ancient China*, 4th ed. (Yale University Press, 1987), and *Shang Civilization* (Yale University Press, 1982); Michael Loewe, John K. Fairbank, and Denis C. Twitchett, eds., *The Ch'in and Han Empires, 221 B.C.–A.D. 220* (Cambridge University Press, 1986); and Patricia Buckley Ebrey, *Cambridge Illustrated History of China* (Cambridge University Press, 1996).

The following are excellent treatments of intellectual and religious traditions: Benjamin Schwartz, *The World of Thought in Ancient China* (Harvard University Press, 1985); Frederick W. Mote, *Intellectual Foundations of China*, 2nd ed. (McGraw-Hill, 1989); A. C. Graham, *Disputers of the Tao* (Open Court Publishing, 1989); Isabelle Robinet, *Daoism: Growth of a Religion*, trans. Phyllis Brooks (Stanford University Press, 1997); and Daniel Overmyer, *Religions of China* (Harper and Row, 1986). On the fine arts, see Michael Sullivan, *The Arts of China*, 4th ed. (University of California Press, 2000), and Wen Fong, ed., *The Great Bronze Age of China* (Metropolitan Museum of Art/Knopf, 1980).

Ancient India

From Origins to 300 C.E.

The Indian subcontinent since ancient times has functioned as a matrix for networks of trade and culture. It has been the target of conquerors and empire builders and the origination point of philosophical and artistic trends that have radiated outward along the land-based routes linking Asia with Europe and the seaborne routes connecting South Asia to Africa, the Middle East, Southeast Asia, and East Asia. The civilizations of classical India have had a profound effect that endures to this day on the arts, literature, religion, and philosophical beliefs of the world.

The subcontinent called India was a land of sometimes dense settlement as early as the Stone Age, dating back 500,000 years. An area diverse in climate, geography, language, and ethnicity, it was, like all premodern societies, primarily a village-based agricultural society. In the ancient times discussed here, India produced an extensive civilization in the Indus valley of the northwest that ultimately declined, adopted culture and language from people who immigrated from the Iranian plateau, and later generated a second large-scale state, centered in the northeast but including large blocks of territory elsewhere throughout much of the subcontinent. Other empires rose and fell, especially in the south, throughout antiquity. Synthesizing the social ideas and the philosophical and religious beliefs and practices arising from immigration and temporary contact with those of indigenous people, India developed three major religious traditions during this time, Hinduism, Jainism, and Buddhism, the last of which spread far beyond the bounds of India to become a pan-Asian and today global religion.

2500 B.C.E.

c. 2500 Indus valley civilization develops

c. 1900–1000 Composition of the early *Rig-Veda*

c. 1900–1700 Growth of Aryan culture

1000

c. 600 Composition of the earliest *Upanishads*

500

c. 481 (perhaps as late as 400) Death of Gautama Buddha

c. 468 (perhaps as late as 447) Death of Jain Tirthamkara Mahavira

c. 400 Composition of early *Mahabharata* and *Ramayana*

321 Chandragupta Maurya establishes Mauryan kingdom

269–232 Reign of Ashoka

1

40 C.E.–200 C.E. Kushana Empire rules northern India

First century Development of Mahayana Buddhism

EARLY INDIA

■ *How did indigenous culture and outside influences come together to create ancient Indian civilization?*

In this chapter we trace the important threads of Indian history to the third century C.E. This period was the formative age of Indian civilization, when its basic institutions and cultural patterns were determined.

Early Civilization in India

The term *India* is used here to refer to the entire subcontinent, an area encompassing the modern nations of Pakistan, India, Nepal, Bhutan, Bangladesh, and Sri Lanka. The term *subcontinent* is frequently used to refer to this large area. It could also be used to refer to other discrete parts of Eurasia, such as China or Europe, but such uses are not common. The Indian subcontinent is a large, irregular diamond, the lower sides of which are bounded by the warm waters of the Indian Ocean and the upper sides by the mountain walls of the Himalayas on the north and several smaller ranges on the west. The highest mountains in the world, the Himalayas, and their western counterparts divide India from the rest of Asia, making it a geographically discrete area, though never cut off from the great movements of civilization and culture. Through the Khyber Pass and other mountain passes in the northwest and across the Indian Ocean have come the armed conquerors, restless tribes, merchants, and travelers who did much to shape India's turbulent history.

In addition to the northern mountain belt, which shields India from arctic winds, the subcontinent comprises two other major geographical regions. In the north is the great plain (which came to be known as *Hindustan* after the Muslim invasions), extending from the Indus valley to the Bay of Bengal. It spans the watersheds of two great river systems, the Indus and the Ganges, which have their sources in the Himalayas. South of this great plain and separated from it in the west by the Vindhya mountain range, rises a semiarid plateau, the Deccan ("southland").

India's climate and the rhythms of Indian life are governed by the dry northeast monsoon wind of the winter and the wet southwest monsoon wind of the summer. Most parts of India receive the majority of their rainfall during the summer and autumn months of the southwest monsoon, which blows in from the Arabian Sea. The Western Ghats cause the summer monsoon to drop most of its rain on the thin Malabar Coast, making it one of the wettest areas of the globe, but the western Deccan, directly east of the Ghat range, has a semiarid climate.

India comprises an area comparable to Europe in size and internal diversity. The regions and peoples of India came to be roughly divided into two major language groups, the Indo-European in the north and the Dravidian in the south; each group embraces a number of separate languages. In the centuries between 1900 B.C.E. and 300 C.E., the emerging Hindu cultural synthesis, though modified by diverse philosophies and religions, gave the subcontinent a general cultural

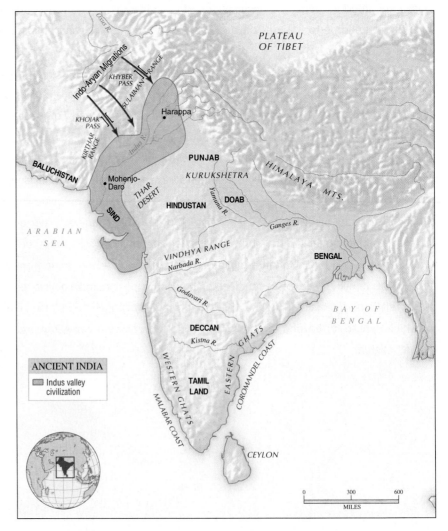

India is a peninsula protected on its northern frontiers by the Himalaya, Kirthar, and Sulaiman mountain ranges.

unity similar to the unity afforded to Europe by the spread of the Christianity in the first millennium C.E.

The Indus Civilization, c. 2500–1500 B.C.E.

Sometime before 2500 B.C.E., a counterpart of the civilizations that had emerged along the Tigris and Euphrates and the Nile appeared along the Indus River in northwestern India. This area, called the Punjab (poon-JAHB) or "land of the five rivers, is made up of an alluvial plain watered by the upper Indus and its tributaries, and the region of the lower Indus (called Sind, from *sindhu*, meaning "river," and the origin of the terms *Hindu* and *India*). This Indus valley civilization flourished until about 1700 B.C.E. Among its major cities, Mohenjo-Daro (moh-HEN-joh dah-ROH), located north of Karachi in present-day Pakistan, is believed to have been one of the largest Bronze Age cities of the world.

Archaeologists believe that the Indus valley civilization began declining sometime around 1900 B.C.E. Around that time, or perhaps a few hundred years earlier, migrants began to move into the subcontinent from the Iranian plateau. Their culture and language gradually came to dominate the north of India, as people adopted important aspects of the migrants' culture and intermixed with them. The migrants' religion, cultivated by their **Brahmans** (BRAH-muhns; seers and priests), became the foundation for much of the later cultural development of the entire subcontinent.

The rise of civilization in the Indus valley around 2500 B.C.E. resembled what had occurred in Mesopotamia nearly a thousand years earlier. In India Neolithic farmers had been living in food-producing villages situated on the hilly flanks of large river valleys since around 4000 B.C.E. These settlements spread out along the river valleys, capitalizing on their abundant water and fertile soil. Here they developed the more complex way of life we call a civilization. Some of these farming villages had grown into large cities with as many as 40,000 inhabitants by 2300 B.C.E. Excavations of two of these cities, Mohenjo-Daro in Sind and Harappa (hah-RAP-pah)

Brahmans—The priestly *varna*; highest in Hindu caste hierarchy.

The ruins at Mohenjo-Daro, a city of an estimated 30,000 to 50,000 people, are still impressive more than four millennia after the city was established. There has been much speculation concerning the function of Mohenjo-Daro's largest buildings. Were they temples, administrative centers, or perhaps granaries? Only the function of the large public bath seems at least relatively clear.

This tiny figure of a girl who may be dancing was unearthed at Mohenjo-Daro and probably dates from around 2000 B.C.E.

The economy of the Indus civilization, like that of Mesopotamia and Egypt, was based on irrigation farming. Wheat and barley were the chief crops, and the state collected these grains as taxes and stored them in huge granaries. For the first known time in history, chickens were domesticated as a food source during the Indus civilization, and cotton was grown and used in making textiles. Cotton textiles would ultimately become a world trade good and an important source of wealth for South Asia. The spinning and weaving of cotton remains today one of the subcontinent's chief industries.

The nature of the society that produced Indus valley civilization is the subject of considerable controversy. Unlike Egyptian hieroglyphics, which were deciphered by modern scholars using the Rosetta Stone, the Indus valley script (400 pictographic signs) has never been deciphered. Thus, the Indus valley writings, used on engraved stamp-seals, have given rise to modern claims and counterclaims about their "true" meaning. Indus stamp seals depict bulls, rhinoceroses, and crocodiles—but they also depict horned humans, unicorns, and large figures that may or may not be gods, generating considerable speculation about the beliefs and social organization of Indus peoples.

Numerous clay mother goddess figurines have been unearthed, indicating an early version of mother-goddess worship still important in India. Such figures are also found in various forms throughout the Mediterranean world, although their exact meaning in India and elsewhere is the subject of

Excavations at Mohenjo-Daro have unearthed what are often called "mother goddess figurines" such as this terra-cotta female. The figure, with her elaborate headdress, may well be a symbol of fertility but that conclusion is speculative.

considerable debate. Another controversial question is whether the Indus valley peoples were peaceful or warlike. Copper and bronze were used for tools and weapons, but the rarity of weapons has been used by some scholars to suggest that Indus society was peaceful. An interesting archaeological find is a set of three double graves, each with

in the Punjab, have provided much of our knowledge of the Indus valley civilization, but other sites were widely dispersed across the whole of northwestern India. Reaching its height in the centuries around 2000 B.C.E., the Indus valley civilization produced highly organized towns and uniform weights, measures, and pottery.

Although Mohenjo-Daro and Harappa were 400 miles apart, similarities in the cities' construction and layout suggest that the Indus River made possible the maintenance of a uniform administration and economy over the entire area. The cities appear to have been carefully planned, with residential blocks arranged on a north-south grid and an elaborate drainage system with underground channels. The spacious two-storied houses of the well-to-do contained bathrooms and were constructed with the same type of baked bricks used for roads. Indeed, it was the durable bricks produced by Indus valley builders that led, in part, to the discovery of Harappa after a nineteenth-century work crew found and "recycled" its ancient bricks for a railway project.

a male and a female. These may be married couples buried in single graves, which may suggest an early form of a wife's duty to her husband, called *sati,* so strongly praised in later centuries.

We cannot yet solve the Indus valley controversies, but what the archaeological evidence does make clear is that the Indus valley civilization was prosperous and well organized. Trade was sufficiently well organized to obtain needed raw materials—copper, tin, silver, gold, and timber—from the mountain regions to the west; and there were active trade contacts with Mesopotamia, some 1500 miles away, as early as 2300 B.C.E. (the time of Sargon of Akkad). In addition, Indus valley seals have been found in Sumerian sites.

Excavations at Mohenjo-Daro show that decline was well underway when a series of great floods caused by earthquakes altered the course of the Indus around 1700 B.C.E and apparently severely affected the settlements along it. Other Indus valley cities, such as Harappa to the north, appear to have suffered a similar fate, although some others continued to carry on long after the decline of these two great cities. The culture of migrants entering the Indus valley through the northwest passes around 1900 B.C.E. was thus able to influence the language, religion, and culture of north India as the great Indus valley civilization was on the decline.

The Introduction of Aryan Ways in the Early Vedic Age, 1900–1000 B.C.E.

The question of the end of the Indus valley civilization and its replacement in north India by different languages and customs is a topic of heated debate among historians. While some assert that a large wave of people called Aryans invaded and conquered north India, bringing their culture with them, other historians stress that Indians already living in the north adopted the culture of a much smaller though influential group of people who immigrated from the Iranian plateau and merged with them. Thus, those who called themselves Aryans included many local people who used the term to distinguish themselves from those who did not share their culture; the distinction, these historians assert, was not between an indigenous ethnic group and immigrants from outside India, but was based more on cultural differences.

People of Aryan culture who lived in northeastern India and eastern Afghanistan inhabited tribal villages and herded cattle, sheep, goats, and horses. Their language, an early form of Sanskrit, belonged to a group of languages called Indo-European, which include Sanskrit, Persian, Celtic, English, Germanic, Italian, and Greek languages. Whether one accepts the view that a wave of semibarbaric Aryan nomads skilled at chariot warfare contributed to the weakening of the

Indus valley civilization or accepts the increasingly common view that local people gradually adopted Aryan culture as they mixed with them, Aryan language and culture certainly became indigenized and dominant in northern India in the first five or six centuries after their arrival. Not all indigenous populations of the subcontinent adopted Aryan languages and cultures. Some, located in the Deccan, retained their own, which were part of the Dravidian language group. The Aryans referred to these people as *Dasas,* which had a negative connotation of "dark" enemies.

During the centuries in which Aryan culture was absorbed in north India, Aryans worshipped their gods with sacrificial rituals that were accompanied by specially composed "verses of praise and adoration," *ric* verses, which would be recited together in "hymns." The *ric* verses and the hymns they made up were regarded as the sacred compositions of inspired seers (the Brahmans), who could see the gods and understood their ways and were thus able to compose verses that could influence the gods to favor and bless Aryan men and their families. Over 1000 such hymns were gathered together in the *Rig-Veda* (reeg-VAY-dah), a collection that has been memorized and used in worship continuously for over 3500 years. (*Veda* means "knowledge," a reference to the Brahman's knowing all the hymns by memory.) The earliest part of the *Rig-Veda* was probably composed between 1900 and 1500 B.C.E., and later portions were added until about 1000 B.C.E. Both religious and secular hymns are included in the *Rig-Veda;* in the latter, the structure of society, with its occupational classifications, is revealed. Thanks to the *Rig-Veda* we know more about the Aryans than we know about the Indus civilization, for which we must still rely only on archaeological evidence because their writings have not yet been deciphered.

The early Aryan religion involved making sacrificial offerings of grain, cakes, dairy products, and animals to the gods, who embodied and controlled the forces of what we today call "nature," in return for such material gains as long life, health, many offspring, victory in war, and life in the "bright place in the sky" (heaven). The god worshipped most in the *Rig-Veda* was Indra, storm-god and patron of warriors, who is described as leading the Aryans in destroying the forts of the Dasas. Virile and boisterous, Indra personified the heroic virtues of the Aryan warrior aristocracy as he drove his chariot across the sky, wielded his thunderbolts, ate the meat of dozens of sacrificed bulls and buffaloes, and quaffed entire lakes of the stimulating ritual drink *soma,* which might have been alcoholic, narcotic, or psychedelic.

Next to Indra in popularity was Agni, the benevolent god of fire, who performed many services for the

IMAGE

Statue of Indra, God of War

Document   *Rig-Veda:* Creation and the Kinds of Men

Like other ancient peoples, the societies of India developed a variety of creation myths. Such myths often involve stories of sacrifice and explanations for the hierarchy of beings. The Purusha Sutra of the *Rig-Veda* provides the first suggestion in ancient Vedic texts of the notion of the *varnas*, the idea that humankind is divided into four classes and their differences are based in Creation itself. The four classes are priests (Brahmans), rulers and warriors (Rajanyas or Kshatriyas), herders and merchants (Vaishyas), and the low-class workers or servants (Shudras). In this Vedic story, Purusha (the "primordial cosmic man") serves as the victim in the cosmic sacrifice from which the universe originates.

The sacrificial victim, namely Purusha, born at the very beginning, they [the gods] sprinkled with sacred water upon the sacrificial grass. With him as oblation, the gods performed the sacrifice, and also the *Sadhyas* [a class of semidivine beings] and the *rishis* [ancient seers].

From that wholly offered sacrificial oblation were born the verses and the sacred chants. . . . From it the horses were born and also those animals who have double rows of teeth; cows were born from it, from it were born goats and sheep.

When they divided Purusha, in how many different portions did they arrange him? What became of his mouth, what of his two arms? What were his two thighs and his two feet called?

His mouth became the brahman; his arms were made into the rajanya; his two thighs the vaishyas; from his two feet the shudra was born.

The moon was born from his mind, from the eye the sun was born; from the mouth Indra and Agni [Vedic gods], from the breath the wind was born.

From the navel was the atmosphere created, from the head the heaven issued forth; from the two feet was born the earth and the quarters [the four cardinal directions] from the ear. Thus did they fashion the worlds.

. . . With this sacrificial oblation did the gods offer the sacrifice. These were the first norms [dharma] of sacrifice. These greatnesses reached to the sky wherein live the ancient *Sadhyas* and gods.

Questions to Consider

1. Think about the many different ways that people can be divided. What is the system of division in this myth based on?
2. What does this myth suggest about the roles of the gods and of sacrifice in Indian society?
3. Think about other creation myths you have heard or read. How is this one similar or different?

From Ainslie T. Embree, ed., *Sources of Indian Tradition,* Vol. 1, 2nd ed. (New York: Columbia University Press, 1988), pp. 18–19.

Aryans, not least of which was conveying their ritual offerings up to the other gods. Another major Aryan god was Varuna, the sky-god. Viewed as the king of the gods, he lived in a great palace in the heavens where one of his associates was a sun-god, Mitra, known as Mithras to the Persians and, a thousand years later, widely worshipped in the Roman Empire. Varuna was the guardian of *rita*, the "right order of things." *Rita* was both the cosmic law of nature (the regularity of the seasons, for example) and the customary tribal law of the Aryans. Varuna was, thus, the divine judge.

The *Rig-Veda* is the earliest surviving work of literature in an Indo-European language, and it gives some insight into the institutions and ideas of the Early Vedic Age. Each tribe was headed by a war leader called *raja,* a word related to the Latin word for king, *rex.* Like the early kings of Sumer, Greece, and Rome, the raja was only the first among equals. Two tribal assemblies, one a small council of the great men of the tribe and the other a larger gathering of the heads of families, approved his accession to office and advised him on important matters.

The hymns in the *Rig-Veda* mention three social categories **(varnas),** the Brahmans or priests, the **Kshatriyas** (kuh-SHAH-tree-yas) or nobility, and the **Vaishyas** (VAI-shas) or commoners. A fourth class, the **Shudras,** the non-Aryan population of workers and serfs, was then added at the bottom of the social scale.

varnas—Originally occupational groups; later also four status groups connected to purity and prestige at sacred rituals.

Kshatriyas—The *varna* associated with governing and military power; second in the *varna* hierarchy.

Vaishyas—Commoner *varna;* merchants and landlords; third in the *varna* hierarchy.

Shudras—Menial workers; lowest in *varna* hierarchy.

In one of the later hymns of the *Rig-Veda*, these four social categories are described as emerging from the sacrifice of the Cosmic Man, Purusha, with priestly Brahmans coming from his mouth, ruling Kshatriyas from his arms, Vaishyas from his thighs, and Shudras from his feet.

The Later Vedic Age, c. 1000–600 B.C.E.

Most of our knowledge about the years between 1000 and 600 B.C.E. derives from religious texts the Brahmans composed during this period or from later texts such as the two great epics of **Hinduism,** the *Mahabharata* (mah-hah-BAH-rah-tah) and the *Ramayana* (rah-mah-YAH-nah). All these texts tell us a great deal about religious and philosophical thought during this time, but what we know of this period's political, social, and economic institutions we must glean from religious texts or infer from the convergence of the archaeological record with later texts.

By about 1000 B.C.E. Aryans and their culture had moved into the critical territory that lies between the Indus watershed and the Ganges watershed. During the Later Vedic Age, they continued their movement both to the east, passing into the Doab ("land of two rivers") between the Yamuna and the Ganges and on down the Ganges valley, and to the south, toward the Vindhya Mountains. The area between the two watersheds came to be known as *Kurukshetra* ("the field of King Kuru"), and it became the sacred heartland of the Aryans in the Later Vedic Age. Kurukshetra (koo-roo-KSHET-rah) was the site of the fabled Bharata (BAH-rah-tah) war (the story of which is told in the *Mahabharata*), and many other battles critical to the history of India over the next 3000 years were fought in this vicinity. The sense of space, particularly sacred space, is very important in Indian thought, and the ways such spaces have been articulated remain a critical factor in Indian politics today.

This era seems to have been a golden age for the Brahmans and their Vedic religion. During this period, some of the hymns of the *Rig-Veda* were set to melodies (called *samans*) collected in a separate *Veda* called the *Sama-Veda*. The *Yajur-Veda* was a compilation of prayers and instructions for priests performing sacrifices. Different families of Brahmans would specialize in learning one or the other of these three *Vedas;* and spectacularly large *soma* sacrifices developed that employed Brahmans of each kind. A fourth *Veda*, the

Atharva-Veda, was formed from a large collection of sacred formulas that, when correctly uttered, were supposed to solve many of life's mundane problems: baldness, impotence, skin rashes, and so on. These hymns and prayers suggest the ways in which the Brahmans, as keepers of the *Vedas,* gained power in Indian society.

As the number of Brahman priests and *Vedas* increased, the focus of Vedic religion shifted from the gods to the power of the sacrifice itself, and especially to the holy energy contained in the sacred words of the different Vedic songs, chants, recitations, and prayers. The Brahmans' perfect singing or chanting of Vedic verses (now called *mantras*) came to be regarded as the embodiment of the sacred energy at the heart of the ritual—the energy, called **brahman** (not to be confused with the priestly Brahmans; the energy force will be italicized in this text), that kept the world going, the energy that had brought the world into being. Even kings, those with the power over violence, had to depend on the spiritual power of the priestly Brahmans.

The Brahmans also composed, now in prose rather than verse, a whole new kind of text, the *Brahmanas* (bra-MAH-nahs), which explained the philosophy of the rituals and the background meaning and use of the Vedic mantras employed in the rituals. During the Early Vedic Age sacrifice had been a means of influencing the gods in favor of the offerer; now in the later Vedic Age the Brahmans regarded sacrifices to the gods as working automatically to produce the good results people wanted, provided that the ritual was performed exactly right. The sacrifices were supposed to bring long life, many sons, victory over one's enemies, general prosperity, and heaven; they made the world a good place for all beings. Since only the priests possessed the knowledge to perform the complex and lengthy rites of sacrifice (a few of which could last for months), and since the slightest variation in ritual was thought to bring harm to the people and the land, the Brahmans gained great prestige and power.

By the beginning of the Later Vedic Age the Aryans had learned iron metallurgy, possibly from people of the Iranian plateau. As in other parts of the world, iron-based tools increased the potential for agricultural exploitation and made warriors with access to iron weapons more deadly and effective. These developments set the stage for the emergence in the eastern Ganges valley of cities, territory-based kingdoms, standing armies, and stronger institutions of kingship.

Although some Indian kingdoms in this period were oligarchic republics, most were ruled by rajas, maharajas (mah-hah-RAH-jas, "great kings"), or samrajas ("universal kings," as some called themselves).

Hinduism—The largest religion in India, this heterodox faith stresses adherence to sacred texts such as the *Vedas* and *Upanishads* and the proper ritual worship of gods, Vishnu, Shiva, and Devi and their various manifestations being the most prominent. Hinduism emphasizes proper behavior for one's station in life and the eventual release *(moksha)* from the cycle of rebirth.

brahman—As first described in the *Upanishads*, the divine force or energy that created and sustains the universe.

Despite the preservation of advisory councils of nobles and priests, the kings' powers were greater than those of the Aryan tribal leaders of the earlier period. They now lived in palaces and collected taxes—in the form of goods from the villages—in order to sustain their courts and armies. The cities that arose were often administrative centers connected to a palace, and some were also commercial centers. Of course, cities did not just appear. They had to be built; and large building projects meant the mobilization of labor: some people doing the work while others gave the orders.

Village, Caste, and Family

In the Later Vedic Age, the three pillars of traditional Indian society—the autonomous village, caste, and the joint or extended family—were established. India has always been primarily agricultural, and its countryside is still a patchwork of villages. The ancient village was made up of joint families governed by a headman and a council of elders. Villages enjoyed considerable autonomy; the raja's government hardly interfered at all as long as it received its quota of taxes.

As noted earlier, Hindu society came to be divided into four occupational categories, or *varnas*—Brahmans (priests), Kshatriyas (nobles), Vaishyas (commoners), and Shudras (workers or servants). The Portuguese in the sixteenth century labeled this the *caste system*, and the name stuck in Western descriptions of Indian society. Medieval Brahmans wrote that within the framework of these four *varnas* society was divided into thousands of subgroups, or **jatis** (literally, "species"), each with a special social, occupational, or religious character. For example, they wrote, occupational groups of merchants or shopkeepers formed many *jatis* within the Vaishya caste.

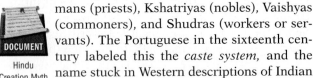

DOCUMENT

Hindu Creation Myth and the Caste System

In ancient times, however, and even today, *varna* and *jati* had different meanings. *Varna* categories described one's actual occupation and could change when one changed jobs. In antiquity, *varnas* were important during rituals involving the whole community because they determined one's task or physical placement for those rituals or sacrifices. *Jati*, on the other hand, were originally kinship groups and, thus, were not changeable as were *varnas*. In time, certain occupations became associated with certain *jati*, and the *jati* came to be ranked by the level of respect each occupation had. Later, the *jati* were associated with particular *varnas*. But there was never a consensus as

to which *varna* a *jati* belonged; disagreement continues today. Those whose occupations were the most menial and degrading—scavengers (who remove human waste) and tanners (because they handle the carcasses of dead animals)—also formed numerous *jatis* but were perceived as outside and beneath the people of the four *varnas*. These outcasts were called *Untouchables* because their touch was considered defiling to members of the *varnas*.

The third pillar of Indian society was the three-generation household, a patriarchal system. In these households, seniority brought status to both men and women. Sons were subordinate to their fathers, and young wives were subordinate to their mothers-in-law. When a woman married, she went from the house of her father to the house of her husband's father. As in many traditional societies, children were considered the property of the father, not the mother. When the patriarch died, his authority was transferred to his eldest son, but his property was divided equally among all his sons. Women were subordinate to men and required a male protector: father, husband, brother, or son. They could not inherit property, nor could they participate in sacrifices to the gods; their presence at the sacrifice was considered a source of pollution. A common Vedic prayer asked for "manly, heroic" sons. Daughters, who needed a dowry to get married, were seen as having little value to their families. Senior women, however, had status as elders and bearers of sons. Ideally, they were revered and served by their daughters-in-law.

DOCUMENT

Women in Classical India

The emphasis placed on communal interests rather than on the individual is a common denominator of the three pillars of Indian society. Thus, Indian society has always been concerned with stability, respect for elders, and family and group solidarity.

DRAMATIC DEVELOPMENTS IN RELIGION AND CULTURE, 600–320 B.C.E.

■ *What characteristics of Indian religion and culture of this era made them so appealing far beyond India's borders?*

Out of all these new political and economic developments came dramatic cultural changes that after 600 B.C.E. elevated an entirely different kind of religion to highest status and eventually gave rise to whole new religions that challenged Brahman hegemony and created important new institutions. The first of these

---

jatis—Literally "species"; originally a term meaning kinship groups, later associated with occupation. Usually what Indians mean by the Western concept of caste.

developments, beginning around 600 B.C.E, was the composition of texts called the **Upanishads** (oo-PAHN-ee-shads). The second was the rise of the new non-Vedic, even anti-Vedic, monastic religions of Jainism and Buddhism sometime in the fifth century B.C.E.

In the 600s B.C.E. a radical minority of Brahmans began to embrace ascetic and mystical religious ideas and practices (early forms of yoga, meaning "spiritual discipline" and usually involving some kind of meditation) that ultimately rejected the goals and means of Vedic ritual religion and the settled village and family life that Vedic religion presumed. Some of these radical mystics recorded the *Upanishads,* which taught "secret, mystical understandings" of the human body, the breath, the mind, and the soul. The most important of these understandings was the assertion that the light of consciousness within a person was nothing less than the undiluted energy of *brahman,* the eternal, sacred creative energy that is the source and the end of all that exists (equivalent to God in monotheistic religions).

Most of the *Upanishads* taught that all things that exist—from the most sublime ideas a person could think to the crudest forms of matter—came from *brahman* energy and eventually returned to *brahman,* the only permanent reality. Beyond these ideas, the *Upanishads* taught a way for ethically pure, worthy persons (usually only Aryans, but not necessarily just Brahmans) to immerse themselves into *brahman,* which the *Upanishads* described as unsurpassably blissful. These ideas gained great power after their presentation in the *Upanishads.* A relatively tiny minority of people followed this yoga (most Aryan people continued to make use of Brahman priests and Vedic rituals). But the basic ideas, values, and meditative techniques over time greatly influenced South Asian society and came to be regarded as the supreme form of Brahman religion.

The Vedic Brahmans had thought that people live only once and that the fate of their soul is determined in that one life. (The same general idea is found in all three of the Western Abrahamic religions: Judaism, Christianity, and Islam.) Vedic Aryans hoped to live up in the heavens with the sky-gods after their death. The *Upanishads,* however, introduced the idea of the transmigration of the soul, which was entirely new in Brahman thought. (Some scholars have speculated that this idea was part of pre-Aryan culture, but there is no solid evidence of this.) Then, in texts called the *Brahmanas,* the idea was put forward that a person's deeds stayed with him or her in the form of an unseen power that would act after that person's death and condition the

Upanishads—Sacred Brahmanic scriptures collected in sixth century B.C.E. that stress *brahman* force and idea of cyclical rebirth until release through *moksha.*

Developments in Culture and Religion in India

c. 600 B.C.E.	Earliest *Upanishads*
c. 481 (perhaps as late as 400) B.C.E.	Death of Gautama Buddha
c. 468 (perhaps as late as 447) B.C.E.	Death of Mahavira
c. 300 B.C.E.	Jainism gains support in North and South India

fate of the departed soul. A deed or action was called *karman* in Sanskrit, and the unseen power of past deeds was called *karman* as well (karma in contemporary English).

The latest *Brahmana* texts sometimes express a fear that people "die again"—the accumulation of their good works, their good karma, supports them in heaven when they die, but the karma gets used up keeping the soul in heaven, and the soul then "dies" again, in heaven. This fear leads directly to the idea that when the soul dies in heaven, it descends to earth, reincarnated in another body. This new person lives and dies, and the soul goes to heaven once again, if the earthly actions of this latest lifetime have been good (that is, if they conformed with the law, or dharma [DAR-mah] as revealed in the *Vedas*). Bad deeds, bad karma, lead the soul to hell.

Eventually, the idea emerged that rebirth in sub-human forms of life was a natural consequence of violating dharma. After living a life as some kind of animal, a soul automatically moves up the ladder of life forms toward an eventual human incarnation because animals cannot violate dharma. The rebirth of the soul in a new body is called *samsara* (sam-SAH-rah), and the *Upanishads* regarded continual, unending samsara as dreary and unpleasant. The *Upanishads* taught that good deeds, including Vedic rituals, could do nothing more for a person than provide a temporary spell in heaven between incarnations. Bad deeds, of course, had far more unpleasant consequences; but worse than either hell or heaven was the prospect of living, acting, and dying over and over, forever without end. In the face of this bleak prospect, the *Upanishads* said the only truly good thing a person can do is try to escape perpetual samsara through release from desire and eventually from rebirth. That release was called *moksha* (MOHK-sha). Achieving *moksha* involves permanently escaping from karma, from

DOCUMENT

Transmigration of Souls in the *Upanishads*

samsara, and from all the pain and suffering encountered in countless lives. According to the *Upanishads,* by permanently immersing oneself in *brahman* through meditation, a person can dissolve the soul back into the holy oneness that is its ultimate source and end. The soul has "returned home"—its journey through samsara is over.

The *Upanishads* depict the first Indian gurus wandering in the forests as ascetics; there they meditated and taught their disciples. One of them summed up their quest as follows:

> From the unreal lead me to the real!
> From darkness lead me to light!
> From death lead me to immortality!

Of course, most Indian people did not become gurus or devote their lives to meditation and asceticism; most Indians lived the life of the agriculturalist. But the powerful ideas of rebirth and *moksha* presented in the *Upanishads* and the *Brahmanas* had an enormous impact on subsequent Indian thought and social organization.

The Jains, Defenders of All Beings

Beyond the changes just noted in Vedic religious thought, two non-Vedic religions also emerged in South Asia during this time: Jainism and Buddhism. Jainism contributed to all of India (and today to the rest of the world) the unique ethical claim that the most important duty of a person is **ahimsa** (ah-

ahimsa—The practice of nonviolence toward all living things; a belief central to Jainism initially but also adopted by Buddhism and Hinduism.

Document   The Jains on the Souls in All Things

The Jains, like the Buddhists, believe in conquering desire as a way of achieving Enlightenment and escaping from the cycle of rebirth. But the Jains emphasize the existence of souls in all living things. They believe all beings experience pleasure, pain, terror, and unhappiness. Hence Jain texts reveal a heightened sensitivity to the pain man can inflict by harming all things, animate and inanimate. This verse passage is taken from a Jain text depicting the speech of a prince who is trying to persuade his parents to allow him to take up a life of religion. He tries to express to them the terrible agonies suffered by beings at various levels of creation.

> From clubs and knives, stakes and maces,
>   breaking my limbs,
> An infinite number of times I have suffered
>   without hope.
> By keen edged razors, by knives and shears,
> Many times I have been drawn and quartered,
>   torn apart and skinned.
> Helpless in snares and traps, a deer,
> I have been caught and bound and fastened, and
>   often I have been killed.
> A helpless fish, I have been caught with hooks and
>   nets;
> An infinite number of times I have been killed and
>   scraped, split and gutted.
> A bird, I have been caught by hawks or trapped in
>   nets,
> Or held fast by birdlime, and I have been killed an
>   infinite number of times.
> A tree, with axes and adzes by the carpenters
> An infinite number of times I have been felled,
>   stripped of my bark, cut up, and sawn into
>   planks.
> As iron, with hammer and tongs by blacksmiths

> An infinite number of times I have been struck
>   and beaten, split and filed. . . .
> Ever afraid, trembling in pain and suffering,
> I have felt the utmost sorrow and agony. . . .
> In every kind of existence I have suffered
> Pains that have scarcely known reprieve for a
>   moment.

Questions to Consider

1. What problems might the Jain teachers have encountered in trying to persuade others to accept their beliefs?

2. If someone truly believed that such suffering was endured by all beings, how might it affect that person and change his or her behavior?

3. Like the Buddha, the "speaker" in this text is a prince going against the wishes of his family. What does this speech suggest about generations, change, and a family's ambitions for its sons?

From Ainslie T. Embree, ed., *Sources of Indian Tradition,* Vol. 1, 2nd ed. (New York: Columbia University Press, 1988), pp. 62–63.

HEEM-sah), which is to practice nonviolence and to cause no harm or pain to any being. Buddhism also adopted the idea of ahimsa, and, over time, many, but not all, Brahmans and their followers eventually did likewise.

Jainism places a special emphasis on the idea that all beings (including plants, insects, and minerals) have "souls" *(jiva)* and experience pain. Thus, causing pain to any other sentient beings is the biggest source of the worst possible karma. Jain texts, for example, explain in graphic detail the suffering caused to the tiny beings living in wood when it is cast upon the fire. While it is inevitable that a believer will cause pain (by drinking water and the beings that are in it, for example), a person should avoid such destructive acts as much as possible. Some Jains, who practice their faith most rigorously, gently sweep the path before them with a broom as they walk to avoid stepping on living things; they may tie cloths over their mouths to avoid inhaling any small creatures in the air.

The most significant figure in Jain belief is Mahavira (mah-hah-VEE-rah; c. 559–c. 468 B.C.E.), the faith's founder. Mahavira means "great hero." He is called the *Jina* (JEE-nah, "victor," "conqueror"), and his followers are called *Jainas* (those who "follow the Jina"), hence the Western name *Jainism* for the religion as a whole. According to Jain tradition, Mahavira was a Kshatriya prince who at the age of 30 renounced the world—his home and family and all property and status that went with them.

For over a dozen years Mahavira followed the teachings of an earlier religious teacher, Parshvanatha (parsh-vah-NAH-tah). During those years Mahavira wandered naked from place to place, lived on handouts, engaged in meditation, debated with other men who were also on holy quests, observed celibacy, and engaged in various painful ascetic practices in order to purify his soul of past karma. Nudity was a form of asceticism because it exposed the genitals and invited the painful ridicule of ordinary people. The practice of nudity was the subject of debate among later Jain ascetics and gradually died out.

Mahavira gained a great reputation as a wise and holy man, attracting many followers. Thirteen years after he resolved to starve himself to death to achieve release from the bondage of his past karma, he died after seating himself in the posture of meditation with the intention of never moving again. This deliberate form of death by inaction is seen not as an act of suicide but as the most heroic and ascetic form of non-action humanly possible. For those whose souls were still fouled with karma, this mode of death was regarded as highly purifying, and many Jain saints have died this way throughout history.

The Jains accept the reality of samsara and karma and regard *moksha* (release from rebirth) to be the only sensible goal to pursue in life; but their way of pursuing *moksha* was very different from that of the Brahmans of the *Upanishads*. The path to *moksha* that Mahavira preached centers on the practice of asceticism, although one does not have to practice the most rigorous forms to be considered a pious Jain. To gain *moksha* a Jain must sooner or later, in this life or a future life, renounce the world and become a wandering monk or nun. But a person may be a pious lay Jaina, supporting the monks and nuns with handouts of food, clothing, and shelter and living a life that conforms to the Jain ethic (which emphasizes nonviolence but also forbids liquor, sex outside of marriage, lying, and stealing) until he or she is convinced that the time for renunciation has come.

Jains believe Mahavira died in 527 B.C.E., but modern, non-Jain historians believe he died 60 to 80 years later. Jains believe Mahavira was the twenty-fourth and last great *tirthamkara* (teer-tahm-KAH-rah; a "ford-maker," who aids his followers in crossing the swirling flood of samsara, the cycle of rebirth) in a long series of wise and powerful men in this current age. For Jains time revolves in endless cycles like a great cosmic wheel. In every age, *tirthamkara*s like Mahavira are born to teach the doctrines of Jainism to humanity. Every era consists of millions of years. The Jains also believe that when a soul gains *moksha* and escapes the cycle of rebirth forever, it ascends to the topmost point of the universe, where it exists in complete purity forever. This differs dramatically from the idea of the *Upanishads* that every individual's soul is completely submerged into *brahman*, the single "soul" of the whole universe.

DOCUMENT

Jainism: From *The Book of Sermons, The Book of Good Conduct*

Socially, Jainism was distinctive. It rejected the sacredness of the *Vedas* and thereby rejected the social stratification that assigned preeminence to the Brahmans. Interestingly, Jainism was also the first Indian religion formally to allow women to become renouncers and pursue *moksha* as nuns. The Buddha only reluctantly and belatedly allowed Buddhist laywomen to become nuns; and although some Hindu women did renounce the world from time to time, the Hindu dharma (sacred law) never formally sanctioned their doing so.

In the centuries after Mahavira the number of Jains has always been significant but never tremendously large. In spite of always being a minority religion in India, the Jains have consistently exerted greater influence than their numbers would lead anyone to expect. By 300 B.C.E. Jainism had gained significant political recognition in various kingdoms of north and south India. Also, because the ethics of their religion basically forbade farming for pious lay followers of the Jina (because tilling the soil kills so many small creatures), lay Jains were usually merchants living in cities. They often became wealthy and poured much of their wealth into the support of their religion. As a result, the Jain religion has contributed a great number of learned Jain scholars and libraries to India's cultural history.

The Middle Way of Gautama Buddha

About the same time that Mahavira lived, another ascetic and monastic religion arose in northern India. This religion, Buddhism, became popular and important in India and remained influential there for many centuries. It also spread outside India to all of Asia and today continues its expansion around the globe. Buddhism had some basic similarities to Jainism, but its root ideas were profoundly different. Both religions derive from the life and teachings of a great man; both stress the humanity of their teacher and do not rely on gods or divine rites to pursue the highest goal of life; both developed monastic institutions in which celibate men and women lived in spiritual communities, supported by a devoted laity. There is an archaic quality to many Jain doctrines, probably due to the fact that the Jain religion was never taken up by people outside of India. Buddhist doctrines, by contrast, seem very modern in certain ways, which may in part account for Buddhism's appeal to non-Indian peoples, including Europeans and Americans in the twenty-first century.

Whereas Jainism stresses purification of the soul and ascetic pain and its leader is described in military terms as a "great hero" and "victor," Buddhism's founder was a man whose leadership was the result of his "waking up," having his understanding boosted to a higher level of insight. The word *buddha* means basically "someone who has awakened from sleep." Buddhists see the Buddha's Great Awakening *(Bodhi)* as the greatest discovery of the truth of life that has ever been made. As Jains follow Mahavira's soldierly example, Buddhists seek to use the Buddha's example and his teachings so that they too may wake up and realize the benefits of Awakening (often also called Enlightenment).

The man who became the Buddha was born Siddhartha Gautama (sid-HAR-ta gow-TAH-ma), a prince of the Shakyas (SHA-kee-ahs), whose small oligarchic state was located at the foot of the Himalayas. As with many of the world's great figures, the traditional accounts of the Buddha's life contain many legends and miracles. Accordingly, Gautama was conceived when his mother dreamed one night that a white elephant entered her right side. Later the baby was born from her right side, and right after birth the baby stood up and announced that this would be his last life. Seers predicted that Gautama would become either a great king or a great sage who would see four special sights of human suffering—a sick man, an old man, a dead man, and an ascetic holy man seeking to escape suffering—after which he would renounce the world and discover a way to relieve the world's suffering.

This seated Buddha from Sarnath shows the elongated earlobes, heavy-lidded eyes, knot of hair, hand gestures, and expression of deep repose that are symbolic of the Buddha.

The traditions tell us that Gautama's father, King Shuddodana (SHOOD-doh-DAH-nah), raised him in luxury and went to great lengths to prevent the prince from ever seeing the sick, the old, or the dead.

In the prince's twenty-ninth year, however, all his father's protections proved vain in the face of fate: On three separate occasions the prince happened to see a sick man, an old man, and a dead man. These sights shocked him, and he was troubled to learn, from his chariot driver, that all people suffer sickness, old age, and death. He then happened to see a wandering ascetic who was in quest of *moksha*, and this encounter made him think very deeply about how to free himself from life's suffering. To his father's great disappointment, Gautama decided to follow that ascetic's example. He renounced his wealth and position, forsaking his wife and child.

Gautama studied meditation for a year with two different teachers, abandoning both after a while because their doctrines did not satisfy him. Then, like Mahavira, he took up the most painful and demanding forms of asceticism and practiced them with great determination and devotion. Gautama almost died from this fasting and self-torture, and after five years he concluded that these ascetic practices weakened the mind and would not lead to the end of suffering.

Gautama left his ascetic companions, who ridiculed him for his "weakness," walked down to a river and had his first bath in five years, then sat down under an expansive banyan tree (the Indian fig tree) to rest in the cool shade. (Asceticism was regarded as a kind of purifying heat by ancient Indians.) Gautama was then given a refreshing meal by a rich woman who offered a special meal once a year to the spirit of that tree. Clean, refreshed, and reinvigorated by food, Gautama was vibrantly awake as night fell. He sat up meditating all through the night; as the night progressed, his mind examined the world and its workings, and he came to understand more and more the fundamental causes for all that happens. Shortly before the dawn, he attained the key insights for understanding and then eliminating suffering, but not, according to legendary tradition, before the demon Mara (Death) and his daughters Greed, Lust, and Anger did all in their powers to prevent his grasping the truth.

Gautama summarized the truth to which he "woke up" during this Great Awakening as the Four Noble Truths, which succinctly express the entire system of Buddhist thought. The religious way of life to which the Four Noble Truths lead is often called the Middle Way. It is the way of life that is in between the normal human life of sensation, desire, and action, on the one hand, and the life of harsh asceticism, on the other. The Middle Way

DOCUMENT

Buddha's Sermon at Benares and The Edicts of Ashoka

involves the moderate asceticism of renunciation, celibacy, and the Buddhist monastic way of life as opposed to the much more rigorous asceticism of Indian groups such as the Jains. The whole philosophy, which the Buddha taught to others, and the religious way of life to which those ideas lead is referred to in Buddhism as the *Dharma*. (The root sense of *dharma* for Hindus is "religious law" or "religious good deeds leading to a good afterlife"; Dharma, for Buddhists, has a broader meaning.)

Buddha's Four Noble Truths are these:

1. Suffering dominates our experience.
2. The cause of suffering is desire or craving.
3. It is possible to extinguish suffering by extinguishing its cause, thereby attaining nirvana. (*Nirvana* originally referred to a fire's going out; the Buddha's idea was to let the fire of desire go out by depriving it of its normal fuel. It resembled *moksha*.)
4. The Noble Eightfold Path leads to the extinction of desire—that is, it leads to nirvana.

The Noble Eightfold Path consists of pursuing the following eight ideals:

1. *Right views*—the intellectual conviction that the Four Noble Truths are "the Truth."
2. *Right resolve*—the decision to act according to the Four Noble Truths.
3. *Right speech*—having words be governed by the Five Moral Precepts of right conduct: do not harm any living being (ahimsa); do not take what is not given to you; do not speak falsely; do not drink intoxicating drinks; do not be sexually unchaste.
4. *Right conduct*—having deeds, like words, be governed by the Five Moral Precepts.
5. *Right livelihood*—conducting oneself ethically even in earning a living; hence such occupations as farming (which could lead to the killing of small creatures), soldiering, prostitution, and tavern keeping are disallowed.
6. *Right effort*—following the path with all one's heart and energy by renouncing the world and becoming a monk or nun.
7. *Right mindfulness*—a form of meditation that eventually produces "wisdom"; wisdom undermines desire because the wise person no longer sees his or her own self as particularly important in the world.
8. *Right concentration*—a form of meditation that uses trances to make the nonrational and unconscious layers of the person completely calm and tranquil.

Buddhism claims that desire is extinguished and nirvana attained when steps 7 and 8 of the path have been perfected—that is, when the person on the path has the wisdom to see that he or she is just one more sentient being among many and is no more valuable or important than any other (this removes the natural instinct to fight for success and even survival) and when "concentration meditation" has stilled all the powerful impulses and drives that condition every sentient being's mind. A person who has reached this nirvana of desire simply looks at his or her own condition at any given moment as "what is" and does not wish it to be otherwise, is not driven to improve it, does not envy anyone else, and does not suffer. Physical pain may be present, but the person who has reached nirvana is dissociated from it and simply sees it as one more fact of the situation of the moment. Nirvana is a happy, friendly state (in which the Buddha lived for 45 years after his Awakening), but it is not an "altered state" of consciousness and certainly not a paradise or any kind of heavenly world. Later developments in Chinese and Japanese Buddhism did create ideas about rebirth in paradise and suffering in hell, but the Buddha himself did not suggest these.

In Buddhist thought the essential element of action is the desire to get something for oneself. So, the Buddhists believe that a person who has extinguished desire no longer really performs actions, even if his or her body may be going through the motions. In other words, such a person accumulates no karma and has escaped the round of samsara. For Buddhists this nirvana amounts to gaining *moksha*.

Many peoples over time have struggled with the question of what, if anything, comes after death. The Buddha's followers were no exception. But when they asked him what happens after the devotee escapes the cycle of rebirth, the Buddha told them that the question could not be answered and was pointless anyway. Such a question, he said, "tends not to edify"; that is, it does not contribute to the one important goal. The only important thing a person can do in life is deal with suffering.

Dressed in a simple yellow robe, with begging bowl in hand, Gautama wandered through the plain of the Ganges, speaking with everyone (regardless of social class) and attracting disciples to a growing community (called the *Sangha;* SAN-gah) of monks walking the Path. He taught many sermons (the Sutras; SOO-trahs) and laid down the Rules specifying many details of the monks' daily life (the Vinaya [vee-NAH-yah] analogous to the much later Rule of St. Benedict in Medieval Europe). Resisting at first, the Buddha eventually acquiesced to demands that women be allowed to renounce the world and pursue the path and its advanced meditations on a full-time basis as nuns. Buddhist history states that while the Buddha lived, it was relatively easy to accomplish the nirvana of desire and suffering and that a great number of disciples actually did so.

At last, 80 years old and enfeebled, the Buddha was invited by a poor blacksmith to a meal. According to legend, the food included tainted mushrooms, but Gautama ate the meal rather than offend his host. Later in the day the Buddha had severe pains, and he knew death was near. Calling his disciples together, he gave them this parting message: "Be ye lamps unto yourselves. Be a refuge to yourselves. Hold fast to the truth as to a lamp. Look not for refuge to anyone beside yourselves." The Buddha had instructed that his body be burned. According to legend, his followers quarreled over possession of his ashes, which were divided into eight parts and ensconced in shrines called *stupas* (STOO-pas). Buddhist tradition credits the third century B.C.E. king Ashoka with construction of tens of thousands of stupas all over his realm, into which the ashes from the eight original stupas were subdivided. Whether or not Ashoka actually carried out this holy task, there are now stupas all over South Asia.

The Buddha stressed the fact that each person could overcome suffering only through her or his own efforts, another aspect of Buddhism that would be modified a millennium after his death by Buddhists in East Asia. Nonetheless, his followers developed a profound affection for him and were very attached to him. After his death (even to some extent during his life) many of his followers believed that mere contact with him would somehow benefit them. What the Buddha taught is a philosophy, but the movement developed by his followers, which we call Buddhism, is a religion. That religion has had a profound effect on the society, politics, and economy of South Asia and other areas, like China, Japan, and Vietnam, where Buddhism spread.

The Buddha, the Dharma he taught, and the Sangha, the community of Buddha's followers, are regarded by Buddhists as the Three Precious Jewels. Historically, as in the Jain religion, the majority of the Buddhist community are laypeople who live in the world until they sense the time is right to take the sixth step of the path, right effort, and become a monk or a nun. (In some Buddhist countries, lay Buddhists often make short retreats to a monastery for instruction from the monks and practice in meditation.) In addition to restricting their speech, conduct, and livelihood by the Five Moral Precepts, they cultivate the virtues of generosity, friendliness, and compassion. Buddhists believe that only people with great amounts of good karma ever hear the Buddhist teachings; and only those with even more good karma possess the courage and determination actually to become a monk or a nun. In the end one does not want any karma at all, good or bad, but whatever good karma a lay Buddhist accumulates will help carry that person further along the Path in this or a future life.

Buddhists who became monks or nuns donned the yellow (or orange) robe worn by all renouncers in India except the Jains (who wore white if they wore anything). Unlike their Hindu and Jain counterparts—who usually lived alone or in small assemblies without any Rule—Buddhist renouncers created the world's first monastic communities, in which people pursuing spiritual goals lived together under strict rules.

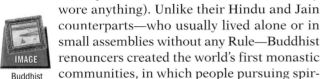

Buddhist Religious Site

Often the Buddhists lived in caves that rich lay Buddhists had cut into the sides of mountains or rock cliffs. Their only possessions were their sandals, robe, and begging bowl. They ate only one meal a day and ate only what they had received from begging. Periodically all the monks in a given area recited together all the rules of monastic life, and anyone who had violated any rule was required to make a public confession. Four sins warranted permanent expulsion from the community: fornication, stealing, murder, and making false claims of one's spiritual attainments. Large parts of the day were given over to meditation, and monks who had accomplished nirvana were known as *arhats* (AHR-hahts; "worthy ones").

The Buddha was a critic of all religious and philosophical thinkers who came before him. He censured the *Vedas* and the rites of the Brahmans, considered the *Upanishads* wrong about *brahman,* and thought Mahavira's religion of ascetic purification futile. The Buddha took an agnostic stance on what really might lie beyond this world; he claimed that we, as finite, conditioned beings, had no way of knowing anything about infinite, unconditioned beings. He thought that anyone, regardless of social status, could gain nirvana, but he did not himself try to change Indian society. Though Shudras and women were admitted to Buddhist monasteries, those monasteries still tended to mirror the social structures and habits of the larger Indian society.

As with Mahavira, there is great uncertainty about exactly when the man who became the Buddha died. Buddhists have traditionally taught that he died in 526 B.C.E. Modern, non-Buddhist historians believed for many decades that 481 B.C.E. was a more accurate date. Current historical scholarship is energetically reconsidering this date and pushing it down toward 400 B.C.E. or possibly even later. Whatever the exact dates of Gautama Buddha and his contemporary Mahavira, both lived and taught in eastern India as powerful new kingdoms were in the process of turning into the Mauryan (MOW-ree-ahn) Empire (inaugurated about 320 B.C.E.). Buddhism in particular

would have a significant impact on the organization of that empire.

THE MAURYAN EMPIRE AND OTHER KINGDOMS, 320 B.C.E.–300 C.E.

■ *Why was Ashoka ancient India's most revered king?*

By the sixth century B.C.E., 16 major kingdoms and tribal oligarchies stretched across northern India, from modern Pakistan to Bengal. The richest and most powerful kingdom was Magadha (mah-GAH-dah), located in the eastern region that included the Ganges River. The Magadha kingdom's support of Buddhism was key to the new religion's survival and growth. The kingdom's important role in trade is seen in the presence of its coins in the far northwest of India as well. Nevertheless, it took an outside stimulus for the Magadha kingdom to attempt to build an empire. Two centuries later, a conquering general, Alexander the Great, appeared in the region. Son of a Macedonian warlord, this famous general conquered the Persian Empire (see Chapter 4), and in 326 B.C.E. brought his phalanxes into the Indus valley, defeating local Punjabi rulers. Despite his apparent ambitions to conquer India, the Punjab proved to be the easternmost territory of Alexander's empire. His weary troops refused to advance farther eastward. So, Alexander constructed a fleet and sailed to the mouth of the Indus; he then returned overland to Babylon while his fleet skirted the coast of the Arabian Sea, sailing west to the Persian Gulf.

After Alexander's death in 323 B.C.E., the empire he had built so rapidly quickly disintegrated, and within two years his kingdom in the Punjab had completely disappeared. He had, however, helped open routes between India and countries to the West and,

MAP

Classical India

The Mauryan Empire

326 B.C.E.	Alexander the Great invades India
321 B.C.E.	Chandragupta seizes Magadha
305 B.C.E.	Chandragupta defeats Seleucus
269–232 B.C.E.	Reign of Ashoka
c. 185 B.C.E.	Brahman-led revolt against last Mauryan emperor

by destroying the petty states in the Punjab, facilitated the conquests of India's own first emperor.

The Founding of the Mauryan Empire (326–184 B.C.E.)

A new era began in India in 321 B.C.E., when Chandragupta (chahn-drah-GOOP-tah) Maurya seized Pataliputra (pah-tah-li-PU-trah), capital of the state of Magadha in the Ganges valley. Chandragupta conquered northern India from this sophisticated city and founded the Mauryan dynasty, which endured until about 184 B.C.E. At its height, the empire spanned most of the subcontinent except the extreme south, although many of its territories were separated by lands ruled by other kings.

India's first empire reflected the imperial vision of its founder. Chandragupta created an administrative

DOCUMENT

Lessons in Statecraft

system of remarkable efficiency. He was also a brilliant general who extended his control westward beyond the Indus River. In 305 B.C.E. he concluded a treaty with Seleucus, the general who had inherited the major part of Alexander the Great's empire in western Asia, that ceded all territories east of Kabul to the Mauryans in return for an exchange of ambassadors and a gift of 500 war elephants to Seleucus.

Life in the Mauryan Empire

Seleucus's ambassador to the court of Chandragupta, Megasthenes, wrote a detailed account of his experiences in India in his diary, fragments of which have survived. They give a fascinating picture of life in the empire. Chandragupta's capital, Pataliputra (known today as *Patna*), covered 18 square miles and was probably the largest city in the world at the time. Outside its massive wooden walls was a deep trench used for defense and the disposal of sewage.

The remarkably advanced Mauryan Empire was divided and subdivided into provinces, districts, and villages whose headmen were appointed by the state. The old customary law, preserved and administered by

CASE STUDY

Hinduism and the Mauryan Empire

the Brahman priesthood, was superseded by an extensive legal code that provided for royal interference in all matters. A series of courts, ranging from the village court presided over by the headman to the emperor's imperial court, administered the law. So busy was Chandragupta with the details of his highly organized administration that, according to Megasthenes, he had to hear court cases during his daily massage.

Two other factors struck Megasthenes as important in the administration of the empire. One was the professional army, which he reports was an enormous force of 700,000 men, 9000 elephants, and 10,000 chariots. The other was the secret police, whose numbers were so large that the Greek ambassador concluded that spies constituted a separate class in Indian society. Chandragupta, fearing conspiracies, was said to have lived in strict seclusion, attended only by women who cooked his food and in the evening bore him to his apartment, where they lulled him to sleep with music.

Of course, the historian cannot take literally the details or the numbers in Megasthenes's account. They were impressionistic and designed to create certain effects on his audience at home. Ambassadors had limited knowledge of and exposure to the daily lives of kings, and the stories of rulers and their female companions are often myths based on hearsay and conjecture. Furthermore, the counts of armies, especially of one's enemies, tended to be inflated. Nonetheless, it is clear that Megasthenes was impressed by the urban development, political organization, and military force of Chandragupta's empire.

An important indigenous source of information on Chandragupta's reign is a remarkable book, called the *Arthashastra* (ar-tah-SHAS-trah), or *Treatise on Material Gain*, written by Kautilya (kow-TIL-ya) as a guide for the king and his ministers. Said to be Chandragupta's chief adviser, Kautilya exalted royal power as the means of establishing and maintaining political and economic stability. The great evil, according to the *Arthashastra*, is anarchy, such as had existed among the small warring states in northern India. To achieve the aims of statecraft, a single authority (the king), who must employ force when necessary, was needed. Kautilya advised the king to make war on weaker kings and make peace with those who had equal or greater power. Attacking a stronger king, he said, is like "engaging . . . in a fight on foot with an elephant," while attacking an equal was like striking two unbaked jars together—both would be smashed. The king must also be wary of sons, "who are inclined to devour their begetters." Kautilya advised the king that princes should be carefully trained; but he also suggested making sacrifices in advance while the queen was pregnant and arranging for specialists to supervise her nourishment and childbirth.[1]

The *Arthashastra* is an early example of a whole genre of literature, sometimes called "mirrors for princes," that provided advice to monarchs on the best and most effective ways to rule. Later examples are found in the Middle East and Europe—for example, the medieval Persian work of Qai Qa'us and that of the Renaissance author Machiavelli. Machiavelli, like Kautilya, would advocate deception or unscrupulous means to attain desired ends. The *Arthashastra* remains in print today and has been translated into many languages. Modern leaders have been known to consult its pages.

The Mauryan state controlled and encouraged economic life. Kautilya's treatise, which is thought to reflect much actual practice, advises the ruler to "facilitate mining operations," "encourage manufacturers," "exploit forest wealth," "provide amenities" for cattle breeding and commerce, and "construct highways both on land and on water." Price controls are advocated because "all goods should be sold to the people at favorable prices," and foreign trade should be subsidized: "Shippers and traders dealing in foreign goods should be given tax exemptions to aid them in making profits."[2] Foreign trade did flourish, and the bazaars of Pataliputra displayed goods from southern India, China, Mesopotamia, and Asia Minor. Agriculture, however, remained the chief source of wealth. In theory, all land belonged to the state, which collected one-fourth of the produce as taxes. Irrigation and crop rotation were practiced, and Megasthenes states that there were no famines. The ability of the ruler to insure a regular supply of food for his kingdom was, of course, a primary measure of success.

Ashoka, India's Greatest King

Following Chandragupta's death, his son and grandson expanded the Mauryan Empire southward into the Deccan peninsula. His grandson, Ashoka (ah-SHOH-kah; r. 269–232 B.C.E.), the most renowned of all ancient Indian rulers, however, gained a reputation for being more committed to peace than to war. After eight years of expansion by military means, Ashoka attacked the kingdom of Kalinga with great brutality. The cruelty of that campaign horrified him, and he resolved never again to permit such acts of butchery. Ashoka adopted the Buddhist law of nonviolence (ahimsa) in his realm in the tenth year of his reign. The story of Ashoka's horror at the carnage of war is similar in some ways to the account of Yudhishthira (yoo-deesh-TEE-rah) in the *Mahabharata*, which also relates a king's remorse in the aftermath of battle. Scholars have pointed out that Ashoka did not renounce violence until he had completed his conquest. But for our purposes, the story of Ashoka illustrates the inherent contradictions between the idea of nonviolence and the idea that a king was by nature a warrior whose duty it was to preside over violence and death.

Throughout his empire, Ashoka had his edicts carved on rocks and stone pillars. They remain today as the oldest written documents in India yet deciphered (the Indus valley texts have not yet been deciphered) and are especially valuable for appreciating Ashoka's own construction of the spirit and purpose of his rule. For example, they contain his conception of the duty of a ruler:

He shall . . . personally attend the business . . . of earth, of sacred places, of minors, the aged, the afflicted, and the helpless, and of women. . . . In the happiness of his subjects lies his happiness.[3]

Although Ashoka made Buddhism Maurya's state religion, he did not persecute the Brahmans and Hindus but proclaimed religious toleration as an official policy:

The king . . . honors every form of religious faith . . . whereof this is the root, to reverence one's own faith and never to revile that of others. Whoever acts differently injures his own religion while he wrongs another's.[4]

Ashoka was a successful propagator of Buddhism. He supported the building of temples and stupas all over his empire, and the remains of many are still standing. He sent Buddhist missionaries to various lands—the Himalayan regions, Tamil Land (India's far south), Sri Lanka (Ceylon), Burma, and even as far away as Syria and Egypt, transforming Buddhism from a small Indian sect to a missionary faith. Modern Indians revere his memory, and the famous lion on the capital of one of his pillars has been adopted as the national seal of the present Indian republic.

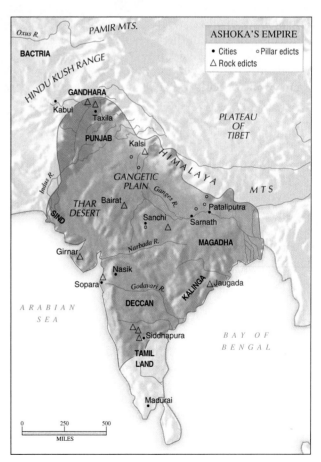

Ashoka (c. 268–233) left a written record of his reign inscribed on rocks and stone pillars all over the Mauryan Empire.

Fall of the Mauryan Empire

As so often happens, almost immediately after Ashoka's death in 233 B.C.E., the Mauryan Empire began to disintegrate. The last emperor was assassinated about 185 B.C.E. in a palace uprising led by a Brahman general. Once again, the subcontinent was politically fragmented. Northern India was overrun by a series of invaders, and the south, never controlled by the north, maintained its separate status.

The sudden collapse of the powerful Mauryan state and the grave consequences that ensued have provoked much scholarly speculation. Some historians have believed that the fall of the Mauryans can be traced to a hostile Brahman reaction against Ashoka's patronage of Buddhism. Others believe that Ashoka's inclination toward nonviolence curbed the military ardor of his people and left them vulnerable to invaders. More plausible explanations for the fall of the Mauryan state take into account the transportation and communications problems facing an empire that spanned much of the Indian subcontinent, with unsubdued areas separating territory under Mauryan control; the difficulty of financing a vast army and bureaucracy; and the intrigues of discontented regional groups within the empire.

In fact, one might argue that political division is a more natural state for large multiethnic, multilingual landmasses with diverse terrain; empires that endure and unite vast expanses of territory are the exception. No one person could directly rule all of the subcontinent; like the later Roman and Ottoman empires elsewhere, the Mauryan kingdom survived through a combination of talented leadership, economic success, flexible rule, and delegated authority.

Bactrian Greeks and Kushanas

The Mauryan Empire was the first of two attempts to unify much of north and even central India in ancient times. The second—the work of the Gupta dynasty (c. 320–550 C.E.)—was more limited in its geographical reach, but was a glorious empire nonetheless (see Chapter 10). In the five centuries between these two eras of imperial splendor, a succession of foreign invaders entered South Asia from the northwest and added new cultural elements to the Indian scene.

The first of the new invaders of India were Greeks from Bactria. They were descendants of the soldiers settled there by Alexander the Great to serve his empire in the East. After Alexander, Bactria continued as a province of the Seleucid Empire, a bastion against the attacks of nomadic tribesmen from the north and a center for trade with India to the southeast. The decline of the Seleucid Empire allowed the Bactrian Greeks to establish an independent kingdom about 245 B.C.E.

In 183 B.C.E., two years after the death of the last Mauryan emperor of India, the fourth Bactrian king, Demetrius, crossed the Hindu Kush mountains as Alexander had done 150 years earlier and occupied the northern Punjab. From his base at Taxila, Demetrius and his successors ruled Bactria and the entire Pun-

Coins provide interesting evidence of cross-cultural artistic influences and of the self-definitions of rulers and peoples. This Bactrian coin from 170–159 B.C.E. shows the influence of Greek portraiture on South Asian money.

jab (modern Afghanistan and northern Pakistan), while Taxila functioned as an important nexus of both the east-west and north-south trade.

The Greeks in India established the farthest outpost of Hellenism in the Hellenistic Age (see Chapter 4). Their cities were not Greek enclaves in a hostile land, like Alexandria in Egypt and Antioch in Syria. The South Asian peoples were enrolled as citizens, a bilingual coinage was issued bearing Greek inscriptions on one side and Indian on the other, and at least one king, Menander, became a Buddhist. The Indo-Greek Buddhist art in the Gandhara (gahn-DAHra) was the greatest legacy of the era of Greek control. Some other Greeks in Bactria adopted aspects of Indian culture, including Hindu worship.

But soon after 150 B.C.E. Bactria was overrun by nomadic tribesmen. Thereafter, Greek rule in the northern subcontinent steadily declined until the last remnants disappeared late in the first century B.C.E. Hordes of nomadic peoples, migrating out of Central Asia, replaced the Greeks in Bactria and northwestern India. First to arrive were the Indo-European Scythians, who had been pushed out of Central Asia by other Indo-European nomads known in Chinese sources as the Yuezhi (yoo-EH-zhih). In their turn, the Yuezhi occupied Bactria, and about 40 C.E. they crossed the

Hindu Kush and conquered the Punjab. The Yuezhi divided into four tribes, and one, Kushana (koo-SHAH-na), took over in north India, expanding eastward to the middle Ganges valley and southward perhaps as far as the borders of the Deccan.

In contrast to the more centralized Mauryan Empire, the Kushana state was more like a loose federation—its kings were overlords rather than direct rulers—yet it gave northern India two centuries of peace and prosperity. The Kushana kingdom acted as a hub for trade routes linking India, China, and the West. Its greatest ruler, Kanishka (kah-NEESH-ka; fl. c. 120 C.E.), produced a multicultural coinage that employed Chinese, Greek, Persian, Hindu, and Buddhist devices. Kanishka gained fame as a patron of the arts and of a new form of Buddhism called **Mahayana** (MAH-hah-YAH-nah).

South India

To a large extent, India can be divided culturally into north and south. Although the south was often penetrated by northern conquerors, in general its civilizations developed in a fashion distinct from those of the north. The vast tableland of South India—the Deccan—and its fertile coastal plains remained outside the main forces of political change in the north, except, in some cases, for the 150 years of Mauryan imperial rule. The peoples of this area differed in appearance, culture, and very importantly, language—their languages were part of the Dravidian language family rather than Aryan—from the Aryan-speaking peoples of the north. Gradually, however, as Brahman priests and Buddhist monks infiltrated the south, Hinduism and Buddhism were grafted onto the existing Dravidian culture.

Politically, the south remained divided into numerous warring states. Prominent among them were three well-developed Tamil (an old Dravidian language) kingdoms in the southern third of the Deccan peninsula. These three kingdoms—Chera, Pandya, and Chola—alternated between allying to fend off northern attacks and rivalrous warfare among themselves. In the early fourth century C.E., a new dynasty, the Pallavas, took over in Chola. Under the patronage of the kings of these three states, the Tamil language developed a classically exquisite literature in the first few centuries of the Common Era. This tradition, known as the *Sangam* ("Academy") tradition, was based in the old city of Madurai in Tamil Nadu ("Tamil Land"), and it produced several anthologies of poetry, several unique epics, and a superb handbook of lan-

guage and poetics. Love was an important theme in the Tamil poetry:

> As a little white snake
> with lovely stripes on its young body
> troubles the jungle elephant
> this slip of a girl
> her teeth like sprouts of new rice
> her wrists stacked with bangles
> troubles me.[5]

Tamil society differed in several key respects from northern society. The divisions among groups of Tamils were based on their geographic origin as hill people, forest people, coastal people, and so on. Social structure was possibly matriarchal rather than patriarchal, and matrilineal inheritance was practiced until recently. Both men and women took part in the production of art, music, and dance.

By the first century B.C.E., Tamil Nadu had become an intermediary in the maritime trade extending eastward to the East Indies and westward to the Hellenistic kingdoms. Indeed, a major factor that distinguishes south India from north India is the former's orientation toward the sea. On the east and west coasts of southern India, ports developed that became important entrepots for the East-West trade and important points of cultural contact with foreign states and peoples. There, large jugs called *amphorae* have been found, evidence either of South Asian taste for Roman wine or of the Roman traders' need to bring their favored drink with them on voyages to India. The ships that brought these amphorae, as well as copper, lead, tin, and large numbers of gold coins, sailed back bearing South and Southeast Asian pepper, cotton goods, silks, cinnamon, cloves, and jewels.

EMERGENT HINDUISM AND BUDDHISM, 200 B.C.E.–300 C.E.

■ *How did Hinduism develop as a religion based on worship of deities and Buddhism branch into two major divisions?*

Hinduism and Buddhism were not static or fixed in time; they were evolving during the classical era. In the years 200 B.C.E. to 300 C.E. the religion called Hinduism was formulating a synthesis and meeting the challenge of Buddhism. Buddhism, in turn, split into two distinct strands of interpretation. These developments were set in the context of the Indian social order that was wedded to village life, caste hierarchies, and a household based on the extended family.

Mahayana—"Greater Vehicle" branch of Buddhism; focuses on bodhisattvas who lead others to nirvana.

The Hindu Synthesis

Hinduism is not one single doctrine. It is an array of highly diverse beliefs that include the various texts of the Vedic Age, pre-Aryan Indian practices, and an evolving set of deities and rituals. Essential to Hinduism are the beliefs in the cycle of birth, death, and rebirth (samsara) and a society structured by social status and proper behavior. Beings may be born as humans in various *jatis* or as lesser creatures, depending on their actions in the previous life. A believer who accumulates good actions ascends in the hierarchy of beings in subsequent births and may ultimately escape rebirth and be absorbed into *brahman* energy.

Three Traditions of Worship and Theology: Vishnu, Shiva, and Devi

Early Aryan religion had focused on sacrifices and rituals, but later Brahmanic religion stressed personal devotion to a deity. This marked the emergence of Hinduism as a religion with increasing popular appeal. The first steps toward this were taken by Brahmans who incorporated Upanishadic thought into their teaching. In doing so, they gave the caste system additional religious support by linking it to karma and the process of reincarnation. The priests made individual salvation, now a conspicuous part of Indian religion, dependent on the uncomplaining acceptance of one's position at birth and the performance of one's dharma, which varied by caste. The belief that a person was born into a caste and died in that caste was given religious support. Marriage outside one's caste was forbidden. Of course, in practice, as in all religious systems, social reality did not always match religious ideals. In fact, some people did marry across caste lines, and some groups did apparently change caste over time. But Brahman and social sanctions against violating caste boundaries made such changes difficult.

The Upanishadic doctrine of salvation by absorption of the individual soul into *brahman* was too intellectual and remote for the average person to grasp fully. Thus, devotion to personal savior gods also emerged as an important element in Hinduism. This devotion centered on anthropomorphic deities with rich personalities and long histories.

The major Vedic gods gradually faded into the background, and three virtually monotheistic gods emerged as paramount in Hinduism: Vishnu (VISH-noo); Shiva (SHEE-va); and Devi (DAY-vee), the Goddess (sometimes called Kali (KAH-lee)). Each one of these gods became immensely popular in Hindu worship. Vishnu, Shiva, and Devi evolved from Vedic and indigenous Indian origins, and each came to be regarded by one or several different traditions as the uniquely supreme and holy God, creator of the universe. The theologies of Vishnu and Shiva were already well developed by about 200 B.C.E.; that of the Goddess was not fully developed until some time later. The theologies of these gods, as in other religious traditions, did not remain static and fixed over the ensuing centuries. In the old Vedic pantheon of the Aryans, Vishnu was a relatively minor god associated with the sun. He then developed into a pacific father-god, comforter, and savior who works continuously for the welfare of humanity. "No devotee of mine is lost," is Vishnu's

Vishnu and his consort, Lakshmi, recline upon the serpent Shesha floating on the waters of creation. Emerging out of Vishnu's navel is a lotus that serves as a throne for the god Brahma, who creates the world. This is a representation of just one of the varied Hindu creation myths. It suggests lushness, fertility, and water as the source of life. Some variants of this particular creation story note that Vishnu also created two demons who were arrogant and boastful. These demons tormented Brahma while he was trying to meditate and attacked Vishnu, thinking they were stronger than he.

promise. His followers believe that he has appeared in nine major "descents" in human form to save the world from disaster. (A predicted tenth descent has yet to happen.) Two of Vishnu's incarnations are described in the great Indian epics, as Krishna in the *Mahabharata* and as Rama (RAH-ma), the hero of the *Ramayana*. Rama saves the human race from the oppressions of a great demon, rules for many years in the city of Ayodhya, and then returns to the "City of the Gods," resuming the form of Vishnu.

Shiva, the other great popular god of classical and modern Hinduism, evolved from a minor Aryan Vedic god who was the guardian of healing herbs but whose arrows also brought disease. It is possible that another prototype of Shiva was a pre-Aryan fertility god who was worshipped in the cities of the Indus civilization. Shiva is often associated with phallic symbols. His spouse, Parvati, is the earliest expression in the Brahman texts of a powerful female goddess who was eventually recognized as a separate deity in her own right (under other names) and elevated to the status of a unique supreme and holy divinity.

Shiva's followers believe he is superior to the other gods. He personifies the cosmic force of change that destroys in order to build anew; he is often depicted with a necklace of skulls. Some representations show Shiva as the Lord of Dancers; the rhythm of his dance is that of a world continuously forming, dissolving, and reforming. He also exemplifies another major characteristic of Hinduism, the reconciliation of extremes: violence and passivity, eroticism and asceticism. Shiva is portrayed as remaining unmoved in meditation for years on end. When he emerges from his meditations, however, he is often lustful and violent.

As already noted, Shiva's wife, Parvati (followed by Vishnu's wife, Lakshmi (LAHKSH-mee)), marked the first appearance in Hinduism of a powerful female divinity. Archaeological and other evidence suggests that goddesses were worshipped in India from the time of the Indus valley civilization. But only toward the Gupta period (fourth and fifth centuries C.E.) did fully developed theologies of a supreme Goddess, Devi (the word *devi* simply means "goddess"), begin to appear. As with the development of Shiva and Vishnu, the development of Devi involved the fusion of numerous local deities into a single complex figure. The Goddess presents two faces to the world: She is a tender mother to her devotees and a ferocious warrior to those who threaten her devotees. Called "Mother" or "Bestower of Food" (Annapurna) in her benevolent moods, she can also be "the Black One" (Kali), wearing a necklace of the skulls of her victims, or Durga, a many-armed warrior riding on the back of a lion to do battle with demons. As the creative power of the universe (similar to the Vedic idea of *brahman*), she is

Lakshmi, Vishnu's consort and goddess of prosperity, beauty, and precious things, emerged from the foam of the ocean. This statuette was found half a world away from India in the ruins of ancient Pompeii in Italy, thus demonstrating the extent of trade both in Indian cultural objects and Indian ideas in the first century C.E.

referred to as Shakti ("Power," "Creative Energy"), and theologies focused on Devi as the Supreme Being of the universe are referred to as Shaktism.

As mentioned earlier, there is no centralized authority in Hinduism. The resulting "flexibility" makes Hinduism seem extremely complicated to outsiders who are used to more structured religious traditions. One aspect of this flexibility is that many versions of the theology and mythology of these deities are mixed together. For example, worshippers of Shiva often recognize Vishnu as an important and exalted creature fashioned by Shiva but who in no way rivals Shiva's divine supremacy. Worshippers of Vishnu often fit Shiva into their theology in similar ways. They also eventually included the Buddha as one of Vishnu's incarnations, and in modern times some Hindus have incorporated the Christians' Jesus into their devotions. Today many Hindus worship Jesus as a divine incarnation, but they do so as Hindus in Hindu ways; they are not Christian converts.

Most Hindus today are devotees of either Vishnu, Shiva, or Devi and their respective incarnations. But animals (especially the cow), vegetation, water, and even stones are also worshipped by some as symbols of the divine. Over time, literally thousands of deities, demigods, and lesser spirits came to form the Hindu pantheon, the world's largest.

Because the authority to teach normative ideas in Hinduism was vested in the Brahmans as a class, Hinduism is probably the world's most flexible religion. Brahmans were present in villages and towns throughout the subcontinent, and many local ideas and practices were "normalized" as "compatible with the *Vedas.*" Hinduism possesses no canon, such as the Bible or the Qur'an; no single personal founder, such as Christ or Muhammad; and no precise body of authoritative doctrine. Hindu beliefs vary dramatically among the faithful.

The Epics

The *Mahabharata* is the great Hindu epic. Composed in verse, it contains over 75,000 stanzas, the longest work of literature in the world. It tells the tale of an all-encompassing war between rival sets of cousins, the Pandavas (pahn-DAH-vas) and the Kauravas (kow-RAH-vas). These cousins are fighting for the throne of the Bharata kingdom, in the upper Ganges plain in the region of modern Delhi. But in the epic, this great battle, lasting 18 days, is not simply a struggle for an earthly kingdom; it is ultimately a cosmic struggle between virtue and evil, a battle to set the world right.

As in the Greek *Iliad*'s account of the Trojan War, the *Mahabharata* presents a dramatic tale of heroism, vengeance, and sacrifice in which the gods directly intervene in the affairs of men. In the great Indian epic, however, it is duty that must govern the actions of kings; only through war will the proper order of the universe be restored. When the war is over and the victorious Pandavas view the horrendous slaughter of their sons, cousins, teachers, and friends, Yudhishthira, the intended king, is so shocked and horrified by the carnage that he refuses to accept the throne and wishes to retreat into the forest. Eventually, however, he is persuaded to become king. It is not his own desires or wishes that Yudhishthira must follow, but his duty.

The *Mahabharata* was shaped and embellished over time. It was incorporated into royal sacrificial ritual, and a long succession of priestly editors added many long passages on religious duties, morals, and statecraft. One of the most famous additions, incorporated into the *Mahabharata* around 200 B.C.E., was the *Bhagavad-Gita* (BAH-gah-vad GEE-tah, "The Lord's Song"), a philosophical dialogue that stressed the performance of duty (dharma) and the overcom-

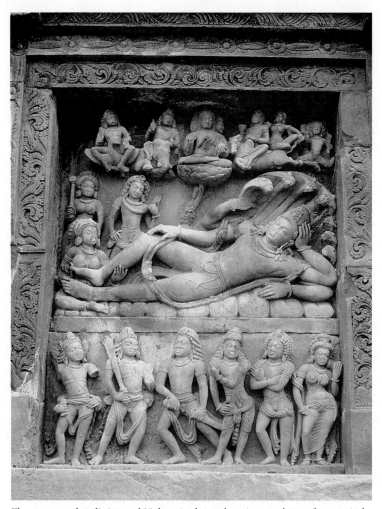

The serene and reclining god Vishnu is shown here in a sculpture from a sixth-century C.E. Hindu temple. Beneath Vishnu are the five Pandavas, heroes of the Mahabharata, *and their shared wife, Draupadi. Draupadi, along with Sita, stands as a model of Hindu womanhood: virtuous, honorable, and strong.*

ing of passion and fear. It is still the most treasured piece in Hindu literature.

The dialogue in the *Bhagavad-Gita* takes place between Arjuna (AR-joo-na), the greatest warrior of the Pandava brothers, and Krishna, an incarnation of the god Vishnu, who takes human form and acts as Arjuna's charioteer. Arjuna is shaken by the prospect of killing his kinsmen. But Krishna, who gradually reveals himself as no ordinary charioteer, instructs Arjuna that he must give up worldly desire and personal attachment and devote himself to discipline and duty. In so doing, he will be able to attain freedom, overcome despair, and act according to his dharma, fulfilling his role in the cosmic struggle. Krishna tells Arjuna:

> Knowledge is obscured
> by the wise man's eternal enemy
> which takes form as desire,
> an insatiable fire, Arjuna.
> The senses, mind, and understanding
> are said to harbor desire;

with these desire obscures knowledge
and confounds the embodied self.
Therefore, first restrain
your senses, Arjuna,
then kill this evil
that ruins knowledge and judgment.[6]

The universal appeal of Arjuna's internal struggle and Krishna's advice has made the *Bhagavad-Gita* a world classic; it has been translated into many languages. Once Arjuna realizes that he is receiving advice from a god, he wants to know more. He wants to see the god as he really is, so he asks Krishna to reveal himself in all his majesty. Krishna obliges the unwitting Arjuna by giving him a "divine eye" with which he can see the whole universe inscribed in the god's body. But this fearful vision of world-devouring time is too much for the awestruck Arjuna. So Krishna takes mercy on him and reverts to his human form.

The other great Hindu epic, the *Ramayana*, which appears to predate the *Mahabharata*, has been likened to the Greek *Odyssey*. It recounts the tale of the exiled prince Rama and his faithful wife Sita (SEE-ta). During their banishment to the forest, Sita is kidnapped by the demon Ravana. Rama searches valiantly for his wife, whom he eventually finds, and vanquishes the

---

Document   The *Ramayana:* The Trial of Sita

In the great Hindu epic, the *Ramayana,* King Rama rescues his wife Sita from her captor, the demon Ravana, after a lengthy struggle. Rama is overjoyed to see Sita but tormented by the shame of knowing she was touched by another male. The doubt thus cast upon her virtue forces him to repudiate her. Devastated at this rejection by her lord, Sita nevertheless proudly answers in her own defense. In a dramatic speech, she demands that a pyre be built on which she can immolate herself. The ideas of devotion, sexual purity, and masculine and feminine honor expressed here are not limited to the society of classical India. They are common in many traditional societies and continue to influence gender relations in the present day.

Rama speaks to his beloved Sita: Oh illustrious Princess, I have re-won thee and mine enemy has been defeated on the battlefield; I have accomplished all that fortitude could do; my wrath is appeased; and the insult and the one who offered it have both been obliterated by me. . . . As ordained by destiny the stain of thy separation and thine abduction by that fickle-minded titan has been expunged by me, a mortal. . . . [However] a suspicion has arisen with regard to thy conduct, and thy presence is as painful to me as a lamp to one whose eye is diseased! Henceforth go where it pleaseth thee, I give thee leave, O Daughter of Janaka. O Lovely One, the ten regions are at thy disposal; I can have nothing more to do with thee! What man of honor would give rein to his passion so far as to permit himself to take back a woman who has dwelt in the house of another? Thou hast been taken into Ravana's lap and he has cast lustful glances on thee; how can I reclaim thee, I who boast of belonging to an illustrious House [family]? . . .

Sita replies with passion: Why dost thou address such words to me, O Hero, as a common man addresses an ordinary woman? I swear to thee, O Long-Armed Warrior, that my conduct is worthy of thy respect! It is the behavior of other women that has filled thee with distrust! Relinquish thy doubts since I am known to thee! If my limbs came in contact with another's it was against my will, O Lord, and not through any inclination on my part; it was brought about by fate. That which is under my control, my heart, has ever remained faithful to thee. . . . If despite the proofs of love that I gave thee whilst I lived with thee, I am still a stranger to thee, O Proud Prince, my loss is irrevocable. . . . Raise a pyre for me, O Saumitri, this is the only remedy for my misery! These unjust reproaches have destroyed me, I cannot go on living! Publicly renounced by mine husband, who is insensible to my virtue, there is only one redress for me, to undergo the ordeal by fire!

Questions to Consider

1. Why might such an abduction be considered equivalent to a rape, even though Ravana never had sexual relations with Sita?

2. Ordeal by fire is an idea and practice found historically in a variety of regions. What does Sita's willingness to undergo such an ordeal suggest about ancient Indian society's beliefs? Why fire?

3. Why are both male and female honor so dependent upon a woman's sexual purity?

4. Why must Rama, as a king, be particularly conscious of his reputation and that of his wife?

From *The Ramayana of Valmiki*, Vol. 3, trans. Hari Prasad Shastri (London: Shanti Sadan, 1970), pp. 336–337.

enemy. Rama then gains his rightful throne. In the course of time, priestly editors transformed this simple adventure story into a book of devotion. Rama, like Krishna in the *Bhagavad-Gita*, was an incarnation of the great god Vishnu. He was viewed as the ideal ruler: a truly virtuous, mighty man who exemplifies "proper conduct and is benevolent to all creatures. Who is learned, capable, and a pleasure to behold."[7] Sita emerged as the perfect woman, devoted and faithful to her husband, yet strangely powerful. Her words were memorized by almost every Hindu bride:

> *Car and steed and gilded palace,*
> *vain are these to woman's life;*
> *Dearer is her husband's shadow*
> *to the loved and loving wife.*

Sita's abduction by the demon Ravana launches another cosmic battle between the forces of good and evil. Rama, though victorious, is dishonored because Ravana had touched his wife and taken her to his palace. He feels compelled to repudiate Sita; her abduction is viewed as a rape even though she rejected Ravana's advances. One of the most moving scenes of the *Ramayana* is that in which the loyal Sita proposes to immolate herself rather than live separated from her lord. The gods save her from the flames, thus allowing Rama honorably to take her back. But years later, wagging tongues revive the question of her "tainted" virtue, and the heroine is once again prompted to prove her purity. The figure of Sita endures as an emblem of ideal Hindu womanhood. In the Indian nationalist struggles of the twentieth century, Sita served as a symbol of femininity and of the nation itself.

Counting Time

There are many ways to understand a civilization: through its art, its buildings, its political systems, its religions, its gender relations. One interesting way to envision a people is to examine its imaginings of time. Past societies have counted time in diverse ways, and those ways then shape the people's myths. Christians and Muslims, for example, trace their histories from a creation that includes the first man, Adam. Then each faith begins counting time from the life of its particular savior or prophet, Jesus and Muhammad, respectively. Of the three great religious traditions that emerged earlier in India, Jainism and Buddhism also focus on the lives of particular holy men who taught the way of Enlightenment. But the belief in reincarnation, shared by Hindus, Buddhists, and Jains, makes Indian notions of time radically different from those of traditions in which humans have only one lifetime. In the Indian traditions, humans

can and will have thousands of lifetimes. The question "What comes after death?" is intimately linked to the imagining of time.

Hindu civilization is unique among ancient world civilizations in its crafting of a particularly grand and elaborate scheme for counting time. There are many Indian creation myths, and these stories merged and shifted over time. One common Indian notion of the creation and destruction of the universe is that time is counted in eras called *mahayugas* (mah-hah-YOO-gahs). Just as individuals die and then are reborn, at the end of each era the world dissolves and then reemerges to begin a new era. Each era consists of one complete cycle of four ages: the Golden Age (1,440,000 human years), in which all beings are good and all life is comfortable; the Age of Trey (1,080,000 human years), in which some evil appears along with some suffering and difficulty in life; the Age of Deuce (720,000 human years), in which there is more evil, pain, and suffering; and the Age of Dissolution (360,000 human years), in which evil, pain, and distress predominate in human life. Before and after each age are "twilight periods" of varying length that altogether add another 720,000 years to the length of a whole cycle.

This vast expanse of human time, however, is nothing compared to the life of the god Brahma. One thousand *mahayugas* make up only one day in his existence, which lasts for 100 years of 360 days each; and as each Brahma dies, a new one is born from an egg that grows within *brahman*. In this Hindu cosmology, there have already been billions of Brahmas. According to certain ancient Hindu texts, the world is currently in an Age of Dissolution; in other words, we are approaching the end of a *mahayuga* and the halfway point in the current day of the current Brahma.

Buddhism After the Buddha

Buddhism was increasingly supported by rulers and wealthy merchants in the third century B.C.E. Its compelling message of escape from suffering and its rejection of the caste system later enhanced its popularity among other segments of society. It maintained an important position for several hundred years after that and, although other religions surpassed it in popular appeal, it survived in India until it was exterminated in the thirteenth century C.E. in the aftermath of the Muslim invasions.

The Brahmans did not sit quietly by while Buddhism challenged their power. They launched a countermovement in the second century B.C.E., reasserting their authority in the face of Buddhist successes and winning back political and economic support. This Brahman effort played a major role in giving rise to a movement of Buddhist rejuvenation, called Mahayana that began to flower about 100 B.C.E. Its followers called this movement the "Great Vehicle." Mahayana Buddhism stressed that pious Buddhists should not just seek their own personal nirvana or release from rebirth. Rather, they should imitate the Buddha directly by trying to relieve others' suffering with the message of the Dharma.

Earlier forms of Buddhism focused on the salvation of the pious individual. Mahayana Buddhism stressed the centrality of bodhisattvas (boh-dee-SAT-vas), those who postpone their own entry into the final nirvana in order to act as a compassionate and loving guide to others still suffering in the world. The Mahayana movement criticized the older forms of Buddhism calling them *Hinayana* (HEE-nah-YAH-nah) or "Lesser Vehicle" because, it said, their focus on salvation was selfish. One school of older Buddhism, Theravada (TAY-rah-VAH-dah), the so-called Doctrine of the Elders, did continue to thrive in India, but Mahayana Buddhism became more popular.

Buddhism, of course was not just a set of religious and philosophical ideas; it was a way of life. Thousands of men and women became monks and nuns, while many other lay Buddhists contributed to their support. Over time, Buddhists built monasteries, some of which became important centers of learning and way stations for traders and travelers. Monks transcribed Buddhist texts, which made their way to China and beyond, and Indian artisans carved thousands of statues of the Buddha to meet burgeoning demand. Gifts of the seven treasures (the luxury trade items gold, silver, lapis lazuli, crystal, pearl, rubies, and coral) were presented to monasteries by donors hoping to secure religious merit, good health, or nirvana for their loved ones. Some devotees venerated the Buddha along with Hindu deities, demonstrating that the lines dividing one religion from another were never as rigid in actual social practice as they often seemed. Even Roman merchants offered gifts to Buddhist monasteries; and some scholars have suggested that certain monasteries functioned as centers of trade and finance.

Buddhism (both the older Theravada and the newer Mahayana) spread outside of India and thrived in all parts of Asia. According to Sri Lankan chronicles, Buddhism was brought to Sri Lanka by missionaries sent there by the Mauryan emperor Ashoka around 250 B.C.E. After 100 B.C.E. Buddhists spread the Dharma beyond the boundaries of the subcontinent into China and central, western, and southeastern Asia. In most of those areas it took permanent root, establishing Buddhist societies, states, and monasteries that function to this day. Today the older form of Buddhism survives only in Sri Lanka and Southeast Asia, and the Mahayana is absent there; Mahayana survives in Tibet, Korea, Japan, and China. The translation of the very

numerous books of the Buddhist scriptures from Sanskrit into Chinese took place during the second, third, and fourth centuries C.E., an intellectual achievement as fascinating as it is staggering. A small revival of Buddhism occurred in Maharashtra, India, in the 1950s when the Untouchable leader Dr. B. R. Ambedkar led a mass conversion of 50,000 Untouchables to Buddhism so that they might escape the oppression of Hindu "untouchability."

THE MEETING OF EAST AND WEST: NETWORKS OF EXCHANGE

▪ *What role did India play in Eurasian trade?*

In the centuries immediately preceding and following the birth of Christ, the great civilizations of the world—Indian, Chinese, and Roman—were connected by a complex network of commercial, intellectual, and diplomatic exchanges. North India and south India played different roles in these networks of exchange, one oriented primarily towards the land and the other towards the sea. Travelers and monks from China visited the holy sites in India, the monsoons carried merchants to and fro across the Indian Ocean, and the goods and ideas of the East continued to enhance and alter the societies of the Mediterranean world.

Buddhist Sculpture and Architecture

Indian thought and art would have a profound effect on the eastern and western ends of Eurasia. Conversely, the most lasting Western influence on India in the Classical Age was the influence of Greek art on Buddhist sculpture. Before the Kushana period, Indian artists were influenced by the Buddha's prohibitions against idolatry, and they refrained from portraying the Buddha in human form. His presence was indicated by symbols only, such as his footprints, his umbrella, or the tree under which he attained Enlightenment. Beginning in the first century C.E., however, the Buddha himself was portrayed in numerous statues and reliefs. Most of these early Buddha figures come from Gandhara, the center of the Kushana Empire and the earlier Greco-Bactrian kingdom.

The primary inspiration for this Gandharan Buddhist art came from Mahayana Buddhism, which viewed the Buddha as a savior. This devotional form of Buddhism used images for worship, and statues of the Buddha as well as of many bodhisattva saints were produced in large numbers. Indeed the demand for images of the Buddha and bodhisattvas was so great that it affected the economy and artistic production of South Asia. Wealthy patrons like the Kushana king Kanishka hoped to gain spiritual favor or answers to their prayers by patronizing Buddhist monks and nuns. They paid artisans to create statues, build monasteries, and carve cells in rock cliffs to accommodate the flourishing communities of monks. The overland routes which carried traders, monks, and the message of Buddhism into China are marked by these monasteries, statues of the Buddha, and rock-carved caves. A second inspiration for Gandha-

ran art came from Greece. Apparently, Hellenistic sculptors and craftsmen migrated to Gandhara via the Central Asian trade routes. The result was an execution of Indian themes through the use of Greek artistic techniques. Thus Mahayana Buddhism and Greco-Buddhist images of the Buddha, both of which developed in the Kushana Empire, spread together throughout eastern Asia.

The magnificent buildings of the Mauryan emperors have disappeared, although archaeologists have found the ruins of a huge pillared hall at the site of the Mauryan capital which probably dates from the time of Chandragupta. Buddhist stupas, the dome-shaped monuments that were used as funeral mounds to enshrine the relics of the Buddha and Buddhist saints or to mark a holy spot, remain in great numbers. Originally made only of earth, more elaborate mounds were later fashioned out of earth faced with brick and surrounded by railings and four richly carved gateways of stone. On top of the dome was a boxlike structure surmounted by a carved umbrella, the Indian emblem that symbolizes the Buddha's princely birth. As centuries passed, the low dome was heightened in some areas into a tall, tapered structure more like a tower. Later, when Buddhism spread to other countries, the stupa type of architecture went along. Its gateway was widely copied, and the stupa itself was the prototype of the multistoried Buddhist pagodas that are common in East Asia today.

Beyond the Indian Frontiers

The Mauryan Empire had already declined by the time the Han dynasty arose in China and the Roman Empire emerged in the Mediterranean. Both empires were connected to India through trade, and the Tamil states, with their excellent ports, were well positioned to promote international commerce. While Rome experienced the prosperous years of the Pax Romana during the first and second centuries C.E., Indian merchants supplied goods to the Roman entrepots in the Middle East. South Asian ports acted as staging points for sales of Chinese silk and Indian cottons demanded in the West. Indian traders exchanged textiles for African gold and ivory and traded rice, oils, precious woods, jewels, and spices in the ports of the Arabian Sea.

Even earlier, in the years after Alexander the Great's death, India had maintained trade contacts with the Seleucid and Ptolemaic kingdoms of the Hellenistic Age over two routes, one by land and the other by sea. The most frequented route was the caravan road that extended from West Asia and Syria, crossed Mesopotamia, and then skirted the Iranian plateau to either Bactria or Kandahar before crossing the Hindu

The Great Stupa at Sanchi, built in the first century B.C.E., contains this detailed and elegant scene from the life of the Buddha. Numerous stupas were built by King Ashoka, starting in the third century, to hold the funeral relics of the Buddha.

South and Southeast Asia were famous for metalworking. Bronze objects used for practical and ritual purposes (like this ceremonial blade) were highly prized and widely traded throughout the Indian Ocean region.

Vessel in the Form of an Ax. Bronze. The Metropolitan Museum of Art, Purchase, George McFadden Gift and Edit Perry Chapman Fund, 1993. (1993.525) Photograph by Bruce White © 1993 The Metropolitan Museum of Art.

Kush to reach Taxila in South Asia. The sea route that linked the eastern and western ends of Eurasia extended from China and Southeast Asia across the Bay of Bengal to India and Sri Lanka and thence across the Indian Ocean to the Red Sea ports or to the head of the Persian Gulf. From those two waterways, goods then proceeded overland and via the Mediterranean to the Middle East and into Africa and Europe.

The courts of kings and seats of power were great consumers of the goods of the East-West trade. The Mauryan and Kushana kings developed the trade passing through northern India in order to provide the foreign commodities that embellished their palace life. The Roman appetite for luxury goods from India and Southeast Asia—ivory, pearls, spices, dyes, and cotton—greatly stimulated trade in the southern kingdoms of India. Rulers vied to control and tax this lucrative commerce.

But no monarch, however great, could maintain control over the whole vast expanse of territory crossed by these trade routes. There were always middlemen. The Parthians, whose kingdom extended from the Euphrates to the borders of Bactria, levied heavy tolls on the caravan trade. The Kushanas acted as middlemen for the Chinese silk trade, selling the silk to the Parthians and later to Mediterranean merchants coming by sea to India. The Sabaean Arabs of southwestern Arabia seized the Red Sea route at Aden and were in control of much of the Mediterranean world's overseas trade with India. From Aden, the Sabaeans sent Indian goods north by caravan to Petra, which grew rich as a distribution point to Egypt via Gaza and to the north via Damascus.

So great was the demand and so lucrative the trade in Indian goods that the Roman emperor Augustus Caesar tried to break the hold of the Parthian and Arab middlemen on the Eastern trade, establishing direct commercial connections by sea with India. By 1 B.C.E. he had gained control of the Red Sea, forcing the Sabaeans out of Aden and converting the city into a Roman naval base. Ships were soon sailing from Aden directly to India across the Arabian Sea, blown by the monsoon winds.

From May to October the monsoon blows from the southwest across the Arabian Sea; between November and March the counter-monsoon blows from the northeast. Thus direct round-trip voyages, eliminating middlemen and the tedious journey along the coasts, could be made in eight months. Strabo, a Greek geographer during the time of Augustus, stated that 120 ships sailed to India every year from Egyptian ports on the Red Sea. This was an era in which early circuits of world trade developed.

When Augustus became head of the Roman world, the Tamil and Kushana rulers sent him congratulatory embassies. At least nine other embassies from India visited the Roman emperors, and Roman-Indian trade flourished. Indian birds (particularly talking parrots, costing more than human slaves) became the pets of wealthy Roman ladies, and Indian animals (lions, tigers, and buffaloes) were used in the wild beast shows of Roman emperors.

During the first century C.E., when Roman-financed ships reached the rich markets of southern India and Sri Lanka, Christianity may have accompanied them. Indian Christians today claim that their small group of about two million was founded by St. Thomas, one of Jesus' original 12 disciples, who may have sailed to India about 50 C.E. Thus, the trade routes carried more than goods. They bore travelers, envoys, pilgrims, and missionaries. Though the story of St. Thomas in India may be legendary, Buddhist philosophy was certainly spreading east and south into China and Southeast Asia.

The Balance of Trade

The balance of trade between the east and west of Eurasia from ancient times until the modern era tended to favor the countries of the East. Although Western trade with the East grew immensely in the first two centuries C.E., Roman exports such as wool, linen, glass, and metalware to the East did not match in value Rome's imports of silk, spices, perfumes, gems, and other luxuries. To make up the difference, gold and silver had continually to be exported to Asia. The discovery of large hoards of Roman coins in India seems to support claims that the Romans had to pay cash for some significant portion of their Indian goods.

Beginning in the third century, contacts between the eastern and western countries gradually declined. India entered a period of change and transition after the Mauryan Empire fell and the Kushana Empire in northeast India collapsed. In China, the Han dynasty in China broke apart. At the Western end of the trade routes, the Roman Empire's power was also circumscribed, and the hegemony of the Romans challenged. These political upheavals disrupted long-range cultural and commercial interchange but certainly did not eliminate it. The desire for diverse goods, commercial profits, and information insured the continuity of trade.

CONCLUSION

During India's formative age, three major religions were evolving on the subcontinent. Hinduism became the dominant social and religious force in India, with its notions of dharma (duty) allocated by caste. Jainism fostered the notion of ahimsa (nonviolence), which would play a powerful role in the twentieth-century Indian independence movement. Buddhism challenged the Brahman order and spread beyond the frontiers of India, ultimately to become a world religion. The great bulk of Indian thought sought not to challenge the existing social order but to explain and justify it; dharma dominated. Individual rights and desires in this world were ideally overshadowed by the requirements of eternal salvation, and freedom meant escape from the cycle of birth, death, and rebirth.

As in China, both local indigenous cultures and new languages, ideas, religions, and cultures came together to form the Indian society of antiquity. Forces of cultural and political integration at various times produced empires that spread across north India and penetrated the south. Unlike China, the written historical record can only be deciphered to the fourth century B.C.E., leaving historians more dependent on archaeological remains and engendering more heated debates about India's cultural origins.

India is today the heir of one of the longest-living civilizations in the world. By the beginning of the third century C.E., this civilization had produced a set of religious, philosophical, and literary traditions that endures to the present day. Television broadcasts of the *Ramayana* and the *Mahabharata* have been enormously successful in India in recent years. Rama and Sita remain as significant models for the virtuous male and female. Although the caste system has been challenged by the nation-state politics of modern India, it remains an essential element of Hindu identity: shaping social convention, determining political allegiance, and providing a framework for the practice of religion.

Suggestions for Web Browsing

You can obtain more information about topics included in this chapter at the websites listed below. See also the companion website that accompanies this text, http://www.ablongman.com/brummett, which contains an online study guide and additional resources.

Itihaas: Chronology—Ancient India
http://sify.com/itihaas/fullstory.php?id=13225643
> *Lengthy chronology of ancient India, 2700 B.C.E. to 1000 C.E.; most entries include subsites with text and images.*

India
http://www.art-and-archaeology.com/timelines/india/india.html
> *Site discussing the history, sites and monuments, and classical texts of India, 600 B.C.E. to 1256 C.E.*

Jainism
http://www.cs.colostate.edu/~malaiya/jainhlinks.html
> *Extensive site discusses the principles, traditions, and practices of Jainism and includes numerous related links.*

The Buddhist Age, 500 B.C.E. to 319 C.E.
http://www.stockton.edu/~gilmorew/consorti/1cindia.htm#religdone
> *Text and images detail Buddha's life, the Four Truths, and the evolution of Buddhism. Related links offer analyses of Buddhist texts and a lengthy list of primary texts.*

Ancient Indian History
http://www.fordham.edu/halsall/India/indiasbook.html
> *Comprehensive collection of documents, secondary sources on India.*

The *Ramayana*: An Enduring Tradition
http://www.maxwell.syr.edu/maxpages/special/ramayana/

The Ramayana is one of the most important literary and oral texts of South Asia. This extensive site from Syracuse University offers both a short and complete story of Rama, history, images, and maps.

Literature and Film

On Indian literature, see *The Rig-Veda,* trans. Wendy Doniger (Penguin, 1986); *Upanisads,* trans. Patrick Olivelle (Oxford University Press, 1996); and *The Laws of Manu,* trans. George Bühler (Cosmo Books, 2004). For the *Mahabharata,* see J. A. van Buitenen, ed. and trans., *The Mahabharata,* 3 Vols. (University of Chicago Press, 1973–1978), and the theatrical adaptation by Jean-Claude Carrière, *The Mahabharata* (Harper & Row, 1985). The scholarly edition of the *Ramayana* is Robert P. Goldman, et al., trans., *The Ramayana of Valmiki: An Epic of Ancient India,* 7 vols. (Princeton University Press, 1984–1998). See also Nigel Frith, *The Legend of Krishna* (Schocken, 1976). Ancient Indian literature also treats intimate matters; see, e.g., Wendy Doniger and Sudhir Kakar, trans., *Kamasutra* (Oxford University Press, 2002)

Tamil literature can be sampled in A. K. Ramanujan, trans., *The Interior Landscape: Love Poems from a Classical Tamil Anthology* (Oxford University Press, 1994); and R. Parthasarathy, trans., *The Cilappatikaram of Ilanko Atikal: An Epic of South India* (Columbia University Press, 1993).

Mahabharata, directed by Peter Brooks, is based on the version by Jean-Claude Carrière. The six-hour film (1989) is highly stylized, and its interpretation of the Indian epic has been controversial. The opera *Satyagraha* by composer Philip Glass and librettist Constance De Jong premiered in 1980; a film version was made in 1983. It focuses on Gandhi but is based on the *Bhagavad-Gita. Satyagraha* was Gandhi's idea of vehemently holding to the truth against all odds and temptations.

Suggestions for Reading

Excellent surveys of ancient India may be found in Romila Thapar, ed., *Recent Perspectives of Early Indian History* (Popular Prakashan, 1995), and Stanley A. Wolpert, *A New History of India,* 7th ed. (Oxford University Press, 2004).

On pre-Aryan society see, Gregory L. Possehl, *The Indus Civilization: A Contemporary Perspective* (Altamira Press, 2003). The question of who the Aryans were is discussed in Frank Raymond Allchin, ed., *The Archaeology of Early Historic South Asia* (Cambridge University Press, 1995); Edwin Bryant, *The Quest for the Origins of Vedic Culture* (Oxford University Press, 2001); and George Erdosy, ed., *The Indo-Aryans of Ancient South Asia* (Walter de Gruyter Press, 1995). On Bactria see Frank Lee Holt, *Thundering Zeus*: *The Making of Hellenistic Bactria* (University California, 1999). The Mauryan civilization is analyzed by Romila Thapar, *Ashoka and the Decline of the Mauryas,* 2nd ed. (Oxford University Press, 1997).

On seafaring and India's trade, see Kenneth MacPherson, *The Indian Ocean* (Oxford University Press, 1998), and Xinru Liu, *Ancient India and Ancient China: Trade and Religious Exchanges 1–600* (Oxford University Press, 1988).

There are a number of studies of Indian religions. On Buddhism, Edward Conze, *A Short History of Buddhism* (Allen & Unwin, 1980), is a good introduction. See also Edward J. Thomas, *The Life of Buddha as Legend and History* (Routledge, 1975); Richard H. Robinson, Willard L. Johnson, and Sandra A. Wawrytko, *The Buddhist Religion: A Historical Introduction,* 4th ed. (Wadsworth, 1996); T. W. Rhys Davids, trans., *Buddhist Suttas* (Book Tree, 2000); and John S. Strong, *The Experience of Buddhism* (Wadsworth, 1995). On Hinduism, see Gavin Flood, *An Introduction to Hinduism* (Cambridge University Press, 1996); Pratima Bowes, *The Hindu Religious Tradition* (Routledge, 1978); and Sarvepalli Radhakrishnan, *The Hindu View of Life* (Allen & Unwin, 1980). For primary documents, see Ainslie Embree, ed., *Sources of Indian Tradition,* Vol. 1, 2nd ed., (Columbia University Press, 1988).

On Indian art, see Benjamin Rowland, *The Art and Architecture of India: Buddhist, Hindu, Jain,* 3rd ed. (Penguin, 1970); John Marshall, *The Buddhist Art of Gandhara* (Cambridge University Press, 1960); Heinrich Zimmer, *The Art of Indian Asia* (Princeton University Press, 1960); and Michael W. Meister, *Encyclopedia of Indian Temple Architecture,* 2 Vols. (Princeton University Press, 1983–1992).

MIGRATION

Why do people move from one place to another?

Spanish Civil Guard watching over illegal immigrants from North Africa.

The history of migration is in a sense the history of humankind. All migrations involve the movement of peoples, cultures, languages, and ideas. As a result, they have shaped history around the world and played a major role in the growth of civilization. The reasons why people migrate vary. Changing environmental conditions, population pressures, economic shifts, political and religious controversies, and war and violence have all compelled people to move from one place to another.

Migrations have been an integral part of human experience since our early ancestors took their first tentative steps on the African savanna and began exploring and adapting to new environments. *Homo erectus* migrated from the African continent to Eurasia. Members of *Homo sapiens* followed their predecessor out of Africa and traveled further still, showing considerable ingenuity in overcoming obstacles such as the open sea to reach Australia and the cold of the northern latitudes to traverse the Bering Strait and enter the Americas.

These earliest human movements were small in scale. Extended families or clans would move into a new area and live off the land. Even with small populations, humans often placed considerable environmental strain on the land after only a short time. From 3000 B.C.E. to 500 C.E., Bantu communities migrating into central, eastern, and southern Africa could cultivate an area for only a few years before the soils were exhausted and they had to move to new land.

While environmental degradation caused by human activity has often forced people to migrate, so too have acts of nature such as droughts, floods, cold spells, and crop failures. Severe drought from around 1300 to 1100 B.C.E. likely initiated political disruptions in the eastern Mediterranean and the migrations of the Sea Peoples, Philistines, Sicilians, Sardinians, and Etruscans that followed.[1] More recently, potato blight destroyed the potato crops in Ireland between 1846 and 1850, creating widespread famine and economic hardship. Ireland's population dropped from 8.5 to 5 million as about a million people died of starvation and disease and hundreds of thousands migrated to Britain and the United States. In the United States, as the Great Depression took hold in the 1930s and a 7-year drought hit the Great Plains states, tenant farmers went deeply into debt and banks called in their loans. In the hope of generating more income, farmers cultivated their fields more intensively, leading to soil erosion. Hundreds of thousands of migrants fled the "Dust Bowl" and headed west along Route 66 seeking a "promised land" in California.

From the sixteenth century onward, an important component of European conquests around the globe was the migration of its citizens to new colonies. European languages and cultures left deep imprints on the colonized societies. English settlers were especially adept at creating "Little Englands" in places such as Australia, New Zealand, Canada, and the American colonies. A common feature of these settler colonies and the states that grew out of them was the expulsion of indigenous peoples from their lands. As American settlers pushed westwards, they moved Amerindian peoples to reservations. In 1838 the U.S. government went a step further by expelling Cherokees from Georgia and sending them on the Trail of Tears to Oklahoma, a territory initially set aside for Indians. This forced migration claimed some 4000 lives.

The largest forced migration in history was the trans-Atlantic slave trade, which, over the span of 300 years, wrenched an estimated 12 million people from West and Central Africa to work as slaves on sugar plantations in Latin America, the Caribbean, and the United States. Many more millions of African slaves were taken from West Africa across the Sahara and from East Africa across the Indian Ocean to states in North Africa and the Middle East.

War and conflict have also triggered huge shifts in populations. In the fourth century C.E. the nomadic Huns of Central Asia drove westwards across the steppes into the lands occupied by Germanic tribes. The violent movement of the Huns, in turn, caused German tribes to flee further westward and eventually confront and overrun the declining western Roman Empire. The subsequent resettling of the former Roman domains by the Germanic tribes eventually led to the creation of nations such as France and England.

In the last century, wars and political conflicts have continued to be a major cause of migration. Before and during World War II, Jews in Germany and eastern Europe fled to escape persecution by the Nazis; many of those who did not manage to escape were killed. After the war millions of ethnic Germans were forcibly relocated from eastern Europe to Germany. When Communist regimes took over in Russia, China, Vietnam, and Cambodia, huge numbers of political refugees sought asylum in other countries. In the 1970s and 1980s, as civil wars erupted between guerilla groups and repressive regimes throughout Central America, hundreds of thousands of refugees fled the fighting, many of them to the United States. This trend shows no signs of abating. In 2003 the UN High Commissioner of Refugees put the total number of refugees around the world at 20.5 million.

Religion has also brought about migrations as religious minorities have sought places to practice their faiths without persecution. After the Muslim conquest of Persia in the seventh century C.E., a group of Zoroastrians migrated to India in the tenth century to escape a forced conversion to the Islamic faith. In 1685 Louis XIV of France revoked the Edict of Nantes of 1598 that guaranteed Protestant Huguenots the right to freedom of worship and made them liable to torture or jail for their beliefs. As a result, about 300,000 Huguenots left France. In 1947, the partition of British India into the new nations of India and Pakistan led to the migration of at least 10 million people who feared religious oppression. Muslims in Hindu India fled for Pakistan while Hindus and Sikhs in Muslim Pakistan fled for India. The resulting religious violence left hundreds of thousands dead.

Economic changes and population growth have also generated migrations of people from rural areas to urban centers. As European nations industrialized in the nineteenth century, rural people seeking work in factories swelled the populations of many cities and leading to problems in housing, sanitation, law enforcement, and transportation. Dramatic population growth and unemployment late in that century also led 40 million Europeans to migrate from the continent to the Americas and Australia. The ethnic makeup and national identity of countries such as Argentina were transformed as a result.

Not all economic migrations, however, have been to cities. A century ago the economic policies of European colonizers in Africa heavily favored exports from coastal areas, which forced seasonal migrants from the interior to seek work on plantations nearer the coast. With the discovery of mineral resources in southern Africa in the late nineteenth century, hundreds of thousands of male migrant workers flocked to the mines for short periods of time leaving their families behind. In both cases, the movements of these migrants between home and places of employment have continued to the present day.

In recent years, migrant workers in foreign countries have been called by many names, for example, "guest workers," "illegal aliens," and "temporary sojourners." Local people have often resented the presence of economic migrants because they are seen as threats to their jobs or way of life. Many governments have been challenged to define the status of foreign migrants and to devise policies for controlling how they enter and where and how long they stay. During the apartheid era (1948–1994) in South Africa, the white-ruled government tried to control the movements of black adults by issuing them passbooks that contained permits allowing them to work and live in areas reserved for whites.

Migration has been an integral feature of history as individuals and groups of people have moved from one place to another for a host of reasons. Some people have moved voluntarily, but over the last five centuries, many migrants have been forced to leave their homes because of war and conquest, oppressive regimes, religious intolerance, and exploitative economic systems. The result is that migration has left few countries in the modern world untouched. The United States often prides itself on being a "nation of immigrants," but as one considers the global reach of migrations, have we reached a point where it is more accurate to refer to a "world of immigrants"?

Questions

1. Why have so many people emigrated to the United States in the last 25 years?

2. How has migration been a part of your own family's history?

3. What were the causes of the world's largest migrations?

Greece

Minoan, Mycenaean, Hellenic,
and Hellenistic Civilizations,
2000–30 B.C.E.

S carred by time, war, weather, and modern pollution, the ruins of the Athenian Acropolis stand today under a smoggy sky and overlook the trees and buildings of a vibrant city that has been modernized and beautified for the 2004 Olympic games. Because of the recent Olympics in Athens, ancient Greek civilization has received renewed attention worldwide. The renovation of the highways and subway system and new construction in preparation for the games have resulted in archaeological discoveries that add greatly to our knowledge of life in this ancient city. Celebration of contemporary Olympics in their birthplace has brought global recognition to the ancient Greeks and the significance of their cultural achievement.

In the fifth century B.C.E. the temples and statues of the Acropolis were new and gleaming, fresh from the hands of confident architects and sculptors. Today those temples, civic centers, and works of art remain ruins, yet ancient Athens and the civilization that was centered there have retained a lasting significance. The accomplishments of the ancient Greeks proved to be enduring. Their magnificent intellectual and artistic legacy helped shape much of the cultural heritage of western Europe and effect political and cultural development in Asia and Africa.

In the past historians and other scholars who specialize in western European civilization have generally tended to overemphasize the originality of Greek civilization and the positive contributions the Greeks made to their cultural heirs. Now we are able to reconstruct a more balanced picture of the ancient Greeks: one that more accurately assesses their cultural inheritance along with their original contributions. We are now much more aware of the formative influences of earlier neighboring civilizations in Africa and Asia that played an important role in influencing the shape of Greek history and culture. Our image of the ancient Greeks has become more balanced, and the recent focus of world attention on modern Athens has resulted in a renewed appreciation of the ancient Greek achievement.

MINOAN AND MYCENAEAN CIVILIZATIONS, C. 2000–1200 B.C.E.

■ *In what ways did these two early Aegean societies interact with each other?*

More than one thousand years before the emergence of the Greek civilization we call classical, two advanced cultures, one on the mainland of Greece and another centered on the island of Crete, had taken shape. Minoan (mi-NO-an) civilization with Crete as its center and the surrounding Aegean (ay-GEE-an) islands its commercial partners, was highly developed by 2000 B.C.E.; Mycenaean (mai-se-NEE-an) civilization on the mainland seems to have reached its greatest power between 1450 and 1200 B.C.E. Both civilizations appear to have collapsed shortly after 1200 B.C.E. And both of them contained elements that were to influence the development of the later so-called classical civilization of Greece.

The Minoans

The earliest of these Aegean cultures to reach a high degree of sophistication is now referred to as Minoan

civilization, named after the legendary king of Crete, Minos (MEE-nos). From its center on Crete, Minoan civilization spread to the surrounding Aegean Islands, the coast of Asia Minor, and to mainland Greece itself. A narrow, 160-mile-long island, Crete served as a stepping-stone for extensive trading contacts with Europe, Asia, and Africa. Established by immigrants from Asia Minor, and made prosperous and powerful by economic and cultural contacts with Mesopotamia, Egypt, and more southern Africa, Minoan civilization achieved a high level of sophistication by 2000 B.C.E.

Minoan prosperity was based on a large-scale trading network that ranged throughout the Mediterranean: from Sicily, Greece, Asia Minor, and Syria to Africa, Sicily, and probably even Britain. The Minoans employed well-constructed ships capable of long voyages over the open sea. Chief exports were olive oil, wine, metalware, and magnificent pottery. This trading network was overseen as the monopoly of an efficient bureaucratic government under a powerful ruler whose administrative records came to be written on clay tablets, first in a form of picture writing **(hieroglyphics)**

---

hieroglyphics—Written characters that are pictorial in nature such as the ancient Egyptian written script. The word is Greek in origin (hieros="holy"; glyphos="writing").

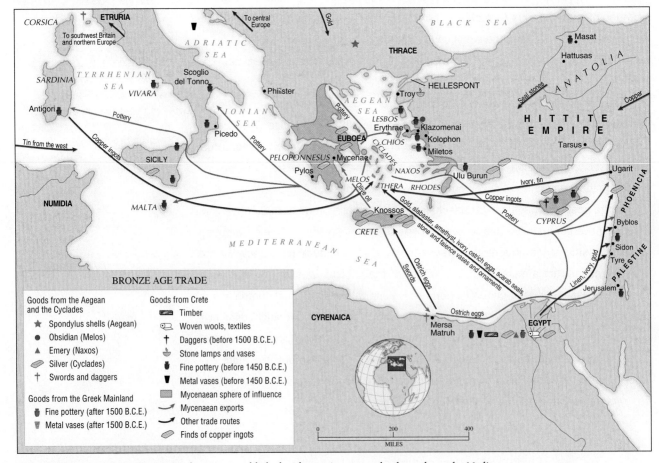

Both the Minoan and Mycenaean civilizations established wide-ranging networks throughout the Mediterranean. Evidence of trading contacts from as far away as Kush (south of Egypt) and Afghanistan has been found in Aegean Bronze Age archaeological sites.

Preclassical Greece

c. 2000–1200 B.C.E.	Minoan and Mycenaean civilizations
1628? B.C.E.	Eruption of Thera
1450–1200 B.C.E.	Mycenaeans in Crete
1150–750 B.C.E.	Greek Dark Ages

and later in a script known as Linear A, whose 87 signs represented syllables. Since neither of these early scripts has been deciphered, our knowledge of the earliest stages of Minoan civilization is incomplete and imprecise; most of what we know is derived from the material remains—walls, temples, houses, and pottery and tablet fragments—uncovered by archaeologists.

The spectacular discoveries of English archaeologist Sir Arthur Evans a century ago first brought to light this impressive civilization, whose existence had previously only been mentioned in the epics of Homer and in Greek legends such as that of the Minotaur, half bull and half man, who devoured young Greek men and women sent to it as tribute from subject Greek cities. Between 1900 and 1905 Evans excavated the ruins of a great palace at Knossos, the largest and most prosperous city in Crete after 1700 B.C.E. Rising at least three stories high and sprawling over nearly 6 acres, this "Palace of Minos," built of brick and limestone and employing unusual downward-tapering columns of wood, was a maze of royal apartments, storerooms, corridors, open courtyards, and broad stairways. Equipped with running water, the palace had a sanitation system that surpassed anything else constructed in Europe until Roman times. Walls were painted with elaborate frescoes in which the Minoans appear as a happy, peaceful people with an enthusiasm for dancing, festivals, and athletic contests. Women are shown enjoying a freedom and prominence rarely matched either in the ancient Near East or even in later classical Greece. They are not secluded in the home but are portrayed sitting with men and taking an equal part in public festivities—even as athletes and participants in religious rituals. Their dresses are very elaborate, with bright patterns and colors, pleats, and puffed sleeves.

Their dresses are open in front to the waist, and their hair is carefully curled and arranged—a certain indication that Minoan women of high standing had sufficient time and wealth to devote to elaborate fashion.

One of the most notable features of Minoan culture was its art, varied in its themes, full of color, motion, and even humor. Art seems to have been an essential part of everyday life and not, as in the ancient Near East, intended to impart a religious or political message. What little is known of Minoan religion also contrasts sharply with earlier religious patterns in the Near East: There is no evidence of great temples, powerful priesthoods, or large cult statues of the gods. The principal deity was probably a Mother Goddess; her importance seems to reflect the prominence women held in Minoan society. A number of recovered statuettes show her dressed like the fashionable Minoan women who are portrayed in the murals that decorated the palace at Knossos. The Minoan Mother Goddess was perhaps an early inspiration for such later Greek goddesses as Athena, Demeter, and Aphrodite.

The Mycenaeans

Around or shortly after 2000 B.C.E., the first Indo-European Greek tribes, usually called Achaeans (ah-KEE-ahns), invaded Greece from the north, either conquered or absorbed the earlier settlers, and ruled from palaces on fortified hills at Mycenae, Pylos, Athens, and other sites in the south of Greece. By 1600 B.C.E. these Greeks—or Mycenaeans, as they are called today, after the richest of their fortresses at Mycenae—had absorbed much of the culture of the Minoans through trading contacts. But unlike

Vivid frescoes decorated the walls of many of the rooms in the Palace of Knossos. This famous Dolphin Frieze in the so-called Queen's Chamber illustrates the importance of the sea and of animals in Minoan life and art.

In contrast to some of the rigid and grandiose Mesopotamian and Egyptian statues, those of the Minoans were small and animated. This little priestess holds snakes, possibly reflecting Minoan religious rituals.

the Minoans, the Mycenaeans seemed to have been a more warlike people and sailed the seas as raiders as well as traders. Mycenaean women adopted Minoan fashions and added to Minoan styles their own cultural preferences in cosmetics, dress, and jewelry.

The Mycenaeans accumulated their wealth through agricultural production, the manufacture of superior pottery and metal tools and weapons, international trade, and probably piracy. Some of the great wealth accumulated by the kings of Mycenae—the greatest single hoard of gold, silver, and ivory objects found anywhere before the discovery of Tutankhamen's tomb—was excavated in 1876 by the amateur German archaeologist Heinrich Schliemann (1822–1890), a few years after his sensational discoveries at Troy. The royal palace on the acropolis, or citadel, of Mycenae had spacious audience

rooms and apartments, fresco-lined walls, floors of painted stucco, and large storerooms. Impressive also were the royal tombs constructed by Mycenaean kings after 1500 B.C.E. These beehivelike tombs, constructed of cut stones over several tons in weight and averaging over 40 feet in height, show proof of the power and control these Mycenaean kings exercised.

The desire to expand wealth and power led the Mycenaeans to establish colonies in the eastern Mediterranean (Hittite sources refer to Achaeans in Asia Minor) and even to the conquest of Knossos about 1450 B.C.E. This Mycenaean takeover was made possible by the destruction of the mazelike palace at Knossos by fire, perhaps in the aftermath of an earthquake that weakened the palace's defenses. Minoan dominance in the Aegean and prosperity on Crete had already been reduced by the destruction caused by the spectacular eruption of the volcanic island of Thera (modern Santorini), 80 miles north of Crete, and a resultant massive tidal wave that may have struck the northern shore of the island at a height of nearly half a mile. Archaeologists and **volcanologists** now place this great eruption in 1628 B.C.E., but the resulting damage to buildings, crops, and the merchant fleet of the Minoans probably contributed to making the civilization vulnerable to Mycenaean raids. The palace at Knossos was rebuilt by the Mycenaeans only to be destroyed about 1380 B.C.E. by earthquake and fire, after which the center of civilization in the Aegean shifted to the Greek mainland.

Many of the details regarding Minoan-Mycenaean relations were unknown until after 1952, when a young English architect, Michael Ventris, startled the scholarly world by deciphering a late type of Minoan script known as Linear B, many examples of which had been found by Evans at Knossos and by later archaeologists at mainland Greek sites such as Pylos, Mycenae, and Tiryns. Before Ventris's translation, most scholars thought that Linear B had to be a written version of the Minoan language. But Ventris proved that Linear B was actually an early form of Greek written in syllabic characters. Since Linear B was Greek, the rulers of Knossos after 1450 B.C.E. must have been Mycenaean Greeks who had come to power in Crete through invasion or piracy and adopted the Minoan script to write their own language.

The Linear B texts, which are administrative documents and inventories, add greatly to our

---

volcanologists—Those who study the formation, distribution, and classification of volcanoes and their eruptions.

knowledge of Mycenaean life. The Mycenaean centers were fortified palaces and administrative offices and not, as in Crete, true cities. The bulk of the population lived in scattered villages where they worked either communal land or land held by nobles or kings. The nobles were under the close control of the kings, whose administrative records were kept daily by a large number of scribes. Prominent in these records are details of the distribution of grain and wine as wages and the collection of taxes. The most important item of income was olive oil, the major article in the wide-ranging network of Mycenaean trade, which was operated as a royal monopoly. Perhaps it was their role as merchant adventurers that led the Mycenaean kings about 1250 B.C.E. to launch an expedition against Troy to eliminate a powerful commercial rival.

Troy—Site of Homer's *Iliad?*

DOCUMENT
Homer, *The Iliad*

The city most authorities believe to have been Troy, as described to us first by the poet Homer, occupied a strategic position on the Hellespont (the strait from the Aegean to the Black Sea, now known as the Dardanelles). In such an important location, this city could command both sea traffic through the straits and land routes between Asia and Europe. For many years scholars thought that Troy existed only in the epic poems of Homer; however, Heinrich Schliemann believed otherwise. As a young man he had read Homer's *Iliad*, and he became firmly convinced that the city had truly existed. At the age of 48, having made fortunes in the California gold rush and in worldwide trade, Schliemann retired from business to prove that his dreams of ancient Troy's existence were real.

In 1870 Schliemann began excavations at the legendary site of Troy, where he unearthed nine buried cities, built one on top of the other. He discovered a treasure of golden earrings, hairpins, necklaces, and bracelets in the second city (Troy II), which led him to believe that this was the city described by Homer. Excavations in the 1930s, however, showed that Troy II had been destroyed about 2200 B.C.E., far too early to have been the scene of the Trojan War. Scholars now believe that Troy VI or VII (c. 1200–1125 B.C.E) was probably the city made famous by Homer.

Homer's account tells us that the Trojan War began because of the abduction of Helen, queen of Sparta, by the Trojan prince Paris. Under the leadership of Agamemnon, king of Mycenae, the wrathful Achaeans besieged Troy for ten long years. Homer's *Iliad* actually describes only a period of a few weeks during the tenth year of the supposed siege. There is no archaeological proof of Homer's account. But we do know that Troy VII was destroyed by fire, and there are indications that the city was besieged. Were the attackers from Greece, or perhaps did the city fall victim to the piracy and disorder associated with the coming of the Sea Peoples or the collapse of the Hittite empire around 1200 B.C.E.? Folktales of the demise of the great city passed from Mycenaean times through oral tradition and elaboration down to the eighth century, when the account attributed to the poet Homer took written form. But the facts behind the destruction of the great city on the Hellespont remain clouded in mystery.

In 1876, when Heinrich Schliemann found this gold death mask at Mycenae, he excitedly telegraphed a friend: "I have looked upon the face of Agamemnon." The mask, however, dates from about 1500 B.C.E., nearly three centuries before the Trojan War, during which Agamemnon is said to have reigned.

The Fall of Mycenaean Civilization

Greek traditions recorded that around 1200 B.C.E. a new wave of Greek invaders, materially aided by weapons made of iron instead of bronze, invaded Greece from the north and conquered the Mycenaean strongholds. These newcomers may have followed in the path of the devastation caused by raiding Sea Peoples (see Chapter 1); some archaeologists suggest that invasions of new peoples caused less damage to Mycenaean sites than did the revolts of the lower classes against their powerful and autocratic overlords. First of the Mycenaean strongholds to fall was Pylos, whose Linear B archives contain numerous references to quickly undertaken preparations to meet military emergencies. We find orders directing women and children to places of safety and instructions given to makers of weapons, the navy, and food suppliers. The preparations were not in time. Pylos was sacked and burned, and all of the other major Mycenaean citadels were likewise destroyed.

THE RISE OF HELLENIC CIVILIZATION, c. 1150–500 B.C.E.

■ *How did a distinct Hellenic civilization evolve out of the Greek Dark Ages?*

The four centuries from around 1150 to 750 B.C.E., called the Greek Dark Ages, were marked by drastic depopulation and the disappearance of the major characteristics of Mycenaean civilization—centralized and bureaucratic administration, wide-ranging commerce, sophisticated art forms, monumental architecture, and writing. Although the fall of Mycenaean civilization was a catastrophic event, the end of Mycenaean dominance eventually gave rise to the emergence of a new and different civilization, called the Hellenic. Hellenic civilization receives its name from the Greek hero Hellen, a mortal who is credited with bringing humans to first inhabit Greece (Greeks ancient and modern call their country Hellas).

The Influence of Geography

The Early Aegean

Geographical factors played an important part in shaping the events of Greek history. The numerous mountain ranges that crisscross the peninsula, which is about the size of the state of Maine, severely restricted internal communication and led to the development of fiercely independent city-states and the reluctance of the Greeks to unite into a single nation. The mountains cover two-thirds of the peninsula, and along the west coast, they come close to the sea, leaving few harbors or arable plains. Elsewhere the deeply indented coast provides many natural harbors. A narrow isthmus at the Gulf of Corinth made southern Greece almost an island—in fact, it was called the Peloponnesus (pe-loh-poh-NEE-sus) for "Pelop's island." The jagged coastline and the many islands offshore stimulated seagoing trade, and the rocky soil (less than a fifth of Greece is agriculturally productive) and few natural resources encouraged the Greeks to establish colonies abroad.

The Homeric Age

Most of our information about the Greek Dark Ages comes from the epic poems put in written form around 750 B.C.E. and attributed to a supposedly blind Greek poet named Homer. Controversy surrounds the question of Homer's existence and whether he alone or several poets composed the *Iliad* and the *Odyssey*. The Homeric epics retain something of the material side of the Mycenaean period, handed down to Homer's time by a continuous oral tradition. But in terms of the details of political, economic, and social life, religious beliefs and practices, and the ideals that gave meaning to life, the poet could only describe what was familiar to him in his own age, probably soon after 800 B.C.E.

The values held by Homer to give meaning to life in the Homeric Age were predominantly heroic values—the strength, skill, and valor of the dominating warrior. Such was the earliest meaning of *arête* (AH-re-te), "excellence" or "virtue," a term whose meaning changed as values changed during the course of Greek culture. To obtain *arête*—defined by one Homeric hero as "to fight ever in the forefront and outdo my companions"—and the undying fame that was its reward, men would endure hardship, struggle, and even death. Honor was the just reward for one who demonstrated *arête*, and the greatest of human injustices was the denial of honor due to a great hero. Homer makes such a denial the theme of the *Iliad*, "The ruinous wrath of Achilles that brought countless ills upon the Achaeans," when Achilles, insulted by Agamemnon, withdraws from battle.

The Homeric king was essentially a war leader, hardly more than the "first among equals" among his companions—his fellow nobles who sat in his council to advise him and to check any attempt he might make to exercise arbitrary power. There was also a popular

---

The Development of Hellenic Civilization

c. 1150–c. 750 B.C.E.	Greek "Dark Ages"
c. 800–750 B.C.E.	Establishment of the Greek *polis* (city-state)
c. 750–550 B.C.E.	Great age of Greek colonization
c. 650 B.C.E.	Age of Greek tyrants; *helot* revolt in Sparta
c. 600 B.C.E.	Coinage introduced in Greece
594 B.C.E.	Solon named sole *archon* in Athens
c. 560 B.C.E.	Pisistratus is tyrant in Athens
508–502 B.C.E.	Cleisthenes establishes democracy in Athens

Document   Homer—*The Iliad:* Andromache and Hector

Homer's *Iliad* is mostly a story of war and carnage. Yet this great work also contains vivid and moving accounts of life and even love during the respites between battles. Homer's work served as inspiration to the Greeks of the classical period; much of the actions of heroic men and women were held up as examples of ideal conduct in times of crisis. Such inspiration can be taken from the description of an interaction between the Trojan hero Hector and his loyal wife Andromache (an-DRO-ma-kee) before Hector went out to meet certain death at the hands of the Greek Achilles:

A flash of his helmet
And off he strode and quickly reached his sturdy,
well-built house. But white-armed Andromache—
Hector could not find her in the halls.
She and the boy and a servant finely gowned
were standing on the tower, sobbing, grieving.
. . . Hector spun and rushed from his house,
back by the same way down the wide, well-paved
*   streets*
throughout the city until he reached the Scaean
*   Gates,*
the last point he would pass to gain the field of
*   battle.*
There his warm, generous wife came running up to
meet him,
. . . She joined him now, and following in her steps
a servant holding the boy against her breast
in the first flush of life, only a baby
Hector's son, the darling of his eyes
and radiant as a star . . .
The great man of war breaking into a broad smile,
his gaze fixed on his son, in silence. Andromache,
pressing close beside him and weeping freely now,
clung to his hand, and urged him, called him:
"Reckless one,
my Hector—your own fiery courage will destroy
*   you!*
Have you no pity for him, our helpless son? Or me,
and the destiny that weighs me down, your widow

now so soon. Yes, soon they will kill you off,
all the Achaean forces massed for assault, and
*   then,*
bereft of you, better for me to sink beneath the
*   earth.*
What other warmth, what comfort's left for me,
once you have met your doom? Nothing but
*   torment!*
I have lost my father. Mother's gone as well.
. . . You, Hector—you are my father now, my noble
*   mother,*

a brother too, and you are my husband, young
*   and*
warm
and strong."

Questions to Consider

1. Do you think Hector and Andromache are displaying ideal conduct in this exchange?

2. Is Andromache in any way receptive to concerns *other* than her own security? What seem to be Andromache's primary goals in her conversation with Hector?

3. Is Andromache helpless to do something other than her husband's bidding? Why?

From Homer, *Iliad,* 6, 439–509, trans. Robert Fagles (New York: Penguin, 1990).

assembly of arms-bearing men, whose consent was asked whenever a crisis occurred, such as war or the recognition of a new king.

Noble women were freed from agricultural labor, but still had major responsibility for maintaining the order of the household and its accounts, supervising the upbringing of the children, and overseeing the activities of any servants attached to the estate. In most circumstances noble women had to manage the estates of their husbands when war or other duties

demanded their attention. They are described by Homer as active participants in the life of their communities and even in the banquet hall conversations alongside the men. But the opportunity for leisure like that possessed by their Minoan and Mycenaean predecessors was a luxury most of these noble women probably could not enjoy.

Society was clearly aristocratic; nobles were recognized as such because of their ownership of larger estates, and their resulting influential position within

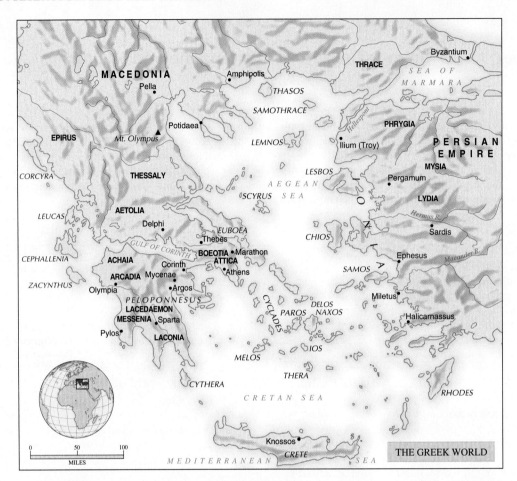

Greek civilization flourished in the mountainous lands of the eastern Mediterranean. Mainland Greece lacked arable land and navigable rivers, but its extensive coastline and fine harbors drew the Greeks to the sea for sustenance and commerce. All of the eastern Mediterranean became involved in the war between Athens and Sparta. The Spartans, surrounded by Athens's growing power, concluded that they had to go to war to prevent eventual Athenian dominance.

the tribes. Only the nobles, the *aristoi* ("best"), possessed *arête*—and the common man was reprimanded and beaten when he dared to question his superiors. Yet the commoners had certain political rights as members of the tribes; they were able to sit in the popular assembly, own land, and enjoy the protection of law as interpreted by the king.

The economy was a simple, self-sufficient agricultural system in which private ownership of land replaced the collective group ownership of Mycenaean times. Slavery was not a widely employed institution in the Greek Dark Age. Most of the estates were small, and most agricultural and domestic labor was provided by free, landless peasants. Slaves were not numerous; if slaves were to be found they were mostly employed as domestic servants on the estates of the wealthiest of the nobles.

From Oligarchy to Tyranny

The *polis* (pl. *poleis*), the term which later comes to mean the city-state—the political unit comprising the city and its people— did not carry the same meaning for the Greeks of Dark Ages. The word originally described only the physical city itself. The center of every polis was the high, fortified site, the *acropolis*, where people could take refuge from attack. In time this defensive center took on added significance as the focus of political and religious life. When commerce revived in the eighth and seventh centuries B.C.E., a trading center *(agora)* developed below the acropolis. The two areas and the surrounding territory, usually smaller than a modern county, in combination with its citizens, came to give new meaning to the word *polis*: the city and the people who share a common citizenship.

The political development of the polis was so rich and varied that it is difficult to find of a form of government not experienced—and given a lasting name—by the Greeks: monarchy, oligarchy, tyranny, and democracy. For most of the Greek Dark Ages, monarchy had been the typical form of government. But by the middle of the eighth century B.C.E., the nobles, who wished to share in the authority exercised by monarchs, had taken over the government of most city-states, ushering in an age of aristocracy ("government by the best") or **oligarchy** ("government by the few"). Exercising their superior power, the nobles in many locations abolished the popular assembly, acquired a monopoly of the best land, reduced many commoners to virtual serfdom, and forced others to seek a living on rocky, barren soil. Often the poor found relief only by emigrating overseas. In many city-states the wealthy promoted colonization as a safety valve to ward off a threatened political and economic explosion from the lower classes.

But the colonization movement was much more than just an effort to relieve the distress of the landless poor. From 750 to 550 B.C.E. the Greeks planted colonies throughout most of the Mediterranean world. Colonies were founded along the northern coast of the Aegean and around the Black Sea. So many Greeks migrated to southern Italy and eastern Sicily that the region became known as *Magna Graecia,* Great Greece. Col-

VIDEO
Ephesus

onies were also founded as far west as present-day France—at Massilia (modern Marseilles), for example—and Spain and on parts of the African coast. Unique was Naucratis (NAH-krah-tis) in Egypt, not a true colony but a trading post whose residents gained extraterritorial rights (their own magistrates and law courts) from the Egyptians.

Colonization not only lessened some of Greece's social problems but also stimulated rapid and significant economic development. By 600 B.C.E. economic progress and the use of coined money, probably inspired by the Lydians, had fostered the beginnings of a middle class. The Greek poleis gradually became "industrialized" as a result of concentrating on the production of specialized goods—vases, metal products, textiles, olive oil, and wine—for export in exchange for

food and raw materials. But before this economic revolution was completed, the continuing land hunger of the poor contributed to a political revolution.

After 650 B.C.E. rulers known as *tyrants* seized power in many Greek states and, supported by both poorer citizens and the rising middle classes, took control of government from the nobility. Tyrants were supported also by the newly developed heavily armed infantry force: the hoplite phalanx—a formation of foot soldiers carrying overlapping shields and long spears, which replaced the aristocratic cavalry as the most important element in Greek warfare. Most tyrants were commanders of the hoplite phalanx. The hoplites, common citizens wealthy enough to furnish their own equipment, supported their commander's efforts to seize power in turn for the promise of more partici-

---

A sixth-century B.C.E. amphora from the polis of Corinth. Corinthian pottery was the most popular of all such merchandise produced in Greece for two hundred years, and many examples of it are found throughout the Mediterranean region, even as far into Asia as modern Iran.

---

pation in the affairs of the polis once the tyranny was established.

The tyrants (the word meant simply "absolute ruler" and did not at first have today's connotation of brutality) sometimes distributed land to the landless poor and, by promoting further colonization, trade, and industry, increased economic prosperity and generally made their poleis better places to live for all residents. At first exceptionally popular leaders, tyrants attempted to keep a dynastic control of their poleis by passing on their power to their sons. Within a few generations, these dynastic tyrannies tended to grow more autocratic and unpopular with the citizens, and almost all were eventually overthrown. Most Greek poleis then reverted to an aristocratic form of government with control in the hands of the nobility. The two notable exceptions to this pattern are two of the most unique of poleis: Athens and Sparta.

Athens to 500 B.C.E.

Athens and Sparta, the two city-states destined to dominate the political history of Greece during the classical period (the fifth century B.C.E. and most of the fourth), had radically different courses of development during the period prior to 500 B.C.E. The

---

oligarchy—Government by the few, from the Greek word oligos ("few"); political domination by a limited number of families or individuals.

political, economic, and social evolution of Athens was typical of most Greek states, but Sparta's development produced a unique way of life that inspired the admiration of other Greeks, and often their astonishment as well.

In Athens during the seventh century B.C.E., the council of nobles became most influential. The popular assembly rarely met, and the king's authority was replaced by nine magistrates, called *archons* ("rulers"), chosen annually by the aristocratic council to exercise the king's civil, military, and religious powers. While the nobles prospered on their large estates, the small farmers and sharecroppers suffered. Bad years and poor land forced them to borrow seed from the wealthy nobles, and when they were unable to repay their debts, they were sold into slavery. Small farmers called out for the cancellation of debts and the end to debt slavery, and those without any land demanded a redistribution of the land claimed by the aristocrats.

The majority of Athenian nobles finally realized that their failure to address the demand for reform might result in the rise of a tyrant, and they agreed to a policy of compromise advocated by the aristocrat Solon. In 594 B.C.E. Solon was made sole archon, with broad authority to revise the constitution of Athens in order to avoid class conflict. Solon, widely respected in Athens for his wisdom and fair dealing, instituted middle-of-the-road reforms intended to save Athens from social revolution and economic disaster.

For the lower classes, Solon agreed to canceling all debts and forbidding future debt slavery, but he rejected as too radical the demand for the redistribution of the land. His long-range solution to the economic problem was to seek full employment by stimulating trade and industry. To achieve this goal, Solon required fathers to teach their sons a trade, granted citizenship to foreign artisans and merchants who settled in Athens, and encouraged the intensive production of wine and olive oil for export.

All citizens in Athens, women included, were encouraged to work—most Athenian women citizens who did so worked at home-based small industries. Solon regulated prostitution in Athens, although such an occupation was considered unacceptable for any but foreign noncitizens.

Moderation also characterized Solon's political reforms—the common people were granted important political rights but not complete equality. Although laws continued to originate in a newly instituted Council of Four Hundred controlled by the nobles, they now had to be ratified by the popular assembly, to which Solon gave more power. And since wealth, not birth, became the qualification for membership in the new council and for the archonships, wealthy commoners could acquire full political equality. Furthermore, the assembly could now act as a court to hear appeals from the decisions of the archons and to try the archons for misdeeds in office.

Solon's reforms were very popular with the middle classes but did not completely satisfy the rich or the poor. The poor had received neither land nor full political equality, while the nobles thought Solon too radical of a reformer who had betrayed his own class. But both classes were given more political power and a sense of participation and involvement in the life of the polis. Solon's reforms moved Athens closer to the implementation of a more fully democratic constitution.

Solon advised the Athenians to accept his reforms, and then left the city and its politics for ten years, in the hope that his new constitutional reforms would take root without his interference. But rivalries between the nobles, the middle class, and the poor resulted in years of civil conflict. In 560 B.C.E., after several attempts to dominate Athens, Pisistratus (pai-SIS-tra-tus), a military hero and champion of the commoners, seized power as tyrant. He addressed the economic problems by banishing many nobles, whose lands he distributed among the poor, and by promoting commerce and industry. Together with extensive public works projects and state sponsorship of the arts—starting Athens on the road to cultural leadership in Greece—these reforms gave rise to a popular saying that "life under Pisistratus was paradise on earth." Like Solon, Pisistratus moved Athens closer to the acceptance of a more fully developed democracy by giving both the middle class and especially the commoners a real possibility to participate in governing the polis.

Pisistratus was succeeded by his son, Hippias (HIP-i-as), who proved unable to retain his father's popularity and soon became tyrannical in the modern sense of the word. The nobles, aided by a Spartan army, took the opportunity to restore aristocracy, but the majority of Athenian citizens by this time supported establishing a more democratic form of government that empowered the middle and lower classes to a greater degree than the nobles supported. The leader of the democrats, a noble named Cleisthenes (KLAIS-the-neez), established order in Athens with the cooperation of even the nobles when they were faced with the possibility of further Spartan interference.

From 508 to 502 B.C.E. Cleisthenes was given power to enact constitutional reforms that greatly reduced the remaining power of the nobility. He disbanded the old noble-dominated tribes and created ten new ones, each embracing citizens of all classes from widely scattered districts. The popular assembly acquired the right to initiate legislation and became the sovereign power in the state; there could be no appeal from its decisions. A new democratic Council of the Five Hundred, selected by lot from the ten tribes, advised the assembly and supervised the administrative actions of the archons.

Cleisthenes also has been credited with instituting the institution of *ostracism*, an annual referendum in which a quorum of citizens could vote to exile for ten years any individual thought to be a threat to the new Athenian democracy. (A quorum consisted of 6000 of the 50,000 male citizens over the age of 18. The average attendance at an Athenian assembly, whose ordinary meetings were held every ten days, was about 5000.) By 500 B.C.E. the Athenian polis had established a form of government more thoroughly democratic than in any other city in the ancient world.

The establishment of democratic government at Athens owed a great debt to the reforms of Solon and to the policies of Pisistratus, as both Athenian leaders encouraged greater participation in governance by the commoners. But the idealism of Cleisthenes was mainly responsible for establishing the democracy. Cleisthenes diminished the power and influence of the nobles in Athenian politics by reducing their ability to influence voting through their control of the tribal structure and their neighborhoods. He abolished the four Athenian tribes into which all Athenian citizens were born, and instituted in their place ten new tribes, based on neighborhood units called *demes*, which were distributed among the new tribes in such a way that no tribe could dominate a region. All citizens were enrolled on lists kept by the demes, and even if a citizen moved away from the deme in which in which he was originally enrolled, he had to return to that deme to vote and to register for military service. Cleisthenes also awarded citizenship to many resident aliens, most of whom were productive members of the middle classes. A council of 500 was established to replace the old council of 400; now 50 citizens from each of the new 10 tribes constituted this new body that was charged primarily to prepare legislation for the assembly's consideration. But final authority was given to the assembly of all citizens over the age of 18, in which any member might propose legislation, initiate debate, or argue for or against a proposal.

By the beginning of the fifth century B.C.E., Athens was fully involved in the implementation of its new democratic institution but unsure of its security against the threat of Spartan intervention and the possibility of Persian expansion into the Aegean. Its large population and great potential for economic advantage through international trade gave the city-state great potential for growth and prosperity. But the greatest test the polis would face came from the Persian suppression of the revolt of the Greek poleis on the coast of Asia Minor and the subsequent Persian invasion of Greece.

Sparta to 500 B.C.E.

The early history of Sparta seems very similar to that of many Greek poleis. Sparta took steps to move from a powerful monarchy to oligarchy when the nobles installed five annually elected aristocratic magistrates, called *ephors* ("overseers"), to supervise the kings' activities. Instead of sending out colonists to satisfy the Spartans' desire for more land, the Spartans turned instead to the conquest of the neighboring region of Messenia, whose residents were forced to become state slaves *(helots)*. Around 650 B.C.E., however, the Messenians revolted, and it took Sparta nearly 20 years to crush the rebellion. During this emergency that threatened the very existence of the polis, the aristocrats were forced to seek the aid of the Spartan commoners. In return, the nobles agreed to the commoners' demand for land division and more political participation. Private ownership of land was abolished, and the land allotments were divided equally among the 9000 Spartan male citizens. These land allotments were to remain with the original claimants and often came to be held by women when no male heirs to the property remained alive to claim inheritance.

DOCUMENT

Plutarch on Life in Sparta

In addition, the nobles established an assembly of all Spartan citizens with the right to elect the ephors and to approve or veto the proposals of the 30-member Council of Elders. While the Athenian state required only two years of military training for young men, the Spartan system—traditionally attributed to a legendary lawgiver named Lycurgus (lai-KUR-guz)—was designed to make every Spartan man a professional soldier and to keep him in a constant state of readiness for war, especially the ever-present danger of a helot revolt. To this end, Spartan society enforced an absolute subordination of the individual to the preservation of the state.

Spartan officials examined all newborn children, and any found sickly or deformed were abandoned. At the age of 7 a boy was taken from his family and placed in the charge of state educators, who taught him to bear hardship, endure discipline, and devote his life to the state. At 20 the young Spartan enrolled in the army and continued to live in barracks, where he contributed food from his allotment of land

CASE STUDY

Comparing Athens and Sparta

granted by the state and worked by helots. He was allowed to marry, but he continued to live in barracks, sneaking back to visit his wife only at night. After 30 he could live at home, but continued to take his meals with his company of male comrades. Finally, at 60, he was released from the army and could live at home with his family. This lifelong pattern of discipline produced some of the most formidable soldiers in human history and inspired Spartan citizens with the sense of purpose, obedience, and respect for Spartan law.

Spartan girls also received state training in order to become healthy mothers of warrior sons. Their primary service to the state was thought to be giving birth to male babies, and to that end they were instructed to strengthen their bodies for childbirth. Clad in short tunics, which other Greeks thought immodest, they engaged in running, wrestling, and throwing the discus and javelin. Their characters were to be as strong and resolute as their husbands'. As their men marched off to war, Spartan women gave them a **laconic** farewell (Laconia was another name for the Spartan homeland): "Come back *with* your shield—or *on* it."

Although many Greeks admired the Spartan way of life, few would ever desire to be a part of the Spartan regimen. The typical Spartan was an unsophisticated, uncultured fighting machine. Spartan discipline was almost universally admired, although no other Greek would wish to trade places with a Spartan who avoided the corruptions of fine food and good wine.

Although Sparta developed the finest infantry force in Greece, the state purposely remained backward culturally and economically. Trade and travel were prohibited because the city fathers feared that foreign ideas might threaten Spartan discipline. Sparta is a classic example of how intellectual stagnation accompanies rigid social conformity and military regimentation. But, through conscious design to preserve the state and the privileged status of the citizen elite, the Spartans purposely froze the natural evolution of their political and cultural institutions.

To provide additional assurance that its helots remained uncontaminated by democratic ideas, Sparta allied itself with oligarchic parties in other Peloponnesian (pe-le-pon-NEE-si-an) states and aided them in suppressing their democratic opponents. The resulting Spartan League of oligarchic states, in operation by the end of the sixth century B.C.E., was shortly to be opposed by an Athenian-led alliance of more democratic states.

---

laconic—Using few words, but expressing much. From Laconia, the region in which Sparta was located. Esessentially, to be laconic is to speak in a terse manner, as a Spartan did.

Persian Wars

before c. 540 B.C.E.	Persian control of Greek cities in Asia Minor
499–495 B.C.E.	Rebellion of Ionian cities in Asia Minor
490 B.C.E.	Battle of Marathon
480–479 B.C.E.	Xerxes' invasion of Greece
480 B.C.E.	Battles of Thermopylae and Salamis
479 B.C.E.	Battle of Plataea

THE GOLDEN AGE OF GREECE, 500–336 B.C.E.

■ *What about this period justifies the idea of a Greek "Golden Age"?*

The leaders of a Greek economic and cultural revival after 750 B.C.E. were the Ionian Greeks, who had settled on the Aegean coast of central Asia Minor and the nearby offshore islands and the mainland region of Attica—the Athenians were also Ionian Greeks. Influenced by contacts with Phoenician traders (from whom they borrowed the alphabet in the eighth century B.C.E.) and neighboring Lydia and Egypt, the Ionians became innovators in art, science, philosophy, and literature. Ionian creativity was also evident in their commercial ventures, which spread throughout the Aegean region. It was especially because of their economic prosperity that they became the first of the Greeks to face conflict with the great powers of the Near East.

The Persian Wars

When the Persian empire and its young king Cyrus conquered Lydia in 547 B.C.E., they also took over the Ionian poleis, which had been fairly content under moderate Lydian rule. In open opposition to their Persian-appointed overlords, the Ionian cities revolted in 499 B.C.E., established democratic regimes, and appealed to the Athenians, their kinsmen, for assistance. Athens sent 20 ships—token help, and far too few to prevail over the Persians. By 494 B.C.E. the Persian king Darius I had crushed the revolt, burning the Greek polis of Miletus in revenge.

King Darius knew that Ionia was insecure as long as Athens remained free to incite the Ionian Greeks to revolt again. In 490 B.C.E. a Persian force of about 20,000 infantry and cavalry sailed across the Aegean, conquering the Greek island states along their path, and eventually encamped on the plain of Marathon, 24 miles northwest of Athens. Darius's attempt to eliminate the interference of Athens was ended when the Athenian army, half the size of the Persian force, won an overwhelming victory, slaying as many as 6400 of the invaders while losing only 192 themselves.

The battle of Marathon was one of the most decisive in ancient history. It destroyed the Greek suspicion of Persian invincibility and demonstrated, according to a contemporary Greek historian, that "free men fight better than slaves." Ten years later the Greeks were forced to prepare for a new Persian invasion under Xerxes, Darius's successor, whose objective this time was the subjection of all of Greece. Athens now had 200 warships, the largest fleet in Greece, and Sparta had agreed to head a defensive alliance of 31 states.

The Persian army was too huge to be transported by ship. Crossing the swift-flowing, mile-wide Hellespont near Troy on two pontoon bridges—a notable feat of engineering—the army marched along the Aegean coast accompanied by a great fleet carrying provisions. The Spartans wanted to abandon all of Greece except the Peloponnesus to the invaders but finally agreed to a holding action at the narrow pass of Thermopylae (ther-MO-poh-lee) in central Greece. Here 300 Spartans and a few thousand other Greeks held back the Persians for three days until the Persians discovered a mountain path to the rear of the Greek position. The Spartans fought magnificently until all were killed, along with at least 700 other Greeks. The Spartan dead were immortalized on a monument erected later at the pass, with the inscription "Go Stranger, and tell the Spartans that we lie here, obedient to their word."

The Persians then sacked Athens, whose inhabitants had been evacuated to the Peloponnesus and the islands near the bay of Salamis. Themistocles (the-MI-stoh-kleez), the leader of the democrats at Athens, had long been a strong advocate for the construction of a strong naval force, and now the Athenians were prepared to put their confidence in their ships to defeat the Persian navy in the Bay of Salamis. The battle that took place in the spring, after the Persians had spent the winter in Athens preparing for the event, was an overwhelming Greek victory. Taking full advantage of the Persians' ignorance of the tides and the inability of their ships to outmaneuver the heavier Athenian vessels designed for ramming and close combat, the Persian navy suffered near complete defeat. With 200 of his 350 ships destroyed and his lines of communication cut, Xerxes saw no alternative but to retreat to Asia, although he left a strong force in Greece. The following summer (479 B.C.E.) the Greek army, with the Spartan army in the forefront, defeated the Persian force in central Greece at Plataea. The Persian threat to the Greek mainland was ended, and the Greeks immediately began plans for campaigns to drive the Persians from the Aegean island and the Ionian coast of Asia Minor.

Athens After the Persian Wars

The prominent role the Athenians played in the Greek victory over the mighty Persian Empire exhilarated the polis and gave Athens the confidence and energy to try to assert their leadership of the Greek world during most of the remainder of the fifth century B.C.E. During this period, often described as the Golden Age of Greece, the Athenians also achieved the fullest development of their democracy, and at the same time established a formidable empire on both land and sea.

For more than 30 years (461–429 B.C.E.) during this period, the great statesman Pericles (PE-ri-kleez) guided Athenian policy. In Pericles' time actual executive power no longer resided in the archons, who were chosen by lot, but in a board of ten generals elected annually. The generals urged the popular assembly to adopt specific measures, and the success or failure of their policies determined whether they would be reelected at the end of their annual term. Pericles failed in reelection only once, and so great was his influence on the Athenians that, in the words of his contemporary, the historian Thucydides (thu-SI-di-deez), the Athenian democracy was in reality completely dominated by Pericles and his policies.

To enable even the poorest citizen to participate in government, Pericles extended payment to jurors (a panel of 6000 citizens chosen annually by lot) and to members of the assembly. Although his conservative opponents called this political bribery, Pericles insisted that it was essential to the success of democracy that all the citizens be able to participate, and so those who could not afford to miss a day's wage would be compensated at state expense.

Athenian Society

Despite the many democratic aspects of Athenian society, not all residents of Athens were given the opportunity to be fully participating citizens. Women, slaves, and resident foreigners (with the exception of those to whom Cleisthenes had granted it) were denied citizenship and had no voice in the government. Legally, Athenian women were first the property of their fathers and then of their husbands. They could not possess property in their own name, make legal contracts, testify in the courts, or initiate divorce proceedings. The exclusion of Athenian women from public life seems significant, given the extent to which the participation in the democracy was extended to males of every social class.

An Athenian wife's function was to bear children and manage the home, where she was restricted to the women's quarters when her husband entertained his friends. Men did not marry until they were about 30, and they usually married girls half their age or less. Marriages were normally arranged through agreements between families, and prospective brides and bridegrooms seldom met before their marriage was agreed upon. Families were small, with usually no more than two children, and infanticide, usually by exposure, of unwanted infants was practiced as a means of population control. The average life expectancy in Athens was little more than 30 years, but if one were able to survive childhood, a longer life could be anticipated.

Sexual activity for men outside marriage was not a matter for negative public comment in Athens, and prostitution was common. An acceptable social institution intended to serve the needs and desires of upper-class Athenian men was spending one's leisure time with female "companions" (*hetaerae;* he-TAI-rai). These prostitutes were normally resident foreigners and therefore not subject to the social restrictions imposed on Athenian women. A few of the *hetaerae,* such as Aspasia (as-PAY-zhah), the mistress and later wife of Pericles, were cultivated women who entertained at gatherings frequented by prominent Athenian political and cultural leaders.

Although there are representations of outspoken and assertive women left for us by Athenian dramatists, actual examples of Athenian women who were publicly prominent are almost nonexistent, and the women themselves accepted their status. Athenian women enjoyed less freedom of movement and participation in the public life of the polis than most other Greek states, even Sparta. Veiled from public view, forbidden to converse with men other than their husbands, restricted to their own quarters in the home when their husbands entertained their guests—the private life of an Athenian wife was known only to her household. Yet married life seems to have been stable and peaceful. Athenian gravestones in particular attest to the love spouses felt for one another. The tie to their children was strong, and the community set high store on the honor owed by sons and daughters to their parents.

Homosexuality was an acceptable form of social conduct for Athenian men during certain periods of their lives. A sexual relationship between a mature man and a young boy just before or after the youth attained puberty was common practice. The relationship was viewed not only as sexual, but educational—a rite of initiation into adult society—and such relationships were most common among Athenian soldiers. However, male homosexuality that continued into the years when Athenians were expected to marry and produce children, as well as homosexual prostitution at any time, was not condoned. Such relationships were regarded as unnatural, and the Athenian government issued strong legal prohibitions against them.

In fifth-century Athens scholars estimate that one out of every four persons was a slave. Some were war captives and others were children of slaves, but most came from outside Greece through slave dealers. No large collections of slaves were used on agricultural estates. Small landowners might own one or more slaves, who worked in the fields alongside their masters. Those who owned many slaves—one rich Athenian owned a thousand—hired them out to private individuals or to the state, where they worked alongside Athenian citizens and received comparable wages.

Other slaves were taught a trade and set up in business. They were allowed to keep one-sixth of their wages, and many of them were able to purchase their freedom. Although a very few voices argued that slavery was contrary to nature and that all people were equal, the Greek world as a whole agreed with Aristotle that some people—non-Greeks in particular—were incapable of full human reason, and so they were by nature of inferior status and likely in need of the guidance of a master.

Athenian Imperialism

The Greek victory over Persia had been made possible by a temporary cooperation of the leading Greek city-states, but that unity quickly dissolved after the war when Sparta, envious of Athenian naval superiority and fearful of helot rebellion at home, recalled its troops and resumed its policy of isolation. Because the Persians still ruled the Ionian cities and another invasion of Greece seemed possible, Athens in 478 B.C.E. invited the city-states of the Aegean to join them in forming a defensive alliance called the Delian League. The small island of Delos, sacred to the Ionian Greeks, was chosen to be the league's headquarters and the

Document   Aristophanes on the Shortcomings of Athenian Democracy

In *The Frogs*, the comic dramatist Aristophanes (445–385 B.C.E.) exhorts the Athenians to elect better-quality leaders.

[The leader of the chorus comes forward and addresses the audience.]

We chorus folk two privileges prize:
To amuse you, citizens, and to advise.
So, mid the fun that marks this sacred day,
We'll put on serious looks, and say our say. . . .
But if we choose to strut and put on airs
While Athens founders in a sea of cares,
In days to come, when history is penned,
They'll say we must have gone clean round the
*   bend. . . .*
I'll tell you what I think about the way
This city treats her soundest men today:
By a coincidence more sad than funny,
It's very like the way we treat our money.
The noble silver drachma, that of old
We were so proud of, and the recent gold,
Coins that rang true, clean-stamped and worth
*   their weight*
Throughout the world, have ceased to circulate.
Instead, the purses of Athenian shoppers
Are full of shoddy silver-plated coppers.
Just so, when men are needed by the nation,
The best have been withdrawn from circulation.
Men of good birth and breeding, men of parts,
Well schooled in wrestling and in gentler arts,

These we abuse, and trust instead to knaves,
Newcomers, aliens, copper-pated slaves,
All rascals—honestly, what men to choose!
There was a time when you'd have scorned to use
Men so debased, so far beyond the pale,
Even as scapegoats to be dragged from jail
And flogged to death outside the city gate.
My foolish friends, change now, it's not too late!
Try the good ones again: if they succeed,
You will have proved that you have sense indeed.

Questions to Consider

1. What do you think the reaction of the Athenian theatergoers might have been to this sort of criticism?

2. What elements of Aristophanes' criticism of Athens' situation seem timeless? In what ways could a modern day satirist get by with making the same remarks?

3. Aristophanes complains that the Athens of his time is not as good as the "good old days." Are you able to understand why Aristophanes might make that remark from the section given above, and the fact that he lived and wrote during the Peloponnesian War?

From Aristophanes, *The Frogs and Other Plays*, trans. David Barrett (Baltimore: Penguin, 1964), pp. 181–183.

location of the league treasury. To maintain a 200-ship navy that would drive the Persians out and then police the seas, each state was assessed an annual payment of either ships or money, in proportion to its wealth, to the league treasury. From the beginning, Athens dominated the league. Since almost all of the 173 member states paid their assessments in money, which Athens was eager to collect, the Athenians furnished the necessary ships by building them to Athenian specifications in Athenian harbors, with cash collected from their allies.

By 468 B.C.E., after the Ionian cities had been set free and the Persian fleet had been destroyed, various league members thought it unnecessary to continue league membership. In putting down all attempts to withdraw from the league, the Athenians were moti-vated to some extent by the fear that a Persian danger still existed but mainly by the desire to maintain and protect the large free trade area necessary for Greek—and especially Athenian—commerce and industry. The treasury of the league was moved from Delos and incorporated into that of Athens—further indication to the league's members that Athens was in total control. The Athenians created an empire because they dared not disband the Delian League and because the league was very beneficial to a vibrant Athenian economy. By aiding in the suppression of local aristocratic factions within its subject states and at times imposing democratic governments on the allied states, Athens both eased the task of controlling its empire and emerged as the leader of a union of "democratic" states subject to Athenian control.

To many Greeks—above all to the Spartans and their allies—Athens had become an autocratic and arrogant state interested only in extending its own authority. Athens' leaders, however, justified Athenian **imperialism** on the grounds that it brought freedom, security, and prosperity to the states that recognized Athenian leadership.

The Peloponnesian War

In 431 B.C.E. the Peloponnesian War broke out between the Spartan League and the Athenian Empire. Although commercial rivalry between Athens and Sparta's major ally, Corinth, was an important factor, the conflict is a classic example of how fear of an enemy's growing power can generate a war unwanted by either side. Several incidents served to ignite the underlying tension, and Sparta finally felt it unavoidable to declare war on the Athenians, whom they considered to be the aggressors.

Sparta's hope for victory lay in its army's ability to lay siege to Athens and destroy the crops in the Athenian countryside. Pericles, for his part, relied on Athens's unrivaled navy to import sufficient food and to harass its enemies' coasts.

But Pericles' careful plans to defeat the Spartans were upset by an unexpected turn of events. In the second year of the war a plague, probably an outbreak of **typhus,** killed a third of the Athenian population, including Pericles himself. His death was a great blow to Athens, for leadership of the government passed to leaders of lesser vision and talent.

Eight more years of indecisive warfare ended in 421 B.C.E. with agreement on a compromise peace treaty. During the succeeding period Athenian imperialism was revealed in its worst form through the actions of Pericles' less able successors. In 416 B.C.E. an expedition embarked for Melos (MEE-los), a neutral Aegean island, to force it to join the Athenian Empire. When the Melians refused to join the Empire and argued that they preferred merely to be left alone, the Athenians executed all the men of military age and sold the women and children into slavery.

The war resumed in 415 B.C.E. with an Athenian expedition against Syracuse, the major Greek state in Sicily. The campaign was hastily put together and badly planned, with complete disaster as a result.

---

imperialism—The policy of a government to build and widen its authority by controlling other states or regions through military, political, and economic domination.

typhus—A disease characterized by exhaustion, fever, and the eruption of reddish spots on the body. Probably spread by a microorganism carried by lice and fleas.

Acting on the invitation of states that feared Syracusan expansion, the Athenians hoped to add Sicily to their empire and so become powerful enough to control nearly the entire Mediterranean. But bad luck and incompetent leadership resulted in the destruction of two Athenian fleets and a large Athenian army by the Syracusans, who were also supported by Sparta. The war dragged on until 404 B.C.E., when Athens surrendered after its last fleet was destroyed by a Spartan fleet, which was built with money received from Persia in exchange for possession of the Greek cities in Ionia. At home, Athens had been weakened by the plots and schemes of oligarchic politicians to whom Sparta now turned over the government. The once powerful city-state was stripped of its empire, its fleet, the defense walls that led to the port, and its army and navy.

Aftermath of the War

Anarchy and depression were the political and economic legacies of the Peloponnesian War. Having ended the threat of Athenian domination of Greece, the Spartans substituted their own form of rule that made Athenian imperialism seem mild in comparison. Everywhere, democracies were replaced by oligarchies supported by Spartan troops. The bloody regimes of these unimaginative oligarchs soon led to successful democratic revolutions at Athens and elsewhere. As one of their generals admitted, the Spartans did not know how to govern free people. Incessant warfare between city-states involved in a bewildering series of shifting alliances became typical of Greece in the fourth century B.C.E. Some alliances were even financed by Persia, which wanted to keep the Greek states disunited and weak.

Political instability in turn contributed to the economic and social problems that plagued Greece during this period. Commerce and industry lagged, and the unemployed who did not go abroad as soldiers of fortune supported authoritarian leaders and their radical schemes for redistribution of wealth. The wealthy, for their part, became increasingly reactionary and uncompromising. Many intellectuals and philosophers—including Plato and Aristotle—lost faith in democracy and joined with the wealthy in looking for an inspirational leader who would bring order and security to Greece. They found him, finally, in the person of the king of Macedonia.

The Macedonian Unification of Greece

To the north of Greece was Macedonia (ma-si-DOH-ni-ah), a region inhabited by people of the same

Forensic facial reconstruction of Philip II, father of Alexander the Great, based on remains of his skull found in his tomb in Macedonia. The king had suffered an arrow wound to the eye during battle.

After unifying all of his home country—including a number of Greek colonies that had been established along the Macedonian coast during the earlier centuries of Macedonia's weakness—Philip turned to the Greek city-states, whose wars afforded him the opportunity first to participate through intervention and then to dominate by military superiority. Demosthenes (de-MOS-the-neez), a prominent Athenian orator and an advocate of democracy, warned constantly of the threat he believed Philip to be to Greek freedom, and urged the Athenians and other Greeks to stop the king's expansion before it was too late. Ultimately, Athens and Thebes did attempt to stop Philip's advance, but their combined forces were shattered at Chaeronea (KAY-ro-NEE-yah) in 338 B.C.E. Philip then forced the Greeks to form a league in which each state, while retaining self-government, swore to make peace and to furnish Philip with men and supplies for a campaign against Persia. Two years later, before setting out for Asia Minor, Philip was assassinated by a Macedonian noble, leaving the war against Persia as a legacy for his gifted son Alexander.

With the Macedonian victory in 338 B.C.E. and the formation of the league of Greek states firmly under the control of King Philip, the warfare between Greek states that had been almost constant for more than one hundred years came to an end. But one of the costs of this peace was the independence and self-government so prized by Greek poleis. With the Macedonian victory came changes not only in the political fabric of traditional Greek life, but cultural adaptations so significant that many scholars detect in them the beginnings of a new political and cultural order in the Mediterranean world.

THE GREEK CULTURAL ACHIEVEMENT

▪ *How did the cultural achievements of the Greeks have an impact on Western civilization and other succeeding world cultures?*

The Greeks were the first to formulate many of the Western world's fundamental concepts in politics, philosophy, science, and art. How was it that a relatively small number of people could leave such a great legacy to later civilizations? The definitive answer may always escape students, but a good part of the explanation might be found in environmental and social factors.

Unlike the older Near Eastern monarchies, the polis was not governed by a "divine" ruler, nor were the thoughts and activities of its citizens restricted by

descent as the Greeks in the south who spoke a Greek dialect. But the Greeks considered the Macedonians backward and almost barbaric. No city-states had ever developed in Macedonia, and the land continued to be ruled by kings who were often assassinated by their own nobles if they attempted to assert too much power. But in the fourth century Macedonia emerged as a centralized, powerful state under a young and brilliant King Philip II (359–336 B.C.E.), who created the most formidable Greek army yet known by joining the well-trained Macedonian cavalry of nobles with the hoplite infantry used by the Greeks. When he was a youth, Philip had been held as a hostage at Thebes, where he acquired an appreciation of Greek culture, an understanding of Greek political weaknesses, and a desire to win for Macedonia a place of honor and power in the Greek world.

Classical Greek Literature and Culture

c. 800 B.C.E.	Homer, *The Iliad*
c. 700–480 B.C.E.	Archaic period of Greek art
c. 700 B.C.E.	Hesiod, *Works and Days*
c. 600 B.C.E.	Thales of Miletus, "father of philosophy"
525–456 B.C.E.	Aeschylus, *Oresteia*
c. 496–406 B.C.E.	Sophocles, *Oedipus*
c. 484–c. 425 B.C.E.	Herodotus, "father of history"
c. 480–406 B.C.E.	Euripides, Athenian tragedian
c. 470–399 B.C.E.	Socrates' quest for truth
460–400 B.C.E.	Thucydides, scientific historian
c. 445–385 B.C.E.	Aristophanes, *The Frogs*
427–347 B.C.E.	Plato, *Republic*
c. 420 B.C.E.	Hippocrates' medical school
384–322 B.C.E.	Aristotle's Lyceum

powerful priesthoods. Many Greeks, and most notably the Athenians, were fond of good, wide-ranging conversation and loved debate and argument. The Greeks were religious people, but in most regards they were not overpowered by their gods and regulated by their priests. Their most creative thinkers believed that most significant questions about the world and their place within it could be answered through human resourcefulness and speculation.

The Greek Character

The Greeks felt a need to discover order and meaning both in nature and in human life. This outlook produced exceptional results in science, philosophy, and the arts. As early as the poet Hesiod (c. 700 B.C.E.), the Greeks stressed the virtue of *sophrosyne* (soh-froh-SEE-nay), moderation and self-control, as the key to happiness and fulfillment in life. Working against this virtue was *hubris*, meaning pride, arrogance, and unbridled ambition. The result of human excess and the basic cause of personal misfortune and social injustice, hubris always inspired *nemesis*, or retribution. According to the Greeks, an unavoidable law would cause the downfall or disgrace of anyone guilty of hubris. The

Athenian dramatists emphasized this theme in their tragedies, and Herodotus attributed the Persian defeat by the Greeks to Xerxes' overpowering pride.

The Greeks had all the usual human frailties and failings—at times they were irrational, vindictive, and cruel. But at their best they were guided by the ideals that are described in their intellectual and artistic legacy. The philosopher Protagoras (proh-TA-goh-rahs) is credited with the statement, "Man is the measure of all things"—a statement that typifies the fundamental humanistic character of Greek thought and art.

Greek Religion

Early Greek religion, like almost all religious expressions of early civilizations, abounded in gods and goddesses who personified the forces of nature. Zeus, sky-god and wielder of thunderbolts, ruled the world from Mount Olympus with the aid of lesser deities, many of whom were his children. His power was limited only by the mysterious decrees of Fate. These gods and goddesses as described by Homer act like humans—capable of evil deeds, favoritism, and jealousy, differing from ordinary people only in their immortality. Zeus was often the unknowing victim of the plots of his wife, Hera, and other deities, and he asserted his authority through threats of violence. Hades, the place of the dead, was a subterranean land of dust and darkness, and Achilles, as Homer tells us in the *Odyssey*, would prefer to be a slave on earth than a king in Hades.

By the time of Hesiod, a more sophisticated religious interpretation had changed the vengeful and unpredictable gods of Homer into more rational dispensers of justice who rewarded the good and punished the wicked. Zeus's stature was increased when he was newly identified as the source of Fate, which was no longer considered a separate mysterious power. And from the famous **oracle** at Delphi the voice of Zeus's son Apollo urged all Greeks to follow the ideal of moderation: "Nothing in excess" and "Know yourself."

A century after Hesiod, the Orphic and Eleusinian (el-eu-SI-ni-uhn) mystery cults emerged as a type of Greek higher religion. Their initiates *(mystae)* were promised salvation in an afterlife of bliss in Elysium,

---

oracle—In ancient Greece, a divine message made by a god through a priest or priestess, or even through the rustling of wind through trees. Oracles were usually delivered in answer to an inquiry from an individual or polis, and the response was typically given in a form that was open to several interpretations. At Delphi, the oracle sometimes refers to the priestess who delivered the god's message.

formerly the home after death of a few heroes only. The basis of the Orphic cult was an old myth about Dionysus, a son of Zeus, who was killed and eaten by the evil Titans before Zeus arrived on the scene and burned them to ashes with his lightning bolts. Orpheus, a legendary figure, taught that Zeus then created man from the Titans' ashes. Human nature, therefore, is composed of two distinct and opposing elements: the evil Titanic element (the body) and the divine Dionysian element (the soul). Death, which frees the divine soul from the evil body, is therefore to be welcomed.

Early Greek Philosophy

What the Greeks were the first to call *philosophy* ("love of wisdom") arose from their curiosity about nature. The early Greek philosophers were called *physikoi* ("physicists") because their main interest was the investigation of the physical world. ("It is according to their wonder," wrote Aristotle, "that men begin to philosophize, pursuing science in order to know.") Later, and primarily due to the influence of Socrates, the chief concern of philosophy was not natural science but *ethics*—how people ought to act in light of moral principles.

The Mesopotamians, as noted in Chapter 1, were skilled observers of astronomical phenomena, which, like the early Greeks, they attributed to the action of the gods. But early Greek philosophers, beginning with Thales of Miletus around 600 B.C.E., changed the course of human knowledge by insisting that the phenomena of the universe could be explained by natural rather than supernatural causes. This rejection of mythological explanations led the Greeks to emphasize the use of human reason to explain the world around them.

Called the "father of philosophy," Thales speculated about the nature of the basic substance of which everything in the universe is composed. He concluded that it was water, which exists in different states and is indispensable to the maintenance and growth of organisms. Thales's successors in Ionia proposed elements other than water as this primal substance in the universe. One called it the "boundless," apparently a general concept for matter; another proposed "air," out of which all things come by a process of "rarefying and condensing"; a third asserted that fire was the "most mobile, transformable, most active, most life-giving" element. This search for a material substance as the first principle or cause of all things culminated two centuries after Thales in the atomic theory of Democritus (de-MO-kri-tus). To Democritus (c. 460–370 B.C.E.), reality was the mechanical motion of indivisible particles, which differed in shape, size, position, and arrangement but not in quality. Moving about continuously, these particles combined to create objects.

While these and other early Greek philosophers were proposing some form of matter as the basic element in nature, Pythagoras of Samos (c. 582–500 B.C.E.) countered with the profoundly significant idea that the "nature of things" was something nonmaterial: numbers. By experimenting with a vibrating chord, Pythagoras discovered that musical harmony is based on arithmetical proportions, and he intuitively concluded that the universe was constructed of numbers and their relationships. His mystical, nonmaterial interpretation of nature, together with his belief that the human body was distinct from the soul, greatly influenced the thinking of Plato.

An important result of early Greek philosophical speculation was the further questioning of conventional beliefs and traditions. In religion, for example, Anaximander argued that thunder and lightning were caused by blasts of wind and not by Zeus's thunderbolts. Xenophanes (ze-NO-fah-neez) went on to ridicule the traditional view of the gods: "If oxen and lions had hands, . . . they would make portraits and statues of their gods in their own image."

The eroding of traditional beliefs was intensified during the last half of the fifth century B.C.E. by the activity of professional teachers, called Sophists ("intellectuals"). They taught a variety of subjects—the nucleus of our present arts and sciences—that they claimed would lead to material success. The most popular subjects they taught were methods of persuasion and successful argumentation; some even claimed to be able to teach virtue and wisdom to students who paid for their knowledge. The Sophists tried to put all conventional beliefs to the test of rational criticism and subjected human beliefs, customs, and even laws to rational analysis. Some even concluded that truth itself was relative, having no firm existence other than in the decisions and institutions of society. Such speculation questioned the existence of fixed universal standards to guide human actions.

The Contribution of Socrates

A contemporary of the early Sophists but opposed to many of their conclusions was the Athenian Socrates (SO-kra-teez). Like the Sophists, Socrates (c. 470–399 B.C.E.) turned from concern with the gods to human affairs. But unlike them, Socrates believed that by asking meaningful questions and subjecting the answers to logical analysis, agreement could be reached about ethical standards and rules of conduct in human affairs. And so he would question his fellow citizens who possessed a certain skill or particular talent in hopes of learning more about the principles that determine human behavior. He found that his fellow citizens possessed no such knowledge. Instead, he found that he was accused of undermining the institutions and values of the city-state through his constant questioning of socially accepted customs and institutions. His dislike of democracy, which he believed to be a government in which important decisions were usually made by badly informed or even totally ignorant participants, earned him the hostility of most of his fellow citizens. In spite of the growing suspicion that he was a subversive, he continued to emphasize his own individualism and his belief that the pursuit of philosophy was the best way to improve the soul and to assert that he was an ignorant man in search of knowledge, rather than a teacher of others.

In time Socrates' quest for truth led to conflict with the state. In 399 B.C.E. the Athenians, unnerved by their defeat in the Peloponnesian War and concerned about subversion from within, put Socrates on trial for introducing new gods into Athens and corrupting the youth. He was found guilty and was condemned to death. Although he was given a chance to escape that fate, he refused to do so, choosing instead to observe the polis's laws, but still retaining the right to question and analyze them.

Plato and His Theory of Ideas

After Socrates' death, philosophical leadership passed to his most famous student, Plato (427–347 B.C.E.). Like Socrates, Plato believed that truth exists, but only in the realm of thought, the spiritual world of ideas or forms. Such universal truths as beauty, good, and justice exist apart from the material world, and the beauty, good, and justice encountered in the world of the senses are only imperfect reflections of eternal and changeless ideas. The task for humans is to come to know the true reality—the eternal ideas—behind these imperfect reflections. Only the soul and the "soul's pilot," reason, can accomplish this goal, for the human soul is spiritual and immortal, and in its original state it existed beyond the "heavens" where ultimate truth also is found.

Disillusioned with the democracy that had led Athens to ruin in the Peloponnesian War and that had condemned Socrates to death, Plato put forward his concept of an ideal state in the *Republic*, the first systematic work on political science. The state's basic function, founded on the idea of justice, was the satisfaction of the common good. Plato described a kind of ideal polis in which the state regulated every aspect of life, including thought. Accordingly, poets and forms of music considered unworthy were prohibited. Private property was abolished on the grounds that it bred selfishness. Plato believed there was no essential difference between men and women; therefore, women received the same education and held the same occupations as men, including military training. Individuals belonged to one of three classes and found happiness only through their contribution to the community: workers by producing the necessities of life, warriors by guarding the state, and philosophers by ruling in the best interests of all the people.

Plato founded the Academy in Athens, the famous school that existed from about 388 B.C.E. until 529 C.E., when it was closed by the Christian emperor Justinian. Here Plato taught and encouraged his students, whom he expected to become the intellectual elite who would go on to reform society.

Aristotle, the Encyclopedic Philosopher

Plato's greatest pupil was Aristotle (384–322 B.C.E.), who set up his own school, the Lyceum (lai-SEE-um), at Athens. Reacting against the otherworldly directions of Plato's thought, Aristotle insisted that ideas have no separate existence apart from the material world—knowledge of universal ideas is the result of the painstaking collection and organization of particular facts. Aristotle's Lyceum, accordingly, became a center for the analysis of data from many branches of learning.

DOCUMENT
Aristotle on Slavery

Aristotle's works remain among the most influential contributions to Western thought. Much of his speculation deals with what he called the "philosophy of human affairs," whose object is the acquisition and maintenance of human happiness. Two kinds of virtue *(arête)*, intellectual and moral, which produce two types of happiness, are described in the *Ethics*. Intellectual virtue is the product of reason, and only such people as philosophers and scientists ever attain it. Much more important for the good of society is moral virtue—virtues of character, such as justice, bravery, and temperance—which is the product less of reason than of habit and thus can be acquired by all. In this connection Aristotle introduced his "doctrine of the mean" as a guide for good conduct. He considered all moral virtues to be means between extremes; courage, for example, is the mean between cowardice and rashness. In the *Politics* Aristotle viewed the state as necessary "for the sake of the good life," because its laws and educational system provide the most effective training needed for the attainment of moral virtue and, as a result of that moral virtue——happiness. To Aristotle, the viewpoint that the state stands in opposition to the individual would not be valid.

There have probably been few geniuses whose interests were as widespread as Aristotle's. He investigated such diverse fields as biology (his minute observations include the life cycle of the gnat), mathematics, astronomy, physics, literary criticism (the concept of **catharsis**—art as a release of emotion), rhetoric, logic (deductive and inductive), politics (he analyzed 158 Greek and foreign constitutions), ethics, and metaphysics. His knowledge was so encyclopedic that there is hardly a college course today that does not take note of what Aristotle had to say on the subject. Although his works on natural science are now mostly historical curiosities, they held a place of undisputed authority until the scientific revolution of the sixteenth and seventeenth centuries. But in no important sense are his humanistic studies, such as the *Ethics* and the *Politics*, out of date.

Medicine

Superstitions about the human body held back the development of medical science until 420 B.C.E., when Hippocrates (hip-PO-kra-teez), the "father of medicine," founded a school in which he emphasized the value of observation and the careful interpretation of symptoms. Such modern medical terms as *crisis*, *acute*, and *chronic* were first used by Hippocrates. He was firmly convinced that disease resulted from natural, not supernatural, causes. The Hippocratic school also gave medicine a sense of service to humanity that it has never lost. All members took the famous Hippocratic Oath, still in use today.

Despite using the empirical approach, the Hippocratic school adopted the theory that the body contained four liquids or *humors*—blood, phlegm, black bile, and yellow bile—whose proper balance was the basis of health. This popular doctrine was to impede medical progress in Europe until the seventeenth century.

The Writing of History

If history is defined as an honest attempt to find out what happened and then to explain why it happened, Herodotus (he-RO-doh-tuhs) of Halicarnassus (c. 484–c. 425 B.C.E.) deserves to be called the founder of that discipline. In his well-researched and highly entertaining history of the Persian Wars, he identified the clash of two distinct civilizations, the Greek and the Near Eastern. His portrayal of both the

DOCUMENT
Herodotus, *Histories*

Greeks and the Persians was in most cases impartial, but his fondness for a good story often led him to include tall tales in his work. As he stated more than once, "My duty is to report what has been said, but I do not have to believe it."

The first truly scientific historian was Thucydides (460–400 B.C.E.), who wrote a notably objective account of the Peloponnesian War. Although Thucydides was a contemporary of the events and a loyal Athenian, a reader can scarcely detect whether he favored Athens or Sparta. Thucydides believed that his history would become a useful tool for those who desire a clear picture

DOCUMENT
Thucydides on Athens

of what has happened and, human nature being as it is, what is likely to be repeated in the future. His belief was based on his remarkable ability to analyze and explain human behavior and the nature of politics.

Greek Poetry and Drama

Greek literary periods can be classified according to the dominant poetic forms that reflect particular stages of the culture's development. First came the time of great epic poems, followed by periods in which lyric poetry and then drama flourished.

Sometime during the eighth century B.C.E. in Ionia, the *Iliad* and the *Odyssey*, the two great epics attributed to Homer, were set down in their present form. The *Iliad*, describing the clash of arms between the Greeks and Trojans, glorifies heroic bravery and physical strength against a background of divine intervention in human affairs. The *Odyssey*, relating the adventure-filled wanderings of Odysseus on his return to Greece after Troy's fall, places less stress on divine intervention and more on the cool resourcefulness of the hero in escaping from danger and in regaining his kingdom. These stirring epics have provided inspiration and source material for many generations of poets.

As Greek society continued to develop and seek new varieties of artistic expression, a new type of poetry, written to be sung to the accompaniment of a small stringed instrument called a lyre, became popular among the Ionian Greeks. Unlike Homer, authors of this lyric poetry sang not of legendary events but of present delights and sorrows.

DOCUMENT
Greek Poetry

Drama (also in verse) developed from the religious rites of Dionysus (son of Zeus from an affair with the daughter of the king of Tyre) in which a large chorus and its leader sang and danced. The legendary Thespis, supposedly a contemporary of Solon, added an actor called the "answerer" (*hypocrites*, the origin of our word *hypocrite*) to converse with the chorus and its leader. This innovation made dramatic dialogue possible. By

---

catharsis—A word which means "cleansing" in Greek, but in its application to ancient Greek tragedy, its meaning is more specifically "a purging of pity and fear"—the desired effect of the performance on the audience.

The World According to Herodotus, c. 450 B.C.E.

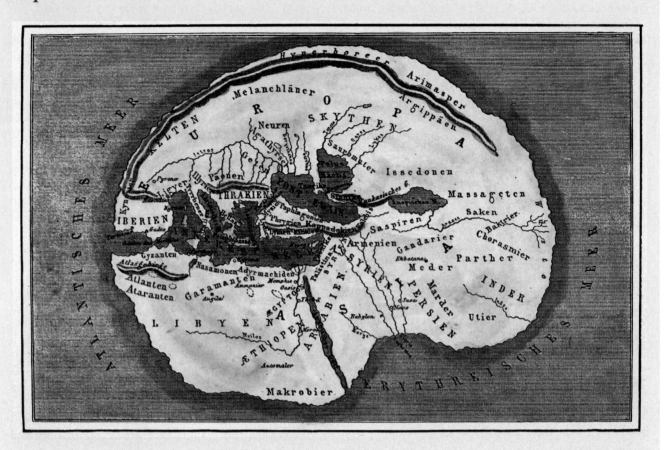

This map depicts the known world at the time of the Greek historian Herodotus, who lived and worked around 450–425 B.C.E. The map is a modern rendition of what we know Herodotus thought to be the world, as described in his writings, the *Histories*. The *Histories* was written to describe the events and circumstances that led the Greeks and the Persians to engage in war—a war that Herodotus believed changed the direction of human history. To understand why these two great powers came into conflict, the historian believed he would have to examine the origins, geographical setting, culture, and traditions of the whole empire of the Persians, as well as the background of the Greek city-states. The *Histories* became not just a listing of chronological events but an exploration of geography, sociology, and anthropology as well.

We are certain that Herodotus himself traveled extensively throughout his world in order to learn firsthand of the people he described. Most of his geographical knowledge came from his own observations or from interviews with the people he met. He seems to have believed that the earth was a flat disk, although he must have been familiar with contemporary theories that the world might be a sphere. He differed from most of his contemporaries in not picturing Europe, Africa (which he called Libya), and Asia as approximately the same size. He described Europe as being as long as both Asia and Africa put together. Yet Herodotus did not travel to the farthest reaches of the continent but relied on accounts of others; he knew nothing of the existence of Britain or Scandinavia, for example, and he did not know if Europe was surrounded by water to the west or north. His knowledge of Asia was limited to the lands of the Persian Empire. He knew that the Caspian Sea was an inland sea and not, as most of his contemporaries believed, a sea that emptied into the band of ocean that encircled the earth. He also knew that Africa was surrounded by water—a fact that the geographer Ptolemy missed 500 years later.

Questions to Consider

1. How might you account for some of the major errors in Herodotus's geographical knowledge?

2. Are there any features of the map which you find to be remarkably accurate for Herodotus's time?

3. Do you see any significance in the proportions of the map, and what region is placed in the center?

the fifth century B.C.E. in Athens, two distinct forms, tragedy and comedy, had evolved. Borrowing from the old familiar legends of gods and heroes for their plots, the tragedians reinterpreted them from the point of view of the values and problems of their own times.

In reworking the old legends of the heroic age, Aeschylus (ES-kuh-luhs; 525–456 B.C.E.) attempted to present the new values being considered regarding Greek religion, first expressed in Hesiod's work, by showing how following the old unsophisticated beliefs leads to suffering. In his trilogy, the *Oresteia*, for example, he concerned himself with hubris as applied to the murder of the hero Agamemnon by his queen following his return from the Trojan War. Aeschylus then proceeded to work out its effects—one murder after another murder until people, through suffering, learn to substitute the moral law of Zeus for the primitive law of the blood feud.

A generation later, Sophocles (c. 496–406 B.C.E.) continued to explore the themes of divine justice, morality, and ethics, while concentrating, in addition, on character development and psychological themes. Euripides (eu-RI-pi-deez; c. 480–406 B.C.E.), the last of the great Athenian tragedians, reflects the rationalism and critical spirit of the late fifth century B.C.E. His plays concentrate more on the personalities of his characters and their interesting behavior, rather than on the overriding power of fate or the gods.

Greek comedies were full of satire and scathing criticism of contemporary prominent citizens. There were no libel laws in Athens, and Aristophanes (a-ri-STO-fah-neez; c. 445–385 B.C.E.), the famous comic-dramatist and a conservative in outlook, brilliantly satirized Athenian democracy as a mob led by demagogues, the Sophists (among whom he included Socrates) as subversive, and Euripides as an opponent of civic spirit and traditional values.

Greek Architecture

During the formative, archaic period of Greek art (c. 700–480 B.C.E.), architecture flourished in Ionia, Greece, and the Greek colonies in Sicily and southern

In the Parthenon, great care was taken to design a perfect building, both structurally and visually. The topics of the Doric columns lean toward the center, and the columns are more widely spaced in the middle of each row than at the ends. All these refinements create an illusion of perfect regularity that would be lacking if the parts were actually regular. Sculpture adorned the triangular gables and part of the frieze just below the gables; another sculptured frieze ran around the walls inside the colonnade. The whole building was once painted in bright colors.

Italy. Reflecting the prosperity produced by colonization, large stone temples were constructed. Their form may have developed from wooden structures that had been influenced by the remains of Mycenaean palaces, and perhaps by Egyptian temples or the religious architecture of the Near East.

The classical phase of Greek architecture reached its zenith in Athens during the second half of the fifth century B.C.E. The Parthenon, the Erechtheum (e-rek-THEE-um), and the other temples on the Acropolis in Athens exhibit the highly developed features that make Greek structures so pleasing to the eye. All relationships, such as column spacing and height and the slight curvature of floor and roof lines, were calculated and executed with remarkable precision to achieve the illusion of a perfect balance, both structurally and visually. The three orders, or styles, usually identified by the characteristics of the columns, were the **Doric,** which was used in the Parthenon; the **Ionic,** seen in the Erechtheum; and the later and more ornate **Corinthian.**

Erectheion,
Athens

Greek temples afford an interesting comparison with those of Egypt. Egyptian temples were enclosed by walls and only priests and royalty could enter the inner rooms, but the Greek temple was open, with a colonnade porch and an inside room containing a statue of the god or goddess. Animal sacrifice and ritual took place outside the temple, where the sacrificial altar was placed.

Other types of buildings, notably the theaters, stadia, and gymnasia, also express the Greek spirit and way of life. In the open-air theaters, the circular shape of the spectators' sections and the plan of the orchestra section set a style that has survived to the present day.

Greek Sculpture and Pottery

Greek sculpture is usually described as having passed through three stages of development: the archaic, the classical, and the Hellenistic periods. Greek sculpture of the archaic period, although crude in its representation of human anatomy, displays the freshness and liveliness of youth. Influenced clearly by Egyptian models, the statues of nude youths and draped maidens usually stand stiffly with clenched fists and with one foot thrust awkwardly forward. The fixed smile and formalized treatment of hair and drapery also reveal the sculptors' struggle to master the technique of their art.

The mastery of technique by 480 B.C.E. began the classical period of fifth-century Greek sculpture, whose principles of harmony and proportion shaped the development of art in the West for centuries after the Greeks. Sculpture from this period displays both the end of technical immaturity and the beginning of idealization of the human form, which reached its culmination in the dignity and poise of Phidias's (FI-dee-uhs) figures in the continuous **frieze** and **pediments** of the Parthenon. Carved with restraint and proportion, the frieze represents the citizens of Athens participating in a procession in honor of their patron goddess, Athena, which took place every four years.

The more relaxed nature of fourth-century B.C.E. Greek sculpture, while still considered classical, lacks some of the grandeur and dignity of fifth-century art. Charm, grace, and individuality characterize the work of Praxiteles (prax-IT-el-eez), the most famous sculptor of the century. These qualities can be seen in his flowing statues of the god Hermes holding the young Dionysus and of Aphrodite stepping into her bath.

The making of pottery, the oldest Greek art, started at the beginning of the Greek Middle Age (c. 1150 B.C.E.) with crude imitations of late Mycenaean forms. Soon the old Mycenaean patterns were replaced by abstract geometrical designs. With the coming of the archaic period came paintings of scenes from mythology and daily life. We are able to form an impression of what Greek painting, now lost, must have been like from surviving Greek pottery and mosaics. The buildings and sculpture we observe today as stark white marble creations were in all likelihood lavishly and brightly painted in the colors the Greeks obviously loved.

THE HELLENISTIC AGE, 336–30 B.C.E.

■ *How did the Hellenistic Age differ from the Greek civilization that preceded it?*

The Hellenistic Age is the three-century period beginning with the career of Alexander the Great to the rise

---

Doric—Specific form of the capital (or crown) of a Greek column. A capital in the Doric order is squat and simple without elaborate decoration and originated in wooden temples.

Ionic—Specific form of the capital (or crown) of a Greek column. A capital of the Ionic order is usually decorated with scrolls (or volutes).

Corinthian—Specific form of the capital (or crown) of a Greek column. Corinthian capitals are the most highly decorated of the three orders of Greek columns, with carved acanthus leaves and scrolls.

---

frieze—In Greek architecture, a long, narrow, horizontal panel often decorated with relief sculpture and placed around the walls of a room or a temple.

pediment—The most dominant feature of the front of a Greek temple. A triangular construction that sits on top of the temple's facade.

Macedonia and Alexander

359–336 B.C.E.	Reign of Philip II
338 B.C.E.	Philip conquers Greek city-states
336–323 B.C.E.	Reign of Alexander the Great
334 B.C.E.	Alexander invades Persian Empire
331 B.C.E.	Battle at Gaugamela
327 B.C.E.	Alexander enters India
323 B.C.E.	Alexander dies

Alexander the Great and the Hellenistic Age

of Augustus Caesar, the first of the Roman emperors, who completed Rome's domination of the Mediterranean world by adding Greek-ruled Egypt to Rome's empire in 30 B.C.E. The Hellenistic Age, begun by the creation of Alexander the Great's vast conquests, was a period of economic expansion, cosmopolitanism, striking intellectual and artistic achievements, and the wide distribution of Greek culture.

Alexander the Great

When Philip of Macedonia was assassinated in 336 B.C.E., his authority was claimed by his 20-year-old son, Alexander. Alexander proved himself a remarkably gifted individual from the very beginning of his reign by gaining the support of the Macedonian nobles, even though some of them suspected the young man of being involved in Philip's murder. Alexander persuaded his father's old generals and comrades to swear their loyalty to him and proceeded to demand the loyalty of the Greek League, which had been founded by his father. When the Greek city of Thebes responded to a rumor that Alexander had been killed in battle by rebelling against the Macedonians, the young king marched his army quickly to the south and ruthlessly crushed the city, selling its remaining inhabitants into slavery. The Greeks were horrified at such brutal action, but a lesson was learned, and few states dared consider rebellion in the years ahead.

Alexander is one of history's most remarkable individuals. Of average height and looks for a Macedonian, he nevertheless impressed his contemporaries as a gifted athlete, a charismatic personality, and a natural leader. Both his father, Philip, and his mother, Olympias, a princess from Illyria, were strong influ-

This small but expertly crafted ivory is thought to be a representation of King Philip, his second wife Olympias, and their young son Alexander (the Great). The three figures are probably represented as participants in a religious ritual dedicated to the god Dionysus. The object was found among the royal graves of the Macedonian monarchs in Vergina.

ences on him. Philip earned his son's respect as a king and a general, and Olympias was a forceful woman who wished great things for her son and who constantly assured the boy that his true father was not Philip, but the god Zeus.

Having been tutored by Aristotle, Alexander was taught the superiority of Greek culture and wished to be the fulfillment of the Greek ideal. Reveling in the heroic deeds of the *Iliad*, which he always kept at his bedside, Alexander saw himself as a new Achilles waging war against barbarians when he planned to complete his father's desire to avenge the Persian attacks on Greece by conquering the Persian Empire. In 334 B.C.E. he set out with an army of 35,000 soldiers recruited from Macedonia and the Greek League. In quick succession he subdued Asia Minor, Syria, and Palestine, defeating the Persians in two great battles. He marched into Egypt, where the Egyptians welcomed him as a deliverer from their Persian masters and recognized him as pharaoh, the living god-king of Egypt.

Greatly impressed with Egypt and its traditions, Alexander wished to spend more time there. But Darius III, the Persian king, was gathering one more massive army to oppose the invader, and Alexander marched into Mesopotamia to meet the Persians for a final battle. In 331 B.C.E., at Gaugamela, near the ancient city of Nineveh, the Macedonians defeated the Persian forces. Darius III was executed by his own relatives as he fled, and Alexander became Great King of the Persian Empire. Alexander led his victorious troops to the ancient Persian capital city of Persepolis (per-SE-poh-lis), but his campaigns did not end there. He wished to command the loyalty of all Persian lands and to extend the great empire to even farther reaches. He led his troops north through Media and Bactria, then south and east into present-day Afghanistan, finally venturing as far east as the rich river valleys of India. There his weary and frightened soldiers, many of whom had been away from home for more than ten years, forced him to turn back.

In 323 B.C.E. Alexander fell ill with a mysterious fever. Perhaps he had contracted malaria in India; perhaps he fell victim to his accumulated battle wounds;

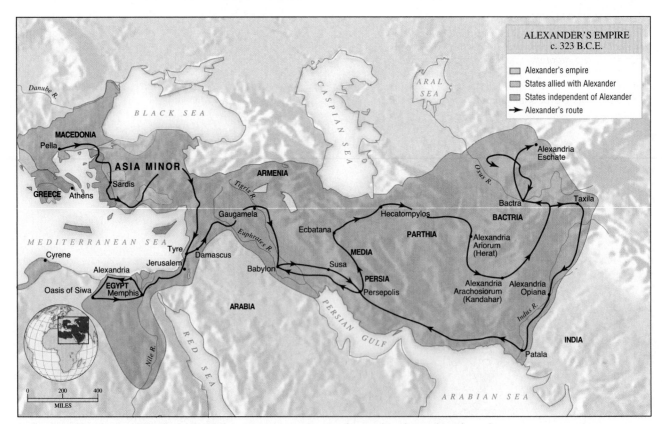

At the time of his death, Alexander had laid claim to a vast empire. One biographer claims that Alexander was planning more conquests when he recovered from his illness—perhaps north into what is now Russia or along the northern coast of Africa and eventually to Rome.

Document   Arrian: Alexander the Leader

Arrian wrote his account of Alexander's campaigns in the second century C.E., almost 500 years after Alexander's death. Yet we can have great trust in most of his account, since Arrian evidently had access to accounts and diaries contemporary with Alexander. The following is a description of Alexander's inspirational leadership during an extremely difficult crossing of the southern Iranian desert in hopes of returning to Babylon:

The army was crossing a desert of sand; the sun was already blazing down upon them, but they were struggling on under the necessity of reaching water, which was still far away. Alexander, like everyone else, was tormented by thirst, but he was nonetheless marching on foot at the head of his men. It was all he could do to keep going, but he did so, and the result (as always) was that the men were better able to endure their misery when they saw that it was equally shared. As they toiled on, a party of light infantry which had gone off looking for water found some—just a wretched little trickle collected in a shallow gully. They scooped up with difficulty what they could and hurried back, with their priceless treasure, to Alexander; then, just before they reached him, they tipped the water into a helmet and gave it to him. Alexander, with a word of thanks for the gift, took the helmet and gave it full view of his troops, poured the water on the ground. So extraordinary was the effect of this action that the water wasted by Alexander was as good as a drink for every man in the army. I cannot praise this act too highly; it was a proof, if anything was, not only of his power of endurance, but also of his genius for leadership.

Questions to Consider

1. Do you think that this account could be factual, or is it most likely propaganda? Why?
2. How could such an act of wastefulness be an inspiration to an army?
3. Do you think that the myth of Alexander was, and is, perhaps more important than the historical reality of the man? Give several reasons for your answer.

From Arrian, *Anabasis*, 6.26 in A. de Selincourt, *The Campaigns of Alexander* (New York: Penguin Books, 1958).

---

perhaps his years of heavy drinking had taken their toll; perhaps, as rumor had it, he had been slowly poisoned by his enemies in the Macedonian camp. Whatever the case, after a short illness, and without designating an heir to his empire, Alexander died in Babylon at the age of 32.

Alexander the Great is a puzzling figure to modern historians. Some view him as a ruthless conqueror who never lost a battle and a despot who ordered even his fellow Macedonians to prostrate themselves in his presence. Others picture him as a farsighted visionary hoping to unite East and West in one world and seeking the eventual "brotherhood of man" by establishing equality for all individuals through the unity of a common Greek culture.

Some of Alexander's military and administrative policies sought to unify the lands he conquered and to promote what he himself called "concord and partnership in the empire" between easterners and westerners. He blended Persians with Greeks and Macedonians in his army and administration; he founded numerous cities—70, according to tradition—in the East and settled many of his followers in them; and he married two oriental princesses and encouraged his officers and men to take foreign wives. Finally, for perhaps egotistical and certainly for political reasons, he ordered the Greek city-states to accord him "divine honors."

Alexander was a remarkable blend of the romantic idealist and the practical realist, contrasting traits that he may have inherited from his parents. His mother, Olympias, who practiced the rites of the cult of Dionysus and claimed to be a descendant of the Greek hero Achilles, instilled in her son the consciousness of a divine mission that drove him onward, even to seeking the end of the earth beyond India. Much like his father, he demonstrated

IMAGE
Mosaic of Alexander the Great

remarkable abilities as military commander, expert diplomat, and able political administrator. Alexander was a self-confident idealist who was excited by challenges, but meeting those challenges forced him to take actions that were practical and pragmatic. For example, he could not merely conquer the Great King of Persia; he had to act as his successor as well. Alexander ruled for only 13 years, but in many ways a large part of the world was never again the same.

The Division of Alexander's Empire

With the Greeks now masters of the ancient Near East, a new and distinctly **cosmopolitan** period in their history and culture began—the Hellenistic ("Greek-like") Age. For several decades following Alexander's sudden death, his generals competed against each other for the spoils of empire. Three major Hellenistic kingdoms emerged and maintained an uneasy balance of power until the Roman conquests of the second and first centuries B.C.E.: Egypt, ruled by Alexander's friend and general Ptolemy (TO-le-mee) and his successors; Asia, comprising most of the remaining provinces of the Persian Empire and held together with great difficulty by the dynasty founded by Seleucus (se-LEU-kus); and Macedonia and Greece, ruled by the descendants of Antigonus (an-TI-go-nuhs) the One-Eyed.

While the Antigonids in Macedonia followed the model of Alexander's father, Philip, in ruling as national kings selected by the army, the Ptolemies ruled Egypt as divine pharaohs, and some of the Seleucids attempted to have themselves recognized as "saviors" and "benefactors" of their subjects. Ptolemaic and Seleucid administrations were centralized in bureaucracies staffed mainly by Greeks, an arrangement that created a vast gulf between rulers and ruled.

Plagued by native revolts, dynastic troubles, and civil war, the Hellenistic kingdoms eventually began to crumble. Macedonia lost effective control of Greece by 250 B.C.E. when Athens asserted its independence and most of the other Greek states resisted Macedonian domination by forming two federal leagues, the Achaean and the Aetolian (a-TOH-li-an). Toward the end of the third century B.C.E. the Romans became involved in the rivalries

of the city-state and Macedonian monarchy and eventually added all Greece and Macedonia into their growing empire.

The eastern reaches of Alexander's empire—Parthia, Bactria, and India—gradually broke out of Seleucid control. Pergamum, in northwestern Asia Minor, renounced its allegiance to the Seleucids and became an independent kingdom famous for its artists and scholars. By 200 B.C.E. the Romans had entered the scene, and by 30 B.C.E. Rome had annexed all but the last remaining Hellenistic state, Egypt; in that very year Cleopatra, the last reigning member of the dynasty founded by Ptolemy, was captured by the Romans and committed suicide.

HELLENISTIC SOCIETY AND CULTURE

■ *What were the results of the expansion of Hellenistic civilization?*

The Hellenistic Age was a time of economic expansion and social change. In the wake of Alexander's conquests, thousands of Greeks moved eastward to begin a new era of Greek colonization, ending the long economic depression that followed the breakup of the Athenian Empire. An economic union of East and West permitted the free flow of trade, and prosperity was stimulated further when Alexander put into circulation huge amounts of Persian gold and silver and introduced a uniform coinage. The result was a much larger and more affluent middle class than had existed previously. The condition of the poor, however, was made worse by rising prices.

VIDEO

Greek Heritage in Turkey

By the third century B.C.E. the center of trade had shifted from Greece to the Near East. Largest of the Hellenistic cities, and much larger than any cities in Greece itself, were Antioch, in northern Syria, and Alexandria, in Egypt. The riches of India, Persia, Arabia, and the Fertile Crescent were brought by sea and land to these Mediterranean ports.

Alexandria outdistanced all other Hellenistic cities as a commercial center. Its merchants supplied the ancient world with wheat, linen, papyrus, glass, and jewelry. Boasting a population of nearly a million, the city had a double harbor in which a great lighthouse, judged one of the wonders of the ancient world, rose to a height estimated at 370 feet. Its busy streets were filled with a mixture of peoples—Greeks, Macedonians, Jews, and Egyptians. As in all other Hellenistic cities in the Near East, the privileged

---

cosmopolitan—A person or thing that belongs to all the world; free from local or national prejudices or limitations. From Greek *cosmopolites* ("citizen of the world").

Greeks and Macedonians were at the top of the social scale and the mass of native population at the bottom; the large Jewish population lived apart and was allowed a significant degree of self-government. Labor was so cheap that slavery hardly existed in Hellenistic Egypt. As a consequence, worker-organized strikes were frequent.

Hellenistic Philosophy

Developments in philosophical thought reflected the changed conditions of the Hellenistic Age. With a growing sense that individual significance was decreased in the large Hellenistic states, in which the vitality of the polis seemed to give way to a more isolated existence, philosophers concerned themselves less with the reform of society and more with the attainment of happiness for the individual. "There is no point in saving the Greeks" is the way one Hellenistic philosopher summed up the new outlook, quite in contrast to that of Socrates, Plato, and Aristotle. This emphasis on peace of mind for the individual living in an insecure world led to the rise of four principal schools of Hellenistic philosophy, all of which had their beginnings in Athens.

The Skeptics and Cynics reflected most clearly the doubts and misgivings of the times. The Skeptics hoped to achieve freedom from anxiety by denying the possibility of finding truth. The wise, they argued, will suspend judgment and not preach to others because they had learned that sensory experience, the only source of knowledge, is deceptive. They believed that real knowledge was impossible to achieve, and that it was not crucial to achieve it anyway. The Skeptics busied themselves with pointing out the errors they identified in the other opposing schools of philosophy. The Cynics believed that withdrawing from the world was the best way to deal with the miseries life held for humans. They advocated rejection of virtually all social conventions, traditions, and religious values. Cynic philosophers, most notably Diogenes of Sinope (c. 400–325 B.C.E.), wandered from city to city, dressed in rags, begging, and performing lewd acts in public to call attention to his rejection of conformity.

More socially acceptable and popular were the schools of Epicureanism and Stoicism. The Athenian Epicurus (342–270 B.C.E.) taught that happiness could be achieved simply by freeing the body from pain and the mind from fear—particularly the fear of death. To reach this dual goal, people must avoid bodily excesses, including sensual pleasures, and accept the scientific teaching of Democritus that both body and soul are composed of atoms that fall

apart at death. Beyond death there is no existence and nothing to fear. Epicurus maintained that the finest pleasures are intellectual and that the gods do not concern themselves with humans, but instead spend their time pursuing true pleasure, like good Epicureans.

The Stoics, followers of Zeno (c. 336–c. 264 B.C.E.), a Semite who settled in Athens, argued in contrast to Epicureanism that the universe is controlled by some power—variously called destiny, reason, natural law, providence, or God—that determines everything that happens. Fortified by this knowledge, wise Stoics conform their will to be in harmony with natural order and "stoically" accept whatever part fortune gives to them in the drama of life. The Epicurean retreated from worldly responsibilities, but the Stoic urged participation. Stoicism's stern sense of duty and belief in the equality of all people under a single ruling force made it particularly attractive to the Roman successors to power in the Hellenistic world conquerors of the ancient world.

Science and Mathematics

The Greek concern for rational, impartial inquiry reached a high level of development in the Hellenistic period, particularly in Alexandria, where the dynasty of the Ptolemies subsidized a great research institute, the Museum, and a library of more than half a million books. Emphasizing specialization and experimentation and enriched by the inheritance of Near Eastern astronomy and mathematics, Greek science in the third century B.C.E. achieved results unmatched until the seventeenth century.

The expansion of geographical knowledge resulting from Alexander's conquests inspired scientists to make more accurate maps and to estimate the size of the earth, which had been identified as a globe through observation of its shadow in a lunar eclipse. Eratosthenes (e-rah-TOS-the-neez), the outstanding geographer of the century, drew parallels of latitude and longitude on his map of the inhabited world and calculated the circumference of the globe (within 1 percent, an error of 195 miles) by measuring the difference in the angles of the noonday sun's shadows at Aswan and Alexandria. In astronomy, Aristarchus (a-ri-STAR-kus) put forward the radical theory that the earth rotates on its axis and moves in an orbit around the sun. Most of his contemporaries, however, held to a belief in the prevailing geocentric theory, which stated that the earth was stationary and the sun revolved around it. Not only was this view supported by the powerful authority of Aristotle, but it also seemed to explain all the known facts of celestial motion. This was particularly true after Hipparchus (hi-PAR-kus) in the next century added the new idea of *epicycles*—each planet revolves in its own small orbit while moving around the earth. Aristarchus's **heliocentric theory** was forgotten until the sixteenth century C.E., when it was revived by Copernicus.

Mathematics also made great advances in the third century B.C.E. Euclid (EU-klid) systematized the theorems of plane and solid geometry, and Archimedes (ar-ke-MEE-deez) of Syracuse, who had studied at Alexandria, calculated the value of *pi*, invented a terminology for expressing numbers up to any magnitude, and established the rudiments of calculus. Archimedes also discovered specific gravity by noticing that he displaced water when submerged in his bath. And, despite his dislike for making practical use of his knowledge, he invented the compound pulley and the windlass—a lifting device consisting of a horizontal cylinder turned by a crank on which a rope or cable is wound.

The Hellenistic Greeks also contributed to the advances in medicine made earlier by Hippocrates and his school. By dissecting bodies of dead criminals, they were able to trace the outlines of the nervous system, to understand the principle of the circulation of the blood, and to ascertain that the brain, not the heart, is the true center of consciousness.

Hellenistic Art and Literature

The large number of new cities that sprang up in Hellenistic times served as a tremendous impetus to new developments and experiments in architecture. These new municipalities benefited from town planning; the streets were laid out on a rectangular grid. The great public buildings were elaborate and highly ornamented; this was an age that preferred the ornate Corinthian column to the simpler Doric and Ionic styles of decoration.

Hellenistic sculptors continued and intensified the realistic, dramatic, and emotional approach that began to appear in late classical sculpture. Supported by rulers and other rich patrons in such affluent cities as Alexandria, Antioch, Rhodes, and Pergamum, they displayed their technical virtuosity by representing violent scenes, writhing forms, and dramatic poses, all

This representation of the goddess of erotic love, Aphrodite (Venus in Latin), being defended by her young son Eros (Cupid) from the advances of the god Pan, was crafted around 100 B.C.E. and is now in the Acropolis Museum in Athens. It is an excellent example of the realism, emotion, and even humor conveyed by much of Hellenistic sculpture.

with a realism that could make stone simulate flesh. Like most postclassical art, little evidence remained of the balance and restraint of classical Greek sculpture. Much of Hellenistic sculpture, with its twisted poses, contorted faces, and swollen muscles, stands in obvious contrast to the works of classical Greece seeking balance, harmony, and restraint.

Literature produced in the Hellenistic Age was generally more narrow and scholarly in its appeal than the earlier literary forms of the classical period. Scholarship flourished, and we are in debt for the

---

heliocentric theory—An astronomical theory, now proven as fact, that the sun resides at the center of the planetary system. *Heliocentric* in Greek literally means "sun centered."

Late Hellenistic sculptors avoided the stylized and perfect bodies preferred by the artists of the classical period and chose instead to portray the realistic and commonplace in their work. This famous sculpture of a drunken old woman shows not only the great skill of the artist, but also the radical shift in artistic themes now more popular and acceptable in the Hellenistic Age.

preservation of much of Greek classical literature to the subsidized scholars who worked at the Library of Alexandria. They composed epics in imitation of Homer (one new feature was romantic love, not found in Homer), long poems on fundamental subjects like the weather, and short, witty epigrams—all in a highly polished style. These sophisticated scholars also invented a new type of romantic, escapist literature: pastoral poetry extolling the unspoiled life and loves of shepherds and their rustic love interests. Some of the best of the new poetry was written at Alexandria in the third century B.C.E. by Theocritus (thee-OH-kra-tus), who also composed very realistic verses.

The Hellenistic Contribution

The greatest contribution of the Hellenistic Age was the diffusion of Greek culture throughout the

ancient East and the newly rising Roman West. In the East, the cities that Alexander and his successors built were the agents for spreading Hellenistic culture from the Aegean Sea to India. Literate Asians learned Greek to facilitate trade and to read Greek literature. In Judea, upper class Jews built Greek theaters and **gymnasia** and adopted Greek speech, dress, and names.

For a time the Seleucid Empire provided the peace and economic stability necessary to ensure the partial Hellenization of a vast area. But with an insufficient number of Greeks to colonize so large an area as the Near East, the Greek cities remained only islands in an Asian ocean. As time passed, this ocean encroached more and more on the Hellenized outposts.

The gradual weakening of the loosely knit Seleucid Empire eventually resulted in the creation of independent kingdoms on the edge of the Greek world. In the middle of the third century, a nomad chieftain founded the kingdom of Parthia, situated between the Seleucid and Bactrian kingdoms. Claiming to be the heirs of the more ancient Persians, the Parthians expanded until 130 B.C.E., when they were able to take Babylonia away from Seleucid control. Although Parthia was essentially a native Iranian state, its inhabitants absorbed some Hellenistic culture. Cut off from Seleucid rule by the Parthian kingdom, Bactria also became independent. Its Greek rulers, descendants of Alexander's veterans, controlled the caravan route to India and issued some of the most beautiful of Greek coins. In 183 B.C.E. the Bactrians crossed into India and conquered the province of Gandhara. One result of the conquest was a strong Greek influence on Indian art (see Chapter 3).

In the history of western European civilization, there are few developments of greater significance than Rome's absorption of Hellenistic Greek culture and its transference of that Greek cultural heritage to later European tradition. The culture of the cosmopolitan Hellenistic Age, drawn mainly from its Greek origins, served as the vehicle through which Greece left its imprint on the Roman world. The process by which the Roman West absorbed the cultural legacy of the Greeks will be described in the next chapter.

---

gymnasia—The plural of gymnasium—an area or a room in which Greeks, usually younger men, came to exercise and converse. From Greek *gymnos* ("naked") and *gymnazein* ("to train").

CONCLUSION

The civilization developed by the ancient Greeks is certainly one of the most outstanding in the history of humanity at any time and at any place on our planet. Those cultures we usually call Western correctly look upon the ancient Greeks as one of the most significant influences in the formation of their cultures. For centuries, these Western cultures considered the Greeks to have been the sole originators of Western civilization, but more recent generations have properly recognized that the Greeks, although highly creative and original, still were influenced by the earlier civilizations of Asia and Egypt. Trade and commerce with these peoples brought knowledge of their skills and past achievements, from metalworking, war, and art to religion. The Greeks did not invent Western civilization in a vacuum.

But the ancient Greeks do deserve great admiration. They developed a culture that was quite different than any previous social achievement. Theirs was a culture that was human-centered; although observant of religion, the Greeks did not believe they were owned by the gods. The Greeks rivaled their own gods in their attempts to gain true knowledge of the secrets of philosophy and science, to produce perfection in art, architecture, and even government. Human self-confidence had never been as high, and the resulting achievements of Greek culture still remain as timeless contributions to human cultures worldwide.

Often it seems the most significant factor explaining the success of a culture contains the seeds of its greatest liability. One might propose that the independence of both individuals and city-states led to outstanding achievements. But that individuality also seems to have made it impossible for the Greeks to unify for any significant length of time or to avoid bitter rivalries and destructive war. In time, the Macedonian king Philip, and later his son Alexander, forced the Greeks to cooperate with the formation of a unified Greece, but much of the originality and creativity of that earlier vibrant Greek culture was lost in the process.

The final chapter of ancient Greek history is called the Hellenistic Age, in which Alexander and then his successors hoped to rule their new subjects in Greek fashion, imposing a superior Greek culture over their new subjects. The attempt was eventually unsuccessful. Alexander's conquest of the Persian empire has been hailed throughout the history of the West as a remarkable achievement, and largely as a noble effort to bring a superior civilization to a broader world. Even today the memory of that Western conquest of the East is remembered in Asia as one of the first of many attempts of the West to impose its brand of civilization on unwelcoming victims. Cultural exchange as well as suspicions over cultural motivations is as old as the ancient civilizations of both East and West. Yet in spite of the complexities brought about when the modern world attempts to find explanations of its difficulties in ancient rivalries, the lasting achievements of the Greeks deserve the admiration of us all. Their creativity, vitality, and humanness have left to the whole world a timeless cultural legacy.

Suggestions for Web Browsing

You can obtain more information about topics included in this chapter at the websites listed below. See also the companion website that accompanies this text, **http://www.ablongman.com/ brummett,** which contains an online study guide and additional resources.

Minoan Palaces
http://dilos.com/region/crete/minoan_pictures.html

Images and text from major Minoan archaeological sites, including Knossos.

Ancient Greek World
http://www.museum.upenn.edu/Greek_World/Index.html

A presentation by the University of Pennsylvania Museum of Archaeology and Anthropology. Text and museum artifacts tell the vivid story of life in ancient Greece: land and time; daily life, economy, religion, and death.

Perseus Project
http://www.perseus.tufts.edu/

An impressive compilation of information on Greek art, architecture, and literature. One of the most useful but also scholarly sites dealing with ancient Greece.

Vatican Museum: Greek Collection
http://www.christusrex.org/www1/vaticano/GP-Profano.html

The excellent works in the Vatican's Greek collection are displayed and discussed in this outstanding site.

Daily Life in Ancient Greece
http://members.aol.com/Donnclass/Greeklife.html

A wonderfully entertaining site on ancient Greek life—gives a feel for what life would be like in a variety of Greek city-states.

Women's Life in Greece and Rome
http://www.stoa.org/diotima/anthology/wlgr/

> *Details about the private life and legal status of women, in addition to biographies of prominent women of ancient Greece and Rome.*

Diotima: Women and Gender in the Ancient World
http://www.stoa.org/diotima/

> *An excellent site for information on women in ancient Greece—their political influence, occupations, dress, diet. A great range of information.*

Alexander the Great
http://united-states.asinah.net/american-encyclopedia/wikipedia/a/al/alexander_the_great.html

> *Web page detailing the life of the king of Macedonia and conqueror of the Persian Empire.*

Ancient Olympics
http://www.perseus.tufts.edu/Olympics/

> *Compare ancient and modern Olympic sports and read about the Olympic athletes who were famous in antiquity.*

Greek Warfare
http://www.dean.usma.edu/history/web03/atlases/ancient%20warfare/ancient%20warfare%20index.htm

> *Informative site for ancient Greek battles, logistics, and tactics. Excellent maps and diagrams of military campaigns.*

Literature and Film

Mary Renault, *The King Must Die* (Bantam, 1974), is an absorbing novel set in Mycenaean times. Several new and excellent works of historical fiction are Steven Pressfield, *Gates of Fire* (Bantam, 1999) and *The Tides of War* (Doubleday, 2000), dealing with the battle of Thermopylae and the general Alcibiades, respectively. Also outstanding are Tom Holt's *The Walled Orchard* (Warner, 1997) and *Olympiad* (Abacus, 2001). Anna Apostolou, *A Murder in Macedon* (St. Martin's, 1998), is a well-done novel dealing with the assassination of Philip, Alexander's father.

Some excellent video presentations dealing with ancient Greece are *The Mystery of the Minoans* (1999), *Atlantis—In Search of a Lost Continent* (1996; 2 tapes, Questar Edition), and *The Greeks: Crucible of Civilization* (2000; 2 tapes, PBS Home Video). Greek art and architecture are beautifully reviewed in *Art in Ancient Greece* (1994; 2 tapes, Kultur Video). *In the Footsteps of Alexander the Great* (1996; 2 tapes, PBS Home Video) is a modern trek over Alexander's ancient route through Asia.

Suggestions for Reading

John Boardman, Jasper Griffin, and Oswyn Murray, eds., *The Oxford History of the Classical World* (Oxford University Press, 1986) is one of the most comprehensive studies of ancient Greece and its culture. A shorter yet still excellent history is J. V. A. Fine, *The Ancient Greeks: A Critical History* (Belknap/Harvard University Press, 1983). John Chadwick's *The Mycenaean World* (Cambridge University Press, 1976) and Robert Drews's *The Coming of the Greeks* (Princeton University Press, 1988) are both excellent studies of the early Greek experience. For the classical period, some outstanding studies are Donald Kagan, *The Peloponnesian War* (Viking Press, 2003), and Sarah Pomeroy, *Goddesses, Whores, Wives, and Slaves: Women in Classical Antiquity* (Schocken, 1975). James Davidson's *Courtesans and Fishcakes* (St. Martin's, 1998) is a delightful study of Athenian manners and private life. Mark Munn, *The School of History: Athens in the Age of Socrates* (University of California Press, 2002) is an outstanding cultural history. For the Hellenistic period, see Peter Green's *Hellenistic History and Culture* (University of California Press, 1993) and his excellent biography of Alexander, *Alexander of Macedon: 356–323 B.C.* (Praeger, 1970).

CHAPTER 5

Roman Civilization

The Roman World, c. 900 B.C.E. to 476 C.E.

The remains of the Roman Forum stand today in the center of a vibrant city of more than a million people—in the capital of Italy, a center of world commerce, diplomacy, and culture. That same description holds true for the Forum and the city as it was more than two thousand years ago. Originally used as a cemetery as early as the ninth century B.C.E., the Forum became a marketplace and a center of political activity two hundred years later. As Roman conquests in Italy and throughout the Mediterranean world grew, so did the importance of the Forum as the symbolic center of Rome's dominance.

Over centuries, the Romans decorated the Forum with triumphal arches and columns commemorating military conquests—constant reminders that Rome was the capital of a world state that extended from Britain to Persia, from Africa to Germany. The public buildings and temples in the Forum were Greek in style and inspiration, although more monumental and immense in appearance. And in that very design and presentation, we see two important elements of Roman culture: they readily borrowed ideas from others, especially the Greeks, if they found those ideas preferable to their own, and they very often modified and made improvements on what they borrowed. Roman ability to adapt and modify may be observed even in the empire's structure: Rome brought political stability to the Mediterranean world and in the same process perpetuated the intellectual and cultural contributions of their conquered subjects. As Rome's empire expanded, the cultural legacies of the ancient world were preserved and spread westward throughout most of Europe.

From their beginning as a simple farming community on the banks of the Tiber River to the largest and longest lasting empire of the ancient world, the Romans met one challenge after another by attempting practical solutions and efficient governmental approaches—and almost always prevailed. In the company of its formidable legions went engineers and architects, so that today, throughout the lands that were once under the rule of Rome, the remains of walls, baths, temples, amphitheaters, and aqueducts survive as reminders of the Roman contribution to shaping European civilization.

EARLY ITALY AND THE ORIGINS OF ROME: c. 900–509 B.C.E.

■ *What impact did Italian geography and the various peoples of Italy have on the development of Rome?*

The history of Rome begins with small agricultural settlements in the region that eventually became the city of Rome around 900 B.C.E. The Romans themselves, however, believed that the city actually began in 753 B.C.E.—the traditional date for the founding of the city by Romulus, Rome's legendary first king. It is equally difficult to assign an end date to Rome, because long after the political dominance of Rome came to an end, the social and cultural legacies of the empire continued to influence life in lands impacted by Roman occupation. A great variety of dates might be offered to indicate the end of the empire; one such significant milestone took place in 476 C.E., when the German chieftain Odovacer (c. 435–493 C.E.) assassinated Romulus Augustulus, the last emperor to ruler the western half of the Roman world. The first period in this remarkable span of more than a thousand years of dominance, however, ended in 509 B.C.E., according to Roman tradition, with the expulsion of the Etruscan monarch Tarquin the Proud, the seventh and last of Rome's kings, and the establishment of an aristocratic republic.

Geography and Early Settlers of Italy

Geography was crucial in shaping the course of events in Italy. The Italian peninsula is 600 miles long and about four times the size of Greece, or two-thirds that of California. A great mountainous backbone, the Apennine range, runs almost the entire length of the peninsula. But the land is not as rugged as Greece, and the mountains did not create a formidable barrier to political unification. Unlike in Greece, a network of roads could be built to link the peninsula. Furthermore, the plain of Latium (LAH-tee-um) and its major city, Rome, occupied a strategic position. The hills near what became Rome were relatively easy to defend, and once

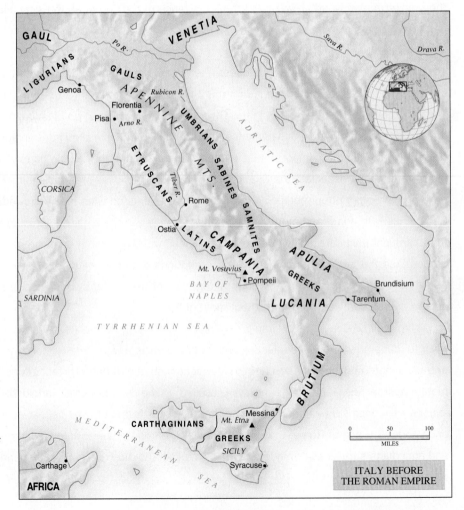

The great variety of peoples and cultures of early Italy are portrayed on this map. Roman institutions and culture were influenced greatly by these early residents.

ITALY BEFORE THE ROMAN EMPIRE

the Romans had begun to establish themselves as successful conquerors, they occupied a central position on the peninsula, which made it difficult for their enemies to unite successfully against them. The important central position of Rome was duplicated on a larger scale by the location of Italy itself. Italy juts into what is almost the center of the great Mediterranean sea. Once Italy was unified, its central position aided Rome in dominating the entire Mediterranean region.

Italy's most imposing valleys and useful harbors are on the western slopes of the Apennines, and the Italian peninsula extends into the western Mediterranean, not eastward. For much of its early history, therefore, cultural development in Italy was not as rapid as it might have been if the two peoples had come into close cultural contact sooner.

Both Greeks and Romans were descendants of a common Indo-European stock, and settlement of the Greek and Italian peninsulas followed broadly parallel stages. Between 2000 and 1000 B.C.E., when Indo-European peoples invaded the Aegean world, a western wing of this nomadic migration filtered into the Italian peninsula, then inhabited by indigenous Neolithic peoples. The first invaders, skilled in the use of copper and bronze, settled in the Po valley. Another wave of Indo-Europeans, equipped with iron weapons and tools, followed; in time the newer and older settlers intermingled and spread throughout the peninsula. One group, the Latins, settled in the plain of Latium, in the lower valley of the Tiber River.

As the Iron Age began in the western Mediterranean, the cultures of Italy became increasingly complex. During the ninth century B.C.E., a people known as the Etruscans established dominance throughout most of central Italy. The exact origin of the Etruscans remains uncertain. Some experts believe them to have been a non-Indo-European people who came to Italy by sea from Asia Minor. Others believe that their origin is explained through a rapid and creative growth of already resident iron-using peoples in northern Italy. Perhaps a combination of the two explanations is most likely—that native creativity fueled by contact with immigrants from the East resulted in a distinctly vibrant and creative culture. Expanding from the west

Etruscan tombs were often elaborately painted with scenes of feasting and entertainment. On these tombs youths celebrate with music and wine.

coast up to the Po valley and south to the Bay of Naples, the Etruscans organized the less-advanced and disparate Italic peoples into a loose confederation of Etruscan-dominated city-states.

In the sixth century B.C.E., Rome became one of the cities controlled by the Etruscans, at a time when that city was not highly developed politically or culturally. The Etruscans brought with them a highly effective political system under the strong direction of kings, an aristocracy of landholding nobles, and a military organization superior to any they encountered among the Italic peoples. Etruscan cultural influence was particularly strong among their Roman subjects. Much of the area around the city was made more useful through Etruscan engineering skill, marsh drainage, and agricultural technology. Their religion, which included many Eastern elements such as the worship of numerous gods and goddesses, powerful priesthoods, rituals, and sacrifices to please the gods and ward off evil, also greatly influenced the development of Roman religious belief. Their funeral customs, which helped to shape Roman practices, show the prominent role of women in Etruscan society. They are usually portrayed in Etruscan tomb paintings as appearing in public, participating in banquets along with their husbands, and in general sharing in the pleasures of life on an equal footing with men.

After 750 B.C.E. Greek colonists migrated to southern Italy and Sicily, where their colonies provided a protective buffer against powerful and prosperous Carthage, a Phoenician colony established in North Africa about 800 B.C.E. The Greeks, along with the Etruscans, had a lasting influence on Roman culture—particularly with regard to religion and their sophisticated accomplishments in art and architecture.

Rome's Origins

Legend held that Rome was founded in 753 B.C.E. by Romulus. He and his twin brother, Remus, were sons of a nearby king's daughter who had been raped by Mars, the god of war. Thrown into the Tiber River by their wicked uncle who had seized the throne, they were rescued and nurtured by a she-wolf. Other legends told the story that Romulus's ancestor was Aeneas (ay-NEE-uhs), a Trojan hero who, after the fall of Troy, founded a settlement in Latium, near what came to be Rome. The Aeneas story, perhaps invented by later mythmakers, pleased the Romans because it linked their history with that of the Greeks, whose culture they thought more sophisticated than their own.

Turning from fable to fact, modern scholars believe that in the eighth century B.C.E. the inhabitants of some small Latin settlements on hills in the Tiber valley united and established a common meeting place, the Forum, around which the city of Rome grew. Situated at a convenient place for fording the river and protected from invaders by surrounding hills and marshes, Rome was strategically located on excellent passes to both north and south. Because of their interest in gaining access to trade with the Greeks in the south, the expanding Etruscans conquered Rome about 625 B.C.E., and under their direction Rome became an important city.

Rome, Italy, and Empire

The Roman Monarchy, 753–509 B.C.E.

Rome's political growth followed a pattern of development similar to that of the Greek city-states: monarchy similar to that described by Homer, oligarchy, modified democracy, and, finally, the permanent dictatorship of the Roman emperors. In moving from oligarchy to democracy, the Romans succeeded in avoiding the intermediate Greek stage of tyranny.

The executive power, both civil and military, of Rome's seven kings (the last three were Etruscans) was called the *imperium,* (the root word for both *imperialism* and *empire*) which was symbolized by an ax bound in a bundle of rods (*fasces;* FAS-kees). Imperium was officially conferred on the king by a popular assembly made up of male citizens, and the king was expected to turn for advice to a council of nobles called the Senate. Senators held their positions for life, and they and their families belonged to the *patrician* class, the fathers of the state (*pater* means "father"). The other class of Romans, the *plebeians,* or commoners, included small farmers, artisans, and many clients, or dependents, of patrician landowners. In 509 B.C.E. the patricians, with some plebeian assistance, overthrew the Etruscan monarchy and established an aristocratic form of government, known as the Republic.

THE REPUBLIC AND THE ROMAN CONQUEST OF ITALY: 509–133 B.C.E.

■ *How did the Romans conquer all of Italy and much of the Mediterranean by 130 B.C.E.?*

The history of the Roman Republic can be divided into two distinct periods. During the first, from 509 to 133 B.C.E., two themes are dominant: a change from aristocracy to a more democratic constitution, the result of the gradual extension of political and social equality to the plebeian lower class; and the expansion of Roman military and political control, first in Italy, and then throughout the Mediterranean region.

The Early Wars of Rome	
509 B.C.E.	Etruscans expelled from Rome
390 B.C.E.	Gauls attack and plunder Rome
338 B.C.E.	Rome emerges victor in wars with members of the Latin League
264–241 B.C.E.	Rome wins Sicily in First Punic War
218–201 B.C.E.	Rome defeats Hannibal in Second Punic War
149–146 B.C.E.	Carthage destroyed in Third Punic War

Establishment of the Republic

In 509 B.C.E. the patricians forced out the last Etruscan king, Tarquin the Proud (Tarquinius Superbus), claiming he had acted despotically. According to the Roman historian Livy, Tarquin was the first of the Roman kings to ignore the advice of the Senate and govern in a selfish and irresponsible manner. The patricians replaced the monarchy with an aristocracy they called a *republic* (*res publica*, "commonwealth"). The imperium of the one king was shared by two new magistrates, called *consuls*. Elected annually from the patrician class, the consuls exercised power in the interest of that class. In the event of war or serious domestic emergency, an "extraordinary" magistrate called a *dictator* could be substituted for the two consuls, but the man was given absolute power for six months only. The popular assembly was retained because the patricians could control it through their plebeian clients who, in return for a livelihood, voted as their patrons directed them.

Struggle of the Orders

For more than two centuries following the establishment of the Republic, the plebeians struggled for political and social equality. Outright civil war was avoided by the willingness of the patricians to accept the demands of the plebeians, even though patrician acceptance was often reluctant and usually slow. Much of the plebeians' success in this struggle was due to their having been granted the right to organize themselves as a corporate body capable of collective action. This permission to organize, granted by the Senate early in the fifth century B.C.E., after the plebeians threatened to leave Rome and found a city elsewhere, established a sort of state within a state known

as the *Concilium Plebis* (kun-SIL-I-um PLAY-bis) or "gathering of the plebeians." This assembly was presided over by plebeian leaders called *tribunes* and could pass *plebiscites* ("plebeian decrees") that were binding only on the plebeian community. The tribunes were given sacred status, *sacrosanctitas* (sak-roh-SANG-ti-tahs), by the plebeian assembly in an effort to furnish them protection from any bodily harm that might come their way from patrician opponents. Tribunes also assumed the right to stop unjust or oppressive acts of the patrician consuls and Senate by uttering the word *veto* ("I forbid.").

Another major concession to plebeian interests was in the field of law. Because the consuls often interpreted Rome's unwritten customary law to suit patrician interests, the plebeians demanded that it be written down and made available for all to see. As a result, about 450 B.C.E., the law was inscribed on a dozen tablets of bronze and set up publicly in the Forum. This Code of the Twelve Tables was the first landmark development in the long history of Roman law.

In time the plebeians acquired other fundamental rights and safeguards: the rights to appeal a death sentence imposed by a consul and to be retried before the popular assembly were secured; marriage between patricians and plebeians, prohibited by the Code of the Twelve Tables, was legalized; and the enslavement of citizens for debt was abolished.

That their service in the Roman army was indispensable to the patricians greatly increased the plebeians' bargaining position in the state. Since Rome was almost constantly at war during these years, the patrician leaders of the state were more ready to accommodate plebeian demands than to face the possibility of a withdrawal of military participation by the commoners. In addition, trade and commerce in early Rome came to be dominated by the plebeian class, since the patricians avoided commercial activities in favor of concentrating their wealth on the acquisition of land and country estates.

Little by little the plebeians acquired more power in the government. In 367 B.C.E. one consulship was reserved for the plebeians, and before the end of the century, plebeians were eligible to hold other important magistracies that the patricians had created in the meantime. Among these new offices, whose powers had originally been held by the consuls, were the *praetor* (PREE-tor; in charge of the administration of justice), *quaestor* (KWEE-ster; treasurer), and *censor* (supervisor of public morals and the granting of state contracts).

The long struggle for equal status ended in 287 B.C.E. when the *Concilium Plebis* was recognized as a constitutional body, which then became known as the Tribal Assembly, and its plebiscites became laws binding on all citizens, patrician as well as plebeian.

The Roman Republic was technically a democracy, although in actual practice a senatorial aristocracy of noble patricians and rich plebeians continued to control the state. Having gained political and social equality, the plebeians were usually willing to allow the more experienced Senate to run the government from this time until 133 B.C.E., a period of almost constant warfare.

After 287 B.C.E. conflict in Roman society gradually assumed a new form. Before this time, the issue of greatest domestic importance had primarily been social and political inequality

This statue of a patrician with busts of his ancestors dates from either the first century B.C.E. or the first century C.E. The patricians were the aristocracy of Rome, and during the later Republic they came increasingly into conflict with senators and generals who took the part of the plebeians.

between the classes of patricians and plebeians. After equal political status was achieved, many rich plebeians were elected to the highest offices and became members of an expanded senatorial aristocracy. The new Roman "establishment" was prepared to guard its privileges even more fiercely than the old patricians had done. This fact became evident in 133 B.C.E. when a popular leader, Tiberius Gracchus (tai-BEE-ri-uhs GRAH-kuhs), arose to challenge the establishment.

The Conquest of Italy

The growth of Rome from a small city-state to the dominant power in the Mediterranean world in less than 400 years (509–133 B.C.E.) was a remarkable achievement. Roman expansion was not deliberately planned; rather, it was the result of dealing with unsettled conditions, first in Italy and then abroad, which were thought to threaten Rome's security. Rome always claimed that its wars were defensive, waged to protect itself from potentially hostile neighbors—Etruscans in the north, land-hungry hill tribes in central Italy, and Greeks in the south. Rome subdued them all after a long, determined effort and found itself master of all Italy south of the Po valley. In the process the Romans developed the administrative skills and traits of character—both fair-mindedness and ruthlessness—that would lead to the acquisition of an empire with possessions on three continents.

Soon after driving out their Etruscan overlords in 509 B.C.E., Rome and the Latin League, composed of other Latin peoples in Latium, entered into a defensive alliance against the Etruscans. This new combination was so successful that by the beginning of the fourth century B.C.E., it had become the chief power in central Italy. But at this time (390 B.C.E.), a major disaster almost ended the history of Rome. A raiding army of Celts, called *Gauls* by the Romans, invaded Italy from central Europe, wiped out the Roman army, and almost destroyed the city by fire. The elderly members of the Senate, according to the traditional account, sat awaiting their fate with quiet dignity before they were massacred. Only a garrison on the Capitoline Hill held out under siege. After seven months and the receipt of a huge ransom in gold, the Gauls withdrew. The stubborn Romans rebuilt their city and protected it with a stone wall, part of which still stands. They also remodeled their army by replacing the solid line of fixed spears of the phalanx formation, borrowed from the Etruscans and Greeks, with much more maneuverable small units of 120 men, called *maniples*, armed with javelins instead of spears. It would be 800 years before another barbarian army would be able to conquer the city of Rome. In the years that followed Rome's recovery from the attack of the Gauls, the Latin League grew more and more alarmed at Rome's increasing strength, and war broke out between the former allies. Upon Rome's victory in 338 B.C.E. the league was dissolved, and the Latin cities were forced to sign individual treaties with Rome.

But soon after the Roman victory over the Latin League, border clashes with aggressive mountain tribes of Samnium led to three fiercely fought Samnite wars and the extension of Rome's frontiers to the Greek colonies in southern Italy by 290 B.C.E. Fearing Roman conquest, the Greeks prepared for war and called in the mercenary army of the Greek king, Pyrrhus (PEER-uhs) of Epirus, who dreamed of becoming a second Alexander the Great. Pyrrhus's war elephants, unknown in Italy, twice defeated the Romans, but at so heavy a cost that such a triumph is still called a "Pyrrhic victory." When a third battle failed to persuade the Romans to make peace, Pyrrhus returned to his homeland. By 270 B.C.E. the Roman army had subdued the Greek city-states in

Italy, and the peninsula south of the Po River was under their control.

Treatment of Conquered Peoples

Instead of killing or enslaving their defeated opponents in Italy, the Romans treated them fairly, a policy which in time created a strong loyalty to Rome throughout the peninsula. Roman citizenship was a prized possession that was not extended to all peoples in Italy until the first century B.C.E. Most defeated states were required to sign a treaty of alliance with Rome, which bound them to accept Rome's foreign policy and to supply troops for the Roman army. No tribute was required, and each allied state retained local self-government. Rome did, however, annex about one-fifth of the land its **legions** conquered in Italy, on which nearly 30 colonies were established by 250 B.C.E.

CASE STUDY

Greek and Roman Slavery

The First Punic War

After 270 B.C.E. Rome's only serious rival for dominance in the western Mediterranean was the city-state of Carthage. This prosperous state located near the modern city of Tunis began as a Phoenician colony on the northern African coast in the ninth century B.C.E. By the sixth century, Carthage had become not only independent but also the dominant commercial power in the western Mediterranean. Much more wealthy and populous than Rome, Carthage's magnificent navy controlled the northern coast of Africa, Sardinia, Corsica, western Sicily, and much of Spain. The city and its empire were governed by a commercial oligarchy of Semitic descendants of Carthage's founders. The native population was forced into service in agriculture or in the army and navy; mercenaries were also hired to secure the interests of the ruling minority.

There had been almost no conflicts of interest between Rome and Carthage before the First Punic War (from *Punicus*, Latin for "Phoenician") broke out in 264 B.C.E. In that year, Rome answered an appeal from a group of Italian mercenaries who were in control of the city of Messana, on the northern tip of Sicily next to Italy. These mercenaries were opposed by a Carthaginian force, and when the Roman Senate agreed to send an army to aid the mercenaries, a war between Carthage and Rome was the obvious result.

The First Punic War was a costly one for both combatants. Roman ground forces were quickly successful

---

legion—A military organizational division, originally the largest permanent unit in the Roman army. The legion was the basis of the military system by which imperial Rome conquered and ruled its empire.

in gaining control of most of Sicily, but the Carthaginian navy was unopposed, since the Romans had no need of a navy in their conquest of Italy. Rome constructed its fleet in hurried fashion and sent it against the Carthaginians with surprising initial success. Roman engineers furnished their new vessels with an invention called the *corvus*, or "crow," a boarding bridge at the bow of a ship that, when lowered, turned a naval engagement into a land battle. After a stunning defeat of the Carthaginian navy, the Romans invaded the African coast, lost decisively, and suffered the losses of large numbers of ships through violent storms in attempting to return home. Eventually, victory for Rome came through another victory over the Carthaginian navy, but the costs of victory were high; Rome and its Italian allies lost more than 500 ships in naval engagements and storms before Carthage asked for peace in 241 B.C.E. Sicily, Sardinia, and Corsica were annexed as the first prizes in Rome's overseas empire, regulated and taxed—in contrast to Rome's allies in Italy—by Roman officials called *governors*.

The Contest with Hannibal

Stunned by its defeat in the First Punic War, Carthage concentrated on enlarging its empire in Spain. Rome's determination to prevent this led to the most famous and most difficult war in Roman history. While both powers sought a position of advantage, a young Carthaginian general, Hannibal, precipitated the Second Punic War by attacking Saguntum, a Spanish town claimed by Rome as an ally. Rome declared war, and Hannibal, seizing the initiative, in 218 B.C.E. led an army of about 40,000 men, 9000 cavalry troops, and a detachment of African elephants across the Alps into Italy. Although the crossing had cost him nearly half of his men and all but one of his elephants, Hannibal defeated the Romans in three major battles within three years, while ranging throughout Italy but not attacking Rome.

Hannibal's forces never matched those of the Romans in numbers, and the Carthaginian general was never given the reinforcements he requested from his home state. Nevertheless, Hannibal's brilliance as a commander was obvious. At the battle of Cannae (KAN-ee), in 216 B.C.E., Hannibal won his greatest victory by surrounding an army of nearly 80,000 Romans with 50,000 Carthaginians. Almost the entire Roman force was killed or captured. Even at this darkest hour of defeat, the Senate displayed the determination that was to become legendary. When the one consul who survived the battle returned to Rome to give his report, he was congratulated by the senators for "not despairing of the Republic."

The Romans ultimately produced a general, Scipio (SI-pee-oh), who was Hannibal's match in military strategy and who was bold enough to invade Africa. Asked to return home after 15 years spent on Italian soil, Hannibal clashed with Scipio's legions at Zama, where the Carthaginians suffered a complete defeat. The power of Carthage was broken forever by a harsh treaty imposed in 201 B.C.E. Carthage was forced to pay a huge **war indemnity,** disarm its forces, and turn Spain over to the Romans. Hannibal fled to the Seleucid Empire, where he attempted to encourage anti-Roman sentiment, and eventually committed suicide in order to avoid Roman capture.

Roman Intervention East and West

The defeat of Carthage freed Rome to turn eastward and deal with King Philip V of Macedonia. Fearful of Rome's growing power, Philip had allied himself with Hannibal during the Second Punic War. In 200 B.C.E., Rome was ready to act, following an appeal from Pergamum and Rhodes for aid in protecting the smaller Hellenistic states from Philip, who was advancing in the Aegean, and from the Seleucid emperor, who was moving into Asia Minor. The heavy Macedonian phalanxes were no match for the mobile Roman legions, and in 197 B.C.E. Philip was soundly defeated in Macedonia. His dreams of empire were ended when Rome destroyed his navy and military bases in Greece. The Romans then proclaimed the independence of Greece and were praised as liberators by the grateful Greeks.

A few years later Rome declared war on the Seleucid emperor, who had moved into Greece, urged on by Hannibal and number of Greek states that resented Rome's interference. The Romans forced the emperor to move out of Greece and Asia Minor, pay a huge indemnity, and give up his warships and war elephants. The Seleucids were checked again in 168 B.C.E. when a Roman ultimatum halted their invasion of Egypt. A Roman envoy met the advancing Seleucid army and, drawing a ring in the sand around the emperor, demanded that he decide on war or on peace with Rome before stepping out of it.

DOCUMENT

Plutarch, *The Life of Cato the Elder*

In the middle of the second century B.C.E. anti-Romanism became widespread in Greece, particularly among the poorer classes, who resented Rome's support of conservative governments and the status quo in general. In 146 B.C.E., after many Greeks had supported an attempted Macedonian revival, Rome destroyed Corinth, a hotbed of anti-Romanism, as an object lesson. The Romans also supported the oligarchic factions in all Greek states and placed Greece under the watchful eye of the governor of Macedonia, a recently established Roman province.

In the West, meanwhile, Rome's more aggressive imperialism led to suspicion of Carthage's reviving prosperity and to a demand by Roman extremists for war—*Carthago delenda est* ("Carthage must be obliterated."). Obviously provoking the Third Punic War, the Romans besieged Carthage, which resisted for three years. Rome destroyed the city in 146 B.C.E. (the same year they destroyed Corinth), killed or enslaved almost all of its surviving inhabitants, leveled the buildings, and poured salt over its borders so that nothing would ever take root on its soil again. The powerful state that had dared to defy Rome was now obliterated, and the province of Africa was created in its place.

In 133 B.C.E. Rome acquired its first province in Asia when the king of Pergamum, dying without an heir, left his kingdom to Rome. The Senate accepted the bequest and created a new province, called Asia. With provinces on three continents—Europe, Africa, and Asia—the once obscure Roman Republic was now supreme in the ancient world.

Society and Religion in Early Rome

The most important unit of early Roman society was the family. The power of the family father *(pater familias)* was absolute, and strict discipline was imposed to instill in children the virtues to which the Romans attached particular importance—loyalty, courage, self-control, and respect for laws and ancestral customs. The Romans of the early Republic were stern, hard-working, and practical. The conservative values of an agrarian society formed the values of both Roman men and women. With much of a Roman man's time taken up with military or political concerns, women had great responsibilities in supervising the upbringing of children and maintaining estates and farms.

In contrast to the frequency of divorce in the late Republic, marriage in the early Republic was viewed as a lifelong union; patrician marriages were usually arranged between families and were undertaken primarily for the creation of children, but on many occasions such marriages resulted in mutual affection between husband and wife. Nonetheless, the authority of the Roman male within his own household was usually unchallenged.

The religion of the early Romans, before their contacts with the Etruscans and Greeks, is very difficult for scholars to describe with confidence. Available evidence for their views on life after death is vague. Religious practices were concerned with appeasing and honoring the spirits *(numina)* of the family and the state by the repetition of complicated rituals and formulas. Mispronunciation of even a sin-

---

war indemnity—A payment to compensate for losses sustained or expenses incurred as a result of war. The Romans regularly imposed such war indemnities on their conquered enemies.

gle syllable was enough to cause the ritual to become ineffective. Under Etruscan influence, major gods and goddesses were personified. The sky-spirit Jupiter became the patron god of Rome; Mars, spirit of vegetation, became god of war and agriculture; and Janus, whose temple doors remained open when the army was away at war, was originally the spirit guarding the city gate.

Although early Roman religion did not have great concern with morals, it had much to do with morale. It strengthened family solidarity and enhanced a patriotic devotion to the state and its gods. But the early Romans' respect for hard work, frugality, and family and state gods was to be challenged by the effects of Rome's expansion in Italy and over much of the Mediterranean area during the early Republic.

THE LATE REPUBLIC: 133–30 B.C.E.

■ *What were the main reasons for the failure of the Roman Republic and the consolidation of power by Augustus?*

The century following 133 B.C.E. during which Rome's frontiers reached the Euphrates and the Rhine, witnessed the failure of the Republic to solve problems generated in part by the acquisition of an empire. These years serve as a good example of the failure of a democracy and its replacement by a dictatorship. The experience of the late Republic gives support to Thucydides' judgment that a democracy is incapable of running an empire. Athens kept its democracy but lost its empire; Rome would keep its empire and loss its democracy.

Effects of Roman Expansion

The political history of Rome to 133 B.C.E. possessed two dominant themes: the gradual extension of citizenship rights in Italy and the expansion of Roman dominion over the Mediterranean world. Largely as a result of this expansion, Rome faced critical social and economic problems by the middle of the second century B.C.E.

One of the most pressing problems Rome faced was the decline in the number of small landowners, whose service and devotion had made Rome great. Burdened by frequent military service, their farms and buildings destroyed by Hannibal, and unable to compete with the cheap grain imported from the new Roman province of Sicily, small farmers sold out and moved to the great city. Here they joined the unemployed and discontented *proletariat,* so called because

The Late Republic	
133–123 B.C.E.	Reform movement of the Gracchi
88–82 B.C.E.	First Civil War (Marius vs. Sulla)
58–49 B.C.E.	Caesar conquers Gaul
49–45 B.C.E.	Second Civil War (Pompey vs. Caesar)
44 B.C.E.	Caesar assassinated
31 B.C.E.	Third Civil War (Octavian vs. Antony)
27 B.C.E.	Octavian (Augustus) becomes ruler of Rome

their only contribution was *proles,* "children." The proletariat soon were the majority of the citizens in the city.

At the same time, improved farming methods learned from the Greeks and Carthaginians encouraged rich aristocrats to buy more and more land. Abandoning the cultivation of grain, they introduced large-scale scientific production of olive oil and wine, sheep, and cattle. This change was especially profitable because an abundance of cheaply purchased slaves from conquered territory was available to work on the estates. With the increase in the availability of slave labor came worsening treatment of the labor force, as well as deteriorating conditions for the declining numbers of free laborers on these large estates. These large slave plantations, called *latifundia* (lah-ti-FUN-dee-uh), became common in many parts of Italy.

The land problem was further complicated by the government's practice of leasing part of the territory acquired in the conquest of the Italian peninsula to anyone willing to pay a percentage of the crop or animals raised on it. Only the wealthy could afford to lease large tracts of this public land, and in time, they treated it as if it were their own property. Plebeian protests led to an attempt to limit the holdings of a single individual to 320 acres of public land, but the law enacted for that purpose was never enforced.

Corruption in the government was another sign of the growing problems of the Roman Republic. Provincial officials took advantage of the opportunity to engage in graft for great profit, and aggressive Roman businessmen scrambled selfishly for the profitable state contracts to supply the armies, collect taxes and loan money in the provinces, and lease state-owned mines and forests.

Although in theory the government allowed for an unhindered participation of all male citizens, in practice it remained a senatorial oligarchy. Wars tend to strengthen the executive power in a state, and in Rome the Senate traditionally had such power. Even the tribunes, guardians of the people's rights, became, for the most part, tools of the Senate. By the middle of the second century B.C.E. the government was in the hands of a wealthy, self-serving Senate, which became increasingly incapable of coping with the problems of governing a world-state. Ordinary citizens were mostly impoverished and landless, and Rome swarmed with fortune hunters, imported slaves, unemployed farmers, and discontented war veterans. The poverty of the many, coupled with the great wealth of the few, contrasted dramatically with the old Roman traits of discipline, simplicity, and respect for authority. The next century (133–30 B.C.E.) saw Rome torn apart by internal conflict, which led to the establishment of a permanent dictatorship and the end of the Republic.

Document — Columella: Roman Farm Women

Columella was a Roman citizen from Spain in the first century C.E. He served with the Roman legions and later retired to an agricultural estate, where he wrote his suggestions for how Roman farming could most efficiently be undertaken. The following excerpt from his works on agriculture describes the duties he believes should be given to the forewomen on Roman estates. Such women were usually under the supervision of a foreman; both were often slaves. Columella's listing of the forewoman's tasks gives us an insight into the wide range of duties for which such Roman farm women were held responsible:

The forewoman must not only store and guard the items which have been brought into the house and delivered to her; she should also inspect and examine them from time to time so that the furniture and clothing which have been stored do not disintegrate because of mold, and the fruits and vegetables and other necessities do not go rotten because of her neglect and slothfulness. On rainy days, or when a woman cannot do field work out of doors because of cold or frost, she should return to wool-working. Therefore, wool should be prepared and carded in advance so that she can more easily undertake and complete the required allotment of wool-working. For it will be beneficial if clothing is made at home for her and the stewards and the other valued slaves so the financial accounts of the *paterfamilias* are less strained. She ought to stay in one place as little as possible, for her job is not a sedentary one. At one moment she will have to go to the loom and teach the weavers whatever she knows better than them or, if she knows less, learn from someone who understands more. At another moment, she will have to check on those slaves who are preparing the food for the *familia*. Then she will also have to see that the kitchen, cowsheds, and even the stables are cleaned. And she will also have to open up the sickrooms occasionally, even if they are empty of patients, and keep them free of dirt, so that, when circumstance demands, a well-ordered and healthy environment is provided for the sick. She will, in addition, have to be in attendance when the stewards of the pantry and cellar are weighing something, and also be present when the shepherds are milking in the stables or bringing the lambs or calves to nurse. But she will also certainly need to be present when the sheep are sheared, and to examine the wool carefully and compare the number of fleeces with the number of sheep. Then she must turn her attention to the slaves in the house and insist that they air out the furniture and clean and polish the metal items and free them from rust, and take to the craftsmen for repair other items which require mending.

Questions to Consider

1. How do you think the responsibilities of Roman forewomen compare to modern positions of responsibility on farms?

2. Do you find it surprising that such heavy responsibilities were often given to slave women? What might be the reasons for this?

3. What duties are omitted from the list of responsibilities given by Columella, and do you see any significance in their omission?

From Columella, *On Agriculture*, 12.3.5, 6, 8, and 9, in Jo-Ann Shelton, *As the Romans Did*, 2nd ed. (New York: Oxford University Press, 1998), p. 304.

Reform Movement of the Gracchi

An awareness of Rome's serious social and economic problems led to the reform program of an idealistic and ambitious young aristocrat named Tiberius Gracchus. His reforming spirit was partly the product of newly imported philosophical arguments from Greece and an awareness that the old Roman values and customs were fast slipping away. He sought to stop Roman decline by restoring the backbone of the old Roman society, the small landowner. Supported by a **faction** of senators, Tiberius was elected tribune for the year 133 B.C.E. at the age of 29.

Tiberius proposed to the Tribal Assembly that the act limiting the holding of public land to 320 acres per male citizen, plus 160 acres for each of two grown-up sons, be reenacted. Much of the public land would continue to be held by the present occupants and their heirs as private property, but the rest was to be taken back and granted to the poor in small plots of 9 to 18 acres. The recipients were to pay a small rent and could not sell their holdings. When it became evident that the Tribal Assembly would adopt Tiberius's proposal, opposing senators persuaded one of the other tribunes to veto the measure. On the ground that a tribune who opposed the will of the people had no right to his office, Tiberius took a fateful—and, the Senate claimed, unconstitutional—step by having the assembly depose the tribune in question. The agrarian bill was then passed.

To ensure the implementation of his agrarian reform, Tiberius again violated custom by standing for reelection in the Tribal Assembly after completing his one-year term. Claiming that he sought to make himself king, partisans of the Senate murdered Tiberius and 300 of his followers.

Tiberius's work was taken up by his younger brother, Gaius Gracchus, who was elected tribune for 123 B.C.E. In addition to the allocation of public land to the poor, Gaius proposed establishing Roman colonies in southern Italy and in Africa—his enemies said near the site of Carthage. To protect the poor against speculation in the grain market (especially in times of famine), Gaius committed the government to the purchase, storage, and distribution of wheat to the urban poor at about half the actual market price. Unfortunately, what Gaius intended as a relief measure later became a dole, through which nearly free food was distributed—all too often for the advancement of astute politicians—to the entire proletariat.

Another of Gaius's proposals would have granted citizenship to Rome's Italian allies, who felt they were being mistreated by Roman officials. This proposal

cost Gaius the support of the Roman proletariat, which did not wish to share the privileges of citizenship or share its control of the Tribal Assembly. In 121 B.C.E. Gaius failed to be reelected to a third term as tribune. In a further effort to guard against Gaius's leadership, the Senate again resorted to force. It decreed that the consuls could take any action deemed necessary "to protect the state and suppress the tyrants." Three thousand of Gaius's followers were killed in rioting or were arrested and executed, a fate Gaius avoided by committing suicide.

Through these actions, the Senate had shown that it had no intention of initiating needed domestic reforms or of allowing others to do so, and the deaths of Tiberius and Gaius were ominous signals of the way the Republic would decide its internal disputes in the future. In foreign affairs as well, the Senate demonstrated ineptness. Rome was forced to grant citizenship to its Italian allies after the Senate's failure to deal with their grievances pushed them into open revolt (90–88 B.C.E.). Other shortsighted actions led to the first of the three civil wars that assisted in the destruction of the Republic.

The First Civil War: Marius Against Sulla

Between 111 and 105 B.C.E. Roman armies, dispatched by the Senate and commanded by senators, failed to protect Roman business interests in Numidia, a kingdom in North Africa allied to Rome. Nor were they able to prevent Germanic tribes from overrunning southern Gaul, then a Roman province, and threatening Italy itself. Accusing the Senate of neglect and incompetence in directing Rome's foreign affairs, the Roman commercial class and common people joined together to elect Gaius Marius consul in 107 B.C.E., and the Tribal Assembly commissioned him to raise an army to put down the foreign danger. Marius first pacified North Africa and then crushed the first German threat to Rome. In the process, he created a new-style Roman army that was destined to play a major role in the turbulent history of the late Republic.

Unlike the old Roman army, which was composed of conscripts who owned their own land and thought of themselves as loyal citizens of the Republic, the new army created by Marius was recruited from landless citizens for long terms of service. These professional soldiers identified their own interests with those of their commanders, to whom they swore loyalty and looked to for bonuses of land and money, since the Senate had refused their requests for such support. Thus the character of the army changed from a militia of draftees to a "personal army" in which loyalty to the state was replaced with loyalty to the commander.

faction—A like-minded, organized group that operates within another group or government. In Rome, various factions rivaled each other for political power in the state.

In 133 B.C.E., a tribune named Tiberius Gracchus proposed a solution to a major crisis in the Roman state. Redistribution of land to the landless and unemployed residents of the city would allow these individuals to become productive citizens, strengthen the economy, and enable the Roman system of military service, which was dependent on land-owning citizens, to function more effectively. Even though such reform was thought to be necessary by many in the Roman aristocracy, Tiberius was resented for the power and prestige his land law gave him, and he was assassinated by rival aristocrats. The tradition of nonviolent domestic reform through compromise and debate was ended in Rome; many students of Roman history see in the assassination of Tiberius, and of his younger brother Gaius ten years after, the first indications of the breakdown of the Roman Republic:

. . . Flavius got to (Tiberius), and informed him that the rich men, in a sitting of the senate, seeing they could not prevail upon the consul to espouse their quarrel, had come to a final determination amongst themselves that he should be assassinated, and to that purpose had a great number of their friends and servants ready armed to accomplish it. Tiberius no sooner communicated this confederacy to those about him, but they immediately tucked up their gowns, broke the halberts which the officers used to keep the crowd off into pieces, and distributed them among themselves, resolving to resist the attack with these. Those who stood at a distance wondered, and asked what was the occasion; Tiberius, knowing they could not hear him at that distance, lifted his hand to his head wishing to intimate the great danger which he apprehended himself to be in. His Adversaries, taking notice of that action, ran off at once to the senate-house, and declared that Tiberius desired the people to bestow a crown upon him, as if this were the meaning of his touching his head. This news created general confusion in the senators, and Nasica at once called upon the consul to punish the tyrant, and defend the government. The consul mildly replied that he would not be the first to do any violence. . . . But Nasica, rising from his seat, "Since the consul," said he, "regards not the safety of the commonwealth, let every one who will defend the laws, follow me." He then, casting the skirt of his gown over his head, hastened to the capitol; those who bore him company, wrapped their gowns also about their arms, and forced their way after him. And as they were persons of the greatest authority in the city, the common people did not venture to obstruct their passing but were rather so eager to clear the way for them, that they tumbled over one another in haste. The attendants they brought with them had furnished themselves with clubs and staves from their houses, and they themselves picked up the feet and other fragments of stools and chairs, which were broken by the hasty flight of the common people. Thus armed, they made towards Tiberius, knocking down those whom they found in front of him, and those were soon wholly dispersed and many of them slain. Tiberius tried to save himself by flight. As he was running, he was stopped by one who caught hold of

him by the gown; but he threw it off, and fled in his under-garment only. And stumbling over those who before had been knocked down, as he was endeavouring to get up again, Publius Satureius, a tribune, one of his colleagues was observed to give him the first fatal stroke, by hitting him upon the head with the foot of a stool. The second blow was claimed, as though it had been a deed to be proud of, by Lucius Rufus. And of the rest there fell above three hundred killed by clubs and staves only, none by an iron weapon.

This, we are told, was the first sedition amongst the Romans, since the abrogation of kingly government, that ended in the effusion of blood. . . . Tiberius himself might then have been easily induced, by mere persuasion, to give way, and certainly, if attacked at all, must have yielded without any recourse to violence and bloodshed. . . . But it is evident, that this conspiracy was fomented against him, more out of the hatred and malice which the rich men had to his person, than for the reasons which they commonly pretended against him. In testimony of which we may adduce the cruelty and unnatural insults which they used to his dead body. For they would not suffer his own brother, though he earnestly begged the favour, to bury him in the night, but threw him, together with the other corpses, into the river. Neither did their animosity stop here; for they banished some of his friends without legal process, and slew as many of the others as they could lay their hands on; amongst whom Diphanes, the orator, was slain, and one Caius Villius cruelly murdered by being shut up in a large tun with vipers and serpents.

Questions to Consider

1. Do you think that Tiberius's assassination could represent a crucial step in the decline of the Roman Republic?

2. Does Plutarch's description of the assassination give you the impression that the assassination was a well-thought-out plan, or action taken in haste? Why?

3. If Tiberius Gracchus's assassination was planned by the Senatorial opposition, what did this group have to gain by Tiberius's death? Why did they resort to violence?

From Plutarch, *Life of Tiberius Gracchus*, 16–20, in *Readings in Ancient History*, vol. 2, ed. William Davis (Boston: Allyn and Bacon, 1913) pp. 108–109.

Ambitious generals were in a position to use their military power to seize the government.

Encouraged by growing anti-Roman sentiment in the province of Asia and in Greece caused by corrupt governors, tax collectors, and moneylenders, in 88 B.C.E. the king of Pontus, in Asia Minor, declared war on Rome. The Senate ordered Cornelius Sulla, an able general and a strong supporter of the Senate's authority, to march east and restore order. As a countermove, the Tribal Assembly chose Marius for the eastern command. In effect both the Senate and the Tribal Assembly, whose power the Gracchi had revived, claimed to be the ultimate authority in the state. The result was the first of a series of civil wars between rival generals, each claiming to champion the cause of either the Senate or the Tribal Assembly. The first civil war ended in a complete victory for Sulla, who in 82 B.C.E. was appointed dictator by the Senate, not for a maximum of six months but for an unlimited term as "dictator for the revision of the constitution."

Sulla intended to restore the preeminence of the Senate. He drastically reduced the powers of the tribunes and the Tribal Assembly, giving the Senate virtually complete control of all legislation. Having massacred several thousand of the opposition, Sulla was convinced that his constitutional improvements would be permanent, and in 79 B.C.E., he voluntarily resigned his dictatorship and retired from public life.

The Second Civil War: Pompey Against Caesar

The first of the civil wars and its aftermath increased both discontent and division in the state and fueled the ambitions of younger individuals eager for personal power. The first of these men to come forward was Pompey (106–48 B.C.E.), who had won fame as a military leader. In 70 B.C.E. he was elected consul. Although he was a former supporter of Sulla, he won popularity with the commoners by repealing Sulla's laws limiting the power of the tribunes and the Tribal Assembly. Pompey then put an end to disorder in the East caused by piracy (the result of the Senate's neglect of the Roman navy), the continuing threats of the king of Pontus, and the political uncertainty caused by the collapse of the Seleucid Empire. New Roman provinces and **client states** set up by Pompey brought order eastward as far as the Euphrates. These included the province of Syria—the last remnant of the once vast Seleucid Empire—and the client state of Judea, supervised by the governor of Syria.

Marcus Crassus (MAR-kuhs KRAS-suhs) was another ambitious member of the Senate who was also reputed to be the richest man in Rome resulting from his shrewd business dealings throughout the empire. Crassus was given special military command in 71 B.C.E. to crush the rebellion of nearly 70,000 slaves in southern and central Italy led by the gladiator Spartacus.

A magnificent and idealized representation of Julius Caesar (100–44 B.C.E.), consummate politician, military strategist, and the first Roman to be awarded the title Dictator for Life. Caesar, in possession of more power than any previous Roman political leader, was assassinated in 44 B.C.E. by opponents who feared that he would destroy the Republic.

Still another ambitious and able leader beginning his public career in the 60s was Gaius Julius Caesar (100–44 B.C.E.) From a noble family, Caesar nonetheless chose to appeal to the commoners for most of his support.

Pompey, Crassus, and Caesar all found that the Senate stood in the way of their desires for more control in the state. To negate senatorial opposition, these three politicians agreed to cooperate with one another in an informal arrangement later called the First Triumvirate. All three politicians would pool their resources to help each individual member reach his personal goals in the state and subvert the opposition of the Senate. In 59 B.C.E. Julius Caesar was elected consul and worked to enact legislation favored by Pompey and Crassus. Following his consulship, Caesar spent nine years conquering Gaul, under the pretext of protecting the Gauls from the Germans across the Rhine. He accumulated a fortune in plunder and trained a loyal army of veterans. During his absence from Rome, he kept his name before the citizens by publishing an attractively written account of his military feats, *Commentaries on the Gallic War.*

---

client state—A kingdom or region that Rome considered to be dependent on Rome's patronage. Such states enjoyed some measure of independence but were expected to seek approval from Rome for any major undertaking. If client states failed to satisfy Roman expectations, Rome usually moved to establish permanent control.

Crassus was killed in battle against the Parthians of Persia in 53 B.C.E. Steadily becoming more fearful of Caesar's growing power, Pompey associated himself with the Senate in order to limit Caesar's authority. When the Senate demanded in 49 B.C.E. that Caesar disband his army, he crossed the Rubicon, the river in northern Italy that formed the boundary of his province, and in effect declared war on Pompey and the Senate. He marched on Rome while Pompey and most of the Senate fled to Greece, where Caesar eventually defeated them at Pharsalus (FAR-sa-luhs) in 48 B.C.E. Pompey was killed in Egypt when he sought refuge there. By 45 B.C.E. Caesar had eliminated all military threats against him, and he returned in triumph to Rome to exercise what he hoped would be unlimited power.

As he assumed the title of "dictator for the administration of public affairs," Caesar initiated far-reaching reforms. He granted citizenship to the Gauls and packed the Senate with many new non-Italian members, making it a more truly representative body as well as a rubber stamp for his policies. In the interest of the poorer citizens, he reduced debts, inaugurated a public works program, established colonies outside Italy, and decreed that one-third of the laborers on the slave-worked estates in Italy be persons of free birth. As a result, he was able to reduce from 320,000 to 150,000 the number of people in the city of Rome receiving free grain. (The population of Rome is estimated to have been 500,000 at this time.) His most enduring act was the reform of the calendar in the light of Egyptian knowledge; with minor changes, this calendar of 365 1/4 days is still in use today.

Caesar realized that the Republic was dead. In his own words, "The Republic is merely a name, without form or substance." He believed that only intelligent autocratic leadership could save Rome from continued civil war and collapse. But Caesar inspired the hatred of many, particularly those who viewed him as a high-handed egomaniac who not only had destroyed the Republic but also even aspired to having himself recognized as a god. On the Ides (fifteenth day) of March, 44 B.C.E., a group of conspirators, led by Brutus and other ex-Pompeians whom Caesar had pardoned, stabbed him to death in the Senate, and Rome was once more drawn into conflict.

The Third Civil War: Antony Versus Octavian

Following Caesar's death, his 18-year-old grandnephew and heir, Octavian (63 B.C.E.–14 C.E.), allied himself with Caesar's chief lieutenant, Mark Antony, against the conspirators and the Senate. The conspirators' armies were defeated at Philippi in Macedonia in 42 B.C.E. Then for more than a decade, Octavian and Antony exercised dictatorial power and divided the Roman world between them. But the ambitions of each man proved too great for the alliance to endure.

Antony, who took charge of the eastern half of the empire, became completely infatuated with Queen Cleopatra, the last of the Egyptian Ptolemies. He even went so far as to transfer Roman territories to her control. Octavian took advantage of Antony's blunders to propagandize Rome and Italy against Antony and his foreign lover-queen. The resulting struggle was portrayed by Octavian as a war between the Roman West and the "oriental" East. When Octavian's fleet met Antony's near Actium in Greece, first Cleopatra and then Antony deserted the battle and fled to Egypt. There Antony committed suicide, as Cleopatra did soon afterward when Alexandria was captured by Octavian in 30 B.C.E.

THE ROMAN EMPIRE AND THE *PAX ROMANA*: 30 B.C.E.–476 C.E.

■ *What were the most significant achievements of the Roman Empire, and what were its greatest failures?*

At the end of a century of civil violence, Rome was at last united under one leader, Octavian, who was hailed by the grateful Romans as the "father of his country." The Republic gave way to the permanent dictatorship of the empire, and two centuries of imperial greatness, known as the *Pax Romana* ("Roman Peace"), followed. But in the third century, the empire was beset with challenges that proved disastrous: economic stagnation, Germanic invasions, and finally the loss of imperial control of the empire in the west.

Reconstruction Under Augustus

Following his triumphal return to Rome, Octavian in 27 B.C.E. announced that he would "restore the Republic." But he did so only outwardly by blending republican institutions with his own strong personal leadership. He consulted the Senate on important issues, allowed it to retain control over Italy and half of the provinces, and gave it the legislative functions of the nearly unused Tribal Assembly. The Senate in return bestowed on Octavian the title *Augustus* ("The Revered," a title previously used for gods), by which he was known thereafter.

DOCUMENT

Excerpt from Suetonius, *The Life of Augustus*

During the rest of his 45-year rule, Augustus never again held the office of dictator, and he seldom held the consulship. Throughout his career he kept the powers of a tribune, which gave him the right to initi-

The Roman Empire

14–68 C.E.	Period of the Julio-Claudian emperors
64 C.E.	Rome destroyed by fire; Emperor Nero attributes fire to Christians
69–96 C.E.	Period of the Flavian emperors
79 C.E.	Mount Vesuvius erupts, destroying Pompeii
96 180 C.E.	Period of the Antonine emperors
313 C.E.	Emperor Constantine issues Edict of Milan; Christians free to worship
378 C.E.	Battle of Adrianople; Germanic invasions into Roman Empire begin
395 C.E.	Roman Empire divided into eastern and western empires
476 C.E.	Last Roman emperor in the West assassinated

challenged. From his military title, *imperator* ("victorious general"), is derived our modern term *emperor*.

Augustus constructed a constitution in which his power was in reality almost unlimited, yet disguised through his masterful use of the institutions of the old republic. He preferred the modest title of *princeps*, "first citizen" or "leader," that he felt best described his position, and his form of virtual dictatorship is therefore known as the Principate. At the beginning of the empire, then, political power was in appearances divided between the princeps and the senatorial aristocrats. This arrangement was continued by most of Augustus's successors during the next two centuries.

Seeking to heal the scars of more than a century of civil strife, Augustus concentrated on internal reform. He annexed Egypt and extended the Roman frontier to the Danube as a defense against barbarian invasions, but he failed in an attempt to conquer Germany up to the Elbe River. As a result, the Germans were never Romanized, as the Celts of Gaul and Spain were.

Through legislation and propaganda, Augustus attempted to check moral and social decline and revive the old Roman ideals and traditions. He rebuilt deteriorated temples, revived old priesthoods, and restored religious festivals. He attempted to reestablish the integrity of the family by legislating against adultery, the chief grounds for divorce, which had become quite common during the late Republic. A permanent court

ate legislation and to veto the legislative and administrative acts of others. He also kept for himself the governorship of the frontier provinces, where the armies were stationed. Augustus's nearly total control of the army meant that his power could not be successfully

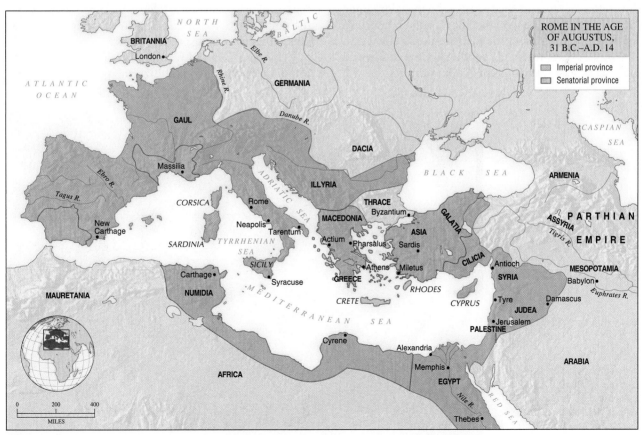

The Roman Empire at the time of Augustus.

was set up to prosecute adulterous wives and their lovers. Among those found guilty and banished from Rome were Augustus's own daughter and granddaughter. Finally, to disarm the gangs that had been terrorizing citizens, he outlawed the carrying of daggers.

DOCUMENT

Augustus on his accomplishments

Augustus greatly reduced the corruption and exploitation that had flourished in the late Republic by creating a well-paid civil service, open to all classes. He also established a permanent standing army, stationed in the frontier provinces and kept out of politics. More than 40 colonies of retired soldiers were founded throughout the empire. Augustus's reforms also gave rise to a new optimism and patriotism that were reflected in the art and literature of the Augustan Age.

The Julio-Claudian and Flavian Emperors

Augustus was followed by four descendants from among his family, the line of the Julio-Claudians, who ruled from 14 to 68 C.E. Augustus's stepson Tiberius, whom the Senate accepted as his successor, and Claudius were fairly efficient and devoted rulers; in Claudius's reign the Roman occupation of Britain began in 43 C.E. The other two rulers of this imperial line disregarded the appearance that they were only the first among all citizens: Caligula (Ka-LIG-eu-lah), Tiberius's nephew and successor, was a megalomaniac who demanded to be worshiped as a god and considered the idea of having his favorite horse elected to high office in Rome; Nero, Claudius's adopted son and successor, was notorious for his immorality, for the murders of his wife and his mother, and for beginning the persecutions of Christians in Rome. Caligula and Nero have been immortalized through history for their excesses and depravity, yet both functioned effectively as emperors for at least some duration of their reigns. Nero in particular was recognized to be intelligent and accomplished by some of his contemporaries.

The Julio-Claudian line ended in 68 C.E. when Nero, declared a public enemy by the Senate and facing army revolts, committed suicide. In the following year, four emperors were proclaimed by rival armies, with Vespasian (ves-PAY-si-an) the final victor. For nearly 30 years (69–96 C.E.) the Flavian dynasty (Vespasian followed by his two sons, Titus and Domitian) provided the empire with effective but autocratic rule. The fiction of republican institutions gave way to a scarcely veiled monarchy as the Flavians openly treated the office of emperor as theirs by right of conquest and inheritance.

The Antonines: "Five Good Emperors"

An end to autocracy and a return to the Augustan principle of an administration of equals—emperor and Senate—characterized the rule of the Antonine emperors (96–180 C.E.), under whom the empire reached the height of its prosperity and power. Selected on the basis of proven ability, these "good emperors" succeeded in establishing a spirit of confidence and optimism among the governing classes throughout the empire. Two of these emperors are especially worthy of mention.

Hadrian reigned from 117 to 138 C.E. His first important act was to stabilize the boundaries of the

The villa of the emperor Hadrian at Tivoli, a short distance away from Rome's congestion. Hadrian had the villa landscaped and decorated with replicas of famous Greek and oriental monuments.

empire. He gave up as indefensible recently conquered Armenia and Mesopotamia and erected protective walls in Germany and Britain. Hadrian traveled extensively, inspecting almost every province of the empire. New cities were founded, old ones were restored, and many public works were constructed, among them the famous Pantheon, still standing in Rome.

The last of the "five good emperors" was Marcus Aurelius (MAHR-kuhs ah-REE-lee-uhs), who ruled from 161 to 180 C.E. He preferred the study of philosophy and the quiet contemplation of his books to the blood and brutality of the battlefield. Yet he was repeatedly troubled by the invasions of the Parthians from the east and Germans from across the Danube. While engaged in his Germanic campaigns, he wrote his *Meditations*, a collection of personal thoughts notable for its Stoic idealism and love of humanity. Like a good Stoic, Marcus Aurelius died at his post at Vindobona (Vienna); at Rome his equestrian statue still stands on the Capitoline Hill.

The Pax Romana

In its finest period, the empire was a vast area stretching from Britain to the Euphrates and populated by more than 100 million people. It was welded together into an orderly and generally peaceful state, bringing stability and prosperity to the Mediterranean region and beyond. Non-Romans were equally conscious of the rich benefits derived from the Pax Romana, which began with Augustus and reached its fullest development under the Five Good Emperors. They welcomed the peace, prosperity, and administrative efficiency of the empire. Cities increased in number and were largely self-governed by their own upper-class magistrates and senates.

DOCUMENT

Excerpt from Aelius Aristides, *The Roman Oration*

Economic Prosperity

Rome's unification of the ancient Mediterranean world had far-reaching economic consequences. The

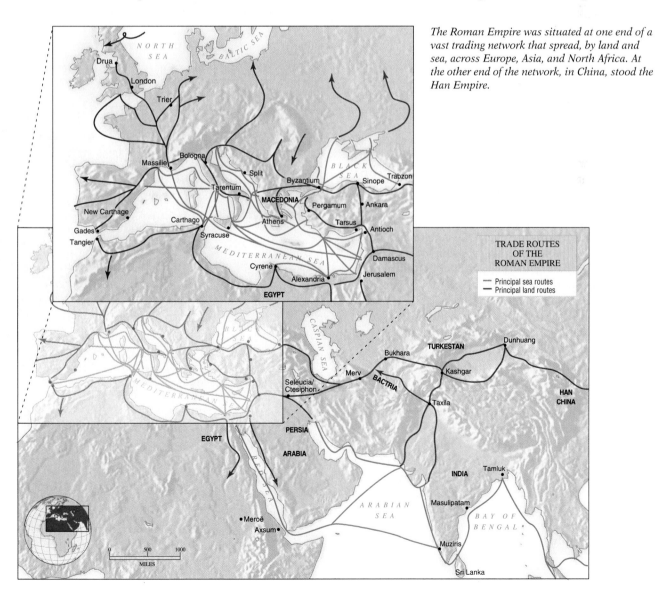

The Roman Empire was situated at one end of a vast trading network that spread, by land and sea, across Europe, Asia, and North Africa. At the other end of the network, in China, stood the Han Empire.

Pax Romana was responsible for the elimination of tolls and other artificial barriers, the suppression of piracy and lawlessness, and the establishment of a reliable coinage. Such factors, in addition to the longest period of peace the West has ever enjoyed, explain in large measure the great expansion of commerce that occurred in the first and second centuries C.E. Industry was also stimulated, but its expansion was limited since wealth remained concentrated and no mass market for industrial goods was created. Industry remained organized on a small-shop basis, with producers widely scattered, resulting in self-sufficiency.

The economy of the empire remained basically agricultural, and huge estates, the *latifundia*, prospered. On these tracts, usually belonging to absentee owners, large numbers of *coloni*, free tenants, tilled the soil as sharecroppers. The *coloni* were replacing slave labor, which was becoming increasingly hard to secure with the disappearance of the flow of war captives.

Early Evidence of Economic Stagnation

Late in the first century C.E. the first sign of economic stagnation appeared in Italy. Italian agriculture began to suffer from overproduction as a result of the loss of Italy's markets for wine and olive oil in Roman Gaul, Spain, and North Africa, which were becoming self-sufficient in those products. To aid the Italian wine producers, the Flavian emperor Domitian created an artificial scarcity by forbidding the planting of new vineyards in Italy and by ordering half the existing vineyards in the provinces to be plowed under. A century later the Five Good Emperors sought to solve the continuing problem of overproduction in Italy by subsidizing the buying power of consumers. Loans at 5 percent interest were made to ailing landowners, with the interest to be paid into the treasuries of Italian municipalities and earmarked "for girls and boys of needy parents to be supported at public expense." This system of state subsidies was soon extended to the provinces.

Also contributing to Roman economic stagnation was the continuing drain of money to the East for the purchase of such luxury goods as silks and spices and the failure of city governments within the empire to keep their finances in order, thus making it necessary for the imperial government to intervene. Such early evidence of declining prosperity foreshadowed the economic crisis of the third century C.E., when political anarchy and monetary inflation caused the economy of the empire to collapse.

Roman Society During the Empire

The social structure of Rome and of the entire empire underwent slow but significant change in the early centuries of the Common Era. At the top of the Roman social order were the old senatorial families who lived as absentee owners of huge estates and left commerce and finance to a large and wealthy middle class. In contrast to the tenements of the poor, the homes of the rich were palatial, as revealed by excavations at Pompeii, which was buried and so preserved by the eruption of the volcano Vesuvius in 79 C.E. These elaborate villas contained courts and gardens with fountains, rooms with marble walls, mosaics on the floors, and numerous frescoes and other works of art. An interesting feature of Roman furniture was the abundance of couches

Wall painting of an imaginary garden, recently excavated in the villa of Livia Drusilla, the wife of the emperor Augustus. The scene is painted on the wall of Livia's triclinium, a large living and dining area within the villa, and dates to circa 10 B.C.E. Trees, fruits, birds, and flowers of all varieties are portrayed to create a perfect natural setting.

A fresco portrait of a young woman from Pompeii. She seems to be caught in thought as she prepares to make an entry in her diary.

and the scarcity of chairs. People usually reclined, even at meals.

Roman women in the early empire were still very much the subjects of their fathers or husbands. They could not vote, they had almost no opportunity to represent their own interests in the law courts, nor could they initiate divorce proceedings unless a husband could be convicted of sorcery or murder. Women of very high social status continued to be looked upon as valuable assets in creating marriage alliances between families for eventual political or economic advantage. Wives of many emperors were regarded as representations of the ideal Roman woman, but most such highborn women were given little actual power. With the steady increase in the west of the number of noble women from the eastern empire, where women were permitted more independence of character and action, and through the growing popularity of eastern **mystery religions,** which highlighted the significance of women, the western empire began slowly to grant more rights to its female citizens.

The lower classes in the cities found recreation in social clubs, or guilds, called *collegia* (co-LEE-gee-ah), each comprising the workers of one trade. The activity of the collegia did not center on economic goals, like modern trade unions, but on the worship of a god and on feasts, celebrations, and decent burials for members. The social conditions of slaves varied greatly. Those in domestic service were often treated humanely, with their years of efficient service sometimes rewarded by emancipation or a less demanding retirement from service. Freed slaves were sometimes able to rise to positions of significance in business, letters, and the imperial service. But conditions among slaves on the large estates could be indescribably harsh. Beginning with Augustus, however, legal restrictions protected slaves from mistreatment.

Slaves in Roman Law

---

mystery religion—Secret religious cults popular in both Greece and Rome. They reached their peak of popularity in the first three centuries C.E. Their members met secretly to share meals and take part in dances and ceremonies, especially initiation rites. Observance of the proper rites and rituals were thought to provide the initiated with a blessed and blissful existence in the afterlife.

Portrait of a young Egyptian man flanked by folding doors depicting the goddess Isis (left) and the god Serapis, both of whom were associated with death and the afterlife. These paintings on wood panels date to circa 180–200 C.E. and are some of the very few remaining representations of Greco-Roman portraiture used in connection with Egyptian rites for the dead.

Recreation played a key role in Roman social life. Both rich and poor were exceedingly fond of their public baths, which in the capital alone numbered 800 during the early days of the empire. The larger baths contained enclosed gardens, promenades, gymnasia, libraries, and famous works of art as well as a sequence of cleansing rooms through which one moved—the sweat room, the warm room where sweat was scraped off by a slave (soap was unknown), the tepid room for cooling off, and the invigorating cold bath. Another popular room was the lavatory, with its long row of marble toilets equipped with comfortable arm rests.

Footraces, boxing, and wrestling were popular sports, but chariot racing and gladiatorial contests were the chief amusements. By the first century C.E. the Roman calendar had as many as 100 days set aside as holidays, the majority of which were given over to games furnished at public expense. The most spectacular sport was chariot racing. The largest of six racecourses at Rome was the Circus Maximus, a huge marble-faced structure seating about 150,000 spectators. The games, which included as many as 24 races each day, were presided over by the emperor or his representative. The crowds bet furiously on their favorite charioteers, whose fame equaled that of the sports heroes of our own day.

Of equal or greater popularity were the gladiatorial contests, organized by both emperors and private promoters as regular features on the amusement calendar. These spectacles were held in arenas, the largest and most famous of which was the Colosseum, opened in 80 C.E. The contests took various forms. Ferocious animals were pitted against armed combatants

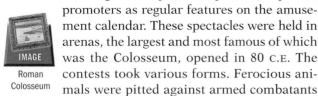

IMAGE

Roman Colosseum

or occasionally even against unarmed men and women who had been condemned to death. Another type of contest was the fight to the death between gladiators, generally equipped with different types of weapons but matched on equal terms. It was not uncommon for the life of a defeated gladiator who had fought courageously to be spared at the request of the spectators. Although many Romans considered these bloodletting contests barbaric, they continued until the fifth century, when Christian rulers outlawed them.

THE RISE OF CHRISTIANITY

■ *How did Christianity grow from humble beginnings to become the sole religion of the Roman Empire?*

The growth of the Christian religion, from its modest beginnings in an obscure part of the Roman Empire to its eventual dominance as the one and only religion tolerated by that same empire that had once persecuted its followers, is a remarkable story. The rise and ultimate victory of Christianity in the Roman world has even been identified by many observers throughout Europe's history as perhaps the most significant reason for the ultimate decline and fall from dominance of the Roman Empire itself. Whether Christianity was the primary cause of Rome's demise remains a highly debated topic, but there is no controversy about the fact that the religion's growth and development in the ancient world changed not just the course of European but also of world history.

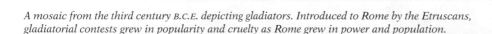

A mosaic from the third century B.C.E. depicting gladiators. Introduced to Rome by the Etruscans, gladiatorial contests grew in popularity and cruelty as Rome grew in power and population.

A partially unrolled section of the texts known as the Dead Sea Scrolls, now preserved and displayed at the Hebrew University in Jerusalem. The Scrolls were preserved by the Essenes, a sect of Jewish militant and religious zealots, whose nearby monastery was destroyed by the Romans in the Jewish revolt of 66–70 B.C.E.

The Jewish Background

Following the conquests of Alexander the Great in the Near East, the Ptolemies and then the Seleucids ruled Palestine. After the Jews returned from exile in Babylonia in 538 B.C.E. (see Chapter 1), they attempted to create a theocratic community based on God's law (the *Torah*) as contained in the *Pentateuch* (PEN-tah-teuk), the first five books of the Old Testament. Later they added to this record the teachings of the prophets and the writings of priests and scholars.

Jewish religious life in Jerusalem centered on the Temple at Jerusalem, and Jewish groups outside Palestine—the Jews of the Diaspora, those who did not return to Palestine after the Babylonian exile—met in local *synagogues* (from the Greek word for "assembly") for public worship and instruction in the Scriptures.

During the Hellenistic Age, Greek philosophy and culture constantly influenced the Jews outside Palestine, most of whom spoke Greek, and contributed to factionalism among the Jews in Palestine. Religious conflict often developed into open warfare.

It was in the midst of a civil war that the Roman legions first made their appearance. In 63 B.C.E. Pompey, who was then completing his pacification of Asia Minor and Syria, made Judea a Roman dependency, subject to the Roman governor of Syria. Later, Herod the Great, a half-Jewish, half-Arab leader from Edom, was appointed king of Judea by Mark Antony and reigned from 37 to 4 B.C.E. Soon after Herod's death, Judea became a Roman administrative unit ruled by officials called *procurators*. The best-known procurator was Pontius Pilate, who ruled from 26 to 36 C.E. and under whose government Jesus was crucified. The Jews remained unhappy and divided under Roman domination. For centuries the prophets had taught that God would one day create a new Israel under a Messiah—a leader anointed by God. Many Jews lost hope in a political Messiah and an earthly kingdom and instead began to hope for a Messiah who would lead all the righteous to a spiritual kingdom.

The Life and Teaching of Jesus

The Jewish sect that became Christianity bears the unmistakable imprint of the personality of its founder, Jesus of Nazareth. According to the biblical accounts pieced together from the four Gospels, he was born in Bethlehem during Herod's reign; therefore, he must have been born by the time of Herod's death in 4 B.C.E.— probably not in the year that traditionally begins the Christian or Common Era, 1 C.E. After spending the first years of his adult life as a carpenter in the village of Nazareth, Jesus began preaching love for one's fellow human beings and urging people to turn away from sin.

DOCUMENT

Excerpt from the Gospel According to Luke

Reports of Jesus's miracles, such as casting out demons, healing the sick, raising the dead, and walking on water, spread among the Jews as he and his 12 apostles traveled from village to village. When he came to Jerusalem to observe the feast of the Passover, huge crowds greeted him enthusiastically as the promised Messiah. But his opponents, most importantly the influential sect of the **Pharisees,** accused him of distortion

Pharisees—Jewish religious party that emerged c. 160 B.C.E. in Palestine. The Pharisees believed that the Jewish oral tradition was as valid as the law presented in the Old Testament. Their belief that reason must be applied in the interpretation of the Old Testament and its application to contemporary problems has now become basic to Jewish theology.

of Jewish religious law, and with treason for claiming to be king of the Jews. He was crucified, a standard Roman penalty for treason, probably in 30 C.E.

The Spread of Christianity

Soon after Jesus's death, word spread that he had been seen alive after his crucifixion and had spoken to his disciples, giving them comfort and reassurance. Initially, there were few converts in Palestine, but the Hellenized Jews living in foreign lands, in contact with new ideas and modes of living, were less firmly committed to traditional Jewish **doctrines.** The new faith first made rapid headway among the Jewish communities in such cities as Damascus, Antioch (where its followers were first called "Christians" by the Greeks), Corinth, and Rome.

The Spread of Christianity to 300 C.E.

The first followers of Jesus had no thought of breaking away from Judaism. But because they adhered to the requirements of the Jewish law, their new message did not easily attract non-Jews. These obstacles were largely removed through more liberal and cosmopolitan teachings of an early Christian convert now known as Saint Paul. Because of his powerful influence, he has been called the second founder of Christianity.

Originally named Saul, Paul was of Jewish ancestry but a Roman citizen by birth. He was raised in the cosmopolitan city of Tarsus, in Asia Minor, and possessed a thorough knowledge of Greek culture. He was also a strict Pharisee who considered Christians to be traitors to the sacred law, and he took an active part in their persecution. One day about 33 C.E., while traveling to Damascus to prosecute the Christian community there, Saul experienced a conversion to the very beliefs he had been vigorously opposing. His conversion caused him to change his name, and also the whole course of his life—from an opponent of the new religion into the greatest of the early Christian missionaries.

Paul taught that Jesus was the Christ (from the Greek *Christos,* "Messiah"), the Son of God, and that he had died to atone for the sins of all people, and to bring salvation to Jews and Gentiles (non-Jews) alike. Adherence to the complexities of the Jewish law was unnecessary.

After covering 8000 miles teaching and preaching, Paul supposedly was put to death in Rome about 65 C.E., the same year as Peter, founder of the church at Rome, during the reign of Nero. By that time Christian communities had been established in all the major cities in the East and at Rome. Paul had performed a very important service to these infant communities of

believers by instructing them, either through visits or letters, in the fundamental beliefs of the new religion. He had served as an authority by which standardization of belief could be achieved.

Reasons for the Spread of Christianity

The popular mystery religions that the Romans had embraced from Greece and the Near East during the troubled last century of the Republic gave spiritual satisfaction not provided by Rome's early ritualistic forms of worship. These mystery religions included the worship of the Phrygian Cybele (Si-BEH-lee), the Great Mother *(Magna Mater);* the Egyptian Isis, sister and wife of Osiris; the Greek Dionysus, called Bacchus by the Romans; and the Persian sun-god Mithras, the intermediary between humans and Ahura-Mazda, the great Lord of Light, whose sacred day of worship was called Sunday and from whose cult women were excluded. Common to all the mystery religions were the notions of a divine savior and the promise of everlasting life.

Followers of these mystery cults found Christian beliefs and practices familiar enough to convert easily to the new faith. But Christianity had far more to offer than the mystery religions did. Its founder was not a creature of myth, like the gods and goddesses of the mystery cults, but a real person whose ethical teachings were preserved by his followers and later written down. Shared with the Jews was the concept of a single omnipotent God, the God of the Hebrew Scriptures, now the God of all humanity. Moreover, Christianity was a dynamic, aggressive faith. It upheld the spiritual equality of all people—rich and poor, slave and freeborn, male and female. Women were among Jesus's audiences, and Paul's letters give much evidence of women active in the early church. One of Jesus's closest and favored followers was said to have been Mary Magdalene, a former prostitute. According to the so-called Gnostic Gospels, which the church declared heretical in the early fourth century and ordered destroyed, "Christ loved her more than all the disciples."

Christianity taught that God, the loving Father, had sent his only Son to atone for human sins and offered a vision of immortality and an opportunity to be "born again," cleansed of sin. Its converts were bound together by faith and hope, and they took seriously their obligation of caring for orphans, widows, and other unfortunates. The courage with which some of their number faced death and persecution impressed even their bitterest enemies.

Persecution of the Christians

The Roman government tolerated any religion that did not threaten the safety and stability of the empire. Christianity, however, initially was perceived as a sub-

---

doctrine—A specific position that is taught or advocated. In a religious context, a doctrine is an official position that must be accepted by those who wish to consider themselves believers.

versive danger to society and the state. Christians, as monotheists, refused to offer sacrifice to the state cults on behalf of the emperor—not even a few grains of incense cast upon an altar. Offering sacrifice to the state cults was considered an essential patriotic rite uniting all Roman subjects in common loyalty to the imperial government. For Christians, however, there was only one God: they could sacrifice to no others. In the eyes of many Roman officials, this attitude branded them as traitors.

To the Romans, the Christians were a secret antisocial group forming a state within a state—"walling themselves off from the rest of mankind," as a pagan writer observed. Many were pacifists who refused to serve in the army, denied the legitimacy of other religious sects, and refused to associate with pagans or take part in social functions that they considered sinful or degrading.

During the first two centuries after Jesus's crucifixion, persecution of Christians was sporadic and local, such as that at Rome under Nero. But during the late third and fourth centuries, when the empire was in danger of collapse, three organized efforts were launched to suppress Christianity throughout the empire. By far the longest and most systematic campaign against the Christians, who made up perhaps one-tenth of the population in the early fourth century, was instigated by the emperor Diocletian (dai-o-KLEE-shan) from 303 to 311. He stringently imposed the death penalty on anyone who refused to sacrifice to Roman gods. But the inspired defiance of the Christian **martyrs,** who seemed to welcome death, had a persuasive effect on many observers. "The blood of the martyrs is the seed of the church" became a Christian slogan.

Church Organization

Viewing the present world as something that would end quickly with the imminent second coming of Christ and the last judgment of the living and the dead, the earliest Christians saw no need to build a formal religious bureaucracy. But after it became clear that the second coming would not be immediate, a church organization emerged to manage the day-to-day business of defining, maintaining, and spreading the faith.

At first there was little or no distinction between laity and **clergy.** Traveling teachers visited Christian communities, preaching and giving advice. But the steady growth in the number of Christians made necessary special church officials who could devote all their time to religious work, clarifying the body of Christian doctrine, conducting services, and collecting money for charitable purposes.

The earliest officials were called *presbyters* ("elders"), *deacons* ("servers"), or *bishops* ("overseers"). By the second century, the offices of bishop and presbyter had become distinct. Christian communities in villages near the main church, which was usually located in a city, were administered by priests who were responsible to a bishop. The *diocese,* a territorial administrative division under the jurisdiction of a bishop, usually corresponded to a Roman administrative district of the same name. The bishops were reputed to be the direct successors of the apostles and, like them, the guardians of Christian teaching and traditions.

A number of dioceses made up a *province.* The bishop of the most important city in each province enjoyed more prestige than his fellows and was known as an *archbishop* or *metropolitan.* The provinces were grouped into larger administrative divisions called *patriarchates.* The title of *patriarch* was applied to the bishop of such great cities as Rome, Constantinople, and Alexandria.

The bishop of Rome rose to a position of preeminence in the hierarchy of the church in the western empire. At first only one of several patriarchs, the Roman bishop gradually became recognized as the leader of the church in the West and was given the title of *pope,* from the Greek word for "father." Many factors explain the emergence of the papacy (the office and jurisdiction of the pope) at Rome. As the largest city in the West and the capital of the empire, Rome had an aura of prestige that was transferred to its bishop. After political Rome had fallen, religious Rome remained. When the empire in the West collapsed in the fifth century, the bishop of Rome emerged as a stable and dominant figure looked up to by all. The primacy of Rome was fully evident during the pontificate of Leo I, the Great (440–461), who provided both the leadership that saved Italy from invasion by the Huns (see page 158) and the major theoretical support for papal leadership of the church, the Petrine theory. This doctrine held that because Peter, whom Jesus had made leader of the apostles, was the first bishop of Rome, his authority over all Christians was handed on to his successors at Rome. The church in the East, insisting on the equality of all the apostles, never accepted the Petrine theory.

Foundations of Christian Doctrine and Worship

While the administrative structure of the church adapted to changing conditions in the West, a combination of theologians and church administrators

---

martyrs—Those who voluntarily suffer death rather than deny their religious convictions. The early Christian church saw the suffering of martyrs as a test of their faith. Many saints of the early church underwent martyrdom during the persecutions imposed by Roman authorities.

clergy—The recognized group or body of persons who are officials of a religious organization. In the early Christian church, the clergy were ordained (recognized as officials through ceremonial appointment) and considered apart from the laity, or the believers who were not officials of the church.

defined and systematized Christian beliefs, sometimes by arbitrary means. This process of fixing Christian doctrine, or *dogma,* began with Paul, who stressed Jesus's divinity and explained his death as an atonement for the sins of all humanity.

In time, differences of opinion over doctrinal matters caused many controversies. One of the most important was over a belief called *Arianism.* At issue was the relative position of the three persons of the Trinity: God the Father, God the Son, and God the Holy Spirit. The view that Father and Son were equal was vigorously denied by Arius (256–336), a priest from Alexandria. He believed that Christ logically could not fully be God because he was not of a substance identical with God and, as a created being, was not coeternal with his creator. The controversy became so serious that in 325 the emperor Constantine convened the first ecumenical church council to resolve the problem. This Council of Nicaea (ni-SEE-a) was the first of such councils in early church history. With Constantine presiding, the council found the Arian position to be a **heresy**—an opinion or doctrine contrary to the official teaching of the church—and Christ was declared to be of the same substance as God, uncreated and coeternal with him. This mystical concept of the Trinity, essential to the central Christian doctrine of the *incarnation*—God becoming man in Christ—received official formulation in the Nicene Creed. However, Arius's views found acceptance among the Germans, and his version of the doctrine of the Trinity was adopted throughout Europe and North Africa.

The **liturgy** of the early churches was plain and simple, consisting of prayer, Scripture reading, hymns, and preaching. Early Christians worshiped God and sought salvation through individual efforts. Following the growth of church organization and proclamation of official dogma, however, the church came to be viewed as the indispensable intermediary between God and humans. Without the church, the individual could not hope for salvation.

The development of the church's dogma owed much to the church fathers of the second through fifth centuries. Since most of them were intellectuals who came to Christianity thoroughly equipped with a classical education, they maintained that Greek philosophy and Christianity were compatible. Because reason (*logos* in Greek) and truth came from God, philosophy was considered a proper tool with which one could discover God's perfection. Thus Christianity was viewed as a superior philosophy that could supersede all pagan philosophies and religions.

In the West three church fathers made highly significant contributions to the formation of Christian dogma and organization. The scholarship of Jerome (340–420) made possible the church-authorized translation of the Bible into Latin. In a revised form, it is still the official translation of the Roman Catholic Church. Jerome also justified Christian use of the literature and learning of the classical world.

Another of the church fathers, St. Ambrose (340–397), resigned his government post to become bishop of Milan, where he employed his great administrative skills to establish a model bishopric. By criticizing the actions of the strong emperor Theodosius I and forcing him to do public penance, Ambrose was the first to assert the church's superiority over the state in spiritual matters.

St. Augustine (354 – 430) was the most influential of all the church fathers in the west. At the age of 32, as he relates in his *Confessions,* one of the world's great autobiographies, he found in Christianity the answer to his long search for meaning in life. Before, he had shared the doubts of men who search for spiritual satisfaction. He blended classical logic and philosophy with Christian belief to lay the foundation of much of the church's theology.

The Regular Clergy

The secular clergy moved through the world (*saeculum;* SAI-keu-lum), administering the church's services and communicating its teachings to the laity, the common people. But another type of clergy also arose: the regular clergy, so called because they lived by a rule (*regula*) within monasteries. These monks sought seclusion from the distractions of this world in order to prepare themselves for the next. In so doing, they helped preserve and spread the heritage of the classical world along with the faith.

The monastic way of life was older than formalized Christianity, having existed among the Essenes, a militant Jewish communal group. Christian ascetics, who had abandoned worldly life to live as hermits, could be found in Egypt and the East as early as the first century C.E. They pursued spiritual perfection by denying their physical feelings, torturing themselves, and fasting. In Syria, for example, St. Simeon Stylites sat for 33 years atop a 60-foot-high pillar. A disciple then surpassed his record by three months.

---

heresy—Any belief rejected as false by religious authorities. In Christianity, the official teachings of the church were believed to be based on divine revelation, and so heretics were viewed as perversely rejecting the guidance of the church. Numerous Christian heresies appeared from the second century onwards.

liturgy—The organization of services for public worship. A standardized and formal presentation of services usually associated with public worship. In the early Christian context, the formal organization of services usually connected with the Eucharist.

In a more moderate expression of **asceticism,** Christian monks in Egypt developed a monastic life in which, seeking a common spiritual goal, they lived together under a common set of regulations. St. Basil (330–379), a Greek bishop in Asia Minor, drew up a rule based on work, charity, and a communal life that still allowed each monk to retain most of his independence. The Rule of St. Basil became the standard system in the eastern church.

In the West the work of St. Benedict (c. 480–543) paralleled St. Basil's efforts in the East. About 529 Benedict led a band of followers to a high hill between Rome and Naples, named Monte Cassino, where they erected a monastery on the site of an ancient pagan temple. For his monks Benedict composed a rule that gave order and discipline to western monasticism. Benedictine monks took three basic vows—of poverty, chastity, and obedience to the *abbot,* the head of the monastery. The daily activities of the Benedictine monks were closely regulated: They participated in eight divine services, labored in fields or workshops for six or seven hours, and spent about two hours studying and preserving the writing of Latin antiquity at a time when illiteracy was widespread throughout western Europe. Benedictine monasticism was to be one of the most dynamic civilizing forces in early medieval Europe.

Women also played an important role in monastic Christianity. In Egypt an early-fifth-century bishop declared that 20,000 women—twice the number of men—were living in desert communities as nuns. In the West several fourth-century biographies of aristocratic women describe how they turned their villas and palaces into monasteries for women of all classes and remained firmly in control of their institutions. These communities became famous for their social and educational services, in addition to providing a different way of life for women who sought alternatives to the usual pattern of marriage, motherhood, and family life.

Official Recognition and Acceptance of Christianity

In 311 the emperor Galerius (ga-LEH-ree-uhs) recognized that persecution of Christians had failed to eliminate the belief and issued an edict of toleration, making Christianity a legal religion in the East. Two years later Constantine granted Christians freedom of worship throughout the empire by issuing, in 313, the Edict of Milan, an order decreeing that Christianity would be tolerated throughout the empire.

Why Constantine did this is open to debate. His Christian biographers assert that the night before a decisive battle at the Milvian Bridge, he looked to the sky and saw a cross with the words *"Hoc vinces"* ("By this, conquer") written on it. The next day, Constantine led his troops to victory, raising the cross as his symbol. The victory also played a role in his embrace of Christianity, which allowed him to build on the support of Christians, who, at 20 percent of the empire, constituted the most organized and unified segment of the population. His actions at the Council of Nicaea (see p. 154) as a self-proclaimed "thirteenth apostle" showed that the Christian Church was to be his state church. Constantine and his mother, Helena, remained deeply committed to Christianity, but he waited until just before his death to be baptized. All of his successors but one were Christian.

This sole exception was Julian the Apostate (361–363), a military hero and scholar who had been raised a Christian but then renounced his faith and sought to revive paganism. But Julian did not persecute the Christians, and his efforts to revive paganism failed.

The emperor Theodosius I (379–395) made Christianity the official religion of the empire. Paganism was now persecuted, Christian authorities sentenced large numbers of pagan philosophers to death, pagan philosophical schools (including Plato's Academy) were closed, and non-Christian works of art and literature were destroyed. Even the Olympic games were suppressed. One famous victim of this persecution *by* Christians was the philosopher Hypatia (hi-PAY-shi-ah), who in 415 was killed by a Christian mob in Alexandria. By the age of 25, she had become famous throughout the eastern half of the empire as a lecturer on Greek philosophy. Her popularity and beauty aroused the resentment of Cyril, the archbishop of Alexandria, who had already led a mob in destroying the homes and businesses of the city's Jews. He incited the mob to abduct Hypatia, who was dragged into a nearby church and hacked to death.

The Roman Crisis of the Third Century

In the third century C.E., internal anarchy and foreign invasion drastically transformed the Roman Empire. Augustus's constitutional monarchy, in which the emperor shared power with the Senate, had changed to a despotic absolute monarchy, in which the emperors made no attempt to hide the fact that they were backed by the military and would tolerate no senatorial influence. By the late third century, the emperor was no

---

asceticism—The denial of physical or psychological desires in order to achieve a spiritual ideal or goal. The quest for spiritual purity, the need for forgiveness, and the wish to earn merit or gain access to supernatural powers all are reasons for ascetic practice. Common forms of ascetic self-denial include celibacy, abstinence, and fasting.

longer addressed as *princeps*, "first among equals," but as *dominus et deus*, "lord and god." The Principate had been replaced by the absolute rule known as the Dominate.

The transformation of the Roman Empire in the third century was foreshadowed by the reign of Commodus (KOM-moh-duhs), who in 180 C.E. began a 12-year rule characterized by incompetence, corruption, cruelty, and neglect of affairs of state. He was strangled in 192, and civil war followed for a year until the establishment of the Severan dynasty (193–235). The Severan dynasty was intimidated by the military, whose commanders the emperors attempted to placate through bribes and exorbitant favors.

After 235, when the last member of the Severan dynasty was murdered by his own troops, 50 years of bloody civil wars, Germanic invasions, and new foreign threats ensued. Of the 26 men who claimed the title of emperor during this time, only one died a natural death. Prolonged economic decline was equally deadly to the well-being of the empire as military anarchy and foreign invasions. The economy became static, inflation set in, and the concentration of land ownership in the hands of the few destroyed the small farming classes. The *latifundia*, with their fortified villas, grew as the number of *coloni*—sharecroppers—grew. As the rural tax base declined, chaotic conditions took their toll on trade, and by the end of the period, the government refused to accept its own money for taxes and required payment in goods and services.

A much needed reconstruction of the empire was accomplished by Diocletian (285–305), a rough-hewn soldier and shrewd administrator. To increase the strength of the government, he completed the trend toward autocracy, leaving the Senate in a greatly diminished role. He attempted to restructure the empire to ensure better government and an efficient succession scheme. Diocletian also tried to stop the economic decay of the empire by issuing new coins based on silver and gold and by imposing a freeze on prices and wages.

Diocletian's succession scheme collapsed when Constantine (306–337) overcame his rivals to take power. Constantine continued

Diocletian's attempts to ensure the production of essential goods and services as well as the collection of taxes. He imposed decrees tying people and their children to the same occupation in the same place. Most important, he moved the capital to the site of the old Greek colony of Byzantium, renaming it Constantinople (see Chapter 6). By doing so, he, in effect, left Rome open to the attacks of the advancing Germanic peoples but ensured the continuation of Roman government in a new, safer location.

The Germanic Tribes

Waves of restless and diverse Germanic tribes were drawn into the power vacuum created during the two centuries of Rome's decline after 180. While the west-

Bust of the emperor Commodus (177–192 C.E.) portrayed as Hercules. The son of the philosopher-emperor Marcus Aurelius, Commodus was physically impressive and often dressed as Hercules and performed as a gladiator. He was one of Rome's most corrupt and despised rulers.

ernmost German tribes (Franks, Angles, and Saxons) had achieved a settled agricultural life in the third and early fourth centuries, the Goths, Vandals, and Lombards remained largely nomadic.

The economic and legal practices of the Germanic tribes set them apart from the Romans. They engaged in so little commerce that cattle, rather than money, sufficed as a measure of value. A basic factor behind Germanic restlessness seems to have been land hunger. Their numbers were increasing, much of their land was forest and swamp, and their agricultural methods were inefficient. In an effort to eliminate blood feuds, the tribal law codes of the Germans encouraged the payment of compensation as an alternative for an aggrieved kin or family seeking vengeance. For the infliction of specific injuries, a stipulated payment, termed a *bot,* was required. The amount of compensation varied according to the severity of the crime and the social position of the victim.

Lack of written laws made it necessary to hold trials to determine guilt or innocence. A person standing trial could produce oath-helpers who would swear to his innocence. If unable to obtain oath-helpers, the accused was subjected to trial by ordeal, of which there were three kinds. In the first, the defendant had to lift a small stone out of a vessel of boiling water; unless his scalded arm healed within a prescribed number of days, he was judged guilty. In the second, he had to walk blindfolded and barefoot across a floor on which lay pieces of red-hot metal; success in avoiding the metal was a sign of innocence. In the third, the bound defendant was thrown into a stream; if he sank he was innocent, but if he floated, he was guilty because water was considered a divine element that would not accept a guilty person.

According to the Roman historian Tacitus, the Germans were notorious as heavy drinkers and gamblers, but Tacitus praised their courage, respect for women, and freedom from many Roman vices. A favorite amusement was listening to the tribal bards recite old tales of heroes and gods. Each warrior leader had a retinue of followers who were linked to him by personal loyalty. The war band—*comitatus* (ko-mi-TAH-tus) in Latin—had an important bearing on the origin of medieval political patterns, which were based on similar personal bonds between vassals and their lords. The heroic values associated with the *comitatus* also continued into the Middle Ages, where they contributed to the basis of the value system of the nobility.

DOCUMENT
Tacitus,
Germania

During the many centuries that the Romans and Germans faced each other across the Rhine-Danube frontier, there was much contact—peaceful as well as warlike—between the two peoples. Roman trade reached into German territory, and Germans entered the Roman Empire as slaves. During the troubled third century, many Germans were invited to settle on vacated lands within the empire or to serve in the Roman legions. By the fourth century, the bulk of the Roman army and its generals in the west were German.

The Germans beyond the frontiers were kept in check by force of arms, by frontier walls, by diplomacy and gifts, and by playing off one tribe against another. In the last decades of the fourth century, however, these methods proved insufficient to prevent a series of new invasions.

The Germanic Invasions

The impetus behind the increasing German activity on the frontiers in the late fourth century was the approach of the Huns. These nomads—superb horsemen and fighters from central Asia—had plundered and slain their Asian neighbors for centuries. In 372 they crossed the Volga River and soon subjugated the easternmost Germanic tribe, the Ostrogoths. Terrified at the prospect of being conquered, the Visigoths, who found themselves next in the path of the advancing Huns, petitioned the Romans to allow them to settle as allies inside the empire. Permission was granted, and in 376 the entire tribe of Visigoths crossed the Danube into Roman territory. But corrupt Roman officials soon cheated and mistreated them, and the proud Germanic tribe went on a rampage. Valens (VAH-lens), the East Roman emperor, tried to stop them, but he lost both his army and his life in the battle of Adrianople in 378.

Adrianople has been described as one of history's decisive battles since it destroyed the legend of the invincibility of the Roman legions and ushered in a century and a half of chaos. For a few years, the emperor Theodosius I held back the Visigoths, but after his death in 395, they began to migrate and pillage under their leader, Alaric. He invaded Italy, and in 410 his followers sacked Rome. The weak West Roman emperor ceded southern Gaul to the Visigoths, who soon expanded into Spain. Their Spanish kingdom lasted until the Muslim conquest of the eighth century.

To counter Alaric's threat to Italy, the Romans had withdrawn most of their troops from the Rhine frontier in 406 and from Britain the following year. A flood of Germanic tribes soon surged across the unguarded frontiers. The Vandals pushed their way through Gaul to Spain and, after pressure from the Visigoths, moved on to Africa, the granary of the empire. In 455 a Vandal raiding force sailed over from Africa, and Rome was sacked a second time. Meanwhile, the Burgundians settled in the Rhone valley, the Franks gradually spread across Gaul, and the Angles, Saxons, and Jutes invaded Britain. Although each of these tribes set up a German-ruled kingdom within the confines of the empire, only the Franks in Gaul and the Angles and Saxons in Britain managed to establish kingdoms that lasted longer than a few generations.

Meanwhile, the Huns pushed farther into Europe. Led by Attila, the "scourge of God," the mounted nomads crossed the Rhine in 451. The remaining Roman forces in Gaul, joined by the Visigoths, defeated the Huns near Troyes, France. Attila then plundered northern Italy and planned to take Rome, but disease, lack of supplies, and the dramatic appeal of Pope Leo I, whose actions brought great prestige to the papacy, caused him to return to the plains of eastern Europe. The Huns' threat disintegrated after 453, when Attila died on the night of his marriage to a Germanic princess.

The End of the West Roman Empire, 395–476 C.E.

After the death of Theodosius I in 395, the Roman Empire was divided between his two sons. The decline of Roman rule in the West was hastened as a series of weakened emperors abandoned Rome and sought safety behind the marshes at the northern Italian city of Ravenna. The leaders of the imperial army, whose ranks were now mainly German, exercised the real power.

In 475 Orestes, a German army commander, forced the Senate to elect his young son Romulus Augustulus ("Little Augustus") emperor in the West. The following year another German chieftain, Odovacar, murdered Romulus Augustulus and named himself head of the government. The murder of this boy, who ironically bore the names of the legendary founder of Rome and the founder of the empire, marks the traditional "fall" of the Roman Empire in the West, since no emperor was named to carry on the succession. Instead, the emperor in Constantinople commissioned Theodoric (thee-O-doh-rik), king of the Germanic tribe of the Ostrogoths, to lead his people into Italy and establish order. The Ostrogothic Kingdom of Italy, with its capital now at Ravenna, restored order on the peninsula, but the political unity of the western empire fell into steady decline. Because he appreciated the culture he had seen at Constantinople, Theodoric attempted to preserve much of the culture of the Roman West, but the basic fabric of society in western Europe was in gradual transition into a new construct which combined useful institutions of both older Roman and new Germanic elements. A new society was evolving.

THE ROMAN LEGACY

■ *What seem to be the greatest cultural achievements of the ancient Romans, and what effects, if any, do they continue to have on the modern world?*

The Romans left a remarkable legacy to their successors. They excelled in the art of government and created a workable and enduring world-state that brought peace and order to extensive lands on three continents. For a time during the empire, probably one-third of the world's population owed allegiance to the Roman superpower. In addition to their skills in administration, the formulation and application of law, and their gifts as architects and engineers, Roman achievements in the arts, literature, philosophy, and religious thought were also greatly influential on the peoples and cultures that were the heir of their accomplishments.

Evolution of Roman Law

Of the many contributions made by the Romans in government, Roman law is one of the most significant. Roman law evolved slowly over a period of about a thousand years. At first, as in all early societies, the law was unwritten custom, handed down from the remote past, and harsh in its judgments. As noted earlier, in the fifth century B.C.E. this law was put in writing in the Code of the Twelve Tables, as the result of plebeian demand. During the remainder of the Republic, the body of Roman law (*jus civile*, "law of the citizen") was enlarged by legislation passed by the Senate and the assembly and by judicial interpretation of existing law to meet new conditions. By the second century C.E. the emperor had become the sole source of law, a responsibility he entrusted to scholars "skilled in the law" (*jurisprudentes*). These scholars were loyal to the principle of equity ("Follow the beneficial interpretation"; "The letter of the law is the height of injustice") and to Stoic philosophy with its concept of a "law of nature" (*jus naturale*) common to all people and obtainable by human reason. As a result, the absolute power of the Roman father over the family was weakened, women gained control over their property, and the principle that an accused person was innocent until proven guilty was established. Finally, in the sixth century C.E. the enormous bulk of Roman law from all sources was codified and so preserved for the future.

Roman Engineering and Architecture

Always at the hub of the sprawling empire was Rome, with close to a million inhabitants by the early days of the empire. Augustus boasted that he had found a city of brick and had left it one of marble. Nonetheless, Rome presented a great contrast of magnificence and slums, of splendid public buildings and poorly constructed tenements, which often collapsed or caught fire.

The empire's needs required a communication system of paved roads and bridges as well as huge public buildings and aqueducts. As road builders, the Romans surpassed all previous peoples. Constructed of layers of stone and gravel according to sound engineering principles, their roads were planned for the use of armies and messengers and were kept in constant repair. The earliest and best-known main Roman highway was the Appian Way. Running from Rome to the Bay of Naples, it was built about 300 B.C.E. to facilitate Rome's expansion southward. It has been said that the speed of travel possible on Roman highways was not surpassed until the early nineteenth century. In designing their bridges and aqueducts, the Romans placed a series of stone arches next to one another to provide mutual support. At times several tiers of arches were used, one above the other. Fourteen aqueducts, stretching a total of 265 miles, supplied some 50 gallons of water daily for each inhabitant of Rome.

At first the Romans copied Etruscan architectural models, but later they combined basic Greek elements with distinctly Roman innovations. By using concrete—a Roman invention—faced with brick or stone, they developed new methods for enclosing space. The Greeks' static post-and-lintel system was replaced by the more dynamic techniques of vaulting derived from the arch, also borrowed from the Etruscans.

Heavy concrete barrel vaults, cross (or groin) vaults, and domes—all so solid that they exerted no sidewise thrust—made possible the vast interiors that distinguish Roman architecture. The barrel vault was essentially a series of connected arches resembling a tunnel, and the cross vault consisted of two barrel vaults intersecting at right angles. The largest Roman domed structure is the Pantheon, the oldest massive roofed building in the world that is still intact. As its name indicates, it was dedicated to "all the gods" by the emperor Hadrian as a symbol of the union of Greeks and Romans on equal terms. The great dome rests on thick round walls of poured concrete with no window openings to weaken them. The only light enters through a great hole, 30 feet wide, at the top of the dome. The size of the dome remained unsurpassed until the twentieth century.

IMAGE

The Interior of the Pantheon, Rome

The typical Roman **basilica,** which served as a social and commercial center and as a law court, was not domed or vaulted. It was a rectangular structure with a light wooden ceiling held up by rows of columns that divided the interior into a central **nave** and side aisles. The roof over the nave was raised to admit light. The Roman basilica would eventually evolve into the Christian church.

Roman buildings were built to last, and their size, grandeur, and decorative richness aptly symbolized the proud imperial spirit of Rome. Whereas the Greeks designed the temple, theater, and stadium, the Romans contributed the triumphal arch, bath, basilica, amphitheater, and multistoried apartment house. Perhaps the most famous Roman building is the Colosseum, a huge amphitheater about 1/4 mile in circumference and with a seating capacity of about 45,000. On the exterior, its arches are decorated with Doric, Ionic, and Corinthian columns.

Marble representation of a dying Gallic woman and her husband committing suicide rather than be taken prisoner by the Romans. The Romans regarded the Gauls as courageous but unsophisticated in politics and culture.

Sculpture and Painting

After the conquest of Greece, many Romans acquired a passion for Greek art. The homes of the wealthy were filled with statues, either brought to Rome as plunder or copied in Greece and shipped to Rome in great number.

Although strongly influenced by Etruscan and Greek models, the Romans developed a distinctive sculpture of their own, particularly portrait sculpture, which was remarkably realistic. Their skill in

basilica—Originally a secular public building in ancient Rome, typically a large rectangular structure with an open hall and a raised platform at one or both ends. "Basilica" is also a title of honor given to a Roman Catholic or Greek Orthodox church distinguished by its antiquity or its role as an international center of worship.

nave—Main part of a Christian church, extending from the entrance (the narthex) to the transept or chancel (area around the altar). In a basilican church (see basilica), which has side aisles, nave refers only to the central section.

portraiture probably originated in the early practice of making and preserving wax images of the heads of important deceased family members. During the Principate, portraiture and relief sculpture tended to idealize the likenesses of the emperors. The Romans developed a great number of decorative motifs, such as cupids, garlands of flowers, and scrolls of various patterns, which are still used today.

What little Roman painting has been preserved clearly reflects the influence of Hellenistic Greek models. The Romans were particularly skilled in producing floor mosaics—often copies of Hellenistic paintings— and in painting frescoes. The frescoes still to be seen in Pompeii and elsewhere show that the artists drew objects in clear though idealized perspective.

Literary Rome

In literature as in art, the Romans originally turned to the Greeks for their models. Roman epic, dramatic, and lyric poetry forms were usually written in conscious imitation of the Greek masterpieces. Although first conforming to Greek examples and standards, Latin prose and poetry developed an originality and substance that ensure its value as one of the world's great literatures. Its influence was extremely strong on medieval and Renaissance literary efforts, and it continues even now on western literary themes and styles.

The Golden and Silver Ages of Latin Literature, c. 100 B.C.E.–138 C.E.

106–43 B.C.E.	Cicero: Orations and letters
c. 87–54 B.C.E.	Catullus: Poems and epigrams
c. 99–55 B.C.E.	Lucretius: Philosophical poem *On the Nature of Things*
70–19 B.C.E.	Virgil: Epic poem *Aeneid*
65–8 B.C.E.	Horace: Poems
43 B.C.E.–17 C.E.	Ovid: *The Art of Love; Metamorphoses*
59 B.C.E.–17 C.E.	Livy: *History of Rome*
c. 55 B.C.E.–117 C.E.	Tacitus: *Annals, Histories, Agricula*
c. 50 B.C.E.–127 C.E.	Juvenal: *Satires*
c. 46–c. 126 C.E.	Plutarch: *Parallel Lives*

Formal Latin literature did not begin until the mid-third century B.C.E. when a Greek slave named Livius Andronicus translated Homer's *Odyssey* and several Greek plays into Latin. By the end of that century the first of a series of Latin epics dealing with Rome's past was composed. Only a few fragments have survived.

The oldest examples of Latin literature to survive intact are the 21 comedies of Plautus (c. 254–184 B.C.E.), which were adapted from Hellenistic Greek originals but with many Roman allusions, colloquialisms, and customs added. Plautus's comedies are bawdy and vigorously humorous, and their rollicking plots of illicit love and character portraits reveal the level of culture and taste in early Rome. The works of Plautus suggest many of the types that modern comedy has assumed, including farce, burlesque, and comedy of manners.

Literature of the Late Republic and Empire

Latin literature came of age in the first century B.C.E., when an outpouring of intellectual effort coincided with the last years of the Republic. This era is often called the Ciceronian period because of the stature and lasting influence of Marcus Tullius Cicero (106–43 B.C.E.), one of the greatest masters of Latin prose and an outstanding intellectual force in Roman history.

Acclaimed as the greatest orator of his day, Cicero found time during his busy public life to write extensively on philosophy, political theory, and rhetoric. Some 900 of his letters survive. Together with 58 speeches, they give us insight into Cicero's personality as well as life in the late Republic. Cicero also made a rich contribution by passing on to the Romans and to later ages much of Greek thought—especially that of Plato and the Stoics—and at the same time interpreting philosophical concepts from the standpoint of a Roman intellectual and practical man of affairs.

Two notable poets of the Ciceronian period were Catullus (Kah-TUHL-luhs) and Lucretius (loo-KREE-shuhs). Catullus (c. 87–54 B.C.E.) was a socially active young man who wrote highly personal lyric poetry. His best-known poems are addressed to "Lesbia," an unprincipled noblewoman ten years older than he, with whom he carried on a passionate affair. Catullus's contemporary Lucretius (c. 99–55 B.C.E.) found in the philosophy of Epicurus (e-pee-KEU-ruhs) an antidote to his profound disillusionment with his fellow citizens, whom he criticized for their lack of morals and obsession for wealth and sensual pleasures.

Augustus provided the Roman world with a stability and confidence that encouraged a further outpouring of literary creativity. The literature of the Augustan Age was notable particularly for its poetry. Virgil (70–19 B.C.E.) is considered the greatest of all Roman poets. His masterpiece, the great epic poem called the *Aeneid* (ay-NEE-id), glorified the work of Augustus and emphasized Rome's destiny to conquer and rule the world. Using Homer's *Iliad* and *Odyssey* as his models, Virgil recounted the fortunes of Aeneas, the legendary founder of the Latin people, who came from Troy to Italy to fulfill his destiny.

As the most noted poet after Vergil, Horace (65–8 B.C.E.) often praised the work of Augustus and the emperor's great mission. But most of Horace's poetry is concerned with everyday human interests and moods, and succeeding generations up to the present have been attracted by his serene outlook on life.

Quite a different sort of poet was Ovid (43 B.C.E.–17 C.E.). His preference for themes of sensual love in his *Art of Love* and other poems caused Augustus to exile him from Rome. But Ovid was also a first-rate storyteller, and it is largely through his *Metamorphoses*, a witty verse collection of Greek stories about the life of the gods—not neglecting their love lives—that classical mythology was transmitted to the modern world.

The literature of the later empire, especially the period between the deaths of Augustus and Hadrian (14–138 C.E.), substituted a more critical and negative spirit for the patriotism and optimism of the Augustan Age. Despite a great emphasis on artificial stylistic devices, the period was memorable for the moral emphasis of much of its literature, seen in the historical works of Tacitus and Plutarch, the philosophical works of Seneca, and especially the poetry of Juvenal (c. 50 B.C.E.–127 C.E.), who has been called one of the greatest satiric poets, who attacked the shortcomings of Roman society and its overwhelming concern for material gain and sensual pleasures.

DOCUMENT

Juvenal, *Satires*

The Writing of History

Two Roman historians produced notable works of lasting significance during the Augustan age and the early empire. The first, Livy (59 B.C.E.–17 C.E.), was a contemporary of Vergil. His immense *History of Rome,* like the *Aeneid,* is of epic proportions and glorifies Rome's conquests and ancestral greatness. By assembling the legends and traditions of early Roman history and folding them into a continuous narrative, Livy, like Vergil, intended to advance Augustus's program of moral and social regeneration. He praised the virtues of the ancient Romans and sought to draw moral lessons from an idealized past.

Tacitus (55–117 C.E.), like his contemporary Juvenal, was concerned with the declining morality of both the Roman nobility and common citizens. In his *Germania* he contrasted the life of the idealized, simple Germanic tribes with the corrupt and immoral existence of the Roman upper classes. In the *Annals* and *Histories* he used his vivid, succinct prose to depict the shortcomings of the emperors and their courts from the death of Augustus to 96 C.E. Tacitus idealized the earlier Republic, and because he viewed the emperors as tyrants, he could not do justice to the positive contributions of imperial government.

The most famous Greek author in the empire was Plutarch (c. 46–c. 126 C.E.). He lectured on philosophy in Rome before retiring to his small hometown to pursue research on the outstanding figures in Roman and Greek history in order to discover what qualities make people great or unworthy. His *Parallel Lives*, containing 46 biographies of famous Greeks and Romans arranged in pairs for the purpose of comparison, is one of the great readable classics of world literature. Because many of the sources Plutarch used have been lost, his *Lives* is a treasure house of valuable information for the historian.

Religion and Philosophy

The turmoil of the late Republic helped erode the traditions, values, and religion of earlier Rome. For spiritual satisfaction and salvation, many Romans turned increasingly to the mystery cults of Greece (see Chapter 4) or to the Near East. Among the latter were Cybele, the Great Mother, and the Egyptian goddess Isis, who attracted the greatest number of women followers. A faithful mother herself, she extended a mother's arms to the weary of this world.

But the more intellectually sophisticated of Romans turned to Greek philosophy, particularly Epicureanism and Stoicism, for meaning. As young men, both Vergil and Horace embraced Epicureanism, but Lucretius became the most important Roman interpreter of this philosophy. In *On the Nature of Things*, Lucretius followed Epicurus in basing his explanation of the "nature of things" on materialism and atomism. He called on people to free themselves from the fear of death—which was drawing them to the emotional mystery religions of Greece and the East—since souls, like bodies, are composed of atoms that fall apart when death comes. Lucretius urged his readers to seek pleasure in the study of philosophy and not from material gain or such sensual excitements as love.

More in line with Roman taste, especially in the days of the empire, was Stoicism. The emphasis of Roman Stoicism was on living a just life, constancy to duty, courage in adversity, and service to humanity. Stoic influence had a humanizing effect on Roman law by introducing such concepts as the law of nature and the brotherhood of all, including slaves. The law of nature, as defined by Cicero, was an eternal truth that ordered all the rational thought upon which human law must be based.

One of the outstanding Roman Stoics was Seneca (4 B.C.E.–65 C.E.), Nero's tutor and a writer of moral essays and tragedies. He was regarded with high favor by the leaders of the early Christian church, for his Stoicism, like that of the ex-slave Epictetus (eh-pik-TEE-tuhs) (d. 135 C.E.) and the emperor Marcus Aurelius, had the appearance of a religious creed. He stressed an all-wise Providence, or God, and believed that each person possessed a spark of the divine.

Science in the Roman Empire

The Romans were accomplished at putting the findings of Hellenistic science to practical use, and they became extremely skilled in engineering, applied medicine, and public health. The Romans pioneered in public health service and developed the extensive practice of *hydrotherapy*, the use of mineral baths for healing. Beginning in the early empire, doctors were employed in infirmaries where soldiers, officials, and the poor could obtain free medical care. Great aqueducts and admirable drainage systems also indicate Roman concern for public health.

Characteristic of their utilitarian approach to science was their interest in amassing large encyclopedias. The most important of these was the *Natural History*, compiled by Pliny (PLI-nee) the Elder (23–79 C.E), an enthusiastic collector of all kinds of scientific odds and ends. In writing his massive work, Pliny is reputed to have read more than 2000 books. The result is an intriguing mixture of fact and fable thrown together with scarcely any method of classification. Nevertheless, it was the most widely read work on science during the empire and the early medieval period in Europe.

Two of the last great scientific minds of the ancient world were two Greeks, Claudius Ptolemy and Galen, both of whom lived in the second century C.E., an era succeeding the greatness of Hellenic civilization and the growing dominance of Rome. Ptolemy resided at Alexandria, where he became celebrated as a geographer, astronomer, and mathematician. His maps show a comparatively accurate knowledge of a broad section of the known world. But he exaggerated the size of Asia, an error that influenced Columbus to underestimate the width of the Atlantic and to set sail from Spain in search of Asia. His work on astronomy, usually called the *Almagest* ("The Great Work") from the title of the Ara-

bic translation, presented the geocentric (earth-centered) view of the universe that prevailed until the sixteenth century. In mathematics, Ptolemy's work in improving and developing trigonometry became the basis for modern knowledge of the subject.

Galen, born in Pergamum, in Asia Minor, was a physician for a school of gladiators. His fame spread, and he was called to Rome, where he became physician to the emperor Marcus Aurelius. Galen was responsible for notable advances in physiology and anatomy; for example, he was the first to explain the mechanism of respiration. Forbidden by the Roman government to dissect human bodies, Galen experimented with animals and demonstrated that an excised heart can continue to beat outside the body and that injuries to one side of the brain produce effects in the opposite side of the body. Galen's medical encyclopedia, in which he summarized the medical knowledge of antiquity, remained the standard authority until the sixteenth century.

CONCLUSION

The story of Rome's rise from a collection of insignificant and unsophisticated villages along the banks of the Tiber to the mighty capital of an empire that included most of western Europe, the Mediterranean region, and the Near East will always remain one of the most fascinating stories in world history. Through the creation of a unified and cosmopolitan empire, the heritage of earlier near Eastern and Greek cultures was preserved, synthesized, and disseminated—and of course the Romans made significant original contributions of their own. They excelled in political theory, governmental administration, and jurisprudence. Roman military might, conquest, and pacification also enabled the growth and development of trade and commerce throughout the Mediterranean and beyond. The security of the empire, and its vast network of roads, fostered a thriving exchange of ideas as well as tangible goods. The growth and triumph of the Christian religion in the West was due in large part to the material benefits provided by the empire's infrastructure, along with the Roman capacity to adapt and refine the innovations of others.

Rome's greatest achievement was perhaps the establishment of peace and prosperity over a vast area for long periods under a stable and acceptable government. The long-enduring empire and its success in uniting a great variety of cultures and peoples under one system of government had a lasting effect on nations and peoples that came after the fall of the empire in western Europe. The cosmopolitan nature of the Roman experience and Rome's long lasting success in bringing unity and peace for centuries, and to a vast amount of terri-

tory and diverse peoples, might also serve as an example that such achievements are not impossible accomplishments.

Suggestions for Web Browsing

You can obtain more information about topics included in this chapter at the websites listed below. See also the companion website that accompanies this text, www.ablongman.com/brummett, which contains an online study guide and additional resources.

Museums of the Vatican: Gregorian Etruscan Museum
http://www.christusrex.org/www1/vaticano/ET1-Etrusco.html
http://www.christusrex.org/www1/vaticano/ET2-Etrusco.html

Two sites within the extensive pages of the Museums of the Vatican offer numerous images from the Etruscan period.

Timeline
http://www.exovedate.com/ancient_timeline_one.html

The history of ancient Rome, with a chronological index and links to Internet resources. Emphasis is placed on the roles of women in ancient times.

Roman Empire
http://library.advanced.org/10805/rome/html

The history of the empire is illustrated through maps and timelines. Examinations of the sources of our knowledge through Roman writers is emphasized. An extensive history of ancient Rome.

Online Encyclopedia of the Roman Empire
http://www.roman-emperors.org/

A massive site emphasizing the study of Roman history through coins and through maps of the empire.

Pompeii Forum Project
http://pompeii.virginia.edu/forummap.html

Constructed by historians and archaeologists from the University of Virginia, this site examines ancient Pompeii through a variety of photographs.

Vesuvius
http://volcano.und.nodak.edu/vwdocs/volc_images/img_vesuvius.html

A beautiful exploration of Mount Vesuvius in ancient Rome and as it appears today. Speculation on the next eruption as well.

Women's Life in Greece and Rome
http://www.stoa.org/diotima/anthology/wlgr/

Details about the private life and legal status of women, in addition to biographies of prominent women of ancient Rome.

Roman Art and Architecture
http://harpy.uccs.edu/roman/html/romarch.html

A collection of images of Roman architecture.

Literature and Film

Recommended historical novels dealing with Republican and Imperial Rome are a continuing series of mystery novels set in late Republican Rome by Steven Saylor, the most recent of which is *The Judgment of Caesar* (St. Martin's Press, 2004); Thornton Wilder, *The Ides of March* (Avon, 1975); John Williams, *Augustus* (Penguin, 1979); Robert Graves, *I Claudius* (Vintage, 1977); Marguerite Yourcenar, *Memoirs of Hadrian* (Modern Library, 1984); Lindsey Davis, *Time to Depart* (Warner, 1995); and a continuing series of novels dealing with the Roman Republic by Colleen McCullough, beginning with *The First Man in Rome* (Morrow, 1990).

A number of excellent videos available deal with Roman and early Christian themes. Outstanding Hollywood movies, spectacular for their recreations of ancient scenes, are *Ben Hur* (1959), *Spartacus* (1960), and most recently *Gladiator* (2000). More scholarly in content are *Ancient Rome: Story of an Empire* (1998; 4 tapes); *Rome: The Power and the Glory* (2001; Questar); *Catacombs of Rome* (2001; A&E Home Video); and *Rome's Lost Harbor* (2000, A&E Home Video), an excellent account of ancient Ostia. *From Jesus to Christ: The First Christians* (1998; 4 tapes, PBS Home Video) is a very good account of the beginnings of the religion. Finally, *I, Claudius* (1996; 7 tapes, BBC Production) is a classic presentation of the novel by Robert Graves.

Suggestions for Reading

H. H. Scullard, *A History of the Roman World, 753–146 B.C.*, 5th edition (Methuen, 1980); and Michael Grant, *History of Rome* (Scribner, 1979), are highly recommended general historical accounts. Also an excellent general study is Max Cary and Howard H. Scullard, *A History of Rome: Down to the Reign of Constantine*, 3rd ed. (St. Martin's Press, 1976). Ellen Macnamara, *The Etruscans* (Cambridge, 1991), is an informative study of these intriguing people. Three valuable studies of Roman society and morals are Keith Bradley, *Slavery and Society at Rome* (Cambridge University Press, 1994); Florence Dupont, *Daily Life in Ancient Rome* (Oxford University Press, 1992); and Roland Auguet, *Cruelty and Civilization: The Roman Games* (Routledge, 1994). Tom Holland, *Rubicon: The Last Years of the Roman Republic* (Doubleday, 2003) is an outstanding study of the fall of the Republic and Julius Caesar.

For the beginnings of Christianity see J. H. Hexter, *The Judeo-Christian Tradition*, 2nd ed. (Yale University Press, 1995), a brief but valuable survey; Rodney Stark, *The Rise of Christianity* (HarperCollins, 1996); and Richard E. Rubenstein, *When Jesus Became God: The Struggle to Define Christianity during the Last Days of Rome* (Harvest Books, 2000). For the later Roman Empire see Averil Cameron, *The Later Roman Empire: A.D. 284–430* (Harvard University Press, 1993), and Peter Brown, *The Making of Late Antiquity* (Harvard University Press, 1978).

Byzantium and the Orthodox World

Byzantium, Eastern Europe, and Russia, 325–1500

At its height the Roman Empire controlled the Mediterranean world, a zone that extended from the Straits of Gibraltar on the Atlantic Ocean to the Red Sea and the Black Sea. Roman bureaucrats ran a centralized administration that dictated details as small as mosaic patterns on floors in cities as distant as the present-day Constanta, Romania, and Colchester, England. Roman military leaders carried on battles in present-day Persia and along the Danube.

In the power vacuum that followed in the wake of Rome's decline, three civilizations, each sharing common Judeo-Christian roots, emerged to occupy the Mediterranean world. The civilization of western Europe, initially the weakest and most fragmented of the three civilizations, developed under the creative tension between the religious center at Rome and the political structures, such as France, north of the Alps (see Chapter 9). The Islamic world dominated the region in southwest Asia and North Africa (see Chapter 7). The Byzantine Empire, dominating the northwestern part of the Mediterranean world, carried on and modified the Roman traditions, in time transmitting a political and civilizational legacy to the peoples of the Balkans and Russia—the Orthodox world.

In this chapter we will consider the origins and development of the Orthodox world, from the founding of the Eastern Roman capitol at Constantinople—the Second Rome—to the rise of the Russian state at Moscow, the city that claimed the title of the Third Rome after the Ottoman Turks took Constantinople in 1453. When the *tsar* (the Russian word for caesar) Ivan III proclaimed Moscow to be the arena for the playing out of God's divine plan, the end of the world, and the second coming of Christ, he was embracing ideas established first in the Byzantine Empire.

300 C.E.

325 Constantine the Great establishes his capitol in Constantinople (city dedicated May 11, 330)

361–363 Reign of Julian the Apostate

500

527–565 Reign of Justinian

c. 590 Slavic invasions begin

610–641 Heraclius saves Constantinople, defeats Persians

674–678 Arab sieges of Constantinople

700

700–1014 First Bulgarian Empire

797–802 Reign of Empress Irene

842–1071 Golden Age of Byzantium

900

900 Serbian Conversion to Christianity

988 Russian Conversion to Christianity

1071 Byzantine defeat at Manzikert

1096 First Crusade

1100

1204 Fourth Crusade; Crusaders sack Constantinople; Byzantine state disappears until 1261

1354 Turks begin to settle in Europe

1389 Battle of Kosovo

1400

1453 Fall of Constantinople, end of East Roman Empire

1462–1505 Reign of Ivan III, the Great

BYZANTIUM: THE LATIN PHASE, 325–610

■ *Why did the East Roman—and not the West— part of the Empire survive the Germanic invasions in the two centuries after 325?*

In his wide-ranging reforms, the Roman emperor Diocletian (die-oh-KLEE-shun; r. 285–305) had wanted to bring order to the governing of the empire. To that end he imposed a new autocratic model for the emperor. He also wanted to make the transfer of power more systematic by dividing up the empire into eastern and western parts, governed by two caesars and two *augusti.* In theory, as each *augustus* would retire, the caesar-in-waiting would advance to take his place. Instead of resolving the problems of civil wars and regime change, Diocletian's solution led to yet another conflict, this one over control of the western half of the empire to be decided in a conflict between Maxentius and Constantine (306–337) at the battle of the Milvian Bridge in 312.

Constantine and Constantinople

Constantine's biographers assert that during the night before the battle, Constantine looked to the sky and saw a cross with the words, *"In hoc signo vinces"* ("By this, conquer") written on it. The next day, after Christ is said to have appeared in his dreams, Constantine led his troops to victory, raising the cross as his symbol. Thereafter he made an alliance with the Christians that turned a minority, though active, sect into a state religion.

DOCUMENT

Eusebius on Constantine The Great

The Roman political tide had turned quickly in the favor of the Christians at the beginning of the fourth century, a time in which they constituted only 20 percent of the empire, though its most organized and motivated population. Diocletian had sanctioned widespread persecution of the Christian faithful but he had succeeded only in creating more martyrs. In 311, the emperor Galerius recognized that persecution had failed to stop the growth of Christianity and issued an edict of toleration, making Christianity a legal religion in the East. Two years later, Constantine and Licinius granted Christians freedom of worship throughout the empire by issuing, in 313, the **Edict of Milan.**

---

augusti—Plural of *augustus,* the title granted the first Roman emperor by the Senate in 27 B.C.E. The title passed to all of his successors. Under Diocletian's plan, the empire would be split into eastern and western parts, governed by two caesars and two *augusti.*

Edict of Milan—Constantine and Licinius in 313 granted Christians the freedom openly to worship their religion throughout the Roman Empire.

In 325, a number of factors convinced Constantine to move his capitol to the site of the old Greek city of Byzantium, including his new affiliation with the Christians (who were then primarily concentrated in the East), the political and defensive disadvantages of Rome, and the wealth of the eastern part of the empire. Constantine named the city after himself and dedicated it as the first Christian city on May 11, 330. He chose a site on the frontier of Europe and Asia dominating the waterway connecting the Mediterranean and Black Seas and protected on three sides by cliffs. The emperor and his successors fortified the fourth side with an impenetrable three-wall network. In the first two centuries, Visigoths, Huns, and Ostrogoths unsuccessfully threatened the city. In the seventh, eighth, and ninth centuries first Persians, then Arab forces, and finally Bulgarians besieged but failed to take Constantinople. The fortress city withstood all assaults until the Fourth Crusade in 1204. The East Roman Empire survived more 1000 years because of the security and wealth provided by Constantinople's setting.

Constantine set out enthusiastically to defend his new faith. At the Council of Nicaea, a gathering of religious leaders held to combat the **Arian heresy,** Constantine declared himself to be the "thirteenth apostle." By combining the function of head of church with that of head of state, Constantine established **caesaropapism,** a system which bestowed on the Byzantine ruler the power to impose his control over all aspects of life in his realm, both spiritual and temporal. Despite his commitment to the church, Constantine waited until just before his death to be baptized. All of his successors but one would be Christian.

Aside from his embrace and use of Christianity, Constantine continued the basic trend of Diocletian's economic and social policies. Upon his death in 337, his three sons took power as coemperors. They, in the tradition of the late Roman Empire, fell into dispute with each other until one, Constantius, emerged victorious. As they built on their father's advances, the successors faced challenges not only from the Germans, but also from the Persians. The East Romans alternately fought with and bribed the Persians, who would remain a continual threat to the East until the rise of Islam.

Arian heresy—The theological doctrine that affirmed that Christ demonstrably, by his suffering on the cross, was not of the same substance as God the father and therefore was less than his father.

caesaropapism—The political system in which the ruler controls all aspects of life in his realm, both secular and spiritual—he is both caesar and pope.

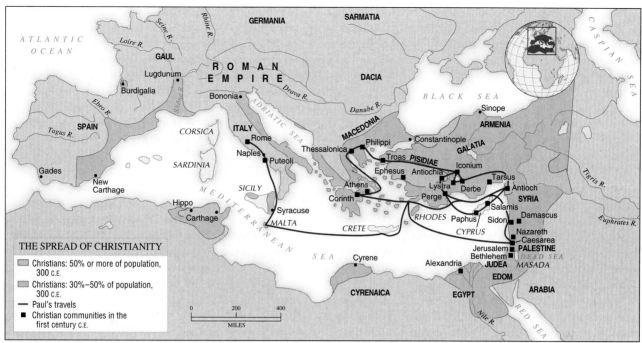

THE SPREAD OF CHRISTIANITY

- Christians: 50% or more of population, 300 C.E.
- Christians: 30%–50% of population, 300 C.E.
- — Paul's travels
- ■ Christian communities in the first century C.E.

Christianity spread rapidly as the result of missionary activity along the Roman road system. The first major theological centers were Alexandria, Antioch, Ephesus, and Corinth.

This colossal head of Constantine captures the emperor's vision of himself as a strong man in control.

Julian: The Last Pagan

By aligning himself with Christianity, transferring his capitol to Constantinople, and installing a new form of government, Constantine began the Roman world's transition from a pagan to a Christian world. But, in going from Rome to the East, Constantine moved from the Latin world—centered around law, government, and public works—to the Greek, more specifically the pagan, Hellenistic world, home of the synthesis constructed by Alexander the Great that combined grandeur, polytheistic mystery cults, and Hellenic civilization. As the role of the Christian church grew between Constantine and Theodosius, the pagan world made some counterattacks.

The most prominent attempt to turn back the Christian tide was that made by Julian, called the **Apostate** (r. 361–363). Julian, a nephew of Constantine, saw three of his brothers killed by their uncles during the succession crisis after 337. Because of his age he was spared and sent into exile in the far-off city of Cappadocia. There, he received a classical Greek education, along with a thorough grounding in the study of Christianity. Even though he was baptized, he remained true to pagan Greek literature and not the Christian catechism. In 347, at the age of sixteen, he was allowed to come back to Constantinople,

Apostate—A person who abandons or renounces his religion.

where he continued his studies in Greek philosophy. In 351, he secretly renounced Christianity and continued the pursuit of **Neo-Platonism.** Four years later he went to Athens, where he was initiated into the Eleusinian cults.

In 357 Julian set out to do battle in Gaul, winning several battles along the Rhine and—at the same time—the love and loyalty of his troops, who proclaimed him to be the new Augustus. In 360 he led his forces back to Constantinople, ready to launch a revolt. Constantius, the emperor, died, however, and Julian took power peacefully. Inspired by the example of Marcus Aurelius and Octavian, he set out to be a modest and humane ruler, clearing out corrupt bureaucrats and imposing a just system of taxes. Because he served as emperor only two years, however, his style of government did not make any significant changes in the East Roman system.

Julian saw himself as a divine person, who was descended from the sun god, and carried out his rule as a religious leader. Even though he declared himself to be openly pagan, he advocated a policy of religious tolerance for all, including the anathematized Arians in Alexandria. The longer he ruled, however, the more he became opposed to the Christians, and he began to exclude them from serving in public offices. In the schools he removed Christian teachings and blocked Christians from teaching literature and philosophy. But Julian did not persecute the Christians, and his efforts to revive paganism failed. In 363, he died from wounds suffered in combat with the Persians. The two years of his reign were not enough to turn the Christian tide.

Thereafter the East Roman state resumed its attack on paganism. Theodosius the Great suppressed the Olympic Games in 393. Individual pagans faced attacks by Christian mobs. One well-known victim of this persecution was the philosopher Hypatia of Alexandria, who in 415 was killed by a Christian gang. Justinian made another attack on the 1000-year-old Greek literary and artistic traditions. He gave pagan professors an ultimatum to convert or lose the right to teach. In 528–530, when they refused to convert to Christianity, he closed Plato's Academy along with other schools in Athens. Justinian made the Christian victory complete.

Orthodoxy and Heresies

Continual theological crises occupied most of the 1128 years of the East Roman state. By establishing the precedent of the emperor as the "thirteenth apostle," Constantine gained important support from the

church, and the church itself profited by becoming a state church. In a single-centered-society, heresy was not only a religious issue, but—by definition—a political crime as well. Therefore, the East Roman leaders became embroiled in the theological controversies involved in defining Orthodox Christian theology until the eighth century. Thereafter, Rome and Constantinople competed on questions of doctrine and conversions until the **Great Schism** of 1054, which split European Christianity into Roman and Greek Orthodox communities and remains to the present day.

From its origins, Christianity has been a religion that has produced important controversies. The notions of the composition of the **Trinity,** the nature of Christ, and the **Incarnation** are difficult concepts to define, let alone agree on. Added to these theological controversies was the political competition posed by the establishment of the new Christian city of Constantinople, which had no apostolic traditions such as those found at the older centers at Alexandria, Ephesus, Chalcedon, Antioch, and Rome. The head of the Orthodox church in Constantinople, the **Patriarch,** and the head of the Catholic church in Rome, the Pope, were in general accord for the first four centuries as they constructed the basis of Orthodox Christianity through their readings of the scriptures and the deliberations of the first seven ecumenical councils, which are: "assembl[ies] under the presidency of the Emperor, where every inter-communicating church was represented [and which] was the inspired body whose decisions were binding on Christendom."

In the modern, pragmatic age, the arguments over the Trinity, the nature of Christ, and the Incarnation strike secular people as being particularly abstruse and abstract. But these theological differences had important consequences, not only for the East Roman Empire but also for the development of Christianity. The Arian heresy remained strong in the West—especially in Spain—until the eighth century, and made church unity difficult. When the Muslims began their expansion in 632, people believing in **Monophysite,** Nestorian, and other heretical beliefs—especially the

---

Great Schism—In 1054, the last in a series of breaks between the churches of Rome and Constantinople occurred. After over 950 years the two churches remain separated.

Trinity—The Christian doctrine asserting that the Father (God), the Son (Jesus Christ), and the Holy Spirit exist as a perfect unity in one godhead.

Incarnation—The putting into human form of a spirit or god. In Christianity, the appearance of the son, Jesus Christ, in human form.

Patriarch—The head of the Orthodox Church in Constantinople, or the head of the churches of Alexandria, Antioch, Moscow, and Jerusalem among others.

Monophysite—A person who believes that God the son has one single, divine nature. This is against the Orthodox view that asserts that Christ was perfect God and perfect man.

Neo-Platonism—A fusing of Plato's philosophy with Aristotelian, Jewish, and Near-Eastern concepts that led logically to the belief in a universal, perfect One with which the individual soul could commune.

Document The Ecumenical Councils and Heresies

First Ecumenical Council: Nicaea I, 325

Attacked the widely followed Arian heresy that asserted Christ was not of the same substance, and therefore less than the father. Instead, affirmed the full divinity of Jesus and of His being of the same substance as God the father.

Produced the creed defining Orthodox Christianity, which, with changes added in the Second Council and in the fifth century is essentially the same as that recited by Christians today. Established the date on which Easter would be celebrated.

Second Ecumenical Council: Constantinople I, 381

Once again, Arianism condemned.

Defined the nature of the Trinity, affirmed the divinity and equality of the Holy Ghost in the Trinity.

Constantinople recognized as second in status among Christian cities, after Rome.

Third Ecumenical Council: Ephesus, 431

Declared Mary to be Mother of God and reaffirmed the single nature of Christ, in opposition to the Nestorian view of the two natures—human and divine—and two persons of Christ, with the implied, reduced role of the Virgin Mary.

Position of Constantinople within the hierarchy of the Church strengthened.

Fourth Ecumenical Council: Chalcedon, 451

Established the Orthodox definition of Christ as having two natures (divine and human) coexisting in one person—perfect God and perfect man, and not one single, divine nature as advanced by the Monophysites living in the east of the empire.

Fifth Ecumenical Council: Constantinople II, 553

Another unsuccessful attempt to reconcile the Nestorian and Monophysite beliefs and bring unity to the empire.

Sixth Ecumenical Council: Constantinople III, 680

In an attempt to heal the divisions within the empire over the Christological controversies, the doctrine of Monotheletism had emerged. In an attempt to bridge the gap between those affirming that Christ had one single, divine nature and the Orthodox position of the two natures of Christ, Monotheletism split the difference and said that Christ had one nature, but that His will was divine-human. This approach was popular in the East, but was found to be heretical at this council.

Seventh Ecumenical Council: Nicaea II, 787

Allowed and encouraged the use of holy images in churches, thus temporarily ending the iconoclastic crisis.

Taken from Steven Runciman, *Byzantine Civilization* (Cleveland and New York: World Publishing Company, 1961), *The Cambridge Medieval History*, Vol. IV, pts. 1 and 2, (Cambridge: Cambridge University Press, 1966).

Copts in Egypt and the Syrians—accepted and even welcomed the invaders, because Islam was more tolerant to them than were the Orthodox Christians. Deeply held differences over the nature of Christ produced substantial political and diplomatic impacts.

The German Challenges

As we saw in Chapter 5, after the end of the first century, the Roman Empire faced the continual pressure of the German migrations. The Rhine-Danube frontier held for the better part of the second century C.E., but the pressure of these migrations, themselves part of a larger, 1000-year-long movement that saw people continually moving to the West from the Chinese frontier to the Atlantic, eventually caused the Rhine-Danube defensive perimeter to fall apart. During the fifth century the western part of the empire became a region dominated by the various German tribes.

The Eastern Roman capitol at Constantinople also found itself on the path of these huge and continuous population movements. Toward the end of the fourth century the Huns, a nomadic tribe of skilled horseman, left Central Asia and began moving to the West. They conquered the Ostrogoths and forced the terrified Visigoths to flee to the West. The Visigoths petitioned the Romans to allow them to settle as allies in the empire. Permission was granted in 376, and the entire tribe crossed the Danube into Roman territory. They were badly treated by corrupt Roman officials, and soon they revolted. The Emperor Valens led his forces from the safe haven of the walls of Constantinople in 378 and tried to stop them at the battle of Adrianople. Aided by the use of the stirrup and long, slashing swords, Visigoth cavalry slaughtered both the emperor and his army. This ended what was left of the Roman army's prestige. The Visigoths soon moved on to the West into Italy, and the eastern capital recovered behind its impenetrable walls. With the exception of Valens's defeat, the Germanic tribes never seriously threatened Constantinople.

Valens' successor, the Spaniard Theodosius (later called "The Great"), pacified the Visigoths and the Ostrogoths who came after them, converting a hostile invasion into a peaceful one. He agreed to make Christianity the official religion of the empire, sought to suppress other beliefs and religions, and advocated conversion of the Jews. After his death, the western portion of the Empire went into a rapid decline, until its final "fall" in 476.

East Rome, however, became stronger, maintaining its defenses against the waves of migration, codifying its laws, and becoming wealthier. Those fortunate enough to live in Constantinople enjoyed the highest standard of living in medieval Europe. The city became a world trade center by the end of the fifth century and enjoyed the continuous use of a money economy in contrast to the barter system found in western Europe. The Byzantines' wealth and taxes supported a strong military force and financed an effective government. The city built excellent sewage and water systems that permitted an increased life span. Food was abundant, with grain from Egypt and Anatolia and fish from the Aegean. Constantinople could feed as many as 1 million people when it was difficult to find a city in Europe able to sustain more than 50,000. Unlike Rome, Constantinople had several industries producing luxury goods, military supplies, hardware, and textiles. Until Justinian's reign (r. 527–565), all raw silk had been imported from China, but after

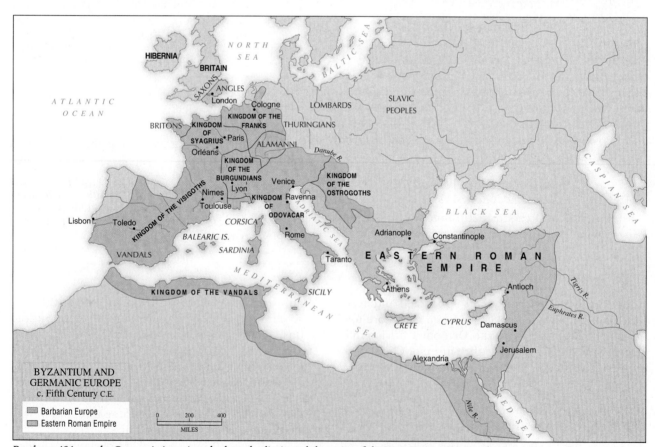

By about 481 c.e. the Germanic invasions had nearly eliminated the unity of the West Roman Empire, but the fate of the East was quite different.

silkworms were smuggled out of China about 550 C.E., silk production flourished and became a profitable state monopoly. The state paid close attention to business: controlling the economy through a system of guilds to which all tradesmen and members of professions belonged; setting wages, profits, work hours, and prices; and even organizing bankers and doctors into compulsory corporations.

Justinian and Theodora

The dream of reclaiming the Mediterranean basin and reestablishing the Roman Empire to its former glory, however, did not die until the end of the reign of Justinian (r. 527–565). Aided by his forceful wife, Theodora, and a corps of competent assistants, he made long-lasting contributions to Byzantine and Western civilization, but gained only short-term successes in his foreign policy.

In the 520s and 530s, after earthquakes devastated much of his realm, Justinian carried out a massive

Emperor Justinian bequeathed a splendid architectural and legal legacy to Europe. However, his attempt to reclaim the former glory of the Roman Empire gained only temporary success and bankrupted his treasury.

Hagia Sophia remains intact today, and visitors can share the awe of the Russians who visited the structure in the tenth century and said, "We knew not whether we were in heaven or on earth."

project of urban renewal throughout the empire. He strengthened the walls defending Constantinople and built the monumental Hagia Sophia, which still stands. Forty windows circle the base of this great church's dome, producing a quality of light that creates the illusion that the ceiling is floating.

Justinian also reformed the government and ordered a review of all Roman law. This project led to the publication of the **Code of Justinian,** a digest of Roman and church law, texts, and other instructional materials that became the foundation of modern Western law. Following Constantine's example, Justinian saw himself as the thirteenth apostle and participated actively in the religious arguments of his day.

The costs of Justinian's ambitious projects triggered violence among the gangs of Constantinople. Since ancient times, groups throughout the Mediterranean

Code of Justinian—A review of all Roman laws since the beginning of the Roman Republic led to the publication of the Code, a digest of Roman and church law, texts, and other instructional materials. This became the basis of modern Western law.

pushed competitively for their own economic, social, and religious goals. Much like contemporary urban gangs, they lived in separate and well-defined neighborhoods, moved about in groups, and congregated at public events. When the factions had complaints with the emperor's policies, they chanted them in unison when Justinian was present at the circus. The most important of these were the Greens and the Blues, factions that often came to the Hippodrome—a structure that could hold 80,000 people—to support competing chariot racers in the circus.

A general dislike of Justinian's wife, Theodora, the daughter of a circus animal trainer (a background that made her almost untouchable in polite society), provided another point of contention. Her enemies believed that she behaved in an outrageous manner, espoused a heretical variant of Christianity, and had too much influence over her husband. Usually, the gangs neutralized each other's efforts. In 532, however, the Blues and the Greens joined forces to try to force Justinian from the throne. The so-called Nika rebellion, named after the victory cry of the rioters, almost succeeded. We know from Procopius's *Secret Histories* that Justinian was on the verge of fleeing until Theodora stopped him and told the emperor:

> *I do not choose to flee. Those who have worn the crown should never survive its loss. Never shall I see the day when I am not saluted as empress. If you mean to flee, Caesar, well and good. You have the money, the ships are ready, the sea is open. As for me, I shall stay.*[1]

Assisted by his generals, the emperor remained and destroyed the rebellion.

Justinian momentarily achieved his dream of reestablishing the Mediterranean rim of the Roman Empire. To carry out his plan to regain the half of the empire lost to the Germanic invaders, Justinian first had to buy the neutrality of the Persian kings who threatened not only Constantinople but also Syria and Asia Minor. After securing his eastern flank through diplomacy and bribery, he took North Africa in 533 and the islands of the western Mediterranean from the Vandals. His generals also reclaimed the southern part of Spain from the Visigoths, but no serious attempt was ever made to recover Gaul, Britain, or southern Germany.

The grandeur of the Byzantine court can be seen in this mosaic presentation of the Empress Theodora in the St. Vitale Church in Ravenna, Italy.

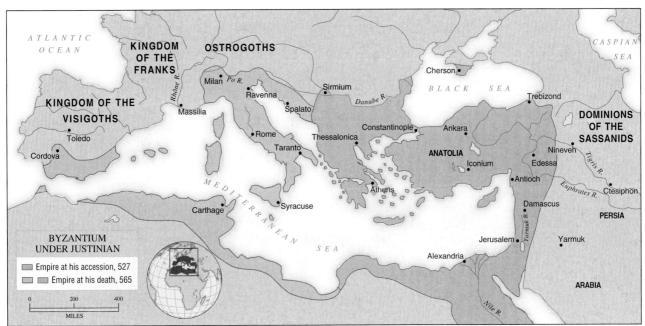

The old Roman tradition of the Mediterranean as Mare Nostrum *("Our Sea") died hard for Justinian. Twenty years of fighting allowed one last glimmer of the old days but exhausted his army and his treasury. A half-century after his reign, the western holdings would be lost, and the East Roman Empire would be redefined around an Anatolian, not a Mediterranean, base.*

Following Theodoric's death without a male heir in 526, civil war broke out in Italy, paving the way for Justinian's 20-year war of reconquest (535–555). Italy was ravaged from end to end by the fighting, and the classical civilization that Theodoric had carefully preserved was in large part destroyed in Rome, with Ravenna suffering extensive damage. To achieve this victory Justinian drained his treasury. Ironically, in 568, three years after his death, the last wave of Germanic invaders, the Lombards, reputed to have been the most brutal and fierce of all the Germans, poured into Italy. The emperor in the East held on to southern Italy, as well as Ravenna and Venice, but left Rome to the pope, who became the most powerful person in the city.

By a decade after Justinian's death, most of the territory he had reconquered had been lost. The Moors in Africa, Germanic peoples across Europe, and waves of nomadic tribes from Asia threatened Byzantium's boundaries. Ancient enemies such as the Persians, who had been bribed into a peaceful relationship, returned to threaten Constantinople when the money ran out, setting in motion a half-century-long battle. In addition, the full weight of the Slavic migrations came to be felt. Peaceful though they may have been, the Slavs severely strained and sometimes broke the administrative links of the state in the Balkans. Finally, the empire was split by debates regarding Christian doctrine.

The stress of trying to maintain order under these burdens drove two of Justinian's successors insane.

THE AGE OF CONSOLIDATION: 610–1071

■ *What were the institutional changes made by Heraclius that permitted the Byzantine Empire to maintain its dominance for the next four centuries? Why did the system finally fall?*

At the beginning of the seventh century, the East Roman Empire appeared to be on the brink of extinction. Salvation appeared from the west when Heraclius (r. 610–641), the Byzantine governor of North Africa, returned to Constantinople in 610 to overthrow the mad emperor Phocas (r. 602–610). When Heraclius arrived in the capital, conditions were so bad and the future appeared so perilous that he considered moving the government from Constantinople to Carthage in North Africa. Heraclius abandoned the hope of reunifying the old Roman Empire around its Mediterranean base and, instead, determined that Anatolia would be the foundation of the empire. During this time the use of Latin as an official language came to an end, and Greek—the language of the great majority of the population—took its place. But even with

Discovery Through Maps

A Sixth-Century Map: The Madaba Mosaic

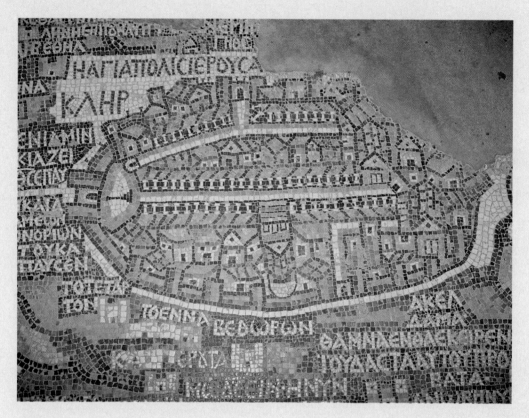

During the first part of Justinian's reign a series of earthquakes shattered buildings around the eastern Mediterranean. The emperor, who had a full treasury, embarked on a massive reconstruction program that adhered to a classical style that was copied all over the empire, even in places that had not suffered from natural disasters. One of the most impressive results of this architectural explosion was Hagia Sophia Church in Constantinople. Another, more subtle but equally revealing, was the Madaba mosaic map, found in present-day Jordan.

Although Justinian was one of the last Latin-speaking emperors of East Rome, the language used in the mosaic map is Greek, a testimony to the existence of the Greek cultural zone established by Alexander the Great in the fourth century B.C.E. that at its height extended from Gibraltar to the Indus River.

Just as Hagia Sophia spoke volumes about the wealth and power of the Christian church, this map, roughly 50 feet by 18 feet, gives remarkable detail about the eastern part of the empire. More than 150 places in present-day Israel, Jordan, Saudi Arabia,

Syria, Lebanon, and part of Egypt—the area of the 12 biblical tribes, or the boundaries of Canaan promised to Abraham—are identified, along with an accurate portrayal of the roads, rivers, deserts, seas, and mountains of the region. Unlike modern maps, which are constructed with a north-south orientation, this map points to the east—toward the altar. The importance of a town can be seen by the way it is described—a small town is depicted as having a small church, whereas the unique qualities of the larger places such as Jerusalem are given more elaborate representations.

There are also other details, such as precise illustrations of places mentioned in the Bible, palm trees to indicate oases, and points at which to cross rivers on foot or by ferry boat. It is obvious that the mosaic map profited from the accounts of travelers. The care with which the unique qualities of various sites are illustrated shows that the map had more than just a decorative function: it was also to be used by Christians making pilgrimages—both those from the West and locally.

A little more than a century later, the region would be swept up in the Islamic advances, and Arabic would begin to replace Greek as the dominant language of the region. Even with that, pilgrims would continue to make their quest through the coming centuries, and the Madaba Mosaic would speak clearly to them.

To gain some notion of a modern perspective, see the map of the Spread of Christianity.

Questions to Consider

1. Locate the five patriarchates. How many are located in the eastern Mediterranean? How many in the West?
2. Why was the use of the Latin language dominant in the western half of the empire, but not the east?
3. Why do you think pious people in a number of religions make pilgrimages?

this linguistic change, the rulers referred to themselves as Romans.

Heraclius

The situation did not improve soon for the Byzantines after Heraclius's arrival. The Persians marched seemingly at will through Syria, took Jerusalem, capturing the "true cross"—the cross on which Christians believed Christ was crucified—and advanced into Egypt. The loss of Egypt to the Persians cost Constantinople a large part of its grain supply. Two fierce Asiatic invaders, the Avars and the Bulgars, pushed against Byzantium from the north. Pirates controlled the sea-lanes, and the Slavs, who had begun to move into southeast Europe in the sixth century, cut land communication across the Balkans. Facing ultimate peril, the emperor abandoned the state structure of Diocletian and Constantine.

Byzantium

325	Constantine the Great establishes capitol in Constantinople (city dedicated May 11, 330)
378	Battle of Adrianople; Visigoths defeat Roman armies, Emperor Valens killed
410	Alaric invades Italy
527–565	Reign of Justinian, construction of Hagia Sophia Cathedral
674–678	Arab sieges of Constantinople
842–1071	Golden Age of Byzantine culture and power
1054	Great schism between the Eastern Orthodox and Roman Catholic churches
1204	Fourth Crusade; Byzantium disappears until 1261
1453	Fall of Constantinople, end of East Roman Empire

Heraclius instituted a new system that strengthened his armies, tapped the support of the church and the people, and erected a more efficient, streamlined administration. He determined that the nucleus of the empire would be Anatolia (Asia Minor, the area of present-day Turkey) and that the main source of fighting men for his army would be the free peasants living there rather than mercenaries. Instead of the sprawling realm passed on by Justinian, Heraclius designed a compact state and an administration conceived to deal simultaneously with the needs of government and the challenges of defense.

This system, the **theme system,** had been tested when Heraclius ruled North Africa. Acting on the lessons of the past four centuries, he assumed that defense was a constant need and that free peasant soldiers living in the theme ("district") they were defending would be the most effective and efficient force. He installed the system in Anatolia, and his successors then spread it throughout the empire over the next two centuries. Heraclius's scheme provided sound administration and effective defense at half the former cost. As long as the theme system—with its self-supporting, landowning, free peasantry—endured, Byzantium remained strong. When the theme system and its free peasantry were abandoned in the eleventh century, the empire became weak and vulnerable.

Heraclius, buttressed by the church, fought a holy war to reclaim Jerusalem. During the 620s he applied some of the lessons of Hannibal's mobile warfare to attack Persian strength and took the enemy heartland. In 626 Heraclius stood ready to strike the final blow and refused to be drawn away by the Avar siege of Constantinople. He defeated the Persians at Nineva, marched on to Ctesiphon, and finally—symbolic of his victories—reclaimed the "true cross" and returned it to Jerusalem in 630.

The Byzantines were unable to savor their victory for long, however, because the advance of a new force, the Muslims, posed an even more dangerous threat to

---

theme system—Heraclius divided his realm, first in Asia Minor and then in other regions, into districts called "themes." Understanding that defense would be a continual necessity, he empowered the free peasant soldiers living in the theme to be responsible, under the leadership of a district commander, for the protection of their homelands.

The Byzantine navy coupled its prowess in battle with the secret and powerful weapon known as Greek fire, depicted here in a fourteenth-century manuscript illumination.

Byzantium than the Persians. Byzantium and Persia had previously dominated the Near East, but they were exhausted after 20 years of war. Aided by a superior cavalry, the Muslims took Syria and Palestine at the battle of Yarmuk in 636. Persia fell to them in 637, Egypt in 640. In Syria and Egypt, their advances were assisted by the anti-Constantinople sentiment provoked during the Christological controversies. Under the more tolerant Muslims, those who had a different view of the nature of Christ could freely follow their faith. A millennium of Greco-Roman rule in the eastern Mediterranean ended in a mere five years.

Constantinople's walls and the redefined Byzantine state withstood the challenge, enduring two Arab sieges in 674–678 and 717. Both times the capital faced severe land and naval attack. The Byzantines triumphed by using new techniques such as Greek fire and germ warfare. Greek fire was the medieval equivalent of napalm. It caught fire on contact with water and stuck to the hulls of the Arabs' wooden ships. The germ warfare was accomplished by sending people with small pox and other diseases into enemy camps. At the same time, the Byzantines faced the serious threats of the Bulgarians—continuing their four-century-long pressure on Constantinople—and the Slavs. Heraclius's successors built on his strong foundations by extending the theme system and protecting the free peasants—a source of taxes and soldiers.

The Heraclian dynasty saved the Byzantine state three times: in 610 and during the two Arab sieges. In the end, however, this dynasty proved the point that the political succession in East Rome was never an orderly process. Beginning with the conflicts among the sons of Constantine and continuing at least once in every century thereafter, civil war erupted around the issue of succession, usually with great violence. Notable among these episodes was that of Justinian II, Rhinometus (r. 685–695 and 705–711). His opponents removed him in 695 and, to insure that he wouldn't return, slit his nose and his tongue. He was sent off to exile across the Black Sea, in Crimea. His expulsion led to a 22-year period in which Byzantium had seven different rulers, including the exiled Justinian Rhinometus for a second tour as emperor in 705.

The Iconoclastic Period

As we have seen, from Constantine on, the Byzantine emperors played active roles in calling church councils to debate the questions concerning the nature of Christ and His relationship with the Father and the Holy Spirit. In a structure in which the emperor was both the political and spiritual leader an Orthodox Christian doctrine had to be established as a base to deal with both the secular and spiritual opponents of Constantinople. During times of war, such as the Persian invasions during Heraclius's reign, the combined force of church and state provided great strength. At other times, as in the eighth century, when arguments raged between Rome and Constantinople over the use of icons and the propagation of their particular branches of the faith, the emperor's mixing in matters of faith hurt the East Roman state.

Byzantine Emperors

306–337	Constantine the Great
361–363	Julian the Apostate
364–378	Valens
527–565	Justinian I
610–641	Heraclius I
717–741	Leo III, the Isaurian
797–802	Irene
829–842	Theophilus
867–886	Basil I, the Macedonian
886–912	Leo VI, the Wise
912–959	Constantine VII, Porphyrogenetus
963–1025	Basil II, Bulgaroctonus
1449–1453	Constantine XI

When Constantinople faced a three-sided invasion from the Arabs, Avars, and Bulgarians in 717, another powerful leader, Leo the Isaurian (r. 717–741), came forward to turn back the invaders. Over the next decade Leo rebuilt the areas ruined by war and strengthened the theme system. He reformed the law, limiting capital punishment to crimes involving treason and increasing the use of mutilation for a wide range of common crimes.

Leo took seriously his role as religious leader. He vigorously persecuted heretics and Jews, decreeing that the latter group must be baptized. In 726 he launched a theological crusade against the use of icons, pictures, and statues of religious figures such as Christ and the saints. He was concerned that icons played too prominent a role in Byzantine life and that their common use as godparents, witnesses at weddings, and objects of adoration went against the Old Testament prohibition of the worship of graven images. Accordingly, the emperor ordered the army to destroy icons. The destruction of the icons caused a violent reaction in the western part of the empire, especially in the monasteries. The government responded by mercilessly persecuting the iconophiles ("icon lovers"). The eastern part of the empire, centered in Anatolia, supported the **iconoclasm.** By trying to

iconoclasm—The breaking of images. Under the reign of Leo the Isaurian, the empire split over the role of icons (holy images) in the life of believers. Leo wanted to destroy icons, seeing them as a worship of graven images.

remove what he saw to be an abuse, Leo split his empire in two and drove a deeper wedge between the church in Rome and the church in Constantinople.

In Byzantium the religious conflict over destruction of the icons had far-reaching cultural, political, and social implications. Pope Gregory II condemned iconoclasm in 731. Leo's decision to attack icons stressed the fracture lines that had existed between East and West for the past four centuries, typified by the linguistic differences between the Latin West and Greek East. As Leo's successors carried on his religious and political policies, Pope Stephen II turned to the north and struck an alliance with the Frankish king, Pepin, in 754. This was the first step in a process that a half-century later would lead to the birth of the Holy Roman Empire and the formal political split of Europe into East and West.

Empress Irene and Iconophilism

Women played a prominent role in Byzantine political life, whether openly as was the case with Justinian's wife Theodora, or more commonly as powers behind the throne. When succession led to the ascendancy of a minor, a regency council or a single regent would exercise power. Several times in Byzantine history, the Dowager Empress—the mother of the emperor in power—ruled. In 1042 the last of the Macedonian dynasty, sisters Zoe and Theodora, ruled briefly. Later on, Theodora ruled on her own in 1055. Anna Comnena (see Document), wrote of the importance of her mother and grandmother in the affairs of state.

The best-known woman who ruled in her own right was the Empress Irene. Irene was from Athens and an iconophile, a curious choice for the wife of Leo IV. She became regent for—and coemperor with—her 10-year-old son Constantine VI at Leo's death in 780, at the age of 30. She resisted attempts to overthrow her and her son and consolidated their power. In addition, she slowly worked to reverse the iconoclastic policies of her predecessors and called the Seventh Ecumenical Council to bring concord with Rome and reinstall the use of icons.

Irene extended her power during the latter part of the 780s and even after her son reached the age at which he was eligible to rule, she refused to yield any of her power. The iconoclasts rallied around Constantine VI while the iconophiles supported Irene, and finally she was forced out after the army declared its loyalty to her son in 790. Two years later, she was back after Constantine suffered defeat in several battles and proved to be incompetent and even vicious in his actions—when he sensed a potential coup from his uncles, he blinded them and cut their tongues out. His personal behavior, including openly adulterous

Document Anna Comnena

Anna Comnena, the first woman historian, was a prominent representative of the rich Byzantine intellectual life. She entered this calling after being blocked by the birth of her brother in her drive to become Byzantium's second empress and in other, later political activities. At the age of 55 she was sent off to a forced retirement and began to write a number of books, the best known of which is *The Alexiad*. She lived at the time of the first crusades, seen by the Byzantines as a western European barbarian invasion, and her descriptions of events show a marked disdain for the crusaders so revered in Western accounts. As she described herself, she was "nurtured and born in the purple, not without my full share of letters, for I carried to its highest point the art of writing Greek, nor did I neglect the study of rhetoric: I read with care the system of Aristotle and the dialogues of Plato, and fortified my mind with the quadrivium of sciences." (Quoted in Norman Baynes, *Byzantium*, Oxford: The Clarendon Press, 1961, p. 258).

On Peter the Hermit and the First Crusade

A Celt named Peter, called "Peter the Hermit," left to worship at the Holy Sepulcher. After having suffered much bad treatment at the hands of the Turks and the Saracens who were ravaging all of Asia he returned to his home only with great difficulty. Since he could not bear to have failed in his aim, he decided to begin the same voyage over again. But he understood that he should not retravel the route to the Holy Sepulcher alone for fear that a worse mishap might occur to him; and he thought up a clever scheme, which was to preach throughout all the countries of the Latins as follows: "A divine voice has ordered me to proclaim before all the nobles of France that they should all leave their homes to go worship at the Holy Sepulcher and try with all their ability and with all their passion to free Jerusalem from the domination of the [Saracens]."

Since they did [not] march in ranks or troops, they [later] fell into a Turkish ambush near Drakon and were wretchedly massacred. So many Celts and Normans were victims of the[ir] . . . swords that when the bodies of the slaughtered warriors which were scattered about were [put together they formed] a high mountain of considerable dimensions, so great was the mass of bones.

From Paul Brians, trans., in *Reading About the World*, Vol. I, eds. Paul Brians et al., published by Harcourt Brace Custom Books.

Anna Comnena also wrote compellingly of the brilliance of her grandmother.

It may cause some surprise that my father the Emperor had raised his mother to such a position of honor, and that he had handed complete power over to her. Yielding up the reins of government, one might say, he ran alongside her as she drove the imperial chariot. . . .

My father reserved for himself the waging of wars against the barbarians, while he entrusted to his mother the administration of state affairs, the choosing of civil servants, and the fiscal management of the empire's revenues and expenses. One might perhaps, in reading this, blame my father's decision to entrust the imperial government to the gyneceum (the quarter of the palace reserved for women). But once you understood the ability of this woman, her excellence, her good sense, and her remarkable capacity for hard work, you would turn from criticism to admiration.

For my grandmother really had the gift of conducting the affairs of state. She knew so well how to organize and administer that she was capable of governing not only the Roman Empire but also every other kingdom under the sun. . . . She was very shrewd in seizing on whatever was called for, and clever in carrying it out with certitude. Not only did she have an outstanding intelligence, but her powers of speech matched it. She was a truly persuasive orator, in no way wordy or long-winded. . . .

She was ripe in years when she ascended the imperial throne, at the moment when her mental powers were at their most vigorous. . . .

As for her compassion toward the poor and the lavishness of her hand toward the destitute, how can words describe these things? Her house was a shelter for her needy relatives, and it was no less a haven for strangers. . . . Her expression, which revealed her true character, demanded the worship of the angels but struck terror among demons. . . .

From "The Writings of Medieval Women," Vol. 14, ed. and trans. M. Thiebaux, *Garland Library of Medieval Literature* (New York, 1987).

behavior—not a thing usually expected from the thirteenth apostle—led to his being increasingly isolated. Finally, in 797, Irene ordered him taken to the Purple Room, the place in which he was born, and blinded. Irene now ruled the empire in her own name—but as emperor, not empress.

Once in power she cut many taxes to gain the support of her people, gave lucrative gifts to the monasteries, and cut import duties. She gained a moment of popularity, but the state treasuries were drained. She failed to

The Empress Irene (r. 797–802) sought to change the anti-icon policies of her realm and make an alliance with Charlemagne, before being deposed.

win lasting support among the eastern part of the empire for her pro-icon policies; nor could she arrange a marriage alliance with the newly proclaimed western emperor, Charlemagne, before being overthrown—a union that would have brought together the forces of East and West. As Irene spent the treasury into bankruptcy, her enemies increased. Finally, in 802 they deposed her and sent her into exile on the island of Lesbos.

The iconoclastic controversy and Irene's failed policies placed the empire in jeopardy once again. Her successor, Nicepherous (r. 802–811), after struggling to restore the bases of Byzantine power, was captured in battle with the Bulgarians in 811. Khan Krum beheaded him in July and turned his skull into a drinking cup. The iconoclasts had made a comeback, but this phase of image-breaking lacked the vigor of the first, and by 842 the policy was abandoned.

The clash over icons marked the final split between East and West. Eastern emperors were strongly impressed by Islamic culture, especially with its prohibition of images. The Emperor Theophilus (r. 829–842), for example, was a student of Muslim art and culture, and Constantinople's painting, architecture, and universities benefited from the vigor of Islamic culture. This focus on the East may have led to the final split with the West, but, by the middle of the ninth century, it also produced an East Roman state with its theological house finally in order and its borders fairly secure.

Missionary Activities

During the ninth and tenth centuries, Constantinople made its major contributions to eastern Europe and Russia. Missionaries from Constantinople set out to convert the Bulgarians and Slavic peoples in the 860s and, in the process, organized their language, laws, aesthetics, political patterns, and ethics as well as their religion. But these activities did not take place without competition. Conflict increasingly marked the relationship between the Byzantine and Roman churches. A prime example of this conflict was the competition between Patriarch Photius and Pope Nicholas I in the middle of the ninth century.

Photius excelled both as a scholar and as a religious leader. He made impressive contributions to schools in the Byzantine Empire and worked to increase Orthodoxy's influence throughout the realm. Nicholas I was Photius's equal in ambition, ego, and intellect. They collided over the attempt to convert the pagan peoples, such as the Bulgarians, caught between their spheres of influence.

Khan Boris of Bulgaria, who was as cunning and shrewd as Photius and Nicholas, saw the trend toward conversion in Europe that had been developing since the sixth century and realized the increased power he could gain with church approval of his rule. But he also wanted a separate patriarch and church for his own people and dealt with the side that gave him the better bargain. From 864 to 866 Boris changed his mind three times on the question of following Rome or Constantinople. Finally, the Byzantines gave the Bulgarians the equivalent of an autonomous (independent) church, and in return the Bulgarians entered the Byzantine cultural orbit. The resulting schism proclaimed between the churches in 867 set off a sputtering sequence of Christian warfare that continued for centuries.

The work of the Byzantine missionary brothers Cyril and Methodius was more important than Bulgarian ambitions or churchly competition. The men were natives of Thessalonica (thes-sa-LON-ee-ka), a city at the mouth of the Vardar-Morava water highway that gave access to the Slavic lands. Versed in the Slavic language, the two led a mission to Moravia, ruled by King Rastislav. He no doubt wanted to convert to Orthodoxy and enter the orbit of distant Constantinople in order to preserve as much independence for his land as he could in the face of pressure from his powerful German neighbors. Cyril and Methodius carried the faith northward in the **vernacular.** Cyril adapted Greek letters to devise an alphabet for the Slavs, and the brothers translated the liturgy and many religious books into the Slavic language. Although Germanic missionaries eventually converted the Moravians, the work of Cyril and Methodius profoundly affected all of the Slavic peoples.

Byzantium's Golden Age, 842–1071

For two centuries, a period coinciding roughly with the reign of the Macedonian dynasty (867–1056), Byzantium enjoyed political and cultural superiority over its western and eastern foes. Western Europe staggered under the blows dealt by the Saracens, Vikings, and Magyars, and the Arabs lost the momentum that had carried them forward for two centuries. Constantinople enjoyed the relative calm, wealth, and balance bequeathed by the theme system and promoted by a series of powerful rulers. The time was marked by the flowering of artists, scholars, and theologians as much as it was by the presence of great warriors. Byzantium's security and wealth encouraged an active political, cultural, and intellectual life. The widespread literacy and education among men and women of various segments of society would not be matched in Europe until eighteenth-century Paris. Unfortunately this time of well-being would come to an end at the beginning of the twelfth century.

During the Golden Age, the population lived within the theoretical stability of the autocratic framework in which all things—political, religious, military, economic, and social—flowed from the emperor. Underneath that caesaropapistic unity, however, were the political, social, and economic struggles found in all societies. In Anatolia, the theme system based on the free soldier-peasants remained until the end of the eleventh century. The rich soil of the area combined with the dignity of self-defense to produce proud and independent families. Life was difficult, but from time to time there were religious feasts, fairs, and the occasional wandering entertainers. Still, there was always the possibility of an early frost that would wipe out a harvest and bring debt, and there were always the tax collectors. Women guaranteed the functioning of the home while also carrying on the work of the farm when their husbands were fulfilling their military obligations.

In Constantinople, a dependable supply of affordable food was guaranteed by the state and the church, again until the end of the eleventh century. Despite the wars and upheavals, the population levels remained constant in Constantinople through to 1204 and the Fourth Crusade. Among the 800,000 or so inhabitants of the city there were of, course, the homeless, numbering perhaps 30,000, and the criminal element, numbering perhaps the same. The population of the city was divided into three major groups: those who worked for the state, those who were in commerce and manufacturing, and the workers, poor people, and slaves.

The civil servants in the ninth century were the foremost proponents of Greek language and civilization, and—like the Chinese scholar gentry—their learning was as essential to their work as to the advancement of their civilization. Their pride in their position made them intolerant of foreigners, especially people from western Europe. The civil servants also carried a deep contempt for the military, who in their eyes were barbarians. For the clever and ambitious from all levels of society, the means to upward mobility was through education in the Greek classics.

Those in the second category, who made and sold things, remained subject to strict governmental controls over their work. They were frozen into a system of guilds and price controls until the theme system died at the end of the eleventh century. But with all of that, the living conditions were comparatively good—even for those who worked for the owners and merchants. The government remembered its Roman past and worked hard to keep the loyalties of the citizens of the capitol. As long as bread was cheap, the emperors had the support of the citizens of Constantinople. Free bread had ended with the loss of Egypt. The cost of food was kept low afterwards, as the supplies from Anatolia were consistent. Along with bread, a diet of

---

vernacular—Using the language of the people of a local, particular region.

dried peas and beans, green vegetables, and fish was possible even for the poorest inhabitant. If food was plentiful and cheap, clothing and shelter were less available and expensive. The homeless were the first to suffer from the bubonic plague of the eighth century and the Black Plague of the fourteenth—not to mention the always-constant small pox.

At the lower levels of society, few lived beyond the age of 60—but this was a longer life span than that found in western Europe at the same time. The life of the common laborer was difficult, jobs were aggressively sought after, and pay was low. Threatening their status from below were the large numbers of slaves kept in the Byzantine Empire. The status of slave, beyond removing one's legal identity, applied equally to some who lived very well, doing important work for their masters, as well as to those who lived an abusive life, performing the most brutal manual labor.

Except for members of the elite, such as the historian Anna Comnena, the social role of women was

DOCUMENT

Anna Comnena, *The Alexiad*

limited. For the most part, women of the top levels of society remained secluded and rarely went out of their houses without wearing a veil. At home it was rare for a woman to share a meal with a stranger. Within this seclusion, however, there was a lively society, an often-rich family life, and a comparatively high level of literacy and knowledge of the Greek classics. At the lower levels, women rarely were permitted by the guild structure to pursue a craft. Prostitution, which had a restricted legal standing under Constantine the Great, was practiced by a large number of women—in the thousands—in all periods of the Byzantine Empire. For women at all levels, death in childbirth was a common tragedy, and those that lived often saw their babies unable to survive the first winter, as infant mortality rates were extremely high.

Byzantium continued its military as well as its theological dynamism. Arab armies made repeated thrusts, including one at Thessalonica in 904 that led to the loss of 22,000 people. But during the tenth century, a decline in Muslim combativeness, combined with the solidity of Byzantine defenses, brought an end to that chapter of conflict. Basil II (r. 963—1025), surnamed Bulgaroctonus (bul-ga-ROK-to-nus) or "Bulgar slayer," stopped Bulgarian challenges for more than a century at the battle of Balathista in 1014. At the same time, the Macedonian emperors dealt from a position of strength with western European powers, especially where their interests clashed in Italy. Western diplomats visiting the Byzantine court expressed outrage at the benign contempt with which the eastern emperors treated them. But the attitude merely reflected Constantinople's understanding of its role in the world.

The Byzantines continued their sometimes violent political traditions. Emperor Romanus Lecapenus I

(r. 920–944) was overthrown by his sons, and in the eleventh century, succession to the throne degenerated into a power struggle between the civil and military aristocracies. Yet through all the political strife, the secular and theological schools flourished, and the emperors proved to be generous patrons of the arts. Basil I (r. 867–886) and Leo VI (r. 886–912) oversaw the collection and reform of the law codes. Leo, the most prolific lawgiver since Justinian, sponsored the greatest collection of laws of the medieval Byzantine Empire, a work that would affect jurisprudence throughout Europe. Constantine VII Porphyrogenitus (por-phi-ro-GEN-ee-tus; r. 912–959) excelled as a military leader, lover of books, promoter of an encyclopedia, and surveyor of the empire's provinces. At a time when scholarship in western Europe was almost nonexistent, Constantinople society featured a rich cultural life and widespread literacy among men and women of different classes.

The greatest contribution to European civilization from Byzantium's Golden Age was the preservation of ancient learning, especially in the areas of law, Greek science and literature, and Platonic and Aristotelian philosophy. Whereas in the West the church maintained scholarship, the men and women of Byzantium perpetuated the Greek tradition in philosophy, literature, and science. Perhaps because of this rich secular intellectual life, Byzantine monasteries—which produced many saints and mystics–showed little interest in learning or teaching about this world.

WESTERN AND TURKISH INVASIONS: 1071–1453

■ *Why did the Byzantine Empire pass from being the dominant power in the region in 1015 to being so weak by 1095?*

Empires more often succumb to internal ailments than to external takeovers. This was the case with the Byzantine Empire. As long as Constantinople strengthened the foundations laid by Heraclius—the theme system and reliance on the free soldier-peasant—the empire withstood the military attacks of the strongest armies of the time. When the Byzantine leaders abandoned the pillars of their success, the state succumbed to the slightest pressure.

Byzantine Decline and the Seljuk Advance

Inflation and ambition ate away at the Heraclian structure. Too much money chased too few goods during the Golden Age. Land came to be the most profitable investment the rich could make, and the landowning magnates needed labor. Rising prices meant increased taxes. The peasant villages were collectively responsible for paying taxes, and the rising tax burden overwhelmed them. In many parts of the empire, villages sought relief by placing themselves under the control of large landowners, thus taking themselves out of the tax pool and lowering the number of peasant-soldiers. Both the state treasury and the army suffered as a result.

Until Basil II, the Macedonian emperors had tried to protect the peasantry through legislation, but the trend could not be reversed. Even though the free peasantry never entirely disappeared and each free person was still theoretically a citizen of the empire, economic and social pressures effectively destroyed the theme system. An additional factor contributing to the empire's decline was the growth of the church's holdings and the large percentage of the population taking holy orders, thus becoming exempt from taxation.

For 50 years following Basil II's death in 1025, the illusion that eternal peace had been achieved after his defeat of the Bulgarians in 1014 encouraged the oppor-

tunistic civil aristocracy, which controlled the state, to weaken the army and neglect the provinces. The next time danger arose, no strong rulers appeared to save Byzantium, perhaps because no enemies massed dramatically outside the walls of Constantinople.

New foes challenged Byzantium. The Turkish peoples, who had migrated from the region north of China to southwestern Asia around the sixth century, converted gradually to Islam. Warrior bands that formed among them fought first with and then against the Persians, Byzantines, and Arabs. The first of these Turkish bands to invade the Middle East and, eventually Anatolia, were the Seljuks (SEL-yukes). When the Seljuk Turk leader Alp Arslan (the "Victorious Lion") made a tentative probe into the empire's eastern perimeter near Lake Van in 1071, the multilingual mercenary army sent out from Constantinople fell apart even before fighting began at Manzikert. With the disintegration of the army, the only thing that could stop the Seljuk Turks' march for the next decade was the extent of their own ambition and energy.

Byzantium lost the heart of its empire when it lost Anatolia, and with it the reserves of soldiers, leaders, taxes, and food that had enabled it to survive

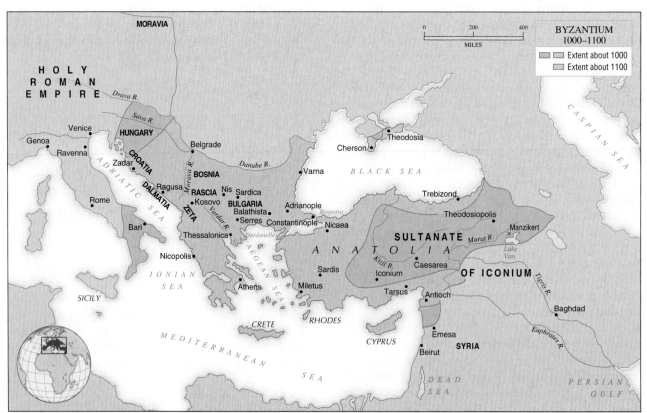

The Byzantine Empire went from a major to a minor power in the century and a half portrayed on this map. After the Turkish defeat at Manzikert in 1071, the Byzantines maintained effective control of only a small fringe of Anatolia to the east and to the north, giving in to the pressure of the Slavic migrations which had begun around the fifth century C.E. The arrival of the Hungarians in the ninth and tenth centuries drove a wedge that prevented the Slavs from unifying.

for four centuries. From its weakened position, the empire confronted Venice, a powerful commercial, and later political, rival. By the end of the eleventh century the Venetians had achieved undisputed trading supremacy in the Adriatic and turned their attention to the eastern Mediterranean. The Byzantines also faced the challenges of the Normans, led by Robert Guiscard, who took the last Byzantine stronghold in Italy.

The Western Crusades

The fracture in the relationship between Rome and Constantinople that had been opened during the iconoclastic controversy steadily grew into a theological gulf during the conversion competition of the ninth century. Thereafter, Rome and Constantinople developed in different ways. The Pope stood at the head of a growing community of independent states while the Emperor and his Patriarch could look to the west and north and see their allied Orthodox countries. The events leading up to the Great Schism in 1054 centered around the competition between Pope Leo IX and Patriarch Michael Cerularius. Each was ambitious for his own cause; neither cared further to maintain the fiction of Christian unity. The issues had been previously discussed: the western doctrine of the double procession of the Holy Ghost and fasting on Sunday and the eastern practices of a married clergy and the use of leavened bread in the communion service. The face-off between Pope and Patriarch led, in July of 1054, to the Roman excommunication of the eastern church's leaders and Constantinople's excommunication of the Roman church's officials. The schism between the two has never been healed.

In 1081 a politically astute and brilliant family, the Comnenians, claimed the Byzantine throne. In earlier times, with the empire at its strongest, these new rulers might have accomplished great things. But the best they could do in the eleventh and twelfth centuries after the defeat at Lake Van was to play a balance-of-power game between East and West, so well described by Anna Comnena in *The Alexiad*. In 1096 the first crusaders appeared, partly in response to the Council of Clermont, partly in response to the lure of gold and glory (see Chapter 9). Alexius Comnenus (r. 1081–1118) had appealed to Pope Urban II for help against the Seljuks, but he did not bargain on finding a host of crusaders, including the dreaded Normans and fanatic and disorganized peasants, on his doorstep. Alexius quickly got the crusaders—both peasant and noble—across the Straits of Bosporus and Dardanelles, where they won some battles that allowed the Byzantines to reclaim land lost in the previous 15 years.

Dueling Crusaders

The envy, hatred, and frustration that had been building up between the Byzantines and the Crusaders during the twelfth century finally erupted during the Fourth Crusade. The Venetians, who wanted to extend

The Crusades, viewed from the Western perspective as an epoch of bravery, were for the Byzantines and the Arabs a time of barbaric invasions. The crusaders not only failed in the long term to reclaim the Holy Land but also failed to stem the Islamic advance. By the sixteenth century, Turkish forces would be threatening Vienna.

their trade dominance in the eastern Mediterranean and the Black Sea, had control of the ships and money for this crusade. When the crusaders proved unable to pay for Venetian services rendered, they persuaded the crusaders to attack the Christian city of Zadar in Dalmatia—a commercial rival of Venice and Constantinople—before going on to the Holy Land. Constantinople itself was paralyzed by factional strife, and in 1204 for the first time an invading force captured and sacked the city. A French noble described the scene:

> The fire . . . continued to rage for a whole week and no one could put it out. . . . What damage was done, or what riches and possessions were destroyed in the flames, was beyond the power of man to calculate. . . . The army . . . gained much booty; so much, indeed, that no one could estimate its amount or its value. It included gold and silver, table-services and precious stones, satin and silk, mantles of squirrel fur, ermine and miniver, and every choicest thing to be found on this earth. . . . So much booty had never been gained in any city since the creation of the world.[2]

The Venetians made sure they got their share of the spoils, such as the bronze horses now found at St. Mark's Cathedral in Venice, and played a key role in placing a new emperor on the throne. The invaders ruled Constantinople until 1261. The Venetians put a stranglehold on commerce in the region and turned their hostility toward the Genoese, who threatened their trade monopoly.

The Ottoman Victory

The empire's last two centuries under the final dynasty, the Paleologus (1261–1453), saw the formerly glorious realm become a pawn in a new game. Greeks regained control of the church and the state, but there was precious little strength to carry on the ancient traditions. Byzantine coinage, which had retained its value from the fourth through the eleventh centuries, fell victim to inflation and weakness. The church, once a major pillar to help the state, became embroiled in continual doctrinal disputes. Slavic peoples such as the Bulgarians and the Serbs under Stephen Nemanja (r. 1168–1196) and Stephen Dushan (r. 1331–1355), who had posed no danger to the empire in its former strength, became threats. After Mongol invasions in the thirteenth century destroyed the exhausted Seljuk Turks, a new more formidable foe, the Ottoman or Osmanli Turks, appeared.

The Ottomans emerged from the groups of elite Turkish warriors, the *ghazis*, which came together on the northwestern frontier of Anatolia. They participated in the complex political and diplomatic relations in the Aegean area in the wake of the Fourth Crusade and were ready to take advantage of the weakened Byzantine Empire. Blessed after 1296 with a strong line of male successors and good fortune, the Ottomans rapidly expanded their power through the Balkans. They crossed the Straits into Europe in 1354 and moved up the Vardar and Morava valleys to take Serres (1383), Sofia (1385), Nis (1386), Thessalonica (1387), and finally Kosovo from the South Slavs in 1389.

The Ottoman Turks' overwhelming infantry and cavalry superiority gave them their military victories. But their administrative effectiveness, which combined strength and flexibility, solidified their rule in areas they conquered. In contrast to the Christians, both Roman and Byzantine, who were intolerant of theological differences, the Turks allowed monotheists or any believers in a "religion of the book" (the Bible, Torah, or Qur'an) to retain their faith and be ruled by a religious superior through the **millet system,** a network of religious ghettos.

In response to the Ottoman advance, the West mounted a poorly conceived and ill-fated crusade against them. The confrontation at Nicopolis on the Danube in 1396 resulted in the capture and slaughter of 10,000 knights and their attendants. Only the overwhelming force of Tamerlane (Timur the Magnificent), a Turco-Mongol ruler who defeated the Ottoman army in 1402, gave Constantinople and Europe some breathing space.

DOCUMENT
Kritovoulos on the Fall of Constantinople

The end for Constantinople came in May 1453. The last emperor, Constantine XI, and his force of 9000, half of whom were Genoese, held off 160,000 Ottomans for seven weeks. Finally, with the help of Hungarian artillerymen, the Turks breached the once impenetrable walls of the depopulated city. After 1123 years, the shining fortress fell.

DOCUMENT
Nestor-Iskander on the Fall of Constantinople

SOUTHEASTERN EUROPE TO 1500

■ *What role did religion play in the formation of the various Balkan nations?*

Following in the wake of the Germanic tribes' westward march, the dominant people of eastern Europe, the Slavs, spread from the Pripet marshes west to the Elbe, east to the Urals, north to Finland, and south to the Peloponnesus. As they settled throughout eastern

---

millet system—The Ottoman Turks ruled in accord with religious law and governed their holdings as a theocratic state. Non-Turks were ruled according to their religious faith, and responsibilities for governance were handed over to the chief figures of each religious area, or millet.

East European and Russian Romes

c. 700–1014	First Bulgarian Empire
862–867	Cyril and Methodius's mission to the Moravians
865–870	Bulgarian conversion to Orthodoxy
867	First "Russian" attack on Constantinople
c. 900	Serb conversion to Orthodoxy
925	First Croat state, conversion to Catholicism
988	Russian conversion to Orthodoxy
988–1240	Kiev Rus'
1169–1389	Serbian Empire
1197–1393	Second Bulgarian Empire
1220–1243	Mongol invasions in Russia and eastern Europe
1240–1480	Mongol domination of Russia
1300s–1400s	Emergence of Wallachia and Moldavia
1389	Battle of Kosovo, Ottoman Empire begins dominance of the Balkans
1450–1468	Albanian state reaches peak under Skanderbeg
1462–1505	Reign of Tsar Ivan III, the Great

and southern Europe from the sixth through the ninth centuries, they absorbed most of the original inhabitants of the region. This mixing of peoples produced the resulting blends of nations that make up the present-day complexity of eastern Europe and Russia.

Compared to the wealth and sophistication of the Byzantines, the Slavs' economic and cultural lives were primitive, and their political and military structures were weak. Outsiders—Byzantines, Germans, Magyars, Mongols, or Turks—often ruled the various Slavic groups. Yet, before the imposition of Ottoman control, each of the Balkan peoples would have a moment of glory—the two Bulgarian empires, the Serbs under Stephen Nemanja and Stephen Dushan—in which each would create its own image of Byzantium.

Bulgaria

During the great migrations of the peoples, a warlike Finno-Tatar group arrived in the late seventh cen-

tury—at a time when the Byzantine Empire was fighting for its life against the Arabs—and occupied the lands between the Balkan and the Rhodope Mountain ranges of the Balkans. Like the Huns, they were fighters and not farmers, and so after easily conquering the Slavic peoples of the region, they lived off the fruits of their subjects' labors while consolidating their positions against other invaders.

As was the case with other nomadic warrior bands, the Bulgarians within a couple of generations were absorbed by the more numerous Slavs, and became, for all intents and purposes, like other South Slavs in language and culture. They still retained their military tradition and their leadership by their Khans, however. And during the ninth and tenth centuries they posed a constant challenge to Constantinople. The great Khan Krum defeated the Emperor Nicepherous, and he led his armies far to the south of the Balkans. He even reached the walls of Constantinople, but as other leaders in the previous half-millennium, he did not possess the strength or technology to take the city.

Khan Boris cleverly set Roman and Byzantine missionaries against each other in order to gain the most advantageous terms for his conversion to Christianity. In fact he was given a national church with its own hierarchy of bishops and archbishops. Once he had joined the Byzantine side, Boris encouraged the work of missionaries from Constantinople to convert his people, and in the process accepted a Slavonic alphabet for the translations of scripture and church documents.

The First Bulgarian Empire hits its high point in the reign of Symeon (r. 893–927), a person who had been educated in Constantinople and had developed not only an appreciation for, but also a mastery of, Greek culture. Bulgaria served as the main transmission line for the spreading of Orthodoxy throughout the Balkans and into Russia. Symeon's admiration for Byzantine culture did not stop him from attempting to set up his own, independent empire however. He controlled most of the land south of present day Belgrade, up to the suburbs of Constantinople. His empire was short-lived, however, because he was in the path of yet another set of invaders coming from the east to the west: the Magyars (Hungarians), the Pechenegs, and the rising power of Russia. Finally Basil Bulgaroctonus defeated the major Bulgarian force and blinded all those who survived the battle 1014.

Bulgaria remained subdued for the next two centuries until 1185 when Peter and John Asen rebelled against Byzantine authority and successful established the Second Bulgarian Empire, and Bulgaria was a serious competitor with the weakened Byzantine Empire. Until the 1240s, Bulgaria briefly became the most important state in the Balkans, with its imitation Byzantine court and ritual. In the middle of the

In the Balkans, the new Serbian, Bulgarian, and Hungarian states grew powerful. Even though the Byzantines claimed control over the region and farther to the north and east, the Bohemian and Polish states and Russia came into existence.

thirteenth century, it fell to the Serbian Empire, and then a century later was overrun by the Ottoman Turks. Despite these reversals, the Bulgarians remained important missionaries and teachers in the spread of the Orthodox Church.

Serbia

The Serbs, a Slavic people, converted to Orthodox Christianity at roughly the same time as the Bulgarians. They too were caught in the Rome-Constantinople conversion competition, and their brothers the Croats and the Slovenes became Catholics. Despite their linguistic and ethnic similarities, the fact that the Serbs became Orthodox and the Croats and Slovenes Catholics established the foundation for centuries of tragic conflict right up to the wars in the former Yugoslavia in the 1990s.

At first the Serbs were dominated by the Bulgars, but by the 1180s, Stephen Nemanja, the Grand Zhupan, united the Serbian people. He successfully

fought off both the Bulgarians and the weakened Byzantines to establish a kingdom along the Vardar and Morava river basins. His son, Stephen Nemanja II (r. 1196–1228) took advantage of the chaos created by the Fourth Crusade to consolidate his power. Like Khan Basil centuries earlier, he skillfully gained the status of king and also a Serbian national church by appealing to Rome and Constantinople for legitimacy.

Stephen Dushan (r. 1308–1355—at various times king and tsar) brought Serbia to its historic high point geographically, politically, and culturally. The Serbian ruler gained control over most of the Balkans north of Saloniki and south of the Sava River. Politically, he raised himself to the dignity of a *tsar*, or caesar—even to the point of challenging the weakened Byzantines in 1355, seeking help from both the Pope and the Turks. He died as his troops marched to Constantinople, and after that his empire fell apart. The legacy of his empire was a rich Serbian culture, based on Byzantine models, but also combining indigenous qualities and Italian influences.

As the Turks patiently advanced in the Balkans in the 1380s, the usually feuding Slavs finally united at the battle of Kosovo. After a long day of valiant fighting, which saw both the Turkish Sultan and the Serbian king die, the Ottomans emerged victorious—with control of the Balkans for the next five centuries. For the Balkan Slavs, especially the Serbs, the memory of the battle of Kosovo would be passed from generation to generation to be used by politicians in the 1990s as a tragedy to unite their people.

The collapse of Dushan's empire created such instability in the Balkans that the Ottoman Turks advanced with very little challenge. Under Sultan Murad (r. 1359–1389) they defeated the South Slavs in 1389 at the Battle of Kosovo—a date of mourning that still unites Serbian patriots today.

Romania

The Romanians, who see themselves today as "an island of Latins in a sea of Slavs," entered history as the Dacian people, settled on both sides of the Carpathian Mountain chain. They stood in the way of the Roman advance in the first century C.E. and irritated the caesars by their incursions into Roman-controlled provinces south of the Danube. The Emperor Trajan managed to defeat the Dacians and to turn the province into a productive part of the empire. These people remained under Roman rule from circa 100 to circa 275 B.C.E. and became thoroughly latinized, so much so that the Dacian culture and language died out.

The area served as a crossroads for the waves of migrating peoples coming from East to West—following the natural geographic path from the steppe frontier to the Danube valley, and from the end of Roman times to the thirteenth century, the Romanians essentially disappeared from history. After the thirteenth century the regions they inhabited became provinces: Moldavia, Wallachia, Bukovina, Bessarabia, and Transylvania. After the thirteenth century two independent, but weak, states emerged—Moldavia and Wallachia. They were threatened on all sides by the Mongols, the Russians, the Hungarians, the Bulgarians, and the Serbs. By the end of the fifteenth century they rested firmly under Ottoman control.

The Romanians were drawn into the religious orbits of whichever dominant power was the closest to where they lived. Thus, the Transylvanians became Catholic, the Wallachians became Orthodox following Serbian and Bulgarian models, and Moldavians became Orthodox with very strong influences from Russia.

Albania

The Albanians are the only indigenous Bronze Age people in the Balkans who have managed to preserve their own unique language and some of their culture. With a small population and little political and military power, they were from the first caught up in the Greek political strife of the Hellenic age, when they were subjects of the Macedonians under Philip and Alexander. In the second century B.C.E., they fell under Roman domination and their homeland became the province of Illyria (EE-lee-ree-ah). Albanians served in the Roman armies and bureaucracy—even providing several emperors, including Diocletian.

The Albanians were overwhelmed by first the Germanic and the Slavic migrations but did not assimilate with either group. They passed from being dominated by the Byzantines, to being harassed by the Bulgarians and then dominated by the Angevines during the early Crusades. Finally, after the death of Stephen Dushan, Albania entered a period of strife-filled independence, having to fight off the attentions of the Venetians and the Turks, until the arrival of their national hero Skanderbeg (r. 1443–1468). Led by Skanderbeg, Albania became a major player in Balkan affairs for one of the few times in its history. After Skanderbeg's death, however, Albania fell to the Turks. With most of the population eventually adopting Islam, Albania earned a favored position within the Ottoman Empire.

RUSSIA TO 1500

- *Of all the Slavic peoples in the Byzantine zone, why did Russia become the Third Rome and, eventually, a great power?*

Like that of eastern Europe, Russia's history is largely a product of its geography. The vast expanse of land combined with a comparatively small population has made the domination of the peasants by the landed interests, both individuals and state, one of the continuing themes in Russian history. Russia's difficulty in gaining access to the sea has had important economic and cultural consequences, stunting the growth of a merchant class and encouraging the formation of an inward-looking population.

Russia's waterways, however, have played a key role in the development of the country. The rivers, which flow north or south across the land, have served as thoroughfares for trade and cultural exchange as well as routes for invasion. Unconnected to the western European region, the rivers dictated a line of communication that led early Russian traders south to Constantinople rather than to the West. The Volkhov and Dnieper network tied together the Varangians (also known as the Vikings) and the Greeks through Russia, while the Volkhov and Volga system reached toward Central Asia.

Kiev Rus' and Vladimir

In the sixth century C.E. the eastern Slavs began moving out of the area near the Pripet marshes. The various clans went as far north as the White Sea, as far east as the Urals, and to the region south of Kiev. (Kiev Rus' describes the Kievan phase of Russian history, especially the introduction of a stronger Ukrainian historiographical tradition. The apostrophe stands for a diacritical mark in the writing of the word *Rus'* in Russian and Ukrainian.) To the north, around Lake Ilmen, the Slavs established a number of trading towns such as Novgorod, from which they founded other trading bases. By the ninth century they had accumulated sufficient wealth to attract the attention of the Varangians, who came down from the Baltic to dominate the trading routes, especially those going from the Dvina to the Dnieper to Constantinople.

Russian history is said to begin with the entry of the Varangians into eastern Slavic affairs in the 860s. One of the key controversies in Russian history revolves around the question of the Varangians' role. Did they impose themselves on the Slavs and form them into their first political units, or were the Varangians invited in by the already sophisticated, though feuding, Slavic tribes? Varying interpretations of the so-called Norman controversy can best be addressed by noting that the Slavs, like most other Europeans, fell under the wave of the northern invaders but, within two generations, assimilated them and incorporated their capabilities.

The Varangian Oleg (c. 882–913) established his seat of government at Kiev, at the transition point between the forest and steppe zones. During the tenth century Oleg and Sviatoslav (SVYAH-toe-slaf; r. 964–972) created a state that was the equal of contemporary France. Oleg took control of both Kiev and Novgorod and, with the strength gained, launched an attack on Constantinople. Sviatoslav carried Kievan power to the Danube and the lower Volga. He fell victim to the knives of Asiatic invaders, the Patzinaks. However, he left a state strong enough to endure almost a decade of internal power struggles.

The most important ruler in the Kievan phase of Russian history was Vladimir, who overcame his brothers to dominate his country from 980 to 1015. Vladimir learned his political lessons dealing with the Byzantines, and he consolidated his power in Kiev. At first, he based his rule on the pagan religion and erected statues to gods such as Perun (the god of thunder) and Volos (the god of wealth). He made peace with the Volga Bulgars to the east and worked with the Byzantines against the Bulgarians in pursuit of his diplomatic and political goals.

CASE STUDY

Constantine I, Vladimir, and the Selection of Christianity

Vladimir acknowledged the fact that the nations surrounding him were converting to one organized

Document   The Acceptance of Christianity

The Christian conversion of European pagan leaders involved a complex formula of political advantage, internal rivalries, and piety. Beginning with Constantine's conversion, as described by Eusebius, the spiritual element is always emphasized as the primary cause for becoming Christian. Vladimir's conversion to Orthodoxy was a fundamental step in the division of Europe between East and West, perhaps a far more important step than any other taken in Russian history. This excerpt from the *Russian Primary Chronicle* explains in touching, if naive, detail how the decision was made.

6494 (986). Vladimir was visited by Volga Bulgars of Mohammedan [Muslim] faith. . . . Then came the Germans, asserting that they came as emissaries of the Pope. . . . The Jewish Khazars heard of these missions, and came themselves. . . . Then the Greeks sent to Vladimir a scholar. . . .

6495 (987). Vladimir summoned together his vassals and the city elders, and said to them, "Behold, the Volga Bulgars came before me urging me to accept their religion. Then came the Germans and praised their own faith; and after them came the Jews. Finally the Greeks appeared, criticizing all other faiths but commending their own, and they spoke at length, telling the history of the whole world from its beginning. . . ."

. . . The Prince and all the people chose good and wise men to the number of ten, and directed them to go first among the Volga Bulgars and inspect their faith. The emissaries went their way, and when they arrived at their destination they beheld the disgraceful actions of the Volga Bulgars and their worship in the mosque; then they returned to their own country. Vladimir then instructed them to go likewise among the Germans, and examine their faith, and finally to visit the Greeks. They thus went into Germany, and after viewing the German ceremonial, they proceeded to Tsargrad [Constantinople], where they appeared before the Emperor. . . .

Thus they returned to their own country, and the Prince called together his vassals and the elders. Vladimir then announced the return of the envoys who had been sent out, and suggested that their report be heard. He thus commanded them to speak out before his vassals. The envoys reported, "When we journeyed among the Volga Bulgars, we beheld how they worship in their temple, called a mosque, while they stand ungirt. The Volga Bulgar bows, sits down, looks hither and thither like one possessed, and there is no happiness among them, but instead only sorrow and a dreadful stench. Their religion is not good. Then we went among the Germans, and saw them performing many ceremonies in their temples; but we beheld no glory there. Then we went on to Greece, and the Greeks led us to the edifices where they worship their God, and we knew not whether we were in heaven or on earth. For on earth there is no such splendor or such beauty, and we are at a loss how to describe it. We only know that God dwells there among men, and their service is fairer than the ceremonies of other nations. . . ." Then the vassals spoke and said, "If the Greek faith were evil, it would not have been adopted by your grandmother Olga, who was wiser than all other men." Vladimir then inquired where they should all accept baptism, and they replied that the decision rested with him. . . .

By divine agency, Vladimir was suffering at that moment from a disease of the eyes, and could see nothing, being in great distress. The Princess declared to him that if he desired to be relieved of this disease, he should be baptized with all speed, otherwise it could not be cured. . . . The Bishop of Kherson, together with the Princess' priests, after announcing the tidings, baptized Vladimir, and as the Bishop laid his hand upon him, he straightway received his sight. Upon experiencing this miraculous cure, Vladimir glorified God, saying, "I have now perceived the one true God." When his followers beheld this miracle, many of them were also baptized.

Questions to Consider

1. Why do you think that Vladimir felt compelled to convert to one religion or another? Were spiritual or secular concerns more important? What did he gain by conversion?

2. Which of the possible options—Catholicism, Islam, Judaism, Orthodoxy—gave the most important advantages to Vladimir? Consider each choice and make a list of negative and positive points for the Russian ruler.

3. If you have access to a genealogy of your family, try to identify how your ancestors come to find their particular religious—or nonreligious—persuasions.

From *The Russian Primary Chronicle*, trans. Samuel H. Cross. In *Harvard Studies and Notes in Philology and Literature*, Vol. 12 (Cambridge, Mass.: Harvard University Press, 1953), pp. 183–213 passim. Reprinted by permission.

religion or another: the Poles and Hungarians to Roman Catholicism, the Khazars to Judaism, the Volga Bulgars to Islam, and the Bulgarians to Orthodox Christianity. His shrewd grandmother, Olga, had accepted Orthodox Christianity from Constantinople in 956, as had other members of his family. During the 980s Vladimir sent observers to judge the various religious alternatives. According to *The Russian Primary Chronicle,* they visited Hagia Sophia at Constantinople in 988 and were impressed with the power and wealth of the city. The observers recommended that Vladimir choose the Orthodox faith.

DOCUMENT
Vladimir's
Acceptance
of Christianity

The story, though interesting, ignores the many concrete advantages Vladimir derived from his decision. As part of the negotiation package, Vladimir agreed to help the Byzantine emperor Basil against his enemies. In return, upon converting to Orthodoxy, he would receive the hand of the emperor's sister in marriage. After a successful campaign, Basil delayed in carrying out his part of the bargain. Vladimir moved quickly to make his point and marched into the Crimea and took the Byzantine city of Cherson. The Kiev-Byzantine arrangements were finally carried out in 990. Vladimir, now a member of the Byzantine royal family, brought his country into the Byzantine, Orthodox orbit. Even before "becoming a saint," the Chronicle tells us he destroyed the pagan statues, converted his many concubines to nuns, and forced his people to become Christians.[3] Eventually the Russians gained their own church, received their own metropolitan, and adapted Byzantine ritual, theology, and monastic practices to their own use. They also applied Byzantine governmental theories to their own social hierarchy.

After Vladimir, few great monarchs ruled during the Kievan period of Russian history. Instead, political fragmentation began to intensify. During the reign of Yaroslav the Wise (r. 1019–1054), the Kievan state reached its high point. It was the cultural and economic equal of any government in Europe, with cities larger than those found in the West. Yaroslav undertook major building projects, revised the law code, and promoted the growth of the church. He formed a dynastic alliance with Henry I of France. Unfortunately, Kiev did not long maintain its prestigious position. Yaroslav introduced a principle of succession based on the seniority system, passing the rule of Kiev from brother to brother in a given generation. This practice is in contrast with the Western one of primogeniture, under which rule is handed down to the eldest son of the ruler. Within two generations, the seniority system led to the political breakup of Kiev, although the city maintained its theoretical superiority within Russia.

Kiev also came under attack from both east and west and suffered as well from the economic decline of Constantinople. Under Vladimir Monomakh

For Christians of all denominations and beliefs, the Archangel Gabriel is one of the most beloved angels. He is the angel of mercy, the messenger of the incarnation and resurrection, and the bringer of consolation. It is no wonder that he figured heavily in the iconography of the Orthodox Church.

(r. 1113–1125), Kiev reemerged briefly as a center of power, but a half-century of decline soon followed. Competing centers arose at Suzdal; Galicia, where the local aristocracy dominated; Vladimir, where the prince emerged all-powerful; and Novgorod, where the assembled citizens—the *veche*—were the major force. Even before the Mongols totally destroyed the city in 1240, Kiev's era of prominence was effectively over.

Novgorod, Moscow, and the Mongols

For more than two centuries, from 1240 to 1480, Mongols dominated Russia, and during that time, much of the land was cut off from contact with the outside world. During this period a new center of power, Moscow, emerged to serve for most of the time as collector of tribute for the Mongol court. New internal markets developed, and the Orthodox Church, unhampered by the Mongols, grew in strength and influence. The Russian city of Novgorod also managed to carry on despite the oriental overlord.

Novgorod had come under the control of the Varangians in the ninth century. However, in 997, the citizens received a charter granting them self-government, and for the next five centuries this *veche* elected its own rulers. The city boasted an aggressive and prosperous merchant class, which exploited the region from the Ural Mountains to the Baltic Sea and held its own against German merchants from the Baltic area. Novgorod was the equal of most of the cities found along the Baltic and North seas. In the middle of the thirteenth century, Alexander Nevsky, the prince of Novgorod, led his fellow citizens in struggles to repel the Teutonic Knights and the Swedes. A few years later, he showed exceptional diplomatic skill in paying homage to the Mongols, even though they had halted 60 miles outside the city and left Novgorod untouched. At a time when the rest of Russia suffered mightily under the first phase of Mongol domination, the *veche*-elected oligarchy continued to rule Novgorod.

The city's wealth and traditions permitted the *veche* to rule. These male citizens elected their princes and forced them to sign a contract setting out what they could and could not do. In the words of a typical document between ruler and city, the citizens could show their prince "the way out" if he failed to live up to the terms of his agreement. The prince could act as a leader of Novgorod only when he remained within the city's limits. The city's method of government permitted the rise of class divisions that led to more than 20 major outbreaks of violence in the thirteenth and fourteenth centuries. Changes in trade routes in the fifteenth century led to a decline in Baltic commerce, and Novgorod became dependent on Moscow for its grain supply. That dependence, in addition to the class conflict, weakened Novgorod, and in 1478 Moscow absorbed the town.

The obscure fortress town of Moscow, first mentioned in records in 1147, became the core of the new Russia. Even before the Mongol invasion, a large number of Slavs moved toward the north and east, and this migration continued for centuries as that frontier offered opportunities for the oppressed. Moscow was well-placed along a north-south river route in a protective setting of marshes and forests.

The Rise of Moscow

One of Alexander Nevsky's sons, Daniel, founded the Grand Duchy of Moscow, and he and subsequent rulers inherited Nevsky's ability to get along with the Mongols. As the Moscow princes skillfully acknowledged their inferior position to the Mongol khans, who sought tribute and recruits, the Muscovites improved their political position in relation to the other Russians by monopolizing the tax collection function for the

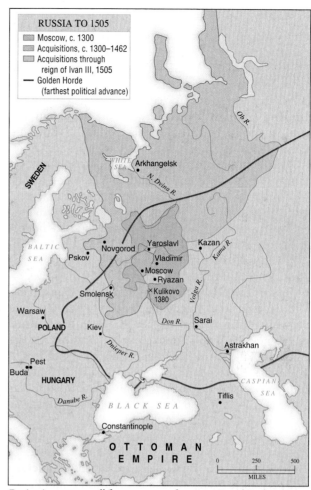

Beginning as a small fortress town, first mentioned in the chronicles in the mid-twelfth century, Moscow grew rapidly by 1500.

Mongols. In addition, at the beginning of the fourteenth century they made sure that the seat of the Russian Orthodox Church would be in Moscow, a reflection of the city's prestige.

In the first century after the Mongol invasion, the Muscovite princes showed a great deal of ambition and ability, albeit in a sometimes unattractive way. For example, during his reign Ivan I Kalita (r. 1328–1341), whose surname means "moneybags," greatly increased the wealth and power of Moscow through aggressive tax collection practices.

On the surface, the fourteenth century appeared to be a time of decline, of Mongol domination and gains by the European states at Russian expense along the western boundary. The reality, however, was that Russia was laying foundations for its future with Moscow as the country's religious and political center. In 1380 Dmitri Donskoi (r. 1359–1389) defeated the Mongols at Kulikovo. Although Mongol strength was far from broken, the Russian victory had great symbolic significance.

St. Basil's Cathedral, Moscow

Ivan III and the Third Rome

Civil war and invasions threatened the Moscow-based country throughout the fifteenth century. Finally, Ivan III (r. 1462–1505) made major strides to build the modern Russian state. He took Novgorod and two years later ceased acknowledging Mongol domination. He then began to advance toward the south and east against the Turks and Mongols, setting in motion a drive of expansion that lasted for centuries.

In developments of considerable symbolic importance, the Russians embraced many elements of the Roman tradition. Ivan III married the niece of the last East Roman emperor, an alliance arranged by the pope. Russians espoused the theory that Moscow was the Third Rome, the logical successor to Constantinople as the center of Christianity. In 1492 (the year 7000 in the Orthodox calendar and the beginning of a new millennium), the Muscovite metropolitan, Zosima, stated that Ivan III was "the new Emperor Constantine of the new Constantinople Moscow." Zosima for the first time called Moscow an imperial city. Philotheus of Pskov (SKOV) expounded the theory of Third Rome in full detail in the 1520s. Ivan began to use the title *tsar* ("caesar") and adopted the Roman two-headed eagle as the symbol of the Russian throne.

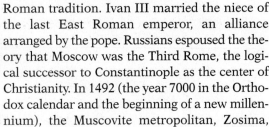

DOCUMENT
Filofei and the Christian Role of Moscow

Ivan opened the doors to the West ever so slightly. He established diplomatic relations with a number of European powers. He brought in Italian technicians and architects such as Aristotele Fieravanti and Pietro Antonio Solari to work on the churches, palaces, and walls of the Kremlin: the vastly expanded site of the original fortress that was the center of the town three centuries earlier. The Italian artistic tradition had no lasting cultural impact on Russia, but use of Italian artists nonetheless signified an awareness of the West. In recognition of the need to establish a standing army, Ivan began the difficult process of building up a modern state structure and increased restrictions on the Russian peasants. During the fifteenth century, Ivan was the equal of his western European colleagues Henry VII of England and Louis XI of France. After three centuries of isolation under the Mongols, the Russians were again interacting with Europe.

CONCLUSION

Byzantium made important contributions to European civilization: Greek language and learning were preserved for posterity—especially after the transmission of documents and texts to Italy, an important stage in the opening of the Renaissance; the Roman imperial system was continued and Roman law codified; and missionary activity spread Christianity throughout much of eastern Europe and Russia and fostered the development of a splendid new art dedicated to the glorification of the Christian religion. Situated at the crossroads of the East and the West, Constantinople acted as the disseminator of culture for all peoples who came in contact with the empire. This rich and turbulent city was to the early Middle Ages what Athens and Rome had been to classical times. Most importantly, by merging Roman political institutions with the Christian Church, Constantine created the form of political legitimacy that would last in Europe until the French Revolution in 1789.

From the fourth through the ninth centuries, as the Slavs moved to their new homelands, they came under the influence of dominant outside forces. In Russia and the Balkans, Byzantine patterns and traditions shaped their lives. After its initial Kievan phase, in which Vladimir made the choice to follow East Roman precedents, the Russians remained under Mongol domination even when Russia's political and religious center moved to Moscow. When the Russians regained their independence in the fifteenth century, they redefined their polity in Roman and Christian terms, claiming the legacy of the fallen city of Constantinople.

From Constantine onward, ambitious Christian leaders strengthened their control through the powerful fusion of Roman symbolism and the Christian Church. Not until the development of modern political ideologies after the French Revolution did a more potent combination of theories and symbols help governments motivate and dominate their people. In its turn, the politicians' embrace of Christ's message profoundly altered the form, if not the substance, of Christianity.

Suggestions for Web Browsing

You can obtain more information about topics included in this chapter at the websites listed below. See also the companion website that accompanies this text, **http://www.ablongman.com/ brummett**, which contains an online study guide and additional resources.

Access to the Metropolitan Museum of Arts Byzantine Collection
http://www.metmuseum.org/explore/Byzantium/byzhome.html
A site providing a wide-ranging selection of Byzantine architectural and artistic triumphs.

Byzantium Studies on the Internet
http://www.fordham.edu/halsall/byzantium/

Byzantine Art
http://www.fordham.edu/halsall/byzantium/images.html

This site includes many images of icons, monasteries, Ravenna, and Hagia Sophia; it details Byzantine life in Jerusalem and offers links to related websites.

Byzantine Architecture
http://www.byzantium1200.com

See a unique experience at computer reconstructions of major Byzantine structures as they might have been in the year 1200.

Historical Tour of Jerusalem: Byzantine Period
http://gurukul.ucc.american.edu/TED/hpages/jeruselum/byzantin
.htm

Short history of Jerusalem, from 324 to 638 C.E., including an image and discussion of the Madaba mosaic showing the Jerusalem Gate.

Women in Byzantium
http://www.wooster.edu/ART/wb.html

Extensive bibliography of primary and secondary sources regarding women in Byzantium.

Byzantium Through Arab Eyes
http://www.fordham.edu/halsall/source/byz-arabambas.html

An original account of a mission to Constantinople by an Arab ambassador in the late tenth century.

Literature and Film

One of the finest novels written about Byzantium is Gore Vidal's celebration of the last pagan emperor, *Julian* (Vintage, 2003). Superbly written, it is unabashedly pro-Julian and makes the fourth-century Christian hierarchy appear to be narrow and even backward in the face of the emperor's learning and sophistication. Michael Ennis gives a lively view of the tenth century in his *Byzantium* (Atlantic Monthly Press, 1989). The fortress city is seen through Viking eyes. A classic, time-travel science-fiction treatment of the reign of Justinian and his Italian campaign is provided by L. Sprague de Camp in *Lest Darkness Fall* (Prime Press, 1949), available in combined edition with David Drake's *To Bring the Light* (Baen, 1996). The author is very good at picking up the religious competition between the Arian Goth and the Orthodox Byzantines. For the most complete selection of novels, poetry, plays, movies, and music of and about Byzantium go to http://www.fordham.edu/halsall/byzantium/texts/byznov.html.

Suggestions for Reading

Two works by Arnold Hugh Martin Jones, *The Decline of the Ancient World* (Longman, 1977), and *The Later Roman Empire, 284–602: A Social, Economic, and Administrative Survey*, 2 vols. (Johns Hopkins University Press, 1986), are indispensable. Two recent and valuable studies on the impacts of the German infiltration and, later, invasions of the Roman Empire are Herwig Wolfram, *The Roman Empire and its Germanic Peoples* (University of California Press, 1998), and Leslie Webster and Michelle Brown, eds., *The Transformation of the Roman World: AD 400–900* (University of California Press, 1997).

For an exhaustive treatment of all aspects of Byzantine life, see *The Cambridge Medieval History* (Cambridge University Press, 2004, replacing Vol. 4 of the 1966–1967 edition). George Ostrogorsky, *History of the Byzantine State* (Rutgers University Press, 1957), provides a clear institutional overview. Joan M. Hussey's *The Orthodox Church in the Byzantine Empire* (Oxford University Press, 1986) is the best introduction in English to the development of the eastern variant of Christianity. Warren Treadgold provides a view of the sophistication of one period of medieval Byzantium in his *The Byzantine Revival, 780–842* (Stanford University Press, 1991). Francis Dvornik, *The Photian Schism: History and Legend* (Rutgers University Press, 1970), and *The Slavs in European History and Civilization* (Rutgers University Press, 1970), address the matters of conversion.

Charles M. Brand, *Byzantium Confronts the West, 1180–1204* (Harvard University Press, 1968), and Donald E. Queller, ed., *The Latin Conquest of Constantinople* (John Wiley & Sons, 1971), describe the tragedy of the Crusades for Byzantium and complement Steven Runciman's three-volume *History of the Crusades* (Cambridge University Press, 1987). For a view from the other side, see Amin Maalouf, *The Crusade Through Arab Eyes* (Shocken Books, 1989). Donald Nicol, *The Last Centuries of Byzantium*, 2nd ed. (Cambridge University Press, 1993), discusses the empire in its state of weakness. For an excellent discussion of the military reorganization that made the survival of the Byzantine Empire possible, see Warren Treadgold, *Byzantium and Its Army: 284–1081* (Stanford University Press, 1995). Paul Stephenson's study, *Byzantium's Balkan Frontier: A Political Study of the Northern Balkans: 900–1204* (Cambridge University Press, 2000), is a much-needed contribution to the opening chapters of the political history of the peoples of the Balkans.

John Fennell, *The Crisis of Medieval Russia, 1200–1304* (Longman, 1983), and Robert O. Crummey, *The Formation of Muscovy, 1304-1613* (Longman, 1987), are two first-rate surveys of the early phases of Russian history. Oscar Halecki, *Borderlands of Western Civilization* (Random House, 1984), gives the outlines of eastern European history, especially the northern region.

Islam

From Its Origins to 1300

A rabia was the birthplace of the Islamic religion; out of this desert peninsula with its commercial entrepots and oases there emerged a new vision of the world and of people's relation to the divine. That vision was based on a single, powerful god, a final prophet, and a belief in revelation. It provided a system of law, a guide for social organization, and a framework for what would become a highly diverse cultural synthesis. Human time began with the first man and woman, Adam and Eve; each believer lived in expectation of a Judgment Day, while the afterlife promised a gardenlike heaven and a fiery hell. For kingdoms and their rulers, Islam provided a universal law extending to all subjects, Muslim and non-Muslim alike. It legitimized sovereigns and promised justice to subjects. The ideal society envisioned in its sacred text, the Qur'an (or *Koran*), was one in which marriage was a preferred state, women were subordinate to men, the wealthy took care of the poor, and competing allegiances were set aside in favor of a primary allegiance to the community of believers (the *umma*). This worldview both challenged and reflected the social order of Arabia. Of course, societies and states never adhere absolutely to the ideals embedded in their sacred texts, and religious messages are interpreted in diverse ways as they extend over time and across space. Like other religious messages, the message of Islam was codified and contested. But the unity embodied in the idea of the *umma* and in the universal Sharia law has prompted some scholars to call Islamic civilization the "first world civilization." Within one century after Muhammad disseminated its message in the seventh century C.E., the power of Islam would be felt from the Indian Ocean to the Atlantic; it would transfigure age-old religious, intellectual, and political patterns.

195

ARABIA BEFORE THE PROPHET

■ *How did the desert environment of Arabia influence Arabic culture?*

The Arabian peninsula is one-third the size of the continental United States. Most of its land is desert; rainfall is scarce, vegetation is scant, and very little of the land is suitable for agriculture. Arabia before the birth of Muhammad was a culturally isolated and economically underdeveloped region. In the relatively more fertile southwestern corner of the peninsula, however, several small Arab kingdoms once flourished in the area now known as Yemen. The most notable of these early kingdoms, Saba' (the biblical Sheba), existed as early as the eighth century B.C.E. and lasted until the third century C.E., when it was taken by the Himyarites (HEEM-yar-aits) from the south.

Aided by the domestication of the camel and the expanding trade in frankincense and spices, these kingdoms became prosperous; they formed part of a commercial network of kingdoms within and beyond the Arabian peninsula. In the north of Arabia, several kingdoms were able to establish contacts with the Byzantine and the Persian (Sassanid) empires as early as the fifth century C.E. Among the most notable of these small kingdoms were Nabataea in northwestern Arabia, which dominated Arabian trade routes until the Romans annexed the kingdom in the second century C.E., and the realm of the Lakhmids in the northeast, whose prominence was greatest around 250 to 600 C.E., until the kingdom was destroyed by the Sassanids. But in the interior of Arabia, a vast desert dotted sparsely with oases, a nomadic life based on herding was the only successful existence.

The Bedouin

The desert nomads, or *Bedouin* (BED-eu-in), lived according to ancient tribal patterns; at the head of the tribe was the male elder, or *shaykh* (SHAYK), elected and advised by the heads of the related families comprising the tribe. These men claimed authority based on family connections and personal merit. Tribes tended to be made up of three-generation families employing a gendered division of labor. The Bedouin led a precarious existence, moving their flocks from one pasture to the next, often following set patterns of migration. Aside from maintaining their herds, these nomads traded animal products for goods from the settled areas. They also relied on plunder from raids on settlements, on passing caravans, and on one another.

Their nomadic existence, its hardships, and the beauty of the desert landscape are all celebrated in the poetry of pre-Islamic Arabia.

The Bedouin enjoyed a degree of personal freedom unknown in more agrarian and settled societies. They developed a code of ethics represented in the word *muru'a* (moo-ROO-ah), or "manly virtue." Far from being abrasive and rough, men proved *muru'a* through grace and restraint, loyalty to obligation and duty, a devotion to do what must be done, and respect for women. The tribe shared a corporate spirit, or '*asabiyya* (AHS-ahb-ee-yah), which reflected the shared interests and honor of the tribe.

Although Bedouin society was patriarchal (dominated by the senior males), women enjoyed a great degree of independence. They engaged in business and commerce and could sometimes wed men of their own choosing. As in all traditional agricultural societies, however, women were under the protection of men, and the honor of the tribe was vested in the sexual honor of the women. The relative freedom of the Bedouin sprang from the realities of life in the desert, as did their values and ethics. One rule of conduct was unqualified hospitality to strangers. A nomad never knew when the care of a stranger might be essential to provide the necessary water and shade to save his or her own life.

The Bedouin of the seventh century did not have a highly structured religious system. They apparently looked at life as a brief time during which to take full advantage of daily pleasure. Ideas of an afterlife were not well defined or described. The Bedouin were animists; they worshipped a large number of gods and spirits, many of whom they believed to inhabit trees, wells, and stones. Each tribe had its own gods, sometimes symbolized by sacred stones.

The Bedouin of the Arabian interior led a relatively primitive and isolated existence, but it was not in their herding camps that the message of Islam was first spoken. In the Arabian cities along the trade routes, the people came into contact with traders and travelers who brought a complex mix of artistic, religious, and philosophical influences. Among these were the monotheistic beliefs of Judaism and Christianity. Some parts of Arabia were greatly influenced by the neighboring and more highly sophisticated cultures of Byzantium, Sassanid Persia, and Ethiopia. It was out of this more urban and commercial context that the early Islamic state would emerge.

Early Mecca

On the western side of the Arabian peninsula along the Red Sea is a region known as the Hijaz, or "barrier."

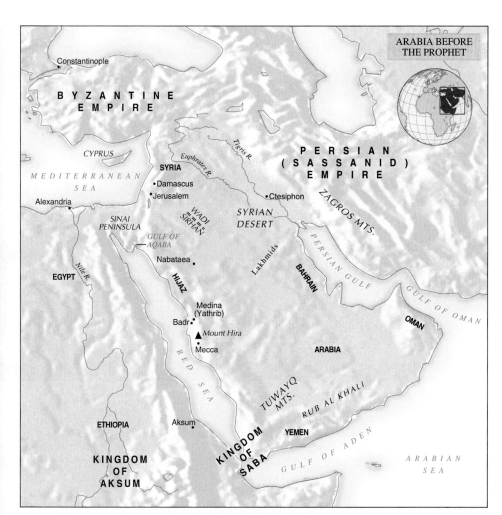

ARABIA BEFORE
THE PROPHET

Geography played a key role in Arab history. The severity of the Arabian environment heavily influenced Bedouin social, economic, religious, and political life.

The Hijaz extends along the western coastal plain from Yemen in the south to the Sinai peninsula in the north. One of the oases in the Hijaz is Mecca, set among barren hills 50 miles inland from the sea. This site had several advantages: Mecca possessed a well (the Zamzam) of great depth, and two ancient caravan routes met there. One route ran from Africa through the peninsula to Iran and central Asia, and another, a southeast-northwest route, brought the textiles and spices of India and Southeast Asia to the Mediterranean world.

A second significant advantage for Mecca was its importance as a religious sanctuary. An ancient temple, an almost square structure built of granite blocks, stood near the well of Mecca. Known as the *Ka'ba* ("cube"), this square temple contained the sacred Black Stone. According to tradition, the stone, probably a meteorite, was originally white but had become blackened by the sins of all those who touched it. Later Muslim historians would attribute the building of the Ka'ba to the prophet Abraham or even to Adam. The Ka'ba itself was draped with the pelts of sacrificial animals and supposedly held the images and shrines of 360 gods and goddesses. For centuries, the Ka'ba had been a holy place of annual pilgrimage for the Arab tribes and a focal point of Arab culture and ritual practice. As a pilgrimage site, it also brought prestige and wealth to the tribes who controlled the city of Mecca.

By the sixth century, Mecca was controlled by the Quraysh (KOO-raysh) tribe, whose rulers organized themselves into an aristocracy of merchants and wealthy businessmen. The Quraysh engaged in lucrative trade with Byzantium and Persia, as well as with the southern Arabian tribes and the kingdom of Aksum across the Red Sea in what is now Ethiopia. In addition, a number of annual merchant fairs, such as one usually held at nearby Ukaz, were taken over by the Quraysh to extend the economic influence of Mecca. The Quraysh were also concerned with protecting the religious shrine of the Ka'ba, in addition to ensuring that the annual pilgrimage of tribes to the holy place would continue as a source of revenue for the merchants of the city.

This nineteenth-century engraving depicts the city of Mecca with, at its center, the Ka'ba, a square building of stone draped with black cloth that became the focal point of Muslim worship. Each year Muslims make the pilgrimage to celebrate their unity and to worship at this most sacred shrine of Islam. The site itself and its buildings (as shown here) have been greatly expanded over the centuries since the Prophet Muhammad's time, and the number of pilgrims has dramatically increased.

MUHAMMAD, PROPHET OF ISLAM

■ *What role did Muhammad play in the creation of Islam?*

Into this environment at Mecca was born a man who would revolutionize the religious, political, and social organization of his people. Muhammad (c. 570–632) came from a family belonging to the Quraysh. An orphan, he suffered the loss of both his parents and his grandfather, who cared for him after his parents' death. He was then raised by his uncle, Abu Talib, a prominent merchant of Mecca. His early years were spent helping his uncle in the caravan trade. Even as a young man, Muhammad came to be admired by his fellow Meccans as a sincere and honest person who earned the nickname al-Amin, "the trustworthy." When he was about 25 years old, he accepted employment from a wealthy widow, Khadija (cah-DEE-jah), whose caravans traded with Syria. He later married Khadija and began to take his place as a leading citizen of Mecca. Muhammad's marriage to Khadija was a long and happy one that produced two sons, who both died as infants, and two daughters. The younger, Fatima,

would play an important role in the future of the fledgling Islamic state.

Biographies of the Prophet, written after his death by his followers, describe him as a handsome, large man with broad shoulders and black, shining eyes, a man who was reserved and gentle but possessed of impressive energy. Tradition relates that Muhammad was an introspective man. Often he would escape from Meccan society, which he considered too materialistic and irreligious, and spend long hours alone in a cave on nearby Mount Hira. During these hours of meditation, Muhammad searched for answers to the metaphysical questions that many thoughtful people have pondered. Muhammad's meditations sometimes produced nearly total mental and physical exhaustion. During one such solitary meditation, Muhammad heard a call that was to alter history. This initial communication from heaven came in the form of a command:

> *Recite! In the name of your Lord, who created*
>   *all things, who*
> *created man from a clot [of blood].*
> *Recite! And your Lord is Most Bounteous*
> *Who teaches by the Pen,*
> *Teaches man that which he would not have*
>   *otherwise known. (Qur'an 96:1–5)*

The collected revelations given to Muhammad are known as the **Qur'an** (or Koran), an Arabic word meaning "recitation" or "reading." The revelations that continued to come over the next 20 years or so were sometimes terse and short, at other times elaborate and poetic. The early revelations did not immediately persuade Muhammad that he was a messenger of God. In fact, his first reactions were fear and self-doubt. Anxious about the source and nature of his revelations, he sought the comfort and advice of Khadija.

As the revelations continued, Muhammad was persuaded that he had been called to be a messenger of divine revelation. He began to think of himself and his mission as one similar to those of prophets and messengers who had preceded him in announcing the existence of the one God, **Allah**. Allah, *"the* God," was the same God worshipped by the Christians and Jews, but Allah had now chosen Muhammad to be his last and greatest prophet to perfect the religion revealed earlier to Abraham, Moses, the Hebrew prophets, and Jesus. The religion Muhammad preached is called **Islam,** which means "submission" to the will of God. The followers of Islam are called *Muslims,* "those who submit" to God's law.

Muhammad's Message and Its Early Followers

At first Muhammad had little success in attracting followers in Mecca. The early message he brought to the Arabs was strong and direct: that Allah was the one God and majestic, all-powerful, and demanding of the faith of his followers. Furthermore, Allah decreed that his followers be compassionate, ethical, and just in all their dealings:

> *In the name of Allah, the most Beneficent, the*
> *Most Merciful*
> *by the night as it enshrouds*
> *by the day as it illuminates*
> *by Him Who created the male and female*
> *indeed your affairs lead to various ends.*
> *For who gives [of himself] and acts righteously,*
> *and conforms to goodness,*
> *We will give him ease.*

Qur'an—Literally "recitation" or "reading" in Arabic; the Islamic holy book containing the word of God (Allah) as revealed to the Prophet Muhammad through the angel Gabriel. Written in Arabic and to be read only in this language by believers.

Allah—"The God" in Arabic; the Arabic word for the same God worshipped in Christianity and Judaism.

Islam—The religion founded by the Prophet Muhammad in the seventh century A.D., a monotheistic faith drawing on elements from Judaism, Christianity, and the indigenous beliefs of the Arabian peninsula; literally "submission" in Arabic, as in "submission" to God's will.

> *But as for him who is niggardly deeming*
> *himself self-sufficient and rejects goodness,*
> *We will indeed ease his path to adversity.*
> *Nor shall his wealth save him as he perishes*
> *for Guidance is from Us*
> *and to Us belongs the Last and First.*
> *(Qur'an 92:1–14)*

Muhammad was able to win the early support of some of his relatives and close friends. His first converts were his wife, his cousin Ali, and Abu Bakr, a leading merchant of the Quraysh tribe, who was highly respected for his integrity. Abu Bakr remained the constant companion of the Prophet during his persecution and exile and later succeeded him as the leader of Islam. But opposition to Muhammad's message was very strong, especially from Mecca's leading citizens. Many thought Muhammad was an ambitious poet attempting to pass on his own literary creations as the word of God. Others believed him to be possessed by demons. Muhammad challenged the status quo; his strong monotheism threatened the polytheistic beliefs of Mecca and the people who obtained their income from the pilgrims to the Ka'ba. Many of Muhammad's early converts were among the poorest of the city's residents, and Mecca's leading citizens feared the possibility of social revolution.

Since Muhammad was himself a member of the Quraysh tribe, its leaders first approached his uncle Abu Talib to persuade his nephew to stop preaching. Next they tried to bribe Muhammad with the promise of a lucrative appointment as an official. When he rejected such offers, actual persecution of Muhammad's converts began, and the Quraysh attempted a commercial and social boycott of the Prophet's family. During this time of trial, Abu Talib and Khadija both died, and Muhammad's faith and resolution were greatly tested. But inspired by the spirit and example of earlier prophets such as Abraham and Moses, who were also tested and persecuted, Muhammad persevered in his faith and continued his preaching.

The Hijra

To the north of Mecca is the city of Medina, which was then called Yathrib. The residents of Medina were somewhat familiar with monotheistic beliefs, in part because of the Jewish community in residence there. While visiting Mecca, some pilgrims from Medina judged Muhammad to be a powerful and influential mediator and invited him to come to Medina to settle differences among that city's tribal chiefs. As opposition to his message increased in Mecca, Muhammad sent some of his followers to take up residence in Medina in order to escape persecution. Finally, Muhammad and Abu Bakr fled Mecca when it became known that the Quraysh intended to kill the Prophet. They were followed, but escaped, the story goes, by hiding in a narrow cave whose entrance was quickly covered by a spider's web. The Quraysh pursuers saw the web and passed on, thinking that the cave had been abandoned for a long time.

The **Hijra** (or *Hegira*), Muhammad's "migration" from Mecca to Medina, took place in September in the year 622. The event was such a turning point in the history of Islam that 622 is counted as year 1 of the Islamic calendar, because it marked the beginning of the Islamic state. In Medina, the Prophet met with entirely different circumstances from those in his birthplace. Muhammad's leadership turned Medina (*Madinat al-Nabi*, "City of the Prophet") into the major center of power in the Arabian peninsula.

The Community at Medina

Muhammad was received in Medina as a leader and a spiritual visionary. There, he and his followers set about the establishment of the Muslim **umma** or community. This new community established relations with the Medinan tribes, including the Jewish and Christian residents. Those who did not choose to accept Muhammad's faith were allowed to continue their way of life, since Christians and Jews were thought to be "people of the Book" to whom God had made himself known through earlier prophets. Ultimately, however, the Prophet's new polity came into conflict with some of the Jewish tribes of Medina and the tribes were expelled. This conflict illustrates the tension between the expansionist political policies and generally tolerant religious policies of the new state.

Hijra—The departure of the Prophet Muhammad from Mecca for Medina in 622 A.D.; considered to be the formal starting point for Islam.

umma—The community or nation of believers in Islam.

The Early Islamic State

622   The Hijra, Muhammad's migration from Mecca to Medina, year 1 of the Islamic calendar

630   The Prophet returns and takes control of Mecca, Ka'ba consecrated to Allah

632   Death of the Prophet

632–661   Rule of the first four caliphs: Abu Bakr, Umar, Uthman, Ali

638   Muslim armies take Jerusalem

651   Defeat of the Sassanids in Persia

Muhammad and his followers became steadily more aggressive in their attempts to win converts to Islam. The word **jihad,** meaning "struggle," was applied to the early efforts of the *umma* to win converts and conquer territory. Military encounters with the opponents of Islam began in 624, with the battle of Badr. Muhammad defeated a stronger Quraysh troop from Mecca, and the victory reinforced the resolve of the new religion's followers. Succeeding battles established the Muslims as the dominant force in Arabia, and a truce with Mecca was arranged, under which the Muslims could visit the holy city.

Return to Mecca

In 630 Muhammad returned to take control of the city of Mecca and to cleanse the Ka'ba of idols. The temple itself, together with the Black Stone, was preserved as the supreme religious center of Islam and rededicated to the One God. It is to this shrine that all devout Muslims, if able, make pilgrimage during their lifetime. Muhammad urged unbelievers and his old enemies to accept Islam and become part of the *umma*. By 632 almost all of the Arabian peninsula had (at least nominally) accepted Islam, and Muhammad had even sent ambassadors to the neighboring Byzantine and Persian Empires to announce the new religion and encourage converts. Just as Christianity began as a religion of the Jews, Islam began as a religion of the Arabs. But, over time, like Christianity, and unlike Judaism, Islam became a universal religion with a missionary spirit.

The Death of Muhammad

Muhammad died on June 8, 632, in Medina. Muslims at first refused to accept his death but were reassured by Abu Bakr, who recited this verse from the Qur'an: "Muhammad is only a messenger: many are the messengers who have died before him; if he dies, or is slain, will you turn back on your heels?" (3:144).

Muhammad had no surviving son and had not designated a successor. On the day of his death, his close companions solved the question of leadership of the faithful by agreeing on the election of Abu Bakr, who became the first successor, or **caliph** (kal-IF). Abu Bakr could not really replace Muhammad, the last prophet. However, as caliph, he was regarded as the head of the Islamic *umma*; he combined the roles

---

jihad—Literally "struggle" in Arabic; an Islamic term with broad meaning, ranging from the internal struggle of an individual to overcome sin to the external struggle of the faithful to address a social challenge or to fight against enemies and unbelievers in what is essentially a holy war.

caliph—The religious and political leader of the Islamic nation; successor of Muhammad.

of religious leader and head of state. Abu Bakr and his three successors in the office, Umar, Uthman, and Ali, are often referred to as the *Rashidun* (RAHSH-ee-deun), the "Rightly Guided" caliphs.

The significance of Muhammad to the birth and growth of Islam is impossible to overestimate. The Prophet and his message inspired his followers to create and work for the betterment of a society united by the Islamic faith. Ideally, tribal loyalties were replaced by loyalty to the *umma* and faith in the One God, who chose to speak to his people in their own language through a messenger who was also one of their own.

Soon after Muhammad's death, his followers began to collect and codify his teachings and actions. The result of their efforts was the **hadith,** or reports of the sayings and activities of Muhammad. The hadith have

hadith—A collection of the sayings, deeds, and traditions of the Prophet Muhammad, compiled by the Prophet's followers after his death to further clarify Islamic values and ethics.

This miniature depicts one of the legends of the Prophet, the Miraj or Night Journey. Muhammad, mounted on a winged part-human, part-horse steed, is believed miraculously to have ascended to heaven from Jerusalem, there enjoying a vision of God, and returning in a single night.

become an important source of values and ethical paths of behavior for the Islamic world. The **sunna,** the custom or practice of the Prophet, is grounded in the hadith and serves as a pattern for a model way of life to be imitated by the faithful.

ISLAMIC FAITH AND LAW

■ *What is the relationship between the Qur'an and Islamic faith and law?*

Islam places great emphasis on the necessity of obedience to God's law in addition to faith. The Qur'an is the fundamental and ultimate source of knowledge about Allah. This holy book contains both the theology of Islam and the patterns of ethical and appropriate conduct to which a Muslim must subscribe. Included in the Qur'an are some basic concepts that the Islamic community holds in common as fundamental to the faith.

The Qur'an

Muslims believe that the Qur'an contains the actual word of God as it was revealed to Muhammad through divine inspiration. These revelations to the Prophet took place over a period of more than 20 years. Before Muhammad's death, many of these messages were written down. Muhammad himself began this work of preservation, and Abu Bakr, as caliph, continued the process by compiling revelations that up to that time had been memorized by the followers and passed on by word of mouth. A complete written text of the Qur'an was produced some years after Muhammad's death, with particular care taken to eliminate discrepancies and record only one standard version. This "authorized" edition was then transmitted to various parts of the new Islamic Empire and used to guide the faithful and assist in the conversion of unbelievers. The text of the Qur'an has existed virtually unchanged for nearly 14 centuries.

The Qur'an was intended to be recited aloud; anyone who has listened to the chanting of the Qur'an can testify to its beauty, melody, and power. Much of the power of the Qur'an comes from the experience of reciting, listening, and feeling the message. The Qur'an is never to be translated from the Arabic for the purpose of worship because it is believed that translation distorts the divine message. But over time, the Qur'an was indeed translated into many languages to facilitate

DOCUMENT

The Holy Qur'an

sunna—The custom or practice of the Prophet Muhammad, grounded in the hadith; intended to serve as a model by which Muslims should conduct their lives.

Document   The Qur'an

The Qur'an is one of the most significant of all religious works and one of the world's most beautiful works of literature. The following is a selection celebrating God's creation, from sura 23, titled "The Believers." It illustrates Islam's connection, through the prophets Moses and Jesus, to the sacred texts and beliefs of Judaism and Christianity. But it also points out the Islamic doctrine that God has no son. The Qur'an makes a point of rejecting the notions that God had either sons (e.g., Jesus) or daughters (goddesses in the Arabian pantheon). Note too, that the Qur'an urges men, as well as women, to "guard their modesty."

In the name of Allah, the Beneficent, the Merciful.
Successful indeed are the believers
Who are humble in their prayers,
And who shun vain conversation,
And who are payers of the poor-due;
And who guard their modesty—
Save from their wives or the [slaves] that their
*   right hands possess, for then they are not*
*   blameworthy,*
But whoso craveth beyond that, such are
*   transgressors—*
And who are shepherds of their pledge and their
*   covenant, and who pay heed to their prayers.*
These are the heirs
Who will inherit Paradise. There they will abide.
Verily We created man from a product of wet
*   earth;*
Then placed him as a drop [of seed] in a safe
*   lodging;*
Then fashioned We the drop a clot, then fashioned
*   We the clot a little lump, then fashioned We*
*   the little lump bones, then clothed the bones*
*   with flesh, and then produced it as another*
*   creation. So blessed be Allah, the Best of*
*   Creators!*
Then lo! after that ye surely die.
Then lo! on the Day of Resurrection ye are raised
*   [again].*
And We have created above you seven paths, and
*   We are never unmindful of creation.*
And We send down from the sky water in
*   measure, and We give it lodging in the earth,*
*   and lo! We are able to withdraw it.*
Then We produce for you therewith gardens of
*   date-palms and grapes, wherein is much fruit*
*   for you and whereof ye eat;*
And a tree that springeth forth from Mount Sinai
*   that groweth oil and relish for the eaters.*
And lo! in the cattle there is verily a lesson for
*   you. We give you to drink of that which is in*
*   their bellies, and many uses have ye in them,*
*   and of them do ye eat;*
And on them and on the ship ye are carried.
Then We sent Moses and his brother Aaron with
*   Our tokens and a clear warrant*

Unto Pharaoh and his chiefs, but they scorned
*   [them] and they were despotic folk.*
And they said: Shall we put faith in two mortals
*   like ourselves, and whose folk are servile unto*
*   us?*
So they denied them, and became of those who
*   were destroyed.*
And We verily gave Moses the Scripture, that haply
*   they might go aright.*
And We made the son of Mary and his mother a
*   portent, and We gave them refuge on a height,*
*   a place of flocks and water-springs.*
O ye messengers! Eat of the good things, and do
*   right. Lo! I am Aware of what ye do.*
And lo! this your religion is one religion and I am
*   your Lord, so keep your duty unto Me.*
Say: In Whose hand is the dominion over all
*   things and He protecteth, while against Him*
*   there is no protection, if ye have knowledge?*
They will say: Unto Allah [all that belongeth]. Say:
*   How then are ye bewitched?*
Nay, but We have brought them the Truth, and lo!
*   they are liars.*
Allah hath not chosen any son, nor is there any
*   God along with Him; else would each God*
*   have assuredly championed that which he*
*   created, and some of them would assuredly*
*   have overcome others. Glorified be Allah*
*   above all that they allege.*
Knower of the invisible and the visible! and
*   exalted be He over all that they ascribe as*
*   partners [unto Him]!*

Questions to Consider

1. What kind of God is suggested in these verses? Characterize him.
2. What clues do these verses give us about the society and environment of Arabia?
3. Compare this account of creation to other creation accounts you are aware of.

From Marmaduke William Pickthall, *The Meaning of the Glorious Koran: An Explanatory Translation* (London: Unwin Hyman/HarperCollins). Reprinted by permission.

scholarship and the spread of the Islamic message. As Islam spread, so too did the Arabic language. Arabic replaced many local languages as the language of administration, and gradually, some of the conquered territories adopted Arabic as the language of everyday use. The Qur'an remains the basic document for the study of Islamic theology, law, social institutions, and ethics. It forms the core of Muslim scholarship, from legal and linguistic inquiry to scientific and technical investigation.

IMAGE

The Holy Qur'an

The Tenets of Islamic Faith

Monotheism is the central principle of Islam. Muslims believe in the unity or oneness of God; there is no other God but Allah, and this belief is proclaimed five times daily as the believers are called to prayer with these words:

> *God is most great. I testify that there is no God but Allah. I testify that Muhammad is the Messenger of Allah. Come to prayer, come to revelation, God is most great! There is no God but Allah.*

Allah is the one and only God, unchallenged by other false divinities and unlike all others in the strength of his creative power. All life—all creation—is the responsibility of Allah alone. His nature is described in many ways and through many metaphors:

> *Allah is the light of the heaven and the earth. . . . His light is as a niche wherein is a lamp. The lamp is in a glass. The glass is as it were a shining star. [The lamp is] kindled from a blessed tree, an olive neither of the East nor of the West, whose oil would almost glow forth [of itself] though no fire touched it. Light upon light, Allah guided unto His light whom He will. And Allah speaketh to mankind in allegories, for Allah is Knower of all things.*
>
> *[This lamp is found] in houses which Allah hath allowed to be exalted and that His name shall be remembered therein. Therein do offer praise to Him at noon and evening. (Qur'an 24:35–36)*

Islam also recognizes the significance and the contributions of prophets who preceded Muhammad. From the beginnings of human history, Allah has communicated with his people either by the way of these prophets or by written scriptures:

> *Lo! We inspire thee as We inspired Noah and the Prophets after him, as We inspired Abraham and Ishmael and Isaac and Jacob and the tribes, and Jesus and Job and Jonah and Aaron and Solomon and as We imparted unto David the Psalms. (Qur'an 4:164)*

Twenty-eight such prophets are mentioned in the Qur'an as the predecessors of Muhammad, who is believed to have been Allah's final messenger. Muhammad is given no divine status by Muslims; in fact, Muhammad took great care to see that he was not worshipped as a god. He told his followers, for example, that it was not appropriate for them to bow down before him.

The creation of the universe and of all living creatures within it is the work of Allah; harmony and balance in all of creation were ensured by God. In addition to humans and other creatures on the earth, angels exist to protect humans and to pray for forgiveness for the faithful. Satan, "the Whisperer," attempts to lead people astray, and mischievous spirits called *jinn* can create havoc for believers and unbelievers alike.

Men and women are given a special status in the pattern of the universe. They can choose to obey or to reject Allah's will and deny him. Allah's message includes the belief in a Day of Resurrection when people will be held responsible for their actions and rewarded or punished accordingly for eternity. The Qur'an graphically describes heaven and hell. Those who have submitted to Allah's law—the charitable, the humble, and the forgiving—and those who have preserved his faith shall dwell in the Garden of Paradise, resting in cool shade, eating delectable foods, attended by "fair ones with wide, lovely eyes like unto hidden pearls," and hearing no vain speech or recrimination but only "Peace! Peace!" This veritable oasis is far different from the agonies of the hell that awaits sinners, the covetous, and the erring. Cast into a pit with its "scorching wind and shadow of black smoke," they will drink boiling water and suffer forever.

The Five Pillars

Over time, the Muslim community developed doctrines, laws, and institutions (like schools and courts) to put into practice its evolving religious ideals. As in other religious traditions, the spread and institutionalization of Islam was a gradual and contested process. And, as in all societies, government and social practice did not always match the religious ideals expressed in the sacred texts. But certain practices became basic to the believers.

Islam is united in the observance of the **Five Pillars,** or five essential duties that all Muslims are required to perform to the best of their abilities. These obligations are accepted by Muslims everywhere and thus serve further to unite the Islamic world. The first obligation is a basic *profession of faith,* by which a

---

Five Pillars—The five essential duties of all Muslims: (1) a profession of faith *(shahada)*; (2) prayer *(salat)* five times a day; (3) giving of alms *(zakat)*; (4) fasting *(sawm)* during the holy month of Ramadan; and (5) making a pilgrimage *(hajj)* to Mecca at least once during one's lifetime if possible.

These illustrations from a sixteenth-century Persian manuscript depict scenes from the lives of the prophets: Jesus multiplying the loaves and fishes and the staff of Moses transformed into a dragon. Artistic representation of people, events, and landscapes varies considerably from place to place, culture to culture, and over time. Moses is depicted in Jewish, Christian, and Muslim texts, but the same story can be "told" artistically in very different ways.

believer becomes a Muslim. The simple proclamation *(shahada)* is repeated in daily prayers. Belief in the One God and imitation of the exemplary life led by his Prophet are combined in the profession of faith.

Prayer (salat) is said five times a day, when Muslims are summoned to worship by the *muezzin* (myeu-EZ-in), who calls them to prayer from atop the minaret of the mosque (*masjid*, meaning "place of prostration"). During prayer, Muslims face Mecca and in so doing give recognition to the birthplace of Islam and the unity of the Islamic community. Prayer can be said alone, at work, at home, or in the mosque.

A Muslim is required to give *alms (zakat)* to the poor, orphans, and widows and to assist the spread of Islam. The payment of alms is a social and religious obligation to provide for the welfare of the *umma*. Muslims are generally expected to contribute annually in alms a percentage (usually 2.5 percent) of their total wealth and assets.

Muslims are requested to *fast (sawm)* during the holy month of Ramadan, the ninth month of the Islamic lunar calendar. From sunrise to sunset, adult Muslims in good health are to avoid food, drink, tobacco, and sexual activity. Finally, every Muslim able to do so is called to make a *pilgrimage (hajj)* to Mecca at least once in his or her lifetime, in the twelfth month of the Islamic year. The focus of the pilgrimage is the Ka'ba and a series of other sites commemorating events in the lives of the prophets Muhammad and Abraham. The *hajj* emphasizes the unity of the Islamic world community and the equality of all believers regardless of race or class.

Islamic Law

Islam is a way of life as well as a religion, and at its heart is the **Sharia,** the law provided by Allah as a guide for a proper life. The Sharia is based on the Qur'an and hadith; it gives the believers a perfect pattern of human conduct and regulates every aspect of

---

Sharia—Islamic law based on the word of God as manifested in the teachings of the Qu'ran and hadith.

a person's activities. God's decrees must be obeyed even if humans are incapable of understanding them, since the Sharia is greater than human reason. Those who study, interpret, and administer the Sharia are called *ulama*, "those who know." These men emerged, in the era after the Prophet's death, as religious scholars and leaders who administered the institutions of worship, education, and law. But there is no priesthood in Islam; all believers are equal members of the community.

Islamic law, then, permeates all aspects of human conduct and all levels of activity, from private and personal concerns to those involving the welfare of the whole state. The Sharia became the universal law of the Islamic lands. In practice, it worked in conjunction with the decrees of rulers and with customary laws that varied from region to region. Family law, set forth in the Qur'an, is based on earlier Arab tribal patterns. Islamic law emphasizes the patriarchal nature of the family and society. Marriage is expected of every Muslim man and woman unless physical infirmity or financial inability prevents it. Muslim men can marry non-Muslim women, preferably Christians or Jews, since they too are "people of the Book," but Muslim women are forbidden to marry non-Muslim men. This law reflects the notion, common in traditional societies, that the children "belong" to the father and his family. Thus, the children of a Muslim father and non-Muslim mother would be Muslims. The Qur'an had the effect of improving the status and opportunities of women, who could contract their own marriages, keep and maintain their own dowries, and manage and inherit property (unlike many Western Christian women at that time).

The Qur'an allows Muslim men to marry up to four wives, but only if each wife is treated with equal support and affection. Many modern-day Muslims interpret the Qur'an as encouraging monogamy. Polygamy, in any case, is not required; it is a practice that may have arisen to provide protection and security in early societies where women may have outnumbered men because of the toll of constant warfare.

Islamic law is considered to be God's law for all humankind, not only for the followers of Islam. Non-Muslim citizens of the Islamic state were called *dhimmis* (DHEE-mees); they received protection from the state and paid an extra head tax called the *jizya* (JIZ-yah). The Sharia courts were open to *dhimmis*,

Women associated with the Prophet are revered by the Muslim community. This manuscript image shows Fatima, Muhammad's daughter, along with Aisha and Umm Salama, two of his wives. Their fiery halos and veiled faces suggest their religious significance. Fatima is often held up as a model of Islamic womanhood and Aisha was a prominent political figure and transmitter of Islamic tradition (hadith).

who could also appeal to juridical authorities, such as rabbis or priests, within their own communities. Disputes between Muslims and *dhimmis* were handled in the Sharia court, but a dispute between Christians might be handled within the Christian community. Islamic law sometimes designated certain dress markers for *dhimmis* to set them apart. Bearing arms, engaging in ostentatious religious displays, and corrupting Muslims (by selling them wine, for example) were also prohibited. But repeated allusions to such violations in court records suggest that these laws often were not enforced.

Thus, in addition to its theology, Islam offers to its believers a system of government, a legal foundation, and a pattern of social organization. The Islamic *umma* was, and is, an excellent example of a theocratic state, one in which power ultimately resides in God, on whose behalf political, religious, and other forms of authority are exercised. Ideally, the role of the state is to serve as the guardian of religious law. Islamic monarchs ruled in the name of Allah and called on the Sharia law to legitimize their rule. Of course, as the Islamic state evolved, some rulers were more pious than others. Some came into conflict with the *ulama* over matters of law (as happened with brahmans and kings in India and priests and kings in Europe). But all Muslim kings, like all Christian kings in this era, claimed to be defenders of their faith.

THE EXPANSION OF COMMUNITY AND STATE

■ *What factors contributed to the rapid expansion of Islam?*

The Islamic state expanded very rapidly after the death of Muhammad through remarkable successes in the form of military conquest and conversion. Immediately after the Prophet's death in 632, Caliph Abu Bakr continued the effort to abolish polytheism among the Arab tribes and also to bring all of Arabia under the political control of Medina. The Muslim polity succeeded in strengthening its power throughout the Arabian peninsula and even began to launch some exploratory offensives north toward Syria.

Expansion Under the First Four Caliphs

Under the first four caliphs (632–661), the Islamic state rapidly expanded the territory under its control. The wars of expansion were aided by the devotion of the faithful to the concept of *jihad*, a term that is sometimes glossed as "holy war" and sometimes interpreted to mean simply "struggle." Muslims were obliged to extend the faith to unbelievers and to defend Islam from attack. *Jihad* was responsible in part for Islam's early conquests beyond the Arabian peninsula.

Arab Expansion and the Islamic World, 570–800 C.E.

But various factors account for the triumph of the early Muslim armies. A long series of wars waged between the Byzantine and Persian (Sassanid) Empires to the north left both sides exhausted and open to con-

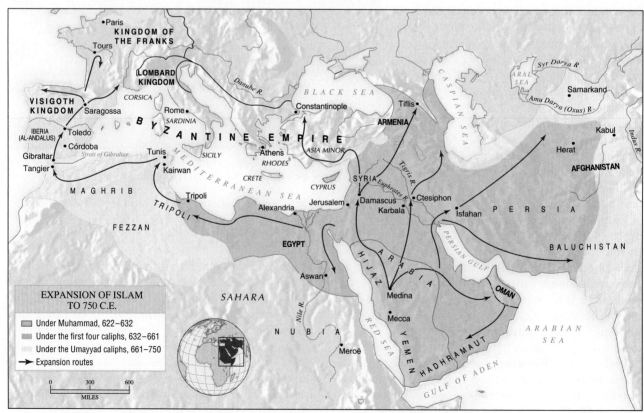

The Islamic conquests were rapid and far-reaching. By 750 Islamic monarchs controlled kingdoms stretching from central Asia to Spain.

quest. In addition, the inhabitants of Syria and Egypt, alienated by religious dissent and resenting the attempts of the Byzantine Empire to impose its brand of Christianity on the population, sought freedom from Byzantine rule. The Arabs' combined use of camels for long distance travel and swift horses for attacks was extremely effective. In 636 Arab armies conquered Syria and occupied the city of Damascus. Jerusalem was taken in 638. The Muslims then won Iraq from the Persians and in 651 defeated the last Sassanid ruler, thereby ending the 400-year-old Persian Empire. Most of Egypt had fallen with little resistance by 646, and raids had begun into the lands the Muslims called the Maghrib (MUG-reb) in North Africa west of Egypt and north of the Sahara. Within 30 years of Muhammad's death, Islam had become the dominant faith of a vast empire connecting western Asia with the Mediterranean and Africa. This area possessed a certain cultural unity under Islam, but it was politically divided.

The new Islamic territories were governed with remarkable efficiency and flexibility. The centralization of authority typical of effective military organization aided in the incorporation of new peoples. Unbelievers in the conquered territories became increasingly interested in the new religion and accepted Islam in great numbers. In addition to the power of the religious message of Islam, the imposition of a head tax on all non-Muslims and some restrictions on unbelievers' holding political office encouraged many to become converts. Accounts of the coercive imposition of Islam on conquered peoples are inexact: Jews and Christians outside Arabia generally enjoyed tolerance because they worshipped the same God as the Muslims, and many non-Muslims were active participants in the Islamic state and prospered financially and socially.

Islam was and remains one of the most effective religions in overcoming the potential barriers of race and nationality to conversion. In the early days of the spread of Islam, apart from a certain privileged position allowed Arabs and the Prophet's earliest supporters, distinctions were mostly those of economic and political rank. The new religion converted and included peoples of many ethnic origins and cultures. This egalitarian ideal of Islam undoubtedly aided its rapid and successful expansion.

Defining the Community

All Muslims shared belief in the unity of God and the practice of the Five Pillars. But Islamic civilization, like other traditions, was marked by debate and conflict over the interpretation of the law. As Islamic law was codified and as the Islamic state expanded, four main schools of legal interpretation emerged. Schol-

ars struggled with questions of faith and reason, just as their Christian and Buddhist counterparts did. Inspired in part by the spiritual thought and practices of India, Islam also developed a set of mystical traditions that challenged the orthodoxy of the *ulama*. Meanwhile, in the political realm, not long after the death of the Prophet, the new Islamic state underwent a crisis that split the community over the question of authority.

Islam's first three caliphs—Abu Bakr (632–634), Umar (634–644), and Uthman (644–656)—were chosen in consultation with the elders and leaders of the Islamic community, setting a pattern for selecting the caliph exclusively from the Quraysh tribe of Mecca. When Uthman was assassinated by a fellow Muslim, the ensuing struggle for power ultimately split the community into two major divisions, **Sunni** and **Shia** (or Shi'ites). The Shi'ites believed that only descendents of the Prophet could command authority in the Islamic state. Because Muhammad had no surviving sons, his bloodline passed through his grandsons, the sons of his daughter Fatima and her husband Ali, the fourth caliph. Thus for the Shi'ites, the first three caliphs before Ali had been usurpers. Ali and his descendents were the only legitimate heads of the community, *imams*, who were believed to have a special knowledge of the inner meaning of the Qur'an. The Sunnis, rather than insisting on a caliph who was a direct descendant of the Prophet, accepted the first three caliphs and upheld the principle that the caliph owed his position to the consent of the Islamic community. The Sunnis argued that they followed the *sunna* of the Prophet, the patterns of behavior modeled on Muhammad's life.

The Shi'ites did not refute the validity of the sunna, but they insisted on the Qur'an as the sole and unquestioned authority on the life and teachings of the Prophet. Though originally an Arab party, the Shia in time became a more widespread Islamic movement that stood in opposition to the ruling Umayyad dynasty. That the Shia remained, in general, a minority and opposition party in part explains the evolution of its doctrine of opposition to political authorities. Notwithstanding the several major Shi'ite dynasties in Islamic history, Sunni Muslims have remained numerically dominant. Some 85 percent of the modern world's Muslims are Sunnis,

---

Sunni—The largest division within Islam, comprising more than 85 percent of all Muslims; the form of Islam embraced by the Umayyad state, which accepts the legitimacy of the first three caliphs and holds that the caliph's authority stems from the consent of the Islamic community.

Shia—A division in Islam representing some 10 to 15 percent of all Muslims, principally in Iran, Iraq, and Lebanon; Shi'ites deny the legitimacy of the first three caliphs and hold that the true caliphs were descended from the Prophet Muhammad through Ali, his cousin and son-in-law.

The Early Islamic Dynasties

661	Umayyad dynasty established; Damascus becomes capital
680	Muhammad's grandson Husayn killed by Umayyads at Karbala in Iraq
711	Tariq ibn Ziyad invades Spain from North Africa
750	Abbasids defeat the Umayyads and establish a new dynasty
756	Umayyads set up a new dynasty in Spain; Córdoba later becomes capital
786–809	Reign of Abbasid caliph Harun al-Rashid
909–1171	Fatimid Shi'ite dynasty in North Africa, Egypt, and Syria
1055	Seljuk Turks gain control of Baghdad but leave Abbasid caliph in place
1095	First Crusade mobilized
1250	Mamluk kingdom established in Egypt, will endure until 1517
1258	Mongols conquer Baghdad and kill Abbasid caliph, ending Abbasid dynasty

although large Shi'ite communities exist, particularly in Iran, Iraq, and Lebanon.

Umayyad Rule

Ali and his followers were opposed first by Muslims under the leadership of Muhammad's widow and favorite wife, Aisha, daughter of Abu Bakr, and later by the forces of Muawiya (MOO-AH-wee-ah), the governor of Syria and a relative of the third caliph. The power struggle for leadership in the Muslim community thus erupted into civil war. In 661, after Ali was assassinated, Muawiya proclaimed himself caliph, made Damascus his capital, and founded the Umayyad (oo-MAI-yad) dynasty, which lasted until 750. In this manner the Umayyads made the caliphate in fact, although never in law, a hereditary office rather than one chosen by election.

The Umayyads expanded the borders of Islam, but not with the spectacular successes of the years immediately after Muhammad's death. The Umayyads held

Cyprus, Rhodes, and several Aegean islands, which served as bases for naval attacks on the Byzantine Empire. The Byzantines successfully defended Constantinople against persistent Umayyad attacks, and the Islamic advance toward eastern Europe was checked for the first time. The Umayyads established garrisons in central Asia to further their conquests northward across the Oxus River and southwest into India. Westward across North Africa, Umayyad armies were eventually victorious. The Berbers, a nomadic tribal people inhabiting the Maghrib, initially resisted stubbornly but eventually converted to Islam. The Berbers then aided the Umayyad armies in expanding across the Strait of Gibraltar into the weak Visigoth kingdom in Spain. General Tariq ibn Ziyad (TAHR-ik ib-in zee-YAHD) led an army across the strait into Spain in 711 (according to legend, the name *Gibraltar* is derived from *Jabal Tariq*, or "Mountain of Tariq"). After the kingdom of the Visigoths swiftly crumbled, the Muslims were able to make conquests throughout the Iberian peninsula, which they called *al-Andalus*.

The Muslims in Spain seem never to have had serious intentions of expanding their territorial holdings across the Pyrenees into what is now France, but they did engage in seasonal raids to the north. One such raiding party was defeated by Charles Martel near Tours in 732 in a battle that Europeans portrayed later as a decisive blow to Muslim expansion in Europe. But the Byzantines indeed delivered such a blow: In 717 the Byzantine emperor Leo III won a major victory over the Muslims that halted the Umayyad advance into eastern Europe.

To the east, however, the Umayyads successfully extended their rule into central Asia; by the middle of the eighth century they could claim lands as far east as Turkestan and the Indus valley. To celebrate the enduring power of Islam in the 690s the Umayyads built the Dome of the Rock in Jerusalem on the site of the old Jewish Temple. This sacred shrine is built around an enormous rock where, according to tradition, God asked Abraham to sacrifice his son Isaac. A monumental building, it reflected the power of the dynasty and its god; its interior is decorated with Qur'anic inscriptions. The Dome of the Rock has endured to the present day and has become a major site of struggle between Muslim and Jewish claims to the city they both consider holy.

The mainstay of the Umayyad dynasty's power was the ruling class, composed of an Arab military aristocracy. The Arabs formed a privileged class greatly outnumbered by non-Arab converts to Islam. Many of these converted peoples had cultures much more highly developed than that of the Arabs, and the economic and cultural life of this Islamic empire came to be dominated by these non-Arab Muslims, called **mawali**, or

Arabs on Horseback

Document   The Early Islamic Conquests

Traditional Western historiography used the rhetorics of medieval Christian writers to portray the early Islamic conquests as sweeping and brutal. The following two excerpts from the Arabic chronicle of al-Tabari (839–923) suggest that wisdom, pragmatism, mercy, and intimidation all played a role in the early Islamic conquests. The Qur'an enjoined mercy as well as warfare, and Abu Bakr's rules of war suggest that the wise conqueror did not kill the citizens and livestock of the lands he wished to rule. In the first reading, the people who have "shaved the crown of their heads" may well be monks. But, earlier on, the passage admonishes the conquerors to leave those in hermitages alone—so the reference here is unclear. In the second passage, although the general initially calls upon God (customary in military and diplomatic messages of this era), he focuses on the power and violence of men. The Arab general Khalid ibn al-Walid's letters to the Persians offer mercy in exchange for submission, but they follow up that offer with a challenge. The *jizya* is the head tax that all non-Muslim citizens must pay to the Muslim state.

Abu Bakr (Muhammad's successor) on the Rules of War (632)

Oh People! I charge you with ten rules; learn them well!

Do not betray, or misappropriate any part of the booty; do not practice treachery or mutilation. Do not kill a young child, an old man, or a woman. Do not uproot or burn palms or cut down fruitful trees. Do not slaughter a sheep or a cow or a camel, except for food. You will meet people who have set themselves apart in hermitages; leave them to accomplish the purpose for which they have done this. You will come upon people who will bring you dishes with various kinds of food. If you partake of them, pronounce God's name over what you eat. You will meet people who have shaved the crown of their heads, leaving a band of hair around it. Strike them with the sword. Go, in God's name, and may God protect you from sword and pestilence.

Letters to the Persians (633)

In the name of God, the Merciful and the Compassionate.

From Khalid ibn al-Walid to the kings of Persia.

Praise be to God who has dissolved your order, frustrated your plans, and split your unanimity. Had he not done this to you, it would have been worse for you. Submit to our authority, and we shall leave you and your land and go by you against others. If not, you will be conquered against your will by men who love death as you love life.

In the name of God, the Merciful and the Compassionate.

From Khalid ibn al-Walid to the border chiefs of Persia.

Become Muslim and be saved. If not, accept protection from us and pay the jizya. If not, I shall come against you with men who love death as you love to drink wine.

Questions to Consider

1. Why would Abu Bakr urge his soldiers to exercise restraint and curb the destructive impulses of war?
2. Think about the idea of submission. Why does the general insist that his enemy submit and what do you think submission means for the conquered peoples?
3. What does Khalid ibn al-Walid mean when he says he shall attack "with men who love death as you love to drink wine"?

From *Islam: From the Prophet Muhammad to the Capture of Constantinople, Volume 1: Politics and War*, ed. Bernard Lewis. Translation copyright © 1974 by Bernard Lewis. Used by permission of Oxford University Press, Inc.

"affiliates." Because they were not Arab by birth, they were treated to a certain extent as citizens of inferior status. They were granted fewer privileges and received less from the spoils of war than did the Arabs. Resent-ment grew steadily among some of the non-Arab Muslims, who objected to their inferior status as a violation of the Islamic laws advocating equality. Eventually the resentment of the *mawali* and the opposition of the Shi'ites, who had been forced from power on the accession of Muawiya, helped bring about the downfall of the Umayyads.

mawali—Non-Arab Muslims; resentment against discrimination by Arab Muslims led them to oppose Umayyad rule.

The Dome of the Rock, a Muslim edifice from the seventh century, is built above the Temple Mount in Jerusalem, the site of Solomon's Temple. According to tradition, the site is also the place where Muhammad ascended into heaven on his "Night Journey." Intricate mosaic decoration covers the outer walls of the building.

Support for Umayyad rule was never universal. Hostility to the Umayyads was inflamed in 680 when an Umayyad troop massacred Husayn, the second son of Ali, and his followers at Karbala in Iraq. The killing of the grandson of the Prophet was considered a horrible affront to the Islamic community. It helped spur resentment against the ruling dynasty and made it appear illegitimate. This event introduced the theme of martyrdom into Shi'ite tradition around which opposition party unity could be mobilized. To this day, a "passion play" commemorating Husayn's death is a dramatic and important element in Shi'ite ceremonial in many communities.

THE ABBASID ERA, ZENITH OF CLASSICAL ISLAMIC CIVILIZATION

■ *What roles did the cities of Baghdad, Cairo, and Córdoba play in classical Islamic civilization?*

A new dynasty, the Abbasid, was founded when a rebel army, with Shi'ite support, defeated the Umayyads. The first Abbasid caliph was Abu al-Abbas, a descendant of Muhammad's uncle, Abbas. His dynasty ruled most of the Muslim world from 750 to 1258 and built the city

of Baghdad in 762 as a symbol of its wealth, power, and legitimacy. The Abbasids owed their initial support and successes in part to the discontent of the non-Arab Muslims, many of whom had become prominent leaders in Islam's cities.

The fall of the Umayyad dynasty marked the end of Arab domination within Islam. The Arab "aristocracy" had led the forces of conquest during the great period of Islamic expansion, but over time, as new dynasties established themselves, the dominant status previously held only by Arab soldiers was shared with non-Arab administrators, merchants, and scholars.

Under the Abbasids, traditional Arab patterns of tribal organization and warfare gave way to patterns of military organization and governance based on the imperial traditions of the conquered lands. The new

This sixteenth-century Persian manuscript depicts the gendered division of space in a mosque scene. Women of various ages and their children are shown in an area separated from the main mosque area by a barrier. Cultural practice has varied from region to region, but today one will often see such a separation of females and younger children from the males in rituals of worship.

Abbasid polity fostered economic prosperity, the growth of town life, and the promotion of the merchant class.

The founding of the new capital at Baghdad shifted Islam's center of gravity to the province of Iraq, whose soil, watered by the Tigris and Euphrates Rivers, had nurtured the earliest civilizations. Here the Abbasid caliphs set themselves up as potentates in the traditional style of the ancient East (particularly Persia), so that they were surrounded by a lavish court that contrasted sharply with the simplicity of the lifestyle of the Prophet and the first caliphs. One historian described the amazement of the Byzantine envoys who, on entering the Abbasid court, found a magnificent tree of silver and gold, with singing birds, also of silver and gold, perched in its leaves. The Abbasid caliph forecast that Baghdad would become the "most flourishing city in the world"; indeed, it rivaled Constantinople for that honor, situated as it was on the trade routes linking East and West. Furthermore, Abbasid patronage of scholarship and the arts produced a rich and complex culture far surpassing that in western Europe at the time. In Baghdad they founded one of the great medieval libraries, the House of Wisdom.

The Abbasid dynasty marked the high point of classical Islamic power and civilization. The empire ruled by the Abbasid caliphs was greater in size than the Roman Empire at its height; it was the product of an expansion during which the Muslim state assimilated peoples, customs, cultures, learning, and inventions on an unprecedented scale. This Islamic empire, in fact, drew from the resources of the entire known world.

Abbasid power, however, did not go unchallenged, even in the Muslim world. While the Abbasids ruled in Baghdad, rival dynasties established their sovereignty in other areas that had been incorporated into the Islamic state during the early conquests. Members of the deposed Umayyad dynasty established a new dynasty in Muslim Spain in 756 and eventually set up a glorious court in Córdoba, famous for its scholarship and patronage of the arts. In Egypt the Fatimids established a Shi'ite ruling house and developed a formidable navy that dominated the eastern Mediterranean. To bolster their legitimacy, the Fatimids claimed descent from the Prophet's daughter, Fatima; hence, the name of the dynasty. They, too, founded a new and glorious capital at Cairo, where they established al-Azhar, the famous institution of Islamic learning that has attracted scholars from throughout the Muslim world since the tenth century. Thus, the eighth to the twelfth centuries were not only the period of the classical glory of the Islamic state but also an era during which rulers in three different Muslim capitals all claimed the title "caliph." This political division stood in contrast to the Islamic world's civilizational unity, which was based on the universal Sharia law and the spread of the Arabic language.

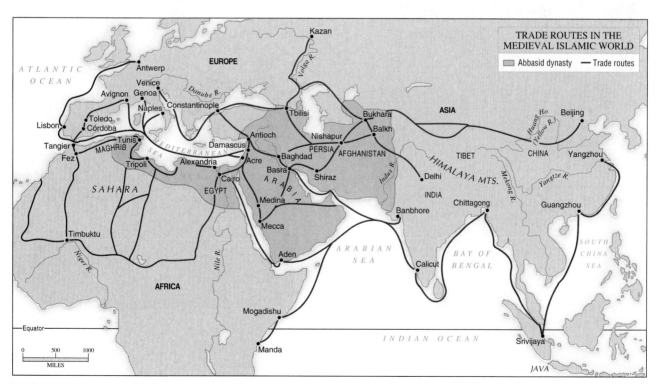

The Islamic world was embedded in a network of trading connections extending from the Atlantic to the Pacific.

Trade, Industry, and Agriculture

From the eighth century to the twelfth, the Muslim world enjoyed enormous prosperity. In close contact with three continents, merchants from the Islamic lands could move goods back and forth from China to western Europe and from Russia to central Africa. The absence of tariff barriers within the empire and the tolerance of the caliphs, who allowed non-Muslim merchants and craftsmen to reside in their territories and carry on commerce with their home countries, further facilitated trade. The presence of such important urban centers as Baghdad, Cairo, and Córdoba stimulated trade and industry throughout the Muslim world; the courts of the monarchs were great consumers of textiles, foodstuffs, arts, and crafts.

The cosmopolitan nature of Baghdad was evident in its bazaars, which contained goods from all over the known world. There were spices, minerals, and dyes from India; gems and fabrics from central Asia; honey, furs, and wax from Scandinavia and Russia; and ivory and gold from Africa. Muslim trade with Southeast Asia increased, and a large Muslim trading community established itself in the Chinese port of Guangzhou (GWANG-JOH; Canton). One bazaar in Baghdad specialized in goods from China, including silks, musk, and porcelain. In the slave markets Muslim traders bought and sold Scandinavians, Mongolians from central Asia, and Africans. Joint-stock companies flourished along with branch banking organizations, and checks (an Arabic word) drawn on one bank could be cashed with commercial agents throughout this vast network of traders. Muslim textile industries turned out excellent cottons (muslins) and silks. The steel of Damascus and Toledo, the leather of Córdoba, and the glass of Syria became internationally famous. Notable also was the art of papermaking, learned from the Chinese. Under the Abbasids, vast irrigation projects in Iraq increased cultivable land, which yielded large crops of fruits and grains. Wheat came from the Nile valley, cotton from North Africa, olives and wine from Spain, wool from eastern Asia Minor, and horses from Persia.

By the tenth century Islam was also making inroads into Africa south of the Nile and the Maghrib. Trade routes through the Sahara brought spices, leatherwork, and eventually slaves from the south to the northern coast, and, in return, caravans from the north brought luxury goods, salt, and the Islamic reli-

In the Muslim world, merchants transported goods by both land and sea. Camels carried merchants and goods on the overland routes, as shown in this manuscript illumination from the thirteenth century (above left). Sound vessels with space for both passengers and cargo, like the Indian ship depicted in this Iraqi manuscript from 1238 (above right), and reliable navigation techniques facilitated the sea trade.

gion to the early African kingdoms of Ghana and Mali. Commercial agents and missionaries carried Islam along the sea routes to central and southeastern African ports such as Mogadishu and Manda and to South and Southeast Asia.

Because the Islamic realms encompassed such a great expanse of territory, languages, and cultures, it is difficult to generalize about Islamic society. Most of the population of the Islamic world was illiterate and engaged in subsistence agriculture. In part because Muhammad was a merchant, trade was considered an honorable profession, and some merchants became quite wealthy. In general, however, the military and administrative classes possessed the greatest wealth and status. Religion, profession, gender, and class could be more important determinants of status than race (even though racism of different varieties was common here as it was in the rest of the world).

The Spectacular Reign of Harun al-Rashid

The rule of Harun al-Rashid (786–809), hero of the tales of *The Arabian Nights,* was the most spectacular of the Abbasid reigns. A contemporary of Charlemagne, who had revived the idea of a Roman Empire in the West (see Chapter 9), Harun was surely the more powerful of the two and the ruler of the more advanced culture. The two monarchs were on friendly terms, based on self-interest. Charlemagne wanted to exert pressure on the Byzantine emperor to recognize his new imperial title. Harun saw Charlemagne as an ally against the Umayyad rulers of Spain, who had broken away from Abbasid dominion. The two emperors exchanged embassies and presents. The Muslim sent the Christian rich fabrics, aromatics, and even an elephant named Abu-Lababah, meaning "the father of intelligence." Another gift, an intricate water clock from Baghdad, seems to have been regarded as miraculous in the West.

Relations between the Abbasid caliphate and the Byzantine Empire were never very cordial, and conflicts often broke out along the shifting borders that separated Christian and Muslim territories. Harun al-Rashid once responded to a communiqué from the Byzantine emperor with the following answer:

In the name of God, the Merciful, the Compassionate. From Harun, Commander of the Faithful, to Nicepherus, the dog of the Greeks, I have read your letter, you son of a she-infidel, and you shall see the answer before you hear it.

This response was followed up with Abbasid raids on Byzantine possessions in Asia Minor.

In the days of Harun al-Rashid, Baghdad's wealth and splendor equaled that of Constantinople, and its chief glory was the royal palace. With its annexes for offi-cials, the harem, and eunuchs, the caliph's residence occupied one-third of the city of Baghdad. The caliph's audience chamber was the setting for an elaborate ceremonial, which mirrored that of the Byzantines and Persians. Such court ceremonial was designed to impress the Abbasid citizens with the justice, power, and magnificence of the caliph and to intimidate foreign envoys.

Challenges to Abbasid Authority

In the tenth century a movement of migration and conquest out of central Asia began that would have a dramatic impact on the political and cultural configuration of the central Islamic lands. By the early eleventh century, Turkish peoples had moved from central Asia into the Abbasid lands, where, over time, they converted to Islam. One group, the Seljuks, after annexing most of Persia, gained control of Baghdad in 1055 and subjugated Iraq. Subsequently, they conquered Syria and Palestine at the expense of the Fatimids and proceeded to take most of Asia Minor from the Byzantines. The Seljuks permitted the Abbasids to retain nominal authority, in part to secure political legitimacy for their reign, but they themselves ruled the state. By the time of the First Crusade in 1095, which was provoked in part by the Seljuk advances, the Abbasid dynasty had lost much of its power and status in the Islamic world.

Seljuk dominance of much of the old Abbasid Empire was later challenged by the arrival of Turco-Mongol invaders from the northeastern steppes of central Asia. Early in the thirteenth century Chinggis (Genghis) Khan succeeded in uniting the animistic, tribal horsemen of Mongolia and conquering much of China and Russia; he and his successors moved on to eastern and central Asia (see Chapter 10) and ultimately conquered Persia and Iraq. In 1258 a grandson of Chinggis Khan captured Baghdad and had the caliph executed. Unlike the Seljuks, the Mongols were contemptuous of the caliph and felt no need to preserve an Abbasid successor as a figurehead to secure their legitimacy. Not only did the Abbasid dynasty come to an end, but so did most of the vast irrigation system that had supported the land. The dynasty established there by the Mongols survived for almost a century, but the Mongol invaders were eventually acculturated and absorbed into the local population.

Egypt was "saved" from the Mongol advance by the Mamluks (1250–1517). The Fatimids had been replaced by one of their own commanders, Salah al-Din, who established a new dynasty, the Ayyubids (ay-YOO-bids), who reigned from 1169–1252. Famed in the West as Saladin, it was Salah al-Din who took Jerusalem from the crusaders. The Ayyubids were in turn overthrown by their own elite "slave" guard, called *mamluks. Mamluk* literally means "slave," but these men were not slaves in the sense of people of low status who did menial tasks. Taken as captives or purchased as young men in the slave market, they were trained in the military and political arts to serve their commanders. They were converted to Islam and hence could not be held as true slaves. Indeed, they often wielded great power and wealth. After overthrowing the Ayyubids and founding their own ruling group, they formed the elite military caste of Egypt. It was the Mamluks who stopped the Mongol advance in Syria and later ejected the last of the crusaders in 1291. They ruled in Egypt and Syria until 1517, claiming the title "Protector of the Holy Places" as a result of their governance of Mecca, Medina, and also Jerusalem, the three holy cities of Islam.

ISLAMIC CULTURE

■ *What were the achievements of Islamic culture in medicine, science, mathematics, literature, art, and architecture?*

The attainments of the Muslims in the intellectual and artistic fields can be attributed not only to the Arabs but also to the peoples who embraced Islam in Persia, Iraq, Turkey, Syria, Egypt, North Africa, and Spain. Muslim

MAP
The Spread of Islam

learning benefited both from Islam's ability to absorb other cultures and from the native talents of the Islamic peoples. Under Abbasid rule, a great synthesis of culture and scholarship emerged, strands of which were then transmitted by traveling scholars, traders, and missionaries throughout the known world from the Mediterranean to the Indian Ocean.

The cosmopolitan spirit permeating the Abbasid dynasty supplied the tolerance necessary for a diversity of ideas, so that the science, philosophies, and literatures of ancient Greece and India alike received a cordial reception in Baghdad. Under Harun al-Rashid and his successors, the writings of Aristotle, Euclid, Ptolemy, Archimedes, Galen, and other great Greek philosophers and scientific writers were translated into Arabic. This knowledge, together with the teachings of the Qur'an, formed the basis of Muslim learning, which was in turn transmitted to scholars in Europe and Asia. In addition to being valuable transmitters of learning, Muslim scholars crafted a unique synthesis based on the genius of Arab civilization and on a continuing dialog among Muslim and non-Muslim thinkers and artists.

Advances in Medicine

The years between 900 and 1100 can be regarded as the golden age of Muslim learning. This period was particularly significant for its medical advances. Muslim students of medicine were by all measures far superior to their European contemporaries. Muslim cities had excellent pharmacies and hospitals, where physicians received instruction and training. Muslim scholars perfected surgical techniques, figured out the mode for the spread of the plague, and described the course of many diseases.

Perhaps the greatest Muslim physician was the Persian Abu Bakr Muhammad al-Razi (d. 925), better known in the West as Rhazes. Chief physician in Baghdad, he wrote more than 100 medical treatises, in which he summarized Greek medical knowledge and added his own clinical observations. His most famous work, *On Smallpox and Measles,* is the first clear description of the symptoms and treatment of these diseases.

The most influential Muslim medical treatise is the vast *Canon of Medicine,* in which the great scholar Ibn Sina, or Avicenna (d. 1037), systematically organized all Greek and Muslim medical learning. In the twelfth century, the *Canon* was translated into Latin. It was so much in demand in the West that it was issued 16 times in the last half of the fifteenth century and more than 20 times in the sixteenth, and it continued to be used until the modern era.

Progress in Other Sciences

Muslim physicists were also highly creative scientists. Al-Hasan ibn al-Haytham, or Alhazen (d. 1038), of Cairo, developed optics to a remarkable degree and challenged the theory of Ptolemy and Euclid that the eye sends visual rays to its object. The chief source of all medieval Western writers on optics, Alhazen was interested in optical reflections and illusions and examined the refraction of light rays through air and water.

Although astronomy continued to be strongly influenced by astrology, Muslim astronomers built observatories, recorded their observations over long periods, and achieved greater accuracy than the Greeks in measuring the length of the solar year and in calculating eclipses. Interest in alchemy—the attempt to change base metals into precious ones and to find the magic elixir for the preservation of human life—produced the first chemical laboratories and caused attention to be given to the value of experimentation. Muslim alchemists prepared many chemical substances (sulfuric acid, for example) and developed methods for evaporation, filtration, sublimation, crystallization, and distillation. The process of distillation, invented around 800, produced what was called *al-kuhl* ("the essence"), or alcohol, a new liquor that brought its inventors great honor in some circles.

In mathematics the Muslims were indebted to the Hindus as well as to the Greeks. From the Hindus

In an empire that straddled continents, where trade and administration made an accurate knowledge of lands imperative, the science of geography flourished. The Muslims added to the geographical knowledge of the Greeks, whose treatises they translated, by producing detailed descriptions of the climate, manners, and customs of many parts of the known world. Developments in mapping went hand in hand with the progress of Arab seafaring, which aimed at exploiting commercial possibilities along the seaborne routes of trade.

Islamic Literature and Scholarship

To Westerners, Islamic literature may seem somewhat alien. Early Western literary styles tried to emphasize restraint and simplicity, but Muslim writers have long enjoyed literature that makes use of elegant expression, subtle combinations of words, and fanciful and even extravagant imagery.

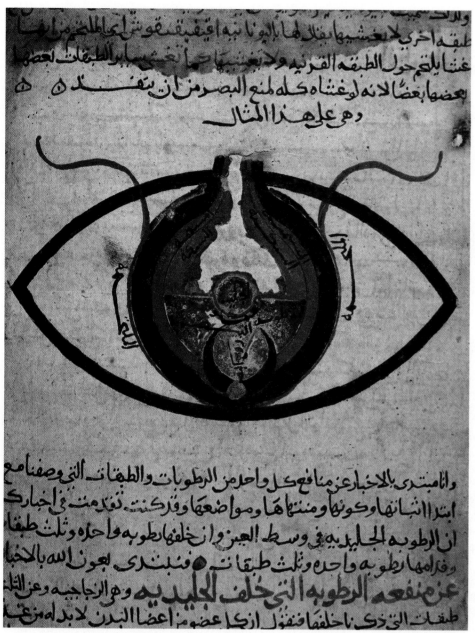

Husayn ibn Ishaq's Book of the Ten Treatises on the Eye *shows the Islamic scientist's outstandingly accurate understanding of the anatomy of the eye. Written in the tenth century, the work was still standard in the thirteenth century, when the copy shown here was made.*

Westerners' knowledge of Islamic literature tends to be limited to *The Arabian Nights* and the poetry of Omar Khayyám. The former is a collection of often erotic tales told with a wealth of local color that sheds light on racial and gender relations and on practices of food, dress, and cleanliness. Although *The Arabian Nights* professedly covers different facets of life at the Abbasid capital, the story is in fact often based on life in medieval Cairo. It took the literary influences of India and Persia, combined them with conventions of Arabic literature, and passed them on to the West, where they can be seen in the works of Chaucer and Boccaccio. These tales present an interesting combination of the courtly and the vulgar. The fame of Omar Khayyám's *Rubáiyát* (reu-BAI-yaht) is due at least in part to the musical (though rather free) translation of Edward Fitzgerald. The following stanzas indicate the poem's beautiful imagery and gentle resignation:

DOCUMENT
The Rubáiyát of Omar Khayyám

A Book of Verses underneath the Bough,
A Jug of Wine, a Loaf of Bread—and Thou

came arithmetic, algebra, the zero, and the nine signs known in the West as Arabic numerals. From the Greeks came the geometry of Euclid and the fundamentals of trigonometry, which Ptolemy had established. Two Muslim mathematicians made significant contributions: al-Khwarizmi (al-KWAHR-iz-mee; d. c. 844), whose *Arithmetic* introduced Arabic numerals and whose *Algebra* first employed that mathematical term, and Omar Khayyám (d. c. 1123), the mathematician, astronomer, and poet whose work in algebra went beyond quadratics to cubic equations. Other Islamic scholars developed plane and spherical trigonometry.

Discovery Through Maps

An Islamic Map of the World

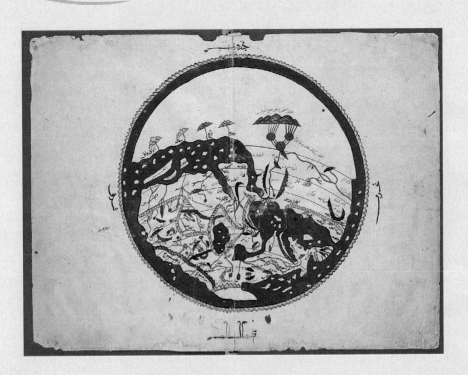

Which way is up? We tend to take the orientation of maps for granted, with north as up. For example, American world maps often depict the United States at the center and north at the top. But not all maps make those same assumptions. The world map of al-Idrisi, an Arab geographer, is a case in point. Al-Idrisi's map is oriented, as was common in Arab maps of his time, with south at the top. It is centered on the world of his own experience, the sacred city of Mecca in Arabia and the civilized realm of the Mediterranean. The map includes several distinctive features typical of this type of medieval map. The world is shown as an island encircled by a world sea. The extent of Africa is unknown; it is depicted as a giant mass occupying the upper half of the map. The Americas are not included at all.

Al-Idrisi was born in Morocco in 1100. Educated in Córdoba, he began his travels as a youth and ended up at the cosmopolitan court of King Roger of Sicily around 1138. There the king asked him to construct a world map complete with written commentary. In collaboration with other scholars, al-Idrisi crafted the map, which was engraved on silver, around the year 1154. Although the original is lost, there are various manuscript versions of al-Idrisi's world map, one of which is shown here. The Arab scholar's map was very influential and widely copied in Europe and Asia for centuries after his death in 1165. Al-Idrisi's map suggests one type of medieval worldview, and his life confirms the notion that cartographers were a valuable commodity in the Afro-Eurasian courts of the time. Rulers valued cartographers because they provided information that was practical and enlightening. They pieced together information about the world from classical sources, old maps, and the accounts of seamen, traders, and travelers. But, cartographers were also artists who made images of the ways in which peoples envisioned their own world and regions beyond their reach. Maps legitimized the power of rulers, cultures, kingdoms, and religions.

Turn the map upside down and see if you can identify the Mediterranean Sea, the Arabian Peninsula, and the Maghrib.

Questions to Consider

1. What does the world "look like" when *you* imagine it? Where and how did you learn your vision of the world?

2. The ways in which the world is represented change over time and place. Not all peoples depict land and sea in the same way. Try drawing a map of your childhood "world." What would it look like?

3. Are maps depictions of reality or do they suggest points of view?

Beside me singing in the Wilderness—
Oh, Wilderness were Paradise enow!—
Some for the Glories of This World; and some
Sigh for the Prophet's Paradise to come;
Ah, take the Cash, and let the Credit go,
Nor heed the rumble of a distant Drum! . . .
The Moving Finger writes; and, having writ,
Moves on: nor all your Piety nor Wit
Shall lure it back to cancel half a Line,
Nor all your Tears wash out a Word of it.
And that inverted Bowl they call the Sky,
Whereunder crawling coop'd we live and die,
Lift not your hands to It for help—for It
As impotently moves as you or I.[1]

DOCUMENT
A Mirror for Princes

The same rich imagery characterizes much Islamic prose, but *The Arabian Nights* and the *Rubáiyát* merely hint at the breadth and diversity of Islamic literature. As the first important prose work in Arab literature, the Qur'an set the stylistic pattern for all Arabic writers. With classical Arabic then "fixed" in the Qur'an, Muslim writers, spurred on by the generosity of the Islamic kings, produced a great corpus of literature. Arabic and then Persian were the languages of high culture. Poetry contests were a standard of the early Islamic courts, where the poets who contrived the most beautiful or wittiest verses received honors and rich rewards. Poetry was also used for satire. Poets used pointed verse to wound or defame their rivals, and kings used the talents of their poets to send insulting messages to their enemies. Muslim philosophy, essentially Greek in origin, was developed and modified by Islamic scholars. Like the medieval Christian philosophers, Muslim thinkers were largely concerned with reconciling the rationalism of Aristotle on the one hand and religious faith on the other. Some sought to harmonize Platonism, Aristotelianism, and Islam. The philosopher Ibn Sina (980–1037) sought to extract what was purely Aristotelian from later additions and to articulate the truths of Islam in terms of Aristotelian logic. His work had a profound effect on Islamic philosophy and was widely read in the West, where it was translated into Latin in the twelfth century.

Another great Islamic philosopher, Ibn Rushd, or Averroës (ah-VEHR-oh-eez; d. 1198), lived in Córdoba,

DOCUMENT
The Sea of Precious Virtues

where he was the caliph's personal doctor. He is famous for his marvelous commentaries on Aristotle. Ibn Rushd rejected the belief in the ultimate harmony between faith and reason along with all earlier attempts to reconcile Aristotle and Plato. He argued that parts of the Qur'an were to be taken metaphorically, not literally. But Ibn Rushd thought that most people were unable to understand either philosophy or the metaphorical meanings of the Qur'an. Those were questions for the philosophers.

In contrast, Moses Maimonides (mai-MON-e-deez), Ibn Rushd's contemporary who was also born in Muslim Spain, sought, in his still influential *Guide to the Perplexed*, to harmonize Judaism and Aristotelian philosophy. St. Thomas Aquinas, who in the next century undertook a similar project for Christianity, was influenced by these earlier attempts to reconcile faith and reason. Although Western historiography has focused on the clash of Muslim and Christian armies in Spain, it might be better to view that territory in particular as a place where Muslim, Christian, and Jewish thinkers and writers interacted and learned from each other through a series of ongoing debates.

Islamic historiography found its finest expression in the work of Ibn Khaldun of Tunis (d. 1406), who has been called the "father of sociology." Ibn Khaldun wrote a large general history dealing particularly with human social development, focusing on the interaction of society with the physical environment. He delineated guidelines for the writing of history and ridiculed earlier historical writing, saying it was often full of stupid or thoughtless errors. Ibn Khaldun defined history in this manner:

> *It should be known that history, in matter of fact, is information about human social organization, which itself is identical with world civilization. It deals with such conditions affecting the nature of civilization as, for instance, savagery and sociability, group feelings, and the different ways by which one group of human beings achieves superiority over another. It deals with royal authority and . . . with the different kinds of gainful occupations and ways of making a living, with the sciences and crafts that human beings pursue as part of their activities and efforts, and with all the other institutions that originate in civilization through its very nature.*[2]

Ibn Khaldun conceived of history as an evolutionary process, in which societies and institutions change continually. He traveled widely in the Islamic world, serving as a judge and scholar in the courts of the Mamluks and other rulers. When he beheld the city of Cairo, he described it as a pinnacle of Islamic civilization, full of shops, gardens, scholars, and institutions of higher learning.

The Sufis

As Islamic civilization produced traditions of scholarship and philosophy, it also produced a tradition of mysticism that came to be a significant factor in the spread of Islam throughout the world. The Arabic word *tasawwuf* (tah-SAHW-woof, "mysticism") is related to the word *suf*, for the coarse woolen clothes some of the early mystics wore. The early sufis were lone ascetics who practiced physical and spiritual dis-

Document   Ibn Sina's Path to Wisdom

The ways in which a person obtains an education vary considerably over time and from place to place. In the medieval Islamic world, it was customary for students to go from teacher to teacher or even from city to city seeking knowledge. Recitation and memorization were important elements of learning. Rather than working on a fixed "semester" system, a student often studied with a teacher until he mastered a particular text or body of knowledge (whether it took three months or three years). Only affluent students could afford their own books. As in many societies, formal education was reserved primarily for men; and, even among men, only an elite few were literate. Although some Muslim women became distinguished scholars and poets, girls generally received only a rudimentary education.

Ibn Sina, the famous Muslim philosopher who died in 1037, recorded the progress of his own education. His diligence, but not his pride, might in some ways serve as a model for modern students. As a young boy, Ibn Sina began his education in religion and the sciences. He remembers himself as a determined and independent student who had little patience with or respect for some of his teachers. By the time he was 16, his education was already far-reaching. Ibn Sina was raised in Bukhara, an important center of Islamic learning in Central Asia. There, he writes:

I was put under teachers of the Qur'an and of letters. By the time I was ten I had mastered the Qur'an and a great deal of literature, so that I was marvelled at for my aptitude. . . . My father sent me to a certain vegetable-seller who used the Indian arithmetic, so that I might learn it from him. Then, there came to Bukhara a man called Abu 'Abd Allah al-Natili who claimed to be a philosopher; my father invited him to stay in our house, hoping I would learn from him also. I had already occupied myself with Muslim jurisprudence, attending Isma'il the Ascetic; so I was an excellent enquirer, having become familiar with the methods of expostulation and the techniques of rebuttal according to the usages of the canon lawyers. . . . Whatever problem he [al-Natili] stated to me, I showed a better mental conception of it than he. So I continued until I had read all the straightforward parts of Logic with him; as for the subtler points, he had no acquaintance with them. From then onwards I took to reading texts by myself; I studied the commentaries, until I had completely mastered the science of Logic. Similarly with Euclid I read the first five or six figures with him, and thereafter undertook on my own account to solve the entire remainder of the book. . . . I now occupied myself with mastering the various texts and commentaries on natural science and metaphysics, until all the gates of knowledge were open to me. Next I desired to study medicine, and proceeded to read all the books that have been written on this subject. Medicine is not a difficult science, and naturally I excelled in it in a very short time, so that qualified physicians began to read medicine with me. I also undertook to treat the sick, and methods of treatment derived from practical experience revealed themselves to me such as baffle description. At the same time I continued between whiles to study and dispute on law, being now sixteen years of age.

Questions to Consider

1. Ibn Sina does not focus on the idea of learning as something that takes place in a specific building or one location. In what terms does he describe the learning process?

2. Think about writing an autobiography. When adults think back and describe their student days, is that history? What roles do memory and sense of identity play in the process?

From A. J. Arberry. *Aspects of Islamic Civilization* (Ann Arbor: University of Michigan Press, 1967), pp. 136–137.

cipline in order to transcend the material world and gain a special kind of closeness to Allah. Later, sufi orders were founded in which the devotees practiced rules of discipline, followed the path shown them by a spiritual master or *shaykh*, divorced themselves to some extent from the community, and developed rituals that ranged from the simple to the elaborate. There are many similarities between some of the sufi orders and the medieval monastic orders of Christian Europe. To be a sufi, however, one does not need to join a spiritual order; many sufis live and work in the community. What is essential to **Sufism** is the belief

Sufism—A broad term used to designate any of ascetic and mystic movements within Islam. Sufi movements have borrowed elements from Christian monasticism and Indian mysticism. The essential aim of Sufism is to achieve mystical communion with Allah.

in following a path of discipline that leads to mystical communion with Allah.

The early Muslim mystics expressed their desire for union with God in a language of love, longing, and ecstasy. This longing came to be embodied in the mystical poetry of sufis like that of the famous Jalal al-Din Rumi (1207–1273), who compared the sufi to a man "drunk with God." The *dhikr*, collective repetition of the name of God, sometimes accompanied by rhythmic movements and breathing, became part of sufi practice. It was a way of both glorifying God and transcending (like yoga) the distractions of the body and the world. In their quest for communion with God, the sufis also ran afoul of Islamic orthodoxy, because their beliefs and practices were sometimes considered extreme or blasphemous.

In the ninth century, sufis began systematically to write down the ways of the path. Communion with God meant the losing of self, however briefly. That losing or merging of self with God smacked of polytheism to many members of the *ulama*. Thus the sufis were accused of claiming to be divine and of believing they were above the law. In 922 al-Hallaj, a famous teacher and sufi in Baghdad, was executed for blasphemy after he claimed, "I am the Truth." Al-Hallaj had also alienated the authorities by claiming that the *hajj*, the pilgrimage to Mecca, was not necessary, because the sufi could pursue the pilgrimage to God from his own room. The pathos of the death of al-Hallaj is graphically described in the words of his servant, Ibrahim ibn Fatik, who wrote that al-Hallaj asked Allah to forgive those who were preparing to kill him:

> *Then he was silent. The Headsman stepped up and dealt him a smashing blow which broke his nose, and the blood ran onto his white robe. The mystic al-Shibli, who was in the crowd, cried aloud and rent his garment, and Abu Husayn al-Wasiti fell fainting, and so did other famous sufis who were there, so that a riot nearly broke out. Then the executioners did their work.*[3]

Al-Hallaj gave the sufi community in Baghdad a martyr. But in the end, the message of Sufism was too powerful and compelling for Islamic orthodoxy to ignore. Sufis were very effective in spreading the message of Islam beyond its Middle Eastern heartlands. In South and Southeast Asia, sufi asceticism and belief in mystical communion found resonances in the ascetic and mystical practices of those areas and aided the conversion of non-Muslims to Islam. By the end of the Abbasid era, Sufism had been brought into the mainstream of Islamic thought as a result of its widespread appeal and through the systematic efforts of scholars like al-Ghazali (1058–1111), who legitimized the sufi way as an acceptable path toward God. Sufism remains a powerful tool in the spread of Islam. In the United States today, Rumi's poetry remains popular, and American college students may get their first taste of Islam through the words of sufi masters.

Art and Architecture

Religious attitudes played an important part in shaping Islamic art. Because the Prophet warned against idols and their worship, there was a prohibition against pictorial representation of human and animal figures; that prohibition, however, was not always obeyed. The effect of this injunction was to encourage the development of stylized and geometrical designs. Islamic art, like other artistic traditions, borrowed extensively to forge a new and unique synthesis. Artists and craftspeople followed chiefly Byzantine and Persian models, but Central Asian, South Asian, and African motifs were also integrated into Islamic styles.

The ultimate stage of refinement of Moorish architecture, which combines Spanish and Islamic elements, is the Alhambra in Granada, the last Islamic stronghold in Spain during the Middle Ages. Slender, rhythmically spaced columns and arches covered with an intricate design of molded stucco frame the Court of the Lions, the most luxurious portion of the palace.

The Muslims excelled in the fields of architecture and the decorative arts. That Islamic architecture can boast of many large and imposing structures is not surprising; monumental building was a natural extension of the power and glory of the Islamic dynasts who wanted to celebrate their own power and glorify God. In time, original styles of building evolved; the great mosques embody such typical features as domes, arcades, and minarets, the slender towers from which the faithful are summoned to prayer. The horseshoe arch is another graceful and familiar feature of Muslim architecture.

On the walls and ceilings of their buildings, the Muslims gave full rein to their love of ornamentation and beauty of detail. The Spanish interpretation of the Islamic tradition is particularly delicate and elegant. A superb artistic example of the sophistication and wealth of the Muslim world is the Alhambra, built between 1248 and 1354 by Muslim kings in Granada, Spain. Some authorities consider it the apogee of Muslim architecture.

Restricted in their subject matter, Muslim craftspeople conceived beautiful patterns from flowers and geometrical figures. The Arabic script, one of the most graceful ever devised, was often used as a decorative motif. Muslim decorative skill also found expression in such fields as carpet and rug weaving, brass work, and the making of steel products inlaid with precious metals.

CONCLUSION

The great power of Islam's message enabled the fragmented Arab tribes to unify and expand across three continents in an astoundingly brief period. During the reigns of the first four caliphs and the century of dominance by the Umayyad dynasty, great gains were made in conquering new territories and peoples. But the Umayyad dynasty was based on a ruling hierarchy of Arabs, and the resentment of the non-Arab Islamic community helped establish the Abbasid dynasty in a new caliphate in Baghdad.

While traders, scholars, and sufis exported variants of the Islamic worldview, the Abbasid Empire provided the security, patronage, and institutional framework for a great cultural synthesis and an expanding network of international trade. As in all traditional empires of the time, agriculture provided the base for the economy of the Abbasid state, but its prosperity evolved from a combination of successful agriculture, trade, and industry.

The Islamic worldview both challenged and integrated the worldviews of the peoples it encountered in Asia, Africa, and Europe. Intellectual life was a product of that evolving synthesis. Muslim scholars participated in the rediscovery of classical (Greek) learning and the emergence of the Renaissance in Europe. They elaborated their cosmology in the course of a contentious but continuing dialog with the scholars, texts, and customs of other traditions.

Islam remains an extremely powerful force in the world. The Islamic community today is made up of leading industrialized societies as well as nations just emerging from colonialism. Present-day Muslims still derive great meaning from the teachings of Muhammad and the community he and his disciples constructed. They face the challenge of melding the world-view embedded in Islam's sacred text with the evolving conditions of the modern era, where the power of the ancient message still plays a dominant role.

Suggestions for Web Browsing

You can obtain more information about topics included in this chapter at the websites listed below. See also the companion website that accompanies this text, http://www.ablongman.com/brummett, which contains an online study guide and additional resources.

Internet Islamic History Sourcebook: Muhammad and Foundations—to 632 C.E.
http://www.fordham.edu/halsall/islam/islamsbook.html
Extensive online source for links about the early history of Islam, including a biography of Muhammad and the many aspects of Islam, including the role of women.

Islam and Islamic History in Arabia and the Middle East: The Message
http://www.islamic.org/Mosque/ihame/Sec1.htm
Islam and Islamic History in Arabia and the Middle East: The Golden Age.

http://www.islamic.org/Mosque/ihame/Sec7.htm
Extensive site details the origins of Islam and provides information and images about Muhammad, the Hijra, the Qur'an, Arabic writing, science and scholarship, Arabic literature, and Arabic numerals.

The Qur'an
http://islam.org/mosque/arabicscript/1/1.htm
The entire text of the Qur'an, with audio.

Islamic and Arabic Arts and Architecture
http://www.islamicart.com/
A rich and attractively designed general site, with information and images regarding architecture, calligraphy, and textiles. Includes a glossary of terms and names of important artists and architects. A subsite offers a portfolio of shrines and palaces including the Ka'ba, the Mosque of the Prophet Muhammad, the Dome of the Rock, and the Alhambra.

http://www.georgetown.edu/labyrinth

A wonderful site on medieval history which includes sections on texts and cartography.

Literature and Film

For literary sources suitable for class reading assignments and available in paperback, see the following: Robert L. Mack, ed., *Arabian Nights' Entertainments* (Oxford University Press, 1995), an annotated and historigraphically grounded edition of the Arabian Nights. Nizami, *The Story of Layla and Majnun*, trans. Rudolph Gelpke (Omega Publications, 1997), a twelfth-century classic Persian version of an Arabian folk epic of poetry, renunciation, and forbidden love. *The Legend of Seyavash* (Penguin, 1992)—one episode of the famous Persian Epic of Kings, penned in the eleventh century by Ferdowsi—is a wonderful study in notions of kingship, virtue, womanly wiles, and the mingling of Islam and animism. Usamah Ibn Munqidh, *An Arab-Syrian Gentleman and Warrior in the Period of the Crusades*, trans. P. K. Hitti (Princeton University Press, 1987), is an engaging memoir that reveals the mechanisms of cross-cultural exchange in twelfth-century Syria. Ruzbihan Baqli, *The Unveiling of Secrets: Diary of a Sufi Master*, trans. Carl Ernst (Parvardigar Press, 1997), records the personal reflections of a twelfth-century Persian Sufi. *The Adventures of Sayf Ben Dhi Yazan*, trans. Lena Jayyusi (Indiana University Press, 1999), is a folk romance composed during the medieval period of Mamluk rule in Egypt (magic, weddings, heroic feats, and day-to-day life). Ross E. Dunn, *The Adventures of Ibn Battuta: A Muslim Traveler of the 14th Century* (University of California, 1989), and Amin Maalouf, *Leo Africanus* (Dee, Ivan R., 1992), are also good student reading selections.

Films suitable for classroom presentation include *Mohammed, Messenger of God*, by Moustafa Akkad (Anchor Bay, 1976; also known as *The Message*), a popular commercial film, but one that has been acceptable in general to the Muslim community in the United States; and *Islam: Empire of Faith* (PBS, 2001), a historical assessment with commentary by various scholars of Islam.

Suggestions for Reading

Major scholarly surveys are Marshall Hodgson, *The Venture of Islam: Conscience and History of a World Civilization*, 3 vols. (University of Chicago Press, 1974), Ira Lapidus, *A History of Islamic Societies* (Cambridge University Press, 1988), and Albert Hourani, *A History of the Arab Peoples* (Warner, 1992). See also Philip K. Hitti, *The Arabs: A Short History* (Regnery, 1996), an excellent abridgment of a scholarly general history; and H. A. R. Gibb, *Mohammedanism: A Historical Survey*, 2nd ed. (Oxford University Press, 1969). See also the clear introduction to Islam by John L. Esposito, *Islam: The Straight Path*, 3rd ed. (Oxford University Press, 1998); Nehemia Levtzion and Randall Pouwels, eds., *The History of Islam in Africa* (Ohio University Press, 2000); J. Spencer Trimmingham, *The Sufi Orders in Islam* (Oxford, 1998); and Richard Fletcher, *Moorish Spain* (University of California Press, 1991).

W. Montgomery Watt, *Muhammad: Prophet and Statesman* (Oxford University Press, 1974), is a brief account of the Prophet's life and teachings. See also Karen Armstrong, *Muhammad: A Biography of the Prophet* (Harper Collins, 1992); Frederick Denny, *An Introduction to Islam*, 2nd ed. (Macmillan, 1996); and Martin Lings, *Muhammad: His Life Based on the Earliest Sources* (Inner Traditions International, 1983). For an interpretation and translation of the Qur'an, see Marmaduke William Pickthall, ed., *The Meaning of the Glorious Koran: An Explanatory Translation* (Unwin Hyman/HarperCollins). For primary source selections in translation, see James Kritzeck, ed., *Anthology of Islamic Literature* (Meridian, 1975). John Renard, *Islam and the Heroic Image* (University of South Carolina Press, 1994), is an excellent introduction to heroic Muslim personalities.

RELIGION AND GOVERNMENT

How do societies manage the relationship between their spiritual concerns and their temporal concerns?

Byzantine wall mosaic, *Christ Pantocrator Between Emperor Constantine IX Monamachus and Empress Zoe.*

Throughout history, religion and government have served as foundational institutions in the world's many societies. These two institutions (often referrred to as "church" and "state" in the West) may seem to deal with different areas of human experience, but in reality the goals of both institutions are similar. Each in its own way seeks to maintain social order, foster a sense of community, and provide hope for a more satisfying future. Nevertheless, the relationship between these two institutions has varied significantly. Some societies fused religion and government into one entity. Other societies chose to maintain mutually cooperative relationships between the two institutions. Yet in further instances, societies consciously strove to separate one institution from the other.

The origins of religion are found in humanity's spiritual concerns while the origins of government stem from humanity's temporal (worldly) concerns. Humans' spiritual concerns essentially attempt to resolve the questions of how and why the universe came into being, what humans' proper role is in the world, and what the significance is of suffering and death. Temporal concerns, on the other hand, focus at their most basic level on how best to address humans' needs for food, water, and shelter. The answers to this question involve the specialization of tasks and social organization, which inevitably form the foundation of government.

The earliest humans made little if any distinction between their spiritual concerns (religion) and their temporal concerns (government). Our earliest ancestors believed that everything in the world around them and the heavens above, both animate and inanimate, possessed a spiritual essence. Because human beings were an integral part of this holistic universe, everything they did, particularly the activity of food gathering and production, was steeped in spiritual significance.

The earliest forms of separation between religion and government probably came about as human societies grew larger, more complex, and required greater specialization from their members. Because of the increasing interdependence of individuals that naturally results from specialization, some groups or individuals within a given society showed greater ability to address the community's spiritual concerns and became their society's priests. Similarly, others showed greater ability in addressing people's temporal concerns and became their society's chiefs. These two new social groups stood at the top of their societies' social hierarchies because of the vital significance of each of their responsibilities. While the two may have often competed with one another for power, they also tended to support each other's authority. We know of only a small number of early human societies in which primary spiritual and temporal roles were likely exercised by one individual.

Many of the world's earliest civilizations, however, eventually combined religious and political authority in the person of one ruler—a priest-king. In Egypt, a truly theocratic state evolved, in which the pharaoh was seen to be a living god who governed the state. In Mesopotamia, it is likely that initially the *patesi* was both a temporal ruler and a religious authority, administering the city-state as its patron god's representative on earth. Throughout most of the history of ancient Mesopotamia, rulers were held to be mortals governing on behalf of the gods.

In ancient China, the emperor, as head of the imperial government, used a religious concept to justify his rule. "The mandate of heaven" held that the emperor ruled with the blessing of heaven, and that if the emperor ruled wisely heaven would reward the nation; if, however, he ruled unwisely, heaven would be displeased and the mandate would pass to another. In Japan, ancient tradition held that the emperor was a divine being, descended from the great sun goddess Amaterasu, the supreme deity of the Shintō religion and queen of all the *kami*, the forces inherent in nature. As civilization emerged in South Asia, the forces of religion and government became permanently intertwined in the development of the caste system, which formally enshrined priests (Brahmans) and rulers (Kshatriyas) at the top of the Hindu socioreligious hierarchy. The earliest pre-Columbian civilizations in the Americas all appear to have combined religious and governmental authority in the person of priest-kings or emperors who functioned as temporal rulers and intermediaries to the gods.

The three monotheistic religions of Judaism, Christianity, and Islam have each had different relationships with government over the course of their histories. Judaism, in its formative stages, combined many religious responsibilities of the community with the political leadership. Moses served as both a temporal leader and a prophet with religious obligations to lead his people according to God's commands. The later kings of Israel and Judah constantly sought to influence the actions of priests and prophets, who, in turn, never hesitated to involve themselves in the politics of the monarchy.

The first Christians were much more focused on spiritual matters than on temporal matters, yet they were not blind to political authority. A strong advocacy of separation of religion and government may be found in Christ's own admonition to "Leave unto Caesar that which is Caesar's, and to God the things that are God's." As Christianity became established and institutionalized in Europe, both Roman emperors and the church realized the mutual benefit of cooperation. At times that cooperation could be more accurately called dependence, especially as strong emperors such as Constantine effectively unified religious and governmental authority, giving rise to caesaropapism—the domination of the church by the emperor. As Rome fell from influence and various European monarchies were established, the church, under the direction of its popes, exerted what political influence it could. Later, as Christian Europe moved through the Renaissance, Reformation, and Enlightenment, religious influence over government weakened, ultimately giving rise to the call for separation of church and state.

Islam, from its origins, sought to unify the two institutions of religion and government. Muhammad served as both political and religious leader of the community of believers. The Prophet's successors, the caliphs, shared the same responsibility: to govern in accordance with the word of Allah as written in the Qur'an.

Religion and government, of course, continue to stand at the foundation of the world's societies today, and the appropriateness of each institution's proper or improper influence over the other is still a matter of debate. In some Islamic countries, the institutions of religion and government still overlap. The political course of Iran is currently determined by its ayatollahs (religious leaders). In Afghanistan, the mullahs, authorities on the Qur'an and Sharia (Islamic law), have strong political influence through their status as tribal spokesmen. In India, while the constitution formally separates religion and government, Hindu nationalism remains a strong force in politics. In 1998, the Hindu nationalist Bharatiya Janata party won the national elections, giving rise to new fears that non-Hindu minorities would suffer under Hindu majority rule.

In western Europe and the United States, tension continues between the two institutions on a number of levels. The French government recently banned religious dress and ostentatious display of religious symbols from its schools in an attempt to assimilate the children of Muslim immigrants into French secular culture. In the United States, religion and government run up against each other over issues such as abortion, stem cell research, public prayer, and religious symbolism in public places.

The tension between the two institutions of government and religion has been present in human society throughout history. Today, the manner in which these two institutions interact can shape a society in profound ways. In general, the separation of religion and government is thought to be more conducive to the democratic principles of equality and pluralism because such a relationship prevents religious majorities from imposing their faith on others through the power of the state. On the other hand, the unification of religion and government may promote political stability and cohesion in societies where members of one religion make up the vast majority of the population. Every society in the modern world continues to grapple with the problems related to one institution's influence over the other, with the appropriate influence of government on religion and religion on government. It is most likely that the disagreement over the proper impact each institution should have on the other will be debated into the foreseeable future.

Questions

1. Why are religion and government such powerful social institutions?
2. Should religion have some influence over government and vice versa, or should the two institutions be separated from one another?
3. What has history taught us regarding the separation of religion and government?

African Beginnings

African Civilizations to 1500 C.E.

> "Unless you know the road you've come down, you cannot know where you are going." This proverb from the Temne people of West Africa reflects the importance that Africans place on understanding the past. And, in Africa's case, there is an extraordinarily vibrant history to consider, stretching from the emergence of our human ancestors to the development of major kingdoms and empires to the creation of modern states. Africa's geography and environment presented formidable challenges to human development, but African peoples have displayed a remarkable genius for adaptation, innovation, and ingenuity and have developed a rich tapestry of cultures, societies, and civilizations. Although there are certain cultural traits that most Africans share, Africans have created a diverse variety of social and political systems, ranging from small-scale communities in which extended families and lineages met most of their needs to large states such as Nubia, Mali, and Great Zimbabwe, with hereditary rulers, elaborate bureaucracies, and extensive trading networks.

An enduring image of Africa is that it is a collection of unchanging societies that were isolated and unaware of developments in other parts of the world. This depiction is erroneous. Africans have shared ideas and innovations with each other and been receptive to technological advances and influences from outside the continent. The trans-Saharan trade linked West African Sudanic states to the Mediterranean and Middle East; Indian Ocean trade tied the East African coastal city-states and southern Africa kingdoms to Arabia, Persia, and Asia; and the Red Sea served as a bridge connecting Aksum and Ethiopia to the Mediterranean and the Indian Ocean.

3000

c. 3000 B.C.E. Beginning of Bantu migrations

1000

700–400 B.C.E. Ironworking introduced in Nok culture, Nigeria

1 C.E.

c. 100 C.E. Establishment of kingdom of Aksum

First century Camel introduced from Asia into trans-Saharan trade

300s Rise of kingdom of Ghana, West Africa

320–350 Reign of Ezana, king of Aksum

1000

1000–1500 Peak of Swahili civilization along East African coast

1076 Almoravid attack on Ghana

1100 Building of rock churches in Ethiopia

c. 1234–1260 Reign of Malinke ruler, Sundiata Keita, founder of Mali Empire

1270 Beginning of Solomonid dynasty, Ethiopia

1290–1450 Peak of kingdom of Zimbabwe

1300s Founding of kingdom of Kongo

1307–1337 Reign of Mansa Musa in Mali

1400–1600 Rise of Edo kingdom of Benin

1434–1468 Reign of Zar'a Ya'kob, emperor of Ethiopia

THE AFRICAN ENVIRONMENT

■ *How did African farmers adapt to different environmental zones?*

Many Americans have thought of the African continent as a place of two extremes: oceans of sand dunes in the north and, to the south, an immense "jungle" teeming with wild animals. In reality, more than half of the area south of the Sahara consists of grassy plains, known as **savanna,** whereas "jungle" or tropical rain forests make up only 7 percent of the continent's land surface.

The most habitable areas have traditionally been the savannas, as their grasslands and trees favor both human settlement and long-distance trade and agriculture. The northern savanna, a region sometimes called the Sahel or Sudan (not to be confused with the modern state by the same name), stretches across the continent just south of the Sahara. Other patches of savanna are interspersed among the mountains and lakes of East Africa and another belt of grassland that runs east and west across southern Africa, north and east of the Kalahari Desert.

Between the northern and southern savannas, in the region of the equator, is dense rain forest. Although the rain forest is lush, its soils are poor because torrential rains cause soil erosion and intense heat leaches the soil of nutrients and burns off humus or organic matter that are essential for soil fertility. The rain forests also harbor insects that carry deadly diseases. Mosquitoes transmit malaria and yellow fever, and the tsetse fly is a carrier of sleeping sickness to which both humans and animals such as horses and cattle are susceptible.

Whether they sustained a living through hunting, gathering, fishing, **pastoralism,** or farming, Africans had to contend with the continent's harsh and fragile environments. Thus, African cultivators accumulated sophisticated knowledge of what food crops to grow in particular areas and how to manage their environments and sustain a living from marginal or poor soils. Permanent cultivation was a luxury that few Africans farmers were able to practice. A more prevalent approach in sparsely populated areas was "slash and burn," or **shifting cultivation.** Farmers knew that they could stay on a piece of land for a few growing seasons before soils were exhausted. Thus, every growing season, they would clear land with iron hoes and machetes and fertilize it by burning natural vegetation

such as brush and tree leaves for ash. Usually after two to three years, the land lost its fertility and a family had to move on and start the cycle in another area. Shifting agriculture was especially necessary in the rain forests, where, as noted, heavy rainfall and high temperatures produced poor soils.

Cultivators learned what crops were best suited for the soils and rainfall in certain climatic zones. In rain forest areas where vegetation was dense, they favored root crops such as yams and cassava, while in the grasslands of the savanna, they grew cereal crops such as sorghum and millet.

AFRICAN CULTURAL PATTERNS

■ *What is the connection between kinship relations and African political systems?*

Although African societies are remarkably diverse, they often share common values, belief systems, and aesthetic styles that are reflected in their family and kinship relations and political, economic, religious, and cultural institutions.

Africans place great importance on family and kinship ties. The primary unit of social organization is the extended family, which includes not only parents and children but also a network of wives and relatives—grandparents, aunts, uncles, and cousins. Relations within families are based on descent patterns. Most African societies are patrilineal, with descent traced through the father to his sons and daughters who belong to their father's kin group. When a woman marries, she becomes part of her husband's kin group and usually no longer shares in the economic resources of her father's group. About 15 percent of African societies are matrilineal, in which descent is passed through the mother's side of the family to a mother's brother. In matrilineal societies, when a man marries, he usually goes to live at his wife's family homestead and has to work for her family for a number of years. In these societies, women live with their own kin and have at least some independent access to economic resources such as land. Many of the matrilineal societies are found in forest areas with poor soils. Because farming required large numbers of laborers, an advantage of matrilineal relationships is that they can bring together a wide network of families from both the mother's and father's side who contribute laborers to agricultural production.

Historically, families also played an important role in decisions about marriages. Marriage was not solely a private issue between a bride and a groom but was a uniting of two larger groups, such as families or clans. Strict rules stipulated whether a person could marry outside a clan or lineage. Marriage was typi-

---

savanna—A flat grassland dotted with trees.

pastoralism—The raising of grazing animals such as sheep and cattle.

shifting cultivation—An agricultural system in which cultivators farm land for a few growing seasons; as the soil loses its fertility, they move to another area.

cally accompanied by an exchange of **bridewealth,** the husband's payment of money, goods, services, or cattle to his new wife's family. Bridewealth gave a husband certain domestic rights—to establish a homestead with his wife, to use his bride's labor in his household and fields, and to attach their offspring to his kinship group. Bridewealth also cemented a social relationship between a husband and his wife's family. If a wife could not bear children or deserted her husband, her parents had to return the bridewealth. This gave the wife's family a vested interest in preserving the marriage.

Another characteristic of both matrilineal and patrilineal African societies is that they accepted **polygyny,** a man's marrying more than one wife. Although a minority of men actually took a second wife, polygyny was seen as a necessity because of high infant mortality, the need for more manpower in farming, and the desire to express status and wealth.

The family household was the foundation for building larger identities and communities—one's *lineage* contained people who could trace their descent to a common ancestor, and one's *clan* contained many lineages or people who shared kinship. Within a society, lineages and clans could be used to mobilize people for self-defense and work parties, to allocate rights to land, to raise bridewealth, and to perform religious rituals. African societies also contained groups of people who were not bound by kinship and who created larger social identities. These were secret societies that often guarded medicines, performed ritual activities, and organized defense and were cohorts of people of roughly the same age who had gone through rites-of-passage ceremonies such as circumcision.

The lineage and clan also provided the basis for political units, ranging from the most basic to the largest kingdoms. Many African societies were formed without chiefs, rulers, or centralized political institutions and operated at the village level. These are known as "stateless" societies. Authority was usually vested in a group of elders or senior members of families and lineages who conferred to work out approaches to common concerns such as deciding when to plant and to harvest, whether to move or migrate, and how to resolve disputes within a community or handle conflicts with other communities. In these egalitarian societies, reaching a consensus was an essential part of the decision-making process.

Other African societies developed slowly into chiefdoms and kingdoms that incorporated larger populations, featured elaborate hierarchies and extensive bureaucracies, and engaged in long-distance trade with other states. Even though kingdoms could be made up of many lineages or clans, they were usually dominated by one. These kingdoms were governed by hereditary rulers who wielded religious as well as political power. However, their tendencies to abuse power were often held in check by councils and courts.

There were many ways in which women shared or influenced decision-making with men. On occasion women served as officials and advisers, religious leaders, and even soldiers, and some states had women rulers. The king's wife (the queen), his sisters, and the queen mother were often powers behind the throne. In the kingdom of Abomey in West Africa, each wife of a king represented one of the kingdom's lineages and advocated its interests to the king.

The queen mother could be the actual mother of a king, or she could be an in-law, an appointee, an influential person in a society, or the wife or sister of a former ruler. She was responsible not only for looking after the king's interests, but also for serving as a unifying presence. She mediated rivalries between court factions, maintained alliances, and represented groups who were excluded in succession disputes.

Work within communities was carried out by families and kinship groups. However, specific tasks were usually determined by sex and age. Women were primarily responsible for maintaining the homestead, cultivating the fields, preparing the food, and running local markets, while men took the lead in building houses, constructing paths and roads, clearing fields, raising livestock, hunting, and conducting long-distance trade. Work parties consisting of age-mates of one or both sexes could be mobilized for communal tasks such as harvesting and planting, clearing fields, weeding, threshing, and house building. Although men usually controlled technological advances such as ironworking and blacksmithing, there were exceptions to this practice. Among the Pare of eastern Africa, women were given the responsibility for gathering and smelting iron.

An important aspect of the African heritage was its value system, which shaped all aspects of life. Paramount were a profound awareness of human interdependence and an appreciation for communal harmony and unity within the family and the larger society. The African conception of land ownership, for instance, stressed that individuals had the right to cultivate untilled land but that they could not sell or rent the land to others or pass it on to their children. Land was held in trust by the larger community.

Religion permeated the everyday experiences of Africans and was an integral part of their social and political life. Specific religious beliefs and institutions varied from society to society, but several tenets were

---

bridewealth—A payment a groom and his family make to the bride's family to arrange for a marriage.

polygyny—A system of marriage that allows a man to have more than one wife.

shared. African societies were polytheistic. Most had a belief in a high god or creator who was usually remote and rarely concerned with the everyday affairs of humans. Therefore, Africans were more directly engaged with other divinities, such as nature and ancestral spirits that maintained an active interest in the affairs of the living and could intercede for humans with the high god. Political leaders were often imbued with ritual authority to approach the ancestors, who provided legitimacy to the moral order and reinforced political authority.

As individuals and as communities, Africans were concerned with identifying the causes of illness and disasters such as drought, crop failures, and plagues. One way of explaining misfortune was that the high god or the ancestors were unhappy with the actions of humans. Thus, people sought the goodwill of the ancestors with prayers and ritual offerings and sacrifices at shrines. Africans also attributed misfortune to witches, who wielded evil powers and inflicted suffering on people. Those afflicted by witchcraft appealed to specialists such as diviners to diagnose the sources of evil and provide remedies for them. Women enhanced their status and prestige by serving in religious rituals as priestesses, healers, rainmakers, diviners, and spirit mediums.

Some African religious systems were extremely complex, with elaborate priesthoods and cults. The Yoruba traditionally had four levels of spiritual beings. At the top was the supreme being, Oludumare, who was served by his subordinate gods on the second level. The secondary gods had their own priests, who presided over temples and shrines. Then came the ancestors, known as *Shango*. Finally, there were the nature spirits found in the earth, mountains, rivers, and trees.

Africans were traditionally skilled and sensitive artists, particularly in sculpture, which they used to record historical events. They carved expertly in wood, ivory, and soapstone. They also fashioned statues from baked clay and cast them in bronze. An innovative technique was the *cire perdue* (SIR purdee; "lost wax") technique, which involved making a cast of the object in wax, covering it with clay, and then melting the wax and replacing it with molten bronze. The famous bronze statuary of Benin, which drew on a long tradition of metalworking in the region of present-day Nigeria, has gained international recognition for its craftsmanship and beauty. Other specific artistic traditions, producing naturalism and symbolism in a rich tapestry of styles, flourished in many early African cultures.

Many African religious ceremonies featured masked male dancers. In this photo of the Dogon people of West Africa, the masked dancers performing at a funeral ceremony are driving the spirit of the dead person from its home. The dancers also act out the Dogon myth explaining how death entered the world through the disobedience of young men.

THE PEOPLING OF AFRICA

■ *How did the knowledge of pastoralism and agriculture spread throughout Africa?*

During the late Stone Age, human communities in Africa were small bands of foragers who based their existence on hunting wild animals and gathering wild plants. Their technology was relatively simple but effective. Small bands of hunters, armed with bows and arrows with stone barbs treated with poisons, tracked down and killed the small and large game that roamed the plains of Africa. While men conducted hunts, women were primarily responsible for gathering. With a tool kit of digging sticks, gourds, and carrying bags, they "collected a variety of wild fruits, nuts, and melons, and dug up edible roots and tubers from the ground."[1] For many foraging groups all over the world, hunting and gathering satisfied all their dietary requirements and remained a preferred way of life long after the invention of agriculture.

About 15,000 to 20,000 years ago foraging groups along the Nile River added more protein to their diets by fishing in rivers and lakes and gathering shellfish. From 10,000 B.C.E. to 6000 B.C.E., the northern half of Africa went through a wet phase known as the Aquatic Age. The region that is now the Sahara became a savanna of grassland and woodland, with an abundance of rivers and lakes. Lake Chad, for instance, formed part of a large inland sea. By fashioning bone harpoons and fishnets, people lived off the rich aquatic life. Around 3000 B.C.E. an extended dry phase set in and the vast barren area that we know now as the Sahara began to form.

Agriculture

The dry period largely cut off sub-Saharan Africa from developments in the Mediterranean, but it was also likely a major stimulus for the development of agriculture in West Africa as communities experimented with new crops to supplement their diets. They began growing barley, wheat, and flax with simple tools such as digging sticks and wooden hoes.

In the past it was widely assumed that sub-Saharan African communities acquired agriculture by diffusion from Nile civilizations, but more recent scientific investigations have shown that plant domestication began independently in four regions: the Ethiopian highlands, the central Sudan, the West African savanna, and the West African forests. In all cases African farmers adapted crops suited to particular environments that were tested over long periods of time. For instance, around 5000 B.C.E. in the dry West African savanna, farmers developed sorghum and pearl millet, both crops requiring short growing sea-

Before the Sahara became a desert, the region was home to pastoralists who herded cattle, sheep, and goats. On a plateau at Tassili n-Ajjer in the central Sahara, these pastoralists left an impressive array of wall paintings depicting their lifestyles and the wild animals that roamed the region. In this painting from the Tassili frescoes, women ride oxen as their community migrates to a new settlement.

sons and minimal rainfall. Around 3000 B.C.E. in the grasslands of the Ethiopian highlands, farmers began cultivating *teff* (a tiny grain), finger millet, *noog* (an oil plant), sesame, and mustard. In the forests they planted *ensete* (a source of starch that looks like a banana), coffee, and qat. People chewed coffee and qat leaves as a stimulant. Around 1000 B.C.E. wheat and barley were imported from across the Red Sea. In the central Sudan agricultural communities began producing sorghum, millet, rice, cowpeas, and groundnuts as far back as 4000 B.C.E. In the West African forests, oil palms, cowpeas, and root crops such as yams were produced.

Africans also began to use domesticated animals about the same time as they adopted agriculture. The

Early African Civilizations

10,000–6000 B.C.E.	Aquatic Age
c. 4000 B.C.E.	Domestication of food crops in central Sudan
c. 3100 B.C.E.	Beginning of unification of Upper and Lower Egypt
c. 3000 B.C.E.	Sahara region begins changing into desert
c. 730 B.C.E.	Kushite conquest of Egypt
c. 700 B.C.E.	Spread of knowledge of ironworking from Egypt to Kush

earliest evidence of livestock is found in the western Egyptian desert about 8000 B.C.E. Cattle, sheep, goats, and pigs were introduced from western Asia to Egypt and North Africa and then spread much later to western, eastern, and southern Africa.

Iron Technology

Another major breakthrough for sub-Saharan African cultures was the introduction of ironworking. Although bronze and copper toolmaking had developed in western Asia, the technology had not spread to sub-Saharan Africa. This was not the case with iron technology, which reached sub-Saharan Africa by two routes. It moved first from Assyria to Egypt around 700 B.C.E. and from Egypt to Nubia in the seventh century B.C.E. Ironworking then spread southward to the Lake Victoria area around 250 B.C.E. It also appeared in West Africa around 1000 B.C.E., apparently brought south across the Sahara by Berbers, in contact with Phoenician or Carthaginian traders.

The production of several pounds of iron requires ten to 15 trees to fuel smelters. Hence, two of the earliest centers of iron smelting were in forested areas at Meroe (MEHR-oh-wee), in the Nubian kingdom of Kush, and Nok, situated on the Jos plateau in central Nigeria. Located on the Nile River in a region rich in iron ore deposits, Meroe became well-known in the fourth century B.C.E. for iron smelting and making iron tools and weapons that were key to the kingdom's success. Huge iron slag heaps still exist around the ruins of Meroe.

Archaeologists have dated ironworking sites at Nok from 1000 to 500 B.C.E. Although some contend that ironworking was an independent invention at Nok, other ironworking sites of about the same time period have recently been identified in Mauritania, southern Mali, and central Nigeria. Nevertheless, it is clear that Nok had one of the earliest ironworking sites. The Nok workers' preheating techniques and their ability to produce steel with a high carbon content were equal to those of Egypt and Rome. The Nok population included ironsmiths, craftspeople, and artists, who produced terra-cotta sculptures of remarkable realism that were strikingly similar to later art forms among the Yoruba kingdoms of Ife and Benin.

Iron production in most African societies usually took place in the dry months when rain and floods were not disruptive and agriculture was less intensive. Because their products were highly valued and could be exchanged for animals and food, ironworking specialists were persons of wealth and status who usually passed on their knowledge to close kin. Magical, ritual, and spiritual powers were often attributed to them. In some societies the ironworking craft assumed such ritualistic significance that the furnaces were hidden in secluded places.

Some scholars see the ironworking process as a metaphor that reinforced age and gender relationships. Ironworking was a preserve of the elders who

This stylized terra-cotta head, dating from about 500 B.C.E., is an outstanding example of a sculpture from the Nok culture of central Nigeria. The head, which has a human face, was probably used for religious purposes.

passed on their knowledge to young apprentices, while the smelting process was likened to a woman conceiving and giving birth. The Phoka, an ethnic group in Malawi, "described their smelting furnace as a fertile young woman while under construction, and as their 'wife' once smelting began."[2] To ensure success, male ironworkers had to observe strict abstinence while smelting, and menstruating and pregnant women were not allowed near the furnaces.

Ironworking allowed African societies to make the transition from stone to metal tools. Iron tools such as hoes, knives, sickles, spearheads, and axes made a significant difference in clearing forests and thick vegetation for agriculture, in hunting, and in waging war. When combined with the introduction of agriculture and pastoralism, the knowledge of ironworking contributed to population growth, craft specializations, trade between communities, and more complex political and economic systems. Ironworking was also a factor in the spread of Bantu groups to central, eastern, and southern Africa.

search of new areas to farm and fish. Another explanation is that the acquisition of ironworking gave Bantu groups access to iron tools that they could use in clearing the thicker vegetation of the forest regions. However, archaeological evidence now suggests that Bantu groups did not use iron tools until after their migrations began.

Using archaeological and linguistic data, historians have had some success in reconstructing the complex movements of Bantu groups. Around 3000 B.C.E., bands of Bantu began slowly moving out of their original homeland. These Bantu groups had common lifestyles—they lived in scattered homesteads and villages and farmed root crops, foraged for food, and fished. One stream of peoples moved south into the equatorial rain forests of west Central Africa and settled in present-day Angola and Namibia. Their agriculture relied heavily on root crops and palm trees. The other stream moved east through the Congo basin and eventually settled in the area east of Lake Victoria

THE BANTU DISPERSION

▪ *Why did Bantu-speaking groups migrate from their original home area?*

One of the striking features of many African societies from central to eastern to southern Africa is that their languages (called Niger-Congo) and cultures have many similarities. How these societies—known as **Bantu** ("people")—came to spread over this vast area is a question that has long vexed scholars.[3]

Authorities generally agree that the original homeland for Bantu speakers was an area in present-day Cameroon near the Nigerian border. They are still not sure, however, what prompted Bantu groups to start migrating from their homeland. One explanation relates to environmental changes—as the Sahara region dried up, small groups were forced to move southward in

Around 3000 B.C.E. groups of Bantu speakers began migrating from west Central Africa and establishing farming and pastoral communities in eastern, central, and southern Africa.

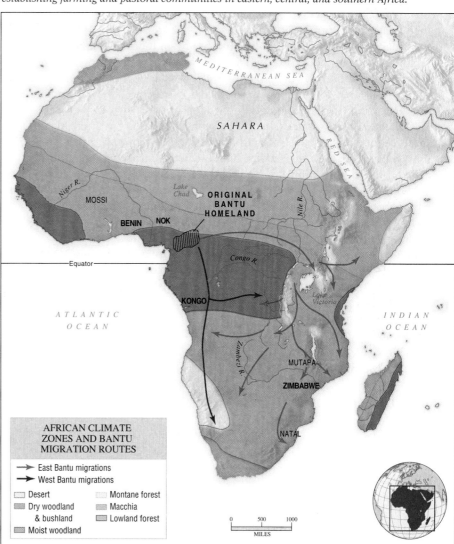

Bantu—A word meaning "people," it refers to a family of related languages spoken in central, eastern, and southern Africa.

in East Africa. There they came into contact with Cushitic-speaking peoples that had migrated from the Ethiopian highlands. The Bantu adopted their mixed farming practices—growing cereal crops such as millet and sorghum and herding cattle, sheep, and goats.

From that point, wherever Bantu groups migrated, they searched for areas that had enough summer rainfall to support cereal cultivation and their animal herds. As soils were not rich and could not support farmers for long periods, groups of people practiced shifting cultivation. The need to move on after two or three years in an area may explain why some Bantu groups, after spreading throughout East Africa, migrated southward, along tributaries of the Congo River, through the equatorial rain forest to present-day southern Congo and Zambia, where they settled in the savannas and woodland areas. Others migrated south, crossing the Zambezi and Limpopo Rivers by the fourth century of the Common Era.

As Bantu communities moved into eastern and southern Africa, they also acquired knowledge of ironworking and adopted new food crops such as the banana and the Asian yam, brought to Africa by sailors from Malaysia and Polynesia who settled on the island of Madagascar several thousand years ago. The banana had many attractive qualities. It could be grown more abundantly than root crops such as yams and without as much labor. Farmers did not have to clear out all the trees in an area for the banana to thrive. Moreover, bananas did not collect standing water and thus attracted fewer mosquitoes. In moist regions, it became a staple food and a source of mash for beer.

Throughout their migrations, Bantu societies came into contact with hunting and gathering groups. Although some scholars have portrayed the Bantu as a superior culture that overwhelmed hunting and gathering groups, recent scholarship has shown that the relationship was complex rather than one-sided. At the same time that Bantu were practicing agriculture and pastoralism, they relied on foraging for subsistence and turned to hunting and gathering bands for assistance and knowledge of local conditions. In addition, hunters and gatherers married into Bantu groups or attached themselves to Bantu groups for periods of time.

ETHIOPIA AND NORTHEASTERN AFRICA

■ *What role did the church play in strengthening the rule of Ethiopia's Solomonid dynasty?*

Situated along and inland from Africa's Red Sea coast, Ethiopia has been one of Africa's most enduring and richest civilizations. Indeed, the region between the Nile River and the Red Sea had been recognized as a major source of trade goods several thousand years before the kingdom of Ethiopia came into existence. To the Egyptians the area on the southern Red Sea coast was known as the Land of Punt, and from the Fifth Dynasty (c. 2494–2345 B.C.E.) on, Egypt's rulers regularly sent expeditions to trade for frankincense, myrrh, aromatic herbs, ebony, ivory, gold, and wild animals. The Egyptian queen Hatshepsut's funerary temple recorded a major expedition that she sent to Punt around 1470 B.C.E.

Around 800 B.C.E. traders from Saba', a kingdom on the southwestern Arabian peninsula, crossed the Red Sea, first founding trading settlements on the Eritrean coast and later a kingdom, Da'amat. The Sabaeans tapped into the ivory trade in the interior highlands, but because they were also proficient at farming in arid environments, they interacted well with farming communities of the coastal interior. The Sabaean language was similar to the Semitic languages spoken in the area, and a language called Ge'ez evolved that became the basis for oral and written communication of the elites.

By the start of the Common Era, a new state, Aksum, emerged to dominate the Red Sea trade. Taking advantage of its location between the Mediterranean and the Indian Ocean, Aksum developed extensive trading ties with Ptolemaic Egypt and the Roman Empire as well as with Asia as far east as Sri Lanka and India. In the fourth century Aksum captured elephants for Ptolemaic rulers to use in warfare against Babylon, which was

DOCUMENT
Strabo on Africa

Aksum and Ethiopia

c. 800 B.C.E.	Sabaean traders establish trading settlements on the Eritrean coast
320–350 C.E.	Reign of Ezana, king of Aksum
c. 350	Aksum conquers Kush
700–800	Aksum's control of Red Sea trade ended by Persian and Muslim forces
c. 1185–1225	Reign of Lalibela, emperor of the Ethiopian Zagwe dynasty; beginning of construction of rock churches
c. 1314–1344	Reign of Amde-Siyon, emperor of Ethiopia
1434–1468	Reign of Zar'a Ya'kob, emperor of Ethiopia

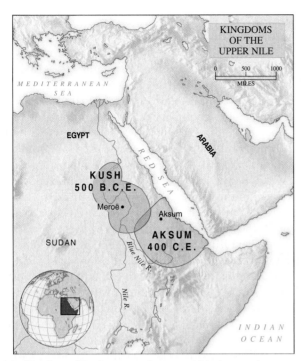

KINGDOMS
OF THE
UPPER NILE

0   500   1000
MILES

The kingdom of Kush was northeastern Africa's preeminent power until the rise of Aksum in the third and fourth centuries C.E.

importing elephants from India. The elephants were transported on specially constructed vessels.

Aksum also controlled trade with its interior, exporting slaves, gold, ivory and exotic items such as tortoise shells and rhinoceros horns in exchange for cloth, glassware and ceramic items, spices, vegetable oils, sugarcane, and wine. Aksum's capital, also called Aksum, was a major entrepot for the trade with the interior, while its bustling seaport, Adulis, prospered as the middleman for trade between the Mediterranean and the Indian Ocean. Monsoon winds dictated the rhythm of Indian Ocean trade. After July, when the summer monsoon winds were favorable, Adulis's traders set forth on their journeys. They returned in October when the prevailing winds reversed direction.

By the third and fourth centuries C.E., Aksum was at its zenith as a trading power, conquering its rival, Meroe, on the Nile, and replacing Rome as the dominant trading power on the Red Sea. Aksum minted its own bronze, silver, and gold coins with Greek inscriptions, something that only a handful of other states, such as Persia and Rome, were doing.

Aksum's best-known ruler was Ezana (320–350), who converted to Christianity toward the end of his reign, about the same time as the Roman emperor Constantine the Great. Some historians contend that Ezana conveniently converted to strengthen trading relations with the Greek-speaking world. Two Syrian brothers, Frumentius and Aedisius, have been credited with winning over Ezana to the Christian faith. Shipwrecked on the Red Sea coast, the brothers were brought to Aksum's royal court as slaves when Ezana was a child. Frumentius became an influential figure in the royal court, serving as main adviser to Ezana's mother, the queen regent. Following Ezana's conversion, Frumentius was chosen Aksum's first bishop, and Christianity was made the official state religion. Subsequently, the head of the Ethiopian church *(abuna)* was traditionally chosen by leaders of the Coptic Church in Egypt, even after Muslims gained control over Egypt.

Although Aksum's court language remained Greek, Ge'ez assumed a new prominence as the language of the Ethiopian church. The Old and New Testaments were translated into Ge'ez, which, much like Latin in the Catholic Church, became the primary language of literature and the liturgy. Several centuries after Ezana's conversion, a group of Syrian monks called the Nine Saints played a major role in spreading Christianity among rural people. The Nine Saints were known for their belief in the **Monophysite** doctrine, which held that Christ's human and divine qualities were inseparable.

The key to Aksum's continued prosperity was maintaining control over Red Sea trade. However, the Aksumites' influence in the Arabian peninsula ended in the late seventh century when a Persian expeditionary force ousted them. In 615 C.E. the Aksumite king El-Asham gave refuge to followers and family of the prophet Muhammad, who were being persecuted in Arabia. Although Muhammad directed Muslims to "leave the Abyssinians in peace,"[4] Islamic expansion late in the eighth century totally removed Aksum as a trading force in the Red Sea.

Despite Aksum's decline, some Ethiopian products such as perfume and coffee were still highly sought after. A highly prized musk was made from the glandular secretions of the civet cat. Coffee originated in Ethiopia. The coffee bean was initially chewed as a stimulant but then was made into a drink by brewing the coffee plant's leaves and berries in boiled water. Another quick-energy snack was a blend of ground coffee beans and animal fat. Finally, after someone came up with the idea of grinding roasted coffee beans, the drink rapidly spread to Arab cultures. Muslim monks drank coffee to stay awake during long periods of meditation and prayer, while coffee houses became popular gathering places throughout the Muslim world. *Qahwa* is the Arabic word from which the name *coffee* is derived.

Aksum's decline as a Red Sea power forced its rulers to migrate to the central highlands of the interior,

Monophysite—The doctrine that held that Christ has only one nature and that Christ's human and divine natures are inseparable.

where their rule continued to be plagued by conflict and warfare. There they mixed with a Cushitic-speaking people, the Agaw, who were assimilated into Aksum's political elite and also converted to Christianity. Some historians contend that the loss of commerce and revenues from the Red Sea trade led Aksum's rulers to develop a form of feudalism based on tribute from peasants that subsequent dynasties based their rule on.

The highland nobility formed the core of the Zagwe dynasty that took over in the mid-twelfth century. The Zagwes stressed their continuity with the Aksumite political order by claiming that they were descendants of Moses and encouraging the faithful to make pilgrimages to Jerusalem and Palestine. In this regard, the most enduring cultural expressions of the Zagwe dynasty were its churches, the most famous of which are the 11 awe-inspiring rock-hewn cathedrals of Roha, commissioned by the legendary Emperor Lalibela (law-lee-BAY-lah; c. 1185–1225). These impressive architectural feats, with ornate decorations and intricate workmanship, drew on Byzantine, Greek, and Roman motifs. The rock churches became the sites of

pilgrimages by Christians cut off from Jerusalem by Muslim forces.

Lalibela's reign was the high point of Zagwe rule. Rivalries between feudal nobles and Muslim merchants and kingdoms were fierce, and Lalibela's successors were unable to maintain the kingdom. Yikunno-Amlak, a southern noble once imprisoned by the Zagwes, led the rebellion that overthrew them in 1270 and founded a new dynasty, the Solomonids. Like the Zagwes, the Solomonid emperors (each known as *negus*, or "king of kings") legitimized their rule by claiming a direct tie to the Aksumite past. In their royal chronicle, the *Kebre Negast* ("Glory of the Kings"), they gave an epic account of their dynasty's direct descent from the Old Testament's King Solomon. The tale related how Makeda, the queen of Sheba (Saba'), had visited Solomon to learn his techniques of rule. Instead, Solomon seduced Makeda, who bore him a son, Menelik. When Menelik later visited his father's court, he tricked Solomon and spirited the Ark of the Covenant out of Israel to Ethiopia—which church officials claim is in the Church of St. Mary of

Ethiopia's Emperor Lalibela oversaw the construction of 11 churches carved out of red volcanic rock at Roha. Shaped in the form of a Greek cross, the Church of St. George was an impressive architectural feat. Workers chipped away at the stone until they reached 40 feet down and then molded the church and hollowed out its interior.

Seyon (Zion). This story was interpreted as a sign of the covenant God was establishing with Ethiopia. Thus to the kings of the Solomonid dynasty, it was an article of faith that they were directly descended from Solomon.

To avoid the same fate as the Zagwes, the Solomonid rulers set strict rules to ensure orderly successions. To insulate royal princes from palace infighting and forming alliances with nobles in the countryside, the first Solomonid emperor crowned in 1285, Yikunno-Amlak, took the bold step of placing the princes in a remote retreat, Mount Geshen (the "mountain of the kings"). The princes lived a comfortable but monastic existence, totally isolated from the outside world. Many of them followed an ascetic life, absorbed in religious issues and gaining reputations as accomplished writers of Ge'ez poetry and composers of sacred music. When an emperor died without a designated heir, the princes provided a pool of candidates for the throne.

The first Solomonid rulers concentrated on consolidating their rule over the central highlands of Ethiopia and refrained from carrying out aggressive wars of expansion. These goals changed dramatically during the reign of Emperor Amde-Siyon ("Pillar of Zion"; c. 1314–1344), who conquered territories to the west and toward the coast and carried out aggressive campaigns against Muslim principalities to the south and east. Amde-Siyon's army had to be in a constant state of readiness because of his repeated campaigns. His soldiers were recruited from two elements: fiercely loyal regiments attached to the royal court and militias from Christian provinces that were called out for specific campaigns. The latter were based on ethnic identities and were commanded by local chiefs. Many women also followed armies, providing food for their husbands.

Amde-Siyon's campaigns against the Muslims were aimed not only at securing control over the lucrative trade in slaves and ivory but also at putting pressure on the Muslim rulers of Egypt to allow the Coptic church to send a new bishop to Ethiopia. Amde-Siyon was so successful in vanquishing his opponents that an Arab historian reported, "It is said that he has ninety-nine kings under him, and that he makes up the hundred."[5]

The Ethiopian emperor had to be constantly on guard against potential revolts against his authority by local hereditary rulers. Although he generally allowed local rulers to remain in place, he strategically placed his officials around the kingdom. Because all land within the kingdom belonged to the emperor, he maintained loyalty by granting **gults,** or fiefs, to nobles and

to soldiers who distinguished themselves in his service, especially in newly conquered areas.

Gult-holders were bound to the emperor because he could revoke a *gult* at any time. Moreover, a *gult* owner did not own the land; he had to pay regular tribute to the emperor. In turn, the *gult* owner had the right during his lifetime to exact tribute and taxes in the form of grain, honey, cattle, and sheep from peasants who owned and worked the land. In Ethiopia tribute cattle were called "burning" because the cows were branded or "touched with fire" before they were handed over. Peasants were also expected to support any soldiers and clergy residing in their area. The major difference between the Ethiopian and European feudal systems was that the European nobility owned large estates and lived off the labor of tenants and serfs, while Ethiopian peasants kept their lands and gave up a portion of their production to the nobility.

Until Gondar was designated as the capital in the seventeenth century, Ethiopian emperors did not have a centralized bureaucracy or a fixed capital for more than a few decades at a time. Rather, they created a mobile court of family members, high officials, soldiers, priests, and retainers that moved regularly around the kingdom. This mobile court allowed the emperor to show off his power as well as encourage trade with outlying regions and to collect tribute from all his subjects. Mobile courts encamped in areas for up to four months, but they put such a strain on local resources that they were encouraged not to return for many years.

The Ethiopian monarchy assumed even greater power during the reign of Zar'a Ya'kob ("Seed of Jacob"; r. 1434–1468). Kings were usually crowned in the area where they found themselves when they took power. But Zar'a Ya'kob resurrected the tradition of kings' being crowned at the ancient capital of Aksum and stayed there an additional three years.

Within his immediate environs Zar'a Ya'kob ruled as an absolute monarch, surrounded by hundreds of courtiers and servants. To consolidate his rule, he dismissed provincial governors and replaced them with his own daughters and other female members of his family. When he held audiences at his court, he was positioned behind a curtain and communicated through a royal spokesman. When he traveled about his kingdom, his subjects had to avert their eyes on the penalty of death.

When Zar'a Ya'kob launched new campaigns of conquest to expand Ethiopia's boundaries, he was faced with the challenge of governing a diverse kingdom of many ethnic, linguistic, and religious backgrounds. He achieved his goal by exploiting the traditional feudal relationships his predecessors established with their nobles and also by reorganizing and aggressively promoting the Ethiopian church.

---

gult—The right to collect tribute granted to nobility and clergy by a king.

A characteristic art form of Ethiopia is wall murals. In this painting the bishop of Aksum confers a blessing on the emperor of Ethiopia at the Cathedral of St. Mary of Zion. When Zar'a Ya'kob became emperor in 1434, he chose to be crowned in Aksum because he wanted to link the monarchy with the historical prestige of that kingdom.

Under previous emperors, the state had perceived churches and monasteries as centers of Zagwe influence and struggled to win them over with gifts and land grants. Monks were especially difficult to influence because they led unpretentious lives and took their commitment to the poor seriously. Turning down a generous gift of gold and fine cloth from the Emperor Dawit, the abbot of the Dabra Halle Luya monastery in central Ethiopia provided an explanation for his decision: "We have no need for this. We have food which God ordered for us, the green of the earth and the roots of the trees. As for grain [it has] to be from the labour of our own hand." The emperor replied. "You say, 'We consume the fruit of our own labour,' but a church does not stand without land. Would it not be like a woman who has no husband?"[6] Dawit's persistence and more gifts eventually wore down the abbot's resistance.

Under Zar'a Ya'kob the Ethiopian church became a royal church, an extension of the crown that actively promoted its expansion throughout the kingdom. He granted the church extensive estates in newly conquered provinces. He appointed several bishops in these provinces. Clerics, who had previously led ascetic lives more concerned with their personal salvation, were now expected to play active roles in spreading the Christian faith. Monks recruited from monasteries were commissioned to establish churches and wage evangelical crusades to convert "pagans" and Muslims. At the same time, Zar'a Ya'kob declared war on traditional religious cults and imposed death sentences on those who practiced divination and sacrifices to gods.

The monarchy also sponsored monastic schools. The schools, mostly for boys, primarily accepted children from clerical families and the royal elite. Education typically consisted of reading and reciting religious tracts.

This was a period of the blossoming of the arts in which priests—and even Zar'a Ya'kob—played a leading role. They produced innumerable biblical translations, theological treatises, biographies of saints, historical chronicles, illuminated manuscripts, and mural paintings.

Although Zar'a Ya'kob's policies may have revived the church, they came at a cost. The church became intimately identified with imperial power and less able to develop deep roots among the common people.

Zar'a Ya'kob's reign was a high point in the Solomonid dynasty. His successors did not have the skills to hold the kingdom together, and Ethiopia went into a decline. Provincial officials and nobles seized on the weakness of the emperor to refrain from paying taxes and build up their own power. The Oromo, a pastoral people, began challenging Ethiopian control of the highland areas, and Muslims stopped sending tribute. Muslim states also grew restive. Under the military leadership of Ahmad al-Ghazi Ahmad Gran, the state of Adal launched a holy war against the Christian kingdom in 1527 that continued until 1543, when Ahmad was killed in battle.

EMPIRES OF THE WESTERN SUDAN

■ *How did trans-Saharan trade influence West African Sudanic states?*

Muslim writers called the savannas of West Africa *Bilad al-Sudan* ("Land of the Blacks"), and this region has been characterized by the long-standing trans-Saharan trade between the western savanna and the Mediterranean coast. Large camel caravans made regular trips across the dangerous desert carrying North African salt in exchange for West African gold. To the Berbers who organized these caravans,

African Empires in the Western Sudan

Document   Emperor Zar'a Ya'kob's Coronation and His Concern for the Church

Beginning with the Solomonid dynasty in the twelfth century, Ethiopian monarchs commissioned courts scribes to record their accomplishments in royal chronicles. Although the chronicles were produced to glorify and lionize the ruler, they do provide valuable insights into Ethiopian political and economic life. The following passages come from the chronicles of Zar'a Ya'kob, who centralized royal administration and reshaped the church as an institution of imperial rule. They describe his coronation at Aksum and his involvement in church affairs.

When our King Zar'a [Ya'kob] went into the district of Aksum to fulfill the law and to effect the coronation ceremony according to the rites followed by his ancestors, all the inhabitants, including the priests, came to meet him and welcomed him with great rejoicing; the chiefs and all the soldiers of Tigre were on horseback carrying shield and lance, and the women, in great numbers, gave themselves up, according to the ancient custom, to endless dancing. When he entered the gates of the town the King had on his right and left the governors of Tigre and Aksum who, according to custom, both waved olive branches.... After arriving within the walls of Aksum the King had gold brought to him which he scattered as far as the city gate on the carpets spread along his route. This amount of gold was more than a hundred ounces....

On the twenty-first of the month of Ter [January 16] the day of the death of our Holy Virgin Mary, the coronation rite was carried out, the King being seated on a stone throne. This stone, together with its supports, is only used for the coronation. There is another stone on which the King is seated when he receives the blessing, and several others to the right and left on which are seated the twelve chief judges. There is also the throne of the metropolitan bishop.

While at Aksum the Emperor made a number of regulations for the church.

During his stay at Aksum our King regulated all the institutions of the church and ordered that prayers which had up to that time been neglected should be recited each day at canonical hours. For this purpose he convened a large number of monks and founded a convent, the headship of which he entrusted to an abbot with the title of Pontiff of Aksum, who received an extensive grant of land called Nader. The King accomplished this work through devotion to the Virgin Mary and to perpetuate his own memory and that of his children and his children's children. He summoned some catechists and presented to the church a great number of ornaments and a golden ewer, revived all the old traditions, spread joy in these places, and returned thence satisfied.

Zar'a Ya'kob also founded churches and regulated religious affairs in other provinces.

Arriving in the land of Tsahay in Amhara, he went up a high and beautiful mountain, the site of which he found pleasing; at the top of this mountain and facing east he found a wall which had been raised by his father, King Dawit, with the intention of erecting a shrine. His father, however, had not had the time to complete the work, in the same way that the ancient King David, who planned to build a temple to the Lord, could not accomplish his task which was completed by his son Solomon. Our king Zar'a Ya'kob fulfilled his father's intention by building a shrine to God on the west of the mountain. Everyone, rich and poor alike and even the chiefs, were ordered to carry the stones with the result that this edifice was speedily erected. They embellished this locality, which underwent a great transformation; two churches were built there, one called Makana Gol and the other Dabra Negwadgwad. The King attached to them a certain number of priests and canons to whom he gave grants of land. He also founded a convent and placed in it monks from Dabra Libanos, whom he endowed in a similar manner.

Questions to Consider

1. Why do you think Zar'a Ya'kob selected Aksum as the site for his coronation?

2. What do these passages tell us about the relations between the Ethiopian monarchy and the church?

3. What comparisons can be made between church-state relations in Ethiopia and in European kingdoms during the same time period?

From Richard K. Pankhurst, ed., *The Ethiopian Royal Chronicles* (Oxford: Oxford University Press, 1967), pp. 34–36.

West African Sudanic Kingdoms

c. 250 B.C.E.	Jenne-jeno on Niger River settled
c. 100–40 B.C.E.	Camel introduced to trans-Saharan trade
c. 900 C.E.	State of Kanem founded
1000–1200	Hausa city-states founded
1076	Almoravid attack on Ghana
c. 1200–1235	Reign of Sumaguru, Sosso king
1300–1400	Rise of kingdom of Oyo
1307–1337	Reign of Mansa Musa in Mali
1352	Visit of Berber geographer Ibn Battuta to Mali
1464–1492	Reign of Sunni Ali, Songhai emperor
1493–1528	Reign of Askia Muhammad, Songhai emperor
1591	Morocco invades Songhai

the bend of the Niger River offered a secure watering and resting place. Here they found people who had conducted local trade for centuries before the caravans came, who knew the savanna well, and who could acquire gold from distant places. Their resulting control of the lucrative gold and salt trade brought great accumulations of wealth and was a key factor in the rise of major West African kingdoms.

Before the formation of these kingdoms, there was already a thriving interregional trade among the savanna communities. Archaeological evidence shows that in the ninth century B.C.E. some savanna communities began harnessing the floodwaters of the Niger River and started raising livestock and cultivating cereals. They formed settlements of 800 to 1000 people. The villages they lived in were unwalled and in open areas, an indication that relations between communities were mostly peaceful and cooperative. However, between 600 and 300 B.C.E., the pattern changed as villages erected walls and retreated to more remote and defensible sites—a sign that they were responding to external threats, possibly from nomadic Berbers who roamed the Sahara and occasionally raided savanna societies.

One of the earliest urban settlements, Jenne-jeno, was begun around 250 B.C.E. Situated on an inland delta of the Niger River, Jenne-jeno was ideally located because it was surrounded by water during the rainy season and was much safer for trade than other settlements. Over time, Jenne-jeno became an interregional trade center for farmers, herders, and fishermen that long predated any involvement in the trans-Saharan trade. Jenne-jeno exported food via the Niger to points to the east.

Although the Sahara was not easy to traverse, it was not impenetrable. As early as 1000 B.C.E., Carthaginians, Romans, and perhaps Greeks began establishing several routes across the Sahara for their horse- and ox-drawn chariots. One route stretched from Libya and Tunisia through the Fezzan, while the other connected Morocco to Mauritania. Trade declined with the collapse of the Roman Empire in the fourth century C.E. but was revived several centuries later, first by the Byzantine Empire and then by Arabs.

The camel, introduced from the Middle East in the first century B.C.E., became the main conveyor of goods in the trans-Saharan trade. As pack animals, camels had several advantages over horses and oxen. Carrying loads of 250 to 300 pounds, camels could travel extended distances with little water. However, they were slow and inefficient. Averaging about 20 to 30 miles a day, they generally took over two months to cross the Sahara. Moreover, attendants had to load and unload their cargo once or twice each day, and much of the provisions were used to feed attendants. Whatever the camel's liabilities, its introduction boosted the vol-

Introduced from the Middle East in the first century B.C.E., the camel was the main transporter of goods in the trans-Saharan trade between North Africa and the West African savanna.

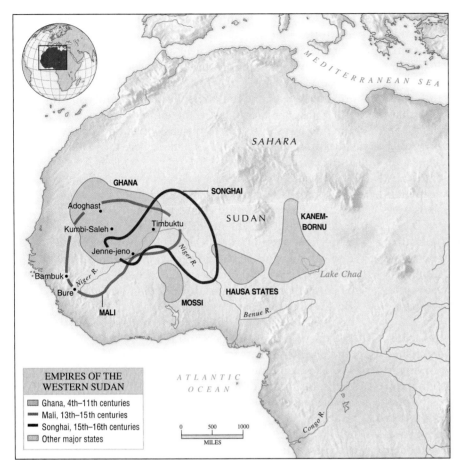

Sudanic kingdoms such as Ghana, Mali, Songhai, and Kanem-Bornu owed their power and wealth to controlling the southern part of the trans-Saharan trade.

ume of trade. The camel remained an essential part of the trans-Saharan trade until the twentieth century, when it was replaced by the automobile.

Ghana

The earliest of the Sudanic kingdoms, first known as *Aoukar* or *Wagadu*, later took the name of its war chief, Ghana (not to be confused with the modern nation of the same name). It arose on the upper Niger during the fourth century C.E. as a loose federation of village-states, inhabited by Soninke farmers. This set a pattern for future kingdoms of the savanna as a lineage or a clan asserted its authority over other groups.

The introduction of ironworking allowed the Soninke farming communities to form larger political systems. In the face of drier conditions, they applied iron tools to improving agricultural production and devised iron swords and spears to conquer neighboring groups. They also used these weapons to fend off Saharan nomads who grazed their animals in the Sahel (the southern fringe of the Sahara) and occasionally raided Soninke communities.

By about 800 C.E. Ghana had established itself as a powerful kingdom able to exact tribute from vassal states in the region. Although agricultural production contributed to Ghana's wealth, it was the expanding trans-Saharan trade with Europe and the Mediterranean world that gave Ghana even more influence. From their strategic position on the upper Niger River, the Soninke were well positioned as intermediaries to barter the salt produced from the Taghaza salt mines in the Sahara, the gold coming from Bambuk, and kola nuts and slaves captured from areas south of the savanna.

Ghana's king controlled the supply of gold within his kingdom and claimed every gold nugget coming into the country, leaving ordinary citizens the right to buy and sell only gold dust. The king was reputed to own a gold nugget so large that he bragged he could tether his horse to it. In addition, taxes were levied on every load of goods entering and leaving the country.

Ghana's gold was actually mined in Bambuk, a region eight days' journey to the west of Ghana's capital, Kumbi-Saleh, from the beds of the Senegal and Faleme Rivers. Ghana's rulers did not have direct control over Bambuk, and the persons who worked the goldfields jealously guarded information about where and how they produced the gold. They devised a strategy for negotiating with Mande traders without actually coming into direct contact with them. Al Masudi, a noted Arab traveler, described this "silent trade" around 950:

> *They have traced a boundary which no one who sets out to them ever crosses. When the merchants reach this boundary, they place their wares and cloth on the ground and then depart, and so the people of the Sudan come bearing gold which they leave beside the merchandise and then depart. The owners of the merchandise then return, and if they are satisfied with what they have found, they take it. If not, they go away again, and the people of the Sudan return and add to the price until the bargain is concluded.[7]*

Outsiders who tried to interfere in gold production soon found that less gold was offered for trade.

Traders avidly sought salt from the trans-Saharan trade because it was a crucial element in diets and a preservative for foods and skins. It was also a scarce commodity in savanna communities. A certain amount of salt could be extracted from vegetable matter or from soil, but not enough to satisfy the requirements of these savanna communities. However, in the Sahara there were large salt deposits, the best known at Taghaza, in the middle of the Sahara, about a three-week journey from both Mediterranean and Sudanese trading centers. Salt was quarried in huge 200-pound slabs, loaded on camels, and transported to trading centers like Timbuktu (tim-buk-TOO), where these slabs were distributed to other places.

Another item featured in the trade was kola nuts, which were primarily grown in the forest areas to the south of the savanna. Used to quench thirst, kola nuts were consumed mainly in the drier savanna. They did not become a major staple of the trans-Saharan exchange.

Slaves were the final component of the trans-Saharan trade. Although slavery was an established practice in some, though not all, sub-Saharan African societies, it took many shapes and forms. A common practice was that a family sent a family member—usually a child or a young adult—to serve in another household to pay off a debt or some other obligation (such as compensation for a crime) or to raise food in times of famine. In those cases, slaves were integrated into a master's family. Servile status could be of limited duration, and the slave would be sent back home as soon as the debt was repaid.

With centralized kingdoms such as Ghana and, later, Mali, slaves were bought and sold in trading transactions and were called on to perform a variety of roles—as servants, farm laborers, porters, traders, and soldiers. Most household slaves were women and children; slave women were often selected as marriage partners or concubines because a man did not have to pay bridewealth for them. Their children had all the rights of free persons.

Slave warriors had a privileged status; they could serve in high capacities as military officers, administrators, and diplomats in a king's court. Slave soldiers were the mainstays of armies and were used in raids to kidnap and capture more slaves. Most slaves were kidnapped or captured in raids on weaker communities by the stronger savanna states, especially in the forest region to the south. Muslim law enjoined Muslims from enslaving other Muslims, but this was not always observed when raiding parties were sent out.

Although savanna kingdoms created their own internal trade in slaves, the trans-Saharan slave trade was fueled primarily by demands from North African Mediterranean states. Slaves were typically taken in caravans, where they were exchanged for salt and horses. In Senegambia (si-neh-GAM-bee-ah) in the mid-fifteenth century, nine to 14 slaves could fetch one horse, while in Kanem-Bornu a horse would cost 15 to 20 slaves. In later centuries some slaves, especially those sold in Libya, were traded on to the eastern Mediterranean, the Italian peninsula, and other southern European areas. From the eighth century, when the trade was initiated, to the early twentieth century, an estimated 3.5 to 4 million slaves were taken across the Sahara.[8]

The 1200-mile journey across the desert was as perilous as the trans-Atlantic slave trade's infamous Middle Passage. Many slaves lost their lives to the harsh conditions. The majority of slaves were women who worked as domestic servants in royal households and courts or were designated as concubines. Male slaves were pressed into service in the salt mines and as caravan porters, agricultural labor, and soldiers. Because many slaves were freed or died of diseases and because so few children were born in captivity, there was a constant demand for more slaves to be sold on the market.

To reconstruct the histories of the Sudanic kingdoms, historians draw heavily on the accounts of Arab geographers, travelers, holy men, and scholars. One Arab chronicler, Al-Bakri, described Ghana at its peak in 1067. He claimed that the army was some 200,000 strong, with many contingents wearing chain mail. The king, who had not converted to Islam, was considered divine and able to intercede with the gods. He appointed all officials and served as supreme judge. His government was organized under ministers, with one responsible for his capital, Kumbi-Saleh. Princes of tributary states were held hostage at his court. When the king appeared in public, he was surrounded by highborn personal retainers holding gold swords, horses adorned with gold cloth blankets, and dogs wearing gold collars.

Ghana's capital, Kumbi-Saleh, was situated on the edge of a crop-growing area and had 15,000 to 20,000 residents. The capital was really two towns, 6 miles apart. One was a large Soninke village, where the king and his retinue lived. Close to the village was a sacred grove where traditional religious cults were practiced. The other town was occupied by Muslim merchants. The merchants' town had 12 mosques, two-story stone houses, public squares, and a market. Besides the traders, the town was also home to religious and legal scholars. Ghana's king relied on literate Muslims as treasurer, interpreters, and counselors. However influential the Muslims were, the king had to make sure that his own religious leaders were regularly consulted and that he participated in shrine and other religious activities. The first king to convert to Islam did not do so until after the Almoravid invasion in 1076.

Document   Ghana, as Described by Al-Bakri

Accounts by Muslim scholars and travelers are important sources for writing the history of West Africa's Sudanic kingdoms. A Muslim geographer and theologian who lived in Spain, Al-Bakri's account of the kingdom of Ghana appeared in his *Kitab al-maslik wa-'l-mamalik ("The Book of Routes and Realms")*, published in 1040 C.E. Al-Bakri relied extensively on people who traveled to the places he describes. The following passages describe contending religious factions at Ghana's royal capital, Kumbi-Saleh.

The city of Ghana consists of two towns situated on a plain. One of these towns, which is inhabited by Muslims, is large and possesses twelve mosques, in one of which they assemble for the Friday prayer. There are salaried imams and muezzins, as well as jurists and scholars. . . . Between these two towns there are continuous habitations. The houses of the inhabitants are of stone and acacia *(sunt)* wood. The king has a palace and a number of domed dwellings all surrounded with an enclosure like a city wall *(sur)*. In the king's town, and not far from his court of justice is a mosque where the Muslims who arrive at his court *(yafid 'alayh)* pray. Around the king's town are domed buildings and groves and thickets where the sorcerers of these people, men in charge of the religious cult, live. In them too are their idols and the tombs of their kings. These woods are guarded and none may enter them and know what is there. . . . The king's interpreters, the official in charge of his treasury and the majority of his ministers are Muslims. Among the people who follow the king's religion only he and his heir apparent (who is the son of his sister) may wear sewn clothes. All other people shave their beards, and women shave their heads. The king adorns himself like a woman [wearing necklaces' round his neck] and [bracelets] on his forearms, and he puts on a high cap *(tartur)* decorated with gold and wrapped in a turban of fine cotton. He sits in audience or to hear grievances against officials *(mazalim)* in a domed pavilion around which stand ten horses covered with gold-embroidered materials. Behind the king stand ten pages holding shields and swords decorated with gold, and on his right are the sons of the [vassal] kings of his country wearing splendid garments and their hair plaited with gold. The governor of the city sits on the ground before the king and around him are ministers seated likewise. . . . The audience is announced by the beating of a drum which they call *duba*, made from a long hollow log. When the people who profess the same religion as the king approach him they fall on their knees and sprinkle dust on their heads, for this is their way of greeting him. As for the Muslims, they greet him only by clapping their hands.

Their religion is paganism and the worship of idols *(dakakyr)*. When their king dies they construct over the place where his tomb will be an enormous dome of *saj* wood. Then they bring him on a bed covered with a few carpets and cushions and place him beside the dome. At his side they place his ornaments, his weapons, and the vessels from which he used to eat and drink, filled with various kinds of food and beverages. They place there too the men who used to serve his meals. They close the door of the dome and cover it with mats and furnishings. Then the people assemble, who heap earth upon it until it becomes like a big hillock and dig a ditch around it until the mound can be reached at only one place.

They make sacrifices to their dead and make offerings of intoxicating drinks.

Question to Consider

1. What insights does Al-Bakri provide into how Sudanic kings balanced their Islamic faith with traditional religious institutions?

From N. Levtzion and J. F. P. Hopkins, *Corpus of Early Arabic Sources for West African History* (Cambridge: Cambridge University Press, 1981), pp. 79–81.

The Almoravid invasion followed Ghana's conquest of Adoghast, a Sanhaja Berber trading center, when Sanhaja Berbers rallied around an Islamic revivalist movement called the Almoravid and attacked Ghana. Although it is still a subject of debate whether the Almoravid attack was a full-scale invasion or a series of raids, Ghana had to give up Adoghast and its dominance over trade. Ghana's dominance over the gold trade was further weakened when the Bure goldfield opened up on the Niger River.

Mali

In the early thirteenth century Ghana's rule was ended by an uprising led by Sumaguru (c. 1200–1235) of the Sosso, who were related to the Soninke. Oral traditions characterize Sumaguru as a tyrant who wielded magical powers over his people. Sumaguru was overthrown in 1235 by Sundiata (SOON-dee-AH-tah), a noted hunter and magician of the Malinke Keita clan, who forged an alliance of Malinke clans and chiefdoms for that purpose. Lengthy wars followed in which Sundiata's army defeated and killed Sumaguru and routed the Sosso. Sundiata's army then embarked on campaigns of conquest throughout the territory that had been Ghana.

From
Sundiata: An
Epic of Old
Mali

Eventually, Sundiata's Malinke created a vast empire called Mali that stretched from the Atlantic south of the Senegal River to Gao on the middle Niger River. Mali gained control of the desert gold trade and the gold-producing regions of Wangara and Bambuk. When Europeans made gold a currency in 1252, West Africa became Europe's leading supplier of gold. Several tons of gold were produced annually. Two-thirds of it was exported, while the rest was kept for conspicuous display by Mali's ruling elites.

The kingdom of Mali was at the height of its power and prosperity during the reign of Sundiata's nephew, Mansa Musa (1307–1337). Musa was perhaps the most widely known sub-Saharan African ruler throughout western Asia and Europe. He was an accomplished soldier who consolidated his kingdom's control over a vast domain. Malian and Arab merchants carried on trade with the Mediterranean coast, particularly with Algeria, Tunisia, Egypt, and the Middle East.

Mansa Musa ruled over an efficiently organized state. On the north and northeast were loosely held tributary kingdoms of diverse populations, including some Berbers. To the south were more closely controlled tributary states under resident governors appointed by the king. Elsewhere, particularly in the cities such as Timbuktu, provincial administrators governed directly in the king's name and at his pleasure. Mali's central government included ministries for finance, justice, agriculture, and foreign relations. Agricultural settlements produced food for the court, the army, and the administration, and taxes and tribute were collected from subject communities.

A devout Muslim, Musa lavishly displayed his wealth and power on a pilgrimage he took to Mecca in 1324–1325. His retinue included thousands of porters and servants and a hundred camels bearing loads of gold. In Egypt he spent so lavishly and gave away so much gold that its value in that country plummeted and did not recover for a generation:

This man spread upon Cairo the flood of his generosity. . . . So much gold was current in Cairo that it ruined the value of money. Let me add that gold in Egypt had enjoyed a high rate of exchange up to the moment of their arrival. But from that day onward, its value dwindled. That is how it has been for twelve years from that time, because of the great amounts of gold they brought to Egypt and spent there.[9]

When he returned to his kingdom, Musa brought along an architect who designed mosques in Gao and Timbuktu as well as an audience chamber for Musa's palace. Musa sent students to study at Islamic schools in Morocco. They returned to found Qur'anic schools, the best known of which was at Timbuktu.

Mansa Musa's pilgrimage also caught the attention of Muslim scholars. Among them was the Moroccan geographer and traveler Ibn Battuta, who visited Mali in 1352 during the reign of Musa's brother, Mansa Sulayman (1336–1358). Battuta's account is one of the key sources for understanding the kingdom of Mali. He was favorably impressed by Mali's architecture, literature, and institutions of learning but was most laudatory about its law and justice, which guaranteed that no person "need fear brigands, thieves, or ravishers" anywhere in the vast domain. Battuta praised the king's devotion to Islam but was disappointed that so many subjects of Mali were not Muslims. He noted also that the unveiled women were attractive but lacking in humility. He was astounded that they might take lovers without arousing their husbands' jealousy and could discuss learned subjects with men.

As Mali's empire grew, Islam became an important unifying element among the political and commercial elite. Key agents for the spread of Islam were Mande traders known as Dyula (DJOO-lah), Jahanke, and Wangara, which created an extensive trading network that stretched from Senegambia on the Atlantic coast to the kingdom of Bornu to the east. Although they were largely responsible for the trade in such items as gold and kola nuts, they were Muslim teachers as well. Wherever they went, they became the lifeblood of small Muslim communities, establishing Qur'anic schools and arranging for the faithful to make pilgrimages to Mecca.

Islam and
Africa: East
and West

Since they operated in areas where most people were not Muslims, the Mande traders formulated religious precepts that allowed them to coexist with and accept the rule of non-Muslims. However, because there were concerns that the traders would not remain devout Muslims, they were encouraged to visit centers of Islamic learning periodically to deepen their faith.

One of the few regions where Muslims actively converted people in the countryside was in Senegambia. Despite the devoutness of kings such as

Mansa Musa and The Catalan Atlas of 1375

Mali's King Mansa Musa literally put himself on the map on his pilgrimage to Mecca in 1324–1325. During a lengthy stay in Cairo, he advertised his kingdom's wealth to the Mediterranean commercial world in a way that modern-day business people would appreciate. He spent extravagantly and gave away large quantities of gold. This reinforced Europe's awareness of Mali's special status—that it was a major source of gold at a time when Europe was exchanging silver for gold as its principal hard currency. Thus, when the Portuguese began exploring the African coast, one of their objectives was to establish direct contact with Mali's king.

Mansa Musa's actions left an indelible impression on outsiders' perceptions of his kingdom. Thus, it was not surprising that when Abraham Cresques, a cartographer from Majorca, was drawing the Catalan Atlas a half-century later, he made a point of highlighting Mansa Musa and his kingdom.

The Catalan Atlas was designed to promote trade between Europe and different parts of the world. For each of the atlas's 12 leaves, Cresques depended on information provided by travelers and traders, even if it was outdated. For instance, the map of Asia drew heavily from Marco Polo's travels a century earlier, while the map of West Africa relied on information passed on by Moroccan Jews who were familiar with trans-Saharan trade routes.

The map of West Africa contained several inscriptions. One was placed next to a Tuareg trader mounted on a camel. "All this region is occupied by people who veil their mouths; one only sees their eyes. They live in tents and have caravans of camels." Cresques clearly believed that Islam had a strong presence in the Sudan, as evidenced by the domes that identified Muslim centers such as Timbuktu and Gao. The map also gave an exaggerated importance to Mali's king, Mansa Musa, who is depicted holding a gold nugget in one hand and a scepter in the other as he awaits the arrival of a Muslim trader. The inscription beside him reads: "The Negro lord is called Musa Mali, lord of the Negroes of Guinea. So abundant is the gold which is found in his country that he is the richest and most noble king in all the land."

Questions to Consider

1. Why was King Mansa Musa of Mali so prominently featured in this map of the Catalan Atlas?

2. The maps in the Catalan Atlas were drawn before the European "Age of Discovery." What sources did the Catalan cartographers rely on for their knowledge of West Africa and other regions of the world?

Musa and the presence of Muslim traders in many areas, Islam was mainly a religion of court and commerce. Most people in the countryside remained faithful to their traditional religious beliefs. Muslim rulers who neglected their people's spiritual practices did so at the risk of provoking opposition. Hence, Islamic festivals were usually celebrated alongside traditional rites.

After Mansa Musa's death, his successors found the large empire increasingly difficult to govern. They were plagued by dynastic disputes, raids by desert nomads such as the Tuaregs and Sanhaja, and the restlessness of tributary states. One of the rebellious states was Songhai, centered around the bend of the Niger. Songhai had been in existence for many centuries before it was absorbed into the Malian Empire in the thirteenth century, and its principal city, Gao, was an entrepot for trade with the Maghrib and Egypt. Before the end of the fifteenth century, Songhai had won its independence, and, within another century, it had conquered Mali.

After Sunni Ali drowned in the Niger River, his son ruled for a few months before Askia Muhammad, who came from Sunni Ali's slave officer corps, deposed him and established his own dynasty. Askia Muhammad set about consolidating and reorganizing the whole empire. Although his armies seized control of the Taghaza saltworks in the Sahara, their attempts to expand control over the Hausa states to the east were not successful.

Reigning from his capital at Gao, Askia Muhammad created a centralized bureaucracy to manage finances, agriculture, and taxation, appointed administrators (usually relatives) to oversee newly created provinces, and built up a professional army featuring a cavalry of chain-mailed horsemen and an enlarged fleet of canoes, which constantly patrolled the Niger.

Unlike Sunni Ali, Askia Muhammad made peace with Muslim scholars and became their benefactor. He declared Islam the official religion. During his reign Timbuktu, Jenne-jeno, and Walata achieved recognition as centers of Islamic scholarship. Several hundred

Songhai

Songhai became the largest of the Sudanic empires, reaching its zenith during the reigns of Sunni Ali (1464–1492) and Askia Muhammad (1493–1528). Sunni Ali is remembered for his military exploits. His armies ventured out on constant campaigns of conquest, largely to the west along the Niger in what had been Mali's heartland, and captured the trading centers of Timbuktu, Walata, and Jenne-jeno.

Sunni Ali regularly feuded with Muslim scholars and clerics who accused him of not observing Muslim practices such as praying in public. They issued a condemnation of his behavior and ruled that because he was not a Muslim, he could not be recognized as a legitimate ruler. He tried to suppress his dissidents and expelled Muslim scholars from Timbuktu.

The Sankore mosque is the oldest surviving mosque in West Africa. Its pyramidlike minaret rises above the city of Timbuktu, the center of Islamic culture in the kingdom of Mali.

Muslim schools were established in Timbuktu, whose scholars developed extensive links and exchanges with scholars in the Middle East and North Africa. Its Sankore mosque became so renowned that a contemporary Arab traveler noted that more profits were being made from selling books and manuscripts there than from any other trade.

Like Mansa Musa, Askia Muhammad made a much publicized pilgrimage to Mecca. Traveling in 1497 with a large group of pilgrims, he brought thousands of gold pieces, which he freely distributed as alms to the poor and used to establish a hostel in Mecca for pilgrims from the western Sudan. Muhammad was not just expressing his faith; he was also drumming up trade with Songhai and shoring up his credentials with Muslims throughout his far-flung empire. On Muhammad's return home the Egyptian caliph recognized him as the **Caliph** of the lands of Takrur, an important distinction for any Muslim ruler.

Although a son deposed Askia Muhammad in 1528 and the kingdom was weakened by internal rivalries, Songhai remained a savanna power until 1591, when Morocco's King Ahmad al-Mansur launched an invasion of Songhai to prevent European rivals from gaining access to Sudanese gold. Taking offense at Songhai's refusal to pay a tax on salt from the Taghaza mines, al-Mansur sent a contingent of 4000 mercenaries to secure control over the Sudanic goldfields. Many died in the harsh march across the Sahara, but the survivors, armed with arquebuses (firearms mounted on a forked staff) and muskets, proved superior to the spears, swords, and bows and arrows of Songhai's soldiers. Although Morocco's impact was fleeting, Songhai was not able to recover, and the empire fragmented into many smaller kingdoms.

Kanem, Bornu, and the Hausa States

In the central Sudan, which stretches from the bend of the Niger to Lake Chad, a series of Muslim states emerged that took advantage of the fertile agricultural lands and their strategic location between the trans-Saharan trade routes to the north and the forest regions to the south. The kingdoms of Kanem and Bornu and the Hausa city-states became the most important dominant political actors.

Kanem, which lay to the northeast of Lake Chad, had been formed around 900 C.E. when groups of nomadic pastoralists unified and established the Saifawa dynasty. The ruling elite converted to Islam in the late eleventh century. As in other Sudanic states, Saifawa power and wealth were based on control of the Saharan trade. The main trade route cut through the central Sahara to the Fezzan and on to Tripoli and Egypt. Because Kanem was too far away from any sources of gold, its rulers exported ivory, ostrich feathers, and, especially, war captives from societies to the south. In return Kanem received horses that its rulers used to create a cavalry that fueled further raiding. Under Mai (king) Dunama Dibalemi (1210–1248), Kanem boasted a cavalry of 40,000 horsemen.

In the fourteenth century, one of Kanem's tributary states, Bornu, became a power in its own right, organizing its own trade and refusing to pay tribute to Kanem. During this period, Kanem's rulers were challenged by the Bulala, a non-Muslim clan, and by the deterioration of their pasturage. About 1400, the Saifawa dynasty came under attack from peoples living east of Lake Chad and moved to Bornu west of Lake Chad, where they gained access to new trading networks. At first they paid tribute to Bornu, but during the sixteenth century, Kanem's leaders gradually took over the Bornu state and began carrying out raids over an extensive area. Their rule was financed by tribute, taxes on peasants and customs levies on the trade in slaves, gold, salt and weapons between Bornu and Tripoli and Cairo.

Bornu's rulers maintained excellent relations with the Muslim world. In the early thirteenth century they established a **madrasa** in Cairo for their students studying at al-Azhar University. They developed a strong relationship with the Ottoman rulers of Tripoli and imported firearms and contracted Turkish mercenaries to train Bornu's army.

To the west of Kanem and Bornu, a group of Hausa city-states had been founded by nomadic cattle-keepers and farmers between 1000 and 1200. A common feature of Hausa villages was wooden stockades for protection. When villages grew into larger towns, they were enclosed by large walls.

Hausa city-states became important political and economic forces in the fifteenth century. All of the Hausa states were centralized, with a king and council making decisions. Islam was an important part of the trading and merchant class and the political elite.

Kano was one of the most powerful of the city-states. In the late fourteenth and fifteenth centuries, Kano's rulers made Muslim officials an integral part of their administration and invited scholars from Egypt, Tunis, and Morocco to establish centers of scholarship.

One way in which Kano's rulers thwarted lineages that were contesting for power was by appointing slaves to important state offices such as treasurer and as palace guards. They also relied on a cavalry with an officer corps to maintain their power and to raid for the slaves who labored on large royal farms. The cavalrymen wore iron helmets and coats of mail.

Caliph—The religious and political leader of the Islamic nation; successor of Muhammad.

madrasa—A theology school, usually for Sunni Muslims.

Ceremonial cavalry procession in contemporary northern Nigeria. Historically the military strength of kingdoms of the western Sudan was partly based on cavalry.

Kano produced and exported textiles, dyed cloth, and leatherwork through an extensive network in the trans-Saharan trade as well as with Yoruba and Akan states to the south.

Other significant Hausa city-states were Zazzau (ZA-zow), a supplier of slaves to Hausa states and to North Africa; Gobir, which traded with Songhai and Mali; and Katsina, an important terminus for the trans-Saharan trade. Katsina also successfully produced textiles from its cotton fields and leather goods from goat, sheep, and cattle hides. However prosperous they were, some of the Hausa states still had to pay tribute to Songhai to the west and Kanem and Bornu to the east. The Hausa states usually coexisted peacefully, although Kano and Katsina carried on a periodic war for almost a century.

A legendary Hausa ruler of the sixteenth century was Zazzau's Queen Amina. She led her armies on campaigns all the way to the banks of the Niger River and conquered Kano and Katsina. Under her rule, Zazzau controlled not only the intra-regional trade but also the region's trans-Saharan trade. Her reign is associated with the building of earthen walls around Hausa cities. She is remembered in a popular song still sung in contemporary Nigeria: "Amina, daughter of Nikatau, a woman as capable as a man."[10]

WEST AFRICAN FOREST KINGDOMS

■ *How did trade in the forest kingdoms compare with those in the savannah region?*

Between the savanna grasslands and the Atlantic was forest land. Some of the forests were extensions of the savannas and were suitable for extensive human settlements; closer to the coast were rain forests that required considerable energy to clear for settlement and cultivation. The rain forests were also the home of the tsetse fly, the carrier of sleeping sickness, which limited the herding of highly susceptible livestock.

IMAGE

Yams as Sources of Traditional Power in West Africa

Most forest societies were built around villages and small chiefdoms sustained by agriculture and hunting. Root crops such as yams and, later, cassava were the main staples. Although they did not approach the same size as the savanna empires, some of these small chiefdoms merged and formed vibrant kingdoms.

In southwestern Nigeria, a Yoruba city-state, Ife, emerged around the eleventh century C.E. According to oral traditions, the Yoruba god of the sky, Olorun, had sent a founding ancestor, Oduduwa, to establish Ife. Anyone who subsequently made a claim to the kingship of Ife or other Yoruba states had to trace descent from Oduduwa.

To the southeast of Ife was the Edo kingdom of Benin, which rose to prominence in the fifteenth and sixteenth centuries. Benin's prosperity was based not only on commerce with the Hausa states, trading food, ivory, and kola nuts for copper and possibly salt, but also on the strength of its fishing communities on the Niger delta.

Benin was ruled by hereditary kings, known as *obas*. Advising the king was the *ozama*, a council composed of hereditary leaders who represented the main Edo lineages. They acted as a restraint on the *oba's* powers until a thirteenth-century *oba* named Ewedo undermined the *ozama's* powers by creating a court of men who were not members of the royal elite and who were given nonhereditary titles.

Benin remained a minor state until the rule of *Oba* Ewuare, who usurped the throne by killing his younger brother in 1440. He took over in a period of instability following the conquest of Benin by a neighboring state. Ewuare ensured that his line would succeed him by arranging that his heir be added to the *ozama* council.

Noted for his magical and healing powers, Ewuare was famous for rebuilding the capital, surrounded by a wall and featuring a broad avenue. He constructed an extensive royal palace that provided quarters for his family as well as for advisers, guilds of craftsmen, and servants. All of his freeborn subjects were expected to spend a period in the service of the palace. During Ewuare's three decades of rule, his armies expanded Benin's borders, conquering some 200 towns and extending Benin's influence far to the north and to coastal regions to the east and west. However, Ewuare did not tightly control his empire. Although he placed loyal officials in subject territories, he gave local rulers autonomy as long as they paid tribute on a regular basis. Ewuare's successors did not fare so well. The *ozama* chiefs asserted themselves and replaced, exiled, or killed a series of *obas*.

Other states developed along the forest fringe of the northern savanna. Most of them profited from the long-distance Saharan trade through the Hausa states to the north, exchanging slaves and forest products such as kola nuts for salt, leather goods, and glassware. In the Niger River region, the kingdom of Oyo emerged in the fourteenth century. The kings *(alafins)* of Oyo presided over a complex of palace councils, subkings, secret organizations, and lineage organizations at the village level. Although *alafins* claimed absolute power, they were held in check by a prime minister *(basorun)* and a council of ministers *(oyo mesi)*, composed of men from the seven wards of the city of Oyo. If an *alafin* abused his authority, the prime minister could rebuke him, "The Gods reject you, the people reject you, the earth rejects you." The *alafin* then had to commit suicide.[11] This happened rarely because an *alafin's* suicide meant that a member of the council also had to take his life. This system of checks and balances worked well until the seventeenth and eighteenth centuries.

The *alafins'* wealth was built on tolls collected from traders and their control of a slave labor force that they placed on royal farms. Oyo's rise as a regional power was due to its permanent officer corps and its cavalry, assembled with horses traded from the savanna. Because horses did not survive in the tsetse-infested forests, the cavalry was most effective in the open savannas to the southwest of Oyo.

All of these forest states are noted for their artistic achievements. Yoruba artisans created sculptures in bronze, copper, brass, and terra-cotta. Most of these artworks were used in religious contexts, as funereal pieces placed in tombs to honor ancestors and in temples. These objects showed continuity with the artistic styles of earlier civilizations such as the Nok culture of central Nigeria.

SWAHILI CITY-STATES IN EAST AFRICA

▪ *Why were small city-states established on the East African coast rather than the large states in West Africa?*

For the past 2000 years the East African, or Swahili, coast has been part of a much wider maritime trading network that linked Africa with the Near East, India, and Asia. Indeed, one scholar argues that the Indian Ocean would be better named the Afrasian Sea.[12] However, unlike the trans-Saharan trade that opened up extensive trade throughout western Africa, trade along the East African coast, with some exceptions, did not have the same impact on the East African interior until the nineteenth century.

The historical and cultural development of the East African coast was intimately linked to the creation of a coastal culture that dates from 100 B.C.E. to 300 C.E. with the establishment of Bantu-speaking communities along the coast north of the Tana River.

MAP
Trade Routes in Africa

They took advantage of the fertile soils and forests along the coast to pasture their animals and to raise a great variety of food crops. They also found the creeks, rivers, lagoons, mangrove swamps, and seas ideal for fishing. Although Bantu farmers relied on subsistence agriculture and fishing, they began to expand their local and regional trading contacts and eventually linked up with merchants from the Arabian peninsula and the Persian Gulf.

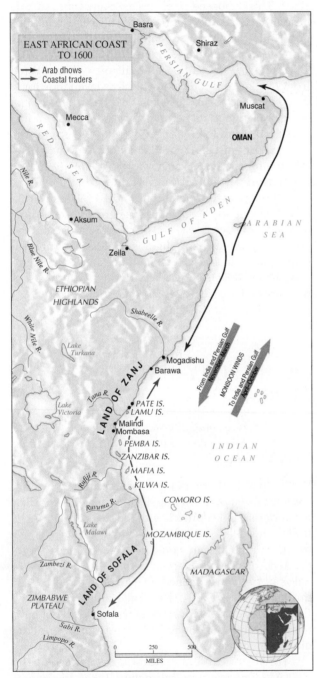

Trade between the coastal Swahili city-states and Indian Ocean trading partners was regulated by monsoon winds that blow in a southwesterly direction between November and March and in a northeasterly direction between April and October.

The language that evolved on the coast and islands was Swahili, which was based on a Bantu language spoken on the Kenyan coast. Indeed, the word *Swahili* is taken from an Arabic word *sawahil*, meaning "coast." As the language evolved, it adopted Arabic loan words, especially after the seventeenth century.

The earliest known record of the East African trade is *The Periplus of the Erythrean Sea*, a navigational guide written by a Greek trader in Alexandria, Egypt, around the first century C.E. The *Periplus* chronicles shipping ports of the Red Sea and the Indian Ocean and identifies a string of market towns on the "Azanian" (East African) coast that actively participated in the Indian Ocean trade, especially with Arabia. The most important was a port named Rhapta. Market towns exported such goods as ivory, rhinoceros horn, copra, and tortoise shells in exchange for iron tools and weapons, cloth, glass, and grain.

The Indian Ocean trade continued between 300 and 1000, but it was given a great stimulus by the spread of Islam and the settling of Muslims from Arabia and the Persian Gulf along the East African coastline from the ninth century C.E. onward. This was about the same time as Islam reached western parts of North Africa, but the spread of Islam in eastern Africa was not associated with conquest. Muslims intermixed with African communities and helped expand trading links with the Arab world. An Arab traveler described this trade on a visit to the "land of Zanj" (the East African coast) in 916:

> *The land of Zanj produces wild leopard skins. The people wear them as clothes, or export them to Muslim countries. They are the largest leopard skins and the most beautiful for making saddles. . . . They also export tortoise-shell for making combs, for which ivory is likewise used. . . . There are many wild elephants in this land but no tame ones. The Zanj do not use them for war or anything else, but only hunt and kill them for their ivory. It is from this country that come tusks weighing fifty pounds and more. They usually go to Oman, and from there are sent to China and India.[13]*

Arab boats or dhows made the Indian Ocean trade possible. They had the ability to cross the Indian Ocean three times as fast as a camel could cross the Sahara, and, with a capacity of up to 200 tons, they could carry a thousand times as much. The dhows' lateen (triangular) sails made it possible for sailors to take advantage of seasonal monsoon winds in the Indian Ocean that blow in a southwesterly direction between November and March and northeasterly between April and October. As with the Red Sea trade, the monsoon winds governed the trading calendar. It took about a month for a dhow to make the 2000-mile journey from East Africa to the Persian Gulf, and the

The Arab dhow was the primary transporter of trade goods in the Indian Ocean. The dhow's lateen sails made it possible to navigate the monsoon winds that dictated the direction of trade at different times of the year.

traders had to carry out their business according to the favorable winds, or they could not transport their goods at all. Along the East African coast itself, however, it was possible to move between the islands at most times of the year. Because the coastal trade was conducted in shallower waters, traders built small dhows with capacities of about 50 tons. These dhows typically had no deck, one mast, and palm-leaf mats for sails.

Swahili civilization flourished between 1000 and 1500, when hundreds of city-states, many of them on offshore islands, sprang up along the 1800-mile stretch from Mogadishu to Sofala on the Mozambique coast. They began as fishing villages and gradually evolved into trading centers. Most were short-lived, but those that were situated at the mouth of a river or had deep harbors and were connected to established trade routes on the African mainland—such as Malindi, Pemba, Pate, Mombasa, Mafia, and Kilwa—became regional trade centers and thrived for centuries.

Kilwa peaked as a trading center between 1250 and 1330 C.E. Kilwa had the advantage of a good supply of fresh water and several natural harbors that could handle large ships. But it became the wealthiest of the city-states because of its near monopoly over gold exported from the Zimbabwe interior. Kilwa's merchants claimed a sphere of influence over the East African coast from Kilwa southward to Sofala on the Mozambique coast, where they established an outpost to facilitate the gold trade with Africans from the interior.

The Swahili city-states were never part of an empire, nor were they dominated by any one of the city-states. Indeed, they usually competed fiercely with one another. The lack of high walls around the cities suggests that they were more concerned with protecting themselves from stray elephants than from rivals. At times, one city might exact tribute from its neighbors or a number of states might federate in time of war. Commercial competition made such cooperation difficult to maintain and curtailed political expansion on the African mainland, where kingdoms like Great Zimbabwe played one coastal city against another. Indian Ocean trade was largely free from major conflicts until the Portuguese arrived in the early sixteenth century.

Within the city-states, a Muslim commercial aristocracy exercised exclusive control over political institutions. Although they provided the capital, skills, and boats for their piece of the Indian Ocean trade, they always remained in the shadow of the Indian Ocean trading powers. The Swahili commercial elite was primarily descended from Arab and Indian settlers and indigenous Africans. A myth developed that that they were descendants of Shirazi Persians. Because the Persian Empire had once been an Indian Ocean trading power, Swahili elites probably manufactured a connection to the Persians who settled along the coast many centuries earlier. Many scholars question whether this claim has any validity.

As the Muslim Middle East became the commercial center of Eurasia, the maritime trade of the Swahili city-states figured significantly in the commercial networks of three continents. Gold, ivory, mangrove poles, amber, and slaves were the main exports. Other products commonly exported were hides and skins, cloth, rhinoceros horn, spices, and grain, in exchange for cloth, silk, beads, porcelain, gum, incense, spices (i.e., cinnamon, nutmeg, and cloves), glass, cloth, perfume, bronze, copper, and silver. Copper and silver coins were minted at Kilwa, Pate, and Mogadishu and used up and down the coast.

Kilwa, with its access to the Zimbabwean gold fields, became the major port for gold sent to Indian Ocean states and through Egypt to Europe. Gold was a mainstay of Swahili trade until gold and silver began to flow in the sixteenth century from Spanish possessions in the Americas. After that, Swahili traders turned more to exporting ivory. Iron ore, exported from Malindi and Mombasa, supplied the iron industries of India. Mangrove trees, typically found where rivers emptied into the Indian Ocean, were stripped of their branches and shipped to treeless areas throughout the southern Persian Gulf. Because mangrove poles are straight and sturdy, they made excellent materials for house construction. This trade remained healthy until the late twentieth century when oil revenues allowed Persian Gulf states to turn to steel for building materials. Slaves were shipped to the Arabian peninsula and Cambay, the capital of Gujarat, in India. There they served as domestic slaves or, as in southern Iraq, as laborers draining marshes. Their oppressive work conditions sparked off a revolt in 869 C.E. that lasted for nearly two decades. One consequence of the revolt was that few Persian Gulf households continued to rely on Africa as a source of slaves.

DOCUMENT

Excerpts from "A Description of the Coasts of East Africa and Malabar" by Duarte Barbosa

The Swahili coast attracted trading expeditions from as far away as China. In the early 1400s, a Chinese fleet under the command of Admiral Zheng He (JUHNG HUH) visited Swahili towns such as Malindi and Mogadishu, bearing porcelain, silks, lacquerware, and fine art objects and exchanging them for ivory, rhinoceros horns, incense, tortoise shell, rare woods, and exotic animals such as ostriches, zebras, and giraffes.

In the early 1400s, the Chinese commissioned seven expeditions to visit all the lands of the Indian Ocean to promote trade. A Chinese fleet under the command of Admiral Zheng He visited some of the Swahili towns and took back several envoys from Malindi who brought along a giraffe as a gift to the Chinese court in 1414. The presentation of this giraffe was memorialized in a tapestry.

Zheng He's ships also took back African envoys, who stayed at the Chinese court for several years.

The governments of the city-states were usually headed by monarchs or sultans, assisted by merchant councils and advised by holy men or royal relatives. Political leadership was equated with commercial success. The king of Pate, for instance, "owned much wealth, . . . acted as an entrepreneur in ship building, trading and even mining and relied for emergency on a private army as distinct from the regular troops which he also commanded. . . ."[14] Elite families maintained their privileged status by building political and commercial alliances through intermarriage and exchanging gifts.

Although the sultans were typical Muslim rulers in most respects, the common order of succession was according to matrilineal rules. When a sultan died at Kilwa, Pate, or any of numerous other cities, the throne passed to one of the head queen's brothers. Swahili civilization was an urban culture. Most towns had a central mosque, a Qur'anic school, a marketplace, a palace, and government buildings. Some towns, such as Kilwa, Mombasa and Lamu, were densely settled; in others, settlements were dispersed. The towns were the preserves of the commercial elite, who lived in houses made of wood with coral stone foundations until the mid-fifteenth century when they replaced wood with coral rag (broken coral stone) with lime mortar. Some of the homes were two or three stories high and reflected the wealth, status, and rank of their owners. A Portuguese account of the late fifteenth century described the layout of Kilwa, a prosperous city of 12,000 people: "The streets of the city are very narrow, as the houses are very high, of three and four stories, and one can run along the tops of them upon the terraces, as the houses are very close together. . . ."[15]

With the exception of the most loyal household slaves, the Swahili traders were the only ones who lived inside the walled cities. Most slaves slept outside the city in houses made of sun-dried mud and palm-matted roofs. They came into the city to work every day. Because the towns were not self-sufficient, the traders relied on the farmers and fishermen on the mainland for foodstuffs and meat.

Swahili masons and craftsmen were celebrated for building ornate stone and coral mosques and palaces, adorned with gold, ivory, and other wealth from nearly every major port in southern Asia. Perhaps because it borrowed architectural styles from the Middle East, Kilwa impressed the famous Muslim scholar-traveler Ibn Battuta in 1331 as the most beautiful and well-constructed city he had seen anywhere. Archaeological excavations have confirmed this evaluation, revealing the ruins of enormous palaces, great mansions, elaborate mosques, arched walkways, town squares, and public fountains. The Husuni Kubwa (hoo-SOO-nee KOO-bwah) palace and trade emporium at Kilwa, built on the edge of an ocean cliff, featured domed and vaulted roofs and contained over 100 rooms, with eight to ten apartments for visiting merchants as well as their goods, and an eight-sided bathing pool in one of its many courtyards.

Constructed in the thirteenth century by the Muslim sultans of Kilwa, the Great Mosque was built from coral blocks. In the mosque's center, its arches supported a domed ceiling.

KINGDOMS OF CENTRAL AND SOUTHERN AFRICA

■ *How were southern African kingdoms tied to the Indian Ocean economy?*

By the third century C.E. central and southern Africa had been settled by migrating groups of Bantu farmers who lived in scattered homesteads or small villages and subsisted on cereal crops and animal herds. Around 1000 C.E. some of these societies began to grow in size and complexity. States were formed with ruling elites that displayed their wealth through their cattle herds. They accumulated cattle through a variety of means—raids, tribute, death dues, court fines, and bridewealth exchanges for marriages. Cattle exchanges through marriages and loans gave ruling families the opportunity to establish broader social and political networks with other powerful families. Cattle herds also financed their participation in regional trading networks and links with the Indian Ocean economy.

A common feature of the ruling elites of these new states was that they built walls, dwellings, palaces, and religious centers made of stone. Throughout the region north and south of the Limpopo River archaeologists have identified more than several hundred political centers. An early state was Mapungubwe, situated south of the Limpopo River. Mapungubwe's rulers lived in stone residences on a hilltop, while commoners lived in their traditional settlements in the surrounding valley. An estimated 3000 to 5000 people lived at Mapungubwe's political center. The elites maintained their privileged status through their control over cattle herds; the trade in such metals as tin, copper, iron, and gold; and the hunting of elephants for ivory. Tin, copper, and iron were traded regionally, but ivory and gold were designated primarily for the expanding trade with the Indian Ocean coast. Mapungubwe peaked during the thirteenth century, but its main settlement had to be abandoned soon thereafter because farmers were not able to sustain production when a climatic change produced a colder, drier environment.

Mapungubwe's successor was Great Zimbabwe ("houses of stone"), centered on a well-watered plateau north of the Limpopo. Its grandeur as a state is symbolized by its imposing granite structures, left after its rulers were forced to move northward to the Zambezi. Extending over 60 acres and supporting about 18,000 residents, the complex at Great Zimbabwe contained many structures built over several centuries. At its center was a large complex of stoneworks where the political and religious elite lived. The most impressive structure was the Great Enclosure, which likely served as the royal family's main residence. Over 800 feet in circumference, the Great Enclosure was built without mortar and featured massive freestanding walls 12 feet thick and 20 feet high. Undoubtedly, Great Zimbabwe's rulers intended their monumental architecture to enhance their power and prestige among their subjects.

Zimbabwe's king presided over an elaborate court and administration. His key advisers included the queen mother and a ritual sister, a half-sister who was appointed when a king was installed. She had to give her consent to decisions made by the royal coun-

The Great Enclosure was Great Zimbabwe's most impressive structure and likely served as the royal family's main residence. Over 800 feet in circumference, the Great Enclosure was built without mortar and featured massive, freestanding granite walls 12 feet thick and 20 feet high.

cil before they could be enacted, she kept the ritual medicines that protected the well-being of the king, and she had considerable input into the choice of a new king.

Zimbabwe's rulers combined political and sacred power. Great Zimbabwe contained a rainmaking shrine, where its rulers prayed for abundant rainfall. On a nearby hillside was a temple where they prayed and offered sacrifices to the high god Mwari and the ancestors to ensure the fertility of the land and the prosperity of the people.

Great Zimbabwe's political elite based their power on their vast cattle herds as well as the control of regional trade, particularly copper and gold. The principal sources of gold were located on the plateau west of Great Zimbabwe. Women and children were responsible for mining most gold, which they did during the dry season, when they could take time off from their farming responsibilities. They sank narrow shafts as deep as 100 feet, brought the ore to the surface, crushed it, and sifted out the gold in nearby streams. Although some of the gold was fashioned into ornamental bangles and jewelry for Zimbabwe's rulers, most of the gold was transported as a fine powder for the external trade with the coastal Swahili cities, especially Kilwa, whose prosperity depended on its ties to Zimbabwe. One historian has estimated that 7 to 10 million ounces of gold were exported from this region from the late tenth to the nineteenth centuries. Besides gold, ivory and animal skins were traded for glass beads, Indian cloth, ceramic vessels from Persia, and blue-and-white porcelain from China.

Great Zimbabwe's zenith was between 1290 and 1450. A common explanation for its sudden collapse is environmental degradation. The land no longer supported large numbers of people living in a concentrated area; trees, chopped down for firewood, had become scarce; and many wild animals had been hunted down. However, part of this interpretation is not supported by data showing that rainfall actually increased around that time. A more likely explanation for the kingdom's decline is the rise to prominence of two of its former tributary states: Torwa to the northwest and Mutapa to the north.

Oral tradition relates that Mutapa's founder was Nyatsimbe Mutota, whom Great Zimbabwe's rulers had sent north to search for an alternative source of salt. He founded the Mutapa kingdom in the well-watered Mazoe Valley south of the Zambezi River. By 1500 Mutapa's ruler, the *mwene mutapa* ("conqueror"), and his army held sway over a vast part of the upper Zimbabwe Plateau. The *mwene mutapa* did not adopt the stone building traditions of Great Zimbabwe. Instead, he lived in a palace complex within a wooden palisade. With his family, military, bureaucracy, and representatives of tributary chiefdoms, he ruled over a federation

of tributary states through governors that he appointed. They paid tribute in the form of agricultural produce, iron, cattle, and especially gold, which was still the mainstay of the trade with the East African coast.

Another notable kingdom in west Central Africa was Kongo, located in a fertile agricultural area near the Atlantic coast at the mouth of the Congo River. It was formed in the fourteenth century when a petty prince named Wene led a migration, married into the local ruling family, and began developing a loose federation of states. Wene took the title of *Mani-kongo* ("lord of Kongo"). However, as kings of Kongo centered their political rule at their capital, Mbanza Kongo, they developed a centralized state. By the time the Portuguese arrived in the late fifteenth century, Kongo had already developed a sophisticated political system. The king, who had a professional army resident at his capital, appointed officials, usually close relatives, as his provincial administrators. The Kongo kingdom also controlled interregional trade, exchanging its cloth, woven from fibers of the raffia palm, for salt and seashells from neighboring societies.

Loango, the Capital of the Congo (Kongo)

CONCLUSION

By 1500 C.E. Africans had successfully adapted to the opportunities and constraints of Africa's challenging environments by creating a diverse range of communities and states. Critical turning points in the histories of African cultures occurred with the introduction of agriculture, herding, and ironworking. These developments spurred population growth, migrations, craft specialization, trade between communities, and more complex political and economic systems. Most Africans in 1500 still lived in scattered homesteads and small communities and earned their livelihoods from farming, herding, and hunting. However, because of trading relations with one another and with other continents, Africans began to establish kingdoms and empires in all parts of the continent and in a variety of environments. Like other early world civilizations, Egypt and Nubia evolved in the Nile River valley, but Aksum and Ethiopia emerged on a mountain plateau; Ghana, Mali, Songhay, and Great Zimbabwe in savannas; Oyo and Benin in rainforests; and the Swahili city-states on the Indian Ocean.

While Africans created their own distinct cultures and traditions, states in the West African Sudan, northeastern Africa, and the East African coast carried on vigorous commercial, technological, and intellectual exchanges with the cultures of the Indian Ocean, the Mediterranean, the Near East, and Asia, largely by tapping Muslim trading networks. The kingdom of Aksum became a major Red Sea power, serving as a bridge between the Mediterranean and the Indian Ocean. The Swahili city-states on the East African coast and the states of the Zimbabwe Plateau carried on extensive relations with Indian Ocean trading networks. West African savanna kingdoms created the most extensive trading network through their position overseeing trade between North Africa, the savanna, and forest regions to the south. However, within these long-distance trading networks, African states were primarily producers of raw materials.

Although most Africans remained faithful to their traditional religious beliefs and practices, many converted to Christianity and Islam in specific areas. Egypt became an early center of Christianity, while Ethiopia's rulers firmly established Christianity as their kingdom's state religion. Islam became the dominant religion of North Africa, while some rulers and traders in the West African savanna, northeastern Africa, and along the Swahili coast adopted Islam. However, until the eighteenth century, Islam remained primarily a religion of court and commerce in sub-Saharan Africa. It won few followers in small-scale societies that did not have ruling elites. This pattern is similar to other places such as Indonesia where Muslim traders established themselves but did not initially win many converts.

Suggestions for Web Browsing

You can obtain more information about topics included in this chapter at the websites listed below. See also the companion website that accompanies this text, http://www.ablongman.com/brummett, which contains an online study guide and additional resources.

Internet African History Sourcebook
http://www.fordham.edu/halsall/africa/africasbook.html

Extensive online source for links about the history of ancient Africa, including the kingdoms of Ghana, Mali, and Songhai.

Art of Benin
http://www.si.edu/ofg/Units/sorsnmafa.htm

Site of the Smithsonian Institution's National Museum of African Art displays art objects from the kingdom of Benin before Western dominance.

Great Zimbabwe
http://www.mc.maricopa.edu/~reffland/anthropology/
anthro2003/legacy/africa/zimbabwe/

A 23-slide series, with commentary, that will take you through the ruins of Great Zimbabwe in southern Africa.

The Story of Africa
http://www.bbc.co.uk/worldservice/africa/features/storyofafrica/
index.shtml

The radio service of the BBC presents a history of Africa from the origins of humankind to modern nation-states.

African Voices
http://www.mnh.si.edu/africanvoices/

The African Voices exhibit at the Smithsonian Institution's Museum of Natural History features discussions of history, culture and politics.

Literature and Films

The Sundiata epic of the Malian Empire is recorded in D. T. Niane, *Sundiata: An Epic of Old Mali* (Longman, 1995). For Ethiopian royal literature, see G. W. B. Huntingford, ed., *Royal Chronicles of Abyssinia: The Glorious Victories of Ama Seyon King of Ethiopia* (Clarendon Press, 1965).

Caravans of Gold (Home Vision, 1984) treats the gold trade between the Sudanic kingdoms of West Africa and the Muslim and European worlds. It is one film in an eight-part series, *Africa: The Story of a Continent,* presented by Basil Davidson, a British writer on African issues. *Lost Cities of the South* (PBS, 1999) presents a discussion of African civilizations of southern Africa, such as Mapungubwe and Great Zimbabwe. It is part of a six-part series, *Wonders of the African World,* narrated by Harvard professor Henry Louis Gates, Jr.

Suggestions for Reading

The best detailed coverage of African history can be found in two multivolume series, each containing chapters by leading scholars: *The Cambridge History of Africa,* 8 Vols. (Cambridge University Press, 1982–1984) and *The UNESCO General History of Africa.* Among other general surveys of African history are Robert July, *A History of the African People,* 4th ed. (Waveland Press, 1992); Erik Gilbert and Jonathan Reynolds, *Africa in World History from Prehistory to the Present* (Pearson Education, 2004); and Christopher Ehret, *The Civilizations of Africa: A History to 1800* (University Press of Virginia, 2002).

The best general reference work on early African history is Joseph Vogel, ed., *Encyclopedia of Precolonial Africa: Archaeology, History, Languages, Cultures, and Environments* (AltaMira Press, 1997). Another general work that examines Africa's history with a disciplinary focus is James Newman, *The Peopling of Africa: A Geographic Interpretation* (Yale University Press, 1995). A general synthesis on women in African history is Iris Berger and E. Frances White, *Women in Sub-Saharan Africa: Restoring Women to History* (Indiana University Press, 1995).

On Ethiopia, see Richard K. Pankhurst, *The Ethiopians* (Blackwell, 1998).

General works on West Africa include J. F. Ajayi and Michael Crowder, eds., *History of West Africa,* 3rd ed., Vol. 1 (Longman, 1985). A comprehensive study on Islam in Africa is Randall Pouwels and Nehemia Levtzion, eds., *The History of Islam in Africa* (Ohio University Press, 2000).

The East African coast and Swahili city-states are well covered in John Middleton, *The World of the Swahili: An African Mercantile Civilization* (Yale University Press, 1992).

The best general study on early central and southern African history is David Birmingham, ed., *History of Central Africa to 1870* (Cambridge University Press, 1981). The kingdom of Great Zimbabwe is extensively treated in Joseph Vogel, *Great Zimbabwe: The Iron Age in South Central Africa* (Garland, 1994). A detailed study of central and eastern African states is David Schoenbrun, *A Green Place, a Good Place: Agrarian Change, Gender, and Social Identity in the Great Lakes Region to the 15th Century* (Heinemann, 1998).

The European Middle Ages, 476–1348 C.E.

The absence of the political unity and military security once provided by the Roman Empire became an obvious fact of life in almost all of western Europe in the fourth and fifth centuries. As the unity and security of the old Roman order collapsed and Germanic chieftains claimed lands and asserted what authority they could, very slowly the civilization of Rome evolved into a culture that was a unique blending of Roman and Germanic institutions. Out of this blending of cultures emerged a distinct pattern of life in western Europe.

One of the institutions that survived the collapse of Roman order was the Christian Church, which, by the beginning of the sixth century, was still in the process of unification under the direction of the bishop of Rome, the Pope. The church increased its efficiency through the centralization of its administration, and unified its efforts to convert all of Europe and eliminate rival religions. Christian efforts to preserve knowledge and learning centered on saving art and literature of the past that was supportive exclusively of the Christian faith; for the most part the art and literature of the non-Christian past was destroyed, suppressed, or ignored—much of the intellectual heritage of the ancient world was lost forever.

The first significant state to emerge out of the fragmentation of old Roman order was that established by the Germanic tribe of the Franks, who gave northern Europe an interim of stability and progress. Military and political security was improved, and Roman Christianity was extended among the barbarian tribes of the north.

But the accomplishments of the Franks were not to be permanent. Their empire did not endure, partly because it lacked the solid economic foundation that had supported the Romans, and because of new and violent invasions. Viking, Magyar, and Muslim incursions had to be addressed through local resistance, since no effective response existed on a national or international level.

Out of the disintegration of the Frankish empire evolved an alternative political order sometimes described as feudalism. Based on formally stated agreements between individuals, this method of government was designed to provide social stability and military security in Europe. And the manorial system, the economic foundation of medieval life, provided stability to the rural economy of Europe. Both institutions attempted to insure security by resisting change and fostering self-sufficiency.

Gradually, the political and military goals of the feudal nobility became aggressive and expansionist. Monarchs once again attempted to increase their authority over the feudal nobility. The growth of trade and commerce slowly provided an economic alternative to the manorial system, and the society of the West changed in the process. In addition, the church increased its power as a political and economic force in European society, in addition to its religious leadership. The church's sponsorship of the Crusading movement of the later Middle Ages was indicative of that power and influence.

The culture of the Later European Middle Ages emerged as greatly distinct from that of the period before 500. The collective and conservative society of the earlier period gave way to a culture becoming more familiar with religious challenge, economic growth, and political centralization. The cultural conservatism and conformity that typified the earlier patterns of medieval life gave way to a society that had to adjust to a more rapid rate of change and challenge in virtually all facets of life. The roots of modern European society are easily found in the civilization of the Late Middle Ages.

THE CHURCH IN THE EARLY MIDDLE AGES

■ *What role did the Church play in stabilizing western European society after the fall of the Roman Empire?*

As Europe formed a unique culture out of the remnants of Roman influence and the injection of Germanic peoples and their traditions, the church played a formative role in shaping this new social fabric. In the Early Middle Ages (500–1000), the administration of the church was centralized through the efforts of the popes and the ever more efficient bureaucracy at Rome. Missionary activity spread Christianity to the borders of the continent and provided a unified cultural and religious foundation for early European society. And, in large part, the church, its missionaries, and its copyists in monasteries should be credited with keeping at least some of the intellectual heritage of the ancient world alive in an age when learning, other than that which supported Christian belief, was considered useless and unnecessary.

The Early Medieval Papacy, 500–1000

Chapter 5 examined the growing authority of the bishops of Rome, the popes, over the Christian Church in western Europe. Not only were the bishops of Rome able to establish control over the church's hierarchy and supervise the spiritual concerns of the believers; often the early popes were looked to for political leadership and guidance in troubled times. During the pontificate of Gregory I, the Great (590–604), the papacy aggressively began to assert its political as well as its spiritual authority. After his election as pope, Gregory assumed the task of protecting Rome and its surrounding territory from the threat of invasion from the Germanic tribe of the Lombards. After successfully negotiating a peace treaty with this tribe, Gregory became the first pope to conduct himself as actual ruler of a part of what later became the Papal States.

Gregory also laid the foundation for the papal machinery of church government. He took the first step in asserting papal control of the church outside Italy by sending a mission of Benedictine monks to convert the non-Christian Anglo-Saxons. The pattern of church government that Gregory established in England—bishops supervised by archbishops, who reported to the pope—became standard.

The task of establishing papal control of the church and extending the pope's **temporal** authority was continued by Gregory's successors. In the eighth century English missionaries transferred to Germany and France the pattern of papal government they had known in England; the Donation of Pepin, a sizable grant of territory in Italy given to the pope by the Merovingian (meh-roh-VIN-gee-ahn) king (see p. 261), greatly increased the pope's temporal power by creating the Papal States.

Missionary Activities of the Church

The early Middle Ages were years of widespread and intense missionary activity. By spreading Christianity,

---

temporal—Having to do with time, or the present life and this world. Worldly or transitory concerns.

The bejeweled front cover of the Lindau Gospels, a work dating from the third quarter of the ninth century, is an example of Carolingian art. The Celtic-Germanic metalwork tradition has been adapted to the religious art produced during the era of Charlemagne. The main clusters of semi-precious stones adorning the gold cover have been raised so that light can penetrate beneath them to make them glow.

faith and erase the effects of worldly corruption. Irish monks also eagerly pursued scholarship and the preservation of early Christian literary works, and their monasteries became storehouses for priceless manuscripts and exquisite copies of original works.

Early in the seventh century, the papacy, along with the monasteries, took a more aggressive part in directing Christian missionary efforts. Under the direction of the pope, Roman Catholicism was established throughout England, and the Irish church acknowledged the primacy of Rome.

The English church, in turn, played an important role in the expansion of Roman Catholic Christianity on the European mainland. Boniface, the greatest English missionary in the eighth century, spent 35 years among the Germanic tribes and established several important monasteries and bishoprics before he turned to the task of reforming the church in France. There, he revitalized the monasteries, organized a system of local **parishes** to bring Christianity to the countryside, and probably was instrumental in forming the alliance between the papacy and the Carolingian dynasty of kings of the Franks. Roman Catholic missionaries were also sent to work among the Scandinavian peoples and the Slavs.

missionaries contributed to the confluence of Germanic and Roman cultures. Monasteries, many of which were established in remote territories far from urban centers, served not only as missionary outposts, but also as refuges for those seeking a life of contemplation and prayer, as centers of learning for scholars, and even as progressive farming centers. The dedication and enthusiasm with which many of these monks approached their faith often extended beyond the monastic walls, and resulted ultimately in the virtual elimination of paganism in Europe.

One of the most successful of early Christian missionaries was Ulfilas (OOL-fi-lahs) (c. 311–383), who spent 40 years with the Visigoths and translated most of the Bible into Gothic. Ulfilas and many other early missionaries were followers of Arius, and the heresy of Arianism (see p. 154) was adopted by all the Germanic tribes in the empire, with the exception of the Franks and the Anglo-Saxons.

Missionary activities in Ireland resulted in the founding of numerous monasteries on that island, many of them in remote and isolated locations. In the late sixth and seventh centuries, many of these Irish monks, moved by a passionate devotion to Christianity and dedicated to the elimination of heresy, traveled to Scotland, northern England, the kingdom of the Franks, and even Italy as missionaries to renew the

The Preservation of Knowledge

One of the great contributions of the monasteries was the preservation of the learning of the early church, and some of the literature of the Greek and Roman world that early Christian leaders found compatible with the Christian faith. After the fall of Rome, learning did not entirely die out in western Europe; the knowledge of the classical world was preserved through the efforts of a small number of concerned intellectuals who recognized its lasting value. Seeing that the ability to read Greek was quickly disappearing, the sixth-century Roman scholar Boethius (boh-EE-thee-uhs) (c. 480–525) determined to preserve Greek learning by

parish—A local church, with its own priest, and the people under the religious care of that priest.

translating all of Plato and Aristotle into Latin. But only Aristotle's treatises on logic were translated, and these works remained the sole writings of that philosopher available in Europe until the twelfth century. Unjustly accused of treachery by the emperor, Boethius was thrown into prison, where he wrote *The Consolation of Philosophy* while awaiting execution, which eventually became a medieval textbook on philosophy.

Cassiodorus (cah-si-oh-DOH-ruhs; c. 490–c. 585), a contemporary of Boethius, devoted most of his life to the collection and preservation of classical knowledge. By encouraging the monks to copy valuable manuscripts, he was instrumental in making the monasteries centers of learning. Following his example, many monasteries established *scriptoria*, departments concerned exclusively with copying manuscripts.

During the early Middle Ages, most education took place in the monasteries. In the late sixth and seventh centuries, when political stability was not yet reestablished throughout much of the European continent, Irish monasteries provided a safe haven for learning. There, men studied Greek and Latin, copied and preserved manuscripts, and, in illuminating them, produced masterpieces of art. The *Book of Kells* is a surviving example of their skill. In the early Middle Ages, women were provided no opportunities for such pursuits; the Church limited access to reading and writing to men involved in clerical and business occupations.

DOCUMENT

Rule of St. Benedict

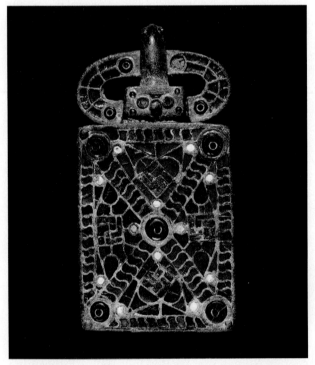

Visigothic belt buckle, circa 525–560. This elaborately crafted buckle is inlaid with finely polished red garnets and was probably worn by a prominent Spanish Visigothic woman. Most Visigothic belt buckles are of the same shape, but the patterns of decoration vary greatly, perhaps to signify the family or clan of the owner.

THE MEROVINGIANS AND CAROLINGIANS

■ *How successful were the Merovingian and Carolingian monarchs in preserving Roman institutions and culture?*

In the blending of Roman and Germanic customs and institutions, the Franks played a particularly significant role. Not only was the kingdom of the Franks the most enduring of the early Germanic states, but it became, with the active support of the church, the first European kingdom that attempted to take the place of the Roman Empire in the West.

The Kingdom of the Franks Under Clovis

Before the Germanic invasions of the fourth century, the Franks lived close to the North Sea; late in the fourth century they began to migrate south and west into Roman Gaul. By 481 they occupied the northern part of Gaul as far south as the old Roman city of Paris, and in that same year, Clovis I of the Merovingian dynasty became ruler of one of the small Frankish kingdoms. By the time of his death in 511, Clovis had united the Franks into a single kingdom that stretched south to the Pyrenees.

Clovis was an intelligent manipulator of alliances and a shrewd diplomat who also used religion for political gain. He was converted to Christianity—perhaps through the influence of his Christian wife—and was baptized together with his whole army. He thus became the only Orthodox Christian ruler in the West, since the other Germanic tribes were either still pagan or followers of Arian Christianity (the heresy that maintained that Jesus was not equal to the Father and thereby not completely divine). This conversion of the Franks to Roman Christianity ultimately led to a close alliance of the Franks and the papacy.

Decline of the Merovingians—Rise of the Carolingians

Clovis's sons and grandsons extended Frankish control south to the Mediterranean and east into Germany. But after Clovis's death, the Merovingian dynasty began to decay. The Germanic tradition of treating the kingdom as personal property and dividing it among all the king's sons resulted in constant and bitter civil wars. But most importantly, the Merovingian kings proved themselves incompetent and ineffectual. Soon the Frankish state broke up into three separate kingdoms; in each, power was

The Merovingians and the Carolingians

481–511	Clovis unites Franks; beginning of Merovingian dynasty
714–741	Charles Martel mayor of the palace
732	Charles defeats Muslims at Tours
741–768	Pepin the Short mayor of the palace
751	Pepin crowned king of the Franks; beginning of Carolingian dynasty
768–814	Reign of Charlemagne
800	Charlemagne crowned emperor by the pope; beginning of Carolingian Empire
814–840	Reign of Louis the Pious
843	Treaty of Verdun divides Carolingian Empire

concentrated in the hands of the chief official of the royal household—the mayor of the palace, a powerful noble who hoped to keep the king weak and ineffectual. The Merovingian rulers became puppets—"do-nothing kings."

By the middle of the seventh century, the Frankish state had lost most of the essential characteristics of Roman civilization. The Roman system of administration and taxation had collapsed. The dukes and counts who represented the Merovinginan king received no salary and usually acted on their own initiative in commanding the fighting men and presiding over the courts in their districts. International commerce had ceased except for a small-scale trade in luxury items carried on by adventurous Greek, Syrian, and Jewish traders. The old Roman cities served mainly as centers housing the local bishops and their staffs. The virtual absence of a middle class meant that society was composed of the nobility, a union through intermarriage of aristocratic Gallo-Roman and German families who owned and exercised authority over vast estates, and, at the other end of the social scale, the peasants *(coloni)* who worked the land and were considered bound to that estate. These peasants included large numbers of formerly free German farmers. Only about 10 percent of the peasant population of Gaul maintained their status as free individuals.

Coinciding with the Merovingian decay, new waves of invaders threatened every region of Europe. A great movement of Slavic peoples from the area that is now Russia had begun around 500 C.E. From this region the Slavs pushed west, inhabiting the areas left by the Germanic tribes when they advanced into the Roman Empire. By 650 the western Slavs had reached the Elbe River, which they crossed to raid German territory. Another danger threatened western Europe from the south: in the late seventh century the Muslim Moors prepared to invade Spain from North Africa.

The kingdom of the Franks gained strength when Charles Martel became mayor of the palace (or the king's court) in 714. His military skill earned him the surname Martel, "The Hammer." Charles was responsible for introducing a major innovation in European warfare. To counteract the effectiveness of the quick-striking Muslim cavalry, Charles recruited a force of professional mounted soldiers. He rewarded his soldiers with land to enable each of them to support a family, equipment, and war horses. With such a force, Charles Martel won an important victory over the Muslim cavalry at Tours in 732.

Charles's son, Pepin the Short (741–768), legalized the power already being exercised by the mayors of the palace by requesting and receiving from the pope a decision that whoever exercised the actual power in the kingdom should be the legal ruler. In 751 Pepin was elected king by the Franks; the last Merovingian was sent off to a **monastery,** and the Carolingian dynasty came to power. In 754 the pope reaffirmed the election of Pepin by personally anointing him as king of the Franks.

Behind the pope's action was his need for a powerful protector against the Lombards, who had conquered the **Exarchate** of Ravenna (the center of Byzantine government in Italy) and were demanding tribute from the pope. Following Pepin's coronation, the pope secured his promise of armed intervention in Italy and his pledge to give the Exarchate to the papacy, once it was conquered. In 756 a Frankish army forced the Lombard king to withdraw, and Pepin gave Ravenna to the pope. The so-called Donation of Pepin made the pope a temporal ruler over the Papal States, a strip of territory that extended diagonally across northern Italy.

The alliance between the Franks and the papacy affected the course of politics and religion for centuries. It furthered the separation of the Roman from the Greek Christian Church by giving the papacy a dependable Western ally in place of the Byzantines, previously its only protector against the Lombards.

---

monastery—A house or residence of a community of religious men (monks), who live in seclusion from the world and maintain a self-sufficient communal lifestyle.

Exarchate—In the Byzantine empire, the office and/or the area ruled by an official named an exarch—a bishop ranking below the patriarch of the Eastern Orthodox Christian church.

Charlemagne and His Achievements

Under Pepin's son Charlemagne (CHAHR-leh-mayn), or Charles the Great, the Frankish state and the Carolingian dynasty reached the height of its power. Although he was certainly a successful warrior-king, leading his armies on yearly campaigns, Charlemagne, who ruled from 768 to 814, also tried to provide an effective administration for his kingdom. In addition, he had great appreciation for learning; his efforts at furthering the arts produced the revival in learning and letters known as the Carolingian Renaissance.

Charlemagne sought to extend his kingdom southward against the Muslims in Spain. He crossed the Pyrenees and eventually drove the Muslims back to the Ebro River, establishing a frontier area known as the Spanish March, centered near Barcelona. French immigrants moved into the area, later called Catalonia, giving it a character culturally distinct from the rest of Spain.

Charlemagne conquered the Bavarians and the Saxons, the last of the independent Germanic tribes, on his eastern frontier. Even farther to the east, the empire's frontier was continually threatened by the Slavs and the Avars (AY-vahrs), Asiatic nomads related to the Huns. In six campaigns, Charlemagne nearly eliminated the Avars and then set up his own military province in the Danube valley to guard against any future advances by eastern nomads. Called the East March, this territory later became Austria. Like his father Pepin, Charlemagne was deeply involved in Italian politics. The Lombards resented the attempts of the papacy to expand civil control in northern Italy. At the request of the pope, Charlemagne attacked the Lombards in 774, defeated them, and named himself their king.

One of the most important events in Charlemagne's reign took place on Christmas Day, 800. In the previous year the Roman nobility had removed the pope from office, charging him with corruption. But Charlemagne came to Rome and restored the pope to his position. At the Christmas service, Charlemagne knelt before the altar and the pope placed a crown on his head while the congregation shouted: "To Charles Augustus crowned of God, great and pacific Emperor of the Romans, long life and victory!"

This ceremony demonstrated that the memory of the Roman Empire still survived as a meaningful tradition in Europe and that there was a strong desire to reestablish political unity. In fact, Charlemagne had named his capital at Aix-la-Chapelle (AX-lah-shah-PEL), "New Rome," or Aachen (AH-ken), and considered taking the title of emperor in an attempt to revive the idea of the Roman Empire in the West.

The Carolingian Empire

The extent of Charlemagne's empire was impressive. His territories included all of the western area of the old Roman Empire except north Africa, Britain, southern Italy, and the majority of Spain. Seven defensive provinces, or *marches,* protected the empire against hostile neighbors.

The Carolingian territories were divided into some 300 administrative divisions, each under a count *(graf)* or, in the marches along the border, a margrave *(markgraf).* In addition, there were local military officials, the dukes. In an effort to supervise the activities of local officials, Charlemagne issued an ordinance creating the *missi dominici,* the king's envoys. Pairs of these itinerant officials, usually a bishop and a lay noble, traveled throughout the realm to check on the local administration. So that the *missi* were immune to bribes, they were chosen from men of high rank, were frequently transferred from one region to another, and no two of them were teamed for more than one year.

Charlemagne's Legacy

Charlemagne is considered one of the most significant figures of early European history. He created a state in which law and order were again enforced

This gold bust of Charlemagne was made in the fourteenth century and is housed now in the treasury of the Palace Chapel of Charlemagne in Aachen, Germany. The reliquary bust contains parts of the emperor's skull.

Document   Charlemagne: A Firsthand Look

Einhard, born in the kingdom of the Franks in circa 770 C.E., was the emperor Charlemagne's secretary and biographer. The following is an excerpt from Einhard's *Life of Charlemagne,* which he completed some years after the emperor's death. Einhard's biography of the emperor is considered one of the finest works of biography produced in the early Middle Ages. It was modeled after Roman biographies of the later emperors, and intended to give its readers an intimate glimpse of Charlemagne's character, as well as to convince them of the emperor's wisdom and majesty. The following except deals mainly with the emperor's physical appearance and private pleasures:

Charles was large and strong, and of lofty stature, though not disproportionately tall (his height is well known to have been seven times the length of his foot); the upper part of his head was round, his eyes very large and animated, nose a little long, hair fair, and face laughing and merry. Thus his appearance was always stately and dignified, whether he was standing or sitting; although his neck was thick and somewhat short, and his belly rather prominent; but the symmetry of the rest of his body concealed these defects. His gait was firm, his whole carriage manly, and his voice clear, but not so strong as his size led one to expect. His health was excellent, except during the four years preceding his death, when he was subject to frequent fevers; at the last he even limped a little with one foot. Even in those years he consulted rather his own inclinations than the advice of physicians, who were almost hateful to him, because they wanted him to give up roasts, to which he was accustomed, and to eat boiled meat instead. In accordance with the national custom, he took frequent exercise on horseback and in the chase, accomplishments in which scarcely any people in the world can equal the Franks. He enjoyed the exhalations from natural warm springs, and often practiced swimming, in which he was such an adept that none could surpass him; and hence it was that he built his palace at Aix-la-Chapelle, and lived there constantly during his latter years until his death. He used not only to invite his sons to his bath, but his nobles and friends, and now and then a troop of his retinue or bodyguard, so that a hundred or more persons sometimes bathed with him. . . . Charles was temperate in eating, and particularly so in drinking, for he abominated drunkenness in anybody, much more in himself and those of his household; but he could not easily abstain from food, and often complained that fasts injured his health. He very rarely gave entertainment, only on great feastdays, and then to large numbers of people. His meals ordinarily consisted of four courses, not counting the roast, which his huntsmen used to bring in on the spit; he was more fond of this than of any other dish. While at table, he listened to reading or music. . . .

Charles had the gift of ready and fluent speech, and could express whatever he had to say with the utmost clearness. He was not satisfied with command of his native language merely, but gave attention to the study of foreign ones, and in particular was such a master of Latin that he could speak it as well as his native tongue; but he could understand Greek better than he could speak it. He was so eloquent, indeed, that he might have passed for a teacher of eloquence. He most zealously cultivated the liberal arts, held those who taught them in great esteem, and conferred great honors upon them. He took lessons in grammar of the deacon Peter of Pisa, at that time an aged man. Another deacon, Albin of Britain, surnamed Alcuin, a man of Saxon extraction, who was the greatest scholar of the day, was his teacher in other branches of learning. The King spent much time and labor with him studying rhetoric, dialectics, and especially astronomy; he learned to reckon, and used to investigate the motions of the heavenly bodies most curiously, with an intelligent scrutiny. He also tried to write, and used to keep tablets and blanks in bed under his pillow, that at leisure hours he might accustom his hand to form the letters; however, as he did not begin his efforts in due season, but late in life, they met with ill success.

Questions to Consider

1. What do you suppose is Einhard's real purpose in writing this biography? Do you think it is an impartial account?

2. What could such a biography be used for, especially since it appeared after Charlemagne's death?

3. Do you think there are some exaggerations contained in this except? If so, what might they be, and why do you think they were included?

From Samuel Epes Turner, trans., *Life of Charlemagne by Einhard* (Ann Arbor: University of Michigan Press, 1960), pp. 50–57.

after three centuries of disintegration. His patronage of learning began a cultural revival that later generations would build on, producing a European civilization distinct from the Byzantine to the east and the Muslim to the south.

Charlemagne's empire was not long-lived, however, for its territories were too vast and its nobility too divisive to be held together after the dominating personality of its creator was gone. Charlemagne had no standing army; his foot soldiers were essentially the old Germanic war band summoned to fight by its war leader. The king did not have a bureaucratic administrative machine comparable to that of Roman times. The Frankish economy was agricultural and localized, and there was no system of taxation adequate to maintain an effective and permanent administration. Under Charlemagne's weak successors, the empire collapsed in the confusion of civil wars and devastating new invasions. Progress toward a centralized and effective monarchy in Europe ended with Charlemagne's death.

When he died in 814, Charlemagne was succeeded by his only surviving son, Louis the Pious, a well-meaning but ineffective ruler. Louis, in accordance with Frankish custom, divided the kingdom among his three sons, and bitter rivalry and warfare broke out among the brothers even before Louis died in 840.

In 843 the three brothers met at Verdun, where they agreed to split the Carolingian lands among themselves. Charles the Bald obtained the western part of the empire, and Louis the German the eastern; Lothair, the oldest brother, retained the title of emperor and obtained an elongated middle kingdom, which stretched 1000 miles from the North Sea to central Italy.

The Treaty of Verdun contributed to the shaping of political problems that continued into the twentieth century. Lothair's middle kingdom soon collapsed into three major parts: Lorraine in the north, Burgundy, and Italy in the south. Lorraine included Latin and German cultures, and, although it was divided in 870 between Charles and Louis, the area was disputed for centuries. Lorraine became one of the most frequent battlegrounds of Europe.

Europe Under Attack

During the ninth and tenth centuries, coinciding with the collapse of the Carolingian Empire, western Europe came under attack by Scandinavians from the

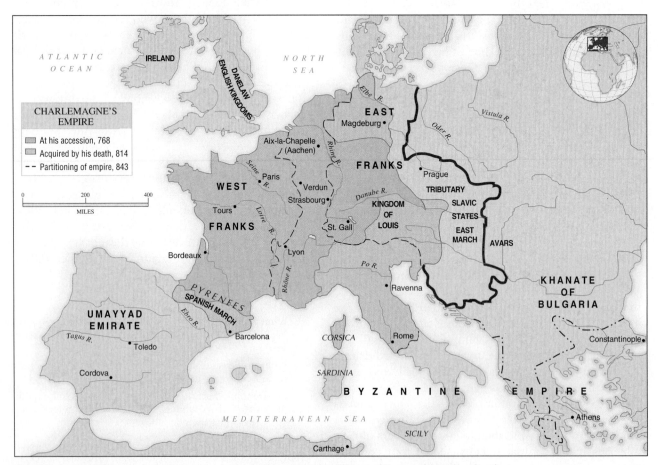

Charlemagne was able to rule the largest empire in the West since the collapse of Rome. Although today the emperor is probably remembered most for his administrative and cultural contributions, he conducted campaigns to enlarge his empire during nearly all of his reign.

north and Muslims from the south, while the Magyars, a new band of Asiatic nomads, conducted destructive raids on central Europe and northern Italy. Christian Europe was hard pressed to repel these warlike newcomers who were more threatening to life and property than the Germanic invaders of the fifth century.

From bases in North Africa, Muslim adventurers, in full command of the sea, raided the coasts of Italy and France. In 827 they began the conquest of Byzantine Sicily and southern Italy. From forts erected in southern France they penetrated far inland to attack merchant caravans even in the Alpine passes. What

New invasions in the ninth and tenth centuries threatened the stability of western Europe in much the same way the Germanic invasions had challenged the Roman Empire. Muslim, Viking, and Magyar attacks posed serious threats to Christian European political stability.

trade still existed between Byzantium and western Europe, except for that undertaken by Venice and several other Italian towns, was now almost totally cut off, and the Mediterranean Sea came under almost complete Muslim control.

The most widespread and destructive raids, however, came from Scandinavia. Swedes, Danes, and Norwegians—collectively referred to as Vikings—began to move south. Overpopulation and a surplus of young men are possible reasons for this expansion, but some scholars suggest that these raiders were defeated war bands expelled from their homeland by the emergence of strong royal power. The Vikings had developed seaworthy ships capable of carrying 100 men, powered by long oars or by sail when the wind was favorable. Viking sailors had also developed expert sailing techniques; without benefit of the compass, they were able to navigate by the stars at night and the sun by day.

The range of Viking expansion reached as far as North America to the west, the Caspian Sea to the east, and the Mediterranean to the south. Between 800 and 850, Ireland was raided repeatedly. Many monasteries, the centers of the flourishing Irish Celtic culture, were destroyed. The Icelandic Norsemen ventured on to Greenland and, later, to North America. Other raiders traveled the rivers of Russia as merchants and soldiers of fortune and founded the nucleus of a Russian state. Danes raided Britain and the shores of Germany, France, and Spain. By 840 they had occupied most of Britain north of the Thames. They devastated northwest France, destroying dozens of abbeys and towns. Unable to fend off the Viking attacks, the weak Carolingian king accepted the local Norse chieftain as duke of a Viking state, later called Normandy. Like Viking settlers elsewhere, these Northmen, or Normans, became Christian converts and eventually played an important role in shaping the future of medieval Europe.

FEUDALISM AND MANORIALISM

■ *What influences did feudalism and manorialism have in shaping European society during the Middle Ages and beyond?*

Europe's response to the invasions of the ninth and tenth centuries was not uniform. By 900 the Viking occupation of England had initiated a strong national reaction, which soon led to the creation of a united British kingdom. Germany in 919 repelled the Magyar threat through the efforts of a new and able line of kings who went on to become powerful European monarchs. But Viking attacks on France accelerated a political fragmentation. Since the monarchy could not hold together its vast territory, small independent landowners surrendered both their lands and their personal freedoms to the many counts, dukes, and other local lords in return for protection and security. The decline of trade further strengthened the position of the landed nobility, whose large estates, or manors, sought to become economically self-sufficient. In addition, the nobility became increasingly dependent on military service provided by a professional force of heavily armed mounted knights, many of whom lived in the houses of their noble retainers in return for their military service.

In most parts of western Europe, where an effective centralized government was entirely absent, personal safety and security became the primary concerns of most individuals. Many historians have used the term *feudalism* to apply to the individual and unique political and social patterns resulting from political decentralization and the resulting attempts to ensure personal security.

Feudalism can be described as a system of rights and duties in which political power was exercised locally by private individuals rather than through the bureaucracy of a centralized state. In general, western European feudalism involved three basic elements: (1) a personal element, called *lordship* or *vassalage*, by which one nobleman, the *vassal*, became the follower of a stronger nobleman, the *lord;* (2) a property element, called the **fief** or *benefice* (usually land), which the vassal received from his lord to enable him to fulfill the obligations of being a vassal; and (3) a governmental element, the private exercise of governmental functions over vassals and fiefs.

Feudal Society

In theory, feudalism was a vast hierarchy. At the top stood the king; all the land in his kingdom in theory belonged to him. He kept large areas for his personal use (royal or crown lands) and, in return for the military service of a specified number of mounted knights, invested the highest nobles—such as dukes and counts (in Britain, earls)—with the remainder. Those nobles, in turn, in order to obtain the services of the required number of mounted warriors owed to the king, parceled out large portions of their fiefs to lesser nobles. This process, called *subinfeudation*, was continued in theory until the lowest in the scale of vassals

---

fief—A grant made to a vassal by a feudal lord in exchange for services. The grant usually consisted of land and the labor of the peasants who were bound to that estate. The income the land provided supported the vassal. Dignities, offices, and money rents were also given in fief.

was reached—the single knight whose fief was just sufficient to support one mounted warrior.

By maintaining the king at the head of this theoretical feudal hierarchy, the justification for monarchy was preserved, even though some feudal kings were little more than figureheads who were less powerful than their own vassals.

Relation of Lord and Vassal: The Contract

Personal bonds between lord and vassal were sometimes formally recognized. In the ceremony known as **homage,** the vassal knelt before his lord, or **suzerain,** and promised to be his "man." In the *oath of fealty* that followed, the vassal swore on the Bible or some other sacred object that he would remain true to his lord. Next, in the ritual of *investiture,* a lance, a glove, or even a clump of dirt was handed to the vassal to signify his jurisdiction over the fief. As his part of the contract, the lord was usually obliged to give his vassal protection and justice. In return, the vassal's primary duty was military service. But in addition, the vassal could be obliged to assist the lord in rendering justice in the lord's court. At certain times, as when the lord was captured and needed to be ransomed, the lord also had the right to demand special money payments, called *aids.*

The lord also had certain rights, called feudal *incidents,* regarding the administration of the fief. These included *wardship*—the right to administer the fief during the minority of a vassal's heir—and forfeiture of the fief if a vassal failed to honor his feudal obligations.

Feudal Warfare

The final authority in the early Middle Ages was force, and the general atmosphere of the era was one of potential violence. Aggressive vassals frequently made war upon their lords. But warfare was also considered the normal occupation of the nobility, for success offered glory and rich rewards. If successful, warfare might increase a noble's territory; and, if they produced nothing else, wars and raids kept nobles active. To die in battle was an appropriate end for a warrior, much preferred to death in restful circumstances.

Medieval society essentially consisted of three classes: nobles, peasants, and the clergy. Each of these

groups had its tasks to perform. The nobles were primarily fighters, belonging to an honored level of society distinct from peasant workers—freemen or serfs. In an age of violence, society obviously accorded prominence to the man with the sword rather than to one with a hoe. The church drew on both the noble and peasant classes for the clergy. Although most higher churchmen were sons of nobles and held land as vassals under the feudal system, the clergy formed a class that was considered separate from the nobility and the peasantry.

The Church and Feudalism

A natural development linked to the decentralization of political power in the early Middle Ages was the involvement of the church in feudalism. The unsettled conditions caused by the Viking and Magyar invasions forced church officials to enter into close relations with the only power able to offer them protection—the feudal nobles in France and Germany. Bishops and abbots often became vassals, receiving fiefs for which they were obligated to provide the usual feudal services. The papacy was also affected; during much of the tenth and early eleventh centuries, the papacy became a political prize sought by Roman nobles.

In spite of its inevitable involvement in politics, the church also sought to influence for the better the behavior of the feudal warrior nobility. In addition to attempting to add Christian virtues to the code of knightly conduct (chivalry), the church sought to impose limitations on feudal warfare. In the eleventh century bishops urged the knights to observe the "Peace of God" and the "Truce of God." The Peace of God banned from the sacraments all those who pillaged sacred places or harmed noncombatants. The Truce of God established "closed seasons" on fighting: from sunset on Wednesday to sunrise on Monday and certain longer periods, such as Lent. These attempts to impose peace, however, were generally unsuccessful.

Chivalry

One of the most interesting legacies of the Middle Ages is its concept of chivalry, a code of conduct that was to govern the behavior of all knights. Early chivalric conduct, emerging during the eleventh century, stressed the warrior virtues that were essential in medieval society: prowess in combat, courage, and loyalty to one's lord and fellow warriors. By the twelfth and thirteenth centuries, many of the rigorous aspects of earlier feudal life had given way to a more peaceful and relaxed lifestyle made possible in a more settled and secure Europe. In a sense, when feudal knights began to occupy themselves with chivalric deeds and

---

homage—A pledge by a vassal to be the lord's "man" (*homo* in Latin means "man"), vowing loyalty and service to his superior. Homage created an unconditional bond between a vassal and his lord.

suzerain—A ruler, or even a state, that exercises political control over a dependent individual or state; a feudal overlord.

gentlemanly pursuits of court life, feudalism itself became a dying institution.

At the height of its development, chivalry was a combination of three elements: warfare, religion, and reverence toward women. It required the knight to fight faithfully for his lord, champion the church, aid the humble, and honor women. Unfortunately, practice often differed from theory. The average knight was more superstitious than religious, and he continued to fight, plunder, and abuse women, especially those of the lower class.

From boyhood, men of the nobility underwent a rigid training for knighthood. At the age of seven, a boy was usually sent to the household of a relative, a friend, or the father's lord. There he became a page, learning the rudiments of manners, hawking, and hunting and undergoing training in the fundamentals of religion. At about 15 or 16, he became a squire and prepared himself seriously for the art of war. He learned to ride a war house with dexterity and to handle a sword, shield, and lance correctly. The squire also waited on his lord and lady at the table and learned music, poetry, and games.

If not already knighted on the battlefield for valor, the squire was usually considered eligible for knighthood at the age of 21. By the twelfth century, the church claimed a role in the ceremony, investing it with impressive symbolism. The future knight took a bath to symbolize purity and washed his weapons before the altar in an all-night vigil, confessing his sins and making a resolution to be a worthy knight. During the solemn Mass that followed, his sword was blessed on the altar by a priest. The climax of the ceremony came when the candidate, kneeling before his lord, received a light blow on the neck or shoulder (the *accolade*). The ceremony was designed to impress upon the knight that he must be virtuous and valiant, loyal to his overlord and his God.

The Lives of the Nobles

Life for the nobles centered around the castle. The earliest of these structures, mere wooden blockhouses, were built in the ninth century. Not until the twelfth and thirteenth centuries were massive castles constructed entirely of stone.

The donjon, or central tower, was the focal point of the castle; it was surrounded by an open space that contained storerooms, workshops, and a chapel. The outside walls of the castle were surrounded by turrets from which arrows, boiling oil, and various missiles might be showered upon attackers. Beyond the wall was the moat, a steep-sided ditch filled with water to deter the enemy. The only entrance to the castle lay across the drawbridge. The portcullis, a heavy iron grating that could be lowered rapidly to protect the gate, was a further barrier against intrusion.

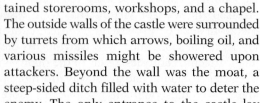

IMAGE

Bodiam Castle, England

Life in the castle was anything but comfortable or ideal. The lord at first dwelt in the donjon, but by the thirteenth century, most had built more spacious quarters. Because the castle was designed for defense, it possessed no large windows, and the rooms were dark and gloomy. The stone walls were bare except for occasional tapestries hung to cut down on drafts and dampness, and a huge fireplace provided the only warmth.

The average noble derived his pleasures primarily from outdoor sports, among which warfare might be included. In peacetime the joust and tournament substituted for actual battle. The joust was a conflict between two armed knights, each equipped with a blunted lance with which one attempted to unseat the other. The tournament was a general melee in which groups of knights attacked each other. Often fierce fighting ensued, with frequent casualties.

The nobles were fond of hunting, and the constant demand for fresh meat afforded a legitimate excuse for galloping over the countryside. Most hunting was done in the nearby forests, but at times an unlucky peasant's crops might be ruined during hunts.

A similar outdoor pastime, which lords, ladies, and even high church dignitaries delighted in, was falconry: hunting with predatory birds. The hawks were reared with great care, and large groups of lords and ladies spent many afternoons eagerly wagering with one another as to whose falcon would bring down the first victim. Nobles often attended Mass with hooded falcons on their wrists.

Indoor amusements included the universally popular diversions of backgammon, dice, and chess. Nights were sometimes enlivened by the entertainment of jesters. At other times, a wandering minstrel entertained his noble hosts in exchange for a bed and a place at the table.

Noble women generally shared the lifestyles of their husbands. Even the nobility had to make the most of life in a crude and often brutal age devoid of many refinements. Like her husband, a medieval woman was expected to devote herself to days of hard work with little time for leisure. Many a noble woman was charged with the administration of the manor and the regulation of its peasants while the lord was otherwise occupied. She may also have presided over the court of the lord's vassals on occasion and generally been charged with the control of the finances for the manor.

The Early Medieval Economy: Manorialism

The economy of the early Middle Ages reflected the localism and self-sufficiency that resulted from the

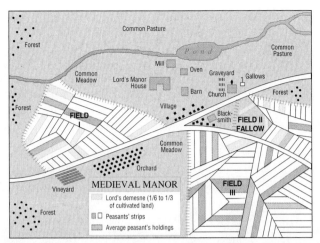

The manor, the self-contained economic unit of early medieval life, operated on a system of reciprocal rights and obligations based on custom. In return for protection, strips of arable land, and the right to use the nonarable common land, the peasant paid dues and worked on the lord's demesne. Under the three-field system, one-third of the land lay fallow so that intensive cultivation did not exhaust the soil.

lack of an effective central government in Europe. The economic and social system based on the manors, the estates held by the nobles, was referred to as *manorialism.*

The manor usually varied in size from one locality to another; a small one might contain only about a dozen households. Since the allotment of land to each family averaged about 30 acres, the smallest manors probably had about 350 acres of land suitable for farming, not counting meadows, woods, wasteland, and the lord's **demesne**—the land reserved for the lord's use alone. A large manor might contain 50 families in a total area of 5000 acres.

The center of the manor was the village, in which the thatched cottages of the peasants were grouped together along one street. Around each cottage was a space large enough for a vegetable patch, chicken yard, haystack, and stable. An important feature of the landscape was the village church, together with the priest's house and the burial ground. The lord's dwelling might be a fortified house or a more modest dwelling.

Distribution of the Land

Every manor contained arable and nonarable land. Part of the arable land was reserved for the lord and was cultivated for him by his serfs; the remainder was held by the villagers. The nonarable land, consisting of meadow, wood, and wasteland, was used in common by the villagers and the lord.

---

desmesne—Part of the land that is owned by the lord. The demesne is the land upon which the lord built his manor house.

From one-sixth to one-third of the arable land was given over to the lord's demesne. The arable land not held in demesne was allotted among the villagers under the open-field system, in which the fields were subdivided into strips. The strips, each containing about an acre, were separated by narrow paths of uncultivated land. The serf's holding was not all in one plot, for all soil throughout the manor was not equally fertile, and an attempt was made to give each of the villagers land of the same quality. Each tenant was really a shareholder in the village community, not only in the open fields but also in the meadow, pasture, wood, and wastelands.

Wooded land was valuable as an area to graze pigs, the most common animal on the manor. Tenants could also gather dead wood in the forest, but cutting down green wood was prohibited unless authorized by the lord.

Medieval Farming Methods

It is difficult to generalize about agricultural methods, because differences in locality, fertility of soil, crop production, and other factors resulted in a variety of farming approaches. Farming as practiced in northwestern Europe was characterized by some common factors. The implements the peasants used were extremely crude; the plow was a cumbersome instrument with heavy wheels, often requiring as many as eight oxen to pull it. (By the twelfth century the use of plow horses had become common.) Other tools included crude harrows, sickles, beetles for breaking up clods, and flails for threshing.

Inadequate methods of farming soon exhausted the soil. The average yield per acre was only 6 to 8 bushels of wheat, one-fourth the modern yield. In classical times farmers had learned that soil planted continually with one crop rapidly deteriorated. As a counteraction, they employed a two-field system: half of the arable land was planted while the other half lay fallow to recover its fertility. Medieval farmers learned that wheat or rye could be planted in the autumn as well as in the spring. As a result, by the ninth century, they were dividing the land into three fields, with one planted in the fall, another in the spring, and the third left lying fallow. This system not only kept more land in production but also required less plowing in any given year.

Both peasant men and women usually had to endure backbreaking labor. While the men usually attended to the daily manual labor of farming, peasant women cooked, cleaned, made clothing, maintained the animals, milked cows, made butter and cheese, brewed ale and beer, and nurtured the gardens. Women assisted the men during planting and

Both peasant men and women toiled in the fields. Here women reap with sickles, while behind them a man binds the sheaves.

harvesting seasons and with any seasonal or special projects endorsed by the lord. The sexes were treated fairly equally on the lower social levels in the Middle Ages—there was not much difference in the demanding lifestyle all had to endure.

Administration of the Manor

Although the lord might live on one of his manors, each manor was usually administered by such officials as the steward, the bailiff, and the reeve. The steward was the general overseer who supervised the business of all his lord's manors and presided over the manorial court. It was the bailiff's duty to supervise the cultivation of the lord's demesne; collect rents, dues, and fines; and inspect the work done by the free peasants (freemen) and the nonfree peasants (serfs). The reeve was the "foreman" of the villagers, chosen by them and representing their interests.

Freemen often lived on the manor, although they constituted only a small portion of its population. Freemen were not subject to the same demands as the serfs. The freeman did not have to work in the lord's fields himself but could send substitutes. Serfs, however, were bound to the manor and could not leave without the lord's consent. Serfdom was a hereditary status; the children of serfs were attached to the soil, just as their parents were.

The lord of the manor was bound by custom to respect certain rights of his serfs. As long as they paid their dues and services, serfs could not be evicted from their hereditary holdings. Although a serf could not appear in court against his lord or a freeman, he could appeal to the manor court against any of his fellows. To the serfs, the manor was the center of their very existence, but to the lord the manor was essentially a source of income and subsistence.

Life of the Peasants

On the manors of the Middle Ages, the margin between starvation and survival was narrow, and the life of the peasant was not easy. Famines were frequent; warfare was a constant threat; and grasshoppers, locusts, caterpillars, and rats repeatedly destroyed the crops. Men, women, and children alike had to toil long hours in the fields.

Home life offered few comforts. The typical peasant dwelling was a cottage with mud walls, clay floor, and thatched roof. The fire burned on a flat hearthstone in the middle of the floor; unless the peasant was rich enough to afford a chimney, the smoke escaped through a hole in the roof. The window openings had no glass and were stuffed with straw in the winter. Furnishings were meager, usually consisting of a table, a kneading trough for dough, a cupboard, and a bed, often either a heap of straw or a box filled with straw, which served the entire family. Pigs and chickens wandered about the cottage continually; the stable was often under the same roof, next to the family quarters.

The peasants, despite their hard, monotonous life, enjoyed a few pleasures. Wrestling was popular, as were cockfighting, a crude type of football, and fighting with quarterstaves, during which contestants stood an excellent chance of getting their heads bashed in. Dancing, singing, and drinking were popular pastimes, especially on the numerous holy days and festivals promoted by the church.

THE REVIVAL OF TRADE AND TOWNS

■ *How did the revival of trade and towns impact the feudal and manorial systems?*

Even though manorialism attempted to secure economic self-sufficiency, an increase in trade and commercial activity in Europe was obvious after the tenth century. The opening of the Mediterranean to European trade was instrumental in increasing trade and commerce. In the eleventh century Normans and Italians broke the Muslim hold on commerce in the eastern Mediterranean, and the First Crusade (see p. 275) revived trade with the Near East. Early in the fourteenth century an all-sea route connected the Mediterranean with northern Europe via the Strait of Gibraltar. The old overland route from northern Italy through the Alpine passes to central Europe was also reopened.

Along the main European trade routes, lords set up fairs, where merchants and goods from Italy and northern Europe met. During the twelfth and thirteenth centuries the fairs of Champagne in France functioned as the major clearinghouse for this international trade.

Factors in the Revival of Towns

The resurgence of trade in Europe was a prime cause of the revival of towns; the towns arose because of trade, but they also stimulated trade by providing greater markets and by producing goods for the merchants to sell. Rivers were important in the development of medieval towns; they were natural highways on which articles of commerce could be easily transported.

Another factor contributing to the rise of towns was population growth. In Britain, for example, the population more than tripled between 1066 and 1350. The reasons for this rapid increase in population are varied. The ending of bloody foreign invasions and, in

some areas, the stabilization of feudal society were contributing factors. More significant was an increase in food production brought about by the cultivation of wastelands, clearing of forests, and draining of marshes. Medieval towns were not large by modern standards. Before 1200 a European town of 20,000 was considered very large, in contrast to such cities as Baghdad, Cairo, and Constantinople—all of which were well over 50,000 in population.

Merchant and Craft Guilds

In each town the merchants and artisans organized themselves into **guilds**. There were two kinds of guilds: merchant and craft. The merchant guild, whose members were the more prosperous and influential of the town's commercial leaders, existed to ensure a monopoly of trade for its members within a given locality. All foreign merchants were supervised closely and made to pay tolls. Disputes among merchants were settled at the guild court according to its

---

guilds—An organization of people who practice a similar occupation and come together to protect their own professional standards and social interests.

A guild master judges the work of two craftsmen, a mason and a carpenter.

own legal code. The guilds also tried to ensure that the customers were not cheated: they checked weights and measures and insisted on a standard quality for goods. To allow only a legitimate profit, the guild fixed a "just price," which was fair to both producer and customer.

With the increase of commerce in the towns, artisans and craftspeople in each of the medieval trades—weaving, cobbling, tanning, and so on—began to organize as early as the eleventh century. The result was the craft guild, which differed from the merchant guild in that membership was limited to artisans in one particular craft.

The craft guild also differed from the merchant guild in its recognition of three distinct classes of workers: apprentices, journeymen, and master craftsmen. The apprentice was a youth who lived at the master's house and was taught the trade thoroughly. Although the apprentice received no wages, all his physical needs were supplied. Apprenticeship commonly lasted seven years. When the apprentice's schooling was finished, the youth became a journeyman. He was then eligible to receive wages and to be hired by a master. About age 23, the journeyman sought admission into the guild as a master. To be accepted he had to prove his ability. Some crafts demanded the production of a "master piece," for example, a pair of shoes that the master shoemakers would find acceptable in every way.

Very few women, usually widows of guild members, were allowed admittance into a craft guild. In Paris in 1300, for instance, there were approximately 200 craft guilds, with nearly 80 including members of both sexes. There were, however, about a dozen guilds restricted to female trades, such as the making of garments, silk, and lace.

In spite of restrictions placed on women's full participation in the guild structure, women played a vital role in the functioning of every craft guild. The home remained the center of production in every medieval town, and the wife and daughters of the master craftsman assisted him in every facet of his profession. Not only did they oversee domestic household duties, they also were relied upon to assist in the production of whatever goods the guildsman produced. They would work with the apprentices and the journeymen; if girls were placed as apprentices, they were usually supervised directly by the wife of the guildsman. The wife of the master craftsman was essential to the operation of business; in most cases, she sold merchandise, kept the financial records, and fed and paid the employees. Because of their experience and skills, such women often took over the shop after their husband's death.

The guild's functions stretched beyond business and politics into charitable and social activities. A guild member who fell into poverty received aid from the guild. The guild also provided financial assistance for the burial expense of its members and looked after their dependents. Members attended social meetings in the guildhall and periodically held processions in honor of their patron saints.

The guilds played an important role in local government. Both artisans and merchants were subject to the feudal lord or bishop in whose domain the city stood. Gradually, the citizens of the towns came to resent their overlord's collecting tolls and dues as though they were serfs. The townspeople demanded the privileges of governing themselves—of making their own laws, administering their own justice, levying their own taxes, and issuing their own coinage. The overlord resisted these demands for self-government, but the towns were able to win their independence in various ways.

THE CHURCH IN THE HIGH MIDDLE AGES: 1000–1348

■ *How did the church and its leaders hold such power and influence over European society?*

During the High Middle Ages the church became more extensively involved in the structure of society and, of necessity, more concerned with temporal affairs. Always a spiritual force in Europe, the church grew in political and economic importance through the assertive and able leadership of the papacy and the bureaucracy that served the popes in Rome. By the middle of the fourteenth century, the church had emerged as a dominant political as well as spiritual force in European life.

Monastic Reform

A religious revival, often called the "medieval reformation," began in the tenth century and grew to exercise strong influence in the twelfth and thirteenth centuries. The first manifestation of the revival was the reformed Benedictine order of monks at Cluny (KLOO-nee), in present-day France, founded in 910. The ultimate goal of these Cluniac reformers was to free the church from secular control and subject it to papal authority.

CASE STUDY

Monks and Warriors

The most aggressive advocate of church reform in the High Middle Ages was Pope Gregory VII (1073–1085), who claimed unprecedented power for the papacy. In 1075 Gregory VII formally prohibited lay investiture (bestowal of the symbols of the churchman's office by a secular official such as a king) and threatened to excommunicate (expel from the Roman Catholic Church) any layman who performed it. The climax to the struggle occurred in Gregory's clash with the German emperor Henry IV (see p. 282).

Late in the eleventh century a second wave of monastic reform produced several new orders of monks, among which were the Cistercians. The Cistercian movement received its greatest inspiration from the efforts of St. Bernard of Clairvaux (klahr-VOH; 1091–1153). This order's abbeys were intentionally located in solitary places, and their strict discipline emphasized fasts and vigils, manual labor, and a vegetarian diet. Their churches contained neither stained glass nor statues, and Bernard denounced the beautification of churches in general as unnecessary distraction from spiritual dedication.

The Papacy's Zenith: Innocent III

Under Innocent III (1198–1216) a new type of administrator-pope emerged, and papal power reached an unprecedented height. Unlike Gregory VII and other earlier reform popes, who were monks, Innocent and other great popes of the late twelfth and thirteenth centuries were lawyers trained in the newly revived and enlarged church, or canon, law.

The unity and power of the church rested not only on a systematized, uniform religious creed but also on the most highly organized and efficient administrative system in western Europe. The church was far ahead of secular states in developing a system of courts and a body of law. Canon law was based on the Scriptures, the writings of the church fathers, and the decrees of church councils and popes. But the papacy's chief weapons to support its authority were spiritual penalties. The most powerful of these was excommunication. A person who

was excommunicated was deprived of the sacraments of the church and in effect condemned to hell should a person die while excommunicated.

Interdict was also a powerful instrument of punishment and control. While excommunication was directed against individuals, interdiction suspended all public worship and withheld most sacraments in the realm of a disobedient subject. Pope Innocent III successfully applied or threatened the interdict 85 times against disobedient kings and princes.

Heresy

Heresy, the belief in doctrines officially condemned by the church, once again became a great concern in the High Middle Ages. Numerous spiritual ideas found new audiences particularly in the newly revived towns, where changing social and spiritual needs went largely ignored by churchmen more traditional in outlook.

For ten years Innocent III tried to combat the growth and popularity of new heretical groups. Unsuccessful, he instigated a crusade against the prosperous and cultured French region of Toulouse, where

Giotto, Pope Innocent III (1198–1216) Approves the Franciscan Rule. *In this predella (part of a series of paintings on the base of an altar) by the Florentine painter Giotto (1266–1337), Innocent III, accompanied by high-ranking churchmen, is shown approving the Franciscan order of monks by giving the approving document to St. Francis (center) and his humble followers. Legend says that the pope had a dream in which he was instructed by God to give approval to the Franciscans.*

the heretics were attacked in 1208 with the approval of the pope. Soon, the original religious motive was lost in a selfish rush to seize the wealth of the accused.

In 1233 a special papal court, the Inquisition, was established to cope with the rising tide of heresy and to bring about religious conformity. Those accused were tried in secret without the aid of legal counsel. Those who confessed and renounced heresy were "reconciled" with the church on performance of penance. Those who did not voluntarily confess could be tortured. If torture failed, the prisoners could be declared heretics and turned over to the secular authorities, usually to be burned at the stake.

Franciscans and Dominicans

As a more positive response to the spread of heresy and the conditions that caused it, Innocent III approved the founding of the Franciscan and Dominican orders of *friars* ("brothers"). Instead of living in remote monasteries, the friars of these orders moved among the people—especially in the quickly growing towns—ministering to their needs, preaching the Gospel, and teaching in the schools.

The Franciscans were founded by St. Francis of Assisi (c. 1182–1226), who rejected riches and emphasized a spiritual message of poverty and Christian simplicity. Love of one's fellow human beings and all God's creatures, even "brother worm," was basic in the Rule of St. Francis.

The second order of friars was founded by St. Dominic (1170–1221), a well-educated Spaniard who had fought the heretics in southern France. There, he decided that to combat the strength and zeal of its opponents, the church should have champions who could preach the Gospel with the dedication of the apostles. The friar-preachers of Dominic's order dedicated themselves to preaching as a means of maintaining the doctrines of the church and of converting heretics.

The enthusiasm and sincerity of the friars in their early years made a profound impact on an age that had grown increasingly critical of the worldliness of the church. But after they took charge of the Inquisition, became professors in the universities, and served in the papal bureaucracy in a variety of capacities, the original simplicity of the spiritual message became lost. Yet their message and zeal had done much to provide the church with moral and intellectual leadership at a time when such leadership was badly needed.

Education and the Origins of Universities

Before the twelfth century, almost all education was under the control and direction of the church. When schools run by monasteries began limiting their admissions to men preparing for church careers, students interested in educations for careers outside the church began to pressure for admittance to schools administered by cathedrals. Although the cathedral schools were still run by churchmen and taught a curriculum centered on religion, these schools steadily expanded their subject offerings to attract students who were pursuing secular careers. Cathedral schools were also more accepting of the new knowledge made available to western Europe by Byzantine and Moslem scholars. Translations of classical works of philosophy (most importantly the works of Aristotle on logic), medicine, and Roman law, accompanied by analyses and commentaries by Islamic scholars, were reintroduced to western Europe. Much of this revived interest can be attributed to an increasing interest in Islamic culture, brought about partially through contacts established during the crusades, and through the revival of international trade. The result was an intellectual revival that invigorated the interest of scholars and students in the cathedral schools.

The development of professional studies in law, medicine, and theology led to the development of universities, which soon eclipsed or expanded the cathedral schools as centers of learning. The word *university* meant a group of persons pursuing a common purpose—a guild of learners, both teachers and students, similar to a craft guild with their masters and apprentices. In the thirteenth century universities had no campuses and little or no money, and the masters taught in rented rooms or religious buildings. If the university was dissatisfied with its treatment by townspeople or the administration, it could move elsewhere. The earliest universities—at Bologna, Paris, and Oxford—were not officially founded, but in time popes or kings granted them and other universities charters of self-government.

Scholasticism

Most medieval scholars did not think of truth as something to be discovered by themselves: They saw it as already existing in the authoritative Christian and a select few non-Christian texts of antiquity. By employing reason (through the use of logic or **dialectic**), scholars of the twelfth and thirteenth centuries attempted to understand and express truth through this process of explanation. Since this task was carried out almost exclusively in the schools, these scholars are known as Scholastics, and the intellectual method they designed is called *Scholasticism*.

Scholasticism reached its highest development in the works of Thomas Aquinas (ah-KWAI-nahs;

---

dialectic—Logical discussion or logical argumentation.

c. 1225–1274). In his *Summa Theologica* ("summation of theology") this brilliant Dominican philosopher and theologian attempted to reconcile the works of Aristotle with church **dogma**—in other words, the truths obvious through natural reason with the truths held through faith. There can be no real contradiction between the two, he argued, since all truth comes ultimately from God. In case of an unresolved contradiction, however, faith won out because of the possibility of human error in reasoning.

Women and Learning

In the early Middle Ages, and especially after the eighth century, the convents of Europe served as centers of learned activity for a very select group of aristocratic and middle-class women who pursued an intellectual life as well as one devoted to faith. But outside the convents, a life devoted to scholarship was almost impossible for a medieval woman; the church taught that a woman should be either a housewife or a virgin in service to her God. Rarely was it possible for a woman to write, compose, or create works of scholarship or literature in such a society.

But intellectual achievement by some exceptional medieval women was possible. One such remarkable example was Hildegard of Bingen (1098–1179), the leader of a community of Benedictine nuns in Germany. Hildegard wrote a mystical work describing her visions, which she began to receive at the age of 42. She was also a skilled composer and the author of a morality play and several scientific works, which cataloged nearly 500 plants, animals, and stones, assessing their medicinal values.

THE CRUSADES

■ *What was the influence of the Crusades on European and world history?*

The Crusades, a series of campaigns that began toward the end of the eleventh century, were a remarkable expression of European self-confidence and expansion in the High Middle Ages. The church was instrumental in beginning these efforts to recapture the Holy Land from Muslim control. But by the conclusion of the crusading era, the church, and the papacy in particular, had suffered a serious loss of prestige, largely because of its actions related to the crusading movement.

DOCUMENT

An Arab-Syrian Discusses the Franks

dogma—A set of beliefs that are accepted as true by a church. A doctrine put forward with authority. From a Greek word meaning "to seem (good)."

For hundreds of years peaceful pilgrims had been traveling from Europe to worship at the sites held to be significant to events described in the New Testament. But during the eleventh century, Christian pilgrims to the Holy Land became especially concerned when the Seljuk Turks, recent and fervent converts to Islam, took over Jerusalem from the more lenient Abbasid Muslims.

In 1095 Pope Urban II proclaimed the First Crusade to establish Christian control of the Holy Land. Preaching at the Council of Clermont in that year, he called on Christians to take up the cross and strive for a cause that promised not merely spiritual rewards but material gain as well. Following Urban's appeal, there was a spontaneous outpouring of religious enthusiasm. The word *crusade* itself is derived from "taking the cross," after the example of Christ.

The Crusading Expeditions

From the end of the eleventh through the thirteenth century, seven major crusades, as well as numerous small expeditions, warred against the Muslims, whom the crusaders called *Saracens*. The First Crusade, composed of feudal nobles from France, parts of Germany, and Norman Italy, marched overland through eastern Europe to Constantinople. Expecting the help of skilled European mercenaries against the Seljuk Turks, the Byzantine emperor Alexius Comnenus was shocked when confronted by a disorderly mob of crusaders and quickly ushered them out of Constantinople to fight the Turks. This First Crusade was the most successful of the seven; with not more than 5000 knights and infantry, it overcame the resistance of the Turks, who were at the time no longer united. It captured Jerusalem and a narrow strip of land stretching from there to Antioch, which became known as the Latin Kingdom of Jerusalem, and over which crusaders and Islamic armies continued to battle until the region was finally retaken by the Muslims in 1291.

IMAGE

Crusaders Besieging a Medieval Castle

The fall of Jerusalem to the Muslims, reinvigorated under the leadership of Salah-al-Din (SAH-lah-ahl-DEEN) or Saladin, the sultan of Egypt and Syria, inspired the Third Crusade in 1189. Its leaders were three of the most famous medieval kings—Frederick Barbarossa of Germany, Richard the Lion-Hearted of England, and Philip Augustus of France. Frederick drowned in Asia Minor, and, after many quarrels with Richard, Philip returned home. Saladin and Richard remained to fight but finally agreed to a three-year truce and free access to Jerusalem for Christian pilgrims.

The Fourth Crusade (1202–1204) was a disaster from both a religious and economic perspective. No kings answered the call of Pope Innocent III for the crusade, and the knights who did participate were unable to pay the Venetians

MAP

The Crusades

the agreed-on transport charges. The Venetians persuaded the crusaders to pay off their debts by capturing the Christian town of Zara on the Adriatic coast, which had long proved a successful rival to Venetian trading interests. Then, in order to eliminate Byzantine commercial competition, the Venetians pressured the crusaders to attack Constantinople itself. After conquering and sacking the great city, the crusaders set up the Latin Empire of Constantinople and forgot about their intentions of recovering the Holy Land.

The thirteenth century produced other crusading failures. The boys and girls participating in the Children's Crusade of 1212 fully expected the waters of the Mediterranean to part and make a path from southern France to the Holy Land, which they would take without fighting; instead, thousands of them were sold into slavery by the merchants of Marseilles. The Seventh Crusade was the last major attempt to regain Jerusalem; the crusading movement ended in 1291 when Acre, the last stronghold of the Christians in the Holy Land, fell to the Muslims.

The Crusader States

Four crusader states, with the kingdom of Jerusalem dominant, were established along the eastern Mediterranean coast as a result of the crusading movement. By the time Jerusalem fell to Saladin in 1187, however, only isolated pockets of Christians remained, surrounded by Muslims. The crusader states were able to cling to survival only through frequent delivery of supplies and manpower from Europe.

The crusader states were defended primarily by three semimonastic military orders: the Templars, or Knights of the Temple, so called because their first headquarters was on the site of the old Temple of Jerusalem; the Hospitalers, or Knights of St. John of Jerusalem, who were founded originally to care for the sick and wounded; and the Teutonic Knights, exclusively a German order. Combining monasticism and militarism, these orders served to protect all pilgrims and to wage perpetual war against the Muslims.

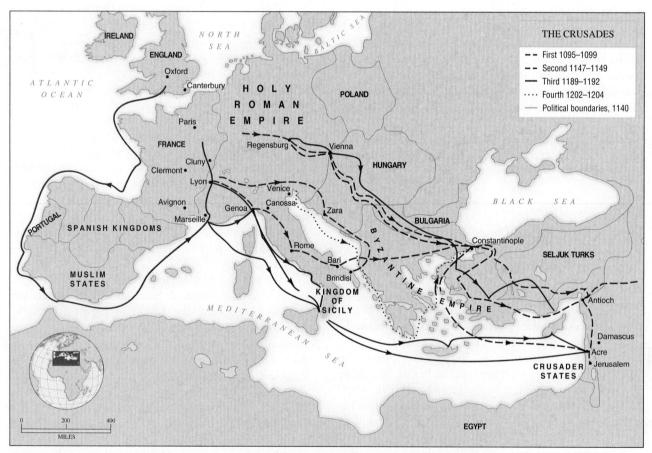

From the eleventh to the thirteenth century, seven major crusades were launched from western Europe for the purpose of taking possession of the Holy Land—portions of the eastern Mediterranean significant to Christians because of their association with the life of Jesus. Although the Crusades eventually failed to annex large amounts of territory for western states, they brought about a broadening perspective and appreciation for Byzantine and Muslim culture on the part of many western Europeans.

Muslim and Christian: Two Contemporary Perspectives

This first selection describes the bloody fall of Jerusalem to the Christians during the First Crusade in 1099, as witnessed by the author, a Frankish knight. He writes with the certainty of religious justification for his cause, and cultural superiority to the Muslim enemy.

In comparison to the Frankish evaluations of their Islamic rivals, the second account, from the Muslim perspective, appears in the writings of a Muslim physician who encountered the crusaders and obviously found their culture not as impressive as his own.

During this siege, we suffered so badly from thirst that we sewed up the skins of oxen and buffaloes, and we used to carry water in them for the distance of nearly six miles. We drank the water from these vessels, although it stank, and what with foul water and barley bread we suffered great distress and affliction every day, for the Saracens used to lie in wait for our men by every spring and pool, where they killed them and cut them to pieces; moreover they used to carry off the beasts into their caves and secret places in the rocks.

At last, when the pagans were defeated, our men took many prisoners, both men and women, in the Temple. They killed whom they chose, and whom they chose they saved alive. After this our men rushed round the whole city, seizing the gold and silver, horses and mules, and houses full of all sorts of goods, and they all came rejoicing and weeping from excess of gladness to worship at the Sepulchre of our Savior Jesus, and there they fulfilled their vows to him. Next morning they went cautiously up on to the Temple roof and attacked the Saracens, both men and women, cutting off their heads with drawn swords. No-one has ever seen or heard of such a slaughter of pagans, for they were burned on pyres like pyramids, and no-one save God alone knows how many there were.

From Rosalind Hill, ed., *Gesta Francorum* (London: Nelson, 1962). Reprinted by permission of Oxford University Press, Oxford.

Glory be to Allah, the creator and author of all things! Anyone who is acquainted with what concerns the Franks can only glorify and sanctify Allah the All-Powerful; for he has seen in them animals who are superior in courage and in zeal for fighting but in nothing else, just as beasts are superior in strength and aggressiveness.

I will report some Frankish characteristics and my . . . surprise as to their intelligence. . . .

Among the curiosities of medicine among the Franks, I will tell how the governor of Al-Mounaitira wrote to my uncle to ask him to send him a doctor who would look after some urgent cases. My uncle chose a Christian doctor named Thabit (?). . . . Thabit replied: "They brought before me a knight with an abscess which had formed in his leg and a woman who was wasting away with a consumptive fever. I applied a little plaster to the knight; his abscess opened and took a turn for the better; the woman I forbade certain food and improved her condition." It was at this point that a Frankish doctor came up and said: "This man is incapable of curing them." Then, turning to the knight, he asked, "Which do you prefer, to live with one leg or die with two?" "I would rather live with one leg," the knight answered. "Bring a stalwart knight," said the Frankish doctor, "and a sharp hatchet." Knight and hatchet soon appeared. I was present at the scene. The doctor stretched the patientís leg on a block of wood and then said to the knight, "Strike off his leg with the hatchet; take it off at one blow." Under my eyes the knight aimed a violent blow at it without cutting through the leg. He aimed another blow at the unfortunate man, as a result of which his marrow came from his leg and the knight died instantly. As for the woman, the doctor examined her and said, "She is a woman in whose head there is a devil who has taken possession of her. Shave off her hair!" His prescription was carried out, and like her fellows, she began once again to eat garlic and mustard. Her consumption became worse. The doctor then said, "It is because the devil has entered her head." Taking a razor, the doctor cut open her head in the shape of a cross and scraped away the skin in the centre so deeply that her very bones were showing. He then rubbed the head with salt. In her turn, the woman died instantly. After having asked them whether my services were still required and obtained an answer in the negative, I came back, having learnt to know what I had formerly been ignorant of about their medicine.

—*Usamah Ibn-Munqidh*

From G. R. Potter, trans., *The Autobiography of Ousama (1095–1188)* (London: George Routledge and Sons, 1929), pp. 172–175, 181–182, in Perry M. Rogers, *Aspects of Western Civilization*, Vol. I, 4th ed. (Prentice Hall, 2000), pp. 311–312.

Questions to Consider

1. What seem to be the most significant obstacles to cultural understanding and tolerance in these two accounts of contact between Christian and Muslim cultures?

2. How might we, as modern analysts of this medieval clash of cultures, misinterpret the sentiments expressed in these two documents? What insights might be gained from a comparison of these two viewpoints?

Significance of the Crusades

Even though the Crusades failed to achieve their permanent objective, they were much more than mere military adventures. Much of the crusading fervor spilled over into the Christian attacks against the Muslims in Spain and the Slavs in eastern Europe. The Crusades crucially weakened the Byzantine Empire and accelerated its fall. Although the early Crusades strengthened the moral leadership of the papacy in Europe, the misadventures of the later Crusades, together with the church's preaching of Crusades against Christian heretics and political opponents, weakened both the crusading ideal and respect for the papacy.

But contact with the East through the crusading movement widened the scope of many Europeans, ended their isolation, and exposed them to a civilization with much within it to be admired. The Crusades did influence the reopening of the eastern Mediterranean to Western commerce, a factor that in itself had an effect on the revival of cities and the emergence of a money economy in the West.

THE DEVELOPMENT OF EUROPEAN STATES: 1000–1348

■ *How successful were European monarchs in establishing authority over their territories?*

The first three centuries of the Later Middle Ages in Europe are often described as the High Middle Ages, since many experts see in this period the full development of the earlier culture of post-Roman Europe. In this era, European monarchies struggled to emerge from the decentralized feudal organization of an earlier time. The church rose to great heights of power and authority. The revival of trade and the rebirth of towns altered the economy of Europe and offered an alternative to manorialism. And this period gave birth to developments in art, architecture, and literature that stand as some of the most significant achievements in European civilization.

The High Middle Ages witnessed the efforts of kings to assert themselves once again as forceful rulers of their lands. As we have seen, feudalism was a system founded on the decentralization of authority; the king was often no more than a figurehead in the feudal order. Now, the monarchs of most European states gradually increased their powers at the expense of their feudal nobility. Through such efforts, several of which took centuries to bear results, national monarchies began to take form on the European continent.

The Capetians and the Beginnings of France

In France, by the beginning of the tenth century, more than 30 great feudal princes were vassals of the king, but they gave him little or no support. When the last Carolingian monarch died in 987, the nobles elected one of their number, Hugh Capet (kah-PAY), count of Paris, as successor. The territory that Hugh Capet (987–996) actually controlled was a small feudal county, the Île-de-France (EEL-duh-FRAHNS), extending from Paris to Orléans. These royal lands were surrounded by many large duchies and counties, such as Flanders, Normandy, Anjou, and Champagne, which were fiercely independent.

The major accomplishment of the first four Capetian (kah-PEE-shi-ahn) kings was their success at keeping the French crown within their own family and at slowly expanding their influence, largely through marriage alliances and the efficiency of the royal courts. With the support of the church, the Capetians cleverly arranged for the election and coronation of their heirs. For 300 years the House of Capet never lacked a male heir.

Philip II Augustus

The first great expansion of the royal domain was the work of Philip II Augustus (1180–1223). Philip's great ambition was to seize from the English kings the vast territory they held in France. Philip took Normandy, Maine, Anjou, and Touraine from the English, and by doing so, he tripled the size of the monarchy's land holdings.

After the brief reign of Philip II's son Louis VIII, France came under the rule of Louis IX (1226–1270), better known as St. Louis. Louis's ideal was to rule justly, and in so doing, he became one of the most beloved kings of France. The king believed himself responsible only to God, who had put him on the throne to lead his people out of a life of sin. Just, sympathetic, and peace-loving, Louis IX convinced his subjects that the monarchy was the most important agency for ensuring their happiness and well-being.

Nation-Building in France

987–996	Reign of Hugh Capet
1108–1137	Reign of Louis VI
1180–1223	Reign of Philip II Augustus
1226–1270	Reign of Louis IX
1285–1314	Reign of Philip IV, the Fair

Height of Capetian Rule Under Philip IV

The reign of Philip IV, known as Philip the Fair (1285–1314), culminated three centuries of Capetian rule. The opposite of his saintly grandfather, Philip was a man of violence and cunning, tireless in his effort to make the monarchy supreme in France. Aware that anti-Semitism was growing in Europe in the wake of the Crusades, he expelled the Jews from France and confiscated their possessions.

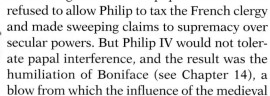

DOCUMENT

Summa de legibus

Philip's need for money also brought him into conflict with the last great medieval pope. Boniface VIII refused to allow Philip to tax the French clergy and made sweeping claims to supremacy over secular powers. But Philip IV would not tolerate papal interference, and the result was the humiliation of Boniface (see Chapter 14), a blow from which the influence of the medieval papacy never recovered. In domestic affairs, the real importance of Philip's reign lay in the king's ability to increase the power and improve the organization of the royal government. Philip's astute civil servants, recruited mainly from the middle class, sought to make the power of the monarch absolute.

Philip enlarged his feudal council to include representatives of the third "estate" or class, the townspeople. This Estates-General of nobles, clergy, and burghers was used to obtain popular support for Philip's policies, including the announcement of new taxes. Philip did not ask the Estates-General's consent for his tax measures; thus, this body did not acquire a role in decisions affecting taxation. By the middle of the fourteenth century, France was well organized, unified in support of a strong monarch, and ready to assert itself as a power on the continent.

England to 1348

Most of England in 1000 was ruled by an Anglo-Saxon monarchy threatened by conquest from the Danish king Canute (ka-NOOT). In 1016 Canute conquered the island and ruled it until his death in 1035, when England returned to an Anglo-Saxon monarchy that was challenged both by the Danes and by William, the duke of Normandy, who claimed the throne on a questionable hereditary right.

William and his army of 5000 men crossed the English Channel to enforce his claim to the throne. In 1066 the duke's mounted knights defeated the English infantry at Hastings, and William became king of England (1066–1087), where he began to introduce the Norman, feudal style of administration. The new king retained some land as his royal domain and granted the remainder as fiefs to royal vassals called *tenants-in-chief*. In return for their fiefs, the tenants-in-chief provided William with a number of knights to serve in his royal army. From all the landholders in England, regardless of whether they were his immediate vassals, William exacted an oath that they would "be faithful to him against all

The Bayeux tapestry, a woolen embroidery on linen, dates from the eleventh century. Over 230 feet long, it depicts the events in the Norman conquest of England in 1066, accompanied by a commentary in Latin and surrounded by a decorative border portraying scenes from fables and everyday life.

other men." Both tenants-in-chief and lesser vassals owed their first allegiance to William.

Henry II

William was succeeded by a number of average or ineffectual rulers, but the monarchy was strengthened by Henry II (1154–1189), the founder of the Plantagenet (plahn-TAH-jehn-et), or Angevin, dynasty. As a result of his inheritance (Normandy and Anjou) and his marriage to Eleanor of Aquitaine (AH-kwi-tayn), the richest heiress in France, Henry's possessions extended from Scotland to the Pyrenees. Henry's great military skill and restless energy were important assets to his reign. He quickly began rebuilding the power of the monarchy in England.

Henry's chief contribution to the development of the English monarchy was to increase the jurisdiction of the royal courts at the expense of the feudal courts. Henry's courts also used the jury system to settle private lawsuits; circuit judges handed down quick decisions based on evidence sworn to by a jury of men selected because they were acquainted with the facts of the case. His judicial reforms stimulated the growth of the common law, one of the most important factors

Henry II's claims to lands in France threatened to absorb the kingdom of France. Note the sizable territory claimed by the English king through his marriage to Eleanor of Aquitaine, once wife of the French king. Though it took hundreds of years, the French eventually gained control of all of the French territories claimed by England.

in unifying the English people; the decisions of the royal justices became the basis for future decisions made in the king's courts and became the law common to all English people.

Thomas à Becket

Although Henry strengthened the royal courts, he was not as successful in regulating the church courts. When he appointed his trusted friend Thomas à Becket archbishop of Canterbury, the king assumed that Becket could easily be persuaded to cooperate, but the new archbishop proved stubbornly independent in upholding the authority of the church courts over the king's. After a number of disagreements in which Becket defended the independence of the English church from royal authority, Henry was reputed to have remarked that he would be relieved if someone would rid England of the troublesome Becket. Responding to this angry remark, four knights went to Canterbury and murdered Becket before the high altar of the cathedral. Popular outrage over this murder destroyed Henry's chances of reducing the power of the church courts.

The Successors of Henry II

Henry's many accomplishments were marred by the mistakes of his successors. Richard the Lion-Hearted (1189–1199) spent only five months of his ten-year reign in Britain, which he regarded as a source of money for his overseas adventures. Richard's successor, his brother John (1199–1216), was an inept and cruel ruler whose unscrupulousness cost him the support of his barons, at the time he needed them most, in his struggles with the two ablest men of the age, Philip II of France and Pope Innocent III. As feudal overlord of John's possessions in France, Philip declared John an unfaithful vassal and his claims to lands in France unwarranted. He also became involved in a struggle with Innocent III that ended in John's complete surrender.

In the meantime, the king alienated the British barons, who rebelled and in 1215 forced him to agree to the Magna Carta, a document that bound the king to observe all feudal rights and privileges. Although in later centuries people looked back on the Magna Carta as one of the most important documents in the history of political freedom, to the English nobility of John's time, the Magna Carta did not appear to break any new constitutional ground. It was essentially a feudal agreement between the barons and the king, the aristocracy and the monarchy. However, two great principles were contained in the charter: The law is above the king, and the king can be compelled by force to obey the law of the land.

A detail of the Carrow Psalter depicts the murder of Thomas à Becket by the knights of Henry II in Canterbury Cathedral. One knight has broken his sword over the archbishop's head.

The Origins of Parliament

The French-speaking Normans commonly used the word *parlement* (from *parler,* "to speak") for the great council. Anglicized as *parliament,* the term was used interchangeably with *great council* and *Curia Regis.*

Nation-Building in England

871–899	Reign of Alfred the Great of Wessex
1016–1035	Reign of Canute
1066	Battle of Hastings
1066–1087	Reign of William the Conqueror
1154–1189	Henry II begins Plantagenet dynasty
1189–1199	Reign of Richard I, the Lion-Hearted
1199–1216	Reign of John I
1215	Magna Carta
1272–1307	Reign of Edward I

Modern historians, however, generally apply the term to the great council only after 1265, when its membership was radically enlarged. Parliament first became truly influential during the reign of Edward I (1272–1307), one of England's most outstanding monarchs. Beginning with the so-called Model Parliament of 1295, Edward followed the pattern of summoning representatives of shires and towns to meetings of the great council. In calling parliaments, Edward had no intention of making any concession to popular government; rather, he hoped to build popular consensus to support his own policies.

Early in the fourteenth century the representatives of the knights and the townsmen, called the Commons, adopted the practice of meeting separately from the lords. This resulted in the division of Parliament into what came to be called the House of Commons and the House of Lords. Parliament, particularly the Commons, soon discovered its power as a major source of revenue for the king. It gradually became the custom for Parliament to exercise this power by withholding its financial grants until the king had redressed grievances, made known by petitions. Parliament also presented petitions to the king with the request that they be recognized as statutes (laws drawn up by the king and his council and confirmed in Parliament). Gradually, Parliament assumed the right to initiate legislation through petition.

Edward I was the first English king with the goal of being master of the whole island of Great Britain—Wales, Scotland, and England. In 1284, after a five-year struggle, English law and administration were imposed on Wales, and numerous attempts were made to conquer the Scots, who continued to offer Edward serious resistance up to the time of his death. By the time of Edward's death in 1307, England was efficiently organized under a strong monarchy and ready to assert itself in the quest for power on the continent.

Spain to 1348

Unification in Spain took a different course from that in either France or England. Customary rivalry between the Christian feudal nobles and royal authority was complicated by another element: religious fervor. Unification of Christian Spain was not thought possible without the expulsion of the Muslims, with their non-Christian religion and culture.

During the long struggle to drive the Muslims from Spain, patriotism blended with fierce religious devotion. This movement became known as the *Reconquista* (ree-kon-KEE-stah)—the reconquest of Spain from Muslim control. As early as the ninth century, northern Spain became committed to a religious effort to drive all Muslims out of territory Christian Spaniards considered theirs. In the early thirteenth century they captured first Cordova and Seville. The conquest of Seville effectively doubled the territory of the Spanish kingdom. From the end of the thirteenth century, when the Reconquista slowed, until the latter part of the fifteenth century, Muslim political control was confined to Granada. Until the fifteenth century, the Christian victors usually allowed their new Muslim subjects to practice their own religion and traditions. Muslim traders and artisans were protected because of their economic value, and Muslim culture—art in particular—influenced Christian designs and preferences.

Disunity in Germany and Italy

When the last Carolingian ruler of the kingdom of the East Franks died in 911, the great German dukes elected the weakest of their number to hold the title of king. But an exceptionally strong ruler inherited the throne in 936—Otto the Great (936–973), duke of Saxony and

Ivory plaque of Christ and the Emperor Otto I (962–968). This ivory carving shows Christ on a throne and in the process of blessing a model of a church presented to him by the German emperor Otto I (left) and a number of saints (right), including St. Peter, who holds his symbolic keys to the kingdom of heaven. The artist was probably influenced by both Carolingian and Byzantine artistic traditions.

founder of the Saxon dynasty of kings. Otto attempted to control the great dukes by appointing his own relatives and favorites as their rulers. Through alliance with the church, he constructed a stronger German monarchy. Otto himself appointed German bishops and abbots, a practice known as lay investiture; since their offices were not hereditary, he expected that their first obedience was to the king.

Otto the Great wanted to establish a German empire, modeled after Roman and Carolingian examples. The conquest and incorporation of the Italian peninsula into that empire were Otto's primary objectives. He proclaimed himself king of Italy, and in 962 he was crowned emperor by the pope. His empire later became known as the Holy Roman Empire.

The Saxon rulers were the most powerful in Europe. They had permanently halted Magyar advances and, by utilizing the German church as an ally, reduced feudal fragmentation in their homeland. They also fostered economic progress. German eastward expansion had begun, and the Alpine passes had been freed from Muslim control and made safe for Italian merchants.

The Salian Emperors

The Saxon kings were succeeded by the Salian dynasty (1024–1125), whose members also tried to establish a centralized monarchy. Under the emperor Henry IV (1056–1106) the monarchy reached the height of its power, but it also experienced a major reverse. The revival of a powerful papacy led to a bitter conflict with Henry, centering on the king's right to appoint church officials who were also his most loyal supporters (lay investiture). This disagreement between state and church culminated in Henry's begging the pope's forgiveness at Canossa in 1077. This conflict, the Investiture Controversy, resulted in the loss of the monarchy's major sources of strength: the loyalty of the German church, now transferred to the papacy; and the support of the great nobles, now openly rebellious and insistent on their "inborn rights."

The second emperor of the new Hohenstaufen (HOH-hen-stahw-fen) dynasty, Frederick I Barbarossa ("Redbeard"), who ruled from 1152 to 1190, also sought to force the great nobles to acknowledge his overlordship. To maintain his hold over Germany, Frederick needed the resources of Italy. But encouraged by the papacy, the cities of northern Italy had joined together in the Lombard League to resist him. Frederick spent about 25 years fighting intermittently in Italy, but the final result was failure: opposition from the popes and the Lombard League was too strong. Frederick did, however, succeed in marrying his son to the heiress of the throne of the kingdom of Naples and Sicily.

The Holy Roman Empire

962	Otto the Great crowned emperor by the pope
1056–1106	Reign of Henry IV
1152–1190	Frederick I Barbarossa begins Hohenstaufen dynasty
1212–1250	Reign of Frederick II

Barbarossa's grandson, Frederick II (1212–1250), was a remarkable individual. Orphaned at an early age, Frederick was brought up as the ward of Innocent III, the most powerful medieval pope. With the pope's support, Frederick was elected emperor in 1215, one year before Innocent's death. Frederick sacrificed Germany in his efforts to unite Italy under his rule. He transferred crown lands and royal rights to the German princes in order to win their support for his Italian wars. Born in Sicily, he remained devoted to the southern part of his empire. He shaped his kingdom there into a vibrant state. Administered by paid officials who were trained at the University of Naples, which he founded for that purpose, his kingdom was the most centralized and efficiently administered in Europe.

After Frederick's death in 1250, the Holy Roman Empire never again achieved the brilliance it had once enjoyed. Later emperors usually did not try to interfere in Italian affairs, and they ceased going to Rome to receive the imperial crown from the pope. In German affairs the emperors no longer even attempted to assert their authority over the increasingly powerful nobles. By the middle of the fourteenth century Germany was hopelessly divided into more than two hundred political units, each striving for separation from the control of the other.

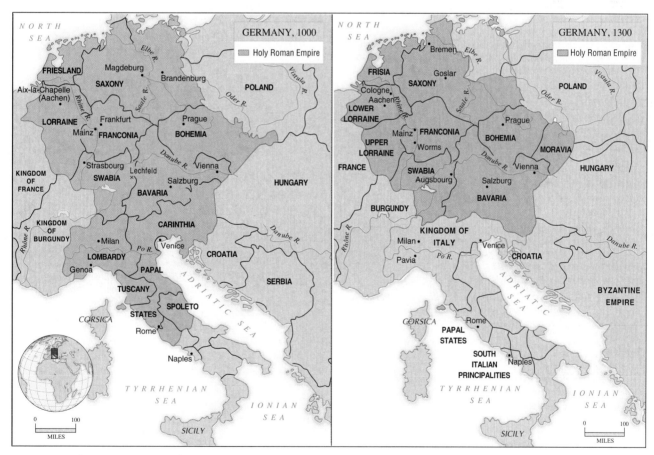

In 962, Otto the Great was crowned as Holy Roman Emperor by the pope. The dreams of recreating a Christian empire to rival the achievements of ancient Rome were never to be realized. Resistance from powerful German nobles and forceful opposition from the northern Italian communes continually frustrated the ambitions of Otto and his successors, so that the Holy Roman Empire was never able to achieve political centralization.

CONCLUSION

This chapter discusses almost one thousand years of European history: from the collapse of Roman political and economic organization, the migrations of new peoples into the old empire, and the growth in influence of a new religion and culture, to the emergence of strong European states under the leadership of ambitious monarchs. Most of the centuries that we call the European Middle Ages were times typified by conservatism and preservation. Political and economic disunity gave rise to institutions that sought to provide protection and security to all segments of society. That quest for security and stability was also evident in early European Christianity, which rejected the cultural heritage of the ancient world in return for a uniform orthodoxy of belief which sought to provide stability in troubled times. But by the eleventh century European self-imposed isolation and the quest for changelessness was challenged on several fronts. Monarchs disrupted the feudal order by setting in motion the drive toward creation of the modern nation-state. The growth of towns and revival of trade brought about new economic and social priorities. The church, once the partner of the state and the unchallenged authority in matters of spirituality and culture, came under increasing examination and challenge. The unique circumstances brought about in Europe by the collapse of Rome, the rise of Christianity, and the Germanic migrations had produced a society unlike any other in world history—one that would emerge by the fourteenth century as vibrant, creative, aggressive, and about to take a more active part in events on a world stage.

Suggestions for Web Browsing

You can obtain more information about topics included in this chapter at the websites listed below. See also the companion website that accompanies this text, http://www.ablongman.com/brummett, which contains an online study guide and additional resources.

Medieval Studies
http://labyrinth.georgetown.edu/

The Labyrinth project at Georgetown University offers numerous links categorized by national cultures and by artistic genre.

Women in the Middle Ages
http://info-center.ccit.arizona.edu/~ws/ws200/fall97/grp7/grp7.htm

An excellent site for examining the many activities and responsibilities of medieval women, from peasants to nobility.

Internet Medieval Sourcebook
http://www.fordham.edu/halsall/sbook.html

Extremely helpful site containing original course materials from medieval authors and secondary sources dealing with a large variety of medieval subjects.

Middle Ages
http://www.learner.org/exhibits/middleages/

This site, under the direction of the Annenberg/CBS Project, features information and exhibits illustrating what daily life was really like during the Middle Ages.

Medieval Women
http://labyrinth.georgetown.edu/display.cfm?Action=View&Category=Women

Site details the individual lives and works of medieval women, including Hildegard of Bingen; women rulers and creators; and the impact of the Crusades on women, in addition to numerous general resources.

Women Writers of the Middle Ages
http://lib.rochester.edu/camelot/womenbib.htm

Site offers bibliographies of primary and secondary sources by and about medieval women writers.

World of the Vikings
http://www.worldofthevikings.com/

This well-indexed site provides links to almost everything there is to know about these medieval seafarers—their everyday life, their travels, their influence.

Literature and Film

An excellent new edition of the Beowulf epic is Seamus Heaney, ed., *Beowulf: A New Verse Translation* (W. W. Norton, 2001). Outstanding video presentations on the Middle Ages are *Charlemagne* (2000; 5 tapes, Acorn Media); *Landmarks of Western Art: The Medieval World*, Vol. I (Kultur Video, 1999); *The Vikings* (Nova, 2000); *Just the Facts—The Middle Ages* (Goldhil Home Media, 2001); *Music of the Middle Ages* (Timeless Multimedia, 1994); *Sienna: Chronicle of a Medieval Commune* (Home Vision Entertainment, 2000); *Living in the Past: Life in Medieval Times* (Kultur Video, 2000); and *Medieval Warfare* (2000; 3 tapes, Kultur Video). An award-winning feature film set in France during this period is *The Return of Martin Guerre* (Nelson Entertainment, 1982).

Suggestions for Reading

Three excellent surveys of the early Middle Ages are Robert Bartlett, *The Making of Europe: Conquest, Colonization, and Cultural Change, 950–1350* (Princeton University Press, 1993); Rosamond McKitterick, ed., *The Early Middle Ages: Europe 400–1000* (Oxford University Press, 2001); and Richard W. Southern, *The Making of the Middle Ages* (Yale University Press, 1992). For economic and social history, see Werner Roesener, *Peasants in the Middle Ages* (Polity Press, 1996) and Frances Gies and Joseph Gies, *Women in the Middle Ages* (Perennial, 1991), *Life in a Medieval Village* (HarperPerennial, 1991), and *Marriage and Family in the Middle Ages* (HarperPerennial, 1989). For the history of the church, see Peter Brown et al., *The Rise of Western Christendom*, 2nd ed. (Blackwell, 2003), and Jaroslav Pelikan, *The Growth of Medieval Theology*, Vol. 3: The Christian Tradition (University of Chicago Press, 1978), and Michael Haren,

Medieval Thought (Dublin University Press, 1992). On the Crusades, see Jonathan Riley-Smith, ed., *The Oxford History of the Crusades* (Oxford University Press, 1997), and Malcolm Billings, *The Cross and the Crescent* (Sterling, 1987). John Burrow, *The Ages of Man: A Study in Medieval Writing and Thought* (Oxford University Press, 1989) is an outstanding review of medieval literature.

Culture, Power, and Trade in the Era of Asian Hegemony, 220–1350

300

c. 300 Yamato clan emerges in central Japan

320–515 Gupta dynasty in India

380s Buddhism adopted in Korea

400

439–534 Northern Wei dynasty in China

500

515 Huna seize northwestern India

600

606–647 Reign of Harsha in north India

618–907 Tang dynasty in China

676 Tang driven out of Korea; Silla unifies Korea

700

710–784 Nara period in Japan

755–763 An Lushan Rebellion in China

788–820 Hindu philosopher Shankara

794–1181 Heian period in Japan

900

960–1279 Song dynasty in China

c. 978–1016 Murasaki Shikibu, writer of *The Tale of Genji*

1100

1130–1200 Zhu Xi, Neo-Confucian scholar in China

1185 Minamoto clan establishes Kamakura Shogunate in Japan

1200

1206 Beginning of Delhi Sultanate in India; Chinggis Khan launches invasions that create Mongol Empire

1279–1368 Yuan dynasty in China

Asia served as an incubator and transmitter of cultures and religions with global reach from 220 to 1350. As empires consolidated and expanded their boundaries, trade and commerce accompanied cultural diffusion. Human cultures had long migrated globally, but during this long millennium, the pace of international contacts accelerated. Religions, philosophies, and arts deepened their roots in areas that had spawned them, and at the same time, new ideas spread throughout the region.

The first half millennium was, in some ways, Asia's Buddhist Age. In South Asia, Hinduism, and in East Asia, Daoism and Confucianism as well as indigenous religions continued to play important roles. But a Buddhist traveler from East Asia would find co-religionists in lands with remarkably distinct cultures. Buddhism was spread by both missionary activity and commercial activity along the Silk Roads. The second half of the millennium was likewise influenced by a global religion—Islam. South and Southeast Asian rulers either adopted Islam or resisted it, and power and trade networks were influenced by Islamic missionary and commercial activities. China and Northeast Asia felt the impact of nomadic cultures throughout the millennium, and in the twelfth and thirteenth centuries much of East and Central Asia was integrated into a trade and power network controlled by originally nomadic Mongols. Disease—bubonic plague—took advantage of these networks to spread the hand of death throughout Eurasia in the mid-fourteenth century, and ironically, fatally weakened the Mongols, whose dominance in China created fourteenth-century globalism. While Asian power and culture were in many ways hegemonic until that time and Asia would continue to grow and dominate world trade until the eighteenth century, the door was open to the rise of new sites of power, particularly in Europe, during the next few hundred years.

Each Asian civilization produced significant contributions to the world's common culture. India made remarkable advances in mathematics, medicine, chemistry, textile production, and literature, and Buddhism continued its dramatic spread to East and Southeast Asia. China excelled in political organization, scholarship, and the arts, and at the same time produced such revolutionary technical inventions as printing, gunpowder, and the mariner's compass. Maritime trade flourished as Arab, Jewish, and Indian traders crisscrossed the Indian Ocean to the west of the subcontinent, while Indian and Southeast Asian traders plied the waters to the east as far as China and Japan.

Growth in the old Asian centers led naturally toward outward cultural diffusion and a varied exchange of goods, philosophies, literatures, and fashions with bordering civilizations. In Southeast Asia these arose from increasing contacts with India and China through trade, missionary efforts, colonizing, and conquest. First Korea, and then Japan, imported cultural bases from China. Similarly, nomads of Central Asia—Turks, Uighurs (WEE-ghers), Mongols, and numerous other steppe peoples—engaged in a vigorous exchange with China and India (often assimilating the cultural patterns of those civilizations) as merchants, subjects, or conquerors. The conquest of China by the Mongols during the thirteenth and fourteenth centuries facilitated the passing of those influences to the peoples of the Middle East and Europe. Nor was the diffusion of cultural influences and material culture a one-way process. The great cultural centers of Persia, India, and China adapted dress styles, military tactics, literature, and the hardy Mongol horse from the Central Asians.

INDIA IN THE CLASSICAL AND MEDIEVAL ERAS

■ *What factors contributed to a diversity of religions and cultures in classical and medieval India?*

The Classical Age

The political fragmentation of India during the 500 years from 184 B.C.E. to 320 C.E. permitted the spread of new Indian religions and the introduction of ideas and technologies from east and west of India. But it was not until the reunification of India's north under the Guptas that the classical age of Hindu culture emerged. India's cultural renaissance took root in the Gupta dynasty (320–500) and attempted to recapture the territorial and cultural grandeur of the Mauryas (MOW-ree-yahs). Its monarchs gained control over northern India while fostering traditional religions, Sanskrit literature, and indigenous art. Hindu and Buddhist culture also spread widely throughout Southeast Asia in this period.

The Gupta state began its rise in 320 with the accession to power of Chandra Gupta I (not related to his earlier Mauryan namesake). His son Samudra Gupta (r. 335–375) and grandson Chandra Gupta II (r. 375–415) were successful conquerors, extending the boundaries of an original petty state in Maghada (mah-GAH-dah) until it included most of northern India, from the Himalayas to the Narmada River and east to west from sea to sea. Within this domain the Gupta monarchs developed a political structure along ancient Mauryan lines, with provincial governors, district officials, state-controlled industries, and an imperial secret service. This centralized system, however, was effective only on royal lands, which were much less extensive than in Mauryan times. With a smaller bureaucracy, the Gupta rulers depended on local authorities and communal institutions. Peasants were obligated to pay as taxes to the state one-fourth of their harvest, one-fiftieth of their cattle and gold, one-sixth of their wealth in meat, fruit, honey and trees, and a day of labor per month for road repair or irrigation maintenance. Despite such high taxes, Indian farmers appeared in reports by foreign visitors to successfully produce an abundance of food. Artisans were organized in guilds which negotiated relationships with state and religious institutions. Military forces were raised by feudal levy.

Gupta India

320	Accession of Chandra Gupta I
c. 335–375	Reign of Samudra Gupta
c. 376–414	Reign of Chandra Gupta II
515	Huna (Huns) seize northwest India; Gupta Empire collapses

Marriage alliances aided the Guptas' rise to power. Chandra Gupta I married a princess from the powerful Licchavi (leek-CHAH-vee) clan; his coins show the king and his queen, Kumaradevi (koo-MAH-rah-DEH-vee), on one side and a lion with his queen's clan name on the other. Chandra Gupta II gave his daughter, Prabhavati (prah-bah-VAH-tee) Gupta, in marriage to Rudrasena II (roo-DRAH-seh-nah), king of the powerful Vakataka dynasty in central India. Rudrasena died after a short reign, and his wife then took control of his kingdom for about 20 years as regent for her minor sons. The two kingdoms maintained close ties even after her death.

Peace and stable government under the later Guptas increased agricultural productivity and foreign trade. Commerce with Rome brought a great influx of gold and silver as well as Arabian horses into the Gupta Empire in exchange for Indian textiles, jewels, spices, perfumes, and wood. In fact, Rome's net deficit in gold exports led to the weakening of its economy. Indian traders were also active in Southeast Asia, particularly in Burma, Vietnam, and Cambodia, where they brought not only new products but also Buddhist culture. India's resulting prosperity was reflected in great public and religious buildings and in the luxuries of the elite, particularly at the Gupta court.

Although the Gupta rulers generally favored Hinduism, they practiced religious pluralism, patronizing and building temples for Hindus, Buddhists, and Jains. The Brahmans provided the Guptas with religious legitimacy, and the Guptas rewarded them with significant grants of land. Hinduism dominated the subcontinent. The Hindu revival of this period brought a great upsurge of devotion to Vishnu, Shiva, and Durga. This religious fervor was reflected in a series of religious books, the *Puranas*, which emphasized the compassion of the personal gods. The *Puranas* are a collection of myths, philosophical dialogues, ritual prescriptions, and dynastic genealogies gathered in the third and fourth centuries. The tales of the gods were popular. Among their legends, for example, is a recounting of the deeds of the goddess Durga and her fight against the buffalo demon. By promoting the devotional Hinduism reflected in these tales, the Gupta monarchs gained great favor among all classes of their subjects.

The *Bhagavad-Gita* (BAH-gah-vahd-GHEE-tah; *Song of the Blessed One*), written during this time, assured Hindus that salvation was possible, regardless of one's station in life. **Bhakti** (BAHK-tee; "devotion") was introduced as a path to salvation. Revealing himself as the Divine Savior Vishnu, the *Gita*'s protagonist Krishna explained: "Those who revere me with devotion (bhakti), they are in me and I too am in them. . . . Even those who may be of base origin, women, men of the artisan caste, and serfs, too."[1] Though inequality remained embedded in the status system that differentiated one's religious duties by caste, Hindu salvation was, in the *Bhagavad-Gita*, made accessible to all.

Much of our knowledge of Gupta society comes from the journal of a Chinese Buddhist monk, Faxian (fah-SHEN), who traveled in India for 14 years at the opening of the fifth century. Despite the Guptas' preference for Hinduism, thousands of Buddhist monks and nuns practiced their religion. Buddhist stupas (funerary mounds) dotted the landscape. In the fourth century, only Sri Lanka was more Buddhist than India. Buddhism was an important bridge linking China and India and stimulating commerce in both East and Southeast Asia.

Faxian was primarily interested in Buddhism in India, but he also commented on social customs. He reported the people to be happy, relatively free of government oppression, and inclined toward courtesy and charity. He mentions the caste system and its associations with purity and impurity, including "untouchability," the social isolation of a lowest class that is doomed to menial labor. Of course, travelers' accounts never tell the entire story and must be read with some caution. Each traveler sees bits and pieces of the society he or she is visiting and looks at the society in ways that may be very different from those of other travelers of different

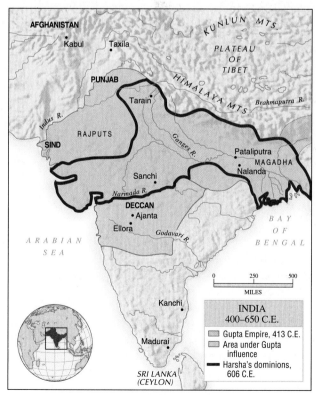

The Guptas extended their rule over northern and central India but never managed to control the southern peninsula.

---

bhakti—Hindu devotion.

Document   Faxian: A Chinese Buddhist Monk in Gupta India

Faxian is an important source on India around 400 C.E. A Buddhist monk, he left China as a pilgrim to India in search of spiritual knowledge and Buddhist texts; he was away from home for 14 years. Faxian reached northern India on foot, via the grueling route over the mountains from China. When he returned home, he translated various Indian works and wrote the account of his travels. Faxian's story and long arduous journey illustrate both the effects of the spread of Buddhism and the draw that the Indian heartland had on Buddhists abroad. Here he describes Pataliputra (modern Patna), where Ashoka once reigned. The festival illustrates the amalgamation of Buddhist and Hindu ritual and suggests the joyous nature of some popular urban religious celebrations. Faxian's account of hospitals gives us some insight into the quality of medical care available free to the poor.

By the side of the tower of King Ashoka is built a monastery belonging to the Great Vehicle [Mahayana Buddhism], very imposing and elegant. There is also a temple belonging to the Little Vehicle [Theravada Buddhism]. Together they contain about 600 or 700 priests; their behavior is decorous and orderly. . . . Of all the kingdoms in Mid-India, the towns of this country are especially large. The people are rich and prosperous; they practice virtue and justice. Every year on the eighth day of the second month, there is a procession of images. On this occasion, they construct a four-wheeled cart, and erect upon it a tower of five stages, composed of bamboos lashed together, the whole being supported by a center post resembling a large spear with three points, in height twenty-two feet or more. So it looks like a pagoda. They then cover it with fine white linen, which they afterward paint with gaudy colors. Having made figures of the *devas* [gods], and decorated them with gold, silver, and glass, they place them under canopies of embroidered silk. Then at the four corners [of the vehicle] they construct niches in which they place figures of Buddha in a sitting posture, with a Bodhisattva [a Buddha in the making] standing in attendance. There are perhaps twenty cars thus prepared and differently decorated. During the day of the procession both priests and laymen assemble in great numbers. There are games and music, whilst they offer flowers and incense.... Then all night long they burn lamps, indulge in games and music, and make religious offerings. Such is the custom of all those who assemble on this occasion from the different countries round about. The nobles and householders of this country have founded hospitals within the city, to which the poor of all countries, the destitute, cripples, and the diseased may repair. They receive every kind of requisite help gratuitously. Physicians inspect their diseases, and according to their cases order them food and drink, medicine or decoctions, everything in fact that may contribute to their ease. When cured they depart at their convenience.

Questions to Consider

1. What does this story suggest about the institutionalization of Buddhism and its integration into city life in India?
2. Why might the people in Patna place figures of the Hindu gods and of the Buddha on the same float or cart used in a festival procession?

From Samuel Beal, ed., *Buddhist Records of the Western World*, translated from the Chinese of Hiuen Tsiang (629) (Delhi: Oriental Books, 1969), pp. lvi–lvii.

class, gender, upbringing, or motive for travel. Nonetheless, travelers like Faxian, who wrote down their observations in some detail, often provide us with the clearest glimpse we can obtain of past societies.

Gupta Art and Literature

Indian art of the Gupta period depicts a golden age of classical brilliance, combining stability and serenity with an exuberant love of life. The Gupta artistic spirit is well expressed in the 28 monasteries and temples at Ajanta, hewn out of a solid rock cliff and portraying in their wall frescoes not only the life of Buddha but also life in general: lovers embracing, beds of colorful flowers, musicians, and dancers. These sculptures reveal the beauty of the human form and provide us with a sense of Indian culture beyond that found in theological texts. The various incarnations of Vishnu and the deeds of the goddess Durga were also common subjects of Gupta sculpture. Hundreds of workers and artisans were employed in this work of building and

IMAGE

Classical
Indian
Sculpture

The Gupta era is justly renowned for its sculpture. This fifth-century terra-cotta piece shows the young Lord Krishna fighting the horse demon. According to Hindu religious tradition, Krishna, even as a baby, was formidably powerful; he battled a whole assortment of demons before reaching adolescence.

of many Eurasian peoples in this era— the Arabian story of *Layla and Majnun*, for example.

Gupta Scholarship and Science

The Gupta era brought a great stimulus to learning. Brahman traditions were revitalized, and Buddhist centers, which had spread after the Mauryan period, were given new support. The foremost Indian university, founded in the fifth century, was the Buddhist university at Nalanda in northeastern India. Accomplishments in science were no less remarkable than those in art, literature, scholarship, and philosophy. The university had a diverse population, with students from China and Southeast Asia also attending classes. The most famous Gupta scientist was the astronomer-mathematician Aryabhatta (AH-ree-ah-BAHT-tah), who lived in the fifth century. He elaborated (in verse) on quadratic equations, solstices, and equinoxes, along with the spherical shape of the earth and its rotation. Other Hindu mathematicians of this period popularized the use of a special sign for zero, passing it on later to the Arabs. Mathematical achievements were matched by those in medicine. Hindu physicians sterilized wounds, prepared for surgery by fumigation, performed cesarean operations, set bones, and were skilled in plastic surgery. They used drugs then unknown in the West, such as chaulmoogra oil for leprosy, a treatment still used during the first half of the twentieth century. With these accomplishments in pure science came many effective practical applications by Gupta craftsmen, who made soap, cement, superior dyes, and the finest tempered steel in the world.

decorating temples that might, as Faxian points out, house hundreds of monks.

The Gupta era was also a golden age for literature, written in Sanskrit, the ancient language of the Brahmans. Authors supported by royal patronage poured forth a wealth of sacred, philosophical, and dramatic works in prose and poetry, including fables, fairy tales, and adventure stories featuring a wide range of characters—thieves, courtesans, hypocritical monks, and strange beasts. The *Panchatantra* is a manual of political wisdom employing animal tales to advise the king on proper rule.

The most renowned literary figure of the Gupta era was India's greatest poet and dramatist, Kalidasa, who wrote at the court of Chandra Gupta II. His best-known work in the West is *Shakuntala,* a great drama of lovers separated by adversity for many years and then by chance reunited. This universal theme of separated lovers is found in the epic stories

DOCUMENT
Tales of Ten Princes

India is famous for its rock carved temples. Kings or affluent families often financed such temples (both Hindu and Buddhist) with spectacular carvings as acts of devotion. This is the Kailasanatha Temple at Ellora, dedicated to the Hindu god Shiva and dating to approximately 765 C.E.

New Political and Religious Orders

Gupta hegemony began to collapse in the second half of the fifth century with attempted invasions by the Huna (called Xiongnu (SHONG-noo) in China and Huns in Europe) from the north. Although the Guptas held out for several decades, they ruled only in parts of northern India after 497. In 515 the Huna—who had already menaced the Roman Empire and successfully invaded Persia—seized first northwestern India and then the Ganges plain. Huna rule did not endure, but it led to several smaller kingdoms breaking free of the Gupta and prompted the migration of more Central Asian tribesmen into India. This resulted in a period in which India was generally divided into regional kingdoms rather than more expansive empires like that of the Guptas. The Central Asian tribesmen also intermarried with local populations to produce a class of fighting aristocrats known as *Rajputs* (RAHJ-poots). These fierce warriors carved out kingdoms among the Hindu states of northern India. Extensive intermarriage was common in frontier areas, blurring the boundaries between ethnolinguistic groups and even creating new identities.

In the seventh century the unity of northern India was revived for a short while by Harsha (r. 606–647), a strong leader. In 6 years he reconquered much of what had been the Gupta Empire, restoring order and partially reviving learning. However, Harsha failed in his bid to conquer the Deccan, and no ruler would do so until 1206. A tolerant leader, he was a strong supporter of Buddhism; during his reign Hinduism also grew in popularity. Harsha's support for Buddhism made possible several successful visits by Chinese ambassadors. In 643 the large delegation sent by the Tang court was received by Harsha who held a Buddhist ceremony in their honor. This diplomatic mission visited Buddhist sites and brought along an artisan to copy Buddhist architecture and sculpture. In addition to making spiritual overtures, the Chinese mission had a key commercial success—acquiring sugar-making technology from the South Asians.

When Harsha died in 647, regional kingdoms again prevailed. The period of the regional kingdoms was not a sterile one. In this era the great Hindu philosopher Shankara (c. 788–820) brilliantly argued a mystical philosophy based on the *Upanishads;* literature, especially in Tamil in the south, flourished; and Brahmans and

Buddhist monks continued to carry their religious and cultural ideas to Southeast Asia and China. Their crucial role in the "Indianization" of Southeast Asia is reflected in the great temples there. It is also reflected in Chinese sources that note 162 visits of Buddhist monks from the fifth to the eighth centuries.[2]

The Chola kingdom on India's southeastern coast played a significant role in the commercial and cultural exchange with Southeast Asia as well. The Chola had long lived in the Tamil south but were apparently a tributary lineage to the more powerful Pallavar dynasty. They began to challenge the Pallavars in the late ninth century and emerged as a ruling force in their own right within a century. Chola rulers in the eleventh century exchanged embassies with China, Sumatra, Malaya, and Cambodia; Chola fleets took Sri Lanka (Ceylon) and challenged the power of the Southeast Asian kingdom of Srivijaya (SHREE-vee-JAH-yah). When a Chola king conquered Bengal, he ordered the defeated princes to carry the holy water of the Ganges River to his new capital to celebrate his victory. Through this ceremony, he not only forced his enemies to perform a ritual act of submission but enhanced his legitimacy in Hindu terms by linking his own lands to those watered by the sacred Ganges.

Muslims in India

The prophet Muhammad founded an Arab Muslim state in Arabia in the seventh century (see Chapter 7); soon the Arab conquerors had defeated the Sassanids in Persia, and Muslim armies arrived at the boundaries of the Indian subcontinent. In 712 an Arab force seized Sind, a coastal outpost in northwestern India. During the next 300 years, Arabic-speaking Muslims established trading posts throughout the Indian Ocean region. Although the existence of the Muslim kingdom at Sind did not serve as a springboard for Arab Muslim penetration of India, Muslim traders did facilitate the integration of India into an Islamic world system. This system was a trading network that did not require participants to be Muslim but did take advantage of Muslim political expansion. The significant expansion of Muslim political control in India 300 years later, beginning in 997, had Turkish, Persian, and Afghan rather than Arabian roots.

Armies of Central Asian and Turkish slaves, originally purchased to support Muslim rulers at Baghdad, began to form independent kingdoms in Afghanistan and Persia. One of them, a kingdom ruled by Mahmud of Ghazni (MAH-mood, GAHZ-nee), launched a series of campaigns into northwestern India. He gained a reputation as a destroyer for his 17 campaigns over the course of 25 years that devastated northern India. One notable episode during these campaigns was Mahmud's destruction of Shiva's large temple complex

DOCUMENT
Al-Biruni on
India's Hindus

in Gujarat and the slaughter of its defenders who, according to legend, numbered 50,000 men. These campaigns of pillage rather than conquest made Mahmud a name that to the present day evokes powerful emotions among Hindus.

Mahmud is also known for the famous scholars at his court, among them Firdawsi (feer-DOW-see; 940–1020), who wrote the great epic Persian poem the *Shahnamah* (SHAH-NAH-mah), and al-Biruni (b. 973), author of a major history of India. Al-Biruni wrote that it was the caste system that prevented Muslims and Hindus from ever reaching any understanding because the Muslims considered "all men as equal, except in piety."[3] Of course, al-Biruni was minimizing the hierarchies that existed in Muslim society. But the caste system did indeed serve as a significant barrier between Hindus and Muslims (although, over time, Hindus and Muslims intermarried and some Muslim groups adapted castelike social divisions).

Firdawsi's career is an illustration of the vagaries of life at court. He spent many years writing the 60,000 verses of the *Shahnamah* but was then disappointed when the king did not reward him properly. So he penned a savage satire of Mahmud and fled to his home region of Khurasan in Persia. Legend has it that Mahmud later realized the value of Firdawsi's work and sent a large reward after him, but by the time it arrived, the poet was already dead.

The date 1206 stands out as the next significant marker of Muslim conquest in India. In the same year that the Mongol Chinggis (Genghis) Khan mobilized his campaigns of conquest and expansion in Central Asia, the general Qutb ud-Din Aibak (KOOT-buh ood-DIN ai-BAHK) seized power as sultan at Delhi. Qutb ud-Din had been a commander in the army of the Afghan ruler Muhammad of Ghur, who seized Delhi in 1193 from the Rajputs, Hindus who mounted a staunch defense in the northwest. Qutb ud-Din founded a new dynasty in 1206 that lasted for 320 years. He was followed on the throne by his son-in-law, Iltutmish (il-TOOT-mish; r. 1211–1236), and by the latter's daughter, Raziyya (ra-ZEE-yah; r. 1236–1240). According to the Muslim chronicler Minhaju-s Siraj, Sultana Raziyya was "wise, just and generous. . . . She was endowed with all the qualities befitting a king, but she was not born of the right sex, so in the estimation of men all these virtues were worthless."[4] Raziyya's father Iltutmish had himself been formally consecrated in 1229 as sultan of Delhi by a representative of the Abbasid sultan in Baghdad. Even though the Abbasid sultan wielded little power at this time, he was still a source of Islamic legitimacy for South Asian Muslim rulers. Less than 30 years later, the Abbasid caliphate would fall prey to the Mongol descendants of Chinggis Khan.

At the peak of its power in the thirteenth century, the Delhi Sultanate held not only the north but also part of the Deccan Plateau in the south. When Sultan

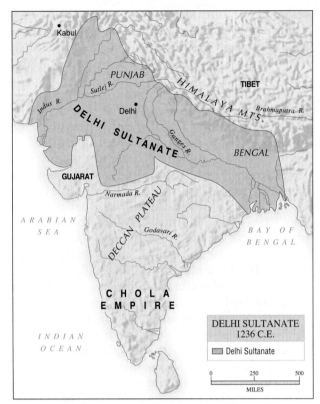

Muslim rulers established a sultanate in northern India, and Delhi flourished as its imperial capital.

Ala ud-Din (r. 1296–1316) invaded the Deccan, he called himself the "Second Alexander," a title that was emblazoned on his coins. The Delhi Sultanate also managed to ward off the Mongol invaders who seized the Punjab (poon-JAHB), thus avoiding the fate of Persia and Iraq. Delhi, under the sultanate, emerged as a great imperial capital. The Delhi sultans were patrons of the arts, builders of splendid monuments, and proponents of philosophy. The Tughluks (TOOG-looks), a Muslim dynasty who ruled Delhi for most of the fourteenth century, held an uneasy rule over the majority Hindu populace as well as over rival Muslim rulers. Ibn Battuta (IH-buhn bah-TOO-tah), the famed Muslim world traveler from north Africa, served the Tughluk court as its chief judge, observing it closely and leaving a detailed historical record. By the middle of the fourteenth century, the Tughluks had lost control of the south (upon the rise of the Hindu Vijayangar (vee-JAH-yahn-gahr) Empire in 1336) and the northeast (Sufi Muslim leaders there declared their independence of Delhi in 1338). Although experiencing brief periods of revival, the regime continued to decline internally before it was terminally fragmented by the brutal destruction of Delhi at the hands of the Turco-Mongol Timur (Tamerlane) in 1398. Timur's army wrought such destruction in Delhi that in his autobiography he denied

DOCUMENT

The Ideal Muslim King

DOCUMENT

A World Traveler in India

responsibility and blamed the slaughter on his soldiers. Numerous rulers, espousing a variety of religious faiths, emerged throughout India as Delhi declined, until a century later, when Timur's great-grandson Babur would return to establish the Mughal dynasty.

Pre-Mughal Muslim rule in India brought some cultural integration as local lords and warriors were incorporated into the new Muslim court. Some Hindus found emotional appeal in the Muslim faith, which had no caste system, or sought to lighten their taxes and qualify for public service by converting to Islam. Others formed new religious groups synthesizing aspects of Hinduism and Islam—for example, **Sikhism.** Another typical example of cultural integration was the spread of Urdu, a spoken Indian language incorporating Persian, Arabic, and Turkish words. The Sikh religion and the Urdu language illustrate how difficult it is to maintain strict boundaries (whether ethnic, linguistic, or spiritual) between peoples who regularly interact with each other, especially in frontier areas.

Cultural synthesis, however, could not eliminate Hindu-Muslim contention over polytheism, religious images, and closed castes. Many aristocratic Hindu leaders continued to resist Islam. The Muslim centuries should not be seen as a takeover of Indian society and culture by foreigners. Scholars today stress that though the rulers were Islamic, their governments ruled in ways similar to non-Islamic Indian rulers. Religion and caste remained significant barriers to assimilation, and mass conversions did not occur. The Delhi Sultanate remained a Muslim military-administrative class that ruled over a predominantly Hindu population. The impact on Buddhism was, however, far greater. The university at Nalanda and other major Buddhist centers were destroyed in 1202, driving thousands of monks and scholars to Nepal and Tibet. Buddhism was, then, effectively erased from India.

DOCUMENT

Indian Poetry

MAP

The Delhi Sultanate and Mughal India

CHINA: CULTURAL AND POLITICAL EMPIRES

■ *How did cross-cultural interaction with indigenous culture and ideology define China as a nation?*

The fall of the Han in 220 was followed by three and a half centuries of political disunity. Unity was regained under the Sui dynasty (589–618), consolidated under the Tang (618–907), maintained precariously under the Song (960–1279), and reasserted

---

Sikhism—Indian religion blending elements of Hinduism and Islam.

under the Yuan (1279–1368). Despite periods of internal disruption, this political system, recreated from Han precedents, survived repeated invasions and civil wars. For the 90-year Yuan dynasty, China was ruled by Central Asian invaders, the Mongols, but despite foreign control at the top, Chinese culture survived and reclaimed the emperorship in 1368. Throughout the millennium, stability resulted from a common written language, a strong family structure, an enduring Confucian tradition, an elite of scholar bureaucrats who shared power while contending for dominance, and the strength of China's economy and material culture. In the first half millennium, including the centuries of political disunity, China was part of the expanding Buddhist world. In the second half, the efforts of China's Confucian scholars promoted a flowering of Chinese culture during the expansionist Tang period, when China was the largest state in the world; during the ensuing economic prosperity of the Song; and in the Yuan period, in which China's economy dominated Eurasian trade.

Period of Division

No single dynasty was able to unite North and South China and establish a long-lasting dynasty from the fall of the Han to the rise of the Sui more than 360 years later. Yet this was a vibrant age of artistic creation, intellectual growth, and profound religious development. The divisions between north and south created dynamic differences in the two regions over time, and the reuniting of the two in the late sixth century led to a fertile synthesis of ideas and practices. Following the fall of the Han Empire various nomadic peoples, mainly Xiongnu and Yuezhi (yoo-EH-juh; "Turks"), interacted with Chinese in the border areas. At the same time, Chinese claimants to power—the ideal of a unified country persisted throughout the age of division—struggled with other Chinese as well as with sinified non-Chinese for dominance. (*Sinification* or *sinicization* meant adopting varying degrees of Chinese civilization, culture, governance, philosophy, and economic organization.) During the third century, three kingdoms vied for supremacy, and one, Jin, seemed to be on the verge of reuniting China in 280. Soon, however, succession disputes pitted Jin factions, joined by Chinese and non-Chinese allies, against one another. Unity was not to be at that time.

Xiongnu and other northern people had been invited inside the Han dynasty's borders in the second century as a way of gaining their support and decreasing the possibility of barbarian conquest. Many were used as soldiers by Chinese generals. By 304, some Xiongnu, sensing an opportunity during the fratricidal wars of the Jin, rose up, declared themselves the new kings of Han, and sacked Luoyang and Chang'an.

For the next century (304–439), China was involved in constant warfare during the period known as the Sixteen Kingdoms. Many aristocrats fled southward, populating the south and bringing Chinese culture with them. This was a demographically significant move, extending the reach of Chinese civilization and developing the south's fertile agricultural economy. When, centuries later, the Grand Canal was built, food could be transported from this "rice basket" to the north, where China's defensive armies had long been dependent on either growing their own food or striking bargains with their barbarian neighbors.

In the North, a clan originally from Manchuria but sinified by the fifth century established the Northern Wei dynasty (439–534). Like other successful outsiders, the Northern Wei had adopted Chinese methods, creating an effective administration by blending their indigenous ways with Chinese ways. Throughout history, China was challenged by the question of maintaining Chinese culture and institutions—especially rule by scholars according to Confucian principles—while learning from the outsider (or barbarians, as they were ungenerously called) to create a hybrid culture, economy, and military. The question of how to maximize borrowing without compromising Chinese culture was most evident in times of strong central government. But religious, cultural, and economic blending occurred at all times. The Northern Wei instituted an **equal-field system** of land tenure that resembled the ancient "well-field" system to overcome the rise of powerful land owners whose control of land and serfs cut the tax roles. They also adopted Chinese language and dress. Their capital at Luoyang was a grand Chinese city, with palaces, 500,000 inhabitants, and 1000 Buddhist temples.

While the Northern Wei controlled the North, other rulers controlled the South. Northern aristocratic families contributed to state building through their interest in Confucianism, while leading southern families were more focused on religion and the arts. Southerners seemed somewhat effete to northerners, but when the two regions reunited in 589, the blend of both styles led to a stronger and more cultured civilization. Each region was differently influenced by foreign cultures as well, stimulating intellectual inquiry and encouraging trade.

The hallmark of the period of political disunity was its cultural growth. At the beginning of the period, the incessant military struggles led many intellectuals to abandon public service. Why bother being a serious Confucian scholar in such times, many concluded, giving themselves up to hedonism and artistic performance, often simultaneously expressing itself in

---

equal-field system—Division of land to peasants, who tilled it, rather than to wealthy landholders; adopted in China, spread to Korea and Japan.

Huge Buddhist rock carvings (these are around 50 feet tall) were commissioned by the Northern Wei at the end of the fifth century. These large figures are part of a collection of thousands of carvings at Yungang in North China. They may have been inspired by earlier Buddhist carvings, recently destroyed by the Taliban in Afghanistan.

poetry or unconventional behavior. The Seven Sages of the Bamboo Grove were the most famous of many talented poets and although one was executed for scandalous behavior, they continue to be celebrated to this day.

Buddhism and Daoism emerged as more spiritual alternatives to Confucian government service. While Daoism had indigenous roots, Buddhism came to China as part of a great expansion of a universal religion. From its origins in India, Buddhism traveled along trade routes to China, bringing international (Greek, Afghan, and Indian) arts and ideas. Missionaries aided the transmission of Buddhism as did Chinese travelers like Faxian.

Buddhism provided comfort in times of crisis. Its promise of salvation (to all, including common people), special appeal to the supposed natural compassion of women and men, offer of monastic security to men in troubled times, and long incubation within Chinese culture all ensured its popularity. China's dominant form of Buddhism, Mahayana, focused on **bodhisattvas** (BOH-dee-SAHT-vahs), individuals who had achieved salvation but chose to postpone their release from the cycle of birth and rebirth in order to save others. Bodhisattvas were technically sexless beings (though identified in popular forms of religion as female) and transcended class and culture as well as gender. The notion of salvation through faith was developed in the **Pure Land** sect of Buddhism in the fourth century; this made Buddhism increasingly appealing to those not able to enter

bodhisattvas—In Mahayana Buddhism, an enlightened being who chooses to postpone salvation to aid others in reaching enlightenment.

Pure Land—A place for those saved by faith in the Amida Buddha.

monastic life. Developments in the Tang dynasty would broaden Buddhism's appeal further.

Daoism was encouraged to enhance its dogma and organization by the rise of Buddhism. Like Buddhists, Daoists formed monastic communities and wrote scriptures, although many of these scriptures were kept hidden from non-Daoists, unlike the widely circulated Buddhist texts. Daoists were particularly important in the study of alchemy as a route to immortality; alchemy, in turn, led to scientific discoveries. Although challenged by native Daoism, scorned by some Confucian intellectuals, and periodically persecuted by rulers jealous of its strength, Buddhism ultimately won adherents throughout China. The monarchs of the North patronized Buddhism by building splendid temples and generously endowing monasteries. From the fourth to the ninth centuries, Buddhism interacted with Chinese religious and philosophical traditions to create a complex new synthesis of ideas and art.

The Sui dynasty (589–618), descended from the Northern Wei, presented themselves as Chinese defenders of Buddhism. Emperor Wendi (r. 581–604), the first Sui ruler, and his son Yangdi (r. 604–618) established an imperial military force and a land-based militia, centralized the administration, and revived the civil service system. Between 605 and 609, Yangdi built a great waterway, the Grand Canal, to link the rice-growing Yangzi basin with northern China; this helped to overcome regional differences. This canal eventually stretched 1200 miles and permitted some later governments to locate their seats of power in the less productive but strategically important North. Building this canal, in addition to a massive conscription of soldiers (over one million) to fight in Korea, took huge amounts of labor. Disgust with this exploitation led to numerous rebellions, and in 618 Yangdi's cousin overthrew the Sui. The new Tang dynasty, like the Sui, was a hybrid of North and South, Chinese and foreign.

Political Developments Under the Early Tang Dynasty, 618–756

During the first half of the Tang period, China attained a new pinnacle of glory. The first three emperors, Gaozu (GOW-dzuh; r. 618–626), Taizong (TAI-dzong; r. 626–649), and Gaozong (GOW-dzong; r. 650–683), subjugated Turkish Central Asia and conquered Annam (northern Vietnam). Tang cultural influence extended north to Manchuria, east to Korea and Japan, and south to parts of Southeast Asia. It controlled Central Asia all the way to Afghanistan during the seventh century and maintained extensive trade routes. Along with territorial expansion came a deepening of state power.

The legal code of 653 combined northern and southern legal traditions, and the reemphasized **examination system** recruited officials from all regions and, in theory, all classes. This system was based on Confucian texts that were, in principle, accessible to all men (women were not allowed to take the examinations), but in reality were more likely studied in families financially able to educate their sons. This bought the elite's loyalty and focused the ideology of those who wished to be rulers, who were selected by their answers on exams based on the Confucian classics, on a unified body of scholarship. Thus, although the expansion of the empire depended on the promotion of *wu* (military), its maintenance was even more dependent on its promotion of *wen* (civil arts). Though strong supporters of Buddhism, early Tang rulers elevated the principles of Confucianism to rule the state and to define its Chinese nature.

The era of growth and grandeur was marked by the extraordinary reign of the able Empress Wu (r. 690–705), a concubine of the second and third emperors, who controlled the government for 20 years after the latter's death, eliminating her political opponents and firmly establishing the Tang dynasty. She greatly weakened the old aristocracy by favoring Buddhism and strengthening the examination system for recruiting civil servants. Moreover, she decisively defeated the Koreans, making Korea a loyal vassal state. As a woman and a widow, she was considered a usurper and was later criticized by Chinese historians and politicians who emphasized her vices, particularly her many favorites and lovers. She was overthrown in 705. Her grandson, Emperor Xuanzong (SHWAHN-dzong; r. 712–756), was also known for his long reign filled with cultural growth.

Tang rulers perfected a highly centralized government, using a complex bureaucracy organized in specialized councils, boards, and ministries, all directly responsible to the emperor. Local government functioned under 15 provincial governors, aided by subordinates down to the district level. Military commanders supervised tribute collections in semiautonomous conquered territories. Officeholders throughout the empire were, by the eighth century, usually degree-holders from government schools and universities who had qualified by passing the regularly scheduled examinations. These scholar-bureaucrats were steeped in Confucian conservatism but were more efficient than the remaining minority of aristocratic hereditary officials. The Tang retained the nationalized land register under the equal-field system, designed to check the growth of large estates, guarantee land to peasants, and relate their land tenure to both their taxes and their militia service. Until well into the eighth century, when abuses began to appear, the system worked to merge the interests of state and people.

Tang Economic and Social Changes

The early Tang economy was extremely prosperous, supported by thriving cities and the always busy trade routes through Central Asia, along the southeastern coast, and up and down the Grand Canal. Economic productivity, both agricultural and industrial, rose steadily during the early Tang period. The introduction of tea and wet rice from Annam turned the Yangzi area into a vast irrigated food bank and the economic base for Tang power. Tea became a staple throughout China during the Tang. More food and rising population brought increasing manufactures. Population growth was most impressive in the south, where it increased form one-quarter of the realm's population in the early seventh century to half by 742. Chinese techniques in the newly discovered craft of paper-making, along with iron casting, porcelain production, and silk processing, improved tremendously and spread west to the Middle East.

Foreign trade and influence increased significantly under the Tang emperors in a development that would continue through the Song era (960–1279). Chinese control in Central Asia facilitated trade along the old overland silk route; but as porcelain became the most profitable export and could not be easily transported by caravan, it swelled the volume of sea trade through Southeast Asia. Most of this trade left from southern ports, particularly from Guangzhou (gwahng-JOH; Canton), where more than 100,000 non-Chinese Indians, Persians, Arabs, and Malays handled the goods. Foreign merchants were equally visible at Chang'an, the Tang capital and eastern terminus of the silk route. Chang'an, a planned city of 30 square miles, not counting the imperial palace, was the largest planned city in the world, and the most populous. The imperial palace at the north of the city was flanked on either side by a market. The "West Market" dealt in foreign goods, food, and wine and exhibited foreign entertainers and magi-

---

examination system—The selection of scholar-officials through examination in Confucian texts.

cians; the "East Market" was for domestic items. The city was vibrant, but it was also controlled, for Chang'an was planned on a grid, and every resident lived in a rectangular ward, surrounded by walls. The gate to the ward was locked at night.

Although largely state-controlled and aristocratic, Tang society was particularly responsive to new foreign stimuli, which it swiftly absorbed. A strongly pervasive Buddhism, a rising population, and steady urbanization fostered this cross-cultural exchange. Many city populations exceeded 100,000, and four cities had more than a million people. Their cosmopolitan residents enjoyed products from foreign lands, including luxury goods, musical instruments, and textiles. The foreign practice of sitting on chairs replaced sitting on floor mats. Hairstyles and games were adopted from abroad. Foreign religions, including Islam, Nestorian Christianity, Judaism, Zoroastrianism, and Manichaeism (MAN-ih-KEE-ism), were practiced freely by the thousands of international residents in Chang'an and Luoyang, though few Chinese converted to these religions as they had earlier to Buddhism. Merchants clearly benefited, but despite their wealth, they were still considered socially inferior. They often used their wealth to educate their sons for the civil service examination, thus promoting a rising class of scholar-bureaucrats. The latter, as they acquired land, gained status and power at the expense of the old aristocratic families. Conditions among artisans and the expanding mass of peasants improved somewhat, but life for them remained hard and precarious.

By the eighth century, Tang legal codes had imposed severe punishments for wifely disobedience or infidelity to husbands. New laws also limited women's rights to divorce, inheritance of property, and remarriage as widows. Women were, however, still active in the arts and literature. Although some wielded influence and power at royal courts, many were confined to harems. This subordinate position was partly balanced by the continued high status and authority of older women within families.

Class and education played an important role in women's status. Women poets were sought after by men of distinction, and one father of a poet, himself a writer of note, was promoted to a prestigious government position on the strength of his daughter's writing. Empress Wu wrote powerful poetry, some of it recalling her mother, some longing for her late husband, some expressing political ideas. Other women wrote of love and longing, military events, affairs at court, and a wide variety of topics. Not all Tang women poets were genteel. In a poem entitled "Getting It Off My Chest," Xu Yueying (SHOO yoo-eh-YING), a late Tang poet wrote: "I've broken the rules—obedience to father, husband, son. That's why I cry so much. This body? What way, what use to stick to what proper people do?"[5]

Fashions in female beauty change from place to place and over time. Figurines like this one of a mounted woman, possibly playing polo, show that physical activity and a plump physique were esteemed. This style also influenced standards of beauty in Korea and Japan at that time.

Tang Religion and Culture

Buddhism and Daoism blossomed alongside Confucian scholarship and government service. Poets, artists, architects, and painters were all inspired by religious as well as secular themes. Buddhism was particularly dynamic in the early Tang dynasty. Buddhist monasteries and temples educated children in their schools, rural temples gave lodging to travelers, and monasteries ran large-scale farms. Buddhist themes permeated folk tales. Most important, faith-based Buddhist sects, especially Pure Land, spread throughout China, offering peasants a route to salvation. Pure Land Buddhism was a vastly different form of devotion from the earlier sects that required years of good living and often many rebirths on earth before attaining salvation. **Chan** (Zen in Japanese) Buddhism developed in the Tang as well. Chan appealed more to the elite and focused on sudden enlightenment rather than scripture.

Chan—A form of Buddhism that seeks sudden enlightenment through techniques and rituals intended to quiet the mind. Known as Zen in Japan.

A fresh flowering of literature occurred during the early Tang period. It followed naturally from a dynamic society, but it was also furthered by the development of papermaking and the invention, in about 600, of block printing, which soon spread to Korea and Japan. Movable type, which would later revolutionize Europe, was little used in China during this period because it was less efficient in printing Chinese characters. Printing helped meet a growing demand for the religious and educational materials generated by Buddhism and the examination system.

Tang scholarship is best remembered for historical writing. Chinese of this period firmly believed that lessons from the past could be guides for the future. As an early Tang emperor noted, "By using a mirror of brass, you may . . . adjust your cap; by using antiquity as a mirror you may . . . foresee the rise and fall of empires."[6] In addition to universal works, the period produced many studies of particular subjects. History itself came under investigation, as illustrated by *The Understanding of History*, a work that stressed the need for analysis and evaluation in the narration of events. Writers produced works of all types, but poetry was the accepted medium, composed and repeated by emperors, scholars, singing courtesans, and common people in the marketplaces. Tang poetry was marked by ironic humor, deep sensitivity to human feeling, concern for social justice, and a near-worshipful love of nature. Two of the most famous among some 3000 recognized poets of the era were Li Bo (701–763; also known as Li Bai) and Du Fu (712–770). The former was an admitted lover of pleasure, especially of wine. A famous story about him is that during a drinking party on a lake, he leaned over the side of the boat in order to scoop out the moon and drowned. But he also had his philosophical side as seen in the following poem inspired by Daoism:

DOCUMENT

Poems by Li Bai (also known as Li Bo) and Du Fu

> *Zhuangzi in a dream*
> *became a butterfly,*
> *And the butterfly became*
> *Zhuangzi at waking.*
> *Which was the real, the*
> *butterfly or the man?*[7]

Du Fu, one of the great landscape poets, also wrote of suffering, especially suffering brought about by rebellions toward the end of his life.

> *The war-chariots rattle,*
> *The war-horses whinny.*
> *Each man of you has a bow and quiver at his*
> *   belt. . . .*
> *At the border where the blood of men spills like*
> *   the sea—*

> *And still the heart of Emperor Wu is beating for*
> *   war. . . .*
> *In thousands of villages, nothing grows but*
> *   weeds,*
> *And though strong women have bent to the*
> *   ploughing,*
> *East and west the furrows are all broken down*
> *   . . .*
> *It is very much better to have a daughter*
> *Who can marry and live in the house of a*
> *   neighbor,*
> *While under the sod we bury our boys. . . .*[8]

The Tang literary revival was paralleled by movements in painting and sculpture. The plastic arts, dealing with both religious and secular subjects, became a major medium for the first time in China. Small tomb statues depicted both Chinese and foreign life with realism, verve, and diversity. These figures—warriors, servants, and traders—were buried with the dead and believed to serve them in the afterlife. Religious statuary, even in Buddhist shrines, showed strong humanistic emphases, often juxtaposed with the naive sublimity of Buddhas carved in the Gandaran (Greek Hellenistic) style of northwestern India. Similar themes were developed in Tang painting, but the traditional preoccupation with nature prevailed in both the northern and southern landscape schools. The most famous Tang painter was Wu Daozi (WOO DOW-zuh), whose landscapes and religious scenes were produced at the court of the emperor Xuanzong in the early eighth century.

Tang Decline and the Transition to Premodern China

The cultural flowering of Xuanzong's reign was matched, in its early years, by vigorous and effective leadership. He fixed problems in the tax system, curbed the power of imperial relatives, and strengthened defenses against the Turks, Uighurs, and Tibetans. His method of strengthening border defenses by giving authority to commanders of military provinces backfired, however. One of these commanders, a protégé of the emperor's favorite concubine, Yang Guifei (YAHNG gwei-FAY), was doted on by the emperor to please his concubine. The commander, An Lushan, built up an army of 160,000 troops along the border, but then turned and marched on Chang'an and Luoyang in 755.

The aged emperor Xuanzong, while fleeing for his life from the capital, was forced by his troops to approve the execution of Yang Guifei, who was seen as having dominated him and his court. According to legend, he died of sorrow less than a month later. Yang

Document   Bo Juyi (772–846): "The Song of Everlasting Sorrow"

This poem by one of the late Tang dynasty's most respected poets recounts the love of Emperor Xuanzong and his beloved concubine, Yang Guifei, who was blamed by her contemporaries for the An Lushan Rebellion. Bo Juyi's poem was esteemed not only in China but also in Japan. Lady Murasaki cited it repeatedly in *The Tale of Genji*.

China's Emperor, craving beauty that might shake
    an empire,
Was on the throne for many years, searching,
    never finding,
Till a little child of the Yang clan, hardly even
    grown,
Bred in an inner chamber, with no one knowing
    her,
But with graces granted by heaven and not to be
    concealed,
At last one day was chosen for the imperial
    household.
If she but turned her head and smiled, there were
    cast a hundred spells,
And the powder and paint of the Six Palaces faded
    into nothing.
. . . There were other ladies in his court, three
    thousand of rare beauty,
But his favours to three thousand were
    concentered in one body.
. . . Her sisters and her brothers all were given
    titles;
And, because she so illumined and glorified her
    clan,
She brought to every father, every mother through
    the empire,
Happiness when a girl was born rather than a
    boy.
. . . The Emperor's eyes could never gaze on her
    enough—
Till war-drums, booming from Yuyang, shocked
    the whole earth
And broke the tunes of The Rainbow Skirt and the
    Feathered Coat.
The Forbidden City, the nine-tiered palace, loomed
    in the dust
From thousands of horses and chariots headed
    southwest.
The imperial flag opened the way, now moving
    and now pausing—
But thirty miles from the capital, beyond the
    western gate,
The men of the army stopped, not one of them
    would stir
Till under their horses' hoofs they might trample
    those moth-eyebrows.
Flowery hairpins fell to the ground, no one picked
    them up,
And a green and white jade hair-tassel and a
    yellow gold hair-bird.

The Emperor could not save her, he could only
    cover his face.
And later when he turned to look, the place of
    blood and tears
Was hidden in a yellow dust blown by a cold
    wind.
. . . And people were so moved by the Emperor's
    constant brooding
That they besought the Daoist priest to see if he
    could find her.
. . . He searched the Green Void, below, the Yellow
    Spring;
But he failed, in either place, to find the one he
    looked for.
And then he heard accounts of an enchanted isle
    at sea,
. . . And the lady, at news of an envoy from the
    Emperor of China,
Was startled out of dreams in her nine-flowered
    canopy.
. . . She took out, with emotion, the pledges he
    had given
And, through his envoy, sent him back a shell box
    and gold hairpin,
But kept one branch of the hairpin and one side of
    the box,
Breaking the gold of the hairpin, breaking the shell
    of the box;
Our souls belong together," she said, "like this gold
    and this shell—
Somewhere, sometime, on earth or in heaven, we
    shall surely meet."
. . . Earth endures, heaven endures; some time
    both shall end,
While this unending sorrow goes on and on for
    ever.

Questions to Consider

1. Why did the Emperor's soldiers execute Yang Guifei, and why was the Emperor unable to protect her?

2. What does this poem suggest about the role of women in the Emperor's court in the Tang?

3. Why was this poem loved not only in China but also throughout East Asia?

Excerpted from Bo Juyi (Po Chi-yi), "A Song of Unending Sorrow," in Cyril Birch, ed., *Anthology of Chinese Literature: From Early Times to the Fourteenth Century* (New York: Grove Press, 1965), pp. 266–269.

Guifei became a model of female perfidy, fueling misogynistic notions of women's control over men.

It took 8 years to put down An Lushan's rebellion, but the ensuing disruption was so extensive that the late Tang emperors never recovered their former power. In several key areas, military governors acted as independent rulers, paying no taxes to Chang'an. In the rest of China, the equal-field system was replaced with twice yearly taxation on the value of the land. This **two tax system** persisted for the next 700 years in China. Regions were allowed to fill their tax responsibilities as they wished with little government supervision. In addition, the government instituted salt, wine, and tea monopolies to raise revenues. Government receipts to merchants came to be used as a kind of currency, becoming the antecedent for paper money that was developed during the Song dynasty. Though private trade was stimulated by the government's declining economic role, government revenues declined, and taxes on peasants were raised. Falling revenues brought deterioration of the state education establishment and a corresponding drop in administrative efficiency. The government further alienated some groups by seizing Buddhist property and persecuting

two tax system—Twice yearly tax payment based on value of land rather than on output as under the earlier equal field system.

all "foreign" religions. Buddhism was suppressed in 841. Tens of thousands of monasteries and temples were destroyed and 250,000 monks and nuns were returned to lay life. Except for the popular sects of Pure Land and Chan, most other sects of Buddhism soon declined.

In response to the threat posed by autonomous regional commanders, the court created armies led by eunuchs, originally personal servants to the emperor or to his women's quarters. In time, these eunuchs gained their own power, manipulating and even murdering emperors and scholar-officials. Bandits and other gangs ravaged the country after 860. Chang'an was captured in 881, and the brutal warlord who took the city killed all the foreign residents. Chang'an would never again be capital of China. In 907, the pretense of Tang rule was ended.

Political Developments During the Song Era, 960–1279

For a half-century after the fall of the Tang dynasty, China experienced political division, at times approaching anarchy. During this period of five dynasties in the north and ten kingdoms in the south, attacks by "barbarian" raiders alternated with internal con-

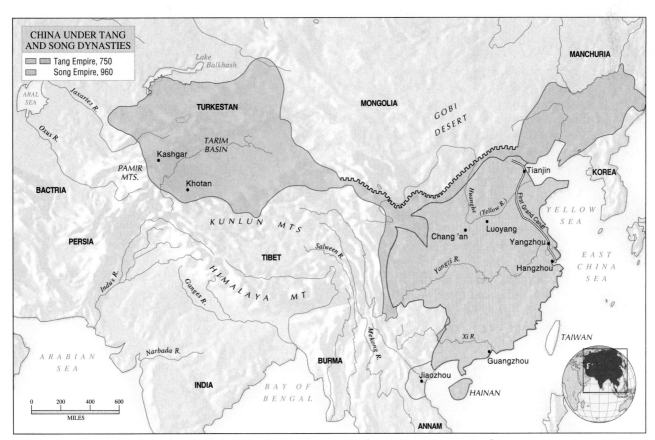

China expanded to the south, west, and north during the Tang dynasty. Northern Vietnam (Annam) and Turkish Central Asia came under Chinese control.

flicts among contending warlords. One military leader in the north—who reigned as Song Taizu (r. 960–76)—was finally able to unify all of China, founding the Song dynasty in 960. Taizu and his successors were never able to regain all the territories, however. Militarily powerful non-Chinese states bordered the Song, and the new rulers had to devise ways to keep them in check. Several were hybrid states, using Chinese methods of governance to rule over populations that included many Chinese immigrants. The Song responded by building a large military—their army had 1.25 million men by 1040—and producing large quantities of armaments. Military technology advanced as well; after using gunpowder to launch grenades, the Song invented the cannon. At the same time, scholar-officials were used to strengthen the centralizing power of the state. While this did help consolidate Song authority, in time excessive bureaucratization crept in, and rules and regulations began to impede creative governing.

Another consequence of the Song's strong focus on rule by scholar-officials was the rise of factionalism. As the state experienced mounting budgetary deficits and confronted peasant unrest, the emperor Shenzong (SHEN-dzhong; r. 1067–1085) called on an eminent statesman, Wang Anshi (WAHNG ahn-SHUH), to resolve these difficulties. Wang sponsored a thoroughgoing—and therefore threatening—reform program that granted interest-bearing agricultural loans to peasants, fixed commodity prices, provided unemployment benefits, established old-age pensions, converted labor service to monetary taxes, mobilized local militias, increased the number of schools, and reformed the examination system by stressing practical rather than literary knowledge. Although these measures brought some improvements, they evoked fanatical opposition from scholars, bureaucrats, and moneylenders. The internal debate resembled that of more than 1000 years earlier (the Salt and Iron Debates of the Han dynasty) over the propriety of the government's involvement in the economy. In the next generation most of Wang Anshi's reforms were rescinded.

Song ministers faced continuous threats along their northern and western frontiers. To placate their neighbors, the Liao (around Beijing) and the Xia (in the northwest), the Song paid them annual tribute payments in silk and silver. These payments indicated Song subordination or at least a desire for peace. In 1115, the Jurchen, a nomadic people from Manchuria, challenged the Liao. Believing the Jurchen would be good allies against their old rivals in Liao, the Song made a pact with them to divide Liao. Soon the alliance broke apart, and the Jurchen took the Song capital at Kaifeng (kai-FUHNG) in 1126. Ruling northern China, the Jurchen became increasingly sinified,

ruling according to Chinese ways and intermarrying with Chinese. The Song court fled in panic to Nanjing and later set up a new capital at Hangzhou (hahng-JOH), thus bringing to an end the Song effort to govern a realm united from north to south. The period from 960 to 1127 is often called the Northern Song, and that from 1127 to 1279 the Southern Song.

After a decade of indecisive war, a treaty in 1142 stipulated that the Song had to pay tribute of silk and silver to the Jurchen whose new dynasty was called Jin (1115–1234). It also prescribed that the Jin monarch be addressed as "lord" and the Song emperor as "servant" in all official communications. The subordination of the Song was thus formalized in language and in tribute payments.

Despite these disasters, the Song rulers enjoyed somewhat better economic conditions. The country experienced unprecedented economic and cultural advances, particularly after its territory was reduced to only southern China, and it turned increasingly toward using the many canals and streams throughout the South to move products. In addition, trade with the Jin state continued as before. One and a half centuries later, a new band of Central Asian nomads, the Mongols, conquered the Jin and went on to take

Tang, Song, and Yuan China

618–907	Tang dynasty
c. 690–705	Reign of Empress Wu
701–763	Poet Li Bo
712–756	Cultural flowering under Emperor Xuanzong
712–770	Poet Du Fu
755–763	An Lushan Rebellion
960–1279	Song dynasty
1005, 1042	Song sign treaties of subordination with Liao and Xia
1019–1086	Sima Guang, historian
1067–1085	Emperor Shenzong and Wang Anshi Reforms
1126–1134	Jin dynasty established in north
1162–1227	Chinggis becomes Mongol Khan (Supreme King)
1260–1294	Khubilai becomes Khan
1279–1368	Yuan dynasty

all of the Southern Song. From 1279 to 1368, China was ruled by Mongols who established a dynasty they called Yuan.

Song Economic and Social Conditions

Economic growth was rapid. Agricultural growth sustained a population that doubled between 750 and 1100. Farmers used their surpluses to buy charcoal, tea, and wine. Many raised and sold silk, sugar, vegetables, cotton, fruit, and wood products. The government maintained some monopolies, taxed trade moderately, built great water-control projects, and aided intensive agriculture, but otherwise loosened control over individual enterprise. Rice production doubled within a century after 1050, and industry grew rapidly, pouring out, for home and foreign markets, fine silk, lacquer wares, porcelain, and paper for writing, books, money and wrapping gifts. Heavy industry, especially iron, grew rapidly, and was used for tools, suspension bridges, and nails for construction. Song economic advances were furthered by such technical innovations as water clocks, explosives for mining, hydraulic machinery, paddleboats, seagoing junks, the stern post rudder, and the mariner's compass. These commercial developments were paralleled by the development of an oceangoing navy. The resulting commercial expansion prompted banks to depend on paper currency and specialized commercial instruments. Trade with the outside world, formerly dominated by Indians and Southeast Asians, was taken over by the Chinese, who established trading colonies throughout East Asia.

The Song economic revolution exerted tremendous foreign influence abroad. Paper money, dating from the eleventh century in the south, was soon copied in the Liao state and issued by the Jin government in 1153; its use then spread steadily in all directions. Other Song economic innovations appeared quickly in coastal areas from Japan and Korea to the East Indies, where Chinese merchants were immigrant culture carriers. Song technology also spread to India, the Middle East, and even Europe. From China, Europe acquired metal horseshoes, the padded horse collar, and the wheelbarrow. Chinese mapping skills, along with the compass and the stern post ship rudder, helped prepare the way for Europe's age of expansion. Later, gunpowder and movable type, both pioneered in Song China, arrived in Europe via Asian intermediaries.

Profound and rapid change brought many tensions to Song society. Some arose from urban expansion in a population that swelled from 60 to 115 million, a growth rate of more than twice the world average. A rise in population unaccompanied by a rise in the number of officials meant that passing the exams to enter officialdom became increasingly, and frustratingly, difficult. On the other hand, life was dynamic and cosmopolitan. Cities offered residents and travelers alike access to international culture, restaurants, plays, artwork, and civic organizations. Rural life was far less exciting, but farmers could go to regularly scheduled rural markets and read printed books published on a variety of topics, including agriculture, rituals, and childbirth. The spread of books and literacy created a national culture that transcended the localism of most rural societies. Unlike Europe, cities were not islands of merchant liberation in a rural sea of aristocratic domination; rather, scholar-officials ruled everywhere. Merchants did not have power, although they could take the exams to enter the scholarly class.

Women's lives were varied though lacking in power. While lively physical activity had been encouraged in the Tang—as evidenced in art work showing women playing vigorous sports like polo—a more demure and modest demeanor was expected of women in the Song. To be sure, the extant records of the Song show women who ran inns, delivered babies as midwives, worked as entertainers, sold their sewing and weaving, wrote poetry, and served as shamans (religious mediums). As wives and mothers, women had a voice in childrearing and spouse selection for their children, despite Confucian ideas that called for women to take a back seat to men in the family. Court records in inheritance cases indicate that judges made sure that daughters received money for dowries by which they could make more successful marriages. The availability of a great number of printed materials opened doors to literature for women of educated families.

At the same time, however, the resurgence of Confucian thinking reinforced a view that demure and even physically weak women were attractive. Women were told to be modest, which limited their public role, and footbinding carried this injunction to an extreme. Begun by dancers in the tenth century, the tight binding of a little girl's feet till they were broken, bent, and ideally just three inches long came to be a symbol both of beauty and of a girl's modesty and refinement. Bound feet attracted better marriage prospects but did little to expand girls' horizons. Though it began in the Song, footbinding was still uncommon at that time and was never mentioned by the Song's greatest woman poet, Li Qingzhao (LEE ching-JOW; 1094–1152). Female infanticide, restriction on remarriage of widows, and harsh legal penalties, including death, for violating the accepted code of prescribed wifely conduct were also Song social phenomena. Women were told to put their families first, but so, too, were men. All family members were under the rule of the patriarchal (male) family head, but women were additionally burdened by their sub-ordinate position in society as a whole.

Song Philosophy, Literature, and Art

The rapidly changing Song society was reflected in its philosophy, literature, and art. Poets wrote of people's inner lives, joys, and misfortunes. Song aesthetic expression encouraged versatility; as during the later European Renaissance, the universal man, public servant, scholar, poet, or painter was the ideal. Song's most famous woman poet, Li Qingzhao, whose work was enthusiastically promoted by her scholar husband, wrote personalized verse describing the early years of her marriage in which she and her husband engaged in lively intellectual discussions. Su Shi (1037–1101) was a northern Song poet who excelled in painting and calligraphy as well as writing. Writing his poems on his paintings, he combined the three arts of the Confucian gentleman-scholar in a single work. In another genre, Sima Guang (SUH-muh GWAHNG; 1019–1086) was an outstanding Confucian historian. Known for his bitter attacks on his contemporary Wang Anshi, he also was an astute observer of the past, looking to it for moral guidance, and a critic of those who misread historical sources. Artists depicted the beauty of nature in

This Song landscape painting, Snow Mountain and Forest, *was painted by the artist Fan Kuan.*

widely varied styles, all involving great attention to detail. Landscapes embraced all of nature in a single work, removing humans from the central position they had had in earlier works. Darker tones and sharper lines replaced the decorative lightness of Tang works. The greatest Song landscape painter was Fan Kuan (FAHN KWAHN; active 990–1020).

Buddhism lost its appeal to Song's rulers as it was associated with their Liao, Xia, and Jin rivals, all of whom were ardent Buddhists. Confucianism, as a result, had a revival. The brothers Cheng Hao (1032–1085) and Cheng Yi (1033–1108) developed metaphysical approaches to Confucianism. They asserted that *li* (principle or pattern) was inherent in all things. *Qi* (CHEE; material force or energy) gives substance to things for which *li* is the blueprint. Mencius's contention that humans are fundamentally good (see Chapter 2) was always hard to explain in light of people's bad behavior. The Song **"Neo-Confucians"** could now claim that humankind's blueprint *(li)* was good but *qi* was sometimes impure and in need of cleaning. The Cheng brothers' most important follower was Zhu Xi (JOO SHEE; 1130–1200). His White Deer Grotto Academy was one of many that trained students in new approaches to Confucianism. He differed from the Chengs by ascribing greater importance to *li* over *qi* and by positing the existence of a Supreme Ultimate to which all *li* was connected. Zhu Xi contended that self-cultivation required the extension of knowledge, best achieved by the "investigation of things." In time, Neo-Confucianism was identified with Zhu Xi's philosophy, though it had many varieties and proponents.

The Song renaissance in scholarship was accompanied by significant advances in the experimental and applied sciences. Chinese doctors introduced inoculation against smallpox, and their education and hospital facilities surpassed anything in the West. In addition, there were notable achievements in astronomy, chemistry, zoology, botany, cartography, and algebra.

The Yuan Dynasty (1279–1368)

The Mongol conquest of the Song followed three-quarters of a century of Mongol growth and expansion in Central and Western Asia. The Mongol Khubilai's (1215–1294) takeover of the southern Song in 1279 furthered China's position as the center of Eurasia. Thus, although the Mongol era was a short dynasty despised by many Chinese and having a relatively minor impact on Chinese culture, it played a very significant role in world history. More than during the

Neo-Confucianism—Metaphysical form of Confucianism developed by the Cheng brothers and Zhu Xi; later became the dominant form of Confucianism throughout East Asia.

Song dynasty, with its lively international trade, and the early Ming, with its unprecedented maritime explorations, during the Yuan the five main areas of Eurasia—China, Southeast Asia, South Asia, Central Asia, and Europe—were part of a single world trading system. Europe was able to acquire Asian goods at low cost during this period; thus, when the Ming drove the Mongols out of China in 1368 and the Turks came to dominate western Asian trade routes, Europeans were inspired to seek maritime access to Asia. This, in turn, led to Europe's encounter with the Americas. Therefore, the brief Mongol period has an importance that belies both its brevity and its very limited demographic extent (the total Mongol population of about 1.5 million ruled over 100 times as many non-Mongols). Some background on earlier Central Asian tribes is helpful to understand the rise of the Mongols.

An earlier precedent for invasions out of Central Asia came from the Turkic peoples, who had figured in Eurasian history for a thousand years before the emergence of the Mongols. Between the sixth and eighth centuries, Turkic and Chinese regimes competed for control of the steppes. With Chinese support, the first Turkish Empire emerged in 552 and extended its dominion over much of Central Asia before it was conquered by the early Tang emperors. (An Lushan was of Turkish background.) During and after their imperial expansion, the Turks absorbed and transmitted much of the culture from their more advanced neighbors. Trade, religion, and warfare facilitated the process. Eastern Turks borrowed early from China, adopting

Buddhism and converting their western kinsmen in far distant Ferghana. After the eighth century, when the Abbasid caliphate brought Islam to the steppes, Turkic invaders launched conquests in the Middle East and India. Through the fifteenth century, there were waves of migration and conquest out of Central Asia and into the settled territories of Eurasia. Such incursions usually brought short-term disaster to occupied regions, but effected a great synthesis of peoples and cultures and ultimately led to the establishment of Turkic regimes from India to the Middle East.

For more than five centuries before the Mongol conquests, this process had been growing in intensity. Westward and to the north of the Chinese frontiers, a series of large states, partially settled but still containing nomadic or seminomadic populations, rose and fell. Among them were the Uighur Empire of the ninth century and the Tangut state. Both of these regimes prospered by providing goods, protection, and transport for the overland trade with China, which continued to grow. For many peoples of Central Asia—Turks, Uighurs, Tanguts, Tibetans, Mongols, and a host of others—trade, especially the silk trade, was one of many stimuli that turned their attention toward the outside world in the thirteenth century.

Debate continues over what sparked Mongol expansion: climatic changes that ruined Mongol pasture lands, military capability, or the inspiration of an ambitious warlord. The Mongols, horse- and sheep-raising nomads and formidable mounted warriors, began conquering cities and trade routes in the early

Two views of Mongols as seen by their contemporaries. Left is a Persian miniature showing Mongols preparing food at their tents. Right is a Chinese painting of a mounted Mongol archer. Tents and horses were critical elements of Mongol life and status. The Mongol khans gave tents and horses as gifts to honor their subordinates and Central Asian horses were in great demand in China and Japan. In Central Asian culture a warrior was, by definition, a horseman.

thirteenth century on the way to establishing an empire that controlled most of Eurasia a century later. Beginning with Temujin, known in the West as Chinggis (1162–1227), who was selected Great Khan (Supreme King) in 1206, they claimed that they were destined by "heaven" to subdue all peoples. Chinggis was likely motivated to begin his quest for power to avenge his father's death. The Mongols were remarkably successful in launching large-scale military operations throughout Eurasia. They seized Persia, toppled the Islamic Abbasid caliphate in Baghdad, established their rule in Russia, and sacked Delhi, though they made no further inroads into India before moving on to China. From North China, they invaded Korea (1231 and 1258) and attempted unsuccessfully to invade Japan (1274 and 1281) and Java (1281 and 1292).

The Mongols have often been represented as destroyers par excellence, sacking cities, disrupting trade, and building towers of the heads of their conquered foes. The Mongols often used terror to control conquered peoples, particularly during the early conquests. Mongol commanders regularly imposed mass murder, torture, and resettlement on resisting populations. One million residents of the Chinese city of Chengdu (chuhng-DOO) were slaughtered in 1236 although that city had already been taken with little fighting. But Mongol presence also facilitated trade and diplomatic activity by providing security and postal service on Eurasian trade routes.

The Mongols Before the Conquest of the Song

Prior to their expansion in the early thirteenth century, Mongols had ranged widely in Central Asia, pitching their black felt tents, pasturing their animals, and fighting the elements much like other peoples who had raided and traded with settled Eurasian populations since the fourth century B.C.E. Mongol chiefs contended to be the "first among equals," decisions were made by councils of warriors, and women enjoyed a high degree of respect and influence. Polygamy was practiced among the warriors, but not all marriages were polygamous, and marital fidelity was enforced equally for men and women. Wives sometimes rode and fought beside their husbands; in a harsh environment where raiding and warfare were common, women as well as men had sometimes to defend the hearth and livestock.

At the opening of the thirteenth century, the Mongols began their campaign of conquests and empire building. Within less than a century, they had subdued most populations from the Pacific to the Caspian Sea,

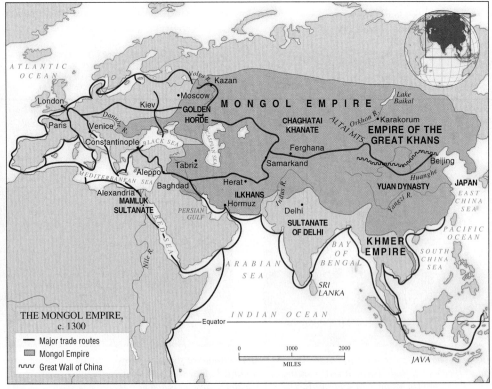

The Mongols extended their hegemony over a major part of Eurasia from the Danube to the Pacific from the mid-thirteenth to the mid-fourteenth centuries.

terrorized the rest, and gained luxuries beyond their imaginings. Trade and travel across Eurasia were facilitated. In most cases, however, they left a light cultural footprint. While the population of China did, indeed, decline from 120 million in 1207 to 60 million in 1290 (after the Mongol conquest), the cultural effects were less drastic. Chinese religion, painting, poetry, and social structure were not touched by the Mongols. Tolerance for foreign religions was promoted, but few Chinese changed their religious beliefs because of the presence of new sects.

During the first stage of their empire building, to 1241, the Mongols concentrated on the Central Asian steppe and its less developed border areas. Chinggis subordinated the Uighurs and Tanguts, seized Turkestan and Afghanistan, and invaded Persia. After his death in 1227, the campaigns halted and the Mongol forces reassembled in Mongolia to elect Chinggis's designated successor, his son Ögödei (EU-guh-dai; 1229–1241). Ögödei was granted Mongolia, from which he took the Jin Empire in northern China in 1234.

Between 1251 and 1259, during the reign of Ögödei's son, Möngke (MUHNG-kuh), Mongol armies conquered eastern Tibet (1252) and Korea (1259) while Möngke's brother, Hülegü (hoo-LEH-goo), toppled the Abbasid caliphate, absorbing every subsidiary state in Persia, Palestine, and Syria. Hülegü's campaign reflected the cosmopolitan nature of the Mongol army, with its Chinese catapult operators, and its court, with its Chinese physicians. The Mongols integrated the commanders, bureaucrats, artisans, and professionals of the conquered peoples into their armies and courts, thereby enhancing their ability to conquer and govern through borrowing the best practices of the conquered people.

Khubilai Khan (r. 1260–1294) emerged as dominant following a struggle from power among Mongol kings in 1260. After 1264 the empire broke up into four parts with only nominal central administration: Mongolia and China under Khubilai; and three other khanates in western Turkestan, Russia, and Persia and Iraq.

Mongol rulers of the mid-thirteenth century were forced to learn quickly how to organize and operate the largest imperial state that had ever existed. Although the ultimate base of authority in the sprawling Mongol territories was military power whose nucleus was a cavalry force of potentially 130,000 Mongols, civil administration and taxation were necessary. They developed a complex courier system linking the empire and created a written form of their language by using the script of the conquered Uighur people to transmit messages and records. The nomadic methods of the steppes were obviously no longer effective and had to be integrated with those of more experienced conquered bureaucrats.

Khubilai Khan hunting with his wife or a consort in a scroll painted in the late thirteenth century. Mongol women and men were expected to be vigorous and talented equestrians.

Before the conquest of the Song dynasty, Möngke revised the law code of Chinggis Khan to accommodate native cultural differences and meet practical needs. He minted coins, issued paper currency, collected taxes in money, and perfected a census system as a basis for taxes and military service. To support military operations, his state industries mined ores and produced arms. Other measures regularized trade tolls, improved roads, and provided for the safety of travelers, especially merchants. These reforms encouraged support from subject peoples, many of whom were now employed in the khan's service. Other areas were under lighter Mongol control. In these, local rulers proclaimed their submission publicly, left hostages with the khans, paid annual tribute, and provided troops for military campaigns. Such tributary rulers who served the khans loyally were guaranteed political security, honored publicly, and rewarded with lavish gifts (e.g., horses, daggers, furs, or silk garments).

China Under the Yuan Dynasty

Khubilai, who reigned as Great Khan from 1260 to 1294, turned his sights to the conquest of the Southern Song. After moving his capital to Beijing in 1264, he adopted a Chinese name for his dynasty in 1271. Like other Central Asian rulers who sought power in the east, Khubilai relied heavily on the advice of his Chinese and non-Chinese sinified advisors. One Song general offered advice on the construction of boats capable of navigating the many rivers and canals of South China. Khubilai, who had relied on cavalry and massive armies for his earlier conquests, thus became the first Central Asian conqueror of South China. Making use of a multiethnic force of Jurchen, Mongols, Persians, Uighurs, Koreans, and Chinese, Khubilai's forces laid siege to the Song. When the Yuan conquered all of China in 1279, Khubilai had gained the richest empire on earth. But even as he gained the wealth of China, the Mongol Empire had already ceased to be a unified Asian empire. Each of the four major khanates had developed its own state, and these were often at odds with one another. Though it is inaccurate to consider the Mongol realm a single political entity, the Mongol bonds of the khanates facilitated trade across the numerous Central Asian routes. Moreover, Turks and other West-Central Asians who had tried to take advantage of the commercial caravans themselves were suppressed during this period, making transport cheaper and easier.

Life under the Mongols was hard for most Chinese. While the Mongols did not prevent Chinese cultural expression, they did treat ethnic Chinese as distinctly inferior. A hierarchy dominated by foreigners was established: Mongols at the top, other peoples of Central Asia on the next rung, northern Chinese in lower positions, and southern Chinese almost completely excluded from office or public life. Taxation of Chinese was high. Many southern Chinese were subjected to serfdom or slavery. Though Khubilai retained the traditional ministries and local governmental structure, he staffed them with those in higher hierarchical positions. Generally, Mongol law prevailed, but the conquerors were often influenced by Chinese legal precedents, as in the acceptance of brutal punishments for loose or unfaithful women. Most religions were tolerated unless they violated Mongol laws.

According to Marco Polo, a Venetian traveler who arrived at Khubilai's court around 1275 and served

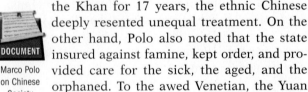

DOCUMENT

Marco Polo on Chinese Society

the Khan for 17 years, the ethnic Chinese deeply resented unequal treatment. On the other hand, Polo also noted that the state insured against famine, kept order, and provided care for the sick, the aged, and the orphaned. To the awed Venetian, the Yuan state appeared fabulously wealthy, as indicated by the khan's 12,000 personal retainers, bedecked in silks, furs, fine leathers, and sparkling jewels.[9] Polo's fabulous story, dictated to a fellow prisoner of war in Genoa, reported the wondrous world of Cathay (China)—its canals, granaries, social services, technology, and such customs (strange to much of Europe) as regular bathing. Polo's account, like many travelogues of the period, is an interesting mix

of fact and fantasy based on impressionistic observations and probably prompted by the desire to entertain as well as inform a specific audience. Polo was not the only observer of China, but his work at the court gave him an unusual vantage point.

The Yuan court's social practices, in addition to the discriminatory ethnic hierarchy, included the requirement that individuals register by occupation in order to pay labor services. In the realm of culture, the Yuan borrowed some Chinese traditions. At first, Daoism and Confucianism were subordinated to Buddhism, but both were revived during Khubilai's reign. The examination system was sporadically revived after 1315 but was weighted in favor of Mongols, so ethnic Chinese grew disillusioned. Chinese drama remained popular, influenced somewhat by the dance of Central Asia. Interest in drama encouraged the development of classical Chinese opera, a combination of singing, dancing, and acting, which reached maturity in the Yuan period. Some of the most influential Chinese painters were also producing at this time, and the novel emerged as a reflection of Chinese concerns. An example is *Romance of the Three Kingdoms*, a long and rambling tale set in late Han times but written in the fourteenth century.

During the Yuan dynasty, hosts of missionaries, traders, and adventurers continued to journey to and from Asia, Africa, and Europe. These travelers describe the opulence of China and the Mongol court. Even before the Polos, Christian missionaries had proceeded eastward, encouraged by hopes of converting the Mongols and, more important, gaining allies against the Muslims. John of Plano Carpini (PLAH-noh car-PEE-nee), dispatched by Pope Innocent IV, visited the Great Khan in 1246 but failed to convert the ruler or enlist him as a papal vassal. In fact, the khan sent him home with a letter demanding that Europe's monarchs submit to him and that the pope attend the khan's court to pay homage. Later, a Flemish Franciscan, William of Rubruck, visited Möngke's court in 1254 and 1255 and met with similar results; but another Franciscan, John of Monte Corvino, attracted thousands of converts to Christianity between his arrival in Beijing in 1289 and his death in 1322. Meanwhile, Mongol religious toleration had drawn Christians into Central Asia and Buddhists into the Middle East.

In addition to the missionaries, swarms of other people visited China and Mongolia. One was Guillaume Boucier, a Parisian architect, who trekked to Karakorum, where he constructed a palace fountain capable of dispensing four different alcoholic beverages. Other adventurers, equally distinct, moved continuously on the travel routes. Between 1325 and 1354, Ibn Battuta, the famous Muslim globetrotter from Morocco, visited Constantinople, every Middle Eastern Islamic state, India, Sri Lanka, Indonesia, and China. In Hangzhou he encountered a man from

Discovery Through Maps

Gog and Magog in the Ebstorf Mappamundi

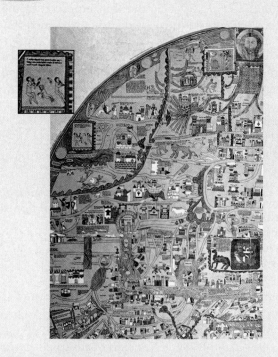

Maps depict more than geographical observations; they tell us the beliefs and imaginings of the people who produce them and reflect the point of view of the mapmaker. Historically, when people lacked a clear picture of far-off lands, they employed fantastic stories to describe what lay beyond their own known world. Like myths and folktales, maps from different eras illustrate some of the ways that societies have imagined apparently "strange" or "foreign" lands. We have seen that there was considerable commercial and intellectual exchange among Europe, India, China, and Central Asia in the years 220–1350 C.E. Nonetheless, the "Orient" remained a mysterious place in the imagination of many Westerners, a sometimes frightening place inhabited by strange creatures.

The thirteenth-century Ebstorf Mappamundi (map of the world), discovered in a Benedictine monastery in Germany, presents a geographical vision that combines Christian historiography, geographical observation, biblical mythology, the legends of Alexander the Great, and ancient tales of beastlike races inhabiting the "ends of the earth." It incorporates the idea of Gog and Magog, the homelands of apocalyptic destroyers, drawn from the New Testament (Revelation 20:7–8), into the description of the territory of northeastern Asia, the Mongol territory to the north of the Caucasus Mountains. On medieval Christian maps

Gog and Magog were equated with barbarian races, with the Ten Lost Tribes of Israel, and with the armies of the Anti-Christ. According to legend, these ferocious peoples had been trapped by Alexander the Great, who built a great wall to contain them; they would break out at the end of time and overwhelm civilized societies. On the Ebsdorf map the people of Gog and Magog are tribes of savages who are shown eating human body parts and drinking blood. They are walled off in the far northeast of the world. Their identification with the Tartars suggests the fear of Turco-Mongol invaders that pervaded the mapmaker's society in the thirteenth century. Given the striking success of the Mongols' conquests in this era, it is no wonder that they came to be associated with Gog and Magog. Gog and Magog also appear on the twelfth-century Islamic world map of al-Idrīsī (see Chapter 7).

Questions to Consider

1. Why might medieval Europeans have imagined that a "hero" like Alexander the Great put a wall around such fearsome peoples?
2. Do you think the mapmakers took the idea of Gog and Magog literally? Why or why not?
3. What other examples do you know reflecting ideas about frightful peoples that live in far-off lands or about terrible events occurring at the "end of time?"

Morocco whom he had met before in Delhi. Some travelers went the opposite way. Rabban Sauma, a monk from Central Asia, traveled to Paris; and a Chinese Christian monk from Beijing, while in Europe as an envoy from the Persian khan to the pope, had audiences with the English and French kings.

Eurasian traders—Persians, Arabs, Greeks, and western Europeans—were numerous and worldly wise travelers. They were enticed by Mongol policies that lowered tolls in the commercial cities and provided special protection for merchants' goods. Land trade between Europe and China, particularly in silk and spices, increased rapidly in the fourteenth century. The main western terminals were Nizhni Novgorod, east of Moscow, where the China caravans made contact with merchants of the Hanseatic League, a coalition of German merchant companies; Tabriz, in northeastern Persia, which served as the eastern terminal for Constantinople; and the Syrian coastal cities, where the caravans met Mediterranean ships, mostly from Venice.

Expanding land trade along the old silk route did not diminish the growing volume of sea commerce. Indeed, the Mongol devastation of Middle Eastern cities provided a quick stimulus, particularly to the spice trade, which was partly redirected through the Red Sea and Egypt to Europe. Within a few decades, however, the Mamluk monopoly in Egypt drove prices up sharply, and the European demand for cheaper spices helped revive overland trade. By now, however, the southern sea route was thriving for other reasons. The Mongol conquest of China had immediately opened opportunities to Japanese and Malayan sea merchants, causing a modest commercial revolution. Later, after the government in China stabilized and became involved in the exchange, the volume of ocean trade between northeastern Asia and the Middle East surpassed that of Song times.

Although their conquests were accompanied by horrifying slaughter and wrought considerable havoc, Mongol control also spread knowledge of explosives, printing, medicine, shipbuilding, and navigation from China to the West. In the Middle East they furthered art, architecture, and historical writing. To China they brought Persian astronomy and ceramics, in addition to sorghum, a new food from India.

In the end, the Yuan dynasty was short-lived. Khubilai was its last effective leader. A powerful chancellor attempted to build a new canal to transport southern grain after the Yellow River burst its dikes in the 1340s, but his conscription of 150,000 laborers strained China's resources. In response, a messianic religion, the **White Lotus Society,** claimed numerous adherents anxious for Maitreya, the messiah Buddha, to bring about an end to suffering and injustice. Devastating epidemics hit cities already weakened by Mongol subjection; in 1232, Kaifeng lost one million people to the plague in three months. By mid-century, plague ravaged China and spread via the trade routes to the rest of Eurasia. A great rebellion, beginning in southern China and led by Zhu Yuanzhang (JOO yoo-ahn-JAHNG; 1328–1398)—known to history as Taizu, the first emperor of the Ming dynasty—ultimately ended the weakened Yuan. After the Chinese reconquered most of Mongolia and Manchuria, many northern Mongols reverted to nomadism. Others, on the western steppes, were absorbed into Turkic states.

KOREA: FROM THREE KINGDOMS TO ONE

■ *How did Buddhism and Confucianism contribute to Korean culture and politics?*

Southeast Asia, Japan, and Korea

In the third century C.E. the land inhabited by modern Koreans was divided in three kingdoms—one in the north and two in the south. Despite the common stereotype of Korea as an isolated "hermit kingdom," these three kingdoms were very much part of East Asian international culture. They adopted religion, arts, philosophy, and means of governance from China, transmitted culture and material goods to Japan, and fought battles against and in alliance with Chinese and Japanese rulers at various times. The fate of Koreans was closely integrated with the rise and fall of empires on the continent. By the fourteenth century, domestic and international influences led to the merger of the Korean kingdoms into one kingdom.

According to legend, Ko Chosŏn (KOH CHO-son), the earliest kingdom of Korea, was established in the third millennium B.C.E., but bronze age remnants date it from about 1500 B.C.E. Archaeological remains show that Koreans grew millet, soybeans, red beans, and rice; used ploughs and knives; developed metallurgy; and had an animistic form of religion in which all natural objects had spirits. Labor became specialized into peasant and artisan categories. In 109 B.C.E., this productive territory attracted the attention of the Han dynasty in China. Emperor Wudi conquered Ko Chosŏn and established four Chinese provincial commanderies in the north, permitting the introduction of Chinese culture. The decline of the Han allowed the newly arising Korean states to push the Chinese out and compete for dominance.

Koguryŏ (KOH-goo-ree-oh) was founded in 37 B.C.E. and by the first century C.E. had adopted a Chi-

---

White Lotus Society—Messianic religion that blended Manichaeism, Maitreya Buddhism, Daoism, and Confucianism. Appealed to people in times of crisis.

Korea

57 B.C.E.	Silla established
37 B.C.E.	Koguryŏ established
200s C.E.	Paekche established
383	Buddhism adopted in Korea
668	Silla defeats Paekche and Koguryŏ, unites Korea
936–1392	Koryŏ dynasty
1238	Mongol Invasion

nese style of kingship. Free peasants, living in villages under headmen, formed the bulk of society. Legal codes punished murder, theft, and bodily injury as well as female (though not male) adultery and jealousy—underscoring the importance of life and property in addition to the centrality of the polygamous, patriarchal family. The rise of the southern state of Paekche (PAIK-cheh) in the third century led Koguryŏ to strengthen its institutions: Koguryŏ's King Sosurim (r. 371–384) adopted Buddhism, set up a National Confucian Academy, and developed an administrative law code, all of which made Koguryŏ a centralized aristocratic state. In 433 Paekche formed an alliance with Silla (SHIL-lah; founded 57 B.C.E.), the other southern state. Koguryŏ fought against its Korean neighbors, sometimes in alliance with Chinese or Japanese forces. Koguryŏ was a powerful kingdom, later launching attacks on the Sui in China. (Its victories against the Sui army are part of the Korean annals of resistance.)

All three kingdoms were culturally Buddhist; Paekche adopted Buddhism in 384 and Silla in 528. Their poetry and arts followed Buddhist themes. Because most buildings were made of wood, none remain, but paintings and sculpture from this period, many with religious themes, are plentiful. A major **pagoda** (the East Asian form of the stupa) was built in Silla in 645, and lasted till it was destroyed by the Mongols in the thirteenth century.

Silla began to assert its power in the fifth century. Silla had an aristocratic society in which officials' positions were determined by "bone-rank" (that is, one's bloodline or status). Officials met in the Council of Nobles, and young men were placed in the Flower of Youth Corps, a powerful military organiza-

tion. Silla allied with the Tang to defeat Koguryŏ and Paekche in the 660s, but, worried about Tang expansionism, Silla decided to push the Tang out of the Korean peninsula in 676. Lively trade between Silla and the Tang ensued, taking the place of conquest. Koreans were drawn into the international system promoted by the Tang; a Silla general in service to the Tang conquered Tashkent and Silla monks traveled to India. The eighth century, in which Pure Land Buddhism and Zen were introduced to Korea and the agricultural output was plentiful and varied, was the high point of Silla rule. By the ninth and tenth centuries, powerful landowners emerged, breaking apart the equal-field system applied in Silla.

In 936, one of many rebels succeeded in unifying the peninsula under a new dynasty he called the Koryŏ (KOH-ree-oh). This leader, King Taejo, and his immediate successors emancipated slaves (while retaining some forms of labor taxes), instituted an examination system (though preserving some aristocratic privilege), collected all arms held by private individuals, built a major university, supported Buddhism, and attempted to model the kingdom on Song Confucianism. Throughout its early years, Koryŏ faced threats from the Liao. The Jurchen's defeat of Liao and then of the northern Song left Koryŏ temporarily at peace with its neighbors. Domestically, however, the civilian leadership of Koryŏ was removed by a bloody coup by military officials in 1170, and peasant uprisings

This crown made of gold and jade is from the Kingdom of Silla and was made in the fifth or sixth century. Its opulence is a symbol for the national unification of Korea under a monarch.

---

pagoda—A Buddhist reliquary/monument, the East Asian equivalent of the Indian stupa.

around the same time weakened, but did not destroy, the state.

The Mongols invaded the weakened Koryŏ state in 1238. In the 1270s and 1280s, Koryŏ joined the Mongols in two unsuccessful invasions of Japan. Destructive Mongol rule led to uprisings throughout Korea in the 1340s, and soon King Kongmin (r. 1351–1374) restored Koryŏ rule. But he was doomed to failure. His bold initiatives at land reform were resisted by officials, tensions between Buddhists and Neo-Confucians of the Zhu Xi school erupted, and Japanese pirates plagued coastal trade. When he was assassinated in 1374, uprisings broke out all over Korea. The newly risen Ming dynasty in China took advantage of Koryŏ's instability, and was poised to invade in 1392. The Koryŏ general facing the Ming saw the writing on the wall, negotiated a treaty that made Korea a Ming tributary state, and marched back to the court to take over as the founder of the Yi or Chosŏn dynasty (1392–1910).

Even in times of trouble, however, Korean culture blossomed. When the great royal library was burnt in 1126, a new collection of Buddhist works was commissioned. Movable type to print this great collection was cast and used three centuries before Gutenberg first used movable type in Europe. Buddhist works of literature, painting, and sculpture as well as a beautiful stone pagoda were also produced during the Mongol era.

of aristocratic society that developed in the classical age that followed the tomb period. How did Japan develop before the tomb period?

Classical Asian culture—religions, philosophies, arts, and means of governance developed on the continent—flowed into Japan first from Korea and later from China. During the Ice Age, land bridges had connected Japan with the continent. Tools dating from 30,000 B.C.E. and pottery dating from 10,000 B.C.E. (the world's oldest examples of pottery) have been found by archaeologists. Whether these were developed in Japan itself or transmitted from elsewhere is uncertain. An increasingly sophisticated Neolithic culture, called Jōmon (JOH-mon) by scholars, developed distinctive pottery and, between 5000 and 3500 B.C.E., the ancient Japanese language. But it was around 300 B.C.E. that a large migration of Koreans to Japan's westernmost large island, Kyūshū, brought about a revolution in agricultural technology (paddy-field rice) as well as bronze and iron technology. By the time the Chinese observers commented on life in Japan in the late third century, the civilization that blended the new continental ideas with indigenous culture had been established for over 600 years. The period from about 300 B.C.E. to 300 C.E. is called the Yayoi (yah-YOI) period for the district in Tokyo in which the period's pottery was first unearthed.

THE EMERGENCE OF JAPAN IN EAST ASIA

■ *Did Japan's distance from the continent allow it to retain more of its indigenous culture than the other countries of Asia in the classical and medieval eras?*

Separated from the Asian mainland by more than 100 miles of open sea since the end of the last Ice Age (around 12,000 B.C.E.), Japan was something of a curiosity to Chinese observers in the late third century C.E. These Chinese chroniclers found the Japanese law-abiding, adept at farming, fond of alcohol, expert at weaving and fishing, interested in divination, and perhaps most surprising, governed by both male and female shamanistic rulers. They described one of these rulers, Queen Himiko (also known as Pimiko), as a powerful priestess/monarch who, after her death, was interred in a remarkably large funeral mound. These tombs, some of which were twice the volume of the Great Pyramid in Egypt, tell historians that Japan was likely a hierarchical society able to mobilize labor during the tomb period, c. 300–645 C.E. The existence of religious leadership, especially female religious leadership, helps to explain the type

Clay figures like this happy dancing peasant couple were placed in the huge tombs built for Japanese uji *leaders in the third, fourth, and fifth centuries.*

The following era, the tomb period, gave birth to what might be called Japan's first organized governments, ruled by those whose remains are in the great tombs. At first, the extent of a leader's control was likely no more than a clan located in one village, but in time, successful leaders brought more and more villages under their control until they had something like a province. Political authority was intimately connected to religious authority. The original clans, called *uji*, were led by a head priest or priestess believed to be descended from the clan's own deity or *kami*. In ancient Japanese religion—later called **Shintō** ("Way of the Gods") when the introduction of Buddhism made it obvious that Japan's intrinsic belief system deserved a religious name—*kami* were believed to be everywhere in nature. The world of the living was seen as connected to the world of the gods, and governance was a part of religious ritual. Thus, women were not barred from what we would consider administrative leadership, and the Chinese observers found that fact sufficiently interesting to comment on it.

The *uji* in the Yamato region, near the area in which the cities of Nara and Kyoto were later built, possessed the most fertile agricultural land in ancient Japan. It is small wonder that the Yamato leaders, able to build on their productive wealth to support military strength, emerged as the most powerful *uji* by the fifth century. The Japanese language did not yet have its own written form, so historians rely on Chinese observers' reports from the fifth century, rich archaeological remains in tombs, and Japanese histories (*Kojiki*—Records of Ancient Matters—and *Nihongi*—Records of Japan), written in the early eighth century and based on orally transmitted tales, for evidence about people's lives at that time. Tomb artifacts throughout the period included jewels, mirrors, and, most interestingly, clay statues of human figures like warriors, musicians, courtiers, and dancing peasants, all showing expressions of joy, as well as of horses, boats and model houses. From the fifth century on, these tombs increasingly held military objects brought in by a new wave of people from the Korean peninsula. Outside the tombs, archaeological remains of peasant villages suggest farmers lived in pit dwellings.

The power of the Yamato *uji* vis-à-vis the other *uji* throughout Japan was bolstered by its alliance with Paekche. Korean artisans and scribes brought a wealth of Korean and Chinese culture with them to Japan, strengthening the prestige, authority, and administrative competence of the Yamato state. Imported weapons allowed the Yamato warriors to hold sway over their neighbors. As in Korea, Chinese characters were used to transcribe Japanese. Confucian scholarship was introduced around 513, and Buddhism made

Japan	
c. 300 B.C.E.–300 C.E.	Yayoi period
late 200s	Queen Himiko of Yamato
c. 300	Yamato clan dominates central Japan
c. 538	Buddhism introduced to Japan
645	Taika Reform
710–784	Nara period
760s	Compilation of *Man'yōshū*
794–1181	Heian period
c. 800	Introduction of Tendai and Shingon Buddhism
995–1027	Regency of Fujiwara Michinaga
c. 1000	Lady Murasaki, *The Tale of Genji*
1185–1333	Kamakura Shogunate
1274, 1281	Mongol Invasions

a grand entrance, possibly in 538, when the king of Paekche sent Yamato a statue of the Buddha and copies of Buddhist scriptures. Though the ties with Paekche soon ended, the coming of continental culture in general and Buddhism in particular set in motion a cultural and intellectual revolution in Japan. After Silla's unification of the Korean peninsula in the 670s, the Yamato leaders turned to the Tang dynasty for cultural models, diplomatic ties, and trade. At the same time, the Japanese retained significant indigenous customs. These included marriage practices that emphasized the central role of the bride and her family, practices that would later play an important political role. They also included the old religions of Japan. The Yamato family, while welcoming Buddhism following a sixth-century struggle between Shintō ritualists and proponents of Buddhism that was won by the latter, nevertheless retained the worship of the Shintō gods. At some earlier time, as the Yamato were rising to power, a myth of Japan's creation that blended several *uji*'s founding myths and placed the Yamato's ancestral deity Amaterasu (AH-mah-teh-RAH-soo), the sun goddess, at the top of the hierarchy, developed. The Yamato would use this to legitimize their political dominance for many centuries to come.

The victorious proponents of Buddhism, the Soga family, greatly influenced the Yamato family. During

Shintō—Indigenous Japanese religion focused on innumerable gods in nature; animistic belief system tied to government in antiquity.

his aunt's reign as the Yamato ruler, Prince Shōtoku (SHOH-toh-koo), head of the Soga, apparently undertook so many reforms that Japan was forever changed. He is credited with scholarly commentary (in flawless Chinese) on Buddhist scriptures; with building many temples, including, in 607, Hōryūji (hoh-ree-OO-jee), which contains the world's oldest extant wooden buildings; with opening diplomatic relations with the Sui and later Tang; with adopting the Chinese calendar; with reorganizing the Yamato governing structure on the model of the Confucian state to make it the central monarchy of Japan; and with writing, in 604, the "Seventeen-Article Constitution." These accomplishments were detailed in one of the eighth-century histories of Japan and undoubtedly exaggerated the Prince's personal contributions, but most of them did take place either during his service as regent to the throne or in the decades after his death. Shōtoku's death in 622 led to a struggle for power, ending with the victory of one courtly faction led by the head of the Nakatomi family (renamed Fujiwara in 645). The Yamato family retained the throne, as they do to this day, but the Fujiwara family replaced the Soga as their main advisors. In 645, the Fujiwara carried out the Taika (Great change) Reforms, which centralized economic control under the equal-field system imported from China and Korea. Two rulers, Emperor Temmu (r. 672–686) and Empress Jito (r. 686–697), implemented additional changes; they and their successors were simultaneously continental-style rulers empowered by the prestige of Confucian authority and Shintō rulers legitimized by descent from Amaterasu.

Government in the Classical Era— Nara and Heian

An important step toward Chinese-style centralization was the building of a permanent capital. In 710, the Yamato, by then considered the imperial family, built the city of Nara on the model of Chang'an. Although today's Nara is located in a different site, the eighth-century capital's grid of streets and ancient Buddhist temples are still evident in the Japanese countryside. The rise of powerful Buddhist monasteries and temples may have challenged the power of the court sufficiently to force it to abandon Nara in 784 and build a new capital, Heian (now called Kyoto), in 794. Like Nara, Heian was originally laid out on a grid pattern preserved in modern Kyoto's downtown boulevards and streets. Historians designate the years 710–784 as the Nara Period and 794–1181 (or 1185) as the Heian Period.

To make the capital the sole seat of power, the court enticed all *uji* leaders, who might be potential rivals for power, to live there by granting them titles of nobility and making the court too glamorous to avoid. Many of these *uji* families' provincial lands were con-

A fine example of architecture during the mid-Heian period in Japan is Phoenix Hall, near the modern city of Kyoto. Used by Fujiwara Michinaga as a villa, it later became a temple honoring Amida.

fiscated and redistributed under the equal-field system in the seventh and eighth centuries, but the *uji* were allowed to retain some lands, as were religious institutions and individual farmers who opened new fields to cultivation. Such private estates, unlike the lands farmed by average peasants, were exempt from taxation by the court. Though these estates, called **shōen,** were but a small percentage of Japan's cultivated fields in the eighth century, during the next several centuries peasants wishing to escape taxation commended their lands to private estate owners. This led to the gradual reduction in taxable lands, as farmers paid rents to large owners rather than the often higher taxes to the court. The replacement of tax revenues by rents did not at first appear problematic, however. The great families not only lived at or near the court but also, as we shall see, were often tied by blood to the imperial family. By the eleventh century, however, the gradual erosion of the tax base undermined the central authority of the court. In addition, the absence of a government-run military—a conscript army was one of the Chinese institutions not implemented by the Japanese court because Japan appeared not to face external enemies as did the Chinese—induced estate owners to hire guards to protect their provincial economic interests. These guards eventually became the samurai or warrior class. When they served as guards, they presented no threat to the throne, but when they banded together, as they did in the tenth century and then, most disastrously for the court, in 1181, they could become an alternate political authority to the throne.

Even during the height of the throne's power, its authority was dependent on a balance with one great family, the northern branch of the Fujiwara family. The Fujiwara had earned a special role as advisors at the time of the Taika Reform, but they preserved their dominant position through Japan's traditional marriage practices. Japanese couples married extremely young by today's standards—often as young as 12 or 13. Though girls of the elite spent most of their time indoors and spoke with men not of their immediate families from behind a screen to maintain their propriety, they were very well educated and could communicate easily by letters. Literature describes the lives of women and girls at the court as much more open, and these courtly women communicated more freely with men and with one another. In either case, women and girls played an important role in selection of their sexual and marital partners.

CASE STUDY

Women in the Imperial Courts of China and Japan

A young man interested in a woman at court might find few barriers to a liaison with her. If the young woman lived at home with her parents, courtship was a bit more complicated. The suitor would call on a potential lover by slipping, under cover of night, through the windows of her room, taking care not to wake her parents. She would speak to him, exchanging poetry and observing his character and attractiveness, from behind her screen. If his clothes, language, scholarly ability, scent, musical talent, and sensitive heart were sufficiently appealing, it was proper for her to invite him behind her screen. If not, she sent him packing, and her propriety was not compromised. If he spent the night, he would have to sneak out at the first rays of morning light. Repeated visits would trigger the parents' investigation of the young man and his career prospects, and if they approved, they would indicate the couple's marriage by leaving ritual food and drink outside their daughter's bedroom door. Thereafter, the young man could come and go during the day, as he was now part of the family as the daughter's husband. The young man would be known as the husband of his bride's house, her parents would make sure he was beautifully outfitted to present himself well at court, and in some cases, once the bride was mature enough to run her own household, the parents and other children might move to another house and leave the teenage bride in charge of her own home. Most likely, she would already have one or two children, raised in their early years by their maternal grandparents, as women usually had their first child in their teens. Grandparents thus had a particularly strong bond with their grandchildren. Property was inherited by daughters, children were their mothers' and maternal grandparents' responsibility, and respectable men and women—though not *married* women—could have more than one sexual partner. Once married, a woman should be unavailable to other men, but serial monogamy was practiced.

Fujiwara influence over the throne depended on marriage customs and family relations. When an 8-year-old boy ascended the throne as emperor in 858, his maternal grandfather, a Fujiwara who was already Grand Minister to the court, assumed even greater control as regent for his grandson. This pattern of Fujiwara patriarchs' control of child emperors, and even some adult emperors who were their grandsons or other relatives, continued for the next 200 years. The pinnacle of Fujiwara dominance was in the early eleventh century. Fujiwara Michinaga (MEE-chee-NAH-gah), who held dominion over the court from 995 to 1027, was the brother of two empresses and the father of four, the uncle of two emperors, the grandfather of two more, and the great-grandfather of another. Some non-Fujiwara protested, but until an emperor whose mother had not been a Fujiwara ascended the throne in the late eleventh century, the Fujiwara controlled the throne. Through this control, the Fujiwara were able to have the tax-free ownership status of their shōen estates confirmed, as only an official could grant that status. For the next century, retired emperors took the place of the Fujiwara as

---

shōen—A tax-free estate in Heian Japan.

regents for their youthful sons whom they placed on the throne. In the late twelfth century, disputes over succession to the throne led to the development of factions at court, and with each faction backed by a powerful samurai family, civil war raged throughout the country from 1181 to 1186. When it was over, the imperial institution survived, but it no longer had the authority to rule Japan. That power fell to the victorious samurai leader, Minamoto Yoritomo (MEE-nah-MOH-toh YOH-ree-TOH-moh; 1147–1199), his wife, Hōjō Masako (HOH-joh MAH-sah-ko; 1157–1225), and her family, who exercised their power from the medieval town of Kamakura in eastern Japan.

Classical Arts and Literature

Japanese emperors sent numerous embassies to the Tang court and brought back a continuing stream of up-to-date culture and material goods. New developments in Chinese poetry were reflected in Japanese verse; new schools of Buddhism influenced Japanese religion; and plump Tang beauties set the standard for female pulchritude at the Japanese court. Yet Japan preserved many of its own practices, including an emphasis on aristocracy, a rejection of eunuchs at court, and unique marriage customs. In 839, as the Tang dynasty was clearly declining, the court ceased to send embassies to China.

Courtly society from the Nara through the Heian periods was extraordinarily refined. The record left from those centuries includes great volumes of poetry, diaries, the world's first novel—the massive *Tale of Genji* by Lady Murasaki—as well as paintings, sculpture, temples, monasteries, and other buildings. Art

works from distant lands in Eurasia, brought to Japan by travelers to China, show Japan's integration with the international culture of the Buddhist Age in the Nara and early Heian eras. And music preserved in Japan's court until the present day is the only extant record of Tang musical styles borrowed in the classical era. Impressive though this body of culture is, it was the creation of just a tiny group of people; aristocrats were no more than one tenth of one percent of the population, with urban residents influenced by those aristocrats perhaps an additional several percent.

Unlike aristocrats, farmers were not literate. Tax rates appear high, as evidenced by peasants' attempts to escape the tax roles. Pestilence devastated farmers and city-folk alike. Men, women, and children worked hard. Despite these difficulties, folk tales and written stories abound with examples of farm women's high status relative to their husbands. Women likely selected their own spouses, and many made important economic contributions to their households. Wives' infidelity was treated as a joke rather than as a capital crime in folk tales.

The poetry of the literate elite reflected the importance of sentiment. The *Man'yōshū* (mahn-YOH-shoo; *The Collection of Ten Thousand Leaves*), compiled in the 760s, contains over 4000 poems, many of which date to the fifth century, composed by emperors, empresses, courtesans, frontier guards, and commoners. These brief and direct compositions covered such themes as parting of lovers, loyalty to one's lord, love of nature, grief over the death of a child, and the Buddhist theme of the fleeting nature of human life, give us a rich sense of early Japanese society and culture. Two *Man'yōshū* poems, the first a love poem by a woman, the second a poem of grief for his wife by a man, give a sense of this collection:[10]

Court ladies and their maids in The Tale of Genji. *Heian court women were ideally plump, had hair longer than their bodies, and wore many layers of robes. The* Genji *scrolls integrated text and images.*

Oh, how steadily I love you—
You who awe me
Like the thunderous waves
That lash the seacoast of Ise!

Lady Kasa

In our chamber, where our two pillows lie,
Where we two used to sleep together,
Days I spend alone, broken-hearted:
Nights I pass, sighing till dawn.
Kakinomoto Hitomaro

The imperial treasury at Nara, built in the eighth century, contains works of art by both Japanese and continental artists, indicating Japan's increasing international contacts in the Nara period. This small silver jar depicts a hunting scene that includes a deer, still one of the symbols of Nara.

Because the Japanese language did not have a written form, it was represented with Chinese characters. Aristocratic men and some women were able to read and write in Chinese and thus sought to use characters to record Japanese. The two languages are not related linguistically, so the characters were used in several different ways. One was to represent meaning—the Chinese character for "tree," for example, would be applied to the Japanese word for "tree." The other was to represent sounds without any consideration for the meaning of the character. This led to a virtually indecipherable script, so *kana*, a syllabic script, was devised in the early ninth century. Soon poetry, diaries, essays, and novels were written in this script. Aristocratic authors, especially but not exclusively women, produced an outpouring of creative works. Women's dominance in the literary arts at that time was due, in part, to the fact that men spent a lot of their time writing government documents in Chinese. But the fact that creativity, including calligraphic, artistic, and sensory abilities, was not gendered at that time, as well as the leisure time their aristocratic privilege gave them, may have had more to do with offering women opportunities to produce fine works.

The most important work of the Heian period—and some might say of the entire body of Japanese literary arts—was *The Tale of Genji*, written over the course of perhaps two decades by Lady Murasaki, who

DOCUMENT
Excerpt from Lady Murasaki Shikibu's Diary

was sometimes praised, sometimes ridiculed for her exceptional knowledge of both Japanese and Chinese scholarship.[11] *The Tale of Genji* describes the life, loves, escapades, and sorrows of the sensitive and talented Prince Genji, a paragon of male virtue; his son Kaoru; Genji's steadfast male friends; and his beloved wife Murasaki. The novel is an intriguing look into courtly life around the year 1000. An excellent parallel to *Genji* is *The Pillow Book* by Sei Shōnagon (SAY SHOH-nah-gon), a contemporary and professional rival of Lady Murasaki at another empress's court. *The Pillow Book* contains often racy, amusing and satirical essays that give good insight into the life of the court.

From the sixth century through the first half of the Heian period, religious themes predominated in the arts. Statues and paintings of various manifestations of the Buddha, indicating changes in artistic style and notions of physical beauty over the centuries, were common. But decorated items for aristocratic pleasure, such as musical instruments, boxes, and tables are also among the treasury of early Japanese art. By the tenth century, paintings of highly secular themes emerged. Fans with themes from literature were made and used by court ladies, and the *Genji* scrolls of the eleventh century were a multimedia production interspersing gorgeous paintings with Murasaki's text. Comic scrolls appeared by the late Heian period. The architecture of the court and of private mansions was elegant, with raised floors of polished wood, sliding screen doors, wooden buildings connected to one another by covered corridors, windows with hinged shutters (through which suitors could climb), all surrounded by carefully landscaped gardens with streams and ponds.

Japanese Buddhism in the Classical and Early Medieval Eras

Mahayana Buddhism reached entered Japan in the sixth century and was well established among the aristocracy by the eighth. To further the secular reach of the Nara state, the court established branch temples throughout the country, staffed by monks trained in the capital. Most commoners, especially those in the countryside, continued to carry out Shintō rituals. Except for the struggles in the sixth century, there was little conflict between Buddhism and either indigenous Shintō and the imported philosophy of Confucianism as there had been in China, and Buddhism was eventually

Document   Sei Shōnagon: *The Pillow Book*

Sei Shōnagon was a contemporary and literary rival of Lady Murasaki. The two served different empresses of the reigning emperor; Sei Shōnagon's court was considered more fashionable and Lady Murasaki's more erudite. Sei Shōnagon was a witty and talented writer. In her diary, Murasaki describes Sei Shōnagon as "a very proud person. She values herself highly and scatters her Chinese writings all about. . . . How can such a vain and reckless person end her days happily!"[11] Below is an excerpt from Sei Shōnagon's *Pillow Book* in which she describes distressing things.

One has been expecting someone, and rather late at night there is a stealthy tapping at the door. One sends a maid to see who it is, and lies waiting, with some flutter of the breast. But the name one hears when she returns is that of someone completely different, who does not concern one at all. Of all depressing experiences, this is by far the worst.

It is very tiresome when a lover who is leaving at dawn says that he must look for a fan or a pocketbook that he left somewhere about the room last night. . . . Instead of experiencing the feelings of regret proper to such an occasion, one merely feels irritated at his clumsiness. . . . It is important that a lover should know how to make his departure. To begin with, he ought not to be too ready to get up, but should require a little coaxing. . . . He should not pull on his trousers the moment he is up, but should first of all come close to one's ear and in a whisper finish off whatever was left half-said in the course of the night. . . . If he springs to his feet with a jerk and at once begins fussing around, one begins to hate him.

I like to think of a bachelor . . . returning at dawn from some amorous excursion. . . . As soon as he is home . . . he begins to write his next-morning letter. . . . When he has washed and got into his court cloak . . . he takes the sixth chapter of the Lotus Sutra and reads it silently. Precisely at the most solemn moment of his reading, the messenger returns. . . . With an amusing if blasphemous rapidity the lover transfers his attention from the book he is reading to the business of framing an answer.

Questions to Consider

1. How important was romantic love to Heian aristocrats?
2. The ideal bachelor Sei Shōnagon describes reads Buddhist scriptures before heading off to work at the court. What other tasks take priority over his religious practice?
3. Did women have a choice in the selection of their suitors?

From "The Pillow Book of Sei Shōnagon," in Donald Keene, *Anthology of Japanese Literature* (New York: Grove Press, 1955), pp. 137–139.

---

indigenized as the dominant religion of Japan following new theological directions in the Heian period.

Two new sects of Buddhism were brought to Japan by student monks who had journeyed to China in 804. Tendai, introduced by Saichō in 805, and Shingon, brought back by Kūkai in 806, both made it possible to

Buddhist Monks

develop mass participation in Buddhist worship. Tendai doctrine stated that those who led a life of purity and contemplation could realize enlightenment and their "Buddha nature." Saichō established an important monastery at Mt. Hiei (HEE-ay), which several centuries later became a source of trouble for the court as it supported not only devotion and learning but also a large army of warrior-monks who demanded land rights and privileges. Shingon was an esoteric faith, with secret and seemingly magical rites. It was extremely popular in the Heian period, as it encouraged art, medicinal use of herbs, incantations, and pageantry. It also appealed to Shintō adherents, as its

central deity was Dainichi (DAI-nee-chee), the "Great Sun" Buddha, who was identified with the Sun Goddess in the popular mind.

In the mid-tenth century, itinerant monks spread a simplified version of the Tendai doctrine of enlightenment, stating that salvation was possible only for those who called on the name of Amida, the Buddha of the Pure Land. But it was not until the end of the Heian period, with its natural disasters, earthquakes, fires, and fearsome warfare that a proponent of Pure Land Buddhism succeeded in establishing a new type of Buddhism. The monk Hōnen (1133–1212) preached that faith in Amida alone, without relying on good works, was the only route to salvation. He endured persecution for his propagation of Pure Land ideas. His follower Shinran (1173–1262) took these ideas even further. He said that perfect faith was shown by uttering the name of Amida just once, and that an evil man of perfect faith was able to enter the Pure Land. Shinran broke with Buddhist tradition—eating meat,

The pagodas of Yakushi-ji at Nara. Built in the eighth century, Yakushi-ji is one of Japan's earliest wooden temple compounds. Buddhist temples of that era challenged the secular power of the government, so the emperor's court moved to Heian in 794.

marrying a nun, and advocating the equality of all occupations if performed with a pure heart. His True Pure Land sect eventually became the largest in Japan. The other important faith sect was Nichiren (NEE-chee-ren) Buddhism, founded by the monk Nichiren (1222–1282), who stated that one should place faith in the Lotus Sutra, a key Buddhist scripture, rather than Amida. Known for his Japanese nationalism, he predicted the Mongol invasions. By the twelfth century, Buddhism had spread to all classes of society.

Two major **Zen** sects were also brought back to Japan by Japanese student monks. Eisai (1141–1215) introduced the Rinzai sect and Dōgen (1200–1253) the Sōtō sect. Rinzai stressed complicated riddles to achieve enlightenment, while Sōtō emphasized long hours of meditation. Both methods were increasingly popular with samurai who were attracted to the sudden enlightenment they promised.

Early Medieval Government and Culture

Minamoto Yoritomo's victory over the other major warrior band, the Taira, in 1185 ushered in the era of warrior dominance. He never claimed the throne, as victorious generals elsewhere in Asia had, but rather had the emperor confer on him a new position, *shōgun* (great general), a title which would remain in use for most of the next 700 years. The shōgun theoretically served at the pleasure of the emperor, but (until 1868) when emperors attempted to assert their rights, the struggle was always won by the shōgun, who, of course, claimed to be serving the emperor. (An

attempted imperial uprising in 1221 was suppressed.) The shōgun set up his seat of power in Kamakura, away from the capital, and the era of Kamakura dominance is called the Kamakura Period (1185–1333).

Minamoto Yoritomo's legitimacy as a ruler was based on his own institutions in addition to his symbolic subordination to the emperor. First, he made use of the loyalty of his samurai. Like feudal lords in Europe, he used a bond of loyalty to motivate his samurai warriors, whom he called "honorable house men" or vassals. These vassals were appointed constables of provinces, with the duty to raise up armies if necessary, and stewards or overseers on the shōen estates owned by the rich old Heian families. To show his authority over the estates, he allowed the stewards to collect a small amount of revenue—so small that owners did not bother to contest it as they had contested the imperial court's ability to collect taxes on private lands. By paying the small fees, however, owners acknowledged the legitimacy of Kamakura's right to collect it. During the next century, the stewards would use these locally collected resources to establish their own landed power base in the countryside, and they would eventually turn on their supposed overlords in Kamakura. Second, Minamoto Yoritomo and his successors made use of much of the provincial governing structure of the old imperial system for most of the next century. The vassal samurai were too few in number to rule on their own, so the previous system was retained in many places. Third, Minamoto established three new offices: the samurai board, which controlled the vassals; the judicial board, which settled suits over land holdings as well as criminal issues; and the administrative board, to carry out his policies. The judicial board was particularly important in gaining the support of the people, as it was known for its impartiality in settling disputes. The administrative board was headed by his Hōjō in-laws, and was used by them to increase their power after Yoritomo's death in 1199. Indeed, power passed into Hōjō hands, where it remained until the Kamakura shogunate (government by shōgun) was overthrown.

Zen—The Japanese form of Chan Buddhism. Popular with the samurai.

By the end of the thirteenth century, samurai ties to Kamakura had become attenuated. Allegiance to the dominant Hōjō was not as certain as allegiance to the Minamoto had been earlier. Far from Kamakura, samurai stewards out in the provinces developed local ties, both political and economic. When the Mongols attacked in 1274 and again in 1281, the samurai, especially those of the western island of Kyūshū, where the attack came, fought bravely, but none was rewarded, because there were no spoils of war to divide. The invasion in 1274 threw 30,000 attackers against Japan; the second invasion was mounted by 140,000. Commoners built a sea wall whose remnants are still visible today to keep the Mongols out; it helped the Japanese warriors hold the Mongols out until typhoon winds, called *kamikaze* (divine winds), blew many of the Mongol vessels out to sea, forcing them to withdraw. Japan was saved, but the invasions had some very significant outcomes. Disgruntled warriors who had fought, commoners whose labor had built the fortifications, and religious people who claimed their prayers brought about the divine winds eventually moved against Kamakura when succession disputes at court gave them an excuse to join one side or the other in the 1330s. Also, the practice of daughter inheritance and multiple inheritance gave way to unigeniture or inheritance by one son in order to keep samurai lands intact to support a mounted warrior now deemed necessary for national defense. Single inheritance weakened family ties, as younger sons sought new patrons to protect them. This strengthened the lord-vassal bond at the heart of feudalism, which became increasingly important in the next three centuries.

Kamakura was home to numerous beautiful temples, built in harmony with the verdant hills, a new style of construction. A huge outdoor Great Buddha statue that still attracts thousands of tourists every day was cast in the early Kamakura period. But much of Japan's culture in this era emanated from Heian (now increasingly called Kyoto). The court commissioned great collections of poetry as they had in earlier centuries, and court ladies wrote, for an aristocratic readership, tales of great emotional depth. Periodic markets began to bring rural people into a larger national culture, but the arts were still fairly elite. This would change in the next century, as a national culture, enhanced by new infusions of Asian styles, entered Japan.

CONCLUSION

During the centuries following the collapse of the Mauryan dynasty in India (184 B.C.E.) and, much later, the Han dynasty in China (220 C.E.), significant cultural revivals occurred in Asia. First India and then China experienced golden ages when political unity was restored and social systems were revitalized. In India, the Gupta era encouraged the development of Hindu thought, along with notable advances in painting, architecture, literature, drama, medicine, and the physical sciences. At the same time, India continued to be part of an emerging international Buddhist culture, helping to link it to other Buddhist countries along the East-West trade routes. Later, international Islam tied rising Indian dynasties, some of them Islamic, to other centers of power and trade. China experimented with blending "barbarian" and indigenous means of government in the millennium from the fall of the Han to the fall of the Mongols. Cosmopolitan blending of culture made China the East Asian center of both cultural consumption and production. Scholarship and art blossomed even in the period of disunity and flourished in the lively international Tang dynasty and the technologically sophisticated early modern Song dynasty. Korea and Japan, while retaining much of their own culture, adopted a number of aspects of Chinese governance, art, philosophy, religion, and means of communication. Rivalries at times impeded trade, but diffusion of material and other forms of culture made Eurasia a single system, often dominated by its eastern side, during much of the millennium. Over the centuries, cultural diffusion gained increasing momentum throughout Eurasia. Goods and cultural patterns spread through migrations, invasions, missionary activities, and trade to China, India, Southeast Asia, Japan, Korea, the Asian steppes, and Europe.

Suggestions for Web Browsing

You can obtain more information about topics included in this chapter at the websites listed below. See also the companion website that accompanies this text, **http://www.ablongman.com/ brummett**, which contains an online study guide and additional resources.

Ancient and Medieval India
http://www.fordham.edu/halsall/india/indiasbook.html
Extensive collection of materials on ancient and medieval India; most entries include subsites with text and images.

Gupta Period
http://www.wsu.edu:8080/~dee/ANCINDIA/GUPTA.HTM
Indian history in the Gupta era.

Medieval India
http://www.goindiago.com/history/medieval.htm
Site discussing the history, sites and monuments, and classical texts of medieval India, 600 B.C.E.–1526 C.E.

Chinese Empire
http://www.wsu.edu/~dee/CHEMPIRE/CHEMPIRE.HTM
Chinese history from 256 B.C.E. to 1300 C.E., with details about philosophy and culture.

The Heian Era
http://www.wsu.edu:8080/~dee/ANCJAPAN/HEIAN.HTM
This site gives a valuable context to the Heian era.

Ancient Japan

http://www.wsu.edu:8080/~dee/ANCJAPAN/ANCJAPAN.HTM

Website on ancient Japan includes political, religious, and cultural history, details about women and women's communities, and a portfolio of art from the era.

Samurai Archives

http://www.samurai-archives.com/

Extensive collection of information about individuals and events in the samurai millennium.

Empires Beyond the Great Wall: The Heritage of Chinggis Khan

http://web.archive.org/web/20000815214514/http://vvv.com/khan/

A rich site (now archived) offering a biography of Chinggis Khan and information about the history and culture of the Mongol Empire.

Literature and Film

The following works give the flavor of this long millennium in India: *The Panchatantra,* trans. Arthur W. Ryder (University of Chicago, 1967); Prince Ilangô Adigal, *Shilappadikaram (The Ankle Bracelet),* trans. Alain Daniélou (New Directions, 1965); Somadeva, *Tales from the Kathäsaritsägara,* trans. Arshia Sattar (Penguin, 1994); Cornelia Dimmitt, ed., *Classical Hindu Mythology: A Reader in Sanskrit Puranas,* trans. J. A. Van Buitenen (Temple University, 1994).

For a fictional treatment about Empress Wu that offers a picture of Tang court opulence and intrigue see Evelyn McCune, *Empress* (Fawcett Columbine, 1994). For Japan, Lady Murasaki's *Tale of Genji* is available in several excellent translations. The newest is by Royall Tyler (Penguin Publishers, 2002). A 1991 animated film (subtitled) is a good introduction to the first third of the book.

Suggestions for Reading

Informative surveys of India's medieval history include Hermann A. Kulke, *A History of India,* 3rd ed. (Routledge, 1998); and Tej Ram Sharma, *The Political History of the Imperial Guptas* (Concept, 1989). On the Delhi Sultanate, see Peter Jackson, *The Delhi Sultanate: A Political and Military History* (Cambridge University Press, 2003). On women, see Tracy Pintchman, *The Rise of the Goddess in the Hindu Tradition* (State University of New York Press, 1994); and Leslie Orr, *Donors, Devotees, and Daughters of God: Temple Women in Medieval Tamilnadu* (Oxford University Press, 2000).

Two of many fine general histories of China in the post-Han, Tang, Song, and Yuan periods are Patricia Buckley Ebrey, *Cambridge Illustrated History of China* (Cambridge University Press, 1996); and Charles O. Hucker, *China's Imperial Past* (Stanford University Press, 1975). A comprehensive work on Chinese painting is *Three Thousand Years of Chinese Painting,* eds. Richard M. Barnhart, Nie Chongzheng, Lang Shaojun, James Cahill, and Wu Hung (Yale University Press, 1998). Dorothy Ko, Jahyun Kim Haboush, and Joan R. Piggott's *Women and Confucian Cultures in Premodern China, Korea, and Japan* (University of California Press, 2003) is an excellent overview of the role of women in each of the three countries. For a classic though still excellent introduction to the Song, see Jacques Gernet, *Daily Life in China on the Eve of the Mongol Invasion, 1250–76* (Stanford University Press, 1962). Valerie Hansen, *The Open Empire: A History of China to 1600* (W. W. Norton, 2000) explicates Tang and Song foreign relations and the domestic repercussions of economic expansion. On women and family relationships see Patricia Buckley Ebrey, *The Inner Quarters: Marriage and the Lives of Chinese Women in the Sung Period* (University of California Press, 1993). Katherine Bernhardt's *Women and Property in China, 960–1949* (Stanford University Press, 1999) gives us a legal history of family law in Song China with its social repercussions. On the Yuan dynasty see Elizabeth Endicott West, *Mongolian Rule in China* (Harvard University Press, 1989).

An excellent study of networks of trade and communication in the Mongol era is Janet Abu-Lughod, *Before European Hegemony: The World System, A.D. 1250–1350* (Oxford University Press, 1989). A recent work that treats Asia as an interacting unit is Warren I. Cohen, *East Asia at the Center: Four Thousand Years of Engagement with the World* (Columbia University Press, 2000).

A solid survey of Korean history is Carter J. Eckert, et al., *Korea Old and New: A History* (Harvard University Press, 1990). Surveys of Japanese history in the classical and medieval eras include *The Cambridge History of Japan: Ancient Japan,* eds. Delmer M. Brown, John Whitney Hall, Marius B. Jansen, Madoka Kanai, and Denis Twitchett (Cambridge University Press, 1993); John W. Hall, *Government and Local Power in Japan, 500–1700* (University of Michigan Press, 1999); and Wayne Farris, *Heavenly Warriors: The Evolution of Japan's Military, 500–1300* (Harvard University Press, 1996). Karen Brazell's translation of *The Confessions of Lady Nijo* (Stanford University Press, 1976) offers a fascinating account by an itinerant woman, once a court lady, now a nun, in the early thirteenth century, and is a wonderful addition to the larger body of work on women writers in the Heian period.

The Americas to 1492

CHAPTER CONTENTS

40,000

c. 40,000–10,000 B.C.E. Movement back and forth across the Bering Strait land bridge

10,000

10,000 B.C.E. Nomadic migrations from Asia reach tip of South America

c. 5000 B.C.E. Development of maize agriculture

2000

c. 2000 B.C.E. Divergence of Inuits and Aleuts

c. 1200 B.C.E.–150 C.E. Formative period of Mesoamerica culture (Olmec)

c. 800 B.C.E.–600 C.E. Adena and Hopewell cultures

1 C.E.

c. 150–900 Classical period in Mesoamerica culture (Maya)

c. 300 Beginning of Anasazi culture

500

c. 500–600 Beginning of Mississippian culture

c. 900–1500 Postclassical period of Mesoamerican culture (Toltec, Aztec)

1000

c. 1100–1500 Development of Inca empire

c. 1300 Height of Cahokia culture

1500

c. 1500s Inca Empire in South America reaches maturity

Early civilizations in the Americas followed a social sequence similar to that found in Africa and Eurasia. As agriculture became more diversified, food supplies increased and some cultures became more and more able to support cities, highly skilled crafts, expanding commerce, complex social structures, and the emergence of powerful states. The most noteworthy were the civilizations of the Mayas in Yucatán and Guatemala, the Aztecs in central Mexico, and the Incas in Peru. The Mayas are particularly recognized for their mathematics, solar calendar, and writing system—70 percent of which has only recently been deciphered. The Aztecs and Incas conquered large populations and governed extensive states. Each civilization produced distinctive customs, values, art, and religion, many of which have become part of the Latin American heritage. Spanish adventurers who invaded these civilizations were shocked by the religious sacrifices of human beings but astonished by the wealth, grandeur, technical efficiency, urban populations, and institutional complexity they saw in Central America and Peru. For example, Tenochtitlán (te-nohch-teet-LAHN), the Aztec capital with its 150,000 inhabitants, was larger and probably better administered than any European city of its time.

To the north of Mesoamerica, hundreds of Amerindian tribes developed diverse social patterns, languages, and economic pursuits as they adapted to the differing environments they faced. Around 4000 B.C.E. Amerindians in the southwestern part of present-day Florida founded villages along the coast in which they enjoyed a rich diet of fish, shellfish, grains, and berries and lived in accord with a sophisticated religious system that included the burial of the dead in funeral mounds. Recent archaeological finds indicate that still earlier in the present-day state of Washington, Amerindians founded villages with their own unique cultures and economic activities. The Amerindians to the north never attained the centralized power or wealth of the Mayas, Aztecs, and Incas. However, they left behind a variety of archaeological sites that attest to their sophistication and creativity.

ORIGINS OF AMERICANS AND THEIR CULTURES

■ *Does the development of Amerindian cultures support or negate the theory of parallel development?*

Many of the American cultures can be traced back to nomadic migrations from Asia to Alaska, across the Bering Strait land bridge. During the Pleistocene epoch, coinciding with the last great ice age, humans established themselves in Siberia where they built underground shelters and hunted large mammals such as mammoths. The most recent ice advance, beginning some 65,000 years ago, locked up immense amounts of global water and lowered sea levels, creating a land bridge that enabled Paleolithic people to follow the animals they hunted into North America. Later, as increasing global temperatures melted the ice and raised water levels, the bridge slowly disappeared around 10,000 years ago, after an estimated 30,000 years of sporadic human migrations. Recent discoveries indicate that there also may have been other routes of entry into the Americas, including those by sea from Iceland and Greenland and across the Pacific into Chile and Peru.

Archaeological work throughout the twentieth century continually pushed back the estimates of the time of the first permanent residents. Artifacts known as Clovis spear points, the oldest of which are about 11,200 years old, were found from Mexico to Nova Scotia. Continued discoveries across North America revised the estimates of when human beings settled in the Americas to around 20,000 years ago. Some archaeologists think humans could have lived in North America even earlier. However, the most widely accepted estimates of the first human settlement in the Americas are 14,000 years ago, with humans reaching southern Chile by circa 12,500 years ago. Recent discoveries in Peru indicate that the first city in the Americas was that at Caral, founded around 2600 B.C.E. Archaeologists believe that the pyramids built there were constructed a century before the Great Pyramid at Giza in Egypt.

Over this protracted period the Amerindians split into eight major ethnolinguistic groups and hundreds of subgroups and adapted to numerous physical environments. New research has shown the Americas to be far more densely populated in the fifteenth century than the European invaders believed—perhaps by as many as 75 million people before the massive population decline caused by climatic changes and foreign diseases such as small pox in the fifteenth and sixteenth centuries.

The development of agriculture in the Mexican highlands, along the Peruvian coastal plain, and in what is now the southwestern United States caused major changes in indigenous American culture after 7000 B.C.E. This development occurred considerably later than in the Near East, and the plants that the Amerindians domesticated were different from those in other parts of the world. They also domesticated animals such as alpacas and llamas in the Andes—there were no cattle, sheep, or horses until the Europeans arrived in 1492. The major agricultural contribution came with the cultivation of maize (corn), shortly before 5000 B.C.E., in the Tehuacán (ti-wah-CAN) valley of Mexico. From this center, maize culture spread widely. After 1000 B.C.E. it became the staple food for hundreds of societies, from the Mississippi River valley to the Argentine pampas. The Aztec Confederacy and Inca Empire, which so awed the Spanish *conquistadores* after 1500, were dependent on the raising of maize.

Beyond these mature civilizations, cultural levels varied widely among the Amerindians by the end of the fifteenth century. Some powerful cultures, like that of the Mound Builders of the Mississippi valley, borrowed heavily from Mexico. Cahokia, a major capital and trade center near contemporary St. Louis, Missouri, housed approximately 25,000 people during the thirteenth century. Other sophisticated cultures north of the Rio Grande ranged from the Pueblo of the southwest to the large Iroquois Confederacy of the eastern woodlands. In South America, complex cultures lived along the north coast and near the mouth of the Amazon. Other societies developed on Caribbean islands, in the South American pampas, and in Chile. Other Amerindians—probably a majority of them—were still hunters and gatherers. These included the Eskimo peoples of Alaska and the Inuit peoples of Arctic Canada; jungle groups such as the Jivaro (he-VAR-oh) of the upper Amazon; and the peoples of Tierra del Fuego, at the southern tip of South America.

Despite differing timeframes, Amerindian cultures differed little from cultures in Africa and Eurasia in their progression from Paleolithic hunting and food gathering to Mesolithic semifixed communities to Neolithic food production and settled communal life and then to urban centers and the emergence of political states. They also displayed common traits with other civilizations in their theocratic systems, sun cults, and human sacrifices. Like the African cultures, they were in transition from matriarchal to patriarchal institutions, although further along in the process. Finally, a common belief in monarchy among Aztecs and Incas was also typical of many other peoples in the ancient river civilizations of Eurasia.

EMERGING CIVILIZATIONS IN MESOAMERICA

▪ *What geographical and climatic factors permitted the rise of Mesoamerican civilization?*

Central and South American Civilizations

A variety of related cultures flourished in **Mesoamerica,** a zone ranging from roughly 100 miles north of Mexico City to Costa Rica. The region varies greatly in landforms, climate, and vegetation. Two mountain ranges run through northern Mexico to join a central highland block in the region of the Valley of Mexico. The Pacific coastal region is relatively narrow while that on the Atlantic side is wide. The north and west have dry lands with sparse vegetation; the south and east are marked by tropical rain forests and savannas.

Despite these physical differences, the early cultures were unified by their economic interdependence, because no one region was self-sufficient. They shared a complex calendar, hieroglyphic writing, bark paper, deerskin books, team games played with balls of solid rubber, chocolate bean money, widespread upper-class polygamy, large markets, and common legends. A popular one featured a god-man symbolized by a feathered serpent. We may conveniently divide Mesoamerican history into three main periods: formative (to 150 C.E.), classical (150–900), and postclassical (900–1492).

The Formative Period

For a millennium after 1500 B.C.E., villages in the regions of Mexico and Central America grew steadily to become cities. Scattered throughout this region at the beginning of this period were some 350,000 people, living in relatively sparsely populated ceremonial trading centers and villages. Labor and stone for the massive construction projects, jade for carving, luxury goods, raw materials for the crafts, and food were brought to the centers often from distant places—without the use of horses, mules, or oxen. These goods were probably not the spoils of conquest; Olmec society left little evidence of war or violence, although some security would have been present to protect trading missions.

In these settlements artisans worked at pottery making, weaving, feather design, and masonry. Merchants ranked second only to the priesthood in social status, as they conducted trade among the temple cities. As population increased and society became

Mesoamerica—A cultural zone in Central America ranging from roughly 100 miles north of Mexico City to Costa Rica.

Mesoamerican and South American Civilizations	
2500s B.C.E.–400s C.E.	Olmec
300s–900s C.E.	Mayas
900s–1200s C.E.	Toltecs
1100s–1500s C.E.	Incas
1300s–1500s C.E.	Aztecs

more complex, priests came to dominate governments. They governed by enjoying respect and exploiting fear rather than relying on force. The general theocratic orientation is reflected most clearly in the great temple mounds; in the huge stone conical pyramid at La Venta, rising some 100 feet; and in the characteristic carved statuary that represented the dominance of the Olmec cults.

In time the common culture, known as the Olmec, centered in five geographical areas. One was in the Oaxaca (wah-HAHK-ah) region of western Mexico; another was in the inland Valley of Mexico; a third straddled the present Mexican-Guatemalan border; and a fourth (the later Mayan) arose in the southern highlands and lowlands of Yucatán, Honduras, and Guatemala. The fifth, and at the time most significant, area spread over some 125 miles of the eastern Mexican coast and its hinterlands, near present-day Veracruz.

Archaeological research in Olmec sites reveals exceptional wealth, technical efficiency, and artistic sensitivity. In many Olmec sites, the oldest at San Lorenzo, there were great stone buildings and pyramids dating from 1200 B.C.E. The culture is perhaps best known for its colossal heads and its fine jade carving, featuring jaguars. This cultural maturity was not matched by military advancements: San Lorenzo was destroyed by invaders about 900 B.C.E.; another ceremonial center at La Venta, in Tabasco, assumed leadership until it, too, fell, six centuries later.

Olmec influence permeated most of present-day Mexico and Central America. A few independent Olmec centers may have been established farther to the north, but it was probably more common for a number of Olmec priests and traders to live among native populations, conducting religious rites and arranging for the transport of goods to the homeland. Such enclaves were typical of regions as distant as the Pacific coast of Central America. In other places, such as the Oaxaca valley to the west, the southwestern

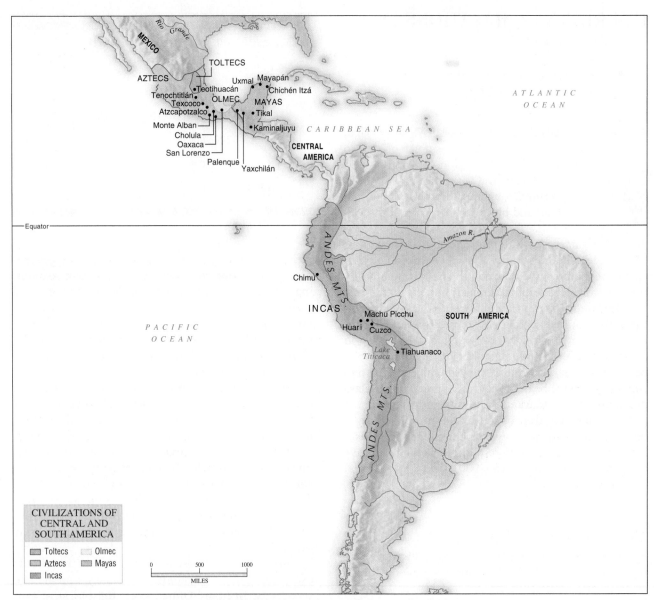

Ranging from the lowland and jungles of Central America to the arctic cold of the Andes, the civilizations of Central and South America exhibited a rich and sophisticated diversity.

Mexican highlands, or the southern Mayan regions, Olmec influence was more indirect, possibly resulting from trade or Olmec marriage into local elites. By such varied means, Olmec foundations were laid for the religion, art, architecture, and characteristic ball games—and possibly for the calendars, mathematics, and writing systems—of later civilizations, including the Mayan and the Aztec.

The Classical Period

After the fall of La Venta, Olmec prestige waned, but by the second century C.E., cultural developments progressed to a point known as the classical period, which

would last until the tenth century. This was a golden age when, across the region, written communication, complex time reckoning, a pantheon of gods, interregional trade, and a 40-fold population increase over the Olmec period occurred. Hundreds of communities raised great buildings, decorated them with beautiful frescoes, produced pottery, figurines, and sculptures in large quantities. Although classical Mayan culture of the Yucatán lowlands is perhaps best known, Teotihuacán (te-oh-tee-wah-*KAHN*), in the northeastern valley, also generated an impressive culture.

At its peak about 500 C.E., Teotihuacán was the sixth largest city in the world, with a population of 125,000 to 200,000. Three and a half miles long and nearly two miles wide, it was laid out in a grid of sorts

The colossal Pyramid of the Sun rose above the metropolis of Teotihuacán. Measuring 650 feet at its base and 213 feet high, the structure is more than four times larger than the Great Pyramid of Khufu (Cheops) in Egypt.

and paved with a plaster floor on which clusters of imposing edifices were erected. This ceremonial center is dominated by the temple-pyramids dedicated to the moon and the sun. The first pyramid was cut off at the top to provide for a temple with a broad step ascending from a wide rectangular court. Running south is a long ceremonial axis, and adjacent to it the Pyramid of the Sun. Also truncated, it measures 650 feet at the base and rises in four terraces to 213 feet above the valley floor. The interior contains more than a million cubic yards of sun-dried bricks, and the exterior was once faced entirely with stone. As with other pyramids throughout Mesoamerica, these structures, with their ceremonial staircases, led to temples at the summit where rites and sacrifices were offered to the gods.

Teotihuacán was noted for its specialized craftspeople who came from all over Mexico and occupied designated quarters of the city. Its streets were studded with bustling markets, where all types of goods were available from foreign as well as local sources. This wealth permitted a governing elite of priests, civil officials, military leaders, and merchants to enjoy great luxury. Teotihuacán exerted a powerful influence over other states, including some among the lowland Mayas, because of its cultural reputation, social connections, and commercial advantages. When necessary, it used its formidable military power to enforce trade and tribute agreements. Above all, Teotihuacán marks the high point of priestly power over the rest of society. Thereafter, especially with the Toltecs, the cultures came to be far more military in character.

Another impressive classical center in Mexico was located at Monte Alban in the Oaxaca valley. In 200 B.C.E. it already had a population of 15,000, and its fortifications dominated the valley. In Teotihuacán's era, this concentration of temples, pyramids, and shrines was a theocratic state, still drawing tribute from adjacent hill settlements and a valley population of over 75,000 people. Although developed on a smaller scale than Teotihuacán, Monte Alban produced a similar pattern of foreign trade, class distinctions, elaborate religious architecture, artistic creativity, writing, and time reckoning. It derived most of its art styles from Teotihuacán and some from the Mayas but synthesized both in its own traditions. Politically, it remained independent through the classical era, although its elite sought the luxury goods and favor of Teotihuacán.

CLASSICAL MAYAN CIVILIZATION

■ *What were the economic, political, cultural, and religious characteristics of Mayan civilization?*

While Teotihuacán and Monte Alban flourished, Mayan peoples farther south in Yucatán and Guatemala brought artistic and intellectual activity to new heights in more than 100 Mayan centers, each boasting temples, palaces, observatories, and ball courts. Although it borrowed from Teotihuacán before the latter's decay in the eighth century A Mayan Town
C.E., Mayan civilization subsequently cast a brilliant light over the whole of Mexico and Central America.

The earliest Mayas are thought to have migrated from the northwest coast of California to the Guatemalan highlands during the third millennium B.C.E. From that homeland, Yucatec- and Cholian-speaking peoples settled the northern and central lowlands, respectively, between 1500 B.C.E. and 100 C.E. Mayan villages developed steadily, many becoming ceremonial centers by the start of the Common Era. In the highlands, Kaminaljuyu (kah-MEEN-ah-leu-yeu) had by then developed architecture and primitive writing under the influence of Oaxaca and Teotihuacán. But in the early classical period, before 550 C.E., Tikal, in the central lowlands, assumed Mayan leadership as it traded with Teotihuacán and allied itself with Kaminaljuyu. The fall of Teotihuacán brought temporary confusion, soon followed by the glorious renaissance of the late classical era at Tikal, Palenque, Yaxchilán (yahks-chee-LAHN), Uxmal, and other Mayan centers.

A number of distinguished scholars such as Linda Schele and David Friedel, Jeremy Sobloff, and Michael D. Coe have given us a detailed view of the Mayas. Their communities had productive economies based not only on agriculture but also on handicrafts and long-distance trade. In often barren soil, except in some parts of the highlands, Mayan farmers used intensive agriculture, clearing, irrigating, and terracing to raise squash, chili peppers, and many other crops, including maize—which supplied 80 percent of their food. Mayan metalwork, cotton cloth, and chipped stone implements were traded widely, carried in large dugout canoes along the rivers and the Atlantic coast. Exchange was facilitated by the use of common goods as media of exchange, including cocoa beans, polished beads, salt, and lengths of cotton cloth.

Mayan society in this period was a rich mixture of old and new. An ancient kinship system prevailed among all classes, with lands assigned and controlled by the clans. Matriarchal values persisted, as indicated by some queens who retained power and influence. Women were generally respected, held some legal rights, and did some of the most important work, such as weaving. The shift toward patriarchy, however, was definite and unmistakable, as was seen in priorities accorded men in most social situations, such as being served first by women at meals. A more fundamental change involved the rise of social classes. Hereditary male nobles and priests were in most positions of authority and power, but craftspeople and merchants enjoyed privileges and status. Slaves, captured in military campaigns or kidnapped, did most of the hard work, particularly in the continuous heavy construction of ceremonial buildings. They were also subject to being used in religious sacrifice, although this was far less common than among the later Aztecs.

A hereditary priest-king, usually considered to be a descendant of a god, governed each Mayan center. He was assisted by a council of priests and nobles. His government levied taxes, supervised local government in outlying villages, and administered justice. It also was responsible for conducting foreign relations and making war. The Mayas were not very successful in large-scale military operations because their armies were drawn mainly from the nobility and were therefore limited in size. Nevertheless, armed with their obsidian-bladed weapons, they were equal to their neighbors in making war. Indeed, as time passed and

cities vied for supremacy, wars became increasingly common. In the process, some centers remained independent, but most joined loosely organized leagues, based on common religious traditions, dynastic marriages, or diplomatic alignments.

Religion permeated all phases of Mayan life. Like the later Aztecs, the Mayas saw life as a burden and time as its measure, and they deified many natural phenomena, particularly the planets and stars, as powers to be appeased by human pain and suffering. Public bloodletting was part of normal ritualistic worship. Human sacrifice, usually accomplished by decapitation, was common, and wars to obtain prisoners for sacrifice were sometimes waged. The dominance of religion over everyday life is further illustrated by the general interpretation of law as religious principle and taxation as religious offerings. Economic value derived as much from the religious sanctity of a thing as from its material utility or scarcity. Moreover, education was aimed primarily at training priests; reading and writing were considered necessary religious skills, and mathematics and astronomy were valued mainly because they were required in scheduling ceremonies honoring the gods.

The two most significant achievements of the Mayas were their calendar and their writing system. Neither of these was original, but both were more efficient than those of earlier peoples. The Mayan astronomers, using only naked-eye observation, surpassed their European contemporaries. Their constant scanning of the heavens allowed them to perfect a solar calendar with 18 months of 20 days each and a five-day period for religious festivals. Using an ingenious cyclical system of notation known as the "long count," they dated events of the distant past for accurate record keeping and the scheduling of astronomical observations. Their notational mathematics, based on 20 rather than 10 as in the decimal system, employed combinations of dots and bars in vertical sequences, to indicate numbers above 20. For nonnumerical records, they combined **pictographs** and **glyphs,** which have recently been deciphered sufficiently to reveal specific historic events and their human dimensions.

DOCUMENT

Anonymous: Victory over the Underworld

These remarkable accomplishments in mathematics, astronomy, and writing were more than matched by the magnificent Mayan art and architecture. The plaza of each Mayan community was marked by at least one pyramid, topped by a temple. The one at Tikal towered to 229 feet, 16 feet higher than the Pyramid of the Sun at Teotihuacán. With their terraced sides and horizontal lines, Mayan pyramids showed a skilled sense of proportion. The highly stylized sculpture dec-

---

pictographs—Picture symbols.

glyphs—Symbolic characters in writing.

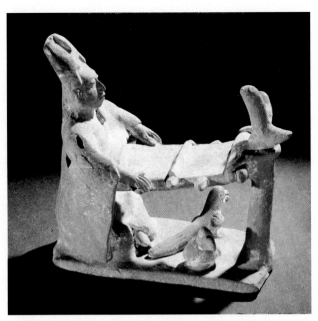

The Mesoamerican societies were at the same time sophisticated, complex, and powerful—and bloody in their human sacrifices to the gods. This seated figure, surrounded by winged messengers, seems to be looking off in the distance to anticipate what the divine powers might next demand from him.

orating their terraces is regarded by some authorities as the world's finest, even though the Mayan sculptors accomplished their intricate carving with only stone tools—there were no bronze or iron implements in the Americas at that time. The Mayas also developed mural painting to a high level of expression. Even their crafts, such as weaving, ceramics, and jewelry making, reveal a great aesthetic sense, subtlety of design, and manipulative skill.

THE POSTCLASSICAL ERA

▪ *Which civilizations rose to prominence after the end of the classical era of Mesoamerican civilization?*

The region's classical artistic development ended during the eighth and ninth centuries. The causes, not yet fully uncovered, have been generally attributed to factors ranging from overpopulation and internal struggles to soil exhaustion and Chichimec invasions from the north. Amid the accompanying upheavals, urban populations dwindled, and most of Teotihuacán's residents scattered in all directions, even into the Mayan lands. But there was no complete collapse; trade continued on a large scale, and the expanded use of writing indicated more social complexity and interstate competition, which contributed to intensified politi-

cal conflict. Consequently, the age produced a new cultural mode, with heavier emphases on militarism, war, and gods thirsting for human blood. Among many smaller but thriving city-states, in addition to the dying Teotihuacán, were the Mayan polities of Tikal, Chichén Itzá (cheech-EN eet-SAH), and Mayapán. Farther north, the Oaxacan centers were still flourishing after the tenth century, as were Atzcapotzalco (ahts-kah-poh-TSAL-koh), Xochicalco (hoh-chee-KAL-koh), and Cholula, with its colossal pyramid.

The Toltecs

Most prominent of all these centers was Tollan, the Toltec capital. Toltec history is unclear before 980, when Topiltzin (to-PIL-tzin), a legendary king, founded the city and created a new power located in the central Valley of Mexico. His subjects were a mixture of Chichimecs and former urbanites of the area, who may have served for a while as peacekeepers in the north. Over the next two centuries, the city became a great urban complex of 120,000 people, a hub of trade, and the center of an evolving Toltec confederacy that assumed the leading role formerly played by Teotihuacán. Meanwhile, Tollan's future was shaped by a struggle for power between Topiltzin and his enemies. The king had early adopted the Teotihuacán god **Quetzalcoatl** (kets-al-koh-AHT-el), who opposed human sacrifice; but followers of the traditional Toltec war god, **Tezcatlipoca** (tez-kat-le-POH-ka), ultimately rebelled and forced Topiltzin into exile. The victorious war cult took over, steadily expanding its hegemony, by conquest and trade, into an empire stretching from the Gulf of Mexico to the Pacific, including some Mayan cities of the south.

The tumultuous political conditions of the early postclassical period finally brought disaster to the Toltecs. Failing crops and internal dissension caused great outward migrations from Tollan and abandonment of the capital at the end of the twelfth century. Shortly after, the city was burned by Chichimecs. For two centuries thereafter, the area was a land of warring states and constantly forming and dissolving federations. Some cultural continuity, however, was maintained by peoples in the Oaxaca valley, notably the Zapotecs, whose culture was as old as the Olmec. Although they struggled constantly with neighboring peoples for supremacy and survival, the Zapotecs maintained towns, temples, ball courts, and art that helped preserve Mesoamerican traditions for later times.

Quetzalcoatl—The Toltec god of the civilization, goodness, and light; literally "plumed serpent."

Tezcatlipoca—The god of the night sky and sorcery; literally "smoking mirror"; initially Toltec in origin but also adopted by subsequent peoples, including the Aztecs.

This Aztec mask is a figure within a figure, and the person wearing the mask would hope to project animal strength and unearthly terror.

Toltec militarism spread from central to southern Mexico. It left the less developed Mayan highlands relatively undisturbed but brought decline and reorientation to the old lowland centers, such as Tikal. Severe droughts also drove migrants into northern Yucatán, where a developing cistern technology provided more water. At Chichén Itzá in the tenth century, a cosmopolitan Mexican-Mayan military elite established their dominance and maintained a trading network, by land and sea, throughout the southern region. From the early thirteenth into the fifteenth century, Mayapán was a fortified center, defended by mercenaries and maintaining leverage over subkingdoms by holding hostages from dependent royal families. Trade continued to grow, along with population, among the postclassical Mayas; but art, cultural pursuits, and even architecture deteriorated. The Spaniards were later to describe the Mayan people as fiercely independent, bloodthirsty, and, like the Aztecs, inclined to sacrifice war captives' hearts on their gods' altars.

The Aztecs

Arising in the confusion of the late postclassical era, the Aztec Confederacy came to conquer and dominate central Mexico from coast to coast in less than two centuries. The Aztecs, like the Toltecs before them, retained many of their old traditions while freely borrowing from the culture, religion, and technology of their neighbors and victims. The most significant example of this borrowing was their hydraulic agriculture. It was the major factor by which they increased population in the central Mexico to more than a million people living in some 50 city-states.

The Aztecs' story really begins with the founding of the capital at Tenochtitlán; their earlier history is quite obscure. They evidently migrated from the north into central Mexico some time before 1200. For a while they were dominated by other peoples, including the Toltecs. About 1325 they settled on an island in Lake Texcoco (the site of present-day Mexico City), later connecting their new town to the mainland by causeways. In its later days Tenochtitlán was an architectural wonder. The Aztecs built a dam to control the lake level, completed a freshwater aqueduct, and created floating artificial islands where irrigated fields supplied food for the capital. Within the imperial metropolis, beautiful avenues, canals, temples, and monuments symbolized increasing Aztec power, particularly after the early fifteenth century.

IMAGE
Aztec Warriors

The Aztecs completed the formation of their confederacy at the same time. During the early decades at Tenochtitlán, the Aztecs had fought as tributaries of Atzcapotzalco, the dominant city-state in the valley. In 1370 they accepted a king of assumed Toltec lineage. For decades they won victories and prospered in concert with their overlords, but in 1427 they rebelled, forming a "triple alliance" with nearby Texcoco and Tlacopán, which defeated Atzcapotzalco and became the major power in the region. For the Aztecs, these events brought great change. Internally, they shifted power from the old clan leaders to a rising military aristocracy. Externally, they started a series of conquests and trading agreements. A new imperial order developed, shared at first by the other two allies but increasingly dominated by Tenochtitlán, whose ruler imposed his will as head of the army, leader of the state, and chief priest. The reigns of the Aztec kings Itzcoatl (1427–1440) and his nephew Montezuma I (1440–1468), ushered in this new era of rising centralism, efficiency, and expansion. It was still in progress under the ninth monarch, Montezuma II (1502–1520), at the time of the Spanish invasion.

DOCUMENT
Xicohtencatl, the Elder: "I Say This"

As the empire expanded, so did the state-controlled economy. Its base was agricultural land, particularly floating plots installed on the lake after the 1430s. Most were built by the government. Some were allotted to the *calpulli* (clans)—made up of the remnants of diverse ethnic groups that came together on the island of Tenochtitlán—for distribution to families. Others were developed as estates for the monarch

---

calpulli—Aztec social units based on family clans.

and the nobility; the latter were worked by tenants under government supervision. Rising agricultural production supported not only the engineering, dredging, stonework, and carpentry required for heavy construction but also artisans turning out weapons, cloth, ceramics, feather work, jewelry, and hundreds of other goods. Porters from distant places backpacked over mountains to the markets of the valley. A later Spanish observer reported that the great market at Tlatelolco (tlah-tel-LOHL-koh), serving Tenochtitlán, attracted 25,000 people daily.

DOCUMENT

"Song of Tlaltecatzin"

Conquest and the increasing wealth that accompanied it modified the ancient social structure. The old *calpulli* developed into city wards, identified largely by occupational specialties. By 1500 most *calpulli* families were headed by men. Women could inherit property and divorce their husbands but were confined mostly to household tasks, except for midwives, healers, and prostitutes. Kinship still promoted social cohesion, but class status provided major incentives. The appointed nobility *(pipiltin)*, along with the priests, held both power and social status, but they were burdened with heavy responsibilities. Moreover, they held appointed rather than hereditary posts, although they could inherit property. Commoners could be made nobles by performing superior service, particularly in war. Craftspeople and merchants paid taxes but were exempt from military service; some long-distance merchants *(pochteca)* served the government as diplomats or spies in foreign states. Peasants worked their plots and served in the army; nonmembers of *calpulli* were tenants. Their lot was hardly better than that of the numerous slaves, except for the latter's potential role as ceremonial sacrifice victims.

Official documents of the period and other written accounts focus mainly on Mesoamerican social and political elites and conditions in the imperial capitals. However, recent archaeological studies throw fresh light on the lives of the Aztec common people and conditions in the provinces. Surveys of settlement patterns show that Aztec society experienced one of the most significant population explosions of premodern times. In the Valley of Mexico, the heartland of the Aztec Empire, population increased from 175,000 in the early Aztec period (1150–1350) to almost one million in the late period (1350–1519). This pattern of growth was duplicated elsewhere in the empire. To cope with this population explosion, the environment was altered: Farmers built dams and canals to irrigate cropland, constructed terraced stone walls on hillsides to form new fields, and drained swamps outside Tenochtitlán to create **chinampas** or

floating gardens. With these changes emerged new villages and towns.

Excavations of rural sites near modern Cuernavaca (kwehr-nah-VAH-kah) disclose that provincial society was much more complex than previously thought. Commoners created a thriving marketing system whereby craft goods produced in their homes were exchanged for a variety of foreign goods. Houses at these sites were small, built of adobe brick walls supported on stone foundations. These houses were furnished with mats and baskets and had a shrine with two or three figurines and an incense burner on one of the walls. In this region the household production of cotton textiles was the major craft. All Aztec women spun and wove cloth, which provided garments, constituted the most common item of tribute demanded by the state, and served as currency in the marketplaces for obtaining other goods and services. In addition to textiles, some residents made paper out of the bark of the wild fig tree, used to produce books of pictographs and to burn in ritual offerings. According to written sources, Aztec commoners were subject to the nobles, who possessed most of the land and monopolized power in the polity. But new archaeological excavations show that the commoners were relatively prosperous people whose market system operated largely beyond state control.

The Aztec polity included subordinated allies and 38 provinces. The latter were taxed directly; most of the former paid tribute in some form; and all were denied free foreign relations. This polyglot empire was headed by a member of the royal family proclaimed to be the incarnation of the sun-god. His household was more lavish than many in Europe and swarmed with servants. A head wife supervised the concubines and scheduled their assignments, but Aztec queens rarely engaged in court intrigues or offered advice to the emperor, for he usually ruled without concern for other opinions. He was assisted in his official duties by a chief minister and subordinate bureaucracies for war, religion, justice, treasury, storehouses, and personnel. The capital and each province were administered directly by governors, most of whom were descended from former kings. They collected taxes, held court, arranged religious ceremonies, regulated economic affairs, and directed police activities. In addition, urban guilds, villages, and tribes had their own local officials. Vassal states were governed under their own laws but observed by resident Aztec emissaries. This whole system was defended by a large military organization, comprising allied forces, local militias, and an imperial guard of elite troops.

Aztec religion developed from the worship of animistic spirits, symbolizing natural forces seeking balance while in constant conflict. A pessimistic obsession with human futility also dominated the Aztec world-

Chinampas—The floating gardens the Aztecs of Tenochtitlán built and tended on Lake Texcoco.

view, perpetuating the common belief that the gods required human blood to sustain life. Thus, as they

assembled their empire, the Aztecs came to envision their sun deity, **Huitzilopochtli** (wheet-tsee-loh-POHCHT-lee), as a bloodthirsty war god with an appetite for warriors captured in battle. In every city, the Aztecs built pyramids, topped by their two temples to the sun deity and Tlatelolco, god of rain. Here they honored Huitzilopochtli in great public ceremonies such as one in 1487 when bloodstained priests at the high altars tore out the living hearts of thousands of victims and held them up, quivering, to the sun. The need for sacrificial victims forced continuing conquests and later weakened the state as it faced the Spanish threat.

Comparing the Aztecs and Mayas with the Romans and Greeks can be an interesting theoretical exercise. The Aztec calendar, mathematics, and writing were derived mainly from Mayan sources, somewhat the way that Roman philosophy and science were based on Greek models. Although Aztec culture spawned skilled sculptors, painters, and craftspeople who produced in great numbers, they lacked the imagination of the Mayas, whom they indirectly copied, just as Roman artists largely imitated their Greek predecessors. Similarly, both Roman and Aztec cultures were characterized by respect for discipline, practicality, directness, and force. Each was highly skilled in engineering, as attested, for example, by their aqueducts and other feats for furnishing copious amounts of water to their respective capitals. They also shared a militaristic ethos and powerful standing armies.

The Inca

The great Inca Empire in the Andean highlands of South America reached its height in the early 1500s.

MAP
Inca Expansion

It extended 3500 miles between Ecuador and Chile, including almost impassable mountain ranges that separate the upper Amazon forests from the Pacific. The empire contained at least ten million people in 200 ethnolinguistic groups. It was six times the size of Texas. The capital, Cuzco, which had an estimated 200,000 inhabitants, was governed in a more centralized way than any city in Europe at the time. The Incas produced fine art and architecture and were superb engineers, but their major achievement was imperial organization. In this respect they compared favorably with the Romans and the Chinese.

A long tradition of scholarship, exemplified by researchers such as Ian Cameron, Richard W. Keating,

Huitzilopochtli—The patron deity of the Aztecs, god of the sun and of war.

and J. Alden Mason, gives us a detailed idea of Inca society. Although it rose very rapidly just before the Spanish conquest, Inca civilization evolved from ancient cultural foundations. Ceremonial and commercial centers had existed on the Peruvian plateau well before the Common Era. About 600 c.e. cities began rising in the highlands of the interior. During the next two centuries, tributary kingdoms drew together formerly isolated ceremonial centers of the Peruvian highlands. Some of the resulting states exercised control over the plain, along with territories in what are now Bolivia and Chile. Two kingdoms had capitals at Huari (WHA-ree) and Tiahuanaco (tee-ah-wah-NAH-koh) in south central Peru. When these states collapsed in the tenth century, they were succeeded by independent agrarian villages, which were nearly consumed by continuous warfare. A completely different situation developed along the northern coast, where the kingdom of Chimu developed a civilization, marked by extensive irrigation, rising population, centralized government, public works, high craft production, widespread trade, and an expanding tributary domain. This polity was conquered and its culture absorbed by the Incas in 1476.

The Incas created their empire while waging ruthless struggles in the highlands. According to their own legends, these "children of the sun" settled the valley of Cuzco, in the heartland of the Andes, about 1200 c.e., having migrated from the south, possibly from the region of Tiahuanaco. During the next hundred years they were a simple peasant people, organized by kinship in clans (ayllu), living in villages, fulfilling mutual labor obligations, and worshipping their local demigods (chuacas). To strengthen their unity and better protect themselves in constant wars for survival, they formed a monarchy, developed their military, and began taking over territory near Cuzco. In this competition they were only moderately successful during the reigns of the first seven kings, to the early fifteenth century.

Like the Aztec state at almost the same time, the Inca polity began a climactic period of rapid development with a memorable series of rulers. Viracocha (veh-rah-CO-cha) (d. 1438), the eighth emperor, turned his ragtag army into a formidable fighting machine, conquered adjoining territories, and instituted a divine monarchy, with his lineage accepted as descendants of the sun-god. His son, Pachacuti (pahch-ah-KEU-tee) (1438–1471), was a reformer, religious leader, and builder who stands among the most powerful people ever to rule in the New World, and received the admiration of the Spanish occupiers. He began arduous campaigns to the north and south, notably against Chimu. Topa Yupanqui (yeu-PAHN-kee) (1471–1493), Pachacuti's son and successor who commanded the Inca armies after 1463, completed the

Document   Father Bernabé Cobo, "Pachacuti, the Greatest Inca"

Bernabé Cobo (1582–1657) spent 61 of his 75 years in the Americas, from his first arrival in the Antilles to his death in Lima. During that time the Jesuit priest combined his duties with his qualities as a scientist and observer to write at great length about the flora and fauna of Latin and southern America. He entered into close relations with the Indians, as he spread the faith, and came to have a deep understanding of respect for them.

This selection is from Chapter 12 of his *History of the Inca Empire*. Cobo relied on Indian legends and contemporary Indian testimony, as well as earlier Spanish writings as he dealt with the civilization his countrymen had attacked. Far from viewing the Incans as barbaric and "uncivilized" as later, nineteenth-century missionaries would do, Cobo showed the capacity to understand and even admire them.

Viracocha Inca left four sons by his principal wife; they were called Pachacuti Inca Yupanqui, Inca Roca, Tupa Yupanqui, and Capac Yupanqui. The first one succeeded him in the kingdom, and concerning the rest, although they were lords and grandees, nothing is said. Pachacuti married a lady named Mama Anahuarque, native to the town of Choco, near Cuzco, and he founded a family that they call Iñaca Panaca. This king was the most valiant and warlike, wise and statesmanlike of all the Incas, because he organized the republic with the harmony, laws, and statutes that it maintained from that time until the arrival of the Spaniards. He injected order and reason into everything; eliminated and added rites and ceremonies; made the religious cult more extensive; established the sacrifices and the solemnity with which the gods were to be venerated, enlarged and embellished the temples with magnificent structures, income, and a great number of priests and ministers; reformed the calendar; divided the year into twelve months, giving each one its name; and designated the solemn fiestas and sacrifices to be held each month. He composed many elegant prayers with which the gods were to be invoked, and he ordered that these prayers be recited at the same time that the sacrifices were offered. He was no less careful and diligent in matters pertaining to the temporal welfare of the republic; he gave his vassals a method of working the fields and taking advantage of the lands that were so rough and uneven as to be useless and unfruitful; he ordered that rough hillsides be terraced and that ditches be made from the rivers to irrigate them. In short, nothing was overlooked by him in which he did not impose all good order and harmony; for this reason he was given the name of Pachacuti, which means "change of time or of the world"; this is because as a result of his excellent government things improved to such an extent that times seemed to have changed and the world seemed to have turned around; thus, his memory was very celebrated among the Indians, and he was given more honor in their songs and poems than any of the other kings that either preceded him or came after him.

After having shown himself to be so devoted to the sun and having taken the care just mentioned that all worship him in the same way that his ancestors had done, one day Pachacuti began to wonder how it was possible that a thing could be God if it was so subject to movement as the Sun, that it never stops or rests for a moment since it turns around the world every day; and he inferred from this meditation that the Sun must not be more than a messenger sent by the Creator to visit the universe; besides, if he were God, it would not be possible for a few clouds to get in front of him and obscure his splendor and rays so that he could not shine; and if he were the universal Creator and lord of all things, sometimes he would rest and from his place of rest he would illuminate all the world and command whatever he wished; and thus, there had to be another more powerful lord who ruled and governed the Sun; and no doubt this was Pachayachachic. He communicated this thought to the members of his council, and in agreement with them, he decided that Pachayachachic was to be preferred to the Sun, and within the city of Cuzco, he built the Creator his own temple which he called Quishuarcancha, and in it he put the image of the Creator of the world, Viracocha Pachayachachic.

Questions to Consider

1. What was there in Pachacuti's quest to understand the universe that would appeal to Bernabé Cobo?

2. Discuss Pachacuti's accomplishments as enumerated by Cobo. Do you think that the Spaniard's admiration came because the Incan chief possessed "European" qualities, or because he chose local solutions to local problems?

3. Would you like to be a citizen in a state led by Pachacuti? Why? Why not?

From *History of the Inca Empire*, trans. and ed. Roland Hamilton from the holograph manuscript in the *Biblioteca Capitular y Colombina de Sevilla*, © 1979. Reprinted by permission of the University of Texas Press.

Machu Picchu, a natural fortress on a narrow ridge between two mountains, was built by the Incas probably after 1440. When the last Inca ruler died, the fortress was abandoned and lost until its rediscovery in 1911.

annexation of Chimu and extended the empire south into central Chile. The next emperor, Huayna Capac (WHAY-nah KAH-pahk) (1493–1527), completed the subjugation of Ecuador, put down rebellions, and attempted to impose order, although the empire was seething with internal discontent when the Spaniards arrived in 1532.

Despite internal problems, intensified by the steep slopes and harsh weather of the Andes, the Incas demonstrated rare technical skills in fashioning their civilization in difficult and often dangerous circumstances. They were master engineers, carrying water long distances by canals and aqueducts, using techniques borrowed from the Chimu Empire, building cities high in the Andes, and constructing networks of roads along the coast and through the mountains, along with suspension bridges and interconnecting valley roadways. All were designed to knit together a vast region that in the Inca Empire covered some 380,000 square miles.

Archaeologists have long known that the Incas gained a knowledge of canals and irrigation systems from the Chimu: Recent excavation have revealed new evidence about their sophisticated use of that technology. Canals are difficult to construct: If the slope is too narrow, the canal silts up; if it is too steep, its sides erode. Inca engineers devised different canal shapes to control the water's speed and prevent its velocity from ruining the canal. One "intervalley" canal carried water to a city from 60 miles away; it was only one of many networks, involving thousands of feeder canals, that stretched for hundreds of miles. These hydraulic

techniques have been described as deserving to stand with Egypt's pyramids and China's Great Wall as among the world's greatest engineering feats. With irrigation canals constructed far removed from the water's source, the Incas farmed 40 percent more land than is achieved today. But if skills fail, land can quickly return to desert conditions. We have yet to learn what caused the destruction or abandonment of these canal systems—was it human or environmental forces, or both?

Hydraulic feats were matched by sophisticated organizational skills. To link the empire together, Inca leaders established a communication service, using state-built roads, runner-messengers, rest houses, and smoke signals. Governing by means of a divide-and-rule technique, they appealed wherever possible to traditional prejudices among conquered peoples, perpetuating feuds, courting native leaders, settling colonies of subjects among their enemies, and generally provoking disunity among potentially rebellious areas. They also relied on a common official language and the cult of divine monarchy to unify their own people, particularly the elite. Every part of their system was fitted together in a highly disciplined and integrated whole. Before the Incas, few other states had succeeded so effectively in regimenting millions of people over such great distances and against such formidable obstacles.

Like all civilized peoples, the Incas faced the problem of population expansion and a limited food supply. They solved it well enough to support large military, bureaucratic, and priestly establishments by developing what economists call a *command economy*. They used no money, no credit, and very little trade beyond local barter. The state planned all economic operations and kept all accounts. Government assigned to families the land to be worked; local family heads, under government supervision, directed workers who produced the crops and saw that harvests were brought to state warehouses. Labor taxes provided work done on public projects, the nobles' estates, and royal lands. A similar approach was used in manufacturing, with craftspeople producing in local guilds, noble households, and palace workshops. From its storehouses, the government distributed goods to individuals, to the military, and to government projects. In the process, it built roads, operated hospitals, and maintained schools. All property, even the nobles' land, was state-owned and assigned, except for distinctly personal possessions, including some luxury goods owned by the privileged classes.

This state-controlled economy functioned by way of a precisely defined class structure, built on the lingering kinship tradition. Commoners were kept loyal and disciplined by identifying the state with their ancient *ayllus*. Inca nobles maintained respect because they were all related directly or indirectly to the royal lineage and therefore shared the divine mandate to rule. They held the highest positions in government, the army, and the priesthood. A notch lower were lesser aristocrats and nobles among conquered peoples, who held local offices, up to subgovernors in the provinces. The two upper classes made up a privileged elite. Trained in special schools, they were rewarded with luxuries in food, dress, and housing. They were also exempted from taxes and cruel punishments. At the third level were common workers. They were generally confined to their villages; their work was prescribed; their dress and food were restricted; and government checked even the cleanliness of their houses. Commoners were thus little better off than the lowest class of slaves, who were often taken as prisoners of war and assigned to serve the upper classes.

The shift from kinship toward class division was accompanied by a decline of matriarchal values. Upper-class women shared some social status with their husbands, and all women could inherit property when they were widowed; but they were generally subordinated and exploited. Indeed, a fifteenth-century royal decree prohibited women from testifying in court because they were by nature "deceitful, mendacious, and fainthearted."[1] Female commoners worked in the fields, while women of all classes were expected to keep house, mind the children, and serve the needs of men. Many were concubines or surplus wives, the number depending on the husbands' wealth and status. The most beautiful and intelligent young girls were drafted as "chosen women." Some would become "virgins of the sun," serving as nuns and weavers in the temple workshops; others would become concubines of the emperor or nobles; a few would be sacrificed. All were honored as servants of the state.

All authority in the Inca state originated with the hereditary divine emperor, who exercised the power of life and death over all his subjects. He was usually aloof, even with his own immediate family, although he might, if he chose, delegate authority to the queen (his full sister after 1438) or take advice from his mother. With its thousands of servants and concubines, his court was a magnificent display of wealth and power. It was also the locus of a central government that included agencies for rituals (religion), war, treasury, accounts, and public works. The chief ministers were advisers to the Imperial Council, consisting of the emperor and four viceroys, who governed the four provinces. Each province, about the size of New York State, was divided into approximately 40 districts, under subgovernors and their assistants. Authority in the districts was further subdivided, ultimately into units of ten families. Officials at each level reported regularly to superiors and were subject to

frequent inspections. This system regulated every aspect of life, including labor, justice, marriage, and even morals.

The power of the ruler depended largely on an excellent military system, which featured compulsory service. Instructors in the villages trained peasant boys for the army; the most promising were marked for advancement when they were called to active service in their twenties. They served for two years before retiring to the labor reserve and militia. The army was organized in units of 10, 50, 100, 1000, and 10,000, under officers who held complete authority over subordinates. A combat force of 200,000, with support units, was always under arms. It was supplied from military storehouses throughout the country and garrisoned in mighty stone fortresses, each with independent water sources. Troops from these centers ruthlessly suppressed any resistance to the regime.

A second base for Inca authority was religion. As the empire grew, its priests appropriated the gods of conquered peoples and included them in a vast pantheon, headed by the Inca sun-god. For example, the virgins of the sun, with their ceremonies and temples, evolved from an earlier moon goddess cult among **matrilineal** societies. War victims would on occasion be sacrificed to the sun, as would some children of "chosen women." In later times the servants of an emperor, as well as his favorite concubines, were sent with him, at his death, to serve him in the hereafter. To emphasize the emperors' divinity and symbolize the state's continuity, dead emperors were mummified, seated on thrones in their sacred palaces, and attended by living servants, wives, and priests. On public occasions these figures were paraded before the people, who bowed before them in reverence. Such ceremonies were conducted by a clerical establishment of 4000 priests in the capital and many scores of thousands more throughout the country.

There was a remarkable exception to this religious mind-set in the person of the emperor Pachacuti. A highly successful military leader who largely laid the empire's foundation by consolidating the area around Cuzco and annexing the rich Titicaca basin, this multitalented innovator established **Quechua** (KECHwah) as the administrative language, reformed the calendar, introduced methods of terracing the hillsides and extending irrigation, and created an efficient public service. Although regarded as a direct descendant of the sun-god, Pachacuti asked himself how the sun could be the supreme deity since it never rested but

CASE STUDY

Death in War
and Childbirth
in the
Americas

---

matrilineal—Tracing hereditary descent through the mother, not the father.

Quechua—A language of the Central Andes, spoken by the Incas and today the most widely spoken indigenous tongue of the Americas.

revolved endlessly around the earth. He concluded that the sun was itself a messenger sent by a more powerful being who from his place of rest could illuminate and command the world. This must be the universal Creator, Viracocha ("Lord"), who governed the sun and had brought into being all other deities. And in his honor the emperor constructed a temple in Cuzco. But, as in the case of Akhenaton, his conceptual forerunner in Egypt, Pachacuti's nascent monotheism did not prevail; later rulers continued to sacrifice victims to the sun-god—though not to the extent practiced by the Aztecs.

Order and security were dominant values in Inca cultural expression, and neither aesthetic concerns nor philosophical speculation received much attention. As we have seen, religious innovation was given short shrift, and any theorizing was subordinated to the practicalities of a state cult and the morality of power—treason and cowardice were considered the worst sins. The Incas had no written records and seem to have lacked even the pictographs of Mesoamerica. Instead they relied on oral traditions, supplemented by mnemonic devices such as the system of knotted strings called *quipus* (KE-peuz). These oral traditions were dealt a lethal blow by the Spanish conquest.

The Inca lunar calendar was inaccurate and provided no starting point for the identification of historical events. Although the Incas were excellent craftspeople, capable of producing fine pottery and metalwork in copper and gold, their most striking technical and cultural accomplishments were in engineering and massive architecture. Without using mortar, they fitted immense slabs of stone into temple and fortress walls. This efficiency is still exhibited in existing roads, bridges, terraced fields, and stone fortresses, such as Machu Picchu.

THE AMERINDIANS OF NORTH AMERICA

■ *Why was there no unification of the North American Amerindians, such as there was in Mesoamerica?*

In the past century Hollywood and the popular media reinforced the fallacy that all Native Americans in North America constituted a single culture with a common lifestyle. The mounted, war-bonneted warrior of the plains has too often been considered the archetype of the "Red Man," presented in the "Wild West Shows" of the last century. Some Plains Indians were indeed fine mounted warriors, but they were only a fraction of the complex family of North American Indians.

European settlers found the Native Americans more diverse in their languages and appearances than the Europeans themselves. Two hundred distinct North American languages have been classified. Amerindian societies presented a wide spectrum of variation: from small bands of hunter-gatherers and farmers to well-organized states. A similar diversity was found in their arts and crafts; various regions excelled in basketry, weaving, sculpture, totem-carving, and boat making.

There is a serious debate among scholars as to the number of Native Americans at the time of the European invasions. Estimates range from as low as 2 million to as many as 18 million people in the area north of Mexico—most estimates fall between these extremes. In any case, much of North America was well populated at the end of the fifteenth century. Amerindians north of the Rio Grande did not produce the massive technological and governmental achievements found in Mesoamerica and South America. As with Paleolithic and Neolithic societies in Asia, Africa, and Europe before the Common Era, their populations were smaller, and consequently, they did not create large cities, with their complex division of labor and urban way of life. More often, they typically survived by hunting and fishing until knowledge of food raising spread north from Mesoamerica.

For North American Indians before 1492, agriculture where it could be practiced had the same effect as elsewhere in the world. A more dependable food supply made possible stable settlements in which men cleared the fields and women tended the crops. Marked population growth, with accompanying large village or town centers, and political and military power occurred in the Rio Grande, Ohio, Mississippi, and St.

North American Civilizations	
c. 3000–2500 B.C.E.	Watson Brake settlements
c. 800 B.C.E.–600 C.E.	Adena and Hopewell cultures
c. 900–1300	Cahokia flourishes
c. 300 B.C.E.–1350 C.E.	Mogollon culture
c. 1100	Establishment of Navajo culture
c. 1300	Arrival of Mandans in Great Plains

---

quipus—A mnemonic system based on knotted strings used by the Inca to keep records and send messages.

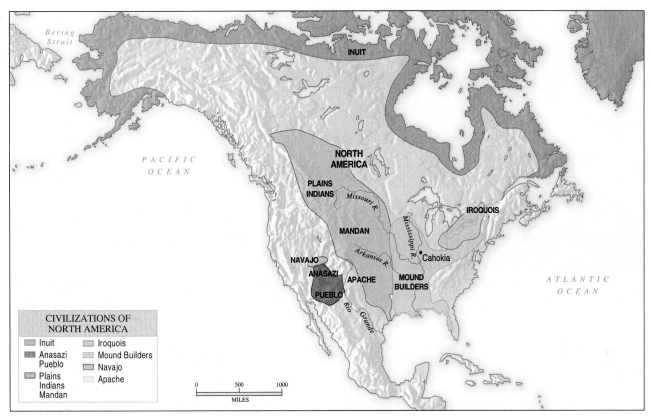

In the vastness of the North American continent, the varied environmental challenges led to the development of hundreds of different Indian tribes—more than 250 alone in the present-day state of California.

Lawrence valleys. In these places, overpopulation exhausted the soil and occasionally created environmental problems that led to the decline of the urban centers. Climate changes and European-borne pandemics in the fifteenth and sixteenth centuries devastated the Native American population, both those settled in the cities and the nomadic peoples.

The Iroquois of the Northeast Woodlands

Europeans arriving in what is now upper New York State found various groups speaking dialects of a common Iroquoian language. They had created a distinctive culture by 1000 C.E. and subsequently formed the League of the Five Nations. They used the metaphor of the longhouse, their traditional communal dwelling, to describe their political alliance: the Mohawk along the Hudson were the "keepers of the eastern door," adjoined in sequence by the Oneida, Onondaga, and Cayuga, with the Seneca, "keepers of the western door." When the Tuscarora joined in the early eighteenth century, the confederacy became known as the Six Nations. The Iroquois eventually extended their control from the Great Lakes toward

the Atlantic by subjugating the nomadic, food-gathering Algonquin people.

The Iroquois had the advantage of being agriculturists with permanent villages. Some of these had several hundred residents and extensive fields where maize, beans, squash, and tobacco were grown. Fish traps were built across streams, and smokehouses preserved joints of game. Related families lived in the longhouses, long rectangular buildings protected by high wooden palisades. Women played a notable part: They owned the homes and gardens, and, since descent was matrilineal, chose the leaders. If the men chosen did not give good leadership, they could be replaced.

The Adena and Hopewell of the Ohio Valley

In the area of present-day Kentucky and Ohio, important Amerindian settlements took root between 800 B.C.E. and 600 C.E. Known generally as the Adena and Hopewell cultures, these Amerindians developed complex societies from the Missouri River to the Appalachians and from the Great Lakes to the Gulf of Mexico. Their settlements were based on the work of Indian women who, over two to three millennia,

The Great Serpent Mound in Ohio is a rich repository of the North American Indian life centered in the Adena culture. Active between 500 B.C.E. and 100 C.E. the Indians of the Adena culture had a well-developed village life and traded with other peoples from Canada to the Gulf of Mexico.

mastered the cultivation of seed plants such as sunflowers and squash and maize that arrived in the area in the fourth century B.C.E. As in Mesoamerica and South America, by 1000, maize cultivation sustained the peoples of the Ohio and Mississippi valley regions. Archaeologists think that the Hopewell and Adena cultures survived on a diet of fish, game, nuts, and other plant life.

The Adena and Hopewell cultures developed differing ways to construct their homes: the Adena chose to live in circular houses made out of poles and covered with mats and thatched roofs, while the Hopewell built round or oval houses with more protective roofs made of skins, bark from trees, and a combination of thatch and clay. They had a sophisticated view of the afterlife, as can be seen in the effort they took to bury their dead. The Native Americans near Watson Brake in northeast Louisiana (3000–2500 B.C.E.) and the peoples of the Adena culture at the beginning of the Common Era built thousands of earthen mounds for their dead. The Adena interred their deceased in vast cone-shaped mounds of earth, sometimes 500 feet around. Sometimes the dead were cremated, and the ashes were placed in the mounds along with all sorts of relics such as carved stone tablets, pipes smoked during religious ceremonies, and jewelry. The Hopewell did the same on an even larger scale for the more distinguished members of their families. Archaeologists have found evidence in these mounds of stone and clay items from both coasts, imported copper from the Great Lakes, and flaked stone items from the Tennessee valley.

Along with the impressive burial mounds, archaeologists have found indications of other projects indicating the combined efforts of hundreds of people in addition to a substantial investment of wealth. At Newark, Ohio, for example, the ceremonial site covers 4 square miles. Such enterprises indicate a long period of relative peace, generations remaining in the same place, and a substantial level of wealth. Archaeologists have also found indications of contacts with tribes across North America. Whether through trading or tribute, the Ohio valley societies had access to metals and goods found only in the Rocky Mountain area and shells from the Gulf coast. They had mastered the manufacture of tools, pottery, and copper jewelry.

The Mississippian Culture

At the end of the sixth century C.E. another major Amerindian culture made its appearance in the area just east of present-day St. Louis. Archaeologists are still investigating the origins and extent of this culture from the various burial sites, the most important of which is that at Cahokia, Illinois. Unlike the Adena and Hopewell cultures, the Mississippian culture lived in houses made out of thin pieces of wood (laths) covered with clay—so-called wattle-and-daub houses. These took various shapes in the large villages of the area. So influential was this culture that it came to dominate most of the region west of the Mississippi to the Plains, as can been seen in the Spiro Mounds in eastern Oklahoma.

The Mississippian peoples benefited from mastering the raising of maize, beans, and squash, and they tied their religion to the planting and harvesting cycles. Their burial mounds took the form of flat-topped pyramids, arranged around a central square. In the most developed regions, fortresslike palisades surrounded the site. The Cahokia complex was constructed over a period of nearly three centuries (c. 900–c. 1150). The centerpiece of the Cahokia site is a pyramid with a base of more than 18 acres, reaching a height of almost 100 feet. This is only one of more than 80 such mounds to be found at Cahokia, a city more than 6 miles long. There was no set burial practice for the Mississippian culture—remains have also been found in cemeteries, in urns, and under the floors of houses.

After the twelfth century the peoples in the Mississippian culture passed a highly complex religion along from generation to generation—an indication of their stability, continuity, and sophistication. The extent of their wealth enabled them to construct temples filled with ceremonial objects such as large stone scepters and copper plates. Their religion used symbols such as the cross, the sun, arrows surrounded by

An artist's creation of what Cahokia might have been like at its height.

semicircles, a sunburst, and—most intriguing—an outstretched hand with an eye in the palm. The art that derived from the religion featured portrayals of gods based on animals, rattlesnakes with feathers and wings, and people portrayed as birds. Vessels found at the sites indicate the presence of human sacrifice: jars with human faces painted on them and portrayals of the heads of sacrificed victims. These are indications that not only adults but also infants were given up to the higher deity the Mississippi culture believed controlled their lives.

Excavations of the Cahokia mounds give evidence of an hierarchical society that maintained order and productivity through brutality. Even though it was far distant from the Aztec and Incan Empires, there were several similarities between the political and religious systems and social repression of Cahokia and the systems in Mesoamerica and South America. For a while at the beginning of the thirteenth century, Cahokia was probably the largest city in North America, with a population larger than that of medieval London. At the end of the fourteenth century Cahokia began to decline. Archaeologists point to climate change, soil exhaustion, and the unification of those peoples Cahokia had repressed as an effective enemy force as likely causes for the end of Cahokia as a major power.

The Mogollon, the Hohokam, the Anasazi, and the Fremont Culture

The southwestern Amerindian cultures lived in the most environmentally challenging part of the continental United States, the dry and rocky regions of present-day Utah, Arizona, New Mexico, and Colorado. In response to their surroundings, they produced the most advanced levels of technology and agriculture around 300 B.C.E. The Mogollon, Hohokam, and Anasazi grew maize, beans, and squash, each group evolving its own techniques. The homes of each group were built out of adobe brick or other techniques of masonry, sometimes on extremely challenging sites.

Each group also produced pottery that could rank in beauty with any in the world.

The Mogollon culture of southwestern New Mexico lasted almost 1600 years, from around 300 B.C.E. to 1350 C.E. Its people built their homes low to the ground along the tops of ridges. Villages were built around large underground buildings used for religious ceremonies and as pit houses until the eleventh century; thereafter, they built these structures at ground level. Because of the constant threat of drought, they developed a diversified economy based on hunting, gathering, and farming. Relatively isolated, they saw little need to change over the centuries.

The Hohokam culture grew along the valleys of the Salt and Gila Rivers. Its architecture was similar to that of the early Mogollon, although the Hohokam built not just ceremonial structures but also their homes inside underground pits. Perhaps learning from the Mesoamerican cultures, the Hohokam constructed an impressive network of canals, some more than 30 miles long, 6 to 10 feet deep, and 15 to 30 feet wide. The extent of these canals proves the existence not only of wealth but also of substantial social organization. The Hohokam also borrowed their religion, their burial practices, and even some of their games from the Mesoamericans.

Deriving from these two cultures was the Anasazi, which appeared around 300 C.E. Of the three cultures, the Anasazi had the most sophisticated and most impressive architecture and the largest area of influence—from the Idaho-Utah border to the Gulf of California. Early on, they built their homes in the shape of beehive-shaped domes made out of logs held together by a mudlike mortar. They grew maize and made pottery, like the Mississippian culture, and stored both in warehouse-like structures. Around 700 C.E. they took their economic development one step further by beginning the manufacture of cotton cloth. Their technological genius is apparent from their use of two forms of irrigation: runoff by building dikes and terracing hills and subsoil by constructing sand dunes at the base of hills to hold the runoff of the

The Cliff Palace of the Anasazi, Mesa Verde National Park, Colorado, is among the important Anasazi ruins to be found in the southwestern United States.

sometimes torrential rains. Their lives revolved around their religion, with ceremonies to placate the gods to hold off storms and to ensure fertility.

The Anasazi are best known today for their architectural accomplishments. Around the eleventh century they began to construct cities, with houses built in the shapes of squares and semicircles. They used all of the available materials to build these settlements; with wood, mud, and stone, they erected cliff dwellings and the equivalent of terraced apartment houses. One such structure, with some 500 living units, was the largest residential building in the North America until the completion of an apartment house in New York in 1882. At their height, these master architects constructed around a dozen towns and nearly 200 villages. The disappearance of the Anasazi around 1300 remains a mystery. It is believed that a combination of a long drought, internecine conflicts, and the arrivals of the Navajo and the Apache led to their demise.

To the north of the Anasazi there were a number of different societies spread across the Colorado Plateau and into Idaho. They were a diverse group: Some depended on farming while others were hunters and they spoke different languages. Anthropologists have labeled this group the Fremont culture. They shared traits with the Navajo in that they raised corn, used the same kinds of tools, and lived in pit houses. The culture flourished between the sixth and the fourteenth centuries. Recently one of the best-preserved settlements of the Fremont culture was revealed to have been found near Horse Canyon, Utah in the Range Creek site.

The Navajo, the Apache, and the Mandan

Three other Amerindian civilizations established their presence before the arrival of Europeans. The Navajo, the largest Native American group in the United States, came down from the north to the Southwest sometime in the eleventh century. There they borrowed extensively from the indigenous cultures.

A century or so later, the Apache, who speak a language close to that of the Navajo, arrived in the southwest and by the end of the 1500s lived in parts of the present states of Arizona, Colorado, and New Mexico. They, too, were heavily influenced by the cultures present there.

Finally, the Mandan, who based their economy on fur trading and hunting, came to the vast valley of the Missouri River from east of the Mississippi in the late 1300s. There had been Amerindians in this region since 12,000–8,000 B.C.E. who hunted on foot on the Great Plains for mammoths, mastodons, and bison using spears tipped with Clovis points. Archaeological sites in Canada indicate that Indians hunted and slaughtered buffalo for more than 7000 years. By 1000 C.E. the use of bows and arrows was common throughout the plains. When the Mandan moved west, they became yet another in a long series of Amerindians who harvested the animal wealth of the mid-continent.

The Far North: Inuit and Aleut

The appearance of the Inuit, also known as the Eskimos, is shrouded in controversy. Some observers assert that they descended from ancient seagoing peoples; others believe that they developed their culture in Alaska after the last ice age. They speak much the same language as the Aleut, whose origins are similarly unclear. It is accepted that the two groups split apart more than 4000 years ago and that they are tied more closely to Asians than the Amerindians are.

The Aleut stayed largely in the area that is now known as the Alaskan peninsula, the Aleutian Islands, and the far eastern portion of Russia. The Inuit spread along the area south of the Arctic Circle from the Bering Strait across the top of Canada to Greenland. Both peoples lived by hunting and fishing. The Aleut hunted sea lions, otters, and seals from kayaks—small boats made of a wood frame over which skins were stretched. The Inuit showed more flexibility, hunting both sea and land animals, fishing in fresh and salt water. Their diet was based primarily on the caribou, musk-ox, walruses, and whales. They used the kayak too, but supplemented it with canoes and dogsleds.

The Navajos constructed houses called hogans *to shelter themselves from the often harsh climate of the high desert in the American Southwest.*

Their greatest accomplishment in seafaring, whaling vessels was the umiak, a larger boat with a wood frame covered with caribou hide, in which several people could row.

By about 100 C.E. the Inuit had established large villages; one of the biggest, with around 400 homes, was near present-day Nome, Alaska. To counter the arctic cold, they dug as much as 20 inches into the permafrost to erect their homes, which they then covered with poles and sod. In settlements such as that near present-day Nome, archaeologists have found large structures for the performance of religious rites, led by shamans who claimed to be able to heal diseases and wounds.

CONCLUSION

Before the European invasions and colonization, the Americas produced a rich variety of highly sophisticated and complex civilizations in response to the varied environmental challenges and opportunities of the Western Hemisphere. Some of these groups made the transition from food hunting to food raising, and some did not.

In Central and South America advanced agriculture supplied the foundation to support growing populations. This in turn led to the establishment of villages, and then cities, and, finally, far-flung states. More food and more wealth made possible leisure and priestly classes who had the time and resources to consolidate their power through control of religion as well as producing an advanced art, architecture, and discoveries in mathematics and astronomy.

In North America, environmental conditions were harsher and did not permit a similar accumulation of wealth as in Central and South America. Some Indian tribes remained hunter-gatherers. Others established settled villages and complex civilizations, but without the power and sophistication of the peoples to the south.

Tragically, a combination of climate changes, pandemics—both indigenous and foreign—and European invasions diminished the population by an estimated 80 percent by 1650. Those who survived were subjugated or later forced from their lands. Although they fought bravely against overwhelming odds, the Amerindians would have to struggle to maintain their identities in the centuries to come.

Suggestions for Web Browsing

You can obtain more information about topics included in this chapter at the websites listed below. See also the companion website that accompanies this text, http://www.ablongman.com/brummett, which contains an online study guide and additional resources.

Mesoweb, including Illustrated Encyclopedia of Mesoamerica
http://www.mesoweb.com/

Mesoweb is devoted to ancient Mesoamerica and its cultures: the Olmec, Mayas, Aztecs, Toltecs, Mixtecs, Zapotecs, and others.

University of Pennsylvania Museum of Archaeology and Art: Mesoamerica
http://www.museum.upenn.edu/new/exhibits/galleries/mesoamericaframedoc1.html

A history of Mesoamerican culture as reflected by the many artifacts in the university's museum.

National Museum of the American Indian
http://www.nmai.si.edu/

Website of the Smithsonian Institution's National Museum of the American Indian offers a look at one of the finest and most complete collections of items from the indigenous peoples of the Western Hemisphere.

Arctic Studies Center
http://www.mnh.si.edu/arctic/

Smithsonian Institution site dedicated to the study of Arctic peoples, culture, and environments includes numerous images, as well as audio and video segments of dance and discussion.

Literature and Film

For a sensitive and moving portrayal of the Indian life before Columbus in North America see Ruth B. Hill's *Hanta Yo: An American Saga* (Doubleday, 1979). Kathleen King's *Cricket Sings: A Novel of Pre-Columbian Cahokia* (Ohio University Press, 1983) gives an imaginative presentation of life in that Mississippian metropolis. An amusing concoction is A. Tanner Smith's *Anasazi and the Viking* (Sunstock, 1992), a not-totally-inconceivable meeting of Europeans and Amerindians. Insights into the Iroquois world can be gained from Joseph Bruchac, *The Boy Who Lived with the Bears and Other Iroquois Stories* (HarperCollins, 1995). A penetrating novel first published in 1826 has been recently translated by Guillermo I. Castillo-Feliis *Félix Varela, Xicoténcatl: An anonymous historical novel about the events leading up to the conquest of the Aztec Empire* (University of Texas, 1999). Another viewpoint on the Spanish conquest from the viewpoint of Atahualpa is given in Suzanne Alles Blom, *Inca, the Scarlet Fringe* (Forge, 2000). David Drew provides a window into the rich Mayan culture in his *The Lost Chronicles of the Maya Kings* (University of California, 1999).

PBS offers presentations on the Incas and the Mayas in their *Odyssey* series. See also the PBS series: *Seeking the First Americans, Surviving Columbus, Myths and Moundbuilders,* and the *Chaco Legacy*.

Suggestions for Reading

For a useful summary of the theories of migration into the Americas, see Sasha Nemecek, "Who were the First Americans," in *Scientific American*, September 2000, pp. 80–87. A sound, in-depth introduction to indigenous cultures in the New World is Alvin M. Josephy, ed., *America in 1492* (Knopf, 1992). See also Robert Wauchope's *Indian Background of Latin American History* (Knopf, 1970).

Among the most informative works on pre-Columbian Mesoamerica are Ross Hassig, *War and Society in Ancient Mesoamerica* (University of California Press, 1992); Richard A. Dieh and Janet C. Berlo, eds., *Mesoamerica After the Decline of Teotihuacán* (Dumbarton Oaks, 1989); and Robert R. Miller, *Mexico: A History* (University of Oklahoma Press, 1989). Special insights into the Mayan experience are provided in Jeremy A. Sobloff, *A New Archeology and the Ancient Maya* (Scientific American Library, 1990). A recent study of the darker side of Aztec society is David L. Carrasco and Micah Kleist, eds., *City of Sacrifice: The Aztec Empire and the Role of Violence in Civilization* (Beacon, 1998). Michael A. Malpass presents *Daily Life in the Inca Empire* (Greenwood Press, 1996).

E. James Dixon's *Bones, Boats, and Bison* (University of New Mexico Press, 1999) guides the reader through complex archaeological questions surround the question of the first colonization in western North America. Colin G. Galloway's documentary survey of American Indian History, *First Peoples* (Bedford/St. Martin's, 1999), is the best introduction to the general discussion of Native Americans in North America.

GLOBAL ISSUES

LOCATION AND IDENTITY

Why do people use location to identify themselves?

Two foreigners on horseback with Mount Fuji and telegraph wires in the background, woodblock print, Hiroshige Utagawa, 1873.

"East is East, and West is West, and never the twain shall meet."
Ballad of East and West, Rudyard Kipling, 1889

Though Kipling's long ballad goes on to reject that assertion, most Europeans and Americans ("West") and perhaps most Asians ("East") of his day would have accepted it. Of course, it is purely arbitrary to designate one area as "West" and one as "East" on a spherical earth rotating on a north-south axis, but historians, politicians, philosophers, generals, and clerics have all done so for millennia. People have long found ways to distinguish themselves from people in other places or even from people in their own backyard, and location has been one of the ways they have done so.

When the line-drawing seems to fail—for example, Morocco, often considered part of the Middle East, is actually west of London, and Japanese maps in the nineteenth century designated the United States as the East because it lies to Japan's east—the East then gets designated as a cultural place rather than one defined by location. But whose culture? Some would say that the culture of the rulers determines the country's identity. But this can be misleading. For instance, largely Hindu (and therefore Eastern) India did not become Middle Eastern under the Muslim Mughals or Western under British rule. Maps in the twentieth century can be equally confusing. They often painted colonies in the hues of their imperialist rulers, which seems to suggest countries could be culturally relocated by a change in rulers. Is Australia Western because its settlers mostly came from Europe, even as its leaders are currently trying to join the lucrative Asian/Eastern economic zone? Are the mostly Christian Philippines Eastern or Western?

For many centuries Europeans associated continents with the cardinal directions. Asia was East, Europe was West, and Africa was South. Later, America was sometimes considered a "new" world and therefore off the directional map, and sometimes part of the West. At first glance, continents seem to be a helpful way to divide the world into areas with some internal similarities. But the continental framework also has some inconsistencies. The Panama Canal now divides North and South America and the Suez Canal divides Africa from Eurasia. Both of those canals were dug through solid ground that had been traversed by people for millennia. And what about Eurasia? If continents have been viewed, since the eighteenth century, as "large space[s] of dry land comprehending many countries all joined together, without any separation by water,"[1] Europe and Asia are no more independent continents than the world's only "subcontinent" of India.

During the Cold War, East and West took on different meanings. The Communist anthem claimed, "The East [was] Red." A line so rigid it was called "an iron curtain" supposedly divided East from West. Many countries did not fit into those categories, however, calling themselves part of the "non-aligned movement." In time, the wealthy capitalist countries, many but not all allied with the United States, came to be called the First World; the Communist countries aligned with the Soviet Union, the Second World; and all others, including Communist China, the Third World. The Second World ended with the break-up of the Soviet Union, and the First and Third Worlds are more commonly referred to as Developed Countries and Developing Countries or by the cardinal directions North and South, with most of the old Second World countries assigned to the North. But many are uncomfortable with these terms, too.

The cardinal directions do not represent the only way that location has been used to identify people and cultures. Until the late nineteenth century, for example, Chinese rulers viewed the world as centered in China, which is reflected in the name for the Chinese realm, Central Kingdom. Chinese maps paralleled this politically inspired world view. (Religiously inspired worldviews differed in China; India was placed at the center of maps by Chinese

Buddhists.) The Chinese view explained what was essentially a power relationship in terms of the ethical virtue of the emperor. Unlike Europeans, the Chinese, who divided the world into cultured and barbarian spheres, did not ascribe these qualities to the cardinal directions East and West. Instead, distance in any direction would lessen the ethical influence of the Chinese center, which was located in the emperor's court.[2] Early modern Indian geographers centered their maps on India. One Indian geographer designated Europe, at his map's margin, as "England, France, and other hat-wearing islands."[3] Medieval Islamic mapmakers centered their world on Dar al-Islam (abode of Islam). Crossing this huge stretch of territory from southern Spain to China, starting in 1325, North African adventurer Ibn Battuta found recognizable Islamic culture throughout the region.[4]

Europeans, however, were more likely to use cardinal directions to define the world's areas. These directions were conflated with cultural characteristics, most of which have been shown by historians to be inaccurate. Thus, geography became destiny—if you're in the West, you must have certain characteristics, and if you're in the East, you have a different set of cultural behaviors. This was constantly inverted as well. When those doing the defining—the "West"—decided a country had cultural characteristics that were undesirable, it could be excluded from the West or Europe by being redefined as Eastern. Even the historical insistence on calling Europe a "continent" when it met none of the usual requirements for that label was a way of setting it aside as a place with a supposedly homogenous culture, distinct from those elsewhere in Africa or the rest of Eurasia. That culture was "Western."

The ancient Greeks had divided the world they knew into three parts, which loosely corresponded to what we call Europe, Asia, and North Africa. They disagreed, however, on the boundaries between those parts. Before 500 B.C.E., the Greeks used the term "Europe" to refer to Greece and the term "Asia" for all foreign lands other than Europe. They soon expanded Europe to include the land north and west of Greece and separated "Africa" from "Asia." Later, that three-part division was given a religious underpinning when Christians asserted that God had divided the world in three parts, giving one to each son of Noah.[5] From the eleventh-century split in Christendom between a Rome-based Catholic Church and a Constantinople-based Orthodox Church, the terms *West* and *East* were increasingly used for Europe and Asia, respectively. While the East was originally a small area in the eastern Mediterranean, it grew in the popular imagination as the Europeans learned more about India and later East Asia. Seeking wealth and riches, spices and textiles, Europeans looked eastward. The East was seen as different, but not necessarily inferior.

Looking for access to the East took Columbus to a "new" world, neither Western nor Eastern but a hybrid—a "West Indies" inhabited by "Indians." In the next several centuries, European countries established relationships of imperialism over many Asians, Africans, Americans, and Australians. But it was concerning Asians that Europeans of the nineteenth century articulated theories of Western superiority. The others were viewed as barbarians, and European dominance did not seem to need explanation. Later, as categories like "Third World" and "South" replaced "East," so-called Eastern characteristics were easily transferred to Africa or South America.

The East came to be seen as the opposite of the West.[6] This was expressed in a series of stereotyped comparisons. For example, where the East contained countries whose people valued irrationality, the West esteemed rationality. Where the West promoted democracy, the East was run by autocratic rulers whose role derived from what was called, as late as the mid-twentieth century, an "Asiatic Mode of Production."[7] While the West was dynamic and thus had a history, Asia was stagnant and unchanging; and even if it had had a history in the murky past, scholars like Karl Marx and G. W. F. Hegel contended that it no longer did. While Europe enjoyed a temperate climate, permitting it to embark on industrialization, the East did not. Many outside of Europe or the United States also absorbed these stereotypes. In the late nineteenth century, Fukuzawa Yukichi, an advocate of modernizing Japan, accepted these supposed characteristics as natural and called on the Japanese to "leave Asia" and join the West. Though scholars have debunked all these notions as having no grounding in historical fact, they continue to influence the meanings of East and West.

A few additional categories were developed in the twentieth century. The Middle East (East of what? The Middle of what?) came into being as a category for military planning during World War II. Its boundaries are as shifting and political as those of Europe and Asia. Africa is also subjected to a number of different slicings—is North Africa separate from sub-Saharan Africa?

Locational designations, groupings by political allegiance, classification by assumed cultural characteristics, and organization by stages of economic development all influence each other. Assumed cultural characteristics today lead to the redrawing of geographic lines in places like the Balkans, where the break-up of Yugoslavia in the 1990s produced warfare over ethnically defined borders. But location may also lead to our ascribing cultural characteristics or history to a country that never even had that history. North-South and East-West are always relative categories and reflect power relations in addition to designations of cultural identity.

Questions

1. Why do people define their world geographically?
2. How are the ways in which people define locations related to politics or power?
3. Do nations' identities change when their rulers, ideology, or dominant religions change?

CHAPTER 12

The Islamic Gunpowder Empires, 1300–1650

By the fourteenth century the waves of migration and conquest out of Central Asia that had established the Mongol Empire and altered the political configurations of the Islamic world had mostly ceased. Late in that century a new Turco-Mongol conqueror called Timur began a campaign that ravaged northern India, Persia, Iraq, and Anatolia, but his empire was not enduring. In the fifteenth and sixteenth centuries, however, three great Turkic empires gained preeminence in the old Mongol and Byzantine domains. The Ottoman, Safavid, and Mughal empires flourished on the bases of preexisting civilizations, Turco-Mongol military organization, and enhanced firepower; in the process they also crafted a new cultural synthesis. These empires are sometimes called the gunpowder empires because, like their European counterparts, they incorporated gunpowder weaponry into their traditional military systems. All three formed parts of a vast trading network reaching from the Pacific to the Atlantic Ocean. At the same time that the Ming Chinese were launching voyages that reached the East African coast, the Ottoman Turks were building an empire in the eastern Mediterranean that, in the sixteenth century, would dominate the region and challenge the Portuguese in the Indian Ocean.

Europeans were active in Asia during this period but exerted relatively little influence. Awed by the wealth and power of Muslim empires, they were generally held in disdain by Asian elites, who considered their own cultures superior. Akbar, the great Mughal emperor, referred to the "savage Portuguese" at his court,[1] Ottoman sultans regarded European envoys as supplicants, and the Safavid shah kept English merchants waiting for weeks while he attended to more important matters.

347

NEW POLITIES IN EURASIA

■ *How did political conditions in Central Asia influence the rise of the Ottoman, Safavid, and Mughal empires?*

For the kingdoms of Europe, the Ottoman conquest of Constantinople in 1453 signaled a catastrophe: the end of the Eastern Roman Empire and a disruption in established commercial patterns. Preachers and writers in Europe depicted the Ottoman victories as a type of divine punishment for the sins of Christendom. Even more significant, the Ottomans symbolized a new Muslim world emerging between the eastern Mediterranean and Southeast Asia. In that expansive territory, the three new Turkic empires would hold sway for centuries. Geographically, this world was centered in Persia, under its Shi'ite Safavid (sah-FAH-weed) dynasty. Culturally, it was influenced by Persian, Arab, and Byzantine courtly traditions. To the east, the magnificent Mughal (moo-GUL) Empire emerged at a crucial crossroads of the east-west and north-south trade. Militarily, this Muslim world was dominated by the forces of the Ottoman Empire,

which were far more formidable than those of any country in Europe at the time. War often raged among these contending states. Nevertheless, they shared the Islamic faith, common steppe antecedents, and Persian artistic and literary traditions.

Background: The Steppe Frontier

After the mid-fourteenth century, tumultuous conditions in Central Asia helped generate the Muslim empires to the south. The fragmented Mongol Empire left the steppe politically divided into states that dissolved and re-formed in new combinations. While the old **khanates** survived for a while, war was almost continuous along the southern steppe frontier, from the Crimea to China.

The continuing steppe influence was well illustrated by the quick rise and collapse of the Timurid (ti-MOR-id) Empire at the close of the fourteenth century. Timur the Lame, the "Tamerlane" celebrated in Western literature, who claimed descent from Ching-

---

khanate—A Turkic state ruled by a khan.

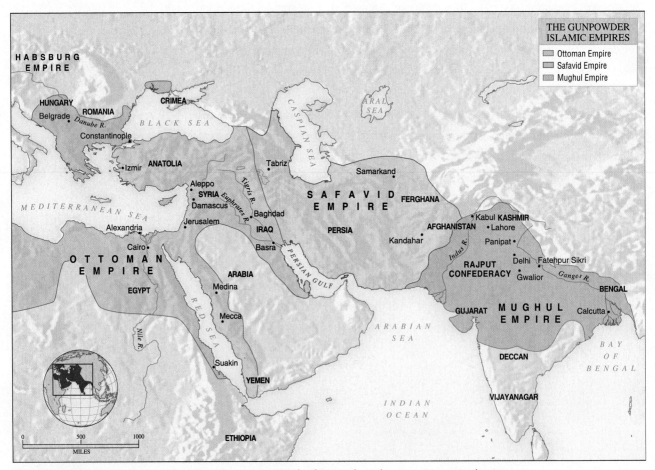

The gunpowder empires dominated south and west Asia, North Africa, and southeastern Europe in the sixteenth century.

gis (Genghis) Khan, rose to power during the 1370s as an *emir* ("commander") in the Chaghatai (chahg-HAH-tai) khanate of Central Asia. In his quest to restore the original Mongol Empire, Timur led whirlwind campaigns through the western steppe, the Crimea, Persia, and Anatolia. He crushed Ottoman resistance and carted the defeated Ottoman sultan, Bayezid I, off across Anatolia in a cage, subjecting him to ridicule. Timur terrorized northern India and was planning to invade Ming China when he died in 1405. But once Timur's army withdrew, the leaders who had submitted to him were less likely to comply

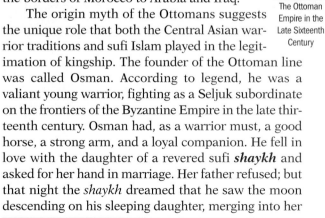

This miniature painting depicts the envoy of Timur at the court of the Ottoman sultan Bayezid I. The sultan is surrounded by his courtiers, with pages to his right and janissaries and officials in the foreground. Bayezid looks imposing, but he was defeated and killed by Timur. Note the fine carpets around the sultan's throne and the soldiers armed with gunpowder weapons in the foreground.

with his demands. A conqueror's real domains were those from which he could effectively collect taxes and levy troops.

For more than a century after Timur had resurrected the spirit of Chinggis Khan, a dream of universal empire—real or imagined—lingered in the minds of his descendants, among the many Turco-Mongol rulers in northern Persia and Transoxiana (trahnz-OX-ee-ahn-ah) to its east. The Ottoman sultans, who had established their hegemony in Anatolia before Timur's time and only barely survived his onslaught, were not direct heirs of his traditions, but they too aspired to the conquests and prestige of Chinggis Khan and Alexander the Great. Russia and particularly northern India, where Muslim regimes took hold after Timur's armies devastated Delhi in 1398, were also sites of a renewed struggle for power.

Drastic change marked the steppe frontier after the late fifteenth century, as populations settled around cities and firearms moderated the advantages of tribal cavalry. Indeed, the Uzbeks, who seized most of Transoxiana in this era, were among the last steppe conquerors. Like their predecessors, they were integrated into the courtly cultures of the lands they conquered. But long after the Uzbek conquest, old nomadic traditions continued to shape the rituals and military ethos of Turco-Mongol dynasties.

THE OTTOMAN EMPIRE

■ *How did the Ottoman Turks create and sustain their empire?*

The most powerful of the new Muslim empires was that of the Ottoman Turks. Centered in Anatolia, its military might cast long shadows over southeastern Europe, western Asia, and North Africa. By the middle of the sixteenth century the Ottoman patrimony stretched from Hungary to Ethiopia and from the borders of Morocco to Arabia and Iraq.

CASE STUDY
The Ottoman Empire in the Late Sixteenth Century

The origin myth of the Ottomans suggests the unique role that both the Central Asian warrior traditions and sufi Islam played in the legitimation of kingship. The founder of the Ottoman line was called Osman. According to legend, he was a valiant young warrior, fighting as a Seljuk subordinate on the frontiers of the Byzantine Empire in the late thirteenth century. Osman had, as a warrior must, a good horse, a strong arm, and a loyal companion. He fell in love with the daughter of a revered sufi **shaykh** and asked for her hand in marriage. Her father refused; but that night the *shaykh* dreamed that he saw the moon descending on his sleeping daughter, merging into her

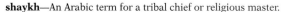

shaykh—An Arabic term for a tribal chief or religious master.

The Ottomans

c. 1281	Osman establishes the Ottoman dynasty
1453	Ottomans capture Constantinople
1517	Sultan Selim conquers Cairo, becomes Protector of the Holy Cities
1520–1566	Reign of Suleiman the Magnificent, Ottoman Golden Age

breast. From this union grew a huge and imposing tree that spread its branches over many lands and many flowing streams. When he awoke, the *shaykh* decided to approve the marriage.

Dreams play an important role in Middle Eastern literatures, and many kings took the interpretation of dreams seriously. The legend of the *shaykh*'s dream linked the warrior tradition to the mystical religious authority of the sufis, thus legitimizing Osman's rule. His dynasty, like the tree, did endure and expand to control many and prosperous territories. As the dynasty grew more powerful, the Ottomans also falsified a genealogy linking them to the prophet Muhammad. This Ottoman claim, like Timur's claim to be a descendent of Chinggis Khan, also lent an aura of legitimacy to their rule. The Ottomans were not the first or the last family to imagine for themselves illustrious ancestors. Osman's line was spectacularly successful; it ruled for over six centuries, from the late thirteenth century until World War I.

Osman's successors won independence from their Seljuk Turk overlords and gradually conquered the surrounding principalities. They had gained control over most of Asia Minor when Timur's army invaded Anatolia, defeated the Ottomans, and forced a half-century of internal restoration. Then two remarkable sultans resumed the Ottoman conquests. The first, Mehmed II (second reign 1451–1481), took Constantinople, Romania, and the Crimea. The second, Selim I (1512–1520), annexed Kurdistan, northern Iraq, Syria,

DOCUMENT
Mehmed II

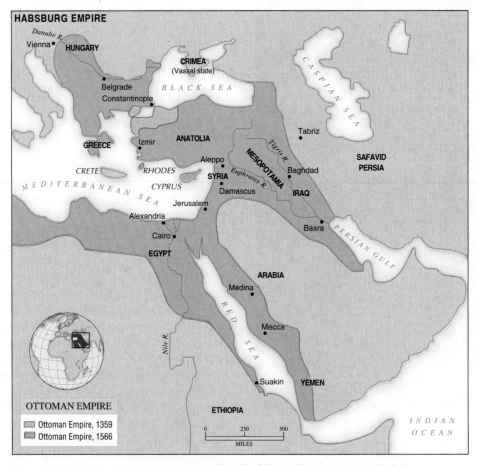

By the mid-sixteenth century the Ottoman Empire encompassed much of the Mediterranean. It included the core territories (excluding Persia) of the Middle East and extended across North Africa and into Europe.

Discovery Through Maps

The World Map of Piri Reis

Western historiography has highlighted Europeans' "discovery" of the New World. But the Age of Discovery produced many visions of the world, only some of which were preoccupied with the Americas. Ottoman cartographers were interested in the Americas, although Ottoman ambitions for conquest were directed primarily eastward to Asia. Mapping in this era was intimately associated with the objectives of merchants and sailors, and the most famous of Ottoman cartographers was a skilled sea captain named Piri Reis. Like other members of the Ottoman military-administrative class, Piri Reis was a man of diverse talents. In 1517, when his sovereign, Sultan Selim, conquered Cairo, Piri Reis presented him with a parchment map of the world, only part of which survives. The segment reproduced here shows the Atlantic Ocean, the western shores of Africa and Europe, and the eastern shores of South and Central America. Piri Reis's map incorporates elaborate illustrations of ships, kings, wildlife, and mythical creatures. It depicts strange tales (like the sailors who landed on a whale's back, mistaking it for an island, at top left) and gives nautical distances. The cartographer provided a list of 20 Western and Islamic sources he consulted, including a map of Christopher Columbus. Piri Reis's map suggests the currents of shared knowledge that linked the scholars, merchants, and sailors of Asia, Africa, and Europe at this time. The boundaries of scholarship were fluid, and learned men eagerly sought out new information. Cartographers like Piri Reis benefited from and contributed to the knowledge assembled by peoples of many nations and religions.

For the sailor or merchant, any map that was more accurate, regardless of its provenance (Portuguese, Ottoman, Christian, Muslim), was a tool for ensuring a more successful and safer journey.

Questions to Consider

1. In the sixteenth century, why would a sea captain be a good mapmaker?

2. Think about the different kinds of maps you have seen in this text and elsewhere. How does the way a map is constructed and illustrated tell us something about the beliefs and objectives of the mapmaker and the people for whom he makes the map?

3. Why do you think there are figures of people and animals on this map?

and Egypt. Mehmed's conquests terrorized European Christendom and brought the Ottoman state considerable wealth and prestige. The sultan repopulated

IMAGE
Mehmet II

Constantinople, renamed Istanbul in the nineteenth century, using a combination of tax breaks and forced population transfers. The declining but intrepid old warrior was planning new campaigns when he died.

Mehmed's son, Bayezid II, acquired further territories and built up a powerful fleet. Then, Selim's conquest of Egypt and Arabia brought added prestige: control of another great imperial capital, Cairo, and claim to the title Protector of the Holy Cities (Mecca and Medina), coveted by all Muslim monarchs. It also gave him control over the wealth and grain of Egypt and all the Mediterranean outlets of the eastern trade in spices, textiles, and jewels. Under Selim, the Ottoman navy dominated the eastern Mediterranean.

Ottoman power increased under Selim's only son, Suleiman (SOO-lay-mahn; 1520–1566). This determined campaigner soon became the most feared ruler among a generation of monarchs that included Henry VIII of England, Francis I of France, and Charles V of Spain. Suleiman's estimation of his own supremacy is illustrated in a letter to the French monarch in which Suleiman claimed glorious and elaborate titles but addressed Francis simply as "King."

Suleiman extended all his borders, particularly those touching Habsburg lands in Europe. After taking Belgrade in 1521 and the island of Rhodes from the Knights of St. John in 1522, he invaded Hungary in 1526 with 100,000 men and 300 artillery pieces. At Mohacs the Turks won an overwhelming victory. Hungary was then integrated into the Ottoman Empire. Although many Hungarian nobles were slaughtered in the war, Suleiman continued the Ottoman practice of integrating nobles and military men from his defeated foe into his own administration. If a governor submitted, he was often allowed to retain his post; this pragmatic administrative flexibility helped ensure the success of Ottoman conquests.

Suleiman aspired to the conquest of even further territory, aiming particularly at the rich agricultural lands,

timber sources, and mines of eastern Europe; he also proposed to control the rich commerce of the Mediterranean. Meanwhile, his forces took Iraq from the Safavids, thus acquiring access to the Persian Gulf. This monarch, who built the great wall around Jerusalem that is still standing today, claimed to be "Lord of the two lands and two seas." His conquests provoked conflicts with the Portuguese in the Red Sea and Indian Ocean. The Portuguese imagined taking Mecca to chastise the "heathen" Ottomans, but no such attack ever materialized.

MAP
The Islamic World: The Ottoman Empire

Suleiman responded harshly to challenges to his authority. He executed his own favorite son and a grandson who rebelled against him. His palace life was marked by pomp and splendor exceeding that of Louis XIV's France. An army of servants attended him, and those men who worked in his palace inner service gained prestige and status because of their proximity to the sultan. The sultan's banquets were served on elaborate tableware of gold, silver, and an expanding collection of fine Chinese porcelain. In the hours between waking and sleeping, Suleiman met with advisers and petitioners, read, or listened to music. For amusement he watched wrestling matches and listened to court poets and jesters. He was trained in the fine art of goldsmithing, also wrote poetry, and had a keen interest in maps. Foreign ambassadors, such as those from the French king or Habsburg emperor, were forced to prostrate themselves before the sultan,

An illuminated tughra *of Sultan Suleiman. The* tughra *was the sultan's signature, used to validate imperial documents and mark coinage. It included the sultan's name and his father's name and designated the sultan as "eternally victorious." The palace employed hundreds of artists, including the designers who fashioned and illuminated such beautiful* tughras.

an indication of the perceived balance of power. European observers commented on the intimidating nature of a visit to Suleiman's court, where thousands of massed troops would stand for hours in absolute silence. In Europe he was known as Suleiman the Magnificent; in the Ottoman Empire he was called Suleiman the Lawgiver.

The sultan's rule was based on an ideal of Persian origin called the "circle of justice." This ideal stated that in order for the kingdom to be prosperous and secure, the sultan required a strong army. To provide for this army, the state needed tax revenues from its citizens, and in order for the citizens to pay their taxes they had to receive in return security and justice from the sultan. Although there were many abuses at various levels of government, the Ottoman sultans did adhere to this ideal. Any of the sultan's subjects could submit a petition to the palace asking redress of wrongs—sometimes the sultan rode out into the streets while his attendants gathered petitions from the crowd. Ottoman court records show many instances in which peasants complained to the local judge *(kadi)* that officials were extracting extra taxes or labor from them. These complaints were then forwarded to the central government, which punished or replaced the offenders.

The Empire Under Suleiman

Suleiman governed the mightiest state of his day. Extending from Poland to Yemen and from Persia to Tripoli, it included 21 provinces and many linguistic and ethnic groups, such as Magyars, Armenians, Bosnians, Albanians, Greeks, Tartars, Kurds, Arabs, Copts, and Jews. "Multiculturalism," often thought of as a twentieth-century concept, was in fact typical of many large agrarian empires of this age.

Economically, Suleiman's empire was nearly self-sufficient, with expanding production and flourishing trade. The Ottoman dominions produced annual revenues greater than those available to any contemporary European monarch and grain surpluses that gave the Ottomans considerable leverage in the Mediterranean region, where grain shortages were endemic. Merchants smuggled grain out despite government attempts to control them, and Ottoman rivals like Venice often purchased grain supplies from the sultan's **pashas.** Indeed, food has been, and still is, one of the most powerful motivating forces in history.

DOCUMENT

An Ambassador's Report on the Ottoman Empire

Power in such a far-flung empire could never be absolute. The sultan delegated authority to local governors and to pashas. Rule in distant provinces, like Egypt, was more flexible and less direct. Conquered lands closer to the capital were given to Ottoman *sipahis* (se-PAH-hee) or "fief" holders, who were expected to bring cavalry contingents for military campaigns. At other times *sipahis* lived on their lands *(timars)*, administering local affairs, collecting taxes, and keeping order. Unlike European feudal lords, they were not usually local residents and were often away in distant wars. Provincial governors *(pashas or beys)* were drawn from the higher-ranking Ottoman commanders. All members of this governing class were thus heavily dependent on the sultan, who might suddenly change their assignments or revoke their land holdings. By Suleiman's reign, the political power of the *sipahis* over their *timars* had been partly usurped by the sultan's central bureaucracy. It functioned under a **vizir,** or chief minister, with a host of subordinate officials. The top officials met regularly as the sultan's **divan** or council to advise the ruler, but his word was law (although top officials and religious authorities—the **ulama**—might use their authority to challenge or moderate his decrees).

The Ottomans developed a unique "slave" *(kul)* system that was a major factor in their success. The system was based on the *devshirme* (dev-SHEHR-me), a levy of boys from the non-Muslim subjects of the empire, which functioned as a special type of "human tax" on the Balkan provinces. These boys were brought to the capital, converted to Islam, and taught Turkish. Most of them went to the **janissaries** (JAN-i-sehr-ees), the famed elite Ottoman infantry corps that was armed with gunpowder weapons. They formed the backbone of the formidable Ottoman armies. The smartest and most talented of the boys, however, were sent to the palace to be educated in literature, science, the arts, religion, and military skills. These boys, when they reached maturity, were given the highest military and administrative posts in the state. Ideally, the *kul* system provided the state with a group of expert administrators who, because they had been separated from their families and homes, would remain loyal to the sultan, to whom they owed everything. These "slaves," rather than occupying the lowest level of the social order, controlled much of the wealth and power in Ottoman society. Many of the buildings they endowed are still standing today. The more common type of domestic or agricultural slave did, of course, also exist in Ottoman society. Slavery and slave markets were scattered

---

pasha—Top military-administrative official (governor) in the Ottoman Empire.

vizir—A chief minister or comparable high-ranking government official in the Muslim world, but most particularly in the Ottoman Empire.

divan—A council or place of administrative assembly within the Ottoman Empire.

ulama—Islamic religious authorities; men versed in Islamic sciences and law.

janissaries—An elite Ottoman infantry corps armed with gunpowder weapons and composed mostly of converted Balkan slaves.

European writers and their audiences were fascinated by the Ottoman harem and often depicted it in exaggerated erotic terms. This engraving from a seventeenth-century French history of the Ottoman palace imagines the sultan taking his bath attended by naked harem women. In fact, this image is pure fantasy; both sexuality and reproduction in the harem were tightly controlled, and the sultan's attendants were male, not female.

throughout the Afro-Eurasian world, although Islam prohibited the enslaving of fellow Muslims.

Western literature has produced an exotic, erotic image of the Ottoman sultan's **harem** (the sacred area of the palace, or of any home, forbidden to outsiders). But much of this image is a myth produced by the overactive imaginations or hostile sentiments of European men inspired by the prospect of several hundred women in one household. In fact, sexuality in the palace was tightly controlled. Like women in other traditional patriarchal societies, most Ottoman women had to work in the fields and towns. Only the women of the elite classes could be fully veiled and secluded. In the palace, the harem women were arranged in a rigid hierarchy much like that of the men; each was paid according to her rank. Most of the women were not destined for the sultan's bed; instead they were married to the sultan's officers to create further ties of loyalty to the palace. A select few were chosen to bear the sultan's heirs.

The harem women wielded power because of their wealth, their connections, and their proximity to the sultan. The most powerful among them was the sultan's mother (the *valide sultan*), not his wife. The *valide sultans* participated actively (although behind the scenes) in court politics. Petitioners, including pashas, applied to these high-ranking women to intercede on their behalf with the sultan. Some *valide sultans* even served a diplomatic function, corresponding with European rulers like the Venetian doge, Catherine de' Medici in France, and Queen Elizabeth in England.

In the Ottoman system, proximity to the sultan was the primary avenue to power, and membership in the royal household or military class brought with it the highest status in society. But pashas, palace women, religious officials, and members of the palace

staff jockeyed for positions of power and formed alliances to advance their own interests. Harem politics, illustrated in Suleiman's reign by the contending influences of his mother and his wife, have often been blamed for weakening the Ottoman state. In fact, however, the factors that compromised Ottoman power were much more complex. Continued conquests produced serious communication and transportation problems, and long wars and failure to pay the troops on time caused rebellions in the ranks. Religious contention, provoked by the rise of the Shi'ite Safavids in Persia, also threatened the empire.

Another important factor in Ottoman politics was the fact that the eldest son had no automatic claim to the throne. The sultan's sons thus contended to succeed him, sometimes producing extended periods of interregnum. That was the case with Bayezid II, whose sons got tired of waiting for him to die and launched a civil war to determine who would sit on the throne in his stead. Once a prince established himself as sultan, he would often have his brothers exe-

---

harem—In Arabic, literally "forbidden." A sacred area of palace or home forbidden to outsiders, often but not always used to protect and sequester women.

valide sultan—The mother of the Ottoman sultan; generally the most powerful and influential woman in the empire.

Document   Evliya Çelebi, "An Ottoman Official's Wedding Night"

Marriages in the Ottoman administrative system were often arranged to link powerful families, consolidate wealth, and secure loyalty. Love matches were also made, but sometimes officials were forced into marriages at the sultan's command. That was the fate of Melek Ahmed Pasha, who, after the death of his beloved first wife, was forced to marry the elderly and intransigent Fatma Sultan, daughter of Sultan Ahmed I. This passage, in which Melek Ahmed tells his tale of woe to the chronicler Evliya Çelebi, suggests that marriage to a princess, however prestigious, could be burdensome. It also illustrates the consumption of goods by royal households and the power and status of royal women, who could supersede the wishes of influential men. Note that Melek Pasha addressed his new wife as "Sultan." That title was used for royal princesses.

As soon as I entered the harem, having uttered a *besmele* [invocation of God's name], I saw her. Now I am supposed to be her husband, and this is our first night—she ought to show me just a little respect. She just sat there stock still, not moving an inch. I went up and kissed her hand.

"Pasha," she says, "welcome."

"God be praised that I have seen my sultan's smiling beauty," say I, and I shower her with all sorts of self-deprecating flatteries. Not once does she invite me to sit down. And she puts on all kinds of virginal airs, as though she weren't an ancient crone who has gone through twelve husbands!

The first pearl from her lips is this: "My dear pasha, if you want to get along with me, whether you are present at court or absent in some government post, my expenses are 15 purses each and every month. Also I owe my steward, Kermetçi Mustafa Agha, 100 purses: pay my debt in the morning. And every year I get six Marmara boatloads of firewood. And my retainers Selman Beg and Ömer Beg and Mukbil Agha and my steward get as a daily stipend 100 bushels of barley each, 10 okkas of coffee, 10 okkas of fine sugar, and nightly 10 okkas of camphor beeswax"—and on and on with suchlike nonsense, spouting these expenses like a talking inventory. Several times she pinched my cheeks. . . .

Now her stewardess and treasuress and ladies in waiting and, in short, 300 or more women came to kiss my hand and stand there in rows. "Well, my dear pasha, these are my servants of the interior. I also have as many or more manumitted [legally freed] slave girls on the exterior. Together with children and dependents, they total 700 souls. You will provide all of them with their annual stipend of silk and gauze and brocade and broadcloth. And you will pay the annual stipend of my halberdiers and cooks and gardeners and coachmen and eunuchs and *begs*, as well as those serving them, numbering 500 people. And if you don't—well, you know the consequence!"

Melek Ahmed replied: "I swear by God, my sultan," say I, "that I have just returned from the Transylvania campaign. I am a vizir who fights the holy war. In that campaign I had 7,000 men to feed. I spent 170,000 goldpieces and 600 purses. I even had to sell quite a lot of equipment and arms and armor and helmets and to borrow money from the janissary corps. . . . I am unable to bear such expenses."

After this "wedding night" Melek prayed for death and complained that he had been asked to "feed the state elephant." He vowed never to see Fatma Sultan again.

Questions to Consider

1. What does this story suggest about the lives and expenses of both males and females in the Ottoman elite class?

2. Does gender or status take precedence in the dealings of Melek and Fatma?

3. When such a story is incorporated into a history such as Evliya's, should we assume that the dialog is reported word-for-word as it occurred? What factors might affect the accuracy of this account? (Remember that Melek was Evliya's patron.)

From Robert Dankoff, trans., *The Intimate Life of an Ottoman Statesman, Melek Ahmed Pasha (1588–1662), as Portrayed in Evliya Çelebi's Book of Travels* (Albany: State University of New York Press 1991), pp. 259–261.

cuted, a grim task designed to ensure the stability of the state and avoid further struggles. A wise prince would try to gain the favor of the janissary corps, for their support might make or break him.

Religion was an integral part of government and society. But as in other Muslim lands, the religious authorities *(ulama)* did not run the government; they were subordinated to the state and the sultan. The grand **mufti,** as head of the Islamic establishment, was also the chief religious and legal adviser to the sul-

mufti—A high-ranking Islamic religious and legal adviser.

tan. The sultan approved religious appointments and might dismiss any religious officer, including the grand mufti. A corps of learned religious scholars represented the sultan as judges *(kadis),* dispensers of charities, and teachers. Non-Muslim subjects or **dhimmis** were regarded as inferior but were granted a significant degree of legal and religious toleration through government arrangements with their religious leaders (rabbis and priests, for example), who were responsible for their civil obedience. Non-Muslim subjects lived under their own laws and customs, pursuing their private interests within limits imposed by Islamic law and Ottoman economic needs. As in other Islamic lands, they had to pay the **jizya,** an additional head tax.

Ottoman society, like other societies, can be divided along different types of lines based on gender, occupation, class, religion, or race. For tax purposes, Ottoman society was divided roughly between tax-paying subjects *(reaya,* or flock) and the military-administrative class *(askeri).* This division between *askeri* and *reaya* was the primary determinant of status, crossing lines of gender, race, and sometimes religion. A woman of the *askeri* class could command authority over a man of lesser status. People of various races could be members of the *askeri* class; the chief black eunuch, for example, was one of the most powerful men in the state. Although merchants and members of the *ulama* might achieve considerable wealth and authority, they did not have access to the same type of power and status as the military administrative class.

Artistic Production

Ottoman success resulted in a vigorous cultural renaissance, most evident in monumental architecture and decorative tile work. Mehmed II rebuilt his decaying capital, from sewers to palaces. His monumental Fatih Mosque and splendid Topkapi Palace, with its fortress walls, fountains, and courtyards, were models of the new Ottoman style, which was influenced by the Byzantine artistic tradition. The palace was divided into three courts that reflected Ottoman concepts of power and space. The outer court was for public affairs, as well as stable and kitchen facilities. The second court provided a dividing line between the public and private life of the sultan. There the sultan met with diplomats and built his library. The inner court was reserved for the sultan and his intimates, a place for relaxation and privacy. Suleiman surpassed Topkapi's splendor with the

beautiful and elegant Suleimaniye, his own mosque and mausoleum. These were but three architectural wonders among thousands scattered throughout the empire, many of which remain today.

In addition, the period was marked by wondrous productions in the realms of decorative arts. Calligraphy could take the form of birds or boats in official documents. Elaborate calligraphy and stunning painted tiles decorated Ottoman mosques and buildings. For example, Suleiman added luminous tiles to the Dome of the Rock in Jerusalem. Ottoman high culture also produced a great outpouring of scholarship and literature, mostly following Persian traditions but also reflecting a unique Ottoman synthesis. Poets, artists,

Portrait of a Sufi, c. 1535, was attributed to the painter Shaykh-Zadeh who studied in Herat and then painted and instructed disciples at the Safavid Court in Tabriz. Talented painters were in great demand in the courts of the gunpowder empires. Sufi shaykhs often served as influential advisors to the sultans and shahs.

---

dhimmis—Non-Muslim subjects of a Muslim state.

jizya—An additional head tax imposed on non-Muslims living under Muslim rule.

and historians vied for the attentions—and rewards (silver, sable furs, robes of honor, even houses)—of the sultan. Some achieved remarkable rank and success; others left the palace disheartened and poor. The great majority of artisans, however, held relatively low status. They lived and worked in the palace or in the cities, grouped often according to their occupations on "the street of the gold-thread makers" or "the street of the coppersmiths."

The Suleymaniye Mosque

Challenges to Ottoman Supremacy

Beginning in Suleiman's reign, cheap silver from the Americas and a population increase led to rising inflation, rebellions, and military mutinies, all of which weakened the government. None of the eight sultans who followed Suleiman before 1648 could duplicate his successes. Selim II was known as "the drunkard"; another sultan gained notoriety by having 19 of his brothers killed on his accession. Increasingly, the sultans did not themselves lead their troops into battle. Other problems plaguing Suleiman's successors were the rising power of the Russians and Habsburgs in Europe, stalemated wars with Persia, and the end of Ottoman naval supremacy in the Red Sea. Nonetheless, the period between 1566 and 1650 should be viewed as one of reorganization and retrenchment rather than decline. The Ottoman Empire was adjusting to newly emerging global configurations of power and commerce, and Ottoman armies still managed to gain important victories in this era, notably the reconquest of Iraq by Murad IV (1623–1640) in 1638.

With Suleiman's death the Ottoman Empire passed its zenith, but it remained a significant contender for power in the Afro-Eurasian sphere well into the eighteenth century. It continued to dominate the overland trade with Asia. Moreover, the sultans moderated Portuguese domination of the Indian Ocean, ultimately aiding the Dutch and English seaborne empires in the East while humbling their Habsburg rivals in Europe.

The Decline of the Ottomans

THE SAFAVID EMPIRE IN PERSIA

■ *What role did Shi'ism play in the Safavid Empire?*

In the beginning of the sixteenth century a new Turkic dynasty came to power in Iran, led by a charismatic, red-headed, adolescent, sufi *shaykh*. This dynasty, emerging out of the Safavid sufi religious order, would unite Iran, challenge the Ottoman empire, and shift Iran's predominantly Sunni population to Shi'ism. The Safavid dynasty had its origins in an Islamic mystical order founded by Safi al-Din (c. 1252–1334). One of his descendants, Ismail (ruled 1501–1524), gathered an army of devoted followers and began a series of lightning campaigns that united Persia, conquered Iraq, and posed a formidable challenge to the Ottomans on their eastern frontiers. Ismail was only 14 when he seized his first territories. Although such precocity may seem unusual today, it was common enough in this era for the sons of powerful men to be trained to fight and rule while still boys.

Ismail was not only a successful military commander; he was also the head of a Shi'ite Muslim sect.

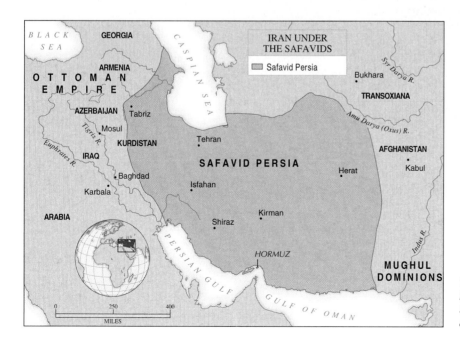

The Safavid Empire was based on the broad, semiarid Iranian plateau. The Safavids and Ottomans contended for control of Iraq and Azerbaijan.

Document   The Coming of Ismail Safavi Foretold

Histories and legends of famous leaders and religious figures often recount the ways in which the coming of these men was predicted or foretold. In this selection, from an anonymous Persian manuscript, the story is told of a sufi mystic named Dede Mohammad. This sufi, or *darwish*, while returning from a pilgrimage to Mecca, becomes separated from his caravan in the desert. Dying of thirst, he is rescued by a mysterious youth who takes him to a magnificent encampment in a flowering plain. There he sees a veiled prince, whom he does not realize is the Twelfth *Imam*, a descendant of the Prophet revered by the Shi'ite Muslims who is believed to be in occultation (that is, he has disappeared but is not dead). In this vision, the Twelfth *Imam* girds and sends forth the young Ismail Safavi, thus legitimizing his reign to the Shi'ites.

After his rescue, Dede Mohammad ... walked by the young man's side, until they came to a palace, whose cupola outrivaled the sun and moon.... Golden thrones were arranged side by side, and on one of the thrones a person was seated whose face was covered by a veil. Dede Mohammad, placing his hand on his breast, made a salutation, whereupon an answer to his salutation came from the veiled one, who having bidden him be seated, ordered food to be brought for him. The like of this food he had never seen in his life before.... As soon as he had finished his repast, he saw that a party of men had entered, bringing a boy of about fourteen years of age, with red hair, a white face, and dark grey eyes; on his head was a scarlet cap.... The veiled youth then said to him, "Oh! Ismail, the hour of your 'coming' has now arrived." The other replied: "It is for your Holiness to command." ... His Holiness, taking his belt three times lifted it up and placed it on the ground again. He then, with his own blessed hands, fastened on the girdle and taking [Ismail's] cap from his head, raised it and then replaced it.... His Holiness then told his servants to bring his own sword which, when brought, he fastened with his own hands on the girdle of the child. Then he said, "You may now depart." [The Arab youth then guided Dede Mohammad back to his caravan, and the sufi asked his guide to reveal the identity of the veiled prince.] He replied, "Did you not know that the prince you saw was no other than the Lord of the Age?" When Dede Mohammad heard this name he stood up and said: "Oh! youth, for the love of God take me back again that I may once more kiss the feet of His Holiness [the Twelfth *Imam*], and ask a blessing of him, perchance I might be allowed to wait on him." But the youth replied: "It is impossible. You should have made your request at first. You cannot return. But you can make your request where you will, for His Holiness is everywhere present and will hear your prayers."

Questions to Consider

1. This manuscript apparently dates from the seventeenth century. Why was it important for the Safavids to relate in this way such stories of the predicted coming of Ismail?

2. The Twelfth *Imam* tied a belt or sash around Ismail's waist, placed his cap on his head, and gave him his own sword. What is the significance of this ceremony? Can you think of similar rituals that take place today?

3. What is the significance of the flowering plain in the middle of a desert and of the miraculous food?

From E. Dennison Ross, "The Early Years of Shah Ismail," *Journal of the Royal Asiatic Society* (1896), pp. 328–331.

Contemporary accounts portray him as a charismatic leader whose army thought him invincible. They followed him into battle crying *Shaykh, Shaykh!* The Safavid troops wore red headgear with 12 folds to commemorate the 12 Shi'ite *imams* (descendants of the prophet Muhammad); because of this headgear, they were called "redheads."

Ismail angered the Ottoman sultan by sending missionaries and agitators to stir up the sultan's subjects on the Ottoman eastern frontiers. He also launched a sometimes violent campaign to convert the Sunni Muslims of his domain to Shi'ism. Because Persia had been predominantly Sunni, he had to import Shi'ite scholars and jurists from the Arab lands, such as Syria and Iraq. Under the Safavid shahs (kings), Persia became overwhelmingly Shi'ite, as it is today.

Power is acquired not only on the field of battle but also in the arenas of reputation and diplomacy. Legends grew up around the youthful leader Ismail because of his many and rapid conquests. He was also supposed to have received the secret knowledge of the Safavi mystical order, passed down from his brother as he lay dying. Hence he had a powerful aura of both political and religious legitimacy. European rulers, including the Portuguese king and the pope, were inspired by the accounts of Ismail's victories and the rumors of his quasi-divine prowess. Hoping that the Safavids would help them defeat the Ottomans, who were Sunni Muslims, these rulers sent envoys to the young shah. Ismail had some interest in exploring possibilities with European powers, but he was apparently more interested in acquiring European artillery and defeating the Ottomans than in a Christian-Shi'ite alliance.

Because transport and communication technology was so primitive in the sixteenth century, rulers often knew little about their rivals. Diplomatic missions were thus crucially important as a means by which a ruler might establish his reputation and gain information about foreign powers. The Portuguese, for example, thought of the Safavids as barbarians, but they were interested in securing an ally against the Ottomans. Their envoy to Ismail was instructed to brag to the Safavids about the fine quality of Portuguese horses, table service, and women (all considered prize possessions). Envoys were also used to send messages of intimidation. When, in 1510, Ismail defeated Shaibani Khan, the Uzbek ruler in Central Asia, he had the Khan's skull gilded and made into a drinking cup. He sent an envoy with the grisly trophy, along with a taunting message, to the Ottoman sultan, Bayezid II. Of course, being an envoy in this era was dangerous, especially for the bearers of rude messages. The Ottoman sultans often imprisoned Safavid envoys, and messengers to the Safavid court were sometimes detained or abused. When Ismail sent another arrogant message to the Mamluk sultan in Egypt, the latter was so enraged that he sponsored a poetry contest to see which of his poets could write the most insulting reply in verse. But he did not harm Ismail's messenger because he was afraid of a Safavid invasion.

The Ottomans were intimidated by Ismail's early successes. In 1514, however, they soundly defeated Ismail's forces on the frontier between Anatolia and Persia. This victory is often attributed to the fact that the Ottomans had more and better gunpowder weaponry. Demoralized, Ismail withdrew to his palace, having lost his reputation for invincibility. After his death, the Safavids fought a series of long wars against the Ottomans to the west and the Uzbeks to the east.

None of his successors wielded the same charismatic religious power as Ismail. They were kings, not *shaykhs* (holy men), even though Ismail's son Tahmasp still claimed the headship of the Safavid sufi order.

Islam shares the story of Adam and Eve with Christianity and Judaism, with certain variations. In this Persian manuscript Adam rides a dragonlike serpent and Eve rides a peacock; these two beasts facilitated the entrance of Iblis *[Satan] into the Garden of Eden.*

Still, the next hundred years of Safavid rule were characterized by a consolidation of state power, lavish patronage of the arts, and an exploration of diplomatic and commercial relations with Europe. European merchants visited the shah's court, trying to gain access to the coveted Iranian silk trade, but they met with little success. Tahmasp ruled for half a century (1524–1576), despite having to contend with foreign invasions, religious factionalism, and power struggles among the tribal leaders.

The Middle East

The Safavids, with the aid of European renegades, developed their gunpowder weaponry but never to the same extent as the Ottomans. Nor did they imitate the elaborate "slave"-based hierarchy and infantry corps (janissaries) that became the basis for Ottoman success. In Persia, the tribal leaders and their cavalry-based militaries retained their position of power.

The Reign of Abbas the Great

The reign of Shah Abbas (1588–1629) is considered a "golden age" of Safavid power, comparable to that of Suleiman in the Ottoman Empire. Ascending the throne at the age of 17, Abbas ultimately became a pragmatic politician, a wise statesman, a brilliant strategist, and a generous patron of the arts. During his reign, Persia acquired security, stability, and a reputation for cultural creativity, symbolized by the shah's splendid new capital at Isfahan.

Abbas directed much of his attention to the threat posed by an Ottoman-Uzbek alliance, which had almost destroyed his country. He held his holy men in political check but labored to project an image of Shi'ite piety. He reorganized his government and army, creating a personal force of "slaves" of the royal household. This force acted as a counterweight to the ambitious and often unruly tribal chiefs. Within the army, Abbas increased his artillery and musket forces, relying less on traditional cavalry. During the 1590s, he slowly recovered territory lost by his less adept predecessors.

Persia prospered under Abbas, and Isfahan was a great center of trade, production, and consumption. The government employed thousands of workers, and the shah, his family, and retainers consumed great quantities of luxury textiles, jade vessels, jeweled weapons, and exotic food items. Government monopolies, particularly in silk, promoted various crafts such as weaving and dying. Hundreds of new roads, bridges, hostels, and irrigation projects promoted agriculture, encouraged trade, and swelled urban populations. These projects also enhanced the prestige of the ruler. Contemporaries noted that a person could travel from one end of the empire to another in safety, without fear of bandits. That was a significant claim in an age when bandits roamed the countryside and merchants traveled at their own risk, often with large retinues of armed guards.

The silk trade was so lucrative that merchants on both sides conspired to get the shipments through, even when the Safavids and the

Ottomans were at war. Persia was an important center in the networks of East-West trade. Its silk was in such demand in Europe that Venetian, French, and other traders would wait in the Syrian entrepots for the caravans of Persian silk to come in. They negotiated with local agents, trying to outbid each other for the rights to purchase each incoming load. One Venetian observer stated that a merchant would willingly pluck out his own eye to triumph over a competitor. The British tried for years to gain concessions from the Safavids on Persian silk. Ultimately, the shah signed a commercial agreement with the British, and the Portuguese were forcibly ejected from Hormuz in the Persian Gulf, moves allowing direct shipment of Persian silk to Europe by sea, and thus the avoidance of Ottoman tolls on the overland routes.

Persia at this time was one of the primary cultural centers of the world. It was a conduit to the West not only for the goods but also for the spiritual and literary influences of India. Meanwhile, sufi Muslim missionaries traveled to South and Southeast Asia, transmitting their own ideas and bringing a synthesis of

Nominally, this image illustrates a story about an elderly dervish who is in love with a handsome young man. But miniatures often depicted scenes of everyday life like this sixteenth-century Safavid scene of a bath house. On the roof, servants shake out towels. In the dressing room men are shown changing their clothes and an attendant brings a man who appears to be the bath keeper some food. A father carries his son into the bath while outside a servant takes care of a horse with rich saddle cloths. Inside the bath (hammam), assisted by bath-attendants, men of various ages wash, get their hair trimmed, or enjoy a massage. The bath was a place for socializing, relaxing, and conducting business. Bathing was a same-sex activity. Women, who either attended separate baths or attended on different days, might bring their children or use the bath as an opportunity to evaluate potential brides for their sons.

mystical ideas and practices back to the Islamic heartlands. Persia's fine arts—ceramics, tapestries, and carpets—were eagerly sought from Alexandria to Calcutta. Persian literary forms, particularly the exquisite imagery of Persian poetry, were imitated at both the Ottoman and Mughal courts, even by the rulers themselves. Persian painters explored realist styles and erotic themes. They were recruited from abroad, as were two émigrés, Khwaja Abdus Samad and Mir Sayyid Ali, who founded the famous Mughal school of painting in India.

Major Middle Eastern courts housed large workshops of artists, sometimes numbering in the hundreds. The Safavid shahs paid their painters to produce lavish manuscripts. Ismail commissioned a wondrous illustrated version of the *Epic of Kings (Shahnamah)*, a long rhyming poem by Firdawsi, that was not finished in the shah's lifetime. Five court calligraphers spent nine years transcribing a single edition of the poet Jami's *Seven Thrones*, for Prince Ibrahim Mirza; it was then turned over to a group of painters who produced its lavish illustrations. When the Ottomans conquered the Persian capital of Tabriz, they carried back many of the Safavid artists and their works as a valuable part of the booty.

Persian architecture, with its jewel-like colors, intricate geometric and floral patterns, luxurious gardens, and artificial streams, exerted considerable influence on the architecture of the Islamic world. Abbas made the capital at Isfahan a showcase for these artistic and architectural talents. One of the largest cities of its time, Isfahan had a million inhabitants. Its public life centered around a broad square (used for assemblies and polo matches), the palace compound, a huge bazaar, and the main mosque. Five hundred years later the beauty of Abbas's surviving monuments still inspires awe in visitors. As one Persian writer put it in his boyhood memoirs, "Isfahan is half the world."

THE MUGHAL EMPIRE IN SOUTH ASIA

■ *How did the Turco-Islamic Mughals modify their rule to accommodate a Hindu majority population?*

The Safavid and Ottoman states were contemporaries of the mighty Mughal Empire in India. It too was ruled by a Turkic dynasty. But unlike the Ottoman sultans and Safavid shahs, the Mughals ruled a population that was predominantly Hindu rather than Muslim. That fact marked the Mughal Empire indelibly and helped craft its distinctive character.

The Mughals	
1525	Babur invades India
1556–1605	Reign of Akbar, Mughal Golden Age
1632	Shah Jahan commissions the Taj Mahal
1658–1707	Reign of Aurangzeb, reasserts Islamic orthodoxy

Origins

The Ottoman Empire emerged out of a warrior principality in what is now Turkey, and the Safavid Empire was established by a sufi boy-king who commanded both political and religious authority in Persia. The origin of the Mughal Empire was different from each of these; one might say it was founded by a determined prince in search of a kingdom.

The establishment of the Mughal Empire was not the first instance of Muslim contact with the diverse, but predominantly Hindu, population of India. Mus-

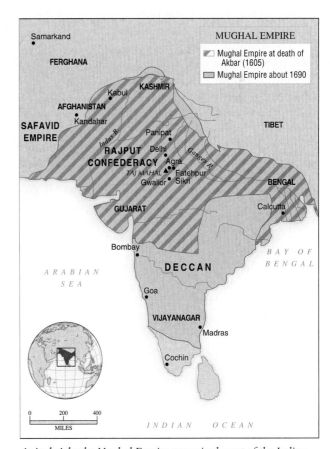

At its height the Mughal Empire comprised most of the Indian subcontinent.

lim merchants and sufi mystics had traveled to India from the Islamic heartlands for many centuries. From the seventh century onward Muslim rulers extended the frontiers of Islam eastward to the borders of South Asia. Then a Turkic warrior, Mahmud of Ghazna (c. 971–1030), gained control of Khurasan province in eastern Persia and Afghanistan and seized control of northern India. Muslim sultanates were also established on the west coast of India, and the Muslim Delhi Sultanate ruled in the thirteenth and fourteenth centuries until Timur's invasion. Thus, by the sixteenth century, much of South Asian society had had some contact with Islamic culture and political power

India is a land of many peoples, many languages, and diverse terrain. At the beginning of the sixteenth century it was politically fragmented. The Delhi Sultanate, having spawned a number of independent contending Muslim states, had been partially resurrected under the Lodi Afghan dynasty. The Rajput Confederacy held sway in the northwest, the Vijayangar Empire controlled much of southern India, and a string of commercial city-states held sway along the southwestern coast. Although many rulers had aspired to unite the entire subcontinent, that goal remained daunting.

Early in the sixteenth century, a new conqueror cast his eye on India. The adventurous Turco-Mongol ruler of Kabul, Babur ("the Tiger"; 1483–1530), was a descendant of both Timur and Chinggis Khan. Babur did not begin his career in India. He inherited the Afghan principality of Ferghana and twice conquered the Timurid capital at Samarkand before losing everything to the Uzbeks. He and his troops finally seized the throne of Kabul in 1504. Babur is a striking historical figure because, unlike many rulers of his time, he compiled his memoirs. They are a tale of triumphs and losses that reveal Babur as a straightforward narrator who built gardens wherever he went, paid careful attention to geography, was solicitous of his mother, and seemed to enjoy good wine and a good fight. He also loved to compose and recite poetry. Babur's memoirs tell of rhinoceros hunts and military relations. He notes, rather ruefully, that he had sworn to give up drink when he reached the age of 40 but now felt compelled to drink out of anxiety because he was already 39. Armed with Turkish artillery, this intrepid warrior mobilized an invasion in 1525, winning decisive battles against the Afghan Sultanate at Delhi and the Rajput Confederacy. Babur was not impressed with Indian culture. He criticized native dress, religion, and the failure of Indians to have running water in their gardens.

> *Hindustan [India] is a place of little charm. There is no beauty in its people, no graceful social intercourse, no poetic talent or understanding, no etiquette, nobility or manliness. . . . There are no good horses, meat, grapes, melons, or other fruit. There is no ice, cold water, good food or bread in the markets.*[2]

Like many travelers, Babur tended to find his own culture superior to those of other peoples. He did, however, admire the Indian systems of numbers, weights, and measures and the country's vast array of craftsmen. Speaking as a prospective ruler, he could not help but remark that "the one nice aspect of Hindustan is that it is a large country with lots of gold and money."[3] When Babur died, soon after the conquest, the hard-living and thoughtful ruler had laid the foun-

Babur, conqueror of northern India, surveying the spectacular rock-cut Hindu sculptures at Urwa fortress in Gwalior, from an illustrated manuscript of Babur's memoirs. Babur ordered these sculptures defaced, probably to fulfill the perceived Islamic prohibition against depicting the human form. Muslim rulers defaced many such Hindu and Buddhist statues, although some Muslim courts also patronized the production of images of the human form.

dations for a Mughal empire that would dominate most of the subcontinent and endure into the eighteenth century.

Babur was succeeded by his able but erratic son, Humayun (hu-MAH-yoon). After ten years of rule during which he expanded Mughal domains, Humayun was overthrown by his vassal Sher Khan. He then fled to the Safavid court of Tahmasp in Persia. The Safavid shah welcomed Humayun. It was always useful for monarchs of the time to shelter in their courts the sons or rivals of neighboring kings, as such refugees gave rulers leverage against their enemies. Rulers also demanded that vassals send their sons to reside at court; it was a practical way to ensure the loyalty of subordinates.

In 1555 Shah Tahmasp helped Humayun regain his kingdom, no doubt presuming that Humayun would prove a significant ally on the Safavids' eastern frontiers. But Humayun died shortly thereafter in a fall down his library steps—perhaps a fitting end for a learned man, but a rather ignominious one for a warrior.

The Reign of Akbar

Humayun's son Akbar (1556–1605) was 14 years old when he succeeded his father, about the same age as Shah Ismail when he commenced his reign. During a half century of rule, Akbar united northern India, advanced against the sultanates in the south of the subcontinent, and presided over a glorious courtly culture. Akbar ruled an empire more populous than those of the Ottoman sultan and the Persian shah; Mughal subjects numbered between 100 and 150 million.

Unlike Ismail, Akbar did not immediately consolidate his power. Initially, he was controlled by a regent. As often happens when a prince comes to power at an early age, powerful men in the court used the prince's youth to advance their own influence and objectives. By the age of 20, however, Akbar took charge and began a determined campaign of conquest that would continue into his old age.

This Mughal potentate was the counterpart of Suleiman in the Ottoman Empire and Shah Abbas in Safavid Persia. His reign is associated with military might, prosperity, and patronage of the arts at a spectacular level. At 13, Akbar led troops in battle; in his thirties, he challenged an enemy commander to personal combat; in late middle age, he still hunted wild animals with sword and lance. Akbar's concern for morality and social justice was indicated by his advice to a son: "Avoid religious persecution; be strong but magnanimous; accept apologies, sincerely given."[4]

A significant aspect of Akbar's reign is that he adapted the Islamic state to the conditions of ruling a non-Muslim population. In so doing, he promoted cultural synthesis, incorporated Hindus and others into the inner workings of government, and showed himself to be a pragmatic monarch. He married a number of Rajput princesses and made alliances with Hindu families, taking the men into his service. The mother of his heir, Jahangir, was a Hindu. He also abolished the *jizya*, the head tax on non-Muslims. This decision may seem like a simple matter, but the *jizya* was a standard of Islamic rule and had been institutionalized in the Sharia Islamic law. By abolishing it, Akbar gave notice to his Hindu subjects that they were granted a more equitable position vis-á-vis the Muslims, who constituted the ruling class.

Akbar also stopped taxing Hindu pilgrims, financed the construction of Hindu temples, and forbade Muslims to kill or eat the cow, which was sacred to Hindus. These measures alienated the *ulama* and the diverse Muslim elite of Turks, Afghans, Mongols, and Persians but won new support among the majority. Akbar, however, also initiated certain measures designed to force Hindu practice into compliance with Islamic law; he issued decrees outlawing Hindu child marriages and **sati** (the self-burning of widows), two reforms that violated Hindu traditions.

Akbar's tolerance in public administration was matched by his pursuit of knowledge and personal explorations of various religious faiths. He was devoted to certain sufi *shaykhs* and launched at his court a "house of worship," a forum for religious discussion to which he invited Muslims, Christians, Jews, Jains, Hindus, and Zoroastrians. In 1582 Akbar proclaimed a new cult, the *Din-i-Ilahi* (deen-i-eel-AH-hee), or "Divine Faith," which centered on Akbar himself and was highly influenced by **Zoroastrianism.** The new creed gained few adherents, but it further antagonized the *ulama* and demonstrated Akbar's religious eclecticism.

DOCUMENT

Akbar and the Jesuits

DOCUMENT

St. Francis Xavier, Jesuit in India

The Mughal State and Its Culture

One of the great accomplishments of the Mughal Empire was its establishment of a highly organized and intrusive central administration. In many ways like that of the Ottomans, it was designed to produce a consistent supply of taxes and troops for the government and to manage distant provinces. Akbar's military administrators, about two-thirds of whom were

---

sati—The practice by Hindu widows of self-immolation on their husbands' funeral pyres.

Zoroastrianism—A religion founded by the Persian prophet and mystic Zoroaster in the fifth century; initially monotheistic, it evolved into a dualistic faith in which the gods of light and good, led by Ahura-Mazda, opposed the gods of darkness and evil, led by Ahriman; influenced the development of Judaism and Christianity; Zoroastrians who migrated to India are known as Parsees.

foreign-born Muslims, were organized in military ranks and paid salaries according to the number of soldiers they commanded. Promotion for these military administrators, who were called ***mansabdars*** (mahn-SAHB-dahrs), was, ideally, based on merit. Their ranks were open to Hindus, and their positions were not hereditary, like those of European nobles. Like the Ottoman *kul* system, the *mansabdar* system was designed to produce loyalty to the state. Officials, in turn, were now made more dependent on the emperor. Like the Ottomans and Safavids, Akbar drew conquered foes into his service as long as they offered their submission. In this way, he took advantage of the military expertise of defeated commanders.

In the early seventeenth century the Mughal Empire was one of the wealthiest states in the world, with revenues ten times greater than those of France. Cities were numerous and large by European standards. Akbar's capital at Agra, for example, housed 200,000 people—twice the population of contemporary London. In the towns and villages, many industries flourished, particularly cotton textiles, which were

mansabdars—Mughal military-administrative official.

exported to most of Asia and Africa. The majority of subjects were Hindu peasants. One-third to one-half of their produce, paid in land taxes, supported the army and kept the administrative elite in considerable luxury.

The early Mughal period saw a new Hindu-Muslim cultural synthesis, well illustrated in literature. Beginning with Babur, each emperor considered himself a poet, a scholar, and a collector of books. Akbar himself could not read, but he founded a great library housing over 20,000 illustrated manuscripts. The Mughals used their wealth to patronize the arts. Their literature was cosmopolitan, reflected a fresh originality, and was expressed in a variety of languages, including Turkish, Persian, Hindi, Arabic, and Urdu (an Indo-Persian fusion).

Despite the Muslim prohibition of representational figures, human or animal, painting developed rapidly as an art in the early Mughal period. Akbar had studied art as a child under Abdus Samad and Mir Sayyid Ali, two Safavid court painters whom Humayan brought to Kabul and later took to India. Akbar's royal studio employed over a hundred artists, mostly Hindus, who created works of great variety including miniatures of courtly life and large murals for Akbar's palaces.

In 1632 the Mughal emperor, Shah Jahan, commissioned the building of the resplendent Taj Mahal as a memorial to his late wife. Tall minarets surround a central dome, and a reflecting pool perfectly mirrors the white marble building, one of the glories of Mughal architecture. The Taj Mahal is one of the more spectacular examples of the ways in which various peoples commemorate their dead.

The royal studio produced beautifully illustrated manuscripts requiring many painters and many years to complete. Foremost among these is the spectacular *Hamzanamah* (hahm-ZAHN-ah-mah), which includes 1400 illustrations on cloth. Akbar also sponsored illustrated versions of Babur's memoirs and of the great Sanskrit epics the *Mahabharata* (MAH-he-BAH-re-te) and the *Ramayana* (rah-MAI-yah-nah). The Mughal school of painters under Jahangir, Akbar's son, produced wonderful animal and bird imagery, developed new strains of sensual and realist representation, and expertly incorporated motifs of European painting into Mughal art.

The most imposing symbols of Mughal glory are to be seen in architecture. Fusing Persian and Indic styles, it featured the lavish use of mosaics, bulbous domes, cupolas, slender spires, lofty vaulted gateways, and formal gardens, all carefully harmonized. Akbar's major building project was his palace complex at Fatehpur Sikri (fe-te-POOR SIK-ree). Akbar wanted to build his new palace on a site dedicated to a famous sufi holy man, *Shaykh* Salim Chishti. But Fatehpur Sikri became a monument to man's vanity and lack of planning. Akbar's court abandoned the complex (which took 15 years to build) after only 14 years because the water supply was inadequate. But visitors still marvel at the red sandstone blocks of the monumental fortress, which were hewn so precisely that they needed no fasteners or mortar.

Akbar's son Jahangir and his grandson Shah Jahan continued the tradition of monumental building. The latter replaced Akbar's sandstone buildings at Delhi with new ones of marble. At Agra, Shah Jahan erected the famous Taj Mahal, a tomb for his favorite wife, Mumtaz Mahal, who died while giving birth to her fifteenth child. This elaborate tomb, set in beautiful gardens, took over 20 years to build. Its luminous white marble, beautiful tracery of semiprecious stones, and elegant lines make the Taj Mahal one of the best-known buildings in the world today.

Akbar's Successors: Contesting the Hindu-Muslim Synthesis

Like most empires, the Mughal polity fared best when its administration was relatively tolerant, its treasury full, and its military successful. Jahangir (1605–1627) and Shah Jahan (1628–1658) continued Akbar's policies of relative tolerance. Jahangir was learned and artistically sensitive (as demonstrated in his memoirs), but he was also a drunkard and a drug addict, often lacking the strength to act decisively and conduct policy. He lost Kandahar to the Persians. Shah Jahan launched three costly and unsuccessful campaigns to retake Kandahar, a disastrous thrust into Central Asia, four costly invasions of the Deccan, and an extravagant expedition to

oust a Portuguese enclave on the Indian coast. To compensate for these military expeditions, he had to raise land taxes, thus oppressing the peasantry.

The tension between Mughal tolerance and Muslim rule culminated in the seventeenth century with Akbar's great-grandsons, Dara Shikoh and Aurangzeb (1658–1707). Dara Shikoh took Akbar's tolerance one step further. He was a devoted sufi and wrote his own mystical works; he also studied Hindu mysticism. In the end this prince's attempt to find a middle ground between Islam and Hinduism provoked a violent response from the empire's Muslims and from his brother, Aurangzeb (OR-ang-zeb). Dara Shikoh was his father's favorite, but in the battle to succeed Shah Jahan, Aurangzeb was victorious. Charging his brother with apostasy, Aurangzeb marched him through the streets of Delhi in humiliation and had him executed.

Both sufi orders and the *ulama* opposed the ecumenicalism of Akbar and Dara Shikoh. With their support, Aurangzeb, having gained the throne, was determined to restore Sunni orthodoxy to the Mughal

Miniatures were not painted solely for artistic expression; they also suggested relationships. In this Mughal painting of Shah Jahangir and the Safavid Shah Abbas, Jahangir's artist portrayed his master as big and powerful, dominating his rather puny-looking Safavid rival. The monarchs stand on the globe, but Jahangir's lion is much more imposing than Abbas' lamb. The angels supporting the rulers' halo show the influence of European art motifs on Mughal imagery. According to the inscription on this miniature, Jahangir commissioned the painting after having a dream about Shah Abbas.

dominions. He reimposed the *jizya* and enforced the Sharia more stringently. Many Hindu temples were destroyed during his reign, and his intolerance and rigid orthodoxy weakened the Mughal hold on its diverse Hindu populations.

The Mughal Social Order

As already noted, Mughal society comprised a series of hierarchies based on a Hindu majority and a predominantly Muslim ruling class. The vast majority of

---

Document   The Idea of Seclusion and Lady Nurjahan

The idea of seclusion (being hidden away from view) is often associated with women in Muslim societies. But historically, we find that women in all Muslim households were clearly not secluded and that "seclusion" itself is a notion that varies over time, place, class, status, and culture. Even when women were considered to be "secluded," they might have been engaged in a variety of activities that we don't ordinarily associate with seclusion. So, one question for historians, of any time, place, and group of women is: "What were those women doing?" Some examples of what elite, secluded women were doing are found in the memoirs of the Mughal emperor Jahangir. Like those of his forefather, Babur, Jahangir's memoirs are full of minute and interesting details, including discussion of the affairs of his principal wife Nurjahan (1577–1645). Nurjahan was the daughter of a Mughal vizir, and, at the end of Jahangir's reign, she, along with her brother, took over effective control of the empire. In her husband's account, we find Nurjahan portrayed as an avid hunter, an owner of estates, and a mover-and-shaker in political affairs. She engaged in all these activities while "secluded." These selections from Jahangir's memoirs (and an appendix by his historian Muhammad-Hadi) give some idea of Nurjahan's activities.

On April 16 [1617] . . . the scouts had cornered four lions. I [Jahangir] set out with the ladies of the harem to hunt them. When the lions came into view, Nurjahan Begam said, "If so commanded, I will shoot the lions." I said, "Let it be so." She hit two of them with one shot each and the other two with two shots, and in the twinkling of an eye the four lions were deprived of life with six shots. Until now such marksmanship has not been seen—from atop an elephant and from inside a howdah [covered seat] she had fired six shots, none of which missed. . . . As a reward for such marksmanship I scattered a thousand ashrafis [coins] over her head and gave her a pair of pearls and a diamond worth a lac [100,000] of rupees.

When Jahangir was suffering from chest pain and shortness of breath, his physicians could not ease his discomfort, so he committed himself to his wife's care:

Nurjahan Begam's remedies and experience were greater than any of the physicians', especially since she treated me with affection and sympathy. She made me drink less and applied remedies that were suitable and efficacious. Although the treatments the physicians had prescribed before were done with her approval, I now relied on her affection, gradually reduced my intake of wine, and avoided unsuitable things and disagreeable food. It is hoped that the True Physician will grant me a complete recovery from the other world.

When Nurjahan's father died, Jahangir awarded his estate to her:

I awarded I'timaduddawla's jagir [a type of fief, revenue from land], household, and paraphernalia of chieftainship and amirship to Nurjahan Begam, and I ordered that her drums should be sounded after the imperial ones.

When Mahabat Khan mounted a rebellion against Jahangir, Nurjahan escaped and mobilized for the emperor's defense:

[She] convened the grandees of the empire and addressed them in rebuke, saying, "It was through your negligence that things have gone so far and the unimaginable has happened. You have been disgraced before God and the people by your own actions. Now it must be made up for. Tell each other what the best thing to do is."

Questions to Consider

1. Nurjahan was a royal woman. What do these stories suggest about class and gender as determinants of women's activities?

2. What do these excerpts suggest about the relationship between Jahangir and his wife?

3. If royal women routinely went on hunting expeditions with the emperor, how could they still be secluded?

From Wheeler Thackston, ed. and trans., *The Jahangirnama: Memoirs of Jahangir, Emperor of India* (New York: Oxford University Press, 1999), pp. xx–xxi, 219, 368, 376, 441.

the populace, as in China, the Middle East, and Europe, consisted of illiterate peasants who provided the bulk of the empire's revenue through agricultural taxes. Wealth was an important factor in determining status, but it was not the primary factor. A merchant could be very wealthy but could not achieve the same status as a member of the elite military-administrative class. Among Hindus, status was intimately linked to caste.

Mughal society, like most societies, was also patriarchal; it allocated family, religious, and political dominance to men. This system of male dominance is often attributed to Islam, but patriarchy predated Islam in India, as it did in the Middle East. In general, it would be more accurate to say that Islam both reinforced preexisting patriarchal structures and improved the position of women by forbidding female infanticide and granting women inheritance rights. In India under Islamic rule, the position of women derived from a synthesis of Hindu custom and Islamic law. Despite Akbar's reform-minded decrees, *sati* and child marriages continued. Formal education of females, as in most societies, was practically nonexistent, except in a few affluent or learned families.

These practices must, of course, be understood in their temporal and social contexts. In Hindu society, as in Muslim society, in which marriage is considered a preferred state (especially for women), early marriage age acted to prevent the girl's sexual purity from being compromised or questioned. By social convention, women were deemed to need male protectors, and when a woman married, she left the protection of her father or brother and became part of her husband's household. By immolating herself on her husband's funeral pyre, a widow prevented herself from becoming a social burden on her husband's family or the family she was born into.

As for female education, we should remember that the overwhelming majority of people, in all the world civilizations of this era, were illiterate. Only certain of the elites could read, and even many people of rank, like Akbar, were illiterate. Men's and women's roles were considered complementary, not equal. Because men were expected to perform the political, religious, and administrative tasks that required literacy, formal education tended to be reserved for them.

The birth of a prince in the Mughal harem. This unusual scene shows the numerous female attendants of the princely court and suggests the ceremonial significance of such an event. Note the varying dress styles of the women and the rich textiles surrounding the princess.

NETWORKS OF TRADE AND COMMUNICATION

▪ *What role do trade and communication play in the maintenance of the Ottoman, Safavid, and Mughal empires?*

The gunpowder empires emerged in a set of interconnected regions that were in turn imbedded in even more extensive networks of trade and communication. The primitive nature of transport and communications technology limited the flow of goods, knowledge, and information. But all three circulated in ways that might seem surprising, given that the only ways to get from one place to another were on foot, on animalback, or aboard oared and sailing vessels. Despite these limitations, scholars traveled from one court to another, enjoying the patronage of Ottoman, Safavid, or Mughal emperors and sharing literary, artistic, and legal traditions. The royal courts consumed prodigiously and supported the exchange of goods and culture on a grand scale. Mehmed II had his portrait painted by the famous Italian painter Bellini. Babur brought Persian artists into India, and the Safavid court imported Arab jurists. Rulers in all three empires drank from Chinese porcelain cups.

The Ottoman, Safavid, and Mughal Empires derived most of their income from agriculture. But trade was their second source of wealth. None of these empires invented the trading routes. Rather, these routes emerged and expanded across a set of well-established commercial networks linking urban centers.

They inherited these networks from their predecessors and competed with rival kingdoms to monopolize goods and collect commercial taxes. To understand how these empires worked, we must abandon the notion of modern boundaries that are marked, fixed, and defended. Rulers could not control frontiers absolutely; instead they defended and taxed key routes, fortresses, and cities. The porous nature of borders encouraged tax evaders. If officials demanded high taxes along one route, merchants might shift to another route. If taxes were collected by the camel-load, merchants stopped their beasts outside of town and repacked in order to have fewer loads.

In this context of flexible boundaries, trading communities developed that facilitated the flow of goods from one place to another. Although the Ottomans fought long wars with both Christian states in Europe and Muslim competitors in Persia and Egypt, trade among these regions was seldom squelched for long. The furs of Muscovy flowed south into the empire and the gold of Africa came north. Armenian merchants played a prominent role in the Persian silk trade, which drew European silver in large quantities into the Safavid Empire. Jewish merchants traded copper to Arab merchants, who sold it to South Asian traders in return for cotton, jewels, and spices.

Many great trading centers were scattered throughout the territories of the gunpowder empires. Babur described the emporium of Kabul, located between Persia and India, as receiving merchant caravans of 15,000 or 20,000 pack animals carrying slaves, textiles, sugar, and spices. Kabul channeled the trade of China and India westward in exchange for goods coming eastward from the Ottoman and Safavid realms.

The merchants in turn served an information function. Because communication technologies were so limited, rulers used travelers of all sorts to gain knowledge about the rest of the world. Scholars, sufis, traders, envoys, and spies all served this purpose. Monarchs used envoys as spies, and their rivals tried to control information by keeping visiting envoys sequestered and by intimidating them with military displays. Response to another ruler's challenge could never be swift because it was often months or years before a monarch received a reply or news about his envoy's fate.

Outside these channels of communication, relations between the gunpowder empires and European or East Asian states were still quite limited. Only the Ottomans had resident consuls from some of the European states in their capital. In this era, the balance of trade was tipped very much in favor of the East, with eastern goods flowing into Europe and cash flowing back. European imports, with the exception of certain kinds of textiles, were negligible by comparison.

DOCUMENT

The English in South Asia

CONCLUSION

In the three and a half centuries before 1650, Europe still lagged behind Asia in many respects. No European state, not even the polyglot empire of Charles V, could compare in manpower and resources with the realms of Suleiman or Akbar. Europeans were impressed by the resources and taxation capabilities of the Ottoman governing system. Opportunities for minorities and toleration for dissenting religions were greater in the Muslim countries than in Europe. Asian cities were usually better planned, more tastefully adorned with works of art, and even better supplied with water and with sewage disposal.

Europe's advantages, which began to be more apparent after the beginning of the seventeenth century, were most evident in the realm of technology, specifically in the production of field artillery and oceangoing ships. These technical assets helped certain of the European states gain leverage in a new age, when powerful states would depend on strategic control of sea lanes and world markets. But in the period from 1300 to 1650 it was the gunpowder empires that tended to dominate, using their resources and militaries to become the great imperial powers of that age.

Suggestions for Web Browsing

You can obtain more information about topics included in this chapter at the websites listed below. See also the companion website that accompanies this text, **http://www.ablongman.com/ brummett**, which contains an online study guide and additional resources.

Islam and Islamic History in Arabia and the Middle East
http://www.islamic.org/Mosque/ihame/Sec11.htm
http://www.islamic.org/Mosque/ihame/Sec12.htm

http://www.islamic.org/Mosque/ihame/Sec13.htm
Related sites detailing the enormous legacy of the early Islamic civilization, a history of Mongol destruction and Mamluk victory, and the rise of the Ottoman Empire.

Ottoman Page
http://ottoman.home.mindspring.com/
Site dedicated to classical Ottoman history, 1300–1600, offering numerous links to other sites.

Topkapi Palace

http://www.ee.bilkent.edu.tr/~history/topkapi.html

A guide to Topkapi Palace, with numerous images of the palace rooms and grounds and its phenomenal artifacts, including portraits of the sultans, manuscripts, clothing, porcelains, and armaments.

Internet Islamic History Sourcebook: The Persians

http://www.fordham.edu/halsall/islam/islamsbook.html

Links to a variety of documents detailing the rise and spread of the Safavid Empire.

Internet Indian History Sourcebook

http://www.fordham.edu/halsall/india/indiasbook.html

Extensive indexed site of primary sources for medieval India.

Mughal Monarchs

http://rubens.anu.edu.au/student.projects/tajmahal/mughal.html

A detailed introduction to the Mughal dynasty and the city of Agra, whose images emphasize the superb architecture of the time.

Literature and Film

A short primary source on Jahangir, available in paperback, is Mutribi al-Asamm, *Conversations with Emperor Jahangir*, trans. Richard Foltz (Mazda, 1998*). The Intimate Life of an Ottoman Statesman: Melek Ahmed Pasha (1588–1662)*, trans. Robert Dankoff (SUNY Press, 1991) is a wonderful portrayal of the realities of Ottoman administration. An excellent selection of Ottoman poetry can be found in *Ottoman Lyric Poetry: An Anthology*, eds. Walter Andrews, Najaat Black, Mehmet Kalpakli (University of Texas Press, 1997).

The University of North Carolina library (Chapel Hill) has a large collection of films on the Islamic world which are cataloged by topic. These include films on the Ottoman Empire and the Modern Middle East. See listings on their website at http://www.lib.unc.edu/house/nonprint.

Suleiman the Magnificent depicts the life, accomplishments and regional significance of this Ottoman sultan.

Isfahan: A City Known as "Half the World" is a great video, in Farsi and English, about Isfahan and its historic sites. For additional information, see http://www.iranianmovies.com/reviews/isfahan.html.

Suggestions for Reading

On Inner Asia and Turkic groups, see Peter Golden, *An Introduction to the History of the Turkic Peoples* (Harassowitz, 1992). Luc Kwanten, *Imperial Nomads, a History of Central Asia, 500–1500* (University of Pennsylvania Press, 1979), is an illuminating study of a subject long neglected in standard texts.

The Ottoman Golden Age is ably depicted in Halil Inalcik, *Phoenix: The Ottoman Empire, the Classical Age 1300–1600* (Phoenix Press, 2001); Norman Itzkowitz, *The Ottoman Empire and the Islamic Tradition* (University of Oklahoma Press, 1980); and Stanford Shaw, *A History of the Ottoman Empire and Modern Turkey*, 2 vols. (Cambridge University Press, 1976–1977). On Sultan Suleiman, see Metin Kunt and Christine Woodhead, eds., *Süleyman the Magnificent and His Age* (Longman, 1995). The harem is covered in Leslie P. Peirce, *The Imperial Harem* (Oxford University Press, 1993).

On medieval Persia, see Ann Lambton, *Continuity and Change in Medieval Persia* (Persian Heritage Foundation, 1988), and David Morgan, *Medieval Persia, 1040–1797* (Longman, 1988). See also Roger Savory, *Iran Under the Safavids* (Cambridge University Press, 1980). Coverage in English of the Safavid period is still limited; an old standard is Percy M. Sykes, *A History of Persia*, (Routledge/Curzon, 2003), first published in 1938 and now in its third edition. On Safavid trade, see Rudolph Matthee, *The Politics of Trade in Safavid Iran: Silk for Silver, 1600–1730* (Cambridge University Press, 1999).

The Mughal system is ably described in John F. Richards, Gordon Johnson, and C. A. Bayly, eds., *The Mughul Empire* (Cambridge University Press, 1996); Douglas E. Streusand, *The Formation of the Mughal Empire* (Oxford University Press, 1990); and Neelam Chaudhary, *Socio-Economic History of Mughal India* (Discovery, 1987). For studies of individual emperors, see Gul Badan Begam, *The History of Humayun*, trans. A. S. Beveridge (B. R. Publishers, 1989); Bamber Gascoigne, *The Great Moghuls* (Harper & Row, 1971); and J. M. Shelat, *Akbar* (Bharatiya Bidya Bhavan, 1964).

CHAPTER 13

East Asian Cultural and Political Systems, 1300–1650

This chapter discusses the development and mutual influences of China, Korea, Japan, and the countries of Southeast Asia from the fourteenth into the seventeenth centuries. During this time, ideologies, religions, and cultural traditions continued to be shared. Trade was maintained, though greatly modified in the middle of the period by the introduction of new players and products from Europe and the Americas and by the severe restriction of Japanese international commerce in the early seventeenth century. China was still the dominant actor in East Asia, but while its power and influence may have seemed paramount, individual nations were forming their own political and cultural traditions and identities.

Throughout its history, Chinese civilization has synthesized outside influences and its own indigenous culture. Culture rather than ethnicity generally defined what it was to be Chinese. Indeed, before the end of the seventeenth century, China was generally seen as a civilization rather than a place inhabited by a dominant ethnic group. Outsiders who adopted Chinese ways could rise to high stations, even rule China. Those who had not sufficiently assimilated Chinese culture were often not viewed as fully Chinese.

China's view of itself as a civilization was just as important as its view of itself as a political entity. Frequently called the "Central Flower," its culture and civilization were seen as having broad universal appeal. As the "Central Kingdom," a term that emphasized *political* unity, China could also justify its international relations based on the tribute system. The tribute system encompassed China's relationships with East Asian nations. It was an unequal system that required peripheral countries to indicate their loyal subordination by donating tribute to China and receiving gifts in return according to a planned schedule of visits—a form of strictly regulated trade. China acted as a protective "parent" toward neighbors who were not entirely independent of China in terms of their foreign relations. The early Ming's place in the larger Eurasian continent was perhaps even more important. It launched the world's largest maritime explorations, dominated world trade, and was deeply connected to the world's silver-based economy.

In Korea, the Koryŏ dynasty, struggling with slave-owning landholders, many of whom had been allied with the Mongols who had themselves just been forced out of China, was overturned by a reformist faction in 1392. The founder of the new Chosŏn dynasty, King T'aejo (1335–1408), sent tribute missions to the Ming, cut all ties to the Mongols, and strengthened Chinese institutions in Korea. The Chosŏn dynasty was known for such cultural advances as the development of an indigenous alphabet, a lively publishing trade, an active scholarly world of competing schools of thought, and refined arts of painting and pottery that blended Korean and Chinese models. Korea retained much of its indigenous aristocratic structure during the long Chosŏn dynasty (1392–1910), but its culture was deeply imbued with neo-Confucianism, originally Chinese but now assimilated into Korean culture.

Japan was also connected with Korea and China in this era. In the first half of the three-century period, refined art collectors revered continental arts. As samurai settled in Kyoto (formerly called *Heian*) in the late fourteenth century, they outdid one another in displaying Chinese, Korean, and Japanese works readily available to wealthy collectors. Although the Ming, in theory, controlled the volume of trade within its tribute system, freebooting Japanese, Chinese, and Korean pirates imported a far greater volume of products through nongovernmental channels. Japanese ships transported products throughout northeast and Southeast Asia, purchased with various currencies, exchange of other goods, and Japanese and New World silver. In the sixteenth century, Japanese silver far surpassed New World silver as the fuel that drove the East Asian trade at the heart of the world economy.

While Confucianism was not yet established in Japan, Buddhism continued to prosper there until the end of the sixteenth century. The breakdown of peace at the end of the fifteenth century and the coming of Iberian missionaries in the sixteenth century, who brought guns along with religion, radically altered Japan's history. In 1600, Japan was once again unified, and by 1640, it would severely restrict its trade to just three partners—China, Korea, and Holland.

The lands and islands southeast of China, today called Southeast Asia, were long influenced by Indian culture and religions. Chinese culture deeply influenced Vietnam. Buddhism, Hinduism, and local religions were celebrated in the kingdoms of Southeast Asia. In Vietnam, a millennium of Chinese rule made the Chinese both despised as overlords and worthy of emulation as bearers of advanced means of governance. With the exception of a period of Mongol attack and, later, a brief occupation by Ming forces, Vietnam was politically independent of China after 939. But Vietnam's government was in many ways an ideal Confucian state, and Vietnam and China were closely bound through the tribute system.

Maritime Southeast Asia—today's Philippines, Malaysia, and Indonesia—was dependent on trade. Important maritime empires, including a succession of rulers on the island of Java, occupied most of modern Malaysia and Indonesia. In the thirteenth century, one of Java's great powers, Majapahit, held off the Mongols' attempted invasion and unified many of the islands of the Indonesian archipelago. In the fourteenth and fifteenth centuries, Islam spread to maritime Southeast Asia as merchants recognized the benefit of Muslim ties in expediting trade in the Indian Ocean. Chinese and Indian traders continued to operate throughout Southeast Asia. The coming of first Portuguese and Spanish and later British and Dutch merchants and missionaries influenced Southeast Asian life by the beginning of the seventeenth century.

CHINA: THE MING DYNASTY

■ *In what ways can Ming China be considered an early modern state?*

Before the modern period, Chinese historians wrote the history of their country as a series of consecutive dynastic waves—as one dynasty declined after a period of growth, another would rise and receive Heaven's mandate (see Chapter 2). The struggle to overthrow the Yuan in the fourteenth century was brutal, but it contained many of the elements of dynastic change identified by contemporaries in China. That is, natural disasters and disease accompanied by religious uprisings suggested Heaven was shifting its sup-

port from the Yuan emperor to new rulers. The traditional dynastic cycle model downplays change over time. The Yuan dynasty's brevity gave it little opportunity to change China in lasting ways, and this seemed to confirm the dynastic cycle's validity. Yet, as we have seen in Chapter 10, the Yuan was at the center of a cosmopolitan Eurasian commercial world which influenced culture far beyond China's borders.

The Yuan dynasty declined after Khubilai's death in 1294. The north of China began to decline economically, and southerners suffered discriminatory treatment. Everywhere, the pre-Yuan power structure had been challenged, as the Mongols had altered civil service recruitment policies. Many peasants were brought to the brink of despair in the face of natural

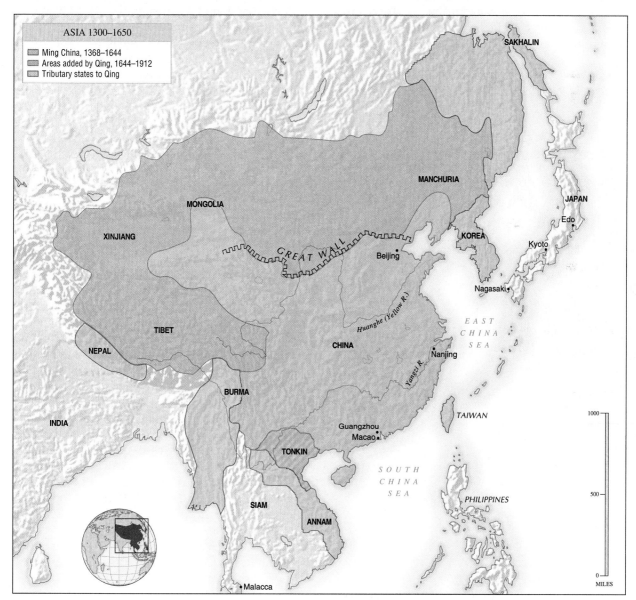

After the first two Ming emperors consolidated and expanded their rule, the rest of the dynasty remained content with the extent of their realm. The Chinese realm was greatly expanded under the Qing, who took power in the second half of the seventeenth century.

disasters in the fourteenth century, especially the Huanghe River's change in course and outbreaks of the plague. Further, the traditionally nomadic Mongol soldiers, now serving in permanent posts, lost some of their toughness and discipline. In the 39 years after Khubilai's death and the installation of the last Mongol sovereign in 1333, disorder also prevailed at the highest level of government. The Mongol royal clan had no orderly method for determining succession, and eight of the nine emperors were either overthrown or killed. Bureaucratic breakdown weakened the base of Yuan power at a time when the Mongols were severely challenged. Religious rebellions sparked by peasant discontent spread throughout southern China in the 1350s.

In 1356, a former Buddhist monk, Zhu Yuanzhang (JOO yoo-ahn-JAHNG), who had taken over the leadership of a religious-based rebel group, the **Red Turbans,** captured Nanjing. Using that city as his capital,

---

Red Turbans—A branch of White Lotus Society, a millenarian Buddhist group that used Confucian and Daoist ideas as well. One of several anti-Yuan religious groups.

Zhu—better known by his reign name, Ming Hongwu (hong-WOO)—conquered other warlords until he was able to march on the Yuan capital at Beijing. The Mongol emperor fled with his court to Mongolia. Hongwu thus founded a new dynasty, the Ming, without actually conquering the old. Hongwu (r. 1368–1398) attempted to assert strong imperial control, even killing thousands of scholars he believed were scheming against or ridiculing him. Neither he nor his successors were model rulers, and the last decades of Ming rule were marked by administrative failure and corruption. The strength of the Ming era lay less in its monarchs and more in the contributions of its artisans, scholars, and philosophers to a Chinese society increasingly claimed by people of all walks of life as their own.

After a period of expansion, the Ming ruled over China until factionalism, corruption, and natural disasters again led to popular uprisings, a symbol of the passage of the Mandate of Heaven, in the middle of the seventeenth century. Although modern historians often judge the Ming a failure, the three centuries were, in fact, an era of population growth, commercial expansion, and a broadening of average Chinese people's participation in the culture of the country.

The Early Ming Era

Hongwu was a rather brutal and paranoid emperor, although he tried to govern effectively. He believed that people should be self-sufficient and motivated to serve their community without having to be paid. He sought to lighten the tax burden of the poor and gave the families of China's 2 million soldiers plots to farm themselves to be self-supporting. More successful villagers were to look out for their less fortunate neighbors, collect village taxes, and serve their communities essentially as administrators but without formal government appointment or pay. At the level of the court, Hongwu tried to cut back the power of the **eunuchs** by forbidding them a role in politics. All these policies failed, however. Village leaders were overworked and undercompensated for their work, soldiers who were unable to support themselves absconded, and eunuchs became more powerful than ever over the next two centuries. The third Ming emperor, Hongwu's son Yongle (YAWNG-luh; r. 1403–1424), moved the capital to Beijing and transformed it into a grand city. He also undertook massive engineering projects, especially the enlarging of the Grand Canal including the construction of fifteen locks, and the expansion of the protective northern wall into the Great Wall of China we know today.

Portrait of Hongwu, the first emperor of the Ming dynasty.

---

eunuchs—Castrated males who served as palace attendants and administrators for the emperor.

Map of China's Ancient Heartland, circa 1500 C.E.

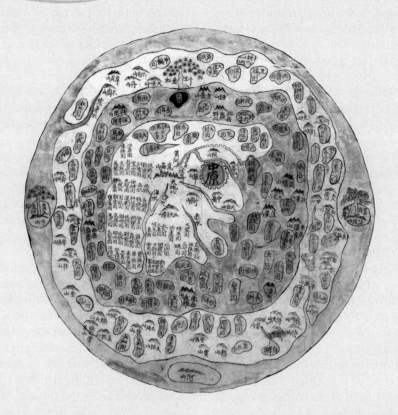

It is one of the marks of human nature that the center of the world is found in one's self-consciousness, and then in concentric circles in the family, community, and nation. This trait extends across civilizations and continents and can be seen not only in this Chinese map depicting the area known as the *Zhongyuan* (ZHONG-yoo-AHN) or heartland of ancient China, but also in maps created around the same time by Europeans as they made their voyages of discovery. The Chinese map is particularly informative because it reminds its viewers that even within China itself, the heartland was the repository of culture and power, and the farther one ventured from the center of that circle, the less likely one was to be influenced by the virtue embodied in the Son of Heaven.

By 1500, the Ming had moved their capital to Beijing, which lay in the northern region in which Chinese civilization was born; thus, the radiance of the Ming emperor was fortuitously in the same region as the birthplace of the culture he represented. In concentric circles around the Central Plain were other areas of China or countries involved in tributary relations with China. The term *central* may also be seen in a common name for China, *Zhongguo* (JONG-gwaw), meaning "Central Kingdom." The Chinese worldview placed it at the center of the world, and it was very much part of the world in terms of cultural and commercial interactions.

The map has political implications, in that it shows its viewers that the original heartland of China was the same place as the home of the Ming. This portrayal is difficult, however, for those trained to see geography in terms of a Mercator projection (see, e.g., p. 467). The Mercator projection, like the Ming map, also reflects a worldview that places the map's creators in the center–in the Mercator case, the center is in Europe. Is there any particular reason, for example, why the Greenwich Meridian (from which all longitudes on the surface of the earth are presently measured) should be the central point of the world's geography and Greenwich Mean Time should be the standard by which most clocks of the world are presently set? English dominance in the eighteenth and nineteenth centuries proved to be only a temporary moment in history, but enough to establish at least a cartographic and chronological centrality.

Questions to Consider

1. Compare and contrast this map with the view of the world on page 467. How are the maps the same? How are they different?

2. Given the particular approach of the China map, draw a simple circular map of the United States. Would Washington, D.C., or some other city be appropriately located at the center of your map? Is the Mercator Projection that is generally used today (see, for example, p. 467) necessarily better in portraying sense and relationship?

Policy in the first century of the Ming reflected a definite interest in border areas and beyond. Non-Chinese tribes, especially the Miao (mee-OW) and the Yao (YOW) in the southwest, were brought under Ming control, engendering a discussion about Chinese identity and cultural blending.

The expansive early Ming invaded Vietnam in 1407, but popular resistance there soon forced them out. The early Ming government, unlike its sixteenth-century successors, encouraged foreign trade with Japan, Southeast Asia, and India. Private trade surpassed the official trade permitted under the tribute system. Yongle regularly sent diplomatic and commercial missions to neighboring states and encouraged Chinese migration south into the Malay Archipelago and north into Mongolia. In 1405 Yongle sponsored a series of naval expeditions to potential tributary states. The greatest were led by Zheng He (JUHNG HUH), a trusted eunuch (see p. 374). The Chinese flotilla of 62 large and 225 small ships (with some ships exceeding 500 tons and carrying crews of 700) visited Sumatra, India, the Persian Gulf, Aden, and East Africa. There they exchanged porcelain for ivory, ostrich feathers, and exotic animals such as zebras and giraffes. These fancy goods were a source of fascination, but the primary purpose of the voyages was neither conquest nor trade but rather the expansion of the tribute system at the heart of Ming foreign relations. China had already penetrated the Indian Ocean while Portuguese captains were just beginning to explore the Atlantic coast of Morocco.

The voyages ended in 1433. They were considered too expensive compared to the potential gains of enrolling additional countries in the tribute system. China maintained a powerful, dominant position in that system with its closest neighbors. These neighbors received Chinese support and reciprocal gifts but were also subjected to Chinese domination—at times even invasion—and to the requirement that they humbly present gifts to the Son of Heaven, the Chinese emperor, as a sign of subordination in an almost parent-child relationship. People in distant lands were far less likely to comprehend that particular Confucian proprieties were at the heart of Chinese identity, and enrolling distant people in a tribute relationship was much less useful than demanding the subordination of a neighbor. In time, maritime exploration came to be seen as an unwise investment when costly defense against land-based border tribes was more crucial. Chinese emperors never again sponsored such path-breaking journeys.

Administration of the realm was seen as central to Ming power throughout the period. While foreign adventures could be curtailed, good government demanded that emperors lead by example and that the examination system bring in loyal and honest bureaucrats.

Yet despite their attempts at eliminating past problems, the Ming emperors perpetuated many of the corrupt and weak practices they wanted to reform. The excesses of court eunuchs—male children sold by their parents to be castrated for court service—continued. At the beginning of the Ming dynasty only 100 eunuchs were employed, and not in direct government posts, but by the end of the dynasty 300 years later, 100,000 were working for the throne. Eunuchs had served as court advisers and servants since the Zhou dynasty; under the Ming, they included men from Annam and Korea, some brought as tribute, and some captured in war. Under the Ming, 28 Korean-born eunuchs served as leaders of missions to Seoul. Although eunuchs served as generals, admirals, explorers, diplomats, architects, secret police, and hydraulic engineers, the majority of them were servants of low and even slave status. The increased number of eunuchs was due not only to the expansion of the imperial family under the Ming but also to the influx of men, many self-castrated, who poured into Beijing, hoping to find a secure livelihood after escaping from poverty or famine in the countryside.

The growth in the number and influence of eunuchs was paralleled by an expansion of Confucian scholarship and scholars. Preparing for a career as a bureaucrat became increasingly attractive despite the danger of repression by paranoid emperors like Hongwu. The Ming decreed that the examinations for entering the civil service be written in a strict, formal style, but at the same time they opened opportunities for students from less advanced regions of the country to pass the exams. A new lower level category was created, permitting locally successful exam candidates to become local leaders even if they were not eligible for a better government post. In time, wealthy families perpetu-

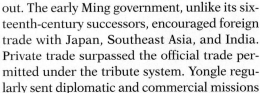

DOCUMENT
A Ming Naval Expedition

MAP
Voyages of Zheng He

Ming China	
1368–1398	Reign of Hongwu
1403–1424	Reign of Yongle, sponsor of encyclopedia
1405–1433	Naval expeditions led by Zheng He
1472–1529	Wang Yangming, philosopher
1583–1610	Matteo Ricci at Ming court
1644	Founding of Qing dynasty

Document   A Censor Accuses a Eunuch

This memorial was submitted to the emperor in 1624 by the official Yang Lien, accusing the eunuch, Wei Zhongxian (WAY jong-shee-AHN). It illustrates how the power of the eunuchs was resented by scholar-bureaucrats while giving a sense of palace politics.

A treacherous eunuch has taken advantage of his position to act as emperor. He has seized control and disrupted the government, deceived the ruler and flouted the law. He recognizes no higher authority, turns his back on the favors the emperor has conferred on him, and interferes with the inherited institutions. I beg Your Majesty to order an investigation so that the dynasty can be saved.

When Emperor Taizu [i.e., Hongwu] first established the laws and institutions, eunuchs were not allowed to interfere in any affairs outside the palace; even within it they did nothing more than clean up. Anyone who violated these rules was punished without chance of amnesty, so the eunuchs prudently were cautious and obedient. The succeeding emperors never changed these laws. Even such arrogant and lawless eunuchs as Wang Zhen (WAHNG JUHN) and Liu Jin (LEE-oh JIN) were promptly executed. Thus the dynasty lasted until today.

How would anyone have expected that, with a wise ruler like Your Majesty on the throne, there would be a chief eunuch like Wei Zhongxian, a man totally uninhibited, who destroys court precedents, ignores the ruler to pursue his selfish ends, corrupts good people, ruins the emperor's reputation as a Yao (YOW) or Xun (SHUN), and brews unimaginable disasters? The entire court has been intimidated. No one dares denounce him by name. My responsibility really is painful. But when I was supervising secretary of the office of scrutiny for war, the previous emperor personally ordered me to help Your Majesty become a ruler like Yao and Xun. I can still hear his words. If today out of fear I also do not speak out, I will be abandoning my determination to be loyal and my responsibility to serve the state. I would also be turning my back on your kindness in bringing me back to office after retirement and would not be able to face the former emperor in Heaven.

I shall list for Your Majesty Zhongxian's twenty-four most heinous crimes. Zhongxian was originally an ordinary, unreliable sort. He had himself castrated in middle age in order to enter the palace. He is illiterate, unlike those eunuchs from the directorate of ceremonial. Your Majesty was impressed by his minor acts of service and plucked him out of obscurity to confer honors on him. . . .

Our dynastic institutions require that rescripts be delegated to the grand secretaries. This not only allows for calm deliberation and protects from interference, but it assures that someone takes the responsibility seriously. Since Zhongxian usurped power, he issues the imperial edicts. If he accurately conveys your orders, it is bad enough. If he falsifies them, who can argue with him? Recently, men have been forming groups of three or five to push their ideas in the halls of government, making it as clamorous as a noisy market. Some even go directly into the inner quarters without formal permission. It is possible for a scrap of paper in the middle of the night to kill a person without Your Majesty or the grand secretaries knowing anything of it. The harm this causes is huge. The grand secretaries are so depressed that they ask to quit. Thus Wei Zhongxian destroys the political institutions that had lasted over two hundred years. This is his first great crime. . . .

One of your concubines, of virtuous and pure character, had gained your favor. Zhongxian was afraid she would expose his illegal behavior, so conspired with his cronies. They said she had a sudden illness to cover up his murdering her. Thus Your Majesty is not able to protect the concubines you favor. This is his eighth great crime. . . .

Questions to Consider

1. Discuss how this document reflects the power politics of the Ming dynasty.

2. Discuss how a similar document might have been phrased if it had been written from the perspective of a eunuch and not the palace scholar-bureaucrat.

From Patricia Buckley Ebrey, *Chinese Civilization: A Sourcebook*, 2nd ed. (New York: Free Press, 1993), pp. 263–266.

ated their status by their sons' success in the examination system. Poor boys, whose work was needed on their parents' farms, were far less likely to devote years to exam preparation. In spite of the system's theoretical openness to boys of all backgrounds, in reality only the rich had the chance to study and enter government service. By the sixteenth century, there were approximately 100,000 students preparing for exams at any given time.

As time passed, Ming rulers became resistant to innovation. Yet even this resistance had a positive aspect, in that it generated an aura of stability through most of the 1500s, when Chinese culture was a model for East Asia. Sixteenth-century European visitors were impressed by Chinese courtesy, respect for law, confidence, and stately ceremonies. They saw material prosperity in the bustling markets, stone-paved roads, and beautiful homes of Ming officials. They noted with awe the breadth of literacy and the availability of books written in vernacular language comprehensible to many readers. The elaborate Ming examination system, with its proclaimed principle of advancement on merit, often evoked favorable surprise. European commentators were lavish in their praise of Chinese justice, an attitude that would change greatly several centuries later.

Ming Society, Scholarship, and Culture

Market towns and commercial networks had been growing in China since the Song dynasty (see Chapter 10). As the population rebounded following its decline during the Yuan dynasty, market towns expanded. The distance between market towns shortened, and commercial links were improved. At the same time, other forms of social interaction developed, especially kinship (lineage) groups and community associations pledging to do good deeds and lead moral lives. Community orientation did not necessarily require that all people be treated equally, but rather humanely. During the Ming era, for instance, women became less visible to the larger society. They were to stay inside the house; widows were not supposed to remarry but rather continue to live with the family of their deceased husband; and the practice of foot binding spread throughout the country, even among commoners. The ideal of the exemplary Confucian woman was institutionalized in the form of written accounts of virtuous widows and of arches built in front of the homes of women widowed before they were 30 who reached the age of 60 without remarrying. Though Ming law, ironically, offered a financial incentive to widows' families to

marry them off—if she remarried, a widow's dowry could be kept by her late husband's family, who would also earn a "bride price" from her next husband's family—widows deemed virtuous did not remarry. Morality tales written during the Ming, while likely exaggerated for didactic effect, portrayed virtuous widows as committing suicide or self-mutilation to show grief or prove their loyalty to dead husbands.

Under Ming rule, legal recognition of **concubinage** also encouraged the sale of young virgins from poor families to families of generally higher status. While women's official legal status, especially that of widows, was lowered because of stricter adherence to Confucian norms, it can also be said that women's independence was encouraged by the same ideology. New Confucian regulations and standards encouraged education for girls as well as boys. Young women, who read the more than 50 works extolling female obedience through accounts of the lives of virtuous women, were also given access to other reading material that could easily have challenged the official vision of a woman as a person confined to a household.

Even foot binding can be seen from several perspectives. The practice mutilated the foot in order to enhance a woman's desirability; mothers bound their daughters' feet to improve their marriage prospects and thus, perhaps, spare their daughters a life of hard physical labor. Farm women often did not have bound feet, as their labor was needed. On the one hand, it could be said that a life of field work liberated a woman from bound feet; on the other, bound feet usually freed a woman from backbreaking field work. Nowhere else in Asia was foot binding practiced, and yet women had subordinate status there as in most parts of the world. Thus, foot binding was a painful, mutilating practice but was itself not a cause of women's second-class status.

The Ming respect for learning and literacy was evident in officially commissioned works as well as popular works. Numerous official works were published, including vast multivolume collections, 1500 local histories, and famous medical works like *The Outline of Herb Medicine*, which took 30 years to complete. The Yongle emperor ordered the compilation of all existing literature, that is, an encyclopedia of all knowledge. It has been surmised that these works added up to more printed works than all the manuscript books throughout the world at that time. (This was also, of course, a half-century before Gutenberg

---

concubinage—A legal relationship of a man and a secondary wife, who usually did not have the rights and protection of a primary wife. Concubines were often obtained by rich men to produce sons.

printed his first book.) The **Yongle Encyclopedia** was produced by over 2000 scholars, who arranged material taken from more than 7000 works, by subject, into over 22,000 chapters bound into half that number of volumes. Although the encyclopedia was too unwieldy to print and distribute, more accessible intellectual developments—not only for the use of the emperor and his officials—were encouraged by the increased printing of books and by the growth of education in private academies that prepared students for public examinations.

During the first half of the Ming, the state considered Zhu Xi (JOO SHEE) Confucianism (see Chapter 10) as orthodox. Zhu Xi's interpretations were reflected in the exam system. Other scholars' views became increasingly important in the sixteenth century, the most important of which was that of the soldier, poet, and philosopher Wang Yangming (WAHNG yahng-MING; 1472–1528), who taught that knowledge is intuitive and inseparable from experience. Wang believed anyone could be a sage and could practice self-cultivation even while doing other tasks. In later centuries, Wang Yangming's ideas inspired reformers and revolutionaries in China, Japan, and Korea.

Ming literature, which embraced romantic notions, evolved in ways similar to scholarship. Written in colloquial language accessible to larger numbers of readers, novels, based on orally transmitted tales, described ordinary life. Three of the best-known Chinese novels date from the sixteenth century. *Journey to the West* (also known as *Monkey*) is a rollicking semisatirical tale about a Buddhist monk traveling to India with his pig and a monkey that had led an earlier human life. The erotic novel *Golden Lotus* recounts the romantic adventures of a merchant, his wife, and his concubines. Perhaps the best-read work is *The Water Margin* (also known as *All Men Are Brothers*), the story of an outlaw band who, like Robin Hood's merry men, broke the law in the name of what they saw as greater justice. Travel literature and adventures found great acceptance among the merchant classes; farmers read treatises on improving their agricultural practices; and students and scholars could cram for exams with study guides. Thousands of titles were available for a wide range of tastes.

Playwrights from the south dominated Chinese drama, which had a golden age of its own during the Ming period. Plays sometimes were as long as ten acts, developing intricate plots and subplots with unexpected endings. Music became more prominent on the stage as solos, duets, and even entire choirs alternated with the spoken word in performances.

Ming artists and architects produced great quantities of high-quality works. The horizontal lines of the Forbidden City, the imperial family's area of temples and palaces constructed from 1403 to 1424, illustrate the period's values of balance and formalism. In Ming painting, naturalistic landscapes were a favorite topic of literati painters Shen Zhou (SHEN JOH; 1427–1509) and his most talented pupil, Wen Zhengming (WEN juhng-MING; 1470–1559). The great later Ming painter Dong Qichang (DONG chee-CHAHNG; 1555–1636) was noted for the formal discipline of his brush strokes.

This subtle work, Whispering Pines on a Mountain Path, *painted by Tang Yin (1470–1523) embodies the artistic ideals of the Ming dynasty.*

Yongle Encyclopedia—Compilation of all known scholarship by Yongle emperor's team of scholars in the fifteenth century.

The period's major artistic achievement was its porcelains, mostly produced at the Ming imperial kilns at Jingdezhen (JING-duh-JEN). While blue pottery had been produced earlier, it so characterized these kilns that Ming pottery is often assumed (incorrectly) to all be blue. Ming porcelain was emulated in Japan and Holland, and it was a major Chinese export item.

The Ming and the Sixteenth-Century World

The Ming's great voyages of exploration and its expansion toward the southwest were completed by the end of the fifteenth century. Though official maritime trade was limited to the ports of Ningbo for Japan, Fuzhou (foo-JOH) for the Philippines, and Guangzhou (gwahng-JOH) for Indonesia, extralegal trade carried on by Japanese, Chinese, Korean, Dutch, Portuguese and Spanish "pirates" enriched Chinese consumers' access to exotic goods. China exported mainly pottery and silk, importing Southeast Asian woods, spices, and food, New World foods like corn, sweet potatoes, and peanuts, and silver from both Mexico and, especially, Japan. The Ming economy became monetized with the huge influx of silver.

The population had expanded from 85 million in 1400 to 310 million by 1650, fueling a rise in the number and size of market towns, particularly in the heavily populated south. Crowded conditions led many to emigrate to Indonesia and the Philippines, where they functioned as cultural and commercial intermediaries. Domestic trade grew alongside foreign trade. Portuguese traders, banned in 1517, were permitted to operate from Macao after 1557. Soon, other European traders were knocking on China's door. They were accompanied by missionaries, at first mostly Jesuits who impressed the Ming imperial court with their scholarly ways and technical expertise in science, medicine, shipbuilding, calendar-making, and mathematics. The primary goal of the Jesuits and other Christian missionaries was to convert the Chinese to their religion, but the court was most impressed by their secular knowledge. Jesuits hoped to influence the top rulers by wearing the clothes of Confucian gentlemen and by speaking Chinese. Matteo Ricci, the best

DOCUMENT

A European View of Asia

DOCUMENT

Matteo Ricci's Journals

DOCUMENT

A Chinese View of Ricci

The blue-and-white pattern on the Ming jar (sixteenth century) is usually associated with the era, but as we can see in the vase at the right red was an equally vivid color in Ming culture. Carved red lacquer ware was produced in palace workshops.

known among them, was extraordinarily erudite, but neither he nor other Christians won over many converts.

Exciting new ideas and products were entering China, and much of the world looked to China as the source of both luxuries and everyday items. China continued to be the center of trade in Eurasia and was one leg of a triangle of trade whose other two legs were the Spanish colonies in the Philippines and in the western hemisphere (the trans-Pacific vessels were called "Manila Galleons"). But governance began to fall apart at the end of the sixteenth century, and the Ming's sophisticated global commerce could not save it from the effects of its shoddy economic mismanagement at home.

Corruption, waste, bureaucratic inertia, and conservatism prevailed at every level of government. The emperor Wanli (wahn-LEE; r. 1573–1619) was known as particularly ineffective, especially in the last decades of his reign. Thousands of his imperial family members lived off the revenues paid by a decreasing number of tax-paying peasants (rich landowners managed to remove themselves from the tax rolls). Peasant discontent with these injustices, combined with the imperial government's inability to respond to weather catastrophes in the 1620s (a "little ice age"), led to tenant uprisings and urban riots. Foreign issues exacerbated the Ming's economic worries at home. In the 1630s, Japan severely restricted its foreign trade, and Japanese silver supplies were rapidly being depleted. Struggles between Chinese and Spanish immigrants in the Philippines cut off access to China's other source of silver—that brought to Asia by the Manila Galleon.

The decline of the military also undermined the Ming. It was badly equipped and, in general, poorly led. The army suffered a serious drop in morale as disorder increased throughout the country: Pirates ravaged the coasts, and Mongol attacks brought near-anarchy along the Great Wall. The Chinese helped defend the Koreans against Japanese attacks in the 1590s, but that was the Ming army's last major stand against an outside threat.

Local governors and commanders, rather than the imperial government, had some success in dealing with these threats. There were even some women among these local leaders. The famous female general Qin Liangyu (CHIN lee-ahng-YOO; 1574–1648) put down local rebellions in southwestern China and later fought the Manchus at the end of the Ming dynasty. Known for her bravery and strength of character, she was also a refined woman who wrote elegant poetry. Meanwhile, the central administration nearly ceased to function. The highly formalized system was insufficiently flexible to deal with new challenges. Moreover, some emperors were puppets of eunuch ministers who pursued policies that were increasingly frivolous and unrealistic.

In the summer of 1644, after attempting to kill his oldest daughter to prevent her inevitable rape, mutilation, and death at the hands of rebels, the last Ming emperor, Chongzheng (chong-JUHNG; r. 1627–1644), hanged himself in his imperial garden, leaving a pitiful note to indicate his shame in meeting his ancestors. An insurgent government had already formed to the west in Sichuan, another rebel army was approaching Beijing, and only a few Portuguese mercenaries and some imperial guards remained nominally loyal. But neither of the Chinese countermovements would succeed. As the Ming regime collapsed, Manchu forces crossed the northern border into Ming territories and began the Qing (Ching) dynasty in 1664.

KOREA: THE MAKING OF A CONFUCIAN SOCIETY

■ *How were Confucian ideas adopted and modified in the early Chosŏn dynasty?*

For fifteen centuries, kingdoms on the Korean peninsula had produced a blend of indigenous and Chinese culture, arts, religions, and statecraft. At the end of the fourteenth century, King T'aejo (TAI-joh), founder of the Chosŏn dynasty, and his successors, especially the fourth Chosŏn king, the brilliant King Sejong (SEH-jong; r. 1418–1450), both enhanced Korean culture and effectively used Chinese governance and political theory. T'aejo continued the practice of sending tribute missions to China, adopted Chinese-style state ministries, and made Confucian learning the basis for government and hence for the exams taken by many

candidates for bureaucratic posts. In spite of T'aejo's respect for the Ming, the Ming refused to recognize the Korean dynasty as legitimate until the third Chosŏn king, T'aejong (TAI-jong; r. 1400–1418).

Unlike in China, in Korea only the sons of the hereditarily elite class, the yangban (YAHNG-bahn), undertook Confucian study and self-cultivation in preparation for a prestigious government post. (The term *yangban* meant "of the two branches," the branches being civil and military.) Other talented young men interested in technical positions as medical doctors, law clerks, scribes, astronomers, and translators came from the hereditary *chung'in* (CHOONG-een) or middle class and took different types of technical exams. In addition, there were nonexam routes to official jobs in Korea. As in China, a comprehensive history of the preceding dynasty was commissioned as a way of asserting one's own dynasty's legitimacy. While Chosŏn Korea became as Confucianized as China, Koreans were also interested in preserving their own culture, arts, religion, and language. Diverging from China in the fifteenth century, they devised a new syllabary called ***han'gul*** (HAHN-gool), to better represent Korean literature.

The Early Years of the Chosŏn Dynasty

In addition to setting up Chinese-style government ministries, King T'aejo made a number of other changes when he came to power. He created a capital with a Chinese-style palace at Hanyang, now the modern city of Seoul. He set up a military controlled by the throne, replacing the armed militias of powerful families. He handed out **Rank Lands** to officials recruited from the yangban class through Confucian examinations. These Rank Lands were intended to be used as

han'gul—Indigenous Korean script, invented by King Sejong.

Rank Lands—Lands granted to yangban officials as pay. They became hereditary, thereby making yangban hereditary aristocracy.

Chosŏn Korea

1392–1910	Chosŏn dynasty
1418–1450	Reign of King Sejong
1501–1570	Yi T'oegye, Confucian scholar
1592, 1598	Invasions by Japan
1627, 1630	Invasions by Manchus

pay during the lifetime of the official, but because the lands tended to become hereditary, they were replaced in the 1450s with salaries. T'aejo also made permanent grants of land to "merit subjects," people who had helped him in his rise to power. Merit lands and the power that went with them were often resented, however, by other yangban without such privileges.

Free and unfree farmers lived on the lands granted to officials or merit subjects. As many as one-third of the farmers were slaves in the Chosŏn period. Actors and entertainers, butchers and hide tanners, and women entertainers called *kisaeng* (kee-SANG)—a Korean version of the Japanese *geisha* (GAY-shah)—were considered to be "lowborn" people as well. Free peasants paid a very low tax on their output (just one-tenth and later one-twentieth of their harvest), but together with local tribute taxes, labor service, military duty, and other requirements, the total tax burden was heavy. Nevertheless, some free but not initially rich peasants eventually became wealthy landholders called commoner-landlords. By the beginning of the seventeenth century, new crops were grown for the expanding urban market. Improved farming technology and irrigation were used by some farmers involved in the production of these commercial crops, and in time, some became wealthy enough to get out of debt and buy enough land to be landlords themselves. The demographic structure of the countryside shifted from one with rich, elite people on top and poor commoners or slaves on the bottom, to a more complicated structure that had some yangban, some rich commoner-landlords, some small peasants, some tenants, and some unemployed homeless people. While the development of the countryside was good for overall economic growth in Korea, the resulting rural stratification would eventually lead to peasant discontent and uprisings.

Chosŏn society was officially divided into four statuses, roughly equivalent to the Chinese status groups (scholars, farmers, artisans, and merchants). In Korea, the yangban were on top followed by farmers, artisans, and the lowborn. In effect, the biggest divide was between the yangban and everyone else. Artisans were, at first, either government employees or government slaves. About 2800 lived in Seoul and 3500 elsewhere in Korea. In addition to doing work for the state, they also took private orders, and in time, these played a more important role in their professions. Eventually, most artisans became independent. Merchants, too, were more restricted than elsewhere in Asia in the early Chosŏn era. Money was used less commonly, and cotton cloth was a major unit of exchange. By the seventeenth century, however, merchants developed a lively commercial scene. They sold new commercial products produced by artisans and farmers—ginseng, cotton, and tobacco, the latter a New World product, were the most common cash crops—and increasing quantities of imported goods. Rows of shops selling a variety of products joined the official Six Licensed Stores that had been permitted since the early years of the dynasty.

In addition to divisions by class and status, Koreans were divided by gender. Women were subordinate to men, and this was particularly true in family law. Inheritance and succession were in the male line, so men with land or any valuables would often have a secondary wife or concubine, believing that could enhance their chances of having a son. Sons of concubines, though educated alongside their "legitimate" brothers, were barred from taking the civil service exams; they could, however, take the specialized exams for the *chung'in*.

Yangban women were more restricted than women of other classes in this period, though no women had rights of inheritance or the ability to decide such family matters as where they would live. Wives had to go along with their husbands and their parents-in-law. Women's most important virtue was preservation of their "chastity." This led to the prohibition of premarital contact with one's fiancée, of a woman having sexual relations with any man other than her husband, and of the remarriage of widows. Some impoverished widows were unable to avoid remarriage, but as in China, it was strongly discouraged. Also, as in China, chastity was encouraged through didactic writings and laws and with rewards. In 1152, *The Register of Licentious Women* stated that when a married woman did some "lustful deed" her position in society should be demoted to that of a sewing woman, a sort of servant. Moreover, her children were to be barred from office. During the Chosŏn dynasty, this sentiment intensified. By the end of the dynasty, yangban women were confined to their homes, had lost ritual duties in ancestral rites, and were not allowed to inherit property. The emphasis on chastity was to have repressive effects on women in Korean society until the end of the twentieth century.

The most effective king of the Chosŏn dynasty was Sejong. Under his rule, Korean borders were extended northward to the present borders. Though Korea was itself in the subordinate position toward China in its tribute system, Sejong established a parallel system with the ruler of the Japanese island of Tsu from whom he required tribute (this relationship eventually played a very significant role in Japanese international trade). A great patron of scholarship, Sejong embodied the **Neo-Confucian** (see Chapter 10) ideal of the scholar-king. He gathered the top scholars of his day

---

Neo-Confucianism—Chinese Confucian school of thought, originated in eleventh century; adopted throughout East Asia; focus on *li* ("principle") and *qi* ("matter" or "energy").

King Sejong of Korea (1418–1450), a member of the Chosŏn dynasty. During his reign, Korea reached the height of cultural achievements, and the modern boundaries of the country were fixed. Sejong is also credited with the creation of the Korean phonetic, or han'gul, alphabet.

but poetry, stressing love of nature, personal grief, and romantic love, was especially popular. Many of the Chosŏn lyric poets were women. The government also sponsored professional painters, most of whom painted landscapes. Confucian gentlemen—often referred to as *literati*—also painted, did calligraphy, and wrote poetry, but always as amateurs. Since artisans were professional artists, it was less appropriate for a gentleman of the yangban class to be a professional artist; it was expected, however, that he would cultivate his skills at the same level as a professional. As in China and Japan, skilled amateurs of this era preferred black ink paintings, sometimes with subdued colors. Other aspects of Korean painting differentiated it from Chinese styles, including humor that made use of bold calligraphy, chromatic contrasts, and an emphasis on vertical expressions rather than on depth.

Among all of the arts, the Chosŏn era is best known for its ceramics. The early Chosŏn blue-green pottery contrasted with the white porcelain produced by the government by the middle of the fifteenth century. The difference was not only one of color. The blue-green ceramics were simple but imaginative and intended for commoners. The white porcelain was made for the aristocratic yangban class.

The sixteenth century was a time of great growth in scholarship as well. One of Korea's best-known philosophers of Neo-Confucianism, Yi T'oegye (YEE TO-eh-ghee-EH; 1501–1570) was a strong supporter of Zhu Xi's learning. Yi T'oegye launched a debate about the relative importance of *i* (EE; Chinese *li*, meaning "principle") and *ki* (KEE; Chinese *qi*, "material force" or "energy"), and other philosophers weighed in. Neo-Confucian scholars have debated this point since the twelfth century. What is interesting about this debate is that many of the philosophers involved went on to establish their own schools. The boys in those schools were fiercely loyal to their teachers. Eventually, this loyalty led to intense school rivalry and the development of factions. The early sixteenth century saw a proliferation of

This Chosŏn era bottle is punchŏng *ware. The attention to detail on an object of daily use indicates the level of Korean sophistication.*

private academies and the increasing role—and factionalism—of men educated in those academies who were advising at the national level.

Korea faced a serious crisis at the hands of Japan in the 1590s. In 1592, soon after consolidating his control over a previously divided Japan,

in a "Hall of Worthies" and commissioned them to create a Korean writing system because, as he wisely noted, the Chinese characters Koreans had been using did not fit the Korean language. Their efforts produced han'gul, which Sejong called "proper sounds to instruct the people." The king then established an Office for Publication, which put out numerous Buddhist texts, geographies, histories, and didactic works of various kinds, including books on medical science and farming. The publication office occasionally used movable copper type, and a number of books were printed with it between 1403 and 1484. Other "Worthies" made advances in mathematics and invented musical instruments, a rain gauge, clocks, and military weapons.

The new han'gul alphabet stimulated cultural expression, particularly in literature and philosophy. Some of these works were prose compositions on simple subjects,

Toyotomi Hideyoshi (TOH-yoh-TOH-mee HEE-deh-YO-shi), Japan's hegemonic military overlord at the time, extended his ambitions to a desire for continental conquest. He took his soldiers, well trained though exhausted from years of conflict in Japan, and invaded Korea with a force of 200,000 soldiers supported by 9000 sailors. Hideyoshi hoped to use Korea as the first stage of his ultimate conquest of Ming China. The official Chosŏn military was no longer effective, and peasants, merchants, yangban, and other ordinary Koreans rose up to defend Korea against an invader armed with guns that the Koreans did not possess. The Chosŏn king was useless, and after he and his high officials fled Seoul, that city's slaves set fire to many government buildings, especially the one where the lists of slaves were kept. The Ming sent soldiers in support of their tributary partner, but it was naval warfare that saved Korea. The hero of the Korean defense was Admiral Yi Sunsin (YEE soon-SHEEN; 1545–1598) who maneuvered his copper-clad ships into narrow waterways where he trapped the invading forces and cut their supply lines. The odd appearance of Yi's armored boats, used almost 300 years before armored vessels were used in the American Civil War, earned them the name "turtle boats." Hideyoshi's forces retreated, but when the terms of the peace treaty were not carried out, the war began again. Again Admiral Yi was called into action. The war was going well for the Koreans, and the Japanese forces withdrew as soon as Hideyoshi died in Japan (of natural causes). The impact on Korea, in spite of its victory, was enormous. The seven years of war diminished Korea's wealth and inflicted terrible hardships on its people. There are few buildings in Korea dating from before the 1590s; unlike other parts of Asia, few ancient Buddhist temples remain. King Kwanghaegun (kwahng-HAI-goong; r. 1608–1623) made determined efforts to rebuild the country, but he was also concerned about maintaining careful foreign relations with new rival continental forces—the Ming dynasty in China and the rising Manchus north of Korea in Manchuria. His successors were not so fortunate or skillful at negotiating. Twice, in 1627 and again in 1636, the Manchus invaded Korea when it appeared the Chosŏn king would side with the Ming. Thousands of Koreans, held hostage by the Manchus, suffered great cruelty and privation before they could be ransomed. Many Korean families rejected female members who had been sexually violated and therefore dishonored. This attitude reflected the intensification of a Neo-Confucian emphasis on female chastity in Chosŏn Korea. When the Manchus conquered China and established the Qing dynasty in 1644, the Koreans had to submit to them until the 1890s. For a long time, Koreans, who had favored the Ming, resented being in a tributary relationship with the Qing.

JAPAN: THE ERA OF SHŌGUNS AND WARRING STATES

■ *How were art, culture, and religion central to the creation of Japanese identity?*

Like Korea and China, Japan had a monarch, the *tennō* (TEN-noh) or emperor, whose dynasty had already reigned for almost a millennium by the fourteenth century. But the emperor's court had not held real power since the late twelfth century, although it had twice attempted in the thirteenth and fourteenth centuries to reassert its authority in the political and economic realms. Instead, military lords and their samurai supporters had created a political system in the eastern town of Kamakura that in many ways resembled medieval European feudalism (see Chapter 10). The Kamakura system was not entirely stable, and internal and external pressures, including the Mongol invasions in the late thirteenth century, undermined the dominance of the shōgun's government.

Renewed warfare in the fourteenth century ended in 1336 with a shaky balance of power among dozens of provincial lords and a new overlord, Ashikaga Takauji (ah-shee-KAH-gah tah-kah-OO-jee), invested with the title of **shōgun** in 1338. Because the Ashikaga set up their shogunal court in the Muromachi (MOO-roh-MAH-chee) section of Kyoto (kee-OH-toh), the period from 1338 to 1568 is called the Muromachi period. The balance of power had actually ended before the end of the Muromachi period, when succession disputes and a struggle for power among newly emerging provincial forces began a 130-year-long Warring States period in 1467. During this period, coalitions of samurai with initially tiny land-

shōgun—The supreme military overlord in Japan from 1185 to 1868.

Japan	
1338–1568	Muromachi period
c. 1368–1443	Zeami Motokiyo, playwright
1467–1600	Warring States period
1568–1582	Oda Nobunaga begins unification, attacks Buddhists
1588	Toyotomi Hideyoshi's Sword Hunt
1600	Tokugawa victory at Sekigahara
1637–1638	Shimabara revolt

KOREA AND JAPAN
BEFORE 1500

Korea was part of the Chinese tribute system throughout the Chosŏn dynasty. Japan also traded with China and Korea, but was able to circumvent the more restricted measures of the tribute system because of its maritime separation from the continent.

enjoyed good relations with villagers, often by being part-time samurai-farmers themselves, were more likely to mobilize the villages' output for their own benefit. Oppressed villagers could run away from their land, and land was worthless without peasants to farm it. Thus, in many areas of Japan, villagers were granted a large degree of autonomy and gradually developed methods of self-government. This does not mean, however, that sixteenth-century villages were democratic entities. Local government varied from village to village; some allowed all families a voice in a village council, while others had a hereditary village headman. Still others were run from the local Shintō shrine or Buddhist temple association.

Just as villages were not run democratically despite their freedom from constant control by warriors or aristocrats, so, too, families were not run democratically. Though women had been able to inherit and make important personal decisions in earlier centuries, inheritance was increasingly in male hands. Village men and women all participated in festivals, and women were responsible for spring planting and often for marketing products. No farm could run without both men and women, as each had necessary chores. But by the Muromachi and Warring States eras, even farm women had to take a back seat to their husbands in ceremonial and political participation in village associations. Wives and daughters of samurai and *daimyō* in the Warring States era had a much more dangerous life than farm women. They were expected to be skilled at defending themselves and their families' interests, but they were also frequently married off by powerful fathers and other relatives in order to cement alliances with other warlords. In those treacherous times, when military alliances shifted frequently, marriage was often not a safe haven for samurai-class women; husbands wondered if their wives were spies on behalf of their fathers or brothers, and many wives were involuntarily divorced, used as hostages, or in a few cases, even executed. Of course, life was hard for male samurai warriors, too; but the decline in the official status of elite women from the early medieval era was quite clear.

The heads of the largest extended families in the villages (families with multiple generations and married cousins or siblings living under one roof) were often samurai-farmers, serving as local notables who settled village disputes and oversaw some of the farming activities of their less fortunate neighbors. Some villages were more independent and powerful than others, particularly those villages, organized around Pure Land (see Chapter 10) temples, which became increasingly militant in the defense of both their faith and their livelihoods during the Warring States period. The first of the "three great unifiers," Oda Nobunaga, found these villages to be one of the greatest challenges to his rise to dominance. After ending the

holdings, supported by villagers whose crops they used to support their troops, fought their samurai neighbors for increasingly larger areas of control. By the mid-sixteenth century, the largest of these warrior lords came to be known as *sengoku daimyō* (SEN-goh-koo DAI-mee-oh) or Warring States lords, and it is from those ranks that three powerful warriors, Oda Nobunaga (OH-dah NOH-boo-NAH-gah; 1534–1582), Toyotomi Hideyoshi (1536–1598), and Tokugawa Ieyasu (toh-koo-GAH-wah EE-eh-YAH-soo; 1544–1616), brought Japan under unified control.

Villages and Towns: The Base of Samurai Power

Villages provided most of the wealth for the rise of these powerful **daimyō** from among the hundreds of small-scale samurai lords. Not all samurai lords survived the warfare of the sixteenth century. Those who

---

daimyō—A military lord, served by samurai.

Muromachi **shogunate** in 1568, he conquered and forced the submission of other *daimyō* lords. But the Pure Land villagers refused to surrender, believing their faith would keep them strong against their enemies' military power. Oda Nobunaga attacked the Buddhists with extreme violence. His forces killed 20,000 men, women, and children in one brutal struggle in 1574. Three years earlier, he had attacked the 700-year-old temple community at Mt. Hiei (HEE-ay), founded by Saichō, burning 300 monastic buildings, including residences, libraries with irreplaceable treasures, and prayer halls.

As a symbol of his power, Oda Nobunaga built the enormous Azuchi (ah-ZOO-chee) Castle (1576–1579). He filled it with art intended to glorify his rule. It was lavishly painted by the great master Kanō Eitoku (KAH-noh AY-to-koo; 1543–1590), using fine colors and gold leaf. Despite his self-aggrandizement, however, Oda Nobunaga was cut down in a most ordinary way—he was assassinated by one of his subordinates in 1582. Nobunaga's assassination afforded Hideyoshi (a man of humble origins who had not yet been awarded the surname Toyotomi at that time) the opportunity to seize power. Intercepting a message not meant for him, Hideyoshi learned that Nobunaga had been killed. Hideyoshi mobilized his forces secretly to attack the perpetrator. This began Hideyoshi's march to power throughout Japan. He conquered rival military leaders and, recognizing that other rural samurai-farmers might become great leaders as he had, decided to neutralize their potential power. In 1588, he issued the famous "Sword Hunt" edict, disarming all villagers and, in the process, gaining them merit in the afterlife:

The farmers of the various provinces are strictly forbidden to possess long swords, short swords, bows, spears, muskets, or any form of weapon. . . . So that the . . . swords collected shall not be wasted, they shall be [melted down and] used . . . in the forthcoming construction of the Great Buddha. This will be an act by which the farmers will be saved in this life, needless to say, and in the life to come. . . . If farmers possess agricultural tools alone and engage [themselves] completely in cultivation, they shall [prosper] unto eternity.

In 1591, Hideyoshi followed up with the Edict on Changing Status, which stipulated that samurai, farmers, and merchants all remain in the status group into which they were born. The same year he carried out surveys of land and its productivity so that he could tax his own lands and gain information about the wealth of other *daimyō* lords. The growth of cities and towns in the seventeenth century shows that the prohibition on mobility was never as rigidly applied as Hideyoshi, and his successors in the Tokugawa shogu-

nate, intended. He got the emperor to name him "regent," an old title from the Heian period, which had no meaning except as a sign of the emperor's recognition. Hideyoshi was never shōgun.

Though Hideyoshi's edicts applied to lands under his own direct control, they were copied by other *daimyō*. Hideyoshi and the *daimyō* lords moved the samurai from the countryside and housed them in barracks around their castles. Merchants and artisans moved nearby to supply the samurai and their lords. In time, these towns, called "castle-towns," became Japan's main cities. Hideyoshi and the *daimyō* built castles, roads, drainage ditches, bridges, port facilities, temples, and countless other structures. Most of the labor force came from the countryside. *Daimyō* ordered farmers to work on their own urban construction projects and on those demanded by Hideyoshi. For example, Hideyoshi requisitioned from his *daimyō* approximately 250,000 workers to build his grand castle at Fushimi (foo-SHEE-mee). After completing their projects, many of these workers settled in the new castle-towns, in spite of Hideyoshi's edict forbidding farmers to permanently change their status.

Art and Culture in Medieval Japan

Hideyoshi's period was an era of grand and colorful art. Like Oda Nobunaga, Hideyoshi used architectural monuments as symbols of his power. Castles and temples, decorated in the most ornate and at times even ostentatious styles, were built by legions of conscripted laborers. The bold and lavish paintings of Kanō Eitoku and his followers, patronized by the rich and powerful, continued to dominate painting for several decades into the next century. The Europeans, with their exotic clothing, appearance, and strange objects of daily life, were another popular theme in artwork patronized by urban connoisseurs.

Townsfolk, whether merchants, samurai, or the highest level elite were not the only ones to patronize and enjoy artistic production. From the fourteenth to the sixteenth century, itinerant storytellers, many of them originally monks and nuns, traveled throughout Japan, to villages and mansions alike, creating what one historian has called a "national literature" that transcended regional and class boundaries. These performances included song, dance, recitation, the playing of stringed instruments, the use of puppets, and the showing of pictures to accompany the text or songs.

Urban elites built permanent theaters to present plays with human actors or puppets. In the Muromachi period, **Nō** (NOH) plays, which had religious and often historical themes and the refined, spare sen-

---

shogunate—The government headed by the shōgun.

Nō— A dramatic form developed in Japan in the fourteenth century; inspired by Buddhist themes.

sibility of Zen, were created by master playwrights like the actor-playwright-critic Zeami Motokiyo (zeh-AH-mee MOH-toh-KEE-yo; c. 1363–1443). Nō developed from thirteenth-century religious rites into a sophisticated theatrical form by the fourteenth century. In the seventeenth century, new forms like puppet plays and kabuki (kah-BOO-kee) plays with human actors emerged (see Chapter 20).

The tea ceremony, intended to be refined, intimate, and meditative, was another artistic form that

---

Document   *Sotoba Komachi*, a Fourteenth-Century Japanese Nō Play

Kan'ami (1333–1384), father of the great playwright Zeami, pioneered the transformation of simple plays and complex court dances into the sophisticated dramatic form of the Nō. Zen aesthetics, Pure Land salvation, and shamanistic spirit possession come together in these dramas. The spare stage and tranquility of action of most of a Nō play culminates in a wild dance, as the main actor is transformed into the tormented soul of another. In this play, Komachi, a poet who had actually lived in the Heian period, is an old woman, no longer the famous beauty of her day. She comes upon two priests who inform her she is sitting on a stupa (*sotoba* in Japanese), whereupon she is possessed by the spirit of a man whose soul cannot cease to be reborn in worldly torment because it is consumed by desire due to the young Komachi's toying with his love. She had told him that if he called on her 100 times, she would consent to see him, but he died after 99 visits, unrequited. The excerpts here are from her conversation with the Buddhist priests at the beginning of the play and from her frenzied comments, as well as those of the Chorus which advances the action of the play, at the end.

KOMACHI: How sad that once I was proud.
   . . . Golden birds in my raven hair
   When I walked like willows nodding, charming
   As the breeze in spring.
   The voice of the nightingale
   The petals of the rosewood, wide stretched. . . .
   I was lovelier than these.
   Now I am foul in the eyes of the humblest creatures
   . . . The wreck of a hundred years . . .
FIRST PRIEST: . . . That old beggar woman sitting on a sacred stupa. We should warn her to come away.

Following some discussion between the priests and the old woman about Buddhist spiritual matters, the priests ask the old woman her name. All three, as well as the Chorus, lament the evanescence of life. Suddenly, Komachi turns into her spurned lover. At times, she speaks as though she is the lover, at other times as herself. The Chorus also speaks as the lover.

KOMACHI: An awful madness seizes me
   And my voice is no longer the same.
   Hey! Give me something you priests!
FIRST PRIEST: What do you want?
KOMACHI: To go to Komachi!
FIRST PRIEST: What are you saying? You *are* Komachi!
KOMACHI: No. Komachi was beautiful.

Many letters came, many messages. . .
But she made no answer, even once. . .
Age is her retribution now
Oh, I love her! . . .
CHORUS: I came and went, came and went
   One night, two nights, three . . .
   I came and carved my mark upon the pillar.
   I was to come a hundred nights,
   I lacked but one . . .
KOMACHI: It was his unsatisfied love possessed me so . . .
   In the face of this I will pray
   For life in the worlds to come . . .
   Before the golden, gentle Buddha I will lay
   Poems as my flowers
   Entering in the Way . . .

Questions to Consider

1. Nō plays were intended as entertainment for samurai and *daimyō*. Why do you think their content was so strongly religious?

2. What Buddhist principles are evident in this excerpt?

3. Why do you think a fourteenth-century playwright would use a tenth-century event as the theme of his play?

From Kan'ami Kiyotsugu, "Sotoba Komachi," in Donald Keene, ed., *Anthology of Japanese Literature* (New York: Grove Press, 1955).

became more popular in the harsh times of the Warring States period. Beautiful teapots and cups were
manufactured in Japan or imported as luxury items
from China or Korea. Hideyoshi had studied with the
greatest tea master of his day, Sen no Rikyō (SEN no
REE-kee-oo), but for reasons historians still cannot
understand, ordered this important artist to commit
suicide in 1591.

Architecture was another art that developed during the three centuries of the Muromachi period and
Warring States period. Ashikaga shōguns,
especially the third, Yoshimitsu (YOH-shee-
MEE-tsoo), and sixth, Yoshimasa (YOH-shee-
MAH-sah), built remarkable religious retreats
of a modest size which blended with their
surroundings. The Temple of the Golden
Pavilion (the photo at the beginning of this
chapter), though rebuilt following a fire after
World War II, and the Temple of the Silver
Pavilion, which still stands, are the finest
examples of Muromachi architecture. Later
buildings might be grandiose, as were the
castles of Oda Nobunaga and Toyotomi
Hideyoshi, or beautiful as well as functional,
like Himeji (Hee-MAY-jee) castle, built by
daimyō during the Warring States period.

Japan was very much part of the international commercial world during the Muromachi and Warring States periods. Arts were
freely imported and exported to the rest of
Asia. As we have seen, the Ming tried to control the volume of trade, but freebooting merchants from China, Japan and Korea, called
"Japanese pirates" by the Ming, got around
the Ming restrictions. Hideyoshi imposed
some restrictions of his own. In 1587, attempting to allay Ming concerns about piracy,
Hideyoshi suppressed many of the Japanese
who had been involved in uncontrolled trade.
But Hideyoshi's other foreign policy initiatives
were decidedly a failure. His invasions of
Korea were disastrous not only for Korea
but also for his own ability to establish long-
lasting rule by his family in Japan. Indeed, though the
invasions were immediately terminated when he died
in 1598, he had so weakened his closest supporters by
sending them to war in Korea that other powerful
men, rivals to his child heir Hideyori (HEE-deh-YOH-
ree), were able to defeat the boy's supporters and take
over Japan in 1600. An additional result of Hideyoshi's
disastrous foreign adventurism was the policy of the
Tokugawa shōguns to minimize and strictly control
foreign relations.

*Himeji Castle, completed in the early seventeenth cen-
tury, is the finest extant example of late Warring States
era castle construction. Like other such castles, it sits
atop a hill and its stone base is capable of defending
against the cannon that began to be used in the late sixteenth century. The lovely living quarters at the top were
vulnerable to fire, but manifested the glory of the
daimyō who commanded the castle.*

Christians presented a related problem. Europeans had been arriving in the islands since a shipwreck in 1543 in which three Portuguese came ashore with arquebuses. These early muskets would soon alter the course of warfare, for Nobunaga and a few other *daimyō* used firearms to great tactical advantage. Thereafter, Portuguese ships began arriving in greater numbers, bringing not only new products, as noted above, but also Jesuit missionaries, starting in 1549. Some *daimyō* converted to Christianity to facilitate trade and often forced their samurai to convert as well. By the 1580s, as many as 200,000 residents of the island of Kyūshū had adopted the foreign faith. Hideyoshi first noticed the divisive role played by Christians in 1586 while fighting his rivals on that island. He issued two edicts, one to expel missionaries and one to limit the propagation of Christianity, but neither edict was effectively carried out. A few years later, Hideyoshi treated Jesuits cordially and offered land in Kyoto to the rival order of Franciscans. Hideyoshi's first expulsion and limitation edicts were apparently not intended to be applied generally but rather were directed at a small group of troublesome Jesuits in Nagasaki who encouraged destruction of Shintō shrines and Buddhist temples and served as currency brokers. Later, however, Hideyoshi became convinced that missionaries were the leading edge of Iberian colonialism and executed several missionaries and converts. But few other actions were taken, as trade was too valuable to jeopardize by offending the Iberians at that time. The systematic expulsion of Christians would come later, under the Tokugawa.

The Road to Sekigahara

In 1590, Tokugawa Ieyasu received a highly productive territory, the Kantō plain in eastern Japan, in exchange for his military assistance to Hideyoshi. The Kantō, which had been the home of the Minamoto shōguns in the Kamakura period (see Chapter 10) and is today the heartland of Japan, was Japan's most productive rice producing area. Tokugawa Ieyasu selected a tiny farming village along Edo creek to build a castle-town, which he called Edo. By 1610, Edo had 5000 houses; by 1620, it had 150,000 residents; and by 1700, with over a million inhabitants, the little fishing village had become the world's largest city. As Hideyoshi and Nobunaga had done, in the 1590s Ieyasu mobilized peasants to clear forests; to cut timber to construct castles, barracks, temples, and buildings for mercantile activities; to lay out roads and canals; and to build bridges and docks. He needed skilled workers of all kinds. He exhausted natural resources, especially lumber, an environmental problem that would be dealt with later in the Tokugawa period.

Ieyasu was one of five regents appointed by Hideyoshi on his deathbed to administer the realm until his son Hideyori came of age. Soon, tensions among the five erupted into a renewal of warfare. Ieyasu and his allies created an army of 80,000 men and challenged the supporters of Hideyori at the battle of Sekigahara (SEH-kee-gah-HAH-rah) in the fall of 1600. Victory in this battle established Tokugawa hegemony and allowed Tokugawa Ieyasu to reward his followers and punish his opponents by either eliminating or reducing their domains. Hideyori and his family were moved to one of the Toyotomi castles, at Osaka, where they remained until the Tokugawa eliminated them in 1615. Tokugawa Ieyasu asked the emperor to declare him shōgun, which he did in 1603. His wealthy domain in the Kantō, his use of natural and human resources, and his military effectiveness led to his victory.

Tokugawa Ieyasu was not known for his kindness, though he was a strong leader. Like his predecessors, Ieyasu manipulated the marriages of women in his family for his own ends. As we have seen, *daimyō* women were expected to act as spies for their fathers or brothers, leading to their husbands' distrust of them. Ieyasu himself was the victim of manipulation at the hands of Nobunaga, whose daughter he married. Hideyoshi forced his sister to divorce her first husband to marry Ieyasu, whereupon the sister's distraught first husband committed suicide. Ieyasu married his granddaughter to Hideyori, son of Hideyoshi; Ieyasu's forces went on to execute the granddaughter's little son (and Ieyasu's own great-grandson) in 1615. The status of women was entirely dependent on their social status, with *daimyō* women the only ones used as marriage pawns. Fortunately, though women's status would remain low during the Tokugawa period, women of other classes were not placed in that kind of jeopardy, and the worst excesses, the use of women as hostages through forced marriages, were terminated with the end of the battles for unification in Japan.

The Early Tokugawa Years

Ieyasu faced some difficult problems in the first years of the Tokugawa shogunate (1600–1868). Even simple public safety was an early problem, as samurai whose *daimyō* had been defeated at the battle of Sekigahara in 1600 roamed the streets of Japan's towns with little to do but make trouble. These masterless samurai, called rōnin (ROH-neen), continued to emerge in times of turmoil in the next several hundred years. For the most part, however, the Tokugawa managed to control them within a few years by offering them alternate forms of employment and amusement. Another problem con-

DOCUMENT

Edicts by Tokugawa Ieyasu

cerned the shogunate's relationship to the loyal *daimyō*. What Ieyasu and his next two successors, his son Hidetada (HEE-deh-TAH-dah; r. 1606–1623) and grandson Iemitsu (EE-eh-MEE-tsoo; r. 1623–1651), did was

Tokugawa Japan, 1600–1800

move the *daimyō* around the country to form layers of protection from those they believed least trustworthy; proclaim a code of conduct for the *daimyō* in 1615; take over control of roads, mines, ports, and international relations; and set up a control system called the "alternate attendance system."

The alternate attendance system had many unanticipated effects, which are discussed in Chapter 20, but it also achieved its primary goal of controlling the *daimyō*. To be a *daimyō* in the Tokugawa era, a lord had to possess a domain that produced at least 10,000 *koku* of rice (a *koku* is a unit of measurement; one *koku* fed approximately one person for one year). Each *daimyō* had to maintain a mansion in the shōgun's capital at Edo in addition to his castle in his home domain. He had to live in the mansion every other year (hence, he *attended* the shōgun in *alternate* years), and his wife and children had to live permanently in Edo, thus making sure he would not raise the banner of rebellion while back at home in his own castle. The alternate attendance system, requiring the movement across the whole country of vast numbers of samurai in the retinues of the *daimyō*, was extremely expensive, as was the maintenance of two homes and two staffs. The impoverishing of the *daimyō* also kept them from rising up against the Tokugawa.

Another area brought under regulation by the first three Tokugawa shōguns was foreign affairs. Some *daimyō*—such as the *daimyō* of Tsu in Korean trade—were

A Japanese View of European Missionaries

involved in foreign relations, but the Tokugawa tried to control it. Ieyasu welcomed trade but not evangelism. Most Europeans wanted both, but the Dutch claimed that religious propagation was not their goal. The English made a similar claim. But unable to compete with Dutch traders, the English abandoned Japan by 1623. The Japanese were finding it more difficult to conduct business as silver supplies began to run low, but trade continued many years into the seventeenth century. Evangelism was another story. Ieyasu's son Hidetada increased

pressure to suppress the Christians in Japan. The end of all missionary activity, and indeed, the closing of Japan to all international contacts excepts those by the Chinese, the Koreans, and the Dutch, was precipitated by a revolt at Shimabara in which Christian banners were raised in 1637–1638, reminding the fearful Tokugawa of the Buddhist-inspired village revolts of the Warring States period.

By the end of the 1630s, peasant starvation and overwork, exacerbated by poor weather due to a devastating El Niño pattern, was at the heart of peasants joining rōnin in demands against the state. Revolts broke out in many places, but the most severe was the Shimabara (SHEE-mah-BAH-rah) revolt. Laying siege to the peasants and rōnin holed up at Shimabara, the Tokugawa starved out 37,000 villagers. The stringent regulation of foreign trade began after this revolt. Japan continued to have a high volume of trade through the rest of the seventeenth century, but its trading partners were limited to the three it could be confident would not try to smuggle in forbidden Christian texts. Japan's foreign policy was then called a *sakoku* (SAH-koh-koo) or closed-country policy, but it would be more accurate to call it a strictly regulated foreign policy.

---

sakoku—Policy of limiting Japan's foreign and trade relations to China, Korea, and the Netherlands from 1640 to 1853. Literally, "closed country."

The shrine at Nikko is one of several built after the death of Tokugawa Ieyasu to legitimate the shogunate's power by designating its founder as a Shintō deity. The ornate construction contrasts with the simplicity of medieval architecture.

By 1650, the Tokugawa had established control of Japan's foreign policy, brought the *daimyō* under their control, and created a regulated society. They continued their control of Japanese politics—the emperor was honored by the Tokugawa but had no power— until the middle of the nineteenth century (see Chapter 24). For the next 200 years, Japan was at peace, and the arts, commerce, scholarship, and the people's livelihood flourished.

SOUTHEAST ASIA: STATES WITHIN A REGION

▪ *How did cultural blending influence Southeast Asian civilizations?*

Situated on the main sea route between East Asia and the Indian Ocean and divided geographically into diverse subregions, Southeast Asia had long been an area of contending states. Although each of these regions had been influenced for centuries by the cultures of India and China, they developed a strong sense of separate cultural identities and statehood. Wars in defense of independence or attempted conquest of neighboring states were, as a result, fairly common.

In the thirteenth century, the powerful land-based Khmer (KMEHR) state, which had dominated southern and central mainland Southeast Asia for four centuries, began to decline. Its very wealth and power were, ironically, factors leading to its decline. With great agricultural wealth derived from its sophisticated irrigation system, Khmer built 20,000 shrines, 102 hospitals, and other monuments. The state supported 300,000 priests and monks. These expenditures sapped the state, as did wars against the neighboring Chams and the encroaching Thais. In the fourteenth century, the Mongols in China encouraged the Thais to move into Khmer territory. The Mongols, who temporarily received tribute from mainland Southeast Asia and parts of Java, seriously disrupted all existing governments. Throughout Southeast Asia, there were ruinous petty wars, often based on Hindu-Buddhist conflicts, each side of which suffered individually under Muslim expansion. Finally, Muslim regimes replaced many traditional Hindu states in Indonesia, which also felt the effects of European empire building, first by the Portuguese and then by the Dutch. Before 1650, however, the total European impact on the mainland was negligible.

Tracing the political interactions among the nations and empires making up the region we now know as Southeast Asia may often seem confusing. Here, what is most significant is that we recognize the

Southeast Asia	
1050	Beginnings of Burmese unification
1283–1317	Rama Khamheng, king of Thailand
1280s	Mongol invasions
1402	Founding of Malacca
1407–1418	Ming invasion of Vietnam
1418	Founding of Le dynasty in Vietnam

important regional influences, such as the roles of religion and trade networks.

Burma and the Thais

In the first millennium C.E., the region of present-day Burma remained an ethnically diverse region, divided into a number of small principalities. Around 1050 a process of political unification began under the Burmese, a group of people who moved to the south from the Tibetan frontier about 900 years earlier. This movement was shattered by the Mongol invasions of the 1280s. The process of unification recommenced after the invasions, but it took till the sixteenth and seventeenth centuries for the Tongoo kingdom to unify most of Burma.

Advancing to the south during the Mongol invasions were the Thais, a group of people from Yunnan, in China. The Mongols' destruction of Burma and the threat to the Khmer helped the expansion of Ayuthaya (AH-yoo-TAI-ya), the Thai state, but it was not the only reason for the rise of the Thais. The weakening of these two other

Thai Statue

states offered opportunities for expansion to the Thais, who had already begun to penetrate the region centuries earlier. Arriving in Khmer and Burma, the Thais—whose name "Thai" meant "free"—also absorbed the richness of the Indian civilization that had for centuries influenced Southeast Asia. In the late thirteenth century, the Thai monarch, Rama Khamheng (RAH-mah KAHM-heng; r. 1283–1317), the head of the small Thai principality of Sukhothai (SOO-koh-THAI), extended Thai power after deciding to establish an independent Thai state. Under Sukhothai rule, the Thai people were given a cultural and political identity derived from several sources in the region. The idea of a divine monarch was borrowed from the Khmer. Burma provided principles of law and Theravada Buddhism. The Thai alphabet was created by Rama Khamheng, based on

South Indian script. In the fifteenth century, the Thai kingdom moved its capital to the agricultural center of the country and brought the various Thai principalities under the king's control. This centralized monarchical system lasted into the nineteenth century.

Under the Tongoo King Bayinnaung (BAI-in-NOWNG) in the 1550s and 1560s, Burma briefly absorbed Laos (LAH-ohs) and conquered Siam (now Thailand) with an army estimated at 500,000, the largest ever assembled in Southeast Asia. Bayinnaung's capital at Pegu was a nucleus of Buddhist culture, a thriving commercial center, and the site of his wondrous palace, which was roofed in solid gold. But his successor wasted resources in unsuccessful wars on its neighbors. Later, the Thai state gained supremacy, humbling Cambodia and Burma after 1595 and profiting from a commercial alliance with the Dutch.

Document   A Traveller's Account of Siam

This description is by a Ma Huan, translator and interpreter for the fourth expedition of eunuch maritime navigator Zheng He, from 1413–1415. The account tells us as much about Chinese attitudes as about "Xian Luo," known to Europeans as Siam, and now known as Thailand.

. . . Travelling from Chan city towards the south-west for several days and nights with a fair wind, the ship comes to the estuary at New Street Tower and enters the anchorage; then you reach the capital.

The country is a thousand *li* in circumference, the outer mountains [being] steep and rugged, [and] the inner land wet and swampy. The soil is barren and little of it is suitable for cultivation. The climate varies—sometimes cold, sometimes hot.

The house in which the king resides is rather elegant, neat, and clean. The houses of the populace are constructed in storeyed form; in the upper [part of the house] they do not join planks together [to make a floor], but they use the wood of the areca-palm, which they cleave into strips resembling bamboo splits; [these strips] are laid close together and bound very securely with rattans; on [this platform] they spread rattan mats and bamboo matting, and on these they do all their sitting, sleeping, eating, and resting.

As to the king's dress: he uses a white cloth to wind round his head; on the upper [part of his body] he wears no garment; [and] round the lower [part he wears] a silk-embroidered kerchief, adding a waist-band of brocaded silk-gauze. When going about he mounts an elephant or else rides in a sedan-chair, while a man holds [over him] a gold-handled umbrella . . . [which is] very elegant. The king is a man of the So-li race, and a firm believer in the Buddhist religion.

In this country the people who become priests or become nuns are exceedingly numerous; the habit of the priests and nuns is somewhat the same as in the Central Country; and they, too, live in nunneries and monasteries, fasting and doing penance. . . .

It is their custom that all affairs are managed by their wives; both the [illegible text] of the country and the common people, if they have matters which require thought and deliberation—punishments light and heavy, all trading transactions great and small—they all follow the decisions of their wives, [for] the mental capacity of the wives certainly exceeds that of the men.

If a married woman is very intimate with one of our men from the Central Country, wine and food are provided, and they drink and sit and sleep together. The husband is quite calm and takes no exception to it; indeed he says 'My wife is beautiful and the man from the Central Country is delighted with her'. The men dress the hair in a chignon, and use a white head-cloth to bind round the head [and] on the body they wear a long gown. The women also pin up the hair in a chignon, and wear a long gown.

Questions to Consider

1. Would the role of Thai women in decision-making have been surprising to a Chinese observer of the Ming dynasty?

2. Did Ma Huan find Thailand exotic? What kinds of exchanges do you think the Ming and Thailand would have made under the tribute system? In this description of Thailand in the fifteenth century can you see cultural or social similarities with any other parts of East Asia during approximately the same time period?

From Ma Huan, *Ying-yai Sheng-lai: The Overall Survey of the Ocean's Shores (1433)*, trans. Feng Ch'eng Chun, intro. by J. V. G. Mills (Cambridge: Cambridge University Press, 1970).

Shwemawdaw Pagoda, Pegu.

Vietnam

Under Chinese rule for a millennium, Vietnam was the Southeast Asian country that was, at the same time, most Sinified and most ardently committed to independence from China. Vietnam used Chinese script, borrowed institutions of government, and adopted Buddhism from Chinese missionaries. Political independence from China was followed by the two countries' continuing tributary relationship and Vietnam's careful study of Confucian scholarship. The Mongol attacks were repulsed by the Vietnamese, but the Ming did briefly rule Vietnam early in the fifteenth century. In 1418, Le Loi (LEH LO-ee), an aristocratic landholder, led an army to push out the Ming. But he and his successors in the Le dynasty adopted Chinese methods; they then succeeded in dominating their Southeast Asian neighbors. These nations were all in decline; indeed, Burma was still broken into a number of principalities. An exception was the Thai polity

under King Trailok (1448–1488), who was more successful in creating an efficient army and establishing a civil administration. By the end of the fifteenth century, the Vietnamese, along with the Thais, momentarily controlled the mainland region of Southeast Asia. Rather than encouraging trade, however, Vietnam's ruling dynasty based its rule on a Confucian approach to national wealth. Stating that commerce was "peripheral," the powerful monarch Le Thanh Tong (leh tahng tong; r. 1460–1497) focused on agriculture, stating: "Concentrate all our forces on agriculture, expand our potential."

Maritime Southeast Asia

The kingdom of Majapahit (mah-JAH-pah-heet), like the Thai state, was able to consolidate its position on the Indonesian island of Java due to Mongol pressure on its neighbors. From the late thirteenth century, Majapahit extended its hegemony over most of the islands of Indonesia, dominating trade and developing a sophisticated and artistic culture. In 1402, Malacca (mah-LAH-ka) declared itself an independent state, and one by one, other Indonesian rulers involved in maritime trade converted to Islam and abandoned Majapahit. Expanding into Indonesia in a gradual and generally peaceful manner, Islam achieved a great success in the fourteenth and fifteenth centuries. Sufi Muslim missionaries were drawn to the area by the expanding India-China trade, particularly when Chinese interests waned in the decade after 1424. Many

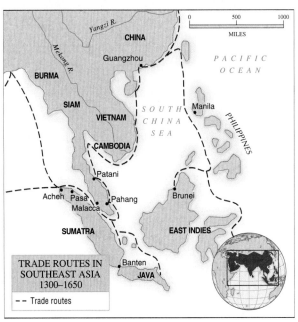

The trade routes across the Indian Ocean served as an arena for the interaction of Chinese, Indian, Arab, and Southeast Asian cultures as well as Hindu, Buddhist, and Muslim religions and eastern and western goods and products.

local rulers embraced Islam to gain independence from the great Hindu state of Majapahit; others sought a share of Indian commerce. The Muslims were tolerant of the Hindu-Buddhist culture of the new converts, and daily practices, rituals, arts, and music, even those contrary to Muslim rules, were allowed to continue. Foreigners, among them the large number of immigrant Chinese and merchants from Egypt, Persia, Arabia, and western India, were accepted. The Muslims mixed easily with the populations of the port cities. As the power of the Majapahit Empire weakened, the influence of Islam grew. Muslim sailors–either pirates or traders, depending on the circumstances–came to control the various straits between the islands and set up their own states.

The indigenous population adopted Islam, as the local princely families intermarried with Muslims in alliances uniting the power and legitimacy of the local nobility with the wealth of the Muslim merchants. From this base in Indonesia, Islam spread throughout present-day Malaysia, the Molucca Islands, and some of the islands of the Philippines. Only Bali remained relatively untouched by the Islamic advance.

The rising Muslim commercial center of Malacca, on the Malay coast opposite Sumatra, best illustrates the entry of Islam into Southeast Asia. Founded in 1402 and by 1404 part of the Ming tribute system, its rulers converted to Islam and built an empire of commercial vassal states in the region. Despite the sultan's profession of Islam, Malacca continued to use the structure of Hindu-Buddhist princely courts. Malacca was multicultural. For example, in 1462, the Arab navigator Ibn Majid described the people of Melaka (Malacca) as follows:

> They have no culture at all. The infidel marries Muslim women while the Muslim takes pagans to wife. You do not know whether they are Muslims or not. They are thieves for theft is rife among them and they do not mind.
>
> The Muslim eats dogs for meat for there are no food laws.
>
> They drink wine in the markets and do not treat divorce as a religious act.

Malacca was the busiest port in Asia, linking China and the Moluccas with India and Africa. Its growing success paralleled Muslim expansion through western Indonesia to the Philippines in the sixteenth century.

Arrival of the Europeans

The Portuguese arrived in maritime Southeast Asia in the early sixteenth century. Butchering its Muslim population, they took the port of Malacca in 1511 and held it for the next 130 years. By 1550, the profits from the trade through Malacca were four times Portugal's internal revenues. But Portuguese rule was arbitrary and cruel and turned increasing numbers of Southeast Asians to convert to Islam to facilitate joining a trade network apart from the Portuguese. Mainland governments in Southeast Asia generally maintained their independence against the Europeans. Portuguese missionaries, at first active in Vietnam, were expelled by the end of the period. Portuguese traders and mercenary soldiers served everywhere, but they were usually controlled. Some were enslaved in Burma; only in weakened Cambodia and Laos did they acquire significant political influence. By the seventeenth century the Portuguese were giving way to the Dutch, who courted the Vietnamese in only partially successful efforts to monopolize trade with Siam and Burma.

Well before 1650, Europeans were becoming very active in Indonesia. The Portuguese used Malacca as a base for dominating trade in the region, but Muslim rulers in nearby states forcefully ejected them from Java and Sumatra and limited their operations in the Molucca Islands. In the late 1500s Spain acquired a foothold in the Philippines. The Spanish established a colonial capital at Manila and sent in missionaries to convert the country to Christianity. The missionaries eventually exerted even greater control over people's daily lives than the Spanish colonial officials in Manila. With the creation of the colony of the Philippines, the triangular trade of the Manila Galleon embraced Mexico, the Philippines, and Japan.

Dutch trading companies merged into the United East India Company in 1602, and initially sought trade, not territory or the conversion of souls, in Southeast Asia. They took control of the Moluccas and expelled the Portuguese in 1641. Soon after that, the Dutch concluded a long war in Java by forcing upon the sultans a treaty that guaranteed a Dutch commercial monopoly in return for native political autonomy. Thereafter, however, Dutch plantation agriculture began undermining Indonesian economies. By the second half of the century, the Dutch had replaced the Muslims as the most powerful merchants in the region. From then on, Europe's demands for the spices and riches of the region would be satisfied by the merchants of Amsterdam. Later, the Dutch would take complete political control of Indonesia.

CONCLUSION

The years after the Mongol conquest of China, which had created a massive Eurasian commercial network, saw the development of diverse nations and cultures. Yet each was tied in some important ways to the others. In China, the tribute system tried to arrange states hierarchically by their proximity and conformity to China's Confucian order. The Confucian emphasis on hierarchy moderated by benevolence (see Chapter 2) was replicated in the obeisance of subordinate states in return for China's protection. The Ming rulers began by trying to expand the tribute system but ended up increasingly inward-directed. At the same time, the people of China began to lay claim to a national culture that defined their identity as Chinese.

In Korea, the Chosŏn dynasty rested under the immediate gaze of its immense neighbor and struggled, in the middle of the period, with calamitous foreign invasions. But, just as the Chinese during the Ming dynasty, the Korean people as a whole gradually laid claim to Korean culture. Japan was part of the East Asian commercial world but, unlike Korea, was only tangentially part of the China-centered tribute system, and even that

involvement continued for only part of the late medieval period. Japan was further differentiated from Korea and Vietnam by being relatively uninfluenced by Confucianism in this period; Buddhism dominated both the popular and the elite culture in medieval Japan.

Southeast Asia, both maritime and mainland, was part of international trading networks. These networks attracted many religions and cultures to the region. For hundreds of years, Southeast Asians have borrowed eclectically from many traditions, enhancing the multicultural nature of the region.

Suggestions for Web Browsing

You can obtain more information about topics included in this chapter at the websites listed below. See also the companion website that accompanies this text, **http://www.ablongman.com/ brummett,** which contains an online study guide and additional resources.

Imperial China: The Ming
http://www.fordham.edu/halsall/eastasia/eastasiasbook.html#I mperial%20China

Map and images pertaining to the Ming dynasty, 1368–1644; a part of the Internet East Asian History Sourcebook.

Chinese History
http://sun.sino.uni-heidelberg.de/igcs

Internet guide to Chinese studies covers all periods and all topics in Chinese history.

Japanese Samurai
http://www.samurai-archives.com

Extensive collection of biographies of important samurai and daimyō in medieval and early modern Japan.

Masterpieces of the Kyoto National Museum
http://www.kyohaku.go.jp/

Numerous images, with descriptions, of the artworks of Japan, Korea, and China.

History of Korea
http://www.lifeinkorea.com/Information/history1.cfm

Text and images documenting the Koryŏ and Chosŏn dynasties of Korea.

Literature and Film

An abridged version of the Chinese classic *Monkey, Journey to the West,* trans. David Kherdian (Shambhala, 2000), offers students a chance to think about Ming era popular beliefs**.** For a translation of *The Romance of the Three Kingdoms* see Moss Roberts, trans. *Three Kingdoms: A Historical Novel* (University of California Press, 1991).

Films include *China's Forbidden City,* produced for the History Channel, A&E TV Network (1997); *Rise of the Dragon: The Genius That Was China, Part One,* produced by John Merson and David Roberts (Coronet Film & Video, 1990); *Japan: Memoirs of a Secret Empire, The Way of the Samurai,* the first of a four-part series on the Tokugawa period produced by Lyn Goldfarb for PBS (2004).

Classic movies by some of Japan's premier filmmakers deal with the Warring States period. See, for example, *Kagemusha,* by Akira Kurosawa (20th Century Fox, 1980) and *Ugetsu Monogatari,* by Kenzo Mizoguchi (Daiei Studios, 1953).

Suggestions for Reading

Fine general histories of early modern China include Charles O. Hucker, *China's Imperial Past* (Stanford University Press, 1975), and the *Cambridge History of China*, Vol. 7 (Cambridge University Press, 1988) and Vol. 8 (Cambridge University Press, 1998), which cover the Ming. Ray Huang, *1587, A Year of No Significance* (Yale University Press, 1981), is noteworthy for its penetrating case study of late Ming weaknesses. For complete coverage of Chinese technology and engineering, see Joseph Needham, *Clerks and Craftsmen in China and the West* (Cambridge University Press, 1970). Dorothy Ko, *Teachers of the Inner Chambers* (Stanford University Press, 1994), is an excellent treatment of women.

On Korea, see Carter J. Eckert et al., *Korea Old and New* (Harvard University Press, 1990); Andrew C. Nahm, *Introduction to Korean History and Culture* (Holly International, 1993); and James Palais, *Politics and Policy in Traditional Korea* (Council of East Asian Studies, 1991). Yung-Chung Kim, *Women of Korea* (Ewha Women's University, 1982), provides a readable and informative treatment of women of the period.

A wealth of material on medieval and early modern Japan has come out in the last several decades. Among these fine studies are Conrad Totman, *Early Modern Japan* (University of California Press, 1993); Jeffrey P. Mass, *Origins of Japan's Medieval World* (Stanford University Press, 1997); Hitomi Tonomura, *Community and Commerce in Late Medieval Japan* (Stanford University Press, 1992); Andrew Goble, *Kenmu: Go-Daigo's Revolution* (Harvard University Press, 1996); and Hitomi Tonomura, Anne Walthall, and Wakita Haruko, eds., *Women and Class in Japanese History* (University of Michigan, 1999). These are also fine studies: John W. Hall et al., *Japan Before Tokugawa* (Yale University Press, 1981), and John W. Hall and Takeshi Toyoda, *Japan in the Muromachi Age* (Cornell University Press, 2001). Two excellent biographies that mirror the time are Mary Elizabeth Berry, *Hideyoshi* (Harvard University Press, 1989), and Conrad Totman, *Tokugawa Ieyasu: Shogun* (Heian International, 1983).

The most comprehensive treatment of Southeast Asia may be found in Nicholas Tarling, ed., *Cambridge History of Southeast Asia*, 2 Vols. (Cambridge University Press, 1992). Anthony Reid, *Southeast Asia in the Age of Commerce, 1450–1680* (Yale University Press, 1995), covers separate cultures and attempts a synthesis of the whole region in terms of commerce. Fine general works include D. R. Sardesai, *Southeast Asia: Past and Present* (Westview Press, 2003), and George Coedes, *The Making of Southeast Asia,* 2nd ed. (Allen & Unwin, 1983). Treatments of individual countries may be found in Michael Aung-Thwin, *Pagan: The Origins of Modern Burma* (University of Hawaii Press, 1985); David K. Wyatt, *Thailand: A Short History,* 2nd ed. (Yale University Press, 2003); David P. Chandler, *A History of Cambodia,* 3rd ed. (Westview, 2000); Barbara W. Andaya and Leonard Y. Andaya, eds., *A History of Malaysia,* 2nd ed. (Macmillan, 2000); and John David Legge, *Indonesia,* 3rd ed. (Prentice Hall, 1980). Barbara W. Andaya, *Other Pasts: Women, Gender and History in Early Modern Southeast Asia* (University of Hawaii Press, 2001) is excellent.

CHAPTER 14

European Cultural and Religious Transformations

The Renaissance and the Reformation 1300–1600

CHAPTER CONTENTS

E ach of the world's civilizations has had a moment when a combination of stability, wealth, and confidence allowed its thinkers, artists, and artisans to create expressions of that civilization's values which not only pleased their contemporaries, but served as models for future generations. These moments are sometimes called "Golden Ages." The two parts of the Han dynasty in China (206 B.C.E.–8 C.E. and 23 C.E.–228 C.E.); the Classical Mayan civilization in Mexico and Central America in the first millennium of the Common Era; the early part of the Tokugawa Shogunate in Japan in the sixteenth through the early eighteenth centuries; and in Africa Great Zimbabwe (1290–1410), the Swahili city-states on the east coast of the continent (fourteenth century), and Benin and Mali in the fourteen and fifteenth centuries: All set standards of excellence for their citizens.

In the Mediterranean world the Hellenic accomplishments in the middle part of the fifth century B.C.E., the Hellenistic variations on Hellenic themes to the end of the first century B.C.E., and the Roman and Byzantine consolidation and transmission of those intellectual and artistic qualities formed the classical basis of European civilization. That precious legacy was enriched by the magnificent accomplishments of the Islamic world from 900–1100. The work of Arab thinkers, artists, and scientists was transmitted through Spain and into Italy in translations to become part of the Western heritage.

In each of the Golden Ages cited above, there was a certain well-being in which philosophical and artistic creation took place. Yet this was not the case for the Italian and Northern Renaissance during the fifteenth and sixteenth century. This period of European history began in crisis: recession, famine, plague, and war; it ended amid similar crises: war, revolutionary economic change, and religious ferment. In spite of, but in part because of these crises, Europe during the centuries of Renaissance and Reformation developed the individualism that marked this Golden Age of European history.

1300

1300s Classical revival, humanism (Petrarch, Boccaccio)

1305–1377 Babylonian Captivity of the church; papacy under French influence

1320–1384 John Wycliffe

1348 Black Death begins to devastate Europe

1350

1378–1417 Great Schism of the Catholic Church

1400

1400s *Quattrocento*, Italian Renaissance (Ghiberti, Brunelleschi, Donatello, Masaccio, Piero della Francesca, Mantagna, Verrocchio, Botticelli)

1414 Council of Constance

1415 John Hus, Bohemian reformer, burned at the stake

1434–1494 Medici family rules Florence

1450

1450s Movable type used in printing

1453 Constantinople falls to Turks

1483–1546 Martin Luther

1500

c. 1500 Northern Renaissance begins (Erasmus, More, Rabelais, von Hutten, Montaigne, Cervantes, Shakespeare, van Eyck, Dürer, Bosch, Holbein, Brueghel)

c. 1500–1530 High Renaissance in Italy (Bramante, da Vinci, Raphael, Michelangelo, Castiglione)

1509–1564 John Calvin, leader of Reformation in Geneva

1517 Luther issues Ninety-Five Theses

1524–1525 German Peasant Revolt

1527 Sack of Rome; Venice becomes center of Renaissance art (Giogione, Titian)

1545–1563 Council of Trent

c. 1530–1600 Mannerist style popular (Tintoretto, Cellini)

SOCIAL UPHEAVAL

■ *What were the most significant reasons for the great social crises in European society in the fourteen and fifteenth centuries?*

The period from 1300 to 1600 in Europe was one of the most disruptive in its history. Among the most significant challenges to European stability were economic depression and the devastation caused by the **Bubonic Plague.** The combination of these two forces provoked an upheaval that changed European society.

Economic Depression and Bubonic Plague

In the three centuries preceding 1300, European agricultural methods had improved, crops were more productive, arable land increased, and the population probably doubled between 1000 and 1300. But the beginning of the fourteenth century saw changing weather patterns bringing drought, famine, and widespread starvation and unemployment. Overpopulation and unsanitary lifestyles contributed to the factors that rendered Europe more vulnerable to the plague which killed probably one-third of Europe's population—around 25 million people—between 1347 to 1350 and continued to reappear sporadically until the seventeenth century.

Called the Black Death because of the discoloring effects it had on the body (especially the lymph nodes), the plague was carried by fleas on infected rats and had worked its way through the trade routes of Asia and India to Europe. Cities were particularly devastated; Florence's population fell from 114,000 to 50,000, London's from 60,000 to 40,000. The outbreak of the Hundred Years' War between France and England in 1337 (see Chapter 15) added to the destruction in both those nations. The Black Death had a very significant formative effect on the development of European history.

Many looked for spiritual explanations for the plague's devastation: that God was punishing a sinful humanity, or perhaps that there was no God at all. Many blamed the Jews for the plague and sought their expulsion from cities throughout Europe. Others found their scapegoats for problems—ranging from the plague, crop failures, economic crises, and religious upheaval—in their searches for witches in the next two centuries. Over 100,000 of these unfor-

tunates were prosecuted during this period, and many were executed by strangling, drowning, burning, or beheading. Seventy percent of those killed were women, nearly half of whom were older single women or widows.

The Plague's Effect on European Society

By devastating the population of Europe, the Plague fundamentally changed the social patterns in Europe. A lack of rural workers effectively ended the remnants of the feudal structure in many places on the continent. Wage payments replaced the centuries-old payments in kind. In the cities in the late fourteenth and early fifteenth century, urban skilled craftsmen and the guilds that gave them security in an earlier age now became beneficiaries of higher prices paid for their goods, and their economic good fortune resulted in increased power and participation in urban politics. The church was also an economic beneficiary of the era; despite the decline of its revenues from its agricultural holdings, its wealth was vastly increased from donations and bequests from those wishing to increase their chances of a heavenly reward. But for those not in the guilds, life in the cities became increasingly difficult as the social problems of urban growth outran the resources of the Catholic Church to deal with them.

The beginning of the sixteenth century marked the beginning of another economic downturn that spread suffering throughout Europe. Economic dislocation accompanying the early development of capitalism added to the strains of transitioning between medieval and modern times, especially for the peasantry. The sixteenth century also marked the end of the relatively favorable situation women had enjoyed in the Middle Ages. The new emphasis on wage labor and competition from men limited their opportunities for outside work. Although women could find some part-time employment as field laborers, this paid very little.

A new global economy brought high rates of inflation and shifting trade routes. The decline of the importance of the Hanseatic League in the Baltic and North Seas, the Mediterranean, and the routes connecting the two hurt the economy of central Europe. Later, the shifting of work to laborers in the surrounding villages—the cottage industry—ruined many old guild industries while swelling the ranks of the urban unemployed. Large-market agriculture weakened the peasants' traditional rights, subjected them to rents beyond their resources, and drove them from the land into the towns, where they joined the idle and the impoverished.

Bubonic Plague—An infectious and usually fatal disease caused by the bacterium *Yersinia pestis*, which is carried and spread by the rat flea. Characteristics include high fever and swollen lymph nodes (buboes).

The poor and out-of-work often increasingly directed their anger against the Church because it was a visible source of authority, and it was rich. For society at large the profit motive overshadowed the church's canon law, which stressed compassion for the weak and the poor and a **"just price."**

In the midst of all of this economic and social upheaval, there began in Italy a cultural movement that touched only the elites but had consequences that would affect the development of Western civilization: It would come to be called the Renaissance, or the "rebirth."

"just price"—A medieval theory of economics supported by the Christian church. The church maintained that a just price should set the standards of fairness in all financial transactions. According to this theory, making interest on any loans was considered improper and labeled as *usury*.

THE ITALIAN RENAISSANCE

■ *Why is this period in Europe's history called a Renaissance—a "rebirth"?*

This cultural rebirth or Renaissance did not take place in a vacuum. Prior to the twelfth century, almost all learning in Europe was under the control of the church, and medieval art and literature reflected the church's influence. Latin was the European language of diplomacy, scholarship, and serious literature. But in the later medieval period the number of literate men and women in secular society began to increase, and the popularity of literature written in the vernacular, or commonly spoken languages of Europe, gained more and more popularity and acceptance, especially in the forms of poetry and song.

This map illustrates Europe in the time of the Italian and Northern Renaissance, as well as some of the cities that served as centers for artistic and humanist activities during the period.

Literary Precedents

DOCUMENT

Dante, *Divine Comedy*

Dante and Chaucer provided a bridge between the medieval and Renaissance worlds. Dante Alighieri (DAHN-teh ah-lig-hi-EH-ree; 1265–1321) was the author of the *Divine Comedy,* one of the great masterpieces of world literature. Combining a deep religious impulse with classical and medieval literature, Dante composed an allegory of medieval man (Dante) journeying through earthly existence (hell) through conversion (purgatory) to a spiritual union with God (paradise). Dante's work is regarded both as a culmination of the medieval intellectual tradition and at the same time as a composition of such unique brilliance that it should be considered one of the first creative works of the Renaissance.

Geoffrey Chaucer (c. 1340–1400), the author of *Canterbury Tales,* wrote an English vernacular account of the journey of 29 pilgrims to the shrine of St. Thomas á Becket at Canterbury. His personality profiles and stories satirized contemporary English customs and lifestyles, and his work solidly established the vernacular as a legitimate literary form of expression in England.

Another voice of the transition was one of the most gifted vernacular poets of the fourteenth century was a woman—Christine de Pizan (pi-ZAHN; 1365–c. 1430), who wrote to support her children after her husband's death. She authored more than ten volumes of poetry and prose, and her allegorical work—*The Book of the City of Ladies*—presented a defense of women's significance in society and a plea for greater compassion to their burdens.

The Italian Setting for the Development of Humanism

In Italy during the fourteenth century, a growing number of literate and artistic individuals began to call themselves *humanists*—citizens of a modern world that would perfect itself through the recovery, study, and transmission of the cultural heritage of Greece and Rome. They believed themselves to be the initiators of a new era—a renaissance (rebirth) of the culture and values of classical antiquity. But this culture historians call the Italian Renaissance did not come into being without tremendous influence from its medieval past—in fact, many historians consider the Renaissance to be more of a natural maturation of medieval society than a radical break with traditional culture. Yet most students of the period agree that the heritage of the past, in combination with a newly found passionate concern with Greece and Rome and emerging political and economic patterns, produced a distinctly different culture.

During the fourteenth and fifteenth centuries, after recovering from the effects of the Black Plague, the city-states of northern and central Italy experienced a tremendous growth in population and expanded to become small territorial states. Eventually five such states emerged: the duchy of Milan; the Papal States, in which the restored authority of the popes crushed the independence of many smaller city-states in central Italy; the republics of Florence and Venice; and the kingdom of Naples. Selling or leasing their country holdings, Italian nobles moved to the cities and joined with the rich merchants to form an urban ruling class. By 1300 nearly all the land of northern and central Italy was owned by profit-seeking urban citizens who produced their goods for city markets. In the large export industries, such as woolen cloth (the industry employed 30,000 in Florence), a capitalistic system of production, in which the merchants retained ownership of the raw material and paid others to finish the product, brought great profits. More great wealth was gained from commerce, particularly the import-export trade in luxury goods from the East.

So much wealth was accumulated by these merchant-capitalists that they turned to money-lending and banking. From the thirteenth to the fifteenth centuries, Italians monopolized European banking (Florence alone had 80 banking houses by 1300). These economic and political successes made the Italian upper-class groups strongly assertive, self-confident, and passionately attached to their city-states. Even literature and art reflected their self-confidence.

Political leaders and the wealthy merchants, bankers, and manufacturers conspicuously displayed their wealth and that of their cities by patronizing the arts and literature. Artists and scholars were provided with governmental, academic, and tutorial positions and enjoyed the security and protection offered by their patrons and the advantage of working exclusively on commission. Among the most famous patrons were members of the Medici family, who ruled Florence for 60 years (1434–1494). Renaissance popes were lavish patrons who made Rome the foremost center of art and learning by 1500.

Humanism and the Classical Revival: Petrarch and Boccacio

Historians are not able to agree on an exact meaning of the Renaissance term known as *humanism.* But they generally agree that humanism consisted of the study and popularization of the Greek and Latin classics and the culture those classics described. The humanists, students of the classics as well as advocates of the Roman concept of a liberal education (or *studia humanitatis*), promoted an education in "humanistic studies," but also advocated civic patriotism and social betterment.

Discovery Through Maps   The Lagoon of Venice

Maps can be designed to illustrate much more than merely the physical features of a geographical area. They may also be designed to serve as vehicles to enhance the image of a particular state—to serve as propaganda. For instance, examine this cartographic rendering of the Lagoon of Venice and the neighboring regions of Friulli and Istria, one of a series of magnificently designed maps painted by Ignazio Danti (1536–1586), a mathematician, astronomer, geographer, and Dominican priest and bishop—another example of the idealized "Renaissance man." Danti was commissioned by Pope Gregory XIII to make a number of maps of ancient and modern Italy, many of which are presently on display in the Vatican Museum in Rome. Danti's map of the Lagoon of Venice depicts an idealized land and seascape that features a bustling harbor, replete with sailing vessels both mythical and contemporary to the sixteenth century. Over the harbor the sun radiates its glory on the land and sea, and a formal inscription in Latin gives testimony to the ancient significance of the harbor and past glories.

The primary purpose of this map was certainly not to provide geographical assistance, but rather to promote the power and glory of the Republic of Venice. Such a map provided its observers with a sense of the historic significance of the Lagoon, its almost mythical role in the history of the Italian peninsula, and the opulence and splendor of one of the most significant republics of Renaissance Italy.

Questions to Consider

1. What seem to be the most significant features emphasized in this map of the Lagoon of Venice? Why does the artist appear to focus most of his attention on the sea rather than the land itself?

2. What effects do you think this map would have had on its viewers in the sixteenth century? What impressions do you believe Danti wanted to impart to his contemporaries who studied this map?

3. Why do you think Danti portrayed such a variety of vessels from different eras and subjects drawn from both pagan mythology and Christian tradition in the harbor?

The classic example of the Renaissance nobleman, statesman, and patron of the arts was the Florentine Lorenzo de' Medici, known as Lorenzo the Magnificent. Under his patronage and guidance, Florence became the leading city of the Italian Renaissance, renowned for the splendor of its buildings and lavish support for the arts.

The humanists were also the founders of modern historical research and linguistics. Humanism was not an anti-Christian movement, and most humanists remained religious, but the church bureaucracy and the extreme authority claimed by the popes received their strongest criticism.

"Father of humanism" is a title given to Francesco Petrarca (frahn-CHEHS-koh peh-TRAHR-kah), better known as Petrarch (1304–1374), by later Italian

DOCUMENT

Petrarch,
*Letter to
Cicero*

humanists because he was the first to play a major role in making people conscious of the attractions of classical literature. He wrote Latin epic poetry and biography in addition to his famous and innovative love sonnets to a married woman named Laura, whom Petrarch admired romantically. Petrarch's works held to his Christian values, but displayed much more of a secular orientation and an involvement with the society and social issues of the day.

Another celebrated early humanist was the Florentine Giovanni Boccaccio (gee-oh-VAH-nee boh-KAH-chee-oh; 1313–1375), a student and friend of Petrarch's who began his career as a writer of poetry and romances. But his masterpiece was the *Decameron*, a collection of one hundred stories told by three young men and seven young women, as they sought to avoid the Black Plague in the seclusion of a country villa. The *Decameron* offers a wealth of anecdotes, portraits of flesh-and-blood characters, and vivid glimpses of Renaissance life.

The *Decameron* was both the high point and the end of Boccaccio's career as a creative artist. Largely through the influence of Petrarch, whom he met in 1350, Boccaccio gave up writing in Italian and turned to the study of antiquity. He began to learn Greek, composed an encyclopedia of classical mythology, and visited monasteries in search of manuscripts. By the time Petrarch and Boccaccio died, the study of the literature and learning of antiquity was growing throughout Italy.

Classical Revival and Philosophy

The recovery and assimilation of Greek and Roman learning was a consuming passion of the humanists. The search for manuscripts became a mania, and before the middle of the fifteenth century, original works, unedited by the church, of most of the important Latin authors had been found. In addition to these Latin works, precious Greek manuscripts were brought to Italy from Constantinople after it fell to the Turks in 1453, and many Greek scholars were welcomed to Italy, in particular to Florence, where the Medici gave their support to a gathering of Florentine

A miniature portrait of Petrarch from his illuminated manuscript of Remedies Against Fortune. *In keeping with a classical tradition, Petrarch composed many letters—which he edited for publication—that were in effect literary essays expressing his own attitudes and humanistic concerns.*

humanists which came to be called the Academy. Under the leadership of the humanists Marsilio Ficino (mar-SEE-lee-oh fee-CHEE-noh) (1433–1499) and Pico della Mirandola (PEE-koh de-lah mee-RAHN-doh-lah; 1463–1494), the Academy focused its study on the works of Plato, and placed particular emphasis on Plato's admiration of human reason and free will. The influence of Aristotle still remained strong among Scholastic thinkers during the Renaissance, especially at the University of Padua, where the study of natural science, logic, and metaphysics continued to be emphasized. Scholasticism was the dominant school of thought in the West from the ninth through seventeenth centuries, drawing its inspiration from Aristotle, St. Augustine, and the declared truths of the church (see Chapter 9).

A growing number of women were well educated, read the classics, and wrote during the Renaissance.

Document ▬ Machiavelli, *The Prince:* On Cruelty and Mercy

Niccoló Machiavelli, born into an impoverished branch of a noble family of Florence, began his pubic life as a diplomat in the service of the Florentine republic. When the Medici family returned to dominate Florence in 1512, Machiavelli was imprisoned and tortured for his supposed plot against the Medici family. He then retired to the countryside to write his most famous works. Machiavelli's best known work is *The Prince* (1532), which presents a description of how a prince might best gain control and maintain power. His ideal prince is calculating and ruthless in his quest to best those who would destroy him in his effort to establish a unified Italian state. The following excerpts from this famous work describe how a prince must decide how, when, and if a prince should use cruelty or mercy to accomplish his aims:

From this arises an argument: whether it is better to be loved than to be feared, or the contrary. I reply that one should like to be both one and the other: but since it is difficult to join them together, it is much safer to be feared than to be loved when one of the two must be lacking. For one can generally say that about men: that they are ungrateful, fickle, simulators and deceivers, avoiders of danger, greedy for gain; and while you work for their good they are completely yours, offering you their blood, their property, their lives, and their sons, as I said earlier, when danger is far away; but when it comes nearer to you they turn away. And that prince who bases his power entirely on their works, finding himself stripped of other preparations, comes to ruin; for friendships that are acquired by a price and not by greatness and nobility of character are purchases but are not owned, and at the proper moment they cannot be spent. And men are less hesitant about harming someone who makes himself loved than one who makes himself feared because love is held together by a chain of obligation which, since men are a sorry lot, is broken on every occasion in which their own self-interest is concerned; but fear is held together by a dread of punishment which will never abandon you.

A prince must nevertheless make himself feared in such a manner that he will avoid hatred, even if he does not acquire love: since to be feared and not hated can very well be combined; and this will always be so when he keeps his hands off the property and the women of his citizens and his subjects. And if he must take someone's life, he should do so when there is proper justification and manifest cause; but, above all, he should avoid the property of others; for men forget more quickly the death of their father than the loss of their patrimony. Moreover, the reasons for seizing their property are never lacking; and he who begins to live by stealing always finds a reason for taking what belongs to others; on the contrary, reasons for taking a life are rarer and disappear sooner. . . . I conclude, therefore, returning to the problem of being feared and loved, that since men love at their own pleasure and fear at the pleasure of the prince, a wise prince should build his foundation upon that which belongs to him, and not upon that which belongs to others: he must strive only to avoid hatred, as has been said.

Questions to Consider

1. Comment on Machiavelli's speculations about the nature of man, and the ways in which a prince should capitalize on the reality of human character as he analyses it. Is he overly cynical, or is he a realist?

2. Does Machiavelli's advice seem out of date given the realities of politics and the quest for power in the modern world?

3. What principles of conduct does Machiavelli advise a prince to cultivate? Is his prince a complete despot, or a more crafty and manipulative, yet ethical, student of man's nature?

From Peter Bondanella and Mark Musa, eds., *The Portable Machiavelli* (New York: Viking Press, 1979), pp. 135–136.

Most of these women were daughters or wives of wealthy aristocrats who could afford private tutoring in liberal studies, since the universities were for the most part still inaccessible to females. But in the works of most humanists—echoing their classical precedents—there is little that supports the participation of women on equal footing with males in scholarly or civic activities. Some historians even maintain that Renaissance women were more restricted in their intellectual pursuits than they had been in the late Middle Ages. Still, some noble women gained great reputation and respect for their political wisdom and intelligence. Battista Sforza (SFOHR-zah), wife of the Duke of Urbino in the fifteenth century, was well known for her knowledge of Greek and Latin and admired for her ability to govern in the absence of her husband. Her contemporary, Isabella d'Este, wife of the Duke of Mantua, was renowned for her education and support of the arts, and for assembling one of the finest libraries in Italy.

ITALIAN RENAISSANCE ART

■ *How did Italian Renaissance artists differ from their medieval predecessors?*

Fourteenth- and fifteenth-century Italy produced innovations in art that culminated in the classic High Renaissance artistic style of the early sixteenth century. These innovations were the products of a new

Major Artists of the Italian Renaissance and Their Works

c. 1266–1337	Giotto: *Life of the Virgin, Life of St. Francis, Life of St. John the Baptist*
1401–1428	Masaccio: *Tribute Money, Trinity, St. Peter*
1447–1510	Botticelli: *Judith and Holofernes, St. Sebastian, The Birth of Venus*
1452–1519	Da Vinci: *Adoration of the Magi, The Last Supper, La Gioconda* (Mona Lisa)
1475–1564	Michelangelo: Ceiling of the Sistine Chapel, *Moses, Pietá, David*
c. 1477–1576	Titian: *The Venus of Zerbine, The Allegory of Marriage, Venus and Adonis*

Giotto, St. Francis Receiving the Stigmata *(c. 1295). Both a painter and architect, Giotto is credited as the first great genius of Italian Renaissance art. Like his medieval predecessors, his subjects were mainly religious, but his human subjects were portrayed as full of life and emotion. One of his favorite subjects was St. Francis of Assisi, who here receives the wounds of Jesus's crucifixion—the stigmata.*

society centered in rich cities, the humanistic and more secular spirit of the times, a revived interest in the classical art of Greece and Rome, and the creativity of some of the world's most gifted artists.

From Giotto to Donatello

The new approach in painting was first evident in the work of the Florentine painter Giotto (JOT-toh; c. 1266–1337). Earlier Italian painters had copied the stylized, flat, and rigid images of Byzantine paintings and mosaics, Giotto observed from life and painted a three-dimensional world peopled with believable human beings moved by deep emotion. He humanized painting much as Petrarch humanized thought and St. Francis, whose life was one of his favorite subjects, humanized religion. Giotto initiated a new epoch in the history of painting, one that expressed the religious piety of his lay patrons, but also their delight in the images of everyday life.

Masaccio, Expulsion from Eden. *Masaccio's mastery of perspective creates the illusion of movement as the angel drives Adam and Eve from Paradise.*

In his brief lifetime the Florentine Masaccio (mah-SAH-chee-oh; 1401–1428) completed the revolution in technique begun by Giotto. As can be seen in his few surviving paintings, Masaccio was concerned with the problems of perspective, and the modeling of figures in light and shade (*chiaroscuro;* CHAH-roh-SKOO-roh). He was also the first Renaissance artist to paint nude figures (Adam and Eve, in his *Expulsion from Eden*), reversing the tradition of earlier Christian art.

Inspired by Masaccio's achievement, most *quattrocento* (quah-troh-CHEN-toh; Italian for "the 1400s" or "fifteenth century") painters constantly sought to improve technique. But the Florentine Sandro Botticelli (sahn-DROH boh-tah-CHEH-lee; 1447–1510) proceeded in a different direction, abandoning the techniques of straightforward representation of people and objects and trying instead to inspire the viewer's imagination and emotion through close attention to strikingly beautiful portraiture and decorative backdrop landscapes.

New directions were also being taken in sculpture, and it, like painting, reached stylistic maturity at the beginning of the *quattrocento*. The Florentine Donatello (1386–1466) produced truly freestanding statues based on the realization of the human body as a coordinated mechanism of bones and muscles; his *David* was the first bronze nude made since antiquity.

Botticelli, The Birth of Venus. *The last great Florentine painter of the early Renaissance, Botticelli did most of his best work for Lorenzo de' Medici and his court. In* The Birth of Venus, *Botticelli blends ancient mythology, Christian faith, and voluptuous representation.*

The High Renaissance, 1500–1530: Leonardo da Vinci, Raphael, and Michelangelo

The painters of the High Renaissance had learned the solutions to such technical problems as perspective space from the *quattrocento* artists. The artists of the earlier period had been concerned with movement, color, and narrative detail, but painters in the High Renaissance attempted to eliminate nonessentials and concentrated on the central theme of a picture and its basic human implications.

The three greatest High Renaissance painters were Leonardo da Vinci, Raphael, and Michelangelo. Leonardo da Vinci (1452–1519) was brilliant in a variety of fields: engineering, mathematics, architecture, geology, botany, physiology, anatomy, sculpture, painting, music, and poetry. Because he loved the process of experimentation more than seeing all his projects through to completion, few of the projects da Vinci started were ever finished. He was a master of soft modeling in light and shade and of creating

groups of figures perfectly balanced in a given space. One of his most famous paintings is *La Gioconda*, known as the Mona Lisa, a portrait of a woman whose enigmatic smile captures an air of tenderness and humility. Another is *The Last Supper*, which he painted on the walls of the refectory of Santa Maria delle Grazie in Milan. In this painting da Vinci experimented with the use of an oil medium combined with plaster, which unfortunately was unsuccessful. The painting quickly began to disintegrate and has been restored several times.

Raphael (1483–1520) was summoned to Rome in 1508 by Pope Julius II to aid in the decoration of the Vatican. His **frescos** there display a magnificent blending of classical and Christian subject matter and are the fruit of careful planning and immense artistic

---

fresco—A type of wall painting in which water-based pigments are applied to wet, freshly laid lime plaster. The dry-powder colors, when mixed with water, penetrate the surface and become a permanent part of the wall. The Italian Renaissance was the greatest period of fresco painting.

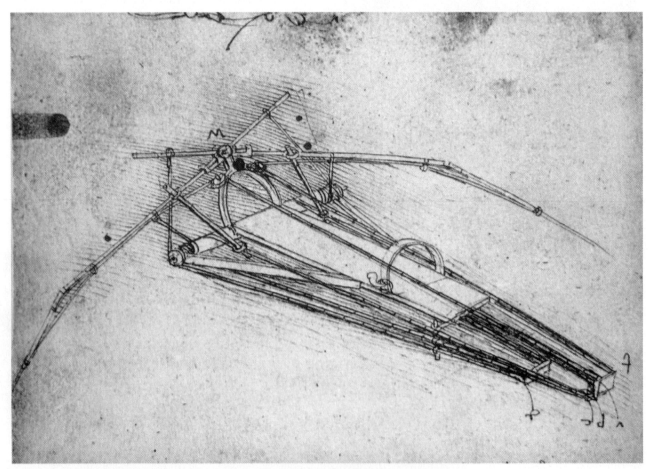

Leonardo da Vinci, Drawing of a Flying Machine. *One of the artist's later designs for a flying machine, which modern engineers speculate could have worked, although it was much too heavy. Da Vinci was convinced that a successful flying machine had to be modeled after the wings of bats and birds, as his numerous sketches of these animals show.*

knowledge. Critics consider him the master of perfect design and balanced composition.

The individualism and idealism of the High Renaissance have no greater representative than Michelangelo Buonarroti (MEE-kel-AHN-je-loh boo-na-ROH-ti; 1475–1564). Stories of this stormy and temperamental personality have helped shape our definition of a genius. His great energy enabled him to paint for Julius II in four years the entire ceiling of the Vatican's Sistine Chapel, an area of several thousand square yards, and his art embodies a superhuman ideal. With his unrivaled genius for rendering the

Raphael, Madonna of the Meadow *(c. 1505/1506). Raphael's painting in oil on canvas is a classic example of a composition based on the figure of a pyramid. The scene is formally balanced yet features the interaction of the figures. The infants portrayed are John the Baptist (left) and Jesus.*

High Renaissance art, Mannerist artists sought to express their own inner vision in a manner that evoked shock in the viewer. Typical are the paintings of Parmigianino (par-me-zhian-NI-no), whose *Madonna with the Long Neck* (1535) purposely shows no logic of structure.

THE NORTHERN RENAISSANCE

■ *How did the Northern Renaissance differ from the Italian Renaissance?*

The Italian Renaissance, by seeking meaning in the classical world, had placed human beings once more in the center of life's stage and infused thought and art with humanistic values. These stimulating ideas spread north to inspire other humanists, who absorbed and adapted the Italian achievement to their own particular national circumstances.

Throughout the fifteenth century, hundreds of northern European students studied in Italy. Though their chief interest was the study of law and medicine, many were influenced by the intellectual climate of Italy with its new enthusiasm for the classics. When these students returned home, they often carried manuscripts—and later printed editions—produced by classical and humanist writers. Both literate laymen and devout clergy in the north were ready to welcome the new outlook of humanism, although these north-

Michelangelo, David. *To Michelangelo, the Florentine painter, sculptor, poet, and architect, sculpture was the noblest of the arts. The large marble statue of the biblical David was commissioned in 1501 to stand in Florence as a symbol of the city, its government, and its culture.*

human form, he devised a wealth of expressive positions and attitudes for his figures in scenes from Genesis. Michelangelo also excelled as poet, engineer, and architect and was undoubtedly the greatest sculptor of the Renaissance. The glorification of the human body was Michelangelo's great achievement. His statue of *David*, commissioned in 1501 when he was 26, expressed his idealized view of human dignity and majesty. He also became chief architect of St. Peter's in 1546, designed the great dome, and was still actively creative as a sculptor when he died, almost in his ninetieth year, in 1564.

From about 1530 to the end of the sixteenth century, Italian artists responded to the stresses of the age in a new style called *Mannerism*. Consciously revolting against the classical balance and simplicity of

Cellini, Saltcellar of Francis I. *The utilitarian purpose of the condiment dish is subordinate to its lavish decoration. Neptune, god of the sea, guards the boat-shaped salt container while a personification of Earth watches over the pepper. Figures around the base represent the four seasons and the four parts of the day. The intricacy of the design is a showcase for the sculptor's virtuosity.*

and new ideas reached a thousand times more people in a relatively short span of time. In the quickening of Europe's intellectual life, it is difficult to overestimate the effects of the printing press.

Major Figures in the Northern Renaissance and Their Works	
c. 1395–1441	Jan van Eyck (painter): *Man with the Red Turban, Wedding Portrait*
c. 1466–1536	Desiderius Erasmus (humanist and scholar): *The Praise of Folly, Handbook of the Christian Knight*
1471–1528	Albrecht Dürer (painter): *Adam and Eve, The Four Apostles, Self-Portrait*
1478–1535	Sir Thomas More (humanist and diplomat): *Utopia*
c. 1483–1553	François Rabelais (writer): *Gargantua and Pantagruel*
1488–1523	Ulrich von Hutten (humanist and poet)
1547–1616	Miguel de Cervantes (writer): *Don Quixote*
1564–1616	William Shakespeare (playwright and poet): *Julius Caesar, Romeo and Juliet, King Lear*

Humanism in France, Germany, Spain, and England

One of the best-known French humanists was François Rabelais (frahn-SWAH RAH-be-lay; c. 1483–1553), who is best remembered for his novel *Gargantua and Pantagruel.* Centering on figures from French folklore, this work relates the adventures of Gargantua and his son Pantagruel, genial giants of tremendous stature and appetite. Rabelais satirized his society while putting forth his humanist views on educational reform and inherent human goodness. He made powerful attacks on the abuses of the church and the

ern humanists were more interested in religious reform than their Italian counterparts.

The Influence of Printing

Very important in the diffusion of the Renaissance and later in the success of the Reformation was the invention of printing with movable type in Europe. The essential elements—paper and block printing—had been known in China since the eighth century. During the twelfth century, the Spanish Muslims introduced papermaking to Europe; in the thirteenth, Europeans, in close contact with China (see Chapter 10), brought knowledge of block printing to the West. The crucial step was taken in the 1440s at Mainz, Germany, where Johann Gutenberg (YOH-hahn GOOT-en-berg) and other printers invented movable type by cutting up old printing blocks to form individual letters. Gutenberg used movable type for papal documents and for the first printed version of the Bible (1454).

Soon all the major countries of Europe possessed the means for printing books. Throughout Europe, the price of books sank to one-eighth of their former cost and came within the reach of many people who formerly had been unable to buy them. In addition, pamphlets and controversial tracts soon began to circulate,

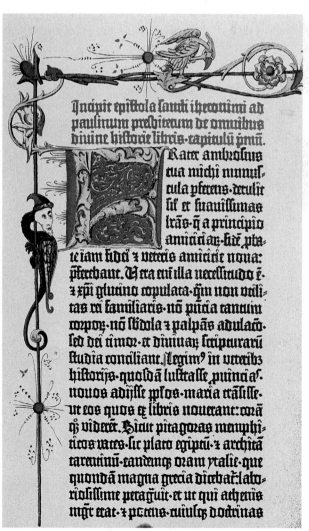

Facsimile copy of a page from the Gutenberg Bible, the Book of Genesis. With the development of printing, learning was no longer the private domain of the church and those few persons wealthy enough to own hand-copied volumes.

hypocrisy and repression he found in contemporary political and religious practice.

Another notable northern humanist was the French skeptic Michel de Montaigne (mee-SHEL de mohn-TANYE; 1533–1592). At age 38, he gave up the practice of law and retired to his country estate and well-stocked library, where he studied and wrote. Montaigne developed a new literary form and gave it its name—the *essay*. In 94 essays he set forth his personal views on many subjects: leisure, friendship, education, philosophy, religion, old age, death. He advocated open-mindedness and tolerance—rare qualities in the sixteenth century, when France was racked by religious and civil strife.

DOCUMENT

Montaigne, *Essays*

One of the most outstanding German humanists was Ulrich von Hutten (HOO-ten; 1488–1523). His idealism combined a zeal for religious reform and German nationalist feelings. This member of an aristocratic family, who wanted to unite Germany under the emperor, supported Martin Luther as a rallying point for German unity against the papacy, to which he attributed most of his country's ills.

In the national literatures that matured during the northern Renaissance, the transition from feudal knight to Renaissance courtier finds its greatest literary expression in a masterpiece of Spanish satire, *Don Quixote de la Mancha*, the work of Miguel de Cervantes (1547–1616). By Cervantes's time, knighthood and ideals of chivalry had become archaic in a world of practical concerns. Cervantes describes the adventures of Don Quixote (ki-HOH-te), a knight who is a representative of an earlier age. Don Quixote appears to be ridiculous old man who desires the great days of the past and has a series of misadventures in his attempts to recapture past glories. But Cervantes's real objective was to expose the inadequacies of chivalric idealism in a world that had acquired new and intensely practical aims. He did so by creating a sad but appealing character to serve as the personification of an outmoded way of life.

The reign of Queen Elizabeth I (1558–1603) was the high point of the English Renaissance and produced an astonishing number of gifted writers. Strongly influenced by the royal court, which served as the busy center of intellectual and artistic life, these writers produced works that were intensely emotional, richly romantic, and often wildly creative in combination with traditional poetic allusions to classical times.

The dominant figure in Elizabethan literature is William Shakespeare (1564–1616). His rich vocabulary and poetic imagery were matched by his turbulent imagination. He was a superb lyric poet, and numerous critics have judged him the foremost sonnet writer in the English language.

Shakespeare wrote 37 plays—comedies, histories, tragedies, and romances. His historical plays reflected the patriotic upsurge experienced by the English after the defeat of the Spanish Armada in 1588. For his comedies, tragedies, and romances, Shakespeare was content, in a great majority of cases, to borrow plots from earlier works. His great strength lay in his creation of characters and in his ability to translate his knowledge of human nature into dramatic speech and action. Today his comedies still play to enthusiastic audiences, but it is in his

Michel de Montaigne, author of the Essays. *Montaigne retired from the business world while in his thirties to reflect on and write about humanity's problems.*

tragedies that the poet-dramatist runs the gamut of human emotion and experience.

Shakespeare possessed in abundance the Renaissance concern for human beings and the world around them. His plays deal first and foremost with the human personality, passions, and problems.

Northern Painting

Before the Italian Renaissance began to influence the artistic circles of northern Europe, the painters of the Low Countries—modern Belgium, Luxembourg, and the Netherlands—had been making significant advances on their own. Outstanding was the Fleming Jan van Eyck (YAHN van AIK; c. 1395–1441), who painted in the realistic manner developed by medieval miniaturists. Van Eyck also perfected the technique of oil painting, which enabled him to paint with greater realism and attention to detail. In his painting of the merchant Arnolfini and his wife, for example, he painstakingly gives extraordinary reality to every detail, from his own image reflected in the mirror in the background to individual hairs on the little dog in the foreground.

The first German painter to be influenced deeply by Italian art was Albrecht Dürer (1471–1528) of Nuremberg. Dürer made several journeys to Italy, where he was impressed both with the painting of the Renaissance Italians and with the artists' high social status— a contrast with northern Europe, where artists were still treated as craftsmen, not men of genius. His own work is a blend of the old and the new and fuses the realism and symbolism of Gothic art with the style and passion of the Italian artists. In his own lifetime and after, Dürer became better known for his numerous engravings and woodcuts, produced for a mass market, than for his paintings.

Another famous German painter, Hans Holbein the Younger (1497–1543), chiefly painted portraits and worked abroad, especially in England. His memorable portraits blend the realism and concern for detail characteristic of all northern painting with Italian dignity.

Two northern painters who remained completely isolated from Italian influences were Hieronymus Bosch (hai-ROH-ni-muhs BAHSH; 1480–1516) and Pieter Brueghel (BROI-gel) the Elder (c. 1525–1569).

Jan van Eyck, Wedding Portrait. *The painting of a merchant named Arnolfini and his pregnant bride is extraordinary for its meticulously rendered realistic detail. Van Eyck painted exactly what he saw— he "was there," as his signature on the painting says (Johannes de Eyck fuit hic). The painting is also filled with symbolism; the dog, for instance, stands for marital fidelity.*

Jan van Eyck, *The Wedding Portrait*, 1434. NG 186. © National Gallery, London.

Hieronymous Bosch, Hell, *from* The Garden of Earthly Delights *(1503/1504). Part of a three-paneled altarpiece (a triptych) depicting the dreams that affect people in a pleasure-seeking world. The panel pictured here displays the horrors that await those sent to hell, where they spend their days tortured by half-human monsters, devils, and demons in a fantastic landscape.*

Brueghel retained a strong Flemish flavor in his portrayal of the faces and scenes of his native land. He painted village squares, landscapes, skating scenes, and peasants at work and at leisure just as he saw them, with an expert eye for detail.

Very little is known about the Dutch master Bosch other than that he belonged to one of the many puritanical religious sects that were becoming popular at the time. This accounts for his most famous painting, *The Garden of Delights*, a triptych whose main panel is filled with large numbers of naked men and women partaking in the sins of the flesh. The smaller left panel, by contrast, depicts an idealized Garden of Eden, while the right panel portrays a nightmarish hell filled with desperate sinners undergoing punishment. Bosch was a stern moralist whose obsession with sin and hell reflects the fears of many of his contemporaries—concerns that contributed to the religious movement known as the Reformation.

Erasmus, Thomas More, and Northern Humanism

The most influential of the northern humanists was Desiderius Erasmus (c. 1466–1536). Dutch by birth, he passed most of his long life elsewhere—in Germany, France, England, Italy, and especially Switzerland. He corresponded with nearly every prominent writer and thinker in Europe and personally knew popes, emperors, and kings. He was *the* scholar of Europe, and his writings and translations of the classics, and the works of the church fathers, as well as a new Latin translation of the New Testament, were eagerly read everywhere.

Perhaps the most famous and influential work by Erasmus was *The Praise of Folly*, a satire written in 1511 at the house of the English humanist Sir Thomas More. This influential work poked fun at and ridiculed a broad range of political, social, economic and religious evils of the day. Erasmus' scholarship and the objects of his literary attention typify the central concerns of the northern humanists. They were interested not only in the classics, but in the Bible and early Christian writings. Their primary focus of reform was not civil society and the state, but morality and a return to the simplicity of early Christianity.

The most significant figure in English humanism was Sir Thomas More (1478–1535), a good friend of Erasmus. More is best known for his *Utopia*, the first important description of an ideal state since Plato's *Republic*. In this work, More criticized his age through his portrayal of a fictitious sailor who contrasts the ideal

DOCUMENT

More, *Utopia*

Portrait of Erasmus *by Hans Holbein the Younger. Erasmus's scholarly achievements include a Greek edition of the New Testament and editions of the writings of St. Jerome and other early church fathers. Erasmus is best known, however, for his popular works, especially* The Praise of Folly.

life he has seen in Utopia (the "Land of Nowhere") with the harsh conditions of life in England. In Utopia, the evils brought on by political and social injustice were overcome by the holding of all property and goods in common. More's economic outlook was a legacy from the Middle Ages, and his preference for medieval collectivism over modern economic individualism was consistent with his preference for a church headed, in medieval style, by popes rather than by kings. This view prompted Henry VIII, who had appropriated the pope's position as head of the Church of England, to execute More, who had been one of Henry's most trusted advisers and officials, for treason.

Erasmus and More transmitted humanist values and research skills throughout Northern Europe. Through their writings they contributed to the increasing demand for reform of the Catholic Church: However, neither man sought the breakup of the church. In some places, such as Spain, the new humanistic linguistic and research skills were used to produce

the Complutensian Bible between 1502–1517, under the supervision of Cardinal Ximenes (HE-men-es). Similar texts in Greek, Latin, and Hebrew were printed on the same page for most of the books of the Bible to assure a proper translation of scripture. In other places, humanism's questioning of authoritative documents, such as Lorenzo da Valla's linguistic research that indicated that the Donation of Constantine was a forgery, emboldened critics of the church to press their case for change. Unfortunately for the church, it went through one of its most stormy periods between 1300 and 1500, and there was much to criticize.

THE CRISIS IN THE CATHOLIC CHURCH: 1300–1517

■ *What factors led to the erosion of church authority from 1300 to 1517?*

The power of the medieval papacy reached its height during the pontificate of Innocent III (1198–1216), who exerted his influence over kings and princes without serious challenge. The church seemed unrivaled in its prestige, dignity, and power. Yet that dominance was challenged on several fronts, and over the next two centuries, the power of the medieval church was diminished and transformed.

Religious Diversity in the Western World

Boniface VIII

Papal power was threatened by the growth of nation-states, whose monarchs challenged the church's temporal power, the papal bureaucracy's maintenance of a separate judicial structure for those under the pope's authority, and the privilege to collect **tithes** destined for Rome. In addition, the papacy became regularly criticized by reformers who questioned the legitimacy of papal authority and its secular power in place of the biblical example of simplicity and otherworldliness in matters of belief. The bourgeoisie, the middle-class workers and craftsmen of the towns whose attitudes were much more pragmatic than those of the rural peasantry of an earlier age, fostered an outlook of growing skepticism, national patriotism, and religious self-reliance.

---

tithes—Contribution of a tenth of one's income to the Church. Tithing dates to the Old Testament and was adopted by the Western Christian church in the sixth century and enforced in Europe by secular law from the eighth century.

Pope Boniface VIII (1294–1303) was an outspoken advocate of papal authority and a strident opponent of any monarch who dared to attempt to tax the church without papal consent. The powerful and popular kings of England, Edward I, and France, Philip IV the Fair, attempted to tax the church and limit the authority of papal courts, and in response Boniface boldly declared in the papal bull *Unam Sanctam* (OO-nam SANK-tam; 1302) that all temporal matters, and even rulers, were ultimately subject to the spiritual power wielded by the pope. Philip demanded that the pope be brought to trial by a general church council. In 1303 French officials and their allies broke into Boniface's summer home at Anagni, roughed the old man up, and attempted to arrest him and take him to France to stand trial, but the pope was rescued by his supporters. Boniface died a month later, perhaps from the shock and physical abuse he suffered during the attack.

DOCUMENT
Boniface VIII, *Unam Sanctum*

CASE STUDY
Role and Authority of the Pope

The Avignon Papacy

Philip's success was as complete as if Boniface had actually been dragged before the king to stand trial. Two years after Boniface's death, a French archbishop was chosen pope; he never went to Rome but instead moved the papal headquarters to Avignon (AH-vin-yahn), a city on the southern border of France, on land technically owned by the papacy, but where the popes and the papal court remained under strong French influence from 1305 to 1377. During this Avignon papacy, also called the Babylonian Captivity of the church, papal prestige suffered enormously. Most Europeans believed that Rome was the only proper capital for the church. Moreover, the English, Germans, and Italians accused the popes and the cardinals, the majority of whom now were also French, of being instruments of the French king.

The Avignon papacy also gave credence to critics who attacked the fiscal and moral corruption of the church bureaucracy and the very obvious lack of spiritual dedication of the Avignon popes. Increasing their demands for income from England, Germany, and Italy and living in splendor in a newly built fortress-palace, the Avignon popes expanded the papal bureaucracy, added new church taxes, and collected the old taxes more efficiently. These actions provoked denunciation of the wealth of the church and a demand for its reform.

Wycliffe and Hus

With the abuses of the church at Avignon all too obvious, reformers began to call for not only an end to cor-

ruption, but change in church teaching and structure. In England, a professor of philosophy and theology at Oxford, John Wycliffe (WIK-lif; c. 1320–1384), attacked not only church abuses but also certain of the church's doctrines. He also worked for the English royal government of Richard II as a cleric attached to foreign missions and was employed to write pamphlets justifying the Crown's seizure of Church property.

Wycliffe was strongly influenced by the writings of St. Augustine and emphasized the primacy of the Bible in the life of a Christian. He believed that God directly touched each person and that the role of the popes was of minor importance. In fact, he asserted, the kings had a higher claim on their subjects' loyalty, and the monarchs themselves were accountable only to God, not the pope. Wycliffe believed that the church is the community of believers, and not the Catholic hierarchy. He even went so far as to question the validity of some of the sacraments. Toward the end of his life, the Roman Church launched a counterattack, and after his death he was declared a heretic. In 1428 his remains were taken from consecrated ground and burned, and his ashes were thrown into a river. In the church's eyes, this act condemned his soul to perpetual wandering and suffering and destroyed the possibility that Wycliffe's followers could preserve any parts of his body as relics. But the influence of his writings took root in England through a group he helped organize called the "poor priests," later known as the Lollards, who were likewise condemned and outlawed, but they continued an underground church that surfaced in the sixteenth century.

In Bohemia, where a strong reform movement linked with the resentment of the Czechs toward their German overlords was under way, Wycliffe's opinions were popularized by Czech students who had studied with him at Oxford. In particular, his beliefs influenced John Hus (c. 1369–1415), a teacher in Prague and later rector of the university there. Hus's attacks on the abuses of clerical power led him to conclude that the true church was composed of a universal priesthood of believers and that Christ alone was its head. In 1402, after becoming the dominant figure at his university, he started to give sermons in the Czech language that soon attracted congregations as large as 3000 people. He preached that the Bible is the only source of faith and that every person has the right to read it in his own language. Like Wycliffe, Hus preached against clerical abuses and the claim of the church to guarantee salvation. This message became more explosive because it was linked with his criticism of the excesses of the German-dominated church at a time of a growing Czech nationalist movement.

In his preaching he openly acknowledged his debt to Wycliffe and refused to join in condemning him in

1410. Hus was later excommunicated and called to account for himself at the Council of Constance in 1415. Even though he had been given the assurance of safe passage, he was seized and burned at the stake as a heretic, and his ashes were thrown into the Rhine. His death led to the Hussite wars (1419–1437), in which the Czechs withstood a series of crusades against them. They maintained their religious reforms until their defeat by the Habsburgs in the Thirty Years' War.

The Great Schism of the Roman Catholic Church

In response to pressure from churchmen, rulers, scholars, and commoners throughout Europe, the papacy returned to Rome in 1377, it seemed for a time that its credibility would be regained. However, the reverse proved true. In the papal election held the following year, the **College of Cardinals** elected an Italian pope. A few months later the French cardinals declared the election invalid and elected a French pope, who returned to Avignon. During the Great **Schism** (1378–1417), as the split of the church into two allegiances was called, there were two popes, each with his college of cardinals and capital city, each claiming complete authority, each sending out papal administrators and collecting taxes, and each excommunicating the other. The nations of Europe gave allegiance as their individual political interests influenced them.

The Great Schism continued after the original rival popes died, and each group elected a replacement. Doubt and confusion caused many Europeans to question the legitimacy and holiness of the church as an institution.

The Conciliar Movement

Positive action came in the form of the Conciliar Movement. In 1395 the professors at the University of Paris proposed that a general council, representing the entire church, should meet to heal the schism. A majority of the cardinals of both factions accepted this solution, and in 1409 they met at the Council of Pisa,

deposed both popes, and elected a new one. But neither of the two deposed popes would give up his office, and the papal throne now had three claimants.

The intolerable situation necessitated another church council. In 1414 the Holy Roman Emperor assembled at Constance the most impressive church gathering of the period. By deposing the various papal claimants and electing Martin V as pope in 1417, the Great Schism was ended and a single papacy was restored at Rome.

The Conciliar Movement represented a reforming and democratizing influence in the church. But the movement was not to endure, even though the Council of Constance had decreed that general councils were superior to popes and that they should meet at regular intervals in the future. Taking steps to preserve his authority, the pope announced that to appeal to a church council without having first obtained papal consent was heretical. Together with the inability of later councils to bring about much-needed reform and with lack of support for such councils by secular

Religious Reforms and Reactions

1415	John Hus, Bohemian reformer, burned at the stake
1437–1517	Cardinal Ximenes carried out reforms of Spanish Catholic Church
c. 1450	Revival of witchcraft mania in Europe
1452–1498	Savonarola attempted religious purification of Florence
1483–1546	Martin Luther
1484–1531	Ulrich Zwingli, leader of Swiss Reformation
1491–1556	Ignatius Loyola, founder of Society of Jesus (Jesuits)
1509–1564	John Calvin, leader of Reformation in Geneva
1515–1582	St. Teresa of Avila, founder of Carmelite religious order
1517	Luther issues Ninety-Five Theses
1521	Luther declared an outcast by the Imperial Diet at Worms
1534–1549	Pontificate of Paul III
1545–1563	Council of Trent
1561–1593	Religious wars in France

College of Cardinals—Cardinals are the highest-ranking churchmen serving under the pope in the Catholic Church. Collectively, they constitute the Sacred College of Cardinals, and their duties include electing the pope, acting as his principal counselors, and aiding in governing the church.

Schism—Literally a split or division (from the Greek *schizein* = to split). The word is usually used in reference to the Great Schism (1378–1417), when there were two, and later three, rival popes, each with his own College of Cardinals.

rulers, the restoration of a single head of the church enabled the popes to discredit the Conciliar Movement by 1450. Not until almost a century later, when the Council of Trent convened in 1545, did a great council meet to reform the church. But by that time the church had already irreparably lost many countries to Protestantism.

While the popes refused to call councils to effect reform, they failed to bring about reform themselves. The popes busied themselves not with internal problems but with Italian politics and patronage of the arts. The issues of church reform and revitalization were largely ignored.

Political Challenges

During the fifteenth century major issues of contention between Rome and the various leaders of Europe dealt with the control of taxes and fees, the courts, the law, and trade. The Catholic Church owned vast properties and collected fortunes in tithes, fees, and religious gifts, controlling, by some estimates, between a fifth and a fourth of Europe's wealth. Impoverished secular rulers looked enviously at the church's wealth. Because the Atlantic states of England, France and Spain were more unified, they were better able to deal with Rome than states of the fragmented Holy Roman Empire.

No longer able to prevail over secular rulers by its religious authority alone after 1300, the papacy fared badly in an era of power politics in foreign relations. Free Italian cities, such as Venice and Florence, had helped build a new balance-of-power diplomacy after the 1450s. But the French invasion at the end of the fifteenth century made the peninsula an arena for desperate struggle between the Habsburg and French Valois (Val-WAH) dynasties that would last until 1559. The Papal States became a political pawn. The papacy's weaknesses were exploited by the troops of Charles V when they sacked Rome in 1527.

Spiritual and Intellectual Developments

The Roman Catholic Church faced more than just social and political challenges by 1500. At the lowest level, popular religion remained based on illiterate believers who worshipped for the magical or practical earthly benefits of the sacraments and the cults of the saints. In their short and grim lives they were far from the political intrigue and sophisticated theological disputes that would trigger the Reformations and much closer to beliefs in the existence of witches, ghosts, phantom grunting swine, and demons who might lurk around the next corner. Arguments between Augustinian and Dominican monks meant little, and dedi-

cation to the opinions of the pope in faraway Rome was weak. Of much greater concern was how to avoid going to Hell, a possibility that was constantly in evidence during this time of fragile life and early death.

At the elite levels, during the fifteenth century, humanist reformers believed that abuses in the Catholic Church resulted largely from misinterpretation of Scripture by late medieval Scholastic philosophers and theologians (see p. 274). Northern humanists like Erasmus and Sir Thomas More ridiculed later Scholastics as pedantic (see p. 412).

Intellectual conflict was not new in Europe. But the means of communicating the nature and extent of the disagreements after the 1450s was new. The printing presses, after their European introduction in the 1350s, produced 6 million publications in more than 200 European towns by 1500. There were better-educated people with a thirst to read these books, which dealt largely with religious themes, and the result was the force of mobilized public opinion.

Some of these readers responded to critics, such as the Augustinian monks, who saw the Scholastics as presumptuous and worldly. Following the teachings of St. Augustine, they believed humans to be such depraved sinners that there could be saved not through "good works," as the Church taught, but only through personal repentance and faith in God's mercy. **Augustinians** accepted only Scripture as religious truth; they believed that faith was more important than the Scholastics' manipulated power of reason. And it was to the Augustinians that Martin Luther would turn to pursue his search for understanding.

LUTHER AND THE GERMAN REFORMATION

■ *Why did the most important fracture in Christendom occur in Germany?*

Martin Luther had no intention of striking the spark that launched more than a century of European conflict. Born in 1483, the son of an ambitious and tough Thuringian peasant turned miner and small businessman, he was raised by his parents under a contradictory regime of Christian love and the attendant harsh physical discipline that would affect his way of dealing with the world after 1521. Like many young boys of his time, he enjoyed the sometimes earthy and profane humor of his peasant society. Unlike many of his friends, he, as did St. Augustine 1200 years earlier, distrusted his own passionate

IMAGE

Martin Luther

Augustinians—Founded in 1256, a religious order dedicated to following of St. Augustine's life and teaching.

nature and became obsessed with fear of the devil and an eternity in hell. Until 1517 Luther's pursuit of his salvation was an intensely personal one, with little regard to the larger context of upheaval in which he lived.

The Search for Salvation

Martin Luther found great comfort in the teachings of the humanists and the Augustinians. After four years of studying the law, he disappointed his father by entering an Augustinian monastery at age 22, following what was to him a miraculous survival in a violent thunderstorm. As a monk, however, Luther was tormented by what he saw as his sinful nature and the fear of damnation. Then, in his mid-thirties, he read St. Paul's Epistle to the Romans and found freedom from despair in the notion of justification by faith: "Then I grasped that the justice of God is that righteousness by which through grace and sheer mercy God justifies us through faith. Thereupon, I felt myself to be reborn and to have gone through open doors into paradise."[1]

As an Augustinian, Luther entered into abstract religious debates that became more spirited because of the widespread problems of the church in central Europe. The buying and selling of church offices and charging fees to give comfort through a variety of theologically questionable ceremonies to superstitious parishioners disturbed him. But the practice that outraged Luther and brought him openly to oppose the Roman Catholic Church was the sale of indulgences. Theologically, these were shares of surplus grace, earned by Christ and the saints and available for papal dispensation to worthy souls after death. Originally, indulgences were not sold or described as tickets to heaven. By the sixteenth century, however, papal salesmen regularly peddled them as guarantees of early release from purgatory.

Luther's immediate adversary in 1517 was a **Dominican** monk named Johan Tetzel (TET-zel), commissioned by the Pope Leo X and Archbishop Albert of Mainz to sell indulgences. At the papal level, this was part of a large undertaking by which Pope Leo X hoped to finance completion of St. Peter's Basilica in Rome: The Archbishop of Mainz received 50 percent of the money for his own purposes. Tetzel used every appeal to crowds of the country people around Wittenberg (vit-en-BERG), begging them to aid their deceased loved ones and repeating the slogan "A penny in the box, a soul out of purgatory."[2] Luther and many other Germans detested Tetzel's methods and his Roman connections. He also rejected Tetzel's Dominican theology, which differed from Augustinian beliefs.

Lucas Cranach, Martin Luther and His Friends. *That Martin Luther (left) and other Protestant reformers did not suffer the same fate as John Hus a century earlier was largely due to the political support of rulers such as the Elector Frederick of Saxony (center).*

There are moments in history when the actions of a single person will link all of the prevailing and contrasting currents of an era into an explosive mixture. In Wittenberg on October 31, 1517, Martin Luther issued his Ninety-Five Theses, calling for public debate—mainly with the Dominicans—on issues involving indulgences and basic church doctrines.

Dominicans—St. Dominic established this religious order in 1215 to go out into the world to teach and preach the word of God.

This document was soon translated from Latin into German and published in all major German cities. The Theses denied the pope's power to give salvation and declared that indulgences were not necessary for a contrite and repentant Christian. Number 62, for example, stated that the "true treasure" of the Church was the "Holy Gospel of the Glory and Grace of God," and number 36 indicated that Christians truly desiring forgiveness could gain it without "letters of pardon." The resulting popular outcry forced Tetzel to leave Saxony, and Luther was almost immediately hailed as a prophet, directed by God to expose the pope and a grasping clergy.

His message was so well received because it satisfied those who wanted a return to simple faith; it also appealed to those, like the humanists, who fought church abuses and irrational authority. Luther's message provided an outlet for German resentment against Rome, and it gave encouragement to princes seeking political independence. The ensuing controversy, which soon raged far beyond Wittenberg, split all of western Christendom and focused and strengthened the social, economic, and political contradictions of the time.

Luther was soon in trouble. Although Rome was not immediately alarmed, the Dominicans levied charges of heresy against their Augustinian competitor. Having already begun his defense in a series of pamphlets, Luther continued in 1519 by debating the eminent theologian John Eck (1486–1543) at Leipzig (LEIP-zig). There Luther denied the **infallibility of the pope** and church councils, declared the Scriptures to be the sole legitimate doctrinal authority, and proclaimed that salvation could be gained only by faith. That same year a last effort at reconciliation failed completely, and in June 1520 Luther was excommunicated by the pope.

Charles V, only recently crowned emperor and aware of Luther's increased following among the princes, afforded the rebellious monk an audience before the **Imperial Diet** at Worms in 1521 to hear his defense of statements against church teachings and papal authority. If Luther recanted, he could perhaps escape his excommunication and execution. After much discussion, when the Orator of the Empire finally asked if he was prepared to recant, Luther responded:

> Your Lordships demand a simple answer. Here it is, plain and unvarnished. Unless I am convicted of error by the testimony of Scripture or (since I put no trust in the unsupported authority of Pope or of councils, since it is plain that they have often

---

infallibility of the pope—The belief that popes cannot be wrong in matters of faith and doctrine.

Imperial Diet—A meeting of the political and religious leaders of the various member states of the Holy Roman Empire.

> erred and often contradicted themselves) by manifest reasoning I stand convicted by the Scriptures to which I have appealed, and my conscience is taken captive by God's word, I cannot and will not recant anything, for to act against our conscience is neither safe for us, nor open to us. On this I take my stand, I can do no other. God help me. Amen."[3]

The Diet finally declared him an outcast. Soon afterward, as he left Worms, Luther was secretly detained for his own protection in Wartburg (VART-burg) Castle by Elector Frederick of Saxony, his secular lord. He would not burn at the stake, as did John Hus, because he enjoyed substantial political and popular support. His message had been spread by the 300,000 copies of his 30 works printed between 1517 and 1520, and he was a German hero.

The Two Kingdoms: God and the State

At Wartburg Luther set his course for the rest of his life as he began organizing an evangelical church distinct from Rome. Although he denounced much of the structure, formality, and ritual of the Catholic Church, Luther spent much of his time after the Diet of Worms building a new church for his followers. It reflected his main theological differences with Rome but kept many traditional ideas and practices. The fundamental principle of the Lutheran creed was that salvation occurred through faith that Christ's sacrifice alone could wash away sin. This departed from the Catholic doctrine of salvation by faith and good works, which required conformance to prescribed dogma and participation in rituals. The Catholic Mass became the Lutheran Communion, involving all who attended services and requiring no priestly blessing to transform the bread and wine into Christ's body and blood, which in Lutheran theory automatically "coexisted" with the wafer and the wine. Other changes included church services in German instead of Latin, an emphasis on preaching, the abolition of monasteries, and the curtailment of formal ceremonies foreign to the personal experiences of ordinary people. The Lutheran Church claimed to be a "priesthood of all believers" in which each person could receive God directly or through the Scriptures. To that end, Luther translated the Bible from Latin into German and composed the sermons that would be repeated in hundreds of Lutheran pulpits all over Germany and Scandinavia.

He took off his clerical habit in 1523 and two years later married a former nun, Katherine von Bora, who bore him six children, raised his nieces and nephews, managed his household, secured his income, entertained his colleagues, and served as his supportive companion. Luther's ideas on marriage and Christian equality promised women new opportunities, which were only partly realized. He stressed the importance of wives as marriage partners for both the clergy and the **laity.** Contrary to Catholic doctrine, he even condoned divorce in cases of adultery and desertion. During the 1520s, his views drew numerous women to Wittenberg, where they found refuge from monasteries or their Catholic husbands. Some Lutheran women became wandering preachers, but they evoked protests from male ministers and legal prohibitions from many German municipal councils, including those of Nuremberg and Augsburg. Although first teaching that women were equal to men in opportunities for salvation and in their family roles, in his later writings, Luther described them as subordinate to their husbands and not meant for the pulpit.

DOCUMENT

Sermon at the Castle Pleissenberg

Lutheranism recognized two main human spheres of human obligation: The first and highest was to God; the other involved a subordinate loyalty to earthly governments, which also existed in accordance with God's will. Luther's idea of "two kingdoms," one of God and one of the world, fit well with contemporary political conditions, winning him support from German and Scandinavian rulers while connecting his movement to dynastic nationalism. Luther's political orientation was clearly revealed in 1522 and 1523 during a rebellion of German knights. When Lutheran support was not forthcoming, the rebellion was quickly crushed. Luther took no part in the struggle but was embarrassed by opponents who claimed his religion threatened law and order.

Another example of Luther's political and social conservatism was provided by a general revolt of peasants and discontented townsmen in 1524 and 1525. Encouraged by Lutheran appeals for Christian freedom, the rebels drew up petitions asking for religious autonomy. At first Luther expressed sympathy for the requests, particularly for each congregation's right to select its own pastor. Then, as violence erupted throughout central Germany in April and May 1525, imperial and princely troops crushed the rebel armies, killing an estimated 90,000 insurgents. Luther had advised rebel leaders to obey the law as God's will; when they turned to war, he penned a virulent pamphlet, *Against the Thievish and Murderous . . . Peasants.* In it he called on the princes to "knock down, strangle, . . . stab, . . . and think nothing so venomous, pernicious, or Satanic as an insurgent."[4]

There was soon a struggle for religious control in Germany between the emperor and the Lutheran princes. When Catholics sought to impose conformity in Imperial Diets during the late 1520s, Lutheran leaders drew up a formal protest (hence the appellation *protestant*). After this Augsburg Confession (1530) was rejected, the Lutheran princes organized for defense in the Schmalkaldic League. Because Charles V was preoccupied with the French and the Turks, open hostilities were minimized, but a sporadic civil war dragged on until after Luther's death in 1546. It ended with the Peace of Augsburg in 1555, when the imperial princes were permitted to choose between Lutheranism and Catholicism in their state churches, thus increasing their independence of the emperor. In addition, Catholic properties confiscated before 1552 were retained by Lutheran principalities, which provided a means for financing their policies. Although no concessions were made to other protestant groups, such as the Calvinists, this treaty shifted the European political balance against the Empire and the church.

Outside Germany, Lutheranism furnished a religious stimulus for developing national monarchies in Scandinavia. There, as in Germany, rulers welcomed not only Lutheran religious ideas but also the chance to acquire confiscated Catholic properties. They appreciated having ministers who preached obedience to constituted secular authority. In Sweden, Gustavus Vasa (goos-TA-vus VAH-sah; 1523–1560) used Lutheranism to lead a successful struggle for Swedish independence from Denmark. In turn, the Danish king, who also ruled Norway, issued an ordinance in 1537 establishing the national Lutheran Church, with its bishops as salaried officials of the state. Throughout Eastern Europe, wherever there was a German community, the Lutheran church spread—for a brief time even threatening the supremacy of the Catholic Church in Poland and Lithuania.

HENRY VIII AND THE ANGLICAN REFORMATION

▪ *What were the political considerations impelling Henry VIII to create the Anglican Church?*

England was affected by the same economic and social crises and changes of the fourteenth and fifteenth centuries as the rest of Europe. But unlike central Europe, England was one of the new Atlantic states characterized by national monarchies, centralized authority, and greater independence from the papacy. The Tudor dynasty adapted itself to the new conditions after the Hundred Years' War with France and the devastating War of the Roses, which destroyed much of the traditional nobility.

Legitimate Heirs and the True Church

During this time of difficult transition, it was necessary that each monarch raise a strong and healthy heir

---

laity—The community of believers in the Christian Church, served by the clergy, the trained and specialized leaders of the community.

to ensure the continuity of the dynasty and the strength of England. Henry VIII (1509–1547) became the heir to the English throne when his older brother Arthur died in 1502. It had not been expected that he would be king, and his education ran to that of a true Renaissance man. He showed talent in music, literature, philosophy, jousting, hunting, and theology. Not only did he become the king of England on his father's death in 1509, but he also soon married the woman who had been his brother's wife, Catherine of Aragon (1485–1536), thus continuing the dynastic alliance with Spain. Catherine was a cultured, strong, respected woman and devoted wife: she successfully conducted a war against Scotland when Henry was campaigning in France.

Henry was a devout Roman Catholic, who gained the title "Defender of the Faith" from the pope for a pamphlet he wrote denouncing Luther and his theology. However, his immediate problem in the 1520s was the lack of a male heir. After 11 years of marriage, he had only a sickly daughter and an illegitimate son. His queen, after four earlier pregnancies, gave birth to a stillborn son in 1518, and by 1527, when she was 42, Henry had concluded that she would have no more children. His only hope for the future of his dynasty seemed to be a new marriage and a new queen. This, of course, would require an annulment of his marriage to Catherine. In 1527 he appealed to the pope, asking for the annulment.

Normally, the request would probably have been granted; the situation, however, was not normal. Because she had been the wife of Henry's brother, Catherine's marriage to Henry had necessitated a papal dispensation, based on her oath that the first marriage had never been consummated. Now Henry professed concern for his soul, tainted by "living in sin" with Catherine. He also claimed that he was being punished, citing a passage in the Book of Leviticus that predicted childlessness for the man who married his dead brother's wife. The pope was sympathetic and

Holbein's portrait of Henry VIII, painted in 1542, shows a man sure of himself in his royal setting. He had by this time broken with Rome, married six times in pursuit of a legitimate male heir, and turned England into a major naval power. What the portrait does not show is all of the suffering and discord he left in his wake.

certainly aware of an obligation to the king, who had strongly supported the church. However, granting the annulment would have been admission of papal error, perhaps even corruption, in issuing the earlier dispensation. Added to the Lutheran problem, this would have doubly damaged the papacy. A more immediate concern for Henry was Catherine's nephew. As the aunt of Charles V, whose armies occupied Rome in 1527, she was able to exert considerable pressure on the pope to refuse an **annulment.**

When the pope delayed a decision, Henry began to rally his support at home. During the three years after 1531, when Catherine saw him for the last time, Henry took control of affairs. Sequestering his daughter Mary (1516–1558) and his banished wife in separate castles, he forbade them from seeing each other. The king forced the clergy into proclaiming him head of a separate, English church "as far as the law of Christ allows," extracted from Parliament the authority to appoint bishops, and designated his willing tool Thomas Cranmer (1489–1556) as archbishop of Canterbury. In 1533 Cranmer pronounced Henry's marriage to Catherine invalid; at the same time, he legalized his union with Anne Boleyn (bo-LIN), a lady of the court who was carrying his unborn child, the future Elizabeth I. Henry even forced his daughter Mary to accept him as head of the church and to admit the illegality of her mother's marriage—by implication acknowledging her own illegitimacy. Parliament also ended all payment of revenues to Rome.

Now, having little other choice, the pope excommunicated Henry, making the breach official on both sides. On his side, Henry divided up the Church's properties—some 25 percent of the wealth of the realm—to distribute to the gentry to consolidate his domestic support. In 1539 Parliament completed its

---

annulment—A religious or political judgment that a marriage was/is not valid, and hence no longer existed/exists.

seizure of monastery lands and the wealth of pilgrimage sites such as Canterbury Cathedral. Meanwhile, Catholics such as the former chancellor and humanist Sir Thomas More (see p. 412), who refused to swear allegiance to the new order, were executed.

There had already been a strong underground resistance movement present in England even before Henry came to power. English theologians, beginning with John Wycliffe and his followers, played an active role in the intellectual and theological debates of the High Middle Age. During the fifteenth and first part of the sixteenth centuries there was an active underground church, the Lollards, in which lay people—especially women—played an important role. William Tyndale's (1494–1536) skillful translation of the New Testament, a work marked by Lutheran influences, served as the basis for the English Bible published in 1537, which made scripture available to all literate English-speaking people. This popular Protestantism was not at all close to the new Anglican Church, which brought about little change in doctrine or ritual. The Six Articles, Parliament's declaration of the new creed and ceremonies in 1539, reaffirmed most Catholic theology except papal supremacy.

Radical Protestants and Renewed Catholics

In his later years, after the decapitation of Anne Boleyn on charges of adultery in 1536 (the year that Catherine of Aragon also died), Henry grew increasingly suspicious of popular Protestantism, which was buttressed by reformist movements spreading into England and Scotland from the Continent. Further, he refused to legalize clerical marriage, which caused great hardships among many Anglican clergymen, including some bishops, and their wives and lashed out indiscriminately at those people such as the protestant Anne Ayscough who dared to question him.

In the decade after Henry's death in 1547, religious fanaticism brought social and political upheaval. For six years, during growing political corruption, extreme protestants ruled the country and dominated the frail young king, Edward VI (1547–1553), born of Henry's third wife Jane Seymour—who died in childbirth. His government was controlled by the Regency Council, dominated first by the duke of Somerset and then, after 1549, by his rival, the duke of Northumberland. The same mix of political opportunism and religious change continued as the council members enriched themselves and pursued their ambitions. At the same time, a radical form of Protestantism swept through many parishes. The government sought political support by courting the religious radicals: it repealed the Six Articles, permitted priests to marry, replaced the Latin service with Cranmer's English version, and adopted the Forty-Two Articles, the expression of extreme Protestantism.

When Edward died in 1553, Mary Tudor came to the throne and tried to restore Catholicism through harsh persecutions, which earned her the name "Bloody Mary" from Protestant historians. The new queen possessed many of the same admirable qualities of her mother, Catherine of Aragon: dignity, intelligence, compassion, and a strong moral sense. Her religious obsession, however, eventually cost her the support of a substantial number of her subjects. Her hopeless love for her Catholic husband, Philip II of Spain—who married her in 1554—led to her being seen as a puppet of Spanish diplomacy. She restored the Catholic Church service, proclaimed papal authority in her realm, and forged an alliance with Spain. In putting down the protestants, she burned 300 of them at the stake—among whom were Cranmer, two other bishops, and 55 women. Mary died pitifully, rejected by her husband and people, but steadfast in her hope to save English Catholicism. Leaving no heir, she was compelled to name Elizabeth, her half-sister, as her successor.

PROTESTANTISM FROM SWITZERLAND TO HOLLAND: ZWINGLI AND CALVIN

■ *Why were the protestants in the Rhine Valley so much more radical in their approaches than Luther or the Anglicans?*

A very different variety of church reforms took place in Switzerland and France. The leaders of these reforms were conscious of the state but not dominated by it, as the Anglicans were. Like the Lutherans, they were also concerned for the salvation of their souls, but in a much more doctrinal and often vindictive way. Calvinism was the most popular and the most conservative of the reforms, but there were many others, including multiple forms of **Anabaptism**. These movements went farther than Lutheranism and Anglicanism in rejecting Catholic dogma and ritual. Generally, they were opposed to monarchy, but their position did not become very apparent until they were deeply involved in religious wars after 1560, when they often found themselves under attack by both the Catholics and the Lutherans.

Anabaptism—A Protestant faith that holds that baptism and church membership come only when one is an adult. Anabaptists also tend to believe in a strict separation of church and state.

Document   Anne Ayscough (Mrs. Thomas Kyme), English Protestant Martyr

Anne Ayscough, the daughter of Sir William Ayscough, received a good education and became remarkably independent at a time when the normal expectation was that a woman's role was to look after the house and be able to entertain guests. She read voraciously, especially Tyndale's version of the New Testament, and participated vigorously in the theological controversies of her time. She did not like the papacy, nor did she much like Henry's VIII's pet theologians and their version of English Catholicism—the Anglican Church. Duty to her family forced her to marry a Catholic husband, but soon he was not pleased when she set out to spread the Gospels by reading from the Bible to the peasants—a practice later forbidden by the law of 1543. For Anne the issues were quite clear: "[T]he papists were the agents of Antichrist and would always be opposed to the Saints of God. . . . " In standing upon her own righteousness and excluding from her heart all love of her enemies, Anne Ayscough was very much a child of her age. In 1545 she was called to London to face charges of heresy. She was then tortured—the only woman in English history put on the rack, tried, and found guilty for her refusal to believe that the wafer literally becomes the body of Christ in the communion, a process called transubstantiation.

On the eve of her execution, she wrote: "O friend most dearly beloved in God, I marvel not a little what should move you to judge in me so slender a faith as to fear death, which is the end of all misery. In the Lord I desire you not believe of me such weakness. For I doubt it not but God will perform his work in me, like as he hath begun. I understand the Council is not a little displeased, that it should be reported abroad that I was racked in the Tower. They say now that what they did there was but to frighten me; whereby I perceive they are ashamed of their uncomely doings and fear much lest the King's majesty should have information thereof. Wherefore they do not want any man to tell it abroad. Well, their cruelty God forgive them."

At the same time, she wrote Henry VIII: "I Anne Ayscough, of good memory, although God hath given me the bread of adversity and the water of trouble (yet not so much as my sins have deserved), desire this to be known unto your Grace. Forasmuch as I am by the law condemned for an evil-doer, here I take heaven and earth to record that I shall die in my innocence. And according to what I have said first and will say last, I utterly abhor and detest all heresies. And as concerning the Supper of the Lord, I believe so much as Christ hath said, therein, which he confirmed with his most blessed blood, I believe so much as he willed me to follow, and I believe so much as the Catholic church of him doth teach. For I will not forsake the commandment of his holy lips. . . ."

And as she was taken out to be executed, her final prayer was written down: "O Lord, I have more enemies now than there be hairs on my head. Yet, Lord, let them never overcome me with vain words, but fight thus, Lord, in my stead, for on thee cast I my care. With all the spite they can imagine they fall upon me, which am thy poor creature. Yet, sweet Lord, let me pay no heed to them which are against me, for in thee is my whole delight. And, Lord, I heartily desire of thee, that thou wilt of thy most merciful goodness forgive them that violence which they do and have done unto me. Open also thou their blind hearts, that they may hereafter do that thing in thy sight, which is only acceptable before thee, and to set forth thy verity aright, without all vain fantasy of sinful men. So be it, O Lord, so be it."

Anne Ayscough was burned at the stake with four companions on July 16 1546. Already viewed as a heroine by many in England, she became the best known English martyr.

Questions to Consider

1. What was there in Anne Ayscough's views that provoked such a harsh response from the leaders of the English Church, such as putting her on the rack?

2. Why were heretics burned at the stake and not, for example, hanged, or decapitated?

3. What qualities earn a person such as Anne Ayscough the accolade of being a "martyr?" What is a martyr? Whom would you consider to be martyrs during the twentieth century?

From Derek Wilson, *A Tudor Tapestry: Men, Women and Society in Reformation England* (London: Heinemann, 1972), pp. 164, 229–232.

Ulrich Zwingli

Popular Protestantism arose early in Switzerland, where many of the same difficult conditions found in the German states favored its growth. During the late medieval period, the country prospered in the growing trade between Italy and Northern Europe. Busy Swiss craftsmen and merchants in Zurich, Bern, Basel, and Geneva suffered under their Habsburg overlords and by papal policies, particularly the sale of indulgences. In 1499 the Confederation of Swiss Cantons won independence from the Holy Roman Empire and the Habsburgs. To many Swiss, this was also the first step in repudiating outside authority.

The Swiss Reformation began in Zurich, shortly after Luther published his Theses at Wittenberg. It was led by Ulrich Zwingli (OOL-rikh ZWING-lee; 1484–1531), a scholar, priest, and former military chaplain, who persuaded the city council to create a regime of clergymen and magistrates to supervise government, religion, and individual morality. Zwingli agreed with Luther in repudiating papal in favor of scriptural authority. He simplified services, preached justification by faith, attacked monasticism, and opposed clerical celibacy. More rational than Luther, he was also more interested in practical reforms, going beyond Luther in advocating additional grounds for divorce and in denying any mystical conveyance of grace by baptism or communion; both, to Zwingli, were only symbols. These differences proved irreconcilable when Luther and Zwingli met to consider merging their movements in 1529.

As Zwingli's influence spread rapidly among the northern cantons, religious controversy separated north from south, rural from urban, and feudal overlords—both lay and ecclesiastical—from towns within their dominions. When, in the 1520s, Geneva repudiated its ancient obligations and declared its independence from the local bishop and the count of Savoy, the city became a hotbed of Protestantism, with preachers streaming in from Zurich. Zwingli was killed in the religious war of 1531, after which it was decided in the Second Peace of Kappel that each Swiss canton could choose its own religion.

John Calvin

Hoping to ensure the dominance of Protestantism in Geneva after the religious wars, local reformers invited John Calvin (1509–1564) to Geneva. Calvin arrived from Basel in 1536. He was an uncompromising French reformer and a formidable foe of the ungodly, but a caring colleague and minister to humble believers. His preaching, based on his study of theology in Paris and law in Orleans, ultimately won enough followers to make his church the official religion. From Geneva, the faith spread to Scotland, Hungary, France, Italy, and other parts of Europe after the early 1540s.

In Basel he had published the first edition of his *Institutes of the Christian Religion* (1536), a theological work that transformed the general Lutheran doctrines into a rational legal system based around the concept of predestination. It also earned Calvin his invitation to Geneva. His original plan for a city government there called for domination by the clergy and banishment of all dissidents. This aroused a storm of opposition from Anabaptists—who believed in adult baptism and separation of church and state—and from the more worldly portion of the population, and Calvin was forced into exile. He moved on to Strasbourg where he associated with other reformers who helped him refine his ideas. Calvin's second regime at Geneva after 1541 involved a long struggle with the city council. His proposed ordinances for the Genevan Church gave the clergy full control over moral and religious behavior, but the council modified the docu-

Margaret of Navarre, a supporter of Protestantism, was the author of the Heptameron, *a collection of tales modeled on Boccacio's Decameron.*

ment, placing all appointments and enforcement of law under its jurisdiction.

Although recognizing the Bible as supreme law and the *Institutes* as a model for behavior, the Geneva city council did not always act on recommendations from the Consistory, Calvin's supreme church committee. For the next 14 years Calvin fought against public criticism and opposition in the council. He gradually increased his power, however, through support from the protestant refugees who poured into the city. His influence climaxed after a failed "revolt of the godless" in 1555. From that year until his death in 1564, he dominated the council, ruling Geneva with an iron hand, within the letter, but not the spirit, of the original ordinances.

Particularly in the later period, the Consistory apprehended violators of religious and moral law, sending its members into households to check every detail of private life. Offenders were reported to secular magistrates for punishment. Relatively light penalties were imposed for missing church, laughing during the service, wearing bright colors, dancing, playing cards, or swearing. Religious dissent, blasphemy, mild heresies, and adultery received heavier punishments, including banishment. Witchcraft and serious cases of heresy led to torture, and then execution—sometimes as many as a dozen or more a year. Michael Servetus (SEHR-vee-tus; 1511–1553), a Spanish theologian-philosopher and refugee from the Catholic Inquisition, was burned for heresy in Calvin's Geneva because he had denied the doctrine of the trinity.

Calvin accepted Luther's insistence on justification by faith; like Luther, he saw Christian life as a constant struggle against the devil, and he expected a coming divine retribution, an end-time, when God would redress the evils that were increasing on every side. Calvin also agreed with Luther in seeing God's power as a relief for human anxiety and a source of inner peace. Both reformers believed man to be totally depraved, but Calvin placed greater emphasis on this point, at the same time emphasizing God's immutable will and purpose. If Calvinism, to human minds, seemed contradictory in affirming man's sinful nature and his creation in God's image, this connection only proved that God's purposes were absolutely beyond human understanding. For depraved humans, God required faith and obedience, not understanding.

God's omnipotence was Calvin's cardinal principle. He saw all of nature as governed by a divinely ordained order, discernible to man but governed by laws that God could set aside in effecting miracles as he willed. Carried to its logical conclusion, such ideas produced Calvin's doctrine of predestination.

DOCUMENT

Calvin on Predestination

By predestination we mean the eternal decree of God, by which he determined with himself whatever he wished to happen with regard to every man. All are not created on equal terms, but some are preordained to eternal life, others to eternal damnation; and, accordingly, as each has been created for one or other of these ends, we say that he has been predestined to life or to death. . . .[5]

In Calvin's grand scheme, as laid out precisely in the *Institutes,* his church served to aid the elect in honoring God. The human purpose was not to win salvation—for this had already been determined—but to honor God and prepare the elect for salvation. As communities of believers, congregations were committed to constant war against Satan. They also functioned to spread the Word (Scripture), educate youth, and alleviate suffering among the destitute.

Calvin was particularly ambivalent in his views on government. Ministers of the church were responsible for advising secular authorities on religious policies and resisting governments that violated God's laws. He believed that all rulers were responsible to God and subject to God's vengeance. But throughout the1540s, when he was hoping to gain the support of monarchs, he emphasized the Christian duty of obedience to secular authorities. Even then, however, he advised rulers to seek counsel from church leaders, and he ordered the faithful, among both the clergy and the laity, to disregard any government that denied them freedom in following Christ. Although willing to support any political system that furthered the true faith, Calvin always preferred representative government.

Another ambiguity in Calvin's social thought involved his attitude toward women. Unlike Catholic theologians, he did not cast women in an inferior light. In his mind, men and women were equally full of sin, but they were also equal in their chance for salvation. As he sought recruits, he stressed women's right to read the Bible and participate in church services. At the same time he saw women as naturally subordinate to their husbands in practical affairs, including the conduct of church business.

Before the Peace of Augsburg, Calvinism was strongest in France, the reformer's own homeland, where the believers were known as *Huguenots.* Calvinism made gains elsewhere but did not win political power. In Italy, the duchess of Ferrara installed the Calvinist church service in her private chapel and protected Calvinist refugees. Strasbourg in the 1530s was a free center for protestant reformers such as Matthew Zell and his wife Katherine, who befriended many Calvinist preachers, including Martin Bucer (BOOT-sur), a missionary to England during the reign of Edward VI. In the same period, John Knox spread the Calvinist message in Scotland.

More extreme than Calvinism were many divergent protestant splinter groups, each pursuing its own "inner lights." Some saw visions of the world's end, some advocated a Christian community of shared wealth, some opposed social distinctions and economic inequalities, some—these Anabaptists—repudiated infant baptism as a violation of Christian responsibility, and some denied the need for any clergy. Most of the sects emphasized biblical literalism and direct, emotional communion between the individual and God. The majority of them were indifferent or antagonistic to secular government, many favored pacifism and substitution of the church for the state.

Women were prominent among the sects, although they were usually outnumbered by men. These women were known for their biblical knowledge, faith, courage, and independence. They helped found religious communities, wrote hymns and religious tracts, debated theology, and publicly challenged the authorities. Some preached and delivered prophecies, although such activities were suppressed by male ministers by the end of the century. More women than men endured torture and suffered martyrdom. Their leadership opportunities and relative freedoms in marriage, compared to women of other religions, were bought at the high price of hardship and danger.

Persecution of the sects arose largely because of their radical ideas. But Catholics and other protestants who opposed them usually cited two revolutionary actions. The first came when some radical preachers took part in the German peasants' revolt of the 1520s and shared in the savage punishments that followed. The second came in 1534 when a Catholic army besieged Münster (MIUN-ster).

Thousands of recently arrived Anabaptist extremists had seized control and expelled dissenters from this German city near the southern Netherlands. Following their radical theology, the "regime of saints" took private property, allowed polygamy, and planned to convert the world. John of Leyden (LI-den), a former Dutch tailor who claimed divine authority, headed a terrorist regime during the final weeks before the city fell. Those who survived the fall of the city suffered horrible tortures and then execution.

Among the most damaging charges against the Münster rebels were their alleged sexual excesses and the dominant role played by women in this immorality. Such charges were mostly distortions. The initiation of **polygamy,** justified by references

---

polygamy—A type of marriage in which a husband has more than one wife.

to the Old Testament, was a response to problems arising from a shortage of men, hundreds of whom had fled the city. Many other men were killed or injured in the fighting. Thus, the city leaders required women to marry so that they could be protected and controlled by husbands. Most Anabaptist women accepted the requirement as a religious duty. Although some paraded through the streets, shouting religious slogans, the majority prepared meals, did manual labor on the defenses, fought beside their men, and died in the fighting or at the stake. Most of the original, Catholic, Münster women, however, fiercely resisted forced marriage, choosing instead jail or execution.

Like Calvin later in Geneva, the Anabaptist regime of John of Leyden closely monitored and controlled private life and public behavior. Their theocratic state found its laws in Scripture. In looking at the laws of the city, capital punishment was applied in the following cases:

> *Whoever curses God and his holy Name or his Word shall be killed (Lev. 24).*
> *No one shall curse governmental authority (Ex. 22, Deut. 17), on pain of death.*
> *Both parties who commit adultery shall die (Ex. 20, Lev. 20, Matt. 5).*
> *. . . Whoever disobeys these commandments and does not truly repent, shall be rooted out of the people of God, with ban and sword, through the divinely ordained governmental authority.*[6]

For more than a century, memories of Münster plagued the protestant sects in general. Although most did not go to the extremes of "the saints," they were almost immediately driven underground throughout Europe, and their persecution continued long after they had abandoned violence. In time, they dispersed over the Continent and to North America as Mennonites, Quakers, and Baptists, to name only a few denominations. Given their suffering and oppression, voices of the radicals were among the first raised for religious liberty. Their negative experience with governments made them even more suspicious of authority than the Calvinists were. In both the Netherlands and England, they participated in political revolutions and helped frame the earliest demands for constitutional government, representative institutions, and civil liberties.

With the exception of Henry VIII's political reformation, the reformers, going back to Wycliffe and Hus and moving on through Luther and Calvin and the Anabaptists, did not believe that they were creating something new. Instead, they were trying to reclaim the purity of the early church.

REFORM IN THE CATHOLIC CHURCH

■ *How successful was the Catholic Church in dealing with the problems that faced it?*

The era of the Protestant Reformation was also a time of rejuvenation for the Roman Catholic Church. This revival was largely caused by the same conditions that had sparked Protestantism. Throughout the fifteenth century, many sincere and devout Catholics had recognized a need for reform, and they had begun responding to the abuses in their church long before Luther acted at Wittenberg. Almost every variety of reform opinion developed within the Catholic Church. Erasmus, More, and other Christian humanists provided precedents for Luther, but none followed him out of the Catholic Church. In a category of his own was Savonarola (sa-vo-na-RO-la; 1452–1498), a Dominican friar, puritan, and mystic who ruled Florence during the last four years before his death. This "Catholic Calvin" consistently railed against the worldly living and sinful luxuries he found: His criticisms of the pope and the clergy were

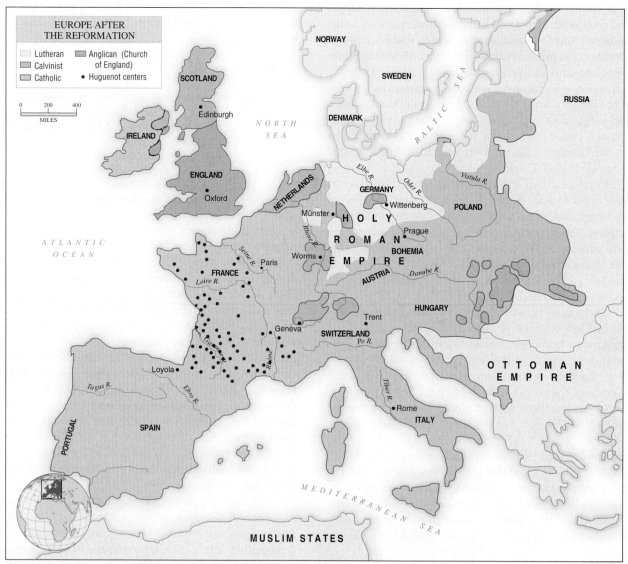

This map illustrates the geographical patterns of the Protestant Reformation. Lutheranism spread through German-speaking areas along the Baltic Sea but rarely crossed the Rhine River. The spread of Calvinism defies linguistic explanation.

much more severe than Luther's. At the other extreme of the Church was Cardinal Ximenes (1437–1517) in Spain, who carried out his own Reformation by disciplining the clergy, compiling the Complutensian Bible—eliminating many of the errors made by medieval copyists and instilling a new spirit of dedication into the monastic orders.

After the protestant revolt began, the primary Catholic reformer was Alessandro Farnese (far-NAY-se), Pope Paul III (1534–1549). Coming into office at a time when the church appeared ready to collapse, Paul struggled to overcome the troubled legacy of his Renaissance predecessors and restore integrity to the papacy. Realizing that issues raised by the protestants would have to be resolved and problems within the church corrected, he attacked the indifference, corruption, and vested interests of the clerical organization. In pursuing these reforms he appointed a commission, which reported the need for correcting such abuses as the worldliness of bishops, the traffic in benefices (church appointments with guaranteed incomes), and the transgressions of some cardinals. Their recommendations led Paul to call a church council, an idea that he continued to press against stubborn opposition for more than ten years.

When Paul died in 1549, he had already set the Roman Church on a new path, although his proposed church council, the Council of Trent, had only begun its deliberations. Perhaps his greatest contribution was his appointment of worthy members to the College of Cardinals, filling that body with eminent scholars and devout stewards of the church. As a result of his labors, the cardinals elected a succession of later popes who were prepared, intellectually and spiritually, to continue the process of regeneration.

The spirit of reform was reflected in a number of new Catholic clerical orders that sprang up in the

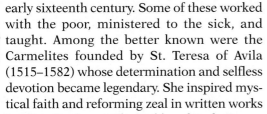

DOCUMENT

Rules for Thinking with the Church

early sixteenth century. Some of these worked with the poor, ministered to the sick, and taught. Among the better known were the Carmelites founded by St. Teresa of Avila (1515–1582) whose determination and selfless devotion became legendary. She inspired mystical faith and reforming zeal in written works such as *Interior Castle* and *The Ladder of Perfection*.

The most significant of the new orders was the Society of Jesus, whose members are known as

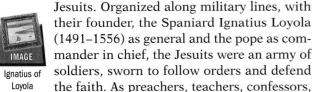

IMAGE

Ignatius of Loyola

Jesuits. Organized along military lines, with their founder, the Spaniard Ignatius Loyola (1491–1556) as general and the pope as commander in chief, the Jesuits were an army of soldiers, sworn to follow orders and defend the faith. As preachers, teachers, confessors,

organizers, diplomats, and spies, they took the field everywhere, founding schools and colleges, serving as missionaries on every continent, and working their way into government wherever possible. Their efforts were probably most responsible for the decided check that Protestantism received after the 1560s, as they zealously defended Catholicism in France, pushed the protestants out of Poland, and reclaimed southern Germany. Jesuit missions also helped Spain and Portugal develop their global empires.

Pope Paul's reform initiatives were given form by the great multinational church council, the first since 1415, which met in three sessions between 1545 and 1563 in the northern Italian city of Trent. Devoting much attention to the external struggle against Protestantism, the council also sought to eliminate internal abuses by ordering changes in church discipline and administration. It strictly forbade absenteeism, false indulgences, selling church offices, and secular pursuits by the clergy. Bishops were ordered to supervise their clergies—priests as well as monks and nuns— and to fill church positions with competent people. The Council of Trent also provided that more seminaries be established for educating priests while instructing the clergy to set examples and preach frequently to their flocks.

Rejecting all compromise, the Council of Trent retained the basic tenets of Catholic doctrine, including the necessity of good works as well as faith for salvation, the authority of church law and traditions, the sanctity of all seven sacraments, the use of only Latin in the Mass, and the spiritual value of indulgences, pilgrimages, veneration of saints, and the cult of the Virgin. The council also strengthened the power of the papacy. It defeated all attempts to place supreme church authority in any general council. When the final session voted that none of its decrees were valid without papal approval, the church became more than ever an absolute monarchy.

The full significance of Trent became evident after the 1560s when the Catholic reaction to Protestantism acquired a new vigor and militancy. Having steeled itself from within, the church and its shock troops, the Jesuits, went to war against protestants and other heretics. The new crusade was both open and secret. In Spain, Italy, and the Netherlands, the Inquisition more than ever before became the dreaded scourge of protestants and other heretics. Jesuit universities, armed with the Index of Forbidden Works, trained scholars and missionaries who would serve as priests and organizers in protestant countries such as England. Many died as martyrs, condemned by protestant tribunals, while others suffered similar fates meted out by pagans whom they sought to convert in America and Asia. But

The devotional works and personal example of St. Teresa of Avila, mystic and visionary, inspired the rebirth of Spanish Catholicism. In 1970 she was proclaimed a doctor of the church, the first woman to be so honored. The sculpture here, The Ecstasy of St. Teresa *(1645–1652), is by the Italian baroque artist Giovanni Bernini.*

Protestantism made no more significant gains in Catholic lands after Trent. Indeed, after Trent, the Catholic Church became a global church.

CONCLUSION

In could be argued that Europe's Golden Age of the Renaissance was no more than a recapitulation of that which had gone before. By resurrecting the gifts of the Greeks and Romans and learning from the sci-ence and history of the Arabs, the elites who partici-pated in the movement were, in fact, reactionaries. But in looking back, they invented new and demand-ing methods of research, and the most important legacy they revived was the old Greek message that "Man Can Know." This individual liberation could be seen immediately in the artistic and architectural works as well as in the writings of Lorenzo da Valla and Machiavelli. The new humanism was not neces-sarily intellectually superior to the best of the scholas-tic thinking. However, it allowed new questions to be posed in critical ways.

Christianity had always been a religion in ferment, and the authorities in Rome and Constantinople after the Seventh Ecumenical Council had sought to stamp out those who were not in accord with orthodoxy. Luther, in many ways, echoed the thoughts of John Wycliffe and John Hus. He succeeded where they failed because of the more favorable political context he found himself in.

In many ways, the Protestant Reformation and Catholic Counter-Reformation helped create the modern world. By breaking the religious monopoly of European Catholicism, Lutheranism and Anglicanism assisted the growth of northern European national monarchies. Later, the Puritan values and "work ethic" of Calvinism helped justify the profit-seeking activities of the middle classes. Even the Catholic Church itself was transformed by the various protestant challenges. After the Council of Trent, the Catholic Counter-Reformation checked the spread of Protestantism, and the Roman Church emerged strengthened to protect and advance itself. Because the Reformation and Counter-Reformation occurred at the same time of the development of the state system (see Chapter 16), faith came to play an integral, and often dangerous, role in politics until 1648.

Because these momentous changes coincided with the beginnings of the European explorations around the world (see Chapter 15), and the construction of Portuguese, Dutch, Spanish, French, and English empires, protestant and Catholic missionaries were able to spread their messages around the globe. Political and economic imperialism were accompanied by a religious imperialism. The Christians had no doubt they were saving the heathen from hell, but this well-intentioned zealousness had mixed, and sometimes destructive, results to the peoples of Asia, Africa, and the Americas touched by European expansion.

Suggestions for Web Browsing

You can obtain more information about topics included in this chapter at the websites listed below. See also the companion website that accompanies this text, http://www.ablongman.com/brummett, which contains an online study guide and additional resources.

Italian Renaissance Art Project
http://www.italian-art.org

One of the very best and most comprehensive sites for reproductions of the major paintings, works of sculpture, and architecture from the Renaissance. An amazing resource of the study of Renaissance art.

Web Museum, Paris: Italian Renaissance (1420–1600)
http://www.ibiblio.org/wm/paint/tl/it-ren/

A useful site for anyone interested in the art of the Italian Renaissance, especially the work of Leonardo da Vinci, Raphael, and Michelangelo.

Florence in the Renaissance
http://www.mega.it/eng/egui/epo/secrepu.htm

A history of the Florentine Republic, with details about the city's influence on Renaissance culture.

Sistine Chapel
http://www.christusrex.org/www1/sistine/0-Tour.html

Photo collection depicting all facets of the Sistine Chapel, including images of Michelangelo's ceiling.

Michelangelo
http://www.michelangelo.com/buonarroti.html

Featuring the works of the artist beautifully illustrated and annotated. An outstanding site.

The Louvre
http://www.paris.org/Musees/Louvre

Website for one of the world's greatest museums offers many paths to some of the most beautiful Renaissance art in existence.

Medieval and Renaissance Women's History
http://womenshistory.about.com/od/medieval/

Site serves as a directory for a wide variety of discussions and references about Renaissance women painters, writers, and women of social standing.

Creative Impulse: Renaissance
http://history.evansville.net/renaissa.html

The University of Evansville's outstanding series of sites on Western civilization includes this compendium of art, history, and descriptions of daily life and culture. Includes one of the very best compilations of other sites dealing with the Renaissance.

Medieval and Renaissance Fact and Fiction
http://www.angelfire.com/mi/spanogle/medieval.html

A useful guide to Web resources for students interested in the history, culture, and literature of the Renaissance.

Northern Renaissance ArtWeb
http://www.msu.edu/~cloudsar/nrweb.htm

A collection of links for exploring the artists and literature of the Northern Renaissance.

Internet Medieval History Sourcebook: Protestant and Catholic Reformations
http://www.fordham.edu/halsall/sbook1y.html

Extensive online source for links about the Protestant and Catholic Reformations, including primary documents by or about precursors and papal critics, Luther, and Calvin and details about the Reformations themselves.

Martin Luther
http://www.wittenberg.de/e/seiten/personen/luther.html

This brief biography of Martin Luther includes links to his Ninety-Five Theses and images of related historical sites.

Tudor England
http://englishhistory.net/tudor.html/

Site detailing life in Tudor England includes biographies, maps, important dates, architecture, and music, including sound files.

Lady Jane Grey
http://www.ladyjanegrey.org/

A biography of the woman who would be queen of England for nine days, and a general history of the time.

Literature and Film

One of the best novels dealing with the Renaissance is Irving Stone, *The Agony and the Ecstasy: A Biographical Novel of Michelangelo* (New American Library, 1996). An outstanding account of the past and present of Florence is given by Mary McCarthy in *The Stones of Florence* (Harvest Books, 2002). There are also many excellent videos available on the art and architecture of the Renaissance. Some of the more notable are *The Art of the Western World: Early and High Renaissance: Realms of Light* (Kultur Video, 1994); *Leonardo Da Vinci: Renaissance Man to the World* (Madacy Entertainment, 1997); *The Art of Renaissance Science: Galileo and Perspective*, by Joseph W. Dauben for Science Television (1991); and *Florence: Cradle of the Renaissance* (Museum City Video, 1992).

The politics of the time provide a rich resource for novels. The activities of this time attracted the best attentions of Alexandre Dumas. Writing about events in France, he published *The Two Dianas*, (dealing with the time of Francis I), *The Page of the Duke of Savoy* (touching the time of the Emperor Charles V), *Ascanio* (France in the middle of the century), and *Marguerite de Valois* (touching the civil wars)—and this is only an incomplete list. Mark Twain wrote about the time of Edward VI in *The Prince and the Pauper*. More recently, Robin Maxwell sheds some light on the reign of Henry VIII in *The Secret Diary of Anne Boleyn: A Novel* (Scribner, 1998).

Filmmakers have been equally attracted to the period, especially the English scene. *A Man for All Seasons* (Columbia/Tristar, 1966), directed by Fred Zinnemann, is a fine telling of the story of Sir Thomas More. Queen Elizabeth has been the subject of films throughout the twentieth century, including *Elizabeth* (Umvd, 1998), directed by Shekhar Kapur, and indirectly in Academy Award winner *Shakespeare in Love* (Miramax, 1998), directed by John Madden. A film dealing with the period after Henry VIII is *Lady Jane* (Paramount, 1985), directed by Trevor Nunn. The 1933 film, *The Private Life of Henry VIII* (AAE Films), directed by Alexander Korda, is worth seeing. From the continent, *The Return of Martin Guerre* (Fox Lorber, 1982), directed by Daniel Vigne, does justice to Natalie Zemon Davis's fine monograph. The film of the life of *Martin Luther* (VCI Home Video, 1953) is a revealing look at the reformer.

Suggestions for Reading

Johnathan Zophy, *A Short History of Renaissance and Reformation Europe*, 2nd ed. (Prentice Hall, 1998) and John Hale, *The Civilization of Europe in the Renaissance* (Scribner, 1994) are both excellent introductions to the period. Jacob Burckhardt, *The Civilization of the Renaissance in Italy*, 2 Vols. (Torchbooks, 1958), first published in 1860, inaugurated the view that the Italian Renaissance of the fourteenth and fifteenth centuries was a momentous turning point in the history of Western civilization. The editors of this edition maintain that Burckhardt's major interpretations remain valid. Donald R. Kelley, *Renaissance Humanism* (Twayne, 1991), and Brian P. Copenhaver, *Renaissance Philosophy* (Oxford University Press, 1992) are excellent surveys. Katharina M. Wilson, ed., *Women Writers of the Renaissance and Reformation* (University of Georgia Press, 1987), is an excellent study of a neglected subject. John White, *Art and Architecture in Italy, 1250–1400*, 3rd ed. (Yale University Press, 1993) is an excellent overview. See also Charles Seymour Jr., *Sculpture in Italy, 1400–1500* (Yale University Press, 1994). Ross King, *Brunelleschi's Dome* (Walker, 2000), is an excellent account of the construction of the famous Florentine's work. Also, Silvio Bedini, *The Pope's Elephant* (Penguin, 2000), is a delightful account of Pope Leo X and his court.

A fascinating study of the attitudes of the Christian laity during the Reformation period can be found in Keith Thomas, *Religion and the Decline of Magic: Studies in Popular Beliefs in Sixteenth and Seventeenth Century England* (Oxford University Press, 1997). A useful context to the religious upheavals of the time is given by John Bossy, *Christianity in the West, 1400–1700* (Oxford University Press, 1985). On the impact of John Hus, see Thomas A. Fudge, *The Magnificent Ride: The First Reformation in Hussite Bohemia* (Ashgate Publishing, 1998). The general background of the Reformation is covered well in Steven E. Ozment, *Protestants: The Birth of a Revolution* (Doubleday, 1992). Brad S. Gregory, *Salvation at Stake: Christian Martyrdom in Early Modern Europe* (Harvard University Press, 2000), is a distinguished work of scholarship that takes the martyrs of the time at their word. Richard Marius, *Martin Luther: The Christian Between God and Death* (Belknap Press of Harvard University Press, 1999), is a superb new study of Luther to 1526. The context for the English Reformation is provided by Richard H. Britnell in *The Closing of the Middle Ages: England, 1471–1529* (Blackwell, 1997). Ulrich Gabler gives a thorough background of Ulrich Zwingli's place in history in his *Huldrych Zwingli: His Life and Work* (Clark, 1995).

William J. Bouwsma, *John Calvin* (Oxford University Press, 1988), is a scholarly portrayal of Calvin's human side, emphasizing his inner conflict against the humanistic trend of his time. On the "left wing" of Protestantism, Anthony Arthur's *The Tailor-King: The Rise and Fall of the Anabaptist Kingdom of Münster* (St. Martin's Press, 1999) is a first-rate history of the radical Reformation city-state in northern Germany. John C.

Olin places the Catholic response in perspective in *The Catholic Reformation: From Savonarola to Ignatius Loyola* (Fordham University Press, 1993). R. Po-chia Hsia, *The World of Catholic Renewal 1540–1770* (Cambridge University Press, 1998), is an innovative study of the history of the Catholic Church from the run up to the Council of Trent to the suppression of the Jesuits.

For the greater part of the period between 1300 and 1500, Europe was militarily and economically inferior to other world civilizations. Europeans were no match for the Turkish armies, did not possess the wealth of China or India, and lacked the centralized efficiency of the Incas. From 1500 to 1650, however, the balance of military and economic power began to change, and Europe began its global expansion, a process that would continue until 1914.

Three influences contributed to this expansion. We have already discussed two of them: the changes in European thought coming out of the Renaissance and the Reformation (see Chapter 14). The third factor in the increase in European power came in the development of the nation-state system.

State structures began to be seen during the origins of modern civilizations, and the variety of state systems throughout history ranges from despotism, to empire, to religious states, to city-states, to loose federations. These states all share the same qualities: they have defined boundaries, possess the power to tax, and monopolize force. As one of the most influential analysts of the origins and dominance of the nation-state system, Charles Tilly, once noted "war made the state, and the state made war." In the thirteenth century, the most successful form of the state, the nation-state emerged, largely sparked by political opposition to the claims of papal power.

Until 1789, the typical European nation-state was inhabited in large part by people of a similar ethnic and linguistic background (the nation) and led by a king or queen who embodied the state. Tilly indicates that the nation-state succeeded because of its capacity to profit from the rise of capitalism and to mobilize the resources within its boundary to fight wars. Some scholars find the approach of linking the changes in military technology to state development to be simplistic. But it cannot be denied that as the age of gunpowder warfare arrived in the fifteenth century, a new infrastructure was demanded to support the standing army and arms factories needed to compete in the international state system. This military efficiency combined with the scientific advances coming out of the new ways of thinking and religious zeal helped propel Europe to a world force.[1]

433

POLITICS IN AN AGE OF CRISIS: 1300–1500

■ *How did the crisis posed by the Black Death and its consequences change European politics?*

Europe saw many changes during the final two centuries of the late Middle Ages, some disastrous, some constructive. The suffering produced by the Black Death (bubonic plague), famine, and economic depression took a massive toll on the population (see Chapter 14) and was compounded by a number of destructive wars. Underway at the same time, however, were political changes that would have lasting effects on the growth and expansion of European power.

England and France: The Hundred Years' War

Nation-making in both England and France was greatly affected by the long conflict that colored much of both nations' history during the fourteenth and fifteenth centuries. The Hundred Years' War (1337–1453) had its origins in a fundamental conflict between the English kings, who claimed much of French territory as theirs, and the French monarchs, whose ultimate goal was a centralized France under the direct rule of the monarchy at Paris.

Another cause was the clash of French and English economic interests in Flanders. This region was falling more and more under French control, to the frustration of both the English wool-growers, who supplied the great Flemish woolen industry, and the

A fifteenth-century portrait of Joan of Arc in battle dress. After leading the French to victory at Orléans in 1429, she was captured by the English, tried and convicted of witchcraft and heresy, and burned at the stake in 1431. The French king, Charles VII, whose kingdom she had helped save, did nothing to rescue her.

Medieval Politics, 1300–1500

1337–1453	Hundred Years' War between France and England
1356	Golden Bull regulates the election of German emperors
1386	Unification of Poland and Lithuania
1454	Treaty of Lodi brings peace to Italian city-states
1455–1485	Wars of the Roses: civil war in England
1479	Marriage of Ferdinand of Aragon and Isabella of Castile
1492	Spain conquers Granada, unifies Spanish nation
1494	France invades Italy

English king, whose income came in great part from duties on wool.

The first years of warfare witnessed impressive English victories. With no thought of strategy, the French knights charged the enemy and then engaged in hand-to-hand fighting. But the English had learned more effective methods. Their greatest weapon was the longbow. Six feet long and made of yew wood, the longbow shot steel-tipped arrows that were dangerous at 400 yards and deadly at 100. The usual English plan of battle called for the knights to fight dismounted. Protecting them was a forward wall of bowmen just behind a barricade of iron stakes planted in the ground to slow the enemy's cavalry charge. By the time the French cavalry reached the dismounted knights, the remaining few French were easily killed.

The revival of the French military effort and a rebirth of national spirit is associated with Joan of Arc, who inspired a series of French victories. Moved by inner voices that she believed divine, Joan persuaded the

Document

The Trial of Joan of Arc

Joan of Arc (1412?–1431) is without doubt one of the most remarkable figures in European history. At the age of 13, Joan was hearing the voices of her "saints," who instructed her to come to the aid of the heir to the French throne and win for him a victory over the English at Orléans. The victory was won, Charles became king, and promptly turned his back on Joan, who was captured by the English and put on trial as a witch, a heretic, and a transvestite, since she now preferred to wear men's clothes even off the battlefield.

The following firsthand accounts were recorded by men who were witness to her trial and ultimate condemnation and execution:

Joan was dressed in men's clothes, that is, a tunic, a cape, and a short robe and other men's clothes, a costume that on our orders she had previously put aside, and had taken on women's clothes. And so we interrogated her to learn when and for what reason she had once more assumed men's clothes: "I did it on my own will," Joan declared; "I took it again because it was more lawful and convenient than to have women's clothes because I am with men; I began to wear them again because what was promised me was not observed, to wit that I should go to mass and receive the body of Christ and be freed from these irons.... I would rather die than stay in these irons; but if it is permitted for me to go to mass, and if I could be freed of these irons, and if I could be put in a decent prison and if I could have a woman to help me [her expression, *avoir femme,* is written on the minutes but not on the official transcript of the trial], I would be good and do what the church wishes."

"Since Thursday, have you heard the voices of St. Catherine and St. Margaret?" [Cauchon asked.]

"Yes."

"What have they told you?"

"God has expressed through St. Catherine and St. Margaret His great sorrow at the strong treason to which I consented in abjuring and making a revocation to save my life, and said that I was damning myself to save my life."

In the margin of the account, the author of this account wrote: "A deadly reply."

Shortly before her execution, another account of a conversation with Joan was recorded by a Dominican monk who visited her very shortly before her death:

The day that Joan was abandoned to secular judgment and delivered to be burned, I found myself in the morning in the prison with Friar Martin Ladvenu, whom the bishop of Beauvais had sent to tell her of her coming death and to induce her to true contrition and penance, and also to hear her confession, which Ladvenu did very carefully and charitably. And when he announced to the poor woman the death that she was to die that day, which her judges had ordered,

and when she had understood and heard the hard and cruel death that was coming, she began to cry out sorrowfully and pitiably to tear and pull her hair. "Alas! That they treat me so horribly and cruelly that my body, clean and whole, which was never corrupted, should be today consumed and reduced to ashes! Ah! I would prefer to be beheaded seven times than to be burned like that! Alas! If I had been in an ecclesiastical prison to which I submitted myself, and if I had been guarded by men of the church, not by my enemies and adversaries, it would not have turned out for me as miserably as it has. Ah! I protest before God, the Great Judge, the great wrongs and grievances that they have done me." She then made marvelous complaint in that place of the oppression and violences that had been done to her in prison by the jailers and by the others they had made enter against her.

After these complaints, the bishop arrived, to whom she said immediately: "Bishop, I die because of you." He began to remonstrate with her, saying: "Ah, Joan, take it patiently, you will die because you have not held to what you promised us and because you return to your first witchcraft." And the poor Maid answered him: "Alas! If you had put me in the prison of a church court and handed me over to the hands of competent and agreeable ecclesiastical caretakers, this would not have happened to me. That is why I complain of you before God." That being done, I went outside and heard no more.

Questions to Consider

1. Do you feel that these accounts of Joan's actions and thoughts as she approached her execution are trustworthy? Do you think that the recorders are unbiased, or swayed toward or against her?

2. What image of Joan is created by these accounts? Does she seem to be a deluded peasant girl, a mystic visionary, or a rational martyr?

3. Are these firsthand accounts of value in illuminating Joan as a historical figure, or do they add to Joan's status as an almost mythological symbol of French resistance to the English?

From Regine Pernoud and Marie Veronique Clin, *Joan of Arc: Her Story,* trans. Jeremy duQuesnay Adams (St. Martin's Press, 1998), pp. 132–133.

A Pilgrim's Map of Canterbury

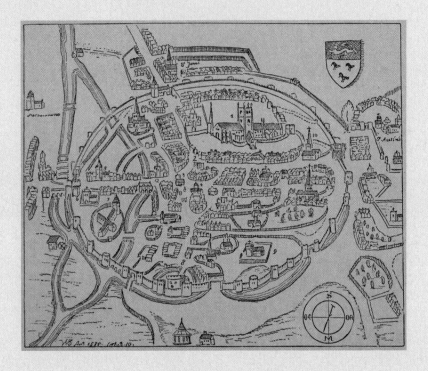

This medieval fifteenth-century map of Canterbury is in many ways a precursor of our modern tourist maps that indicate the "must see" sights of a visitor's destination. Canterbury was an English tourist attraction as early as the Roman occupation of the island—Julius Caesar and the Emperor Claudius were early visitors. But Canterbury's great fame as a pilgrimage site began when the Archbishop of Canterbury, the most influential bishop in the English Catholic Church, was killed in the cathedral by knights who claimed they were sent to conduct the assassination by the King of England, Henry II. The Archbishop, Thomas à Becket, immediately became regarded as a martyr for the cause of religious freedom. King Henry himself visited Canterbury as a pilgrim, asking forgiveness for his sins and walking barefoot to the shrine of the man he may have ordered murdered. Thomas was quickly made a saint, and the site of his murder became a destination for medieval pilgrims seeing forgiveness for their sins.

Such a pilgrimage is described by Geoffrey Chaucer in his Canterbury Tales. Chaucer prefaces this work by describing how he joined near London with a group of 29 pilgrims on their way to Canterbury to visit Thomas à Becket's shrine. To ward off the boredom of the trip, the pilgrims agree to tell tales (two on the way to Canterbury and two on the journey back), and whoever told the best tale was to be rewarded with a supper paid for by the others.

Chaucer's resultant stories still remain as one of the greatest works of English literature.

Canterbury's popularity as a pilgrimage site continued throughout the Middle Ages. Although the most famous landmark remained the cathedral, the church of St. Dunstan attracted the increased attention of pilgrims in the late sixteenth century, since that church became the final resting place of the head of Sir Thomas More (1478–1535). This noted English lawyer, scholar, and humanist served as King Henry VIII's chancellor before refusing to deny the legitimacy of the king's first marriage and later failing to recognize Henry as the head of the church in England in place of the pope. More was imprisoned, refused to change his position, was put on trial, and was convicted of treason. He was beheaded in London, but his head found its final resting place in Canterbury. Henry VIII went on to confiscate much of the wealth of Canterbury, including donations of pilgrims over the centuries, in order to increase revenue. He also discouraged pilgrimage to the shrines, but Canterbury's popularity as a visitor's site has maintained its popularity to the present day.

Questions to Consider

1. How would this map serve the purposes of a visitor unfamiliar with the city of Canterbury?

2. Do you think the lack of great detail would be of concern to viewers of this map?

3. The twelve sites named and numbered on the map are almost all churches. Why do you think that is the case?

French ruler to allow her to lead an army to relieve the besieged city of Orléans. Clad in white armor and riding a white horse, she inspired confidence and a feeling of invincibility in her followers, and in 1429 Orléans was rescued from what had seemed certain conquest. Joan was captured by the enemy, found guilty of bewitching the English soldiers, and burned at the stake. But her martyrdom seemed a turning point in the long struggle.

France's development of a permanent standing army and the greater use of gunpowder also began to transform the art of war. English resistance crumbled as military superiority now turned full circle; the English longbow was outmatched by French artillery. Of the vast territories they had once controlled in France, the English retained only Calais when the war ended in 1453.

The Hundred Years' War exhausted England and fueled discontent with the monarchy in Parliament and among the common people. Baronial rivalry to control both Parliament and the crown erupted into full-scale civil war known as the Wars of the Roses (1455–1485); the white rose was the symbol of the Yorkists, and the red rose the House of Lancaster. Thirty years of bloody civil war ended in 1485 with the victory of Henry Tudor over his rivals. His victory at Bosworth Field enabled him to become Henry VII, the first of the Tudor dynasty. Henry VII (1485–1509) proved to be a popular and effective monarch, bringing national unity and security to the English people.

The Hundred Years' War left France with a new national consciousness and royal power that was stronger than ever. Shortly after the war, Louis XI (1461–1483) continued the process of consolidating royal power. Astute and tireless, yet completely lacking in scruples, Louis XI earned himself the epithet the "universal spider" because of his constant intrigues. In his pursuit of power he used any weapon—violence, bribery, treachery—to obtain his ends. The "spider king" devoted his reign to restoring prosperity to his nation and to reducing the powers of the noble families still active and ambitious after the long war. Like Henry VII in England, Louis XI was one of the "new monarchs" who worked for the creation of a subject-sovereign relationship in their kingdoms, replacing the old feudal ties of personal fidelity.

Spain: Ferdinand and Isabella and the Reconquista

Spain became strongly centralized under an assertive and aggressive monarchy in 1479, when Isabella of Castile and Ferdinand of Aragon began a joint rule that united the Iberian peninsula except for Navarre, Portugal, and Granada. The "Catholic Majesties," the title the pope conferred on Ferdinand and Isabella, set out to establish effective royal control in all of Spain.

Ferdinand and Isabella believed that the church should be subordinate to royal government. By tactful negotiations, the Spanish sovereigns induced the pope to give them the right to make church appointments in Spain and to establish a Spanish court of **Inquisition** largely free of papal control. The Spanish Inquisition confiscated the property of many *conversos* (Jews and Muslims who had converted to Christianity to avoid persecution) and terrified the Christian clergy and laity into accepting royal absolutism as well as religious orthodoxy. Although the Inquisition greatly enhanced the power of the Spanish crown, it also caused many people to flee Spain and the threat of persecution. About 150,000 Spanish Jews, mainly merchants and professional people, fled to the Netherlands, England, North Africa, and the Ottoman Empire. Calling themselves Sephardim (su-faer-DUIM), many of these exiles retained their Spanish language and culture into the twentieth century.

Inquisition—A special Roman Catholic court directed to search out and punish heretics, believers in doctrines other than those prescribed by the Church.

The uniting of Castile and Aragon, represented here by Isabella and Ferdinand, provided the foundation for the dominant Spanish state in the sixteenth century.

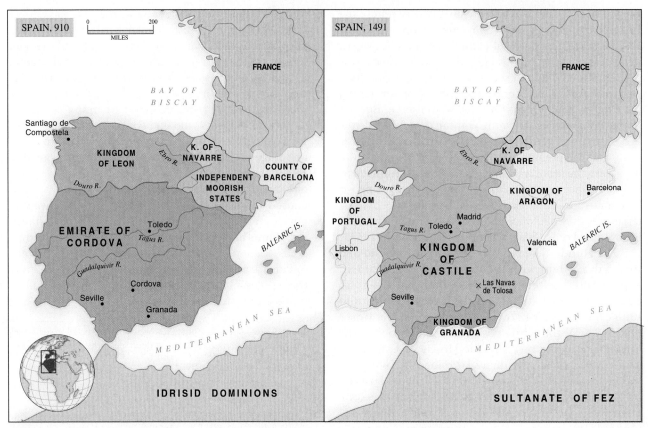

The progress of nation-building in Spain was linked to the Reconquista, the effort to expel the Muslims from the peninsula—in 1492 the kingdom of Granada, the East Muslim stronghold in Spain, fell to the Spanish.

Another manifestation of Spanish absolutism, defined by Isabella herself as "one king, one law, one faith," was the intentional neglect of the Cortes of Castile and Aragon. These representative assemblies, having emerged in the twelfth century, never were allowed by the monarchy to take an effective position as legislative bodies.

One of the most dramatic achievements of the Catholic Majesties was the completion of the *Reconquista* in 1492 with the defeat of Granada, the last Moorish state on the Iberian Peninsula. This occurred in same year that Columbus claimed the New World for Spain. Before Ferdinand died in 1516, a dozen years after Isabella, he seized the part of Navarre that lay south of the Pyrenees. This acquisition, together with the conquest of Granada, completed the unification of the Spanish nation-state.

Portugal

The western part of the Iberian Peninsula, Portugal, had a different historical evolution than did Spain. There was never a classic feudal tradition in the country, in which kings gave grants of land and positions to their vassals; rather the country was dominated by strong regional barons against whom the kings would

struggle during the thirteenth century. But during the fourteenth century the centralizing power of monarchy began to impose its will over the country, and the Avis dynasty would rule Portugal from 1384 to 1580.

As will be shown in Chapter 16, the Portuguese were the first Europeans to venture out into the Atlantic in search of new business and resources. The person most known for this adventure was Prince Henry (1394–1460), the Navigator. He established an observatory where advances in navigation and ship making were made. In 1411, he crossed the Straits of Gibraltar and captured the Moroccan city of Ceuta (SIU-ta). During his life his sailors took the Azores and penetrated as far south as Senegal. In response to the economic stimulus of new markets and resources, Portugal doubled its population between 1400 and 1600 and established a global trading empire, however briefly. Then in 1580, during the reign of the Spanish Habsburg, Philip II, Spain incorporated Portugal into its realm.

Central Europe 1300–1521

Central Europe at this time included the Holy Roman Empire, Italy, and the Catholic nations of Poland, the Czech lands of Bohemia and Moravia, and Hungary. The history of this region was largely one of conflict:

political (Empire-Papacy), ethnic (German-Slav), or religious (Orthodox-Catholic). The region was, however, tied together by economics. It comprised an economic zone anchored on the west by the Rhine river, the primary route of the overland trade from the Mediterranean to the North Sea and beyond to the Baltic Sea and Russia. The cities of the **Hanseatic League** dominated the northern portions of this trade route, trading primarily in beer, wool, wood, and grain. Until the opening of the Atlantic trade routes in the sixteenth century, this zone experienced comparative economic well-being and important cultural exchange, despite the plague and wars.

The Holy Roman Empire

In the late Middle Ages, the Holy Roman Empire lapsed progressively into political disunity. In 1273 the imperial crown was given to the weak Count Rudolf of the House of Habsburg. During the remainder of the Middle Ages, the Habsburgs had amazing success in territorial acquisition; Rudolf himself acquired Austria through marriage, and, thereafter, the Habsburgs ruled their holdings from Vienna.

While the empire grew, however, its authority over its constituent states weakened. In 1356 the German nobility won significant victory in their efforts to avoid the creation of a powerful monarchy. **The Golden Bull,** a document that served as the political constitution of Germany until early in the nineteenth century, established a procedure by which seven German electors—three archbishops and four lay princes—chose the emperor. The electors and other important princes were given rights that made them virtually independent rulers, and the emperor could take no important action without the consent of the imperial feudal assembly, the Diet, which met infrequently. The empire, including 2000 independent lesser nobles, 66 autonomous cities, over 100 imperial counts, 30 secular princes, and 70 quasi-independent bishoprics was loosely governed by the Imperial Diet.

Despite the absence of political unity with the Empire, the Habsburg family managed to vastly expand its power in the fifteenth century. They achieved this primarily through successful marriage alliances and not by battle. Most marriage contracts among royal families involved a clause in which, in the case of the death of one of the participants in the marriage, all of the holdings of that person would pass to the survivor. The Habsburgs started this period of marital expansion

in 1477 when Frederick III, largely ineffectual in the face of attacks by the Hungarians, arranged the marriage of his son Marximilian I to Maria of Burgundy—whose family laid claim to the lands of northeastern France and the Low Countries. Their marriage produced one son, Philip.

When Frederick died, Maximilian picked up his deceased father's Austrian lands, and then put together a marriage alliance between his son Philip and the daughter of the Spanish king, Juana. Although their marriage ended sadly, they produced a number of children, three of whom became important: Charles, Ferdinand, and Maria. Charles (1516–1556) became Holy Roman Emperor in 1519 and controlled the family's central and western holdings—including Spain and its world empire. Ferdinand headed the eastern part of the Empire, and Maria was married off to the king of Hungary, Louis II. When Louis was killed by the Turks at Mohacs in 1526, Maria Habsburg received her late husband's holdings.

The Hapsburgs' rise to power was not unnoticed at the time, and a phrase made the rounds, *Bella gerant alii, tu felix Austria nube* ("Let the others fight wars; you lucky Austrian, marry"[2]).

Because of his long reign and political skill, the Austrian monarch Frederick III (r. 1440–1493) started the successful policy of favorable marriage alliances that led to the Habsburgs ruling over a world empire in the sixteenth century.

Hanseatic League—A commercial league of mostly German cities extending from the English Channel to the eastern end of the Baltic Sea that was active between the thirteenth and seventeenth centuries.

Golden Bull—A document issued from the Holy Roman Emperor King Charles IV in 1356 that served as the political constitution of the German speaking lands until the nineteenth century.

Switzerland

In 1291, citizens in the German-speaking parts of the Alps began the drive to separate themselves from the Habsburg-dominated Empire. In 1291 the three cantons that controlled the access to Italy through the Saint Gothard Pass made an alliance to protect their independence. Fourteen years later they fought off the Habsburgs at the battle of Mortgaten, thus beginning the history of the country of Switzerland.

Because of its location on the overland route between the Mediterranean and the Rhine road to the North Sea, the region became rich. In addition, the Swiss artisans became known throughout Europe for the quality of their weapons. As we saw in Chapter 14, the region became touched by the currents of the Reformation during the career of Ulrich Zwingli.

Italy

After 1300, the middle and southern parts of the Italian peninsula gained a bit of distance from the Germans. In southern Italy, the Angevin dynasty asserted itself, while in the center the papacy worked to extend its holdings. Between Rome and the Alps, the rich and powerful city-states of Genoa, Milan, and Florence joined with Venice to construct their own diplomatic and political structures.

The years between 1300 and 1500 were not stable: As one authority notes, it was a time of threatened cities, kingdoms without kings, feudal holdings in transition to becoming principalities. Throughout the fourteenth and early fifteenth centuries the area was marked by intra-city conflicts fought using mercenary forces known as the **condotierri** (kon-do-TIER-ree). These mercenaries, many of them Spanish, fought for pay and would change sides in mid-battle if a better offer was made by their opponents. Economic developments shifted the political center of gravity during the 1400s to the northern cities from the Kingdom of Sicily and the Papal States.

As we saw in Chapter 14, in the northern Italian cities, new, bourgeois elites led by families such as the Medici accumulated great wealth from the wool business and banking to sponsor the great artists and thinkers of the middle classes. In 1454 they tired of their ongoing conflicts and at the Treaty of Lodi worked out a way of getting along, including exchanges of ambassadors with extraterritoriality. Unfortunately, all of the new peace was destroyed when the French invaded in 1494, and Italy became an object of and no longer a subject in European diplomacy. Incipient steps toward some sort of Italian sovereignty would have to wait nearly four centuries before being realized.

---

condotierri—Mercenaries employed by the Italian city-states during the conflicts of the fourteenth and fifteenth centuries.

The Catholic Frontier: Poland, Bohemia, and Hungary

East of the empire and north of the Italian peninsula, the frontiers of the Roman Catholic zone were to be found. In the tenth century, three peoples along the frontier accepted Roman Catholic Christianity: the Poles (966), the Czechs (864), and the Hungarians (1000). They joined a singular religious community that stretched from the Bug River to the Straits of Gibraltar to Iceland. Common threads uniting this community were the Latin language and a belief in papal authority. Irish and German missionaries had carried the Roman faith to this frontier area, and they were followed and sustained by a Germanic population movement, the *Drang nach Osten* ("drive to the east"). The royal families of the Poles, Czechs, and Hungarians intermarried with those of France, Luxembourg, and Austria and they participated fully in all of the major events and movements of the Western tradition. As converts to Catholicism, they proudly saw themselves, in Oscar Halecki's words, as the borderlands of civilization—facing Orthodox and even Turkish and Mongol attacks.[3]

Unlike the centralizing tendencies in western Europe where kings became stronger than their nobles, in east Central Europe—especially in Poland and Hungary—the nobles jealously guarded their authority in the fourteenth and fifteenth centuries, leading to weakened central power.

The church played a key role in both the uniting of the countries and the formation of the national identity, lending its legitimacy by converting the royal family in each country. In the course of the tenth century the Polish Piasts (895–1306), the Bohemian Přemyslids (PSHEM-ui-sleds; 895–1306), and the Hungarian Arpads (896–1310) formed the dynasties that would rule their respective countries until 1300. The Poles, Czechs, and Hungarians suffered from the Mongol invasions in the 1240s but recovered quickly within a generation. Each of their states had close commercial and cultural ties with the Germans, and—sometimes went to war with them.

The cities of Poland and Hungary tended to be dominated by Germans and Jews, the bulk of the indigenous people living as serfs. In Bohemia, however, urban life was dominated by the Czech people, still with a healthy representation of Germans and Jews. The Czechs would be the only people of eastern Europe to share fully in the urban lifestyle of Central Europe. The three countries had their individual legal traditions— the Hungarians, for example, refer to their Golden Bull of 1222 as the equivalent to the English Magna Carta in terms of its guarantees of liberties.

The region did not suffer as heavily from the Black Plague as western Europe, and as a result Poland, Bohemia, and Hungary experienced a golden age of cultural and economic development in the fourteenth century. There were universities established at Prague (1348), Krakow (1364), and Pecs (1369) and scholars from those schools participate in the humanist movement in the fifteenth century. Even with their economic and cultural progress, the three states argued over a number of issues as their respective kings sought to expand their influences and fought over regions such Silesia.

During that fourteenth century, the originating dynasties died out in Hungary and Bohemia. Foreign kings such as the Angevin Louis the Great of Hungary (1342–1382), and the Luxembourger Charles the Great of Bohemia (1333–1378) were elected by the powerful nobles and bourgeoisie of the area. The last Piast, Casimir the Great of Poland (1333–1370) led his country through its golden age, but after his death the Poles resorted to a system of elective kingship.

This well-being of the fourteenth century, however, would not last long because of the expansion of Russia to the east, Sweden to the north, and the Ottoman Empire to the south. Internal problems also would lead to a weakening of the realms. Elective kings in Poland and Hungary frittered away their central powers to satisfy the demands of the nobles who elected them. The weakening of central power hit its peak in Poland, where successive royal elections cut the powers of the monarchy until the installation of the *Liberum* **Veto**, an act that allowed one member of the nobility, the *szlachta* (SCHLOK-tah), to block a king's program by his negative vote.

In 1386 Poland united with Lithuania—the last pagan country in Europe—and became the largest state in Europe. Invasions from the east and the west, however, eroded the strength of this state. The Poles had earlier added to their own problems in 1225 when they invited the crusading order of the Teutonic knights into Poland to aid in the combat against the indigenous Baltic peoples to the north, the Prus. The Teutonic knights, out of work after failed crusades in the Eastern Mediterranean, slaughtered the Prus, established their own state based around present-day Kaliningrad (Koenigsberg), and called it Prussia. They proved a considerable threat to the Poles and were not defeated until the battle of Tannenberg in 1410. Later the Teutons would turn their territory of West Prussia over to the Poles and keep East Prussia as a fief of the Polish crown. Poland would face competition and eventual destruction by Russia, Prussia, Sweden, and Austria in the seventeenth and eighteenth centuries.

The Bohemians became the richest part of the Catholic orbit and went on to challenge the Germans

politically, economically, and religiously. The Golden Bull of 1356 made the Bohemian king one of the seven electors of the Holy Roman Empire. We have already discussed the religious controversy between the Czechs and the Germans during the late fourteenth century. The creation of the Hussite Church after Jan Hus's immolation led to four crusades being preached by the Catholic Church against the forces at Prague. The Czechs successfully defended themselves under leaders such as John Žižka (ZHISH-kah) and they would continue to progress, growing economically and politically until the seventeenth century—when they were defeated in the first phase of the Thirty Years' War.

The Hungarians experienced a brilliant fifteenth century under János Hunyadi (YAWN-nosh HOON-ia-dee) and his son and successor Mathias Corvinus. As Magyar aristocrats, they ended the period of foreign kings. János Hunyadi, by his wealth and military prowess, paved the way for his son Mathias to be elected king in 1458, who came to be known as Mathias Corvinus. During his 32-year reign, Mathias established close ties with the Italian Renaissance cities, especially Florence. Scholars and artists at his court participated fully in the cultural movements of the

Matthias Corvinus was a true "renaissance man." He was a patron of the arts, supporter of artists and writers, and a collector of books and manuscripts. He was also one of the pioneers in introducing printing to Central and Eastern Europe.

Liberum **Veto**—In order to guard against the potential power of a strong central monarchy, the Polish nobles in 1652 installed the Liberum Veto, an act that allowed one member of the nobility to block the king's program by his single negative vote in the noble assembly.

time. He founded a printing press and had one of the most important libraries in Europe. Although he was unable to increase his central power in competition with the Czechs and the Poles, he did manage to capture Vienna. After he died in 1490 from unknown causes, the Hungarian magnates went back to electing foreign kings. The Hungarians became disunited and were finally defeated by the Ottoman Turks at the battle of Mohacs (1526). Hungary was divided into three zones, the larger part controlled directly by the Ottomans.

THE RELIGIOUS-POLITICAL FUSION

■ *The framers of the American Constitution demanded a total separation of church and state. What examples can you find in the wars of religion between 1517 and 1648 to support their belief in a separation of faith and politics?*

The papacy's political power had been in a continual decline since the thirteenth century. In Central Europe, local elites fought the Catholic clergy and the excluded lower classes for political control. In the Atlantic states of England, France, and Spain, the monarchs became increasingly independent of the Pope's demands. The French invasion at the end of the fifteenth century made the Italian peninsula an arena for desperate struggle between the Habsburg and French Valois dynasties that would last until 1559. The Papal States became a political pawn. The papacy's weaknesses were exploited by the troops of Charles V when they sacked Rome in 1527. Protestant leaders such as Martin Luther profited from the disarray in the Catholic world, and his followers combined religion and politics in a new and explosive way that Catholic leaders quickly learned to emulate. The result would be a series of religious-political conflicts that would last until 1648.

Religious Diversity in Western Europe
MAP

Protestant Politics

The rise of the Protestants finally liberated the nation-state from any claim of authority by the church. As we saw in Chapter 14, Luther spelled out that humans have two obligations: first and most importantly, loyalty to God and second, loyalty to the earthly government. Luther's positions on church-state relations found biblical support in the words of Christ: "Therefore, render unto Caesar, that which is Caesar's and unto God, that which is God's" (Matthew 22:21).

Luther immediately gained support from German and Scandinavian rulers and in every city along the Baltic coast where there was a German-speaking majority—including in Poland and present-day Estonia. Luther supported the repression of the protesting German knights and the crushing of the Peasant's Revolt in 1524–1525. In addition, Luther said little about the Protestant princes' taking the considerable wealth of the Catholic Church

The religious split between Lutherans and Catholics soon took the form of military alliances. Lutheran princes organized for defense in the **Schmalkaldic League** and were not immediately challenged because Emperor Charles V had to deal with the French and Turkish threats. A low-intensity, sporadic civil war dragged on in the empire until after Luther's death in 1546. It ended with the Peace of Augsburg in 1555, when the imperial princes were permitted to choose between Lutheranism and Catholicism in their state churches, thus increasing their independence from the emperor. In addition, Catholic properties confiscated before 1552 were retained by Lutheran principalities, which provided a means for financing their policies.

Henry VIII's Break with Rome

In England, the conflict between the church and state had little if anything to do with differences over religious doctrine. As we saw in Chapter 14, Henry VIII (r. 1509–1547) broke from the church because he needed a legitimate male heir. When Henry's wife Catherine of Aragon failed to provide him with an heir, he sought in 1527 to have his marriage to her annulled so he could remarry. For political reasons, however, the Pope refused to grant an annulment, and Henry forced the clergy into proclaiming him head of a separate, English church.

The Anglican Church was essentially the same as the Catholic Church, with the exception that the English monarch served as the head of the church, the clergy could marry, and English replaced Latin as the official language of the church. Henry also extracted from Parliament the authority to appoint bishops, and Parliament ended all payment of revenues to Rome. In 1539 Parliament completed its seizure of monastery lands and the wealth of pilgrimage sites such as Canterbury Cathedral. While Henry's break from the church left a legacy of turmoil and strife that would last for another 150 years, his actions placed both temporal and spiritual authority in the

---

Schmalkaldic League—A defensive alliance of Lutheran princes organized in 1531 under the leadership of Philip the Magnanimous of Hesse to defend themselves against the Catholic powers of the Holy Roman Empire.

hands of the monarchy, strengthening the power of the English state.

Calvinist Variations

Calvin viewed politics as a theocratic exercise—the laws of God become the laws of the state. His plans for a city government in Geneva called for domination by the clergy—full control over moral and religious behavior—and banishment of all dissidents. Though met with grudging opposition, he gradually increased his power through support from the Protestant refugees who poured into the city. His influence climaxed after a failed "revolt of the godless" in 1555. From that year until his death in 1564, he dominated the council, ruling Geneva with an iron hand, within the letter, but not the spirit, of the original ordinances. As we saw in Chapter 15, he imposed a religious totalitarianism over Geneva, and religious police held the power to investigate every detail of private life.

DOCUMENT

Calvin on Predestination

In advising people from outside of Geneva, he said that political authorities had to consult with the church on policies. He also said, however, that it was the duty of Christians to obey the state in secular matters. When he discussed how governments should be run, he advocated the concept of representative government.

Many of the divergent Protestant splinter groups up and down the Rhine saw different lessons in scripture. The majority of them were indifferent or antagonistic to secular government; many favored pacifism and substitution of the church for the state.

The legacy of the Protestant Reformation on politics was mixed. Luther, Henry VIII, Calvin, and the Protestant radicals all advocated different combinations of the church and the state. Between 1517 and 1564, however, political life in Europe became revolutionized. The change from the concept of Christendom in 1300 to communities based on faith and allegiance imposed by the state brought with it much death, suffering, and destruction.

WARS OF RELIGIONS: THE SPANISH HABSBURGS' QUEST FOR EUROPEAN HEGEMONY, 1556–1598

▪ *Did Philip II of Spain use the powers of the state to spread the influence of the Catholic Church, or did he use the Church for political gain?*

After the 1560s, religious fanaticism, both Protestant and Catholic, combined with pragmatic politics to form a combustible mixture. Sometimes religious conflict caused the reshaping of the old political system to justify movements against royal authority. More often, it popularized centralized monarchies, whose rulers promised to restore order by wielding power. Despite pious declarations, kings and generals in this period conducted war with little regard for moral principles; indeed, as time passed they steadily subordinated religious concerns to dynastic ambitions or national interests. This change, however, came slowly and was completed only in 1648 after Europe was thoroughly exhausted by the human suffering and material destruction of religious wars.

Until the end of the sixteenth century, Spain, led by Philip II, attempted to impose its will over the Continent. When he took power in 1556, he looked across the Pyrenees and across the Mediterranean and saw a Europe split by religious strife and still threatened by the presence of the Ottoman Empire. In Central Europe, the Peace of Augsburg ended a short war in Germany and sought to bring an accord between the Catholics and Lutherans. Even before Calvin died in 1564, however, his movement was spreading rapidly throughout the Continent. The Council of Trent launched a formidable counteroffensive, led by the Jesuits and supported by the Spanish and Austrian Habsburgs, against all Protestants. England remained on the verge of religious civil war after the death of Queen Mary, while France plunged into three decades of conflict after the extinction of the Valois line to the throne in 1559. Religious conflict broke out in the Spanish Netherlands, and in eastern Europe, militant Catholicism reversed the gains made by Protestants in the previous half-century. Philip saw opportunity in

War and Politics in the Age of Philip II	
1556–1598	Reign of Philip II of Spain
1558–1603	Reign of Elizabeth I of England
1561–1593	Religious wars in France
1566	Revolt in the Netherlands
1571	European forces defeat Turks at Lepanto
1572	Massacre of St. Bartholomew's Eve in Paris
1581	Dutch United Provinces declare independence from Spain
1587	Dutch Republic formed
1588	English defeat Spanish Armada

this tumultuous setting where the politics of religion dominated the scene in Europe.

The Era of Spanish Habsburg Dominance

Although it was a relatively underdeveloped and sparsely populated country of 8 million people, Spain, under Philip II (1556–1598), was the strongest military power in Europe. Seven centuries of resistance against the Moors (see Chapter 9) had formed a chivalric nobility that excelled in the military arts, if not also in business. This tradition, in addition to the promise of empire, saw the rigidly disciplined Spanish infantry absorb neighboring Portugal and fan out around the world as conquistadores, bringing back silver in seemingly unlimited quantities from the Americas. Working in tandem with the army was the Spanish Church, whose courts of the Inquisition, which had earlier banished the Jews, were now being used to eliminate the few remaining Moors and Spanish Protestants.

Philip willingly took on the Habsburgs' global burdens of maintaining Catholic orthodoxy, fighting the Turks, and imposing his will on his troublesome European neighbors. He considered this responsibility a part of his inheritance from his father, Charles V, whose long reign ended in 1556 when he abdicated his imperial throne and entered a monastery. At that time, Charles split his Habsburg holdings. His brother Ferdinand acquired control of Austria, Bohemia, and Hungary and became Holy Roman Emperor in 1556. Philip received Naples, Sicily, Milan, the Netherlands, Spain, and a vast overseas empire, which was much more lucrative than the traditional imperial domain in Central and eastern Europe. Indeed, the division of Habsburg lands appeared to be a blessing for Philip, allowing him to shed his father's worrisome "German problem" and concentrate more effectively on his Spanish realm.

Philip was a slightly built, somber, hardworking man. He was totally absorbed by the tasks of running a worldwide empire and rarely broke away to enjoy the luxurious life offered by his position. He seldom delegated authority, and his councilors served more as advisers than as administrators. Philip labored endlessly, reading and annotating official documents and dominating the *Cortes* (the traditional assembly of estates) of Castile. He married each of his four wives—Maria of Portugal, Mary of England, Elizabeth of France, and Anne of Austria, his niece—for political reasons; except for Mary, they bore his children but ate at his table only during official banquets. Elizabeth was his favorite, as were her daughters, who received some of his few open shows of tenderness and loving concern.

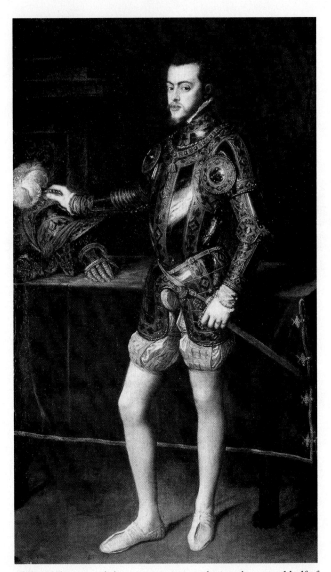

Philip II dominated the European scene during the second half of the sixteenth century. Even though he worked hard to assure Spanish Habsburg dominance, he failed to defeat the Dutch and the British and left Spain in an exhausted condition.

Philip took advantage of his role as defender of the Catholic faith. Although the church was wealthy and had unleashed the Inquisition to wipe out dissent, Philip used it to enforce Spanish traditions, arouse patriotism, and increase his popularity to strengthen the state. He was by no means a tool of the papacy: indeed, he defied more than one pope by denying jurisdiction over Spanish ecclesiastical courts, opposing the Council of Trent on clerical appointments, and fighting the Jesuits when they challenged his authority. He saw the Catholic Church as an arm of his government, and not vice versa.

Throughout his long reign, Philip continually encountered limitations to his authority. Spain had only recently been unified, and powerful nobles opposed him and his viceroys in their local councils. An overworked and overextended bureaucracy and a weak financial, communications, and industrial infrastructure placed the victories gained by the army and the state on a weak foundation. The backward Spanish sociopolitical system caused Philip many economic problems. Tax-exempt nobilities, comprising under 2 percent of the people, owned 95 percent of nonchurch land; the middle classes, overtaxed and depleted by purges of Jews and Moriscos (Spanish Muslims), were diminished; and the peasants were so exploited that production of food, particularly grains, was insufficient to feed the population. State regulation of industry and trade further limited revenues and forced primary reliance on precious metals from the Americas to fill the treasury, which ultimately produced a ruinous inflation. When his income failed to meet expenses, Philip borrowed at rising interest rates from Italian and Dutch banks. In 1557 and 1575 Philip had to suspend payments, effectively declaring national bankruptcy.

Revolt in the Netherlands

Philip's centralized rule encouraged some unity in Spain; the Netherlands, however, with its own traditions, was immediately suspicious of its foreign king who tried to enforce Catholic conformity. The Netherlands ("Low Countries") at the time also included modern Belgium, Luxembourg, and small holdings along 200 miles of marshy northern coast, an area not open to easy conquest. The geographical setting promoted strong local nobilities but also relatively independent peasants and townsmen. Even in medieval times, cities were centers of rapidly expanding commerce: of the 300 walled towns in 1560, some 19 had populations of over 10,000. (At the same time, England had only three or four of that size.) Antwerp was the commercial hub of northern Europe, serving as the crossroads of the Hanseatic League and the Italian-English trade axis. The combination of geography and wealth created a

The inherent logic of balance-of-power politics is readily evident in this map showing the extent of Habsburg—both Spanish and Austrian—holdings.

spirit of independence in religious affairs, as Lutherans, Calvinists, and Anabaptists were found in great numbers. Charles V had attempted sporadically to suppress the Protestants and had even burned a few notable heretics. But his status as a native son allowed him to maintain a tenuous stability in the region.

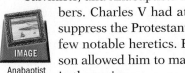

IMAGE
Anabaptist Torture in Muenster

Charles's daughter, Margaret of Parma (1522–1586) served as Philip's first regent for the Netherlands. She was sensitive to the religious complexities of her task; Philip, however, ordered a crackdown on the Protestants. Margaret introduced the Inquisition to fight heresy, a policy that forced leading nobles to leave her council and provoked vocal protests from her subjects. As the Inquisition did its work and executed prominent Protestants, the protests became loud and violent. Finally the so-called Calvinist Fury erupted in 1566, terrorizing Catholics and desecrating 400 churches. Most of the people in the Netherlands were shocked by the excesses of the radicals and voiced their support for Margaret.

Philip's response was to send the duke of Alva to the Netherlands with 10,000 Spanish troops, a great baggage train, and 2000 camp followers to establish order. Alva removed Margaret from her regency and clamped a brutal military dictatorship on the country. By decree, he centralized church administration, imposed new taxes, and established a special tribunal, soon dubbed the Council of Blood, to stamp out treason and heresy. During Alva's regime between 1567 and 1573, at least 8000 people were killed, including the powerful counts of Egmont and Horne. In addition, the Catholic terror deprived 30,000 people of their property and forced 100,000 to flee the country.

By 1568 Alva's excesses had provoked open rebellion—the first national liberation struggle, led by William of Orange (1533–1584), nicknamed William the Silent. Constant early defeats left him impoverished and nearly disgraced, but in 1572 the port of Brielle fell to his privateers, the "sea beggars," an event that triggered revolts throughout the north. Soon thereafter, William cut the dikes near Zeeland and mired down a

In his 1564 rendering of the biblical account of The Massacre of the Innocents *(1566–1567; Matthew 2:16), Pieter Brueghel the Elder anticipated well the horrors of violence that would befall the Netherlands.*

weary Spanish army. The continuing war was marked by savage ferocity, such as the sack of Antwerp by mutinous Spanish soldiers (1576). At the Spanish siege of Maestricht (MICE-treeschte) in 1579, women fought beside their men on the walls, and Spanish soldiers massacred the population, raping women first before tearing some limb from limb in the streets. That same year, in the Pacification of Ghent, Catholics and Protestants from the 17 provinces united to defy Philip, demand the recall of his army, and proclaim the authority of their traditional assembly, the States General.

Unfortunately for the rebel cause, this unity was soon destroyed by religious differences between militant northern Calvinists and Catholic southerners, particularly the many powerful nobles. The Spanish commander Alexander Farnese exploited these differences by restoring lands and privileges to the southern nobles. He was then able to win victories that induced the ten southern provinces to make peace with Spain in 1579. The Dutch, now alone, proclaimed their continued resistance to Spanish persecution and, in 1581, declared their independence from Spain. They persisted after William of Orange was assassinated in 1584, but meanwhile, the Spanish continued their war on heresy, butchering, burning, and burying alive Protestants who would not renounce their faith. The conflict lasted until a truce was negotiated in 1609.

Religious Wars in France

Although frustrated in the Netherlands, Philip did not face his father's French problem. According to the Treaty of Cateau-Cambrésis (KA-tow kam-BRAY-sees) in 1559, France gave up claims in Italy and the Netherlands. This humiliating surrender to the Habsburgs marked a definite turning point in French history. With its government bankrupt, its economy nearly prostrate, and its people disillusioned, France lost its leverage in foreign affairs as civil wars encouraged by Philip wasted the country during the next four decades.

Beneath the prevailing religious contention was another bitter struggle between the haves and have-nots. High prices, high rents, and high taxes drove the lower classes to riot and rebel against urban oligarchies, noble landlords, and government tax collectors. The social unrest continued sporadically throughout the sixteenth century. It brought no improvement of conditions for suffering peasants and town artisans, but it did frighten the wealthy nobles, merchants, and bankers whose mildly divergent interests were unified by threats from below.

By the 1560s Calvinism had become a major outlet for the frustrations of the discontented. Although outlawed and persecuted earlier, the movement grew rapidly during the decade. It converted approximately 15 percent of the population, most of whom were of the lower urban middle class; however, the leadership came mainly from the nobility, 40 to 50 percent of whom accepted Calvinism. Their motives varied—although many were sincerely religious, most pursued political ends. Even among the lesser nobles, the Calvinist side promised military employment, political prominence, and a way for taking advantage of popular discontent. The movement's potential popular support was particularly appealing to contenders for the throne among the high nobility. In 1559 the Huguenots held a secret synod in Paris that drew representatives from 72 congregations and a million members. A distinct minority, they were nevertheless well-placed and well organized with articulate spokesmen and competent military leaders.

Religious, political, and social forces combined when France suffered the loss of King Henry II in 1559, who left his crown to his sickly 15-year-old son, Francis II. His young queen was Mary Stuart (later Mary, Queen of Scots), whose uncles, the brothers Guise, took actual control of the government. They were opposed by noble families from the Huguenot camp. Francis II died in 1560, and the crown passed to his 9-year-old brother Charles. At that time, however, the real power behind the throne was Charles's mother, Catherine de Medici. Single-minded, crafty, and ready to use any means, she was determined to save the throne for one of her three sons, none of whom had produced a male heir. Exploiting the split between the Guises—the champions of the Catholic cause—and their enemies, she assumed the regency for Charles. She then attempted, through reforms of the church, to reconcile the differences between Catholics and Protestants. In this endeavor she was unsuccessful, but she kept her tenuous control, using every political strategy, including a squadron of noble women who solicited information by seducing powerful nobles.

Religious war erupted in 1561; supported by substantial Spanish financial and military interventions, it lasted through eight uneasy truces until 1593. Fanaticism evoked the most violent and inhumane acts on both sides, as destructive raids, assassinations, and torturous atrocities became commonplace. Catherine maneuvered through war and uneasy peace, first favoring the Guises and then the Bourbons. In 1572, fearing that the Huguenots were gaining supremacy, she joined a Guise plot that resulted in the murder of some 10,000 Huguenots in Paris. This Massacre of St. Bartholomew's Eve was a turning point in decisively dividing the country. The final "war of the three Henries" in the 1580s involved Catherine's third son, Henry III, who became king upon the death of Charles in 1574. The king's rivals were Henry of Guise and the

DOCUMENT

Massacre of St. Bartholomew

Protestant Henry of Navarre. When the other two Henries were assassinated, Henry of Navarre proclaimed himself king of France in 1589. Spain would have little to fear from France for the next half-century.

Elizabethan England, 1558–1603

For most of the sixteenth century, Spain built its European foreign policies on the base of an English alliance. Despite Henry's breaking his marriage with Catherine of Aragon, the Spanish ambassadors did not give up their efforts to keep England in their camp. For the better part of his reign, Philip had to deal with England's most outstanding monarch, Elizabeth I, who ruled a country that was, as the earl of Essex put it, "little in territory, not extraordinarily rich and defended only by itself."[4]

Elizabeth, a superb image maker, projected the picture of a country united behind a national church, even as her government suppressed Catholicism, put down a northern rebellion, and avoided serious troubles with Scotland and Ireland. Elizabeth dealt with potential dangers from the great Catholic powers by playing them against each other. Such successes were seen as the natural result of her brilliance and courage. This image only partly reflected reality. The "Protestant Queen" detested most of the Protestants, especially those founded on the heretical traditions of the **Lollards.** Her support for Scottish and Dutch rebels went against her fervent belief in absolute monarchy. Her celebrated coy approach in encouraging but ultimately denying prospective royal suitors, despite the diplomatic advantages of the practice, often ran counter to her emotional inclinations, throwing her into momentary rages against her advisers.

But she had learned her lesson well from Tudor politics—to compromise and discount personal feelings for the larger interests of her realm. Consequently, England became her family and her primary interest. She was especially skilled at judging people, dealing with foreign diplomats in their own languages, and projecting her charisma in public speeches. With these notable talents, she brought the English people a new sense of national pride, often expressed in Shakespeare's plays. In the second half of the sixteenth century—in contrast to France—England gave the impression of having achieved relative peace and prosperity.

Elizabeth's earliest immediate danger emerged in Scotland, where Mary of Guise was regent for her daughter Mary Stuart, queen of both France and Scotland. French troops in Scotland supported this Catholic regime. Because Mary Stuart was also a direct descendant of Henry VII of England, she was a leading claimant for the English throne and a potential rallying symbol for Catholics who hoped to reestablish their faith in England. These expectations were diminished in 1559 when a zealous Calvinist named John Knox (1505–1572), fresh from Geneva, led a revolt of Scottish nobles. Aided by English naval forces, the Scots broke religious ties with Rome, established a Presbyterian (Calvinist) state church, and, with Elizabeth's help, drove out the French soldiers.

Another serious problem loomed in Ireland, where Spanish and papal emissaries used old grievances over taxes and religion to arouse uprisings against English rule. James Maurice, an Irish leader in the southwest, began a series of revolts in 1569. Eight years later, the pope helped raise troops and money for him on the Continent. An expedition in 1579 to aid the Irish rebels was ruthlessly suppressed, but fighting dragged on for four more years. In 1601 a more serious Irish rebellion aided by 3000 Spanish troops cost Elizabeth a third of her revenues. Although never directing a successful Irish policy, as has been true of all of her successors up to the present, she managed to escape catastrophe by her stubborn persistence.

Her innate pragmatism was most beneficial in quieting English sectarian strife. She despised **Puritans** and favored rich vestments for the clergy, but she thoroughly understood the practical necessity of securing Protestant political support. Moving firmly but slowly, Elizabeth re-created a nominal Protestant national church, but one similar to her father's. The queen's policy lessened religious controversy and persecution but failed to end either completely.

Elizabeth also faced a serious danger from abroad. In 1568, after Mary Stuart was forced into exile by her Protestant subjects, she was received in England by her royal cousin. Although kept, for all intents and purposes, a prisoner, she became involved in a series of Catholic plots, which appeared even more dangerous after the pope excommunicated Elizabeth in 1570. Philip of Spain aided the plotters but still hoped to enlist Elizabeth's cooperation in creating a Catholic hegemony in Europe.

Despite all her troubles, Elizabeth's reign showed marked economic improvement. By careful—some said stingy—financial management, her government reduced debt and improved national credit. A new coinage helped make London the financial center of Europe, especially after the Spanish destruction of Antwerp. Monopolies granted to joint stock companies promoted foreign trade and brought wealth into the country. By the end of her reign in 1603, England, despite festering social and religious problems, was the most prosperous state in Europe.

Lollards—Followers of John Wycliffe who spread his doctrines both openly and secretly throughout England in the fifteenth and sixteenth centuries.

Puritans—Those English protestants in the 1500s and 1600s who found the theology and worship services of the Church of England to be not in accord with Holy Scripture.

Lepanto and the Armada

Philip's wars against Turkey—including the destruction of the Turkish fleet at Lepanto off the western coast of Greece—promoted his image as the Catholic champion, boosted Spanish morale, and revived the traditional national pride in defending the faith. When Cyprus, the last Christian stronghold in the eastern Mediterranean, fell to the Turks in 1570, Philip responded to the pope's pleas and formed a Holy League to destroy Turkish naval power. Spanish and Venetian warships, together with smaller squadrons from Genoa and the Papal States, made up a fleet of over 200 vessels that drew recruits from all over Europe. In 1571 the Holy League's fleet and the Turkish navy clashed at Lepanto, off the western coast of Greece. Christian Europe scored a major victory over the Ottoman Empire, which would never pose a naval threat again. The Spanish king could bring all of his resources to bear in northwest Europe.

Philip's diplomatic efforts, particularly his marriage to Mary Tudor in 1558, his next marriage to Elizabeth of Valois in 1560, and his clumsy efforts to court Queen Elizabeth, brought no lasting influence over English or French policies. Indeed, English captains were preying on Spanish shipping in the Atlantic, and Dutch privateers, with English and Huguenot support, were diminishing the flow of vital supplies to northern Europe. In 1580, after nine years of frustration in the Netherlands, Philip launched the first phase of his new offensive policy, using military force to validate his claim to the Portuguese throne. As king of Portugal, he gained control of the Portuguese navy and Atlantic ports, where he began assembling an oceangoing fleet, capable of operations against the Dutch and English in their home waters.

Philip's last hope for an easy solution to his problems was dashed in 1587. Pressed by the pope and the English Catholic exiles, he had tried for years to use

This detail from a painting by artists in the school of Tintoretto dealing with the Battle of Lepanto presents the decisive battle for the control of the Mediterranean in a splendid light.

Mary Stuart to overthrow Elizabeth, regain England for Catholicism, and seize control of the country. But Mary's complicity in a plot against the English queen's life was discovered, and Elizabeth finally signed a death warrant. Mary's execution confirmed Philip's earlier decision that England had to be conquered militarily. In pursuing this end, Philip planned a "great enterprise," an invasion of England blessed by the pope.

The Spanish strategy depended on a massive fleet, known as the Invincible Armada. It was ordered to

DOCUMENT

John Hawkins Reports on the Spanish Armada

meet a large Spanish army in the southern Netherlands and land this force on the English coast. But in 1588, when the Armada sailed for Flanders, Dutch ships blocked the main ports, preventing the Spanish galleons from entering the shallow waters. Philip's project was then completely ruined when the smaller and more maneuverable English ships, commanded by Charles Howard and captained by privateers such Sir Francis Drake and Sir John Hawkins, scattered the Armada in the English Channel. Retreating through the North Sea, the Spanish fleet was then battered by a severe storm, called the "Protestant wind," and forced to make a miserable return to Spain.

Philip II's Failure in Europe

Contrary to English expectations, the defeat of the Armada brought no immediate shift in the international balance of power. Spain retained its military might, built new ships, and defended its sea-lanes. On the ground, the Spanish infantry would not suffer defeat until 1643 at the battle of Rocroi (ruh-KWAH). In fact, all the major combatants were exhausted, a factor that largely explains the Bourbons' acquisition of the French crown and continued Dutch independence. Lingering wars brought new opportunities for France and the Netherlands, but only more exhaustion for England and Spain.

During the last decade of Philip's life, his multiple failures foreshadowed the decline of his country. He encountered rebellion in Aragon, quarreled with Pope Clement VIII over recognizing the Bourbons (see following), and sent two more naval expeditions against England, both of which were scattered by storms. Before he died in 1598, he turned over the Netherlands to his favorite daughter Clara Isabella Eugenia and her husband, Archduke Albert, an Austrian Habsburg. He had also made peace with France. He left Spain bankrupt for the third time during his reign, having wasted the country's considerable resources and sacrificed its future to his dynastic pride. His son Philip III (r. 1598–1621), no match for his father, presided in a lazy, extravagant, and frivolous way over the beginning of the long decline of the Spanish Empire.

England experienced similar difficulties. Though sea raids on Spanish shipping continued and brought

in badly needed money, all of Elizabeth's grand projects failed, such as in 1596 when the earl of Essex plundered Cadiz but missed the Spanish treasure fleet. Conflicts in France, the Netherlands, and Ireland drained her treasury, and Parliament delayed in granting her funds to continue fighting. Social and religious tensions surfaced at the turn of the seventeenth century, and the Puritans proved to be an especially irritating group for the aging queen. At her death in 1603, she left no successors, and the Stuarts took the English throne.

The Dutch declaration of independence in 1581 reflected more concern for aristocratic privilege and national survival than democratic principles, but it served as a basis for holding the northern Netherlands together. After finding no acceptable French or English person to be their king, the Dutch created a republic in 1587 and tenaciously persevered to sign a truce with Spain in 1609. As time passed, their growing maritime trade and naval power guaranteed their security.

The post-Armada stalemate most benefited the French. With the death of the last Valois claimant in 1589, the Bourbon Protestant king of Navarre was proclaimed king of France as Henry IV. This act threw the Catholic Holy League into a fanatical antiroyalist frenzy and encouraged Philip's military intervention in France to support his daughter's claim to the throne. But English aid and Henry's willingness to turn Catholic—he is said to have claimed that "Paris is worth a mass"—led to Philip's withdrawal and the Peace of Vervins in 1598. To pacify his Huguenot allies, Henry issued the Edict of Nantes, which guaranteed them some civil and religious rights and permitted them to continue holding more than a hundred fortified towns. Henry had at last gained peace for his exhausted country.

ORTHODOX EUROPE: RUSSIAN CONSOLIDATION AND OTTOMAN EXPANSION

■ *In the last part of the sixteenth century, the Ottoman Empire was at its peak and Muscovite Russia was in a state of crisis. By 1700 the Turks were in a state of decline and the Russians were on the verge of becoming a major power. How do you account for the differences in the developments of the two empires?*

Russian Autocracy

As we saw in Chapter 6, Ivan III had claimed the Byzantine heritage of the Russian state and used his marriage to the niece of the last ruler of Byzantium to proclaim himself as the tsar (Russian for caesar), and he adopted the use of the two-headed eagle as the symbol for the

Russian throne. His grandson, Ivan IV (1533–1584), later surnamed "the Terrible," tried to take the next step toward the imposition of a truly imperial, autocratic rule. Ivan was three years old when his father died, and during the next decade he learned to distrust the aristocratic boyars, who showed him, his mother, and his tutors no respect as they took advantage of his youth. Once he took power in the late 1540s, he began a series of reforms to put the Russian state on a modern footing. He published a new law code, brought together representatives of the Russian population—the ***Zemski Sobor*** (ZIEM-ski so-BOR)—to reform the administration of the land, saw his forces take Kazan and Astrakhan, and opened trade with the West.

Ivan "the Terrible"

As would be the case with the monarchies in western and Central Europe, Ivan faced the opposition of his nobles, the boyars, to his plans to strengthen the state. After 1560 he launched a full-scale war against them. He declared most of Russia, including Moscow, to be under a martial law, enforced by a group of special forces called the *oprichniki* (oh-PREACH-nee-kee), masked men of legendary cruelty dressed in black, riding black horses, carrying broomsticks topped with dog skulls. He wanted to replace the old independent boyar class with a service nobility loyal to him. To that end he and his *oprichniki* drove 12,000 families from their lands in the dead of winter. To those who opposed him, Ivan responded with an inventive cruelty that gained him his name. As the terror increased, he lost control of himself, accidentally killing his beloved son and heir to the throne. Finally he achieved his goals, and the terror diminished. When he died in 1584, he was succeeded by another son Fedor, who was totally unequipped to face the challenge of a devastated and discontented land.

For a time Fedor ruled with the advice of his brother-in-law, Boris Godunov, a competent and ambitious boyar. For seven years the country recovered from the trauma through which it had been put by Ivan IV; however, in 1591 Ivan's last son,

Zemski Sobor—A meeting of representatives of the Russian population—an assembly of the land—to reform the state in the 1550s and then to approve the choice of the Romanovs as the ruling family in 1613.

Dmitri, died under mysterious circumstances, and when Fedor died in 1598 without an heir, the Rurik line of rulers came to an end. Boris presented himself as the next tsar and received the acclaim of the nobles and church. However, Russia felt the effects of the same famine, economic failure, and discontent that preceded the Thirty Years' War in Central Europe. Boris's policies failed to bring the country back to even minimal prosperity. At the same time, plots against him spread throughout the country, and when he died in 1605, there was no agreed-on successor. Eight years of civil war and Polish intervention, known as the "time of troubles," devastated Russia. Finally, the Russians reunited to drive the Poles out and call a zemski sobor in 1613 to choose a new ruling family, the Romanovs.

Between 1613 and 1676, the first two Romanov tsars, Michael and Alexis, integrated most aristocrats into the state nobility and achieved some degree of stability. As in Prussia, the nobles and the government were reconciled in their common exploitation of the serfs through the Code of 1649, which established serfdom, and the primitive agricultural economy encouraged aristocratic independence. Russian ignorance and

DOCUMENT
Adan Olearius: A Foreign Traveler in Early Russia

In the second part of his reign, Ivan the Terrible lapsed into periods of insanity from time to time. In one of these periods he killed his favorite son and heir. Il'ya Repin captured this tragedy in a nineteenth century painting.

technical deficiencies, along with a conservative-minded nobility, made the country stagnant in comparison with Western states.

The Balkans

As we saw in Chapter 6, the nations of the Balkans took advantage of the reduced status of the Byzantine Empire and the rise of the Italian city-states to consolidate their power in the thirteenth and fourteenth centuries. The Second Bulgarian Empire, the Empire of Stephan Dushan in Serbia, and even Skanderbeg's Albania enjoyed their golden ages in the fourteenth and fifteenth century.

But after 1345, the Ottoman Turks began their biannual incursions into Europe. It was the Byzantines themselves who had invited the Turks to cross the Dardanelles during one of their periodic dynastic disputes. Three hundred years later the Ottomans would be at the gates of Vienna.

The advancing Turks found no obstacle in the weakened government at Constantinople, and as they proceeded up the rivers of the Balkans they found not much in the way of opposition from the Bulgarians, Slavs, and Romanians. In a time of economic difficulties and religious controversies, there was a considerable degree of class conflict in the area. In addition, instead of uniting against the Ottomans, the various Slavic princes squabbled with each other, mirroring the civil wars in the Byzantine world, until it was too late.

The Ottomans were nothing if not patient, and they took advantage of the conflicts within the Balkans. They understood that they did not have enough troops in the 1350s and 1360s to militarily take the area—so they advanced diplomatically, signing treaties, establishing tribute payments, and then rearming for the next advance. Then in 1362 they took Adrianople, present-day Edirne, and from there they proceeded in a measured matter through Macedonia, then to take Sofia in 1384, then Nis 1386, and southward to take Salonika in 1387. Finally on June 15, 1389, Sultan Murad I defeated the Serbian and Bosnian forces at Kosovo and effectively sealed Ottoman control over the Balkans for the next 500 years. The taking of Constantinople in 1453 completed the conquest. Only Montenegro, of all of the Balkan region, would be able to escape Ottoman rule.

Thereafter the Balkans would experience a different historical development from the rest of Europe. The Ottomans ruled through a theocratic model (see Chapter 6)—all were slaves of the sultan who was, himself, the shadow of God. *Sharia* law was to be followed by Muslims, based on the Koran and other religious writings. There was no secular state.

DOCUMENT

An Ambassador's Report on the Ottoman Empire

The nations of the Balkans were ruled either as core provinces or as vassal states. In the core, the different regions were under the command of a governor—who had his miniature version of the Istanbul government. He delegated power to various regional and district authorities, while combining military and civilian authority. Then there were the vassal states—Moldavia, Wallachia, Transylvania, and Ragusa-Dubrovnik (ra-GOOZ-a dew-BROV-nik)—who were allowed to rule themselves in return for loyalty to the sultan and extensive payments in money and grain.

In the core provinces, those who were not Muslims, but followers of a religion of the book—the Bible or the Torah—were governed theocratically, also, through the *millet* system. As Peter Sugar noted, "These were parallel organizations, and each was independent within the limits of its own competence. The Ottomans had no concept corresponding to national lines of differentiation . . . but of religions. . . . The purpose of the . . . system was simply to create a secondary imperial administrative and primary legal structure for the *dhimmis* (non-Muslims in a protected position)." The chief rabbi in Istanbul had his own courts and law enforcers for Jews, as did the leaders of each Christian division—Armenian Catholics, Roman Catholics, and Orthodox Christians. The Phanariote Greeks who dominated the Orthodox structure became extremely powerful in the Balkans during Ottoman rule.

The Ottoman armies remained the most important part of the sultan's government. Before going into Europe, the military was characterized by valiant, independent volunteer horsemen, who fought when there was a war and went home when there was none. Once the empire began to expand in Europe, Sultan Orkhan began to divide the new land among his soldiers, to be given to them for their lifetime. This rewarded the forces for their work but did not create, for the moment, a hereditary service nobility. Orkhan also created a new, slave-based army, the janissaries.

As the empire grew larger, the Ottomans needed more fighters and bureaucrats. They instituted in the core area an arrangement to supply soldiers and bureaucrats, the **devshirme** (dev-SHIR-ma) system. Ottoman officials would go to villages throughout the Balkans and select male children whom they would take from their families and enroll in Ottoman service. The boys thus chosen would be given examinations to determine where they would serve the sultan, whether as janissaries or officials at the highest levels. This levy of Christian male children was carried on between the end of the fourteenth century and the beginning of the seventeenth system, and historians estimate that

---

devshirme—The Ottoman levy of Christian male children in the Balkans. More than 200,000 young boys were taken from their families to serve in the Ottoman army or bureaucracy.

around 200,000 sons were taken from their families during that time. Most of the boys taken came from the Slavic Orthodox populations.

The Balkans participated in none of the formative developments of modern European civilization. They did not experience the Renaissance or the Reformation, the Capitalist and Scientific Revolutions, nor the Enlightenment and Industrialization. The splendor of Constantinople was paid for by the exactions—human and materials—taken from the Balkans peoples. When the region reentered European affairs in the nineteenth century it lagged behind Central and western Europe.[5]

THE AUSTRIAN HABSBURGS' DRIVE FOR SUPERIORITY AND THE THIRTY YEARS' WAR

■ *Why was the Thirty Years' War the most destructive military conflict in Europe until the First World War in the twentieth century?*

By 1600 the Spanish Habsburgs' golden age had ended, but the potent mixture of religious and political competition among dynasties and nations would continue with even greater intensity. Philip had taken on too much and had failed to impose his will. Now, in their turn, his cousins in Central Europe—the Austrian Habsburgs—would attempt to impose their dominance in Europe. Religious passions remained at a high pitch as

---

War and Politics in the Age of Austrian Habsburg Dominance

1589–1610	Reign of Henry IV of France, beginning of Bourbon dynasty
1598	Edict of Nantes guarantees Protestant rights in France
1611–1632	Reign of Gustavus Adolphus in Sweden
1618–1648	Thirty Years' War
1624–1642	Cardinal Richelieu holds power in France
1643	Spanish infantry suffers first defeat at Battle of Rocroi
1648	Peace of Westphalia
1649	Independence of the United Provinces

---

increasing numbers of Calvinists and Lutherans on one side and proponents of the Catholic Counter-Reformation on the other still dreamed of the complete victory of their faith and their realms. It was a dangerous time of disruption, frustration, and fanaticism.

Europeans faced severe economic depression, along with intensified conflict in every sphere of human relations. The first few decades of the seventeenth century brought a marked decline to the European economy, even before the advent of open warfare. Prices continued to fall until about 1660, reversing the inflation of the 1500s. International trade declined, as did Spanish bullion imports from Central and South America. Heavy risks on a falling market caused failures among many foreign trading companies; only the larger houses, organized as joint-stock companies, were able to survive. A climate change, bringing on colder weather, reduced the growing season and agricultural production, and the hard times in the countryside were felt in the cities, where urban craftspeople saw their wages drop.

Tensions accompanying economic depression added to those arising from continuing religious differences. The most dangerous area for religious conflict was in Central Europe, which had directly experienced an increasingly militant Counter-Reformation since the Peace of Augsburg. Although the European power balance in 1618 resembled that of the 1500s, it was much less fixed. The power of the Habsburgs of Vienna drove even normally competitive states to come together in alliances. Underneath the facade of their sixteenth-century dominance there was a sense of vulnerability. Spain was weakening and there were other states— France, the Netherlands, and Sweden—which were growing more powerful. Under these circumstances European opposition against Austrian Habsburg dominance became almost inevitable.

The Bohemian and Danish Phases of the Thirty Years' War: The Habsburgs' High Tide to 1630

The Thirty Years' War, fought between 1618 and 1648, was a culmination of all these related religious and political conflicts. Almost all of western Europe except England was directly involved and suffered accordingly. Central Europe was hit particularly hard, as can be seen in an account by a soldier writing under the name Simplicissimus, suffering population declines that would take two centuries to replace.

Despite the devastation, neither Protestantism nor Catholicism won decisively. What began as a religious war in Bohemia and the German principalities turned into a complex political struggle involving the ambitions of northern German rulers, the expansionist

Document   Simplicissimus on the Horrors of the Thirty Years' War

The Protestant and Catholic armies that ranged throughout Central Europe destroyed entire villages, cities, and districts. Battles were the least of the problems for the unfortunate peasants caught in the way. Accompanying the armies were thousands of camp followers who took what they wanted and destroyed the rest. In some instances it took two centuries for the devastated regions to regain their population levels and recover from the damage done by the competing forces. This account of disaster and suffering by Hans von Grimmelshausen (c. 1622–1676), the son of a German innkeeper who was left an orphan and carried away by soldiers during the Thirty Year's War, gives vivid testimony to the horrors of war. Writing under the name of Simplicissimus, he describes the arrival of an army in his home and the activities of the invaders. These ring as true for his day as they do for recent wars such as those in the Balkans, where destruction for destruction's sake and rape are common fare.

The first thing that the riders did was to stable their horses. After that, each one started to his own business which indicated nothing but ruin and destruction. While some started to slaughter, cook and fry, so that it looked as though they wished to prepare a gay feast, others stormed through the house from top to bottom as if the golden fleece of Colchis were hidden there. Others again took linen, clothing and other goods, making them into bundles as if they intended on going to market; what they did not want was broken up and destroyed. Some stabbed their swords through hay and straw as if they had not enough pigs to stab. Some shook the feathers out of the beds and filled the ticks with ham and dried meat as if they could sleep more comfortably in these. Others smashed the ovens and windows as if to announce an eternal summer. They beat copper and pewter vessels into lumps and packed the mangled pieces away. Bedsteads, tables, chairs, and benches were burned, although many stacks of dried wood stood in the yard. Earthenware pots and pans were all broken, perhaps because our guests preferred roasted meats, or perhaps they intended to eat only one meal with us. Our maid had been treated in the stable in such a way that she could not leave it any more—a shameful thing to tell! They bound the farm-hand and laid him on the earth, put a clamp of wood in his mouth and emptied a milking churn full of horrid dung water into his belly. This they called the Swedish drink, and they forced him to lead a party of soldiers to another place, where they looted men and cattle and brought them back to our yard. Among them were my dad, my mum and Ursula.

The soldiers now started to take the flints out of their pistols and in their stead screwed the thumbs of the peasants, and they tortured the poor wretches as if they were burning witches. They put one captive peasant into the bake-oven and put fire on him. Then they tied a rope around the head of another one, and twisted it with the help of a stick so tightly that blood gushed out through his mouth, nose and ears. In short everybody had his own invention to torture the peasants, and each peasant suffered his own martyrdom. . . . What happened to the captive women, maids and daughters I do not know as the soldiers would not let me watch how they dealt with them. I only very well remember that I heard them miserably crying in corners here and there, and I believe that my mum and Ursula had no better fate than the others.

In the midst of this misery I turned the spit and did not worry as I hardly understood what all this meant. In the afternoon I helped to water the horses and found our maid in the stable looking amazingly dishevelled. I did not recognize her but she spoke to me with pitiful voice:

"Oh, run away, boy, or the soldiers will take you with them. Look out, escape! Can't you see how evil. . . ."

More she could not say.

Questions to Consider

1. What military roles do the physical abuse and rape mentioned by Simplicissimus play in the securing of an area? Are they just instances of bestial behavior or do they reflect military strategy?

2. In considering recent instances of conflict—for example, Yugoslavia, the Palestinian conflict, and Indonesia—do you find that the nature of warfare has changed significantly in the past four centuries?

3. Do you believe that if the local peasantry in the account you have just read had had their own weapons against the occupying army that their villages and property would have been saved?

Mark A. Kishlansky, ed., *Sources of the West: Readings in Western Civilization*, 4th edition, Longman Publishers, New York, 2001, pp. 15–18.

ambitions of Sweden, and the efforts of Catholic France to break the "Habsburg ring."

Despite the general decline of Habsburg supremacy in Spain, the early years of the war before 1629, usually cited as the Bohemian (1618–1625) and Danish (1625–1629) phases, brought a last brief revival of Habsburg prospects. The new Habsburg emperor, Ferdinand II, a fanatical Catholic, was determined to intensify the Counter-Reformation, set aside the Peace of Augsburg, and literally wipe out Protestantism in Central Europe. For a time he almost succeeded.

Ferdinand's succession came amid severe political tension. Spreading Calvinism, in addition to the aggressive crusading of the Jesuits, had earlier led to the formation of a Protestant league of German princes in 1608 and a Catholic league to counter it the next year. The two alliances had almost clashed in 1610. Meanwhile, the Bohemian Protestants had extracted a promise of toleration from their Catholic king, Rudolf II (1576–1612). In 1618 the Bohemian leaders, fearing that Ferdinand would not honor that promise, threw two of his officials out a window after heated discussions—an incident known as the **defenestration of Prague.** When Ferdinand mobilized troops, the Bohemians refused to recognize him and gave their throne to Frederick, the Protestant elector of the Palatinate, in western Germany.

---

defenestration of Prague—The end of negotiations between Bohemia and the Holy Roman Empire in 1618; the Bohemian representatives were so angry with the representatives of the Holy Roman Emperor that they threw them out the window.

In the short Bohemian war that followed, Frederick was quickly overwhelmed. In 1620 Ferdinand deployed two strong armies, one from Spain and the other from Catholic Bavaria, and scattered the Bohemian forces at the battle of the White Mountain, near Prague. Ferdinand gave the Bohemian lands to Maximillian of Bavaria, distributed the holdings of Bohemian Protestant nobles among Catholic aristocrats, and proceeded to stamp out Protestantism in Bohemia. Of the some 3.2 million Bohemians in 1618, mostly Protestants, all that remained 30 years later were less than 1 million people, all Catholics.

War began again in 1625 when Christian IV (r. 1588–1648), the Lutheran king of Denmark, invaded Germany. As duke of Holstein and thus a prince of the empire, he hoped to revive Protestantism and win a kingdom in Germany for his youngest son. Unlike Frederick in Bohemia, Christian had support from the English, the Dutch, and the North German princes. Their help was not enough. Ferdinand dispatched his new general, Albert von Wallenstein, to crush the Protestants in a series of overpowering campaigns. By 1629 Christian had to admit defeat and withdraw his forces, thus ending the Danish conflict with another Protestant debacle. Their successful campaigns of the 1620s gave the Habsburgs almost complete domination in Germany. In 1629 Ferdinand issued his Edict of Restitution, restoring to the Catholics all properties lost since 1552. This step seemed to be only the first step toward eliminating Protestantism

By the simplicity and starkness of his portrayal, the French artist Jacques Callot captured, in a series of 24 etchings, the senseless tragedy of the Thirty Years' War (1633). The dangling bodies in this plate dramatize the tenuousness of life in turbulent times.

completely and creating a centralized Habsburg empire in Central Europe.

The Swedish and French Phases and the Balance of Power, 1630–1648

Fearing the Counter-Reformation and the growing Habsburg power behind it, threatened European states resumed the war in 1630. As the war rapidly spread and intensified, religious issues were steadily subordinated to power politics. This transformation could be seen in the phases of the conflict usually designated as the Swedish (1630–1635) and the French (1635–1648) because these two countries led successive and ultimately successful anti-Habsburg coalitions. By 1648 the Dutch Republic had replaced Spain as the leading maritime state and Bourbon France had become the dominant European land power.

Protestant Swedes and French Catholics challenged Ferdinand's imperial ambitions for similar political reasons. Although Gustavus Adolphus (r. 1611–1632), the Swedish king, wanted to save German Lutheranism, he was also determined to prevent a strong Habsburg state on the Baltic from restricting his own expansion and interfering with Swedish trade. A similar desire to liberate France from Habsburg encirclement motivated Cardinal Richelieu, the powerful minister of Louis XIII. Richelieu offered Gustavus French subsidies, for which the Swedish monarch promised to invade Germany and permit Catholic worship in any lands he might conquer. Thus, the Catholic cardinal and the Protestant king compromised their religious differences in the hope of achieving mutual political benefits.

Gustavus invaded Germany in 1630, while the Dutch attacked the Spanish Netherlands. With his mobile cannons and his hymn-singing Swedish veter-

Sweden's warrior-king Gustavus Adolphus is portrayed here at the battle of Breitenfeld in 1631.

ans, Gustavus and his German allies won a series of smashing victories, climaxed in November 1632 at Lützen, near Leipzig, where Wallenstein was decisively defeated. Unfortunately for the Protestant cause, Gustavus died in the battle. A stalemate for the next three years led to the 1635 Peace of Prague and a momentary compromise between the emperor and the German Protestant states.

The situation now demanded that France act directly to further its dynastic interests. Thus, a final French phase of the war began when French troops moved into Germany and toward the Spanish borders. The French also subsidized the Dutch and Swedes and an army of German Protestant mercenaries. The Paris government continued limiting Protestantism within its borders but gladly allied with Protestant states against Spain, Austria, Bavaria, and their Catholic allies. The war that had begun in religious controversy had now become pure power politics, completing the long political transition from medieval to modern times.

For 13 more years, the seemingly endless conflict wore on. France's allies, the Swedes and northern Germans, kept Habsburg armies engaged in Germany, while French armies and the Dutch navy concentrated on Spain. In 1643 the French beat the Spaniards in the decisive battle at Rocroi, in the southern Netherlands. Next they moved into Germany, defeating the imperial forces and, with the Swedes, ravaging Bavaria.

For all practical purposes, the war was over, but years of indecisive campaigning and tortuous negotiations delayed the peace. Finally, a horde of diplomats met at Westphalia in 1644. Even then, Spain and France could reach no agreement for four years, but a settlement for the empire, the Treaty of Westphalia, was finally completed in 1648.

The Peace of Westphalia

The peace agreement at Westphalia signaled a victory for Protestantism and the German princes while almost dooming Habsburg imperial ambitions: France moved closer to the Rhine by acquiring Alsatian territory; Sweden and Brandenburg acquired lands on the Baltic; and the Netherlands and Switzerland gained recognition of their independence. The emperor was required to obtain approval from the Imperial Diet for any laws, taxes, military levies, and foreign agreements—provisions that nearly nullified imperial power and afforded the German states practical control of their foreign relations. German religious autonomy, as declared at Augsburg, was also reconfirmed, with Calvinism now permitted along with Lutheranism. In addition, Protestant states were conceded all Catholic properties taken before 1624.

In its religious terms the treaty ended the dream of reuniting Christendom. Catholics and Protestants now realized that major faiths could not be destroyed. With this admission, a spirit of toleration would gradually emerge. Although religious uniformity could be imposed within states for another century, it would not again be a serious issue in foreign affairs until the end of the twentieth century.

The Peace of Westphalia is particularly notable for confirming the new European state system. Henceforth states would customarily shape their policies in accordance with the power of their neighbors, seeking to expand at the expense of the weaker and to protect themselves—not by religion, law, or morality, but by alliances against their stronger adversaries. Based on the works of the Dutch jurist Grotius, the treaty also instituted the international conference as a means for registering power relationships among contending states, instituted the principle of the equality of all sovereign states—as seen today in the General Assembly of the United Nations—and put into practice the tools of modern diplomacy such as extraterritoriality and diplomatic immunities.

Both Spain and Austria were weakened, and the Austrian Habsburgs shifted their primary attention from Central to southeastern Europe. German disunity was perpetuated by the autonomy of so many of the microstates. France emerged from this time as the clear winner, the potential master of the Continent. The war also helped England and the Netherlands. No matter the condition of the surviving states, their future relations would be based on the pure calculus of power, both military and economic.

CONCLUSION

Despite almost constant political and religious conflict, the years between 1300 and 1650 saw the nation-state system firmly established in Europe, particularly in the Atlantic states of Spain, France, and England.

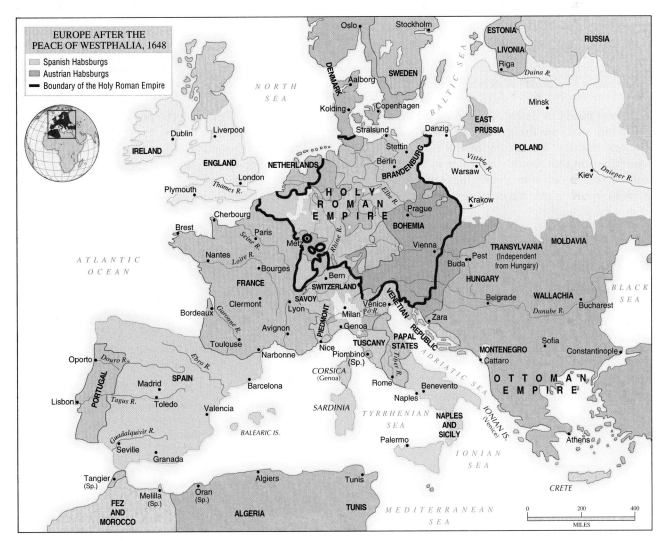

Exhausted Europeans finally agreed to put an end to the Thirty Years' War with the Treaty of Westphalia. This agreement put an end to Habsburg ambitions in Central Europe, marked the emergence of France as the major continental power, and removed religion as a factor in interstate relations. It also laid the foundations for modern international law.

Each of these three countries evolved in different ways. The political evolution of both England and France was affected by the Hundred Years' War. In England, the power of Parliament was increased, and the upsurge in the power of the nobility led to the Wars of the Roses, which ended finally with the accession of the Tudor dynasty; in France, royal power was consolidated under Louis XI, and his abilities in government made possible further progress in national unification. Nation-making in Spain was unique, since the ambitions of the monarchy were combined with the religious fervor of the Reconquista and then the Inquisition. Not until the end of the fifteenth century was the task of Spanish unification completed.

In Central and eastern Europe, state building proceeded in a haphazard and often tragic way. In the last two centuries of the Middle Ages, the Holy Roman Empire remained divided and weak; there, national unification would not be achieved until the nineteenth century. In Italy, the attempt at building a unified structure after 1454 suffered a defeat with the French invasions of a half-century later. The Italian peninsula would remain split into competing areas, also, until the nineteenth century. Poland, the Czech lands, and Hungary all made strong starts toward constructing national states, and then after a brief golden age in the fourteenth century they followed different roads to defeat. Poland opted for elective kingship and saw the growth in the powers of its nobles, and the weakening of the central state—a combination that would culminate in its disappearance from the map in the eighteenth century. The Czechs would mount a true national liberation move-

ment against German dominance in the fifteenth century and withstand numerous attacks. However, they fell victim to Habsburg aggression in the seventeenth century. Hungary, after a shining moment under king Mathias Corvinus in the fifteenth century would be conquered by the Turks in 1526.

In eastern Europe, the Russians under Ivan III attempted to construct a strong central state, before facing chaos in the later years of his rule, and then Polish invasion during the Time of Troubles. The Romanovs slowly began to restore central power thereafter. The Balkans nations fell under the domination of the Ottoman Turks in the fourteenth and fifteenth centuries and would pursue a totally different road to state development.

The 130 years after Luther's stand at Wittenberg was an era of wrenching change for Europe. At the opening of the period, most people in their villages were still imbued with the individual, medieval concern for salvation, which gave meaning to the religious issues of the Protestant Reformation and Catholic Counter-Reformation. In the century after the Peace of Augsburg (1555), the nature of state and society changed. Initially, long and exhaustive religious wars and civil wars dominated the Continent. Later, secular political concerns became increasingly evident. But whether the wars were for faith or for state, or a combination of the two, the period until the Treaty of Westphalia ended the Thirty Years' War was the bloodiest century Europe would endure until the twentieth. Finally, in 1648, the modern state structure emerged. Europeans now lived, for better or worse, in a world of nation-states dominated by secular concerns.

Suggestions for Web Browsing

You can obtain more information about topics included in this chapter at the websites listed below. See also the companion website that accompanies this text, **http://www.ablongman.com/ brummett**, which contains an online study guide and additional resources.

End of Europe's Middle Ages
http://www.ucalgary.ca/applied_history/tutor/endmiddle/

This site is developed to aid students of the late Middle Ages by providing collected links and access to primary sources.

Tudor England
http://tudor.simplenet.com/

Site detailing life in Tudor England includes biographies, maps, important dates, architecture, and music, including sound files.

The Thirty Years' War
http://www.pipeline.com/~cwa/TYWHome.htm
http://en.wikipedia.org/wiki/Thirty_Years'_War
http://www.historylearningsite.co.uk/thirty_years_war.htm

Images and explanations of Europe's bloodiest conflict, until 1914.

Peace of Westphalia
http://www.yale.edu/lawweb/avalon/westphal.htm

Complete text of the peace treaties that together made up the Treaty of Westphalia (1648), which ended the Thirty Years' War.

Literature and Film

Several recent and outstanding translations and/or editions of later medieval literature are available: Geoffrey Chaucer, *The Canterbury Tales in Modern English*, ed. Neville Coghill (Penguin, 2000); Dante Alighieri, *The Divine Comedy*, trans. Allen Mandelbaum (Knopf, 1995); and Giovanni Boccaccio, *Decameron*, trans. G. H. McWilliam (Penguin, 1996) are outstanding presentations.

This is a rich period for novels. The activities of this time attracted the best attentions of Alexandre Dumas. Writing about events in France, he produced *The Two Dianas* (dealing with the time of Francis I), *The Page of the Duke of Savoy* (touching the time of the Emperor Charles V), *Ascanio* (France in the middle of the century), and *Marguerite de Valois* (touching the civil wars), and this is only an incomplete list. Mark Twain wrote about the time of Edward VI in *The Prince and the Pauper* (1881). More recently, Robin Maxwell sheds some light on the reign of Henry VIII in *The*

Secret Diary of Anne Boleyn: A Novel (Scribner, 1998), and Reay Tannahill's *Fatal Majesty: A Novel of Mary Queen of Scots* (Griffin, 2000) offers another recent discussion of the tragic queen.

Some excellent video explorations of the late medieval period are *Siena: Chronicle of a Medieval Commune* (Metropolitan Museum of Art, 1988); *Landmarks of Western Art: The Medieval World* (Kultur Video, 1999); *Living in the Past: Life in Medieval Times* (Kultur Video, 1998); and *Medieval Warfare* (1997; Kultur Video, 3 tapes).

Filmmakers have been equally attracted to the period, especially the English scene. (All of the following are available in VHS.) Fred Zinnemann's *A Man for all Seasons* (Columbia, 1966) is a fine telling of the story of Sir Thomas More. Queen Elizabeth has been the subject of films throughout the twentieth century, including Shekhar Kapur's *Elizabeth* (Channel Four Films, 1998), and indirectly in *Shakespeare in Love* (Miramax, 1998). A film dealing with the period after Henry VIII is Trevor Nunn's *Lady Jane* (Paramount, 1986). The 1933 film, Alexander Korda's *The Private Life of Henry VIII* (London Film Productions) is worth seeing as is *Mary Queen of Scots* (Charles Jarrett, director, Universal Pictures, 1971). On the continent, *The Return of Martin Guerre* (Daniel Vigne, director, European International, 1982) does justice to Natalie Zemon Davis's fine monograph. The film of the life of Martin Luther (Louis de Rochemont Associates, 1953) is a revealing look at the reformer.

Suggestions for Reading

For the spirit of the age see David Nirenberg, *Communities of Violence: Persecution of Minorities in the Middle Ages* (Princeton University Press, 1996). See also S. Harrison Thomson, *Czechoslovakia In European History* (Frank Cass and Co. Ltd., 1965); Lonnie R. Johnson, *Central Europe: Enemies, Neighbors, Friends* (Oxford University Press, 1996); Daniel Herlihy, *The Black Death and the Transformation of the West* (Harvard University Press, 1997); and Richard Kieckhefer, *Magic in the Middle Ages* (Cambridge University Press, 2000). See also C. H. Haskins, *The Rise of Universities* (Cornell University Press, 1965).

Valuable sources of English history include Bell Henneman, ed., *The Medieval French Monarchy* (Krieger, 1973); C.B. Bouchard, *Strong of Body, Brave and Noble: Chivalry and Society in Medieval France* (Cornell, 1998); Nigel Saul, ed., *The Oxford History of Medieval England* (Oxford, 2001); and P.S.P. Goldberg, ed., *Women in Medieval English Society* (Sutton, 1997). See also Edmund King, *Medieval England, 1066–1485* (Salem House, 1989). Bernard T. Reilly, *The Medieval Spains* (Cambridge University Press, 1993), and Richard Fletcher, *Moorish Spain* (University of California Press, 1993), are excellent surveys.

On later medieval society, see Philip Ziegler, *The Black Death* (Sutton, 1998); Christopher Allmand, *The Hundred Years' War* (Cambridge University Press, 1988); Norman Cantor, *In the Wake of the Plague: The Black Death and the World It Made* (Free Press, 2001); Jonathan Sumption, *The Hundred Years' War: Trial by Battle* (University of Pennsylvania Press, 1999); and Daniel Waley, *Later Medieval Europe: From St. Louis to Luther* (Longman, 1985).

Geoffrey Parker, *The Grand Strategy of Philip II* (Yale University Press, 1998), is the best study of the construction of the Spanish world empire. It is still important to read Fernand Braudel's *The Mediterranean and the Mediterranean World in the Age of Philip II,* 2 vols. (Harper Torchbook, 1976), translated by Siân Reynolds,

for its lessons both about the age and about how to understand history in a broader context. The classic treatment of the Armada is Garrett Mattingly, *The Armada* (Houghton Mifflin, 1988).

For the Dutch rebellion see James D. Tracy's, *Holland Under Habsburg Rule* (University of California Press, 1990). Simon Schama, *The Embarrassment of Riches: An Interpretation of Dutch Culture in the Golden Age* (Knopf, 1987), and Charles R. Boxer, *The Dutch Seaborne Empire* (Penguin, 1989), depict the republic at the apex of its struggle for power and wealth. Guido Marnef, *Antwerp in the Age of Reformation* (Johns Hopkins University Press, 1996), gives the texture and detail of this extraordinary time.

French society and politics during the whole era are ably treated in Mack P. Holt, *The French Wars of Religion, 1562–1629* (Cambridge University Press, 1995), a new study of the chaotic period preceding Richelieu, with considerable emphasis on social history. Henry Heller, *Iron and Blood: Civil Wars in Sixteenth-Century France* (McGill-Queen's University Press, 1991), describes the catastrophic religious wars. For a re-creation of life just beneath the religious and political conflict see Natalie Zemon Davis's classic, *The Return of Martin Guerre* (Harvard University Press, 1984).

A revealing survey of English social history is J. A. Sharpe, *Early Modern England: A Social History, 1550–1760,* 2nd ed. (Arnold, 1997). On the growing social and political awareness of English women in the sixteenth and seventeenth centuries, see Katherine A. Henderson and Barbara McManus, *Half Humankind: Contexts and Texts of the Controversy About Women in England, 1540–1640* (University of Illinois Press, 1985), and Mary Prior, ed., *Women in English Society, 1500–1800* (Methuen, 1985). Excellent general interpretations of Elizabethan England are presented in Arthur Bryant, *The Elizabethan Deliverance* (St. Martin's Press, 1982), and David B. Quinn and A. N. Ryan, *England's Sea Empire, 1550–1642* (Allen & Unwin, 1983). Biographies worth consulting include Anne Somerset, *Elizabeth I* (Knopf, 1991), and J. Mary Wormald, *Mary, Queen of Scots* (Philip & Sons, 1988). A noteworthy special work on Elizabethan women is Susan Cahn, *The Transformation of Women's Work in England, 1500–1600* (Columbia University Press, 1987). Wallace T. MacCaffrey, *Elizabeth I, War and Politics 1588–1603* (Princeton University Press, 1992), is the best general survey of her reign.

On the less developed absolutism in eastern Europe, see Robert James Weston Evans, *The Making of the Habsburg Monarchy, 1550–1700* (Oxford University Press, 1984); see also Norman Davies, *A History of Poland,* Vol. 1 (Columbia University Press, 1981). A useful study of Prussian history in this period is Otis Mitchell, *A Concise History of Brandenburg-Prussia to 1786* (University Press of America, 1980). Development of the Romanov state is ably described in Otto Hoetzsch, *The Evolution of Russia* (Harcourt Brace, 1966), and W. Bruce Lincoln, *The Romanovs* (Dial, 1981).

Ronald G. Asch, *The Thirty Years' War, the Holy Roman Empire and Europe, 1618–1648* (St. Martin's Press, 1997), is a brief up-to-date survey with a good appreciation of the historiographical conflicts surrounding this event that adds to, but does not replace, Cicely V. Wedgewood's classic *The Thirty Years' War* (Anchor Books, 1961). Joseph Polisensky discusses the by-products of the war in *War and Society in Europe, 1618–1648* (Cambridge University Press, 1978). Michael Roberts, *Sweden's Age of Greatness* (St. Martin's Press, 1973), gives good coverage of both the political and military events in this conflict.

TECHNOLOGICAL EXCHANGE

How does technology move from one culture to another?

First trial of Maxim machine gun by English troops in Africa, 1887.

Technology has played a decisive role in human history, but its movement between cultures is often overlooked. Indeed, while American society tends to stress the creative genius of individual inventors such as Thomas Edison and the Wright brothers, technological innovations such as the light bulb and the airplane rest on a vast body of knowledge that stretches both back in time and around the world. It is, in fact, a universal tendency for individuals and societies to build on past discoveries, whatever their place of origin.

Traditionally, most world cultures have been open to beneficial new technologies originating from other cultures. Between 800 and 1300 C.E. Islamic civilization became dominant in the sciences in part because it eagerly absorbed the scientific knowledge of other civilizations such as Greece, Persia, and India. Caliphs and wealthy patrons sponsored medical centers, observatories, and libraries that translated foreign scientific treatises and undertook their own scientific investigations. Their efforts helped Muslim scientists make advances in mathematics, astronomy, medicine, and navigation. During this era, Arabic became the language of science, and both technological innovations and classical learning flowed from the Islamic world to Europe, where they helped stimulate the Renaissance.

Technology has often moved from its culture of origin to new cultures only to undergo further development there and then be transmitted on to other cultures and even back to its culture of origin, which was the case with gunpowder technology. A range of societies had experimented with explosives, but it was the Chinese who first invented gunpowder in the mid-ninth century C.E., initially only to make fireworks for religious and entertainment purposes. It would take another three centuries before they applied this technology to warfare, with the invention of rockets, bombs, and mortars. In the thirteenth century, the invading Mongols, in turn, helped to spread gunpowder technology from China across Asia to the Islamic world and Europe. Muslims and Christians alike were quick to recognize the potential of this new technology. When two English nobles in Spain witnessed the battle of Tarifa in 1340, they observed an Arab army fielding cannons against a Spanish force. They took that knowledge back with them to England, where it was immediately put to use in their wars with the French.

The Europeans, in fact, were so quick to embrace and develop gunpowder technology that it was the Portuguese and not the Chinese who first introduced muskets to East Asia in the early sixteenth century. The Japanese quickly accepted the new technology and begun manufacturing their own muskets. In a very short time, they were making guns equal to, if not better than, those made by the Europeans. This trend, however, would not last. In the seventeenth century, the samurai, the warrior class of Japan, opposed production of guns because they recognized that guns would endanger their exclusive status in Japanese society.

The Japanese only changed their view about guns out of necessity some 200 years later when a relatively small British force defeated China in the Opium War during the 1840s and Matthew Perry's warships anchored in Edo Bay in 1853. The Meiji emperor's embrace of modernization came out of the realization that Japan had to rapidly assimilate Western weapons of war if it wanted to fend off Western domination. Japanese scientists and officers studied English, French, and German military science, and the government poured money into the armament industry. Foreigners were admitted as teachers and technicians, and Japanese students were sent to American and European universities. The Imperial University, established in 1886, set up a faculty of engineering with departments specifically for explosives and shipbuilding. Japan's embrace of Western technology paid dividends when it defeated first China in the Sino-Japanese War of 1894–1895 and then Russia in the Russo-Japanese War of 1905.

Given the military and economic advantages offered by many technologies, it should not be surprising that many nations have sought to secure their own technologies and acquire or even steal the "protected" technologies of other nations. The Chinese closely guarded the secrets of silk and porcelain production for centuries until spies finally managed to carry those secrets abroad and break the Chinese monopoly. In the nineteenth century, Europeans may have eagerly sold the finished products of their technologies in the Americas, Asia, and Africa, but they generally kept the most advanced technologies for themselves, particularly weapons. Hilaire Belloc's famous couplet stated the truth bluntly: "Whatever else we have got / The Maxim gun and they have not."

The Europeans also sought to ensure that the manufacture of finished products—and thus the industry and profits—remained in their home countries. The colonized peoples of Africa and Asia, then, became the consumers of finished products and were prevented from developing their own manufacturing capabilities—a legacy that continues to challenge many countries in the developing world today.

Over the last two centuries one way some countries have sought to protect valuable technologies and encourage inventiveness in their people is through the issuing of patents, which give inventors an exclusive monopoly on the production of their invention for a number of years. Patented technologies are generally honored in the developed world, but cases of counterfeiting and piracy are rampant in the developing world. Of course, patent or no patent, if a business or individual is to have any chance of protecting a technology, it must recognize its value in the first place. This wasn't the case of the American company Western Electric and the transistor. American scientists had invented the transistor, but American electronics companies still relied on vacuum tubes in their products and were not prepared to apply the new technology in their manufacturing. Instead, a Japanese firm, Tokyo Telecommunications, recognized the importance of transistors and bought the rights from Western Electric when it sold its patent in 1954. Within a few years, the Japanese company had designed a transistor radio, and, after changing its name to Sony, it became a world leader in mass-producing electronics products.

Today, the dominant new economic technologies of our times are embodied in the Internet and information technology (IT). While these technologies have been exchanged freely around the world, their benefits have not reached all people. Because of the costs of achieving connectivity, a "digital divide" has emerged in which access to the Internet, for example, is often limited to urban elites in developing countries. On the other hand, some new technologies such as cell phones have opened up communications and business opportunities in remote areas of the world and are often even more ubiquitous in developing countries than they are in the West.

With advances to communication and transportation technology making the world smaller and smaller by the day, it seems certain the rate of technological exchange between cultures will only accelerate in the future.

Questions

1. What reasons might a culture have for rejecting a new technology coming from another culture?
2. Can you think of any situations in which counterfeiting and piracy of a technology would be morally acceptable?
3. Why is technological exchange inevitable?

Global Encounters

Europe and the New World Economy, 1400–1650

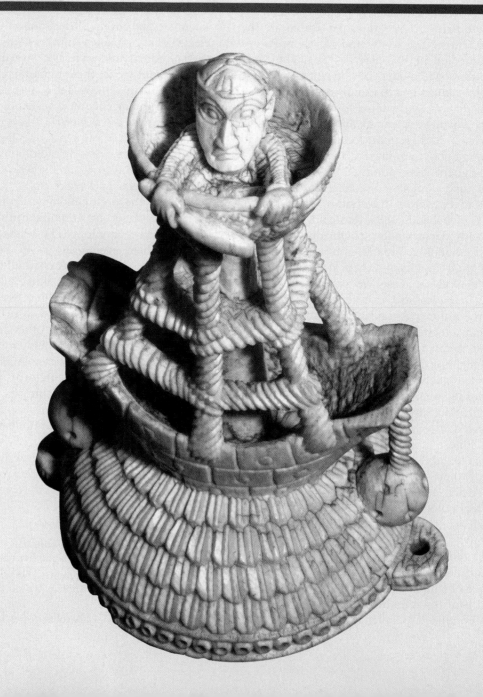

1300

1394–1460 Prince Henry the Navigator

1400

1400s Iberian navigators develop new naval technology; Spain and Portugal stake claims in Asia, Africa, and the Americas; Atlantic slave trade begins

1492 Christopher Columbus reaches San Salvador

1498 Vasco da Gama rounds Cape of Good Hope, reaches India

1500

1513 Vasco de Balboa reaches Pacific Ocean

1519 Hernando Cortés arrives in Mexico, defeats Aztecs

1520 Ferdinand Magellan rounds South America

1600

c. 1600 Second phase of European overseas expansion begins

1609 Henry Hudson establishes Dutch claims in North America; English East India Company chartered

1620 Pilgrims land at Plymouth

During the fifteenth century, European nations began a process of exploration, conquest, and trade, affecting almost all areas of the world. Their activities were mirrored in other parts of the world as Asian and Arab states took the lead in expanding their trading networks and their connections with each other. The processes were furthered by improved navigational technology and the resulting expansion of trade that encouraged long sea voyages by Arabs, Japanese, and Chinese. Likewise, sea power, rather than land-based armies, was the key to Europe's becoming a significant force in various parts of the world, especially the Americas and Africa.

European endeavors overseas were obviously related—both as cause and as effect—to trends set in motion as Europe emerged from the medieval era. The Crusades and the Renaissance stimulated European curiosity; the Reformation produced thousands of zealous missionaries seeking converts in foreign lands and refugees searching for religious freedom; and the monarchs of emerging sovereign states sought revenues, first by trading in the Indian Ocean and later by exploiting new worlds. Perhaps the most permeating influence was the rise of European capitalism, with its monetary values, profit-seeking motivations, investment institutions, and consistent impulses toward economic expansion. Some historians have labeled this whole economic transformation the Commercial Revolution. Others have used the phrase to refer to the shift in trade routes from the Mediterranean to the Atlantic. Interpreted either way, the Commercial Revolution and its accompanying European expansion helped usher in a modern era, largely at the expense of Africans and Amerindians.

Europe's Commercial Revolution developed in two quite distinct phases. The first phase involved Portugal and Spain; the second phase, after 1600, was led by the Netherlands, England, and to some extent France. The second fostered a maritime imperialism based more on trade and finance than the more directly exploitative systems of the first phase.

THE IBERIAN GOLDEN AGE

■ *What motivated the Portuguese and Spanish to develop global commercial networks?*

Portugal and Spain, the two Iberian states, launched the new era in competition with each other, although neither was able to maintain initial advantages over the long term. Portugal lacked the manpower and resources required by an empire spread over three continents. Spain wasted its new wealth in waging continuous wars while neglecting to develop its own economy. In 1503 Portuguese pepper cost only one-fifth as much as pepper coming through Venice and the eastern Mediterranean. Within decades, gold and silver from the New World poured into Spain. Iberian bullion and exotic commodities, flowing into northern banks and markets, provided a major stimulus to European capitalism. This early European impact abroad also generated great cultural diffusion, promoting an intercontinental spread of peoples, plants, animals, and knowledge that the world had never seen before. But it also destroyed Amerindian states and weakened societies in Africa.

Conditions Favoring Iberian Expansion

A number of conditions invited Iberian maritime expansion in the fifteenth century. Muslim control over the eastern caravan routes, particularly after the

Portuguese and Spanish Exploration and Expansion

1470–1541	Francisco Pizarro
1474–1566	Bartolomé de Las Casas
1479	Treaty of Alcacovas
1494	Treaty of Tordesillas
1509–1515	Alfonso de Albuquerque serves as eastern viceroy of Portugal
1510–1554	Francisco de Coronado
1510	Portuguese acquire Goa, in India
1531	Pizarro defeats Incas in Peru
c. 1550	Spanish introduce plantation system to Brazil
1565	St. Augustine founded; first European colony in North America

Turks took Constantinople in 1453, brought rising prices in Europe. At the same time, the sprawling Islamic world lacked both unity and intimidating sea power, and China, after 1440, had abandoned its extensive naval forays into the Indian Ocean. Because Muslim and Italian rivals prevented the Iberian states from tapping into the spice trade in the eastern Mediterranean and the gold trade in West Africa, Portugal and Spain sought alternative sea routes to the East, where their centuries-old struggle with Muslims in the Mediterranean might be continued on the ocean shores of sub-Saharan Africa and Asia.

During the 1400s, Iberian navigators became proficient in new naval technology and tactics. They adopted the compass (which came from China through the Middle East), the **astrolabe,** and the triangular **lateen sail** that gave their ships the ability to take advantage of winds coming from oblique angles and cut weeks off longer voyages. They also learned to tack against the wind, thus partly freeing them from hugging the coast on long voyages. This skill was important because prevailing winds and ocean currents made it impossible for Portuguese sailors to go farther south than Cape Bojador (bo-hyah-DOR) and still return home. In 1434, a Portuguese seafarer learned that it was possible to sail west toward the Canary Islands and catch trade winds that allowed ships to proceed home. This discovery opened up a new era of exploration.

The Iberians, especially the Portuguese, were also skilled cartographers and chartmakers. But their main advantages lay with their ships and naval guns. The stormy Atlantic required broad bows, deep keels, and complex square rigging for driving and maneuvering fighting ships. Armed with brass cannons, such ships could sink enemy vessels without ramming or boarding at close range. They could also batter down coastal defenses. Even the much larger Chinese junks were no match for the European ships' maneuverability and firepower.

A strong religious motivation augmented Iberian naval efficiency. Long and bitter wars with the Muslim Moors had left the Portuguese and Spanish with an obsessive drive to convert non-Christians or destroy them in the name of Christ. Sailors with Columbus recited prayers every night, and Portuguese seamen were equally devout. Every maritime mission was regarded as a holy crusade.

For two centuries Iberians had hoped to expand their influence in Muslim lands by launching a new Christian crusade in concert with Ethiopia. The idea

---

astrolabe—An instrument used in navigation for calculating latitude.

lateen sail—A triangular sail that is set at a 45-degree angle to the mast and takes advantage of winds coming from oblique angles.

originated with twelfth-century crusaders in the Holy Land; it gained strength later with Ethiopian migrants at Rhodes, who boasted of their king's prowess against the infidels. Thus arose the myth of "Prester John," a mighty Ethiopian monarch and potential European ally against Mongols, Turks, and Muslims. In response to a delegation from Zar'a Ya'kob, the reigning emperor, a few Europeans visited Ethiopia after 1450. These and other similar contacts greatly stimulated the determination to find a new sea route to the East that might link the Iberians with the legendary Ethiopian king and bring Islam under attack from two sides.

"The Land of Prester John"

This dream of war for the cross was sincere, but it also served to rationalize more worldly concerns. Both Spain and Portugal experienced dramatic population growth between 1400 and 1600. The Spanish population increased from 5 to 8.5 million; the Portuguese population more than doubled, from 900,000 to 2 million, despite a manpower loss of 125,000 in the sixteenth century. Hard times in rural areas prompted migration to cities, where dreams of wealth in foreign lands encouraged fortune seeking overseas. Despite the obvious religious zeal of many Iberians, particularly among those in holy orders, a fervent desire for gain was the driving motivation for most migrants.

The structures of the Iberian states provided further support for overseas expansion. In both, the powers of the monarchs had been recently expanded and were oriented toward maritime adventure as a means to raise revenues, divert the Turkish menace, spread Catholic Christianity, and increase national unity. The Avis dynasty in Portugal, after usurping the throne and alienating the great nobles in 1385, made common cause with the gentry and middle classes, who prospered in commercial partnership with the government. In contrast, Spanish nobles, particularly the Castilians, were very much like Turkish aristocrats, who regarded conquest and plunder as their normal functions and sources of income. Thus, the Portuguese and Spanish political systems worked in different ways toward similar imperial ends.

Staking Claims

During the late fifteenth century, both Portugal and Spain staked claims abroad. Portugal gained a long lead over Spain in Africa and Asia. But after conquering Granada, the last Moorish state on the Iberian peninsula, and completely uniting the country, the Spanish monarchs turned their attention overseas. The resulting historic voyage of Columbus established Spanish claims to most of the Western Hemisphere.

The man most responsible for Portugal's ambitious exploits was Prince Henry (1394–1460), known as "the Navigator" because of his famous observatory at

Using ships like these broad-beamed carracks, the Portuguese controlled much of the carrying trade with the East in the fifteenth and sixteenth centuries.

Sagres (SAH-greesh), where skilled mariners planned voyages and recorded their results. As a young man in 1415, Henry directed the Portuguese conquest of Ceuta (see-YOO-tah), a Muslim port on the Moroccan coast, at the western entrance to the Mediterranean. This experience imbued him with a lifelong desire to divert the West African gold trade from Muslim caravans to Portuguese ships. He also shared the common dream of winning Ethiopian Christian allies against the Turks. Such ideas motivated him for 40 years as he sent expeditions down the West African coast, steadily charting and learning from unknown waters.

Before other European states began extensive explorations, the Portuguese had navigated the West African coast to its southern tip. Henry's captains claimed the Madeira Islands in 1418 and the Azores in 1421. A thousand miles to the west of Portugal, these uninhabited islands were settled to produce, among other things, wheat for bread-starved Lisbon.

By 1450 the Portuguese had explored the Senegal River and then traced the Guinea coast during the next decade. After Henry's death in 1460, they pushed

Motivated by a desire to find a sea route to India that bypassed the overland caravan routes controlled by Muslim states, Prince Henry the Navigator was a leading figure in promoting Portuguese explorations down the West African coast. Ironically he seldom left Portugal himself. When he died in 1460, his sailors had reached the Canary Islands, but by the end of that century, Vasco da Gama had sailed from Portugal to India.

south, reaching Benin in the decade after 1470 and Kongo, on the southwest coast, in 1482. Six years later, Bartolomeu Dias rounded southern Africa, but his disgruntled crew forced him to turn back. Nevertheless, King John II of Portugal (1481–1495) was so excited by the prospect of a direct route to India that he named Dias's discovery the "Cape of Good Hope."

Spain soon challenged Portuguese supremacy. The specific controversy was over the Canary Islands, some of which were occupied by Castilians in 1344 and others by Portuguese after the 1440s. The issue, which produced repeated incidents, was ultimately settled in 1479 by the Treaty of Alcacovas (ahl-KAHS-ko-vahsh), which recognized exclusive Spanish rights in the Canaries but banned Spain from the Madeiras, the Azores, the Cape Verdes, and West Africa. Spanish ambitions were thus temporarily frustrated until Columbus provided new hope.

Christopher Columbus (1451–1506), a Genoese sailor with an impossible dream, had been influenced by Marco Polo's journal to believe that Japan could be reached by a short sail directly westward. Although he underestimated the distance by some 7000 miles and was totally ignorant of the intervening continents, Columbus persistently urged his proposals on King John of Portugal and Queen Isabella of Spain, who was captivated by Columbus's dream and became his most steadfast supporter until her death in 1504. Having obtained her sponsorship, Columbus sailed from Palos, Spain, in three small ships on August 3, 1492. He landed on San Salvador in the West Indies on October 12, thinking he had reached his goal. In three more attempts he continued his search for an Asian passage. His voyages touched the major Caribbean islands, Honduras, the Isthmus of Panama, and Venezuela. Although he never knew it, he had claimed a new world for Spain.

VIDEO

Christopher Columbus and the Round World

Columbus's first voyage posed threats to Portuguese interests in the Atlantic and called for compromise if war was to be averted. At Spain's invitation, the pope issued a "bull of demarcation," establishing a north-south line about 300 miles west of the Azores. Beyond this line all lands were opened to Spanish claims. The Portuguese protested, forcing direct negotiations, which produced the Treaty of Tordesillas (tordhai-SEE-lyahs) in 1494. It moved the line some 500 miles farther west. Later explorations showed that the last agreement gave Spain most of the New World but left eastern Brazil to Portugal.

The Developing Portuguese Empire

Through the first half of the sixteenth century, the Portuguese developed a world maritime empire while maintaining commercial supremacy. They established trading posts around both African coasts and a falter-

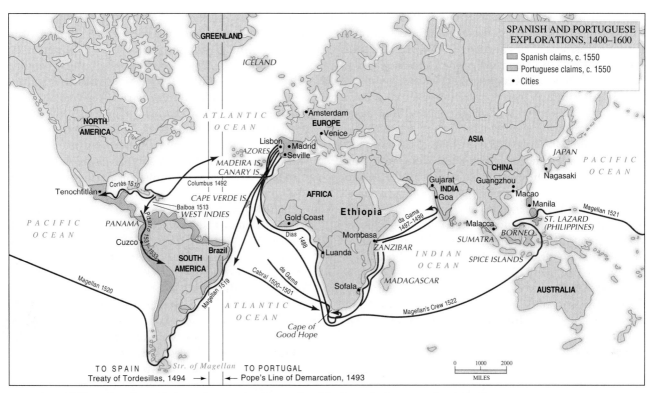

From the mid-fifteenth to the mid-sixteenth centuries, Portugal and Spain took advantage of new naval technology and tactics to become the leading seafaring nations in the world.

ing colony in Brazil, but their most extensive operations were in southern Asia, where they gained control of shipping routes and dominated the Indian Ocean spice trade.

Two voyages at the turn of the sixteenth century laid the foundations for the Portuguese interests in the Americas and the Orient. In 1497 Vasco da Gama (1469–1524) left Lisbon, Portugal, in four ships, rounding the Cape of Good Hope after 93 days on the open sea. While visiting and raiding the East African ports, da Gama picked up an Arab pilot, who brought the fleet across the Indian Ocean to Calicut (KAL-i-kut), on the western coast of India. When he returned to Lisbon in 1499, da Gama had lost two ships and a third of his men, but his cargo of pepper and cinnamon returned the cost of the expedition 60 times over. Shortly afterward, Pedro Cabral (1468–1520), commanding a large fleet on a second voyage to India, bore too far west and sighted the east coast of Brazil. The new western territory was so unpromising that it was left unoccupied until 1532, when a small settlement was established at São Vicente. In the 1540s it had attracted only some 2000 settlers, mostly men, although a few Portuguese women came after the arrival of the lord protector's wife and her retinue in 1535. The colony served mostly as a place to send convicts, and by 1600 it had only 25,000 European residents.

Brazil was neglected in favor of extensive operations in the Indian Ocean and Southeast Asia, where the Portuguese sought to gain control of the spice trade by taking over flourishing port cities, places strategically located on established trade routes. The most striking successes were achieved under Alfonso de Albuquerque, eastern viceroy from 1509 to 1515. He completed subjugation of the Swahili city-states and established fortified trading posts in Mozambique and Zanzibar. After a decisive naval victory over an Arab fleet (1509), Albuquerque's force captured Hormuz (hor-MOOZ) six years later, thus disrupting Arab passage from the Persian Gulf. In 1510 the Portuguese acquired Goa on the west coast of India; it became a base for aiding Hindus against Indian Muslims and conducting trade with Gujerat (goo-ja-RAHT), a major producer of cloth. The next year a Portuguese force took Malacca, a Muslim stronghold in Malaya, which controlled trade with China and the Spice Islands, through the narrow straits opposite Sumatra (soo-MAH-trah). Although a Portuguese goal was to spread the Christian faith at the expense of Islam, the expulsion of Muslim traders had the opposite effect. These traders moved to the Malaysian peninsula and founded new Muslim states.

The Indian Ocean had previously been open to all traders, but the Portuguese network left no room for competitors, and rival traders, especially Muslims, were squeezed out of their previous settlements. Portuguese officials financed their operations from two sources, customs duties and a tax levied on ships trading in the Indian Ocean. All ships were required to stop at Portuguese ports and take a ***cartaz.***

The Portuguese presence was largely felt on the ocean; it had very little impact on the land-based empires and trading networks of the Ottomans, the Safavids, the Mughuls, and the Chinese. On the Asian mainland, for instance, the Portuguese were mostly supplicants because they had to interact with well-established and more powerful states. They acquired temporary influence in Laos and Cambodia but were expelled from Vietnam and enslaved in Burma. In China their diplomatic blunders and breaches of etiquette offended Ming officials, who regarded the Portuguese as cannibals. In 1519 a Portuguese representative angered the Chinese by, among other things, starting to erect a fort in Canton harbor without permission and buying Chinese children as slaves. Chinese officials

cartaz—A license issued by the Portuguese that permitted non-Portuguese traders to operate in areas of the Indian Ocean controlled by the Portuguese.

responded by jailing and executing a group of Portuguese emissaries who had been visiting Beijing. After being banished from Chinese ports in 1522 and 1544, the Portuguese cooperated with Chinese smuggling rings off South China before Chinese officials granted them strictly regulated trading rights in Macao (mah-KOU) in 1554. Although the Chinese generally had little interest in European goods, the Portuguese served a useful purpose by supplying the Chinese economy with Indian manufactures such as cloth and Indonesian spices and silver from the Americas reexported through Europe.

The Portuguese developed an extensive relationship with Japan. The connection was established accidentally in 1542 when three Portuguese traders landed off southern Japan after a storm blew their ship off course. At the time Japanese *daimyo* (feudal lords) were contending with each other for power, and Portuguese traders prospered by selling matchlock muskets to rival factions.

The Jesuit priests who followed the merchants in 1549 had great success in winning converts. While the *daimyo* Nobunaga was gaining mastery over his opponents, he

A Japanese View of European Missionaries

In the sixteenth century a Japanese artist depicted the Portuguese as "Southern Barbarians" in a decorative screen.

encouraged the Catholics because they were useful allies against Buddhist sects opposing him. By the 1580s, the Catholics were claiming as many as 150,000 adherents. However, as Japan became unified in the late sixteenth century, Nobunaga's successors began regarding Christians as a divisive threat. They perceived the arrival of Spanish Franciscan friars in 1592 as an additional danger because they had recently scored major successes in winning converts in the Philippines. Japanese officials issued a series of anti-Christian edicts that led to the persecution and killing of thousands of Christians. Following the suppression of a Christian peasant revolt in 1637–1638, the Japanese government expelled all Europeans except for a small contingent of Dutch traders who were confined to a small island in the Nagasaki harbor.

Long before this expulsion, the Portuguese Empire had begun to decline. It did not have the special skills or fluid capital required by a global empire and had become dependent on the bankers and spice brokers of northern Europe for financing. This deficiency was magnified by Albuquerque's failure to recruit women from home who might have produced a Portuguese governing elite in the colonies. To make matters worse, the home population dropped steadily after 1600. Thus the relatively few Portuguese men overseas mated with local women. Most were concubines, prostitutes, or slaves—regarded generally as household pets or work animals. These conditions contributed largely to a decided weakening of morale, economic efficiency, and military power. After the turn of the seventeenth century, the Portuguese lost ground to the Omani Arabs in East Africa, the Spanish in the Philippines, and the Dutch in both hemispheres. Despite a mild later revival, their empire never regained its former glory.

THE PORTUGUESE AND AFRICA

▪ *How did Africans respond to the opportunities offered by trade with the Portuguese?*

Africa, Europe, and the World

The Portuguese came to Africa as traders rather than settlers. Their original goal was to find a way around Muslim middlemen who controlled the trans-Saharan caravan trade and to gain direct access to the fabled goldfields of West Africa. Muslim kingdoms of the Sudan, such as Mali, Kanem-Bornu, and the Hausa states, dominated trade in the West African interior and were reluctant to open up their trade to Europeans. Therefore, the Portuguese concentrated their efforts on establishing commercial bases along the West African coast.

The Portuguese in West Africa

Africa was not of primary importance to the Portuguese, especially after they opened up sea routes to Asia. Thus, they selectively established links with African states where they could trade for goods of value such as gold, which could be traded anywhere in the world, and slaves, which were initially taken to southern Portugal as laborers. The first bases of operation for Portuguese seafarers were at Cape Verde, Arguin (ahr-GWEEN), and Senegambia.

CASE STUDY

Portuguese Travelers in Africa

Although the Portuguese conducted hit-and-run raids for slaves and plunder, they soon learned that if they expected to sustain a profitable trade in gold, they could not afford to alienate African rulers. When the Portuguese arrived on the Gold Coast (present-day Ghana) in 1471, they found Akan states carrying on a vigorous trade to the north through Muslim Dyula traders. Still hoping to develop trade links with the kingdom of Mali, the Portuguese sent several envoys with Dyula traders to Mali in the late fifteenth century. However, Mali's king sent a clear signal about his lack of interest in ties with Portugal by informing the envoy that he recognized only three kings beside himself—the rulers of Yemen, Cairo, and Baghdad.

From that point on, the Portuguese concentrated on establishing a profitable relationship with Akan leaders, exchanging firearms (that could not be obtained through Mali), copper and brass objects, textiles, slaves, and later cowrie shells for gold. From their fort at Elmina ("the mine"), established in 1482, the Portuguese exported close to half a ton of gold annually for the next half century. Because the Akan required slave labor to clear forests for arable agricultural land, the Portuguese brought slaves from the region of Benin and Kongo. It took several more

The Portuguese and Africa	
1482	Portuguese establish Fort Elmina on Gold Coast; Portuguese reach kingdom of Kongo
1506–1543	Reign of Nzinga Mbemba, king of Kongo
1506	Portuguese seize Sofala
1571	Portuguese establish colony of Angola
1607	King of Mutapa kingdom signs treaty with Portugal
1698	Portuguese driven from East African coast by Omani Arabs

centuries before Akan states actively participated in selling rather than buying slaves.

The Portuguese also initiated contacts with the kingdom of Benin, located in the forests of southwestern Nigeria. The kings of Benin, called *obas*, had governed their land since the eleventh century. When the Portuguese arrived, Benin possessed a formidable army and was at the peak of its power. Edo, the walled capital, was a bustling metropolis with wide streets, markets, and an efficient municipal government. The huge royal palace awed Europeans who chanced to see it, although the Portuguese—and later the Dutch—were generally prohibited from living in the city. The few European visitors who gained entrance were amazed by Benin's metalwork, such as copper birds on towers, copper snakes coiled around doorways, and beautifully cast bronze statues.

Benin artists cast brass plaques that adorned the oba's palace walls. The plaques depicted important events in Benin's history, including the engagement with the Portuguese. The two Portuguese soldiers in this plaque are notable for their long wavy hair and military uniforms.

The first Portuguese emissary who arrived at oba Ozuola's court in 1486 was sent back to Lisbon with gifts, including a Maltese-type cross. The cross excited the Portuguese who interpreted it as a sign that Benin was near Prester John's kingdom and that its inhabitants would be receptive to conversion to Christianity. However, when Ozuola admitted Catholic missionaries to his kingdom in the early 1500s in the hope of securing Portuguese muskets, the Portuguese made acceptance of Christianity a precondition for receiving arms. Although the missionaries converted several of Ozuola's sons and high-ranking officials, their influence ended at Ozuola's death.

Portugal believed that it could manipulate Benin's rulers to extend Portuguese trade over a much wider area, but the obas did not regard trade with the Portuguese as a vital necessity and did not allow them to establish a sizable presence in the kingdom. The obas controlled all transactions, and Portuguese traders duly paid taxes, observed official regulations, and conducted business only with the obas' representatives.

The Portuguese traded brass and copper items, textiles, and cowrie shells for pepper, cloth, beads, and slaves. Because Benin did not have access to sources of gold, the Portuguese took the slaves from Benin and traded them for gold with the Akan states, which needed laborers for clearing forests for farmland. However, in 1516, Benin decided to curtail the slave trade and offered only female slaves for purchase.

Although effectively limited in Benin, Portuguese traders openly operated among nearby coastal states, where they gained some political influence. They were particularly successful in the small kingdom of Warri, a Niger delta vassal state of Benin. Shortly after 1600, the Warri crown prince was educated in Portugal and brought home a Portuguese queen. Warri supplied large numbers of slaves, as did other nearby states, which were now competing fiercely with one another. Before long, even Benin would accept dependence on the slave trade in order to control its tributaries and hold its own against Europeans.

The Portuguese and the Kongo Kingdom

Farther south, near the mouth of the Congo River, the Portuguese experienced their most intensive involvement in Africa. There, Portuguese seafarers found the recently established Kongo kingdom of several million people, ruled by a king who was heavily influenced by the queen mother and other women on his royal council. Although the Kongo initially perceived the Europeans as water or earth spirits, Kongo's king, Nzinga Nkuwu, soon came to regard them as a potential ally against neighboring African

Loango, Capital of the Kingdom of the Congo

Discovery Through Maps

Savage Pictures: Sebastian Munster's Map of Africa

Voyages of exploration in the fifteenth and sixteenth centuries greatly expanded European knowledge of the rest of the world. However, mapmakers who knew very little about the geography and peoples of continents such as Africa still tended to rely on outdated information or stereotypical representations. Thus, when Sebastian Munster (1489–1552 C.E.), a professor of Hebrew and mathematics at Basel, the home of Switzerland's oldest university, developed an interest in maps, he turned to Ptolemy (90–168 C.E.), a celebrated astronomer, geographer, and mathematician of Alexandria, Egypt, whose theories about the universe influenced the European and Arab worlds for many centuries. When Ptolemy's *Guide to Geography* was published in Florence around 1400, it was the first atlas of the world.

Ptolemy's view of the world heavily influenced Munster when he began drawing his own world atlas. First published in 1544, Munster's *Cosmographia Universalis* went through 46 editions and was translated into six languages. It was the first collection to feature individual maps of Europe, Asia, the Americas, and Africa.

Munster's map of Africa relied not only on Ptolemy but also on Portuguese and Arab sources. However, it still contained many errors. The map identified the source of the Nile far to the south and, based on the assumption that the Senegal was connected to the Niger River in West Africa, showed a river flowing westward to the Atlantic.

The *Cosmographia* was also a descriptive geography, providing an accompanying narrative and drawings of prominent figures, the customs and manners of societies, and the products, animals, and plants of regions. Munster's Africa map depicted a lone human figure that bore no resemblance to Africans and a large elephant at the southern end of the continent. His rendering of Africa conformed to Jonathan Swift's satirical lines:

So Geographers in Africa-Maps
With Savage-Pictures fill their Gaps;
And o'er unhabitable Downs
Place Elephants for want of Towns.

Questions to Consider

1. Why do you think Muster chose to rely on Ptolemy's views rather than on more recent information?

2. Compare the portrayal of Africa in Munster's map with that in Abraham Cresque's Catalan map. Why does Cresque's map contain so much more detail than Munster's?

states. In the 1480s he invited the Portuguese to send teachers, technicians, missionaries, and soldiers. His son, Nzinga Mbemba (1506–1543), who converted to Catholicism in 1491, consolidated the control of the Catholic faction at his court, making Portuguese the official language and Catholicism the state religion. He encouraged his court to adopt European dress and manners while changing his own name to Don Afonso. Many friendly letters subsequently passed between him and King Manuel of Portugal.

This mutual cooperation did not last long. While the Portuguese were prepared to assist Afonso's kingdom, their desire for profits won out over their humanitarian impulses. Portuguese traders, seeking slaves for their sugar plantations at São Tomé (SAH-o TO-mai) and Principe, ranged over Kongo. By 1530 some 4000 to 5000 slaves were being taken from Kongo annually. No longer satisfied with treaty terms that gave them prisoners of war and criminals, the traders ignored the laws and bought everyone they could get, thus creating dissension and weakening the country. Driven to despair, Afonso wrote to his friend and ally Manuel: "There are many traders in all corners of the country. They bring ruin. . . . Every day, people are enslaved and kidnapped, even nobles, even members of the King's own family."[1] Such pleas brought no satisfactory responses. For a while, Afonso tried to curb the slave trade; however, he was shot by disgruntled Portuguese slavers while he was attending Mass in 1430. Afonso's successors were no more successful, and Portuguese slavers operated with impunity throughout Kongo and in neighboring areas.

The Portuguese crown also turned its attention to the Mbundu kingdom to the south of Kongo. In 1520 Manuel established contact with the Mbundu king, Ngola. However, when the Portuguese government agreed to deal with Ngola through Kongo, São Tomé slavers were given a free hand to join with Mbundu's rulers to attack neighboring states. Using African mercenaries known as pombeiros equipped with firearms and sometimes allied with feared Imbangala warriors, the slavers and their allies began a long war of conquest. In 1571 the Portuguese crown issued a royal charter to establish the colony of Angola, situated on the Atlantic coast south of the Kongo kingdom. Although Portugal had ambitious plans to create an agricultural colony for white settlement and to gain control over a silver mine and the salt trade in the interior, Angola was never a successful venture. Few settlers immigrated, and Angola remained a sleepy outpost, consisting of a handful of Portuguese men, even fewer Portuguese women, a growing population of Afro-Portuguese, and a majority of Africans. The colony functioned primarily as a haven for slavers. By the end of the sixteenth century, 10,000 slaves were flowing annually through Luanda (loo-AHN-dah), Angola's capital.

The Portuguese in East Africa

Portuguese exploits in East Africa were similar to those in Kongo and Angola. The Swahili city-states along the coast north of the Zambezi (zam-BEE-zee) River were tempting targets for Portuguese intervention because they were strategically well located for trade with Asia. However, because they rarely engaged in wars with each other or supported sizeable militaries, they could not effectively defend themselves against a ruthless Portuguese naval force that sacked and plundered city-states from Kilwa to Mombasa. At Mombasa Portuguese sailors broke into houses with axes, looted, and killed before setting the town afire. The sultan of Mombasa wrote to the sultan of Malindi: "[They] raged in our town with such might and terror that no one, neither man nor woman, neither the old or the young, nor even the children, however small, was spared to live."[2]

DOCUMENT

"Of the Coasts of East Africa and Malabar"

Although a few city-states such as Malindi (mah-LEEN-dee) escaped the wrath of the Portuguese by becoming allies, the Portuguese usually relied on coercion to keep the city-states in line. They constructed fortified stations from which they attempted to collect tribute and maintain trade with the interior. An early station at Mozambique became the main port of call for vessels on the Asia route. In the 1590s the Portuguese built a fort at Mombasa, hoping to intimidate other cities and support naval operations against Turks and Arabs in the Red Sea. Although the Portuguese dominated trade in gold and ivory along the East African coast, they could not control the whole coastline and Swahili merchants continued to trade with their traditional partners. However, local industries such as ironworking and weaving virtually disappeared under Portuguese rule. When Omani Arabs expelled the Portuguese from the Swahili coast in 1698, the Swahili did not lament their departure. A Swahili proverb captured Swahili sentiment: "Go away, Manuel [the king of Portugal], you have made us hate you; go, and carry your cross with you."[3]

On the southeast coast the Portuguese were drawn to the Zimbabwean plateau by reports of huge gold mines. The Portuguese needed gold to finance their trade for spices in the Indian Ocean, while Shona kingdoms desired beads and cotton cloth from India. The Portuguese seized Sofala in 1506, diminishing the role of Muslim traders and positioning themselves as the middlemen for the gold trade with the coast. After establishing trading settlements along the Zambezi River at Sena and Tete, the Portuguese developed a close relationship with the Karanga kingdom of Mutapa, which received Portuguese traders and Catholic missionaries. This relationship soured when the king of Mutapa ordered the death of a Jesuit missionary in 1560. In the 1570s the Portuguese retaliated

Document   Portuguese Encounters with Africans

The Portuguese had very specific objectives in Africa. They usually established amicable relations with stronger states, while they were more likely to coerce weaker states such as the Swahili city-states in East Africa. When Vasco da Gama dealt with the ruler of Kilwa, an island off the East African coast, he showed little patience for the subtleties of diplomacy and quickly resorted to threats to achieve his aims. This document records an exchange between da Gama and the King of Kilwa.

In the case of the Kingdom of the Kongo, the Portuguese were dealing with a state that clearly defined its interests and did not regard Portugal as a superior nation. Kongo's king, Don Afonso, who converted to Catholicism, wrote a series of letters to the king of Portugal in 1526. These letters demonstrate the complex relationship between the Kongolese leadership and the Portuguese. Afonso complains about Portuguese involvement in the slave trade but also conveys a request for doctors and apothecaries to treat illnesses.

KING IBRAHIM OF KILWA: Good friendship was to friends like brothers are and that he would shelter the Portuguese in his city and harbor . . . to pay tribute each year in money or jewelry was not a way to a good friendship, it was tributary subjugation . . . to pay tribute was dishonor . . . it would be like to be a captive . . . such friendship he did not want with subjugation . . . because even the sons did not want to have that kind of subjugation with their own parents.

VASCO DA GAMA: Take it for certain that if I so decide your city would be grounded by fire in one single hour and if your people wanted to extinguish the fire in town, they would all be burned and when you see all this happen, you will regret all you are telling me now and you will give much more than what I am asking you now, it will be too late for you. If you are still in doubt, it is up to you to see it.

KING IBRAHIM: Sir, if I had known that you wanted to enslave me, I would not have come and I would have fled into the forest, for it is better for me to be a fox but free, than a dog locked up in a golden chain.

From Chapurukha M. Kusimba, *The Rise and Fall of Swahili States* (Walnut Creek: AltaMira Press, 1999), pp. 161–162.

Moreover, Sir, in our Kingdom there is another great inconvenience which is of little service to God, and this is that many of our people [*naturaes*], keenly desirous as they are of the wares and things of your Kingdoms, which are brought here by your people, freed and exempt men; and very often it happens that they kidnap even noblemen and the sons of noblemen, and our relatives, and take them to be sold to the white men who are in our Kingdoms; and for this purpose they have concealed them, and others are brought during the night so that they might not be recognized.

And as soon as they are taken by the white men they are immediately ironed and branded with fire, and when they are carried to be embarked, if they are caught by our guards' men the whites allege that they have brought them but they cannot say from whom, so that it is our duty to do justice and to restore to the freemen their freedom, but it cannot be done if your subjects feel offended, as they claim to be.

And to avoid such a great evil we passed a law so that any white man living in our Kingdoms and wanting to purchase goods in any way should first inform three of our noblemen and officials of our court . . . who should investigate if the mentioned goods are captives or freemen, and if cleared by them there will be no further doubt nor embargo for them to be taken and embarked. But if the white men do not comply with it they will lose the aforementioned goods. . . .

[1526] Sir, Your Highness has been kind enough to write to us saying that we should ask in our letters for anything we need, and that we shall be provided with everything, and as the peace and health of our Kingdom depend on us . . . it happens that we have continuously many and different diseases which put us very often in such a weakness that we reach almost the last extreme; and the same happens to our children, relatives and natives owing to the lack in this country of physicians and surgeons who might know how to cure properly such diseases.

And to avoid such a great error and inconvenience, since it is from God in the first place and then from your Kingdoms and from Your Highness that all the good and drugs and medicines have come to save us, we beg of you to be agreeable and kind enough to send us two physicians and two apothecaries and all the necessary things to stay in our kingdoms. . . .

From Basil Davidson, *African Past* (Boston: Little, Brown and Co., 1964), pp. 192–194.

Questions to Consider

1. Why did the Portuguese treat the kings of Kongo and Kilwa in different ways?
2. What do the letters from the King of the Kongo reveal about the involvement of his people and the Portuguese in the slave trade?

by sending several expeditionary forces up the Zambezi to seize control over the gold-producing areas. The Portuguese believed the gold came from rich mines, when, in reality, African peasants recovered most of the gold from riverbeds during the winter months. In any event, these adventures ended disastrously as drought, disease (especially malaria), and African resisters decimated the Portuguese forces.

A series of internal rebellions and wars with neighboring states, however, forced Mutapa's rulers to turn to the Portuguese for assistance. In 1607 they signed a treaty that ceded control of gold production to the Portuguese. For the rest of the century the Portuguese regularly intervened in Mutapa's affairs until the forces of Mutapa and a rising power, Changamire, combined to expel the Portuguese from the Zimbabwean plateau. Along the Zambezi River the Portuguese crown granted huge land concessions **(prazos)** to Portuguese settlers (*prazeros*) who ruled them as feudal estates. Over time, the *prazeros* loosened their ties with Portugal's officials and became virtually independent. In the absence of Portuguese women, *prazeros* intermarried with Africans and adopted African culture.

The tale of Prester John, the mythical Ethiopian Christian monarch who held the Muslims at bay, had long captivated Portugal's monarchs. Thus, they initially responded positively when the astute Ethiopian empress Eleni made diplomatic overtures. Eleni, the daughter of a Muslim king, had married the Ethiopian emperor Baeda Maryam and converted to Christianity. After his death in 1478, she remained an influential figure as regent during the reigns of two of her sons and two grandsons. Recognizing that the interests of both Ethiopia and Portugal would be served by defeating Muslim states on the Red Sea coast, she wrote Portugal's king in 1509 proposing an alliance against the Ottoman Turks. She reasoned that the combination of Ethiopia's army and Portugal's sea forces would be very potent. However, the Portuguese, disappointed that Ethiopia did not meet their grand expectations of a kingdom ruled by Prester John, were reluctant to sign a pact.

After Eleni's death in 1522, her projected alliance was not completed for several decades. In 1541, the army of Muslim leader Ahmad Gran of the kingdom of Adal had come close to conquering Ethiopia. This time, the Portuguese responded to Ethiopian appeals by dispatching 400 Portuguese musketeers who helped to defeat the Muslims. The following year, however, Muslim forces, augmented by Turkish soldiers, rallied and defeated the Portuguese contingent,

killing its commander, Christopher da Gama, Vasco's son. When the Ethiopians eventually pushed the Muslims out, they enticed some of the Portuguese soldiers to stay on by granting them large estates in the countryside. Subsequent Ethiopian rulers called on descendants of the Portuguese in their conflicts with the Turks.

The Portuguese impact on Africa was not as immediately disastrous as Spanish effects on the New World. The Portuguese did not have the manpower or arms to dictate the terms of trade with most African states. However, they did inflict severe damage in Kongo, Angola, Zimbabwe, and the Swahili city-states. Their most destructive involvement was the slave trade.

By the end of the sixteenth century the Portuguese had moved an estimated 240,000 slaves from West and Central Africa; 80 percent were transported after 1575. These trends foreshadowed much greater disasters for African societies in the seventeenth and eighteenth centuries as the Atlantic slave trade expanded (see Chapter 19).

THE GROWTH OF NEW SPAIN

■ *What factors contributed to the Spanish conquest of Amerindian societies?*

While Portugal concentrated on Asian and African trade, Spain won a vast empire in America. Soon after 1492, Spanish settlements were established in the West Indies, most notably on Hispaniola (ees-pah-nee-O-lah) and Cuba. By 1500, as the American continents were recognized and the passage to Asia remained undiscovered, a host of Spanish adventurers—the **conquistadora**—set out for the New World with dreams of acquiring riches. From the West Indies they crossed the Caribbean to eastern Mexico, fanning out from there in all directions, toward Central America, the Pacific, and the vast North American hinterlands.

In Mexico the Spaniards profited from internal problems within the Aztec Empire. By the early 1500s, the Aztecs ruled over several million people in a vast kingdom that stretched from the Gulf of Mexico to the Pacific Ocean and from present-day central Mexico to Guatemala. However, unrest ran rampant among many recently conquered peoples, who were forced to pay tribute and taxes and furnish sacrificial victims to their Aztec overlords.

In 1519 Spanish officials in Cuba, excited by reports of a wealthy Amerindian civilization from two

---

prazo—A land grant from the Portuguese crown to a Portuguese settler (*prazero*) in the Zambezi river valley in Mozambique that gave the settler control over tribute and labor service from local residents.

---

conquistadora—The Spanish soldiers who conquered Mexico and Peru.

expeditions to the Yucatán (yoo-kah-TAHN) peninsula, dispatched Hernando Cortés (1485–1574) with 11

ships, 600 fighting men, 200 servants, 16 horses, 32 crossbows, 13 muskets, and 14 mobile cannons. Before marching against the Aztec capital, he destroyed 10 of his 11 ships to prevent his men from turning back. He had the good luck to secure two interpreters. One was an Amerindian woman, Malitzin, later christened Doña Marina, who became a valuable interpreter and intelligence gatherer as well as bearing Cortés a son. As Cortés's band marched inland, he added thousands of Amerindian warriors to his small force. He easily enlisted Amerindian allies, such as the Cempoala who had suffered under Aztec rule. By contrast, the loyalty of the Tlaxcalan (tlash-KAH-lahn) was secured only after Cortez's force demonstrated the superiority of its firearms, steel swords, and armor and horses (that the Aztecs initially thought were deer).

The Aztec emperor Moctezuma II's initial view of the Spaniards was shaped by an Aztec belief that the

Spaniards were representatives of the white-skinned and bearded Teotihuacán (tay-o-tee-wah-KAHN) god, Quetzalcoatl (KAT-SAL-KWA-tel), who had been exiled by the Toltecs in the tenth century C.E. He forbade human sacrifice and had promised to return from across the sea to enforce his law. However, as reports of Spanish victories came to his attention, Moctezuma had second thoughts as Cortés approached the Aztec capital, Tenochtitlán (te-noch-teet-lahn), a city of more than 150,000 people. Thus, Moctezuma warily welcomed Cortés as a guest in his father's palace. Although surrounded by a host of armed Aztecs, Cortés seized the ruler and informed

him that he must cooperate or die. The bold scheme worked temporarily. But when Cortés left the capital to return to the coast, his commander attacked an unarmed crowd at a religious festival, killing many Aztec notables. The massacre touched off a popular uprising. Cortés returned with reinforcements, but when he placed Moctezuma on a wall to pacify the Aztecs, they renounced their former ruler as a traitor and stoned and killed him. Neither the Aztecs nor the Spaniards showed any mercy in the fierce fighting that followed. The Aztecs ultimately drove a battered band of terrified Spaniards from the city in the narrowest of escapes. Later, having regrouped and gained new Amerindian allies, Cortés wore down the Aztecs in a bloody siege during which some Spanish prisoners were sacrificed in full view of their comrades. The outcome of the fighting was in doubt when a smallpox epidemic, accidentally introduced by a Spanish soldier, broke out, killing many thousands of Aztecs who had no immunity to the disease. Finally, in August 1521, some 60,000 exhausted and half-starved defenders surrendered.

As the inheritors of the Aztec empire, the Spaniards found the Aztec's hierarchical system suited to their needs. They replaced an urbanized Aztec elite with their own and gave privileged positions to Amerindian allies such as the Tlaxcalans. The Spanish ruled from Tenochtitlán, rebuilt as Mexico City, which became the capital of an expanding Spanish empire.

Although *conquistadora* steadily penetrated the interior, the fierce Mayas of Yucatán and Guatemala put up a determined resistance until the 1540s. By then, Spanish settlements had been established throughout Central America. The first colony in North America was founded at St. Augustine, on Florida's

An illustration from the Codex Azacatitlán of the Spanish arriving in Mexico. Standing next to Cortés is Malitzin, the Aztec woman who served as his interpreter.

east coast, in 1565. Meanwhile, numerous expeditions, including those of Hernando de Soto (1500–1542) and Francisco de Coronado (1510–1554), explored what is now California, Arizona, New Mexico, Colorado, Texas, Missouri, Louisiana, and Alabama. Spanish friars established a mission at Santa Fe in 1610, providing a base for later missions. All these new territories, known as New Spain, were administered from Mexico City after 1542.

The viceroyalty of Mexico later sponsored colonization of the Philippines, a project justified by the historic voyage of Ferdinand Magellan (1480–1521). Encouraged by the exploits of Vasco de Balboa (1479–1519), who had crossed Panama and discovered the Pacific Ocean in 1513, Magellan sailed from Spain in 1520, steered past the ice-encrusted straits at the tip of South America, and endured a 99-day voyage to the Philippines. He made an unwise choice by intervening in a conflict between two sheikdoms, and he lost his life in a battle with the inhabitants of Mactan Island. Many of Magellan's crew died after terrible suffering from **scurvy.** This illness explains why only one of Magellan's five ships completed this first circumnavigation of the world. However, the feat established a Spanish claim to the Philippines. It also prepared the way for the first tiny settlement of 400 Mexicans at Cebu in 1571. By 1580, when the Philippine capital at Manila had been secured against attacking Portuguese, Chinese, and Moro fleets, the friars were beginning conversions that would reach half a million by 1622. The colony prospered in trade with Asia but remained economically dependent on annual galleons bearing silver from Mexico. Because the Spanish were excluded from China, they relied on a community of Chinese merchants in Manila to trade the silver in the Chinese market for luxury items such as porcelain, silk, and lacquer ware.

The Development of Spanish South America

As in Mexico, the Spanish exploited unique opportunities as well as epidemics in their process of empire building in Peru. Just before they arrived, the recently formed Inca state had been torn apart by a succession crisis. When the emperor Huayna Capac and his heir apparent suddenly died of smallpox in 1526, the claim of his son Huascar (was-KAR) to the throne was contested by Atahualpa, a half-royal son who had been Huayna Capac's favorite. Their conflict, which soon

destroyed nearly every semblance of imperial unity, was a major factor in the surprisingly easy triumph of a handful of Spanish freebooters over a country of more than ten million people, scattered through Peru and Ecuador in hundreds of mountain towns and coastal cities.

Francisco Pizarro (1470–1541), the son of an illiterate peasant, was the conqueror of Peru. After two earlier exploratory visits, he landed on the northern coast in January 1531 with a tiny privately financed army of 207 men and 27 horses. For more than a year he moved south, receiving some reinforcements as he plundered towns and villages. Leaving a garrison of 60 soldiers in a coastal base, he started inland in September 1532 with a Spanish force of fewer than 200. About the same time, word came that Altahualpa's forces had defeated Huascar's in battle and were poised to capture the imperial capital, Cuzco. Pizarro now posed as a potential ally to both sides. At Cajamarca he met and captured Altahualpa, slaughtering some 6000 unarmed retainers of the Inca monarch. He next forced Altahualpa to fill a room with 26,000 pounds of silver and over 13,000 pounds of gold. Then, having collected the ransom, Pizarro executed his royal prisoner and proclaimed Manco, the young son of Altahualpa's dead brother, as emperor.

Thus, upon arriving in Cuzco with their puppet ruler, the Spaniards were welcomed as deliverers and quickly secured tentative control of the country. Manco, after suffering terrible indignities from the Spaniards, organized a rebellion in 1536. Although his army of 60,000 heavily outnumbered Pizarro's 200 Spaniards, they could not score a decisive victory. Manco and his supporters retreated to the northwest to a mountain outpost at Vilacamba where an independent Inca kingdom survived until the Spanish captured and executed the last Inca emperor in 1572.

Although the *conquistadora* had triumphed over the Incas, political anarchy still reigned in Peru as the *conquistadora* split into two factions led by the Pizarro and Almagro families. When Pizarro was assassinated in his palace in 1542, it touched off a bloody civil war that raged for six years.

The period was marked by an obsessive Spanish rape of the country, along with cruel persecution of its Amerindian population, and by ruthless contention, involving every degree of greed and brutality, among the conquerors. Meanwhile, marauding expeditions moved south into Chile and north through Ecuador into Colombia. Expeditions from Chile and Peru settled in Argentina, founding Buenos Aires. Relationships between *conquistadora* and Amerindian women were common, and they

---

scurvy—A disease contracted on voyages of longer than a month because sailors' diets lacked sufficient quantities of vitamins B and C.

produced a new *mestizo* population in Paraguay. Despite this dynamic activity, there was no effective government at Lima, the capital, until the end of the sixteenth century.

Along with brutality, Spaniards in the post-conquest era also demonstrated unprecedented fortitude and courage. Pizarro's Spaniards were always outnumbered in battle. They faced nearly unendurable torments, including scorching heat, disease-carrying insects, air too thin for breathing, and cold that at times could freeze a motionless man into a lifeless statue. Amid the terrible hardships of this male-dominated era, both Amerindian and Spanish women played significant roles. As in Mexico, Amerindian women were camp-following concubines who prepared food and bore children; in addition to traditional feminine tasks, some Spanish women fought beside the men when necessary. Ines Suarez achieved distinction by donning armor and leading the defense of Santiago, Chile, shortly after its founding in 1541. Some women were present on all the pioneering ventures, and others were direct participants in the terrible sacrifices of the civil wars.

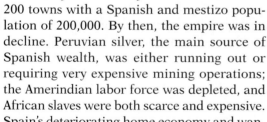

To govern Mexico and Peru the Spanish established two viceroyalties that by 1600 contained over 200 towns with a Spanish and mestizo population of 200,000. By then, the empire was in decline. Peruvian silver, the main source of Spanish wealth, was either running out or requiring very expensive mining operations; the Amerindian labor force was depleted, and African slaves were both scarce and expensive. Spain's deteriorating home economy and waning sea power presented even more serious problems.

European Empires in Latin America, 1660

IBERIAN SYSTEMS IN THE NEW WORLD

■ *What role did Amerindian and African labor play in the Spanish and Portuguese economic systems?*

European expansion overseas after the fifteenth century brought revolutionary change to all the world's peoples, but the Iberian period before 1600 was unique in its violence and ruthless exploitation. Not only were highly organized states destroyed in the New World, but whole populations were wiped out by European diseases,

mestizo—A person of Spanish and Indian descent.

shock, and inhumane treatment. This tragic catastrophe was accompanied by a decided change in the racial composition of Iberian America as an influx of African slaves, along with continued Spanish and Portuguese immigration, led to a variegated racial mixture, ranging through all shades of color between white and black. Fortunately, the

---

The arrival of the Spanish and Portuguese in America led to a mixing of three cultures: European, African, and Amerindian. This painted wooden bottle, done in Inca style and dating from about 1650, shows the mix. The three figures are an African drummer, a Spanish trumpeter, and an Amerindian official.

Amerindian population began recovering in the mid-1600s, and their cultures, combining with Iberian and African, formed a new configuration, to be known later as Latin American.

The General Nature of Regimes

Iberian regimes in America faced serious problems. Their vast territories, far greater than the homelands, contained nearly impassable deserts, mountains, and dense rain forests. Supplies had to be moved thousands of miles, often across open seas. Communications were difficult, wars with indigenous peoples were frequent, and disease was often rampant. Such conditions help explain, if not justify, the brutality of Iberian imperialism.

DOCUMENT

New Laws for the Treatment and Preservation of the Indians

With all their unique features, Iberian overseas empires were similar to Roman or Turkish provinces: they were meant to produce revenues. In theory, all Spanish lands were the king's personal property. The Council of the Indies, which directed the viceroys in Mexico City and Lima, advised him on colonial affairs. The highborn Spanish viceroys were aided (and limited) by councils (*audiencias*), made up of aristocratic lawyers from Spain. Local governors, responsible to the viceroys, functioned with their advisory councils **(cabildos)** of officials. Only the rich normally sat in such bodies; poor Spaniards and mestizos had little voice, even in their own taxation. Most taxes, however, were collected by Amerindian chiefs **(caciques)**, still acting as rulers of Amerindian peasant villages.

---

cabildos—Town councils whose members were usually appointed by the governor.

cacique—An Amerindian chief who assisted the Spanish in collecting taxes from his subjects.

Portuguese Brazil was less directly controlled than the Spanish colonies. It languished for years under almost unrestricted domination of 15 aristocratic "captains" who held hereditary rights of taxing, disposing lands, making laws, and administering justice. In return, they sponsored settlement and paid stipulated sums to the king. This quasi-feudal administration was abandoned in 1548. When Philip II became king of Portugal in 1580, he established municipal councils, although these were still dominated by the hereditary captains.

Iberian Economies in America

Both the philosophies and the structures of the Iberian states limited colonial trade and industry. Most Spanish and Portuguese immigrants were disinclined toward productive labor. With few exceptions, commercial contacts were limited to the homelands; Mexican merchants fought a steadily losing battle to maintain independent trade with Peru and the Philippines. Local trade grew modestly in supplying the rising towns, some crafts developed into large-scale industrial establishments, and a national transport system, based on mule teams, became a major Mexican industry. So did smuggling, as demand for foreign goods rose higher and higher.

Agriculture, herding, and mining silver, however, were the main economic pursuits. The early gold sources soon ran out, but silver strikes in Mexico and Peru poured a stream of wealth back to Spain in the annual treasure fleets, convoyed by warships from Havana to Seville. Without gold to mine, many Spanish aristocrats acquired conquered Amerindian land, raising wheat, rice, indigo, cotton, coffee, and sugarcane. Cattle, horses, and sheep were imported and bred on ranches in the West Indies, Mexico, and Argentina. Brazil developed similar industries, particularly those related to brazilwood (for which the country was given its name), sugar, livestock, and coffee. Although Iberian economic pursuits in America were potentially productive, revealing numerous instances of initiative and originality, they were largely repressed by bureaucratic state systems.

Before 1660, plantations (large estates that used servile labor to grow crops) were not typical for agriculture in Iberian America, although they were developing in certain areas. The Spanish tried plantations in the Canaries, later establishing them in the West Indies, the Mexican lowlands, and Central America and along the northern coasts of South America. Even in such areas, which were environmentally suited for intensive single-crop cultivation, it was not easy to raise the capital, find the skilled technicians, and pay for the labor the system required.

The Spanish initially dealt with the labor problem in Mexico and Peru by forcing Amerindians on the labor market with taxation, but so many died from the devastating impact of European diseases that the Spanish turned to Africans for slave labor. Besides being separated from their families and societies, Africans slaves were mobile and could be shipped anywhere (see p. 563). By the 1550s, some 3000 African slaves were in Peru, working in gold mines and on cattle ranches and participating in a variety of unskilled and skilled occupations in the capital, Lima. At the end of the century, Africans, although replaced in the mines by Amerindians, continued to labor on coastal plantations and serve in elite households. Some 75,000 slaves were in the

Amerindian slaves work a Spanish sugar plantation on the island of Hispaniola. Spanish treatment of the Amerindians was often brutal.

Spanish colonies by 1600; more than 100,000 more arrived in the next four decades.

Portugal established sugar plantations on its Atlantic islands (Madeira, Cape Verde, and São Tomé). São Tomé was uninhabited when the Portuguese settled on it in 1485. Because the island is situated on the equator and receives abundant rainfall, it was an ideal setting to begin sugar production a half century later. São Tomé was also near Angola, a primary source of slaves. This experience created a direct link between the production of sugar and African slave labor. São Tomé also witnessed the resistance of slaves, who, much like the Maroons in Jamaica, fled the sugar plantations for the safety of the mountainous interior.

São Tomé, Cape Verde, and Madeira were the models when the Portuguese introduced the plantation system into northern Brazil around 1550. Like the Spanish, the Portuguese initially recruited Amerindian labor, but after a smallpox epidemic in the 1560s killed off many Amerindians, they began to rely on African slaves as the primary laborers on plantations. By the early 1600s, 30,000 Africans were annually being brought to Brazil. After 1650, as Dutch, British, and French possessions in the Caribbean islands were drawn into the sugar economy, they, as well as Portuguese Brazil, became the largest importers of unfree labor from Africa.

Some slaves were brutally oppressed as laborers in the mines, and others sweated on Spanish or Brazilian plantations. Slaves were also teamsters, overseers, personal servants, and skilled artisans. Particularly in the Spanish colonies, a good many earned their freedom, attaining a social status higher than that of Amerindian peasants. Free blacks, both men and women, operated shops and small businesses. Prostitution was common among black and **mulatto** women, a profession that went hand-in-hand with the sexual exploitation of female slaves as concubines and breeders.

Iberian Effects on Amerindian Life

The Spanish and Portuguese brought terrible disaster to most Amerindians. Having seen their gods mocked and their temples destroyed, many accepted Christianity as the only hope for survival, as well as salvation, while toiling for their Iberian masters. Some died from overwork, some were killed, and others simply languished as their cultures disintegrated. The most dangerous adversity was disease—European or African—to which Amerindians had no immunities.

---

mulatto—A person of European and African descent.

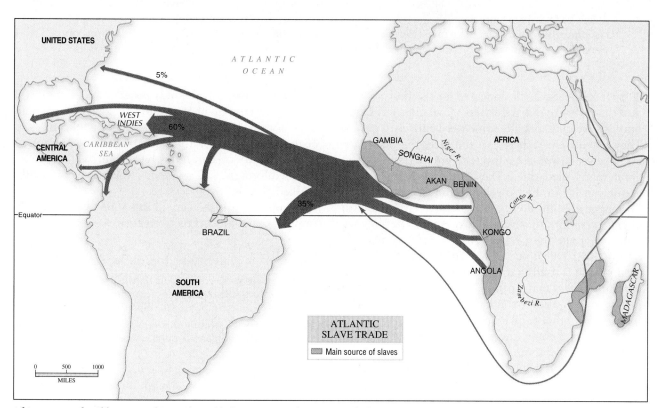

Africans were forcibly captured in raids and kidnappings in the interior of Africa and taken to the coast. After they were sold to European traders, the slaves were transported across the Atlantic to work on sugar plantations in the New World.

Epidemics arrived with Columbus and continued throughout the sixteenth century. Smallpox on Hispaniola in 1518 left only 1000 Amerindians alive there. Cortés's men carried the pox to Mexico, where it raged while he fought his way out of Tenochtitlán. From Mexico the epidemic spread through Central America, reaching Peru in 1526. It killed the reigning emperor and helped start the civil war that facilitated Pizarro's conquest. Following these smallpox disasters in the 1540s and 1570s, a wave of measles, along with other successive epidemics, continued depleting the population.

Depopulation of Amerindians was caused in part by their enslavement, despite disapproval by the Catholic Church and the Spanish government. The worst excesses came early. Original settlers on Hispaniola herded the Arawaks to work like animals; they soon became extinct. A whole indigenous population

of the Bahamas—some 40,000 people—were carried away as slaves to Hispaniola, Cuba, and Puerto Rico. Cortés captured slaves before he took Tenochtitlán; other Amerindians, enslaved in Panama, were regularly sent to Peru. Before Africans arrived in appreciable numbers, the Portuguese organized "Indian hunts" in the forests to acquire slaves.

Another more common labor system in the Spanish colonies was the **encomienda.** This system was instituted in Mexico by Cortés as a way of using Amerindian caciques to collect revenues and provide labor. It was similar to European feudalism and manorialism, involving a royal grant that permitted the holder (*encomendero*) to take income or labor from specified lands and the people living on them. Many

---

encomienda—A system of control over land and Indian labor granted to a Spanish colonist (*encomendero*).

Document   Disease and the Spanish Conquest

Diseases introduced by Europeans had a devastating impact on indigenous societies in the New World. This account of the impact of a smallpox epidemic among the Aztecs appeared in the Florentine Codex, an invaluable history of the Aztecs published in the mid-sixteenth century. Written in Nahuátl, the Aztec language and translated into Spanish, the books were based on information gathered by Aztec scribes under the supervision of a Franciscan priest Bernadino de Sahagún. This story of the smallpox epidemic drew on eyewitness accounts of individuals who lived through the Spanish conquest.

Before the Spanish appeared to us, first an epidemic broke out, a sickness of pustules. . . . Large bumps spread on people, some were entirely covered. They spread everywhere, on the face, the head, the chest, etc. The disease brought great desolation; a great many died of it. They could no longer walk about, but lay in their dwellings and sleeping places, no longer able to move or stir. They were unable to change position, to stretch out on their sides or face down, or raise their heads. And when they made a motion, they called out loudly. The pustules that covered people caused that covered people caused great desolation. very many people died of them, and many just starved to death; starvation reigned, and no one took care of others any longer.

On some people, the pustules appeared only far apart, and they did not suffer greatly, nor did many of them die of it. But many people's faces were spoiled by it, their faces and noses were made rough. Some lost an eye or were blinded.

This disease of pustules lasted a full sixty days; after sixty days it abated and ended. When people were convalescing and reviving, the pustules disease began to move in the direction of Chalco. And many were disabled or paralyzed by it, but they were not disabled forever. . . . The Mexica warriors were greatly weakened by it.

And when things were in this state, the Spaniards came, moving toward us from Tetzcoco.

Questions to Consider

1. What was more responsible for the Spanish conquest of the Aztecs—Spanish weapons, armor, horses or the diseases that accompanied the Spanish?

2. What was the overall impact of diseases such as smallpox on the indigenous populations of the Americas?

From James Lockhart, *We People Here: Nahuatl Accounts of the Conquest of Mexico* (Berkeley: University of California Press, 1993), pp. 180–182.

encomenderos lashed and starved their Amerindian laborers, working men and women to exhaustion or renting them to other equally insensitive masters. Amerindian women on the *encomiendas* were generally used as wet nurses, cooks, or maids or as sex slaves by the owners and the caciques, who served as overseers.

DOCUMENT

From "In Defense of the Indians"

The *encomienda* system was slowly but steadily abandoned after the 1550s largely because of the efforts of a former *conquistadore* and *encomendero*, Bartolomé de Las Casas (1474–1566). A Dominican friar, he protested the cruel treatment of Amerindians and persuaded Charles V that they should hold the same rights as other subjects. His efforts led to the New Law of 1542, which ended existing *encomiendas* upon the death of their holders, prohibited Amerindian slavery, and gave Amerindians full protection under Spanish law. Most of these provisions, however, were rescinded when the law evoked universal protest and open rebellion in Peru. Although later governors gradually eliminated *encomiendas*, many Amerindians were put on reservations and hired out as contract laborers under the direction of their caciques and local officials *(corrigodores)*. This practice eliminated some of the worst excesses of the *encomiendas*, but corrupt officials often exploited their wards, particularly in Peru.

Such physical hardships were matched by others of a psychological nature, which were almost equally damaging to Amerindians. The Spaniards insisted on forcing Christian conversion even while they raped and destroyed, as Pizarro did before executing Atahualpa. Except when they used Amerindian authorities to support their regimes, the Spaniards went out of their way to insult, shame, and degrade their unfortunate subjects. In the new social milieu, Amerindians were constantly reminded of their lowly status, unworthy of human consideration. For example, Cortés, who had multiple Amerindian mistresses, passed off Malitzin to one of his captains; Pizarro forced Manco, while still an ally, to give his young Inca queen to the conqueror. Such indignities, repeated by the hundreds among both Spanish and Portuguese, left many Amerindians demoralized to the point of utter despair.

Their distress was alleviated to some extent by missions, established by the Dominican and Jesuit religious orders. These afforded Amerindians the most effective protection and aid. Las Casas led the way in founding such settlements, where Amerindians were shielded from white exploitation, instructed in Christianity, and educated or trained in special skills. The prevailing philosophy in the missions stressed patient persuasion. Large mission organizations developed in Brazil, Venezuela, Paraguay, and upper California. But even the Amerindians protected by the missions died rapidly in this alien way of life.

Moved by the simplicity and gentle nature of the Amerindians, Bartolomé de Las Casas launched a vigorous campaign to ensure their protection. His Apologetic History of the Indies *(1566) is an indictment of the Spaniards' harsh treatment of the Amerindians.*

Although most Amerindians were demoralized by their misfortunes, some resisted. In Yucatán and Guatemala, where the Mayas did not believe the Spaniards were gods, bloody fighting lasted until the 1540s. About that time, the Spanish put down a revolt on the Mexican Pacific coast with great difficulty. As the silver mines opened in northern Mexico into the 1590s, the Chichimecs, relatives of the Apaches of North America, conducted a border war, using horses and captured muskets. In Peru an Inca rebellion, led first by Manco, was subdued only in 1577. The most stubborn resistance came from the Araucanians of southern Chile, who fought the Spaniards successfully until the close of the sixteenth century.

The full Iberian impact on Amerindian culture is difficult to assess, although there can be no denying that it was disastrous. A conservative estimate of Amerindian population losses puts the proportion at 25 percent during the era to 1650, but some recent figures place losses much higher, up to 95 percent of the pre-1492 total of 100 million. Signs of mental deterioration were also evident in prevalent alcoholism, which began among Amerindians shortly after the conquest.

Spanish Colonial Society and Culture

Spanish colonial society was stratified but somewhat flexible. A small elite of officials and aristocrats contended over politics, policy toward subject peoples, and foreign trade. Merchants and petty officials were on a lower social level but above mestizos, mulattoes, and **zambos.** Amerindians were considered incompetent wards of the home government, and African slaves were legally designated as beneath the law, but there were numerous individual exceptions. Many Amerindians went from their rural homes to the towns, mines, or **haciendas;** some caciques enjoyed wealth and privilege; and a few established Amerindian families retained their nobility as early Spanish allies. Similarly, some African slaves were overseers, privileged personal servants, and involved in urban crafts such as tailoring, shoemaking, carpentry, and blacksmithing; others acquired freedom and became prosperous merchants; still others escaped slavery, organized free communities, and successfully defended their independence.

Women in Spanish American society were a numerical minority. They played ambiguous roles, reflecting the traditional ideal of male superiority. They were excluded from male contacts throughout childhood, not allowed to join in dinner conversations, educated in cloistered schools to become wives and mothers, married in their teens to further family interests, and legally subordinated to their husbands. Most could not serve in public office or qualify as lawyers. Those who did not marry, particularly women of the upper classes, usually entered convents. There was, however, another side to the story. Spanish law guaranteed a wife's dowry rights, a legal protection against the squandering of her wealth, and leverage to limit her husband's activities. The courts recognized separations and at times even granted annulments in cases of wife abuse. Women, particularly widows, operated businesses. Some were wealthy, powerful, and even cruel *encomenderas,* supervising thousands of workers. Whatever their special roles, Iberian matrons defended religion, sponsored charities, dictated manners, and taught their children family values. They civilized the empires conquered by their men.

---

zambo—A person of African and Indian descent.

hacienda—An estate or plantation belonging to elite families.

Both the unique environment and the mix of peoples shaped Spanish colonial culture toward a new distinctive unity. From southwestern Europe came its aristocratic government, disdain for manual labor, a preference for dramatic over precise expression, and ceremonial Catholic Christianity. From Amerindian traditions came characteristic foods, art forms, architecture, legends, and practical garments like the poncho and serape, as well as substantial vocabulary. From Africa came agricultural knowledge, crafts, and animal husbandry. By 1650 this characteristic colonial culture was being preserved in its own universities, such as those at Lima and Mexico City, both founded more than a century earlier.

BEGINNINGS OF NORTHERN EUROPEAN EXPANSION

■ *What were the experiences of the Dutch, French, and British with their colonies of European settlement?*

European overseas expansion after 1600 entered a second phase, comparable to developments at home. As Spain declined, so did the Spanish Empire and that of Portugal, which was unified with Spain by a Habsburg king after 1580 and plagued with its own developing imperial problems. These conditions afforded opportunities for the northern European states. The Dutch between 1630 and 1650 almost cleared the Atlantic of Spanish warships while taking over most of the Portuguese posts in Brazil, Africa, and Asia. The French and English also became involved on a smaller scale, setting up a global duel for empire in the eighteenth century.

The Shifting Commercial Revolution

Along with this second phase of expansion came a decisive shift in Europe's Commercial Revolution. Expanding foreign trade, new products, an increasing supply of bullion, and rising commercial risks created new problems, calling for energetic initiatives. Because the Spanish and Portuguese during the sixteenth century had depended on quick profits, weak home industries, and poor management, wealth flowed through their hands to northern Europe, where it was invested in productive enterprises. Later it generated a new imperial age.

European markets after the sixteenth century were swamped with a bewildering array of hitherto rare or unknown goods. New foods from America included potatoes, peanuts, maize (Indian corn), tomatoes, and fish from Newfoundland's Grand Banks. In an era without refrigeration, imported spices—such as pepper, cloves, and cinnamon—were valued for making spoiled

Marketplace at Antwerp. In the sixteenth century, Antwerp was the leading city in international commerce. As many as 500 ships a day docked in its bustling harbor, and as many as 1000 wagons arrived each week carrying the overland trade.

foods palatable. Sugar became a common substitute for honey, and the use of cocoa, the Aztec sacred beverage, spread throughout Europe. Coffee and tea from the New World and Asia would also soon change European social habits. Similarly, North American furs, Chinese silks, and cottons from India and Mexico revolutionized clothing fashions. Furnishings of rare woods and ivory and luxurious oriental carpets appeared more frequently in the homes of the wealthy. The use of American tobacco became almost a mania among all classes, further contributing to the booming European market.

Imported gold and, even more significant, silver probably affected the European economy more than all other foreign goods. After the Spaniards had looted Aztec and Inca treasure rooms, the gold flowing from America and Africa subsided to a respectable trickle; but 7 million tons of silver poured into Europe before 1660. Spanish prices quadrupled, and because most new bullion went to pay for imports, prices more than tripled in northern Europe. Rising inflation hurt landlords who depended on fixed rents and creditors who were paid in cheap money, but the bullion bonanza ended a centuries-long gold drain to the East, with its attendant money shortage. It also

increased the profits of merchants selling on a rising market, thus greatly stimulating northern European capitalism.

At the opening of the sixteenth century, Italian merchants and moneylenders, mainly Florentines, Venetians, and Genoese, dominated the rising Atlantic economy. The German Fugger banking house at Augsburg also provided substantial financing. European bankers, particularly the Fuggers and the Genoese, suffered heavily from the Spanish economic debacles under Charles V and Philip II. As the century passed, Antwerp, in the southern Netherlands, became the economic hub of Europe. It was the center for the English wool trade as well as a transfer station, drawing southbound goods from the Baltic and Portuguese goods from Asia. It was also a great financial market, dealing in commercial and investment instruments. The Spanish sack of the city in 1576 ended Antwerp's supremacy, which passed to Amsterdam and furthered Dutch imperial ventures.

Meanwhile, northern European capitalism flourished in nearly every category. Portuguese trade in Africa and Asia was matched by that of the Baltic and the North Atlantic. Northern joint-stock companies pooled capital for privateering, exploring, and commercial venturing. The Dutch and English East India companies, founded early in the seventeenth century, were but two of the better-known stock companies. In England common fields were enclosed for capitalistic sheep runs. Throughout western Europe, domestic manufacturing, in homes or workshops, was competing with the guilds. Large industrial enterprises, notably in mining, shipbuilding, and cannon casting, were becoming common. Indeed, the superiority of English and Swedish cannons caused the defeat of the Spanish Armada and Catholic armies in the Thirty Years' War.

The Dutch Empire

By 1650 the Dutch were supreme in both southern Asia and the South Atlantic. Their empire, like that of the Portuguese earlier, was primarily commercial; even their North American settlements specialized in fur trading with the Indians. They acquired territory where necessary to further their commerce but tried to act pragmatically in accordance with Asian cultures rather than by conquest. An exception was their colony in Java, where the Dutch drive for monopolizing the spice trade led them to take direct control of the island. Unlike the Spanish and the Portuguese, the Dutch made little attempt to spread Christianity.

Dutch involvement in the Indian Ocean was the direct result of the Spanish absorption of Portugal in 1580. The Spanish restricted the flow of spices, especially pepper, to Northern Europe, and Dutch seafarers set out to control the sources of the trade. Systematic Dutch naval operations commenced in 1595 when the first Dutch fleet entered the East Indies. Dutch captains soon drove the Portuguese from the Spice Islands. Malacca, the Portuguese bastion, fell after a long siege in 1641. The Dutch also occupied Sri Lanka (SHREE-lahn-KAH) and blockaded Goa, thus limiting Portuguese operations in the Indian Ocean. Although largely neglecting East Africa, they seized all Portuguese posts on the west coast north of Angola. Across the Atlantic,

Dutch Exploration and Expansion

1576	Sack of Antwerp; Amsterdam becomes commercial hub of Europe
1595	First Dutch fleet enters East Indies
1609	Henry Hudson explores Hudson River
1621	Dutch form West India Company
1624	Dutch found New Amsterdam on Manhattan Island
1641	Dutch drive Portuguese out of Malacca

they conquered and held part of Brazil for a few decades, drove Spain from the Caribbean, and captured a Spanish treasure fleet. Decisive battles off the English Channel coast near Kent (1639) and off Brazil (1640) delivered final blows to the Spanish navy. What the English began in 1588, the Dutch completed 50 years later.

Five Dutch trading companies initially conducted trade with Asia, but the Dutch state decided their competition with each other cut into profits and established the Dutch East India Company. Chartered in 1602 and given a monopoly over all operations between the Cape of Good Hope in South Africa and the Strait of Magellan, it conserved resources and cut costs. In addition to its trade and diplomacy, the company sponsored explorations of Australia, Tasmania, New Guinea, and the South Pacific.

The Dutch Empire in the East was established primarily by Jan Pieterszoon Coen, governor-general of the Indies for two periods between 1619 and 1629 and founder of the company capital at Batavia in northwestern Java. At first he cooperated with local rulers in return for a monopoly over the spice trade. When this involved him in costly wars against local sultans as well as their Portuguese and English customers, Coen determined to control the trade at its sources. In the ensuing numerous conflicts and negotiations, which outlasted Coen, the Dutch acquired all of Java, most of Sumatra, the spice-growing Moluccas (mol-U-kuz), and part of Sri Lanka. They began operating their own plantations, overseen by Dutch settlers and worked by thousands of slaves brought in from such diverse areas as East Africa, Bengal, Persia, and Japan. The plantations produced cinnamon, nutmeg, cloves, sugar, tea, tobacco, and coffee, but it was pepper that reaped the highest profits. In the seventeenth century 7 million pounds of pepper were shipped to Europe annually.

Although commercially successful in Asia, the Dutch were not able to found flourishing colonial settlements. Many Dutchmen who went to the East wanted to make their fortunes and return home; those willing to stay were usually mavericks, uninterested in establishing families but instead pursuing temporary sexual liaisons with female slaves or servants. For a while after 1620 the company experimented with a policy of bringing European women to the Indies, but such efforts were abandoned when the venture failed to enlist much interest at home or in the foreign stations. Consequently, the Dutch colonies in Asia, as well as those in Africa, the Caribbean, and Brazil, remained primarily business ventures with less racial mixing than in the Iberian areas.

After resuming war with Spain in 1621, the Dutch formed the West India Company, charged with overtaking the diminishing Spanish and Portuguese holdings in West Africa and America. The company wasted no time. It soon supplanted the Portuguese in West Africa; by 1630 it had taken over the slave trade with America. After driving the Spanish from the Caribbean, the Dutch

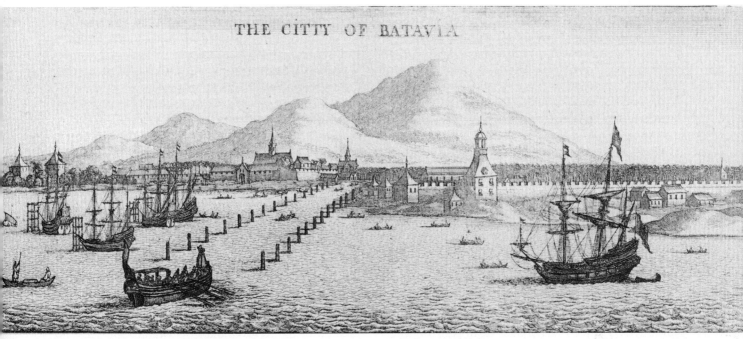

THE CITTY OF BATAVIA

Batavia (present-day Djakarta), on the island of Java, became the headquarters of the Dutch East India Company when the Dutch ousted the Portuguese and took command of the East Indies trade in the seventeenth century.

invited other European planters to the West Indies as customers, keeping only a few bases for themselves. The company then launched a successful naval conquest of Brazil, from the mouth of the Amazon south to the San Francisco River. In Brazil the Dutch learned sugar planting, passing on their knowledge to the Caribbean and applying it directly in the East Indies.

Dutch settlements in North America never amounted to much because of the company's commercial orientation. In 1609 Henry Hudson (d. 1611), an Englishman sailing for the Dutch, explored the river (ultimately named for him) and established Dutch claims while looking for a northwest passage. Fifteen years later the company founded New Amsterdam on Manhattan Island; over the next few years it built a number of frontier trading posts in the Hudson valley and on the nearby Connecticut and Delaware Rivers. Some attempts were made to encourage planting by selling large tracts to wealthy proprietors *(patroons)*. Agriculture, however, remained secondary to the fur trade, which the company developed in alliance with the Iroquois tribes. This arrangement hindered settlement; in 1660 only 5000 Europeans were in the colony.

The French Empire

French exploration began early, but no permanent colonies were established abroad until the start of the seventeenth century. The country was so weakened by

religious wars that most of its efforts, beyond fishing, privateering, and a few failed attempts at settlement, had to be directed toward internal stability. While the Dutch were winning their empire, France was involved in the land campaigns of the Thirty Years' War. Serious French empire building thus had to be delayed until after 1650, during the reign of Louis XIV.

Early French colonization in North America was based on claims made by Giovanni da Verrazzano (1485–1528) and Jacques Cartier (1491–1557). The first, a Florentine mariner commissioned by Francis I in 1523, traced the Atlantic coast from North Carolina to Newfoundland. Eleven years later Cartier made one of two voyages exploring the St. Lawrence River. These French expeditions duplicated England's claim to eastern North America.

French colonial efforts during the sixteenth century were dismal failures. They resulted partly from French experiences in exploiting the Newfoundland fishing banks and conducting an undeclared naval war in the Atlantic against Iberian treasure ships and trading vessels after 1520. In 1543 Cartier tried unsuccessfully to establish a colony in the St. Lawrence valley. No more serious efforts were made until 1605, when a French base was established at Port Royal, on Nova Scotia. It was meant to be a fur-trading center and capital for the whole St. Lawrence region. In 1608, Samuel de Champlain (1567–1635), who had been an aide to the governor of the Nova Scotia colony, acted for a French-chartered company in founding Quebec on the St. Lawrence. The company brought in colonists, but the little community was disrupted in 1627 when

---

patroon—An owner of a landed estate granted by the Dutch West India Company in New York and New Jersey.

British troops took the town and forced Champlain's surrender. Although when Champlain came back as governor the fort was returned to France by a treaty in 1629, growth was slowed by the company's emphasis on fur trading, the bitterly cold winters, and skirmishes with Indians. Only a few settlers had arrived by Champlain's death in 1635, and just 2500 Europeans were in Quebec as late as 1663. Nevertheless, Montreal was established in 1642, after which French trapper-explorers began penetrating the region around the headwaters of the Mississippi.

Elsewhere, the French seized opportunities afforded by the decline of Iberian sea power. They acquired the isle of Bourbon (BOOR-bon), later known as Réunion, in the Indian Ocean (1642) for use as a commercial base. In West Africa they created a sphere of commercial interest at the mouth of the Senegal River, where they became involved in the slave trade with only slight opposition from the Dutch. Even more significant was the appearance of the French in the West Indies. They occupied part of St. Kitts in 1625 and later acquired Martinique, Guadeloupe, and Santo Domingo. Fierce attacks by Carib Indians limited economic development before 1650. However, by the late eighteenth century, Santo Domingo had become the crown jewel of France's Caribbean possessions. Possessing half of the Caribbean's slave population, the island was the largest producer of sugar in America, and—after coffee was introduced in 1723—the world's largest coffee producer until the Haitian revolution of 1791.

British and French Exploration and Colonization

1485–1528	Giovanni da Verrazzano
1491–1557	Jacques Cartier
1497–1498	John Cabot establishes English claims in North America
1567–1635	Samuel de Champlain founds Quebec
1605	French establish base at Port Royal, in Nova Scotia
1607	First English colony in North America founded at Jamestown
1627	British conquer Quebec
1629	Puritans settle near Boston
1632–1635	English Catholics found colony of Maryland
1642	Montreal established

The English Empire

In terms of power and profit, English foreign expansion before 1650 was not impressive. Like French colonialism, it was somewhat restricted by internal political conditions, particularly the poor management and restrictive policies of the early Stuart kings, which led to civil war in the 1640s. A number of circumstances, however, promoted foreign ventures. The population increased from 3 to 4 million between 1530 and 1600, providing a large reservoir of potential indentured labor; religious persecution encouraged migration of nonconformists; and holders of surplus capital were seeking opportunities for investment. Such conditions ultimately produced a unique explosion of English settlement overseas.

During the sixteenth century, English maritime operations were confined primarily to exploring, fishing, smuggling, and plundering. English claims to North America were registered in 1497 and 1498 by two voyages of John Cabot, who explored the coast of North America from Newfoundland to Virginia but found no passage to Asia. For the next century, English expeditions sought such a northern passage, both in the East and in the West. All of them failed, but they resulted in explorations of Hudson Bay and the opening of a northeastern trade route to Russia. From the 1540s, English captains, including the famous John Hawkins of Plymouth, indulged in sporadic slave trading in Africa and the West Indies, despite Spanish restrictions.

After failures in Newfoundland and on the Carolina coast, the first permanent English colony in America was founded in 1607 at Jamestown, Virginia. For a number of years the colonists suffered from lack of food and other privations, but they were saved by their leader, Captain John Smith (1580–1631), whose romantic rescue by the Indian princess Pocahontas (1595–1617) is an American legend. Jamestown set a significant precedent for all English colonies in North America. By the terms of its original charter, the London Company, which founded the settlement, was authorized to supervise government for the colonists, but they were to enjoy all the rights of native Englishmen. Consequently, in 1619 the governor called an assembly to assist in governing. This body would later become the Virginia House of Burgesses, one of the oldest representative legislatures still operating.

Shortly after the founding of Jamestown, large-scale colonization began elsewhere. In 1620 a group of English Protestants, known as Pilgrims, landed at Plymouth. Despite severe hardships, they survived, and their experiences inspired other religious dissenters against the policies of Charles I. In 1629 a number of English Puritans formed the Massachusetts Bay Company and settled near Boston, where their charter gave them the rights to virtual self-government. From this first enclave, emigrants moved out to other areas in present-day Maine, Rhode Island, and Connecticut. By 1642 more than 25,000 people had migrated to New England, laying the foundations for a number of future colonies. Around the same time (1632–1635), a group of English Catholics, fleeing Stuart persecution, founded the Maryland colony. These enterprises firmly planted English culture and political institutions in North America.

Life in the English settlements was hard during those first decades, but a pioneering spirit and native colonial pride was already evident. Food was scarce, disease was ever-present, and conflicts with Amerindians were not uncommon. Yet from the beginning, and more than in other European colonies, settlers looked to their future in the new land because they had left so little behind in Europe. Most were expecting to stay, establish homes, make their fortunes, and raise families. The first Puritans included both men and women; a shipload of "purchase brides" arrived in 1619 at Jamestown to lend stability to that colony. This was but the first of many such contingents, all eagerly welcomed by prospective husbands. In addition, many women came on their own as indentured servants.

Anglo-American colonial women faced discrimination but managed to cope with it pragmatically. They were legally dependent on their husbands, who controlled property and children; a widow acquired these rights, but it was not easy to outlive a husband. Hard work and frequent pregnancies—mothers with a dozen children were not uncommon—reduced female life expectancies. Nevertheless, many women developed a rough endurance, using their social value to gain confidence and practical equality with their husbands, although some did this more obviously than others. This independent spirit was exemplified by Anne Hutchinson (1591–1643), who was banished from Massachusetts for her heretical views and founded a dissenting religious settlement in Rhode Island. Another freethinker was Anne Bradstreet (c. 1612–1672), who, although painfully aware that men considered her presumptuous, wrote thoughtful poetry.

The English government considered the rough coasts and wild forests of North America less important in this period than footholds in the West Indies and Africa, where profits were expected in planting and slave trading. Therefore, a wave of English migrants descended on the West Indies after the Dutch opened the Caribbean. In 1613 English settlers invaded Bermuda, and by the 1620s others had planted colonies on St. Kitts, Barbados, Nevis, Montserrat (mawn-suh-RAHT), Antigua (ahn-TEE-gwah), and the Bahamas. Tobacco planting was at first the major enterprise, bringing some prosperity and the promise of more. The white population expanded dramatically, especially on Barbados, which was not subject to Carib Indian attacks. There, the English population increased from 7,000 to 37,000 in seven years. As yet, there were few African slaves on the English islands, although some were already being imported for the sugar plantations.

This is an anonymous engraving made around 1776 of the Mohawk chief and diplomat Tiyanoga. He was an ally for the British and known to them as "King Hendrick." In this portrait, one can see the influence of European trade goods in Tiyanoga's dress. His shirt is made of linen or calico, and his mantle and breechcloth of English wool duffels.

Meanwhile, English slaving posts in West Africa were beginning to flourish, and English adventurers were starting operations in Asia. Captain John Lancaster took four ships to Sumatra and Java in 1601, returning with a profitable cargo of spices. But expansion outside of the Caribbean was difficult because the Dutch were uncooperative. In the Moluccas, for example, they drove out the English in the 1620s, after repeated clashes. The English fared better in India. By 1622 the British East India Company, which had been chartered in 1600, had put the Portuguese out of business in the Persian Gulf. Subsequently, the English established trading posts on the west coast of India at Agra, Bombay, Masulipatam, Balasore, and Surat. The station at Madras, destined to become the English bastion on the east coast, was founded in 1639. The East India Company prospered from the trade in Indian cotton and silk cloth for the English and European markets.

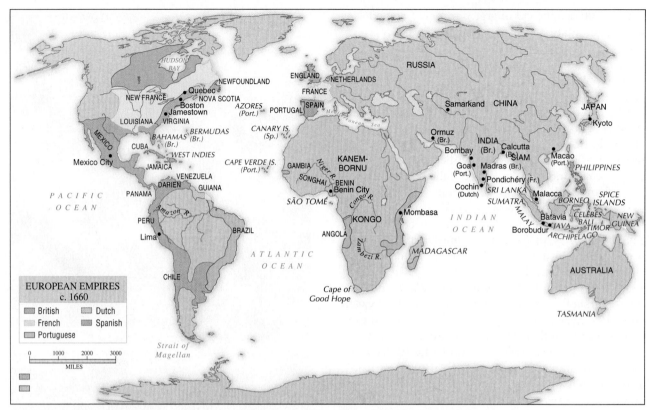

By the late 1600s the Portuguese and Spanish, the pioneers in global exploration, had been displaced in many regions by the English, French, and Dutch.

CONCLUSION

Between 1450 and 1650, the era of the early Commercial Revolution, Europeans faced outwards toward a new world and, following precedents set by earlier Eurasian empires, initiated their own age of oceanic expansion. In the process they stimulated capitalistic development, found a sea route to Asia, became more familiar with Africa, began colonizing America, and proved the world to have a spherical surface. For most of the period Spain and Portugal monopolized the new ocean trade and profited most from exploiting American gold and silver. Only after 1600, when leadership shifted toward the Dutch, French, and English, did European colonialism show signs of developing in new directions.

Overseas expansion exerted a tremendous effect on European culture and institutions. Spain's political predominance in the sixteenth century was largely bought with Amerindian treasure, and Spain's eventual decline was mainly caused by the squandering of wealth on war rather than on investment and the influx of American bullion, which inflated Spanish money and discouraged Spanish economic development. Northern European capitalism, developing in financial organization, shipbuilding, metalworking, manufacturing, and agriculture, brought a new vitality to northern economies in response to Spanish and Portuguese purchasing power. Economic advantages also contributed to Protestant victories in the Thirty Years' War.

By the late seventeenth century, the Europeans had experienced mixed results in their encounters with societies around the world. In the Indian Ocean, where they engaged well-established states, such as in China, Japan, and India, they usually had to respect their laws and authority and even do their bidding and had little impact on land-based trading networks. The Portuguese were run out of China twice before they came to respect Chinese law, and other Europeans fared worse. All were ultimately excluded from Japan. Southern India was not entirely open, as the Portuguese found by the end of the period. In the main, Turks, Arabs, Chinese, Japanese, Thais, and Vietnamese felt superior to Europeans and were usually able to defend their interests with effective action.

Where they dealt with smaller states and city-states, such as in Indonesia and East Africa, Europeans were more likely to directly intervene or dominate their affairs. Sri Lanka and the Spice Islands of the Malay archipelago, which were vulnerable to sea attack, came under domination, direct or indirect, and were exploited by the Portuguese and the Dutch.

In the New World the European impact was both dramatic and tragic. Portuguese captains and Spanish *conquistadora*, as well as diseases such as smallpox, nearly destroyed indigenous peoples and subjected most of the survivors to terrible hardships, indignities, cultural deprivations, and psychological injuries. However, the Portuguese and Spanish in America generated a new cultural synthesis, blending European, Amerindian, and African elements to produce a richness and variety not present in any of the parent cultures. This integration was largely accomplished by racial mixing, which created a new Latin American stock in the Western Hemisphere.

The European impact on Africa was less apparent at the time but perhaps more damaging in the long run than what happened to the Amerindians of Latin America. When the Portuguese began exploring the African coastline, they were more concerned with scoring quick profits through gold exports than with establishing stable, long-term relationships with African states. Moreover, with the exception of Angola or landed estates along the Zambezi River, the Portuguese did not have the manpower or resources to conquer or influence the political affairs of African states. However, as the Atlantic slave trade increased, the Portuguese and African states, especially along the Atlantic and Indian Ocean coasts, became bound up in a destructive process that would run its tragic course over the next few centuries.

Suggestions for Web Browsing

You can obtain more information about topics included in this chapter at the websites listed below. See also the companion website that accompanies this text, **http://www.ablongman.com/ brummett**, which contains an online study guide and additional resources.

Age of Discovery

http://www.win.tue.nl/cs/fm/engels/discovery/#age

An excellent collection of resources that includes text, images, and maps relating to the early years of European expansion.

Internet Medieval History Sourcebook: Exploration and Expansion

http://www.fordham.edu/halsall/sbook1z.html

Extensive online source for links about Western exploration and expansion, including primary documents by or about da Gama, Columbus, Drake, and Magellan.

Columbus Navigation Home Page

http://www1.minn.net/~keithp/

Extensive information regarding the life and voyages of Christopher Columbus.

Internet African History Sourcebook

http://www.fordham.edu/halsall/africa/africasbook.html

Extensive online source for links about African history, including primary documents about the slave trade and by people who opposed it, supported it, and were its victims.

Literature and Film

Two major documentary series marked the quincentennial of Columbus's 1492 voyage in different ways. *Columbus and the Age of Discovery* (1991) is a seven-part series that primarily treats European exploration and expansion in the New World, while *500 Nations* (1995) is an eight-part series that examines Native American history before and after the arrival of Europeans. *Conquistadores* (2001) is Michael Wood's presentation of European explorers/conquerors such as Cortés and Pizarro.

Mexican writer Carlos Fuentes has written a major epic, *Terra Nostra*, trans. Margaret Peden (Farrar, Straus, and Giroux, 1976) and a collection of short stories and novellas, *The Orange Tree*, trans. Alfred MacAdam (Farrar, Straus, and Giroux, 1994), with Spanish exploration and conquest of the New World as their backdrop. James Lackhart's *We People Here: Nahuatl Accounts of the Conquest of Mexico* (University of California Press, 1993) presents indigenous Indian narratives of the Spanish conquest compiled by a Franciscan priest in the sixteenth century.

Suggestions for Reading

Several excellent works, which cover the subject of European exploration and colonization, are Geoffrey V. Scammell, *The First Imperial Age: European Overseas Expansion, 1400–1700* (Unwin Hyman, 1989); Anthony Pagden, eds., *European Encounters with the New World* (Yale University Press, 1993); and Nicholas Canny and Anthony Pagden, *Colonial Identity in the Atlantic World* (Princeton University Press, 1989). European encounters with other peoples are treated in Urs Bitterli, *Cultures in Conflict: Encounters Between European and Non-European Cultures, 1492–1800* (Stanford University Press, 1989), and Stuart Schwartz, ed., *Implicit Understandings: Observing, Reporting, and Reflecting on the Encounters between Europeans and Other Peoples in the Early Modern Era* (Cambridge University Press, 1994).

Books on the Iberian New World are Tzvetan Todorov, *The Conquest of America* (Harper&Row, 1984) and Mark A. Burkholder, *Colonial Latin America* (Oxford University Press, 1989). Works on Columbus include Felipe Fernandez-Armesto, *Columbus* (Oxford University Press, 1992), and John Yewell, Chris Dodge, and Jan De Surey, *Confronting Columbus: An Anthology* (McFarland, 1992).

For a penetrating study of Latin American social conditions, see Louisa Hoberman and Susan M. Socolow, eds., *Cities and Society in Colonial Latin America* (University of New Mexico Press, 1986).

Luis Martin, *Daughters of the Conquistadores* (Southern Methodist University Press, 1989) documents the significant role of women in the grueling process of colonization. Good coverage of the Spanish campaigns in Peru is provided in Susan Ramirez, *The World Upside Down: Cross-Cultural Contact and Conflict in Sixteenth-Century Peru* (Stanford University Press, 1996).

On political, economic, and social conditions, see Leslie B. Simpson, *The Encomienda in New Spain*, 3rd ed. (University of California Press, 1982). Edward Murguca, *Assimilation, Colonialism, and the Mexican American People* (University Press of America, 1989), depicts the racial and cultural synthesis in colonial Mexico.

A respected work on Portuguese exploration and colonization is A. J. R. Russell-Wood, *A World on the Move: The Portuguese in Africa, Asia and America, 1415–1808* (St. Martin's Press, 1992). On the Portuguese in Asia, see Michael Pearson, *The Indian Ocean* (Routledge, 2003).

A sound treatment of Dutch imperial development is Charles R. Boxer, *The Dutch Seaborne Empire* (Penguin, 1989). French colonialism in America is covered in William J. Eccles, *France in America* (Michigan State University Press, 1990), and the British Empire in William R Lewis, Nicholas Canny, P. J. Marshall, and Alaine Low, eds., *The Origins of Empire: British Overseas Enterprise to the Close of the Seventeenth Century* (Oxford University Press, 1998).

Credits

Chapter 1

2 University of Pennsylvania Museum (neg #30-12-702); **3** John Reader/Science Photo Library/Photo Researchers, Inc.; **4** John Reader/Science Photo Library/Photo Researchers, Inc.; **6** Drawing of Paleolithic tools; **7** Des & Jen Bartlett/Bruce Coleman; **8** James Mellaart; **11** Erich Lessing/Art Resource, NY; **16** Courtesy, The Oriental Institute of the University of Chicago. Photo by Victor J. Boswell, Jr. (sm8601); **18** Kurt Scholz/Egyptian National Museum, Cairo/SuperStock; **20** ©The Trustees of the British Museum (EA 921); **21** ©The Trustees of the British Museum; **23** ©The Trustees of the British Museum; **24** ©Sandro Vannini/CORBIS; **26** The Metropolitan Museum of Art, Gift of Norbert Schimmel Trust, 1989. (1989.281.10) Photograph ©1992 The Metropolitan Museum of Art; **32** ©The Trustees of The British Museum

Chapter 2

38 Gansu Provincial Museum,Wang Lu/China Stock; **41** The Avery Brundage Collection, B60P377 ©Asian Art Museum of San Francisco, Chong-Moon Lee Center For Asian Art and Culture. Used by permission.; **43** Imagine China; **44** Musée Cernuschi, Musées des Arts de l'Asie de la Ville de Paris; **48** ©Bettmann/CORBIS; **53** Don Hamilton Photo & Film; **55** Werner Forman/Art Resource, NY; **58** Christie's Images; **58** Robert Harding Picture Library Ltd.

Chapter 3

65 Jean-Louis Nou/akg – images; **67** MacQuitty International Collection, London; **68** Jean-Louis Nou/akg – images; **68** National Museum of India, New Delhi/Bridgeman Art Library; **76** Jean-Louis Nou/akg – images; **82** Burstein Collection/CORBIS; **84** British Library/The Art Archive; **85** Ministero per I Beni e le Attivitá Culturali Soprintendenza Archeologica; **86** Jean-Louis Nou /akg – images; **90** ©Adam Woolfitt/CORBIS; **91** "Vessel in the Form of an Ax," 2nd cent. B.C. to 5th cent. A.D. The Metropolitan Museum of Art, Purchase, George McFadden Gift and Edith Perry Chapman Fund, 1993. (1993.525) Photograph by Bruce White. ©1993 The Metropolitan Museum of Art

Global Issue Essay

94 ©Reuters/CORBIS

Chapter 4

97 Scala/Art Resource, NY; **99** Michael Holford Photographs; **100** Nimatallah/Art Resource, NY; **101** Scala/Art Resource, NY; **105** Réunion des Musées Nationaux/Art Resource, NY; **113** Courtesy, The Manchester Museum, The University of Manchester (Fx 568); **118** akg – images; **119** ©Charles O'Rear/CORBIS; **121** "Dionysos, Ariadne & Pan." Hellenic Ministry of Culture/Archaeological Receipts Fund/TAP Service; **126** Erich Lessing /Art Resource, NY; **127** ©Araldo de Luca/Corbis

Chapter 5

130 Vanni/Art Resource, NY; **133** Scala/Art Resource, NY; **136** Scala/Art Resource, NY; **143** Archivo Fotografico Musei Capitolini/INDEX, Firenze; **146** Werner Forman Archive/Art Resource, NY; **148** The Art Archive/Museo della Civilta Romana Rome/Dagli Orti; **149** Scala/Art Resource, NY; **149** The J. Paul Getty Museum, Villa Collection, Malibu, California. ©J. Paul Getty Museum; **150** Scala/Art Resource, NY; **151** Israel Museum, Jerusalem, Israel/Ancient Art and Architecture Collection Ltd/ Bridgeman Art Library; **156** ©Araldo de Luca/Corbis; **159** Scala/Art Resource, NY

Chapter 6

164 ©Diego Lezama Orezzoli/CORBIS; **167** Duane Preble; **171** ©Christel Gerstenberg/CORBIS; **171** Woodfin Camp & Associates; **172** Ronald Sheridan/Art Resource, NY; **174** akg – images; **176** The Granger Collection, New York; **179** Scala/Art Resource, NY; **183** Bibliothèque Nationale, Paris, France/Bridgeman Art Library; **187** Roger-Violett/Getty Images; **190** ©The State Russian Museum/CORBIS

Chapter 7

194 Bibliotek Nationale/akg – images; **198** By permission of the British Library; **201** "The Night Journey of Muhammad on His Steed, Buraq," 1514. Leaf from the "Bustan" (underline) of Sa'di, copied by calligrapher Sultan-Muhammad Nur. The Metropolitan Museum of Art, Purchase, Louis V. Bell Fund and Astor Foundation Gift, 1974. (1974.294.2) Photograph by Schecter Lee. Photograph ©1986, The Metropolitan Museum of Art; **204** Qisas al-Anibiya, folio 152v, illustration: "Jesus Performs Miracle of Loaves." (Spencer Persian MS 46) Spencer Collection, The New York Public Library, Astor, Lenox and Tilden Foundations; **204** Qisas al-Anibiya, "Moses Turns Staff into a Dragon." Spencer Persian Manuscript, 46, folio 82. Courtesy, the Spencer Collection, The New York Public Library, Astor, Lenox and Tilden Foundations; **205** Reproduced by kind permission of the Trustees of the Chester Beatty Library, Dublin; **210** The Imagebank Films/Getty Images; **210** The Bodleian Library, Uni-

Freer Gallery of Art, Smithsonian Institution, Washington, D.C.: Purchase, (F1945.9a); **367** "Birth of a Prince" from an illustrated manuscript of the Jahangir-nama, Bishndas (Attributed to), Northern India, Mughal, c. 1620. Museum of Fine Arts, Boston, Francis Bartlett Donation of 1912 and Picture Fund (14.657)

Chapter 13

370 ©Craig Lovell/CORBIS; **374** "Portrait of Hung-Wu." National Palace Museum, Taipei. Photograph by Wan-go H. C. Weng; **375** By permission of the British Library, (Maps 33.c.13); **379** National Palace Museum, Taipei, Taiwan, Republic of China; **380** Victoria & Albert Museum, London/Art Resource, NY; **380** National Palace Museum, Taipei, Taiwan, Republic of China; **383**; **383** Courtesy, The Trustees of the Victoria and Albert Museum, Photograph by Ian Thomas; **388** ©Mike Yamashita/CORBIS; **390** ©Michael Maslan Historic Photographs/CORBIS; **393** ©Richard Bickel/CORBIS

Chapter 14

397 Vatican Museums and Galleries, Vatican City, Italy/Bridgeman Art Library; **401** Scala/Art Resource, NY; **402** Scala/Art Resource, NY; **402** Erich Lessing/Art Resource, NY; **404** SCALA/Art Resource, NY; **405** Erich Lessing/Art Resource, NY; **405** Scala/Art Resource, NY; **406** Bibliothèque de l'Institute de France, Paris; **407** Erich Lessing/Art Resource, NY; **408** Scala/Art Resource, NY; **408** Kunsthistorisches Museum, Vienna, Austria/ Bridgeman Art Library; **409** akg –images; **410** Giraudon/ Art Resource, NY; **411** ©National Gallery, London (NG 186); **411** ©Archivo Iconografico, S.A./CORBIS; **412** SCALA/Art Resource, NY; **413** Réunion des Musées Nationaux/Art Resource, NY; **417** Lucas Cranach the Younger, "Martin Luther and the Wittenberg Reformers," c.1543. Toledo Museum of Art (1926.55). Purchased with funds from the Libbey Endowment, Gift of Edward Drummond Libbey; **420** Erich Lessing/Art Resource, NY; **423** Giraudon/Art Resource, NY; **428** Scala/Art Resource, NY

Chapter 15

432 Elizabeth I, Armada portrait, c.1588 (oil on panel), English School, (16th century)/Private Collection/Bridgeman Art Library; **434** Giraudon/Art Resource, NY; **436** Ken Walsh Private Collection/Bridgeman Art Library; **437** ©CORBIS; **439** ©Austrian Archives; Haus-, Hof- und Staatsarchiv, Vienna/CORBIS; **444** Scala/Art Resource, NY; **446** Erich Lessing/Art Resource, NY; **449** ©Archivo Iconografico, S.A./CORBIS; **451** ©Archivo Iconografico, S.A./CORBIS; **455** Wallach Collection, New York Public Library, Astor, Lenox and Tilden Foundations; **456** Les Musées de la Ville de Strasbourg

Global Issue Essay

461 ©Bettmann/Corbis

Chapter 16

462 British Museum, London, UK/Bridgeman Art Library; **465** National Maritime Museum, Greenwich (HC0705); **466** ©Bettmann/CORBIS; **468** The Art Archive/Museo de Arte Antiga Lisbon/Dagli Orti; **470** Werner Forman /Art Resource, NY; **475** Bibliothèque Nationale de France, Paris; **477** ©The Trustees of the British Museum (1950AM22 1); **481** akg – images; **483** Musées Royaux des Beaux-Arts de Belgique; **487** Library of Congress (LC-USZ62-14987)

Notes

Chapter 1

1. Harold C. Conklin, *The Relation of Hanunóo Culture to the Plant World*, doctoral dissertation, Yale University, 1954 (microfilm), p. 9. See also Claude Levi-Strauss, *The Savage Mind* (Chicago: University of Chicago Press, 1970), Chapter 1, "The Science of the Concrete."
2. Rob Stein, *Archaeology: Astronomical Structures in Ancient Egypt* (Washington, D.C.: Washington Post Company, 1998).
3. *The Code of Hammurabi*, Reverse Side, xxiv: 43–48, as quoted in Jean Bottero, *Mesopotamia: Writing, Reasoning, and the Gods* (Chicago: University of Chicago Press, 1992).
4. *The Code of Hammurabi*, Reverse Side, xxiv: 43–48.
5. From the *Epic of Gilgamesh*, trans. E. A. Speiser, in *Ancient Near Eastern Texts Relating to the Old Testament*, 2nd ed., ed. James B. Pritchard. Copyright © 1950, 1955, 1969, renewed 1978 by Princeton University Press. Reprinted by permission of Princeton University Press.
6. From the *Epic of Gilgamesh*, in Pritchard.
7. From Miriam Lichtheim, *Ancient Egyptian Literature: A Book of Readings, Three Volumes*, Vol. 2. Copyright © 1973–1980 Regents of the University of California. Reprinted by permission of the University of California Press.
8. John A. Wilson, *The Burden of Egypt* (Chicago: University of Chicago Press, 1951), p. 117.
9. Lichtheim, *Ancient Egyptian Literature*, Vol. 2, pp. 96, 98.
10. John Foster, *Love Songs of the New Kingdom* (New York: Charles Scribner's Sons, 1974), p. 72.
11. Amy Dockser Marcus, *The View from Nebo* (Little, Brown, and Company: 2000), pp. 22–28.
12. I. Finkelstein and Neil A. Silberman, *The Bible Unearthed* (New York: The Free Press, 2002), pp. 123–145 passim.

Chapter 2

1. From *The Book of Songs*, quoted in Patricia Buckley Ebrey, *The Cambridge Illustrated History of China* (Cambridge: Cambridge University Press, 1996), p. 34.
2. Michael Loewe, *The Pride That Was China* (New York: St. Martin's Press, 1990), p. 99.
3. Loewe, p. 99.
4. Loewe, p. 99.
5. Mencius, VA:5, in W. Theodore de Bary et al., trans., *Sources of Chinese Tradition* (New York: Columbia University Press, 1960), p. 96.

6. From the *Laozi*, quoted in Ebrey, p. 48.
7. Arthur Waldron, *The Great Wall of China: From History to Myth* (Cambridge: Cambridge University Press, 1990).
8. Loewe, p. 106.
9. W. Theodore de Bary, *East Asian Civilizations: A Dialogue in Five Stages* (Cambridge, Mass.: Harvard University Press, 1988), p. 19.
10. R. G. Collingwood, *The Idea of History* (New York: Galaxy Books, 1956), p. 22.
11. Kwang-Chih Chang, *The Archaeology of Ancient China*, 4th ed. (New Haven, Conn.: Yale University Press, 1987), p. 5.
12. Christopher Cullen, *Astronomy and Mathematics in Ancient China: The Zhou bi su an jing* (Cambridge: Cambridge University Press, 1996).
13. Nancy Lee Swann, *Pan Chao: Foremost Woman Scholar of China* (Ann Arbor, Mich.: University of Michigan, 2001).
14. See Loewe, ch. 18.

Chapter 3

1. Kautilya, *The Kautiliyan Arthasastra*, Part II, 2nd ed., trans. R. P. Kangle (Bombay: University of Bombay, 1972), pp. 327, 339–341.
2. Kautilya, pp. 327, 339–341.
3. Quoted in Vincent Smith, *The Oxford History of India* (Oxford: Oxford University Press, 1958), p. 131.
4. Quoted in Charles Drekmeier, *Kingship and Community in Early India* (Stanford, Calif.: Stanford University Press, 1962), p. 175.
5. From *The Interior Landscape: Love Poems from a Classical Tamil Anthology*, trans. A. K. Ramanujan (Bloomington: Indiana University Press, 1975), p. 54.
6. *The Bhagavad-Gita*, trans. Barbara Stoler Miller (New York: Bantam, 1986), pp. 46–47.
7. *The Ramayana of Valmiki*, Vol. 1, trans. Robert P. Goldman (Princeton, N.J.: Princeton University Press, 1984), p. 121.

Global Issues: Migration

1. B. Weiss, "The Decline of Late Bronze Age Civilizations as a Possible Response to Climatic Change," *Climatic Change*, Vol. 4 (1982), pp. 172–198.

Chapter 6

1. Procopius of Caesarea, *History of the Wars*, Vol. 1, 24:36–38, trans. S. R. Rosenbaum, in Charles Diehl,

Theodora: Empress of Byzantium (New York: Ungar, 1972), pp. 87–88.

2. Geoffrey de Villehardouin, "The Conquest of Constantinople," in M. R. B. Shaw, *Chronicles of the Crusades* (Baltimore: Penguin, 1963), pp. 79, 92.

3. *The Russian Primary Chronicle*, trans. Samuel H. Cross and O. P. Sherbowitz-Wetzor (Cambridge: Mediaeval Academy of America, 1953), pp. 110–118.

Chapter 7

1. *Rubáiyát of Omar Khayyám*, trans. Edward Fitzgerald, stanzas 12, 13, 71, and 72.

2. Ibn Khaldun, *The Muqaddimah: An Introduction to History*, Vol.1, trans. Franz Rosenthal (London: Routledge & Kegan Paul, 1958), p. 71.

3. John Williams, ed., *Islam* (New York: Braziller, 1962), p. 142.

Chapter 8

1. Kevin Shillington, *History of Africa* (New York: St. Martin's Press, 1989), p. 10.

2. Terry Childs and David Killick, "Indigenous African Metallurgy: Nature and Culture," *Annual Review of Anthropology* (1993), pp. 326–327.

3. The latest synthesis of research on Bantu migrations is Jan Vansina, "A Slow Revolution: Farming in Subequatorial Africa," *Azania* 29–30 (1994–1995), pp. 15–26.

4. Richard Pankhurst, *The Ethiopians: A History* (Oxford: Blackwells, 1998), p. 40.

5. Al Omari, quoted in Tadesse Tamrat, "The Horn of Africa: The Solomonids in Ethiopia and the States of the Horn of Africa," in D. T. Niane, ed., *UNESCO General History of Africa: Africa from the Twelfth to the Sixteenth Century* (Berkeley: University of California Press, 1984), p. 435.

6. Donald Crummey, *Land and Society in the Christian Kingdom of Ethiopia from the Thirteenth to the Twentieth Century* (Oxford: James Currey, 2000), p. 29.

7. Joseph Vogel, *Encyclopedia of Precolonial Africa: Archaeology, History, Languages, Cultures, and Environment* (Walnut Creek, Calif.: AltaMira Press, 1997), p. 490.

8. Ralph Austen, "Slave Trade: Trans-Saharan Trade," in Seymour Drescher and Stanley Engerman, eds., *A Historical Guide to World Slavery* (Oxford: Oxford University Press, 1998), p. 368.

9. Al Omari, quoted in Vogel, *Encyclopedia of Precolonial Africa*, p. 492.

10. Barbara Callaway, *Muslim Hausa Women in Nigeria: Tradition and Change* (Syracuse University Press, 1989), p. 9.

11. Adu Boahen, *Topics in West African History* (Longman, 1966), p. 9.

12. Michael Pearson, *Port Cities and Intruders: The Swahili Coast, India, and Portugal in the Early Modern Era* (Johns Hopkins University Press, 1998), pp. 36–37. Pearson defines the Afrasian Sea as extending from Sofala in Mozambique to the southern tip of India.

13. Al Masudi, quoted in G. S. P. Freeman-Grenville, *The East African Coast* (Oxford: Oxford University Press, 1962), pp. 15–17.

14. A. H. J. Prins, *The Swahili-Speaking Peoples of Zanzibar and the East African Coast* (International African Institute, 1961), p. 93, quoted in Chapurukha Kusimba, *The Rise and Fall of Swahili States* (AltaMira Press, 1999), pp. 134–5.

13. Eric Gilbert and Jonathan Reynolds, *Africa in World History from Prehistory to the Present* (Upper Saddle River, N.J.: Pearson, 2004), p. 113.

Chapter 10

1. Stanley Wolpert, *A New History of India*, 7th ed. (New York: Oxford University Press, 2004), p. 79.

2. Hermann Kulke and Dietmar Rothermund, *History of India*, 3rd ed. (London: Routledge, 1998), p. 147.

3. *Alberuni's India*, trans. Edward Sachau (New York: Norton, 1971), p. 100.

4. Minhaju-s Siraj, quoted in John Keay, *India: A History* (New York: Grove Press, 2000), p. 245.

5. Excerpt from poem by Xu Yeueying, in Kan-I Sun Chang and Haun Saussy, eds., *Women Writers of Traditional China* (Stanford, Calif.: Stanford University Press, 1999), p. 78.

6. Quoted in H. H. Gowen and H. W. Hall, *An Outline History of China* (New York: Appleton, 1926), p. 117.

7. *The Works of Li Po*, trans. Shigeyoshi Obata (New York: Dutton, 1950), no. 71.

8. Du Fu, "A Song of War Chariots," in Cyril Birch, ed., *Anthology of Chinese Literature* (New York: Grove Press, 1965), pp. 240–241.

9. Marco Polo, *The Travels of Marco Polo* (New York: Grosset & Dunlap, 1931), pp. 30, 133–149.

10. Donald Keene, ed., *Anthology of Japanese Literature: From the Earliest Era to the Mid-Nineteenth Century* (New York: Grove Press, 1955), pp. 39–41.

11. Murasaki Shikibu, "The Diary of Murasaki Shikibu," in Donald Keene, ed., *Anthology of Japanese Literature* (New York: Grove Press, 1960), p. 152.

Chapter 11

1. Quoted by Clements Markham, in Edward Hyams and George Ordish, *The Last of the Incas* (New York: Simon & Schuster, 1963), p. 88.

Global Issues: Location and Identity

1. Emanuel Bowen, *Complete Atlas of the Known World* (London, 1752), cited in Martin W. Lewis and Kären Wigen, *The Myth of Continents: A Critique of Metageography* (Berkeley: University of California Press, 1997), p. 29.

2. Just as the European-initiated paradigm of East and West influenced people outside of Europe in the past century, China's view of itself as the "Middle Kingdom" has influenced non-Chinese views of the

rest of Asia. On maps of Asia, Japan sometimes gets chopped off, and in teaching about East Asia, Korea and Vietnam have only recently joined China and Japan as deserving of treatment.

3. Cited by Lewis and Wigen, p. 69.
4. Robert B. Marks, *The Origins of the Modern World: A Global and Ecological Narrative* (Lanham, Md.: Rowman and Littlefield, 2002), pp. 52–53.
5. Lewis and Wigen, p. 23.
6. An early critic of the arbitrary binary divide between East and West is Edward W. Said, *Orientalism* (New York: Pantheon, 1978).
7. Karl Wittfogel, *Oriental Despotism: A Comparative Study of Total Power* (New Haven, Conn.: Yale University Press, 1957). Because Asian agriculture— uniquely—required irrigation, Wittfogel alleged, autocratic government came into being there. The argument may be logical, but the ecological premise is wrong.

Chapter 12

1. Vincent A. Smith, *Akbar, the Great Mogul,* 2nd ed. (Mystic, Conn.: Verry, 1966), p. 522.
2. Zahiruddin Muhammad Babur, *Baburnama,* trans. and ed. Wheeler Thackston (New York: Oxford University Press, 1996), pp. 350–351.
3. Babur, p. 351.
4. Quoted in Bamber Gascoigne, *The Great Moghuls* (New York: Harper & Row, 1971), p. 128.

Chapter 14

1. Quoted in Roland Bainton, *Here I Stand: A Life of Martin Luther* (New York: Abingdon Cokesbury, 1950), p. 54.
2. Quoted in Heiko A. Oberman, *Luther, Between God and the Devil* (New Haven, Conn.: Yale University Press, 1982) p. 190, see also pp. 187–188.
3. From Henry Bettenson, ed., *Documents of the Christian Church* (New York: Oxford University Press, 1963), pp. 280–283.

4. Quoted in Harold Grim, *The Reformation Era* (New York: Macmillan, 1968), p. 17.
5. From "Institutes of the Christian Religion," in Harry J. Carroll et al., eds., *The Development of Civilization* (Glenview, Ill.: Scott, Foresman, 1970), pp. 91–93.
6. From Lowell H. Zuck, ed., *Christianity and Revolution* (Philadelphia: Temple University Press, 1975), pp. 95–97.

Chapter 15

1. Charles Tilly, ed., *The Formation of the National States in Western Europe* (Princeton, N.J.: Princeton University Press, 1975), p. 42.
2. See Charles Tilly, *Coercion, Capital, and European States, AD 990–1992* (Oxford: Blackwell, 1992).
3. Lonnie R. Johnson, *Central Europe: Enemies, Neighbors, Friends* (New York/Oxford: Oxford University Press, 1996), p. 63.
4. See K. Bosl, A. Gieysztor, F. Graus, M. M. Postan, F. Seibt, *Eastern and Western Europe in the Middle Ages,* ed. Geoffrey Barraclough (London: Thames and Hudson, 1970).
5. Wallace T. MacCaffrey, *Elizabeth I, War and Politics 1558–1603* (Princeton, N.J.: Princeton University Press, 1992), p. 6.
6. Peter F. Sugar, *Southeastern Europe under Ottoman Rule: 1354–1804,* Vol. 5 of Peter F. Sugar and Donald W. Treadgold, eds., *A History of East Central Europe* (Seattle and London: University of Washington Press, 1977), pp. 55–59, 273–274.

Chapter 16

1. Quoted in David Killingray, *A Plague of Europeans* (New York: Penguin, 1973), p. 20.
2. Quoted in Robert Rotberg, *A Political History of Tropical Africa* (New York: Harcourt Brace, 1965), pp. 85–86.
3. Quoted in John Middleton, *The World of the Swahili: An African Mercantile Civilization* (New Haven, Conn.: Yale University Press, 1992), pp. 46–47.

Index

160°W 140°W 120°W 100°W 80°W 60°W 40°W 20°W

80°N

GREENLAND
(KALAALLIT NUNAAT)
(Den.)

Arctic

ALASKA
(U.S.)

ICELAND

60°N

U.
KING

C A N A D A

IRELAND

F

40°N

UNITED STATES

ATLANTIC
OCEAN

AZORES (Port.)

PORTUG

MOR

CANARY IS. (Sp.)

Tropic of Cancer

WESTERN SAHARA
(Mor.)

HAWAII (U.S.)

MEXICO

BAHAMAS

DOMINICAN
REPUBLIC

HAITI

PUERTO RICO (U.S.)

ST. KITTS AND NEVIS
ANTIGUA AND BARBUDA
DOMINICA

CAPE
VERDE

MAURITAN

20°N

CUBA

JAMAICA

BELIZE

GUADELOUPE (Fr.)

MARTINIQUE (Fr.)

SENEGAL

THE GAMBIA

GUATEMALA

HONDURAS

ST. VINCENT AND THE GRENADINES

ST. LUCIA

BARBADOS

GUINEA-BISSAU

EL SALVADOR

NICARAGUA

GRENADA

TRINIDAD AND TOBAGO

GUINEA

SIERRA LEONE

COSTA RICA

VENEZUELA

GUYANA

SURINAME

LIBERIA

PANAMA

FRENCH GUIANA (Fr.)

CÔTE D'IVO

PACIFIC OCEAN

COLOMBIA

BURKINA F

0° Equator

GALÁPAGOS IS.
(Ec.)

ECUADOR

G

PERU

BRAZIL

WESTERN
SAMOA

AMERICAN
SAMOA (U.S.)

BOLIVIA

TONGA

FRENCH
POLYNESIA (Fr.)

20°S

PARAGUAY

Tropic of Capricorn

CHILE

ATLANTI
OCEAN

URUGUAY

0   1,500   3,000 Miles

ARGENTINA

0   1,500   3,000 Kilometers

40°S

**Contemporary
Political Map
of the World**

FALKLAND IS. (U.K.)

60°S

Antarctic Circle

80°S

Primary Source Documents

HOW TO ANALYZE PRIMARY SOURCE DOCUMENTS

Historians study sources to reconstruct the lifestyles and events of previous generations. By examining the ideas and thoughts conveyed in primary sources, we can attempt to understand the past as the people who lived it did. By using sources, historians craft an understanding of the people, events, ideas, trends, and themes of the past based upon interpretation of those sources.

Primary sources are generally first-hand accounts or records. They may have been written or created during the time period under investigation, or they may have been written at a later date by someone who lived through earlier events. Most crucially, primary sources have not been interpreted by anyone else, though they may offer interpretations of the events they describe.

The primary source documents presented here give you the opportunity to put your investigative skills to the test by analyzing the sources yourself, rather than by reading others' interpretations.

WHEN ANALYZING A PRIMARY SOURCE, YOU SHOULD ASK SEVEN KEY QUESTIONS.

1. **Who is the author?**
   Who wrote or created this? Is there a single or multiple authors? An author's identity sometimes helps you answer the later questions.

2. **What type of source is this?**
   All the sources here are documents, but what type? Is it a biography or a government document? This is a simple but crucial step because you must consider what you can expect to learn from the document.

3. **What is the message of this source?**
   What is the author describing? What is happening in the text? What is the story?

4. **Who is the intended audience?**
   Who is the author addressing? Was the source intended for private or public consumption? Identifying the audience will help you answer the next question.

5. **Why was this source created?**
   Does the author have an agenda, a larger purpose? Is the author trying to persuade the audience? Is the document or source simply a compilation or facts, or does it include opinion, inference, or interpretation?

6. **Is this source credible and accurate?**
   Historians must examine every source with a critical eye. What do you know about the author? Does the document make sense? Do the facts presented by the author or what you know about the time period support the thesis, statement, assertion, or story the author is conveying? Why should you trust, or distrust, this source?

7. **How is this source valuable to me?**
   How does the source relate to other sources from the time period or along the same issue or theme? Does it support or contradict them? Does it repeat information from other sources or add new information? How relevant is the source to your topic of inquiry? Does it extensively cover your topic, or only marginally or not at all? Remember, you should explore enough sources to obtain a variety of viewpoints.

Let's take a look at a portion of a document to see how this process works. Reading the full document selection, of course, provides even more clues to understanding this source.

Galileo Galilei, Letter to the Duchess Christina

Galileo Galilei (1564–1642) was one of the primary figures in the Scientific Revolution. In 1608 Galileo, then a professor of mathematics at the University of Pisa, heard of a new technology, the telescope. Galileo quickly built his own telescope and used it to observe the planets and the stars. His observations provided evidence in favor of the Copernican theory of heliocentrism. For a variety of reasons, many religious leaders considered heliocentrism dangerous, and Galileo was initially commanded by the Roman Catholic Church to avoid teaching it. After the publication in 1632 of his most important work, Dialogue on the Two World Systems, *which was supposed to be impartial but favored heliocentrism, he was forced to recant his claim that the earth moves in relation to the sun. He spent the remainder of his life under house arrest. Galileo is also famous for his work in theoretical mechanics, particularly for his formulation of the law of inertia. In the following selection, Galileo describes how the results of the new science can be reconciled with the Bible.*

My goal is this alone; that if, among errors that may abound in these considerations of a subject remote from my profession, there is anything that may be serviceable to the holy Church in making a decision concerning the Copernican system, it may be taken and utilized as seems best to the superiors. And if not, let my book be torn and burnt, as I neither intend nor pretend to gain from it any fruit that is not pious and Catholic. And though many of the things I shall reprove have been heard by my own ears, I shall freely grant to those who have spoken them that they never said them, if that is what they wish, and I shall confess myself to have been mistaken. Hence let whatever I reply be addressed not to them, but to whoever may have held such opinions.

The reason produced for condemning the opinion that the earth moves and the sun stands still is that in many places in the Bible one may read that the sun moves and the earth stands still. Since the Bible cannot err, it follows as a necessary consequence that anyone takes an erroneous and heretical position who maintains that the sun is inherently motionless and the earth movable . . .

. . . Hence I think that I may reasonably conclude that whenever the Bible has occasion to speak of any physical conclusion (especially those which are very abstruse and hard to understand), the rule has been observed of avoiding confusion in the minds of the common people which would render them contumacious toward the higher mysteries. Now the Bible, merely to condescend to popular capacity, has not hesitated to obscure some very important pronouncements, attributing to God himself some qualities extremely remote from (and even contrary to) His essence. Who then, would positively declare that this principle has been set aside, and the Bible has confined itself rigorously to the bare and restricted sense of its words, when speaking but casually of the earth, of water, of the sun, or of any other created thing? Especially in view of the fact that these things in no way concern the primary purpose of the sacred writings, which is the service of God and the salvation of souls—matters infinitely beyond the comprehension of the common people.

This being granted, I think that in discussions of physical problems we ought to begin not from the authority of scriptural passages, but from sense-experiences and necessary demonstrations; for the holy Bible and the phenomena of nature proceed alike from the divine Word, the former as the dictate of the Holy Ghost and the latter as the observant executrix of God's commands. It is necessary for the Bible, in order to be accommodated to the understanding of every man, to speak many things which appear to differ from the absolute truth so far as the bare meaning of the words is concerned. But Nature, on the other hand, is inexorable and immutable: she never transgresses the laws imposed upon her, or cares a whit whether her abstruse reasons and methods of operation are understandable to men. For that reason it appears that nothing physical which sense-experience sets before our eyes, or which necessary demonstrations prove to us, ought to be called in question (much less condemned) upon the testimony of biblical passages which may have some different meaning beneath their words. For the Bible is not chained in every expression to conditions as strict as those which govern all physical effects; nor is God any less excellently revealed in Nature's actions than in the sacred statements of the Bible.

NOW LET'S LOOK AT WHAT WE CAN LEARN FROM THIS TEXT.

1. Who is the author?
From the header we know that the author is Galileo Galilei (1564–1642), a key figure during the Scientific Revolution.

2. What type of source is this?
This is an open letter Galileo wrote to the Grand Duchess Christina to defend his position in the conflict between the scientific community and the Catholic Church.

3. What is the message of this source?
Galileo's message is that the Copernican system, even though it appears to be in conflict with certain Biblical passages, must be viewed as the truth. He wants readers to understand that in spiritual matters the Bible is the unquestioned authority, but in matters of Nature, human observation must be considered the final authority.

4. Who is the intended audience?
The source is titled Letter to the Grand Duchess Christina, as it was written to the Grand Duchess at her request to answer her questions regarding the contradictions between the Bible and science. Letters of this sort were circulated among the elites, so Galileo wrote it with the anticipation that it would be widely distributed.

5. Why was this source created?
As the header suggests, Galileo was in the middle of a controversy surrounding the relationship between science and religion. Galileo intended this document to defend the role of science and to argue man's observational powers should stand alongside Christian doctrine.

6. Is this source credible and accurate?
Galileo was constantly under duress from the Catholic Church, as he was forced to recant some of his scientific claims and was placed under house arrest by the Church. He was writing a letter to someone in a position of power who, although she was Protestant, was certain to circulate his writings among members of the Catholic Church hierarchy. Despite this, Galileo appears to have written a letter outlining his argument that the findings of science must not be constrained by the Church's desire to avoid confusing "the common people." You must weigh the various outside factors and decide if this letter may be taken as an accurate representation of Galileo's position in the matter and what that position means in the overall debate.

7. How is this source valuable to you?
This source would be an invaluable central component if you were researching:
- The debate between science and religion
- Galileo's writings and his position in the debate

It would be an important part of a paper on:
- The resistance to scientific knowledge by the Catholic Church
- The origins of modern science

It would be crucial background information if you were researching:
- The writings and opinions of Galileo
- The evolution of Catholic Church policy regarding scientific discovery

You now have the basic tools to begin analyzing historical documents yourself. As you apply these skills to the documents contained here, you will likely find that your skill level will increase rapidly. You may even find yourself reading others' interpretations of primary source documents with a more critical eye.

DOCUMENT 1.1
Papyrus of Ani, "The Egyptian Book of the Dead" (1200 B.C.E.)
From the translation by E. A. Wallis Budge

In the Egyptian belief system, Ra was the sun god and Osiris was the god of the dead. The excerpt below is from the Papyrus of Ani, a wonderfully preserved papyrus scroll (though Egyptologists describe it as a "book") entombed with the scribe Ani. The purpose of such scrolls was to assist the deceased in the afterlife, where every person possessed three spirits called the Ka, the Ba, and the Akh. These spirits could survive only if the deceased's body did not decay.

A Hymn of Praise to Ra When He Riseth in the Eastern Part of Heaven:

Behold, the Osiris Ani, the scribe of the holy offerings of all the gods, saith: Homage to thee, O thou who hast come as Khepera, Khepera the creator of the gods, Thou art seated on thy throne, thou risest up in the sky, illumining thy mother [Nut], thou art seated on thy throne as the king of the gods. [Thy] mother Nut stretcheth out her hands, and performeth an act of homage to thee. The domain of Manu receiveth thee with satisfaction. The goddess Maat embraceth thee at the two seasons of the day. May Ra give glory, and power, and thruth-speaking, and the appearance as a living soul so that he may gaze upon Heru-khuti, to the KA of the Osiris the Scribe Ani, who speaketh truth before Osiris, and who saith: Hail, O all ye gods of the House of the Soul, who weigh heaven and earth in a balance, and who give celestial food [to the dead]. Hail, Tatun, [who art] One, thou creator of mortals [and] of the Companies of the Gods of the South and of the North, of the West and of the East, ascribe ye praise to Ra, the lord of heaven, the KING, Life, Strength, and Health, the maker of the gods. Give ye thanks unto him in his beneficent form which is enthroned in the Atett Boat; beings celestial praise thee, beings terrestial praise thee. Thoth and the goddess Maat mark out thy course for thee day by day and every day. Thine enemy the Serpent hath been given over to the fire. The Serpent-fiend Sebau hath fallen headlong, his forelegs are bound in chains, and his hind legs hath Ra carried away from him. The Sons of Revolt shall never more rise up. The House of the Aged One keepeth festival, and the voices of those who make merry are in the Great Place. The gods rejoice when they see Ra crowned upon his throne, and when his beams flood the world with light. The majesty of this holy god setteth out on his journey, and he goeth onwards until he reacheth the land of Manu; the earth becometh light at his birth each day; he proceedeth until he reacheth the place where he was yesterday. O be thou at peace with me. Let me gaze upon thy beauties. Let me journey above the earth. Let me smite the Ass. Let me slit asunder the Serpent-fiend Sebau. Let me destroy Aepep at the moment of his greatest power. Let me behold the Abtu Fish at his season, and the Ant Fish with the Ant Boat as it piloteth it in its lake. Let me behold Horus when he is in charge of the rudder [of the Boat of Ra], with Thoth and the goddess Maat on each side of him. Let me lay hold of the tow-rope of the Sektet Boat, and the rope at the stern of the Matett Boat. Let Ra grant to me a view of the Disk (the Sun), and a sight of Ah (the Moon) unfailingly each day. Let my Ba-soul come forth to walk about hither and thither and whithersoever it pleaseth. Let my name be called out, let it be found inscribed on the tablet which recordeth the names of those who are to receive offerings. Let meals from the sepulchral offerings be given to me in the presence [of Osiris], as to those who are in the following of Horus. Let there be prepared for me a seat in the Boat of the Sun on the day wheron the god saileth. Let me be received in the presence of Osiris in the Land of Truth-speaking—the Ka of Osiris Ani.

DOCUMENT ANALYSIS

1. What can we learn about a culture from its funereal rites?

_____

_____

_____

2. What does this document seek to do for Ani?

_____

_____

_____

DOCUMENT 1.2
Hammurabi's Law Code (1792 B.C.E.)
Source: James B. Pritchard, ed. *Ancient Near Eastern Texts Relating to the Old Testament*, trans. Theophile J. Meek (Princeton, NJ: Princeton University Press, 1955), pp. 166–7, 170–7. Language modernized by Wayne Ackerson.

Originally one of many small city-state empires in Mesopotamia, Babylon became the center of a large empire under its king, Hammurabi. Hammurabi ruled from approximately 1792 to 1750 B.C.E., and was a tremendously successful ruler. Not only did he build an empire for his city, he also helped that city become the new Near Eastern cultural center. Hammurabi's scribes carefully maintained old Sumerian records, encouraged literacy among the upper classes, and made religious changes (elevating Babylon's patron god, Marduk, to the top divine position). Notwithstanding Hammurabi's military skill, his most noted contribution was the creation of the world's first written, comprehensive law code. Law codes had always existed (usually passed down orally), and some had been written, but even the previous written ones were not complete and comprehensive. Though usually called Hammurabi's law code, the collection of laws is more a list of decisions made by judges in the past than laws passed by the king himself. Hammurabi claimed that these laws were sanctioned by the gods, and had copies carved on markers to be placed in prominent locations such as temple courtyards. Despite Hammurabi's efforts at empire-building, within a few years of his death his kingdom began to crumble.

1. If an upper class man accused another upper class man and brought a charge of murder against him, but has not proven it, his accuser shall be executed.

3. If an upper class man came forward with false testimony in a case, and has not proven the word he spoke, if that case was a death-penalty case, that man shall be put to death.

4. If he came forward with false testimony concerning grain or money, he shall bear the punishment in that case.

14. If an upper class man has kidnapped the young son of another upper class man, he shall be executed.

15. If an upper class man has helped either a male slave owned by the government or a male slave of a private citizen or a female slave of a private citizen to escape the city, he shall be executed.

17. If an upper class man caught a runaway slave in the open and has taken him to his owner, the slave's owner shall pay him two shekels of silver.

19. If he has kept the slave in his house and later the slave has been found in his possession, that upper class man shall be executed.

21. If an upper class man broke into a home through the wall, he shall be executed in front of the hole and then walled in.

22. If an upper class man is caught committing robbery, he shall be executed.

128. If an upper class man marries a woman but did not draw up the marriage contracts for her, she is not his wife.

129. If the wife of an upper class man has been caught while sleeping with another man, they shall tie them both up and throw them into the water. If the husband of the woman wishes to spare his wife, then the king may in turn order his subject spared.

131. If an upper class man's wife was accused by her husband of adultery, but was not caught while sleeping with another man, she shall swear she is innocent before god and return home.

134. If an upper class man was kidnapped and there was not enough money and food in his home for his wife to survive, she may enter the home of another, with no blame incurred by the wife.

149. If that woman has refused to live in her husband's home, he shall return her dowry to her and she may leave.

153. If an upper class man's wife has caused her husband's death because of another man, the woman shall be impaled on stakes.

154. If an upper class man sleeps with his daughter, he shall be forced to leave the city.

155. If an upper class man chose a bride for his son and his son has slept with her, but later the man is caught sleeping with her, that upper class man shall be tied up and thrown into the water.

157. If an upper class man sleeps with his mother after his father dies, both mother and son shall be burned to death.

162. If, when an upper class man gets married, and his wife bears him children and later dies, the dowry belongs to her children and her father cannot claim it.

185. If an upper class man adopted a boy and has raised him, that foster child shall never be reclaimed.

186. If an upper class man, upon adopting a boy, seeks out the boy's parents, that child may return to his father's home.

188. If an artisan took a son as a foster child and taught him his trade or craft, he may never be reclaimed.

189. If he has not taught him his trade or craft, that child may return to his father's home.

195. If a son hits his father, the son's hand shall be cut off.

196. If an upper class man destroyed the eye of another noble, his eye shall also be destroyed.

197. If he has broken another noble's bone, his bone shall also be broken.

198. If he destroyed the eye or broken the bone of a commoner, he shall pay one mina of silver.

199. If he has destroyed the eye or broken a bone of an upper class man's slave, he shall pay half the slave's value.

202. If an upper class man slaps the face of an upper class man who is superior to him, he shall be whipped sixty times with an oxtail whip in public.

203. If a noble slaps another noble's face who is of the same rank, he shall pay one mina of silver.

204. If a commoner slaps the face of another commoner, he shall pay ten shekels of silver.

205. If an upper class man's slave has slapped the face of a noble, his ear shall be cut off.

228. If a builder built a house for an upper class man and finished it, the man shall pay the builder two shekels of silver per sar (a measurement of about 42 square yards).

229. If a builder built a house for an upper class man but the house falls down due to poor craftsmanship and kills the upper class man, the builder shall be executed.

230. If it has caused the death of a son of the home's owner, the son of the builder shall be executed.

282. If a male slave has said to his master, "you do not own me," his master shall prove him to be his slave and cut off the slave's ear.

DOCUMENT ANALYSIS

1. Are there any business-related laws here?

_____

_____

_____

2. What happens if someone lies in court?

_____

_____

_____

3. What happens to someone who harbors a runaway slave in his home?

_____

_____

_____

4. Would you say that these laws are "fair"? Why or why not?

_____

_____

_____

5. Would you say that women have any rights, according to Hammurabi's code?

_____

_____

_____

DOCUMENT 2.1
Confucius, from *Analects* (441–479 B.C.E.)
Source: *Confucian Analects, the Great Learning, and the Doctrine of the Mean,* in *Chinese Classics Series of the Clarendon Press,* Vol. 1, trans. James Legge (Oxford: Clarendon Press, 1893).

Confucius was a scholar who lived between ca. 551 and 479 B.C.E. During this time, China experienced political decentralization and social instability as a result of rivalry among difference princes. In his search for restoration of social order, Confucius argued that this chaotic situation was due to the breakdown of China's social foundation, which was based on the principle of proper relationships. According to Confucius, the key relationships included those between ruler and subject, father and son, husband and wife, elder brother and younger brother, and friend and friend. Only by fixing these relationships could China regain peace and order. Confucius' ideas, however, were not well accepted by the ruling class of his time, and he spent the rest of his lifetime teaching. After Confucius, China sank into an even worse period known as the Warring States (475–221 B.C.E.). Confucius did not leave any written works, but his disciples recorded and further enriched his ideas by putting together—in a rather unsystematic way—a collection of his teachings and arguments. These Analects, which describe what we commonly know as Confucianism, would reshape the Chinese way of thinking in the millennia to come. Confucius's ideas on good government and proper relationships in the society are clearly reflected in the following arguments.

FILIAL PIETY

Zi, you asked what filial piety was. The Master said, "The filial piety of now-a-days means the support of one's parents. But dogs and horses likewise are able to do something in the way of support;—without reverence, what is there to distinguish the one support giver from the other?"

The Master said, "In serving his parents, a son may remonstrate with them, but gently; when he sees that they do not incline to follow his advice, he shows an increased degree of reverence, but does not abandon his purpose; and should they punish him, he does not allow himself to murmur."

Mang I asked what filial piety was. The Master said, "It is not being disobedient." Soon after, as Fan Chih was driving him, the Master told him, saying, "Mang Sun asked me what filial piety was, and I answered him, 'not being disobedient.'" Fan Chih said, "What did you mean?" The Master replied, "That parents, when alive, should be served according to propriety; that, when dead, they should be buried according to propriety; and that they should be sacrificed to according to propriety."

PROPRIETY

The Master said, "Respectfulness, without the rules of propriety, becomes laborious bustle; carefulness, without the rules of propriety, becomes timidity; boldness, without the rules of propriety, becomes insubordination; straightforwardness, without the rules of propriety, becomes rudeness."

IDEAL GOVERNMENT

The Master said, "When rulers love to observe the rules of propriety, the people respond readily to the calls on them for service."

The Master said, "If the people be led by laws, and uniformity sought to be given them by punishments, they will try to avoid the punishment, but have no sense of shame.

"If they be led by virtue, and uniformity sought to be given them by the rules of propriety, they will have the sense of shame, and moreover will become good."

The Master said, "He who exercises government by means of his virtue may be compared to the north polar star, which keeps its place and all the stars turn towards it."

The duke Ai asked, saying, "What should be done in order to secure the submission of the people?" Confucius replied, "Advance the upright and set aside the crooked, then the people will submit. Advance the crooked and set aside the upright, then the people will not submit."

Ji Kang asked how to cause the people to reverence their ruler, to be faithful to him, and to go on to nerve themselves to virtue. The Master said, "Let him preside over them with gravity;—then they will reverence him. Let him be filial and kind to all;—then they will be faithful to him. Let him advance the good and teach the incompetent;—then they will eagerly seek to be virtuous."

Ji Kang asked Confucius about government. Confucius replied, "To govern means to rectify. If you lead on the people with correctness, who will dare not to be correct?"

. . . . . .

The Master said, "If a minister makes his own conduct correct, what difficulty will he have in assisting in government? If he cannot rectify himself, what has he to do with rectifying others?"

The Master said, "If good men were to govern a country in succession for a hundred years, they would be able to transform the violently bad, and dispense with capital punishments." True indeed is this saying!

THE SUPERIOR MAN

Confucius said, "There are three things of which the superior man stands in awe. He stands in awe of the ordinances of Heaven. He stands in awe of great men. He stands in awe of the words of sages.

"The mean man does not know the ordinances of Heaven, and consequently does not stand in awe of them. He is disrespectful to great men. He makes sport of the words of sages."

Zi Gong asked what constituted the superior man. The Master said, "He acts before he speaks, and afterward speaks according to his actions."

The Master said, "The mind of the superior man is conversant with righteousness; the mind of the mean man is conversant with gain."

The Master said, "If the will be set on virtue, there will be no practice of wickedness."

The Master said, "Riches and honors are what men desire. If it cannot be obtained in the proper way, they should not be held. Poverty and meanness are what men dislike. If it cannot be obtained in the proper way, they should not be avoided.

"If a superior man abandon virtue, how can he fulfill the requirements of that name?

"The superior man does not, even for the space of a single meal, act contrary to virtue. In moments of haste, he cleaves to it. In seasons of danger, he cleaves to it."

The Master said, "By nature, men are nearly alike; by practice, they get to be wide apart."

. . . . . .

The Master said, "By extensively studying all learning, and keeping himself under the restraint of the rules of propriety, one may thus likewise not err from what is right."

The Master said, "The accomplished scholar is not a utensil."

SPIRITS

The subjects on which the Master did not talk, were extraordinary things, feats of strength, disorder, and spiritual beings.

. . . . . .

Ji Lu asked about serving the spirits of the dead. The Master said, "While you are not able to serve men, how can you serve their spirits?"

Ji Lu added, "I venture to ask about death?" He was answered, "While you do not know life, how can you know about death?"

DOCUMENT ANALYSIS

1. From this document, what can be seen as the major themes in Confucianism?

_____

_____

_____

2. Summarize Confucius's idea of an ideal government.

_____

_____

_____

3. What should be the major qualities of a superior man, according to Confucius?

_____

_____

_____

4. Why does Confucius consider propriety important for individuals and family, as well as the state?

_____

_____

_____

5. Why was the Warring States period so important for the development of Confucianism?

_____

_____

_____

DOCUMENT 2.2
Laozi, from *Daodejing* (500s–400s B.C.E.)

Source: *The Sacred Books of the East,* Vol. 39, ed. F. Max Müller, (Oxford: Clarendon Press, 1886). 1.

Daoism was associated with a legendary scholar, Laozi, who was believed to be a contemporary of Confucius. Laozi's view of restoring peace in the face of China's collapsing social order was quite different from that of Confucius. According to Laozi, the proper way to escape from war and political entanglement is to retreat into seclusion and embrace the harmony of nature. Through this contemplation of nature, one could become attuned to the Dao ("the way" in Chinese). Daoist views on government and human relationships were also different from those of Confucius. Daoism suggests a less active role for the government and more freedom for the people. Because of this retreatist attitude toward politics and society, Daoism gradually evolved into a popular religion absorbing its rites and organizational forms from Buddhism and local superstitions.

THE WAY

The Dao that can be trodden is not the enduring and unchanging Dao. The name that can be named is not the enduring and unchanging name.

Conceived of as having no name, it is the Originator of heaven and earth; conceived of as having a name, it is the Mother of all things.

. . . . . .

The Dao produces all things and nourishes them; it produces them and does not claim them as its own; it does all, and yet does not boast of it; it presides over all, and yet does not control them. This is what is called "The mysterious quality" of the Dao.

When the Great Dao ceased to be observed, benevolence and righteousness came into vogue.

Then appeared wisdom and shrewdness, and there ensued great hypocrisy.

Man takes his law from the Earth; the Earth takes its law from Heaven; Heaven takes its law from the Dao. The law of the Dao is its being what it is.

All-pervading is the Great Dao! It may be found on the left hand and on the right.

All things depend on it for their production, which it gives to them, not one refusing obedience to it. When its work is accomplished, it does not claim the name of having done it. It clothes all things as with a garment, and makes no assumption of being their lord;—it may be named in the smallest things; . . . it may be named in the greatest things.

. . . . . .

He who has in himself abundantly the attributes of the Dao is like an infant.

. . . . . .

The Dao in its regular course does nothing, for the sake of doing it, and so there is nothing which it does not do.

THE WISE PERSON

When we renounce learning we have no troubles.

If we could renounce our sageness and discard our wisdom, it would be better for the people a hundredfold. If we could renounce our benevolence and discard our righteousness, the people would again become filial and kindly. If we could renounce our artful contrivances and discard our scheming for gain, there would be no thieves nor robbers.

. . . . . .

The sage manages affairs without doing anything, and conveys his instructions without the use of speech.

. . . . . .

Therefore the sage holds in his embrace the one thing of humility, and manifests it to all the world. He is free from self-display, and therefore he shines; from self-assertion, and therefore he is distinguished; from self-boasting, and therefore his merit is acknowledged; from self-complacency, and therefore he acquires superiority. It is because he is thus free from striving that therefore no one in the world is able to strive with him.

THE IDEAL GOVERNMENT

A state may be ruled by measures of correction; weapons of war may be used with crafty dexterity; but the kingdom is made one's own only by freedom from action and purpose.

How do I know that it is so? By these facts:—In the kingdom the multiplication of prohibitive enactments increases the poverty of the people; the more implements to add to their profit that the people have, the greater disorder is there in the state and clan; the more acts of crafty dexterity that men possess, the more do strange contrivances appear; the more display there is of legislation, the more thieves and robbers there are.

Therefore a sage has said, "I will do nothing, and the people will be transformed of themselves; I will be fond of keeping still, and the people will of themselves become correct. I will take no trouble about it, and the people will of themselves become rich; I will manifest no ambition, and the people will of themselves attain to the primitive simplicity."

Not to value and employ men of superior ability is the way to keep the people from rivalry among themselves; not to prize articles which are difficult to procure is the way to keep them from becoming thieves; not to show them what is likely to excite their desires is the way to keep their minds from disorder.

Therefore the sage, in the exercise of his government, empties their minds, fills their bellies, weakens their wills, and strengthens their bones.

He constantly tries to keep them without knowledge and without desire, and where there are those who have knowledge, to keep them from presuming to act on it. When there is this abstinence from action, good order is universal.

DOCUMENT ANALYSIS

1. How different is the Daoist idea an ideal government from that of Confucianism?

_____

_____

_____

2. How does Daoism portray the relationship between people and nature? Why is harmony between man and nature important?

_____

_____

_____

3. What is the Daoist view of "good order"?

_____

_____

_____

4. What is the Way in Daoist interpretation?

_____

_____

_____

5. What kind of people in China's classical society were likely to be attracted by Daoist teaching?

_____

_____

_____

DOCUMENT 3.1
Buddhist Stories (300 B.C.E.)

*These Buddhist stories or "Jataka tales" are very old and have a long tra-
dition of being passed on from generation to generation serving as source
for moral behavior for humans in general. These stories are stories of
wisdom and morals written around 300 B.C. in a language called Pali,
which were later translated and distributed to people across the world.
They are mainly about past incarnations of Buddha, and are meant to
teach the values of self-sacrifice, honesty, morality, and others to a common person.*

A Poor Man Wins Spiritual Treasure

Should one see, as it were, a revealer of hidden treasures. This religious
instruction was given by the Teacher while he was in residence at Jetavana
with reference to Venerable Rādha. [104]

We are told that before Rādha became a monk he was a poor Brahman
living at Sāvatthi. Deciding to live with the monks, he went to the monastery
and took up his residence there, performing various duties such as cutting the
grass, sweeping the cells, and preparing water for bathing the face. The monks
treated him kindly, but were not willing to admit him to the Order. The result
of this was that he began to lose flesh.

Now one day, early in the morning, the Teacher surveyed the world and
seeing the Brahman, considered within himself what would become of him.
Perceiving that he would become an Arahat, he went in the evening, feigning
that he was making a tour of the monastery, to the Brahman's quarters and
said to him, "Brahman, what are you doing here?" "Performing the major and
minor duties for the monks, Reverend Sir." [105] "Do they treat you kindly?"
"Yes, Reverend Sir, I receive sufficient food, but they are not willing to admit
me to the Order." Accordingly the Teacher convoked an assembly of the
monks and questioned them about the matter, saying, "Monks, is there anyone who remembers any act of this Brahman?"

Said the Elder Sāriputta, "Reverend Sir, I remember something. When I
was making my round in Rājagaha, he brought me a ladleful of his own food
and gave it to me. I remember this good office of his." Said the Teacher,
"Sāriputta, is it not proper to release from suffering one who has performed
such a service?" "Very well, Reverend Sir, I will receive him into the Order."
Sāriputta accordingly received him into the Order. He received a seat in the refectory in the outer circle of seats. Even with rice-porridge and other kinds of
food, he grew weary.

The Elder took him with him on his rounds and constantly admonished
and instructed him, saying, "You must do this; you must not do that." The
monk was amenable to discipline and respectful, and followed his preceptor's
instructions so faithfully that in but a few days he attained the Arahatship. The
Elder went with him to the Teacher, paid obeisance to the Teacher, and sat
down. The Teacher gave him a friendly welcome and said to him, "Sāriputta,
is your pupil amenable to discipline?" "Yes, Reverend Sir, he is thoroughly
amenable to discipline; no matter what fault I mention, he never shows resentment." [106] "Sāriputta, if you could have pupils like this monk, how
many would you take?" "I would take all I could get, Reverend Sir."

Now one day the monks began a discussion in the Hall of Truth: "They
say the Elder Sāriputta is grateful and thankful. When a poor Brahman gave

him but a ladleful of food, he remembered his kindness and made a monk of
him. Moreover the Elder Rādha, patient of admonition, received a patient
teacher." The Teacher, hearing their talk, said, "Monks, this is not the first
time Sāriputta has shown himself grateful and thankful. He showed the same
disposition in a previous state of existence also." And to illustrate his meaning,
he related the Alīnacitta Jātaka, found in the Second Book, as follows:

Because of Alīnacitta, a mighty host was defeated; Alīnacitta captured
alive the king of Kosala, dissatisfied with his army.

Even so a monk alert of will, directed aright,
By cultivating good qualities, by the attainment of Nibbāna,
Will in due time bring about the destruction of all Attachments.

Said the Teacher, "The Elder Sāriputta was at that time the solitary elephant which presented the pure white elephant his son to the carpenters, in
recognition of the service they did him in healing his foot." Having thus related
the Jātaka about the Elder Sāriputta, he said with reference to the Elder Rādha,
"Monks, when a fault is pointed out to a monk, he ought to be amenable to discipline like Rādha; and when he is admonished, he should not take offense.
Indeed he who gives admonition should be looked upon as one who points out
where treasures are to be found." So saying, [107] he joined the connection and,
instructing them in the Law, pronounced the following Stanza,

76. Should one see, as it were, a revealer of hidden treasures, one who
points out what should be avoided, Who administers reproof where there is
occasion for reproof, a man of intelligence, One should follow so wise a man;
It will be better, not worse, for one to follow so wise a man.

The Insolent Monks

Let a man admonish and instruct. This religious instruction was given by
the Teacher while he was in residence at Jetavana with reference to the
Assajipunabbasuka monks. [109] But the story begins at Kītāgiri.

These monks, we are told, were two pupils of the Chief Disciples, but in
spite of that fact were shameless and wicked. While they were in residence at
Kītāgiri with their retinues of five hundred monks, they planted and caused to
be planted flowering trees sand were guilty of all manner of misconduct besides. They violated homes and procured thence the monastic requisites on
which they lived. They rendered the monastery uninhabitable for the amiable
monks.

Hearing of their doings, the Teacher determined to expel them from the
Order. For this purpose he summoned the two Chief Disciples, together with
their retinues, and said to them, "Expel those who will not obey your commands, but admonish and instruct those who will obey. He who admonishes
and instructs is hated by those that lack wisdom, but is loved and cherished by
the wise." And joining the connection and instructing them in the Law, he
pronounced the following Stanza,

77. Let a man admonish and instruct, and forbid what is improper;
For if he do so, he will be loved by the good, but hated by the wicked.
[110]

Sāriputta and Moggallāna went there and admonished and instructed
the Elders and corrected their behavior, others returned to the house-life,
while still others were expelled from the Order.

DOCUMENT ANALYSIS

1. The selection, "A Poor Man Wins Spiritual Treasure," deals with Rādha's efforts to become a monk. What information does it provide about
   Buddhist views concerning the gaining of wisdom and stature?

_____

_____

_____

2. What information do the two selections give about the importance of the proper order of things in Buddhism?

_____

_____

_____

DOCUMENT 4.1
Plutarch on Alexander the Great, from Plutarch, *Lives* (1st c. B.C.E.)

Source: Plutarch, *Lives*. Vol. 7. trans. Bernadotte Perrin (Cambridge, MA: Harvard University Press, 1919), pp. 225, 231, 233, 235, 241, 43, 245, 289, 291, 339, 341, 355, 359, 361, 399, 401.

The Hellenistic Age was an era of great change for the eastern Mediterranean. Ushered in by Philip of Macedon's conquest of Greece in 338 B.C.E. and lasting until Rome's takeover of Egypt in 31 B.C.E., this age saw the spread of a Greek-like culture throughout the Middle East and Egypt. This change was made possible by the empire-building of Alexander III of Macedon, or "Alexander the Great."

Alexander the Great is often cited by military historians as the greatest military figure in human history. It is certainly true that, as a general, he never lost a battle, and he overcame serious obstacles to conquer a huge empire stretching from Greece to western India in just over ten years. As with most major historical figures, however, Alexander is still a subject of controversy. Some historians call him one of the world's great visionaries—a leader who wanted to create a unified, peaceful Greek world. Others call Alexander little more than a drunken brawler, prone to violence and excess. These scholars say that it was after a night of extreme revelry that Alexander died in 323 B.C.E.

One of the surviving sketches written by the Greek historian Plutarch is on Alexander the Great.

It is the life of Alexander the king . . . that I am writing in this book, and the multitude of the deeds to be treated is so great that I shall make no other preface than to entreat my readers, in case I do not tell of all the famous actions of these men, nor even speak exhaustively at all in each particular case, but in epitome for the most part, not to complain.

. . . The outward appearance of Alexander is best represented by the statues of him which Lysippus made, and it was by this artist alone that Alexander himself thought it fit that he should be modelled. For those peculiarities which many of his successors and friends afterwards tried to imitate, namely, the poise of the neck, which was bent slightly to the left, and the melting glance of his eyes, this artist has accurately observed. Appelles, however, in painting him as wielder of the thunder-bolt, did not reproduce his complexion, but made it too dark and swarthy. Whereas he was of a fair colour, as they say, and his fairness passed into ruddiness on his breast particularly, and in his face. Moreover, that a very pleasant odour exhaled from his skin and that there was a fragrance about his mouth and all his flesh, so that his garments were filled with it.

But while he was still a boy his self-restraint showed itself in the fact that, although he was impetuous and violent in other matters, the pleasures of the body had little hold upon him, and he indulged in them with great moderation, while his ambition kept his spirit serious and lofty in advance of his years. For it was neither every kind of fame nor fame from every source that he courted, as Philip did, who plumed himself like a sophist on the power of his oratory, and took care to have the victories of his chariots at Olympia engraved upon his coins; nay, when those about him inquired whether he would be willing to contend in the foot-race at the Olympic games, since he was swift of foot, "Yes," said he, "if I could have kings as my contestants." And in general, too, Alexander appears to have been averse to the whole race of athletes; at any rate, though he instituted very many contests, not only for tragic poets and players on the flute and players on the lyre, but also for rhapsodists, as well as for hunting of every sort and for fighting with staves, he took no interest in offering prizes either for boxing or for the pancratium.

[Alexander's father, Philip, employed Aristotle as his son's tutor.]

. . . Aristotle he admired at the first, and loved him, as he himself used to say, more than he did his father, for that the one had given him life, but the other had taught him a noble life; later, however, he held him in more or less of suspicion, not to the extent of doing him any harm, but his kindly attentions lacked their former ardour and affection towards

him, and this was proof of estrangement. However, that eager yearning for philosophy which was imbedded in his nature and which ever grew with his growth, did not subside from his soul.

. . . Alexander was naturally munificent, and became still more so as his wealth increased. His gifts, too, were accompanied by a kindly spirit, with which alone, to tell the truth, a giver confers a favour. . . . [A] common Macedonian was driving a mule laden with some of the royal gold, and when the beast gave out, took the load on his own shoulders and tried to carry it. The king, then, seeing the man in great distress and learning the facts of the case, said, as the man was about to lay his burden down, "Don't give out, but finish your journey by taking this load to your own tent." Furthermore, he was generally more displeased with those who would not take his gifts than with those who asked for them.

[The Greeks considered anyone who did not speak Greek to be a "barbarian." Alexander and his armies obviously encountered many non-Greek speakers, but here Plutarch is probably referring to the Parthians. Parthia, a Middle Eastern kingdom, was attacked in late 330 B.C.E.]

. . . [H]e marched into Parthia, where, during a respite from fighting, he first put on the barbaric dress, [perhaps] from a desire to adapt himself to the native customs, believing that community of race and custom goes far towards softening the hearts of men. . . . At first he wore this only in intercourse with the Barbarians and with his companions at home, then people generally saw him riding forth or giving audience in this attire. The sight was offensive to the Macedonians, but they admired his other high qualities and thought they ought to yield to him in some things which made for his pleasure or his fame.

Under these circumstances, too, he adapted his own mode of life still more to the customs of the country, and tried to bring these into closer agreement with Macedonian customs, thinking that by a mixture and community of practice which produced good will, rather than by force, his authority would be kept secure while he was far away. For this reason, too, he chose out thirty thousand boys and gave orders that they should learn the Greek language and be trained to use Macedonian weapons, appointing many instructors for this work. His marriage to Roxana [from Bactria, a kingdom to the east of the Persian Empire], whom he saw in her youthful beauty taking part in a dance at a banquet, was a love affair, and yet it was thought to harmonize well with the matters which he had in hand. For the Barbarians were encouraged by the partnership into which the marriage brought them, and they were beyond measure fond of Alexander, because, most temperate of all men that he was in these matters, he would not consent to approach even the only woman who ever mastered his affections, without the sanction of law.

[By late 326 B.C.E., Alexander and his armies had conquered Persia and had crossed the Indus River Valley. After a major battle, Alexander wished to continue eastward.]

. . . [H]aving had all they could do to repulse an enemy who mustered only twenty thousand infantry and two thousand horse, they violently opposed Alexander when he insisted on crossing the river Ganges. . . . For they were told that [local] kings were awaiting them with eighty thousand horsemen, two hundred thousand footmen, eight thousand chariots, and six thousand fighting elephants.

At first, then, Alexander shut himself up in his tent from displeasure and wrath and lay there, feeling no gratitude for what he had already achieved unless he should cross the Ganges, nay, counting a retreat a confession of defeat. But his friends gave him fitting consolation, and his soldiers crowded about his door and besought him with loud cries and wailing, until at last he relented and began to break camp.

DOCUMENT ANALYSIS

1. Do you notice any negative observations in this account?

_____

_____

_____

2. Does Plutarch say anything positive about Alexander, and would you characterize this account as generally positive?

_____

_____

_____

3. Is there any evidence in this selection to support those historians who argue that Alexander wished for peace and unity? If so, what is it?

_____

_____

_____

4. What kinds of leisure activities does Alexander seem to have enjoyed?

_____

_____

_____

5. What reaction did the other Macedonians have when Alexander wore his "barbarian" clothes in public?

_____

_____

_____

DOCUMENT 5.1
Aelius Aristides, from "The Roman Oration" (2nd c. C.E.)
Source: Moses Hadas, *A History of Rome* (1956)

The period of Roman history between the rise of Nerva to the imperial throne in 96 C.E. and the death of the emperor Marcus Aurelius in 180 C.E. is known as the Pax Romana (Roman Peace), and its rulers during that time have been called the "Five Good Emperors." During this time, Rome reached the height of its military expansion and wealth. The pride and confidence of the Roman elite is clearly on display in the following document. The Roman Oration is one of the most important works of one of the most celebrated orators of the period. Aelius Aristides (120–189 C.E.) was a leader of the literary movement to revive the style of the Greek sophists. In The Roman Oration, Aelius praises the accomplishments of Rome. His purpose was not to give an accurate account of Roman conquest and governance, but to dazzle his audience with hyperbolic eloquence. Even so, it gives us a glimpse of how Romans wished to think of themselves.

"If one considers the vast extent of your empire he must be amazed that so small a fraction of it rules the world, but when he beholds the city and its spaciousness it is not astonishing that all the habitable world is ruled by such a capital. . . . Your possessions equal the sun's course. . . . You do not rule within fixed boundaries, nor can anyone dictate the limits of your sway. . . . Whatever any people produces can be found here, at all times and in abundance. . . . Egypt, Sicily, and the civilized part of Africa are your farms; ships are continually coming and going. . . .

"Vast as it is, your empire is more remarkable for its thoroughness than its scope: there are no dissident or rebellious enclaves. . . . The whole world prays in unison that your empire may endure forever.

"Governors sent out to cities and peoples each rule their charges, but in their relations to each other they are equally subjects. The principal difference between governors and their charges is this—they demonstrate the proper way to be a subject. So great is their reverence for the great Ruler [the emperor], who administers all things. Him they believe to know their business better than they themselves do, and hence they respect and heed him more than one would a master overseeing a task and giving orders. No one is so self-assured that he can remain unmoved upon hearing the emperor's name: he rises in prayer and adoration and utters a twofold prayer—to the gods for the Ruler, and to the Ruler for himself. And if the governors are in the least doubt concerning the justice of claims or suits of the governed, public or private, they send to the Ruler for instructions at once and await his reply, as a chorus awaits its trainer's directions. Hence the Ruler need not exhaust himself by traveling to various parts to settle matters in person. It is easy for him to abide in his place and manage the world through letters; these arrive almost as soon as written, as if borne on wings.

"But the most marvelous and admirable achievement of all, and the one deserving our fullest gratitude, is this. . . . You alone of the imperial powers of history rule over men who are free. You have not assigned this or that region to this nabob or that mogul; no people has been turned over as a domestic and bound holding—to a man not himself free. But just as citizens in an individual city might designate magistrates, so you, whose city is the whole world, appoint governors to protect and provide for the governed, as if they were elective, not to lord it over their charges. As a result, so far from disputing the office as if it were their own, governors make way for their successors readily when their term is up, and may not even await their coming. Appeals to a higher jurisdiction are as easy as appeals from parish to county. . . .

"But the most notable and praiseworthy feature of all, a thing unparalleled, is your magnanimous conception of citizenship. All of your subjects (and this implies the whole world) you have divided into two parts: the better endowed and more virile, wherever they may be, you have granted citizenship and even kinship; the rest you govern as obedient subjects. Neither the seas nor expanse of land bars citizenship; Asia and Europe are not differentiated. Careers are open to talent. . . . Rich and poor find contentment and profit in your system; there is no other way of life. Your polity is a single and all-embracing harmony. . . .

"You have not put walls around your city, as if you were hiding it or avoiding your subjects; to do so you considered ignoble and inconsistent with your principles, as if a master should show fear of his slaves. You did not overlook walls, however, but placed them round the empire, not the city. The splendid and distant walls you erected are worthy of you; to men within their circuit they are visible, but it requires a journey of months and years from the city to see them. Beyond the outermost ring of the civilized world you drew a second circle, larger in radius and easier to defend, like the outer fortifications of a city. Here you built walls and established cities in diverse parts. The cities you filled with colonists; you introduced arts and crafts and established an orderly culture. . . . Your military organization makes all others childish. Your soldiers and officers you train to prevail not only over the enemy but over themselves. The soldier lives under discipline daily, and none ever deserts the post assigned him.

"You alone are, so to speak, natural rulers. Your predecessors were masters and slaves in turn; as rulers they were counterfeits, and reversed their positions like players in a ball game. . . . You have measured out the world, bridged rivers, cut roads through mountains, filled the wastes with posting stations, introduced orderly and refined modes of life. . . .

"Be all gods and their offspring invoked to grant that this empire and this city flourish forever and never cease until stones float upon the sea and trees forbear to sprout in the springtide. May the great Ruler and his sons be preserved to administer all things well."

DOCUMENT ANALYSIS

1. In the modern world, most people regard imperialism as unequivocally oppressive. Based on this document, how might the Romans justify their conquests?

_____

_____

_____

2. Pushing past the obvious exaggeration, what does this document tell us about how the Romans ruled?

_____

_____

_____

3. The phrase "rule over men who are free" seems like an oxymoron to a modern person. What does the author mean by this?

_____

_____

_____

4. This speech reflected the opinion of the Roman elite. If you asked a member of the Roman aristocracy what the special abilities of Romans were, how would he respond?

_____

_____

_____

5. What are this author's criteria for the greatness of the Roman Empire?

_____

_____

_____

DOCUMENT 6.1
Nestor-Iskander on the fall of Constantinople (1450s)
Source: *Anthology of Old Russian Literature*, ed. Ad. Stender-Petersen in collaboration with Stefan Congrat-Butlar.
(New York: Columbia University Press, 1954).

Nestor-Iskander was, insofar as we know, a Slav of Orthodox background who converted to Islam. His account of the fall of Constantinople has been preserved in Russian language sources, and tells the story of the battle from the Byzantine perspective—that is, from inside the city. Nestor-Iskander apparently was actually present for the siege and fall of the city.

This document paints a noble picture of the Byzantine Emperor, Constantine XI. More importantly, it highlights the intimate relationship between the Byzantine ruler, the Orthodox Church, and the elite of Byzantine society.

Nestor-Iskander concludes his tale by mentioning an old Byzantine "prophecy" that held that one day a people called the rhusios would gain control of Constantinople. Russian sources interpreted rhusios, which in Greek means "red-haired," as russkii, which means Russian. This "prophecy" would inspire some Russians to understand that Russia would take Constantinople's place as the heir of Rome, and the seat of true Christianity.

The godless [Sultan] Mohammed [II, 1451–1481], son of Murad [II, 1421–1451], who at that time ruled the Turks, took note of all the problems [that plagued Constantinople]. And, although he professed peace, he wanted to put an end to Emperor Constantine [XI, 1449–1453]. Towards that end he assembled a large army and, by land and by sea, suddenly appeared with that large force before the city [of Constantinople] and laid siege to it. . . . [The Emperor], therefore, sent his envoys to Sultan Mohammed in order to discuss peace and past [relations]. But Mohammed did not trust them, and as soon as the envoys departed, he ordered cannons and guns to fire at the city. Others were commanded to make ready wall-scaling equipment and build assault structures. Such city inhabitants as Greek, Venetian, and Genoese [mercenaries] left because they did not want to fight the Turks. . . .

On the fourteenth day, after they had said their heathen prayers, the Turks sounded trumpets, beat their drums, and played on all other of their musical instruments. . . . Because of continued heavy shooting, city defenders could not stand safely on the wall. Some crouched down awaiting the attack; others fired their cannons and guns as much as they could, killing many Turks. The Patriarch, bishops, and all clergy prayed constantly, pleading for God's mercy and for [His help in] saving the city.

When the Turks surmised that they had killed all the defenders on the wall, they ordered their forces to give a loud shout [before the assault]. Some soldiers carried incendiary devices, others ladders, still others wall-destroying equipment, and the rest many other instruments of destruction. They were ordered to attack and capture the city. City defenders, too, cried out and shouted back and engaged them in a fierce battle. The Emperor toured the city, encouraging his people, promising them God's help and ordering the ringing of church bells so as to summon all the inhabitants [to defend their city]. When the Turks heard the ringing of church bells, they ordered their trumpets, flutes, and thousands of other musical instruments to sound out. And there was a great and terrible slaughter! . . .

When Mohammed saw such a multitude of his men killed, and when he was told of Emperor's bravery, he could not sleep. [On May 27, 1453] he called in his Council and informed them that he wanted to lift the siege that night, before a large [Papal] fleet arrived in the city to reinforce [its defenses]. But then there appeared an unexpected miracle of God! The anticipated [Papal] help failed to materialize. Instead, at 7:00 p.m. that evening the entire city was suddenly engulfed by a great darkness. The air suddenly thickened and, in a moaning way, it hovered above the city. Then, big black drops of rain, as large as the eye of a buffalo, began to fall. People were shocked and horrified by this unusual occurrence. Patriarch Athanasius gathered all of his clergy and members of the Imperial Council, went to the Emperor, and told him the following: "Your Illustrious Majesty! All citizens of the city believe in its vitality. But they also think that the Holy Spirit has abandoned it. Now every living creature is foretelling the demise of this city. We beseech you to leave the city. All of us will perish here. For God's sake, please leave!". . . The Emperor did not listen to them. He replied instead: "Let God's will be done!"

. . . When they noticed the determination of the godless [Mohammed], [the Byzantine] military commanders, officials, and nobles joined the battle and implored the Emperor to leave in order to escape death. He wept bitterly and told them: "Remember the words I said earlier! Do not try to protect me! I want to die with you!" and they replied: "All of us will die for God's church and for you!"

Then they escorted him to [relative] safety and many people told him to leave the city. After they pledged their allegiance to him, they lamented and cried and returned to their posts. . . . There was fierce fighting, more vicious than all previous encounters. Many [Byzantine] military commanders, officials, and nobles perished and the few who survived went to the Emperor to report to him about the disaster. There is no way to give an accurate number of Byzantine and Turkish casualties. The select Turkish force of 3000, like wild animals, dispersed and searched all comers of the city in an effort to capture the Emperor.

The impious Mohammed then ordered all of his forces to occupy all city streets and gates in order to capture the Emperor. In his camp he retained only the Janissaries, who readied their cannons and guns in fear of a sudden attack by the Emperor. Sensing God's command, the Emperor went to the Great Church [St. Sophia?], where he fell to the ground pleading for God's mercy and forgiveness for his sins. Then he bade farewell to the Patriarch, the clergy, and the Empress, bowed to those who were present and left the church. . . . As he left the church the Emperor said: "If you want to suffer for God's church and for the Orthodox faith, then follow me!"

Then he mounted his horse and went to the Golden Gate, hoping to encounter there the godless. He was able to attract some 3000 [Byzantine] soldiers. Near the Gate they met a multitude of Turks whom they defeated. The Emperor wanted to reach the Gate but could not on account of many corpses. Then he encountered another large Turkish force and they fought till darkness. In this manner the Orthodox Emperor Constantine suffered for God's churches and for the Orthodox faith. On May 29 [1453], according to eyewitnesses, he killed more than 600 Turks with his own hand. And the saying was fulfilled. *It started with Constantine and it ended with Constantine.* . . .

. . . City inhabitants in streets and courtyards refused to surrender to the Turks. They fought them and on that day [May 29] many died, including women and children. Others were taken into captivity. Brave soldiers stationed themselves in windows and refused to surrender and give up their posts. . . . During daylight they ran and hid themselves in various abysses and at night they came out and fought the Turks. Others, especially women and children, threw bricks, tiles, and burning pieces of wood at them and thereby caused them great trouble.

[This form of resistance] stunned the pashas and sanjak-beys. Because they did not know what to do, they sent a messenger to the Sultan with the following information: "The city will not be pacified until you enter it!" He ordered that a search be made for the Emperor and the Empress. He [the Sultan] himself was afraid to enter the city and that fact troubled him greatly. He then called in [Byzantine] nobles and military commanders who had been captured in the battle and were held as war prisoners by the pashas. He gave them his resolute word and some gifts, and sent them, together with the pashas and sanjak-beys, to deliver the following message to [the defiant] city inhabitants in streets and courtyards: "All fighting must stop! There should be neither fear, nor killings nor taking people into captivity! If you disobey this order, all of you, including your wives and children, will be put to the sword!" And so it was. The fighting stopped. . . .

When he heard this the Sultan was pleased. . . .

. . . [H]eresy caused the downfall of old Rome. The Turks used their axes to shatter the doors of all churches of the Second Rome, the city of Constantinople. Now [in Moscow], the new Third Rome, the Holy Ecumenical Apostolic Church of your sovereign state shines brighter than the sun in the universal Orthodox Christian faith throughout the world. Pious Tsar! Let [people of] your state know that all states of the Orthodox faith have now merged into one, your state. You are the only true Christian ruler under the sky!

DOCUMENT ANALYSIS

1. How do the two sides view the "great darkness" that enveloped the city on 27 May 1543?

2. How does Muhammed II view the Byzantine Emperor, the Orthodox Patriarch, and the other elites of Byzantine society?

3. What role does religion play in the outcome of the conflict, according to this source?

4. What weapons were the most critical to the fall of the city?

5. Which leader is portrayed as the better military commander, Constantine XI or Muhammed II?

DOCUMENT 7.1
From "The Holy *Qur'an*" (7th c. C.E.)
Source: *The Koran Interpreted,* trans. Arthur J. Arberry, 2 vols. (London: George Allen and Unwin, 1955), Vol. 1, pp. 41–46, 50–55, 65, 71–72.

The religion of Islam was revealed to an Arabian merchant named Muhammad in 610 C.E. Within about twenty years, by the time of Muhammad's death in 632, the religion was on firm footing within the Arabian Peninsula. The next few decades would see Islam spread quickly into Egypt and North Africa, as well as into the Middle East.

Shortly after Muhammad's death, in the 650s, an "official" version of God's words to Muhammad, as well as Muhammad's sayings, was written down. The Qu'ran is a document much like the Judeo-Christian Old Testament, containing the mythos of the religion, as well as its basic tenets and practices. Not surprisingly, given the influence of both Judaism and Christianity (or perhaps because, as some scholars suggest, the supreme God in each is actually the same being), there are many things that the three religions share in common. The following excerpt not only discusses some of the basic beliefs of Islam, but also illustrates some of the similarities between these three monotheistic religions.

Those unbelievers of the **People of the Book** and the idolaters wish not that any good should be sent down upon you from your Lord;
but God singles out for His mercy whom he will;
God is of bounty abounding. . . .

Many of the People of the Book wish they might
restore you as unbelievers, after you have believed,
in the jealousy of their souls, after the truth has become clear to them; yet do you pardon and be forgiving, till God brings His command;
truly God is powerful over everything.
And perform the prayer, and pay the alms;
whatever good you shall forward to your souls' account,
you shall find it with God; assuredly God sees the things you do.
And they say, "None shall enter Paradise except that they be Jews or Christians."
Such are their fancies. Say: "Produce your proof, if you speak truly."
Nay, but whosoever submits his will to God, being a good-doer, his wage is with his Lord, and no fear shall be on them, neither shall they sorrow.

The Jews say, "The Christians stand not on anything";
the Christians say, "The Jews stand not on anything";
yet they recite the Book. So too the ignorant say the like of them. God shall decide between them on the Day of Resurrection touching their differences.
And who does greater evil than he who bars God's places of worship, so that His Name be not rehearsed in them, and strives to destroy them?
Such men might never enter them, save in fear; for them is degradation in the present world,
and in the world to come a mighty chastisement.

To God belong the East and the West;
whithersoever you turn, there is the Face of God;

God is All-embracing, All-knowing. . . .
Children of Israel, remember My blessing wherewith I blessed you, and that I have preferred you above all beings. . . .

And when his Lord tested Abraham with certain words, and he fulfilled them.
He said, "Behold, I make you a leader for the people." Said he, "And of my seed?"
He said "My covenant shall not reach the evildoers."
And when We appointed the House to be a place of visitation for the people, and a sanctuary,
and: "Take to yourselves Abraham's station for a place of prayer." And We made covenant with Abraham and Ishmael, "Purify My House for those that shall go about it and those that cleave to it, to those who bow and prostrate themselves." . . .

When his Lord said to him, "Surrender," he said, "I have surrendered me to the Lord of all Being."
And Abraham charged his sons with this and Jacob likewise: My sons, God has chosen for you the religion;
see that you die not save in surrender."

Why, were you witnesses, when death came to Jacob? When he said to his sons,
"What will you serve after me?" They said,
"We will serve thy God and the God of thy fathers
Abraham, Ishmael, and Isaac, One God;
to Him we surrender."
That is a nation that has passed away;
there awaits them that they have earned, and there awaits you that you have earned;
you shall not be questioned concerning the things they did.

And they say, "Be Jews or Christians and you shall be guided." Say thou: "Nay, rather the creed of Abraham, a man of pure faith;
he was no idolater."
Say you: "We believe in God, and in that which has been sent down on us and sent down on Abraham, Ishmael, Isaac and Jacob, and the Tribes, and that which was given to Moses and Jesus

and the Prophets, of their Lord; we make no division between any of them, and to Him we surrender."
And if they believe in the like of that you believe in, then they are truly guided; but if they turn away, then they are clearly in schism,
God will suffice you for them; He is the All-hearing, the All-knowing;
the baptism of God; and who is there that baptizes fairer than God?
Him we are serving.
Say: "Would you then dispute with us concerning God, who is our Lord and your Lord? Our deeds belong to us, and to you belong your deeds; Him we serve sincerely. . . . "

It is not piety, that you turn your faces to the East and to the West.
True piety is this:
to believe in God, and the Last Day, the angels, the Book, and the Prophets, to give of one's substance, however cherished, to kinsmen, and orphans, the needy, the traveler, beggars, and to ransom the slave, to perform the prayer, to pay the alms.
And they who fulfill their covenant when they have engaged in a covenant, and endure with fortitude misfortune, hardship, and peril, these are they who are true in their faith, these are the truly godfearing. . . .
O believers, prescribed for you is the Fast, even as it was prescribed for those that were before you—haply you will be godfearing—
for days numbered; and if any of you be sick, or if he be on a journey, then a number of other days. . . .
And fight in the way of God with those who fight with you, but aggress not: God loves not the aggressors.
And slay them wherever you come upon them, and expel them from where they expelled you;
persecution is more grievous than slaying.
But fight them not by the Holy Mosque until they should fight you there;
then, if they fight you, slay them—
such is the recompense of unbelievers—
but if they give over, surely God is

All-forgiving, All-compassionate.
Fight them, till there is no persecution
and the religion is God's; then if they
give over, there shall be no enmity
save for evildoers.
The holy month for the holy month;
holy things demand retaliation.
Whoso commits aggression against you,
do you commit aggression against him
like as he has committed against you;
and fear you God, and know that God is
with the godfearing.
And expend in the way of God;
and cast not yourselves by your own hands
into destruction, but be good-doers; God
loves the good-doers.
Fulfill the Pilgrimage and the Visitation
unto God; but if you are prevented,
then such offering as may be feasible. . . .
And when you have performed your holy rites
remember God, as you remember your fathers
or yet more devoutly. . . .
God
there is no god but He, the

Living, the Everlasting.
Slumber seizes Him not, neither sleep;
to Him belongs
all that is in the heavens and the earth.
Who is there that shall intercede with Him
save by his leave?
He knows what lies before them and
what is after them,
and they comprehend not anything of
His knowledge save such as He
wills.
His Throne comprises the heavens and
earth;
the preserving of them oppresses Him not;
He is the All-high, the All-glorious.
No compulsion is there in religion.
Rectitude has become clear from error.
So whosoever disbelieves in idols
and believes in God, has laid hold of
the most firm handle, unbreaking; God is
All-hearing, All-knowing.
God is the Protector of the believers;
He brings them forth from the shadows
into the light. . . .

Those who believe and do deeds of
righteousness,
and perform the prayer, and pay the alms—
their wage awaits them with their Lord,
and no fear shall be on them, neither shall
they sorrow. . . .
God charges no soul save to its capacity;
standing to its account is what it has earned,
and against its account what it has merited.
Our Lord,
take us not to task
if we forget, or make mistake.
Our Lord,
charge us not with a load such
as Thou didst lay upon those before us.
Our Lord,
do Thou not burden us
beyond what we have the strength to bear.
And pardon us,
and forgive us,
and have mercy on us;
Thou art our Protector.
And help us against the people
of the unbelievers.

DOCUMENT ANALYSIS

1. From this excerpt, would you say that Islam is similar at all to Judaism and Christianity? If so, how?

_____

_____

_____

2. How are Muslims supposed to fight?

_____

_____

_____

3. What is the "Pilgrimage" referred to in this excerpt?

_____

_____

_____

4. What sorts of good deeds should Muslims do?

_____

_____

_____

5. Will Jews or Christians enter "Paradise" after death?

_____

_____

_____

DOCUMENT 8.1
From *Sundiata: An Epic of Old Mali* (1235)
Source: D. T. Niane, *Sundiata: An Epic of Old Mali*, trans. G. D. Pickett (Essex, England: Longman House, 1988).

A powerful rival to Mandingo power in the Sudan was the pagan people called Soso. In order to check the influence of the Mali Empire, the Soso king, Soumaoro, killed the eleven brothers who were heirs to the throne of Mali. There was a twelfth, Sundiata, whom they spared because he was crippled.

The story of Sundiata's rise to power reveals much of the early history of the Mandingo king and his thrilling defeat of Soumaoro in 1235. The epic of old Mali contains a fascinating description of palace intrigue in the capital city of Niani. Sundiata emerges as the central hero of the tale through magic, cunning, strength and providence. Sundiata becomes a great king noted for his Muslim piety, wisdom, justice and military strength. Under his reign, the Mali Empire recovers from war and returns to prosperity. Caravans of many riches traveled to Niani, and people from distant lands spoke of this great king. Sundiata is still regarded by the Mandingo as their national hero.

The oral history excerpted below is primarily the work of an obscure griot from the village of Djeliba Koro. A "griot" is a member of a hereditary caste in West Africa whose job it is to keep the oral history of the tribe or village. As explained by author D.T. Niane, at one time "griots were the counsellors of kings, they conserved the constitutions of kingdoms by memory work alone; each princely family had its griot appointed to preserve tradition; it was from among the griots that kings used to choose the tutors for young princes. In the very hierarchical society of Africa before colonization, . . . the griot appears as one of the most important of this society, because it is he who, for want of archives, records the customs, traditions and governmental principles of kings."

Soumaoro sent a detachment under his son Sosso Balla to block Sundiata's route to Tabon. Sosso Balla was about the same age as Sundiata. He promptly deployed his troops at the entrance to the mountains to oppose Sundiata's advance to Tabon. . . .

Sundiata was immovable, so the orders were given and the war drums began to beat. On his proud horse Sundiata turned to right and left in front of his troops. He entrusted the rearguard, composed of a part of the Wagadou cavalry, to his younger brother Manding Bory. Having drawn his sword, Sundiata led the charge, shouting his war cry.

The Sossos were surprised by this sudden attack for they all thought that the battle would be joined the next day. The lightning that flashes across the sky is slower, the thunderbolts less frightening and floodwaters less surprising than Sundiata swooping down on Sosso Balla and his smiths. In a trice, Sundiata was in the middle of the Sossos like a lion in the sheepfold. The Sossos, trampled under the hooves of his fiery charger, cried out. When he turned to the right the smiths of Soumaoro fell in their tens, and when he turned to the left his sword made heads fall as when someone shakes a tree of ripe fruit. The horsemen of Mema wrought a frightful slaughter and their long lances pierced flesh like a knife sunk into a paw-paw. Charging ever forwards, Sundiata looked for Sosso Balla; he caught sight of him and like a lion bounded towards the son of Soumaoro, his sword held aloft. His arm came sweeping down but at that moment a Sosso warrior came between Djata and Sosso Balla and was sliced like a calabash. Sosso Balla did not wait and disappeared from amidst his smiths. Seeing their chief in flight, the Sossos gave way and fell into a terrible rout. . . .

The news of the battle of Tabon spread like wildfire in the plains of Mali. It was known that Soumaoro was not present at the battle, but the mere fact that his troops had retreated before Sundiata sufficed to give hope to all the peoples of Mali. Soumaoro realized that from now on he would have to reckon with this young man. He got to know of the prophecies of Mali, yet he was still too confident. When Sosso Balla returned with the remnant he had managed to save at Tabon, he said to his father, 'Father, he is worse than a lion; nothing can withstand him.'. . .

The son of Sogolon had already decided on his plan of campaign—to beat Soumaoro, destroy Sosso and return triumphantly to Niani. He now had five army corps at his disposal. . . .

Sundiata caught sight of him and tried to cut a passage through to him. He struck to the right and struck to the left and trampled underfoot. The murderous hooves of his 'Daffeké' dug into the chests of the Sossos. Soumaoro was now within spear range and Sundiata reared up his horse and hurled his weapon. It whistled away and bounced off Soumaoro's chest as off a rock and fell to the ground. Sogolon's son bent his bow but with a motion of the hand Soumaoro caught the arrow in flight and showed it to Sundiata as if to say 'Look, I am invulnerable.'

Furious, Sundiata snatched up his spear and with his head bent charged at Soumaoro, but as he raised his arm to strike his enemy he noticed that Soumaoro had disappeared. Manding Bory riding at his side pointed to the hill and said, 'Look, brother.'

Sundiata saw Soumaoro on the hill, sitting on his black-coated horse. How could he have done it, he who was only two paces from Sundiata? By what power had he spirited himself away on to the hill? The son of Sogolon stopped fighting to watch the king of Sosso. The sun was already very low and Soumaoro's smiths gave way but Sundiata did not give the order to pursue the enemy. Suddenly, Soumaoro disappeared! . . .

The battle of Neguéboria showed Djata, if he needed to be shown, that to beat the king of Sosso other weapons were necessary.

The evening of Neguéboria, Sundiata was master of the field, but he was in a gloomy mood. He went away from the field of battle with its agonized cries of the wounded, and Manding Bory and Tabon Wana watched him go. He headed for the hill where he had seen Soumaoro after his miraculous disappearance. . . .

But it was time to return to his native Mali. Sundiata assembled his army in the plain and each people provided a contingent to accompany the Mansa to Niani. . . .

Sundiata and his men had to cross the Niger in order to enter old Mali. One might have thought that all the dug-out canoes in the world had arranged to meet at the port of Ka-ba. It was the dry season and there was not much water in the river. The fishing tribe of Somono, to whom Djata had given the monopoly of the water, were bent on expressing their thanks to the son of Sogolon. They put all their dug-outs side by side across the Niger so that Sundiata's sofas could cross without wetting their feet.

When the whole army was on the other side of the river, Sundiata ordered great sacrifices. A hundred oxen and a hundred rams were sacrificed. It was thus that Sundiata thanked God on returning to Mali.

The villages of Mali gave Maghan Sundiata an unprecedented welcome. At normal times a traveller on foot can cover the distance from Ka-ba to Niani with only two halts, but Sogolon's son with his army took three days. The road to Mali from the river was flanked by a double human hedge. Flocking from every corner of Mali, all the inhabitants were resolved to see their saviour from close up. The women of Mali tried to create a sensation and they did not fail. At the entrance to each village they had carpeted the road with their multi-coloured pagnes, so that Sundiata's horse would not so much as dirty its feet on entering their village. . . .

Sundiata was leading the van. He had donned his costume of a hunter king—a plain smock, skin-tight trousers and his bow slung across his back. At his side Balla Fasséké was still wearing his festive garments gleaming with gold. Between Djata's general staff and the army Sosso Balla had been placed, amid his father's fetishes. But his hands were no longer tied. As at Ka-ba, abuse was everywhere heaped upon him and the prisoner did not dare look up at the hostile crowd. . . .

The troops were marching along singing the 'Hymn to the Bow', which the crowd took up. New songs flew from mouth to mouth. Young women offered the soldiers cool water and cola nuts. And so the triumphal march across Mali ended outside Niani, Sundiata's city.

It was a ruined town which was beginning to be rebuilt by its inhabitants. A part of the ramparts had been destroyed and the charred walls still bore the marks of the fire. From the top of the hill Djata looked on Niani, which looked like a dead city. He saw the plain of Sounkarani, and he also saw the site of the young baobab tree. The survivors of the catastrophe were standing in rows on the Mali road. The children were waving branches, a few young women were singing, but the adults were mute. . . .

With Sundiata peace and happiness entered Niani. Lovingly Sogolon's son had his native city rebuilt. He restored in the ancient style his father's old enclosure where he had grown up. People came from all the villages of Mali to settle in Niani. The walls had to be destroyed to enlarge the town, and new quarters were built for each kin group in the enormous army. . . .

After a year Sundiata held a new assembly at Niani, but this one was the assembly of dignitaries and kings of the empire. The kings and notables of all the tribes came to Niani. The kings spoke of their administration and the dignitaries talked of their kings. Fakoli, the nephew of Soumaoro, having proved himself too independent, had to flee to evade the Mansa's anger. His lands were confiscated and the taxes of Sosso were payed directly into the granaries of Niani. In this way, every year, Sundiata gathered about him all the kings and notables; so justice prevailed everywhere, for the kings were afraid of being denounced at Niani.

Djata's justice spared nobody. He followed the very word of God. He protected the weak against the strong and people would make journeys lasting several days to come and demand justice of him. Under his sun the upright man was rewarded and the wicked one punished.

In their new-found peace the villages knew prosperity again, for with Sundiata happiness had come into everyone's home. Vast fields of millet, rice, cotton, indigo and fonio surrounded the villages. Whoever worked always had something to live on. Each year long caravans carried the taxes in kind to Niani.

You could go from village to village without fearing brigands. A thief would have his right hand chopped off and if he stole again he would be put to the sword.

New villages and new towns sprang up in Mali and elsewhere. 'Dyulas', or traders, became numerous and during the reign of Sundiata the world knew happiness.

There are some kings who are powerful through their military strength. Everybody trembles before them, but when they die nothing but ill is spoken of them. Others do neither good nor ill and when they die they are forgotten. Others are feared because they have power, but they know how to use it and they are loved because they love justice. Sundiata belonged to this group. He was feared, but loved as well. He was the father of Mali and gave the world peace. After him the world has not seen a greater conqueror, for he was the seventh and last conqueror. He had made the capital of an empire out of his father's village, and Niani became the navel of the earth. . . .

The griots, fine talkers that they were, used to boast of Niani and Mali saying: 'If you want salt, go to Niani, for Niani is the camping place of the Sahel caravans. If you want gold, go to Niani, for Bouré, Bambougou and Wagadou work for Niani. If you want fine cloth, go to Niani, for the Mecca road passes by Niani. If you want fish, go to Niani, for it is there that the fishermen of Maouti and Djenné come to sell their catches. If you want meat, go to Niani, the country of the great hunters, and the land of the ox and the sheep. If you want to see an army, go to Niani, for it [is] there that the united forces of Mali are to be found. If you want to see a great king, go to Niani, for it is there that the son of Sogolon lives, the man with two names.'. . .

After him many kings and many Mansas reigned over Mali and other towns sprang up and disappeared. Hajji Mansa Moussa, of illustrious memory, beloved of God, built houses at Mecca for pilgrims coming from Mali, but the towns which he founded have all disappeared, Karanina, Bouroun-Kouna—nothing more remains of these towns. Other kings carried Mali far beyond Djata's frontiers, for example Mansa Samanka and Fadima Moussa, but none of them came near Djata.

Maghan Sundiata was unique. In his own time no one equalled him and after him no one had the ambition to surpass him. He left his mark on Mali for all time and his taboos still guide men in their conduct.

Mali is eternal. To convince yourself of what I have said go to Mali.

DOCUMENT ANALYSIS

1. In what manner does the king of Timbuktu (Tombuto) consolidate and maintain political and economic power?

_____

_____

_____

2. Reading the geographic descriptions provided by Leo proved very useful to geographers of the period. What is the importance of the Niger River to kingdom-building in the Sudanic region?

_____

_____

_____

3. The role of merchants is well described by this Arab traveler. What are the most important trade goods of the region? How is the trade conducted, and by whom?

_____

_____

_____

4. What is Leo Africanus' opinion of the people of Mali (Melli)?

_____

_____

_____

5. What is the role of Islam to kingdom-building in West Africa?

_____

_____

_____

DOCUMENT 9.1
Usamah Ibn-Munqidh, "An Arab-Syrian Gentleman and Warrior in the Period of the Crusades" (1100s C.E.)
Source: Usamah Ibn-Munqidh, *An Arab-Syrian Gentleman and Warrior in the Period of the Crusades*, trans. Philip K. Hitti
(New York: Columbia University Press, 2000), pp. 70, 158–61, 163–65.

The Crusades were a crucial series of events for both Europe and the Middle East. Scholars continue to debate exactly how much of Europe's Crusading efforts were truly religious, and how much motivated by other interests. Irrespective of this, the Crusades contributed to an expanding worldview for both Europeans and the peoples they encountered. Just as Westerners were learning about the Middle East, Middle Easterners were learning about Westerners.

In the mid-twelfth century C.E., a Syrian named Usamah Ibn-Muniqidh wrote a memoir about his life and times that included discussions of his experiences with Frankish (French) Crusaders. While other parts of his memoirs address his travels throughout Egypt and Lebanon and include a section eulogizing his father, it is his portrayal of the European Crusaders for which his work is most remembered.

A Moslem cavalier survives a Frankish thrust which cuts his heart vein.—I once witnessed in an encounter between us and the **Franks** one of our cavaliers, named Badi ibn-Talīl al-Qushayri, who was one of our brave men, receive in his chest, while clothes with only two pieces of garment, a lance thrust from a Frankish knight. The lance cut the vein in his chest and issued from his side. He turned back right away, but we never thought he would make his home alive. But as **Allah** (worthy of admiration is he!) had predestined, he survived and his wound was healed. But for one year after that, he could not sit up in case he was lying on his back unless somebody held him by the shoulders and helped him. At last what he suffered from entirely disappeared and he reverted to his old ways of living and riding. My only comment is: How mysterious are the works of him whose will is always executed among his creatures! He giveth life and he causeth death, but he is living and dieth not. In his hand is all good, and he is over all things potent.

An artisan dies from a needle prick.—We had once with us an artisan, 'Attab by name, who was one of the most corpulent and tall of men. He entered his home one day, and as he was sitting down he leaned on his hand against a robe which happened to be near him and in which there was a needle. The needle went through the palm of his hand and he died because of it. And, by Allah, as he moaned in the lower town, his moan could be heard from the citadel on account of the bulk of his body and the volume of his voice. This man dies of a needle, whereas al-Qushayri is pierced with a lance which penetrates through his chest and issues out of his side and yet suffers no harm!

A Shayzar woman captures three Franks.—The following will serve as an illustration of women's love of adventure:

A group of Frankish pilgrims, after making the pilgrimage, returned to Rafaniyyah, which at that time belonged to them. They then left it for Afamiyah. During the night they lost their way and landed in Shayzar, which at that time had no wall. They entered the city, numbering about seven or eight hundred men, women and children. The army of Shayzar had already gone out of the town in the company of my two uncles, 'Izz-al-Dīn abu-al-'Asakir Sultan and Fakhr-al-Dīn abu-Kamil Shafi' (may Allah's mercy rest upon their souls!), to meet two brides, whom my uncles had married, who were sisters and belonged to the banu-al-Sufi, the Aleppines. My father (may Allah's mercy rest upon his soul!) remained in the castle. One of our men, going out of the city at night on business, suddenly saw a Frank. He went back and got his sword, then went out and killed him. The battle cry sounded all over the town. The inhabitants went out, killed the Franks and took as booty all the women, children, silver and beasts of burden they had.

At that time there was in Shayzar a woman named Nadrah, daughter of Buzarmat, who was the wife of one of our men. This woman went out with our men, captured a Frank and introduced him into her house. She went out again, captured another Frank and brought him in. Again she went out and captured still another. Thus she had three Franks in her house. After taking as booty what they had and what suited her of their possessions, she went out and called some of her neighbors, who killed them.

During the same night my two uncles, with the army, arrived. Some of the Franks had taken to flight and were pursued by certain men from Shayzar, who killed them in the environs of the town. The horses of my uncles' army, on entering the town in the nighttime, began to stumble over corpses without knowing what they were stumbling over, until one of the cavaliers dismounted and saw the corpses in the darkness. This terrified our men, for they thought the town had been raided by surprise. In fact, it was booty which Allah (exalted and majestic is he!) had delivered into the hands of our people.

Prefers to be a Frankish shoemaker's wife to life in a Moslem castle.—A number of maids taken captive from the Franks were brought into the home of my father (may Allah's mercy rest upon his soul!). The Franks (may Allah's curse be upon them!) are an accursed race, the members of which do not assimilate except with their own kin. My father saw among them a pretty maid who was in the prime of youth, and said to his housekeeper, "Introduce this woman into the bath, repair her clothing and prepare her for a journey." This she did. He then delivered the maid to a servant of his and sent her to al-Amīr Shihab-al-Dīn Malik ibn-Salim, the lord of the Castle of Ja'bar, who was a friend of his. He also wrote him a letter, saying, "We have won some booty from the Franks, from which I am sending thee a share." The maid suited Shihab-al-Dīn, and he was pleased with her. He took her to himself and she bore him a boy, whom he called Badran. Badran's father named him his heir apparent, and he became of age. On his father's death, Badran became the governor of the town and its people, his mother being the real power. She entered into conspiracy with a band of men and let herself down from the castle by a rope. The band took her to Saruj, which belonged at that time to the Franks. There she married a Frankish shoemaker, while her son was the lord of the Castle of Ja'bar.

Their lack of sense.—Mysterious are the works of the Creator, the author of all things! When one comes to recount cases regarding the Franks, he cannot but glorify Allah (exalted is he!) and sanctify him, for he sees them as animals possessing the virtues of courage and fighting, but nothing else; just as animals have only the virtues of strength and carrying loads. I shall now give some instances of their doings and their curious mentality.

Newly arrived Franks are especially rough.—Everyone who is a fresh emigrant from the Frankish lands is ruder in character than those who have become acclimatized and have held long association with the Moslems.

Franks lack jealousy in sex affairs.—The Franks are void of all zeal and jealousy. One of them may be walking along with his wife. He meets another man who takes the wife by the hand and steps aside to converse with her while the husband is standing on one side waiting for his wife to conclude the conversation. If she lingers too long for him, he leaves her alone with the conversant and goes away.

Here is an illustration which I myself witnessed:

When I used to visit Nablus, I always took lodging with a man named Mu'izz, whose home was a lodging house for the Moslems. The house had windows which opened to the road, and there stood opposite to it on the other side of the road a house belonging to a Frank who sold wine for the merchants. He would take some wine in a bottle and go around announcing it by shouting, "So and so, the merchant, has just opened a cask full of this wine. He who wants to buy some of it will find it in such and such a place." The Frank's pay for the announcement made would be the wine in that bottle. One day this Frank went home and found a man with his wife in the same bed. He asked him, "What could have made thee enter into my wife's room?" The man replied, "I was tired, so I went in to rest." "But how," asked he, "didst thou get into my bed?" The other replied, "I found a bed that was spread, so I slept in it."

"But," said he, "my wife was sleeping together with thee!" The other replied, "Well, the bed is hers. How could I therefore have prevented her from using her own bed?" "By the truth of my religion," said the husband, "if thou shouldst do it again, thou and I would have a quarrel." Such was for the Frank the entire expression of his disapproval and the limit of his jealousy.

DOCUMENT ANALYSIS

1. Does the author seem to favor women using their abilities or not? Why?

_____

_____

_____

2. How diligently do the Frankish men work to keep their wives faithful, according to the author?

_____

_____

_____

3. How does the author view the Franks?

_____

_____

_____

4. Is there anything positive that the author recounts about the Franks?

_____

_____

_____

5. What is the character of the new arrivals from Frankish territory?

_____

_____

_____

DOCUMENT 10.1
Dandin, from *Tales of the Ten Princes* (500s)

Source: Dandin, *Tales of the Ten Princes*, in A. L. Basham, *The Wonder That Was India* (New York: Grove Press, 1954), pp. 444–6.

Much as Latin was long considered the "high" language of Christianity, the learned language of Hinduism is Sanskrit. Though few people could actually read it, scholars, intellectuals, and writers used it frequently in early India. One of the most well-known writers of Sanskrit literature in the early period was Dandin, who lived sometime in the late 500s to early 600s C.E.

Dandin's most noted work is Tales of the Ten Princes, *a collection of tales connected by an ongoing narrative. Focusing on the experiences of Prince Rajavahana, a Hindu prince, the tales are more secular than religious. Many of Dandin's tales tend to be sensual in nature, or deal with leading a virtuous life. Despite being written in a language that most Hindus could not understand, Dandin's stories provide quite a bit of detail about the lives and attitudes of common people. In this excerpt, Dandin uses his story to discuss the characteristics of the perfect wife.*

"In the land of the **Dravidians** is a city called Kañci. Therein dwelt the very wealthy son of a merchant, by name Saktikumara. When he was nearly eighteen he thought: 'There's no pleasure in living without a wife or with one of bad character. Now how can I find a really good one?' So, dubious of his chance of finding wedded bliss with a woman taken at the word of others, he became a fortune-teller, and roamed the land with a measure of unhusked rice tied in the skirts of his robe; and parents, taking him for an interpreter of birthmarks, showed their daughters to him. Whenever he saw a girl of his own class, whatever her birthmarks, he would say to her: 'My dear girl, can you cook me a good meal from this measure of rice?' And so, ridiculed and rejected, he wandered from house to house.

One day in the land of the Sibis, in a city on the banks of the Kaveri, he examined a girl who was shown to him by her nurse. She wore little jewellery, for her parents had spent their fortune, and had nothing left but their dilapidated mansion. As soon as he set eyes on her he thought: 'This girl is shapely and smooth in all her members. Not one limb is too fat or too thin, too short or too long. Her fingers are pink; her hands are marked with auspicious lines—the barleycorn, the fish, the lotus and the vase; her ankles are shapely; her feet are plump and the veins are not prominent; her thighs curve smoothly; her knees can barely be seen, for they merge into her rounded thighs; her buttocks are dimpled and round as chariot wheels; her navel is small, flat and deep; her stomach is adorned with three lines; the nipples stand out from her large breasts, which cover her whole chest; her palms are marked with signs which promise corn, wealth and sons; her nails are smooth and polished like jewels; her fingers are straight and tapering and pink; her arms curve sweetly from the shoulder, and are smoothly jointed; her slender neck is curved like a conch-shell; her lips are rounded and of even red; her pretty chin does not recede; her cheeks are round, full and firm; her eyebrows do not join above her nose, and are curved, dark and even; her nose is like a half-blown sesamum flower; her wide eyes are large and gentle and flash with three colours, black, white and brown; her brow is fair as the new moon; her curls are lovely as a mine of sapphires; her long ears are adorned doubly, with earrings and charming lotuses, hanging limply; her abundant hair is not brown, even at the tips, but long, smooth, glossy and fragrant. The character of such a girl cannot but correspond to her appearance, and my heart is fixed upon her, so I'll test her and marry her. For one regret after another is sure to fall on the heads of people who don't take precautions!' So, looking at her affectionately, he said, 'Dear girl, can you cook a good meal for me with this measure of rice?'

"Then the girl glanced at her old servant, who took the measure of rice from his hand and seated him on the veranda, which had been well sprinkled and swept, giving him water to cool his feet. Meanwhile the girl bruised the fragrant rice, dried it a little at a time in the sun, turned it repeatedly, and beat it with a hollow cane on a firm flat spot, very gently, so as to separate the grain without crushing the husk. Then she said to the nurse, 'Mother, goldsmiths can make good use of these husks for polishing jewellery. Take them, and, with the coppers you get for them, buy some firewood, not too green and not too dry, a small cooking pot, and two earthen dishes.'

"When this was done she put the grains of rice in a shallow wide-mouthed, round-bellied mortar, and took a long and heavy pestle of acacia-wood, its head shod with a plate of iron. . . . With skill and grace she exerted her arms, as the grains jumped up and down in the mortar. Repeatedly she stirred them and pressed them down with her fingers; then she shook the grains in a winnowing basket to remove the beard, rinsed them several times, worshipped the hearth, and placed them in water which had been five times brought to the boil. When the rice softened, bubbled and swelled, she drew the embers of the fire together, put a lid on the cooking pot, and strained off the gruel. Then she patted the rice with a ladle and scooped it out a little at a time; and when she found that it was thoroughly cooked she put the cooking pot on one side, mouth downward. Next she damped down those sticks which were not burnt through, and when the fire was quite out she sent them to the dealers to be sold as charcoal, saying, 'With the coppers that you get for them, buy as much as you can of green vegetables, ghee, curds, sesamum oil, myrobalans and tamarind.'

"When this was done she offered him a few savouries. Next she put the rice-gruel in a new dish immersed in damp sand, and cooled it with the soft breeze of a palm-leaf fan. She added a little salt, and flavoured it with the scent of the embers; she ground the myrobalans to a smooth powder, until they smelt like a lotus; and then, by the lips of the nurse, she invited him to take a bath. This he did, and when she too had bathed she gave him oil and myrobalans [as an unguent].

"After he had bathed he sat on a bench in the paved courtyard, which had been thoroughly sprinkled and swept. She stirred the gruel in the two dishes, which she set before him on a piece of pale green plantain leaf, cut from a tree in the courtyard. He drank it and felt rested and happy, relaxed in every limb. Next she gave him two ladlefuls of the boiled rice, served with a little ghee and condiments. She served the rest of the rice with curds, three spices, and fragrant and refreshing buttermilk and gruel. He enjoyed the meal to the last mouthful.

"When he asked for a drink she poured him water in a steady stream from the spout of a new pitcher—it was fragrant with incense, and smelt of fresh trumpet-flowers and the perfume of full-blown lotuses. He put the bowl to his lips, and his eyelashes sparkled with rosy drops as cool as snow; his ears delighted in the sound of the trickling water; his rough cheeks thrilled and tingled at its pleasant contact; his nostrils opened wide at its sweet fragrance; and his tongue delighted in its lovely flavour, as he drank the pure water in great gulps. Then, at his nod, the girl gave him a mouthwash in another bowl. The old woman took away the remains of his meal, and he slept awhile in his ragged cloak, on the pavement plastered with fresh cowdung.

"Wholly pleased with the girl, he married her with due rites, and took her home. Later he neglected her awhile and took a mistress, but the wife treated her as a dear friend. She served her husband indefatigably, as she would a god, and never neglected her household duties; and she won the loyalty of her servants by her great kindness. In the end her husband was so enslaved by her goodness that he put the whole household in her charge, made her sole mistress of his life and person, and enjoyed the three aims of life—virtue, wealth and love. So I maintain that virtuous wives make their lords happy and virtuous."

DOCUMENT ANALYSIS

1. According to Dandin, what sorts of attributes does an ideal wife possess?

_____

_____

_____

2. Do domestic activities appear to be a primary concern for Indian men? Why or why not?

_____

_____

_____

3. Does the author seem more concerned about the wife's moral nature or her physical appearance?

_____

_____

_____

4. Does this excerpt seem to paint a picture of a "typical" husband and wife relationship throughout much of history? Why or why not?

_____

_____

_____

5. What things does the husband in this excerpt do for his wife?

_____

_____

_____

DOCUMENT 10.2
Marco Polo on Chinese society under the Mongol rule (1270s)
Source: W. Marsden, trans., *The Travels of Marco Polo (1818)*; rendered into modern English by A. J. Andrea.

Marco Polo was the son of an Italian merchant who traveled the Silk Road to Mongol China in the year 1275. A gifted linguist and master of four languages, Marco Polo was appointed by emperor Kublai Khan as an official in the Privy Council in 1277 and for three years he was a tax inspector in Yanzhou, a city on the Grand Canal near the northeastern coast. He also visited Karakorum, the old capital of the original Mongol empire. Marco Polo stayed in Khan's court for seventeen years, acquiring great wealth in gold and jewelry.

Reportedly, Marco Polo kept a detailed dairy about his travels and his experiences in China. He recalled in great detail the moment when he and other members of his family first met the Emperor Kublai Khan: "They knelt before him and made obeisance with the utmost humility. The Great Khan bade them rise and received them honorably and entertained them with good cheer. He asked many questions about their condition and how they fared after their departure . . . Then they presented the privileges and letters which the Pope had sent, with which he was greatly pleased, and handed over the holy oil, which he received with joy and prized very highly."

Marco Polo's account of his life under the Mongols and his personal experience in China's Yuan Dynasty caused both curiosity and doubts among Westerners. Many questioned the validity of his records, wondering if he had ever reached China. The controversy led to a book in 1995 entitled Did Marco Polo Go to China? *by Frances Wood, head of Chinese Studies at the British Library. Wood argued that Marco Polo probably only went as far as Constantinople, where he gathered information on China from Arabs and Persians who returned from their China trip.*

It is their custom that the bodies of all deceased grand khans and other great lords from the family of Chinggis Khan are carried for internment to a great mountain called **Altai.** No matter where they might die, even if it is a hundred days' journey away, they nevertheless are brought here for burial. It is also their custom that, in the process of conveying the bodies of these princes, the escort party sacrifices whatever persons they happen to meet along the route, saying to them: "Depart for the next world and there serve your deceased master." They believe that all whom they kill in this manner will become his servants in the next life. They do the same with horses, killing all the best, so that the dead lord might use them in the next world. When the corpse of **Mongke** Khan was transported to this mountain, the horsemen who accompanied it slew upward of 20,000 people along the way.

Now that I have begun speaking about the **Tartars,** I will tell you more about them. They never remain fixed in one location. As winter approaches they move to the plains of a warmer region in order to find sufficient pasturage for their animals. In summer they inhabit cool regions in the mountains where there is water and grass and their animals are free of the annoyance of gad-flies and other biting insects. They spend two or three months progressively climbing higher and grazing as they ascend, because the grass is not sufficient in any one spot to feed their extensive herds.

Their huts, or tents, are circular and formed by covering a wooden frame with felt. These they transport on four-wheeled carts wherever they travel, since the framework is so well put together that it is light to carry. Whenever they set their huts up, the entrance always faces south. They also have excellent two-wheeled vehicles so well covered with black felt that, no matter how long it rains, rain never penetrates. These are drawn by oxen and camels and serve to carry their wives, children, and all necessary utensils and provisions.

It is the women who tend to their commercial concerns, buying and selling, and who tend to all the needs of their husbands and households. The men devote their time totally to hunting, hawking, and warfare. They have the best falcons in the world, as well as the best dogs. They subsist totally on meat and milk, eating the produce of their hunting, especially a certain small animal, somewhat like a hare, which our people call Pharaoh's rats, which are abundant on the steppes in summer. They likewise eat every manner of animal: horses, camels, even dogs, provided they are fat. They drink mare's milk, which they prepare in such a way that it has the qualities and taste of white wine. In their language they call it *kemurs*.

Their women are unexcelled in the world so far as their chastity and decency of conduct are concerned, and also in regard to their love and devotion toward their husbands. They regard marital infidelity as a vice which is not simply dishonorable but odious by its very nature. Even if there are ten or twenty women in a household, they live in harmony and highly praiseworthy concord, so that no offensive word is ever spoken. They devote full attention to their tasks and domestic duties, such as preparing the family's food, managing the servants, and caring for the children, whom they raise in common. The wives' virtues of modesty and chastity are all the more praiseworthy because the men are allowed to wed as many women as they please. The expense to the husband for his wives is not that great, but the benefit he derives from their trading and from the work in which they are constantly employed is considerable. For this reason, when he marries he pays a dowry to his wife's parents. The first wife holds the primary place in the household and is reckoned to be the husband's most legitimate wife, and this status extends to her children. Because of their unlimited number of wives, their offspring is more numerous than that of any other people. When a father dies, his son may take all of his deceased father's wives, with the exception of his own mother. They also cannot marry their sisters, but upon a brother's death they may marry their sisters-in-law. Every marriage is solemnized with great ceremony.

. . .

Their weapons are bows, iron maces, and in some instances, spears. The bow, however, is the weapon at which they are the most expert, being accustomed to use it in their sports from childhood. They wear armor made from the hides of buffalo and other beasts, fire-dried and thus hard and strong.

They are brave warriors, almost to the point of desperation, placing little value on their lives, and exposing themselves without hesitation to every sort of danger. They are cruel by nature. They are capable of undergoing every manner of privation, and when it is necessary, they can live for a month on the milk of their mares and the wild animals they catch. Their horses feed on grass alone and do not require barley or other grain. The men are trained to remain on horseback for two days and two nights without dismounting, sleeping in the saddle while the horse grazes. No people on the earth can surpass them in their ability to endure hardships, and no other people shows greater patience in the face of every sort of deprivation. They are most obedient to their chiefs, and are maintained at small expense. These qualities, which are so essential to a soldier's formation, make them fit to subdue the world, which in fact they have largely done.

When one of the great Tartar chiefs goes to war, he puts himself at the head of an army of 100,000 horsemen and organizes them in the following manner. He appoints an officer to command every ten men and others to command groups of 100, 1,000, and 10,000 men respectively. Thus ten of the officers who command ten men take their orders from an officer who commands 100; ten of these captains of a 100 take their orders from an officer in charge of a 1,000; and ten of these officers take orders from one who commands 10,000. By this arrangement, each officer has to manage only ten men or ten bodies of men. . . . When the army goes into the field, a body of 200 men is sent two days' march in advance, and parties are stationed on each flank and in the rear, to prevent surprise attack.

When they are setting out on a long expedition, they carry little with them. . . . They subsist for the most part on mare's milk, as has been said. . . . Should circumstances require speed, they can ride for ten days without lighting a fire or taking a hot meal. During this time they subsist on the blood drawn from their horses, each man opening a vein and drinking the blood. They also have dried milk. . . . When setting off on an expedition, each man takes about ten pounds. Every morning they put about half a pound of this into a leather flask, with as much water as necessary. As they ride, the motion violently shakes the contents, producing a thin porridge which they take as dinner. . . .

All that I have told you here concerns the original customs of the Tartar lords. Today, however, they are corrupted. Those who live in China have adopted the customs of the idol worshippers, and those who inhabit the eastern provinces have adopted the ways of the Muslims.

DOCUMENT ANALYSIS

1. Could Marco Polo tell the difference between Chinese culture and Mongol traditions?

_____

_____

_____

2. How Chinese was the Mongol governor in his perspective and his rule?

_____

_____

_____

3. How different or similar are the views of the Mongol governor and Marco Polo concerning the Mongol Empire?

_____

_____

_____

4. To what can you attribute the success of the Mongol rule in China?

_____

_____

_____

DOCUMENT 11.1
Xicohtencatl the Elder, "I Say This" (15th–16th c. C.E.)
Source: Xicohtencatl, the Elder, "I Say This," in *Fifteen Poets of the Aztec World*, ed. Miguel Leon-Portilla
(Norman, OK: University of Oklahoma Press, 1992), pp. 239–40.

*Xicohtencatl, the Elder, was Lord of Tizatlan. He was also a composer of songs. What is known is that he was born in about 1425 and lived until 1522 C.E., after the arrival of the Spanish. Xicohtencatl was also a warrior. It is said he took part in important battles and conquests involving the Mexicas (Aztecs), but in the end Xicohtencatl was forced to come to an agreement making Tizatlan an ally of other chiefdoms in the lake region near Mexico-***Tenochtitlán.***

Warfare for these people, in this era, had very specific rules. A field needed to be marked, and the battle could not go beyond its boundaries. The battles provided an opportunity for sons of lords to practice warfare, but they could not attempt to gain land for chiefdoms out of the war. The warriors captured would be sacrificed to the gods.

Warfare was about the political ambitions of the combatants and brought out the Mexican "worldview" that they were the chosen people of Huitzelopochi, the god of war. Xicohtencatl made a decision to take advantage of the arrival of the Spanish to aid in his fight against surrounding chiefdoms. However, the Spanish were ultimately not interested in helping native groups, but in conquering them.

*The ***Flowery Wars*** *tells of the past struggles of the people of Tlazcala (the wider confederacy of cities of which Tizatlan was a part). The poem speaks to the value of war in the life of Tlazcala, because "flowery war" is sacred war. However, there is irony in telling the glory of wars that eventually, with the coming of the Spanish, brought doom to the people of Tlazcala.*

I say this, I the lord Xicohtencatl:
Do not go forth in vain!
Take up your shield, the vessel of flowery water!
Your little bowl with a handle.
Your precious vessel, color of obsidian, stands upright,
with it, we will bring the water on our shoulders,
we will carry it there in Mexico,
from Chapolco, on the shore of the lake.

Do not go forth in vain,
my nephew, my little children, my nephews,
you, children of the water!
I make the water flow,

O Lord Cuauhtencoztli,
let us all go!

We will bring the water on our shoulders,
truly we are going to carry it!

Captain Motelchiuhtzin wants to announce it,
my friends!
He says it is not yet dawn.
We take up our burden of water:
crystal clear, precious, color of turquoise,
which moves in waves.
Thus you will come there, to the place of the vessels,
do not go forth in vain!

Nanahuatl [the god] will perhaps make noise there.
My little son!
You, leader of men, you, precious creature,
a painting with gold in the Toltec manner,
paint the precious bowl, Lord Axayacatl.
We go together to partake,
we approach the precious waters.
They are falling, drops rain down,
there, close to the small canals.

He who carries my flowery water, Huanitzin,
now comes to give it to me,
O my uncles, Tlaxcalans, Chichimecs!
Do not go forth in vain!

The flowery war, the shield's flower,
have opened their corollas.
They resound,
the sweet-smelling flowers rain down,
Thus perhaps for this,
he came to conceal gold and silver;
for this I take the painted books.
O my little canal, with my vessel the water flows!
O my old ones!

DOCUMENT ANALYSIS

1. Both documents refer to the "field." What is the significance? Why would there be a specific place for warfare?

_____

_____

_____

2. How do the documents speak of the warriors?

_____

_____

_____

3. How do you see the place of warfare in the life of a people? Would it have been the most important thing in a communityís life? What does it tell us about the overall culture?

_____

_____

_____

4. What is the relationship of the gods to the warriors? What part do the gods play in war?

_____

_____

_____

5. What is the significance of flowers? What is the connection between flowers and warfare?

_____

_____

_____

DOCUMENT 11.2

Anonymous Aztec (mid-1500s), "The Midwife Addresses the Woman Who Has Died in Childbirth"

Source: "The Midwife Addresses the Woman Who Has Died in Childbirth," trans. John Bierhorst in Nahuatl (1994).

The Florentine Codex was one of several permanent records of Aztec culture. Like other codices, the Florentine Codex was written down by the Spanish, who had Aztec elders tell them the stories of the Aztec people. It is known as the General History of the Things of New Spain.

In Aztec culture, the parents of a married couple who are expecting a child choose a midwife for the pregnant mother. After some ritualistic protests, the midwife accepts the task of delivering the child and assumes care of the expectant mother. The midwife and the woman prepare for the birth. The midwife prepares the "flower house," or birthing room. The expectant woman is urged to be like Cihuacoatl Quilaztli, source of the human race, and bring forth another human in, to the world. The woman is also likened to a warrior in battle.

If the woman successfully gives birth, she is addressed as a great warrior, but reminded to be humble. She should respect the Creator who gives life and takes it away. If she dies in childbirth, she is spoken of as one of the great warriors in the sky. She will become one of the women who accept the sun at midday and lead it down to the west.

In the document that follows, the midwife addresses a woman who has died in childbirth. We see that the midwife treats the woman as a god. She prays to the woman, who lies silent in death in front of her.

Precious feather, child,
Eagle woman, dear one,
Dove, daring daughter,
You have labored, you have toiled,
Your task is finished.
You came to the aid of your Mother, the noble lady, Cihuacoatl Quilaztli.
You received, raised up, and held the shield, the little buckler that she laid in your hands: she your Mother, the noble lady, Cihuacoatl Quilaztli.
Now wake! Rise! Stand up!
Comes the daylight, the daybreak:
Dawn's house has risen crimson, it comes up standing.
The crimson swifts, the crimson swallows, sing,
And all the crimson swans are calling.
Get up, stand up! Dress yourself!
Go! Go seek the good place, the perfect place, the home of your Mother,
your Father, the Sun,
The place of happiness, joy,
Delight, rejoicing.
Go! Go follow your Mother, your Father, the Sun.
May his elder sisters bring you to him: they the exalted, the celestial women,
who always and forever know happiness, joy, delight, and rejoicing, in the company and in the presence of our Mother, our Father, the Sun; who make him happy with their shouting.
My child, darling daughter, lady,
You spent yourself, you labored manfully:
You made yourself a victor, a warrior for Our Lord, though not without consuming all your strength; you sacrificed yourself.
Yet you earned a compensation, a reward: a good, perfect, precious death.
By no means did you die in vain.
And are you truly dead? You have made a sacrifice. Yet how else could you have become worthy of what you now deserve?
You will live forever, you will be happy, you will rejoice in the company and in the presence of our holy ones, the exalted women. Farewell, my daughter, my child. Go be with them, join them. Let them hold you and take you in.
May you join them as they cheer him and shout to him: our Mother, our Father, the Sun;
And may you be with them always, whenever they go in their rejoicing.

But my little child, my daughter, my lady,
You went away and left us, you deserted us, and we are but old men and old women.
You have cast aside your mother and your father.
Was this your wish? No, you were summoned, you were called.
Yet without you, how can we survive?
How painful will it be, this hard old age?
Down what alleys or in what doorways will we perish?
Dear lady, do not forget us! Remember the hardships that we see, that we suffer, here on earth:
The heat of the sun presses against us; also the wind, icy and cold:
This flesh, this clay of ours, is starved and trembling. And we, poor prisoners of our stomachs! There is nothing we can do.
Remember us, my precious daughter, O eagle woman, O lady!
You lie beyond in happiness. In the good place, the perfect place,
You live.
In the company and in the presence of our lord,
You live.
You as living flesh can see him, you as living flesh can call to him.
Pray to him for us!
Call to him for us!
This is the end,
We leave the rest to you.

DOCUMENT ANALYSIS

1. How does the midwife address the woman who has just died?

_____

_____

_____

2. How does the midwife describe life for those left behind?

_____

_____

_____

3. How does the midwife describe what it will be like in "the good place"?

_____

_____

_____

4. How is the woman like a warrior?

_____

_____

_____

5. What evidence of Aztec theology is evident in this song?

_____

_____

_____

DOCUMENT 12.1
Gianfrancesco Morosini, "Turkey Is a Republic of Slaves" (late 16th c.)

Source: Gianfrancensco Morosini, "Turkey Is a Republic of Slaves," in *Pursuit of Power: Venetian Ambassadors' Reports on Spain, Turkey, and France in the Age of Phillip II, 1560–1600* (New York: Torchbook/Harper and Row, 1970), pp. 127–9, 131–4.

Constantinople was conquered in 1453 by the Ottoman Empire. The city was renamed Istanbul and was soon on its way back to the greatness it had enjoyed during the height of the Byzantine Empire. Indeed, just as the city had been the cultural, intellectual, and political heart for the Byzantines, so, too, would it be for the Ottoman Empire.

But, in many ways, the history of the Ottoman Empire was of a quick, decisive rise to power followed by a long, steady decline. Even by the seventeenth century, European observers (who admittedly tended to be biased against Muslim institutions anyway) were noticing signs of decay and weakness. One such individual was a Venetian ambassador to Istanbul, who was in Turkey during the 1580s. His reports Gianfrancesco Morosini not only discuss the organization of the military and the government, but also provide a European view of the perceived strengths and weaknesses of the Turkish people. These and other dispatches also describe the Turkish capital.

They succeed to the throne without any kind of ceremony of election or coronation. According to Turkish law of succession, which resembles most countries' laws in this respect, the oldest son should succeed to the throne as soon as the father dies. But in fact, whichever of the sons can first enter the royal compound in Constantinople is called the sultan and is obeyed by the people and by the army. Since he has control of his father's treasure he can easily gain the favor of the janissaries and with their help control the rest of the army and the civilians.

Because this government is based on force, the brother who overcomes the others is considered the lord of all. The same obedience goes to a son who can succeed in overthrowing his father, a thing which bothers the Turks not at all. As a result, when his sons are old enough to bear arms, the sultan generally does not allow them near him, but sends them off to some administrative district where they must live under continual suspicion until their father's death. And just as the fathers do not trust their own sons, the sons do not trust their fathers and are always afraid of being put to death. This is the sad consequence of unbridled ambition and hunger for power—a miserable state of affairs where there is no love between father and sons, and much less between sons and father.

This lord has thirty-seven kingdoms covering enormous territory. His dominion extends to the three principal parts of the world, Africa, Asia, and Europe; and since these lands are joined and contiguous with each other, he can travel for a distance of eight thousand miles on a circuit through his empire and hardly need to set foot in another prince's territories.

The principal cities of the Turks are Constantinople, **Adrianople,** and Bursa, the three royal residence places of the sultans. Buda is also impressive, as are the Asian cities—Cairo, Damascus, Aleppo, Bagdad and others—but none of these have the things which usually lend beauty to cities. Even Constantinople, the most important of them all, which is posted in the most beautiful and enchanting situation that can be imagined, still lacks those amenities that a great city should have, such as beautiful streets, great squares, and handsome palaces. Although Constantinople has many mosques, royal palaces, inns, and public baths, the rest of the city is mazy and filthy; even these [public buildings], with their leaded domes studded with gilded bronze ornaments, only beautify the long-distance panorama of the city.

The security of the empire depends more than anything else on the large numbers of land and sea forces which the Turks keep continually under arms. These are what make them feared throughout the world.

The sultan always has about 280,000 well-paid men in his service. Of them about 80,000 are paid every three months out of his personal treasury. These include roughly 16,000 janissaries, who form the Grand Signor's advance guard; six legions, or about 12,000 cavalry called "spahi," who serve as his rear guard; and about 1,500 other defenders. . . . The other 200,000 cavalry . . . are not paid with money like the others, but are assigned landholdings [called timars].

The timariots are in no way inferior as fighting men to the soldiers paid every three months with cash, because the timars are inherited like the fiefs distributed by Christian rulers.

What about the fighting qualities of these widely feared Turkish soldiers? I can tell you the opinion I formed at Scutari, where I observed the armies of Ferrad Pasha and Osman Pasha (Ferrad's army was there for more than a month, and Osman's for a matter of weeks). I went over to Scutari several times to confer with the two pashas and also, unofficially, to look at the encampment, and I walked through the whole army and carefully observed every detail about the caliber of their men, their weapons, and the way they organize a bivouac site and fortify it. I think I can confidently offer this conclusion: they rely more on large numbers and obedience than they do on organization and courage.

Although witnesses who saw them in earlier times claim they are not as good as they used to be, it appears that the janissaries are still the best of the Turkish soldiers. They are well-made men, and they can handle their weapons—the arquebus, club, and scimitar—quite well. These men are accustomed to hardships, but they are only used in battle in times of dire necessity.

As for the cavalry, some are lightly armed with fairly weak lances, huge shields, and scimitars.

If I compare these men with Christian soldiers, such as those I saw in the wars in France or in the Christian King's conquest of Portugal, I would say they are much better than Christian soldiers in respect to obedience and discipline. However, in courage and enthusiasm, and in physical appearance and weapons, they are distinctly inferior.

The naval forces which the Great Turk uses to defend his empire are vast and second to none in the world. . . . True, at present they do not have at hand all the armaments they would need to outfit the as yet uncompleted galleys, . . . But his resources are so great that if he wanted to he could quickly assemble what he needs; he has already begun to attend to this.

DOCUMENT ANALYSIS

1. From the document, how does it appear that a new king is selected in the Ottoman Empire?

_____

_____

_____

2. How does the author evaluate the Ottoman army?

_____

_____

_____

3. Is Constantinople considered an attractive city by the author?

_____

_____

_____

4. What are the three principal Turkish cities?

_____

_____

_____

5. Would you consider this a positive or a negative account? Why?

_____

_____

_____

DOCUMENT 13.1
Ieyasu Tokugawa, "Closed Country Edict of 1635" and "Exclusion of the Portuguese, 1639" (1630s)
Source: *Japan: A Documentary History,* trans. and ed. David John Lu (Armonk, NY: M. E. Sharpe, 1997).

Ieyasu Tokugawa was granted the title of shogun in 1603 after defeating his rivals by using guns brought into Japan by the Europeans. His successors, however, began to fear that the growing trade with the West and influence of Christianity would directly challenge the Japanese value system. Below are two major shogun edicts intended to force foreign trade and missionaries out of Japan. Japan remained an isolated country for the next two hundred years, until the Americans tried to open relations with Japan in 1853.

CLOSED COUNTRY EDICT OF 1635

1. Japanese ships are strictly forbidden to leave for foreign countries.

2. No Japanese is permitted to go abroad. If there is anyone who attempts to do so secretly, he must be executed. The ship so involved must be impounded and its owner arrested, and the matter must be reported to the higher authority.

3. If any Japanese returns from overseas after residing there, he must be put to death.

4. If there is any place where the teachings of padres is practiced, the two of you must order a thorough investigation.

5. Any informer revealing the whereabouts of the followers of padres must be rewarded accordingly. If anyone reveals the whereabouts of a high ranking padre, he must be given one hundred pieces of silver. For those of lower ranks, depending on the deed, the reward must be set accordingly.

6. If a foreign ship has an objection [to the measures adopted] and it becomes necessary to report the matter to **Edo**, you may ask the **Omura** domain to provide ships to guard the foreign ship. . . .

7. If there are any **Southern Barbarians** who propagate the teachings of padres, or otherwise commit crimes, they may be incarcerated in the prison. . . .

8. All incoming ships must be carefully searched for the followers of padres.

9. No single trading city shall be permitted to purchase all the merchandise brought by foreign ships.

10. Samurai are not permitted to purchase any goods originating from foreign ships directly from Chinese merchants in Nagasaki.

11. After a list of merchandise brought by foreign ships is sent to Edo, as before you may order that commercial dealings may take place without waiting for a reply from Edo.

12. After settling the price, all white yarns brought by foreign ships shall be allocated to the five trading cities and other quarters as stipulated.

13. After settling the price of white yarns, other merchandise [brought by foreign ships] may be traded freely between the [licensed] dealers. However, in view of the fact that Chinese ships are small and cannot bring large consignments, you may issue orders of sale at your discretion. Additionally, payment for goods purchased must be made within twenty days after the price is set.

14. The date of departure homeward of foreign ships shall not be later than the twentieth day of the ninth month. Any ships arriving in Japan later than usual shall depart within fifty days of their arrival. As to the departure of Chinese ships, you may use your discretion to order their departure after the departure of the Portuguese *galeota.*

15. The goods brought by foreign ships which remained unsold may not be deposited or accepted for deposit.

16. The arrival in Nagasaki of representatives of the five trading cities shall not be later than the fifth day of the seventh month. Anyone arriving later than that date shall lose the quota assigned to his city.

17. Ships arriving in Hirado must sell their raw silk at the price set in Nagasaki, and are not permitted to engage in business transactions until after the price is established in Nagasaki.

You are hereby required to act in accordance with the provisions set above. It is so ordered.

EXCLUSION OF THE PORTUGUESE, 1639

1. The matter relating to the proscription of Christianity is known [to the Portuguese]. However, heretofore they have secretly transported those who are going to propagate that religion.

2. If those who believe in that religion band together in an attempt to do evil things, they must be subjected to punishment.

3. While those who believe in the preaching of padres are in hiding, there are incidents in which that country [Portugal] has sent gifts to them for their sustenance.

In view of the above, hereafter entry by the Portuguese galeota is forbidden. If they insist on coming [to Japan], the ships must be destroyed and anyone aboard those ships must be beheaded. We have received the above order and are thus transmitting it to you accordingly.

The above concerns our disposition with regard to the galeota.

Memorandum

With regard to those who believe in Christianity, you are aware that there is a proscription, and thus knowing, you are not permitted to let padres and those who believe in their preaching to come aboard your ships. If there is any violation, all of you who are aboard will be considered culpable. If there is anyone who hides the fact that he is a Christian and boards your ship, you may report it to us. A substantial reward will be given to you for this information.

This memorandum is to be given to those who come on Chinese ships. [A similar note to the Dutch ships.]

DOCUMENT ANALYSIS

1. How would these two edicts affect Japan's relations with the outside world?

_____

_____

_____

2. What was the argument behind the shogun's decision of 1639 to expel the Christians?

_____

_____

_____

3. What was the primary purpose of the 1635 Edict?

_____

_____

_____

4. What were the major restrictions imposed upon the Japanese?

_____

_____

_____

5. What were the major restrictions on foreign traders?

_____

_____

_____

DOCUMENT 14.1
Giorgio Vasari, from "Life of Leonardo Da Vinci" (1550)

This description of Leonardo barely does justice to its brilliant subject. Da Vinci gave meaning to the phrase "Renaissance Man." He was an artist, a scientist, an inventor par excellence. This short piece was written by Vasari, a contemporary of Leonardo, and a keen observer of Renaissance Rome. It is believed that Vasari actually coined the term "renaissance."

The richest gifts are occasionally seen to be showered, as by celestial influence, upon certain human beings; nay, they sometimes supernaturally and marvelously congregate in a single person,—beauty, grace, and talent being united in such a manner that to whatever the man thus favored may turn himself, his every action is so divine as to leave all other men far behind him. This would seem manifestly to prove that he has been specially endowed by the hand of God himself, and has not obtained his preeminence through human teaching or the powers of man.

This was perceived and acknowledged by all men in the case of Leonardo da Vinci, in whom (to say nothing of his beauty of person, which yet was such that it has never been sufficiently extolled) there was a grace beyond expression, which was manifest without thought or effort in every act and deed, and who had besides so rare a gift of talent and ability that to whatever subject he turned his attention, no matter how difficult, he presently made himself absolute master of it.

In him extraordinary power was combined with remarkable facility, a mind of regal boldness and magnanimous daring. His gifts were such that the celebrity of his name was spread abroad, and he was held in the highest estimation not only in his own time but also, and even to a greater degree, after his death,—nay, he has continued, and will continue, to be held in the highest esteem by all succeeding generations.

Truly remarkable, indeed, and divinely endowed was Leonardo da Vinci. He was the son of Ser Piero da Vinci. He would without doubt have made great progress in learning and knowledge of the sciences had he not been so versatile and changeful. The instability of his character led him to undertake many things which having commenced he afterwards abandoned. In arithmetic, for example, he made such rapid progress in the short time that he gave his attention to it, that he often confounded the master who was teaching him by the perpetual doubts that he started and by the difficult questions that he proposed.

He also commenced the study of music, and resolved to acquire the art of playing the lute, when, being by nature of an exalted imagination and full of the most graceful vivacity, he sang to the instrument most divinely, improvising at once both the verse and the music.

[Verocchio, an esteemed artist of the period, upon seeing some of the drawings which Leonardo had made, gladly agreed to take him into his shop.] Thither the boy resorted with the utmost readiness, and not only gave his attention to one branch of art but to all those of which design makes a portion. Endowed with such admirable intelligence and being also an excellent geometrician, Leonardo not only worked in sculpture but in architecture; likewise he prepared various designs for ground plans and the construction of entire buildings. He too it was who, while only a youth, first suggested the formation of a canal from Pisa to Florence by means of certain changes to be effected in the river Arno. Leonardo likewise made designs for mills, fulling machines, and other engines which were run by water. But as he had resolved to make painting his profession, he gave the greater part of his time to drawing from nature.

DOCUMENT ANALYSIS

1. To what does Vasari attribute da Vinci's talents?

_____

_____

_____

2. For many, Leonardo da Vinci embodies the idea of the multi-talented Renaissance man. According to Vasari, in what areas did da Vinci excel?

_____

_____

_____

DOCUMENT 14.2
Dante, from *The Divine Comedy* (1321)

Dante Alighieri's long narrative poem, The Divine Comedy, describes the author's imaginary journeys through hell (Inferno), purgatory (Purgatorio), and heaven (Paradiso). It is considered to be one of the great works of Western literature and it assured its author of celebrity status in Renaissance Italy. Here is a brief excerpt from the Paradiso.

II. Humanism

We were still a little distant from it, yet not so far that I could not partially discern that honorable folk possessed that place. "O thou that honorest both science and art, these, who are they, that have such honor that from the condition of the others it sets them apart?" and he to me, "The honorable fame of them which resounds above in thy life wins grace in heaven that so advances them." At this a voice was heard by me, "Honor the loftiest Poet! His shade returns that was departed." When the voice had ceased and was quiet, I saw four great shades coming to us: they had a semblance neither sad nor glad. The good Master [Virgil] began to say, "Look at him with that sword in hand who cometh before the three, even as lord. He is Homer, the sovereign poet; the next who comes is Horace, the satirist; Ovid is the third, and the last is Lucan. Since each shares with me the name that the solitary voice sounded, they dome honor, and in that do well."

Thus I saw assembled the fair school of that Lord of the loftiest song which above the others as an eagle flies. After they had discoursed somewhat together, they turned to me with sign of salutation; and my Master smiled thereat. And fat more of honor yet they did me, for they made me of their band, so that I was the sixth amid so much wit. Thus we went on

as far as the light, speaking things concerning which silence is becoming, even as was speech there where I was.

We came to the foot of a noble castle, seven times circled by high walls, defended roundabout by a fair streamlet. This we passed as if hard ground; through seven gates I entered with these sages; we came to a meadow of fresh verdure. People were there with eyes slow and grave, of great authority in their looks; they spake seldom and with soft voices. Thus we drew apart, on one side, into a place open, luminous, and high, so that they all could be seen. There opposite upon the green enamel were shown to me the great spirits, whom to have seen I inwardly exalt myself.

I saw Electra with many companions, among whom I knew Hector and Æneas, Cæsar in armor, with his gerfalcon eyes; I saw Camilla and Pentheliea on the other side, and I saw the King Latinus, who was seated with Lavinia, his daughter. I saw that Brutus who drove out Tarquin; Lucretia, Julia, Marcia, and Cornelia; and alone, apart, I saw the Saladin. When I raised my brow a little more, I saw the Master of those who know, seated amid the philosophic family; all regard him, all do him honor. Here I saw both Socrates and Plato, who before the others stand nearest to him; Democritus, who ascribes the world to chance; Diogenes, Anaxagoras, and Thales, Empedocles, Heraclitus, and Zeno; and I saw the good collector of the qualities, Dioscorides, I mean; and I saw Orpheus, Tully, and Linus, and moral Seneca, Euclid the geometer, and Ptolemy, Hippocrates, Avicenna, Galen, and Averroës, who made the great comment. I cannot report of all in full, because the long theme so drives me that many times speech comes short of fact.

DOCUMENT ANALYSIS

1. What does this selection tell us about Dante's views regarding humanism?

_____

_____

_____

2. Who is Dante talking about when he refers to "the Master of those who know"? Who does Dante place around the Master?

_____

_____

_____

DOCUMENT 15.1
James I, "The Divine Right of Kings" (1616)

From *The Political Works of James I*, reprinted from the edition of 1616 with an introduction by Charles Howard McIlwain
(Cambridge, Mass.: Harvard University Press, 1918), pp. 53–70.

James Stuart (James VI of Scotland, 1567–1625; James I of England, 1603–1625) was an intellectual who was rarely able to implement his ideas. He had hoped to unify England, Scotland, and Ireland, but was thwarted by both political realities and his own personal failings. He sought to ease international tensions, but his efforts to prevent the conflict that would become the Thirty Years' War were unsuccessful. The outbreak of the Thirty Years' War also destroyed his hope of brokering a European religious compromise. In addition to his duties as monarch, James I wrote on a variety of topics. His most famous work, the True Law of a Free Monarchy, is a classic argument for divine-right monarchy. Interestingly, although James penned this work in 1598, before he assumed the throne of England, he never tried to implement divine-right rule in England. He firmly believed that his power and authority derived solely from God, but acknowledged that as king of England, he had sworn oaths to govern according to the "laws and customs of England."

As there is not a thing so necessarie to be knowne by the people of any land, next the knowledge of their God, as the right knowledge of their alleageance, according to the forme of governement established among them, especially in a Monarchie (which forme of government, as resembling the Divinitie, approacheth nearest to perfection, as all the learned and wise men from the beginning have agreed upon; Unitie being the perfection of all things,) So hath the ignorance, and (which is worse) the seduced opinion of the multitude blinded by them, who thinke themselves able to teach and instruct the ignorants, procured the wracke and overthrow of sundry flourishing Common-wealths; and heaped heavy calamities, threatening utter destruction upon others. And the smiling successe, that unlaw rebellions have oftentimes had against Princes in ages past (such hath bene the misery, and the iniquitie of the time) hath by way of practise strengthened many of their errour: albeit there cannot be a more deceivable argument; then to judge by the justnesse of the cause by the event thereof; as hereafter shall be proved more at length. And among others, no Common-wealth, that ever hath bene since the beginning, hath had greater need of the trew knowledge of this ground, then this our so long disordered, and distracted Common-wealth hath: the misknowledge hereof being the onely spring, from whence have flowed so many endlesse calamities, miseries, and confusions, as is better felt by many, then the cause thereof well knowne, and deeply considered. The naturall zeale therefore, that I beare to this my native countrie, with the great pittie I have to see the so-long disturbance thereof for lack of the trew knowledge of this ground (as I have said before) hath compelled me at last to breake silence, to discharge my conscience to you my deare country men herein, that knowing the ground from whence these your many endlesse troubles have proceeded, as well as ye have already too-long tasted the bitter fruites thereof, ye may by knowledge, and eschewing of the cause escape, and divert the lamentable effects that ever necessarily follow thereupon. I have chosen the onely to set downe in this short Treatise, the trew grounds of the mutuall deutie, and alleageance betwixt a free and absolute Monarche, and his people.

First then, I will set downe the trew grounds, whereupon I am to build, out of the Scriptures, since Monarchie is the trew paterne of Divinitie, as I have already said: next, from the fundamental Lawes of our own Kingdome, which nearest must concerne us: thirdly, from the law of Nature, by divers similitudes drawne out of the same.

By the Law of Nature the King becomes a naturall Father to all his Lieges at his Coronation: And as the Father of his fatherly duty is bound to care for the nourishing, education, and vertuous government of his children; even so is the king bound to care for all his subjects. As all the toile and paine that the father can take for his children, will be thought light and well bestowed by him, so that the effect thereof redound to their profite and weale; so ought the Prince to doe towards his people. As the kindly father ought to foresee all inconvenients and dangers that may arise towards his children, and though with the hazard of his owne person presse to prevent the same; so ought the King towards his people. As the fathers wrath and correction upon any of his children that offendeth, ought to be by a fatherly chastisement seasoned with pitie, as long as there is any hope of amendment in them; so ought the King towards any of his Lieges that offend in that measure. And shortly, as the Fathers chiefe joy ought to be in procuring his childrens welfare, rejoycing at their weale, sorrowing and pitying at their evil, to hazard for their safetie, travell for their rest, wake for their sleepe; and in a word, to thinke that his earthly felicitie and life standeth and liveth more in them, nor in himself; so ought a good Prince thinke of his people.

As to the other branch of this mutuall and reciprock band, is the duety and alleageance that the Lieges owe to their King: the ground whereof, I take out of the words of Samuel, dited by Gods Spirit, when God had given him commandement to heare the peoples voice in choosing and annointing them a King. And because that place of Scripture being well understood, is so pertinent for our purpose, I have insert herein the very words of the Text.

10. So Samuel tolde all the wordes of the Lord unto the people that asked a King of him.

11. And he said, this shall be the maner of the King that shall raigne over you: hee will take your sonnes, and appoint them to his Charets, and to be his horsemen, and some shall runne before his Charet.

12. Also, hee will make them his captaines over thousands, and captaines over fifties, and to eare his ground, and to reape his harvest, and to make instruments of warre and the things that serve for his charets:

13. Hee will also take your daughters, and make them Apothicaries, and Cookes, and Bakers.

14. And hee will take your fields, and your vineyards, and your best Olive trees, and give them to his servants.

15. And hee will take the tenth of your seed, and of your Vineyards, and give it to his Eunuches, and to his servants.

16. And hee will take your men servants, and your maid-servants, and the chief of your young men, and your asses, and put them to his worke.

17. Hee will take the tenth of your sheepe: and ye shall be his servants.

18. And ye shall cry out at that day, because of your King, whom ye have chosen you: and the Lord God will not heare you at that day.

19. But the people would not heare the voice of Samuel, but did say: Nay, but there shalbe a King over us.

20. And we also will be all like other Nations, and our King shall judge us, and goe out before us, and fight out battles.

As likewise, although I have said, a good king will frame all his actions to be according to the Law; yet is hee not bound thereto but of his good will, and for good example—giving to his subjects: For as in the law of abstaining from eating of flesh in Lenton, the king will, for examples sake, make his owne house to observe the Law; yet no man will thinke he needs to take a licence to eate flesh. And although by our Lawes, the bearing and wearing of hag-buts, and pistolets be forbidden, yet no man can find any fault in the King, for causing his traine use them in any raide upon the Borderers, or other malefactours or rebellious subjects. So as I have alreadie said, a good King, although hee be above the Law, will subject and frame his actions thereto, for examples sake to his subjects, and of his owne free-will, but not as subject or bound thereto.

And the agreement of the Law of nature in this our ground with the Lawes and constitutions of God, and man, already alleged, will by two similitudes easily appeare. The King towards his people is rightly compared to a father of children, and to a head of a body composed of divers members: For as fathers, the good Princes, and Magistrates of the people of God acknowledged themselves to their subjects. And for all other well ruled Common-wealths, the stile of Pater patriae was ever, and is commonly used to Kings. And the proper office of a King towards his Subjects, agrees very wel with the office of the head towards the body, and all members thereof: For from the head, being the seate of Judgement, proceedeth the care and foresight of guiding, and preventing all evill that may come to the body, so doeth the King for his people. As the discourse and direction flowes from the head, and the execution according thereunto belongs to the rest of the members, every one according to their office: so it is betwixt a wise Prince, and his people. As the judgement coming from the head may not onely imploy the members, every one in their owne office, as long as they are able for it; but likewise in case any of them be affected with any infirmitie must care and provide for their remedy, in-case it be curable, and if otherwise, gar cut them off for feare of infecting of the rest: even so is it betwixt the Prince, and his people. And as there is ever hope of curing any diseased member of the direction of the head, as long as it is whole; but by contrary, if it be troubled, all the members are partakers of that paine, so is it betwixt the Prince and his people.

And now first for the fathers part (whose naturally love to his children I described in the first part of this my discourse, speaking of the dutie that Kings owe to their Subjects) consider, I pray you what duetie his children owe to him, & whether upon any pretext whatsoever, it wil not be thought monstrous and unnaturall to his sons, to rise up against him, to control him at their appetite, and when they thinke good to sley him, or to cut him off, and adopt to themselves any other they please in his roome: Or can any pretence of wickedness or rigor on his part be a just excuse for his children to put hand into him? And although wee see by the course of nature, that love useth to descend more than to ascend, in case it were trew, that the father hated and wronged the children never so much, will any man, endued with the least sponke of reason, thinke it lawful for them to meet him with the line? Yea, suppose the father were furiously following his sonnes with a drawen sword, is it lawful for them to turne and strike againe, or make any resistance but by flight? I thinke surely, if there were no more but the example of bruit beasts & unreasonable creatures, it may serve well enough to qualifie and prove this my argument. We reade often the pietie that the Storkes have to their olde and decayed parents: And generally wee know, that there are many sorts of beasts and fowles, that with violence and many bloody strokes will beat and banish their yong ones from them, how soone they perceive them to be able to fend themselves; but wee never read or heard of any resistance on their part, except among the vipers; which prooves such persons, as ought to be reasonable creatures, and yet unnaturally follow this example, to be endued with their viperous nature.

And it is here likewise to be noted, that the duty and alleageance, which the people sweareth to their prince, is not bound to themselves, but likewise to their lawfull heires and posterity, the lineall to their lawfull heires and posterity, the lineall succession of crownes being begun among the people of God, and happily continued in divers Christian commonwealths: So as no objection either of heresie, or whatsoever private statute or law may free the people from their oathgiving to their king, and his succession, established by the old fundamentall lawes of the kingdom: For, as hee is their heritable over-lord, and so by birth, not by any right in the coronation, commeth to his crowne; it is a like unlawful (the crowne ever standing full) to displace him that succeedeth thereto, as to eject the former: For at the very moment of the expiring of the king reigning, the nearest and lawful heire entreth in his place: And so to refuse him, or intrude another, is not to holde out uncomming in, but to expell and put out their righteous King. And I trust at this time whole France acknowl-

edgeth the superstitious rebellion of the liguers, who upon pretence of heresie, by force of armes held so long out, to the great desolation of their whole country, their native and righteous king from possessing of his owne crowne and naturall kingdome.

Not that by all this former discourse of mine, and Apologie for kings, I meane that whatsoever errors and intollerable abominations a sovereigne prince commit, hee ought to escape all punishment, as if thereby the world were only ordained for kings, & they without controlment to turne it upside down at their pleasure: but by the contrary, by remitting them to God (who is their onely ordinary Judge) I remit them to the sorest and sharpest school-master that can be devised for them: for the further a king is preferred by God above all other ranks & degrees of men, and the higher that his seat is above theirs, the greater is his obligation to his maker. And therfore in case he forget himselfe (his unthankfulness being in the same measure of height) the sadder and sharper will be correction be; and according to the greatnes of the height he is in, the weight of his fall wil recompense the same: for the further that any person is obliged to God, his offence becomes and growes so much the greater, then it would be in any other. Joves thunderclaps light oftner and sorer upon the high & stately oaks, then on the low and supple willow trees: and the highest bench is sliddriest to sit upon. Neither is it ever heard that any king forgets himself towards God, or in his vocation; but God with the greatnesse of the plague revengeth the greatnes of his ingratitude: Neither thinke I by the force of argument of this my discourse so to perswade the people, that none will hereafter be raised up, and rebell against wicked Princes. But remitting to the justice and providence of God to stirre up such scourges as pleaseth him, for punishment of wicked kings (who made the very vermine and filthy dust of the earth to bridle the insolencie of proud Pharaoh) my onely purpose and intention in this treatise is to perswade, as farre as lieth in me, by these sure and infallible grounds, all such good Christian readers, as beare not onely the naked name of a Christian, but kith the fruites thereof in their daily forme of life, to keep their hearts and hands free from such monstrous and unnaturall rebellions, whensoever the wickednesse of a Prince shall procure the same at Gods hands: that, when it shall please God to cast such scourges of princes, and instruments of his fury in the fire, ye may stand up with cleane handes, and unspotted consciences, having prooved your selves in all your actions trew Christians toward God, and dutifull subjects towards your King, having remitted the judgement and punishment of all his wrongs to him, whom to onely of right it appertaineth.

But craving at God, and hoping that God shall continue his blessing with us, in not sending such fearefull desolation, I heartily wish our kings behaviour so to be, and continue among us, as our God in earth, and loving Father, endued with such properties as I described a King in the first part of this Treatise. And that ye (my deare countreymen, and charitable readers) may presse by all means to procure the prosperitie and welfare of your King; that as hee must on the one part thinke all his earthly felicitie and happiness grounded upon your weale, caring more for himselfe for your sake then for his owne, thinking himselfe onely ordained for your weale; such holy and happy emulation may arise betwixt him and you, as his care for your quietnes, and your care for his honor and preservation, may in all your actions daily strive together, that the Land may thinke themselves blessed with such a King, and the king may thinke himself most happy in ruling over so loving and obedient subjects.

DOCUMENT ANALYSIS

1. Are there any limits on the power of a king? What are they?

_____

_____

_____

2. What are James's motives in this essay?

_____

_____

_____

DOCUMENT 16.1
Christopher Columbus, Letter from the 'New World' (1493)

There was no more fateful encounter in human history than Columbus's "discovery" of the so-called New World. In this letter, he describes his initial encounters with the native peoples of the Caribbean.

The Discovered Islands.

Because my undertakings have attained success, I know that it will be pleasing to you: these I have determined to relate, so that you may be made acquainted with everything done and discovered in this our voyage. On the thirty-third day after I departed from Cadiz, I came to the Indian Sea, where I found many islands inhabited by men without number, of all which I took possession for our most fortunate king, with proclaiming heralds and flying standards, no one objecting. To the first of these I gave the name of the blessed Saviour, on whose aid relying I had reached this as well as the other island. But the Indians call it Guanahany. I also called each one of the others by a new name. For I ordered one island to be called Santa Maria of the Conception, another Fernandina, another Isabella, another Juana, and so on with the rest. As soon as we had arrived at that island which I have just now said was called Juana, I proceeded along its coast towards the west for some distance; I found it so large and without perceptible end, that I believed it to be not an island, but the continental country of Cathay; seeing, however, no towns or cities situated on the sea-coast, but only some villages and rude farms, with whose inhabitants I was unable to converse, because as soon as they saw us they took flight. I proceeded farther, thinking that I would discover some city or large residences. At length, perceiving that we had gone far enough, that nothing new appeared, and that this way was leading us to the north, which I wished to avoid, because it was winter on the land, and it was my intention to go to the south, moreover the winds were becoming violent, I therefore determined that no other plans were practicable, and so, going back, I returned to a certain bay that I had noticed, from which I sent two of our men to the land, that they might find out whether there was a king in this country, or any cities. These men traveled for three days, and they found people and houses without number, but they were small and without any government, therefore they returned. Now in the meantime I had learned from certain Indians, whom I had seized there, that this country was indeed an island, and therefore I proceeded towards the east, keeping all the time near the coast, for 322 miles, to the extreme ends of this island. From this place I saw another island to the east, distant from this Juana 54 miles, which I called forthwith Hispana; and I sailed to it; and I steered along the northern coast, as at Juana, towards the east, 564 miles. And the said Juana and the other island there appear very fertile. This island is surrounded by many very safe and wide harbors, not excelled by any others that I have ever seen. Many great and salubrious rivers flow through it. There are also many very high mountains there. All these island are very beautiful, and distinguished by various qualities; they are accessible, and full of a great variety of trees stretching up to the stars; the leaves of which I believe are never shed, for I saw them as green and flourishing as they are usually in Spain in the month of May; some of them were blossoming, some were bearing fruit, some were in other conditions; each one was thriving in its own way. The nightingale and various other birds without number were singing, in the month of November, when I was exploring them. There are besides in the said island Juana seven or eight kinds of palm trees, which far excel ours in height and beauty, just as all the other trees, herbs, and fruits do. There are also excellent pine trees, vast plains and meadows, a variety of birds, a variety of honey, and a variety of metals, excepting iron. In the one which was called Hispana, as we said above, there are great and beautiful mountains, vast fields, groves, fertile plains, very suitable for planting and cultivating, and for the building of houses. The convenience of the harbors in this island, and the remarkable number of rivers contributing to the healthfulness of man, exceed belief, unless one has seen them. The trees, pasturage, and fruits of this island differ greatly from those of Juana. This Hispana, moreover, abounds in different kinds of spices, in gold, and in metals. On this island, indeed, and on all the others which I have seen, and of which I have knowledge, the inhabitants of both sexes go always naked, just as they came into the world, except some of the women, who use a covering of a leaf or some foliage, or a cotton cloth, which they make themselves for that purpose. All these people lack, as I said above, every kind of iron; they are also without weapons, which indeed are unknown; nor are they competent to use them, not on account of deformity of body, for they are well formed, but because they are timid and full of fear. The carry for weapons, however, reeds baked in the sun, on the lower ends of which they fasten some shafts of dried wood rubbed down to a point; and indeed they do not venture to use these always; for it frequently happened when I sent two or three of my men to some of the villages, that they might speak with the natives, a compact troop of the Indians would march out, and as soon as they saw our men approaching, they would quickly take flight, children being pushed aside by their fathers, and fathers by their children.

DOCUMENT ANALYSIS

1. Upon what sources did Columbus draw in naming the islands he encountered?

_____

_____

_____

2. What were the key physical attributes of the islands that Columbus noted?

_____

_____

_____

3. How did Columbus view the native peoples he encountered?

_____

_____

_____

DOCUMENT 16.2
Bartolomé de las Casas, from *In Defense of the Indians* (1500)

Source: Bartolomé de las Casas, "In Defense of the Indians," in *In Defense of the Indians,* ed. and trans. Stafford Poole
(Dekalb, IL: Northern Illinois University Press, 1974), pp. 42-46.

As Spain struggled in the mid 1500s to consolidate control over its New World possessions, a great debate erupted over the status and treatment of the Indians. At the heart of the debate lay the issue of whether Indians were civilized. An Aristotle treatise enshrined in Spanish law gave civilized peoples the right to wage war upon uncivilized peoples and take them as slaves. Consequently, assessments of Indians as barbarian benefited many Spanish settlers who sought both to impose their jurisdiction on the Indians and to take advantage of their labor. The Iberian scholar and theologian Juan Ines de Sepúlveda became a spokesperson for such interests.

Sepúlveda faced stiff opposition. Bartolomé de las Casas, who had served several years as a bishop in Mexico, represented the other side of the debate. Arguing that Indians were civilized, the theologian sought on behalf of both Indians and priests outraged at the settlers' excesses to persuade the Spanish Crown to impose stricter controls on its colonists. The debate's outcome would determine and shape Spain's policy toward all of its New World inhabitants.

Now if we shall have shown that among our Indians of the western and southern shores (granting that we call them barbarians and that they are barbarians) there are important kingdoms, large numbers of people who live settled lives in a society, great cities, kings, judges and laws, persons who engage in commerce, buying, selling, lending, and the other contracts of the law of nations, will it now stand proved that the Reverend Doctor Sepúlveda has spoken wrongly and viciously against peoples like these, either out of malice or ignorance of Aristotle's teaching, and, therefore, has falsely and perhaps irreparably slandered them before the entire world? From the fact that the Indians are barbarians it does not necessarily follow that they are incapable of government and have to be ruled by others, except to be taught about the Catholic faith and to be admitted to the holy sacraments. They are not ignorant, inhuman, or bestial. Rather, long before they had heard the word Spaniard they had properly organized states, wisely ordered by excellent laws, religion, and custom. They cultivated friendship and, bound together in common fellowship, lived in populous cities in which they wisely administered the affairs of both peace and war justly and equitably, truly governed by laws that at very many points surpass ours, and could have won the admiration of the sages of Athens, as I will show in the second part of this Defense.

Now if they are to be subjugated by war because they are ignorant of polished literature, let Sepúlveda hear Trogus Pompey:

Nor could the Spaniards submit to the yoke of a conquered province until Caesar Augustus, after he had conquered the world, turned his victorious armies against them and organized that barbaric and wild people as a province, once he had led them by law to a more civilized way of life.

Now see how he called the Spanish people barbaric and wild. I would like to hear Sepúlveda, in his cleverness, answer this question: Does he think

that the war of the Romans against the Spanish was justified in order to free them from barbarism? And this question also: Did the Spanish wage an unjust war when they vigorously defended themselves against them?

Next, I call the Spaniards who plunder that unhappy people torturers. Do you think that the Romans, once they had subjugated the wild and barbaric peoples of Spain, could with secure right divide all of you among themselves, handing over so many head of both males and females as allotments to individuals? And do you then conclude that the Romans could have stripped your rulers of their authority and consigned all of you, after you had been deprived of your liberty, to wretched labors, especially in searching for gold and silver lodes and mining and refining the metals? And if the Romans finally did that, as is evident from Diodorus, [would you not judge] that you also have the right to defend your freedom, indeed your very life, by war? Sepúlveda, would you have permitted Saint James to evangelize your own people of Córdoba in that way? For God's sake and man's faith in him, is this the way to impose the yoke of Christ on Christian men? Is this the way to remove wild barbarism from the minds of barbarians? Is it not, rather, to act like thieves, cut-throats, and cruel plunderers and to drive the gentlest of people headlong into despair? The Indian race is not that barbaric, nor are they dull witted or stupid, but they are easy to teach and very talented in learning all the liberal arts, and very ready to accept, honor, and observe the Christian religion and correct their sins (as experience has taught) once priests have introduced them to the sacred mysteries and taught them the word of God. They have been endowed with excellent conduct, and before the coming of the Spaniards, as we have said, they had political states that were well founded on beneficial laws.

. . . From this it is clear that the basis for Sepúlveda's teaching that these people are uncivilized and ignorant is worse than false. Yet even if we were to grant that this race has no keenness of mind or artistic ability, certainly they are not, in consequence, obliged to submit themselves to those who are more intelligent and to adopt their ways, so that, if they refuse, they may be subdued by having war waged against them and be enslaved, as happens today. For men are obliged by the natural law to do many things they cannot be forced to do against their will. We are bound by the natural law to embrace virtue and imitate the uprightness of good men. No one, however, is punished for being bad unless he is guilty of rebellion. Where the Catholic faith has been preached in a Christian manner and as it ought to be, all men are bound by the natural law to accept it, yet no one is forced to accept the faith of Christ. No one is punished because he is sunk in vice, unless he is rebellious or harms the property and persons of others. No one is forced to embrace virtue and show himself as a good man. One who receives a favor is bound by the natural law to return the favor by what we call antidotal obligation. Yet no one is forced to this, nor is he punished if he omits it, according to the common interpretation of the jurists.

DOCUMENT ANALYSIS

1. How does las Casas's position on the role of Christianity in the New World differ from that which he ascribes to Sepúlveda? What are some of the implications of this division within the Church?

2. In comparing the Spaniards to the Romans, what do you think las Casas was trying to achieve?

3. Las Casas was a master of rhetoric. How does his language in describing the Spanish settlers and their actions incline his audience to accept his bias or position? Do you think he was successful?

4. On what grounds does las Casas argue that the Indians are civilized?

5. Referring to the reading, say how important you think legal and philosophical precedents were in making a successful case before the Spanish Crown? Do you think this form of logic and argument was itself based upon Roman precedent? Why or why not?